Acc 2020/002

Abolitians

WALKER AND WALKER

THE LAW OF EVIDENCE IN SCOTLAND

WALKER AND WALKER

THE LAW OF EVIDENCE IN SCOTLAND

MARGARET L. ROSS

Solicitor; Senior Lecturer in Law, University of Aberdeen

with

JAMES CHALMERS

Lecturer in Law, University of Aberdeen

T & T CLARK
EDINBURGH
2000

T&T CLARK LTD
59 GEORGE STREET
EDINBURGH EH2 2LQ
SCOTLAND

First published 1964

ISBN 0 567 00562 3

British Library Cataloguing-in-Publication Data.
A catalogue record for this book is available from the British Library.

Typeset by Fakenham Photosetting Limited, Fakenham, Norfolk
Printed and bound in Great Britain by MPG Books, Bodmin

For Iain, Alan, Emma and Paul

FOREWORD

The law of evidence is a curious amalgam of general and highly technical rules. For that reason, perhaps, it is one of the hardest areas of the law to absorb. And yet almost everyone involved in the practice of the law, from the conveyancer to the criminal court practitioner, will require to know and apply at least part of this body of law. In 1964 "Walker and Walker", as it quickly became known, appeared on the scene and provided the first definitive survey of our law for decades. The work quickly established itself as the leading authority to which all turned for guidance on those tricky questions which can spring up so suddenly in the course of a proof or trial. Its influence is to be seen in the opinions of the courts.

But for some years now our copies of Walker and Walker have tended to remain on the shelf since the law of evidence has changed so significantly that much of the current text is out of date. The Civil Evidence (Scotland) Act 1988, the Requirements of Writing (Scotland) Act 1995 and the successive reforms of the criminal rules now enshrined in the Criminal Procedure (Scotland) Act 1995 are only the most obvious examples of the alterations introduced by Parliament. It is still too early to predict what the effects of the Human Rights Act 1998 may be. The courts too have been active, especially in criminal law, where the need to explain the rules to a jury means that judges and practitioners constantly have to check that they are formulated in language which is both accurate and readily understood.

With so much in flux, it is good indeed to know that Margaret Ross, with James Chalmers, has restored and rewritten Walker and Walker. The new edition will now provide the same kind of guidance through this changed world as the first edition provided through the very different law of the 1960s. The enormous amount of work involved in updating the text will be obvious to anyone who even glances at the footnotes. In expressing the thanks of the profession to Margaret Ross and James Chalmers, as well as to all those who assisted them, I take this opportunity to wish the new edition every success.

Rodger of Earlsferry

Parliament House
October 2000

PREFACE TO SECOND EDITION

The project of updating and reworking the seminal work on evidence by the Sheriffs Walker has been daunting. Throughout, it has had at its roots a strong commitment to the original, coupled with a desire that the second edition should reflect the developments and restatements of the law that have occurred since completion of that text. The aim of the reworking is restoration: to restore the text to its place as comprehensive leader. An indication of the methods employed in producing the second edition is given in the Introduction to the Second Edition which precedes Chapter 1.

The project has been completed only with invaluable assistance. James Chalmers undertook the reworking of the criminal aspects of Chapter 9 (confessions), and all of Chapter 12 (oral evidence) and the diverse Chapter 19 (proof of public and official documents). He also read other chapters. His timely assistance is greatly appreciated and acknowledged. Christopher Gane read some chapters. Sarah Jackman assisted with research in general and updating of Chapter 3 (presumptions) in particular; Amanda Walton and Kirsty McKnight assisted with converting the original text to digital format. Dr Carole Dalgleish, Managing Editor at T & T Clark Ltd provided encouragement and commitment to completion, and managed the team who provided tabling, proof reading and indexing. The motivation to embark upon and conclude the project was fuelled by colleagues, past and present, at Aberdeen University Law School and at Campbell Connon, Solicitors, Aberdeen (notably the late Frank Clark Connon) and by an irrepressibly enthusiastic family.

The aim has been to state the law as at 2 October 2000, and, in common with the original authors, where the law may be unclear, to offer a view on what most nearly applies, or what questions might arise. Many changes have taken place in the years between publication of the first and second editions, some of which have been disapproved and replaced in a return to basic principles. In the past year processes for the recovery and presentation of evidence have been subject to scrutiny in the domestic courts in the context of fundamental human rights. That scrutiny for conformity with fundamental rights has much further to go, and the text reports the first year's changes, but predicts others only with caution. To do otherwise would have departed from the cautiously reflective approach to the topic from which the text has derived its enduring respect.

M.L.R.
Aberdeen, October 2000

PREFACE TO FIRST EDITION

When Sheriff Dobie died he left the manuscript of a book on Evidence, and we undertook "to see it through the press." As we proceeded, we came to be of opinion that the scheme and treatment could be improved, and we also received advice to that effect. Accordingly we have rewritten the book, a task which would have been very much more difficult without the material which Sheriff Dobie had collected.

For a time Professor D. M. Walker, Regius Professor of Law in the University of Glasgow, was associated with us, but he had to withdraw under pressure of other work. The writing of Chapter XVIII was under-taken by Mr. Peter G. B. McNeill, M.A., LL.B., Ph.D., Advocate. Mr. J. S. Forbes, Advocate, prepared the Table of Cases.

We have to acknowledge the help of Sheriff J. M. Cowan, Q. C., Sheriff C. D. L. Murray, Mr. Robert Macdonald, Procurator-Fiscal of the Lower Ward of Lanarkshire, Mr. J. C. Patterson, O.B.E., formerly Procurator-Fiscal at Hamilton, Mr. C. G. Hogg, Procurator-Fiscal at Cupar, and Mr. Joseph Mellick, Lecturer in Evidence and Procedure in the University of Glasgow, who either read and criticised portions of the manuscript or gave advice upon modern practice.

Dickson's great work was planned over a hundred years ago, and we have taken the bold step of planning *de novo*. We have tried to keep in view the practical situations in which questions of evidence arise, and to deal comprehensively in one place with each of these situations. A reconsideration of some of the rules of evidence is overdue, notably with regard to the need for writing in proof of certain obligations, but we have not attempted to suggest what form any restatement ought to take. Our aim has been to state what the law is. When this was impossible because it has never been decided, we have indicated the general principle which in our opinion most nearly applies. We think that we can safely say that we have cited no case which we have not read and fully considered.

A. G. W.
N. M. L. W.
Glasgow, January 1964

INTRODUCTION TO
SECOND EDITION

The Law of Evidence in Scotland, a skilful work crafted by the Sheriffs Walker from Sheriff Dobie's repository of material and their own expository plans, has been relied upon by those who adjudicate upon, practice and learn the law since publication in 1964. It was written at a time when books on the law of Scotland were few and the intractable subject of evidence had received little attention. Dickson's treatise supplemented the primary sources used by them. Now texts on all areas of law abound, and where, as in their treatment of private international law or in proof of various regularly occurring substantive matters, the authors would now have deferred to a specialist text, that topic has been omitted. An exception was made for family actions. These were included in the original text because of the peculiarities of proof beyond reasonable doubt in many such cases, but have been retained in this edition because such proceedings are still subject to additional evidential requirements, and have been the scene of significant examination of issues of evidence in recent years. Proof of writings quite rightfully remains a substantial part of the text. There is no other detailed coverage of this topic in recent evidence texts, and substantive texts invariably defer to the first edition of *The Law of Evidence in Scotland* in their treatment of the topic.

As work on the second edition proceeded it became increasingly clear that, with some exceptions, that original exposition of basic rules and concepts of evidence had not only withstood the test of time but provided strong formulations to which the court had returned in recent years (some confusing departures having occurred in the intervening years). This strength was evident despite the extensive revision of exclusionary rules and procedures at the behest of the Scottish Law Commission, informed in part by Sheriff Macphail's industrious and scholarly review published in 1987; and the impact of the European Convention on Human Rights in the Scottish courts and in the European Court of Human Rights. Nevertheless, substantial new material had to be worked into the text, and in places the text had to be completely rewritten. However, statements in the first edition are noted regularly in judgments, and words that have been judicially approved have been preserved in so far as they are not superceded by change in the law. Words which, very occasionally, the court has chosen not to approve as a statement of the law, have been examined and, if appropriate, reworked in so far as they have continuing application.

In the main, the second edition follows the organisation of the first. As in any treatment of the law of evidence there is no clear starting point or ending point, and any division of topics is at risk of becoming tangled in the web that is the whole. The first edition dealt with this by extensive cross-referencing, a technique carried forward to the second edition. This assists with locating material that has been touched upon in different chapters but it is worth noting here that the topics interact on a much deeper level for which careful attention to different chapters may be necessary. For example: burdens of proof and presumptions are co-dependent; sufficiency will be dependent upon circumstantial evidence, but also upon admissibility of confessions, oral evidence or affidavits, absence of privilege and confidentiality; documents (now so widely defined) may be recovered, but, if the issue is one for which writing is essential, the requirements of constitution and proof, and scope for admission of evidence extrinsic to the document, must be considered.

Many statutory reforms in relation to the receipt and effect of evidence have been drawn to take effect upon future events or proceedings only, or upon the limited situations to which the statute applies. Accordingly, the prior law had to be updated for application to cases falling outwith the statutory regime. The increase in resolution of disputes outwith the judicial arena, and the transfer of jurisdiction of certain matters from courts to administrative tribunals, has raised new issues, often dealt with by resort to basic principles. The requirement that public authorities (including courts) must act in accordance with the Human Rights Act 1998 poses a challenge for the rules of evidence as they have evolved in Scotland. The principles of fairness and equality of arms enshrined in the Convention Articles and Protocols are likely to support the fundamentals of our law of evidence, if not the detail as it has developed over the years.

The case law of the European Court of Human Rights is cited where it is thought to be directly relevant, bearing in mind that court's view that control of evidence in judicial proceedings is mainly a matter for the domestic courts. In their examination of case and statute law in the context of a rights charter the Scottish courts have considered case law from other jurisdictions such as Canada and South Africa (much more accessible now on internet databases). However, this text does not set out to draw from the law of jurisdictions other than, where relevant, England, the European Court of Justice and the European Court of Human Rights. Reforms originating in the European Union such as recognition of electronic signatures, and those forthcoming provisions intended to facilitate access to evidence from the institutions of the European Union, are considered only in the form in which they are directly effective in Scotland.

Statutes and statutory instruments are cited in their amended form, with specific reference to amendments occurring since June 2000 only, unless the date of amendment is important to the text. Chapter numbers and regnal references appear in the tables alone. Best case references have been used in the text where possible, with alternative references in the tables.

The male descriptor continues to prevail in this edition. The authors of the original edition used the language of their education and experience, including the male descriptor, in a clear and eloquent manner. Where terms used by them have become outmoded or have fallen into disuse these have been changed, but to convert to use of the female descriptor in whole or in part would have appeared artificial in this second edition. Nevertheless, gender neutral language has been introduced where possible. Of course, except where the facts of a case are discussed, "he" implies "she" and the reverse.

CONTENTS

TABLE OF CASES

TABLE OF STATUTES

TABLE OF STATUTORY INSTRUMENTS

CHAPTER 1

ADMISSIBILITY AND RELEVANCY OF EVIDENCE

1.1 ADMISSIBILITY OF EVIDENCE

1.1.1 Admissible evidence is evidence which a court of law may both receive and consider for the purpose of deciding a particular case. To be admissible in this sense, evidence must satisfy two requirements—it must be relevant and it must conform to the peremptory rules of the law of evidence. Relevancy is defined more fully later in this chapter, and it is sufficient to say here that it depends upon the existence of some sort of logical relationship between the evidence and the subject-matter of the case. Irrelevant evidence is never admissible, but even relevant evidence may be made inadmissible by one of the peremptory rules which the law prescribes. The law for reasons of policy imposes these rules, which are mainly negative in character. They spring from the knowledge that the discovery of the truth by a human tribunal from what is said by human witnesses is a difficult task, and they attempt to limit the risk or the evil consequences of error by excluding certain kinds of evidence as being insufficiently reliable, or too remote, or as creating the possibility of unfairness or confusion. So, for example, a statement made by a person who is not a witness may be relevant in a criminal case, because it has a bearing on the subject-matter of the case, but it may nevertheless be necessary to exclude it, because, as hearsay evidence[1] a rule of law declares it to be inadmissible except in certain specified circumstances.

1.1.2 When objection to a line of evidence is taken during the course of an enquiry, it is sometimes impossible for the court to decide as to its admissibility until all the evidence has been heard. In these circumstances it is usual in civil proofs to allow the evidence to be received under reservation of its admissibility.[2] The advantage of this practice is that the evidence is recorded, and is thus available for consideration by the appeal court, even if the judge of first instance decides, after considering all the other evidence in the case, that it is inadmissible. It has also been commanded as the normal and proper practice in summary criminal trials.[3] In a

---

[1] See Chapter 8.
[2] *McDonald v Duncan* 1933 SC 737, per Lord Anderson at 744.
[3] *Clark v Stuart* 1950 JC 8. See, however, *MacLeod v Woodmuir Miners Welfare Society Social Club* 1961 JC 5 at 8.

jury trial, civil[4] or criminal,[5] the judge must accept responsibility for admitting or excluding evidence which is challenged as inadmissible. If evidence, later shown to be inadmissible, is in fact led, the judge must direct the jury to dismiss it from their minds,[6] and if the judge does so the jury are assumed to have followed the directions. It may be clear from the proposed verdict that account must have been taken of evidence, which the jury were charged to disregard, in which case the judge should do whatever possible to clarify the verdict, before it is recorded.[7]

1.2 RELEVANCY OF AVERMENTS

1.2.1 Relevancy of averments must be distinguished from relevancy of evidence. In a civil action, before enquiry is allowed, whether by proof or jury trial, a party must in the written pleadings make averments of facts which are relevant in law to support the claim or defences.[8] The averments are irrelevant when, even if they are proved, the case on that issue must necessarily fail.[9] If they are in this sense irrelevant the action will be dismissed or the defences repelled, without enquiry into the facts. Certain averments may, separately, be deemed irrelevant due to lack of specification. There the issue is not that they disclose a case which is not relevant in law, but that they fail to disclose with sufficient specification the case which the opponent is expected to answer. The effect of successful challenge to the relevancy of averments is to exclude from probation evidence on the issue to which the irrelevant pleadings were directed. A criminal charge, to be relevant, must meet the statutory requirements as to the specification of time and place, and must set forth facts sufficient to constitute a crime.[10] Relevancy of averment, both in civil and in criminal causes, is governed by the substantive law applicable to the cause in question, and not by the law of evidence.

1.2.2 Although relevancy of averment is not part of the subject-matter of the law of evidence, it has a bearing upon the question of evidence in several ways. If averments of fact are remitted to probation, without reservation as to their relevancy, evidence relevant to prove or disprove them is in general relevant evidence.[11] If the

---

[4] *McDonald v Duncan* 1933 SC 737.
[5] For the proper procedure when the admissibility of statements made by an accused person to the police is challenged, see *Chalmers v HM Advocate* 1954 JC 66; *Manuel v HM Advocate* 1958 JC 41; *Thompson v Crowe* 2000 JC 173. See also paras 1.6 and 9.12.
[6] *McEwan v HM Advocate* 1939 JC 26 at 31; *Parker and Barrie* (1888) 16 R (J) 5 at 9. See also *Slater v HM Advocate* 1928 JC 94.
[7] See Renton & Brown, *Criminal Procedure* (6th edn), para 18-89.
[8] It may emerge from the pleadings that a party wishes to prove a collateral issue which is not relevant in logical terms to the issue in the case: see *A v B* (1895) 22 R 402. The debate as to the logical relevance of the issue will arise before probation, although the assessment of relevance calls upon the factors which are considered in more detail in the following paragraph regarding relevance of evidence, para 1.4, rather than matters of relevance in law (sometime termed "materiality" in other jurisdictions).
[9] *Jamieson v Jamieson* 1952 SC (HL) 44, per Lord Normand at 50 and Lord Reid at 63. See also *Miller v South of Scotland Electricity Board* 1958 SC (HL) 20, commented on in *Blaikie v British Transport Commission* 1961 SC 44 at 49–51. A recent example is *Blackfriars (Scotland) Ltd v John Laurie* 2000 SCLR 385, in which detailed consideration of the law applicable to the execution of citations was required before the court, reluctantly, repelled the defences as irrelevant in this sense.
[10] Criminal Procedure (Scotland) Act 1995, Scheds 2 and 5; Renton and Brown, *Criminal Procedure* (6th edn), paras 8-11–8-60.
[11] *Barr v Bain* (1896) 23 R 1090; *Scott v Cormack Heating Engineers Ltd* 1942 SC 159, per Lord President Normand at 162.

court reserves the question of the law and the relevancy of the averments until after evidence has been led, and allows a proof before answer, the reservation applies only to these two matters, and not to the admissibility of the evidence to be led. However, evidence that is not otherwise admissible is not thereby made admissible.[12]

1.3 RELEVANCY OF EVIDENCE—GENERAL

In very general terms relevant evidence may be said to be evidence which is logi- **1.3.1**
cally connected with those matters in dispute between the parties, the *facta probanda*, which are under investigation by the court. These are sometimes called the matters, or the facts, in issue. To allow evidence to be led on other matters is of no assistance to the court, is a waste of time, and is unfair to the other party to the action, who could neither anticipate it nor be prepared to contradict it,[13] and is entitled to expect that adjudication will focus upon the issue libelled.[14] For the purposes of more detailed discussion, relevant evidence may be regarded as being either direct evidence of a fact in issue,[15] or evidence of a fact (*factum probationis*) bearing on the probability or improbability of a fact in issue,[16] or evidence of a fact which has a bearing only on the admissibility of other evidence, or on the credibility of a witness.[17]

1.4 DIRECT EVIDENCE OF FACTS IN ISSUE

Direct evidence is only available when the fact in issue is something appreciable **1.4.1**
by the senses or contained in a document. The evidence of witnesses who saw or heard the thing happen, or the evidence provided by the terms of the document itself, is clearly relevant, and the only question when such evidence is tendered, apart from any specialty as to the witnesses themselves, is whether the witnesses are truthful and reliable—that is to say, whether they have accurately observed and remembered and truthfully related what occurred—or whether the document is genuine.[18]

1.5 INDIRECT EVIDENCE OF FACTS IN ISSUE—GENERAL

Whether or not direct evidence of a fact in issue is available, evidence of any fact, **1.5.1**
which renders probable or improbable the existence of the fact in issue, is relevant. This includes any fact which is consistent or inconsistent with, or which gives rise to a logical inference regarding, the fact in issue. The whole circumstances surrounding the fact in issue are generally regarded as being in this category in so far

---

[12] *Robertson v Murphy* (1867) 6 M 114; *Haldane v Speirs* (1872) 10 M 537; Maclaren, *Court of Session Practice*, pp 552–553.
[13] Dickson, *Evidence* (3rd edn), para 1.
[14] *A v B* (1895) 22 R 402. For examination of the relevance of evidence of conduct other than that libelled, see paras 1.5–1.6 and Chapter 7.
[15] See para 1.4.
[16] See para 1.5.
[17] See para 1.6.
[18] Dickson, *Evidence* (3rd edn), para 63.

as, with or without other evidence, they have a bearing or throw light upon it. So, for example, in a case which concerns the negligent driving of a motor vehicle, evidence of the behaviour of the vehicle shortly before and shortly after the collision is relevant[19]; where the case concerns the dangerous condition of a road and the road authority's knowledge of it, it may be relevant that accidents similar to that in question have occurred at the same place during the previous two months[20]; it is relevant in a trial for housebreaking to show that the accused person was in the vicinity shortly before, and ran away from it immediately after, the time of the commission of the crime.[21] It is also relevant to admit evidence of the attitude of an accused to his conduct after the offence, in order to place light on his attitude at the time of the offence.[22] In order to be relevant, however, evidence of surrounding circumstances must have a reasonably direct bearing on the subject under investigation, and must not be too remote from it either in time, place, or character. What is, or is not, too remote for the purposes of relevancy is a question of degree in each case,[23] and it is difficult to draw general authority from case law in this area.[24]

1.5.2　　Evidence of facts from which the fact in issue can be inferred, especially when it is the whole evidence in the case, is commonly known as circumstantial evidence, and this is mentioned at greater length in a later chapter.[25] Occurrences which are contemporaneous, or roughly contemporaneous, with the main occurrence are part of the *res gestae*, and as such may be proved, even when evidence of them might in other circumstances be inadmissible.[26]

1.6 FACTS AFFECTING ADMISSIBILITY OR CREDIBILITY OF OTHER EVIDENCE

Facts affecting admissibility

1.6.1　　These facts are relevant,[27] not because they are directly associated with the fact in issue, but because they lay the foundation for evidence which is so associated.

---

[19]　*Bark v Scott* 1954 SC 72, per Lord President Cooper at 76.

[20]　*W Alexander & Sons Ltd v Dundee Corporation* 1950 SC 123. See also *Lightways (Contractors) Ltd v Associated Holdings Ltd* 2000 SC 262.

[21]　In a charge of being found on premises without lawful authority contrary to the Civic Government (Scotland) Act 1982, s 57(1), the fact that the section entitles the court to convict if "in all the circumstances it may reasonably be inferred that he intended to commit a crime there" made relevant evidence that there were suspicious circumstances involving the accused some distance away from the locus: *Frail v Lees* 1997 JC 203.

[22]　*Reid v HM Advocate* 1999 GWD 19-871.

[23]　*Bark v Scott* 1954 SC 72, per Lord President Cooper at 75–76; *W Alexander & Sons v Dundee Corporation* 1950 SC 123, per Lord Justice-Clerk Thomson at 131; *HM Advocate v Kennedy* (1907) 5 Adam 347, per Lord Salvesen at 349; *Gallagher v Paton* 1909 SC (J) 50, per Lord McLaren at 55 (see the comment on this decision at para 7.15.1); *HM Advocate v Joseph* 1929 JC 55, per Lord Murray at 56–57.

[24]　However, it may be of particular interest to tribunals—where issues of relevance and admissibility tend to be raised, not as preliminary issues but as points of appeal—to have guidance on relevant evidence. In two recent cases arising from the Employment Tribunal the Inner House has approved of their reliance upon evidence outwith the direct facts in issue, which would cast light upon the primary facts, including assessment of loss: *Lightways (Contractors) Ltd v Associated Holdings Ltd* 2000 SC 262; *Leonard v Strathclyde Buses Ltd* 1999 SC 57.

[25]　See Chapter 6.

[26]　See para 8.5.

[27]　They were characterised as irrelevant but admissible by Phipson, but see Cross & Tapper (9th edn), pp 62–63 where the preferred description is that they are relevant, albeit to a subsidiary matter rather than to an issue in the cause.

Proof of them may be prerequisite to a decision on the admissibility or inadmissibility of other evidence. The death of a person who would have been a witness, for example, or the destruction or irrecoverability of a relevant document, are facts which have no direct bearing on the subject-matter of the cause, but they must be proved if the dead person's statement,[28] or evidence in place of the document,[29] is to be admissible in evidence. Similarly, the circumstances in which an accused person made a statement to the police may have nothing directly to do with the circumstances of the crime, but they must be proved before the admissibility of the statement itself is established.[30] The facts which form the basis of opinion evidence given by expert witnesses are sometimes relevant and admissible only because of the use which the expert witnesses make of them.[31]

Facts affecting credibility

Evidence of such facts may be elicited from the witness himself in cross-examination, and examples of the questions, which may be put to him for the purpose of testing credibility, are given later.[32] Convictions of crimes inferring dishonesty are regarded as legitimate subjects of cross-examination for this purpose, but if the witness denies the convictions, his denial cannot be contradicted by parole evidence.[33] If a witness is examined by either party as to the making of an earlier statement which is different from the evidence given by that witness in court, and denies it, the examiner is authorised by statute to adduce evidence to prove the making of the earlier statement.[34] In civil cases evidence of a prior statement by a person who gives evidence in court is admissible in so far as it reflects favourably or unfavourably on that witness's credibility.[35] In civil cases, although hearsay evidence is generally admissible, there is no express allowance of evidence bearing upon the credibility of that hearsay evidence. By comparison, if hearsay evidence is admitted in a criminal case because a witness is unable to attend court, evidence that would have been admissible in relation to credibility had the witness given evidence is admissible for that purpose in relation to the hearsay evidence.[36] Apart from these statutory rules it is thought that evidence of facts affecting the credibility of a witness, apart from the evidence of the witness himself or herself, is generally inadmissible unless the facts are also relevant to the questions at issue.[37] This is not because the facts are irrelevant, but because it is inexpedient to spend time on the investigation of collateral issues concerning persons who are not necessarily parties to the cause.[38] Thus it may be admissible to lead evidence that a witness was drunk at or about the time when he claims to have been

1.6.2

---

[28] See para 8.6.
[29] See paras 20.1–20.3; 21.15–21.16.
[30] See paras 9.11–9.22.
[31] See para 16.3.6.
[32] See para 12.9.3.
[33] See para 12.10.
[34] Evidence (Scotland) Act 1852, s 3; Criminal Procedure (Scotland) Act 1995, s 263(4). This subject is dealt with at para 12.10 and 8.4.
[35] Civil Evidence (Scotland) 1988, s 3.
[36] Criminal Procedure (Scotland) Act 1995, s 259(4).
[37] In *King v King* (1841) 4 D 124, however, it was held competent not only to cross-examine a witness as to expressions of hostility to a party, but also to prove these by other evidence. In *Green v HM Advocate* 1983 SCCR 42 evidence of the tendency of a complainer to make false allegations of sexual assault was considered relevant to an appeal against conviction.
[38] *Kennedy v HM Advocate* (1896) 23 R (J) 28, per Lord Justice-Clerk Macdonald at 30; *Dickie v HM Advocate* (1897) 24 R (J) 82 at 83. As to the reasons for excluding collateral issues, see para 7.1 and 7.2.

assaulted,[39] or that he was not in a position to witness the commission of the crime which he describes in his evidence, because these facts are relevant to the decision of the case as well as to the credibility or reliability of the witness. On the other hand, in trials for sexual crimes, at common law evidence that the alleged victim had acted immorally on specific occasions years before the commission of the crime was held to be inadmissible,[40] and now such evidence is inadmissible under statute,[41] unless relevant in accordance with criteria specified in the statute.[42]

1.7 ADMISSION OF EVIDENCE ILLEGALLY OBTAINED

General

1.7.1 An example of evidence which, although relevant, may be held to be inadmissible is that which has been obtained illegally or irregularly. Such evidence may be real[43] or documentary,[44] or it may be oral evidence of confessions by an accused person,[45] and mention is made later of the legal and the illegal or irregular methods by which evidence may be obtained.[46] When it has been established that a piece of evidence has been obtained illegally or irregularly, the question as to whether in a particular case it is admissible or inadmissible is frequently one of difficulty.[47]

Criminal causes

1.7.2 It has been said that, from the standpoint of principle:

> "the law must strive to reconcile two highly important interests which are liable to come into conflict—(a) the interest of the citizen to be protected from illegal or irregular invasions of his liberties by the authorities, and (b) the interest of the State to secure that evidence bearing upon the commission of crime and necessary to enable justice to be done, shall not be withheld from Courts of law on any merely formal or technical ground."[48]

When these interests conflict, the rule is that the evidence is inadmissible unless the illegality or irregularity associated with its procurement can be excused by the court.[49]

1.7.3 In practice a distinction has been made between oral statements or admissions

---

[39] *Falconer v Brown* (1893) 21 R (J) 1. It seems to be clearly implied that the evidence, if tendered, ought to have been admitted.
[40] *Reid v HM Advocate* (1861) 4 Irv 124; *Dickie v HM Advocate* (1897) 24 R (J) 82. As to evidence of character generally, see paras 7.4 and 7.7.
[41] Criminal Procedure (Scotland) Act 1995, s 274.
[42] Criminal Procedure (Scotland) Act 1995, s 275, and see para 7.7.2.
[43] See Chapter 18.
[44] See Chapter 21.
[45] See Chapter 9.
[46] See Chapters 9 and 21.
[47] See JTC, "Evidence Obtained by Means Considered Irregular" 1969 JR 55; Finnie, "Police Powers of Search in the Light of *Leckie v Miln*", 1982 SLT (News) 289; Fraser, "Undercover Law Enforcement in Scots Law", 1994 SLT (News) 113; Mackarel and Gane, "Admitting Irregularly or Illegally Obtained Evidence from Abroad into Criminal Proceedings—A Common Law Approach", 1997 Crim LR 720.
[48] *Lawrie v Muir* 1950 JC 19 at 26.
[49] *Lawrie v Muir* 1950 JC 19 at 27.

by an accused person, on the one hand, and real and documentary evidence, on the other. In the case of oral statements or admissions irregularly obtained, there may be an uncertainty as to what was actually said, or as to the proper interpretation of it, which does not exist to the same extent with regard to real or documentary evidence. Evidence of extra-judicial oral statements by an accused person, if irregularly obtained, is in practice regarded as inadmissible,[50] and the inadmissibility has been held also to apply to actings of an accused person, while in the company of police officers, arising from, and closely associated with, a statement irregularly obtained from him by them.[51]

Real or documentary evidence irregularly obtained, on the other band, as far as **1.7.4** the reported decisions disclose, was always in practice admitted prior to the full bench case of *Lawrie v Muir*,[52] in which the earlier decisions are mentioned. In that case, which concerned a relatively trivial statutory prosecution for selling milk in bottles belonging to other persons, the court, not without hesitation, disallowed the evidence, the balance being tilted in this direction by the fact that the milk bottles were obtained without proper warrant by Milk Marketing Board inspectors, who should have been aware that their powers were limited and that they did not have the common law discretionary powers of police officers.

Since that decision, applying the general rule which it laid down, the courts have **1.7.5** disallowed such evidence in some cases, and allowed it in others. The decision as to whether the irregularity is excusable or not is discretionary. In making the decision the court must take into consideration the gravity of the crime with which the accused is charged[53]; the seriousness or triviality of the irregularity[54]; the urgency of the investigation in the course of which the evidence was obtained,[55] to which has been connected the likelihood of the evidence disappearing if time is taken to seek a warrant[56]; the authority[57] and good faith of those who obtained the evidence[58]; and

---

[50] For detail on this, see Chapter 9.

[51] *Chalmers v HM Advocate* 1954 JC 66 at 76. See also *Mahler* (1857) 2 Irv 634 (confession to civilian witness, following upon earlier promise of immunity by police officer, held inadmissible).

[52] *Lawrie v Muir* 1950 JC 19 at 27–28. This matter is also discussed at para 18.2.

[53] *Lawrie v Muir* 1950 JC 19 at 27; *Milford v HM Advocate* 1973 SLT 12. In *HM Advocate v McGuigan* 1936 JC 16 this factor had applied.

[54] See *McGovern v HM Advocate* 1950 JC 33 at 37; *Fairley v Fishmongers of London* 1951 JC 14. This is mitigated by any element of accidental finding: *HM Advocate v Hepper* 1958 JC 39; *Drummond v HM Advocate* 1993 SLT 476; *Hepburn v Brown* 1998 JC 63. See also *HM Advocate v McKay* 1961 JC 47.

[55] *McGovern v HM Advocate* 1950 JC 33; *HM Advocate v Turnbull* 1951 JC 96; *Edgley v Barbour* 1995 SLT 711.

[56] *Walsh v MacPhail* 1978 SLT (Notes) 29; *Burke v Wilson* 1988 SCCR 361; *Edgley v Barbour* 1995 SLT 711.

[57] A search by a steward who had no authority and in circumstances of no particular urgency was not excused: *Wilson v Brown* 1996 SLT 686. Cf *Mackintosh v Stott* 1999 SCCR 291 where the steward's request for the items was complied with and the evidence allowed. A number of cases depend upon whether the investigators had reasonable grounds for suspicion of criminal activity sufficient to justify a statutory power to arrest without warrant, for example under the Criminal Procedure (Scotland) Act 1995, s 14 or the Misuse of Drugs Act 1973, s 23. See, for example, *Weir v Jessop* 1991 SCCR 242, *Cooper v Buchanan* 1997 SLT 54 but *cf Lucas v Lockhart* (1980) SCCR Supp 256. Evidence found in the car of a drink driver while it was held in the police pound was admitted in *Baxter v Scott* 1992 SLT 1125 but *cf Graham v Orr* 1995 SCCR 30. Delay between receiving information and acting upon it to effect a search is a relevant factor: *Weir v Jessop (No 2)* 1991 SCCR 636 (evidence admitted); *cf Ireland v Russell* 1995 SLT 1348 (evidence not admitted).

[58] *McGovern v HM Advocate* 1950 JC 33 at 37; *Fairley v Fishmongers of London* 1951 JC 14; *Hepburn v Brown* 1998 JC 63; *Webley v Ritchie* 1997 SLT 1241.

the question of fairness to the accused.[59] The factors of urgency, authority, and good faith are assessed according to an objective view of the information possessed by the investigator at the time.[60] In some cases the issue has been avoided by the conclusion that the person who possessed the evidence gave it up voluntarily on request,[61] albeit that no caution or warning had been given before the request was made or complied with[62] and the person making the request had no authority to do so.[63]

Procedure for considering an objection to evidence irregularly obtained

1.7.6 When objection is taken to the admission of evidence alleged to have been irregularly obtained, any jury should be excluded, and the evidence bearing upon the attendant circumstances should be heard by the judge alone, including, if desired, the evidence of the accused himself. The evidence of the accused is taken in *voir dire* for this purpose alone, and only if so taken it does not impinge upon the right to silence.[64] If the judge sustains the objection, any evidence so heard should be disregarded. If there is a jury, it should be told nothing about the matter. If the objection is repelled, the case will proceed before the judge or jury, and, if the Crown or the defence thinks it necessary, the evidence bearing upon the attendant circumstances can be the subject of examination and cross-examination a second time. It is then for the judge or jury to decide as to the truth, weight and value of the evidence, in the light of the evidence as a whole, including, in the case of a statement or admission made by the accused person, a decision as to whether it was voluntarily and freely given.[65] The practice which prevailed between 1977 and 1999[66] of allowing the jury to decide upon the fairness of the circumstances in which evidence had been obtained after hearing the evidence from the prosecution and the defence, was disapproved when the matter was considered by a full bench.[67]

Civil causes

1.7.7 It has been held in the Inner House that in a divorce action a letter, written by the defender to the co-defender and stolen by the pursuer, is admissible evidence for the pursuer, the opinion being judicially expressed that the policy of the law is to admit almost all evidence which will throw light on disputed facts and enable justice to be done.[68] Whilst the court has had no difficulty in admitting evidence

---

[59] Considered expressly in *Webley v Ritchie* 1997 SLT 1241, *Brown v Glen* 1997 SCCR 636. In *Namyslak v HM Advocate* 1995 SLT 528 irregularity was not shown not to exist, but if there was any irregularity there was no unfairness to the accused.

[60] As in *Hepburn v Brown* 1998 JC 63; *Houston v Carnegie* 1999 SCCR 605. *Cf Leckie v Miln* 1982 SLT 177.

[61] *Davidson v Brown* 1990 JC 324; *Devlin v Normand* 1992 SCCR 875; *Normand v Cox* 1997 SCCR 24; *Brown v Glen* 1998 JC 4; *Mackintosh v Stott* 1999 SCCR 291.

[62] Examined in *Brown v Glen* 1998 JC 4.

[63] *Mackintosh v Stott* 1999 SCCR 291 (steward at disco).

[64] *Thompson v Crowe* 2000 JC 173. For more detail on this case, see para 9.12.

[65] *Chalmers v HM Advocate* 1954 JC 66, per Lord Justice-General Cooper at 80, Lord Justice-Clerk Thomson at 82; *Manuel v HM Advocate* 1958 JC 41 at 49.

[66] Following the decision in *Balloch v HM Advocate* 1977 JC 23 and applied in *Morley v HM Advocate* 1981 SCCR 250. *Cf McHugh v HM Advocate* 1978 JC 12 at 15–18.

[67] *Thompson v Crowe* 2000 JC 173.

[68] *Rattray v Rattray* (1897) 25 R 315, per Lord Trayner at 318–319, although there was a split of judicial opinion in the case, and only Lord Trayner's short opinion is relied upon.

obtained by irregular means short of criminality,[69] the decision was followed with some reluctance in a later case in the Outer House.[70] In another Outer House case the view was taken that the reasoning applied in criminal cases to the admission of evidence obtained irregularly would form a better basis for consideration of its admission in civil cases, namely that it would be relevant to have regard to the nature of the evidence, the purpose for which it was to be used in evidence, the manner in which it was obtained, fairness to the party from whom it had been illegally obtained, and fairness considered in light of the matters to be determined in the proceedings as a whole.[71] The view taken in that case has been preferred by commentators,[72] and is no doubt preferable, but no subsequent judicial or legislative development has taken place, and the matter may bear further scrutiny having regard to Article 8 of the European Convention on Human Rights.[73]

---

[69] *MacNeill v MacNeill* 1929 SLT 251; *Turner v Turner* 1930 SLT 393; *Watson v Watson* 1934 SC 374.
[70] *MacColl v MacColl* 1946 SLT 312.
[71] *Duke of Argyll v Duchess of Argyll* 1963 SLT (Notes) 42.
[72] Macphail, *Evidence*, para 21.14; Scottish Law Commission Memo No 46, para U.06; Field & Raitt, *The Law of Evidence in Scotland*, para 15-34; Sheldon, *Evidence: Cases and Materials*, p 314; Wilkinson, *Scottish Law of Evidence*, p 118.
[73] For more detail on this point see para 9.10.

CHAPTER 2

BURDEN OF PROOF

2.1 GENERAL

With regard to each disputed issue of fact arising in the course of a litigation, the **2.1.1** burden of proof (*onus probandi*) rests upon either one party or the other. This means, in very general terms, that if on any issue of fact no evidence is led, or the evidence leaves the matter in doubt, the party upon whom the burden of proof rests has not discharged it, and accordingly fails on that issue. It makes no difference to his failure that his opponent may not have proved his own averments. In the simplest of terms one can say that in any civil case the issues which must be proved for a pursuer to succeed are that there is a right of action against the defender by virtue of some obligation or situation giving rise to a legal remedy, and that the criteria exist for the remedy to be granted in the pursuer's favour: for example, there is a contract, it has been breached and there is a resultant loss not yet compensated. In a criminal case the issues are the commission of a crime, and the identification of the accused as perpetrator. These are matters determined by the substance of the law. Unless any of these issues is admitted by the opponent, the burden of proving them falls on the person who initiated the proceedings: that is, the pursuer or the prosecutor. This has been described as the "persuasive" or "legal" burden.[1] It involves not only the presentation of evidence on those issues to the court for consideration, but persuading the court to accept that evidence. In civil cases, by making a judicial admission which proves directly or by inference an issue on which the pursuer had the burden of proof, a defender may assume the persuasive burden of proving a substantive line of defence. In criminal cases the accused never carries a persuasive burden of proof unless founding upon insanity or diminished responsibility. A persuasive burden exists on these issues because they are

---

[1] *Brown v Rolls Royce Ltd* 1960 SC(HL) 22. See also Denning, "Presumptions and Burdens" (1945) 61 LQR 379; Brealey, "The Burden of Proof before the European Court" (1985) 10 EL Rev 250; Cross and Tapper *Evidence* (9th edn), Chapter III.

contrary to the presumption of law that all persons are sane. In all other respects the accused cannot carry a persuasive burden in relation to defence issues because there is a presumption of innocence and at all times during a trial the prosecutor must satisfy the persuasive burden of displacing that presumption beyond reasonable doubt. Burdens in criminal cases are considered in detail below.

2.1.2   Quite apart from the allocation of burdens of proof according to the substantive law or the pleadings, during the course of a case evidence may be led by one party which, if believed, would establish an issue on which that party has the persuasive burden of proof. In that event if there is contradictory evidence available to the other party they will no doubt feel obliged to lead it, because without it the case may succeed against them on that issue. In the past it was common to describe this as the burden of proof "shifting" during the case,[2] but this tended to suggest that the burdens set by the substantive law or the pleadings in the case could move between the parties,[3] which is not the case. Now the preferred description for the process whereby one party may be expected to dispel any adverse inferences raised by the other party's evidence is "provisional"[4] or "tactical"[5] burden. Finally, the term "evidential" burden has been also been used[6] and at times apparently confused with the provisional burden described above.[7] However, the "evidential" burden is merely the requirement to lead some evidence on an issue so that the issue can be open for consideration by the court at all.

2.2 GENERAL PROPOSITIONS AS TO INCIDENCE OF BURDEN OF PROOF—CIVIL CASES

2.2.1 The persuasive burden of proof may be placed by statute upon one or other of the parties. For example, the Contract (Scotland) Act 1997 provides that where a document appears to comprise all the express terms of a contract or unilateral obligation, it shall be presumed until the contrary is proved to contain all the express terms of the contract or obligation.[8] Accordingly, a party seeking to establish that the terms of a contract or unilateral obligation differ from that set down in writing carries the burden of so proving. There are also statutory provisions regarding commercial paper transactions such as bills of exchange and promissory notes.[9] Statutory provisions may (a) expressly state upon whom will fall the burden of proving a particular issue,[10] (b) expressly create a presumption that a certain situ-

---

[2]   As in *Gibson v National Cash Register Co* 1925 SC 500, per Lord Justice-Clerk Alness at 504; *Clyde Navigation Trs v Barclay Curle & Co* (1876) 3 R (HL) 44, per Lord Selborne at 51. In *Mactavish's JF v Michael's Trs* 1912 SC 425 (action against endorser for balance of sum due under a bill of exchange), the burden of proof was held to have shifted twice in the course of the proof. Dickson, *Evidence* (3rd edn), para 35; and the first edition of this text at paras 77–79.

[3]   A suggestion criticised by Lord Pearson in the English case *Henderson v Henry E Jenkins & Sons* [1970] AC 282 at 301. However, "shifting" is used by Lord Hope in *R v DPP, ex parte Kebeline & Ors* [1999] 3 WLR 972.

[4]   In *Brown v Rolls Royce Ltd*, 1960 SC (HL) 22, Lord Denning referred to these as "provisional" or "evidential" burdens although the terms are not synonymous.

[5]   Field & Raitt, *Evidence* (2nd edn), paras 2–25 to 2–44; Cross and Tapper, *Evidence* (9th edn), p 113.

[6]   *eg* in Macphail, *Evidence* at paras 22.03 *et seq*.

[7]   *eg* as by Lord Pearson in *Henderson v Henry E Jenkins & Sons* [1970] AC 282.

[8]   s 1(1).

[9]   Bills of Exchange Act 1882, ss 13(1), 21(3), 30(2), 32(5) and 63(3).

[10]   *eg*, in the Bills of Exchange Act 1882, ss 30(2) and 63(3), and the Mental Health (Public Safety and Appeals) (Scotland) Act 1999, s 1(4).

ation exists, which is rebuttable by evidence, thus placing a burden of proof on the person seeking to rebut,[11] or (c) contain no express guidance on burden of proof, in which case they are open to interpretation as to who must prove the statutory criteria or qualifications.

In the interpretation of these statutes and in considering the incidence of burden of proof in general, some basic propositions have emerged at common law. These in many respects reflect common sense, but in some instances have a foundation in the policy of laying the burden at the feet of the person to whom the evidence is most accessible. The following are suggested as general propositions, one or more of which may indicate where burdens of proof lie, either initially upon the pleadings or at any subsequent stage of the enquiry.[12] They are not mutually exclusive. **2.2.2**

(a) The persuasive burden of proof lies on the party who will fail if no evidence at all is led.[13] This means that in the normal case the burden, initially at least, rests upon the pursuer, since, in accordance with the maxim *melior est conditio possidentis vel defendentis* (the condition of a possessor or defender is better), the pursuer cannot, merely by raising an action, require his opponent to disprove his allegations as a condition of escaping liability. It also means that if, at any stage of the case, the judicial admissions give rise to a presumption or inference of fact, which, if not rebutted, entitles one of the parties to succeed, the burden of rebutting the presumption or inference of fact rests upon his opponent.[14] **2.2.3**

(b) The burden of proof rests on the party who alleges the affirmative. The maxim is *ei qui affirmat, non ei qui negat, incumbit probatio* (on he who asserts, not he who denies, is the obligation to prove).[15] So, if liability for negligence or breach of contract is admitted, but the defender avers that the pursuer's injury or damage is partly attributable to his own subsequent negligence[16] or failure to minimise his loss,[17] the burden of proving these averments rests upon the defender, and it is not for the pursuer to justify his actions. In applying this proposition it is the substance and not the language of the allegation which is considered, so that an allegation of negligence, for example, is regarded as affirmative, whether it charges the other party with an act or an omission.[18] The burden of proving that he has not received a document may rest upon the party making the assertion, if the proved facts raise an inference that he received it in the ordinary course of delivery or posting.[19] Similarly, in an action concerning the delivery of goods to a party in respect of which that party signed a receipt, the burden is on the party alleging non-delivery so to prove.[20] A signed bill of lading creates the inference that the **2.2.4**

---

[11] *eg,* Bills of Exchange Act 1882, ss 13(1), 21(3) and 32(5).

[12] If the parties have erroneously agreed that one of them has the burden of proof on a particular issue and have conducted the proof on this basis the court will be unlikely to allow the issue of burden to be reopened on appeal: *John Thorburn & Sons v Border Harvesters Ltd* 1992 SLT 549.

[13] Dickson, *Evidence* (3rd edn), para 25.

[14] *eg Fennel v Cameron* 1968 SLT (Sh Ct) 30.

[15] Dickson, *Evidence* (3rd edn), para 26. See also *Clyde Navigation Trs v Barclay Curle & Co* (1876) 3 R (HL) 44, per Lord Selborne at 51–52; *Alexander v Philip* (1899) 1 F 985.

[16] *SS "Baron Vernon" v SS "Metagama"* 1928 SC (HL) 21.

[17] *Connal, Cotton & Co v Fisher, Renwick & Co* (1882) 10 R 824.

[18] See *McClure, Naismith, Brodie & Macfarlane v Stewart* (1887) 15 R (HL) 1, per Lord Herschell at 12, and Dickson, *Evidence* (3rd edn), para 34.

[19] *Guthrie v Stewart* 1926 SC 743, per Lord Justice-Clerk Alness and Lord Ormidale at 747, and cases in Dickson, *Evidence* (3rd edn), para 28, notes (d), (e). But it will not fall upon the defender so to prove if the pursuer has led insufficient evidence of dispatch to raise the inference of receipt: *Donald v Cordale Investments* 1996 SLCR 1 (Land Ct).

[20] *eg Potter Cowan & Co Ltd v Allen* 1983 SLT (Sh Ct) 42.

goods detailed in the bill were submitted for shipping and in a dispute regarding the extent or condition of the goods on unloading the burden is on the shipper to prove otherwise.[21]

2.2.5 (c) When a fact is peculiarly within the knowledge of one of the parties, very slight evidence may suffice to satisfy the burden of proof upon the other party on that issue, and to lay upon the party with the knowledge the burden of proving his own averment, whether affirmative or negative, about the fact in question.[22] When, for example, it is proved by the pursuer that his property has been destroyed or damaged while in the possession of the defender under a contract in which the defender has assumed custody of the property, the burden of proving that it was destroyed or damaged without fault on his part rests upon the defender. Examples include a borrower,[23] hirer,[24] depositary,[25] or holder under some similar contract or arrangement.[26] The same rule applies to carriage by land[27] or sea,[28] and has been said to apply to the proper maintenance by bus company proprietors of a tyre which burst in an action raise by an injured passenger.[29] At its least the burden will be to prove that the custodian took all reasonable care while the property was in his custody but may extend to ruling out the defender's negligence,[30] even though the exact cause may not be proved. However, in some instances the custodian bears a strict burden to prove that the damage or destruction came about by act of the pursuer, act of God or *damnum fatale*, and failure so to prove (*eg* because the cause is unknown) entitles the pursuer to success. That strict burden of proof upon the custodian arises from the adoption into Scots law of the praetorian edict *nautae, caupones, stabularii*,[31] and thus applies in the case of stabler,[32] hotel keeper,[33] and carrier by sea.[34]

2.2.6 (d) When a statute provides that an order shall be pronounced or refused if it appears to the court,[35] or if the court is satisfied,[36] that something has or has not occurred, then, in the absence of express statutory provision concerning the burden of proof, it will fall upon the party who will fail if after evidence is heard the court

---

[21] *Horsley v J & A D Grimond* (1894) 21 R 410; *Smith & Co v Bedouin Steam Navigation Co* (1895) 23 R (HL) 1; *cf Craig Line Steamship Co v North British Storage & Transit Co* 1921 SC 114. The Carriage of Goods by Sea Acts 1971 and 1992 now affect statements in a bill of lading.

[22] *McClure, Naismith, Brodie & Macfarlane v Stewart* (1887) 15 R (HL) 1, per Lord Chancellor Halsbury at 2–3; *Cruickshank v Smith* 1949 JC 134, per Lord Jamieson at 151–152. See also *Lockhart v Barr* 1941 SC 578 at 585; 1943 SC (HL) 1.

[23] *Bain v Strang* (1888) 16 R 186.

[24] *Wilson v Orr* (1879) 7 R 266, per Lord Gifford at 269; *Pullars v Walker* (1858) 20 D 1238. Followed in *Leith v Downie* 1996 SCLR 336 (Sh Ct, Notes).

[25] *Taylor v Nisbet* (1901) 4 F 79 (Lord Young dissenting); *cf Sutherland v Hutton* (1896) 23 R 718, per Lord Young at 721–722 (questioned in *Mustard v Paterson* 1923 SC 142 at 149).

[26] *Sinclair v Juner* 1952 SC 35 (motor car in repairer's garage); *Copland v Brogan* 1916 SC 277 (gratuitous mandatory).

[27] *Anderson v North British Railway Co* (1875) 2 R 443.

[28] eg *Williams v Dobbie* (1884) 11 R 982; *Bishop v Mersey & Clyde Navigation Steam Co* (1830) 8 S 558; *Langlands & Sons v McMaster & Co* 1907 SC 1090.

[29] *Elliott v Young's Bus Service* 1945 SC 445, per Lord Mackay at 459.

[30] *MacRae v K & L Ltd* 1962 SLT (Notes) 90.

[31] Inst IV, 5, 3; Dig 44, 5, 6; 47, 5.

[32] *Mustard v Paterson* 1923 SC 142.

[33] *Burns v Royal Hotel (St Andrews) Ltd* 1958 SC 354 (motor car in hotel garage).

[34] *Williams v Dobbie* (1884) 11 R 982; *Bishop v Mersey & Clyde Navigation Steam Co* (1830) 8 S 558; *Langlands & Sons v McMaster & Co* 1907 SC 1090.

[35] *McLaughlin v Caledonia Stevedoring Co* 1938 SC (HL) 31; *cf Moore v Harland & Wolff* 1937 SC 707.

[36] *Kerrigan v Nelson* 1946 SC 388; *McCallum v Arthur* 1955 SC 188 at 197, 198.

is not satisfied.[37] When a right is given by statute subject to a qualification or to an exception, the question arises as to whether the burden of showing that the qualification or exception does not apply rests upon the party seeking the right, or whether his opponent must prove that it is applicable. A number of early decisions were contradictory and left the position in some doubt.[38] Interpretation of analogous provisions in criminal causes provided some guide.[39] Essentially the matter is one of statutory interpretation,[40] but varied and complex styles of drafting[41] militate against general rules. After a series of conflicting decisions[42] clear authority has emerged in relation to the burden of proof in statutory provisions requiring a person to maintain a safe system or premises "so far as reasonably practicable". The House of Lords in *Nimmo v Alexander Cowan & Sons Ltd*[43] held that the pursuer relying on a provision of the Factories Act 1961 in these terms need only show that his workplace was unsafe. The defenders bore the burden of showing that it was not reasonably practicable to make the workplace safer. Effectively the House of Lords decided that as a matter of policy and efficacy the burden should lie upon the defenders.[44] Their reasoning took account of this being something peculiarly within the knowledge of the defenders as proprietors of the factory, the interpretation of such provisions in criminal cases, the English authorities which were to the effect that the defender should bear the burden of showing that there was no reasonably practicable safer system, and what Lord Wilberforce described as "the orthodox principle (common to both the criminal and the civil law) that exceptions etc, are to be set up by those who rely on them."[45] However, the case applies only to provisions drawn in those terms and interpretations of other such provisions have varied.[46]

(e) A burden of proof lies upon the party against whom on the pleadings, or at **2.2.7** any later stage in the enquiry, a presumption operates, or, if there are presumptions

---

[37] In order to be "satisfied" the court may well be exercising a discretion, and it may not be appropriate to think of the matter as one of satisfying a burden, unless the question is whether one party has failed to bring evidence of the factors necessary for a discretion to be exercised: *Sanderson v McManus* 1997 SC (HL) 55, per Lords Hope and Clyde.

[38] In *Coul v Ayr County Council* 1909 SC 422 at 424, Lord President Dunedin observes that the person who stands to gain from the application of the exception should prove it. However, in *Brydon v Railway Executive* 1957 SC 282 at 290–291 Lord Patrick states that it is not enough for a person to prove an unqualified right leaving the opponent to prove the existence of a qualification. He states that it would be for the claimant to prove that the qualification does not apply.

[39] See para 2.12.4.

[40] eg *Glasgow District Licensing Board v Din* 1995 SC 244, re Licensing (Scotland) Act 1976, s 17(1); *Milne v Milne* 1994 SLT (Sh Ct) 57 re Matrimonial Homes (Family Protection) (Scotland) Act 1981, s 19; *Midlothian District Council v Drummond* 1991 SLT (Sh Ct) 67 re Tenants Rights etc (Scotland) Act 1980.

[41] eg *Barclays Bank v RBS Advanta* 1996 RPC 307 re the burden upon a trade mark proprietor to establish that an injunction was justified under the Trade Marks Act 1994, s 10(6).

[42] In *Donno v British Railways Board* 1964 SLT (Notes) 108 the onus was said to be on the pursuer to establish the reasonable practicability of a situation safer than that used by the defenders; in *Fern v Dundee Corporation* 1964 SLT 294 it was observed that onus in a provision such as this was an open question and it certainly did not fall automatically upon the defender to establish that there was not a more reasonably practicable method.

[43] 1967 SC (HL) 79.

[44] If the pursuer has specifically averred reasonably practicable means by which the defenders could have improved safety, this merely enables the pursuer to lead evidence in chief about those means but does not absolve the defenders from the burden of proof set by the *Nimmo* case: *Gibson v British Insulated Callenders Construction Co* 1973 SC (HL) 15.

[45] *Nimmo* 1967 SC (HL) 79 at 109.

[46] eg *Earnshaw v HM Advocate* 1982 SLT 179; cf *McClory v Owen-Thomas* 1990 SLT 323.

operating against both parties, upon the party who must overcome the stronger presumption. Presumptions are considered in more detail in the next chapter.

2.3 IMPORT OF PERSUASIVE BURDENS OF PROOF

2.3.1 The question as to where the persuasive burden of proof rests is important at various stages in proceedings. The parties in framing their pleadings, gathering evidence and preparing for proof must consider it. It may have to be considered by the court before the enquiry commences in order to determine whether a relevant case has been pled. So, for example, if a defender claims that the pursuer's case must fail due to prescription, it is the defender who carries the burden of proof and must have a specific plea to that effect.[47] If the facts underlying that plea are admitted by the pursuer in averment this may lead to the case failing at debate without the need for evidence. However, if the pursuer wishes to argue that the claim falls within an exception to the normal rules of prescription or limitation the pursuer carries the persuasive burden on that issue, and if facts are specifically averred which, if proved, would bring the case within the exception, the case will be able to proceed to proof.[48] A defender who admits the facts averred by the pursuer, which raise an inference of fault, but meets these with a bare denial of negligence may be found liable by summary decree and thus prevented from putting the pursuer to proof on the issue of negligence.[49]

2.3.2   The burden may also determine which party must first lead evidence at the proof. The question of who should lead at the proof is usually unimportant, apart from the supposed tactical advantage, either of making an initial good impression upon the court in favour of the party who leads, or, in the case of the party who follows, of knowing the strength or weakness of his opponent's case before his own evidence need be led. No difficulty arises in the normal case where the persuasive burden of proof rests upon the pursuer, and where he leads in the proof. There is equally no difficulty in the less usual case where the pursuer's averments, if relevant and sufficient to support his conclusions, are admitted by the defender, in which event the initial burden of proving his defence, whatever it may be, rests upon the latter, and he leads in the proof. But where each party, as disclosed by his own averments, must rebut a presumption in order to succeed, the question may be more difficult, and must depend, failing agreement, upon a comparison of the strengths of the two presumptions.[50] So, for example, the party who must rebut a

---

[47] *Strathclyde Regional Council v WA Fairhurst & Partners* 1997 SLT 658 (OH), *Paterson v Geo Wimpey & Co Ltd* 1999 SLT 584 (OH).

[48] *Strathclyde Regional Council v WA Fairhurst & Partners* 1997 SLT 658.

[49] *Struthers v British Alcan Rolled Products Ltd* 1995 SLT 142 (OH).

[50] As an example of such a case, see *Penman v White* 1957 SC 338 (OH), where the pursuer averred that he gave money on loan, and the defender averred that he received the money as a gift. If the pursuer had been ordained to lead in the proof he would presumably have been restricted to proof by writ or oath of the defender, and might have failed because of this restriction. But the presumption against loan was relatively weak and that against donation was strong. (See Lord Ormidale in *Penney v Aitken* 1927 SC 673 at 679.) The initial burden of proof was, therefore, held to rest upon the defender, who was ordained to lead, the pursuer being allowed a conjunct probation *prout de jure*. It therefore became possible, it would appear, for the pursuer to obtain repayment of the sum sued for without having proved the loan by writ or oath. Proof restricted to reference to oath, or by writ or oath, was abolished by the Requirements of Writing (Scotland) Act 1995, s 11(1) and (2). Accordingly, this precise example would no longer arise, but it gives a clear indication of the effect of conflicting presumptions on burdens of proof. Conflicting presumptions arise more commonly now in relation to parentage, on which see para 28.15.

more special presumption as compared with a general presumption may be ordered to lead.[51] The question of who shall lead, however, is usually decided by the court as a matter of convenience upon a *prima facie* view of the incidence of burdens of proof, and without arriving at a concluded view upon it.[52] If nothing to the contrary is said in an interlocutor issued before the proof, the pursuer must lead.[53] An assessment of the court's probable answer to the question of burden of proof may also have to be made by the parties' counsel or solicitors during the course of the enquiry, with a view to deciding whether, or to what extent, further evidence need be led. At the end of the enquiry it may come into play in order properly to consider the effect of the evidence led upon the decision of the case as a whole.

2.4 PERSUASIVE BURDENS OF PROOF AFFECTING FINAL JUDGMENT

It has been said that "questions of onus usually cease to be important once the evidence is before the court".[54] The court is concerned with the question of burden of proof only if it is unable to come to a definite conclusion on the evidence, or some part of it, and must then decide which party has to suffer as a result.[55] When the truth is clear, the question of who had the duty of making it clear becomes unimportant.[56] When it is not clear, either because there is no evidence, or because the evidence is insufficient in quantity or quality for the purpose, the question of where the persuasive burdens lie must usually be decided before judgment can be given. To decide this the court must look at the substantive law upon which the parties found, the issues raised in their pleadings, and, if necessary, the general propositions detailed above. **2.4.1**

2.5 PERSUASIVE BURDENS OF PROOF AS DISCLOSED BY THE PLEADINGS

When both parties make substantive averments, each must normally bear the burden of proving his own, but the burdens do not arise contemporaneously. The persuasive burden rests upon one of them, and the burden upon the other arises only when that persuasive burden has been discharged.[57] The persuasive burden normally rests upon the pursuer. If a pursuer avers negligence, and the defender avers contributory negligence, the burden resting upon the defender of proving contributory negligence need never be discharged if the pursuer fails to discharge the burden resting upon him. Similarly, if a pursuer sues for payment for work done or for the price of goods sold, he must prove that the work was instructed and performed or that the goods were ordered and delivered before the defender **2.5.1**

---

[51] *Millar v Mitchell* (1860) 22 D 833 at 836. See per Lord Neaves at 847. See also para 3.4 as to the relative strengths of presumptions.

[52] See, for example, *Gibson v Adams* (1875) 3 R 144.

[53] Maclaren, *Court of Session Practice*, p 554; Dobie, *Sheriff Court Practice*, p 182. Macphail, *Sheriff Court Practice* (2nd edn), paras 8.64, 8.65. The defender, of course, may agree to lead.

[54] *Sanderson v McManus* 1997 SC (HL) 55, per Lord Hope at 62G.

[55] *Thomas v Thomas* 1947 SC (HL) 45, per Lord Thankerton at 54.

[56] *Milne v Townsend* (1892) 19 R 830, per Lord Adam at 836, Lord McLaren at 837.

[57] Except when there is a counterclaim in which the defender, who is truly the pursuer, may insist, whether the pursuer in the action succeeds, fails or abandons: RCS, r 25.4(2) OCR, r 19.3(2).

need discharge a burden of proving that the work was defective or the goods disconform to contract. The persuasive burden of proof, however, may rest upon the defender if in his pleadings he has admitted some or all of the pursuer's averments. This occurs when the averments so admitted are held to give rise to a presumption or inference of fact which, if not rebutted, must result in the pursuer's success. If in an action of damages in respect of the negligent driving of a vehicle the defenders were to admit in their pleadings that the pursuer, while a passenger, was thrown from his seat and injured as a result of violent braking, the burden of disproving the negligence of the driver of the vehicle would rest initially upon the defenders.[58] Similarly, if a defender admits in his pleadings that the pursuer performed work on his instructions, or sold and delivered goods to him on his order, the burden of proving that he is not liable to pay for the work or for the goods rests upon him.[59] Even when the pursuer's averments disclose that he must rebut a presumption in order to succeed, the persuasive burden of proof may nevertheless rest upon the defender if his own admissions and averments disclose the existence of a stronger presumption operating against him, as where a pursuer avers that he gave money on loan and the defender avers that he received it as a gift.[60]

2.6 PROVISIONAL BURDENS OF PROOF—GENERAL

2.6.1 The party upon whom the persuasive burden of proof rests may discharge that burden by leading evidence which either proves conclusively the fact or facts necessary for his success or gives rise to a presumption that it exists. In the latter case, if the presumption is rebuttable, a provisional burden of proof falls upon the other party, who must either lead evidence to rebut the presumption against him or fail in the action or issue of fact in question. If in the examples suggested in the last paragraph regarding the motor accident, the performance of work and the sale of goods, the defender does not admit the facts which give rise to the presumption in the pursuer's favour, the initial burden of proof rests upon the pursuer. However, a provisional burden falls upon the defender if the pursuer leads evidence and proves the facts which give rise to such a presumption. When this occurs in the case of the injury to the passenger in the vehicle, the defenders, in order to escape liability, must prove that, despite the violent braking, the driver was not negligent, and, in the cases of the performance of work and the sale of goods, the defender must prove that for some good reason he is not bound to pay for the work which was performed on his instructions, or for the goods which were sold and delivered to him.[61] One method by which a party may satisfy the burden of proof on his own shoulders and lay a provisional burden upon those of his opponent is by leading sufficient evidence to bring into operation a presumption in his favour which is stronger than the presumption initially operating against him or to create an inference that what he avers is true. Provisional burdens of proof upon either

---

[58] See para 2.10.
[59] *Carruthers v Macgregor* 1927 SC 816, per Lord Murray at 822; *cf McIntyre v Clow* (1875) 2 R 278 (where the building collapsed before it was completed and handed over, and the builders bore the burden of proving that at the time of its collapse during a severe gale they had undertaken their work conform to contract).
[60] See para 2.3.2, n 50.
[61] For another example, see *Reilly v Beardmore & Co* 1947 SC 275, per Lord President Cooper at 278, Lord Carmont at 280; *Binnie v Rederij Theodoro BV* 1993 SC 71.

party may arise a number of times during a proof depending upon the state of the evidence.

2.7 PROVISIONAL BURDENS OF PROOF—EXAMPLES IN CONTRACT

A pursuer sued a garage proprietor for damages for the loss of his vehicle which **2.7.1** had been left for repair, and which had been destroyed by fire while in the defender's possession. It was held that the pursuer discharged the burden resting upon him by proving (first) that the contract with the defender included an element of *locatio custodiae* (deposit into the defender's safekeeping) and (secondly) that the defender, as its custodier, had failed to return the vehicle to him. A provisional burden then fell upon the defender to establish by evidence at least a *prima facie*[62] case that the fire which destroyed the vehicle was accidental, in the sense that he was not to blame for it. Had the defender been able to do this a provisional burden would lie with the pursuer to prove, if he could, that the fire had in fact been caused by the defender's negligence. If an owner of cargo proves that it was shipped in good condition and, when delivered, was damaged by sea water, a provisional burden of proof falls upon to the shipowner to prove that the damage occurred without fault. He may discharge this by proving that the ship met with unduly severe weather which led to the cargo damage, whereupon there is a provisional burden on the owner of the cargo to prove that, despite the weather, the damage both to ship and cargo was caused by fault on the part of those in charge of the ship, as, for example, by failing to pack the cargo adequately.[63]

2.8 PROVISIONAL BURDENS OF PROOF—NEGLIGENCE

In actions of damages for loss and injury caused by negligence certain presump- **2.8.1** tions or inferences of fact have been accepted by the courts from time to time as placing a burden on the defender. It may be said in general terms that in such cases the burden on the defender arises when an inference of negligence on his part arises from the circumstances, proved or admitted, in which the accident or injury occurred. When there is a burden on the defender he will normally require to establish the cause of the accident before he can dissociate it from his own negligence.[64] However, unless the burden is a persuasive one, placed on the defender by the substantive law, or admissions in the pleadings, it must be remembered that the persuasive burden lies with the pursuer to prove the case. If, after hearing all of the evidence, the court is not satisfied on the balance of probabilities that the defender was negligent the pursuer will fail. On the other hand, if the evidence led by the pursuer has given rise to a presumption of negligence, and no evidence to the contrary is led by the defender, then the inferences to be drawn from the facts proved by the pursuer are those most favourable to him.[65]

---

[62] *Sinclair v Juner* 1952 SC 35, per Lord Keith at 46–47, 48. See also *Macrae v K & L Ltd* 1962 SLT (Notes) 90 (OH).
[63] *Williams v Dobbie* (1884) 11 R 982.
[64] *The Merchant Prince* [1892] P 179; *Marshall & Son v Russian Oil Products Ltd* 1938 SC 773.
[65] *Binnie v Rederij Theodoro BV* 1993 SC 71, per Lord Hope at 87; *O'Donnell v Murdoch McKenzie & Co* 1967 SC (HL) 63 (following *Ross v Associated Portland Cement Manufacturers* [1964] 1 WLR 768).

2.9 PROVISIONAL BURDENS OF PROOF—EXAMPLES IN NEGLIGENCE

2.9.1   When a pursuer's property was damaged by flooding from a burst water pipe in property owned and occupied by the defender, it was held that a presumption of negligence on the part of the latter arose from the fact that the pipe was 30 years old and had needed repairs on six occasions during the year preceding the burst.[66] When a barrel of petrol exploded and set fire to a pursuer's bakery premises while it was being delivered there on behalf of the defenders, the barrel being the property of and under their control, and there being no evidence that the leakage was caused by negligence in unloading, an inference that the defenders were negligent in failing to provide a suitable barrel was held to arise, the burden of rebutting which fell upon them.[67] In the days of horse-drawn transport it had been held that if a horse left unattended or otherwise uncontrolled, bolted and a pedestrian was injured, there was a presumption of fault against the horseman, the burden of rebutting which rested upon him,[68] but this was thought to need reconsideration,[69] and the whole circumstances must probably be considered before the question of onus can be decided.[70] Cases in the first half of the twentieth century indicate that when a pedestrian in daylight is walking steadily along[71] or across[72] a road and is knocked down by a vehicle in circumstances which would have enabled the driver by slowing down or stopping to avoid the collision, the burden is upon the driver to prove that he was not at fault.[73] Drivers of motor vehicles are now obliged to have due care and attention for other road users,[74] and the provisional burden to show that care and attention was taken will fall upon the driver if evidence of the circumstances of the accident raises the inference that he could have avoided the collision by taking care or paying attention. If a bus swerves on to the pavement and collides with an object there and a passenger is injured, there is *prima facie* evidence of negligent driving which the owners of the bus, as defenders, must rebut.[75] Merely proving that the swerve was caused by the bursting of a tyre will not rebut the inference because that fact is neutral on the question of negligence. They must go further and prove that the bursting of the tyre was not the result of a faulty system of tyre maintenance or otherwise due to their negligence.[76] When a public service

---

[66]   *Moffat & Co v Park* (1877) 5 R 13, per Lord Ormidale at 15, Lord Gifford at 17.

[67]   *Marshall & Son v Russian Oil Products Ltd* 1938 SC 773, per Lord Wark at 810.

[68]   *Gunn v McAdam & Son* 1949 SC 31 at 38, 40.

[69]   *Snee v Durkie* (1903) 6 F 42.

[70]   *Ballantyne v Hamilton* 1938 SN 57; 1938 SLT 468, per Lord Moncrieff at 471; *Hendry v McDougall* 1923 SC 378, per Lord Justice-Clerk Alness at 382, Lord Anderson at 387; *cf* Lord Ormidale at 383, Lord Hunter at 386. Civil liability for animals is now subject to the Animals (Scotland) Act 1987, which creates strict liability in relation to animals which are inherently likely to injure. As to damage caused by an unattended and driverless motor vehicle, see *McCusker v Armstrong* 1946 SN 113.

[71]   *Anderson v Blackwood* (1886) 13 R 443.

[72]   *Clerk v Petrie* (1879) 6 R 1076.

[73]   *Craig v Glasgow Corporation* 1919 SC (HL) 1, per Lord Dunedin at 11 (visibility 100 yards during hours of darkness).

[74]   Road Traffic Act 1988, s 3. Drivers are expected to follow the provisions of the Highway Code (HMSO).

[75]   *Elliot v Young's Bus Service* 1945 SC 445, per Lord Justice-Clerk Cooper at 455; *Barkway v South Wales Transport Co* [1948] 2 All ER 460, per Asquith LJ at 471 (revd on another point [1950] AC 185, the House of Lords insisting upon a more stringent proof of a proper system of tyre maintenance than had been required by the Court of Appeal: see [1950] 1 All ER 392).

[76]   *Elliot v Young's Bus Service* 1945 SC 445; *Barkway v South Wales Transport Co* [1948] 2 All ER 460.

vehicle is driven in such a way that the safety of a passenger is imperilled, the peril occurring raises an inference of negligent driving which the driver's employers must rebut in order to escape liability.[77] This general statement has been applied to the sudden application of the magnetic brake of a tramcar which threw a standing passenger[78] and seated passengers[79] to the floor, the sudden swerving to the right of a bus moving gradually to the left, which threw a passenger from the platform on to the road,[80] and the collision of a bus with a roadside fence.[81] It is thought that in order that the inference of negligence may arise when the injury is caused merely by braking or swerving, the passenger must have been taking normal precautions for his own safety.[82] In actions arising out of collisions at sea there are conventions concerning the responsibility of, for example, an overtaking vessel, or a vessel which collides during daylight with a vessel moored or at anchor.[83]

2.10 RES IPSA LOQUITUR

Res ipsa loquitur ("the thing itself speaks") is a maxim which has sometimes been **2.10.1** construed as meaning that the mere occurrence of an accident infers negligence and places the burden of disproving negligence upon the defender. The mere occurrence of an accident, however, cannot by itself give rise to such an inference,[84] whereas the circumstances of and surrounding its occurrence may do so. The maxim is not a legal principle,[85] but merely a presumption of fact depending upon the circumstances of each case.[86] Whether it applies or not depends upon whether the circumstances of the occurrence are enough to infer negligence.[87] So described, the maxim seems to be indistinguishable from the general statement in the previous

---

[77] In Elliot v Young's Bus Service differing reasons are given for placing the onus of proof upon the defenders: (1) an inference of negligent driving arose because the omnibus mounted the pavement (Lord Justice-Clerk Cooper at 455); (2) the facts regarding the maintenance of their tyres being peculiarly within the knowledge of the defenders (see para 2.2.5), the onus of proof was on them (Lord Mackay at 459); (3) an inference of negligence arose from the fact that the tyre burst (Lord Jamieson at 464–465).

[78] O'Hara v Central SMT Co 1941 SC 363, per Lord President Normand at 375; Sutherland v Glasgow Corporation 1951 SC (HL) 1, per Lord Normand at 7. Cf Ballingall v Glasgow Corporation 1948 SC 160, per Lord Jamieson at 168–169.

[79] Sutherland v Glasgow Corporation 1951 SC (HL) 1.

[80] Mars v Glasgow Corporation 1940 SC 202.

[81] O'Hara v Central SMT Co 1941 SC 363.

[82] Doonan v SMT Co 1950 SC 136; O'Hara v Central SMT Co 1941 SC 363, per Lord Fleming at 384 ("a passenger who was taking due care of her own safety"). It was clearly proved that the pursuer was holding on tightly to the handrail (p 366). In Sutherland v Glasgow Corporation 1951 SC (HL) 1, although the pursuer was standing, it was found in fact (p 2) that the driver knew or ought to have known that she had not had time to take her seat. In Mars v Glasgow Corporation 1940 SC 202, the pursuer was seated. Cf, however, Allan v Western SMT Co 1943 SN 69, where the Lord Chancellor (Viscount Simon) said that, at least in crowded wartime conditions, the driver owed a duty of care to standing passengers who were not "holding on".

[83] Owners of the "Hilda" v Owners of the "Australia" (1884) 12 R 76. See the Merchant Shipping (Distress Signals and Prevention of Collisions) Regulations 1989 (SI 1989/1798, as amended by SI 1991/638) made under the Merchant Shipping Act 1979, ss 21, 22 and 49. These incorporate into British law the International Regulations for the Prevention of Collisions at Sea 1972.

[84] O'Hara v Central SMT Co 1941 SC 363, per Lord Carmont at 391; Alexander v Phillip (1899) 1 F 985.

[85] Ballard v North British Railway Co 1923 SC (HL) 43, per Lord Shaw at 56.

[86] O'Hara v Central SMT Co 1941 SC 363, per Lord President Normand at 377. See also Lord Carmont at 391.

[87] Ballard v North British Railway Co 1923 SC (HL) 43, per Lord Dunedin at 53.

paragraph concerning provisional burdens of proof in cases of negligence. However, it has sometimes been regarded as an exception to it, and the courts have expressed limits to its application.[88] It has been said to apply "where the thing is shown to be under the management of the defendant or his servants, and the accident is such as in the ordinary course of things does not happen if those who have the management use proper care",[89] but to be limited to cases in which a state of apparent stability has been disturbed without the intervention of personal activities which can be spoken to by witnesses,[90] or where the thing which causes the injury is outside human control at the moment of the accident.[91] In effect these limitations simply indicate the situations in which there is likely to be an absence of direct evidence as to why the accident happened, but nevertheless an inference of negligence may be drawn from the known fact of the thing happening as it did. The maxim was held to apply in a case where an explosion occurred and an employee working near the site of the explosion was injured when he jumped to a lower floor. His employers were able to present some possible hypotheses for the explosion occurring (including one which involved a third party) but none was more than a possibility nor more probable than the inference of negligence. The employers were thus unable to rebut the presumption of negligence arising from the occurrence of the explosion on their premises.[92] However, if the facts relied upon by the pursuer initially are equally susceptible of two explanations[93] the evidence is neutral on the question of negligence and the maxim does not come into play at all.[94]

2.11 CRIMINAL CASES—PERSUASIVE BURDENS OF PROOF

2.11.1 Because of the presumption of innocence,[95] the burden of proof of a criminal charge rests upon the Crown throughout the trial.[96] It is for the Crown to prove the

---

[88] In *Elliott v Young's Bus Service* 1945 SC 445, Lord Justice-Clerk Cooper described it as "an overdriven metaphor" to be construed in the narrow sense.

[89] Erle CJ in *Scott v London & St Katherine's Dock Co* (1865) 3 H & C 596 at 601, quoted with approval in *Ballard v North British Railway Co* 1923 SC (HL) 43 at 48, 55, 56, and *Milliken v Glasgow Corporation* 1918 SC 857, per Lord Salvesen at 867. It was still so construed in *Devine v Colvilles* 1969 SC (HL) 67.

[90] *O'Hara v Central SMT Co* 1941 SC 363, per Lord Moncrieff at 388, Lord President Normand at 377.

[91] *Inglis v London, Midland and Scottish Railway Co* 1941 SC 551, per Lord President Normand at 559.

[92] *Devine v Colvilles* 1969 SC (HL) 67. The suggestion by Lord Dunedin in *Ballard v North British Railway Co* 1923 SC (HL) 43 at 54 that in certain circumstances it might be enough for the defender to put forward, apparently without proof, an explanation of the accident other than his own negligence, and then "the cogency of the fact of the accident by itself disappears and the pursuer is left as he began, namely, that he has to show negligence" was not shared by the majority of judges in the case, and has not been taken up in later case law. See *Ballard v North British Railway Co* 1923 SC (HL) 43, per Lord Haldane at 49–51, Lord Finlay at 52, Lord Shaw at 56; Lord Carmont's note on this point in *O'Hara v Central SMT Co* 1941 SC 363 at 393, and his opinion on the whole question at 390–394; Lord Moncrieff in *Mars v Glasgow Corporation* 1940 SC 202 at 209, and Lord Wark in *Marshall & Son v Russian Oil Products Ltd* 1938 SC 773 at 810, 811.

[93] *eg* as in *McQueen v Ballater Golf Club* 1975 SLT 160.

[94] That this is the true position seems to be implicit in the words of Lord Dunedin quoted above. See Lord Carmont in *O'Hara v Central SMT Co* 1940 SC 363 at 393, and Evershed MR in *Moore v R Fox & Sons* [1956] 1 QB 596 at 614.

[95] *Slater v HM Advocate* 1928 JC 94 at 105, *McKenzie v HM Advocate* 1959 JC 32, 1960 SLT 41; *Lambie v HM Advocate* 1973 JC 53, 1973 SLT 219. The presumption is preserved in the European Convention on Human Rights, Art 6(2).

[96] *Lambie v HM Advocate* 1973 JC 53. Also *Lennie v HM Advocate* 1946 JC 79 at 80; *Owens v HM Advocate* 1946 JC 119 at 124, although other aspects of these cases are disapproved in *Lambie*.

accused's guilt beyond reasonable doubt.[97] If at the conclusion of the evidence for *both* parties[98] a reasonable doubt exists in the mind of the jury as to the accused's guilt, he must be acquitted. This persuasive burden never moves from the Crown, and even if the accused is pleading a particular line of defence at common law or under statute the burden upon the Crown remains the same.[99]

The main other persuasive burden arising in a criminal case relates to insanity **2.11.2** or diminished responsibility. At common law there is a presumption of sanity which must be rebutted by the party alleging insanity or diminished responsibility. An accused who so pleads carries from the outset the persuasive burden of proving insanity[100] or diminished responsibility[101] but the standard of proof on such an issue is balance of probabilities.[102] The same is the case if the issue of sanity is raised by the Crown rather than the accused.[103] Normally expert evidence of the condition will be needed to satisfy the burden.[104] If no evidence of condition is led, the issue of sanity or diminished responsibility will not be open for the court to consider. Stature may restrict the facts which the Crown must prove in order for criminal conduct to be inferred, and create a burden of proof on the accused. This is examined in the next paragraph.

2.12 DEFENCE BURDENS

General

Although the persuasive burden of proving guilt beyond reasonable doubt rests **2.12.1** upon the Crown throughout the trial, there are occasions when on certain issues or for certain purposes a burden of proof falls upon the defence. The accused may satisfy the burden by leading evidence from more than one source, but is not required to lead corroborated evidence. Uncorroborated exculpatory evidence, if believed, may be sufficient to raise a reasonable doubt in the court's mind, and thus prevent the Crown from satisfying the persuasive burden of proving the charge.[105] Generally this evidence will take the form of the accused's oral testimony in court but it could be in the form of a statement of the accused made extrajudicially in reply to judicial examination or interrogation and tendered as part of the Crown case.[106] No defence issue is subject to the same high standard of proof which the

---

[97] It has been said that the doubt must not be "a strained or fanciful acceptance of remote possibilities"—*Irving v Minister of Pensions* 1945 SC 21; nor "speculative or academic"—*McKenzie v HM Advocate* 1959 JC 32.

[98] *Lambie v HM Advocate* 1973 JC 53; *Seils v HM Advocate* 1997 JC 176.

[99] *Lambie v HM Advocate* 1973 JC 53; *King v Lees* 1993 JC 19. It is a grave misdirection to suggest that the accused carries a burden of proving innocence: *Tallis v HM Advocate* 1982 SCCR 91.

[100] *HM Advocate v Mitchell* 1951 JC 53.

[101] *HM Advocate v Braithwaite* 1945 JC 55 at 58; *HM Advocate v Savage* 1923 JC 49; *Lindsay v HM Advocate* 1997 SLT 67.

[102] *HM Advocate v Mitchell* 1951 JC 53.

[103] *Jessop v Robertson* 1989 SCCR 600. Note Sheriff Gordon's commentary to the case in which he refers to a "general rule that matters adverse to the accused require to be proved beyond reasonable doubt and those favourable to him only on the balance of probabilities".

[104] *HM Advocate v Kidd* 1960 JC 61 at 68–69; *HM Advocate v Braithwaite* 1945 JC 55.

[105] *Lambie v HM Advocate* 1973 JC 53.

[106] *Lambie v HM Advocate* 1973 JC 53 refers to such evidence emerging as part of the Crown case. In *Ridler v HM Advocate* 1995 SLT 1270 where the accused had made a mixed statement which came out in evidence for the Crown the court had to make clear to the jury that the exculpatory parts of the statement might raise a reasonable doubt (following the requirements of *Morrison v HM Advocate* 1990 JC

Crown must satisfy. An issue raised by the defence need only be proved on a balance of probabilities[107] at most. The suggestion that the accused may have to meet a standard of proof may imply that the accused bears a persuasive burden on defence issues (other than insanity and diminished responsibility discussed above) but, because the requirement upon the accused is only to lead enough evidence for the court to consider the issue,[108] which may be sufficient to raise a reasonable doubt, the burden is in effect only an evidential one.[109] However, assuming that the Crown can lead evidence sufficient to prove the charge, an accused seeking to raise a defence issue should be prepared to produce as much supporting evidence as possible. It will not be necessary for the accused to lead any evidence on defence issues if the Crown fails to make a case to answer. Conversely, if an accused pleads guilty but a proof in mitigation is held, the accused bears the burden of proof on the balance of probabilities in repect of the mitigating factors.

The occasions when, subject to what has been said above, a burden of proof lies with the accused are examined in the following sub-paragraphs.

Special defences

2.12.2   As stated in the previous paragraph an accused who pleads insanity or diminished responsibility carries a persuasive burden of proof on these issues. The other special defences—ie alibi, incrimination and self-defence[110]—are special only in the sense that they must be intimated to the court in advance of a solemn trial commencing.[111] There is not a persuasive burden on the accused to prove them. If the accused has intimated such a defence but there is no evidence at all in support of it the court will withdraw it from consideration.[112] If there is any such evidence before the court (whether through Crown evidence or defence evidence) reasonable doubt may be raised and the Crown will risk failure to prove the case unless evidence is led to negative the defence. If the accused has not intimated such a defence the Crown need not lead evidence to negative it. Akin to these special defences are the pleas of coercion and automatism. Whilst not amounting to a special defence, notice of such a defence must be given in advance of solemn trials,[113] and the defence will only be considered by the court if some evidence is led in respect of the requisite elements of the defence.[114]

---

299). See also *Craddock v HM Advocate* 1994 SLT 454, also reported 1993 SCCR 1087: *sub nom Harrison v HM Advocate*.

[107] *Robertson v Watson* 1949 JC 73, per Lord Justice-General Cooper at 88; *HM Advocate v Mitchell* 1951 JC 53 at 53–54.

[108] *Lambie v HM Advocate* 1973 JC 53; *King v Lees* 1993 SLT 1184.

[109] See the discussions by Gordon, "The Burden of Proof on the Accused" 1968 SLT (News) 29–34, 37–43; Sheldon, "Hip Flasks and Burdens" 1993 SLT (News) 33 and also Dean, "Negative Averments and the Burden of Proof" [1966] CrimLR 594.

[110] The accused must now give notice of the intention to argue coercion or automatism in solemn cases "as if it were a special defence": Criminal Procedure (Scotland) Act 1995, s 78(2).

[111] *Lambie v HM Advocate* 1973 JC 53; Criminal Procedure (Scotland) Act 1995, s 78(1). In summary cases alibi should be intimated before the first witness is sworn: Criminal Procedure (Scotland) Act 1995, s 149.

[112] *Crawford v HM Advocate* 1950 JC 67 (self-defence); *Kennedy v HM Advocate* 1944 JC 171 (diminished responsibility due to drunkenness). The same applies to a substantive ground of mitigation: *Parr v HM Advocate* 1991 JC 39 (provocation).

[113] Criminal Procedure (Scotland) Act 1995, s 78(2).

[114] Because one of the elements required for the defence of automatism is "total alienation of reason" (*Ross v HM Advocate* 1991 JC 210) it has been observed that the defence is unlikely to be established without expert evidence (*Sorley v HM Advocate* 1992 JC 102; followed in *MacLeod v Napier* 1993 SCCR 303) and evidence of the accused (*Carrington v HM Advocate* 1995 SLT 341). If coercion is pled, the elements of the defence are as defined in *Thomson v HM Advocate* 1983 JC 69.

Inference of guilt from proved facts

When the facts proved by the Crown raise an inference[115] of the guilt of the   **2.12.3**
accused person, the accused bears a provisional burden of introducing contradictory facts or explanation. The burden arises purely through the state of the
evidence and if the accused remains silent the court may well draw the inference
least favourable to him.[116] This is more likely to arise where the facts are peculiarly
within the accused's own knowledge.[117] When a man was found at 2 am in a house
with three others, all of whom were fully clothed, and the house contained goods
stolen from premises nearby on that night and the preceding night, there being a
trail of oily footmarks between the two properties, the court was entitled, in the
absence of an explanation from the accused, to find him guilty of breaking into
the premises and stealing the goods.[118] When it was proved, in a charge of fishing
for salmon without permission from the proprietors, that the accused were on the
water at 4.50 am in the possession of gear suitable only for illegal salmon fishing,
it was held that an inference arose that the accused had no permission from the proprietors, and that, since the accused had led no evidence to rebut this inference,
they ought to have been convicted.[119] When an accused charged with using a
motor car without licence and insurance was proved to be the registered keeper of
the vehicle and not to possess licence and insurance, it fell to the accused to lead
evidence that it was no longer a motor car because the main motor mechan-
isms had been removed from it, but he did not require to substantiate this with
corroboration.[120]

Burden placed on accused by statute

Two general statutory provisions have the effect of placing a limited burden of   **2.12.4**
proof upon the accused in certain cases. They are as follows: in relation to a statutory offence any exception, exemption, proviso, excuse or qualification, whether
appearing in the same or another enactment, may be proved by the accused, but
need not be specified or negatived in the complaint and the prosecution is not
required to prove it[121]; and where an offence is alleged to be committed in any
special capacity, as by the holder of a licence, master of a vessel, occupier of a
house or the like, the fact that the accused possesses the qualification necessary to

---

[115] It is acceptable to direct a jury that evidence may raise an "inference of guilt" (as in *Dunn v Normand* 1992 SCCR 209), but the court has frowned upon the expression "presumption of guilt": *McLean v Canning* 1993 SCCR 605.

[116] *HM Advocate v Hardy* 1938 JC 144; *Mochan v Herron* 1972 SLT 218; *McLean v Canning* 1993 SCCR 605; *McNeill v Ritchie* 1967 SLT (Sh Ct) 68; *McIntosh v HM Advocate (No 2)* 1997 SLT 1320.

[117] Dickson, *Evidence* (3rd edn), para 32; *HM Advocate v Hardy* 1938 JC 144 at 147; *Cruickshank v Smith* 1949 JC 134, per Lord Jamieson at 151 *et seq*.

[118] The facts of *Mochan v Herron* 1972 SLT 218. See also *Costello v Macpherson* 1922 JC 9. See also *Dewar v HM Advocate* 1945 JC 5. The provisional burden placed upon the accused as a result of his possession of recently stolen property has been mentioned earlier. See para 3.15.

[119] *Cruikshank v Smith* 1949 JC 134.

[120] *McNeill v Ritchie* 1967 SLT (Sh Ct) 68.

[121] Criminal Procedure (Scotland) Act 1995, Sched 3, para 16. This provision (and its predecessors) have been discussed and applied in, *eg*, *Archibald v Plean Colliery Co* 1924 JC 77; *Chalmers v Speedwell Wire Co* 1942 JC 41; *Din v Adair* 1947 JC 145; *Muir v Grant & Co* 1948 JC 42; *Cruickshank v Smith* 1949 JC 134; *British Transport Commission v Dalgleish* 1955 JC 80; *Wood v Allan* 1988 SLT 341; *Lees v Styles* 1997 SLT (Sh Ct) 11; *MacKenzie v Vannet* 1999 JC 44. In *Earnshaw v HM Advocate* 1982 SLT 179, the same outcome was reached although the statutory provision applying at that time was not founded upon.

the commission of the offence, unless challenged by preliminary objection before his plea is recorded, is held as admitted.[122]

2.12.5   In addition to these general provisions many statutes and statutory instruments create presumptions against the accused arising from basic facts proved by the prosecution and the burden of rebutting the presumption falls upon the accused when those basic facts are proved. For example: in a charge against a parent for failing to ensure a child's attendance at school, a certificate to the effect that the child had not attended is sufficient proof of the crime, and the burden of proving that there is reasonable excuse for the non-attendance lies with the accused[123]; in a charge of failure to comply with a traffic sign it is presumed that the sign in question is of prescribed size, colour and type unless the contrary is proved[124]; in a charge under the Prevention of Corruption Act 1906, if the Crown prove gift or consideration between parties who are in a prescribed relationship[125] the gift or consideration is deemed to have been given corruptly unless the contrary is proved.[126] In order to accord with Article 6 of the European Convention on Human Rights the court has considered how much it is necessary for the prosecutor to prove in order to create a burden for the accused, how readily that burden may be discharged, ie is it persuasive or evidential, and what is the threat faced by society which the provision is there to counter.[127] The assumption created by the Proceeds of Crime (Scotland) Act 1995, s 3(2) require minimal proof by the prosecutor seeking an order for confiscation of proceeds of crime[128] and are open to challenge as contrary to Article 6.

2.12.6   Statute may also provide that the accused may prove specific defences in answer to the case proved against him by the prosecution. Examples are: the defence that controlled drugs found in the possession of the accused were legitimately provided to him on prescription[129]; and that a man who had sexual intercourse with a female aged over 13 and under 16 had reasonable cause to believe that she was 16 or over.[130] Any defence burdens need only be satisfied on the balance of probabilities,[131] and uncorroborated evidence will suffice if believed.[132]

---

[122] Criminal Procedure (Scotland) Act 1995, s 255. This provision has been discussed in *Archibald v Plean Colliery Co* 1924 JC 77; *Shiach v Farquhar* 1929 JC 88; *Smith v Grant* 1932 JC 36; *Smith v Ross* 1937 JC 65; *Wilson v Brown* 1947 JC 81; *Frame v Fyfe* 1948 JC 140; *Ross v Simpson* 1995 SLT 956.

[123] Education (Scotland) Act 1980, ss 35 and 42; *Kennedy v Clark* 1970 JC 144; *Buchanan v Price* 1982 SCCR 534; *Ross v Simpson* 1994 SCCR 847.

[124] Road Traffic Act 1988, s 36(3); *Spiers v Normand* 1995 JC 147.

[125] Prescribed in the Prevention of Corruption Act 1916, s 2.

[126] *Beaton v HM Advocate* 1994 SLT 309.

[127] *R v DPP, ex parte Kebeline & Ors* [1999] 3 WLR 972, per Lord Hope at 999–1000, and *Salabiaku v France* (1988) 13 EHRR 379 to which Lord Hope referred at 997.

[128] See, for example, *Donnelly v HM Advocate* 1999 SCCR 508.

[129] Misuse of Drugs Act Regulations 1985, reg 10(2), as in *Wood v Allan* 1988 SLT 341.

[130] Criminal Law (Consolidation) (Scotland) Act 1995, s 5(5). The defence is only open to offenders aged under 24 who have no previous similar charges.

[131] *Robertson v Watson* 1949 JC 73, per Lord Justice-General Cooper at 88; *HM Advocate v Mitchell* 1951 JC 53 at 53–54; *Neish v Stevenson* 1969 SLT 229, per Lord Justice-Clerk Grant at 231; *HM Advocate v McSalley* 2000 JC 485 (confiscation order where a challenge in terms of Article 6 was unsuccessful).

[132] *King v Lees* 1993 SLT 1184. It is thought that the evidence could be in the form of a mixed statement or replies to judicial examination led by the Crown, although opinion was reserved on this point in *Ridler v HM Advocate* 1995 SCCR 655.

CHAPTER 3

PROOF—PRESUMPTIONS

3.1 PRESUMPTIONS—GENERAL

A presumption has been said to be an inference as to the existence of one fact from **3.1.1** knowledge of the existence of another fact,[1] drawn solely by virtue of previous experience of the ordinary connection between the known and inferred facts, and independent of any process of reasoning in the particular case. It has been said to differ from an inference from circumstantial evidence in that the latter is the result of reason exercised upon the facts of the particular case, or of reason and experience combined.[2] Various classifications of presumptions have been attempted, but none is entirely satisfactory or particularly useful. It is proposed to mention only the threefold classification of presumptions *juris et de jure* (irrebuttable and conclusive presumptions of law), *juris tantum* (rebuttable presumptions of, law), and *hominis vel judicis* (rebuttable presumptions of fact). The irrebuttable presumptions of law are rules of one or other of the branches of substantive law, and as such do not fall within the scope of the law of evidence except in the sense that they exclude evidence. The rebuttable presumptions of law and fact may to a greater or lesser degree take the place of evidence and affect the burden of proof,[3] one of their principal uses being to establish facts which, by their nature, are

---

[1] However, two of the most common presumptions—the presumption of innocence and the presumption of sanity—do not arise from proof of facts at all. They are established principles of law, which determine persuasive burdens of proof, but are rebuttable by proof of facts to the contrary. See para 3.7 and paras 2.11–2.12.

[2] Dickson, *Evidence* (3rd edn), paras 64, 109.

[3] Dickson, *Evidence* (3rd edn), paras 27, 115.

incapable of proof by direct evidence. In criminal cases, presumptions "must be confined within reasonable limits which take into account the importance of what is at stake and the rights of the defence",[4] in order to satisfy ECHR requirements.

3.2 IRREBUTTABLE PRESUMPTIONS OF LAW

3.2.1 Irrebuttable presumptions of law cannot be contradicted by evidence to the contrary, however strong.[5] In most cases they are rules of the branches of the substantive law to which they relate rather than of the law of evidence. In some cases they resemble fictions of law,[6] and they arise both from statute and from the common law. They are sometimes based on a reasonable inference from the established facts, but frequently arise only from considerations of public policy.[7] If a statute provides that A "shall be deemed to be B", the court may not hold that A is not in fact B, but is bound by the irrebuttable statutory presumption.[8] The following are a few examples:

> (a) *Prescription*: that a right is satisfied or abandoned if the creditor has abstained from its enforcement for the relevant period of negative prescription[9]; that if there has been possession of heritage for 10 years on a habile title, the earlier title is in order through positive prescription[10];
>
> (b) *Age*: that a person of 16 years of age has capacity to enter into contracts, but has the capacity to make a will at the age of 12[11]; that a child under eight years of age is incapable of committing a crime or offence,[12] that a girl under 16 years of age is not capable of consenting to sexual intercourse,[13] that a person under 16 years of age is not capable of consenting to marriage[14];
>
> (c) *Parentage after assisted reproduction or adoption*: that the husband of a woman who has become pregnant as a result of assisted reproductive techniques involving sperm from a donor other than the husband, is the father of the child,[15] and the woman who carries a child during gestation

---

[4]   *Salabiaku v France* (1991) 13 EHRR 379.

[5]   Stair, iv, 45, 14; Erskine, iv, 2, 35.

[6]   For the distinction between them, see Erskine, iv, 2, 38.

[7]   Dickson, *Evidence* (3rd edn), para 111.

[8]   *Ferguson v Macmillan* 1954 JC 38, per Lord Justice-General Cooper at 44.

[9]   Bell, *Principles*, para 606; now Prescription and Limitation (Scotland) Act 1973, ss 6 and 7.

[10] Bell, *Principles*, para 606; now Prescription and Limitation (Scotland) Act 1973, s 1.

[11] Age of Legal Capacity (Scotland) Act 1991, ss 1 and 2. A child may be considered capable of consent to certain other contracts below the age of 16 but that is a matter for proof. At common law a boy under 14 and a girl under 12 were deemed to be incapable of giving consent to form a legally binding contract: Stair, i, 10, 13; Erskine, iii, 1, 16.

[12] Criminal Procedure (Scotland) Act 1995, s 41. The common law rule is that no child under seven years of age may be punished of crime: Hume, i, 35; Alison, i, 666. A boy of less than 14 years of age has been convicted of rape: *Lord Advocate v Fulton* (1841) 2 Swin 564.

[13] At common law a girl under 12 cannot give such consent (Hume, i, 303) and intercourse with a girl under 12 is rape, but under the Criminal Law (Consolidation) (Scotland) Act 1995 (as amended by the Crime and Punishment (Scotland) Act 1997, ss 2–6), it is an offence to have intercourse with a girl under 13 (s 5(1)) or under 16 (s 5(3)) regardless of apparent consent from the girl.

[14] Marriage (Scotland) Act 1977, s 1.

[15] Human Fertilisation and Embryology Act 1990, s 28(2). A male partner of a woman who is not married may be deemed to be the father if the pregnancy arose from treatment provided to them together by a person licensed in terms of the Act: s 28(3).

after assisted reproduction involving a donated egg or embryo is the mother for all purposes[16]; that a child, once adopted, is the legitimate child of the adopter[17]; and

(d) *Road traffic control*: that for the purposes of proof of failure to comply with a traffic sign at or near a road, the sign is of the prescribed size, colour and type authorised by the responsible Minister and placed lawfully.[18]

3.3 REBUTTABLE PRESUMPTIONS OF LAW OR FACT

A presumption of law differs[19] from a presumption of fact in that the former **3.3.1** has been recognised as such by statute, custom or judicial decision.[20] Unless it has been so recognised it is a presumption of fact only.[21] In general the fact or facts (sometimes termed the "basic facts") which bring a presumption of law into existence are well-defined, easily ascertainable and of general occurrence. When the defined basic facts are proved a presumption will arise, although it may be rebutted by evidence to the contrary. Some are of ancient origin, whilst others are recent creations to address situations in which it has been considered desirable to ease proof of a particular issue.[22] Hence the legislature has introduced legal presumptions facilitating proof: (a) of joint ownership of property acquired during marriage[23] and equal sharing of matrimonial property on divorce[24]; (b) that a dog is of the breed asserted by the prosecutor in proceedings taken under the Dangerous Dogs Act 1991[25]; (c) that where an accused is libelled with committing an offence in a special capacity, such as a licence-holder, master of vessel, occupier of property, prostitute, or person on bail conditions, the accused had that capacity at the date of the crime[26]; (d) that a document which appears to contain all the express terms of a contract or unilateral voluntary obligation does contain all express terms[27]; and (e) that prior judicial findings of criminal or adulterous conduct will be sufficient evidence of the existence of that conduct for the purposes of later proceedings in which the conduct is a relevant issue.[28]

---

[16] Human Fertilisation and Embryology Act 1990, s 29(1). For an excellent discussion of these provisions and their impact on legitimacy and rebuttable presumptions affecting parentage, see Wilkinson & Norrie, *The Law Relating to Parent and Child in Scotland* (2nd edn), paras 3.01–3.44.

[17] Adoption (Scotland) Act 1978, s 39.

[18] Road Traffic Act 1988, s 36(3) and see *Spiers v Normand* 1995 JC 147.

[19] For a discussion of the difference, see *Millar v Mitchell, Cadell & Co* (1860) 22 D 833 at 844–845.

[20] Erskine, iv, 2, 37. For an example of the creation of such a presumption by judicial decision, see *G's Trs v G* 1936 SC 837 (court of seven judges).

[21] *Millar v Mitchell, Cadell & Co* (1860) 22 D 833 at 844–845.

[22] And to ease proof of uncontroversial facts, as in Criminal Procedure (Scotland) Act 1995, s 258. See also paras 5.5.1, 19.16.

[23] Family Law (Scotland) Act 1985, s 25(1). This assists in determining division between the spouses if the marriage ends, but also in proceedings for diligence against a spouse by a third party—*eg Christie v Tayside Regional Council* 1991 SCLR 258; *Kinloch v Barclays Bank Plc* 1995 SCLR 975.

[24] Family Law (Scotland) Act 1985, s 9(1)(a) and *eg Jacques v Jacques* 1997 SC (HL) 20.

[25] Dangerous Dogs Act 1991, s 5(5).

[26] Criminal Procedure (Scotland) Act 1995, s 255 and see para 3.17. For detailed examination of the application of this presumption, see Renton & Brown, *Criminal Procedure* (6th edn), paras 24-104–24-107/1.

[27] Contract (Scotland) Act 1997, s 1(1). An irrebuttable or conclusive presumption may be invoked by including in the document a clause to the effect that it comprises all the express terms: s 1(3).

[28] Law Reform (Miscellaneous Provisions)(Scotland) Act 1968, ss 10 and 11. Section 12 contains a further presumption arising from criminal convictions which are founded upon for limited purposes in defamation proceedings but that presumption is conclusive, not rebuttable.

3.3.2   The court has, in general, steered away from creating new presumptions, whilst adhering to those which are long recognised.[29] For example, the court refused to acknowledge a presumption of fact or law to the effect that a child should have contact with a parent,[30] or that a mother is presumptively preferable to father as primary carer for a very young child.[31] Also, the court refused to acknowledge that there would be any presumption that if traffic lights were working properly to one effect in one direction they were at the same time working properly and with contrary effect in the other direction.[32] More significantly, the House of Lords, in a Scottish case concerning misrepresentation by a husband in inducing his wife to grant security for his business debts, had to consider whether to adopt into Scots law a presumption of constructive notice on the part of a bank creditor of potential undue influence in such a situation, which presumption had been acknowledged a short time before in an English case.[33] The House of Lords accepted that the principle that a creditor should be on guard in such a situation was one which should apply in Scotland as well as in England, but formulated this as a principle of good faith in contract rather than as a presumption.[34]

3.3.3   Presumptions of fact, on the other hand, emerge, if they emerge at all, only after consideration of the particular circumstances of each case,[35] and are frequently difficult to distinguish from the inference drawn from circumstantial evidence.[36] Judicial recognition of a presumption of fact in one case is a precedent for its subsequent recognition in another case only where the circumstances are identical or closely analogous. An example of this distinction between the two types of presumption may be seen by comparing the presumption that (subject to certain exceptions) a woman of 53 years of age is incapable of childbearing,[37] which is a presumption of law, with the presumption of unseaworthiness when a ship breaks down or sinks soon after commencing its voyage, which is a presumption of fact.[38] The presumption regarding childbearing inevitably arises as soon as the basic fact of age of the woman has been proved or admitted. The presumption of unseaworthiness emerges only if it is justified by the whole circumstances, proved or admitted, of the particular case.

---

[29]   These are considered in paras 3.5–3.16. For example, in *Lindsay v HM Advocate* 1997 SLT 67 the court refused to interfere with the presumption of sanity and its effect in placing an onus on the accused to prove diminished responsibility on the balance of probabilities. The court stressed that any reform of a long line of authority on this point was for Parliament and not the court: per Lord Justice-General Hope at 73.

[30]   *Sanderson v McManus* 1997 SC (HL) 55 at 63F–64A.

[31]   *Brixey v Lynas* 1994 SC 606 at 609D–E.

[32]   *Inwar v Normand* 1997 SCCR 6. *Cf Pacitti v Copeland* 1963 SLT (Notes) 52.

[33]   *Barclays Bank Plc v O'Brien* [1994] 1 AC 180.

[34]   *Smith v Bank of Scotland* 1997 SC (HL) 111, per Lord Clyde at 119–122; and Lord Jauncey of Tullychettle, at 115, *dubitante* as to the desirability of introducing presumptions where none existed before, although he accepted that there would be cases in which an inference might be drawn from the facts without difficulty.

[35]   Erskine, iv, 2, 37.

[36]   *Millar v Mitchell, Cadell & Co* (1860) 22 D 833 at 844. An inference which is not sufficiently strong to place upon the party adversely affected by it the burden of displacing it, ought not to be regarded as a presumption but merely as an item of circumstantial evidence. As to circumstantial evidence, see Chapter 6.

[37]   *G's Trs v G* 1936 SC 837.

[38]   For examples of the many facts which may have to be considered before the presumption arises, see Lord Shaw in *Klein v Lindsay* 1911 SC (HL) 9 at 14–15. For a recent unsuccessful attempt to rely on the presumption, see *Stephen v Scottish Boatowners Mutual Insurance Association ("The Talisman")* 1986 SLT 234.

3.4 EFFECT OF REBUTTABLE PRESUMPTIONS ON EVIDENCE AND PROOF

Rebuttable presumptions vary in strength, but can be conclusive in the absence of contradiction.[39] It follows from this that the onus of rebutting such a presumption is on the party who wishes to contradict it, and this may generally be done either by disproving the existence of the presumed fact or by proving facts from which a stronger contrary presumption arises. The strength or weakness of a presumption is important only if there is such contrary evidence or contrary presumption. A presumption of law is not necessarily stronger than a presumption of fact. The presumption of innocence, for example, which is a presumption of law, is displaced in the courts as a matter of everyday occurrence, by presumptions of fact and by circumstantial evidence.[40] However, a general presumption is weaker than, and will be displaced by, a special presumption arising from the facts of the particular case.[41] So the general presumption in favour of seaworthiness[42] may be displaced by a special presumption of unseaworthiness arising from the fact that the ship in question foundered at the commencement of the voyage, the general presumption in favour of sanity by the special presumption arising from the appointment on the ground of insanity of a *curator bonis* to the estate of the person concerned,[43] and the general presumption of innocence by the special presumption of guilt of theft arising from the accused's possession of recently stolen property in criminative circumstances.[44] **3.4.1**

Each branch of substantive law has its own associated group of presumptions, and the statute law in that area of substantive law, together with case authority, should be checked for presumptions, as should textbooks on these subjects. To provide a complete list of presumptions in a book on the law of evidence is neither possible nor particularly helpful. However, an attempt has been made in the following paragraphs of this chapter to indicate some of the main groups of rebuttable presumptions, with examples in each group of the leading presumptions, and of the contrary presumptions where they exist. Reference may also be made to the examples of circumstantial evidence[45] through which inferences of fact have been drawn which have been held to have the same effect as presumptions in discharging or the burden of proof. The standard of proof required for the rebuttal of presumptions, other than the presumption of innocence,[46] is balance of probabilities at the highest.[47] **3.4.2**

---

[39] Erskine, iv, 2, 36, 37; Dickson, *Evidence* (3rd edn), para 112. For recent examples see *Kinloch v Barclay's Bank* 1995 SCLR 975; *MacDonald of Keppoch Petitioner (No 2)* 1994 SLT (Lyon Ct) 2; *Neilson v Stewart* 1991 SC (HL) 212; *Inverness District Council v Highland Universal Fabrications Ltd* 1986 SLT 556.

[40] Dickson, *Evidence* (3rd edn), para 112; *Campbell v Campbell* (1866) 4 M 867, per Lord Ardmillan at 988.

[41] *Millar v Mitchell, Cadell & Co* (1860) 22 D 833, per Lord Neaves at 847. It is thought that this rule in practice will solve most questions arising from the relative strengths of presumptions. It does not assist in the rare case where a conflict between two general presumptions arises from the pleadings to determine the question of who must lead in the proof.

[42] *Klein v Lindsay* 1911 SC (HL) 9, per Lord Shaw at 14–15.

[43] See para 3.5.

[44] See para 3.16.

[45] See paras 2.6–2.9 (civil causes), para 2.12 (criminal causes).

[46] Which the prosecutor must displace beyond reasonable doubt: see paras 3.5 and 4.2.

[47] See the observations of Lord President Hope in *Ward v Chief Constable, Strathclyde Police* 1991 SLT 292. Standard of proof is dealt with in Chapter 4.

3.5 PRESUMPTIONS AS TO PHYSICAL AND MENTAL POWERS OF A HUMAN BEING

General

3.5.1 There is a general presumption that the ordinary course of nature has run, and that human beings possess ordinary powers and faculties both physical and mental.[48]

Duration of life

3.5.2 There is a presumption that human life extends for a period of between eighty and one hundred years.[49] Statutory provision is made for restricting the effect of this presumption by petition to the court after a person has not been known to be alive for seven years.[50] The petition may be taken by any person having an interest, which is usually a family member wishing to proceed to wind up an estate or effect dissolution of marriage.[51] When two or more persons die as a result of a common calamity there is, in the absence of evidence as to who died last,[52] a presumption that the younger or youngest survived longer, unless the victims are husband and wife or the elder had made testamentary provision for the younger who was intestate.[53]

Begetting and bearing of children

3.5.3 Men are presumed to be capable of begetting children between puberty and old age although the degree of improbability increases with age.[54] With regard to childbearing, the law appears to be that there is no age at which a woman is presumed incapable of giving birth to a child, where interests other than those of possible unborn children are affected.[55] However, according to a seven-judge decision from 1953, where no such interests are affected, there is a presumption of law that a woman who has attained 53 years of age is incapable of bearing children.[56] Evidence to the contrary may be led more easily now that biological evidence is more sophisticated and genetic links may be established by DNA profiling.[57]

---

[48] Dickson, *Evidence* (3rd edn), para 114(1). This was applied in the recent case of *Patterson v HM Advocate* 2000 JC 137, in establishing the competence of an adult witness (now deceased) whose hearsay evidence was to be led under the Criminal Procedure (Scotland) Act 1995, s 259.

[49] *Secretary of State for Scotland v Sutherland* 1944 SC 79, per Lord President Normand at 84, Lord Moncrieff at 85; Dickson, *Evidence* (3rd edn), para 116. For circumstances sufficient to rebut the presumption, see *Greig v Merchant Company of Edinburgh* 1921 SC 76; *X v Society of Solicitors in Supreme Courts of Scotland* 1937 SLT 87, and authorities cited in Dickson. This presumption is a manifestation of the general presumption supporting the continuance of an existing condition, examined at para 3.8.

[50] Presumption of Death (Scotland) Act 1977, s 1.

[51] Presumption of Death (Scotland) Act 1977, s 1.

[52] Examined in *Lamb v HM Advocate* 1976 SLT 151.

[53] Succession (Scotland) Act 1964, s 31.

[54] Dickson, *Evidence* (3rd edn), para 114(1). *Munro's Trs v Monson* 1965 SLT 314, applying *G's Trs v G* 1936 SC 837 in which there was held to be a high degree of improbability of issue in men aged 81 and 76.

[55] *G's Trs v G* 1936 SC 837 (seven judges), per Lord President Normand at 844, Lord Justice-Clerk Aitchison at 849; *Rackstraw v Douglas* 1917 SC 284; *Inland Revenue v Bone* 1927 SC 698.

[56] *G's Trs v G* 1936 SC 837.

[57] However, the evidence of genetic link may not be conclusive of parentage if a deeming provision as to maternity applies under the Human Fertilisation and Embryology Act 1990, s 29(1), which would make a surrogate mother the mother for all purposes, even if a genetic link with an egg donor could be proved. For presumptions as to parentage, see para 3.7 and on proof of parentage, see para 28.15. On the general effect of deeming provisions, see para 3.2. For a detailed examination of conflicts of presumptions and deeming provisions in this context, see Wilkinson & Norrie, *The Law Relating to Parent and Child in Scotland*, paras 3.01–3.12.

Sanity

A person is presumed to be sane.[58] There has been a contrary factual presumption **3.5.4** that a person to whom a tutor-at-law[59] or *curator bonis* has been appointed in respect of unsoundness of mind is insane. However, proof of mental disorder for the purposes of mental health legislation would not of itself invoke a presumption of insanity in the broader sense, nor of continuing mental disorder.

3.6 PRESUMPTIONS SUPPORTING REGULARITY AND VALIDITY

General

The general presumption is *omnia rite et solemniter acta praesumuntur* (that **3.6.1** everything is done validly and in accordance with the necessary formalities).[60] This presumption carries particular weight when it is sought to disturb an earlier transaction after a long period of time. When this occurs "every intendment should be made in favour of what has been done as being lawfully and properly done."[61]

Judicial and official actings

There is a presumption that a person purporting to act in a public capacity has auth- **3.6.2** ority to do so. This presumption has been applied to a procurator fiscal,[62] police officers[63] and other officials.[64]

Acts of administrative and public bodies

There is a presumption, when a course of procedure has followed upon the public **3.6.3** act of an administrative body, that the act, and the formalities associated with it, were legally and regularly performed.[65] So for example, when an offence was allegedly committed on a motorway it was presumed that by its designation "M9" the road had in force in relation to it all orders necessary to establish its motorway status.[66]

---

[58] Bell, *Principles*, para 2103; Dickson, *Evidence* (3rd edn), paras 27, 114(1); *HM Advocate v Mitchell* 1951 JC 53. See also *HM Advocate v Braithwaite* 1945 JC 55; *HM Advocate v Lindsay* 1997 SLT 67.

[59] *Dick v Douglas* 1924 SC 787 provides an example of such an appointment.

[60] Dickson, *Evidence* (3rd edn), para 114(4).

[61] *Bain v Assets Co* (1905) 7 F (HL) 104, per Lord Chancellor Halsbury at 106.

[62] *Hill v Finlayson* (1883) 10 R (J) 66.

[63] Who are presumed to act not only with authority but in good faith and without malice: *Beaton v Ivory* (1887) 14 R 1057, followed in *Robertson v Keith* 1936 SC 29 (a court of seven judges) and *Ward v Chief Constable, Strathclyde Police* 1991 SLT 292.

[64] *McAlpine v Campbell* (1840) 2 D 481 (schoolmaster); *McLeod* (1858) 3 Irv 79 (postmaster); *Smith and Milne* (1859) 3 Irv 506 (water bailiff); *Borthwick v Lord Advocate* (1862) 1 M 94 (revenue officer); *Marr v Procurator Fiscal of Midlothian* (1881) 8 R (J) 21 (temporary member of the shrieval bench). In connection with revenue officials there are statutory presumptions to the same effect, founding upon the Inland Revenue Regulation Act 1890, s 24(3).

[65] *Presbytery of Stirling v Heritors of Larbert and Dunipace* (1902) 4 F 1048 (statutory commissioners); *Scott v Mags Of Dunoon* 1909 SC 1093 (local authority); *Hamilton v Fyfe* 1907 SC (J) 79 (statutory order by local authority); *McCallum v Brown* 2000 JC 6 (local authority byelaw). In criminal cases there is a statutory provision to this effect: Criminal Procedure (Scotland) Act 1995, s 279A(3) and (4); and see, for example, *Donaldson v Valentine* 1996 SLT 643.

[66] *Donaldson v Valentine* 1996 SLT 643.

Land tenure

3.6.4 There is a presumption that a building which has existed for a long time was originally constructed in conformity with the titles.[67] There is also a presumption in
favour of freedom *(praesumptio pro libertate)* so feuing conditions, if unclear, are
considered invalid or presumed to have the most liberal effect.[68] There is a presumption that a lease will continue after ish by tacit relocation, rebuttable by proof
of notice in proper form, or, exceptionally, other proof that the tenant knew that
the lease was at an end[69]; that an owner should benefit from occupation by
another[70]; that a danger arising from physical features of land is an obvious and
usual danger[71]; and that ownership and entitlement to the value of timber arises
presumptively in crofting tenure.[72]

Judicial records and other documents

3.6.5 It is presumed that the decrees or other acts recorded in old judicial records were
validly and properly pronounced or performed.[73] When a deed bears to have been
executed in accordance with the statutory solemnities, it is presumed that these
solemnities have been complied with, and that the apparent granter of it has subscribed it.[74] If reference is made in a document to an alteration to it having been
made before signature it is assumed that the alteration forms part of the document
subscribed by the granter.[75] If the terms of a lost deed are proved by secondary evidence, the original deed is presumed to have been duly stamped,[76] and when a deed
bears traces of having been stamped there appears to be a presumption that the
stamp was for the correct amount.[77] Prior to the enactment of the Requirements of
Writing (Scotland) Act 1995 the following documents were afforded special status
and were presumed to have been executed on the dates which they bear: holograph
testamentary writings,[78] bills of exchange and acceptances or endorsements
thereon,[79] and, at least for ordinary commercial purposes, other mercantile documents.[80] However, the special rules applying to these documents are abolished by

---

[67] *Sutherland v Barbour* (1887) 15 R 62.
[68] *Stair Memorial Encyclopaedia*, Vol 18, para 415. It has been said that the presumption in favour of
freedom is applied less strictly in the context of servitudes as compared to burdens: Cusine & Paisley,
Servitudes, paras 12.182, 15.06. For examples of the presumption, see *Alvis v Harrison* 1991 SLT 64;
Heritage Fisheries Ltd v Duke of Roxburghe 2000 SLT 800.
[69] See *Stair Memorial Encyclopaedia*, Vol 13, paras 450–460 and *eg Signet Group plc v C & J Clark
Retail Properties Ltd* 1996 SC 444.
[70] Stewart, *The Law of Restitution in Scotland*, p 41, approved in *Rochester Poster Services v AG Barr
plc* 1994 SLT (Sh Ct) 2.
[71] For an example of successful rebuttal, see *Duff v East Dunbartonshire Council* 1999 GWD 22-1072.
[72] See, for example, *Sutherland v MacKenzie* 1999 SLT (Land Ct) 2.
[73] *Duke of Atholle v Lord Advocate* (1880) 7 R 583 at 589. See also *Heritors of Old Machar v The
Ministers* (1870) 8 M (HL) 168 at 169.
[74] The formalities now required and the presumption as it now applies (in statutory form from 1 August
1995) are contained in the Requirements of Writing (Scotland) Act 1995, s 3: see Chapter 22. For the
common law presumption in use, see *Brown v Duncan* (1888) 15 R 511; *Ferrie v Ferrie's Trs* (1863)
1 M 291 at 298; *Baird's Trs v Murray* (1883) 11 R 153 at 161–162, 164; *Young v Paton* 1910 SC 63.
This is dealt with more fully in Chapter 23.
[75] Requirements of Writing (Scotland) Act 1995, s 5.
[76] See para 21.12.1.
[77] See para 21.12.1.
[78] Conveyancing (Scotland) Act 1874, s 40.
[79] Bills of Exchange Act 1882, s 13(1).
[80] On commercial writings, see Chapter 24.

the 1995 Act[81] and, if the obligation is committed to writing, the writing is subject to the general statutory presumption in favour of validity of a document.[82]

Business books, office administration and execution of service or notices

Business books, if they appear to have been regularly kept, are presumed to be **3.6.6** accurate.[83] When the regular practice of a business with regard to the dispatching of letters has been proved, it is presumed that a particular letter was dispatched in the usual way.[84] There is a presumption that arises on proof that a citation has been properly sent, to the effect that it has been received.[85]

Regular marriages

The general presumption applies to the validity of a regular marriage, which is **3.6.7** proved to have been duly solemnised and registered,[86] so that the onus of proof rests upon the person challenging the marriage to establish its nullity.[87] There is an exception to this rule when the pursuer admits a fact, such as, for example, his own prior marriage, which itself establishes that the marriage on which he founds was a nullity, or from which its nullity must be presumed.[88] In contrast with an irregular marriage, where the person alleging the marriage must prove the matrimonial intention of the parties, the solemnisation of a regular marriage gives rise to a presumption that marriage was truly intended by the parties to the ceremony.[89] The view has been expressed that this presumption may be rebutted by proof that both parties took part in the ceremony without a real intention to marry,[90] and proof before answer of such averments has been allowed,[91] but there appears to be no case in Scotland where a regular marriage was annulled for this reason.[92]

---

[81] s 11(3).

[82] Requirements of Writing (Scotland) Act 1995, s 2, and see para 22.3–22.8.

[83] Erskine, iv, 2, 4; Dickson, *Evidence* (3rd edn), para 114 (2). See also *McLaren v Liddell's Trs* (1862) 24 D 577. Business documents are subject to special rules regarding admissibility and authentication: see Criminal Procedure (Scotland) Act 1995, Sched 8, Civil Evidence (Scotland) Act 1988, s 5 and see Chapter 21.

[84] Dickson, *Evidence* (3rd edn), para 28, 114(2), 304; *Robertson v Gamack* (1835) 14 S 139; *Stock v Aitken* (1846) 9 D 75; *Mackenzie v Dott* (1861) 23 D 1310. For an example in relation to notice in terms of a contract, see *Chaplin v Caledonian Land Properties Ltd* 1997 SLT 384.

[85] Erskine, iv, 2, 5; Citation Amendment (Scotland) Act 1882, ss 3 and 4; Interpretation Act 1978, s 7, Criminal Procedure (Scotland) Act 1995, s 66(3) (solemn) and s 141(7) (summary). For an interesting examination of the requirements for citation and the presumption in effect, see *Blackfriars (Scotland) Ltd v John Laurie* 2000 SCLR 385.

[86] *Burke v Burke* 1983 SLT 331.

[87] See, for example, *CB v AB* (1885) 12 R (HL) 36; *Hooper v Hooper* [1959] 1 WLR 1021.

[88] *Sharp v Sharp* (1898) 25 R 1132; *McDonald v McDonald* 1924 SLT 200 (OH).

[89] *Jolly v McGregor* (1828) 3 W&S 85, per Earl of Lauderdale at 179; *Lockyer v Sinclair* (1846) 8 D 582, per Lord Justice-Clerk Hope at 602; *Robertson v Steuart* (1874) 1 R 532, per Lord Deas at 667; *Lang v Lang* 1921 SC 44, per Lord Justice-Clerk Scott Dickson at 54.

[90] Fraser, *Husband and Wife*, I, 434–436; Walton, *Husband and Wife* (3rd edn), p 38. Lord Eldon in *Jolly v McGregor* (1828) 3 W&S 85 at 190 preferred to express no opinion on the point.

[91] *Orlandi v Castelli* 1961 SC 113 (OH).

[92] *Jolly v McGregor* (1828) 3 W&S 85, which was mentioned in Fraser, *Husband and Wife*, I, 431, 436 as the only example in Scotland, seems not in fact to have been an example, because it was decided by the House of Lords on the footing that the marriage was irregular, the certificate of proclamation of banns being manifestly false: see Earl of Lauderdale at 179, Earl of Eldon at 195, Lord Chancellor Lyndhurst at 202. See, however, *Orlandi v Castelli* 1961 SC 113 (OH). It seems clear that the validity of a regular marriage cannot be disturbed by proof that only one of the parties behaved in this way: Fraser, *Husband and Wife*, I, 436. See also Clive, *The Law of Husband and Wife in Scotland* (4th edn, 1997) para 05.006.

Irregular marriages

3.6.8 Marriages constituted by declaration *de praesenti copula* and promise *subsequente copula* were possible only before 1 July 1940 and, if registered on the warrant of a sheriff following a judicial enquiry,[93] or after a decree of declarator by the Court of Session establishing the marriage,[94] were presumed valid as in the case of a regular marriage. In the unlikely event that such a marriage is challenged nowadays, the onus of proof would rest upon the challenger.[95] However, if the marriage had not been registered, the person who desired to establish it would have to prove that all the essentials of a valid marriage were present[96] in the proceedings to which the proof of the marriage is incidental. In contrast with a regular marriage, where the genuineness of the intention to marry is presumed, the genuineness of the apparent interchange of consent in an irregular marriage must be proved in addition to the fact of consent. Such proof must usually be founded upon an inference from the terms and the circumstances in which consent was apparently interchanged, or from the actings of the parties before and after the alleged marriage, or from both.[97] Irregular marriage after 1940 may still be established by evidence of cohabitation and repute. This form of marriage is constituted neither by the cohabitation of the man and woman, nor by the fact that they hold themselves out, and are habitually regarded, as husband and wife, but by the tacit interchange of consent to marry which is presumed from these facts.[98] The presumption of consent arising from the proof of cohabitation and repute may be rebutted, for example by evidence that there was reluctance to marry at some stage during the cohabitation, and later discussion of marrying in the future.[99]

Contract

3.6.9 There is a presumption in favour of freedom of contract,[100] and against delegation of contractual obligations.[101] It is also presumed that a written contract which bears to contain all express terms of the contract between the parties does contain all of those terms.[102] A party to a contract founding upon an oral warranty must prove by satisfactory evidence the very words spoken.[103] There is a presumption of

---

[93] Under the Marriage (Scotland) Act 1916 (now repealed). As to the enquiry before the sheriff, and its purpose, see *Courtin v Elder* 1930 SC 68, per Lord Ormidale at 75, Lord Anderson at 76.

[94] Such a decree had to be intimated to the Registrar-General by the Principal Clerk of Session in order that the marriage might be registered: Marriage (Scotland) Act 1939, s 6 (now repealed).

[95] See, for example, *Polack v Shiels* 1912 2 SLT 329 (OH).

[96] *Reid v HM Advocate* 1934 JC 7; *Turnbull v Wilsons and Clyde Coal Co Ltd* 1935 SC 580.

[97] *Fleming v Corbet* (1859) 21 D 1034, per Lord Justice-Clerk Inglis at 1044; *Imrie v Imrie* (1891) 19 R 185; *Dunn v Dunn's Trs* 1930 SC 131, per Lord Sands at 146, Lord Blackburn at 151–152, Lord Morison at 159.

[98] *Campbell v Campbell* (1867) 5 M (HL) 115 at 135, 140; *De Thoren v Wall* (1876) 3 R (HL) 28 at 29, 33; *Lapsley v Grierson* (1845) 8 D 34, per Lord Justice-Clerk Hope at 47; *Nicol v Bell* 1954 SLT 314, per Lord Mackintosh at 326; *AB v CD* 1957 SC 415 (OH). Recent examples are *Vosilius v Vosilius* 2000 SCLR 679 (in which the presumption of tacit consent prevailed) and *Walker v Roberts* 1998 SLT 1133 (in which the presumption was rebutted by other evidence). See also Clive, *The Law of Husband and Wife in Scotland* (4th edn), para 05.038.

[99] The example is *Walker v Roberts* 1998 SLT 1133.

[100] Mentioned in *Quantum Claims Compensation Specialists Ltd v Powell* 1998 SC 316.

[101] eg *Harte Construction v Scottish Homes Ltd* 1992 SLT 948.

[102] Contract (Scotland) Act 1997, s 1(1). An irrebuttable or conclusive presumption may be invoked by including in the document a clause to the effect that it comprises all the express terms: s 1(3). On proof of contract, see Chapter 24.

[103] *Robeson v Waugh* (1874) 2 R 63; *Mackie v Riddell* (1874) 2 R 115.

interdependence of contracts when two or more properties are conveyed in one disposition following upon one set of missives, but the terms of the missives may themselves indicate that there are two distinct transactions.[104]

3.7 PRESUMPTIONS SUPPORTING INNOCENCE, MORALITY AND PROPRIETY[105]

There are presumptions favouring innocence of crime[106] and innocence of adul- **3.7.1** tery.[107] There are presumptions in support of paternity,[108] under statute arising from marriage to the mother at any time in the period beginning with conception and ending with the birth of the child,[109] and, should the former not apply, arising from the acknowledgement by both the mother and a man that the man is the father, and registration of that man as the father in the birth register.[110] At common law the presumption is *pater est quem nuptiae demonstrant* (the father is whom marriage demonstrates).[111] Marriage at a date between conception and birth brought the common law presumption into play but it had no effect on proof of the paternity of a child born before marriage.[112] There is a strong presumption of legitimacy arising from birth during the marriage of the mother.[113] A presumption based on recognised status assists to prove marriage by cohabitation with habit and repute.[114]

There is in civil causes a general presumption against delict, such as fraud,[115] and quasi-delict, negligence or breach of duty.[116] With regard to fraud, a contrary presumption may arise from the nature and appearance of articles sold,[117] from the

---

[104] *eg Coomber v Ross* 1987 SLT 266.
[105] Dickson, *Evidence* (3rd edn), para 114(6). The maxim applicable to these presumptions is *odiosa et inhonesta non sunt in lege praesumenda* (unpleasantness and dishonour are not presumed in law). Once again the maxim is an understatement.
[106] Macdonald, *Criminal Law of Scotland* (5th edn), p 339; *Slater v HM Advocate* 1928 JC 94 at 105. Rebuttal requires proof beyond reasonable doubt.
[107] *Currie v Currie* 1950 SC 10 (OH) at 15. Rebuttal now requires proof only on balance of probabilities: Divorce (Scotland) Act 1976, s 1(5). As to standard of proof, see para 4.3. As to proof of adultery, see para 28.13.
[108] For a detailed examination, see Wilkinson & Norrie, *The Law Relating to Parent and Child in Scotland* (2nd edn), paras 3.13–3.26. Rebuttal now requires proof only on the balance of probabilities: Law Reform (Parent and Child) (Scotland) Act 1986, s 5(4). See also para 4.3.
[109] Law Reform (Parent and Child) (Scotland) Act 1986, s 5(1)(a). For the purposes of establishing parentage for the purposes of liability for child support, see Child Support Act 1991, s 26.
[110] Law Reform (Parent and Child) (Scotland) Act 1986, s 5(1)(b).
[111] Stair, iii, 3, 42; Erskine, i, 6, 49. For examples of rebuttal, see *Ramsay v Ramsay's Curator ad litem* 1986 SLT 590 (affirmed at 799); *J v Aberdeen City Council* 1999 SC 405.
[112] *Brooks' Exrx v James* 1971 SC (HL) 77.
[113] Stair, iii, 3, 42; Erskine, i, 6, 49. The presumption is seen in operation in *MacDonald of Keppoch, Petitioner (No 2)* 1994 SLT (Lyon Ct) 2 (in which another presumption arose (*non apparentibus non existentibus praesumuntur*) due to lack of mention in printed family histories. See also Wilkinson & Norrie, *The Law Relating to Parent and Child in Scotland* (2nd edn), para 1.44. The presumption of legitimacy arising after adoption is irrebuttable (Adoption (Scotland) Act 1978, s 39, and see para 3.02), but may interact with the common law presumption (Adoption (Scotland) Act 1978, s 39(2)).
[114] See para 3.6.8.
[115] See, for example, *Gibson v National Cash Register Co Ltd* 1925 SC 500; *Cullen's Tr v Johnston* (1865) 3 M 935, per Lord President McNeill at 937; *Campbell v Aberdeen Fire and Life Assurance Co* (1841) 3 D 1010.
[116] See, for example, *McLure, Naismith, Brodie & Macfarlane v Stewart* (1887) 15 R (HL) 1; *Alexander v Phillip* (1899) 1 F 985. For examples of inferences when negligence is averred, see para 2.9.
[117] *Patterson v Landsberg & Son* (1905) 7 F 675, per Lord Kyllachy at 681 (inference of fraud from fact that alleged antiques, not in fact old, had the appearance of age).

fact that the vendors of two secondhand cash registers, which the purchasers believed to be new, held themselves out as manufacturers and vendors of such registers,[118] and from the fact that the person in whose favour a deed or obligation was granted was a person having, through relationship or official or professional position, a power to influence the granter in his favour.[119] With regard to negligence, if certain facts are proved a factual presumption of negligence may arise due to *res ipsa loquitur*.[120]

3.8 PRESUMPTIONS SUPPORTING CONTINUANCE OF EXISTING CONDITIONS

3.8.1 Conditions proved to have existed are presumed to continue in existence.[121] The effect of this in relation to duration of life has been dealt with in an earlier paragraph.[122] Other particular applications of the general presumption are as follows: a person's domicile of origin is presumed to continue until another domicile has been acquired, with the intention of abandoning the domicile of origin, the burden of proving the change (*animo et facto*) being upon the party asserting it[123]; insanity, when established in an appropriate process, has been presumed to continue[124]; a general mandate is presumed to continue until discharged[125]; the relationship of debtor and creditor is presumed to continue until it is proved to have been terminated[126]; a person in the general employment of a party is presumed to continue in that employment, and the onus of proving that *pro hac vice* that person was in the service of another rests upon the party who makes the assertion.[127] There are statutory presumptions that containers which expressly indicate their contents do contain what is so indicated,[128] but this will not absolve a party from proof of an essential fact which is not clear from the container.[129]

---

[118] *Gibson v National Cash Register Co Ltd* 1925 SC 500.

[119] *Grieve v Cunningham* (1869) 8 M 317 (solicitor); *Gray v Binny* (1879) 7 R 332 (parent and child). For a general discussion of the position of solicitor, clergyman, doctor and parent, see *Forbes v Forbes's Trs* 1957 SC 325 (OH); *Munro v Strain* (1874) 1 R 522 at 525; *McKechnie v McKechnie's Trs* 1908 SC 93 at 97–98.

[120] This is examined at para 2.10.

[121] Dickson, *Evidence* (3rd edn), para 114(5).

[122] para 3.5.

[123] Dickson, *Evidence* (3rd edn), para 27; *Aikman v Aikman* (1861) 3 Macq 854, per Lord Wensleydale at 877. See also *Liverpool Royal Infirmary v Ramsay* 1930 SC (HL) 83; *McLelland v McLelland* 1942 SC 502; *Labacianskas v Labacianskas* 1949 SC 280.

[124] Bell, *Principles*, para 2103; Dickson, *Evidence* (3rd edn), para 35, but this may not accord with modern thinking regarding the assessment of mental disorder and sanity. For the presumptions regarding sanity and insanity, see para 3.5.

[125] Bell, *Commentaries*, I, 488; Dickson, *Evidence* (3rd edn), para 114(5).

[126] Dickson, *Evidence* (3rd edn), para 114(5). Unless there has been an acknowledgement of debt, the relationship may be terminated by short negative prescription in terms of the Prescription and Limitation (Scotland) Act 1973, s 6.

[127] *Malley v London, Midland & Scottish Railway Co* 1944 SC 129 at 137, 149, 152.

[128] *eg* Licensing (Scotland) Act 1976, s 127(1), applied in *Doyle v Ruxton* 1999 SLT 487.

[129] *eg* *Grieve v Hillary* 1987 SCCR 317.

3.9 PRESUMPTIONS FROM POSSESSION OR DESTRUCTION OF DOCUMENTS

There is a strong presumption that a deed found in the grantee's possession has **3.9.1** been duly delivered.[130] The presumption may be rebutted by proof that possession was obtained by fraud, or for some purpose, such as for safe custody, which was not intended to place it outwith the granter's control.[131] When a will, which is known to have been made and to have been in the testator's custody, is not discovered on death, the testator is presumed to have destroyed it *animo revocandi* (intending revocation),[132] and there is a similar presumption when an undelivered deed is found mutilated in the granter's possession.[133]

When a written obligation or document of debt is found in the hands of the **3.9.2** debtor or cautioner[134] or of one of the obligants, it is presumed that payment has been made *or* that the obligation has been implemented or extinguished[135] but the presumption does not apply to bilateral deeds, nor to a heritable right which is not normally extinguished without writing.[136] When the presumption applies the creditor may offer to rebut it by proving that the document was surrendered for some special temporary purpose without abandoning the right to it—the question for decision is whether or not the document was truly delivered as a surrendered document of debt by the creditor to the debtor.[137] When a creditor in a written obligation cannot produce the document of debt, it is presumed that the document was returned to the debtor as cancelled on payment of the debt, or that it was destroyed or cancelled by the creditor in order to extinguish the debt.[138] However, the presumption applies mainly to writings which are usually cancelled or destroyed when their purpose has been served, such as bills of exchange, promissory notes and personal bonds. With regard to a deed which is not normally revoked in this way, such as a deed concerning heritage, the presumption, if it applies at all,[139] is more easily rebutted.[140] Now that few obligations require to be constituted in writing, although parties may commit any obligation to writing by choice, the presumption inevitably will arise even less frequently than it has occured in reported

---

[130] Stair, i, 7, 14; iv, 42, 8; Erskine, iii, 2, 43; Dickson, *Evidence* (3rd edn), paras 114(2), 936.

[131] Dickson, *Evidence* (3rd edn), para 938; Gloag, *Contract* (2nd edn), p 71; *McAslan v Glen* (1859) 21 D 511; *Semple v Kyle* (1902) 4 F 421.

[132] Dickson, *Evidence* (3rd edn), para 114(2); *Bonthrone v Ireland* (1883) 10 R 779, per Lord Young at 790. For facts regarded as insufficient to rebut the presumption, see *Clyde v Clyde* 1958 SC 343 (OH). See also *Lauder v Briggs* 1999 SC 453.

[133] Dickson, *Evidence* (3rd edn), para 114(2).

[134] Stair, i, 7, 14; Erskine, iii, 4, 5.

[135] Stair, i, 7, 14; iv, 45, 24; Erskine, iii, 4, 5; Dickson, *Evidence* (3rd edn), para 173. The maxim is *chirographum apud debitorem repertum presumitur solutum* (a bond not existing is presumed to be discharged).

[136] Dickson, *Evidence* (3rd edn), para 173, and the Requirements of Writing (Scotland) Act 1995, s 1, unless *rei interventus*, homologation or their statutory replacement is relied upon: see Chapters 22, 23 and 26.

[137] *Knox v Crawford* (1862) 24 D 1088, referred to and followed in *Henry v Miller* (1884) 11 R 713, per Lord President Inglis at 716–717. See also *Ferguson, Davidson & Co v Jolly's Tr* (1880) 7 R 500, per Lord Mure at 504.

[138] *Walker v Nisbet* 1915 SC 639; Dickson, *Evidence* (3rd edn), para 175; Gloag, *Contract* (2nd edn), p 717.

[139] Examples in which it might apply would be bonds and dispositions in security, and deeds handed over after public roup.

[140] See the distinction made in *Winchester v Smith* (1863) 1 M 685, per Lord President McNeill, Lord Curriehill and Lord Ardmillan at 689; *Clyde v Clyde* 1958 SC 343 (OH) at 345.

cases in recent years. However, it may have, and continue to have, indirect effect in preventing parties from litigating if a document of debt has passed into the possession of the debtor.

3.10 PRESUMPTIONS FROM POSSESSION OF HERITABLE AND MOVEABLE PROPERTY

3.10.1 The underlying maxim is *in pari causa melior est conditio possidentis* (in an equal case the possessor is in the better position).[141] Long continued possession of heritable property raises a presumption that it has a legal origin, if such an origin is possible,[142] and it is this presumption which underlies the positive prescriptions relating to an estate in land,[143] a right of servitude,[144] or a public right of way.[145] The possessor of corporeal moveables is presumed to be the owner, and the onus of establishing title rests upon anyone who asserts the contrary.[146] In order to discharge this onus it is not enough to prove that the goods were once the property of the person claiming them.[147] He must show that possession was lost by theft, or by granting possession to a liferenter or under a contract of loan, hiring, hire-purchase, deposit or pledge or in other similar circumstances which made it impossible for the present possessor to be the owner.[148] The position of a creditor who seeks to attach by diligence the goods of a third party in the possession of the debtor, in reliance upon the doctrine of reputed ownership, is now dealt with by statute. In executing a poinding an officer of court is entitled to proceed on the assumption that any article in the possession of the debtor is owned by him unless that officer knows or ought to know that the contrary is the case.[149]

---

[141] Erskine, ii, 1, 24; Bell, *Principles*, para 1313.

[142] *Clippens Oil Co v Edinburgh and District Water Trs* (1903) 6 F (HL) 7, per Lord Chancellor Halsbury at 8.

[143] Prescription and Limitation (Scotland) Act 1973, ss 1 and 2.

[144] Prescription and Limitation (Scotland) Act 1973, s 3. In *Mags of Edinburgh v North British Railway Co* (1904) 6 F 620 at 636–637, the establishment of a public right of way has been held to be legally impossible.

[145] Prescription and Limitation (Scotland) Act 1973, s 3. For a recent case of proof of a public right of way see *North East Fife District v Nisbet* 2000 SCLR (Notes, IH) 413. The old law relating to possessory judgments is to be found in Stair, iv, 26, 3; Erskine, iv, 1, 50. See also *Galloway v Cowden* (1885) 12 R 578; *Calder v Adam* (1870) 8 M 645; *McKerron v Gordon* (1876) 3 R 429. For a particular application of the general presumption with reference to 13 years' possession by a minister of any heritable subject as part of his benefice, see Stair, ii, 8, 29; Erskine, iii, 7, 33; Connell, *Parishes*, pp 439 *et seq*.

[146] Stair, ii, 1, 42; Erskine, ii, 1, 24; Dickson, *Evidence* (3rd edn), paras 149–151; Bell, *Principles*, paras 1313, 1314. Although in recent years there has been a trend towards the separation of ownership from possession, including statutory presumption of joint ownership of moveables by husband and wife (Family Law (Scotland) Act 1985, s 25(1) and see para 3.3 above), the common law presumption may be relied upon; for an example see *Pragnell-O'Neill v Lady Skiffington* 1984 SLT 282.

[147] For a recent example in the sheriff court involving landlord's hypothec, see *Novacold v Fridge Freight (Fyvie) Ltd (in receivership)* 1999 SCLR 409.

[148] Stair, ii, 1, 42; Erskine, ii, 1, 24; Dickson, *Evidence* (3rd edn), paras 149–151; Bell, *Principles*, paras 1313, 1314.

[149] Debtors (Scotland) Act 1987, s 19(2). For a discussion of the common law, see *George Hopkinson Ltd v Napier & Son* 1953 SC 139, per Lord President Cooper at 145–149.

3.11 PRESUMPTIONS REGARDING DONATION

There is a strong presumption against donation, the maxim *donatio non praesum-*   **3.11.1**
itur (donation is not presumed) being an understatement of the position.[150] When
moveable property has passed from one person to another the onus placed by the
presumption upon the person alleging donation is to prove it by evidence which is
reasonably convincing, and which is so clear as to displace all other explanations
put forward in evidence as being reasonable in the known circumstances of the
case.[151] If the transfer can on the evidence be ascribed to a purpose other than
donation, the onus has not been discharged.[152] The presumption applies with
additional strength when the transfer is by a debtor to his creditor, the maxim
debitor non praesumitur donare (a debtor is not presumed to make a gift to his
creditor) being once again an understatement.[153] It applies also when services are
rendered or money is lent by one person to another, the presumption being that the
services are to be paid for,[154] and that interest is payable on the loan until repaid.[155]
When the recipient of the services[156] or loan[157] is a near relative, the onus of proving that the services were gratuitous or that the loan was free of interest is more
easily discharged. When payments are made by a parent or by a person *in loco
parentis* (in the role of parent) there may be a presumption, contrary to the general
presumption, that the payments are gifts made *ex pietate* (family devotion), in
which event the onus is upon the person seeking repayment to prove the contrary.[158] Whether or not such a presumption arises must depend upon the exact
relationship of the parties and the whole surrounding circumstances. It has been
said that the presumption against donation *inter vivos* is stronger than the presumption against donation *mortis causa*,[159] but in practical terms it may be more
difficult to secure convincing evidence to contradict the presumption in the latter
situation.[160] There is a presumption of donation in favour of the recipient of unsolicited goods if the statutory conditions are met.[161]

---

[150] Stair, i, 8, 2; iv, 45, 17 (14); Erskine, iii, 3, 92; Dickson, *Evidence* (3rd edn), para 158; *Sharp v Paton*
(1883) 10 R 1000, per Lord President Inglis at 1006; *Dawson v McKenzie* (1891) 19 R 261, per Lord
President Robertson at 271; *Brownlee's Exrx v Brownlee* 1908 SC 232, per Lord President Dunedin at
242.
[151] *Grant's Trs v McDonald* 1939 SC 448, per Lord Carmont at 471. For examples of how donation
may be proved, see the cases cited in support of paras 149 and 150 of the first edition of this text, and
Stair Memorial Encyclopaedia, Vol 8, paras 620–626.
[152] *Grant's Trs v McDonald* 1939 SC 448, per Lord President Normand at 460–461. See also *British
Linen Co v Martin* (1849) 11 D 1004, per Lord Fullerton at 1008, Lord Jeffrey at 1011; *Callander v
Callander's Exr* 1972 SC (HL) 70.
[153] Stair, i, 8, 2; Erskine, iii, 3, 93; Dickson, *Evidence* (3rd edn), para 165; *Johnstone v Haviland* (1896)
23 R (HL) 6, per Lord Herschell at 9.
[154] *Landless v Wilson* (1880) 8 R 289. See also *Taylor v Forbes* (1853) 24 D 19. For the old authorities
regarding the provision of board and lodging, see Dickson, *Evidence* (3rd edn), para 163.
[155] *Smellie's Exrx v Smellie* 1933 SC 725. Interest on an IOU is presumed to be payable from the date
of the demand for repayment of the principal sum: *Winestone v Wolifson* 1954 SC 77.
[156] *Anderson v Halley* (1847) 9 D 1222; *Thomson v Thomson's Tr* (1889) 16 R 333; *Miller v Miller*
(1898) 25 R 995; *Urquhart v Urquhart's Tr* (1905) 8 F 42; *Russel v McClymont* (1906) 8 F 821. For a
slightly more modern case as to the provision of board and lodging, see *Turnbull v Brien* 1908 SC 313.
[157] *Smellie's Exrx v Smellie* 1933 SC 725.
[158] Dickson, *Evidence* (3rd edn), para 159; *Malcolm v Campbell* (1889) 17 R 255 at 257, 259;
Macalister's Trs v Macalister (1827) 5 S 219.
[159] *Grant's Trs v McDonald* 1939 SC 448, per Lord President Normand at 460; *Sharp v Paton* (1883)
10 R 1000, per Lord Deas at 1008. *Cf Macpherson's Exrx v Mackay* 1932 SC 505, per Lord President
Clyde at 513.
[160] See, for example, *Piggott v Piggott* 1981 SLT 269; *Macaulay v Milliken* 1967 SLT (Notes) 30.
[161] Unsolicited Goods and Services Act 1971, s 1.

3.12 PRESUMPTION FROM ACKNOWLEDGEMENT OF RECEIPT OF MONEY

3.12.1   An unqualified[162] written acknowledgement of the receipt of money, signed by the granter, raises a presumption that the money was received on loan, or on some other footing inferring an obligation to repay, and places upon the recipient the onus of proving that it was not so received.[163] It is not easy to reconcile the judicial dicta, but it would appear that the presumption arises not from the mere admission or proof that money has been paid, which by itself has been said to raise no presumption of any kind,[164] but because the written acknowledgement has been granted as a document of debt and is in the grantee's possession as such when repayment is demanded.[165] A judicial admission of the receipt of money does, however, raise a presumption of loan, or of an obligation to repay, if, but only if, the defender avers that the money was received as a gift,[166] unless the relationship between the parties is such as to raise a contrary presumption of the kind referred to in the last paragraph.[167]

3.13 PRESUMPTION THAT PAYMENT IS MADE BY PROPER DEBTOR

3.13.1   When a debt has been paid, the presumption is that it has been paid by the debtor,[168] and when the payment has in fact been made by another, in the event of doubt it will be presumed to have been made with the debtor's funds.[169] The presumption, though it may be weakened, is not displaced if the payment has been made by the debtor's father.[170]

---

[162] For examples of *qualified* acknowledgements which were held not to give rise to the presumption, see *Duncan's Trs v Shand* (1873) 11 M 254, per Lord Justice-Clerk Moncreiff at 257 (qualification that sum received in payment of debt of honour); *Patrick v Patrick's Trs* (1904) 6 F 836 (qualification that sum received on loan bequeathed by borrower to lender in his will).

[163] *Martin v Crawford* (1850) 12 D 960; *Thomson v Geekie* (1861) 23 D 693, per Lord Wood at 698, Lord Cowan at 699, Lord Justice-Clerk Inglis at 701; *Gill v Gill* 1907 SC 532, per Lord Low at 537. An IOU is an acknowledgement producing this result; the payee's endorsement upon a cheque in his favour is not.

[164] *Penney v Aitken* 1927 SC 673, per Lord Ormidale at 680, Lord Anderson at 682; *Gill v Gill* 1907 SC 532, per Lord Low at 537; *Haldane v Speirs* (1872) 10 M 537, per Lord President Inglis at 541; *Duncan's Trs v Shand* (1873) 11 M 254, per Lord Neaves at 259. Cf *Fraser v Bruce* (1857) 20 D 115 at 118–119, and Lord Murray's opinion in *Clark's Exrx v Brown* 1935 SC 110 at 118, that an unqualified judicial admission of the receipt of money gives rise to the presumption.

[165] *Wink v Speirs* (1868) 6 M 657, per Lord Neaves at 658; *Haldane v Speirs* (1872) 10 M 537, per Lord President Inglis at 541; *Duncan's Trs v Shand* (1873) 11 M 254, per Lord Neaves at 259; *Nimmo v Nimmo* (1873) 11 M 446, per Lord Neaves at 449, Lord Cowan at 449–450; *Malcolm v Campbell* (1889) 17 R 255, per Lord Justice-Clerk McDonald at 259; *Dunn's Tr v Hardy* (1896) 23 R 621, per Lord Kinnear at 633; *Clark's Exrx v Brown* 1935 SC 110, per Lord Justice-Clerk Aitchison at 120–121.

[166] *Penney v Aitken* 1927 SC 673 at 681, 683; *Penman v White* 1957 SC 338 (OH); *McVea v Reid* 1958 SLT (Sh Ct) 60. Cf *Malcolm v Campbell* (1889) 17 R 255, per Lord Lee at 257, Lord Kyllachy at 258, Lord Justice-Clerk Macdonald at 259, where, contrary to what is stated in *Penman v White,* the onus of proof was regarded as resting upon the pursuer.

[167] See para 3.11.

[168] Dickson, *Evidence* (3rd edn), para 189; Bell, *Principles*, para 559. An argument made in the sheriff court to the effect that the presumption can be extended by analogy to show that the recipient of the payment was the true creditor was considered doubtful: *McCaig Butler Computing Ltd v Campbell-Lee Computer Services Ltd* 1999 GWD 29-1360.

[169] Erskine, iii, 4, 6.

[170] *Welsh v Welsh's Trs* (1878) 5 R 542.

3.14 PRESUMPTION FROM *APOCHA TRIUM ANNORUM*

In the case of obligations requiring termly payments, such as rents, feu-duties, or **3.14.1**
interest, the production of receipts for three consecutive termly payments has
raised a presumption that all prior instalments have been paid.[171] The presumption
depended upon the reiteration of written discharges without reservation or qualification regarding the earlier period,[172] and a single discharge, though covering three
or more consecutive instalments, did not raise it.[173] Receipts for payments to
account were not enough, though several of these, discharging in aggregate the
amount due at a particular term, would be accepted as a receipt for that term,[174] and
the presumption was held to apply where receipts for the balance of rent for five
consecutive years were produced.[175] The three terms had to be consecutive and the
intervention of an unvouched term elided the presumption. Receipts for occasional
payments not linked to any term, but amounting in aggregate to payment for three
years, probably did not raise the presumption.[176] Where one or more of the later
discharges were by an heir the position was doubtful,[177] but it was immaterial that
one or more of the discharges were to the original debtor, and the rest to a representative or successor.[178] Discharges by a singular successor in lands, or an
assignee of a security, raised no presumption that earlier payments to the original
landlord or creditor have been settled.[179] Receipts by a factor with a general power
of management sufficed, but not by one who merely acted *ad hoc* in receiving
rents.[180] Receipts by successive factors did not raise the presumption.[181] The presumption could be rebutted.[182] The presumption appears to have been used little,
if at all, this century, although it has not been abolished or disapproved. The lack
of use may be because termly payments are relatively uncommon in current times,
although by logical extension the presumption could be applied to any payment
regularly due, since the presumption appears to have been dependent upon a series
of discharges at the hand of the creditor personally or one agent of the creditor. The
presumption will not arise through payments made after a charge or other diligence
for payment, because this would breach the requirement for payment in accordance with a regularly recurring obligation, and because there is now a statutory
scheme for ascription of payments made or recovered in response to diligence,[183]

---

[171] Stair, i, 18, 2; Erskine, iii, 4, 10; Bell, *Principles*, para 567; Dickson, *Evidence* (3rd edn), paras
177–184. The institutional writers deal with yearly or half-yearly payments. Dickson concedes quar-
terly instalments, but there is no authority in regard to payments at more frequent intervals, save
Rankine (*Leases* (3rd edn), p 321), who would extend the rule to even shorter periods.
[172] Stair, i, 18, 2; Dickson, *Evidence* (3rd edn), para 184.
[173] Dickson, *Evidence* (3rd edn), para 177; *Hunter v Kinnaird's Trs* (1829) 7 S 548.
[174] Dickson, *Evidence* (3rd edn), para 177; *Hunter v Kinnaird's Trs* (1829) 7 S 548.
[175] Dickson, *Evidence* (3rd edn), para 177; *Hunter v Kinnaird's Trs* (1829) 7 S 548.
[176] Rankine, *Leases* (3rd edn), p 321.
[177] Gloag, *Contract* (2nd edn), p 719, note 1.
[178] Dickson, *Evidence* (3rd edn), para 179; Rankine, *Leases* (3rd edn), p 321.
[179] Gloag, *Contract* (2nd edn), p 718.
[180] Stair, i, 18, 2; Dickson, *Evidence* (3rd edn), para 180. In Rankine's view it is enough if the granter
of the receipts held the landlord's order to receive the rents (*Leases* (3rd edn), p 820).
[181] Dickson, *Evidence* (3rd edn), para 180.
[182] *Cameron v Panton's Trs* (1891) 18 R 728, per Lord Kincairney at 729; *Stenhouse v Stenhouse's Trs*
(1899) 36 SLR 637. See also Bell, *Principles*, para 567.
[183] Viz poinding and sale, earnings arrestment, arrestment and furthcoming or sale, or conjoined arrestment order: Debtors (Scotland) 1987, s 94(1).

first to the expenses of that or previous diligence, then to interest, then to the principal debt.[184]

3.15 PRESUMPTION AS TO PAYMENT OF HOTEL BILLS

3.15.1 There is a presumption that a hotel bill has been paid before the guest is allowed to leave the hotel, which places upon the hotelkeeper the onus of proving not only the constitution but the subsistence of the alleged debt.[185]

3.16 PRESUMPTION FROM POSSESSION OF STOLEN PROPERTY

3.16.1 Possession of stolen property by itself may be no more than a piece of circumstantial evidence.[186] However, in certain circumstances it may give rise to a factual presumption that the possessor was the thief,[187] so as to throw upon the possessor an onus of providing an explanation of possession which is consistent with innocence of theft, and which the court or the jury is prepared to accept as true, or at least as raising a reasonable doubt in the possessor's favour.[188] Proof of possession depends upon the circumstances of each case and is a crucial fact requiring corroboration.[189] An employee acting in the ordinary course of duties is not a possessor for this purpose.[190] The occupier of premises upon which the stolen property is found is normally the possessor,[191] but this is not necessarily so when other persons also have access to the premises.[192] When a number of persons are associated together in dealing with the stolen property, all may be regarded as its possessors whether physically in possession of it or not.[193] Before the presumption can arise it must be proved that the interval between the crime and the accused's possession of the stolen goods was short,[194] and that there were criminative circumstances[195] associated with the possession.[196] What is regarded as a short interval depends upon the nature of the stolen goods,[197] a longer interval being more

---

[184] Debtors (Scotland) Act 1987, s 94(2).

[185] *Barnet v Colvill* (1840) 2 D 337; Bell, *Principles*, para 568; Dickson, *Evidence* (3rd edn), para 114(2).

[186] Dickson, *Evidence* (3rd edn), para 157. As to circumstantial evidence, see Chapter 6.

[187] The presumption covers any form of theft including theft by housebreaking: *Christie v HM Advocate* 1939 JC 72, and aggravation of theft by violence: *Cameron v HM Advocate* 1959 JC 59.

[188] *Hume*, i, 111; Alison, i, 320; Dickson, *Evidence* (3rd edn), para 157. The evidence of the accused alone, if believed, is enough for this purpose. It was a misdirection for the judge to state that if recent possession was established it was for the accused "to prove his or her innocence from the evidence in the case": *McDonald v HM Advocate* 1989 SCCR 559.

[189] As is evident in *Hassan v Normand* 1993 SCCR 849.

[190] *Simpson v HM Advocate* 1952 JC 1.

[191] See *Brannan v HM Advocate* 1954 JC 87.

[192] *Cryans v Nixon* 1955 JC 1.

[193] *HM Advocate v Browne* (1903) 6 F (J) 24; see also *McAttee* (1903) 5 F (J) 69.

[194] If the interval is long, the chance that the accused obtained it otherwise than by theft is increased to the point that the presumption cannot be relied upon: *L v Wilson* 1995 JC 29.

[195] Substituting the term "suspicious circumstances" was not a material misdirection in *McDonald v HM Advocate* 1989 SCCR 559.

[196] *Fox v Patterson* 1948 JC 104; *Brannan v HM Advocate* 1954 JC 87. But see *McDonald v HM Advocate* 1989 SCCR 559. In *L v Wilson* 1995 JC 29 the existence of criminative circumstances did not compensate for the delay between the theft and the possession.

[197] *Hannah and Higgins* (1836) 1 Swin 289; *HM Advocate v Browne* (1903) 6 F (J) 24; *MacLennan v Mackenzie* 1988 SLT 16; *Druce v Friel* 1994 SLT 1209.

usually regarded as sufficient to raise the presumption when the goods are cumbersome than when they are small and easily negotiable.[198] The criminative circumstances must be such as to suggest that the possession was not innocent but was more than mere reset[199]—for example, that the goods were of a kind or quantity which would not normally be in the accused's possession in that condition[200] at the hour and place at which they were found, that they were of a kind not normally dealt with by the accused in the course of his business,[201] or that the accused's actions at or about the time of his possession were in some other way indicative of guilt, such as the accused ordering his wife to throw the stolen goods out of the window just before the police arrived.[202] The fact that the accused said nothing when cautioned by the police and charged with the crime is not a criminative circumstance for this purpose.[203]

3.17 PRESUMPTION OF SPECIAL CAPACITY IN CRIMINAL CASES

In criminal cases the prosecutor may libel the accused in a special capacity. This **3.17.1** is usually relied upon when the crime is a statutory one requiring some special capacity for its commission.[204] If the prosecutor alleges that the offence has been committed in a special capacity (the examples given in the statute are "holder of a licence, master of a vessel, occupier of a house and the like"),[205] the fact that the accused possesses the qualification necessary for the commission of the offence is held as admitted unless challenged by the accused through preliminary procedure.[206] Other examples of special capacity are a disqualified driver,[207] prostitute,[208] agent,[209] parent[210] and thief.[211] The capacity should be clear from the indictment or complaint.[212] The presumption goes no further than to prove the capacity,[213] and the detail of the use or misuse of that capacity—for example, the technicalities of the licence condition of which breach has been alleged[214]— must be proved.[215] Furthermore, if the prosecutor has mentioned the age of any person in the libel this will give rise to a rebuttable presumption that the accused

---

[198] Dickson, *Evidence* (3rd edn), para 157.

[199] As in *L v Wilson* 1995 JC 29.

[200] *Connelly v Heywood* 1993 SCCR 1026.

[201] cf *Fox v Patterson* 1948 JC 104.

[202] *Cameron v HM Advocate* 1959 JC 59; and see *Cassidy v McLeod* 1981 SCCR 270.

[203] *Cryans v Nixon* 1955 JC 1; *Collins v HM Advocate* 1959 JC 44; 1959 SLT (Notes) 27.

[204] In *Hamilton v Normand* 1994 SLT 184 the Lord Justice-Clerk (Ross) opined that the provision applied only in this situation, but the provision bears no such restriction in its terms.

[205] Criminal Procedure (Scotland) Act 1995, s 255(1).

[206] Criminal Procedure (Scotland) Act 1995, s 255(1). It has been suggested that the section applies only when the crime is a statutory one requiring some special capacity for its commission.

[207] *Paton v Lees* 1992 SCCR 212.

[208] *Allan v McGraw* 1986 SCCR 257.

[209] *Templeton v HM Advocate* 1988 SLT 171.

[210] *Ross v Simpson* 1995 SLT 956.

[211] *Newlands v MacPhail* 1991 SCCR 212.

[212] In both *Wimpey Homes Holdings v Lee* 1991 SCCR 447 and *Ross v Simpson* 1995 SLT 956 the capacity could have been more clearly set out.

[213] As to the effect of the prosecutor leading evidence when the presumption would have sufficed, see Renton & Brown, *Criminal Procedure* (6th edn), paras 24-104–24-106.

[214] *Larkin v Docherty* 1991 SCCR 377; *Young v HM Advocate* 1995 SLT 683.

[215] For presumptions that may assist with proof of conditions set by statutory instruments or byelaws, see para 3.6.

is that age.[216] However, without prejudice to that presumption, in proceedings for offences under the Children and Young Persons (Scotland) Act 1937 or an offence involving bodily injury to, or lewd or libidinous practice or behaviour towards, a child under the age of 17 years, if it appears to the court that the child is a particular age that age may be presumed unless the contrary is proved.[217] Given that the latter presumption of age appears to require some evidence before it applies, as compared to the mere assertion in the libel which will give rise to the former, in a case of conflict between the two the stricter provision may apply.

---

[216] Criminal Procedure (Scotland) Act 1995, s 255A.

[217] Criminal Procedure (Scotland) Act 1995, s 46(3). At common law failure to prove the age of the victim by corroborated evidence was fatal to proof of the crime: *Lockwood v Walker* 1910 SC (J) 3.

CHAPTER 4

STANDARD OF PROOF—DIFFERENCES BETWEEN AVERMENT AND PROOF

4.1 STANDARD OF PROOF—CRIMINAL CAUSES

The standard of proof needed to discharge the onus of proof of a criminal libel is **4.1.1** beyond reasonable doubt. The Appeal Court has cautioned against attempts to describe or exemplify what is meant by "reasonable doubt".[1] It has been said that it must not be "a strained or fanciful acceptance of remote possibilities"[2] nor doubt that is "speculative or academic"[3] but it has been stressed in recent years that it is best to do no more than state that the doubt must be based on reason and that the accused should get the benefit of that doubt.[4]

The effect of this standard upon the prosecutor is that enough evidence must be **4.1.2** led to satisfy the court beyond reasonable doubt that the crime was committed by the accused. The standard should not be applied to each adminicle of prosecution evidence[5] nor, it is submitted, evidence which is merely descriptive of the method of committing the crime,[6] but to such evidence as the court has chosen to accept relating to the crucial facts of the case.[7]

---

[1] In *Shewan v HM Advocate* 1989 SCCR 364 reference in the judge's charge to doubts such as affect commercial decisions was said by the Appeal Court to be unhelpful, and in *Buchanan v HM Advocate* 1998 SLT 13 the sheriff's comparison with the kind of doubt that would "dissuade you from getting married or buying a house" was a misdirection in that it suggested that the level of doubt required to be enough to alter a decision rather than to give cause for pause or hesitation.

[2] *Irving v Minister of Pensions* 1945 SC 21.

[3] *McKenzie v HM Advocate* 1959 JC 32.

[4] *Shewan v HM Advocate* 1989 SCCR 364; *Buchanan v HM Advocate* 1998 SLT 13. In *Stillie v HM Advocate* 1992 SLT 279 reference to "reasonable certainty" was disapproved.

[5] *Martin v HM Advocate* 1993 SCCR 803; but *cf HM Advocate v McGinlay* 1983 SLT 562. In *Thompson v Crowe* 2000 JC 173 at 192B–F it is said that proof that a statement by the accused was obtained fairly is on balance of probabilities—see para 9.12.

[6] In *Smith v Lees* 1997 JC 73 the High Court distinguished such descriptive features of the charge from the crucial facts in respect of which corroboration is necessary. See para 5.11.

[7] When the evidence on a crucial issue, even if accepted, could not meet the standard, it may be appropriate to withdraw the issue from the jury. In *HM Advocate v McGinlay* 1983 SLT 562, two doctors were asked whether an assault brought on a cardiac infarction of which the victim died, to which one replied "possibly" and the other "probably". As the link between the assault and the death was crucial to the charge of culpable homicide the jury could not have reached a conclusion upon that issue to the standard of beyond reasonable doubt. However, *cf Paxton v HM Advocate* 1999 SCCR 895; *Fyfe v HM Advocate* 1998 SLT 195; *Hendry v HM Advocate* 1987 JC 63.

4.1.3   It is not appropriate to say generally that the accused must satisfy a particular standard of proof in his defence. The effect of the criminal standard of proof upon the accused is that if the prosecutor has led evidence which, if believed, would meet the standard, the accused will carry an evidential burden to adduce some evidence which could give rise to reasonable doubt. This general effect remains intact even if the accused introduces a statutory defence, on which the accused would have a persuasive burden on a balance of probabilities,[8] or enters a plea of insanity or diminished responsibility which must also be proved by the accused on a balance of probabilities.[9] At no point does the accused have to meet the standard of beyond reasonable doubt, that being a standard reserved for the prosecutor who must rebut the presumption of innocence.[10]

4.2 STANDARD OF PROOF—CIVIL CAUSES—GENERAL RULE

4.2.1   The standard of proof needed to discharge an onus or to rebut a presumption in a civil cause is not so high or so exacting as that required of a prosecutor in a criminal cause. It does not need to be proof beyond reasonable doubt.[11] When the proved facts give rise to a number of conflicting inferences, the inference which is the more probable will prevail. If all are equally consistent with the proved facts and none is more probable than the others, nothing has been proved, and the party upon whom lies the onus of proof fails.[12] However, if the evidence satisfies the court of the probability of that which must be established, the onus of proof is discharged.[13] The decision has been said to turn upon a balance[14] or preponderance[15] of probabilities, and the simple expression "balance of probabilities" need not be improved upon or explained.[16] The standard of proof applies to every substantive issue which is necessary to prove the case. So, for example, when negligence is in issue the standard of balance of probability applies not only to the proof of negligence, whether that consist in common law fault or breach of statutory duty, but also to the proof that the injury resulted therefrom.[17] This may involve consideration of complex expert evidence, and although it may be appropriate to assess that evidence by exacting standards applying within the sphere of expertise,[18] the overall standard of proof in the case remains the balance of probabilities. A strong presumption, such as the presumption that the police act with authority and without

---

[8]   See para 2.12.

[9]   See para 2.12.

[10]   The same standard applies when the Crown seeks an order under the Proceeds of Crime (Scotland) Act 1995, and any rebuttal by the defence is to be proved on balance of probabilities: *HM Advocate v McSalley* 2000 JC 485.

[11]   *Hendry v Clan Line Steamers, Ltd* 1949 SC 320.

[12]   *Hendry v Clan Line Steamers, Ltd* 1949 SC 320, per Lord Jamieson at 328.

[13]   *Robertson v Watson* 1949 JC 73, per Lord Justice-General Cooper at 88, quoted as applying also to civil causes by Lord Justice-Clerk Thomson in *Hendry v Clan Line Steamers Ltd* 1949 SC 320 at 323–324.

[14]   *Simpson v London, Midland & Scottish Railway Co* 1931 SC (HL) 15, per Lord Dunedin at 20.

[15]   *R v Carr-Briant* [1943] KB 607 at 611.

[16]   *Agar v HM Advocate* 2000 GWD 12-421, a criminal case in which a defence burden requiring proof on the balance of probabilities had to be explained to a jury.

[17]   *Wardlaw v Bonnington Castings* 1956 SC (HL) 26, per Lord Reid at 31, Lord Tucker at 34; *Kenyon v Bell* 1953 SC 125 (OH), per Lord Guthrie at 128.

[18]   As the Inner House had to do in *Dingley v Chief Constable, Strathclyde Police* 1998 SC 548, and the approach was approved by the House of Lords on appeal: *Dingley v Chief Constable, Strathclyde Police* 2000 SC (HL) 77.

malice in the conduct of their duties,[19] may place a burden of proof on a party to rebut that presumption, but the standard of proof will still be the balance of probabilities.[20] Consideration by the jury or by the court of the probability of a party's averments being true must, however, proceed upon evidence supporting these averments, and not upon conjecture as to what would probably have been established if such evidence had been led. Thus a party cannot discharge the onus of proving his case by leading only the evidence of the opponent and his employees which contradicts it, and by arguing that, since the evidence was manifestly false, the opposite of it must be true.[21] Similarly, an onus will not be satisfied by leading evidence which is more probable than that led by the opponent, but nevertheless improbable in itself. The court must be satisfied of the probability, inherent and relative, of what is led in evidence by the party who carries the onus of proof on that issue.

4.3 VARIATIONS OF THE GENERAL RULE

The question as to whether in a civil cause the commission of a crime, such as **4.3.1** fraud, must be proved by the standard of proof appropriate for crime, or whether proof on a balance of probabilities is sufficient, has arisen in some cases in Scotland.[22] Although it appears to have been said that the criminal standard applied[23] this has not been the view taken in England,[24] nor in recent Scottish cases.[25] The suggestion that there is any intermediate standard[26] has been disapproved by the Inner House who have confirmed that there are only two standards in Scotland, viz the criminal standard of beyond reasonable doubt and the civil standard of balance of probabilities.[27] However, the court has acknowledged that the more serious or unusual[28] the allegation made in civil proceedings the more cogent,[29] clear,[30] or careful and precise[31] will be the evidence needed to satisfy the civil standard.

Historically, as exceptions to the standard applying generally in civil cases, **4.3.2** adultery in an action of divorce or of separation and aliment had to be proved beyond reasonable doubt, and so too, it was thought, did guilt of sodomy or bestiality in an action of divorce, when an extract of a conviction was not produced.

---

[19] *Beaton v Ivory* (1887) 14 R 1057.
[20] *Ward v Chief Constable, Strathclyde Police* 1991 SLT 292, and see para 3.6.
[21] *Cameron v Yeats* (1899) 1 F 456.
[22] eg *Arnott v Burt* (1872) 11 M 62; *Sereshky v Sereshky* 1988 SLT 426; *Rehman v Ahmad* 1993 SLT 741. However, in eg *Gibson v National Cash Register Co Ltd* 1925 SC 500 (damages for fraud) the matter is not discussed.
[23] *Arnott v Burt* (1872) 11 M 62, per Lord Neaves at 74.
[24] *Hornal v Neuberger Products Ltd* [1957] 1 QB 247, but cf *Halford v Brookes* [1991] TLR 427. For a discussion of the English decisions, see Cross & Tapper, *Evidence* (9th edn), pp 152–153.
[25] *Sloan v Triplett* 1985 SLT 294; *Rehman v Ahmad* 1993 SLT 741. Cf *Lennon v Co-operative Insurance Society Ltd* 1986 SLT 98; *Sereshky v Sereshky* 1988 SLT 426.
[26] Made in *Lennon v Co-operative Insurance Society Ltd* 1986 SLT 98 and *Sereshky v Sereshky* 1988 SLT 426.
[27] *Mullan v Anderson* 1993 SLT 835.
[28] As in *Dingley v Chief Constable, Strathclyde Police (No 1)* 1998 SC 548 (IH), 2000 SC (HL) 77.
[29] *1st Indian Cavalry Club Ltd v Commissioners of Customs & Excise* 1998 SC 126, per Lord Hamilton at 138B.
[30] *Wink v Speirs* (1867) 6 M 77, per Lord Justice-Clerk Patton at 80; *Cullen's Tr v Johnston* (1865) 3 M 935, per Lord President McNeill at 937.
[31] *Mullan v Anderson* 1993 SLT 835; *Rehman v Ahmad* 1993 SLT 741.

The presumption against illegitimacy, when it arose,[32] could be rebutted only by proof beyond reasonable doubt.[33] All of these exceptions are now superceded by the general application of the general civil standard to all family proceedings regardless of the issues raised.[34]

4.3.3   The only true exceptions apply in cases which are civil in their procedure, but generate a criminal or quasi-criminal outcome. Therefore, in actions for breach of interdict,[35] contravention of lawburrows[36] or contempt of court[37] the standard of proof is beyond reasonable doubt.[38] However, in proceedings for imposition of a civil penalty for evasion of revenue duty, the civil standard applies, assuming that the civil penalty exists separately from potential criminal proceedings for the alleged evasion.[39] In proceedings before the children's hearing, where an offence *by* a child is a ground of referral under dispute, the standard to which it must be proved is the criminal standard,[40] but an allegation of an offence *against* the child is provable on the balance of probability.[41]

4.4 DIFFERENCES BETWEEN AVERMENT AND PROOF—CIVIL CAUSES

4.4.1 The Scottish system of written pleadings is designed to give notice of the facts and of the pleas-in-law which are to be relied upon by each party,[42] to ascertain which of those facts are judicially admitted,[43] and to prevent either from proving other facts or founding upon other legal pleas to the detriment of an opponent who has

---

[32] As to this, see para 3.17.

[33] *Preston-Jones v Preston-Jones* [1951] AC 391 at 400, 412, 417; Dickson, *Evidence* (3rd edn), para 143; *Mackay v Mackay* (1855) 17 D 494, per Lord President McNeill at 500. See also *Imre v Mitchell* 1958 SC 439; *Brown v Brown* 1972 SLT 143; *Docherty v McGlynn* 1985 SLT 237. For historical examples of evidence to satisfy the court that the husband *de facto* was not the father of the child, see *Mackay v Mackay* (1855) 17 D 494; *Brodie v Dyce* (1872) 11 M 142; *Gardner v Gardner* (1877) 4 R (HL) 56; *Montgomery v Montgomery* (1881) 8 R 403; *Steedman v Steedman* (1887) 14 R 1066; *Coles v Homer* (1893) 22 R 716. For the modern approach to proof of parentage, see paras 28.14–28.16, and Wilkinson & Norrie, *The Law Relating to Parent and Child in Scotland* (2nd edn), paras 3.13–3.66.

[34] Divorce (Scotland) Act 1976, s 1(5) and the Law Reform (Parent and Child) (Scotland) Act 1986, s 5(4).

[35] *Eutectic Welding Alloys Co Ltd v Whitting* 1969 SLT (Notes) 79; *Gribben v Gribben* 1976 SLT 266.

[36] Observed in *Morrow v Neil* 1975 SLT (Sh Ct) 65, per Sheriff Macphail at 69, based upon Erskine's description of such proceedings for contravention as "penal" (Erskine iv, 1, 16).

[37] *Gribben v Gribben* 1976 SLT 266; *Nelson v Nelson* 1988 SCLR 663; *Johnston v Johnston* 1996 SLT 499.

[38] The same has been held in proceedings for breach of probation: *Valentine v Kennedy* 1987 SCCR 47.

[39] *1st Indian Cavalry Club Ltd v Commissioners of Customs & Excise* 1998 SC 126.

[40] Children (Scotland) Act 1995, s 68(3)(b). This would apply even if the ground is expressed in different terms, as long as the ground of referral has a basis in the criminal conduct of the child: *Constanda v M* 1997 SC 217 (dealing with the equivalent s 42(6) of the Social Work (Scotland) Act 1968).

[41] *McGregor v D* 1977 SC 330; *Harris v F* 1991 SLT 242. See also para 29.3.2.

[42] Lees, *Handbook of Pleading*, paras 1–2; Macphail, *Sheriff Court Practice* (2nd edn), para 9-03; Walker, "Written Pleadings" (1963) 79 ScLR 161 at 162–163. The averments have no evidential value unless admitted: *Lee v National Coal Board* 1955 SC 151 at 160; *Stewart v Glasgow Corporation* 1958 SC 28. Failure by a party to deny an averment which is within that party's knowledge constitutes an implied admission: *Central Motor Engineering Co v Galbraith* 1918 SC 755. See also para 11.2.5.

[43] Lees, *Handbook of Pleading*, paras 1–2; Macphail, *Sheriff Court Practice* (2nd edn), para 9-03. It has been observed that if a party states in relation to the other's averments that they are "believed to be true" and goes on to deny other averments, the averments which are "believed to be true" do not require evidence: *Binnie v Rederij Theodoro BV* 1993 SC 71. See also para 11.2.5.

had no opportunity of bringing evidence with regard to them.[44] If for any reason evidence of such facts has been received, or argument in support of a plea-in-law not stated has been allowed, judgment ought not to be pronounced until the party concerned has amended,[45] and the opponent has had an opportunity of answering, and of leading further proof, if desired.[46] However, when the opponent has had ample notice of the case made, it may not matter that the facts proved, if they justify the remedy sought, are not entirely in line in matters of detail with what has been averred.[47] As a general rule it is sufficient if a party proves the substance of what he avers.[48] So, in an action of damages for negligent driving of a motor vehicle, when it was averred that a child was struck while both his feet were on the pavement and the evidence showed that one or both were in the gutter, it was held that the discrepancy was not material to the general case of negligent driving which had been averred, and on which evidence had been led, and that the case ought not to have been withdrawn from the jury.[49] On the other hand, exact conformity between the proof and the averment has been held essential in a case of oral slander, as to the precise words of the alleged slanderous statement,[50] and as to the identity of the person in whose presence it was uttered.[51] What is or is not a material divergence is a question of degree in each case.[52] A party need not necessarily prove all his averments. It is sufficient if the party establishes facts consistent with and within the ambit of the supporting averments, which give rise to entitlement in law to the remedy sought.[53] If a party pleads alternative grounds for the remedy sought, the remedy may be granted if only one of the alternative grounds is proved and the others are not.[54] The same rule does not necessarily apply to a cause remitted to a jury, where the pursuer will fail if he does not obtain a favourable verdict on the issue remitted, even if the issue includes more than is necessary for success.[55]

---

[44] *Esso Petroleum Co Ltd v Southport Corporation* [1956] AC 218 at 238 and 241.

[45] *Black v John Williams & Co Ltd (Wishaw)* 1924 SC (HL) 22; *"Vitruvia" SS Co Ltd v Ropner Shipping Co Ltd* 1924 SC (HL) 31. For the court's powers to allow amendment, see RCS Ch 24; OCR Ch 18.

[46] *Oswald v Fairs* 1911 SC 257.

[47] *Gunn v McAdam & Son Ltd* 1949 SC 31. But *cf Lawrence v Sir William Arrol & Co Ltd* 1958 SC 348.

[48] Dickson, *Evidence* (3rd edn), para 41.

[49] *McDonald v Duncan* 1933 SC 737. It must be noted that the evidence referred to was admitted without challenge on the part of the defender. See also *Livingstone v Strachan, Crerar & Jones* 1923 SC 794; *Brown v Ross* 1935 SN 9. *Cf Littlejohn v Brown & Co* 1909 SC 169.

[50] *Martin v McLean* (1844) 6 D 981.

[51] *Broomfield v Greig* (1868) 6 M 992. See also *Walker v Cumming* (1868) 6 M 318.

[52] *McDonald v Duncan* 1933 SC 737, per Lord Murray at 745, Lord Wark at 746. In *Parker v Lanarkshire Health Board* 1996 SCLR 57, a reparation case, evidence as to lifting patients by "pivot lift", although heard under reservation, was not admitted in proof since the pleadings did not give fair notice that such a form of lifting was to be considered.

[53] *Gunn v McAdam & Son Ltd* 1949 SC 31. But *cf Lawrence v Sir William Arrol & Co Ltd* 1958 SC 348.

[54] For example, in an action of damages for negligent driving the pursuer usually avers that the defender has failed in a number of duties, such as the duty to drive at a safe speed, to keep the vehicle under proper control and not to change direction without giving adequate warning of his intention, but will succeed if the negligence is proved by any one of these faults; in an action of reduction, where fraud and undue influence are averred and pleaded, decree may be pronounced on the ground of undue influence although fraud is negatived: *Gray v Binny* (1879) 7 R 332. See also *Petrie v Forsyth* (1874) 2 R 214; *Forbes v Forbes's Trs* 1957 SC 325, per Lord Guthrie at 330.

[55] *Balmer v Hogarth* (1830) 8 S 715; *Black v Duncan* 1924 SC 738 at 744.

4.5 DIFFERENCES BETWEEN LIBEL AND PROOF—CRIMINAL CAUSES

4.5.1   Any discrepancy between the libel and the evidence led was at one time fatal to the prosecutor's success, but this strictness is considerably mitigated by the wide power of amendment now given by statute.[56] Briefly put, the charge may, subject to the discretion of the court, be amended so as to cure any error or defect therein or any discrepancy or variance between it and the evidence, provided that the character of the crime or offence is not changed and that an adjournment is allowed if the accused would, without it, be prejudiced in conducting his defence. Specifications of time, place and quantity, moreover, are read as if subject to a latitude implied by statute,[57] such as "in or near" or "or thereby," unless proof of the exact time, place or quantity libelled is essential to the proof of the crime or offence.[58] Thus, on a charge of theft or reset of a specified number of articles, proof of the theft or reset of only some of them justifies a verdict of guilty as libelled,[59] since the words "or part thereof" are by implication read into all such statements of quantities,[60] but when it is essential to the proof of a statutory offence that, of the articles making up a consignment, those over a certain size shall exceed a specified proportion of the whole, proof that a part of the consignment contained an excessive proportion of over-size articles does not justify a conviction.[61] Latitude is also afforded in the nature of the offence, in respect that the greater offence charged may by implication include a lesser or related offence. Thus, under a charge of robbery, or of theft, or of breach of trust and embezzlement, or of falsehood, fraud and wilful imposition the accused may be convicted of reset; under a charge of robbery, or of breach of trust and embezzlement, or of falsehood, fraud and wilful imposition the accused may be convicted of theft; and under a charge of theft the accused may be convicted of breach of trust and embezzlement or of falsehood, fraud and wilful imposition, or may be convicted of theft although the circumstances proved may in law amount to robbery.[62] Where a completed crime is charged it is competent to convict only of an attempt to commit the crime, and, if the attempt alone is charged, the accused may be convicted of the attempt though the evidence is sufficient to prove completion of the crime.[63] Where a crime is charged as having been committed with a particular intent or with particular circumstances of aggravation it is competent to convict of the crime without the intent or aggravation.[64]

4.5.2   Where an act is charged as a contravention of an enactment it is implied that the enactment[65] applied to the person charged and to the circumstances existing at

---

[56] Solemn procedure—Criminal Procedure (Scotland) Act 1995, s 96; Summary procedure—Criminal Procedure (Scotland) Act 1995, s 159.
[57] Criminal Procedure (Scotland) Act 1995, Sched 3, para 4.
[58] Criminal Procedure (Scotland) Act 1995, Sched 3, para 4(1).
[59] *Gold v Neilson* 1908 SC (J) 5; *Myers v HM Advocate* 1936 JC 1.
[60] Criminal Procedure (Scotland) Act 1995, Sched 3, para 4(6).
[61] *Pattullo, Barr & Co Ltd v McLean* 1947 JC 50. See also *Heatlie v Reid* 1961 JC 70 (sale of milk); *Macdonald v Patterson* (1894) 21 R (J) 38 (sale of exciseable liquor on Sunday); *Sharpe v Donald* 1935 JC 37; *cf Bain v Agnew* 1952 JC 108 (sale of liquor after permitted hours in private room not part of licensed premises).
[62] Criminal Procedure (Scotland) Act 1995, Sched 3, para 8(2)–(4).
[63] Criminal Procedure (Scotland) Act 1995, Sched 3, para 10(1) and (2).
[64] Criminal Procedure (Scotland) Act 1995, Sched 3, para 9(3).
[65] If the contravention is of a statutory instrument it is implied that the instrument was duly made and in force at the time: Criminal Procedure (Scotland) Act 1995, Sched 3, para 12(a); and for challenge to that implication, see *MacGillivray v Johnston (No 2)* 1994 SLT 1012. The same may not apply to a byelaw (*Herkes v Dickie* 1958 JC 51), although it has been said that there is a strong presumption in favour of the validity of a byelaw ostensibly made by a local authority, especially if it was subject to confirmation at a higher level: *McCallum v Brown* 2000 JC 6. See also paras 19.8, 19.10 and 19.19.

the time and place of the offence, and that there existed the circumstances and pre-
liminaries necessary for contravention and prosecution respectively.[66] Where a
statutory offence is also criminal at common law, or where the facts proved in
a case do not amount to a contravention of the statute, but do amount to a crime at
common law, it is lawful to convict of the common law crime.[67] It is not, however,
competent to lead evidence not relevant to the statutory offence charged in order
to establish a common law crime,[68] and the statutory relaxations generally cannot
be extended by analogy to other circumstances which the statutory provisions do
not in terms cover.[69]

It is not necessary in order to justify a conviction that the prosecutor must prove **4.5.3**
all the averments contained in a charge. It is enough to prove facts consistent with
and within the ambit of his averments from which the essential elements of the
crime or offence may be inferred. Hence, evidence of murder by poisoning on a
libel of murder by stabbing would not justify a verdict of guilty as libelled, since
this would not be consistent with the crime as libelled.[70] Proof of any part of what
is charged, if it is itself a crime or offence, justifies a conviction of that crime or
offence.[71] Purely descriptive material in the charge, which is not an essential
element of it, may be proved by evidence from one source only.[72] Wholly superfluous information[73] in the charge need not be proved. Provided evidence is led
which proves identity, particulars given in the charge about any person, corporation, company, place or thing,[74] need not be proved.

---

[66] Criminal Procedure (Scotland) Act 1995, Sched 3, para 12(a).
[67] Criminal Procedure (Scotland) Act 1995, Sched 3, para 14.
[68] *Markland v HM Advocate* (1891) 18 R (J) 50.
[69] Thus, on a statutory charge of theft of an article controlled under defence regulations, a conviction
of the distinct statutory offence of reset of a controlled article was held incompetent: *Mitchell v Adair*
1949 JC 114.
[70] Macdonald, *Criminal Law* (5th edn), p 341.
[71] Criminal Procedure (Scotland) Act 1995, Sched 3, paras 9(1) and (2).
[72] *Smith v Lees* 1997 JC 73 and see para 5.11.
[73] Macdonald, *Criminal Law* (5th edn), p 336; *Henderson v Callender* (1878) 6 R (J) 1.
[74] Criminal Procedure (Scotland) Act 1995, Sched 3, para 15.

CHAPTER 5

SUFFICIENCY OF EVIDENCE

5.1 INTRODUCTORY

"Sufficiency" for the purposes of the law of evidence means sufficiency in law. **5.1.1** Evidence which might satisfy the tribunal as to where the truth lies may not be sufficient in law to entitle the tribunal to come to that opinion.[1] On the other hand, evidence which is sufficient in law may not satisfy the tribunal.[2] When evidence has been led two questions arise. Is there sufficient evidence in law to entitle the tribunal, jury or judge to consider the issue to which the evidence relates? That is a question of law for the decision of the judge, and it is only if it is answered in the affirmative that the second question arises, viz, whether the tribunal is satisfied with the evidence. The first question is the main subject of this chapter. It is now of most significance in criminal cases, where the crucial facts of the Crown case must be corroborated—that is, they must be proved by evidence from two sources. In civil cases, generally, corroboration is not required, but if no evidence is led upon an issue, that issue would have to be withdrawn from consideration by the judge. The second question, as to whether the evidence led satisfies the tribunal on a particular issue, is nevertheless important, and has been considered expressly in consequence of the removal of the requirement of corroboration in civil cases. The second question is discussed at the end of the Chapter under the heading "Weight of evidence".

5.2 PROOF OF CASE OR PROOF OF FACTS

"No person can be convicted of a crime or a statutory offence, except where the **5.2.1** Legislature otherwise directs, unless there is evidence of at least two witnesses implicating the person accused with the commission of the crime or offence with

---

[1] A jury on being directed to acquit because the evidence was insufficient in law, has been known to enquire, "Must we?"

[2] In *Sim v Sim* (1834) 12 S 633 the evidence was sufficient in law, but the tribunal was not satisfied by it, stating that the witnesses were "utterly unworthy of credit".

which he is charged."[3] In civil proceedings the court or jury, "if satisfied that any fact has been established by evidence in those proceedings, shall be entitled to find that fact proved ... notwithstanding that the evidence is not corroborated."[4] To justify a conviction on a criminal charge one or more facts must be proved. The old form of indictment brought this out clearly, since it specified the crime in the major premise and narrated the facts to be proved in the minor. Similarly, in a stated case, while the question whether upon the facts found the lower court was entitled to convict or to acquit is a question of criminal law, the High Court may consider whether upon the evidence a fact or facts ought to have been found proved,[5] the purpose being to enable the High Court to decide whether that evidence was sufficient. In a civil cause several facts may have to be proved to justify the decision. A sheriff court inter-locutor with its findings in fact illustrates this. In summary, whether the facts proved justify the decision is a matter of the particular branch of substantive law. Whether the evidence is sufficient to prove a particular fact is a matter for the law of evidence.

5.2.2 Evidence is thus concerned with proof, not of cases but of facts, and, from this point of view, facts fall into three classes: (1) crucial facts,[6] (2) evidential facts[7] and (3) procedural facts.[8] The opinion evidence of an expert, when led to establish a crucial fact such as cause of death or analysis of a controlled substance, will require corroboration,[9] unless statute has removed the need for corroboration in such circumstances.[10] Expert opinion led otherwise than to establish a crucial fact constitutes an evidential fact which does not require corroboration.[11]

5.3 CRUCIAL FACTS—GENERAL

5.3.1 Crucial facts are the *facta probanda*,[12] the facts which in a criminal cause establish the accused's guilt of the crime charged[13] and must be libelled in an indictment or complaint, expressly or by statutory implication,[14] in order that the libel may be

---

[3]   *Morton v HM Advocate* 1938 JC 50, per Lord Justice-Clerk Aitchison at 55.

[4]   Civil Evidence (Scotland) Act 1988, s 1, replacing the common law requirement as stated in *Maitland v Glasgow Corporation* 1947 SC 20, per Lord President Normand at 25: "Our rule of law is that a case is not to be proved against a defender by the evidence of a single witness ... There must be independent corroboration found in admission or in the testimony of some other witness."

[5]   In *McArthur v Stewart* 1955 JC 71, the court remitted to the sheriff-substitute to state the evidence on which he had made a crucial finding, and on his report held that the evidence was sufficient. So also in *Dow v MacKnight* 1949 JC 38 and *Smith v HM Advocate* 1995 SLT 583. The Criminal Procedure (Scotland) Act 1995, s 179(7) requires the trial judge to append to the stated case a note of evidence relevant to his findings in fact or any proposed adjustment rejected by him, for consideration by the High Court under s 182(5)(g).

[6]   See paras 5.3–5.6.

[7]   See paras 5.7–5.11.

[8]   See para 5.12.

[9]   *McKillen v Barclay Curle & Co Ltd* 1967 SLT 41.

[10]   As in civil cases, or in criminal cases where the reports of forensic scientists or analysts on a crucial fact may be the subject of evidence from a single witness: Criminal Procedure (Scotland) Act 1995, s 281(2), (3) and s 282(1).

[11]   *Davie v Magistrates of Edinburgh* 1953 SC 34.

[12]   Described as "crucial facts" in *Farrell v Concannon* 1957 JC 12 at 17, *Lockwood v Walker* 1910 SC (J) 3 at 5, *Smith v Lees* 1997 JC 73 at 79C; "essential facts" in *Bisset v Anderson* 1949 JC 106 at 110, *Stewart v Glasgow Corporation* 1958 SC 28 at 45; "essential matter" in *Gillespie v Macmillan* 1957 JC 31 at 39; "essential elements" in *McCourt* 1913 SC (J) 6 at 8; and "material facts" in *McArthur v Stewart* 1955 JC 71 at 74.

[13]   Some procedural facts unconnected with the accused's guilt are essential to a conviction—*eg* a private prosecutor's title, which must be libelled and proved: *Lees v Macdonald* (1893) 20 R (J) 55. See para 5.12.

[14]   Those terms implied in criminal charges in general are found in the Criminal Procedure (Scotland) Act 1995, Sched 3.

relevant. In a civil cause they are the facts which a party must, or ought to, aver in order to make a case relevant to be sent to proof.[15]

In criminal cases, unless by statute a single witness is sufficient,[16] such facts require "legal proof "[17] or "full proof",[18] which consists of evidence from at least two separate sources—either the direct evidence of two witnesses,[19] or two or more evidential facts spoken to by separate witnesses[20] from which the crucial fact may be inferred, or of a combination of the direct evidence of one witness and of one or more evidential facts spoken to by other witnesses[21] which support it.[22] The direct evidence of a single witness does not become sufficient proof of a crucial fact because the witness is not cross-examined.[23] It is not corroborated, in so far as corroboration is now required by a false denial by the accused[24] or by a party in the witness box,[25] nor by the silence of an accused when charged,[26] or by selections from the opposite party's unproved, unadmitted averments.[27] Nor is any fact proved merely because witnesses who deny it are not believed.[28]

5.3.2

---

[15] As to averments in civil causes, see para 11.2.4.

[16] See para 5.5.

[17] In *O'Hara v Central SMT Co* 1941 SC 363, Lord President Normand several times used the phrases "full legal proof" and "legal proof" with the meaning stated in the text, corroboration being required then in the civil case.

[18] Used by Dickson, *Evidence* (3rd edn), para 1807, and in *Moore v Harland & Wolff* 1937 SC 707 at 715, 721.

[19] An accused, who chose to give evidence, was in effect the necessary second witness for the prosecution: *McArthur v Stewart* 1955 JC 71. This would not occur if the defence submitted that there was no case to answer at the conclusion of the Crown case: Criminal Procedure (Scotland) Act 1995, ss 97 and 160.

[20] A witness cannot corroborate himself: *Morton v HM Advocate* 1938 JC 50, per Lord Justice-Clerk Aitchison at 54. A complainer's identification of a pullover seen by her in the accused's car which she said had been used to tie her up during a rape, and not identified or spoken to by any other witness, could not be corroborative of her evidence since she was the only source of evidence about it, although it had been produced in court: *Cordiner v HM Advocate* 1993 SLT 2. A conviction based upon the accused's reaction and demeanour while making extra-judicial admissions was quashed on appeal, when the Crown acknowledged that evidence of the accused's own reactions could not corroborate his own admissions: *McGougan v HM Advocate* 1991 SLT 908.

[21] Hume, *Commentary on the Law of Scotland regarding Crimes*, ii, 384.

[22] Hume, ii, 284; Burnett, *Criminal Law*, 519; *Smith v Lees* 1997 JC 73; *O'Hara v Central SMT Co* 1941 SC 363 at 379. Lord McLaren's dictum in *Lees v Macdonald* (1893) 20 R (J) 55 at 58 to the effect that any fact in the case may be proved by the testimony of one credible witness, though cited by the court in *Morton v HM Advocate* 1938 JC 50 and *Gillespie v Macmillan* 1957 JC 31 at 37, is irreconcilable with the decisions cited below.

[23] Criminal causes: *Morton v HM Advocate* 1938 JC 50, expressly disapproving observations in *Strathern v Lambie* 1934 JC 137, and impliedly those of Lord Justice-Clerk Macdonald and Lord Lee in *Lees v Macdonald* (1893) 20 R (J) 55; *Wilson v Brown* 1947 JC 81, per Lord Mackay at 94, Lord Jamieson at 96; *McArthur v Stewart* 1955 JC 71, per Lord Justice-General Clyde at 74. Civil causes: *Stewart v Glasgow Corporation* 1958 SC 28; *Moore v Harland & Wolff* 1937 SC 707.

[24] In *Wilkie v HM Advocate* 1938 JC 128 the alleged lie was not told in the witness box, but the opinions cover the general point; *Quinn v HM Advocate* 1990 SLT 877; *Fisher v Guild* 1991 SLT 253. *Cf* the court's approach to false information given about the use of the accused's motor car: *Winter v Heywood* 1995 JC 60.

[25] *Davies v Hunter* 1934 SC 10; Civil Evidence (Scotland) Act 1988, s 1(2) removed any vestige of a rule of corroboration by false denial, in so far as any had existed in civil cases for affiliation and aliment.

[26] *Robertson v Maxwell* 1951 JC 11. As to the evidential effect of the accused's silence at judicial examination or in court, see para 6.10. Evidence of the silence of an accused in the immediate aftermath of the alleged crime was held to be of corroborative value in *Kay v Allan* (1978) SCCR Supp 188, but the accused had also made a comment akin to an implied admission.

[27] *Stewart v Glasgow Corporation* 1958 SC 28; *Lee v National Coal Board* 1955 SC 151.

[28] *Cameron v Yeats* (1899) 1 F 456.

5.3.3   In civil cases the court may find a crucial fact proved even if evidence on that fact comes from only one source,[29] but in actions of declarator of marriage, nullity of marriage, separation or divorce, that source must be someone other than a party to the case.[30] Proceedings for breach of interdict or contempt of court, whilst requiring proof beyond reasonable doubt because of the quasi-criminal nature of the penalty,[31] are civil proceedings in terms of the Civil Evidence (Scotland) Act 1988 and do not require corroboration.[32] Care proceedings under the Children (Scotland) Act 1995, Part II are also civil proceedings and corroboration is not normally required.[33]

5.4 CRUCIAL FACTS—CRIMINAL CAUSES

5.4.1   In criminal cases the identification of the accused and the commission of the crime are the very least that constitute the crucial facts, and they are examined in more detail in the following sub-paragraphs. The nature of the crime may be such that a number of elements are crucial within it, as are described below. Statutory crimes are frequently made up of a number of different elements which are crucial, and statute may provide that a crime is committed by a person merely because of their special capacity, albeit that they are not physically identifiable as the perpetrator. Hence the master of a vessel or the owner of a motor vehicle may be convicted of using the vessel or the vehicle although another person was in control of it at the time.

5.4.2   Statute has introduced a new issue for corroboration when an appeal is taken on the ground of the existence and significance of evidence which was not heard at the original proceedings.[34] If that evidence is to be from or of a person who gave evidence in the original proceedings and is additional or different to the evidence given then, it may not found an appeal unless there is a reasonable explanation for the evidence not being given at the time, which explanation is supported by independent evidence. In the first case to apply this test[35] judicial opinion differed as to the exact nature of the crucial fact that has to be supported,[36] and what could constitute that support.[37]

Identification of accused

5.4.3   In every criminal cause the fact that the accused was implicated in the commission of the crime or offence is crucial,[38] and therefore requires full legal proof. It may

---

[29] Civil Evidence (Scotland) Act 1988, s 1, previously introduced for personal injury actions only by the Law Reform (Miscellaneous Provisions) (Scotland) Act 1968, s 9.

[30] Civil Evidence (Scotland) Act 1988, s 8(3). This was also the position at common law: *Macfarlane v Macfarlane* 1956 SC 472; *Keenan v Keenan* 1974 SLT (Notes) 10.

[31] para 4.3.3.

[32] *Byrne v Ross* 1993 SLT 307.

[33] Civil Evidence (Scotland) Act 1988, s 9, except when the ground of referral under consideration is criminal conduct by the child which in terms of the Children (Scotland) Act 1995, s 68(3)(b) must be proved to the standard of criminal proceedings and thus, it is submitted, by corroborated evidence. See para 29.3.2.

[34] Under the Criminal Procedure (Scotland) Act 1995, s 106(3)(a) or s 175(5).

[35] *Campbell v HM Advocate* 1998 SLT 923. This was followed in *Mills v HM Advocate* 1999 SLT 680.

[36] Per Lord Sutherland at 955A and Lord McCluskey (dissenting) at 951A.

[37] Per Lord Justice-Clerk Cullen at 941A–L, Lord McCluskey (dissenting) at 950D–951L, and Lord Sutherland at 955B–C.

[38] *Morton v HM Advocate* 1938 JC 50; *Mitchell v Macdonald* 1959 SLT (Notes) 74; *Smith v Lees* 1997 JC 73.

sometimes be proved by the evidence of the same witnesses who speak to the commission of the crime or offence. On other occasions it may have to be proved by the evidence of witnesses who have no knowledge of the commission of the crime or offence. So, for example, in a prosecution of a driving offence, the identification of the accused as the person who committed the offence may be proved by the witnesses who observed the manner of driving and, at the same time, were able to recognise the driver. However, the witnesses to the manner of driving may have been unable to recognise the driver. In this case it may be possible to prove that the accused was the driver at the relevant time by the evidence of a witness who saw him driving the vehicle immediately before, and of a witness who saw him driving it immediately after, the alleged offence, in circumstances which prove beyond reasonable doubt that no other person could have occupied the driver's seat during the intervening period when the offence occurred. Where the offence arises from the presence of a vehicle or vessel, with which the accused has been associated in evidence, the identification of the vessel becomes a crucial fact. So when it was proved that a vessel was trawling illegally a conviction of the master was quashed because only one witness could identify the vessel.[39] An accused may be sufficiently identified by his voice.[40] When an accused was identified visually by one witness and aurally by another the conviction was quashed, not because the aural identification was inadmissible, but because the two witnesses contradicted each other.[41]

The proper practice is that the witnesses who purport to identify the accused as **5.4.4** the person who committed the crime should point him out in court as the person of whom they are speaking.[42] It may not be sufficient that they merely refer to him by name,[43] unless they also state that he is the person in the dock, but this will depend upon all the circumstances of the evidence and identification.[44] Merely to identify the accused as the person named in the indictment or complaint is valueless.[45]

If a witness cannot identify the accused in court it will be sufficient to prove by **5.4.5** other evidence that on an earlier occasion—for example, at an identification parade—he did identify the accused as the person concerned.[46] If the witness is merely unable to recall sufficiently to enable identification in court, reliance upon

---

[39] *Harrison v Mackenzie* 1923 JC 61.
[40] Evidence of identification by voice was admitted in *McGiveran v Auld* (1894) 21 R (J) 69, and applied in *Lees v Roy* 1990 SCCR 310 and in *Farmer v HM Advocate* 1991 SCCR 986, cases relying upon the *Moorov* doctrine.
[41] *Burrows v HM Advocate* 1951 SLT (Notes) 69. There must be a conjunction of testimonies for the sources of evidence to corroborate, which was missing in, *eg, Connolly v HM Advocate* 1958 SLT 79, *McDonald v Scott* 1993 JC 54, *Mitchell v Maguire* 1995 SLT 1277.
[42] *Bruce v HM Advocate* 1936 JC 93, and observed to be best practice in *Robson v HM Advocate* 1996 SCCR 340. It has also been observed that for such identification the accused is entitled to remain sitting and should not be asked to do anything by way of movement, adjustment or speech which might assist the identification process: *Beattie v Scott* 1990 JC 320, but see Sheriff Gordon's commentary at 1990 SCCR 296 at 303.
[43] *Wilson v Brown* 1947 JC 81 at 96; *Bruce v HM Advocate* 1936 JC 93 at 95.
[44] *Robson v HM Advocate* 1996 SCCR 340.
[45] *Bruce v HM Advocate* 1936 JC 93. A statutory presumption that the person who has appeared to stand trial for a crime is the person who was charged by the police (now the Criminal Procedure (Scotland) Act 1995, s 280(9)) is also of limited use in that it does not identify the accused as the perpetrator; but for examples of its use, see *Smith v Paterson* 1982 JC 125, *Rollo v Wilson* 1988 JC 82.
[46] Alison, *Criminal Law*, Vol II, 628; Macdonald, *Criminal Law* (5th edn), 325. In *Wight* (1836) 1 Swin 47, the witness had already identified the accused from the witness box. There was no direct judicial authority until the decision in *McGaharon v Lord Advocate* 1968 SLT (Notes) 99 but no opinions were given in that case. Authority is now found in *Muldoon v Herron* 1970 JC 30.

evidence of identification from an earlier occasion has been said to complete a chain of identification[47] or to fill a gap in the witness's evidence.[48] This is logical if the witness acknowledges having made the earlier identification.[49] However, it has been decided that even if a witness states in court that the accused is not the culprit,[50] or denies the terms of the earlier identification,[51] evidence of the earlier identification may be admitted and can be sufficient evidence of that witness's identification of the accused, it being for the court to assess the relative weight of the evidence of the earlier identification compared to that given by the witness in court.[52]

5.4.6 One source of positive identification[53] may be sufficiently corroborated by a second witness who states that the accused resembles the perpetrator.[54] It has been decided that a statement or concession by the witness that other persons may also resemble the perpetrator[55] does not mean that the evidence of resemblance with the accused is in conflict with the positive evidence of identification.[56] Instead the equivocal nature of the supporting evidence is a matter for the court to consider when assessing its weight.[57]

Commission of the crime

5.4.7 Some crimes consist of a single act, in which case the fact that the act was done is crucial and requires full legal proof. Assaults frequently fall into this category, and another example was the offence of having commercial petrol in the tank of a private car.[58] However, most other crimes and offences are compound—that is to say

---

[47] Alison, *Criminal Law*, Vol II, 628; *Muldoon v Herron* 1970 JC 30 at 36 (identification parade); *Frew v Jessop* 1990 JC 15 (earlier description given to police). *Cf McAllister v HM Advocate* (1975) SCCR Supp 98.

[48] *Muldoon v Herron* 1970 JC 30 per Lord Wheatley at 40. Lord Wheatley delivered a dissenting judgment, but not on this point.

[49] More general authority now exists for adoption of an earlier "statement" by a witness who cannot recall the evidence when the case comes to trial: *Jamieson v HM Advocate (No 2)* 1995 SLT 666, and under the Criminal Procedure (Scotland) Act 1995, ss 260 and 262 provided that the statement is incorporated in a document. See para 8.6.

[50] As did the witness Mrs Miller in *Muldoon v Herron* 1970 JC 30.

[51] As did the witness Mrs Cooper in *Smith v HM Advocate* 1986 SCCR 135.

[52] *Smith v HM Advocate* 1986 SCCR 135; *Neeson v HM Advocate* 1984 SCCR 72; *Maxwell v HM Advocate* 1990 JC 340. For critical examination of this line of authority, see Sheriff Gordon's commentary to *Smith* in 1986 SCCR at 138–139, and "Identification and Credibility" (1987) 32 JLSS 30. These decisions go further than the later statutory provisions regarding adoption into evidence of statements made before the trial (Criminal Procedure (Scotland) Act 1995, ss 260 and 262) but are apparently preserved by s 262(4).

[53] Stating that the accused was "very like" the perpetrator was taken to be a positive identification in *Gracie v Allan* 1987 SCCR 364.

[54] *Ralston v HM Advocate* 1987 SCCR 467; *Nelson v HM Advocate* 1989 SLT 215; *Murphy v HM Advocate* 1995 JC 16; *Mair v HM Advocate* 1997 SLT 817; *Kelly v HM Advocate* 1998 SCCR 660. Without the one positive identification, resemblance expressed as "doesn't look unlike" the perpetrator was held to be insufficient: *MacDonald v HM Advocate* 1998 SLT 37. It has been observed that such identifications rarely stand alone, but are accompanied by descriptions of features or surrounding circumstances: *Fox v HM Advocate* 1998 JC 94 per Lord Coulsfield at 119C–D.

[55] Such as other members of an identification parade, as in *Nelson* 1988 SCCR 536 and *Kelly* 1998 SCCR 600.

[56] This could be said to be another example of the court taking evidence at its best interpretation for the Crown when considering sufficiency, an approach endorsed by the court in *Fox v HM Advocate* 1998 JC 94.

[57] *Kelly v HM Advocate* 1998 SCCR 600.

[58] *Bisset v Anderson* 1949 JC 106. See also *Callan v MacFadyean* 1950 JC 82.

they arise from the coincidence of two or more independent facts, none of which supports any other. Each of these independent facts is crucial and requires full legal proof.[59] The common law crime of using lewd and libidinous practices consists of two crucial facts—the use of the practices and the vulnerability of the victim[60]—and that of obtaining money by fraud of four crucial facts—the representation, its falsity, the payment induced by it and the accused's knowledge of its falsity.[61] In a charge of theft the fact of the theft from the owner or possessor must be proved in addition to identification of the accused as the perpetrator.[62] However, the fact of theft spoken to only by one person (usually the victim) can be corroborated by inference from possession by the accused of the stolen property.[63]

Statutory charges frequently involve compound facts. For example, in various **5.4.8** offences under the Civic Government (Scotland) Act 1982 two crucial facts must be established: it is an offence to be found in possession of tools for theft if one has two unspent previous convictions for theft[64] and both the possession and the record are crucial facts.[65]

5.5 STATUTORY EXCEPTIONS

Some statutes contain a provision that an offence may be proved by the evidence **5.5.1** of one credible witness.[66] If such evidence is led, the court is not entitled to reject it merely because other witnesses, apparently available, were not called.[67] If one witness would suffice, and the prosecution adduces two, who contradict each other, the court may disbelieve one and convict on the evidence of the other.[68] The

---

[59] *Morton v HM Advocate* 1938 JC 50; *Mitchell v Macdonald* 1959 SLT (Notes) 74; *Smith v Lees* 1997 JC 73. For example, in *Smith v Lees* 1997 JC 73 at 79B Lord Justice-General Rodger expressed the crucial facts in a crime of rape as "(1) penetration of the complainer's vagina by, (2) the accused's private member, (3) forcibly, and (4) without the complainer's consent".

[60] *Lockwood v Walker* 1910 SC (J) 3, where the child's evidence as to her age was not corroborated. Whether age is crucial to the crime was later doubted (*eg McLauglan v Boyd* 1934 JC 19) and according to the court in *Batty v HM Advocate* 1995 JC 160, the age of the complainer (to prove that the complainer is below the age of puberty) is not of the essence. Other sexual offences created by statute require the age of the victim to be proved (Criminal Law (Consolidation) (Scotland) Act 1995, ss 5–10, 12 and 13, but proof of age, where required, may now be achieved by statutory presumption in favour of the age libelled unless challenged by the accused prior to trial: Criminal Procedure (Scotland) Act 1995, s 255A.

[61] *Townsend v Strathern* 1923 JC 66, where only one witness spoke to the accused's knowledge of the falsity of her representation.

[62] *McDonald v Herron* 1966 SLT 61. See also *Carson v McGlennan* 2000 SCLR 631.

[63] *McDonald v Herron* 1966 SLT 61. For examples, see *Tudhope v Smellie* (1977) SCCR Supp 186, *Hunter v Heywood* 1993 SCCR 121.

[64] s 58(1). An accused's previous record, when a crucial fact in the case, is admissible under the Criminal Procedure (Scotland) Act 1995, s 266(4)(a).

[65] They must be corroborated unless statute provides otherwise. *Eg* the criminal record of the accused may be treated as a special capacity, which, if specified in the libel, will be proved by statutory presumption unless challenged prior to trial: *Newlands v MacPhail* 1991 SLT 642; Criminal Procedure (Scotland) Act 1995, s 255.

[66] *eg* Game (Scotland) Act 1832, ss 1, 2, 6; Salmon and Freshwater Fisheries (Protection) (Scotland) Act 1951, s 7A(3); Poaching Prevention Act 1862, s 3, as construed in *Anderson v Macdonald* 1910 SC (J) 65; Wildlife and Countryside Act 1981, s 194; Road Traffic Offenders Act 1988, s 21, and a similar provision in earlier legislation considered in *Sutherland v Aitchison* 1970 SLT (Notes) 48.

[67] *Jopp v Pirie* (1869) 7 M 755. *Cf Macrorie v Mackay* 1909 SC (J) 18.

[68] *Coventry v Brown* 1926 JC 20, dealing with a section in the Excise Management Act 1827, which is now repealed.

one witness required may be an accomplice[69] if his evidence is accepted as credible.[70] Under the Food and Drugs (Scotland) Act 1956,[71] the certificate of an analyst is sufficient evidence of the facts stated in it, unless the other party requires the analyst to be called as a witness. If the analyst is not so called, and there is no counter evidence, the certificate becomes conclusive,[72] but, if evidence is led for the other party, the whole evidence must be considered and the certificate may be rebutted.[73] If the analyst is required by the other party to be called as a witness, his oral evidence is sufficient.[74] Similar provisions exist for proof that a substance is a controlled drug or medicinal product[75] and proof of alcohol or drugs found in samples taken from a driver,[76] but vary as to whether contrary evidence may be led in the absence of timeous objection to the certificate.[77] These innovations on the law of evidence are limited to the precise words of the provision in question, so, for example, evidence of one pathologist or forensic scientist in relation to an autopsy will be sufficient unless the accused challenges the Crown's notice of intention to rely upon one such witness, but the written autopsy report must be lodged nevertheless.[78]

5.6 CRUCIAL FACTS—CIVIL CAUSES

5.6.1 The crucial facts in any civil cause ought to be discoverable from the written pleadings. They are the facts which ought to be averred in order that the averments may relevantly support the party's pleas-in-law. So, for example, in *Moore v Harland & Wolff*[79] it was a condition precedent to a relevant statutory claim that the pursuer should have taken all reasonable steps to obtain employment. The pursuer alone gave evidence about his efforts to obtain work, and, since at that time corroboration of crucial facts was required in civil cases, this crucial fact was held not to be proved. In order to prove negligence against a local authority who were in possession and control of a clothes pole in a back court it was essential for the pursuer to prove, not only that the pole was defective through rust at the time when it broke, but that it had been defective at an earlier time when the defenders had an opportunity of discovering the defect. Again this case failed because the defective condition of the pole at the earlier period was not sufficiently proved by the evidence of one witness.[80]

---

[69] *Manson v Macleod* 1918 JC 60; *Dow v MacKnight* 1949 JC 38.

[70] The evidence of an accomplice (*socius criminis*) is no longer subject to any special credibility warning (*ie* it is no longer received *cum nota*) following the decision in *Docherty v HM Advocate* 1987 JC 81.

[71] s 42(1).

[72] *Chalmers v McMeeking* 1921 JC 54. An example can be found in *Milne v Sinclair* (1975) SCCR Supp 89.

[73] *Bisset v Anderson* 1949 JC 106 at 113; *Todd v Cochrane* (1901) 3 Adam 357.

[74] Food and Drugs (Scotland) Act 1956, s 42(1).

[75] Criminal Procedure (Scotland) Act 1995, s 282.

[76] Road Traffic Offenders Act 1988, s 16(5)(a).

[77] See, for example, *Macaulay v Wilson* 1995 SLT 1070, in relation to the Road Traffic Offenders Act 1988, s 16.

[78] Criminal Procedure (Scotland) Act 1995, s 281(2). For examples of the strict interpretation of such provisions, see *Bisset v Anderson* 1949 JC 106, *McMillan v HM Advocate* 1988 SLT 211. As to statutory certificates, see also para 19.16 (opinion).

[79] 1937 SC 707.

[80] The facts in *Stewart v Glasgow Corporation* 1958 SC 28.

Now that the requirement for corroboration has been removed from civil cases **5.6.2** generally, the lack of corroborative evidence on crucial facts such as these examples would not be fatal to the case, the court's satisfaction that the crucial fact had been proved being a matter of weight rather than sufficiency.[81] However, if no evidence was led upon a crucial fact not judicially admitted, the case would breach the requirement of sufficiency in law and could not be found proved.[82] Failure to advance a defence in the pleadings and to take steps to establish it by lodging relevant productions can lead to the grant of summary decree in favour of the pursuer.[83]

5.7 EVIDENTIAL FACTS—GENERAL

These are facts which individually establish nothing but from which, in conjunc- **5.7.1** tion with other such facts, a crucial fact may be inferred. They are frequently described as circumstantial evidence, to which further attention is given below and in the next chapter. The evidence of a single witness is sufficient proof of each fact which is used in this way. It has been explained that two witnesses are unnecessary to establish each of such facts "because the aptitude and coherence of the several circumstances often as fully confirm the truth of the story as if all the witnesses were deponing to the same facts."[84] An evidential fact may also be used in conjunction with, and as providing sufficient corroboration of, the direct evidence of a single witness, so that combined they provide sufficient evidence of the crucial fact. "If one man swear that he saw the pannel stab the deceased, and others confirm his testimony with circumstances, such as the pannel's flight from the spot, the blood on his clothes, the bloody instrument found in his possession, his confession on being taken, or the like; certainly these are as good, nay better even, than a second witness to the act of stabbing."[85] In the example quoted, the flight, the blood on the clothes, the blood on the knife and the confession,[86] are evidential facts, each of which is sufficiently proved by the evidence of one witness, if it is used to support, and receives support from,[87] direct testimony or other evidential facts in order to establish the crucial fact that the deceased was stabbed by the accused.

---

[81] Civil Evidence (Scotland) Act 1988, s 1; *L v L* 1998 SLT 672. The specialties arising in family actions are considered at Chapter 28.

[82] *eg* as occurred on one of the causal issues in the reparation case *Kay's Tutor v Ayrshire and Arran Health Board* 1986 SLT 435.

[83] *eg King v Moore* 1993 SLT 1117 (OH).

[84] Hume, ii, 384. See also Dickson, *Evidence* (3rd edn), para 1811. What is required is a "concurrence of testimonies": Hume, ii, 383.

[85] Hume, ii, 383.

[86] An extra-judicial confession in a criminal cause may be proved by the evidence of one witness: *Mills v HM Advocate* 1935 JC 77; *Innes v HM Advocate* 1955 SLT (Notes) 69. Such a confession, however, is evidence from only one source and is insufficient by itself to justify a conviction unless supported by other evidence. If a confession contains features of special knowledge to the perpetrator and is to be corroborated only by evidence that those features did apply to the crime, the making of the confession should be spoken to by more than one witness (*Low v HM Advocate* 1994 SLT 277), but the witnesses need not accord on each and every element of the confession (*Mitchell v HM Advocate* 1996 SCCR 97), and it is not necessary for an unchallenged tape recording of the admission to be played in court to both such witnesses (*Hudson v Hamilton* 1994 SLT 150). As to the probative effect of extra-judicial confessions and admissions, see para 9.2.

[87] As to this "dual use" of circumstantial evidence, see Lord Justice-General Rodger in *Fox v HM Advocate* 1998 JC 94 at 100E–F.

5.8 EVIDENTIAL FACTS—CRIMINAL CAUSES

5.8.1 Circumstantial evidence is indirect evidence of a fact in issue. It consists of circumstances, admitted or proved, from which the existence of the fact in issue is inferred. Each circumstance by itself may be of little significance.[88] It may be consistent both with the existence of the fact in issue and with some other possibility.[89] But if, despite the other individual possibilities, the circumstances agree in supporting the existence of the fact in issue, it is proper to regard that fact as proved.[90] Examples are given in the next chapter, but here a simple illustration may be given. An unidentified man snatched a bag containing £50 in notes. Soon afterwards the accused was seen to run into a neighbouring back court carrying something, and to run from it carrying nothing. When arrested he had £50 in notes in his pocket, and the stolen bag was found in the back court. From each of these circumstances an innocent inference may be drawn. The accused may have been hurrying by a short cut to catch a train, a parcel may have been dropped unnoticed as he ran, he may have won £50 betting on a horse, while the bag may have been thrown away by another person. But each circumstance also yields an inference against the accused, and in combination point to him as the thief. The strength of the inference against him is increased if it is proved that the trains were not running because of a strike, that no parcel was found in the back court, that he had not won £50 betting on a horse, and that no other person entered the back court during the relevant period. Circumstantial evidence may be as good as if not better than direct testimony,[91] but since it, equally with direct evidence, is tainted by human fallibility[92] failure to produce, without good reason, any direct evidence which is available may impair the probative value of the circumstantial evidence.[93]

5.9 PROBATIVE VALUE OF EVIDENTIAL FACTS

5.9.1 Evidential facts or circumstantial evidence must be considered in two ways during a prosecution. It must be considered by the judge in the context of sufficiency in order to ascertain whether the facts and circumstances are capable of amounting to corroboration,[94] here described as the probative requirement. If deemed sufficient

---

[88] *Little v HM Advocate* 1983 SLT 489.
[89] *Fox v HM Advocate* 1998 JC 94, disapproving *Mackie v HM Advocate* 1994 JC 132. However, see *Gallagher v HM Advocate* 2000 SCCR 634, and the commentary at 636–637.
[90] *Fox v HM Advocate* 1998 JC 94, and see Brown, "Two Cases on Corroboration" 1998 SLT 71.
[91] *Mackinnon v Miller* 1909 SC 373, per Lord President Dunedin at 378; *Withers v HM Advocate* 1947 JC 109, per Lord Justice-General Cooper at 115.
[92] *Mackinnon v Miller* 1909 SC 373.
[93] Dickson, *Evidence* (3rd edn), para 108(7). In *Withers v HM Advocate* 1947 JC 109, the Crown produced the available positive circumstantial evidence (staining on the accused's clothing appearing to match paint from the scene of the crime), in addition to circumstantial evidence to exclude the possibilities of accident and suicide.
[94] At end of the Crown case, as in *Williamson v Wither* 1981 SCCR 214; and again before the evidence is weighed by judge or jury: *Farmer v Guild* 1991 SCCR 174. In *Reilly v HM Advocate* 1981 SCCR 201 the court on appeal held that the evidence in "character, quality and strength" fell short of what was required to corroborate the one direct witness. This terminology has not been taken up in subsequent cases (other than *Rubin v HM Advocate* 1984 SLT 369 where it was said to be inapplicable) and, it is submitted, it is suggestive of a confusion between sufficiency and weight.

in law, it is for the jury, or the judge if sitting alone, to assess whether the facts and circumstances actually do corroborate,[95] here described as the probative effect. The probative requirements of circumstantial evidence were considered in detail in the case of *Fox v HM Advocate*[96] after concern had been expressed about the decision in *Mackie v HM Advocate*.[97] The latter had concluded that circumstantial evidence which was equally consistent with the Crown case and the appellant's exculpatory account was at best neutral and not capable of affording corroboration of the Crown case, a charge of insider dealing contrary to the Company Securities (Insider Dealing) Act 1985. In *Fox* a full bench examined the corroboration requirement in criminal cases and could find no basis for the restriction imposed in *Mackie* upon the probative requirements of circumstantial evidence. By reference to Hume,[98] Burnett[99] and Alison[100] the court confirmed that circumstantial evidence need only be capable of providing that confirmation or support of other evidence which is the essence of the corroboration requirement. In assessing the sufficiency of that evidence at the conclusion of the Crown case, and again at the conclusion of the trial, the judge must take the evidence led at its best interpretation for the Crown.[101] The existence of an alternative or exculpatory account for that piece of circumstantial evidence is therefore not relevant to sufficiency, but must be taken into account by the jury in assessing the weight to attach to direct evidence and to the circumstantial evidence.[102] There is thus no requirement for the circumstantial evidence to be incriminating per se[103] or for it to be "consistent with"[104] or "unequivocally referable to"[105] other evidence of the commission of the crime or more consistent with the crime than with any competing account.[106] It is unclear where this leaves circumstantial evidence which had been ruled out in earlier cases because there was nothing to link it in time with the offence. Hence prints that could have been placed during some earlier contact between the accused and the place where they were found[107] or torn underwear which was not proved to have been intact before an alleged rape[108] were declared not to be capable of affording corroboration. It is submitted that such evidence would still fail the test in that without something to link it in time with the crime it is not clearly

---

95 *Fox v HM Advocate* 1998 JC 94; *Williamson v Wither* 1981 SCCR 214.

96 1998 JC 94.

97 1994 JC 132; the concern was expressed in *Smith v Lees* 1997 JC 73.

98 *Commentaries*, ii, 384.

99 *Treatise on Criminal Law*, 518–519.

100 *Practice of Criminal Law*, 551–553.

101 *Williamson v Wither* 1981 SCCR 214.

102 *Fox v HM Advocate* JC 94 1998 at 103H–104B, 117E–F.

103 *Fox v HM Advocate* JC 94 1998 at 118C. In *Hoy v HM Advocate* 1998 SCCR 8 evidence of animosity between the parties was said to be sufficient to support the occurrence of an assault but not the murder charge. Sheriff Gordon in his commentary to the report suggests that this is requiring the corroborative evidence to be incriminating per se, but this is not clear from the report.

104 *Mackie v HM Advocate* 1994 JC 132. As Lord McCluskey pointed out in *Smith v Lees* 1997 JC 73 and Lord Kirkwood agrees in *Fox v HM Advocate* 1998 LJC 94 at 108H–109A; 112C–E the word "consistent" is ambiguous, and may mean either positive concurrence or possible concurrence of testimonies, when it is the former that is necessary.

105 *Stobo v HM Advocate* 1994 JC 28 (disapproved in *Smith v Lees* 1997 JC 73).

106 Argued by the appellant in *Fox v HM Advocate* 1998 JC 94 by reference to *Mackie v HM Advocate* 1994 JC 41 and *O'Hara v Central SMT Co Ltd* 1941 SC 363; *cf Gallagher v HM Avocate* 2000 SCCR 634.

107 As in *Slater v Vannet* 1997 JC 226; *MacDonald v HM Advocate* 1998 SLT 37.

108 *Gilmour v HM Advocate* 1993 JC 15.

relevant[109] nor indicative of a concurrence of testimony[110] and thus not capable of affording the necessary support or confirmation.

5.9.2 The probative force of circumstantial evidence is considered further in the next chapter but here we should note that it has been described by analogy,[111] which although rarely referred to now in judicial reasoning, may be of assistance in visualisation or conceptualisation of the use of circumstantial evidence.

Cable analogy

5.9.3 The favoured analogy is with a cable whereby individual circumstances of slight moment by their existence and coexistence lead an inference to be drawn, and as others are added which can provide support these give added and increased strength to the cable of which they form a component part. The comparison with a chain of facts had been said to be inept.[112] "The chain is weakened by the increasing number of its links ... not so with circumstantial evidence. The cable gains increased strength by each added strand. The failure of proof as to one circumstance is but one strand from the cable."[113] If, having decided which of the evidence to accept the jury conclude that the accepted circumstances in combination—the strands in the cable—support the fact in issue, it can be regarded as proved. If, on the other hand, there is a single proved circumstance which is incompatible with the fact in issue, the proof of the fact in issue fails.[114] For example, even if the accused's fingerprints are found in the premises which have been broken into, the jemmy used was his, and the stolen goods were found hidden in his bedroom, he must be acquitted of the theft if he was in prison when it occurred.

Chain analogy

5.9.4 As has been indicated above, the cable is usually regarded as the correct analogy with circumstantial evidence, and the view has been expressed that evidence consisting solely of a chain of independent facts, from which another fact inevitably follows, is not truly circumstantial evidence.[115] However, the rule which allows

---

[109] In *Fox v HM Advocate* 1998 JC 94 at 118B, Lord Coulsfield observes that "Since the purpose of requiring corroboration is to eliminate the risk of injustice which might arise from reliance on a single source of evidence, it is important that the requirement should not be held to be satisfied by evidence which is trivial or, properly considered, irrelevant to the fact in issue."

[110] In *Fox v HM Advocate* 1998 JC 94, per Lord Kirkwood at 112E.

[111] Dickson, *Evidence* (3rd edn), para 95.

[112] The inaptness of the chain analogy is commented on in Wills, *Circumstantial Evidence* (7th edn), p 435. It is illustrated in *Forrester v HM Advocate* 1952 JC 28, where what broke was not a link in a chain, which would have been fatal to the conviction, but a strand in a cable, which left the appeal court free to consider whether the conviction might not be sustained.

[113] Quoted by Dickson, *Evidence* (3rd edn), para 95. See also Wills, *Circumstantial Evidence* (7th edn), p 10.

[114] Dickson, *Evidence* (3rd edn), para 108(5). In *Kane v Friel* 1997 JC 69, a prosecution for theft by finding, although there was proof of the finding there was also a finding in fact that no one had reported the goods stolen. This was incompatible with the conclusion that the crime had been proved and the conviction was quashed on appeal.

[115] WA Wilson, "The Logic of Corroboration" (1960) 76 SLR 101. The same opinion is implied in "Corroboration of Evidence in Scottish Criminal Law" 1958 SLT (News) 137. Both these articles deal very fully with the principles underlying the acceptance of circumstantial evidence in Scotland. Full discussion of the use of a single source of circumstantial evidence in support of one direct witness is to be found in *Smith v Lees* 1997 JC and *Fox v HM Advocate* 1998 SLT 335, and see Brown, "Two Cases on Corroboration" 1998 SLT (News) 71.

each of a number of evidential facts, because of their "aptitude and coherence" and their "concurrence", to be proved by the evidence of a single witness was apparently extended, by one line of cases, to include independent facts, having no aptitude, coherence or concurrence, from which, if *all* of them are proved, the fact in issue inevitably follows by a process of, or akin to, mathematical calculation. Facts of this kind are like the links in a chain,[116] failure in any one of which makes the whole chain useless.[117] When a motor vehicle's speed, which was the fact in issue, had to be calculated from the measured distance between two points, the exact time when the vehicle passed the first point and the exact time when it passed the second point, it was held that each of these three essential facts could be proved by the evidence of a single witness.[118] This reasoning has been subjected to sustained criticism[119] and, given that the reasoning is closely entwined with the particular facts of the cases,[120] it has not been followed in subsequent cases.[121]

If facts of this kind can properly be described as circumstantial evidence, they **5.9.5** constitute a very special kind of such evidence, having more in common with the independent facts which must all be proved before a person can be convicted of a compound crime,[122] than with circumstantial evidence as generally understood. A negative variant of this kind of evidence exists when proof of the fact in issue depends solely upon the exhaustive and complete exclusion and elimination of all the other possibilities.[123] In such a case also, if one of the links in the chain is missing, and one of the alternative possibilities has not been eliminated, proof of the fact in issue fails.[124] It would seem to follow that each of the other possibilities may also be excluded by the evidence of a single witness.

5.10 SIMILAR CRIMINAL ACTS

Interrelation of character, circumstances and time

Where an accused is charged with two or more crimes and only one witness[125] **5.10.1**

---

[116] In *Scott v Jameson* 1914 SC (J) 187, Lord Guthrie described them as facts which "require to be proved" and form a "consecutive chain". The Lord Justice-General (Strathclyde) described them as fundamental facts or important facts.

[117] *Gillespie v Macmillan* 1957 JC 31, per Lord Justice-General Clyde at 36. The fact in issue was the speed of a motor car over a measured distance. This required for its proof (a) the exact distance, (b) the exact time of entry and (c) the exact time of departure. All three facts were necessary for the mathematical calculation of the speed of the vehicle, and none of the facts by itself gave rise to any significant inference.

[118] *Gillespie v Macmillan* 1957 JC 31; *Scott v Jameson* 1914 SC (J) 187.

[119] See "Corroboration of Evidence in Scottish Criminal Law" (1960) 76 SLR 101, Wilson, "The Logic of Corroboration" 1958 SLT (News) 137, and more recently Macphail, *Evidence*, paras 23.04–S23.05 and Lord McCluskey during observations in *Smith v Lees* 1997 JC 73 at 103F and 104H.

[120] Facts now unlikely to be repeated given the widespread use of electronic speed recording devices, in respect of which issues of sufficiency are considered in *Scott v MacPhail* 1992 SLT 907.

[121] Noted most recently by Lord McCluskey during observations in *Smith v Lees* 1997 JC 73 at 103F and 104H and previously by Macphail, *Evidence*, paras 23.05 and S23.05.

[122] As to proof of compound crimes, see para 5.4.7.

[123] *Withers v HM Advocate* 1947 JC 109, per Lord Justice-General Cooper at 114.

[124] If an assault is proved to have been committed by one of a number of people, it may be brought home to the accused by proving that none of the others in fact committed it. If exclusion alone is relied upon, each of the other possible assailants must be excluded before the accused may be convicted. See, for example, *Docherty v HM Advocate* 1945 JC 89.

[125] There must be one witness for each crime whom the jury could find credible and reliable: *Coffey v Houston* 1992 JC 80.

implicates him in each,[126] they afford mutual corroboration if the crimes are so interrelated by character, circumstances and time as to justify an inference that they are parts of a course of criminal conduct systematically pursued by the accused.[127] It is difficult, and not as a rule particularly helpful, to consider the character separately from the circumstances of the crimes, and in fact they seldom are so considered.[128] What is required to justify the inference is that the crimes should exhibit common features. The similarity is not dictated by the *nomen iuris*[129] (name in law) of the crime, but by an underlying similarity of character[130] or substance,[131] sometimes termed a nexus,[132] suggesting that they are part of the same[133] systematic course of conduct.[134] General illustrations were given by Lord Sands,[135] by Lord Wark,[136] and by Dickson.[137] Indecent offences having been committed against young children generally, but not exclusively, establish the necessary character.[138] Judicial views as to common character have differed when sodomy was charged alongside incest[139] and rape.[140]

5.10.2   It is possible for the common character to exist between certain charges on an indictment and not between others, in which case the others will require legal proof independently.[141] Furthermore, while evidence on a charge of, for example, incest may be used to corroborate a charge of, say, lewd practices, the converse does not necessarily follow but in some cases the jury will have the choice of convicting on both charges or none at all. The greater will be capable of supporting the lesser, but not the lesser of supporting the greater,[142] and this must be made clear to a jury.[143] Whether the necessary similarity could be found to exist is a

---

[126] Identification on each crime is essential, by direct evidence of the single witness as in *McRae v HM Advocate* 1975 JC 34, or by inference as in *Lindsay v HM Advocate* 1994 SLT 546. Evidence of identification by voice was accepted in *Lees v Roy* 1991 SLT 665 and *Farmer v HM Advocate* 1991 SCCR 986.

[127] *Ogg v HM Advocate* 1938 JC 152 at 157. The principle is set out in Hume, ii, 384.

[128] They were distinguished in *Ogg v HM Advocate* 1938 JC 152 at 159.

[129] As in *McMahon v HM Advocate* 1996 SLT 1139.

[130] *McMahon v HM Advocate* 1996 SLT 1139; *Carpenter v Hamilton* 1994 SCCR 108.

[131] As with charges of breach of the peace and careless driving which, given the particular circumstances, were in substance the same: *Austin v Fraser* 1997 SCCR 775.

[132] *Moorov v HM Advocate* 1930 JC 68, per Lord Justice-Clerk Alness at 80; *Tudhope v Hazelton* 1985 SLT 209; *Hay v Wither* 1988 SCCR 334.

[133] Considered in the reasonable sense of the word: *HM Advocate v Cox* 1962 JC 27.

[134] In *Quinn v Lowe* 1992 SLT 701 the charges could not have been more closely connected in that they arose out of one incident, a fight in which three women were separate victims of crimes of assault and breach of the peace.

[135] *Moorov v HM Advocate* 1930 JC 68 at 88.

[136] *Ogg v HM Advocate* 1938 JC 152 at 160.

[137] *Evidence* (3rd edn), paras 1809, 1810, quoted in *Moorov v HM Advocate* 1930 JC 68 at 80.

[138] *Burgh v HM Advocate* 1944 JC 77 at 80; *Moorov v HM Advocate* 1930 JC 68 at 74, 89.

[139] Held not to have the necessary common features in *HM Advocate v Cox* 1962 JC 27.

[140] *P v HM Advocate* 1991 SCCR 933.

[141] As in *W v HM Advocate* 1997 SLT 51; *McMahon v HM Advocate* 1996 SLT 1139. In *Townsley v Lees* 1996 SLT 1182 this principle was applied between charges 1 and 2 but not charge 3. However, charge 3 was found proved because of its similarity to charges 1 and 2, in accordance with the reasoning described in para 5.10.5.

[142] *HM Advocate v Brown* 1970 SLT 121, per Lord Justice-Clerk Grant at 122.

[143] If not, an appeal court may be unable to rule out the possibility that the jury has used the evidence on the lesser charge incorrectly and a conviction on the greater charge (or perhaps on both) must be quashed: *O'Neill v HM Advocate* 1996 SLT 1121; *Hutchison v HM Advocate* 1998 SLT 679. In *Reid v HM Advocate* 1999 SCCR 769 the jury could only apply *Moorov* to find corroboration, and could not rely on the evidence of one victim to her own assault as circumstantial evidence of the other by using the *ratio* of *Fox v HM Advocate* 1998 JC 94. On *Fox* see para 5.9.1.

matter for the judge initially, who, on considering that the necessary similarity could be found, directs the jury as to the possibility of applying the doctrine, and then it is for the jury to consider whether the similarity does exist to the extent that they can find the similar charges proved on the single source of evidence.[143a] The similarity should be more than one which reveals that the accused has propensity to commit a particular type of crime.[144]

The question of time relationship depends to some extent on the nature of the **5.10.3** crimes. "A man whose course of conduct is to buy houses, insure them, and burn them down, or to acquire ships, insure them, and scuttle them, or to purport to marry women, defraud and desert them, cannot repeat the offence every month, or even perhaps every six months."[145] In the case of *Moorov v HM Advocate* the principle was applied in sustaining a conviction on nine charges of indecent assault (of which six rested on the evidence of a single witness) by an employer on his women employees, within his own premises, over a period of about three years.[146] The principle, which is now described commonly as the "*Moorov* doctrine", was also applied to two charges of attempting within three weeks to bribe professional football players to lose a match by the same method,[147] to one charge of shameless indecency and one of breach of the peace committed within the same park within a three-month period,[148] to six charges of assault (all but one spoken to by only one witness) committed with a razor in a small district in Glasgow within four months, on persons unknown to the accused, and apparently motiveless,[149] and to charges of incest with the accused's two daughters over a period of six years.[150] But the court refused to apply the principle to three charges of indecent conduct, each in different circumstances, at intervals of one year and 18 months.[151] A period of three years has been held to be just within the borderline of the principle when there were two charges with very similar circumstances,[152] but too long in another,[153] particularly if there are material differences in circumstances.[154]

Common purpose

A similar rule applies when the several crimes charged are all directed to the same **5.10.4** end. The most obvious example is subornation of perjury.[155] Where there is

---

[143a] *Paterson v HM Advocate* 1999 SCCR 750, *Russell v HM Advocate* 1992 SCCR 257. See also *Boncza-Tamaszewski (aka fraser)* 2000 SCCR 657, an opinion of the court on a reference by the Scottish Criminal Cases Review Commission.

[144] As in *Mackintosh v HM Advocate* 1991 SCCR 776; *O'Neill v HM Advocate* 1996 SLT 1121, where the trial judge directed the jury that the principle could be applied but the appeal court held that the necessary inference of a course of criminal conduct could not be drawn.

[145] *Moorov v HM Advocate* 1930 JC 68 at 89.

[146] *Moorov v HM Advocate* 1930 JC 68. But for a technical misdirection of the jury, the court would have sustained convictions on six charges of assault of an intimate nature by him on women employees over a period of four years.

[147] *McCudden v HM Advocate* 1952 JC 86.

[148] *Carpenter v Hamilton* 1994 SCCR 109.

[149] *HM Advocate v McQuade* 1951 JC 143.

[150] *HM Advocate v AE* 1937 JC 97. See also *HM Advocate v McDonald* 1928 JC 42; *HM Advocate v Bickerstaff* 1926 JC 65.

[151] *Ogg v HM Advocate* 1938 JC 152.

[152] *Turner v Scott* 1996 SLT 200.

[153] *HM Advocate v Cox* 1962 JC 27. The principle was not applied in *Bargon v HM Advocate* 1997 SLT 1232 and *McHardy v HM Advocate* 1982 SCCR 582 where the gaps were 3 years 7 months and 4 years respectively.

[154] *McRae v HM Advocate* 1975 SLT 174.

[155] *Moorov v HM Advocate* 1930 JC 68 at 74.

subornation or attempted subornation of two or more witnesses at the same trial or proof, each incident spoken to by one witness is corroboration of similar evidence by another. The purpose is clear, to influence the result of the trial or proof. The same reasoning would have been applicable to the case of the professional footballers referred to above, if the bribes had been offered in respect of the same matches. It was applied where the charges were of attempts to induce two partners of a firm to render fraudulent accounts,[156] and the reset of goods stolen by employees of the same warehouse on three occasions within a year.[157] How delicate the subject is appears from the fact that, as an illustration of circumstances in which the principle would *not* apply, Dickson mentions uttering forged notes to different persons at different times.[158]

Similarity of crimes without identification

5.10.5   The categories of similar criminal acts discussed in the preceding sub-paragraphs require identification of the perpetrator of every crime charged. However, a recent line of cases has endorsed corroboration between charges where positive identification is not available on every charge, but where the similarities between the crimes are such that they create the inference that the perpetrators were the same.[159] In one case[160] there were two charges against an accused: one of robbery from a building society in which there was ample evidence of identification, and one of robbery from a bank where only very weak evidence of identification existed, both occurring within a two-week period. There were eight points of similarity between the modes of commission of the two crimes, and the appeal court confirmed that the trial judge was entitled to invite the jury to find support for the weak identification of the accused on the second robbery from the fact of his identification on the first and the similarity of the two incidents.[161] This was said not to involve reliance upon the *Moorov* doctrine, but instead to draw upon all of the circumstantial evidence available in relation to the two charges.[162]

5.11 EVIDENTIAL FACTS—CIVIL CAUSES

5.11.1   The nature and purpose of evidential facts in civil cases is the same as in criminal cases but, since there is no longer a requirement for corroboration in civil cases,

---

[156] *HM Advocate v Tannahill* 1943 JC 150 at 154.

[157] *Harris v Clark* 1958 JC 3.

[158] *Evidence* (3rd edn), paras 1809, 1810. In *McRae v McDowall* 1975 SLT 174, a successful appeal against conviction turned upon application of the *Moorov* doctrine without identification of the male accused on each charge, but the sheriff, in a passage which the appeal court found unclear, may have been applying this principle instead when he held separately from the application of *Moorov* that uttering over a period of two days was part of a "scheme". However, even this principle would not have justified the conviction without corroboration of identification.

[159] *Howden v HM Advocate* 1994 SCCR 19; *Townsley v Lees* 1996 SLT 1182.

[160] *Howden v HM Advocate* 1994 SCCR 19. This reasoning was followed to support a conviction in *Townsley v Lees* 1996 SLT 1182, where three charges of theft involved two perpetrators, one of whom in offering to sell rose bushes to the elderly householder persuaded the householder to go out into the garden while the other entered the property, but positive identification existed in only one of the charges. The *Moorov* doctrine was applied between charges 1 and 2 and the reasoning in *Howden* to support a conviction on charge 3.

[161] The appeal court's reasoning goes so far as to allow this even if one of the crimes had no evidence of identification, other than the inference to be drawn from the similarities between the two crimes: 1993 SCCR 19 at 24E–F. See also Sheriff Gordon's commentary at 24–25.

[162] 1993 SCCR 19 at 24D–E.

they are not distinguishable from crucial facts in requiring only one source of evidence. A civil case may be proved upon circumstantial evidence alone,[163] and an appeal court may consider whether the judge at the proof was entitled to draw those inferences from the facts proved.[164] Reliance upon one source of evidence when another source existed is not an issue of sufficiency[165] but weight.[166]

The direct evidence of one witness to an act of adultery[167] is sufficiently corroborated by evidence of indecent conduct given by another witness,[168] and *a fortiori* by evidence of adultery given by another witness.[169] Since adultery must be proved by evidence other than that of the parties to an action of separation or divorce,[170] this principle is still of some practical import, despite its anomalous nature.[171] **5.11.2**

5.12 PROCEDURAL FACTS

This phrase is used to mean what have been described as incidental facts[172] or matters of procedures in a criminal trial. They are not crucial because they are neither the commission of the crime nor the accused's implication in it; nor are they evidential because they do not yield any inference in support of a crucial fact. Although proof of them may be essential, the evidence of a single witness is sufficient. They include the title of a private prosecutor[173] and the warning preceding medical examination given to a person charged with driving a motor car while under the influence of alcohol to such an extent as to be incapable of having proper control.[174] An aggravation[175] or incidental description[176] of a crime has been held to be within this class. In a charge of theft, or of theft by housebreaking or by opening a lockfast place, the fact that the house or the place was properly **5.12.1**

---

[163] As in *Hamilton v McIntosh Donald* 1994 SC 304, for proof of possession of land during a prescriptive period. The same applies in care proceedings, now under the Children (Scotland) Act 1995, Part II, which are *sui generis*: *Kennedy v F* 1985 SLT 22.

[164] *Hamilton v McIntosh Donald* 1994 SLT 793, where the various opinions reveal differing views as to the inferences to be drawn from the proven circumstances; *M & I Instrument Engineers Ltd v Varsada* 1991 SLT 106 in which part of the circumstantial evidence was in the form of hearsay admissions.

[165] *L v L* 1998 SLT 672; *McCallum v British Railways Board* 1991 SLT 5—although in other cases decided after the removal of the corroboration requirement for personal injury cases the court had indicated that it would be difficult to satisfy the court that the case had been proved when other potential sources of evidence had not been called upon: *Morrison v J Kelly & Sons Ltd* 1970 SC 65, *McGowan v Lord Advocate* 1972 SLT 188. *Cf McLaren v Caldwell's Papermill Co Ltd* 1973 SLT 158.

[166] *L v L* 1998 SLT 672.

[167] See paras 7.3.2 and 28.12.1.

[168] *Whyte v Whyte* (1884) 11 R 710.

[169] *Sim v Sim* (1834) 12 S 633.

[170] Civil Evidence (Scotland) Act 1988, s 8(3).

[171] *Duff v Duff* 1969 SLT (Notes) 53; Macphail, paras 16.03 and 16.04; and see paras 7.3.2 and 28.12.1.

[172] *Lees v Macdonald* (1893) 20 R (J) 55.

[173] *Lees v Macdonald* (1893) 20 R (J) 55 at 56.

[174] *Farrell v Concannon* 1957 JC 12. For a breakdown of the crucial and procedural facts in drink driving prosecutions (then under the Road Traffic Act 1972) see *MacLeod v Nicol; Torrance v Thaw* 1970 JC 58.

[175] *Davidson* (1841) 2 Swin 630.

[176] *Smith v Lees* 1997 JC 73 at 78E; *Stillie v HM Advocate* 1992 SLT 279. In *Campbell v Vannet* 1998 SCCR 207 evidence corroborating part of the detail of an assault charge was held to be sufficient corroboration of the crime, despite the fact that in the circumstances the same corroborating witness might have been expected to know of the rest of the detail.

locked[177] and the ownership of the stolen property[178] are also regarded as procedural or incidental facts.[179]

5.13 WEIGHT OF EVIDENCE

5.13.1 The assessment of the weight of evidence has been said to depend upon common sense.[180] In assessing the value of the testimony of a particular witness much may depend on demeanour,[181] apparent intelligence, means of knowledge, on the coherence of the testimony with facts otherwise established,[182] and also on the manner in which the testimony has been elicited.[183] There is no absolute requirement to put to a witness in cross-examination contradictory assertions that are to be spoken to by the cross-examiner's witness, but failure so to do can be commented upon by the opponent and the judge, in order that it may be taken into account by the court in considering the weight to attach to the witnesses' evidence.[184] The value of expert evidence will depend upon on the authority, experience and qualification of the witness.[185]

5.13.2   The weight to be attached to the evidence adduced for a party as a whole depends only to some extent on its volume. A number of pieces of evidence all pointing to the same result have great weight.[186] No doubt considerable weight attaches to the evidence of a body of witnesses agreeing with each other whose reliability is not suspect.[187] If a witness or witnesses are considered unreliable or not credible the court should proceed to assess the weight of the remaining sources of evidence. In a criminal case at least two credible and reliable[188] sources (whether direct or circumstantial) should exist on each crucial fact for the court to be satisfied that the fact has been proved.[189] In a civil case, where all the witnesses appeared to be honest, the court proceeded on the testimony of the pursuer and one independent witness as against the uncorroborated testimony of the defender.[190]

---

[177] *Davidson* (1841) 2 Swin 630; *Cameron* (1839) 2 Swin 447.

[178] *Lees v Macdonald* (1893) 20 R (J) 55 at 56.

[179] For additional examples of procedural facts, see Macphail, *Evidence*, para S23.01B.

[180] *Lord Advocate v Lord Blantyre* (1879) 6 R (HL) 72, per Lord Blackburn at 85; *L v L* 1998 SLT 672.

[181] For consideration of the issues involved in assessing demeanour, see Stone, *Proof of Fact in Criminal Trials*, Chapter 14.

[182] See para 12.9.2 regarding accuracy of evidence.

[183] *McKenzie v McKenzie* 1943 SC 108 (evidence elicited by leading questions). But in *Gilluley v Greater Glasgow Health Board* 1987 SCLR 431 (Sh Ct) the appellant argued that because cross-examination of a witness had challenged only reliability and not credibility the sheriff had not been entitled to find that the witness was not credible. The sheriff principal noted that the trier of fact is entitled to come to a view on credibility regardless of the aim of the cross-examination.

[184] *Mailley v HM Advocate* 1993 SLT 959.

[185] *Davie v Magistrates of Edinburgh* 1953 SC 34, per Lord President Cooper at 39, Lord Russell at 42.

[186] *Lord Advocate v Lord Blantyre* (1879) 6 R (HL) 72.

[187] *Jordan v Court Line* 1947 SC 29 at 36 (reversing the Lord Ordinary), where failure to cross was founded on. See also *North British Rly v Wood* (1891) 18 R (HL) 27 at 34.

[188] It is the expectation that the trial judge will charge the jury expressly as to the potential for unreliability of eye-witness identification (*McAvoy v HM Advocate* 1992 SLT 46, *Webb v HM Advocate* 1997 SLT 170) but there is judicial discretion not to do so, provided that a general charge as to the need to consider credibility and reliability has been given (*Kearney v HM Advocate* 1999 GWD 19–744).

[189] Hume, ii, 384; *Fox v HM Advocate* 1998 JC 94 at 100D, 108G–H, 117E–F.

[190] *Duncan v Wilson* 1940 SC 221 (reversing the Lord Ordinary).

However, since corroboration is not required in civil cases, the court at first instance has relied upon the uncorroborated but credible evidence of the pursuer even if the corroborative witness is not believed,[191] or in preference to that of the defender and his supporting witness.[192]

It is unnecessary for a party to call every possible witness,[193] but when a court **5.13.3** is assessing weight by application of common sense some importance may attach to failure to call what may be described as an obvious witness or to produce available corroborative material.[194] In two civil cases[195] decided prior to the removal of the corroboration requirement the court *founded* on such failure against the party who might have been expected to call the witness. However, a similar approach taken recently by an Outer House judge[196] was disapproved on appeal where the court observed that the legislature had removed the requirement for corroboration and it was inappropriate for judges to introduce qualifications to this.[197] Nevertheless, it was acknowledged that, in assessing the weight of evidence led, regard could be had to the fact that there were other sources of evidence that might have been led. An appeal court will consider the weight of evidence for itself in so far as it does not depend on factors available only to the judge or jury who saw the witnesses.[198] The assessment of weight is generally a matter for the court at first instance, but if the trier of fact is a judge who finds evidence to be unreliable or unworthy of credit, the reasons for so finding should be made clear in the opinion or stated case so that the reasoning can be reviewed by an appeal court.[199]

---

[191] *Thomson v Tough Ropes Ltd* 1978 SLT (Notes) 5.

[192] *Comerford v Strathclyde Regional Council* 1988 SCLR 67 (Sh Ct); *Airnes v Chief Constable, Strathclyde Police* 1998 SLT (Sh Ct) 15.

[193] *cf* views expressed in *Morrison v J Kelly & Sons Ltd* 1970 SLT 198, *McGowan v Lord Advocate* 1972 SLT 188 and *McLaren v Caldwell's Papermill Co Ltd* 1973 SLT 158, cases decided shortly after the removal of the corroboration requirement in personal injury cases by the Law Reform (Miscellaneous Provisions) (Scotland) Act 1968, s 9, but now doubted: *Lynch v Lynch* 1998 SLT 672.

[194] Observed in *Watson v Adam* 1996 JC 104, a case concerning special reasons for not disqualifying from driving, which can be found without a requirement of corroboration.

[195] *Jordan v Court Line* 1947 SC 29 at 35, 41; *Coles v Homer and Tulloh* (1895) 22 R 716 at 732, 739. In both cases the Lord Ordinary was reversed.

[196] *L v L* 1996 SLT 767.

[197] *Lynch v Lynch* 1998 SLT 672, per Lord President Hope and Lord Coulsfield, doubting *Morrison v J Kelly & Sons Ltd* 1970 SLT 198, *McGowan v Lord Advocate* 1972 SLT 188 and *McLaren v Caldwell's Papermill Co Ltd* 1973 SLT 158.

[198] *Thomas v Thomas* 1947 SC (HL) 45.

[199] *Jordan v Court Line* 1947 SC 29; *Maley v Daylay Foods Ltd* 1998 SC 324.

CHAPTER 6

CIRCUMSTANTIAL EVIDENCE—EXAMPLES OF ITS NATURE AND EFFECT

6.1 INTRODUCTORY

Circumstantial evidence is not in itself directly probative of an issue, and in order **6.1.1** for it to be of evidential value the court must be able to draw an inference from it which supports that issue. As such it requires scrutiny on the part of the party who has to recover the evidence and seeks to lead it, on the part of the court to consider its relevance, and on the part of the judge or jury to consider what inferences may be drawn from the circumstance. It may be helpful to consider here examples of circumstantial evidence used in a wide range of situations from crimes of historical notoriety, via the growth of expert analysis to aid the drawing of inferences from forensic evidence, to the evidential value of reactions of victim and accused after the offence.

6.2 POSSESSION OF INCRIMINATING ARTICLES

An accused's possession, either before or after the commission of a crime, of a **6.2.1** weapon or instrument used in connection with it, or his acquisition of, or attempt to acquire, such a weapon or instrument, is frequently relied upon. In the *Mannings* case, where the body of the murdered man was found embedded in lime, it was proved that about a fortnight before the murder the male accused ordered a quantity of lime of the kind "which would burn quickest".[1] The accused's jemmy may be associated with the commission of a housebreaking by showing that it exactly fits the marks made on a door which was forced, and the nature and characteristics of a wound may show that it was caused by a weapon similar to a weapon found in the accused's possession. Newspapers or periodicals in which articles have been

---

[1] Dickson, *Evidence* (3rd edn), para 103. The purchase by Dr Crippen of hyoscene and by Dr Pritchard of unusually large quantities of tartar emetic, the poisons causing death in each case, was an item of the evidence on which each was convicted of murder: *Notable British Trials.*

wrapped, proved to have been distributed in a particular district on or about a particular date, may justify an inference which associates the article with an accused person. In the case of Dr Ruxton, portions of the victims' bodies, when found near Moffat, were wrapped in pages from an edition of the *Sunday Graphic* which was distributed only in the Lancaster area where Dr Ruxton lived, and a copy of which had been delivered to his house.[2]

6.2.2   When relying upon facts which show some association between a weapon or other article and the accused, it is not sufficient merely to show that the accused person is the owner of the article. Articles are sometimes borrowed or stolen by the thief for use in connection with a crime. For example, it is common practice to steal a vehicle for the purpose of carrying away heavy or bulky stolen goods from the owner's premises. A murderer or a thief may use another person's weapon or instrument deliberately in order to direct suspicion towards the owner or at least away from the perpetrator. In an old English case[3] concerned with the sending of threatening letters, a piece of paper used for the purpose was proved to have been torn from a larger sheet found in the accused's bureau, the ragged edges of which it exactly fitted, and which shared the same watermark. Insufficient attention was paid to the fact that the accused's son, together with other persons in the house, also had access to the bureau, which was kept unlocked. After the accused was convicted it was discovered that his son had been the writer of the letters. Possession of stolen property soon after the theft is frequently founded upon as a fact from which implication in the theft may be inferred.[4]

6.3 EVIDENCE LINKING ACCUSED WITH PREMISES, VEHICLE OR ARTICLE

6.3.1   Articles, such as an accused person's driving licence, found in premises broken into, or a button or piece of cloth apparently torn from an intruder's clothing, which are proved to be identical with the remaining buttons or material of the accused's clothing, are examples of this kind of evidence.[5] The possibility that another person was carrying the accused's driving licence, or wearing his clothing, must not be forgotten. A particular typewriter may be traced by a worn or defective letter, and clothing by a laundry or manufacturer's mark. Evidence of telephone calls made from a call box near the spot where a getaway car crashed, to a house in the street where the accused lived, were linked with the accused's fingerprints on an item found under stolen goods in the car, and forensic samples found at the crime scene, to produce an interesting combination of circumstantial evidence from which guilt of theft was inferred.[6]

---

[2]   *Notable British Trials*; Wills, *Circumstantial Evidence* (7th edn), p 508. See also Glaister's notes on the Ruxton case in *Medical Jurisprudence and Toxicology* (13th edn, 1973) at p 90, regarding the combined effect of circumstantial evidence and medico-legal techniques.

[3]   *Rex v Looker* (1831); Dickson, *Evidence* (3rd edn), para 72.

[4]   This subject is covered more fully at para 3.16.

[5]   In *Sutherland v HM Advocate* 1994 JC 62 the fact that the accused's shoes were found in his own house to which he had allegedly set fire and in which another person died was a piece of circumstantial evidence.

[6]   *Curley v HM Advocate* 1999 SCCR 467. For another example see *Kennedy v HM Advocate* 1999 GWD 15-691.

6.4 FORENSIC EVIDENCE

The advance in scientific and technical aids to the detection of crime, and the **6.4.1**
increased use of camera and microscope to reveal and analyse evidence invisible
to the naked eye, has greatly increased the scope for use of circumstantial evidence. Bloodstains on the accused's clothing or person are relevant and important,
though not in themselves conclusive evidence of association with murder or
assault,[7] and paint[8] stains, identical with, or similar to, paint from premises or vehicles,[9] are frequently founded upon. A bullet may be associated with a particular
weapon by the rifling mark, and dust, mud, hairs or fibres may associate an accused
with a particular locus. Relevant samples of material found on the body may be
taken by a police officer acting under warrant to take prints, samples, impressions
or other information,[10] or, in the case of a person arrested and in custody or
detained under section 14(1) of the Criminal Procedure (Scotland) Act 1995, by a
constable under section 18 of that Act.[11] The statutory power extends to taking
samples of the detainee's hair, other than pubic hair, by cutting, combing or plucking; taking samples of nail or other material from on or under the nail; taking
swabs of blood, body fluids, body tissue or other body material from the external
parts of the body, and taking swabs of saliva or other material from
the mouth.[12] The constable is also empowered to take prints as described below.[13]

Such evidence which cannot be assessed just by the naked eye of the judge or **6.4.2**
jury, must be the subject of evidence not only as to its recovery from the locus of
the crime or from the property or person of the accused, but also as to its analysis.
This is sometimes described as the "chain" of circumstantial evidence,[14] meaning
simply that it must be tracked from its source through its analysis to production in
court. In a trial concerning safe-blowing the accused was convicted on three
elements of circumstantial evidence: (a) the possession soon after the theft of
banknotes stolen from the safe; (b) a cut on the accused's hand at the time of his
arrest which corresponded with a tear on a rubber glove found near the scene of
the crime; and (c) a small piece of pink material found in his coat pocket which
corresponded with fibres said to have been taken from a bedcover used in the safe-blowing. The conviction was quashed only because of a technical failure by the
Crown to identify the fibres examined by the expert witnesses as fibres which had
been taken from the pocket of the accused.[15]

Production of the original item or sample may be possible, but some pro- **6.4.3**
cesses of analysis involve destruction of all or part of the sample.[16] In criminal

---

[7] For example, in *Codona v HM Advocate* 1996 SLT 1100 bloodstains on the accused's clothing were
not consistent with the murder charge although they were consistent with the accused's limited confession to assault (declared inadmissible on appeal), and one would have expected the murderer to have
other blood staining to clothes and footwear.
[8] See *Withers v HM Advocate* 1947 JC 109.
[9] As in *Topping v Scott* 1979 JC 40.
[10] On appropriate cause shown for the grant of a warrant: *eg* measurements of the identical twin of an
accused (*Smith v Cardle* 1994 SLT 514) or dental impressions of a person not yet charged (*Hay v HM
Advocate* 1968 JC 40).
[11] Some samples may only be taken with the authority of an inspector or more senior officer: s 18(6).
[12] s 18(6).
[13] s 18(2) and (7A).
[14] *Forrester v HM Advocate* 1952 JC 28. Not to be confused with the chain analogy in relation to
interpretation of circumstantial evidence, discussed above at para 5.9.4.
[15] *Forrester v HM Advocate* 1952 JC 28.
[16] *eg* a post mortem examination.

proceedings biological material taken from an animal or human does not require to be produced in court for it to be admissible in evidence[17] but unless it is a hazard to health or has been destroyed during analysis it should be made available to the other party for inspection.[18] Some samples are split between prosecution and defence at the outset,[19] so that independent analysis can take place at an early stage if desired. Whilst a sample of biological material need not be produced in court, in its place there is produced the label that had been attached to the sample when it was taken so that relevant witnesses can trace its removal and labelling through to its analysis under that label.[20] However, the necessary link between the material and the analyst's report can be inferred from the facts and circumstances revealed in other evidence before the court.[21]

6.4.4   Forensic analysis for prosecution purposes is generally carried out by two forensic scientists,[22] but procedures exist for their evidence to be produced by written report or certificate[23] without their attendance in court, or for the attendance of only one forensic witness,[24] unless the defence, having had sight of the report or certificate, challenges a qualification, finding or conclusion of the scientist.[25] Calibration or accuracy of testing equipment should also be the subject of direct evidence,[26] but can be inferred from circumstances.[27]

6.4.5   A distinction must be drawn between expert evidence as to fact, such as the group and type of blood found at a scene or the nature of a victim's injury, and the expert's opinion based upon those facts, such as the probability of that blood group occurring in the general population or the likelihood of a particular weapon having caused the injury.[28] Both are items of circumstantial evidence, and it has been held that, provided the expert's qualifications and experience are detailed in evidence, the assessment of probabilities arising from the evidence is a matter for the court[29] rather than the witness and is one of weight rather than sufficiency.[30] This issue arose in the first reported Scottish criminal case to deal with evidence of DNA analysis,[31] where the defence argued that a certain threshold of probability might be set by the judge before that evidence could be put to the jury for assessment of weight. This argument was rejected in favour of the jury hearing all of the expert

---

[17] Criminal Procedure (Scotland) Act 1995 ("1995 Act"), s 276(1); and see *Williamson v Aitchison* 1982 SLT 399.

[18] 1995 Act, s 276(2). For the position at common law re real evidence that is perishable, see *Anderson v Laverock* 1976 JC 9 and para 18.5.2.

[19] *eg* a sample of blood or urine taken from a driver suspected of driving under the influence of alcohol or drugs: Road Traffic Offenders Act 1988, s 16.

[20] When the certificate of analysis referred to a specimen having been provided in one police station and the label referred to a different station the link was not made out: *Douglas v Wilkinson* 1964 SLT (Sh Ct) 68.

[21] *Allan v Ingram* 1995 SLT 1086; *Sproat v McGibney* 1968 SLT 33; *cf O'Brien v Ferguson* 1987 SLT 96.

[22] For the relative roles to be played by the two analysts and evidence of procedures, see *LAW Mining v Carmichael* 1996 SCCR 627.

[23] Criminal Procedure (Scotland) Act 1995, s 280. See also para 19.16.

[24] 1995 Act, s 281.

[25] Under 1995 Act, s 280(6)(b) or s 281(2).

[26] *Wigdor v Hogg* 1974 SLT (Notes) 59.

[27] *Wigdor v Hogg* 1974 SLT (Notes) 59; *Valentine v MacPhail* 1986 JC 131. As to laboratory procedures, see also *LAW Mining v Carmichael* 1996 SCCR 627.

[28] For more detail in relation to expert evidence and opinion, see para 16.3.

[29] *Hendry v HM Advocate* 1988 SLT 25; *cf HM Advocate v McGinlay* 1983 SLT 562.

[30] *Welsh v HM Advocate* 1992 SLT 193.

[31] *Welsh v HM Advocate* 1992 SLT 193.

evidence and drawing its own conclusion from that. There has been considerable academic comment about the scientific evidence used in court, particularly evidence of DNA analysis which purports to link the accused with the crime to a high degree of probability. The issues raised include: methods of presentation of complex scientific information to the jury; how probabilities of DNA fingerprint matches with persons other than the accused are calculated; to what extent these calculations are influenced or challenged by other facts in the case, and the impact of the scientific data upon the court's decision making.[32] The court in England has ruled on some of these issues.[33] The continuing advances in genetic science and analysis may further extend the scope and potential influence of circumstantial evidence derived from samples of body fluids or tissue.

6.5 PRINT EVIDENCE

The police in Scotland are entitled, without a warrant, to take the "relevant physical data" of a person arrested or detained.[34] These include any fingerprint, palm print or print of another external part of the body.[35] These may be compared with impressions found at premises, or on articles, associated with the crime, in order to discover whether they were made by the same person. Evidence resulting from this comparison given by expert witnesses,[36] if accepted by the court or by the jury, is an important, and in many cases a conclusive, example of circumstantial evidence. In the case of fingerprints, for example, the purpose of the comparison is to discover whether certain ridge characteristics, which make up the pattern in the fingerprint, are identically arranged in both prints. An identification can be made on this basis when at least 16 of these identical characteristics can be discovered by those skilled in fingerprint identification.[37] In the leading case in Scotland[38] the facts were that a shop had been broken into, a safe blown open and money stolen. In the shop, after the crime had been committed, was found a wine bottle with certain prints. The bottle had been wrapped up in paper when the shop was closed. Police experts spoke to complete identity between 16 characteristics of a print on the bottle with corresponding characteristics of one of the accused's prints, which was more than sufficient to justify the inference that the print on the bottle was that of the accused. Apart from the fact that he lived in the neighbourhood, which was of no great importance, there was no other evidence against the accused. The jury

6.5.1

---

[32] Some of these issues are considered in, *eg*, Kelly, Rankin and Wink, "Method and Applications of DNA Fingerprinting: A Guide for the Non-Scientist" [1987] CrimLR 105; Young, "DNA Evidence—Beyond Reasonable Doubt?" [1991] CrimLR 264; Alldridge, "Recognising Novel Scientific Techniques: DNA as a Test Case" [1992] CrimLR 687; Balding and Donnelly, "The Prosecutor's Fallacy and DNA Evidence" [1994] CrimLR 711; Redmayne, "Doubts and Burdens: DNA Evidence, Probability and the Courts" [1995] CrimLR 464.

[33] *R v Doheny, R v Adams* [1997] CrimLR 669.

[34] Criminal Procedure (Scotland) Act 1995, s 18; as to fingerprints of persons apprehended, this was established in *Adair v McGarry* 1933 JC 72. As to the circumstances in which a warrant may be granted for the taking of prints and the use to which they can be put, see para 18.2.

[35] Criminal Procedure (Scotland) Act 1995, s 18(7A). A certificate by an authorised officer is sufficient evidence that the prints were taken or provided: Criminal Procedure (Scotland) Act 1995, s 284(1); and see *McBeth v HM Advocate* (1976) SCCR Supp 123.

[36] As to skilled witnesses generally, para 16.3.

[37] *Hamilton v HM Advocate* 1934 JC 1. The whole subject is discussed in Wills, *Circumstantial Evidence* (7th edn), pp 205 *et seq*.

[38] *Hamilton v HM Advocate* 1934 JC 1.

convicted on that evidence, and it was held that they were entitled to do so.[39] In a later case[40] similar evidence as to a palm print was held to be admissible and sufficient, if accepted by the jury, for the identification of the accused with the commission of the crime. Identification by fingerprint is not regarded as infallible, but as providing evidence of a degree of probability which is ample for judicial proof.[41] However, there appears to be no reason why a smaller number of common features should not be deponed to, as part of the evidence in the case, if an imperfect or partial impression at the *locus* of the crime makes a complete comparison impossible, although, in such a case, the fingerprint evidence alone might not be sufficient to justify a conviction.

6.5.2   The correct inference to be drawn from a fingerprint impression found in premises, or on an article, connected with the crime, may depend upon the accused person's normal association with the premises or the article or an alternative explanation for the presence of the fingerprint being possible[42] or being advanced by the accused. If the accused person is normally employed in the shop which is broken into, no inference of guilt arises, unless the impression is found in part of the shop from which he was normally excluded. If the accused person is not so employed, an inference of guilt may arise if the fingerprint is found on the shopkeeper's side of the counter, but does not necessarily arise if it is found on the customers' side. An inference of guilt in charges of reset and uttering was drawn where there was evidence from fingerprint experts that the accused's fingerprints were found on cheques in places consistent with signing, gripping and removing the cheques from a cheque book, the accused having said that she had merely flicked through the cheques when they were shown to her by a third party.[43] Palm prints on plastic carrier bags, matched with those of the accused, found in an indoor market could not give rise to the inference that the accused broke in there, since the possibility could not be ruled out that the accused had been there legitimately and there was no evidence of how long they had been there.[44]

6.6 BEHAVIOURAL CHARACTERISTICS

6.6.1   The normal behaviour and reactions of animals in given situations may find a place in circumstantial evidence. The curious incident of the dog which did not bark in the night-time, and Sherlock Holmes' inference therefrom,[45] were anticipated in a

---

[39] Another example of conviction on the basis of a fingerprint alone is *Langan v HM Advocate* 1989 JC 132.

[40] *HM Advocate v Rolley* 1945 JC 155. A toe-print has been accepted: *Gourlay* 1953 SLT (News) 45.

[41] See *Hamilton v HM Advocate* 1934 JC 1; *HM Advocate v Rolley* 1945 JC 155.

[42] In *Reilly v HM Advocate* 1986 SCCR 417 the presence of a fingerprint belonging to the accused on the rear of the false number-plate of a stolen car was insufficient to justify an inference of guilt in the theft of the car.

[43] *Crowe v Deasley* 1996 SCCR 1 (Sh Ct).

[44] *Slater v Vannet* 1997 JC 226. In *MacDonald v HM Advocate* 1998 SLT 37, the presence of the accused's fingerprint on the trim of the passenger door of a car similar to that used in a robbery was not sufficient when there was no evidence as to how long the fingerprint might have been there and the accused admitted stealing the car three months previously. It is not clear whether situations such as these would be affected by the decision in *Fox v HM Advocate* 1998 JC 94. Do the other potential reasons for the existence of the evidence simply go to weight rather than prevent its use as corroboration? It is suggested that in circumstances such as these, without some evidence of when the prints were placed, the evidence would still be insufficient to lend the support required of a piece of corroborative evidence.

[45] Sir Arthur Conan Doyle, *Memoirs of Sherlock Holmes* (Penguin edn), p 32.

Scottish case[46] when a fierce watchdog in charge of an empty shop was not heard by the neighbours to bark at the time when a theft was committed. It was part of the evidence on which the accused person was convicted that he had been an employee in the shop and was known to the dog. The actions of a police tracker dog were held to justify the conviction of a housebreaker. The dog, after it had been allowed to smell articles which had been disturbed by the housebreaker in the house broken into, was taken to the tenement where the accused resided. It led the police past the other flats in the tenement to the door of the accused's house on the top floor. Later, at a police office, it picked out shoes belonging to the accused from a number of shoes belonging to other persons.[47] In proceedings arising from the conduct of an animal the behaviour complained of will require to be proved, but in most cases the substantive law imposes strict or absolute liability dependent upon the species rather than the nature of the particular animal, although the behaviour of the owner or handler may be relevant.[48]

The capability, training and skill of an accused person, or of the victim of a   **6.6.2** crime, may be elements in circumstantial evidence. For example, a person who cannot read or write is unlikely to have forged or fabricated a document. The mere strength of an accused person may be a factor of importance if the crime could have been committed only by a person of powerful physique.[49] In cases of assault, murder or culpable homicide the nature or direction of the wound may indicate the height and strength of the assailant, and whether the assailant was right-handed or left-handed. The ability to travel in a given time, with the means of transport available, between one place and another, may indicate whether or not an accused had an opportunity of committing the crime.

6.7 DISTRESS OF THE VICTIM

The evidence of a third party to the effect that the victim was in a distressed state after   **6.7.1** the incident in respect of which the accused is charged, is an item of circumstantial evidence. It is a source of evidence independent of the victim, since the third party is speaking to personal observation of the victim's distressed condition. When an accused who was charged with raping a girl by use of threats, including threat to use a knife, admitted having sexual intercourse with the girl, but stated that she had consented, evidence that she was seen in a shocked state shortly after the incident was capable of providing corroboration of the lack of consent.[50] Distress may be particularly valuable in relation to proof of sexual crimes, to corroborate "the broad proposition of force"[51]—that is whether the victim was subjected to force or the victim consented to the conduct. But it has been used in charges of assault,[52] abduction,[53] theft and robbery.[54]

In a line of cases commencing in 1977[55] the court has encountered the main   **6.7.2**

---

[46] *William Young* 1828 (unreported), mentioned in Alison, 1, 323.

[47] *Patterson v Nixon* 1960 JC 42.

[48] *eg* Animals (Scotland) Act 1987; Dangerous Dogs Act 1991.

[49] See *Withers v HM Advocate* 1947 JC 109.

[50] *Yates v HM Advocate* 1977 SLT (Notes) 42.

[51] *Yates v HM Advocate* 1977 SLT (Notes) 42.

[52] *Bennett v HM Advocate* 1989 SCCR 608.

[53] *Horne v HM Advocate* 1991 SCCR 248.

[54] *Stillie v HM Advocate* 1992 SLT 279.

[55] With *Yates v HM Advocate* 1977 SLT (Notes) 42. It has been observed that the case established no new principle: *Smith v Lees* 1997 JC 73, per Lord Justice-General Rodger at 83E.

points of contention concerning the use of distress as circumstantial corroborative evidence. The issue and the case law between 1977 and 1997 were reconsidered by a full bench in 1997,[56] following an apparent extension of the use of distress to corroborate issues other than force or lack of consent.[57] It is now clear that evidence of a third party as to the distress of the victim is capable of confirming only that the victim suffered some distressing event or conduct.[58] It cannot by itself corroborate identification of the accused or the exact nature of the conduct if that is a crucial element of the crime. It is thus capable of corroborating by inference the fact that an admitted or otherwise proven sexual encounter was brought about against the will of the victim and by force.[59]

6.7.3   In order to be capable of providing such corroboration the distress must have been exhibited spontaneously[60] and must not be too remote in time from the event,[61] which is initially a matter for the judge to determine. Some cases had involved consideration of whether the distress had to be "unequivocally referable to"[62] or "consistent with"[63] the crime before it could be capable of corroboration. Generally this point arose in cases where another possible explanation for the distress had been introduced by the defence in evidence or cross-examination, as a result of which the distress might be considered neutral[64] or not sufficiently linked to any one of a number of crimes charged.[65] However, it is now clear that when deciding whether evidence of distress should be put to the jury as potentially corroborative evidence, the judge should take the distress at its best interpretation for the Crown case, as would be done in assessing sufficiency of evidence generally. It is enough that the distress is capable of lending support to the complainer's evidence of a distressing event. The existence of an alternative explanation for the distress is a matter for the jury to consider in assessing the weight to attach to it.[66] Before allowing such evidence to corroborate the proposition of force, the jury must decide whether the distress is genuine.[67]

---

[56] *Smith v Lees* 1997 JC 73.

[57] Seen most vividly in *Stobo v HM Advocate* 1994 JC 28 (overruled in *Smith v Lees* 1997 JC 73), and to a lesser extent in *McLellan v HM Advocate* 1992 SLT 991 and *Begg v Tudhope* 1983 SCCR 32, which were commented upon in *Smith v Lees*.

[58] Per Lord Justice-General Rodger in *Smith v Lees* 1997 JC 73 at 81A.

[59] *Smith v Lees* 1997 JC 73 at 80H.

[60] *Moore v HM Advocate* 1990 JC 371.

[61] As in *Gracey v HM Advocate* 1987 JC 45; *Stephen v HM Advocate* 1987 SCCR 570. *Cf Moore v HM Advocate* 1990 JC 371; *Cannon v HM Advocate* 1992 JC 138. An appropriate period cannot be specified because it depends upon the circumstances of the crime, the opportunities arising for the victim to show the distress, and intervening events as in *Moore v HM Advocate* 1991 SLT 278, *Geddes v HM Advocate* 1997 SLT 392; *Gibson v Heywood* 1997 SLT 101.

[62] *Stobo v HM Advocate* 1994 SLT 28 at 34C.

[63] *Mackie v HM Advocate* 1994 JC 132; *Stobo v HM Advocate* 1994 SLT 28 at 33D. In *Smith v Lees* 1997 JC 73 Lord McCluskey referred to evidence which "separately points to the truth of facts". This point can equally be made of any circumstantial evidence: see para 6.1.

[64] Following *Mackie v HM Advocate* 1994 JC 132 circumstantial evidence which was equally consistent with Crown and defence versions was not capable of providing corroboration, but this has now been overruled by *Fox v HM Advocate* 1998 JC 94. For a critical discussion see Sheldon "Corroboration and Relevance" 1998 SLT (News) 115.

[65] eg *Gibson v Heywood* 1997 SLT 101; *Martin v HM Advocate* 1993 SCCR 803; *MacLean v McClory* 1995 SLT 1316.

[66] *Fox v HM Advocate* 1998 JC 94 at 104A, 117E.

[67] *Gracey v HM Advocate* 1987 JC 45.

6.8 REACTIONS OF THE ACCUSED—CONDUCT

The actions of an accused person before and after the commission of a crime **6.8.1** frequently give rise to inferences which point towards guilt.[68] Attempts to fabricate evidence in order to indicate that no crime, or a crime of a different character, has been committed, are of this kind. So a window may be broken in order to suggest that a theft was committed by housebreaking instead of by a person living or working in the premises, and, if proved to have been done by the accused, may point to guilt. The attempted destruction or disposal of the body of a victim of murder is a further example, and usually gives rise to an inference of guilt, although an innocent person may sometimes destroy incriminating articles in order to avoid the risk of suspicion, arrest and trial.[69] Running away from the scene of the crime may be due to a guilty conscience,[70] but may also arise from fear of wrongful arrest.[71] Motive, or apparent lack of motive, may be proved by circumstantial evidence,[72] and previous animosity[73] or threats of intention to harm the victim may be important,[74] unless it is clear that they were uttered in mere bravado.[75]

Even more important may be remarks made after a crime has been committed, **6.8.2** if they are inconsistent with the innocence of the accused person.[76] These are most commonly admissions of involvement,[77] or "mixed" statements that contain both inculpatory and exculpatory material such as "I hit him in self defence".[78] However, a suspect may be incriminated by too ready a denial of guilt of a crime which only the perpetrator could know to have been committed. The surprised reaction of a witness who was originally a co-accused, to discovery of a firearm in his flat during a police search, has been admitted in evidence against the accused who was the only other occupant of the flat.[79] It would also have been exculpatory of the witness had he remained a co-accused.[80]

---

[68] It was the practice of Smith, the "brides in the bath" murderer, to take the intended victim to a doctor with a history suggesting that she suffered from fits or seizures, and this formed part of the evidence at his trial: *Rex v Smith* (1915) 84 LJ (KB) 2153; *Notable British Trials*.

[69] See *Ronald Light* (1920), *Life of Marshall Hall*, 396; *Green Bicycle Case* by HR Wakefield (1930). In this case the jury accepted the defence proposition that the green bicycle, and other incriminating articles belonging to the accused, who had been shellshocked, were thrown by him into a canal because he was afraid of being wrongly suspected of the murder with which newspaper publicity had associated them.

[70] As was inferred in *Proctor v Tudhope* 1985 SCCR 39, but held insufficient to corroborate in *Gallagher v HM Advocate* 2000 SCCR 634.

[71] Dickson, *Evidence* (3rd edn), para 91.

[72] See para 7.14.

[73] *Hoy v HM Advocate* 1998 SCCR 8.

[74] As in *HM Advocate v Kay* 1970 JC 68, where the murder charge specified that the accused had previously evinced ill-will against the victim, her husband.

[75] More fully discussed in Best, *Evidence*, para 458.

[76] Dickson, *Evidence* (3rd edn), para 92.

[77] See paras 9.2, 9.5 and 9.7.

[78] See para 8.6.6.

[79] *Fulton v HM Advocate* 1999 SLT 1423. Lord Coulsfield dissented on the basis that the surprise could not indicate the reason for the surprise, at p 1427. Sheriff Gordon in his commentary in the report in 1999 SCCR 851 at 858 suggests that the reaction of a witness can do more than affect credibility.

[80] *Fulton v HM Advocate* 1999 SLT 1423 at 1425.

6.9 CIRCUMSTANTIAL EVIDENCE TO CORROBORATE CONFESSIONS

6.9.1 Extra-judicial admissions[81] by the accused are but one source of evidence and they require to be corroborated.[82] The need for corroboration is intended to act as a check that the confession is not "phoney or quixotic".[83] Since the confession is a statement against interest uttered by the accused personally the court may start from the assumption that it is true.[84] It has been said in a number of cases that "very little" is needed to corroborate a confession,[85] but that this is a statement of fact about quality and weight as compared to quantity, and not a rule.[86] It has also been said that what one looks for in corroboration of a confession is something capable of confirming the terms of the confession, rather than the terms of the charge,[87] although the two things will in many cases be the same. Ultimately the quantity and nature of evidence required to corroborate a confession will vary from case to case, and will be influenced by the content and nature of the confession, and the circumstances in which it was made.[88]

6.9.2　　Some confessions are termed "special knowledge" or "circumstantial" confessions, and they differ from "normal" confessions in that the corroboration of them is derived from the information contained in the confession itself. The case of *Manuel v HM Advocate*[89] is a prime example. The accused uttered a confession in which he indicated that he had buried one victim in a particular place in a field and that victim's shoe elsewhere in the same field. He then took the police to the location of the buried items. The trial judge indicated to the jury that they could find corroboration of the confession in the finding of the buried items where the accused had said they would be. On appeal it was noted that the detail provided by the accused *and* the finding of the items constituted a series of quite independent facts which constituted all the corroboration of the confession that was needed.[90]

6.9.3　　Whilst the concept as occurring in *Manuel* is consistent with the requirement of evidence from two sources, the use of "special knowledge" in confessions for corroboration has been extended to an extent which has attracted judicial criticism.[91] In *Manuel* the confession was the source of the detailed information which the police were then able to discover. In subsequent cases the fact that before

---

[81] *ie* any admission other than by a guilty plea accepted by the prosecutor. It therefore includes an admission made, *eg*, at a judicial examination or in evidence in court: *Milne v Whaley* 1975 SLT (Notes) 75. Repetition of a confession to different persons is not corroboration, since the accused is still the only source.
[82] *Sinclair v Clark* 1962 JC 57, per Lord Justice-Clerk Thomson at 62.
[83] *Sinclair v Clark* 1962 JC 57.
[84] *Hartley v HM Advocate* 1979 SLT 26.
[85] *Sinclair v Clark* 1962 JC 57; *Hartley v HM Advocate* 1979 SLT 26; *Lockhart v Crockett* 1987 SLT 551; *Greenshields v HM Advocate* 1989 SCCR 637; *Meredith v Lees* 1992 SLT 802.
[86] *Meredith v Lees* 1992 SLT 802.
[87] *Hartley v HM Advocate* 1979 SLT 26.
[88] *Sinclair v Clark* 1962 JC 57. These factors are considered with differing results in, *eg*, *Hartley v HM Advocate* 1979 SLT 26 and *Codona v HM Advocate* 1996 SLT 1100.
[89] 1958 JC 41. See also *Connolly v HM Advocate* 1958 SLT 79.
[90] Lord Justice-General Clyde at 48, after referring to an almost identical scenario described in Alison, ii, 580.
[91] Per Lord McCluskey in *Smith v Lees* 1997 JC 73 at 104C–D; per Lord Coulsfield in *Fox v HM Advocate* 1998 JC 94 at 118D–E but in neither case was a re-examination necessary or relevant to the precise issue which the full bench had under consideration.

the confession was made the detailed information was already known to the police,[92] to the victim's family and acquaintances, including the accused,[93] and to the public at large,[94] has not prevented the court from ruling that a confession which contains the detailed knowledge can be sufficiently corroborated by proof of the detail. There has also been a weakening of the requisite speciality of the knowledge.[95] The test to be applied by the jury requires them to decide whether the only reasonable explanation for the knowledge of the details of the crime disclosed in the confession is that the confessor was the perpetrator[96] and in so doing the jury would have regard to the other sources from which the accused could have got the detailed information.[97] This leaves little scope for the judge to consider sufficiency, and is far removed from the ratio of *Manuel*. It may be expected that this will be re-examined having regard to the requirements of Article 6(1) of the European Convention on Human Rights.[98] Unlike "normal" confessions which can be proved by the evidence of one witness, "special knowledge" confessions require to be proved by two witnesses,[99] although these witnesses need not accord on each and every element of the confession.[100]

6.10 EVIDENTIAL IMPLICATIONS OF SILENCE OF ACCUSED

Usually the fact that an accused has remained silent in the aftermath of a crime will **6.10.1** not be of evidential value to the prosecution.[101] However, in particular circumstances that call for an immediate explanation the lack of an explanation in those particular circumstances may be an item of circumstantial evidence.[102] An accused charged with setting his dog on two children[103] had been confronted by the father of one of the children at the time of the offence with the question, "Did you set that dog on these children?". He had not replied to that question, but said that the children had no right to be in his garden. This was the only item of corroborative evidence and the court held that, although a narrow case, the corroboration could be drawn from the failure of the accused to deny the conduct. A statement made

---

[92] As in *McAvoy v HM Advocate* 1982 SCCR 263. However, in *Hamilton v Normand* 1994 SLT 184 Lord Justice-Clerk Ross and Lord McCluskey found it difficult to regard knowledge as special when it was elicited by specific questioning from police officers who already had the details.

[93] As in *Wilson v HM Advocate* 1987 SCCR 217. The unusual circumstances of the confessions by the two accused in *Wilson* and the fact that they revealed a motive previously unknown to the police were no doubt important features in the court's decision on sufficiency but such details as they gave regarding the *modus* were well known.

[94] In *Wilson v HM Advocate* 1987 SCCR 217 some of the detail had been broadcast on radio.

[95] See *Macdonald v HM Advocate* 1988 SLT 85; *cf Hamilton v Normand* 1994 SLT 184.

[96] Per Lord Justice-General Emslie in *Wilson v HM Advocate* 1987 SCCR 217 at 222. This is a lesser requirement than proving that only the perpetrator could have known the details: see Sheriff Gordon's commentary to *McAvoy v HM Advocate* 1982 SCCR 263 at 275.

[97] *McAvoy v HM Advocate* 1982 SCCR 263; *Wilson v HM Advocate* 1987 SCCR 217.

[98] Having regard to *Thompson v Crowe* 2000 JC 173, on which see para 9.12. For a critical examination of development of case law on this point, see Gordon, "At the Mouth of Two Witnesses: Some Comments on Corroboration" in Hunter (ed), *Justice and Crime*. See also his commentary to *Wilson v HM Advocate* 1987 SCCR 217 at 223–224.

[99] *Low v HM Advocate* 1993 SCCR 493. Sheriff Gordon asks in his commentary, at 510 whether the corroborating circumstance should now be proved by two witnesses. It is submitted that such questions have only arisen because of the unnatural extension of this concept.

[100] *Mitchell v HM Advocate* 1996 SCCR 97.

[101] *Robertson v Maxwell* 1951 JC 11.

[102] See para 2.12.3.

[103] *Kay v Allan* (1978) SCCR Supp 188.

by one accused which by inference implicated his companion has been corroborated by evidence that the companion heard it and did not deny it then.[104]

6.10.2   However, these cases rest very much upon their particular facts and as a general rule silence of the accused when confronted will not be evidence for the prosecution. It is well known that the accused in a Scottish criminal case is presumed innocent until proven guilty and is entitled to remain silent at trial.[105] Whilst the trial judge can, in the charge to the jury, comment "with restraint" upon the silence of the accused at trial,[106] it must be made clear to the jury that the accused's silence is not capable of affording corroboration of the Crown case.[107] Comment by the prosecutor, formerly prohibited,[108] is now permitted[109] but should also be exercised with restraint.[110] Failure by an accused to answer a question at a judicial examination, separately can be the subject of comment from the prosecutor, co-accused or the judge, but only if the accused personally or through defence witnesses raises at the trial something which could have been "stated appropriately" in answer to a question at judicial examination.[111]

6.10.3   While silence of the accused should not, *per se*, afford corroboration of the prosecution case,[112] the court commonly refers to the absence of an explanation from the accused when assessing the sufficiency of evidence in appeal against conviction.[113] It must be noted that these cases involve review of what was before the jury rather than sufficiency at the conclusion of the Crown case, and at most it can be said that in the absence of an explanation from the accused an inference of guilt is more likely to be drawn from other evidence.[114] So, for example, Crown evidence which the accused has not contradicted by his own testimony is more likely to be believed, or a factual line of defence taken by the accused at trial which could have been disclosed at judicial examination is less likely to be believed. If a "no case to answer" submission is not made or fails and the accused or defence witnesses give evidence, such testimony may provide direct or circumstantial evidence which supports the Crown case.[115]

---

[104] *Annan v Bain & Hamill* 1986 SCCR 60. See also *HM Advocate v O'Donnell* 1975 SLT (Sh Ct) 22 but *cf HM Advocate v Keen* 1926 JC 1, *Hipson v Tudhope* 1983 SLT 659. See also para 9.9.

[105] *eg HM Advocate v Von* 1979 SLT (Notes) 62; Criminal Procedure (Scotland) Act 1995, s 266.

[106] *Scott v HM Advocate* 1946 JC 90; *Knowles v HM Advocate* 1975 JC 6; *Stewart v HM Advocate* 1980 JC 103.

[107] *Stewart v HM Advocate* 1980 SLT 245.

[108] Criminal Procedure (Scotland) Act 1975, ss 141(1)(b), 346(1)(b).

[109] The prohibition was removed by the Criminal Justice (Scotland) Act 1995, s 32.

[110] It must not encroach upon the presumption of innocence and right to silence enshrined in ECHR, Art 6(1). See also para 13.12.

[111] Criminal Procedure (Scotland) Act 1995, s 36(8); *Dempsey v HM Advocate* 1995 JC 84. Failure to answer on legal advice does not preclude such comment: *Alexander v HM Advocate* 1989 SLT 193. *Cf Gilmour v HM Advocate* 1982 SCCR 590, but restraint should be exercised: *McEwan v HM Advocate* 1990 SCCR 401.

[112] *Robertson v Maxwell* 1951 JC 11 and see *Douglas v McNulty* 1999 SCCR 884 where silence after caution in face of an incriminating statement by a co-accused should not have been admitted by the Sheriff. In England the judge now directs the jury that "proper inferences" may be drawn from the silence at questioning or trial: Criminal Justice and Public Order Act 1994, ss 34–38. See also Nash, "Silence as Evidence" 1996 SLT (News) 69.

[113] *eg HM Advocate v Hardy* 1938 JC 144; *Mochan v Herron* 1972 SLT 218; *Sutherland v HM Advocate* 1994 JC 62; *Beattie v HM Advocate* 1995 JC 33.

[114] *Donaghy v Normand* 1992 SLT 666; *Sutherland v HM Advocate* 1994 SLT 634; *McLean v HM Advocate* 1993 SCCR 605. See paras 2.12, 13.12.

[115] *McArthur v Stewart* 1955 JC 71.

CHAPTER 7

RELEVANCY OF EVIDENCE—CHARACTER AND COLLATERAL ISSUES

7.1 GENERAL

Generally speaking evidence of character and evidence regarding an issue which **7.1.1** is collateral to the main issue is inadmissible. A "collateral" issue is one which runs parallel to a fact in issue but evidence of it is generally inadmissible on grounds of relevance, because the existence of the collateral fact does not have a reasonably direct bearing upon a fact in issue and thus does not render more or less probable the existence of that fact, and it is inexpedient to allow an enquiry to be confused and protracted by enquiries into other matters.

> "Courts of law are not bound to admit the ascertainment of every disputed fact which may contribute, however slightly or indirectly, towards the solution of the issue to be tried. Regard must be had to the limitations which time and human liability to confusion impose upon the conduct of all trials. Experience shows that it is better to sacrifice the aid which might be got from the more or less uncertain solution of collateral issues, than to spend a great amount of time, and confuse the jury with what, in the end, even supposing it to be certain, has only an indirect bearing on the matter in hand."[1]

The application in practice of this general proposition and the exceptions to it are considered in this chapter with reference to evidence of similar acts, evidence of character, and evidence of state of mind.

---

[1] *A v B* (1895) 22 R 402, per Lord President Robertson at 404. See also *H v P* (1905) 8 F 232, per Lord President Dunedin at 234. For examples of collateral issues considered relevant, see *Houston v Aitken* 1912 SC 1037, per Lord Skerrington (Ordinary) at 1038; *Swan v Bowie* 1948 SC 46, per Lord President Cooper at 51. The general rule against the admission of collateral evidence was confirmed by Lord Justice-Clerk Ross in *Brady v HM Advocate* 1986 JC 68. For recent comment that the term "collateral" may cloud the basic issue of relevance: *Strathmore Group Ltd v Credit Lyonnais* 1994 SLT 1023.

7.2 EVIDENCE OF SIMILAR ACTS—GENERAL RULE

7.2.1 When the question in issue is whether a person did a particular thing at a particular time, it is in general irrelevant to show that he did a similar thing on some other occasion. "The question being whether A said a certain thing to B," it is irrelevant "to show that A said something of the same sort upon another occasion to C."[2] In an action of damages for rape committed on two specified days it was held irrelevant to prove that on other occasions the defender had attempted to ravish other women.[3] Where a pursuer sought to recover money alleged to have been paid as a result of misrepresentations, he was not allowed to prove that similar misrepresentations had been made by the same person to others.[4] Theft and attempted theft on two specified dates having been charged, it was said to be improper to lead evidence that the accused had been in the premises on earlier occasions when cash shortages had occurred.[5] Where the question in issue on a plea of *veritas* in an action of damages for slander was whether the pursuer, a married woman, had committed adultery with the defender, the latter was not allowed to prove that the pursuer had committed adultery with another man on another occasion.[6]

7.3 EVIDENCE OF SIMILAR ACTS—EXCEPTIONS TO GENERAL RULE

General

7.3.1 Except in the limited situations described in the following sub-paragraphs, case law in this area "is unlikely to be a guide for the decision of any other unless the facts are virtually identical".[7] The circumstances in which evidence of similar acts has been considered relevant are wide-ranging and the following are merely examples. In a case where a husband and wife claimed damages for a slander contained in anonymous letters sent to them by post, the pursuers were allowed to lead evidence about similar letters sent to other persons. This was not a true exception to the rule, since the evidence was allowed, not because it supported the probability of the pursuers' case but because it was relevant to the only question really in issue, viz: whether the letters received by the pursuers were in the defender's handwriting.[8] In an action of reduction of a trust disposition and settlement and two codicils, the instrumentary witnesses for each deed being the same two persons, Lord Justice-Clerk Inglis charged the jury that if they were satisfied regarding one of the deeds that the witnesses did not see the testator sign or hear him acknowledge his signature, that fact was relevant to their consideration of whether in the execution of the other deeds the same irregularity had occurred. The reason for this was said to be that if the testator, when executing one of the deeds, acted

---

[2] *Oswald v Fairs* 1911 SC 257, per Lord President Dunedin at 265.

[3] *A v B* (1895) 22 R 402.

[4] *Inglis v National Bank of Scotland* 1909 SC 1038; *Advertising Concessions (Parent) Co v Paterson, Sons & Co* (1908) 16 SLT 654 (OH). For cases where such evidence has been admitted as relevant only to proof of guilty knowledge or intention in a criminal charge, see para 7.15.

[5] *Coventry v Douglas* 1944 JC 13, per Lord Justice-General Normand at 19.

[6] *H v P* (1905) 8 F 232. See also *C v M* 1923 SC 1.

[7] *Strathmore Group Ltd v Credit Lyonnais* 1994 SLT 1023, per Lord Osborne at 1031J–K.

[8] *Swan v Bowie* 1948 SC 46. This evidence was intended to form the basis for skilled evidence as to handwriting: see para 16.4. See also *Knutzen v Mauritzen* 1918 1 SLT 85 (OH).

upon a mistaken belief as to the legal requirements for testing, it was not improbable that he acted in the same way with regard to the others.[9] Although this is an apparent exception to the general rule, it must be noted that the three deeds were closely related in date and in subject-matter, were under reduction in the same action, and bore to be signed and witnessed by the same three persons, and its use as a precedent should perhaps be restricted to these circumstances. Whilst misrepresentations made by the defender other than to the present pursuer are normally excluded by the general rule, such misrepresentations which appeared to have been part of a single course of conduct, either through closeness in time[10] or in nature[11] to the conduct in issue, have been deemed relevant if expediency did not demand their exclusion.

Divorce on adultery grounds

The general rule has been relaxed in actions of divorce for adultery, and the court **7.3.2** has admitted evidence of attempted adultery or indecent conduct on the part of the defender with persons other than the cited paramour, as supporting the probability of the acts of adultery founded upon.[12] This relaxation has been justified on the basis that it is assumed that a party to a marriage will act faithfully and evidence to the contrary will therefore be relevant to protect the matrimonial bond against injury.[13] However, the logicality of the relaxation has been questioned[14] and courts have resisted requests to extend its application. The relaxation does not extend to the paramour's relationships with persons other than the defender, evidence of which is irrelevant and inadmissible.[15] Evidence of earlier adultery, which has been condoned, between the defender and the paramour,[16] or between the defender and someone other than the paramour,[17] or of adultery committed after the raising of the action,[18] although it cannot be founded upon as a ground of judgment, may be relevant as throwing light on the conduct founded on as proof of adultery, or on the nature of the association between the defender and the paramour. It should be noted that statute provides that if in earlier matrimonial proceedings anywhere in the United Kingdom a finding of adultery has been made, that finding may be relied upon in subsequent civil proceedings in which it is relevant to an issue, and creates a rebuttable presumption that the adultery took place.[19]

Actions concerning parentage

In actions of affiliation and aliment or declarator of parentage evidence of acts of **7.3.3** intercourse between the parties, other than those alleged to have caused the conception of the child, is admissible, and may be relevant as throwing light on the

---

9   *Morrison v Maclean's Trs* (1862) 24 D 625 at 630.
10   *Gallagher v Paton* 1909 SC (J) 50.
11   *Arabian Mechanical Engineering Co Ltd v Beaton* 1988 SLT 180; *Strathmore Group Ltd v Credit Lyonnais* 1994 SLT 1023.
12   *Whyte v Whyte* (1884) 11 R 710; *Wilson v Wilson* 1955 SLT (Notes) 81 (OH).
13   *H v P* (1905) 8 F 232, per Lord President Dunedin at 234; *A v B* (1895) 22 R 402, per Lord President Robertson at 404.
14   *Duff v Duff* 1969 SLT (Notes) 53 and Macphail, *Evidence*, paras 16.02–16.05.
15   *King v King* (1842) 4 D 590; *Johnston v Johnston* (1903) 5 F 659.
16   *Collins v Collins* (1884) 11 R (HL) 19, per Lord Blackburn at 29; *Robertson v Robertson* (1888) 15 R 1001, per Lord Young at 1003–1004.
17   *Nicol v Nicol* 1938 SLT 98 (OH).
18   *Ross v Ross* 1928 SC 600.
19   Law Reform (Miscellaneous Provisions) (Scotland) Act 1968, s 11.

probable relationship between the parties at the date of the conception. Evidence that the mother had intercourse with other men at or about the time of conception is also relevant because it has a direct bearing upon the main question in issue, viz: whether the defender is the father of the child. A judicial suggestion that evidence of intercourse between the defender and other women is also relevant has not been adopted in practice.

Criminal causes

7.3.4 Another exception to the rule occurs when evidence of similar acts of an accused person in a criminal cause is admitted in order to establish motive[20] or guilty knowledge or intention,[21] and examples of such evidence are given later.

7.4 EVIDENCE OF CHARACTER—GENERAL

7.4.1 The good or bad character of a party to a cause is generally a matter which is collateral to the main issue, and evidence of it is accordingly in general inadmissible.[22] With regard to the character of the defender in a civil action there seem to be few exceptions to this rule.[23] So, in an action of damages for rape, evidence that the defender was a man of brutal and licentious disposition was held irrelevant,[24] and evidence regarding the defender's character has been held irrelevant in actions of damages for slander,[25] assault,[26] wrongous imprisonment,[27] and breach of contract,[28] and in an action for reduction of a testamentary deed on the ground of facility, circumvention and fraud.[29] The character of the pursuer, however, is sometimes a fact in issue, or has a direct bearing on such a fact, and evidence regarding it is then admissible. In an action of damages for assault against a police constable who had instructions to remove bad characters from a racecourse and who had forcibly ejected the pursuer, evidence of the pursuer's bad character was allowed in order to establish that the ejection was justifiable and did not constitute an assault.[30] And in other actions of damages the pursuer's character may be relevant to the question of *quantum*, the following being examples: actions founded on slander, seduction and breach of promise of marriage[31]; an action by a widow for solatium in respect of her husband's death, when evidence about her moral conduct before, but not after, his death may be relevant to establish that her life with her husband had not been normally happy[32]; an action of damages for bodily

---

[20] See para 7.14.
[21] See para 7.15.
[22] *Clark v Spence* (1825) 3 Mur 450 at 474; Dickson, *Evidence* (3rd edn), para 6.
[23] There is an apparent exception in the admission of evidence of similar acts of adultery or sexual conduct, which indirectly affects the defender's character, in divorce and parentage actions. See paras 7.3.2, 7.3.3. *Cf* also Lord President Robertson in *A v B* (1895) 22 R 402 at 404, who said that if the defender admitted in cross-examination that he had tried to ravish other women this might properly be regarded as making it more probable that he had ravished the pursuer.
[24] *A v B* (1895) 22 R 402.
[25] *Scott v McGavin* (1821) 2 Mur 484 at 493; *Cooper v Macintosh* (1823) 3 Mur 357 at 359.
[26] *Haddaway v Goddard* (1816) 1 Mur 148 at 151.
[27] *Simpson v Liddle* (1821) 2 Mur 579 at 580.
[28] *Kitchen v Fisher* (1821) 2 Mur 584 at 591.
[29] *Clark v Spence* (1825) 3 Mur 450.
[30] *Wallace v Mooney* (1885) 12 R 710.
[31] See paras 7.5 and 7.6.
[32] *Donnelly v Glasgow Corporation* 1949 SLT 362 (OH).

injury resulting in loss of business profits when evidence that the pursuer's losses were partly due to his intemperate habits was admitted.[33] Evidence of character in criminal causes is dealt with later in this chapter.[34] Even when general evidence as to character or reputation is held to be admissible, evidence of specific criminal or immoral acts may be disallowed on the practical ground of inexpediency[35] unless the specification of those acts is in itself relevant to the case in hand.

7.5 CHARACTER IN SLANDER ACTIONS

It has been said that in actions of damages for slander, the pursuer necessarily puts **7.5.1** his character in issue.[36] The pursuer is entitled to substantiate his claim for damages by proving that he is of good character, and the defender, in order to mitigate damages, is entitled to prove the contrary.[37] In this connection, however, it is more accurate to speak of "reputed character" than of "character", because it is loss of reputation rather than loss of character for which damages are claimed. When the defender seeks to mitigate damages, "the point of such a defence is not that [the pursuer] *is* a bad character, but that she *has* a bad character."[38] So, in a slander action, the defender in mitigation of damages was allowed to prove that the pursuer was well known as a person of loose and immoral character, but not that she had committed adultery on specific occasions.[39] Proof of the truth of allegations of the defender's poor character is only admissible if the defence of *veritas* has been specifically pled.[40]

7.6 CHARACTER IN ACTIONS FOR SEDUCTION AND BREACH OF PROMISE OF MARRIAGE

In these actions also (still competent but now rarely pursued) it has been said that **7.6.1** the pursuer's character is necessarily put in issue.[41] In an action for seduction the pursuer is not bound to prove her own good character, but her character may be considered by the jury as supporting the probability or improbability of her consent to sexual relations with the defender having been obtained by dole.[42] In an action for breach of promise of marriage it has been held relevant to prove as a defence to the action that, unknown to the defender, the pursuer has had a child (in

---

[33] *Butchart v Dundee & Arbroath Railway Co* (1859) 22 D 184.

[34] See paras 7.7–7.10.

[35] *C v M* 1923 SC 1 (slander): Lord President Clyde said that while substantive evidence might not be led about specific acts of adultery committed by the pursuer, they might have a bearing on character and credibility and could be put to her in cross-examination if fair notice, not necessarily on record, was given. This point was not specifically carried forward in *Duff v Duff* 1969 SLT (Notes) 53. Cross-examination was similarly permitted, but in relation only to credibility, in *A v B* (1895) 22 R 402 (damages for rape) and *H v P* (1905) 8 F 232 (slander), per Lord Ordinary at 234.

[36] *Hyslop v Miller* (1816) 1 Mur 43 at 49; *C v M* 1923 SC 1, per Lord President Clyde at 4.

[37] *McNeill v Rorison* (1847) 10 D 15, per Lord Justice-Clerk Hope at 34, Lord Moncreiff at 26, 27.

[38] *C v M* 1923 SC 1, per Lord President Clyde at 4.

[39] *C v M* 1923 SC 1. See also *MacCulloch v Litt* (1851) 13 D 960 (evidence of current rumour allowed in mitigation of damages).

[40] *C v M* 1923 SC 1. On this point, see also *Paul v Jackson* (1884) 11 R 460; *Browne v McFarlane* (1889) 16 R 368.

[41] *Bern's Exr v Montrose Asylum* (1893) 20 R 859, per Lord McLaren at 863.

[42] *Walker v McIsaac* (1857) 19 D 340; Dickson, *Evidence* (3rd edn), para 10.

this case as a result of an extramarital relationship), because on discovering the fact the defender was entitled to resile from the engagement.[43] In these actions, also, evidence as to the pursuer's character is relevant to the question of *quantum* of damages.

7.7 CHARACTER IN CRIMINAL CAUSES

Of victim or complainer

7.7.1 The accused may, if notice has been given,[44] attack the character of the injured person's credibility as a witness if relevant to the crime charged. In cases of murder or assault the accused may prove that the injured person was of a violent or quarrelsome disposition,[45] but not the commission of specific acts of violence[46] unless, exceptionally, these are directly relevant to the crime charged.[47] It has been held that the victim may be cross-examined, apparently without notice, as to his insobriety at the time of the assault, and that evidence may be led for the defence regarding it.[48] The prosecutor is entitled to ask a witness whether the victim was quarrelsome or inoffensive.[49] In an appeal against conviction for rape, the court accepted that reliable evidence that the victim had previously made false accusations of sexual assaults upon her, which evidence had been unavailable at trial, was highly relevant to the issue of the victim's credibility and the accused's defence of consent.[50] The prosecutor may lead evidence that the victim was of good character.[51]

7.7.2 At common law in cases of rape or of similar assaults upon women, the accused could attack the woman's character for chastity, and could lead evidence that at the time she was reputedly of bad moral character,[52] that she associated with prostitutes, but not that her friends were otherwise of bad character,[53] and that she had previously had intercourse with the accused.[54] The accused could not lead evidence to prove specific acts of intercourse with other men, unless, possibly, these were so closely connected with the alleged rape as to form part of the *res gestae*.[55] Since 1985 in cases involving a range of crimes of a sexual or indecent nature, now specified in the Criminal Procedure (Scotland) Act 1995, s 274(2), evidence that the complainer is not of good character in relation to sexual matters, is a prostitute or an associate of prostitutes or has at any time engaged with any person in sexual

---

[43] *Fletcher v Grant* (1878) 6 R 59.
[44] *Dickie v HM Advocate* (1897) 24 R (J) 82, at 83, 87; *Brown* (1836) 1 Swin 293. *Cf Craig v HM Advocate* 1993 SLT 483; *Felber v Lockhart* 1994 SLT 240.
[45] *Blair* (1836) Bell's Notes 294; *Irving* (1838) 2 Swin 109; *Fletcher* (1846) Ark 171.
[46] *Irving* (1838) 2 Swin 109; *Fletcher* (1846) Ark 171.
[47] Such an exception was made in the case of *HM Advocate v Kay* 1970 JC 68 where, the accused being charged with the murder of her husband having previously evinced ill-will against him, in respect of which she pled self-defence, evidence of prior specific assaults by the victim upon the accused were admitted.
[48] *Falconer v Brown* (1893) 21 R (J) 1. It would seem that the evidence was regarded as the possible basis of a defence related to assault or provocation by the complainer (see Lord McLaren at 3), but this is by no means clear.
[49] *Porteous* (1841) Bell's Notes 293.
[50] *Green v HM Advocate* 1983 SCCR 42.
[51] *McMillan* (1846) Ark 209; Dickson, *Evidence* (3rd edn), para 7.
[52] *Dickie v HM Advocate* (1897) 24 R (J) 82.
[53] *Webster* (1847) Ark 269.
[54] *McMillan* (1846) Ark 209; Dickson, *Evidence* (3rd edn), para 7.
[55] *McMillan* (1846) Ark 209; Dickson, *Evidence* (3rd edn), para 7.

behaviour not forming part of the subject-matter of the charge is not admissible either as evidence in chief or by cross-examination[56] except on application to the court, which may in its discretion[57] grant or refuse the application and having granted it may limit the extent of the evidence to be presented. Criteria justifying the grant of such an application are set out in section 275, namely: the evidence is to explain or rebut other evidence in the case; the evidence concerns sexual behaviour on the same occasion as the incident libelled or is relevant to a defence of incrimination; or it would be contrary to the interests of justice to exclude the evidence. Evidence of a prior sexual relationship with the accused will not necessarily be admissible, depending upon the time elapsed between the ending of that relationship and the incident libelled.[58] Evidence of the victim's sexual conduct after the date of the crime is generally inadmissible.[59]

Of persons not present at trial

In certain circumstances evidence has been admitted as to the character of persons **7.7.3** who were neither the victim nor the accused, and who were not witnesses at the trial. In reset cases, in order to establish guilty knowledge, the Crown has been allowed to prove that the persons frequenting the accused's shop were thieves or dealers in stolen property,[60] and that the man from whom the accused, in his declaration, admitted obtaining the stolen watch, was a dealer in stolen watches.[61] On a charge of brothel keeping the prosecutor may lead evidence that women seen by witnesses to enter the premises are known by them to be prostitutes.[62] In sexual crimes, the accused, if permitted by the court, may lead evidence that the accused's associates are common prostitutes,[63] but not that they are otherwise of bad character.[64] In offences under the Misuse of Drugs Act 1971, evidence has been admitted to the effect that the accused has associated with those believed to be involved in the possession or supply of controlled drugs where this has been integral to other relevant evidence against the accused, but evidence of the associates' criminal records for drug offences was held inadmissible on grounds of fairness to the accused, in respect of whom the jury might have put the evidence to improper use.[65]

7.8 CHARACTER OF ACCUSED PERSON—GENERAL

The accused's good character may always be proved for the defence.[66] An **7.8.1**

---

[56] s 274(1).
[57] With which an appeal court will not lightly interfere: *Bremner v HM Advocate* 1992 SCCR 476. *Cf Love v HM Advocate* 2000 JC 1.
[58] *Bremner v HM Advocate* 1992 SCCR 476.
[59] *Leitch* (1838) 2 Swin 112. However, in *Love v HM Advocate* 2000 JC 1 the Appeal Court quashed the conviction when the trial judge had refused to admit evidence that the victim had a sexual relationship from age 12, in a case where sexual offences were alleged to have taken place when the accused was aged between 10 and 14. The evidence could have been relevant to explain the victim's detailed sexual knowledge at the date of trial.
[60] *Burns v Hart and Young* (1856) 2 Irv 571.
[61] *Gracie v Stuart* (1884) 11 R (J) 22.
[62] *Macpherson v Crisp* 1919 JC 1. See also *McLaren v Macleod* 1913 SC (J) 61, per Lord McKenzie at 68.
[63] Criminal Procedure (Scotland) Act 1995, ss 274(1)(b) and 275.
[64] *Webster* (1847) Ark 269.
[65] *Forsyth v HM Advocate* 1992 SLT 189.
[66] Dickson, *Evidence* (3rd edn), para 15. See also *Slater v HM Advocate* 1928 JC 94 at 105.

attack by the Crown, on the other hand, on the accused's character is generally inadmissible,[67] although evidence, otherwise relevant, which may attack the character of the accused will not on that account be excluded. For example, if a man is charged with the murder of his mistress, the relationship between them must necessarily be disclosed. A voluntary statement by the accused, which is admissible in evidence, is not excluded merely because it incidentally betrays his previous bad character[68] but references therein to the accused's previous convictions should be prevented by the prosecutor,[69] in order to avoid breach of the statutory protection against disclosure of the accused's previous convictions, discussed below. In the case of Oscar Slater,[70] who was charged with the murder of an old lady, it was proved that a box in her house had been broken open and that a valuable brooch was missing. Evidence was led for the Crown to show that the accused, who pretended to be a dentist, in fact made money by gambling and dealing in jewels, and it also came out in evidence that he was living on the earnings of prostitution. It was held on appeal that the first item of evidence was relevant as showing a motive for the taking of jewellery, but that the evidence regarding the earnings of prostitution, while it could not have been excluded owing to the nature of the defence, was wholly irrelevant to the issue, and that the jury should have been instructed to ignore it. Where a writing, which is held to be relevant and admissible as a piece of documentary evidence, contains irrelevant matter which is prejudicial to the accused, the judge must warn the jury against allowing their verdict to be affected by the irrelevant matter.[71] It has been held proper to bring out from a reluctant witness for the Crown that an attempt at intimidation was made on her by someone representing the accused, but the jury should be directed that this evidence is relevant only to explain the witness's demeanour, and is not evidence against the accused.[72]

7.9 CRIMINAL RECORD OF ACCUSED PERSON

7.9.1 Apart from questions of character in general, express statutory provision is made for excluding the accused's previous convictions from the knowledge of the court, prior to a conviction or a plea of guilty. In solemn procedure previous convictions may not be laid before the jury before the verdict is returned and the prosecutor has moved for sentence,[73] save where it is competent to lead evidence regarding

[67] eg Burns v Hart and Young (1856) 2 Irv 571 (a reset charge, where the allowance of evidence that the accused was by habit and repute a resetter was held fatal to the conviction). See also Dickson, Evidence (3rd edn), para 15. For circumstances in which the accused's bad character may be mentioned in evidence, see paras 7.9 and 13.13–13.14.

[68] HM Advocate v McFadyen 1926 JC 93.

[69] Graham v HM Advocate 1984 SLT 67 in which it was held that the prosecutor was negligent in allowing a police witness to quote from the accused's reply to caution and charge after a domestic incident, "that cow's got me the jail again!"

[70] Slater v HM Advocate 1928 JC 94.

[71] McEwan v HM Advocate 1939 JC 26 (a letter). This must be distinguished from a report by an expert witness, read by him in the witness box for convenience as part of his parole evidence. In such a case a conviction will be quashed if the expert is allowed to read any part of his report which is inadmissible and prejudicial to the accused: Grant v HM Advocate 1938 JC 7 (report of a medical witness); McEwan v HM Advocate at 32, 33–34.

[72] Manson v HM Advocate 1951 JC 49.

[73] Criminal Procedure (Scotland) Act 1995 ("1995 Act"), s 101(1) and (3).

them *in causa* in support of a substantive charge[74] or, on application to the court, where the accused in eliciting evidence or otherwise in the conduct of his defence attacks the character of the victim, complainer, prosecutor or Crown witness or introduces his or her own character.[75] Similarly, in summary procedure previous convictions may not be laid before the court until the judge is satisfied that the case is proved,[76] unless the same exempting conditions apply.[77] Previous convictions may be proved *in causa* if they are essential to proof of the *actus reus* of the charge, such as proof of conviction and disqualification from driving in a subsequent charge of driving while disqualified,[78] or proof of conviction and length of sentence in a subsequent charge of prison-breaking. In certain situations statute provides that previous convictions may be proof *in causa*. So, for the purpose of proving guilty knowledge in a reset case, the prosecutor, if he gives seven days' notice to the accused in writing, may prove previous convictions of offences inferring fraud or dishonesty obtained during the preceding five years, provided that he has first led evidence to establish that the accused was in possession of stolen property.[79] A person found in possession of tools or objects in circumstances from which it can reasonably be inferred that it was intended to commit theft can only be successfully prosecuted if proved to have two or more convictions for theft.[80] It has been held that accidental or incidental reference by a witness to a previous conviction may not constitute a breach of the statutory prohibition since the test is whether the prosecutor took reasonable steps to ensure that the convictions were not laid before the court by framing questions appropriately.[81] If the prohibition is held to be breached that may not be fatal to the conviction nor contrary to Article 6 of the European Convention on Human Rights.[82] How to deal with a witness's indirect reference to previous convictions during trial is a matter for the trial judge and depends upon the nature of the reference and its likely effect upon the jury.[83] Evidence that a witness examined a photograph of the accused in an album in the police station is not regarded as a disclosure of the accused's criminal record.[84]

7.10 CROSS-EXAMINATION OF ACCUSED AS TO CHARACTER

This subject is dealt with later in connection with specialities of witnesses.[85]   **7.10.1**

---

[74] 1995 Act, s 101(2)(b).
[75] 1995 Act, s 270(1) and (2); *Leggate v HM Advocate* 1988 JC 127. An example is *Sinclair v Macdonald* 1996 JC 145.
[76] 1995 Act, s 166(3).
[77] 1995 Act, s 166(8).
[78] *Mitchell v Dean* 1979 JC 62, but the record of previous convictions produced should not exceed that necessary to prove the current charge.
[79] Prevention of Crimes Act 1871 s 19; *Watson v HM Advocate* (1894) 21 R (J) 26.
[80] Civic Government (Scotland) Act 1982, s 58; *Newlands v MacPhail* 1991 SLT 642.
[81] *Kepple v HM Advocate* 1936 JC 76; *Carberry v HM Advocate* 1975 JC 40; *Johnston v Allan* 1984 SLT 261. See also *Deighan v MacLeod* 1959 JC 25; *Fyfe v HM Advocate* 1989 SCCR 429; *Armstrong v HM Advocate* 1993 SCCR 311.
[82] *Kerr v Jessop* 1991 SCCR 27, *Andrew v HM Advocate* 2000 SLT 402.
[83] *Kepple v HM Advocate* 1936 JC 76; *Armstrong v HM Advocate* 1993 SCCR 311; *Robertson v HM Advocate* 1995 SCCR 497, *Andrew v HM Advocate* 2000 SLT 402.
[84] *Corcoran v HM Advocate* 1932 JC 42.
[85] See para 13.13 and 13.14.

7.11 EVIDENCE OF STATE OF MIND—GENERAL

7.11.1 A party's state of mind at a particular time cannot be proved by direct evidence other than the uncorroborated testimony of that party, who may not be a compellable witness. When state of mind is one of the facts in issue, or is relevant to a fact in issue, it can be proved only by inferences drawn from other facts, and the collateral issues associated with these other facts are in these circumstances relevant and admissible in evidence.[86]

7.12 STATE OF MIND IN CIVIL CAUSES

7.12.1 When in reparation actions the defender's knowledge of the existence of a danger is one of the matters in issue, evidence is admissible of earlier accidents or injuries arising from the same danger from which his knowledge at the relevant time may be inferred. The collateral facts which it is intended to prove must always be averred in the pleadings. Evidence was admitted that a person other than the pursuer had previously fallen down a stairway in public-house premises[87]; that the absence of a sideguard between the wheels of tramcars had caused similar earlier injuries to pedestrians[88]; and, in an action against a road authority, that four earlier skidding accidents had occurred on the street, the dangerous condition of which was blamed for the accident to the pursuers' bus.[89] On the same principle, in an action against the owner of a dog for damages caused to persons or livestock injured by the dog, evidence that it has bitten other persons or endangered other livestock is admissible to establish the owner's knowledge of its vicious disposition.[90] When the defender's malice is one of the facts which must be proved, collateral facts from which malice may be inferred if averred are admissible in evidence. The following are examples of such facts: in a case of judicial slander, the defender's knowledge that the defamatory averments were untrue, and the facts from which that knowledge could be inferred[91]; in other cases of slander uttered on privileged occasions, the defender's failure to make reasonable enquiry into the truth of the defamatory statements,[92] needless publicity given to the slander,[93] prior indications of ill-will,[94] and the fact that the language used was unnecessarily violent, persistent and intemperate.[95]

---

[86] Dickson, *Evidence* (3rd edn), para 19. *Gernmill v HM Advocate* 1979 SLT 217.
[87] *Cairns v Boyd* (1879) 6 R 1004 at 1006.
[88] *Gibb v Edinburgh & District Tramways Co* 1912 SC, 580, per Lord Ordinary (Guthrie) at 582.
[89] *W Alexander & Sons v Dundee Corporation* 1950 SC 123.
[90] *Gordon v Mackenzie* 1913 SC 109; *McIntyre v Carmichael* (1870) 8 M 570 (damages for sheep killing based on common law fault).
[91] *Mitchell v Smith* 1919 SC 664.
[92] *Dinnie v Hengler* 1910 SC 4.
[93] *Ingram v Russell* (1893) 20 R 771, per Lord McLaren at 778.
[94] *Suzor v McLachlan* 1914 SC 306.
[95] *Gall v Slessor* 1907 SC 708; *Riddell v Glasgow Corporation* 1910 SC 693, per Lord Ardwall at 694–700 (revd on another point, 1911 SC (HL) 35).

7.13 STATE OF MIND IN CRIMINAL CAUSES

General

Evidence of collateral facts may be admissible in criminal causes in order to estab- **7.13.1**
lish motive[96] or guilty knowledge and intention,[97] and these subjects are dealt with
in the following paragraphs. The rules regarding the proximity of the collateral fact
to the crime charged, and the necessity for notice being given of the collateral issue
to be raised, are common to the whole of this subject.

Proximity of collateral fact to crime charged

The general test regarding the relevancy of indirect evidence applies. In order to **7.13.2**
be relevant the collateral fact which it is desired to prove must not be too remote
from the crime charged in time, place or character, what is or is not too remote for
this purpose being a question of degree in each case.[98]

Notice of the collateral issue

Evidence of the commission of a crime other than the crime principally libelled has **7.13.3**
for long been considered inadmissible unless the indictment or complaint gives
notice of it, either by libelling the other crime as a substantive charge,[99] or by averring the facts relating to it which the evidence is intended to establish.[100] This rule
has been applied even when the collateral evidence related only to a statutory
offence.[101] Over time some difficulty arose in the expression and application of this
rule, leading to confusion as to the need for notice if the evidence was relevant and
not intended to prove a separate crime against the accused. The rule was reviewed
by a court of five judges in 1994[102] when the authorities[103] were examined and the
High Court restated the rule in the following terms.

> "The Crown can lead any evidence relevant to the proof of a crime charged, even
> though it may tend to show the commission of another crime not charged, unless
> fair notice requires that that other crime should be charged or otherwise referred
> to expressly in the complaint or indictment. This will be so if the evidence sought
> to be led tends to show that the accused was of bad character and that other crime
> is so different in time, place or character from the crime charged, that the libel
> does not give fair notice to the accused that evidence relating to that other crime
> may be led, or if it is the intention as proof of the crime charged to establish that
> the accused was in fact guilty of that other crime".[104]

---

[96] See para 7.14.
[97] See para 7.15.
[98] For judicial dicta on this point, see para 7.3.
[99] *HM Advocate v Pritchard* (1865) 5 Irv 88; *HM Advocate v Wishart* (1870) 1 Couper 463; *HM Advocate v Monson* (1893) 21 R (J) 5; *Robertson v Watson* 1949 JC 73.
[100] *HM Advocate v Joseph* 1929 JC 55; *HM Advocate v Tully* 1935 JC 8; *Griffen v HM Advocate* 1940 JC 1. An exception to this rule seems to have been sanctioned in *Gallagher v Paton* 1909 SC (J) 50. See paras 7.3.1 and 7.15.
[101] *HM Advocate v Tully* 1935 JC 8; *Robertson v Watson* 1949 JC 73.
[102] *Nelson v HM Advocate* 1994 SCCR 192.
[103] *HM Advocate v Monson* (1893) 21 R (J) 5; *HM Advocate v Joseph* 1929 JC 55; *Griffen v HM Advocate* 1940 JC 1; *Robertson v Watson* 1949 JC 73.
[104] *Nelson v HM Advocate* 1994 SCCR 192, per Lord Justice-General (Hope) at 203C–D.

The facts of the case then under review were that the accused had been charged with being concerned in the supply of controlled drugs contrary to the Misuse of Drugs Act 1971, s 4(3)(b). Evidence of police officers who witnessed the circumstances giving rise to his arrest disclosed that the accused had concealed a package of drugs in his possession by swallowing them, which would have amounted to a contravention of section 23 of the 1971 Act but was not libelled in the indictment. Applying the restated test the court found the collateral evidence relevant and that in the terms of the indictment as drawn the accused had fair notice that the police witnesses would speak to all facts surrounding his arrest. Although his attempt to conceal the drugs was relevant to the question of whether he committed the crime libelled it was not essential to its proof, so it was not necessary to libel the concealing charge separately. In a later case the court upheld an appeal against conviction where the charges against the accused for contraventions of the Road Traffic Act 1988 were preceded by a preamble narrating that the offences were committed while the accused had unlawfully removed the vehicle and evidence in support of the preamble had been admitted at trial. The accused had been given the requisite fair notice of the facts referred to in the preamble but these were not necessary or relevant to the proof of the crimes libelled, and the existence of this evidence was grossly prejudicial to the court's assessment of the accused's character without the corresponding rights which he would have if the facts were libelled as a charge against him.[105] Collateral evidence which is relevant, other than that relating to a crime not charged, is usually admissible without notice, in accordance with the general rule that a party need not disclose in advance the evidence by which he hopes to prove his case.[106]

7.14 MOTIVE IN CRIMINAL CAUSES

7.14.1 The Crown need not prove a motive for the commission of a crime[107] and, indeed, it may be impossible to discover a rational motive for some crimes which are clearly proved to have been committed. Apparent absence of motive, however, may be an important element in favour of the defence,[108] and evidence of motive in support of the case for the Crown is admissible.[109] For example, in murder cases evidence of earlier assaults and threats of violence has been allowed as relevant to the motive of hatred or revenge, the proximity in time of the earlier conduct being a matter influencing weight rather than admissibility.[110] Evidence that Oscar Slater[111] was a dealer in jewels was held relevant to a possible motive for the murder of a woman from whom a valuable brooch had been stolen. In all crimes

---

[105] *Slack v HM Advocate* 1996 SLT 1084.

[106] *Ritchie and Morren* (1841) 2 Swin 581 (see para 7.15.1); *HM Advocate v Rae* (1888) 15 R (J) 80 at 81–82; *HM Advocate v Monson* (1893) 21 R (J) 5, per Lord Justice-Clerk Macdonald at 7; *Barr v HM Advocate* 1927 JC 51, per Lord Justice-Clerk Alness at 56.

[107] Hume, i, 254; Macdonald, *Criminal Law* (5th edn), p 1.

[108] Dickson, *Evidence* (3rd edn), para 83.

[109] *Nelson v HM Advocate* 1994 SCCR 192, per Lord Justice-General Hope at 202E–F. Notorious examples are to be found in the early cases of *A A Rouse* (*Notable British Trials*), *Madeleine Smith* (1857) *Notable Scottish Trials*, and *HM Advocate v Pritchard* (1865) 5 Irv 88 at 100 (also reported in *Notable Scottish Trials*).

[110] *HM Advocate v Kennedy* (1907) 5 Adam 347; *Millar* (1837) 1 Swin 483 at 486; *Salt* (1860) 3 Irv 549. In *Stewart* (1855) 2 Irv 166, expressions indicative of violence shortly after the murder were admitted as part of the res gestae. Cf *Platt v HM Advocate* 2000 SCCR 620.

[111] *Slater v HM Advocate* 1928 JC 94.

associated with dishonesty the impecuniosity of the accused is relevant to the question of motive, and evidence that the accused had previously pawned some of his own property was admitted for this purpose in a case of wilful fireraising.[112]

7.15 GUILTY KNOWLEDGE AND INTENTION

Mens rea, dole or intention is a necessary element in crimes at common law.[113] **7.15.1**
Some statutory offences, often termed absolute offences or offences of strict liability, may be committed without *mens rea*, but the question of whether statutory contraventions require proof of intention, culpability, knowledge or wilfulness is determined by statutory interpretation.[114] In all crimes requiring such proof *mens rea* may be inferred from proof of the crime itself, and does not need to be separately established. The Crown may nevertheless lead evidence of collateral facts from which guilty intention or guilty knowledge may be inferred, and such evidence is both admissible and necessary when the act itself is neutral in quality, and is susceptible either of a guilty or of an innocent interpretation such as accident, self defence or unintentional injury or deceit. So, in a charge of wilful fireraising evidence was admitted that shortly before the fire the accused removed some of his own goods from the building,[115] and, in a case of murder of a child by its parents, the Crown, in order to show knowledge and premeditation, was allowed to prove that both accused discussed their concern about the mother's pregnancy with a doctor five months before the child's birth.[116] In charges relating to fraudulent pretences, and the uttering of forged documents, the Crown must establish knowledge that the representations or the documents were false, and for this purpose evidence of the accused's earlier or later actings may be admissible. So, where the accused was charged with defrauding a shop assistant of the cost of an advertisement in a directory, on the pretence that her employer made this payment annually, evidence of other shopkeepers and shop assistants in the same town was admitted to show that similar false representations were made to them on the same day.[117] In that case Lord McLaren said: "A false statement made to one person may be explained away, but when a system of false statements is proved, the probability is very great that the statements were designedly made." When the charge was that of uttering a base shilling, evidence that on the same night the accused had offered coins to other persons, who had rejected them as bad, was admitted to show his knowledge

---

[112] *Rosenberg* (1842) 1 Broun 266.
[113] Hume, i, 21, 22; Macdonald, *Criminal Law* (5th edn), p 1; and for more detail on issues of dole and *mens rea*, see Gordon, *Criminal Law* (2nd edn), Chapter 7.
[114] For example, under the Road Traffic Act 1988 and the Road Vehicles (Construction and Use) Regulations 1986 (SI 1986/1078), reg 100(2) an offence of using a vehicle of defective construction or in dangerous condition in contravention of the regulations may require no *mens rea* (as in *MacNeill v Wilson* 1981 SLT (Notes) 109), but the separate offence of causing and permitting it to be so used requires an element of knowledge, intention or wilful disregard (as in *Smith of Maddiston Ltd v Macnab* 1975 SLT 86). Offences under the Misuse of Drugs Act 1971, ss 4 and 5 do not require *mens rea* per se; however, the defences available to the accused under s 28 introduce issues of knowledge and inference of intention which may require the prosecutor to counter the defence with evidence from which knowledge or intention may be inferred: *Tudhope v McKee* 1988 SLT 153.
[115] *McCreadie* (1862) 4 Irv 214. See also *HM Advocate v Smillie* (1883) 10 R (J) 70 at 71.
[116] *HM Advocate v Wishart* (1870) 1 Couper 463.
[117] *Gallagher v Paton* 1909 SC (J) 50 at 55. The judicial opinions contain no comment on the fact that the evidence of the collateral false representations was allowed without notice. The decision seems to be an exception to the rule mentioned in para 7.13.2.

of their falsity at the time of the act charged.[118] When an accused was charged, as part of a fraudulent scheme, with uttering a forged draft and pretending that it was genuine, evidence was admitted that in the following month he pretended in Belgium that a similar forged draft was genuine.[119] This evidence was allowed, not because the commission of a similar crime made it probable that the accused committed the crime charged, which would have been an irrelevant consideration, but as relevant to show that the act charged was done of design and not by accident. One means of proving guilty knowledge in a case of uttering is to establish that the accused himself forged the document uttered, and evidence to this effect is admissible for that purpose.[120] In order to prove guilt in a charge of reset the Crown must lead evidence from which the accused's knowledge that the articles were stolen can be inferred, the time, place and circumstances of the accused's possession being relevant and sufficient for this purpose.[121]

---

[118] *Ritchie and Morren* (1841) 2 Swin 581. This evidence was allowed without notice, which, if the earlier attempts are to be regarded as criminal, is in conflict with the rule mentioned in para 7.13.2. The court may have thought that they could not be established as criminal without proof of guilty knowledge at the times when they were committed.

[119] *HM Advocate v Joseph* 1929 JC 55.

[120] *Barr v HM Advocate* 1927 JC 51. See also the trial of Donald Merrett, *Notable British Trials.*

[121] Gordon, *Criminal Law* (2nd edn), paras 20–09 to 20–10. Recent examples are *Friel v Docherty* 1990 SCCR 351, *McKellar v Normand* 1992 SCCR 393 and *L v Wilson* 1995 SLT 673.

CHAPTER 8

HEARSAY

8.1 INTRODUCTORY

In literal terms hearsay evidence is evidence of what another person has said **8.1.1** (orally, in writing or by other physical expression). Scotland, in common with most legal systems operates a rule against the admission of hearsay evidence, although that rule is now mainly limited to criminal proceedings, hearsay evidence in civil proceedings having been declared admissible by statute in 1988.[1] An expression of the rule adopted recently is "Any assertion other than one made by a person while giving oral evidence in the proceedings is inadmissible as evidence of any fact or opinion asserted"[2] and this definition, with the word "statement" in place of "assertion", was adopted by the Scottish Law Commission in its *Report on Hearsay Evidence in Criminal Proceedings*.[3] So defined the rule strikes at secondary hearsay, that is the indirect evidence of the truth of the facts alleged in the statement,[4] but does not cover primary hearsay, that is the direct evidence of the fact that the statement was made, irrespective of its truth or falsehood. Some writers prefer to describe this as original evidence that such a statement was made,[5] thus avoiding the terminology of "primary" and "secondary" hearsay. Admission of evidence that a statement was made is unobjectionable provided that it is relevant to an issue in the case,[6] and in that respect it may indeed be desirable

---

[1]   Civil Evidence (Scotland) Act 1988, s 2(1). There are some qualifications to its admissibility, which are considered below.

[2]   For examination of the review of the hearsay definition in England see Cross & Tapper, *Evidence* (9th edn) pp 598–599. The definition approved by the House of Lords in *R v Sharp* [1988] 1 All ER 65 at 68, which was later adopted in *Morrison v HM Advocate* 1990 JC 299 at 312.

[3]   Scot Law Com No 149, para 3.2. The term "statement" is taken there to include expressions made orally, in writing or by conduct.

[4]   Dickson, *Evidence* (3rd edn), para 245. In *Grant v HM Advocate* 1938 JC 7 the conviction was quashed because a passage was read to the jury from a medical report narrating a statement made by a witness implicating the accused.

[5]   *eg* Cross & Tapper, *Evidence* (9th edn) p 599; Field & Raitt at paras 8-05 to 8-10.

[6]   *Subramaniam v Public Prosecutor* [1956] 1 WLR 965 at 970. As to the relevance, or not, of prior consistent statements, see paras 8.4 and 8.6.

to separate it from the hearsay rule. However, while these two approaches to the repetition in court of statements made by someone other than the witness are totally distinct,[7] they have been easily confused,[8] particularly if there is not clear consideration of the purpose for which the evidence was admitted,[9] and the confusion is apparent in the evolution of some of the exceptions to the hearsay rule.[10]

8.1.2   The rationale for the rule,[11] which operates to exclude evidence that would otherwise be relevant, is largely based upon fear as to truthfulness and accuracy[12] since the court is unable to assess the credibility and reliability of the evidence from the maker of the statement in court, on oath, and subject to cross-examination, and instead is faced with second best evidence from a third party who may not be credible or reliable as to what was overheard or seen. There is also fear that juries are unable to bear these factors in mind when assessing the probative value of the evidence. These traditional grounds for excluding hearsay evidence were considered by the Scottish Law Commission,[13] who reported in 1995 that the rule, as it then stood in criminal proceedings with its limited exceptions,[14] did not accord with some of the general principles upon which, they stated,[15] the law of evidence should be based, namely that the rules of evidence should be as clear and simple as possible, and should allow for all relevant evidence to be generally admissible.[16] Instead they considered that the rule excluding hearsay at times operated to withhold from the court evidence potentially more informative or reliable than such evidence, if any, which was admissible.[17] Stopping short of abolition of the rule in criminal cases[18] they recommended that a wider range of exceptions be introduced allowing for the admission of hearsay as evidence of any matter contained in the statement in specified circumstances in which that is the best evidence available, with safeguards such as requirements for prior notice and judicial approval, and entitlement to lead evidence in rebuttal and to challenge the credibility of the maker of the statement.[19] They further recommended admission of the prior statement of a witness who adopted that prior statement to supplement evidence given in court.[20] These recommendations were adopted into legislation which commenced in April 1996,[21] and are discussed further in the following paragraphs. These new statutory provisions for dealing with hearsay evidence in criminal cases do not prejudice the admissibility of a hearsay statement which is admissible otherwise than by virtue of those provisions, that is at common

---

[7]   *Jackson v Glasgow Corporation* 1956 SC 354, per Lord President Clyde at 361, Lord Russell at 363, Lord Sorn at 365.

[8]   See para 8.10.

[9]   As in *Farooq v HM Advocate* 1993 SLT 1271 and *McAllister v HM Advocate* (1975) SCCR Supp 98.

[10]   The history of the rule and its exceptions is considered by Wilkinson in "Hearsay: A Scottish Perspective" in Hunter (ed), *Justice & Crime*, pp 66–75.

[11]   Considered by Macphail at paras 19.03–19.09.

[12]   *Teper v R* [1952] AC 480 at 486; *R v Blastland* [1986] AC 41 at 54.

[13]   In *Report on Corroboration, Hearsay and Related Matters in Civil Proceedings* (Scot Law Com No 100), and in *Report on Hearsay Evidence in Criminal Proceedings* (Scot Law Com No 149).

[14]   Which had developed for the admission of classes of hearsay rather than to permit its admission as the best available evidence as judged on a case by case basis: Scot Law Com No 149, para 3.6.

[15]   In Scot Law Com No 149, Pt I.

[16]   Scot Law Com No 149, para 3.4.

[17]   Scot Law Com No 149, paras 3.20–3.21, 4.1.

[18]   For consideration of the options see Scot Law Com No 149, paras 4.20–4.46.

[19]   Scot Law Com No 149, paras 4.47–4.52 and Pts V and VI.

[20]   Scot Law Com No 149, Pt VII.

[21]   They are now in the Criminal Procedure (Scotland) Act 1995, ss 259–262.

law[22] or in terms of another statutory provision.[23] Whether a statement will be admitted under an exception to the hearsay rule, at common law or under statute, will depend upon satisfaction of the criteria for the exception to apply, and also upon whether the maker of the statement was someone who would have been competent to give oral evidence in the case, and whether the nature of the statement or its contents would render it inadmissible on any ground other than hearsay.

8.2 EVIDENCE THAT A STATEMENT WAS MADE (PRIMARY HEARSAY)

It is frequently necessary to prove that a statement has been made, for example, in **8.2.1** actions based on misrepresentation or for damages for slander or arising from a contract entered into orally, or in a trial for perjury or extortion. The party leading the evidence does so merely to establish that the statement was made. The party may not be concerned with its truth, and indeed may assert that it was untrue. All that the court should consider is whether it is true *that* the statement was made, and not whether *what* the statement asserts is true. Usually a party will decide positively to lead the evidence for this limited purpose, but may be forced into that decision by the inability to use the evidence as proof of the content of the statement because, in a criminal case, the criteria for admission of hearsay have not been met, or, in a civil case, because the party making the statement would not have been competent to give the evidence orally.[24]

It may be proved that a witness has previously made a statement differing from **8.2.2** his evidence.[25] Further, statements proved to have been made by a person, orally or in writing, may be evidence of the maker's state of mind[26] or feelings towards another person,[27] such as a parent with whom a child has contact.[28] Evidence of a statement by a third party to a witness is admissible to explain the witness's actions[29] and frequently to explain grounds on which a medical or other expert witness bases an opinion. Where the defence was that the accused acted under duress, evidence of threats used against him by persons who were not witnesses was held admissible.[30] Evidence of statements was held admissible on the ground that they had no material bearing, except that they rendered the case more intelligible.[31] It may be competent to prove that a conversation took place between people who

---

[22] Such as evidence of a statement forming part of the *res gestae*: see para 8.5.

[23] *eg* the Criminal Procedure (Scotland) Act 1995, s 263(4) allows evidence to show that a witness made a different statement on a previous occasion as part of an attack on credibility, but this is an example of "primary hearsay" or original evidence that the statement was made, rather than "secondary hearsay" or the statement being evidence of any matter contained in it.

[24] As in *Sanderson v McManus* 1997 SC (HL) 55 at 60.

[25] See para 12.7.

[26] *Mackintosh v Fraser* (1859) 21 D 783, 792 (writings by pursuer alleged to be insane); *Cairns v Marianski* (1852) 1 Macq 212 (deceased's books as evidence of facility); *Milne* (1863) 4 Irv 301 at 342 (accused's declaration as evidence of insanity); *Coles v Homer and Tulloh* (1895) 22 R 716 at 737; *Watson v Watson* 1934 SC 374. Evidence of state of mind generally is mentioned at paras 7.12 *et seq.*

[27] *Rose v Junor* (1846) 9 D 12; *King v King* (1841) 4 D 124 (expressions of enmity against a party).

[28] *Sanderson v McManus* 1997 SLT 629 at 633.

[29] *Hunter v Dodds* (1832) 10 S 833.

[30] *Subranamiam v Public Prosecutor* [1956] 1 WLR 965.

[31] *McDonalds Ltd v Adair* 1944 JC 119. It is thought that this case is wrongly rubricked "*res gestae*".

were not witnesses, or at least were not asked about the conversation, merely to establish the subject of discussion,[32] or to prove the character of the premises where it took place.[33] Evidence of statements may be competent as part of proof of character or reputed ownership.[34]

8.3 *DE RECENTI* AND PRIOR CONSISTENT STATEMENTS

8.3.1 At common law evidence may be led of a statement made by a witness shortly after the occurrence. Such evidence is not corroboration of the fact of the occurrence. Its only effect, if the statement tallies with the witness's evidence, is to enhance the witness's credibility, by showing that his story has been the same from the beginning.[35] Although such evidence may theoretically be admissible in any case, it is tendered mainly in cases of physical injury. Probably for this reason it was sometimes said[36] that a *de recenti* statement by the injured party was admissible. But this was inaccurate. Unless the party was a witness, his credibility could not be set up, and evidence of the statement was not admissible, at least as a *de recenti* statement.

8.3.2 The period within which the statement must have been made depends on circumstances. It should be short, so as to reduce the chance of concoction, and it should have been made to the first natural confidant: for example, by a girl to her mother. Where a girl of 13 only saw her mother three days after the alleged assault and told her then, the mother's evidence of the girl's statement was held admissible.[37] When a boy of seven was a witness, evidence was admitted from subsequent witnesses as to what the boy had said to them within 48 hours of the incident.[38] On the other hand, such evidence was rejected in an action of damages for alleged assault where the girl's statement was made to the third person she met and even then not at the first opportunity.[39] In *A v B*[40] evidence was admitted of a statement as to paternity made by a woman at the birth of her child. This was clearly wrong. As was pointed out in *Gilmour v Hansen*,[41] the *de quo* was the intercourse months before the statement was made. A *de recenti* letter written by a witness and sent to his employers describing events may help to set up his credibility.[42] Evidence of a *de recenti* statement by an accused person has been admitted for the purpose of showing that the person's story has been consistent.[43] At common law such a statement by an accused cannot be used to support the

---

[32]   *Ryan v Mill* 1947 JC 28.
[33]   *McLaren v Macleod* 1913 SC (J) 61 (1912–1916) 7 Adam 110 (brothel).
[34]   Dickson, *Evidence* (3rd edn), para 248.
[35]   *Morton v HM Advocate* 1938 JC 50; *Burgh v HM Advocate* 1944 JC 77; *Barr v Barr* 1939 SC 696; *Gilmour v Hansen* 1920 SC 598. In the last two cases the evidence was inadmissible because the statement was not *de recenti*.
[36]   Lewis, *Evidence*, pp 44, 325.
[37]   *Anderson v McFarlane* (1899) 1 F (J) 36.
[38]   *Stewart* (1855) 2 Irv 166 at 179.
[39]   *Hill v Retcher* (1847) 10 D 7. The girl, being pursuer, was not an admissible witness.
[40]   (1858) 20 D 407 at 417.
[41]   1920 SC 598 at 603.
[42]   *Gibson v National Cash Register Co* 1925 SC 500.
[43]   *Pye* (1838) 2 Swin 187; *Forrest* (1837) 1 Swin 404, noted also in *Morrison v HM Advocate* 1990 JC 299; *Khan v HM Advocate* 1992 SCCR 146. See also para 8.4. There is an interesting discussion in Macphail paras 19.38–19.44. Subject to the outcome of *Morrison* and the statutory change in civil cases described in para 8.4 the reforms in this area discussed by Macphail have not taken place.

credibility of a co-accused,[44] but there is potential so to use it under statute.[45] Consistent prior statements are not in general admissible in proof of the truth of their contents,[46] and when admitted to show consistency, this should be only to the extent necessary to rebut an allegation of inconsistency.[47]

8.4 STATUTORY GROUNDS FOR ADMITTING EVIDENCE TO SHOW THAT A STATEMENT WAS MADE

In civil cases the evidence of a hearsay statement of a person examined as to the statement at proof is now expressly admissible under statute in so far as it tends to reflect favourably or unfavourably upon the credibility of that person,[48] and the requirements of proximity to the event expected of *de recenti* statements do not apply. In criminal cases a witness may be examined as to whether he has on any specified occasion made a statement different from the evidence given by him in the trial; and evidence of the statement may be put to the witness and led to prove that the witness made the different statement on the occasion specified.[49] Evidence of statements consistent with that of the witness are not statutorily admissible in criminal cases, but will be admitted for this purpose if they fall within the *de recenti* exception.[50] An exculpatory statement by the accused may be admitted provided that the accused has first given evidence and requires to lead the evidence to rebut an attack upon credibility.[51] Otherwise such statements are inadmissible hearsay. Their admission has been resisted on grounds of superfluity and irrelevance.[52]

8.4.1

8.5 *RES GESTAE*

"*Res gestae*, is the whole thing that happened,"[53] and this includes not only

8.5.1

---

[44] *Murray v HM Advocate* 1996 SLT 648; reported also *sub nom Mathieson v HM Advocate* 1996 SCCR 388.

[45] Criminal Procedure (Scotland) Act 1995, s 261(2).

[46] *Khan v HM Advocate* 1992 SCCR 146.

[47] *KJC v HM Advocate* 1994 SCCR 560, observed at 565, following *Burns v McAndrew & Partners Ltd* 1963 SLT(Notes) 71.

[48] Civil Evidence (Scotland) Act 1988, s 3. This provision stands apart from the general admission of hearsay as proof of its facts in civil cases under s 2. The proviso in s 2 that the evidence would have been competent if led orally does not apply to admission under s 3.

[49] Criminal Procedure (Scotland) Act 1995, s 263(4) and see *McNee v Ruxton* 1997 SCCR 291, *Paterson v HM Advocate* 1997 SCCR 707. The person seeking to lead such evidence must be careful first to elicit the witness's own evidence and only then to lead the evidence of the different statement. The court must also make it clear to the jury that the evidence of the different statement affects credibility only, and is not evidence against the accused. For an example of failure to follow this process, leading to a miscarriage of justice, see *Ogilvie v HM Advocate* 1999 SLT 1068. See para 12.10.

[50] *Pye* (1838) 2 Swin 187; *Forrest* (1837) 1 Swin 404. If they form part of the *res gestae* they will be admissible as proof of their contents: see para 8.5.

[51] *Morrison v HM Advocate* 1990 JC 299; *Khan v HM Advocate* 1992 SCCR 146; *KJC v HM Advocate* 1994 SCCR 560.

[52] *KJC v HM Advocate* 1994 SCCR 560 at 565 states the general proposition. See also para 8.3.

[53] *Greer v Stirlingshire Road Trustees* (1882) 9 R 1069, per Lord Young at 1076. It is thought that the hearsay of the children's statements founded on by Lord Craighill was inadmissible. Lord Rutherfurd Clark had difficulty, Lord Justice-Clerk Moncreiff preferred another ground, and Lord Young dissented.

"exclamations uttered or things done at the time by those concerned"[54] but also exclamations forced from an onlooker[55] by the events.[56] Such exclamations are facts, real evidence,[57] which may found inferences as to the nature of the acts which they accompany or which gave rise to them. Evidence that members of a crowd of which the accused formed part were shouting "A la Bastille" would (assuming French law to be the same as Scots) yield an inference that the accused were guilty of mobbing and rioting.[58] Evidence that one accused had asked a witness "You here for gear frae Hammy?" was evidence against the accused maker of the statement and the co-accused named within it[59] because the expression of one of a number of persons engaged in the common design can yield an inference against the others.[60] Evidence of protests by the alleged victim of an assault would found an inference that the interference was uninvited.

8.5.2   The distinction between *res gestae* and a subsequent account was emphasised by Lord Normand[61]: "It is essential that the words sought to be proved should be, if not absolutely contemporaneous with the action or event, at least so clearly associated with it, in time, place and circumstances, that they are part of the thing being done, and so an item or part of real evidence and not merely a reported statement."[62] His Lordship then described English decisions illustrating the narrow limits of the doctrine.[63] The last of these was a trial for assault by throwing a stone, in which evidence had been wrongly admitted that an unknown woman had pointed to the accused's door and said: "The person who threw the stone went in there." Lord Normand commented: "The words were closely associated in time and place with the event, the assault. But they were not directly connected with that event itself. They were not words spontaneously forced from the woman by the sight of the assault, but were prompted by the sight of a man quitting the scene of the assault, and they were spoken for the purpose of helping to bring him to justice."[64] The phrase "words spontaneously forced from the woman by the sight of the assault" and Lord Moncrieff's words, "an exclamation forced out of the witness[65] by the emotion generated by an event",[66] bring out clearly the reason why such evidence is admissible. The exclamation is an involuntary reaction, made in circumstances which rule out the possibility of concoction.[67] It is generally considered to be an exception to the hearsay rule, since it has the effect of admitting the statement as truth of its contents, although the terminology of *O'Hara* and *Teper* sets it in a class of its own as real evidence. Lords Normand and Moncrieff described it as real evidence, and from this real evidence could be inferred the nature of the incident which gave rise to it.

---

[54] *Greer v Stirlingshire Road Trustees* (1882) 9 R 1069. For a recent example considered on appeal see *Hamill & Gemmill v HM Advocate* 1999 SLT 963.
[55] *Ewing v Earl of Mar* (1851) 14 D 314.
[56] *Teper v R* [1952] AC 480, per Lord Normand at 487; *O'Hara v Central SMT Co* 1941 SC 363, per Lord Moncrieff at 390. For the facts of the latter, see para 8.10.
[57] *Teper v R* [1952] AC 480; *O'Hara v Central SMT Co* 1941 SC 363.
[58] Dickson, *Evidence* (3rd edn), para 256.
[59] *Hamill and Gemmill v HM Advocate* SLT 963.
[60] Dickson, *Evidence* (3rd edn), para 256.
[61] Who explained that what he said applied to Scotland: *Teper v R* [1952] AC 480 at 486.
[62] *Teper v R* [1952] AC 480 at 487.
[63] *Teper v R* [1952] AC 480 at 487
[64] *Teper v R* [1952] AC 480 at 488.
[65] Not necessarily a witness. It may be a person unknown.
[66] *Teper v R* [1952] AC 480; *O'Hara v Central SMT Co* 1941 SC 363.
[67] *Ratten v R* [1971] 3 All ER 801.

The duration of the *res gestae* varies according to circumstances. In a trial on a **8.5.3** charge of conspiracy it was held to include all the acts of conspiracy.[68] The opinion was expressed by Lord Moncrieff that in the case of an accident it might include the victim's recovery of consciousness.[69] This principle was applied in a trial for ravishing a mentally incompetent girl, who was considered unfit to take the oath and was rejected as a witness. Evidence was admitted from her mother as to "the first statement or exclamation she made" when she arrived home, this being likened to the cry of a child.[70] This may also explain why in *O'Hara v Central SMT Co*[71] Lord Moncrieff founded on the fact that a little while after the accident the driver challenged a bystander with getting in the way. It was considered to be the first opportunity for the discharge of the driver's pent-up emotion.[72]

8.6 HEARSAY AS PROOF OF ITS CONTENTS (SECONDARY HEARSAY)—MAKER OF STATEMENT

At common law the only recognised exceptions to the rule against hearsay occur **8.6.1** where there is *prima facie* evidence[73] that the maker of the statement is dead or permanently insane or, at least in a civil cause, a prisoner of war.[74] The fact that the maker has disappeared is insufficient at common law, and a suggestion that hearsay would be admissible where the maker of the statement is permanently disabled by illness from giving evidence was left open.[75] Statute has now extended the scope for admission of hearsay evidence.

In civil cases evidence is not to be excluded solely on the ground that it is **8.6.2** hearsay[76] and a statement made by a person other than in the course of giving oral evidence is now admissible evidence of any matter contained in the statement of which direct oral evidence would have been admissible.[77] Furthermore, since it is evidence of the truth of its contents, it may be preferred to oral evidence of the witness in court.[78] In terms of the Criminal Procedure (Scotland) Act 1995,

---

[68] *Hunter* (1838) 2 Swin 1 at 12. See also *Platt v HM Advocate* 2000 SCCR 620.

[69] *Teper v R* [1952] AC 480; *O'Hara v Central SMT Co* 1941 SC 363.

[70] Or even the scream of an animal: *Murray* (1866) 5 Irv 232.

[71] 1941 SC 363.

[72] This is thought to stretch the *res gestae* to or beyond its limits. See para 8.10. In *AB v CD* (1848) 11 D 289, an action of separation by a wife (who was not then a competent witness), on the ground of cruelty, a witness found the wife in a distressed state and, during the interview, the wife said something. The witness was asked what it was, and the Lord Ordinary sustained an objection. This decision was reversed by a majority in the Inner House, but the difference of opinion arose, not as to whether the utterance formed part of the *res gestae*, but as to what the *res gestae* were. The majority thought they were the interview between the wife and the witness, of which the utterance clearly formed part. The dissenting judge thought that the *res gestae* were some earlier interviews, between the wife and the husband, and no one suggested that the utterance could have formed part of that. The decision is therefore no authority for the view that utterances subsequent to the event are admissible.

[73] Dickson, *Evidence* (3rd edn), para 269.

[74] *HM Advocate v Manson* (1897) 21 R (J) 5 at 9, 10.

[75] *McKie v Western SMT Co* 1952 SC 206 at 215. In *McNair v HM Advocate* 1993 SLT 277 the High Court appeared to imply that hearsay would be admissible if the child whose hearsay it was sought to lead had been proved to be incapable of giving evidence, yet in civil cases failure to establish the child's competence has prevented the admission of hearsay: see, *eg, Sanderson v McManus* 1997 SLT 629.

[76] Civil Evidence (Scotland) Act 1988, s 2(1)(a).

[77] Civil Evidence (Scotland) Act 1988, s 2(1)(b).

[78] *F v Kennedy (No 2)* 1993 SLT 1284.

s 259(1)(a) and (2) an exception to the rule against the admission of hearsay in those proceedings applies if the judge is satisfied that the person who made the statement is dead or is, by reason of bodily or mental condition, unfit or unable to give evidence in any competent manner.[79] Also, if the maker is outwith the United Kingdom and it is not reasonably practicable to secure his attendance at trial or to obtain his evidence in any other manner, or if the maker cannot be found and all reasonable steps which, in the circumstances, could have been taken to find him have been taken, then, provided that the maker is named or otherwise sufficiently identified, hearsay may be admitted.[80] If these are the grounds for seeking to admit hearsay, notice must be given to the other parties to the proceedings[81] of the fact that application to admit hearsay is to be made and the witnesses and productions to be used for that purpose, but if none of the parties objects to the notice it will be admitted without the judge having to be satisfied that one of the exceptions applies.[82] If a witness refuses to take the oath or affirm, or, having been sworn or admonished[83] to tell the truth refuses to give evidence,[84] including refusal on the ground of self-incrimination,[85] hearsay may be admitted. The judge may not admit hearsay under one or more of these exceptions, if the circumstances on which the exception is founded were brought about by or on behalf of the person seeking to have the hearsay admitted.[86]The admission of hearsay *per se* will not breach the requirements of Article 6(1) of the European Convention on Human Rights[87] and any argument based upon that Article would require to address the fairness of the proceedings in totality.[88]

8.6.3   The maker of the hearsay statement must be a person who would have been a competent witness.[89] At common law the question has arisen as to the date on which competency should be tested. The three possible dates are (1) the day when the statement is tendered in evidence, (2) the day the maker of the statement died or became unable to be a witness, and (3) the day when the statement is alleged to have been made. In criminal cases where hearsay is admitted under the statutory provisions the point is specified to be the date when the statement was made.[90] The

---

[79] As to competent manner for evidence to be given, see Chapter 12 and Chapter 14.

[80] 1995 Act, s 259(2)(b) and (c).

[81] 1995 Act, s 259(5), (6)(a) and (8). The court is empowered to waive the requirement for notice: s 259(6)(b).

[82] 1995 Act, s 259(7), but the requirements of s 259(1)(b)–(c) as to admissibility, competence and degree of hearsay must still be met.

[83] In the case of a child witness: 1995 Act, s 259(2)(e).

[84] 1995 Act, s 259(2)(e). "Refusal" cannot be equated with inability or difficulty: observed in *MacDonald v HM Advocate* 1998 SLT 533.

[85] 1995 Act, s 259(2)(d).

[86] 1995 Act, s 259(3). In *R v Radak and Others, The Times*, 7 October 1998, in construing an application under the Criminal Justice Act 1988, s 23 for admission of the written statement of a prosecution witness who was abroad and refusing to give evidence through fear, the court, having regard to Art 6(3)(d) of the European Convention on Human Rights, refused the application when evidence could have been taken on commission under the Criminal Justice (International Co-operation) Act 1990, s 3 (see para 14.6).

[87] *McKenna v HM Advocate* 2000 JC 291, *HM Advocate v Nulty* 2000 SLT 528, following the reasoning in *Ferantelli v Italy* 1996 III Reports of Judgements and Decisions 937.

[88] *McKenna v HM Advocate* 2000 JC 291, *HM Advocate v Nulty* 2000 SLT 528, following the reasoning in *Ferantelli v Italy* 1996 III Reports of Judgements and Decisions 937 and *Doorson v Netherlands* (1996) 22 EHRR 330.

[89] *Deans's Judicial Factor v Deans* 1912 SC 441, per Lord President Dunedin at 448. See also *Lovat Peerage Case* (1885) 10 App Cas 763; Dickson, *Evidence* (3rd edn), paras 266, 267; Civil Evidence (Scotland) Act 1988, s 2(1)(b); Criminal Procedure (Scotland) Act 1995, s 259(1)(c).

[90] Criminal Procedure (Scotland) Act 1995, s 259(1)(c).

point is not specified in the civil statute but it has been decided that the point is the day when the statement is tendered in evidence.[91] Since the categories of competent witness had been extended over the years the point was thought to have decreased in significance but it has persisted in relation to hearsay evidence of a child[92] and could do so in relation to, for example, a mentally disordered witness whose competence to give evidence is in doubt.[93] There is no express prohibition upon the use of hearsay of a witness who is competent but not compellable and this has been admitted in two cases involving spouses.[94]

At common law hearsay of hearsay is probably admissible,[95] provided that each **8.6.4** statement fulfils the necessary conditions as to the makers and the nature of the statement.[96] Under the civil statute there is no express or implied limitation upon the degree of hearsay, but in criminal cases the hearsay is only admissible if contained in a document[97] or if the person repeating the statement orally in court has direct personal knowledge of the making of the statement,[98] that is first hand hearsay.

Evidence that a witness has at some earlier date identified the accused, or a pro- **8.6.5** duction, may either support the identification by the witness at the trial, or if he cannot identify at the trial, may possibly take the place of such identification.[99] If the latter applies, the evidence of the prior identification is effectively being used as truth of its contents and as such goes beyond primary hearsay.[100] A witness in a criminal case may now adopt a prior statement of his or hers into oral evidence

---

[91] *L v L* 1996 SLT 767, in which it was also stated that competency could only be assessed by the judge seeing the child in person. An appeal to the Inner House is reported as *L v L* 1998 SLT 672 but does not deal with this point. This decision accords with the views expressed in *F v Kennedy (No 1)* 1992 SCLR 139 and *Sanderson v McManus* 1997 SC (HL) 55 to the effect that hearsay would be inadmissible as proof of its contents if the child had not been confirmed before the court to be a competent witness. This was the outcome in an appeal before an Extra Division—*R, Petitioner* 1999 SC 380—where the court makes comments as to what is required in a preliminary examination as to competence and where oral evidence of the child had been offered. However, in *Sanderson v McManus* at 60C and *M v Kennedy* 1993 SC 115 the court indicated that the competence of the witness could be satisfied by evidence of competency at the date when the statement was made, which is now the position in criminal cases (Criminal Procedure (Scotland) Act 1995, s 259(1)(c)). In *MT v DT*, 10 July 2000 the Inner House reported the case on this point to a larger court.

[92] *L v L* 1996 SLT 767. For a criticism of the reasoning and conclusion in *L v L*, see Sheldon, "Children's Evidence, Competency and the New Hearsay Provisions" 1997 SLT (News) 1.

[93] Such as in *HM Advocate v Stott* (1894) 1 Adam 386. Adults will be assumed competent normally, see para 13.1.

[94] *Rumping v DPP* [1962] 3 All ER 256; *Lockhart v Massie* 1989 SCCR 421. The Scottish Law Commission chose not to address the issue in their recommendations in the *Report on Hearsay Evidence in Criminal Proceedings* (Scot Law Com No 149): see paras 5.55–5.56.

[95] *Smith v Bank of Scotland* (1826) 5 S 98; *Deans's Judicial Factor v Deans* 1912 SC 441, where hearsay of hearsay was considered without comment. See also *Lovat Peerage Case* (1885) 10 App Cas 763 at 774. But the last two were pedigree cases and possibly unsafe guides in other actions.

[96] The Scottish Law Commission in its Memorandum No 46 at para T.09 recommended that it be made clear that double hearsay is admissible, but this has not been implemented. As to the nature of the statement see para 8.7.

[97] Criminal Procedure (Scotland) Act 1995, s 259(1)(d)(i). For a definition of document, see s 262(3).

[98] Criminal Procedure (Scotland) Act 1995, s 259(1)(d)(ii).

[99] *McGaharon v Lord Advocate* 1968 SLT (Notes) 99; *Muldoon v Herron & Ors* 1970 JC 30; *Neeson v HM Advocate* 1984 SCCR 72; *Smith v HM Advocate* 1986 SCCR 135; *Maxwell v HM Advocate* 1990 JC 340; *Frew v Jessop* 1990 JC 15; *Jamieson v HM Advocate (No 2)* 1994 JC 251. Macdonald, *Criminal Law* (5th edn), p 325. The passage from Dickson, *Evidence* (3rd edn), para 1776 does not go so far, nor does para 263.

[100] See *Report on Hearsay Evidence in Criminal Proceedings* (Scot Law Com No 149), paras 7.2, 7.6–7.8. For critical examination of this line of authority, see Sheriff Gordon's commentary to *Smith v HM Advocate* in 1986 SCCR at 138–139, and "Identification and Credibility" (1987) 32 JLSS 30. See also para 5.4.5.

given in court.[101] Unless that prior statement is in the form of a precognition on oath or evidence in court,[102] it must be proved that it is contained in a document and at the time that the statement was made the person who made it would have been a competent witness.[103]

8.6.6 If the maker of the statement is the accused the statement may be admissible as evidence of the content of the statement (a) when the statement is against the accused's interest and therefore falls within the rules for admissibility of admissions or confessions, dealt with in another chapter,[104] or (b) when the statement is "mixed", that is partly incriminating and partly exculpatory and is led by the Crown, or the defence without Crown objection, in which case the whole statement, both inculpatory or exculpatory, is admissible as proof of its contents.[105] At common law, an accused was not permitted to lead evidence of the hearsay statement of an incriminee.[106] Now it is provided by statute that when the statement is that of an incriminee, whether a co-accused or third party, and is founded upon during the trial of both accused or by the accused who has cited the incriminee, the statement is admissible in proof of the truth of its contents if the co-accused or incriminee does not repeat the statement in court.[107]

8.7 HEARSAY—NATURE OF STATEMENT

8.7.1 Even though the ground for admission of hearsay based upon the maker of the statement is made out and the maker would have been a competent witness on the material date, evidence of the statement is inadmissible if the circumstances raise a presumption that it does not truly reflect what was in the maker's mind[108] or that it may be prejudiced.[109] Such a presumption arises at common law if the statement was made on precognition, other than a precognition on oath,[110] because it is not spontaneous or voluntary.[111] Similarly, under statute in civil[112] and criminal[113] cases an admissible hearsay statement, which includes any representation, however made or expressed, of fact or opinion,[114] including, in

---

[101] Criminal Procedure (Scotland) Act 1995 ("1995 Act"), s 260(1); *Jamieson v HM Advocate (No 2)* 1994 SCCR 610.

[102] 1995 Act, s 260(4).

[103] 1995 Act, s 260(2) and (3).

[104] See Chapter 9.

[105] *Morrison v HM Advocate* 1990 JC 299.

[106] *Perrie v HM Advocate* 1991 SCCR 255; *McLay v HM Advocate* 1994 SLT 873.

[107] 1995 Act, ss 259(2)(e) and 261(2). In the case of co-accused, the first accused is deemed to be refusing to give evidence under s 259(2)(e) and to have been competent when the statement was made: s 261(3).

[108] *Geils v Geils* (1855) 17 D 397 at 404.

[109] As in *William Thyne (Plastics) Ltd v Stenhouse Reed Shaw Scotland Ltd* 1979 SLT (Notes) 93; *Pirie v Geddes* 1973 SLT (Sh Ct) 81; *Miller v Jackson* 1972 SLT (Notes) 31.

[110] *Coll, Petitioner* 1977 SLT 58.

[111] *KJC v HM Advocate* 1994 SCCR 560; *Young v National Coal Board* 1960 SC 6 (OH); *Kerr v HM Advocate* 1958 JC 14; *Macdonald v Union Bank* (1864) 2 M 963; *Stevenson v Stevenson* (1893) 31 SLR 129; *Ormond* (1848) Ark 483. This was a factor in the court's refusal to allow precognition of an accused under the influence of a truth drug: *Meehan, Petitioner* 1969 SLT (Notes) 90. On precognitions see also para 17.1.

[112] Civil Evidence (Scotland) Act 1988, s 9.

[113] Criminal Procedure (Scotland) Act 1995, s 262(1).

[114] Civil Evidence (Scotland) Act 1988, s 9; Criminal Procedure (Scotland) Act 1995, s 262(1)(a).

criminal cases, any part of a statement,[115] does not include a statement in a precognition.[116] It is generally for the judge to assess whether a statement is a precognition, having regard to the circumstances in which it was taken,[117] and whether the maker had the opportunity to check and reuse it,[118] but it has been held that when the question of the status of the statement is sufficiently open, it may be left to the jury for assessment.[119]

This prohibition against admission of precognitions includes a precognition **8.7.2** taken for the purposes of another action.[120] However, a precognition made part of a dying deposition[121] was admitted,[122] and so was oral evidence of what a person said while being precognosced, given from recollection and without reference to the written precognition.[123] Statements made to a solicitor with a view to raising or defending an action are usually not admissible.[124] A statement made to a police officer who is investigating a complaint generally, as compared to seeking particular evidence on the instructions of the prosecutor, is not normally treated as a precognition.[125] Statements made to an insurance investigator[126] and to social workers[127] may be precognitions depending upon the circumstances in which they were taken. The mere fact that the statement was elicited in response to questions will not dictate that it is a precognition.[128]

An averment does not become evidence on the death of the party making it.[129] **8.7.3** A statement made as evidence in another cause is admissible, provided there is

---

[115] Criminal Procedure (Scotland) Act 1995, s 262(1)(b).

[116] In criminal cases precognitions on oath are admissible: Criminal Procedure (Scotland) Act 1995, s 262(1). See also para 17.4.

[117] *Low v HM Advocate* 1988 SLT 97; *Kerr v HM Advocate* 1958 JC 14. This was the approach taken in *Hall v HM Advocate* 1968 SLT 275, *HM Advocate v Sayers* 1981 JC 98, *Thomson v Jamieson* 1986 SLT 72. The court may apply the test more strictly in criminal cases, as in *Pirie v Geddes* 1973 SLT (Sh Ct) 81, but there is widespread interchanging of civil and criminal authorities.

[118] Discussed in *McAvoy v City of Glasgow District Council* 1993 SLT 859 with reference to *Highland Venison v Allwild Gmbh* 1992 SLT 1127.

[119] *Low v HM Advocate* 1988 SLT 97. However, this approach would be suspect in light of *Thompson v Crowe* 2000 JC 173, see para 9.12.

[120] *Graham v Western Bank* (1865) 3 M 617. In *Low v HM Advocate* 1988 SLT 97 the statement had been made for the purpose of earlier proceedings.

[121] See para 15.5.

[122] *Peterson* (1874) 2 Coup 557. On a literal interpretation of the Criminal Procedure (Scotland) Act 1995, ss 259 and 262 if the statement was in the nature of a precognition, other than a precognition on oath, the fact that it formed part of a dying deposition would not render it admissible. The point has not been tested against the statutory background. However, the Scottish Law Commission had failed to see why precognitions should not be admitted as part of dying declarations: Memorandum No 46, para T10.

[123] *Cavanagh v BP Chemicals* 1995 SLT 1287; *Anderson v Jas B Fraser & Co Ltd* 1992 SLT 1129; *Ward* (1869) 1 Coup 186; Dickson, *Evidence* (3rd edn), para 271. *Cf Ferrier's Exr v Glasgow Corporation* 1966 SLT (Sh Ct) 44.

[124] *Traynor's Exrx v Bairds & Scottish Steel Ltd* 1957 SC 311 (OH); *Ferrier's Exr v Glasgow Corporation* 1966 SLT (Sh Ct) 44; *McAvoy v City of Glasgow District Council* 1993 SLT 859. *Cf Highland Venison Marketing Ltd v Allwild GmbH* 1992 SLT 1127; *Anderson v Jas B Fraser & Co Ltd* 1992 SLT 1129. Quite apart from the question of whether they constitute a precognition, they may also be inadmissible because they are confidential on the ground of lawyer–client relationship or *post litem motam*.

[125] *HM Advocate v McGachy* 1991 SLT 921; *Low v HM Advocate* 1988 SLT 97; *HM Advocate v Irving* 1978 SLT 58; *Hall v HM Advocate* 1968 SLT 275; *Kerr v HM Advocate* 1958 JC 14 (in which the enquiry had gone further and the statement was held to be a precognition).

[126] *Thomson v Jamieson* 1986 SLT 72; *cf Moffat v Hunter* 1974 SLT (Sh Ct) 42.

[127] *F v Kennedy (No 2)* 1993 SLT 1284.

[128] *Hall v Edinburgh Corporation* 1974 SLT (Notes) 14; *Dorona Ltd v Caldwell* 1981 SLT (Notes) 91; *F v Kennedy (No 2)* 1993 SLT 1284.

[129] *Cullen's Trustee v Johnston* (1865) 3 M 935.

nothing to discredit it as a full record.[130] Letters written[131] and probably a diary kept[132] by a deceased person are admissible unless they appear to be prejudiced or tendentious.[133] The dying deposition of any person who might have been a competent witness is admissible.[134] In civil cases an affidavit is admissible as secondary evidence of the deponent,[135] and in both criminal and civil cases certificates or reports may be received if provided for by statute.[136]

8.8 HEARSAY—PROOF AND WEIGHT

8.8.1 If the statement was oral it is proved by the evidence of those who heard it, and they are subject to cross-examination as to the circumstances in which it was made: for example, whether it was elicited in answer to leading questions, whether the maker had means of knowledge, or was actuated by some emotion.[137] While the fact that two or more witnesses speak to the statement does not add to its sufficiency in law, for it still remains the evidence of one witness,[138] its reliability will be increased if several people can speak to it, since there is more opportunity to test their recollections.[139] If hearsay has been admitted under the Criminal Procedure (Scotland) Act 1995, s 259 it is expressly provided that evidence may be led to challenge the credibility of the maker of the statement, including evidence of another statement inconsistent with the one led in hearsay, if that evidence would have been relevant and admissible for proof or cross-examination as to credibility had the maker been giving the evidence orally in court.[140] While there is no equivalent provision in the civil statute upon the normal rules of relevance and given the lack of any rule against hearsay in civil proceedings, it is implicit that the hearsay evidence can be challenged by any evidence relevant to its credibility and not rendered inadmissible on some other exclusionary ground (such as confidentiality).

8.8.2 At common law, if the statement is written, it must be proved by whom it was written, and similar questions surrounding the circumstances of it being made may arise as in the case of an oral statement. In civil proceedings, statute permits documentary hearsay without limitation as to degree, and it is not necessary to prove who made the document, but for the proper assessment of weight evidence as to

---

[130] *Geils v Geils* (1855) 17 D 397; *Courts v Wear* 1914 2 SLT 86 (OH); *Gordon v Grant* (1850) 13 D 1 at 10, 27. In *McGowan v Mein* 1976 SLT (Sh Ct) 29 the court refused to allow a shorthand writer to refer to the notes of evidence of a now deceased witness from an earlier case, when there was no proof of the witness's death and no personal recollection of the evidence on the part of the shorthand writer. A tape recording was admitted in *HM Advocate v Nulty* 2000 SLT 528 in preference to the transcript of it.

[131] *McAlister v McAlister* (1833) 12 S 198; *Tennent v Tennent* (1890) 17 R 1205 at 1223, 1224.

[132] However, opinions were reserved in *Hogg v Campbell* (1864) 2 M 1158.

[133] *Madeleine Smith* (1857) 2 Irv 641.

[134] *Stewart* (1855) 2 Irv 166. See para 15.5.

[135] Act of Sederunt (Rules of the Court of Session) 1994, r 36.8. Sheriff Courts (Scotland) Act 1971, s 32(1)(e) and First Schedule as replaced by Act of Sederunt (Sheriff Court Ordinary Cause Rules) 1993 (SI 1993/1956), r 29.3, which provisions were introduced to take account of the removal of the hearsay rule in civil cases. *Cf* common law position: *Tennent v Tennent* (1890) 17 R 1205 at 1225. As to affidavits, see Chapter 15.

[136] eg Criminal Procedure (Scotland) Act 1995, s 280 and Sched 9; Sheriff Courts (Scotland) Act 1971, s 32(1)(e). At common law certificates were received only rarely: *Lauderdale Peerage Case* (1885) 10 App Cas 692 at 707. See also para 19.16.

[137] *Gordon v Grant* (1850) 13 D 1 at 11.

[138] *Deans's Judicial Factor v Deans* 1912 SC 441 at 447; *Wallace v Ross* (1891) 19 R 233.

[139] *A v B* (1858) 20 D 407 at 416.

[140] Criminal Procedure (Scotland) Act 1995, s 259(4).

when the document was made, and by whom, should be led where possible. In criminal cases when the statutory grounds for admission of hearsay are relied upon, the statement is admissible in documentary form only if it is proved that the document was made by the maker of the statement,[141] or made by someone else but then approved by the maker of the statement as embodying the statement,[142] or the document was made by a person who had direct personal knowledge of the making of the statement.[143] The definition of document includes, in addition to traditional text, any map, plan, graph or drawing, photograph, a reproductive recording of sound such as a disc, tape, or sound track and a reproductive recording of visual images such as a film, microfilm, negative, tape or disc.[144] A similar broad definition of "document" is found in the civil legislation[145] and authenticated copies of documents are expressly admissible in place of the original in civil proceedings.[146] However, an unauthenticated copy contract has been held inadmissible under the general provision for admission of hearsay statements.[147] It was held that the best evidence of a contract committed to writing was the contract itself, and not the oral evidence of parties to it, so reliance upon the provisions for admission of hearsay (rather than the admission of documents) was misguided.[148] These facts can be contrasted with a hearsay statement which has been made in, or committed to, written form, which would be admissible.[149]

The fact that evidence led is hearsay will always be brought to the attention of **8.8.3** a jury so that account can be taken of this in assessing the weight to attach to that evidence.[150] The jury must also be told whether the evidence is led as proof of any matter contained in the statement or whether it is led only as proof that the statement was made.[151] If hearsay evidence is ambiguous, it will be read *contra proferentem* (against the person putting it forward),[152] and a court may not be satisfied to the requisite standard that a fact has been proved by hearsay evidence albeit that it is legally sufficient.[153]

8.9 HEARSAY—CASES ALLOWING PROOF OF REPUTATION

In all civil cases hearsay is now admissible, subject to the competence of the maker **8.9.1** of the statement to give admissible oral evidence. The cases mentioned in this paragraph developed as a class apart at common law, though decisions in ordinary hearsay cases were from time to time discussed in the opinions or speeches, and

---

[141] Criminal Procedure (Scotland) Act 1995, s 262(2)(a).
[142] 1995 Act, s 262(2)(c).
[143] 1995 Act, s 262(2)(b).
[144] 1995 Act, s 262(3). See para 21.1.
[145] Civil Evidence (Scotland) Act 1988, s 9. See para 21.1.
[146] Civil Evidence (Scotland) Act 1988, s 6.
[147] *Japan Leasing (Europe) plc v Weir's Trustee (No 2)* 1998 SLT 973.
[148] For a discussion of the implications of the decision, see Poole, "Productions, Hearsay and the Best Evidence Rule" 1998 SLT (News) 211. See also para 20.2.
[149] Civil Evidence (Scotland) Act 1988, s 2(3) and (4).
[150] In *Ridler v HM Advocate* 1995 SCCR 655, the sheriff's directions although overall sufficiently clear, might have gone further in expressing this point.
[151] *Farooq v HM Advocate* 1993 SLT 1271. See also para 8.10.1.
[152] *Walker's Trs v McKinlay* (1880) 7 R (HL) 85 at 98.
[153] *Gordon v Grampian Health Board* 1991 SCLR 213; *TSB Scotland plc v James Mills (Montrose) Ltd (in receivership)* 1992 SLT 519, considering the effect of ss 1 and 2 of the Civil Evidence (Scotland) Act 1988.

points decided in them could apply to ordinary cases. They are, for example, cases for proof of the existence of a marriage by habit and repute, cases concerning peerage[154] or pedigree,[155] and cases to establish usage which may exceed living memory, such as the existence of a crofting title or the extent of an implied servitude.[156] In such cases, in the absence of any direct evidence, the only evidence available might be that passed down through generations by word of mouth. While it was always necessary to consider whether the tale had been adapted in the telling or was never more than myth,[157] the absence of other potential sources of evidence and the nature of the claim were held to justify the admission of hearsay evidence in proof of the truth of the contents of the statements. In some circumstances the court required that the maker of the original statement had special means of knowledge[158] but the issue of the competence of the witness was not generally raised. The Civil Evidence (Scotland) Act 1988 does not expressly retain the common law in relation to admission of hearsay, although categories of hearsay at common law are still potentially relevant if the statutory requirement of admissibility of the witness to give evidence in oral form cannot be met. It is thought that these cases, which are peculiarly concerned with proof of historical states of affairs and in which testing the competency of the original witnesses is impossible, would still constitute authority for admission of hearsay in circumstances which are on all fours.

8.10 CONTRAST BETWEEN PRIMARY AND SECONDARY HEARSAY

8.10.1   A pleader who has successfully secured the admission of hearsay as evidence that the statement was made, may see it treated by the jury, or even the judge, as secondary hearsay, and therefore as evidence of the facts stated in it. Once the evidence has been led, this may easily happen. In *O'Hara v Central SMT* Co[159] a bus swerved suddenly, and the pursuer was thrown off and injured. The defence was that the driver had swerved to avoid knocking down a man who ran in front of the bus. The only direct evidence in support of the defence was that of the driver, but he was held to be corroborated by facts and circumstances. There was, however, evidence as to statements made by a man who was not a witness, first to the bus conductress and then to a police officer, but both after, rather than during, the event. Opinions were delivered *obiter* as to the admissibility and effect of this evidence.[160] The Lord President referred to "the unsworn evidence of someone who

---

[154] *Viscountcy of Dudhope and Earldom of Dundee* 1986 SLT (Lyon Ct) 2.

[155] The principal more modern cases are *Alexander v Officers of State* (1868) 6 M 54; *Macpherson v Reid's Trs* (1877) 4 R (HL) 87; *Deans's Judicial Factor v Deans* 1912 SC 441; *Dysart Peerage Case* (1881) 6 App Cas 489; *Lauderdale Peerage Case* (1885) 10 App Cas 692; and *Lovat Peerage Case* (1885) 10 App Cas 763.

[156] Documentary evidence such as old correspondence has been admitted, together with such oral evidence as is available. See Cusine and Paisley, *Servitudes and Rights of Way* (1998), paras 2.80, 2.81 and 8.21 and cases cited there.

[157] A qualification stressed in *Viscountcy of Dudhope and Earldom of Dundee* 1986 SLT (Lyon Ct) 2.

[158] If family tradition as to propinquity was to be proved, the deliberate statement of a deceased person was admissible only if he had special means of knowledge (such as the personal knowledge of a confidential servant): *Macpherson v Reid's Trs* (1877) 4 R (HL) 87; *Alexander v Officers of State* (1868) 6 M 54.

[159] 1941 SC 363.

[160] The conductress said that after the bus had stopped, which it did immediately, and she and the driver had attended to the pursuer and helped her into a shop, the driver brought a man to her, who admitted

is not adduced as a witness" and then considered the effect of the two statements together just as if they had been evidence.[161] Lord Fleming "preferred" the statement given to the conductress to the later statement given to the policeman.[162] All this was just to treat the statements as evidence of the facts in them. Lord Moncrieff dissented, taking the view that the "event" terminated on the man's arrival on the pavement.[163] In the circumstances of the case, evidence that as, or just before, the bus swerved some unknown spectator had shouted, "Watch the bus" or that the driver had shouted, "Look out, you fool", would clearly have been admissible as part of the *res gestae*. Such evidence would have founded an inference that there was somebody in the way. *O'Hara v Central SMT Co*[164] was referred to without comment in *Teper v R*[165] but it is difficult to see how either of the man's utterances was part of the thing done and not a reported statement which cannot be *res gestae*."[166] The opinions of the majority in *O'Hara*[167] appear irreconcilable with those in *Jackson v Glasgow Corporation*[168] and with their own descriptions of the limited nature of the rule. It might have been thought that the general admission of hearsay evidence in civil cases would remove the scope for difficulty arising as to the evidential value of the hearsay. However, when hearsay is heard, but the competence of the maker to give oral evidence has not been established, the evidence cannot be used as proof of the contents of the statement. When hearsay of a child was led without the court being able to assess the child's competency, the hearsay was admissible only to show that the statement was made, and therefore what was in the child's mind at the time the statement was made, and the sheriff who had incorrectly used the statement as proof of the facts contained in it was overruled on this point.[169]

In spite of Dickson's statement[170] that the principles for admission of *de recenti* **8.10.2** statements and statements forming part of the *res gestae* are akin, they are in fact totally different.[171] Proof of a *de recenti* statement is admitted for its bearing on the credibility of a witness, and is therefore confined to statements by witnesses that may have been made after some interval.[172] It is not corroboration. A statement forming part of *the res gestae*, on the other hand, may have been made by some

---

crossing in front of the bus and gave her a paper containing his name and address. About ten minutes after the accident the paper was handed to a police officer. He interviewed a man at once, and the man told him he did cross the road, but was not in the way of the bus. The view of the majority was that the statement to the conductress was part of the *res gestae*, although it was not made until some time had elapsed. When the majority came to deal with the statement to the police officer, they appear to have lost sight of the ground on which the first statement had been admitted and it became an "admission", while the second became a "qualification" of it.

[161] at 383.

[162] at 386.

[163] at 390.

[164] 1941 SC 363.

[165] [1952] AC 480, and in *Ratten v R* [1971] 3 All ER 801.

[166] *Greer v Stirlingshire Road Trustees* (1882) 9 R 1069.

[167] 1941 SC 363.

[168] 1956 SC 354 at 361, 363, 365. The rule was re-examined in *Ratten v R* [1971] 3 All ER 801, although the court concluded that the evidence of a call made to an emergency operator by an assault victim did not require to be admitted as hearsay in proof of the facts asserted in the call.

[169] *Sanderson v McManus* 1997 SLT 629.

[170] Dickson, *Evidence* (3rd edn), para 258,

[171] It is not very clear under which principle the judges treated a witness's remark in *Jordan v Court Line* 1947 SC 29 at 39, 41.

[172] *Greer v Stirlingshire Road Trustees* (1882) 9 R 1069 seems to be the only exception, apart from old cases where the person was not a competent witness.

unknown person[173]; it must be part of the event; and it is independent, and potentially corroborative, evidence. Indeed, if a *de recenti* statement is one made shortly after the occurrence it cannot by definition be part of the occurrence. This seems to have been overlooked in *O'Hara v Central SMT Co,*[174] where two of the judges in defining *res gestae* said that the statement should be at least *de recenti* and not after an interval which would allow time for reflection and for concocting a story. These are almost the very words used in an earlier case to define a *de recenti* statement,[175] and they leave out of account that no "story" can be part of the *res gestae*.

---

[173] *Ewing v Earl of Mar* (1851) 14 D 314.
[174] 1941 SC 363.
[175] *Gilmour v Hansen* 1920 SC 598, per Lord President Clyde at 603.

CHAPTER 9

ADMISSIBILITY OF EVIDENCE OF EXTRA-JUDICIAL ADMISSIONS AND CONFESSIONS

9.1 GENERAL

An extra-judicial admission or confession made by a party must be distinguished **9.1.1** from a judicial admission. A judicial admission is made within the court proceedings and is generally conclusive against and binding upon the party making it for the purpose of the cause in which it is made. It is considered in detail in another chapter.[1] This chapter examines statements made extra-judicially, that is outwith the court proceedings. Here, "admission" is used to mean a statement against interest in relation to a civil cause, and "confession" to mean a statement against interest in relation to a criminal cause, although in modern practice the terms are interchanged in criminal cases.[2] Confessions disclosing special knowledge on the part of an accused attract special treatment and this is considered in another chapter.[3]

---

[1] See paras 11.2 and 11.3. For an example of the respective effects of judicial and extra-judicial admissions see *Buick v Jaglar* 1973 SLT (Sh Ct) 6. Only judicial admissions concerning the arrangements for care of children are not conclusive, since they are subject to the court's overriding obligation to ensure that issues agreed to or admitted are likely to safeguard and promote the child's interests: see the Children (Scotland) Act 1995, s 11(7); *Lothian v Lothian* 1965 SLT 368; *Milne v Milne* 1987 SLT 45; *Horton v Horton* 1992 SLT (Sh Ct) 37, and see Macphail, *Evidence* (1987), paras 2.16 and S2.16 regarding the position under prior legislation.
[2] See, for example, the wording in the Criminal Procedure (Scotland) Act 1995, s 35(5).
[3] para 6.9.

9.1.2   The general rule is that evidence of a statement against interest, whether oral[4] or written,[5] made extra-judicially by a party to a cause, is admissible against him or her as an exception to the hearsay rule at common law.[6] Such statements, if proved, are not by themselves conclusive against the party making them as in the case of judicial admissions. Evidence of them is relevant either because it may throw light on the party's credibility as a witness,[7] or as an adminicle of evidence in the cause, and must be considered along with all the other evidence led. In a civil case, where corroboration is not now required, in theory at least, an extra-judicial admission when proved in evidence, if it deals with all of the issues in the case, will be sufficient in law for proof of the case.[8] The matter would rest upon credibility of the extra-judicial admission.

9.1.3   The fact that a statement is made against interest is supposed to indicate that it is more likely to be true than false.[9] However, when the statement has been made in the course of a precognition, evidence of it is inadmissible.[10] The rules applicable to the use of a qualified extra-judicial admission are the same as those applying to qualified judicial admissions, namely that the person relying upon the qualified admission bears the burden of contradicting the qualification.[11] Mere concessions made by a party in the course of abortive negotiations for a settlement of the dispute are not admissible in evidence, but unequivocal admissions made in the course of such negotiations are admissible.[12] It appears that an oral admission, which was interrupted before completion, may be proved for what it is worth, but the fact of the interruption must be considered in assessing its value, because it may have prevented the party from adding a qualification or explanation materially altering its meaning.[13]

---

[4]   See, for example, *Foggo v Hill* (1840) 2 D 1322 (statement by party that partial payment made by other party); *Gordon v Stewart* (1842) 5 D 8 (boast by defender that he committed assault sued for); *Morrison v Burrell* 1947 JC 43 (confession of fraud by accused sub-postmaster to Post Office investigators).

[5]   See, for example, Hume, ii, 396; *Anderson v Anderson* (1848) 11 D 118 (newspaper advertisement and correspondence); *British Linen Co v Thomson* (1853) 15 D 314 (excerpts from a bank's deposit journal); *Muir v Goldie's Trs* (1898) 6 SLT 188 (records of payments made towards a debt); *Palestine Transport and Shipping Co Ltd v Greenock Dockyard Co Ltd* 1947 SN 162 (entry in ship's log kept in course of employee's duties). When the admission is contained in a letter, the contents of the letter to which it was a reply may also be proved for the purpose of identifying the subject-matter of the admission: *MacBain v MacBain* 1930 SC (HL) 72 at 75.

[6]   Dickson, *Evidence* (3rd edn), para 297; Macphail, *Evidence* (1987), para 20.01.

[7]   See para 1.6.

[8]   Civil Evidence (Scotland) Act 1988, s 2.

[9]   Dickson, *Evidence* (3rd edn), para 297; Macphail, *Evidence* (1987), para 20.01; *Hartley v HM Advocate* 1979 SLT 26.

[10]   *Kerr v HM Advocate* 1958 JC 14. Precognitions are specifically excluded from the recent statutory relaxations of the hearsay rule: see Civil Evidence (Scotland) Act 1988, s 9; Criminal Procedure (Scotland) Act 1995, s 262(1). The position regarding precognitions on oath was thought to be different (*Coll, Petitioner* 1977 JC 29), and they are not excluded in criminal cases: Criminal Procedure (Scotland) Act 1995, s 262(1). At common law there had been some uncertainty as to whether precognitions could be admitted as admissions in civil cases (see *Fraser v Wilson* (1842) 4 D 1171 at 1173; *Morrison v Somerville* (1860) 23 D 232, per Lord Justice-Clerk Inglis at 238), but the situation is clarified in the later cases which are cited at para 8.7.

[11]   See para 11.2.

[12]   Dickson, *Evidence* (3rd edn), para 305; *Fyfe v Miller* (1835) 13 S 809; *Williamson v Taylor* (1845) 7 D 842; *Daks Simpson Group plc v Kuiper* 1994 SLT 689; *Richardson v Quercus Ltd* 1999 SC 278.

[13]   Dickson, *Evidence* (3rd edn), para 309.

9.2 PROOF AND PROBATIVE EFFECT OF EXTRA-JUDICIAL ADMISSIONS AND CONFESSIONS

The nature and quantity of the evidence needed to prove the terms of an admis- **9.2.1** sion or confession, and the fact that it was made by the party concerned, are governed by the general rules as to sufficiency of evidence.[14] The testimony of a single witness to the making of an admission or confession is an item of evidence which may be considered along with other evidence, direct or circumstantial.[15] An extra-judicial admission or confession, when proved, does not preclude the party who made it from presenting a case which contradicts it. Its probative effect depends upon its terms, its importance in relation to the facts in issue in the cause, the circumstances in which it was made, and on whether the cause is civil or criminal.

In a civil cause the party who made the admission is entitled to establish that **9.2.2** it was made for some secondary reason and was not true, and the whole circumstances in which it was made are relevant to qualify or explain its terms. If it was made in the course of proceedings with a third party, now shown to be as a result of a mistaken view of the law or of facts, it will be of little importance in the subsequent action.[16] In each case the probative weight to be attached to an extra-judicial admission must depend upon the circumstances of the particular case.

The accused in a criminal case is entitled to introduce evidence that a confes- **9.2.3** sion was made in circumstances or for reasons which nullify or reduce its apparently incriminating character.[17] An accused cannot be convicted upon proof of an extra-judicial confession alone, even if the commission of the crime is independently proved.[18] To justify a conviction there must in addition be other evidence, direct or circumstantial, which associates the accused with the commission of the crime. It has been said that what is sought as corroboration of an unequivocal confession is evidence consistent with the terms of the confession rather than evidence of general corroborative value.[19] However, the approach now preferred is to look for corroborative evidence which constitutes a sufficiently independent check of the confession. What precisely is required to corroborate a confession will depend upon the facts and circumstances of the case and the nature and circumstances of the confession.[20] Another extra-judicial confession made by the accused, even if in different terms and made to other persons, is not sufficient for this purpose, since both confessions emanate from the same source (the accused) and repetition of a confession acts as no check against the possibility that it may have been falsely made for an ulterior reason.[21] However, proof of an

---

[14] See Chapter 5.

[15] On corroboration of confessions in criminal cases and the specialities of confessions disclosing special knowledge confessions, proof of the making of which may be required from two sources, see Chapter 5 and para 6.9.

[16] *Beattie and Muir v Brown* (1883) 11 R 250.

[17] For examples of false confessions, see Dickson, *Evidence* (3rd edn), paras 380–383. In *Boyle v HM Advocate* 1976 JC 32 a soldier apparently made a false confession to a robbery in order to be committed to civilian prison instead of the military detention which faced him for being absent without leave, and his conviction was set aside on appeal.

[18] Hume, ii, 333; Dickson, *Evidence* (3rd edn), para 352; *Connolly v HM Advocate* 1958 SLT 79.

[19] *Hartley v HM Advocate* 1979 SLT 26, per Lord Dunpark at 33; *Sinclair v Clark* 1962 JC 57, per Lord Justice-Clerk Thomson at 62.

[20] *Sinclair v Clark* 1962 JC 57.

[21] *Sinclair v Clark* 1962 JC 57.

accused person's incriminating actions at or after the commission of the crime,[22] and even after apprehension,[23] are sufficient to support a confession, particularly when these were associated with real evidence connected with the commission of the crime.[24] Circumstantial evidence capable of corroborating a confession is considered in more detail in another chapter.[25]

9.3 DECLARATIONS—JUDICIAL EXAMINATION

9.3.1 Declarations in this context are statements made by an accused person when appearing before the sheriff on the petition commencing a solemn prosecution. Although in that sense it is not entirely accurate to describe these as extra-judicial,[26] as evidence they are treated similarly to extra-judicial confessions. Historically, a declaration was taken from the accused person by judicial examination in the days when the accused person was not a competent witness, and when in 1898 the accused became a competent witness the practice of taking a judicial declaration from the accused fell into disuse. In 1980 following recommendations of the Thomson Committee[27] a new statutory process for judicial examination by the prosecutor was introduced,[28] and the procedure for carrying out the examination, recording verbatim the questions and declarations in response, submitting the record to defence scrutiny prior to trial, and production of the record in evidence are all controlled by statute.[29]

9.3.2   The examination takes place in the presence of the sheriff but the accused is not put on oath. If there is more than one accused each must be examined individually outwith the presence of the others. It is in the prosecutor's discretion to carry out a judicial examination of any accused, and the examination may be used to question the accused about an extra-judicial confession, whether or not a full admission, which the accused is alleged to have made.[30] If the prosecutor does not carry out a judicial examination, the accused person normally intimates, personally or through a solicitor, that he or she does not desire to emit a declaration.[31] Voluntary emission of a declaration by the accused person is a very rare event.[32]

---

[22] *Costello v Macpherson* 1922 JC 9; *Chalmers v HM Advocate* 1954 JC 66, per Lord Justice-General Cooper at 76.

[23] *Manuel v HM Advocate* 1958 JC 41; Alison, ii, 580. See also *Connolly v HM Advocate* 1958 SLT 79. *Cf Chalmers v HM Advocate* 1954 JC 66, where evidence of the incriminating actings of the accused in leading police to recover items referred to in his confession was held to be indistinguishable from the confession which had been rendered inadmissible due to the unfairness of the circumstances in which it was taken.

[24] *Manuel v HM Advocate* 1958 JC 41; Alison, ii, 580.

[25] See para 6.9.

[26] Although it is accurate in the sense that the solemn proceedings commence formally only with the indictment.

[27] Criminal Procedure in Scotland (Second Report) (Cmnd 6218, 1975), Chapter 8.

[28] Criminal Justice (Scotland) Act 1980, s 6.

[29] See now Criminal Procedure (Scotland) Act 1995, ss 35–38 and Act of Adjournal (Criminal Procedure Rules) 1996, Chapter 5. If the accused wishes to take issue with the record of the declaration he must do so within a time limit after receipt of service of the record and, unless the accused's point is conceded by the prosecutor, the court will deal with the matter by way of preliminary hearing: Criminal Procedure (Scotland) Act 1995, s 38.

[30] Criminal Procedure (Scotland) Act 1995, s 35(5).

[31] Criminal Procedure (Scotland) Act 1995, s 35(3).

[32] See *Robertson v HM Advocate* 1995 SCCR 152. For the procedure to be followed in the taking of a declaration, see Renton and Brown, paras 12–10 *et seq*.

Historically, the prosecutor alone was entitled to put the declaration in evidence,[33] but if the accused wished the declaration to be read in court, the prosecutor usually consented. However, now the prosecutor must lodge as a production the record of the declaration whether made voluntarily[34] or in response to judicial examination, even if the charge on petition in respect of which the declaration was made does not appear in the subsequent indictment.[35] It then becomes evidence either if read out on the instructions of the prosecutor, or if put to the court by an accused.[36] The declaration can never by itself be sufficient evidence of the accused's guilt, as if it were the equivalent of a plea of guilty, and, even if it includes a virtual admission of guilt, it must be corroborated by other evidence before a conviction is justified.[37] The prosecutor, trial judge or co-accused is entitled to make comment at trial if the accused introduces then evidence which he could have stated appropriately in answer to a question at judicial examination but declined to answer.[38]

A declaration is not admissible as evidence against a co-accused,[39] but if it is **9.3.3** lodged as a production a co-accused is entitled to put it in evidence in his own favour.[40] A declaration emitted by an accused in respect of one charge may be used in support of a subsequent charge less serious in character, but involving the same *species facti*.[41] So a declaration taken on a charge of assault, mobbing and rioting was held admissible in a subsequent trial for breach of the peace.[42] Whether it could be used in relation to a more serious charge in the same *species facta* is likely to depend upon the circumstances and fairness to the accused.[43] At one time a declaration was regarded as admissible in evidence against the person who emitted it in a subsequent civil cause to which that person was a party.[44] It was later held that such a use of a declaration is inadmissible on the ground *inter alia* that a judicial examination is held in private.[45] It is thought that this objection could not be held to apply if the declaration had been introduced in evidence in a criminal trial, and, subject to any claim of confidentiality, its admission in a civil case now would depend upon relevance.

9.4 JUDICIAL ADMISSIONS IN ANOTHER CAUSE

A judicial admission made by a party in a civil cause may be used in a subsequent **9.4.1**

---

[33]   Dickson, *Evidence* (3rd edn), para 337; Macdonald, *Criminal Law* (5th edn), p 329.

[34]   As in *Robertson v HM Advocate* 1995 SCCR 152.

[35]   Criminal Procedure (Scotland) Act 1995, s 68(1). This is mandatory (*HM Advocate v Cafferty* 1984 SCCR 444), but the requirement to intimate the record of the declaration to the accused in terms of s 37 has been held in a majority decision to be merely directory: *Robertson v HM Advocate* 1995 SCCR 152. In *Robertson* the declaration related to a charge which had been libelled against the accused on petition but not on indictment.

[36]   Criminal Procedure (Scotland) Act 1995, s 67(6).

[37]   Dickson, *Evidence* (3rd edn), para 339. If it contains exculpatory as well as incriminatory material the rule in *Morrison v HM Advocate* 1990 JC 299 would apply as it does to all mixed statements. See para 8.6.6.

[38]   Criminal Procedure (Scotland) Act 1995, s 36(8).

[39]   *Milne* (1866) 5 Irv 229.

[40]   Criminal Procedure (Scotland) Act 1995, s 67(6).

[41]   *Macdougall v Maclullich* (1887) 14 R (J) 17; Macdonald, *Criminal Law* (5th edn), p 328.

[42]   *Macdougall v Maclullich* (1887) 14 R (J) 17.

[43]   *Willis v HM Advocate* 1941 JC 1.

[44]   For a reference to the earlier cases, see Dickson, *Evidence* (3rd edn), para 289.

[45]   *Little v Smith* (1847) 9 D 737. See the comments on this case in Dickson, *Evidence* (3rd edn), para 290.

civil cause in which that person is also a party, but in that subsequent cause it will be an extra-judicial admission.[46] As with any other extra-judicial admission it is not conclusive against the party making it,[47] and the question as to whether it was authorised by the party,[48] any qualifications attached to it,[49] and the circumstances in which it was made,[50] are all relevant to assessment of its weight. On the same principle a judicial confession of guilt in a criminal cause—that is a plea of guilty, as distinct from the verdict in that cause—is, at common law, admissible in evidence against the person making it in a subsequent civil cause to which that person is a party.[51]

9.4.2   At common law, the decree or verdict in an earlier cause, whether civil or criminal—as distinct from a judicial admission in that cause—is not admissible in evidence in another cause[52] except for some limited purposes. Those purposes are: (a) when it is the foundation of a plea of *res judicata*,[53] (b) when it is a decree *in rem* or declaratory of status,[54] (c) when it is an essential preliminary to the later action (as, for example, a decree constituting a debt which must precede an action of furthcoming), and (d) when the fact of its pronouncement, as distinct from its merits, is part of the relevant background of the later cause. However, statute has provided increasingly for specific circumstances in which a prior relevant conviction or civil decree may be produced in evidence in a later cause, and will create a presumption that the conduct referred to in the conviction or decree is proved.[55] A prior verdict of acquittal is generally inadmissible since it is of no probative value and could only serve to confuse in subsequent proceedings.[56]

9.5 ADMISSIONS AND CONFESSIONS MADE WHILE A WITNESS IN ANOTHER CAUSE

9.5.1 Statements made by a person when giving evidence on oath in another cause,[57]

---

[46] *Jackson v Glasgow Corporation* 1956 SC 354, per Lord President Clyde at 359, Lord Russell at 362 and Lord Sorn at 365. Earlier authorities had been doubtful on this point but recognised that common sense favoured its admission: see *Cairns v Marianski* (1850) 12 D 1286, per Lord Medwyn at 1292, Lord Justice-Clerk Hope at 1296; *Morrison v Somerville* (1860) 23 D 232.

[47] Dickson, *Evidence* (3rd edn), para 293.

[48] *Aitchison v Aitchison* (1877) 4 R 899, per Lord Justice-Clerk Moncreiff at 914. See also *Morrison v Somerville* (1860) 23 D 232 at 238.

[49] *Jackson v Glasgow Corporation* 1956 SC 354, per Lord President Clyde at 359, Lord Russell at 362 and Lord Sorn at 365.

[50] *Aitchison v Aitchison* (1877) 4 R 899, per Lord Justice-Clerk Moncreiff at 914. See also *Morrison v Somerville* (1860) 23 D 232 at 238.

[51] *Mackay v Bolton* (1897) 4 SLT 321; Dickson, *Evidence* (3rd edn), para 389.

[52] *Devlin v Earl* (1895) 3 SLT 166; Dickson, *Evidence* (3rd edn), paras 386, 387; Alison, ii, 67; Bell, *Principles*, para 2215. These authorities were examined and approved in *William Bain & Co (Joinery) Ltd v Gilbert Ash (Scotland) Ltd*, Sheriff Principal Dick at Glasgow, 28 January 1982, unreported, cited by Macphail, *Evidence* (1987) at paras S11.22A and S11.29B; *cf* Bell, *Principles*, para 2216.

[53] See paras 11.4 and 11.5

[54] See paras 11.4 and 11.5.

[55] *eg* for convictions: Divorce (Scotland) Act 1976, s 3(1); Law Reform (Miscellaneous Provisions) (Scotland) Act 1968, ss 10 and 12. For a finding in an earlier civil proceeding for adultery, see the Law Reform (Miscellaneous Provisions) (Scotland) Act 1968, s 11. See para 28.12 and 28.13.

[56] Macphail, *Evidence* (1987), paras S11.18–S11.19A, but see *Dennison v Chief Constable, Strathclyde Police* 1996 SLT 74, in which it was noted that evidence of an acquittal might be admitted if needed for a full narrative of the case, but other circumstances surrounding the acquittal might also then be admitted as relevant, in this case the outcome of other criminal charges against the party seeking to lead evidence of the acquittal.

[57] *Banaghan* (1888) 15 R (J) 39.

whether as a party or witness, are in general admissible against that person in sub-sequent proceedings in which that person is a party.[58] In civil cases they may also be led in evidence for that party.[59] A statement by a witness in a civil proof that he, and not the defender, was the writer of a threatening letter, was held admissible in evidence against him at his subsequent trial on a criminal charge of sending the threatening letter.[60] In a civil action an oath on reference in an earlier action was held admissible against the trustees of the person making it,[61] and a statement made on oath in a party's earlier deposition as a haver,[62] in so far as it was in answer to questions properly put to a haver,[63] was allowed to be used against him on the merits of the action. Evidence of a confession made by an accused in excul-pation of another person, charged at an earlier date with the same crime, was held admissible against her,[64] although a deposition made by an accused in another person's sequestration was excluded when he was charged with embezzlement of the fund referred to in it.[65] The making of the admission or confession will normally be proved by the evidence of the shorthand writer and the production of the shorthand writer's notes,[66] but even when shorthand notes were taken, proof by purely oral evidence has been said to be sufficient.[67] If the earlier statement was recorded by mechanical means rather than by shorthand writer,[68] the mechanically prepared record (usually an audio tape) which has been certified and retained by the clerk of court[69] should be recovered and produced together with a transcript of the recorded material if available,[70] but it is thought that oral evidence of anyone who overheard the earlier statement would be admissible even if the mechanical record is not produced.[71] If the earlier statement was made in summary criminal or civil proceedings where no formal record is kept, the sheriff[72] could be compelled to give evidence supported by his notes of the earlier case. This commonly applies in proceedings for perjury.

---

[58] Dickson, *Evidence* (3rd edn), para 288.

[59] Civil Evidence (Scotland) Act 1988, ss 2 and 3.

[60] *Banaghan* (1888) 15 R (J) 39.

[61] *Hunter v Nicolson* (1836) 15 S 159.

[62] *Home v Hardy* (1842) 4 D 1184.

[63] See *Dye v Reid* (1831) 9 S 342.

[64] *Edmiston* (1866) 1 SLR 107.

[65] *Fleming* (1885) 5 Coup 552 at 581. See now the Bankruptcy (Scotland) Act 1985, s 47(3), which provides that in bankruptcy the debtor or a relevant person may not invoke the privilege against self-incrimination at examination, but that his answers are inadmissible in any subsequent criminal proceedings (except in respect of a charge of perjury relating to such answers).

[66] Corroboration of the making of the statement will not normally be necessary, but as to such other evidence as may corroborate, see *Banaghan* (1888) 15 R (J) 39.

[67] *McGiveran v Auld* (1894) 21 R (J) 69 at 72.

[68] As permitted by the Criminal Procedure (Scotland) Act 1995, s 93(1).

[69] Criminal Procedure (Scotland) Act 1995, s 93(3).

[70] Criminal Procedure (Scotland) Act 1995, s 94 provides for the preparation of transcripts for the pro-ceedings in which the evidence was given, or on the application of other persons (s 94(2)(b)) but see also subss (3) and (4).

[71] As was permitted in relation to a tape-recorded extra-judicial confession in *HM Advocate v Swift* 1983 SCCR 204. The weight to attach to the witness's recollection of the earlier statement would be a matter for the jury.

[72] *Davidson v McFadyean* 1942 JC 95. A supreme court judge could not be so compelled: *Muckarsie v Wilson* (1834) Bell's Notes 99.

9.6 IMPLIED ADMISSIONS AND CONFESSIONS

9.6.1 An admission or confession may in some cases be inferred from a party's silence or inaction in response to a statement made to him orally or in writing, and evidence of such statements is relevant and admissible for this purpose.[73] Whether or not the party's silence or inaction gives rise to such an inference or implication is a question of fact in each case. The general rule is that when the statement made is such that the party to whom it was made would normally repudiate it if untrue,[74] failure to repudiate will imply an admission of its truth.[75] The inference of admission will be drawn more readily, at least in a civil cause, if the statement made was prejudicial, and failure to repudiate it may lead another person to believe in its truth.[76] When an account has been rendered, an implied admission of its accuracy will generally arise if no objection is made within a reasonable time[77] or if a partial payment has been made without explanation,[78] and, if certain items only are challenged, this will generally be regarded as an implied admission that the other items are accurate.[79] However, failure to repudiate statements in a letter relating to a matter with which the recipient is not concerned, does not imply an admission of the truth of these statements,[80] and this applies to any unsolicited mail.[81]

9.6.2   In a criminal cause it is not legitimate to infer an admission of guilt from the fact that the accused, when charged with the crime, either says nothing or says that he or she has nothing to say. The accused is entitled to put the prosecutor to proof, and it must be made clear to a jury that the accused carries no burden of proving innocence.[82] With the exception of the expected declaration of an ostensible defence at any judicial examination,[83] the accused is entitled to reserve his or her defence.[84] Silence at trial, although no longer immune from comment by the prosecutor, may assist the court in reaching a conclusion on the credibility of other evidence led, but does not imply guilt.[85]

---

[73] Dickson, *Evidence* (3rd edn), para 368, but see also para 372. For implied judicial admissions, see paras 11.2–11.3.

[74] In *Wiedemann v Walpole* [1891] 2 QB 534 at 538, Lord Esher MR observed that in the case of letters "charging a man with some offence or meanness ... [t]he ordinary and wise practice is not to answer them—to take no notice of them. Unless it is made out to be the ordinary practice of mankind to answer, I cannot see that not answering is any evidence that the person who receives such letters admits the truth of the statements contained in them."

[75] *Dowling v Henderson & Son* (1890) 17 R 921.

[76] Dickson, *Evidence* (3rd edn), para 367.

[77] Dickson, *Evidence* (3rd edn), para 369; Phipson, *Evidence* (15th edn), para 30-11; *Smith v Maxwell* (1833) 11 S 323, per Lord Cringletie at 324, applied in *Potter Cowan & Co Ltd v Allen* 1983 SLT (Sh Ct) 42.

[78] *George v Scott* (1832) 10 S 443 at 445.

[79] Dickson, *Evidence* (3rd edn), para 370; Phipson, *Evidence* (15th edn), para 30-11. The position may be different where there is a general objection to the account as a whole coupled with a specification of particular items: Dickson, *ibid.*

[80] *British Linen Co v Cowan* (1906) 8 F 704, per Lord Ardwall at 708, Lord Justice-Clerk Macdonald at 710, Lord Stormonth-Darling at 713. In *MacBain v MacBain* 1930 SC (HL) 72 a reply in terms "I should very much like to see you and explain matters" but which did not specifically repudiate a debt mentioned in the letter under reply was held not to be a written admission of the debt.

[81] For the regulation of unsolicited goods, see the Unsolicited Goods and Services Act 1971.

[82] See Chapter 2.

[83] See para 9.3.

[84] *Robertson v Maxwell* 1951 JC 11 at 14. *Cf* Dickson, *Evidence* (3rd edn), para 370; Alison, ii, 518.

[85] *Jack v HM Advocate* 1999 SCCR 296.

Although at common law a statement by a third party incriminating the accused   **9.6.3**
(whether made by a co-accused or not) could not be evidence against the
accused,[86] the reaction of the accused to that statement can be relevant evidence.
The statement is admissible for the limited purpose of establishing the significance
of the accused's reaction.[87] It is a question of fact in each case as to whether an
inference of guilt may legitimately be drawn from the accused's silence in the face
of a statement, and the implied admission can only arise if the circumstances were
such that the accused was reasonably called upon to repudiate the statement.[88] The
fact that a caution had been given prior to absence of reaction to the statement has
been held to deprive the non-reaction of evidential value.[89] In a case where the
accused had complied with requests to provide breath and urine samples for analysis, it was held that this co-operation did not amount to an admission that he had
been driving the car at the relevant time.[90]

9.7 ADMISSIONS AND CONFESSIONS CONTAINED IN WRITINGS

The general principles described in the previous paragraphs[91] apply equally to   **9.7.1**
written admissions and confessions. Thus a statement in a deed or other document,
even if it concerns a transaction with a person who is not a party to the action, is
admissible as an adminicle of evidence against the party who made it,[92] provided
that it is relevant,[93] and not a precognition.[94] An admission contained in a document which had not been uttered,[95] such as a letter not dispatched[96] or a pleading

---

[86] *Black v HM Advocate* 1974 JC 43, per Lord Cameron at 53; *Jones v HM Advocate* 1981 SCCR 192.
Reform in this area has been proposed for some time: see Macphail, *Evidence*, paras 20.34–S20.34.
For the statutory reform, see para 8.6.6.

[87] *Lewis v Blair* (1858) 3 Irv 16; *Glover v Tudhope* 1986 SCCR 49; *Buchan v HM Advocate* 1993
SCCR 1076; *McDonnell v HM Advocate* 1997 SCCR 760; *Douglas v McFadyen* 1999 SCCR 884. See
also the statement of the law in Renton & Brown, *Criminal Procedure* (6th edn), para 24–56, which
was approved in *Buchan*, *McDonnell* and *Douglas*.

[88] Dickson, *Evidence* (3rd edn), paras 370–371. See also *Hipson v Tudhope* 1983 SCCR 247, where
the police stopped a car and one of the occupants said it was stolen. The accused made no comment,
but replied "not guilty" when cautioned and charged. It was held that guilty knowledge could not be
inferred from his silence.

[89] *Douglas v McFadyen* 1999 SCCR 884.

[90] *Douglas v Pirie* 1975 SLT 206.

[91] See paras 9.1–9.6.

[92] See *Macfie v Callander and Oban Railway Co* (1897) 24 R 1156; (1898) 25 R (HL) 19, an action
of declarator that land belonging to the defenders was superfluous to their requirements, where evidence of writings and minutes concerning earlier negotiations by the defenders with other persons, for
the sale or lease of the land, was considered by the court as relevant to the contention that the land was
superfluous. For criminal cases, see *Main and Atchieson* (1818) Hume, ii, 396; *HM Advocate v Fawcett*
(1869) 1 Coup 183. *Cf HM Advocate v Walsh* 1922 JC 82.

[93] The Civil Evidence (Scotland) Act 1988, s 2 so liberalised the admission of hearsay evidence that
relevance will now be the factor determining admissibility.

[94] See paras 8.71 and 17.1. An earlier doubt on this point (see Dickson, *Evidence* (3rd edn), para 299),
is thought to have resulted from confusion between the admissibility as evidence of a statement against
interest, with which this chapter is primarily concerned, and the sufficiency of such evidence as supporting a plea of personal bar. See *Macfie v Callander and Oban Railway Co* (1897) 24 R 1156 at 1168
et seq; (1898) 25 R (HL), per Lord Halsbury Lord Chancellor at 20.

[95] Dickson, *Evidence* (3rd edn), para 303.

[96] *Livingston v Murray* (1831) 9 S 757.

not lodged in court,[97] is admissible in evidence.[98] In actions of divorce for adultery, a diary in the defender's handwriting,[99] and a draft letter written by the defender and found torn up in a bureau,[100] containing statements from which the commission of adultery could be inferred, were held admissible as evidence against the defenders.

9.8 ADMISSIONS MADE VICARIOUSLY

9.8.1 The position of admissions made vicariously depends upon the substantive law governing the relationship between the person who made the admission and the party in respect of whose case the evidence is being proffered. Admissibility is determined by relevance to that relationship and its connection with the admission. An admission made by a predecessor in title may be proved against a party, if the predecessor, at the time when it was made, had the interest in the subject-matter which the party subsequently acquired, and the admission relates to that interest. Thus in an action for recovery of a debt raised by an assignee[101] or by the executor of the original creditor,[102] evidence of an admission by the cedent made before the granting of the assignation, or by the deceased creditor, is admissible against the assignee or the executor. Evidence of an admission by a bankrupt before sequestration, if made without collusion, is admissible against the general body of creditors[103] and admissions made by a trustee in a sequestration may be admissible in evidence against the creditors.[104] An admission by an agent, made with the express authority of a principal, is admissible in evidence against the principal.[105] An admission made by an agent with the principal's implied authority is similarly admissible, and authority will usually be implied if the admission related to a matter in respect of which the agent was employed, and if the agent was still so employed when it was made.[106] An admission, the making of which was outside

---

[97] *Gavin v Montgomerie* (1830) 9 S 213, per Lord President Hope at 218–219. For the evidential value of pleadings lodged in court but subsequently adjusted or amended, see *Lennox v National Coal Board* 1955 SC 438.

[98] Contrary to the view expressed in *Watson v Watson* 1934 SC 374, where *Livingston v Murray* and *Gavin v Montgomerie* were discussed. Since the document has not been uttered, it is not evidence of concluded intention, but it may be evidence of the writer's knowledge or state of mind, or it may bear on some disputed collateral issue.

[99] *Creasey v Creasey* 1931 SC 9; see also *Duke of Argyll v Duchess of Argyll* 1962 SC 140. But see para 1.7.

[100] *Watson v Watson* 1934 SC 374.

[101] Dickson, *Evidence* (3rd edn), para 356.

[102] *Ibid.* It is thought that the same rule would apply in an action for damages for physical injury, pursued by the executor of the person who was injured and subsequently died, in respect of a statement against interest made by the deceased. *Cf Traynor's Exrx v Bairds Scottish Steel Ltd* 1957 SC 311, where the executrix sought to use *in her favour* a statement made in precognition.

[103] Dickson, *Evidence* (3rd edn), para 357.

[104] *Buchanan v Mags of Dunfermline* (1828) 7 S 35; *cf Ellis v White* (1849) 11 D 1347.

[105] Dickson, *Evidence* (3rd edn), para 358. See also para 25.5.2, and *Dryburgh v Macpherson* 1944 SLT 116; *Fisher v Fisher & Ors* 1952 SC 347, per Lord President Cooper at 351. These cases vouch the proposition that a letter written by a solicitor with the authority of his client may be regarded as the client's writ. See also *Healey v A Massey & Son Ltd* 1961 SC 198. A *fortiori*, it is thought, an admission in such a letter may be proved as an adminicle of evidence against the client. *Cf Smith v Smith* (1869) 8 M 239, where the solicitor's letters were not proved to have been authorised by the client.

[106] Dickson, *Evidence* (3rd edn), para 359; *McLean and Hope v Fleming* (1871) 9 M (HL) 38 at 41, 44 (bill of lading signed by shipmaster); *Mitchell v Berwick* (1845) 7 D 382 at 384 (admission by factor as to rent paid by tenant); *Aitchison v Robertson* (1846) 9 D 15 (purchasing agent).

the scope of the agent's authority, or an admission made after the agency has ceased about matters which occurred during the agency, is not admissible in evidence against the principal.[107] In a similar vein, a partner's admission concerning partnership affairs and in the ordinary course of its business is admissible in evidence against the firm.[108]

When a defender is sued in respect of the negligence of an employee in his **9.8.2** service, an extra-judicial admission by the employee regarding the alleged act of negligence is not admissible in evidence against the defender, since the employee had no implied authority to make an admission.[109] On the other hand, a statement or admission by an employee whose normal duty it was to make the statement, such as a receipt contemporaneously issued for goods or money received on his employer's behalf, is admissible in evidence against the employer.[110] An admission by one of a body of trustees may be proved *quantum valeat* (for what it may be worth) against the estate which that trustee represents, unless the trustee has an interest adverse to the estate.[111] However, mere possession of a common interest does not make an admission by one of those interested admissible in evidence against the others, so that an admission made by a part owner,[112] an acceptor of a bill of exchange,[113] or a defender in an action,[114] as such, is not admissible in evidence against a co-proprietor, another acceptor or a co-defender. If a party to an action has referred his opponent for information regarding some transaction to another person (such as to an accountant or technical adviser), a statement regarding the transaction by that person is then admissible in evidence against the party.[115] The admission of a spouse is not admissible in evidence against the other spouse automatically,[116] but either spouse may have express authority as the other's agent to make admissions which will be admissible against the other in accordance with the general principles of agency mentioned above.[117]

9.9 CONFESSIONS MADE VICARIOUSLY

Common law

When concert between two or more accused is in issue, anything said or written by **9.9.1**

---

[107] Dickson, *Evidence* (3rd edn), para 359. The same general principle applies to admissions by directors and officials of limited companies, corporations and public bodies. See Cross and Tapper, *Evidence* (9th edn), pp 559–560.

[108] Partnership Act 1890, s 15. The common law rule was the same: Dickson, *Evidence* (3rd edn), para 353; *Nisbet's Trs v Morrison's Trs* (1829) 7 S 307, per Lord Glenlee at 310.

[109] *Livingstone v Strachan, Crerar & Jones* 1923 SC 794; *Scott v Cormack Heating Engineers Ltd* 1942 SC 159.

[110] See Cross and Tapper, *Evidence* (9th edn), p 559.

[111] Dickson, *Evidence* (3rd edn), para 354.

[112] Dickson, *Evidence* (3rd edn), para 355.

[113] Dickson, *Evidence* (3rd edn), para 355.

[114] *Creasey v Creasey* 1931 SC 9; Dickson, *Evidence* (3rd edn), para 355.

[115] Dickson, *Evidence* (3rd edn), para 358. The principle applied in *Cooper v Hamilton* (1824) 2 S 609 (altd on expenses (1826) 2 W & S 59) was similar to this. See also *Mackay v Ure* (1847) 10 D 89.

[116] For example, an extra-judicial admission of negligence by a husband is not admissible in evidence against his wife in an action in which, as pursuer, she seeks to establish negligence against the other driver: *Jackson v Glasgow Corporation* 1956 SC 354.

[117] The validity of any implied agency which existed between husband and wife at common law is now questionable: Clive, *Husband and Wife* (4th edn), para 13.005. The wife's *praepositura* was abolished by the Law Reform (Husband and Wife) (Scotland) Act 1984, s 7.

one of them in relation to the preparation, execution or completion of their common criminal enterprise is admissible in evidence against all of them.[118] Apart from this, however, at common law a confession of or inferring guilt by one accused is not admissible as evidence for[119] or against another,[120] and dicta which suggest that confessions by two co-accused can be mutually corroborative[121] must be regarded as incorrect. In *Wilson v HM Advocate*,[122] the court appeared to treat the fact that two confessions were "remarkable [and] almost identical" as an adminicle of evidence. This view has been heavily criticised on the basis that neither accused's confession could be admissible in evidence against the other.[123] However, it is arguable that in such a case it is the *similarity* which is the adminicle of evidence and not the confession of the co-accused, which is therefore admissible solely for the purpose of establishing that similarity in the same way that a statement made in the presence of an accused may be admissible solely for the purpose of establishing his reaction to it.[124] If evidence of a confession by one accused is led as admissible against him, and its terms implicate another accused, the jury should be directed to disregard it as evidence against the other accused,[125] but this rule was not always observed in the period immediately preceding the statutory reform mentioned in the next paragraph.[126] A confession by a director of a company has been held to be a confession by the company.[127]

Admissibility under statute

9.9.2 Now it is provided by statute that when the statement is that of a co-accused[128] it may be admitted as evidence in relation to an accused, on the application of that accused, subject to giving pre-trial notice to the other parties in the case.[129] The provision is linked to the more general provision for the admission of hearsay evidence,[130] and the combined effect of the two provisions is unclear.[131] It may be

---

[118] Dickson, *Evidence* (3rd edn), para 363; Macdonald, *Criminal Law* (5th edn), pp 315–316. See also *HM Advocate v Camerons* 1911 SC (J) 110; *Tobin v HM Advocate* 1934 JC 60; *HM Advocate v Docherty* 1980 SLT (Notes) 33; *Hamill v HM Advocate* 1999 JC 190.

[119] *Mathieson v HM Advocate* 1996 SCCR 388.

[120] *Milroy* (1839) Bell's Notes 291; *HM Advocate v Kemp* (1891) 3 White 17; Dickson, *Evidence* (3rd edn), para 363; *Perrie v HM Advocate* 1991 JC 27; *McLay v HM Advocate* 1994 JC 159; *Ridler v HM Advocate* 1995 SLT 1271. The silence of an accused person after a statement made by another person in his presence may be founded on as an implied admission, and evidence of the other person's statement may be admissible only for the purpose of showing the context of that silence: *Buchan v HM Advocate* 1995 SLT 1057; *McDonnell and Smith v HM Advocate* 1998 JC 228. See para 9.6.

[121] See *HM Advocate v Davidson* 1968 SLT 17; *Annan v Bain* 1986 SCCR 60.

[122] 1987 SCCR 217.

[123] See Sheriff Gordon's commentary to *Wilson* at 1987 SCCR 223. See also Griffiths, *Confessions* (1994), para 3.04.

[124] Given that Sheriff Gordon accepts that the similarity of the confessions in *Wilson* was the "most convincing aspect of the case" and "striking and reassuring" (see 1987 SCCR at 223), his view that it is also irrelevant seems undesirable in principle.

[125] *Monson* (1893) 21 R (J) 5 at 9; *Stark and Smith v HM Advocate* 1938 JC 170 at 174; Dickson, *Evidence* (3rd edn), para 366.

[126] See, for example, *McLay v HM Advocate* 1994 JC 159, which is to be compared with *Mathieson v HM Advocate* 1996 SCCR 388.

[127] *Industrial Distributions (Central Scotland) Ltd v Quinn* 1984 SLT 240.

[128] Criminal Procedure (Scotland) Act 1995, s 261(2).

[129] Criminal Procedure (Scotland) Act 1995, ss 261(4) and 259(5).

[130] Criminal Procedure (Scotland) Act 1995, s 259, subs (2)(e) of which is deemed to be satisfied in the case of hearsay of a co-accused.

[131] See Renton & Brown, *Criminal Procedure* (6th edn), paras 24-24–24-25.

different in effect, in so far as that can be determined from examining the provisions, from the proposal of the Scottish Law Commission preceding it, which was concerned with the inability at common law to call upon the extra-judicial statement of an incriminee.[132] It is thought that the statutory effect is that when an extra-judicial statement of a co-accused or an incriminee is to be founded upon during trial by an accused, that statement will be admissible in proof of the truth of its contents in relation to the accused who founds upon it, if the co-accused or incriminee does not repeat the terms of the extra-judicial statement in court.[133] However, it is possible to take a broader interpretation to include all relevant extra-judicial statements of co-accused persons as evidence in the cause.[134]

9.10 ADMISSIONS IMPROPERLY OBTAINED

The admissibility of evidence in civil causes which has been improperly obtained **9.10.1** was mentioned in general terms in an earlier chapter,[135] where it was noted that the policy of the law in civil cases is to admit almost all evidence which will throw light on disputed facts and enable justice to be done. Written admissions obtained by theft have been held admissible by the courts.[136] There appears to be no case in which the Scottish courts have had to consider the admissibility of admissions obtained in some other improper way, as, for example, by threats or compulsion, or by trickery or deceit.[137, 138] It is possible that an admission obtained by threats which were illegal and unwarrantable, or by deceit or trickery, might also be held to be admissible *quantum valeat*, the whole circumstances in which it was obtained being relevant to the question of whether the admission was true or false. These comments must now be read against Article 8 of the European Convention on Human Rights, whereby privacy and family life are respected, and interference by a public authority, including a court, is permissible only if in accordance with the law and necessary, e.g. for protection of the rights and freedoms of others.[139] Admissions intercepted in the course of the post or their transmission via a public telecommunications system are subject to the Interception of Communications Act 1985, which is discussed below in the context of criminal proceedings.[140]

---

[132] *Evidence: Report on Hearsay in Evidence in Criminal Proceedings* (Scot Law Com No 149), paras 5.65–5.69.

[133] Criminal Procedure (Scotland) Act 1995, ss 259(2)(e) and 261(2). The co-accused whose statement is to be used, if not a witness, is deemed to be refusing to give evidence under s 259(2)(e) and to have been competent when the statement was made: s 261(3).

[134] See Renton & Brown, *Criminal Procedure* (6th edn), para 24-25.

[135] See para 1.7.

[136] *Rattray v Rattray* (1897) 25 R 315. This decision has been followed (with reluctance) by trial judges in subsequent cases: *MacColl v MacColl* 1946 SLT 312; *Duke of Argyll v Duchess of Argyll* 1962 SC 140. At the subsequent proof in the *Argyll* case, Lord Wheatley suggested that, as the action was one of divorce for adultery, which was historically a "quasi-criminal" offence and still required proof beyond reasonable doubt in a court action, the test in *Lawrie v Muir* 1950 JC 19 might be applied (1963 SLT (Notes) 42). However, adultery no longer requires to be proved beyond reasonable doubt in a divorce action: Divorce (Scotland) Act 1976, s 1(6).

[137] When the evidence had been obtained inadvertently, the objection was repelled: *McLeish v Glasgow Bonding Co Ltd* 1965 SLT 39. Admissions made in response to a threatened use of legal diligence, even if that includes imprisonment, would probably be held to be admissible in evidence. See Dickson, *Evidence* (3rd edn), para 308; Gloag, *Contract* (2nd edn), pp 489–490.

[138] See Dickson, *Evidence* (3rd edn), para 307.

[139] See Art 8(1). The effects of Arts 8 and 6 (fair trial) may lead to the same outcome as the existing policy at common law, but on a strict interpretation of Art 8 admission may constitute a breach of Art 8 by the court.

[140] See para 9.15.

9.11 CONFESSIONS UNFAIRLY OBTAINED—GENERAL

9.11.1 In modern practice extra-judicial confessions unfairly obtained are held to be inadmissible in evidence against the accused person. The general nature of the "fairness" test remains unclear. While the earlier cases refer simply to "fairness to the accused",[141] the courts have more recently adopted the view that fairness is a bilateral test, and that fairness to the accused should be balanced against fairness to the public.[142] However, in the recent case of *B v HM Advocate*,[143] it was held that it was "entirely out of place" for the sheriff to have directed the jury to have regard to the public interest in the suppression of crime in deciding whether evidence of an alleged confession was admissible.[144]

9.11.2 It is clear, however, that the appropriate question is one of fairness and not of whether the police or other persons who obtained the confession acted properly. A confession may be held to have been unfairly obtained and therefore inadmissible without any impropriety on the part of the police.[145] That said, it should be remembered at all times that the role of the police in this context is to ascertain the facts and not to construct the prosecution case.[146] If the police go beyond that role and attempt to extract a confession from the suspect, there is a strong risk that any evidence obtained will be inadmissible.

9.11.3 Where only part of an interview conducted by the police is inadmissible, the transcript may be edited so as to withhold the inadmissible parts from the jury.[147] In summary procedure, the judge should simply leave those parts out of account.[148] A statement by an accused, otherwise admissible, will not be excluded merely because it discloses his previous bad character.[149] Where a statement is unfairly obtained, not only will it be inadmissible, but it may be that a subsequent statement in the same terms will be considered tainted and therefore itself inadmissible, even if there is no unfairness directly bearing upon it.[150]

---

[141] *HM Advocate v Aitken* 1926 JC 83; *Mills v HM Advocate* 1935 JC 77; *HM Advocate v Olsson* 1941 JC 63; *HM Advocate v Rigg* 1946 JC 1; *Brown v HM Advocate* 1966 SLT 105, per Lord Justice-General Clyde at 107. See also *McAdam v HM Advocate* 1960 JC 1, per Lord Justice-General Clyde at 4: the principle of fairness to the accused "underlies the proper conduct of all trials".

[142] *Miln v Cullen* 1967 JC 21, per Lord Wheatley at 30; *Welsh & Breen v HM Advocate*, unreported, High Court (on appeal), 15 November 1973, excerpted in *HM Advocate v O'Donnell* 1975 SLT (Sh Ct) 22 at 24; *Jamieson v Annan* 1988 JC 62.

[143] 1995 SLT 961.

[144] See also *HM Advocate v B* 1991 SCCR 533 (Sh Ct), which also refers only to fairness to the accused.

[145] *HM Advocate v Lieser* 1926 JC 88; *HM Advocate v Gilgannon* 1983 SCCR 10; *Jack v HM Advocate* 1999 SCCR 296.

[146] Renton & Brown, *Criminal Procedure* (6th edn), para 24-43.

[147] *Tunnicliffe v HM Advocate* 1991 SCCR 623. It was also suggested in *Tunnicliffe* that the tape itself could be edited before being played to the jury, but that suggestion has been heavily criticised and was ignored by the court in *Carmichael v Boyd* 1994 SLT 734. See Griffiths, *Confessions* (1994), para 6.48.

[148] *Carmichael v Boyd* 1994 SLT 734.

[149] *HM Advocate v McFadyen* 1926 JC 93. *Cf HM Advocate v Graham* 1984 SLT 67. As to evidence of character, see paras 7.4–7.10.

[150] See *Robertson* (1853) 1 Irv 219; *Chalmers v HM Advocate* 1954 JC 66, per Lord Justice-General Cooper at 77 and Lord Strachan (trial judge) at 69–70. But see *Honeyman v Smith* (1815) Hume, ii, 315. However, the ratio of *Honeyman* is not clear from Hume's note and it may be that the original statement in that case would itself have been considered perfectly admissible at the time: see *Simpson* (1889) 2 White 298.

9.12 UNFAIRNESS—DETERMINING ADMISSIBILITY

Until very recently, it was thought that whether or not a confession was fairly **9.12.1**
obtained was a question for the jury to determine, and that a judge should not
exclude evidence of a confession unless satisfied that no reasonable jury could
hold that the statement had been voluntarily made and had not been extracted by
unfair or improper means.[151] However, following the full bench decision in
Thompson v Crowe,[152] it is now clear that admissibility of evidence is a question
for the trial judge and not the jury, and that the judge must determine any issues of
fact which are necessary to enable that decision to be taken.[153]

This should be done by means of a trial within a trial, where the Crown must **9.12.2**
prove on the balance of probabilities that the statement is admissible.[154] This procedure is appropriate in summary as well as solemn procedure as it "ring fences"
the evidence and allows the accused to give evidence on matters pertaining to
admissibility without exposure to cross-examination on the merits of the case.[155] If
the evidence is held admissible but doubt is cast on this ruling in the course of the
trial, the judge may reconsider the ruling. If the evidence is held inadmissible at
this stage but has already been led, the judge may direct the jury to disregard it or
desert *pro loco et tempore* if the jury could not realistically be expected to put it
out of their minds.[156] In summary procedure, it will rarely be appropriate to desert
the diet and the judge should simply disregard the inadmissible evidence.[157]

It is important to bear in mind the revolution effected by *Thompson* when con- **9.12.3**
sidering earlier case law. From the 1977 decision in *Balloch v HM Advocate*[158] up
until *Thompson*, the appeal court has asked not whether the trial judge's decision
was correct in law, but whether the judge was correct in holding that no reasonable
jury could have held the evidence to have been fairly obtained. Pre-*Thompson*
decisions where the appeal court has chosen not to interfere with the decision of
the trial judge to admit evidence should not therefore be interpreted as meaning
that the evidence proffered in those cases would be admissible *as a matter of law*
post-*Thompson*. It is probable that future appellate decisions will take a more
strict approach to admissibility as a result of *Thompson*.[159]

---

[151] The leading decisions were *Balloch v HM Advocate* 1977 JC 23; *HM Advocate v Whitelaw* 1980
SLT (Notes) 25 and *Lord Advocate's Reference (No 1 of 1983)* 1984 JC 52. *Cf HM Advocate v Mair*
1982 SLT 471, per Lord Hunter at 472.
[152] 2000 JC 173.
[153] *Thompson v Crowe* 2000 JC 173 at 191H–192A.
[154] *Thompson v Crowe* 2000 JC 173 at 192B–F. *Cf Black v Annan* 1996 SLT 284, which made it clear
that the burden of proof lay with the Crown but ignored the question of the standard of proof required.
Strictly speaking, the *Thompson* court's observations on this point are *obiter* but are likely to be followed. It will be noted, however, that the court's view is out of step with English law: see Police and
Criminal Evidence Act 1984, s 76(2) and Cross and Tapper, *Evidence* (9th edn), pp 169–170. See also
Sheriff Gordon's comments on the issue at 1999 SCCR 1050–1051. *Quaere* as to whether there is an
ECHR issue here: *cf S v Zuma and Others* 1995 (2) SA 642.
[155] *Thompson v Crowe* 2000 JC 173 at 193E–G and 200–201.
[156] *Thompson v Crowe* 2000 JC 173 at 199A–B.
[157] *Thompson v Crowe* 2000 JC 173 at 202H.
[158] 1977 JC 23.
[159] See *Thompson v Crowe* 2000 JC 173, per Lord Justice-General Rodger at 190J–191A: "Not only
does such a system [that used pre-*Thompson*] make it harder to do justice in an individual case, but it
also means that the courts cannot develop meaningful rules for having the issue determined consist-
ently—making it at best difficult for them to fulfil a basic requirement of justice, that like cases should
be treated alike."

9.12.4   Where a confession is held admissible, the evidence of the circumstances in which it was obtained remains relevant to the question of the weight to be attached to it.[160]

9.13 UNFAIRNESS—PERSONAL CHARACTERISTICS

9.13.1 The courts have held a number of factors personal to the suspect to militate against the admissibility of any confession. The factors disclosed by the cases to date are as follows: the youth of the suspect[161]; the fact that the suspect was intoxicated[162] or not fully awake[163] at the time; the mental or physical distress of the suspect at the time[164]; medical or mental impairment or incapacity[165]; and a limited command of English (particularly in the absence of an interpreter).[166]

9.14 UNFAIRNESS—THREATS OR INDUCEMENTS

9.14.1 A confession made as a result of threats, inducement or undue influence is inadmissible.[167] Although it had been suggested that this rule does not apply to threats, inducements or undue influence on the part of persons not associated with the judiciary, prosecutor or police,[168] that view is no longer tenable as it is now accepted that the admissibility of such confessions is subject to the normal test of fairness.[169] The same principle applies to confessions induced as a result of misrepresentation (for example, telling one suspect that another has confessed).[170]

9.14.2   It is open to question whether it is improper for a police officer to use a personal relationship with a suspect in order to encourage them to make a statement.[171] In an older case, it was suggested that a confession by a gunner in response to questions by his commanding officer would be inadmissible, the gunner being under an obligation to account to his commanding officer whilst on duty.[172]

---

[160] *Thompson v Crowe* 2000 JC 173; *Boyne v HM Advocate* 1980 JC 47.

[161] *HM Advocate v Aitken* 1926 JC 83; *Chalmers v HM Advocate* 1954 JC 66; *HM Advocate v B* 1991 SCCR 533 (Sh Ct); *Codona v HM Advocate* 1996 SLT 1100.

[162] *Thomson v HM Advocate* 1989 SLT 170; *McClory v McInnes* 1992 SLT 501. See also *Hay v HM Advocate* 1998 SCCR 634, where the sheriff excluded confession evidence for this reason. The correctness of this decision was not raised on appeal.

[163] *McClory v McInnes* 1992 SLT 501.

[164] *HM Advocate v Aitken* 1926 JC 83; *HM Advocate v Rigg* 1946 JC 1; *Chalmers v HM Advocate* 1954 JC 66.

[165] *HM Advocate v Gilgannon* 1983 SCCR 10; *Blagojevic v HM Advocate* 1995 SLT 1189. See also *HM Advocate v Mair* 1982 SLT 471, where the suspect was a deaf mute.

[166] *HM Advocate v Olsson* 1941 JC 63.

[167] Alison, ii, 581; Dickson, *Evidence* (3rd edn), para 344; *Watt* (1834) Bell's Notes 244; *Mahler* (1857) 2 Irv 634; *Millar* (1859) 3 Irv 406; *Proudfoot* (1882) 9 R (J) 19. The most recent case is *Harley v HM Advocate* 1996 SLT 1075, where the police told the suspect that if he co-operated they would avoid approaching a witness with whom H was having an extra-marital affair in such a way as to alert the witness's husband to the existence of the affair. It was held that the judge should not have allowed the statement to go to the jury. See also *Young v Friel* 1992 SCCR 567 ("I can't offer you any deals at present" held not to be an inducement).

[168] Alison, ii, 581; Dickson, *Evidence* (3rd edn), para 345.

[169] *McCuaig v Annan* 1986 SCCR 535. See also *Robertson* (1853) 1 Irv 219; *Turner* (1853) 1 Irv 285.

[170] *Kerr v Mackay* (1863) 1 Irv 213. *Cf HM Advocate v Campbell* 1964 JC 80, which might be considered to involve an implied misrepresentation.

[171] See *HM Advocate v Anderson* 1980 SLT (Notes) 104; *Fraser v HM Advocate* 1989 SCCR 82.

[172] *Turner* (1853) 1 Irv 284. It is doubtful whether the same view would be taken today.

In *Stewart v Hingston*,[173] the suspect was informed by a police officer that he **9.14.3** intended to detain her. When she pointed out that there was no one available to look after her children, he said that a social worker could be obtained or she could make a statement there and then. She elected to make a statement there and then, and did so after caution. It was held that this did not amount to an inducement as the police officer had acted in good faith and the caution had made it clear that she was not obliged to say anything.[174] This appears to view the question of inducement from the perspective of whether the police officer has acted wrongly rather than from the point of view of the accused.[175]

9.15 UNFAIRNESS—CONFESSIONS OVERHEARD OR INTERCEPTED

Evidence of conversations between persons in custody has been held admissi- **9.15.1** ble,[176] even when obtained by eavesdropping.[177] The rationale appears to be that persons in custody cannot reasonably expect their conversations to be private.[178] Equally, a letter written by a prisoner to his brother and intercepted by the prison authorities was held admissible against him.[179] The fairness test may therefore demand a different result where conversations of a more private nature are eavesdropped on or communications of a more private nature intercepted.[180]

The police may not evade their duty to caution a suspect by engaging a third **9.15.2** party to question them and eavesdropping on the conversation. In one case, a suspect agreed to make a statement to a reporter but insisted the police should not be present. The reporter notified the police. An officer attended in the guise of a second reporter, but took no part in the proceedings and simply listened to the statement being made. The trial judge held that in the circumstances there was a duty upon the policeman to caution the suspect and his failure to do so rendered the statement inadmissible in evidence.[181]

None of this applies to eavesdropping on the commission of a crime itself, **9.15.3** which is considered unobjectionable.[182] The interception of communications

---

[173] 1997 SLT 442.

[174] This conclusion is, with respect, questionable as it had been made clear to S that she would be detained and her child taken into the care of a social worker if she refused to make a statement. It is questionable whether she could be said to have been under "no obligation" in that situation.

[175] *Cf Law v McNicol* 1965 JC 32, where the suspect had been told that he might be kept in custody over Christmas Day if the matter were not cleared up that morning. His confession was held inadmissible, with Lord Strachan stating that he was "not convinced" there would have been good grounds for keeping M in custody over Christmas, but it is notable that the sheriff appears to have excluded the confession as induced without addressing the question of whether or not the police had acted in good faith.

[176] *Brown* (1833) Bell's Notes 244; *Miller* (1837) Bell's Notes 244; *Welsh and Breen v HM Advocate*, unreported, High Court (on appeal), 15 November 1973, excerpted in *HM Advocate v O'Donnell* 1975 SLT (Sh Ct) 22 at 24.

[177] *HM Advocate v O'Donnell* 1975 SLT (Sh Ct) 22; *Jamieson v Annan* 1988 JC 62; *Johnston* (1845) 2 Broun 401. But see *HM Advocate v Keen* 1926 JC 1.

[178] See A D Gibb, "Fair Play for the Criminal" 1954 JR 199 at 219: "Men in a police station who shout their observations must surely be taken to know that policemen will hear them"—a statement quoted with approval by Sheriff Macphail in *HM Advocate v O'Donnell* 1975 SLT (Sh Ct) 22 at 24.

[179] *Fawcett* (1869) 1 Coup 183. *Cf HM Advocate v Walsh* 1922 JC 82, where the court thought it unnecessary to decide the point.

[180] *Khan v UK* (2000) 8 BHRC 310.

[181] *HM Advocate v Campbell* 1964 JC 80, *HM Advocate v Graham* 1991 SLT 416; *Cf Weir v Jessop* 1992 SLT 533, per Lord Justice-Clerk Ross at 573E–G.

[182] *Weir v Jessop* 1992 SLT 533, particularly per Lord Morison at 539E–H; *Hopes and Lavery v HM Advocate* 1960 JC 104; *Ming v HM Advocate* 1987 SCCR 110.

whilst in the course of their transmission by post or by means of a public telecommunication system is now regulated by the Interception of Communications Act 1985. The intentional interception of such communications is a criminal offence unless done in obedience to a warrant issued by the Secretary of State,[183] or under the reasonable belief that one party has consented,[184] or for certain other narrowly defined purposes.[185]

9.15.4   Section 9 of the 1985 Act prevents any evidence being adduced in court which "tends to suggest" either that an offence has been committed by any person holding office under the Crown, the Post Office or any Post Office employee, any public telecommunications operator or any person engaged in the running of a public telecommunications system, or that a warrant has been or is to be issued to any of these persons.

9.15.5   The courts have viewed the logical result of this provision as being that evidence obtained by interception is generally inadmissible,[186] unless it has been obtained legally other than by a warrant (*eg* consensually),[187] or obtained abroad, in which case the 1985 Act is inapplicable.[188]

9.16 UNFAIRNESS—STATEMENTS TO POLICE—GENERAL

9.16.1   It is difficult to deduce general rules on this topic, because each decision depends upon its own facts.[189] A good deal, however, turns upon the stage of the police investigation at which the statement is made.[190] It has been said that there are three relevant stages: (1) before police suspicion has focused on the accused, (2) while the accused is detained on suspicion, and (3) after the accused has been charged.[191]

9.17 UNFAIRNESS—STATEMENTS TO POLICE—BEFORE SUSPICION FOCUSED ON ACCUSED

9.17.1   It appears that, where the police have not identified the accused as the person they believe to have committed a crime, they may question him without administering a caution. This is so even where the accused has attained the status of a "mild

---

[183] Interception of Communications Act 1985, s 1(2)(a).

[184] Interception of Communications Act 1985, s 1(2)(b).

[185] See Interception of Communications Act 1985, s 1(3).

[186] *R v Preston* [1994] 2 AC 130. It should be said that this appears to have been accepted in *Preston* without argument, and is questionable as it is possible to lead evidence obtained by interception without necessarily indicating how that interception came about, and the fact that such evidence has been obtained does not of itself show that an offence has been committed by one of the specified persons or that a warrant has been granted. More problematic, however, is the fact that any material obtained by way of an intercept must be destroyed once the investigation (not the prosecution) is complete: Interception of Communications Act 1985, ss 6(3) and 2(2); *Preston*.

[187] *R v Rasool* [1997] 1 WLR 1092.

[188] *R v Aujla* [1998] 2 Cr App R 16; see also *R v Governor of Belmarsh Prison, ex p Martin* [1995] 1 WLR 412. See also, Mackarel & Gane, "Admitting Irregularly or Illegally Obtained Evidence from Abroad into Criminal Proceedings—A Common Law Approach" [1997] Crim LR 720.

[189] *Chalmers v HM Advocate* 1954 JC 66, per Lord Justice-General Cooper at 77–78.

[190] For an example in which the stage did not preclude admissibility but unfairness existed in respect of one of the admissions made, see *Van Lierop v McLeod* 1999 SCCR 577.

[191] *Bell v HM Advocate* 1945 JC 61.

suspect",[192] has been accused by a member of the public of committing a crime,[193] or is a member of a discrete group of people (such as the crew of a ship[194] or the residents of a house) and the police believe that a member of that group has committed a crime. It has been suggested that to administer a caution at the preliminary stages of an inquiry may be undesirable as it might deter a reasonable exculpatory reply.[195]

9.18 UNFAIRNESS—STATEMENTS TO POLICE—AFTER SUSPICION FOCUSED ON ACCUSED

This category includes any statement made at, or after, the time when the suspicions of the police have focused upon the accused, and when he or she is under serious consideration by them as the perpetrator of the crime.[196] To decide when a particular statement falls into this, rather than the first, category is sometimes difficult. This category necessarily includes cases where the suspect is detained under section 14 of the Criminal Procedure (Scotland) Act 1995, as this power cannot be exercised in the absence of reasonable grounds for suspecting that a person has committed or is committing an offence punishable by imprisonment.[197] It also includes cases where, although technically the accused has accompanied the police voluntarily in response to a request, he is not for practical purposes a free agent.[198] It is not limited to either of these two categories, however. The rule governing the admissibility as evidence of statements falling into this category is discussed in the following paragraphs. **9.18.1**

Breach of statutory detention provisions

It would appear that a breach of the statutory requirements for a lawful detention does not necessarily render answers to questions inadmissible, but is instead simply a factor to be taken into account in applying the overall test of fairness.[199] Where the suspect is detained for longer than the six-hour limit, this will not affect the admissibility of any statements made prior to the expiry of the time limit.[200] **9.18.2**

Failure to give usual caution

The mere fact that a suspected person has been asked questions by the police **9.18.3**

---

[192] *HM Advocate v McPhee* 1966 SLT (Notes) 83.
[193] *Miln v Cullen* 1967 JC 21; *Custerson v Westwater* 1987 SCCR 389.
[194] *Bell v HM Advocate* 1945 JC 61.
[195] *Wingate v Mackinnon*, unreported, High Court (on appeal), 13 June 1989, Crown Office Circular A27/89.
[196] *HM Advocate v Aitken* 1926 JC 83; *Chalmers v HM Advocate* 1954 JC 66, per Lord Justice-General Cooper at 78 and Lord Justice-Clerk Thomson at 81–82.
[197] Criminal Procedure (Scotland) Act 1995, s 14(1). A detainee is under no obligation to answer any question other than to give his name and address: s 14(9). He must be informed of this right (see *ibid*) but such a warning is not a sufficient substitute for a full common law caution: *Tonge v HM Advocate* 1982 JC 130.
[198] *HM Advocate v Rigg* 1946 JC 1; *Chalmers v HM Advocate* 1954 JC 66 at 75, 78.
[199] *Scott v Howie* 1993 SCCR 81. *Cf Wilson v Robertson* 1986 SCCR 700; *Forbes v HM Advocate* 1990 SCCR 69.
[200] *Grant v HM Advocate* 1990 JC 77. It may be that the logical corollary of the approach taken by the court in this case is that statements made after the expiry of the time limit are necessarily inadmissible, but the point is yet to be considered.

without caution does not of itself render any reply inadmissible.[201] This is particularly the case where the suspect has already been cautioned on another matter and can thus be taken to be aware of his right to silence.[202] Equally, the fact that a caution was administered in proper form does not of itself make a confession admissible if the circumstances in which it was obtained were otherwise unfair.[203] Instead, the stage (if any) at which a caution was given falls to be considered as part of the general test of fairness.[204] The caution should warn the suspect both that he is not obliged to say anything and that anything he does say may be recorded or noted and given in evidence against him.[205] A truly voluntary statement (as opposed to one obtained by questioning) at this stage will be admissible even if the suspect has not been cautioned.[206] However, this does not apply where the suspect *indicates* to the police that he wishes to make a voluntary statement (either by an explicit request or by spontaneously embarking on such a statement). Where it appears that the suspect wishes to make such a statement, the police should halt the proceedings and follow the appropriate procedures for voluntary statements,[207] which are noted below.[208]

9.18.4   It had formerly been suggested that if a suspect was not informed of his "basic right" to silence, then this would necessarily render any confession inadmissible,[209] but this is difficult to reconcile with the more recent cases, particularly *Pennycuick v Lees*,[210] where DSS investigators, having already formed the opinion that the suspect had made false benefit claims, told him what the purpose of their visit was but did not caution him until after he had been shown and admitted signing the relevant claim forms. It was held that as there was no suggestion of undue pressure, deception or other device, the sheriff had been entitled to hold that there was no unfairness. It remains to be seen whether the High Court will take a firmer line on such cases now that admissibility is a question of law[211] and thus open to stricter review on appeal.[212]

Manner of questioning

9.18.5   It is commonly said that confessions obtained by way of "cross-examination" are

---

[201] *Jones v Milne* 1975 JC 16; *Murphy v HM Advocate* 1975 SLT (Notes) 17. It has been said that it is "proper practice" for a caution to be given to an individual on whom suspicion has centred before further questioning: *Tonge v HM Advocate* 1982 JC 130, per Lord Cameron at 147. It is not, however, a condition of admissibility that proper practice be followed as long as the requirements of fairness are met: *cf Cordiner v HM Advocate* 1993 SLT 2.

[202] *Wilson v Heywood* 1989 SLT 279; *Young v Friel* 1992 SCCR 567.

[203] *Chalmers v HM Advocate* 1954 JC 66, per Lord Justice-General Cooper at 79.

[204] *Pennycuick v Lees* 1992 SLT 763; *HM Advocate v Middler* 1994 SCCR 838.

[205] *HM Advocate v Docherty* 1981 JC 6.

[206] *Costello v Macpherson* 1922 JC 9; *Hodgson v Macpherson* 1913 SC (J) 68; *Thompson v HM Advocate* 1968 JC 61. Much will depend here on the nature of the statement—the police can hardly be expected to interrupt an unexpected one-sentence admission of guilt in order to follow "voluntary statement" procedures, but a 15-minute monologue is clearly of a different nature.

[207] *Thompson v HM Advocate* 1968 JC 61.

[208] See para 9.20.

[209] *HM Advocate v Von* 1979 SLT (Notes) 62; *HM Advocate v Docherty* 1981 JC 6.

[210] 1992 SLT 763. Although this is not a case involving the police, the point is a general one and the court treated it as such. *Pennycuick* was explicitly applied to police questioning by Lord Marnoch in *HM Advocate v Middler* 1994 SCCR 838.

[211] *Thompson v Crowe* 2000 JC 173.

[212] In this context, it may be worth noting that *Docherty* and *Von*, where confessions were held inadmissible due to the suspect not having been informed of his right to silence, were first instance rather than appellate decisions.

inadmissible,[213] but this is clouded to an extent by differing uses of the term "cross-examination". It is now understood that this refers only to "improper forms of bullying or pressure designed to break the will of the suspect or to force from him a confession against his will."[214] Cross-examination which does not amount to this will not render answers obtained thereby inadmissible.[215] It is acceptable to tell a suspect that charges may or will be preferred against them, and this does not render a confession made thereafter but before charge inadmissible.[216] It has been suggested in the past that statements "made in answer to questions as to the accused's association with the crime for which he is tried" are inadmissible,[217] but this can no longer be regarded as the law.[218]

The "chargeable suspect"

There is no rule that the police must charge a suspect once they have sufficient evidence to do so, and further questioning after this point has been reached is not automatically precluded.[219] It is permissible for the police to question a suspect after arrest but before charge.[220]

9.18.6

Access to a solicitor

A suspect detained under the statutory provisions[221] is entitled to have intimation of his detention sent to a solicitor (and one other person).[222] There is no right for the suspect to consult with the solicitor during the period of detention, nor to have the solicitor present at any interview. It appears that this does not conflict with Convention rights.[223] Failure to inform a suspect of this right will not of itself render any subsequent confession unfairly obtained,[224] but it is a factor to be taken into account. Although there is no right of consultation with a solicitor, failure to allow such consultation may amount to unfairness in some cases, particularly where the suspect is in some way vulnerable and/or charged with a grave offence.[225]

9.18.7

---

[213] See, eg, *Chalmers v HM Advocate* 1954 JC 66, per Lord Justice-General Cooper at 78–79; *Hartley v HM Advocate* 1979 SLT 26, per Lord Avonside at 28; *HM Advocate v Friel* 1978 SLT (Notes) 21.

[214] *Lord Advocate's Reference (No 1 of 1983)* 1984 JC 52 at 58.

[215] *Carmichael v Boyd* 1993 JC 219; *Codona v HM Advocate* 1996 SLT 1100 at 1105K.

[216] *Codona v HM Advocate* 1996 SLT 1100; *Miller v HM Advocate* 1997 SCCR 748. See also *HM Advocate v Penders* 1996 JC 107, where the matter was left to the jury.

[217] See the first edition of this work at para 46.

[218] See, eg, the transcript of the police interview which was held admissible in *Lord Advocate's Reference (No 1 of 1983)* 1984 JC 52. However, in *Van Lierop v McLeod* 1999 SCCR 577 a casual question by a fingerprinting officer of a person who had been arrested on warrant, but not cautioned and charged, to the effect "did you do it?" was unfair and rendered the reply inadmissible.

[219] *HM Advocate v Penders* 1996 JC 107; *Murphy v HM Advocate* 1975 SLT (Notes) 17.

[220] *Hay v HM Advocate* 1998 SCCR 634. Cf *HM Advocate v Caithness and Fraser*, unreported, Dundee High Court, 1985, noted in Griffiths, *Confessions* (1994), para 2.82.

[221] Criminal Procedure (Scotland) Act 1995, s 14.

[222] Criminal Procedure (Scotland) Act 1995, s 15. Similarly, an accused, once charged, is also entitled to have intimation sent to a solicitor: s 17.

[223] *Paton v Ritchie* 2000 JC 271.

[224] *HM Advocate v Fox* 1947 JC 30. Cf *HM Advocate v Olsson* 1941 JC 63.

[225] *HM Advocate v Aitken* 1926 JC 83.

9.19 UNFAIRNESS—STATEMENTS TO POLICE—CHARGE AND THEREAFTER

Reply to charge

9.19.1   A reply to a charge will normally be admissible in evidence.[226] However, a suspect must be cautioned before being charged with an offence or any reply thereto will be inadmissible.[227] This rule is equally applicable where the police simply accuse the suspect of the crime without making a formal charge.[228] A reply may also be inadmissible (although the law is not entirely settled) where it is in substance a repetition of a confession elicited earlier in response to improper cross-examination by the police,[229] or where its terms indicate that the accused misunderstood the nature of the crime with which he had been charged.[230] No adverse inference arises from a failure to reply to a charge.[231] A reply to a charge is admissible even if the police had insufficient evidence to justify the charge at the time, at least where it is not made in bad faith.[232] A reply to a charge is admissible at trial for a different charge provided that both charges fall into the same category (*eg* they both infer dishonesty, or personal violence)[233] and that each charge covers substantially the same facts.[234]

Questioning after charge

9.19.2   Once a suspect has been charged, any further questioning in relation to that charge is improper and any replies will be inadmissible.[235] Any replies made to statements by the police which were "likely to provoke a response" (whether or not the police had that intention) will be equally inadmissible.[236] An answer, made by the accused in a police office after he had been charged, to a question put, not to him but to another police officer, was disallowed on the ground that he might

---

[226] *HM Advocate v Laing* (1871) 2 Coup 23; *HM Advocate v Aitken* 1926 JC 83, per Lord Anderson at 86; *HM Advocate v McFadyen* 1926 JC 93; *Wade v Robertson* 1948 JC 117, per Lord Justice-Clerk Thomson at 120. In leading the reply in evidence, however, the prosecutor must consider whether it would be exceptionable on some other ground, such as in *HM Advocate v Graham* 1984 SLT 67, when it disclosed the previous record of the accused, and was held to be in contravention of statutory provision prohibiting the prosecutor from laying the record before the court before conviction. See also para 7.9.
[227] *Tonge v HM Advocate* 1982 JC 130.
[228] *Tonge v HM Advocate* 1982 JC 130.
[229] *Chalmers v HM Advocate* 1954 JC 66, per Lord Justice-General Cooper at 77 and Lord Strachan (trial judge) at 69–70. See also *Robertson* (1853) 1 Irv 219.
[230] *HM Advocate v McSwiggan* 1937 JC 50.
[231] *Robertson v Maxwell* 1951 JC 11 at 14. See para 9.6.2.
[232] *Heywood v Smith* 1989 SCCR 391.
[233] Note that this may depend on the particular detail of the charge and not simply the *nomen juris*: *cf Sproull v McGlennan* 1999 JC 105. In *HM Advocate v McTavish* 1975 SLT (Notes) 27 a reply to a charge of assault was held admissible in a trial for murder. See also *HM Advocate v Cunningham* 1939 JC 61, but see *James Stewart* (1866) 5 Irv 310; *HM Advocate v Graham* 1958 SLT 167.
[234] *McAdam v HM Advocate* 1960 JC 1. See also *HM Advocate v Taylor* 1963 SLT 53.
[235] *HM Advocate v Aitken* 1926 JC 83, per Lord Anderson at 86; *Stark and Smith v HM Advocate* 1938 JC 170; *Wade v Robertson* 1948 JC 117; *MacDonald v HM Advocate* 1987 SCCR 581; *Carmichael v Boyd* 1993 JC 219; *Aiton v HM Advocate* 1987 JC 41; *HM Advocate v Penders* 1996 JC 107. Earlier suggestions in such cases as *Paterson* (1842) 1 Broun 388, *Wylie* (1858) 3 Irv 218 and *Gracie v Stuart* (1884) 11 R (J) 22 that questions may be put at the time when the charge is made must now be regarded as unacceptable.
[236] *Jack v HM Advocate* 1999 SLT 749. *Cf Aiton v HM Advocate* 1987 JC 41.

mistakenly have thought that the question was addressed to him.[237] Questioning in relation to other matters is acceptable, even where there appears to be a possible connection between the two matters.[238]

9.20 UNFAIRNESS—VOLUNTARY STATEMENTS

Where a suspect indicates to police officers that he wishes to make a voluntary **9.20.1** statement, it is proper practice for this to be taken by officers unconnected with the investigation,[239] and the suspect should be advised that he is entitled to consult with a solicitor before making a statement.[240] A failure to comply with either of these requirements will not necessarily render the statement inadmissible but is a factor to be taken into account in applying the fairness test.[241] It is unlikely that it will be objectionable for the statement to be taken by an officer connected with the investigation whom the suspect specifically requests to speak to,[242] particularly where the suspect is advised that it would be better to speak to another officer.[243] While it is also proper practice for the suspect to be cautioned before making a voluntary statement, a failure to caution will not necessarily render the confession inadmissible if the suspect has previously been cautioned and can be expected to be aware that he is not obliged to say anything.[244] A suspect who elects to make a voluntary statement should not be questioned any more than is necessary to elucidate the meaning of the statement.[245]

9.21 UNFAIRNESS—CONFESSIONS TO UNOFFICIAL PERSONS

It is now accepted that confessions made to persons not associated with the **9.21.1** judiciary, prosecutor or police are subject to the usual test of fairness in determining their admissibility.[246] The courts, however, will bear in mind that such

---

[237] *HM Advocate v Lieser* 1926 JC 88.

[238] *Carmichael v Boyd* 1993 JC 219.

[239] *Tonge v HM Advocate* 1982 JC 130, per Lord Cameron at 147; *Paton v Ritchie* 2000 JC 271 at 276B–C. Cf *Thompson v HM Advocate* 1968 JC 61. The investigating officer should not be present when the statement is taken, but unless he actively participates this is unlikely to render the statement inadmissible: *Rodgers v Hamilton* 1993 GWD 30-1863.

[240] *HM Advocate v Olsson* 1941 JC 63; *Paton v Ritchie* 2000 JC 271 at 276B.

[241] *Cordiner v HM Advocate* 1993 SLT 2; *HM Advocate v Olsson* 1941 JC 63; *HM Advocate v Fox* 1947 JC 30.

[242] *Cordiner v HM Advocate* 1993 SLT 2. See also *HM Advocate v Olsson* 1941 JC 63, where the statement was not objected to on this ground but was held inadmissible for other reasons.

[243] In *Hartley v HM Advocate* 1979 SLT 26, H indicated that he wished to make a statement and was told that it would have to be to an officer unconnected with the investigation. He insisted on speaking to a particular officer who was connected with the investigation and was allowed to do so. No objection appears to have been raised to the admissibility of his statement on this ground.

[244] *Mills v HM Advocate* 1935 JC 77. See also *Wilson v Heywood* 1989 SLT 279; *Young v Friel* 1992 SCCR 567.

[245] *Manuel v HM Advocate* 1958 JC 41, per Lord Justice-General Clyde at 48.

[246] *HM Advocate v Friel* 1978 SLT (Notes) 21 (customs & excise officers); *McCuaig v Annan* 1986 SCCR 535 (store employee); *Irving v Jessop* 1988 SLT 53 (which overrules *Walkingshaw v McIntyre* 1985 SCCR 389 (Sh Ct)) (television licence inspectors); *Pennycuick v Lees* 1992 SLT 763 (DSS investigators); *Williams v Friel* 1999 JC 28 (immigration officer). See also *Morrison v Burrell* 1947 JC 43; cf *Waddell v Kinnaird* 1922 JC 40.

persons may well not know how to administer a caution.[247] Most of the reported cases are concerned with persons who have assumed some kind of investigatory role, but in one case a confession made by an accused to his brother was held admissible.[248]

9.22 CONFESSIONS OBTAINED UNDER STATUTORY COMPULSION

9.22.1 There are a number of statutory provisions which make it a criminal offence not to provide certain information or to answer certain questions when asked by specified persons.[249] The statute may expressly provide that the reply is admissible against the person who gives it, that it is not admissible, or that it is admissible for certain purposes only. Where there is no express provision, "the question whether such answers are admissible evidence must depend on the proper construction of the particular statute."[250]

9.22.2 In *HM Advocate v Von*,[251] Lord Ross drew a distinction between statutory powers to question suspects and non-suspects. In the former case, it is to be presumed that Parliament has not intended to alter the principle against self-incrimination in the absence of clear language to the contrary, and a suspect should be warned that they are not obliged to incriminate themselves before questioning.[252] In the latter, it would appear that there is no such presumption.[253]

9.22.3 However, Parliamentary abrogation of the principle against self-incrimination may conflict with Convention rights,[254] and it was held recently in *Brown v Stott*[255] that where the police invoke section 172 of the Road Traffic Act 1988,[256] under which the owner of a vehicle may be required to state who was driving it at the time an offence was committed, evidence of an incriminating reply may not be led in a subsequent prosecution of the owner. It cannot be said that this decision applies to all similar provisions, as the High Court indicated that the situation might be different where (a) there is something "exceptional, either in the nature of the offence or in the difficulties of proof"[257] justifying such a provision, or (b) the provision can be seen to serve a wider regulatory purpose as opposed simply to the obtaining of incriminating evidence.[258]

9.22.4 Where Convention rights do not require the exclusion of evidence obtained

---

[247] *McCuaig v Annan* 1986 SCCR 535; *Irving v Jessop* 1988 SLT 53.

[248] *HM Advocate v Parker* 1944 JC 49.

[249] See Heydon, "Statutory Restrictions on the Privilege Against Self-Incrimination" (1971) 87 LQR 214.

[250] *Commissioners of Customs & Excise v Harz* [1967] 1 AC 760, per Lord Reid at 816.

[251] 1979 SLT (Notes) 62.

[252] *HM Advocate v Von* 1979 SLT (Notes) 62.

[253] *Foster v Farrell* 1963 JC 46.

[254] The European Court of Human Rights has found the right not to incriminate oneself to be implicit in Article 6 of the Convention: see *Funke v France* (1993) 16 EHRR 297; *Saunders v UK* (1997) 23 EHRR 313.

[255] 2000 JC 328 (under appeal).

[256] The predecessor of which was considered by Lord Ross in *Von* to be a power to question "non-suspects", which meant that it was unnecessary to caution the car's owner before invoking the power.

[257] *Brown v Stott* 2000 JC 328 at 346D.

[258] *Brown v Stott* 2000 JC 328 at 346–353. For example, the statutory obligation, backed up by criminal sanctions, to lodge company accounts with Companies House—which might well be incriminatory—would probably fall into this category: Companies Act 1985, ss 241(3), 243. *Cf Abas v Netherlands* [1997] EHRLR 418.

through the exercise of such powers, any incriminatory statements obtained are still inadmissible if they were unfairly obtained,[259] although a caution is clearly unnecessary and inappropriate as where such powers are invoked there is an obligation to answer.[260]

---

[259] *Styr v HM Advocate* 1993 JC 74.
[260] *Foster v Farrell* 1963 JC 46; *Styr v HM Advoca* 1993 JC 74.

CHAPTER 10

CONFIDENTIALITY

10.1 GENERAL

Evidence of communications, written or oral, may be excluded on the ground that **10.1.1** they were confidential. Except where indicated, the confidentiality discussed here amounts to privilege in the sense that it overrides the relevance of the communication and the desirability of its disclosure. With certain exceptions, communications between husband and wife[1] and professional communications between solicitor and client[2] are confidential, viz they can be withheld from evidence although they are relevant to an issue.[3] Generally speaking, communications between other persons are not confidential in this sense,[4] unless they have passed in connection with the preparation of the case (in other words have been made *post litem motam*: after an action has been commenced or contemplated),[5] or during an attempt to reconcile the parties,[6] or where their confidentiality must be protected in the public interest.[7] Where there is doubt whether communications are confidential the court can decide by reading the documents,[8] or, in the case of oral evidence, by allowing it under reservation.[9] An undespatched letter or a private diary while not a communication is confidential, but confidentiality may be waived

---

[1] See paras 13.7–13.10.

[2] See para 10.2. For a detailed discussion of the position up to 1987, see Ogston and Seager, "Legal Professional Privilege", 1987 JR 38.

[3] In the first edition of this text the authors included communications between partners within the plea of confidentiality, citing as authority for that proposition *Tannett, Walker & Co v Hannay & Sons* (1873) 11 M 931 and *Pearson v Anderson Brothers* (1897) 5 SLT 177 (OH). As Macphail points out at para 18.52, these authorities are explicable on the *post litem motam* ground and there is no other authority before or since, nor academic commentary, in support of this statement. Macphail's interpretation of the case law which follows that of, *inter alia*, Lewis, *Manual of the Law of Evidence in Scotland*, p 193, has been preferred in this edition.

[4] There may be a relationship between persons through which a duty of confidentiality arises in the popular sense. See para 10.6.

[5] See para 10.4.

[6] See paras 10.7 and 10.8.

[7] See para 10.9.

[8] *Clippens Oil Co Ltd v Edinburgh and District Water Trustees* (1906) 8 F 731 at 742; *Munro v Fraser* (1858) 21 D 103; *Hay, Thomson and Blair v Edinburgh and Glasgow Bank* (1858) 20 D 701.

[9] *MacNeill v MacNeill* 1929 SLT 251 (OH).

expressly or implicitly—for example, by leaving it lying about.[10] The question of confidentiality is most frequently raised on a motion for approval of a specification of documents,[11] and the bulk of reported desisions are of the Outer House. Confidentiality is not the only reason for refusing approval[12]: the averments may not justify the call,[13] or, in the exercise of its discretion, the court may refuse the call as unreasonable.[14] In one case reports were held confidential after a certain date, but the significance of the date does not appear from the report,[15] and others are of questionable guidance.[16]

10.1.2   It has been argued that the protection of confidentiality encroaches upon the right of the accused to a fair trial in terms of the European Convention on Human Rights, Article 6.[17] However, the European Court of Human Rights has stated that if a right to seek disclosure exists, albeit that it may be overriden by the confidential interest to be protected, this is consistent with the right to a fair trial[18] and a similar view has been expressed in Scotland[19] and in England.[20]

10.2 SOLICITOR AND CLIENT

Extent of confidentiality

10.2.1   As a general rule, a solicitor is neither entitled nor bound, without the client's consent, to disclose information communicated to the solicitor by the client for professional purposes, viz for the purpose of either seeking advice or giving instructions, nor is the solicitor entitled or bound without such consent to disclose the advice given. After some variations in judicial opinion,[21] it is now settled that such communications "are privileged, although they may not relate to any suit depending or contemplated or apprehended."[22] This dictum was *obiter*, since the

---

[10] *Watson v Watson* 1934 SC 374; *Creasey v Creasey* 1931 SC 9. An admission on record of its existence is not enough: *Duke of Argyll v Duchess of Argyll* 1962 SC (HL) 88. See also para 9.10.

[11] See para 21.10.

[12] See paras 21.3 and 21.5.1. Many of the decisions are what the first Lord President Clyde once described as "waifs and strays from the Outer House". In several there is no opinion, and it is impossible to tell on which of the grounds argued, if these are stated, the Lord Ordinary proceeded.

[13] eg *Earl of Morton v Fleming* 1921 1 SLT 205 (OH); *Northern Garage Ltd v North British Motor Manufacturing Co Ltd* (1908) 16 SLT 573 (OH). See paras 21.5.1 and 21.10.

[14] *William Whiteley Ltd v Dobson, Molle & Co Ltd* (1902) 10 SLT 71 (OH); *Simcock v Scottish Imperial Ins Co* (1901) 9 SLT 234 (OH).

[15] *Sutherland v John Ritchie & Co* (1900) 8 SLT 100 (OH); and, *quoad* reports by servants, see *Tannett, Walker & Co v Hannay & Sons* (1873) 11 M 931.

[16] Confidentiality was reserved in *Logan v Miller* 1920 1 SLT 211 (OH); *Thomson v Thomson* (1907) 14 SLT 643 (OH); *Macbride v Caledonian Railway Co* (1894) 2 SLT 61 (OH), so the decisions are of no guidance. *MacKinnon v National SS Co* (1904) 12 SLT 411 (OH) was decided on the ground that the documents could not be evidence and could only be used in cross, but this decision was influenced by the supposed effect of *Livingstone v Dinwoodie* (1860) 22 D 1333. It is now recognised that this decision had a much more limited effect. See para 21.6.

[17] A point mentioned in *Science Research Council v Nasse; Leyland Cars v Vyas* [1980] AC 1028; and in *McLeod v HM Advocate (No 2)* 1998 JC 67.

[18] *Edwards v United Kingdom* Series A No 247-B (1993) 15 EHRR 417, followed in *Rowe and Davis v United Kingdom* [2000] TLR 147.

[19] *McLeod v HM Advocate* 1998 JC 67.

[20] *Science Research Council v Nasse; Leyland Cars v Vyas* [1980] AC 1028.

[21] See Dickson, *Evidence* (3rd edn), paras 1670–1674.

[22] *McCowan v Wright* (1852) 15 D 229, per Lord Wood at 237. Lord Justice-Clerk Hope said the same at 231, 232. In *Munro v Fraser* (1858) 21 D 103, Lord President McNeill founded on Lord Wood's dictum. Also *Micosta SA v Shetland Islands Council* 1983 SLT 483. In *Leslie v Grant* (1760) 5 Brown's

case was decided on averments of fraud, but it has never been disapproved or criticised, and obviously if the privilege were restricted to communications relating to an action pending or apprehended, a solicitor's position would be no different from that of any other person. The purpose of the rule is to enable a person to consult a solicitor freely, without the risk of what passed between them being revealed to some future opponent. For example, when a tenant made over the crop to his landlord and then sold the turnips to a third party, the landlord consulted his solicitor as to whether he should sue the purchaser for the price of the turnips, but did not sue. It was held in an appeal by the landlord against a deliverance by the trustee in sequestration of the landlord that the communications about the turnips were confidential, although at the time they passed no one could have contemplated that appeal.[23]

The privilege extends only to information obtained in a professional capacity[24] but subsists in relation to anything passing between solicitor and client during that relationship, and should be pled even after the relationship has ended.[25] The effect on the privilege of the relationship ending due to the death of solicitor or client is not the subject of clear authority. A suggestion that the plea cannot be taken if the solicitor is dead[26] is not supported by authority[27] and it is suggested that the solicitor's successors should take the plea unless confidentiality has been waived by the client. It has been suggested that if the client dies, and is thus unable to waive the privilege, the right to waive passes to the client's executors for the sole purpose of fulfilling the executors' functions, but that in all other situations, including claims by third parties on the estate, the solicitor or the executors should assert the privilege.[28] However, in one case for declarator of marriage the plea of confidentiality was repelled on appeal in the special circumstances of the case in respect of communications between the alleged husband (deceased) and his solicitors.[29] **10.2.2**

It has been held that a statement made by an accused to a solicitor who then declined to act was not confidential[30]; however, the judgment was made in the trial court with some reservation, and because the trial resulted in a not proven verdict the question was not referred to the High Court as the trial judge had anticipated when making the judgment. The judgment, if correct,[31] displays a hard doctrine[32] and one which is unlikely to be known or understood by those prospective clients who disclose information to a solicitor only to find that the solicitor declines to act in the matter to which the information relates. It has been suggested that **10.2.3**

Supp 874, cited by Edward in "The Professional Secret, Confidentiality and Legal Professional Privilege in the Nine Member States of the European Community" (1978) 23 JLSS 19 the confidentiality covered "everything the lawyer was informed of" as lawyer in the case.

[23] *Munro v Fraser* (1858) 21 D 103. For another example, see *Lady Bath's Exrs v Johnston*, 12 Nov 1811, FC.

[24] Dickson, *Evidence* (3rd edn), para 1668; Hume, ii 350.

[25] Dickson, *Evidence* (3rd edn), para 1664.

[26] Field & Raitt, *Evidence* (2nd edn), para 12-38.

[27] Perhaps it could be inferred from the outcome in *Davie* (1881) 4 Coup 450 that the professional relationship of solicitor and client would be broken by the solicitor's death—or that on the death of the solicitor the communications inevitably fall into the hands of a third party—but public policy would favour protection of the client's confidentiality until a new solicitor can be appointed.

[28] Wilkinson, *The Scottish Law of Evidence*, p 96, citing *Mackenzie v Mackenzie's Trs* 1916 1 SLT 271.

[29] *Mackenzie v Mackenzie's Trs* 1916 1 SLT 271, a very special case decided partly on the ground that status was in issue.

[30] *Davie* (1881) 4 Coup 450.

[31] For a criticism, see Black, "A Question of Confidence" (1982) 27 JLSS 299 and 389.

[32] The opposite was held in England: *Minter v Priest* [1930] AC 558; Cross & Tapper (9th edn), p 446.

information passed to a solicitor in contemplation of a solicitor–client relationship and which is fairly referable to that relationship, should be confidential.[33] It has also been said that the privilege extends only to what the client has communicated and not what the solicitor has personally observed about the client,[34] such as bloodstained clothing. However, there is only English authority in this respect,[35] and the Scottish and English rules of confidentiality and legal privilege are not the same in many respects.[36] It is submitted that to limit the rule in such a way is not defensible and indeed is subversive of the privilege if the only way in which the solicitor has come to observe the client's bloodstained clothing is through the client seeking legal advice. Surely there can be no distinction between what a client discloses orally and what is physically disclosed; understanding of one may be dependent upon the other. The position would be different if the solicitor saw the client in this condition without any "professional communication" taking place, in which case there would be no confidentiality.

10.2.4   Statements made by a solicitor to the client are not confidential if the only purpose is to show that the statement was made. Where the defenders averred delay on the part of the pursuer in making his claim, confidentiality did not attach to correspondence between the defenders and their solicitors in so far as it tended to instruct an earlier claim.[37] There is no confidentiality when the existence of the relationship of solicitor and client or the extent of the solicitor's authority is in issue. In an action against a solicitor for payment of the expenses of a previous action in which the pursuers averred that the defender had been *dominus litis* and acted without instructions, they obtained a diligence to recover correspondence between the defender and the alleged client, a plea of confidentiality being repelled.[38] Where parties were in dispute as to the terms on which a previous action had been settled, the pursuer obtained a diligence to recover letters between the defender and his solicitor so far as tending to establish the solicitor's authority to settle and the defender's approval of the settlement.[39]

10.2.5   There is no confidentiality if it is averred that the communications were made for the purpose of the client obtaining advice or assistance in committing a crime or other illegal act,[40] and the solicitor was directly concerned or involved in the carrying out of the criminal or illegal transaction.[41] Therefore, in an action of damages for an abuse of power by a local authority in the act of its harbourmaster, communications between the authority and its law agents were confidential since they were no more than advice about the intended act of the harbourmaster, with the law agents playing no part in the execution of the act itself. The court rejected the pursuer's proposal that the confidentiality should be lost if the communications are directly relevant to the intention or state of mind of the defender at the relevant

---

[33] Macphail, *Evidence*, para 18.21, which would accord with the more liberal situation in England.
[34] Wilkinson, p 95; Field & Raitt, para 12-40.
[35] Cited by Wilkinson at p 95, n 5.
[36] *eg Bursill v Tanner* (1883) 13 QBD 691, cited by Wilkinson in partial support of this statement, was not applied in Scotland in *Conoco (UK) Ltd v The Commercial Law Practice* 1997 SLT 372.
[37] *Anderson v Lord Elgin's Trs* (1859) 21 D 654. It is not clear from the report whether solicitors were involved, but the headnote contains the words "agent and client", and Dickson treats it as a solicitor and client case: *Evidence* (3rd edn), para 1677.
[38] *Fraser v Malloch* (1895) 3 SLT 211 (OH).
[39] *Kid v Bunyan* (1842) 5 D 193. Lord Fullerton referred to the Lord Ordinary's "guarded" interlocutor, to which the Inner House adhered.
[40] *McCowan v Wright* (1852) 15 D 229; *Morrison v Somerville* (1860) 23 D 232; *Millar v Small* (1856) 19 D 142.
[41] *Micosta SA v Shetland Islands Council* 1983 SLT 483.

time, as an exception which "would open the door so widely as largely to render worthless the general rule which our law has always regarded as of the highest importance".[42] However, in an application heard in the Outer House,[43] the exception was extended to a communication between client and solicitor in connection with the client's proposal to offer information to an offshore operating company which would enable that company to identify the recipient of an overpayment of more than £1 million made by the company some years previously. The client sought a share of any recovery in exchange for the information, and his proposal had been put in a letter from the solicitor in which the identity of the client was withheld.[44] The facts were held to merit application of the "illegal act" exception because the recipient of the overpayment had acted fraudulently in invoicing for a greater sum than he knew to be due, and the client and solicitor had become involved in the client's attempt to derive benefit from that fraud. While accepting that the facts fell on the very borderline of rule and exception, with no direct precedent, and not obviously meeting the existing test for the exception,[45] the Lord Ordinary nevertheless decided that the public policy underlying the protection of confidentiality was outweighed by the public policy in favour of disclosure.[46] The only communication of which recovery was sought was the identity of the client and the court confirmed that in Scotland identity would normally fall within solicitor and client confidentiality.[47]

The privilege extends to communications with advocates, solicitor-advocates,[48] **10.2.6** their clerks and assistants,[49] solicitors who are also employees of the client as in-house counsel,[50] licensed conveyancers and registered executry practitioners[51] and probably to those made to an intermediary for transmission to or from any of these persons.[52] In England it has been extended to those performing functions usually undertaken by solicitors.[53] The position with communications that fall into the hands of a third party has not been decided authoritatively.[54] If the client intentionally or carelessly passes the communication to a third party this may consititute implied waiver, as might acquiescence in the situation once known to the

---

[42] *Micosta SA v Shetland Islands Council* 1983 SLT 483, per Lord President Emslie at 485.

[43] For recovery under the Administration of Justice (Scotland) Act 1972, s 1(1A), see para 18.3.

[44] *Conoco (UK) Ltd v The Commercial Law Practice* 1997 SLT 372.

[45] As defined in *Micosta SA v Shetland Islands Council* 1983 SLT 483.

[46] *Conoco (UK) Ltd v The Commercial Law Practice* 1997 SLT 372 at 380L. For a discussion of the case, see O'Donnell, "A Question of Privilege: *Conoco v The Commercial Law Practice*" (1997) 2 SLPQ 162.

[47] *Conoco (UK) Ltd v The Commercial Law Practice* 1997 SLT 372 at 378G–K, contrary to the English position as set down in *Bursill v Tanner* (1885) 16 QBD 1 and contrary to comments by Wilkinson at p 95 and Ogston and Seager, "Legal Professional Privilege", 1987 JR 38 at 47.

[48] *ie* solicitors who have been afforded extended rights of audience as provided for in the Law Reform (Miscellaneous Provisions) (Scotland) Act 1990, s 25.

[49] Dickson, *Evidence* (3rd edn), para 1665.

[50] *Alfred Crompton Amusement Machines v Customs & Excise Commissioners* [1972] 2 QB 102. *Cf* the situation under EC law, where the confidentiality cannot be claimed by an in-house laywer: *AM & S Europe Ltd v Commissioners of the European Communities* [1983] QB 878, except when reporting the opinion of external counsel, *Hilti v Commissioners of the European Communities* T30/89, 1991. The policy of protecting the confidentiality of communications with in-house lawyers in proceedings before the ECJ is under review.

[51] Law Reform (Miscellaneous Provisions) (Scotland) Act 1990, s 22(1).

[52] Dickson, *Evidence* (3rd edn), para 1666; *Stuart v Millar* (1836) 14 S 837, per Lord Justice-Clerk Boyle and Lord Medwyn; *contra* Lord Glenlee.

[53] *Prince Jefri Bolkiah v KPMG* [1999] 2 WLR 215 (accountants).

[54] For a discussion, see Macphail, *Evidence*, paras 18.22–18.23

client. If the client plays no part in the information falling into the hands of a third party it is hard to rationalise the loss of the privilege, since the need for its protection has not changed. However, the contrary argument is that once a communication is known beyond the solicitor–client relationship it no longer needs to be protected. This issue has taxed the English courts with contradictory results,[55] apparently dependent upon whether the communication was obtained by the third party improperly. In Scotland communications which are confidential in the popular sense are admissible at the hands of third parties into whose possession they have fallen,[56] although it has been suggested that before admitting such evidence the whole circumstances should be considered and a balance struck between the importance of having all relevant evidence, the excuse for any irregularity and the protection of the confidentiality.[57] The title to plead confidentiality is with the client[58] and, if the client waives it,[59] the solicitor, if a witness, must answer, and, if a haver, must produce.[60] A party who is not the client has taken the plea without objection.[61] If the client calls the solicitor as a witness, there is no confidentiality.[62]

10.2.7 In some circumstances the privilege is affected by statute.[63] It is protected and extended by the Copyright, Designs and Patents Act 1988,[64] the Data Protection Act 1998[65] and the Criminal Law (Consolidation) (Scotland) Act 1995[66] but apparently overridden by the obligation in the Bankruptcy (Scotland) Act 1985 to answer "all lawful questions" in a public examination,[67] and in the context of written communications between prisoners and their lawyers is tempered by the prison governor's power of censorship.[68] Other statutory obligations to reveal information, under pain of prosecution, such as that relating to road traffic

---

[55] For a discussion, see Cross & Tapper *Evidence* (9th edn), p 450, referring particularly to the apparent conflict between *Calcraft v Guest* [1898] 1 QB 759 and *Lord Ashburton v Pape* [1913] 2 Ch 469, but explained to some extent in *Webster v James Chapman & Co* [1989] 3 All ER 939.

[56] *Rattray v Rattray* (1897) 25 R 315.

[57] Per Lord Wheatley in *Duke of Argyll v Duchess of Argyll* 1963 SLT (Notes) 42; Macphail, *Evidence* paras 21.14–S21.15; Scottish Law Commission Memorandum No 46, paras U.05–U.06.

[58] In *Williamson v HM Advocate* 1980 JC 22 an accused person asked in cross-examination why he had lodged, but then withdrawn, a special defence, stated that the solicitor had lodged it contrary to instructions. It was held on appeal that no issue of confidentiality arose when the question was asked of the client, but different considerations would have arisen if the question had been put to the solicitor: per Lord Justice-Clerk Wheatley at 25.

[59] Waiver may be implied from the client's reliance upon part of the communication in their own pleadings or evidence: *Duke of Argyll v Duchess of Argyll* 1962 SC (HL) 88; *Wylie v Wylie* 1967 SLT (Notes) 9, but the fact that the court has already seen the document for a limited purpose does not constitute waiver in relation to its contents: *Barclay v Morris* 1998 SC 74.

[60] Bell, *Principles*, para 2254; Dickson, *Evidence* (3rd edn), para 1682.

[61] *Lady Bath's Exrs v Johnston* 12 Nov 1811, FC.

[62] Evidence (Scotland) Act 1852, s 1.

[63] For a discussion of the position in 1990, see Maher, "Professional Privilege" (1990) 35 JLSS 108–112, 138–142. It should be noted that some statutes define the privilege broadly, in common with English authorities, to include both professional communications between lawyer and client, and communications made in connection with or in contemplation of legal proceedings and for the purposes of those proceedings (*eg* Criminal Law (Consolidation) (Scotland) Act 1995, s 33) and would thus appear to include all communications *post litem motam*.

[64] ss 280–284.

[65] s 35(2)(a) (exemption from non-disclosure) and Sched 7, para 10 (exemption from subject information provisions).

[66] ss 28–33 (investigations of serious or complex fraud and of drug-trafficking).

[67] s 47(3) and *Sawers v Balgarnie* (1858) 21 D 153.

[68] Under the Prison (Scotland) Rules 1952 (SI 1952/565), r 74; noted to cover letters from the prisoner client to the solicitor in *Leech v Secretary of State for Scotland* 1992 SC 89.

offences[69] have not been tested against this privilege.[70] Whether public interest can outweigh the privilege or preclude its operation, such as when a client tells the solicitor that he has committed a crime for which another person has been prosecuted or that he is about to commit a serious crime, has not been tested in the Scottish courts but has been discussed hypothetically.[71] In England the privilege has been upheld against a request for disclosure relevant to the conduct of a defence in criminal proceedings,[72] but apparently has been overridden in proceedings concerning children, on the premise that the court's overriding duty there is to the interests of the child.[73]

10.3 *POST LITEM MOTAM*—MEANING

Communications to or by a litigant in connection with investigations into an accident, an alleged breach of contract, a family dispute, or other event giving rise to the action, are, generally speaking, confidential. "The general rule is that no party can recover from another material which that other party has made in preparing his case."[74] This, it is thought, is the true meaning of the proposition that communications *post litem motam* are confidential. So stated, the proposition is too wide. First, the mere date of the communication is immaterial. Secondly, an admission, confession or indeed a casual remark about the dispute is not necessarily confidential. It must be something said or written with a view to preparation of the case. A report obtained after the action has commenced is, in the ordinary case, confidential,[75] but the rule is much wider. It applies not "merely after the summons has been raised, but after it is apparent that there is going to be a litigious contention,"[76] or, as soon as litigation is "threatened or mooted".[77] There is *lis mota* (here defined as "litigation contemplated") "after an accident, and even before any claim has been made,"[78] "once the parties are at arm's length, or are   **10.3.1**

---

[69] Road Traffic Act 1988, s 172, although the provision has been held to breach an individual's privilege against self-incrimination, *Brown v Stott* 2000 JC 328 (under appeal). See para 9.22. Another, more serious, example was the Prevention of Terrorism (Temporary Provisions) Act 1989, s 18(1).

[70] Maher (1990) 35 JLSS at 139 assumes, following an English decision forcing a doctor to disclose under the Road Traffic provision (*Hunter v Mann* [1974] QB 767), that the same would apply to lawyers, although the only basis for so assuming is that the provision does not expressly preserve the solicitor–client privilege.

[71] Black, "A Question of Confidence" (1982) 27 JLSS 299 and 389.

[72] *R v Derby Magistrates, ex parte B* [1995] 4 All ER 526.

[73] In *Re L (A Minor) (Police Investigation: Privilege)* [1996] 2 All ER 78, the order included disclosure to the police whereas in earlier cases (such as *Oxfordshire County Council v M* [1994] 2 All ER 269) the order had been for disclosure within the proceedings of a report that had in any event been ordered by the court and might therefore be argued to be outwith legal professional privilege.

[74] *Anderson v St Andrews Ambulance Association* 1942 SC 555 at 557.

[75] *Clippens Oil Co Ltd v Edinburgh and District Water Trustees* (1906) 8 F 731 at 740.

[76] *Admiralty v Aberdeen Steam Trawling and Fishing Co* 1909 SC 335 at 340.

[77] *Whitehill v Glasgow Corporation* 1915 SC 1015.

[78] *Young v National Coal Board* 1957 SC 99 at 101, 106, 108. In *Anderson v St Andrews Ambulance Association* 1942 SC 555, photographs of the locus of an accident taken the day after were held confidential; see, too, *Meaney v Plumbe* 1997 SLT (Sh Ct) 87. In *Secretary of State for Trade and Industry v Houston (No 2)* 1995 SLT 196 a report by a liquidator on whether directors of the liquidated company met criteria for possible disqualification under the Company Directors Disqualification Act 1986 was held to be confidential *post litem motam*; but for the opposite outcome in an identical English case see *Secretary of State for Trade and Industry v Baker (No 2)* [1998] 1 All ER 673. *Cf Black v Bairds & Dalmellington* 1939 SC 472, where a report of a post mortem examination was held not confidential *quoad* the facts stated.

obviously going to be at arm's length."[79] These opinions accord with modern conditions, when as soon as an accident occurs the victim personally or through representatives consults a solicitor and the potential payee intimates the possibililty of a claim, in terms of any policy, to the insurance company. A similar extension applies in breach of contract. A dispute under a mining lease arose in 1848, but the action was not raised till 1852. The Lord Ordinary repelled an objection to the confidentiality of engineers' reports obtained by the pursuer in 1848 and 1851, but the Lord Justice-Clerk clearly thought he ought not to have done so, presumably on the ground that there was *lis mota* in 1848.[80]

10.3.2   A communication made in contemplation of litigation does not lose that confidentiality if the litigation never occurs or is concluded.[81] A communication which has fallen into the hands of a third party and thence into the hands of the opposing party may be used by that party on the basis that it has lost its confidentiality on transmission to the third party.[82] This was the decision in an Outer House case in which the communication had been passed on by mistake, but the situation may be the same even if the communication was obtained irregularly.[83] While confidentiality for communications *post litem motam* exists to enable a party to pursue investigations into the cause of an incident without fear of having to reveal that information to the other side,[84] procedural rules require disclosure before proof of reports or other communications upon which a party will wish to found pleadings[85] or lead evidence.[86] In England the view has been taken that procedural disclosure does not *per se* impinge upon confidentiality.[87] The confidentiality is waived by the incorporation into evidence during proof. If a witness is asked in cross-examination about communications *post litem motam* with the party leading that witness which are not founded upon in evidence the plea may be taken,[88] but a party who founds upon part of a privileged communication cannot take the plea in relation to other parts of it.[89] In litigation which the parties elect to have dealt with as a Commercial Action under Chapter 47 of the Rules of the Court of Session,[90] the procedure is accelerated, the role of the judge is interventionist and proactive, and the judge can require parties to reveal the existence of relevant documents, and require presentation of them to the court, all with a view to achieving early determination of the issues. Parties electing for such procedure effectively relinquish

---

[79] *Young v National Coal Board* 1957 SC 99 at 105.

[80] *Wark v Bargeddie Coal Co* (1855) 17 D 526; (1859) 3 Macq 467 at 488.

[81] *Hunter v Douglas Reyburn & Co Ltd* 1993 SLT 637. In this case confidentiality was successfully pled by the defenders in relation to reports obtained for earlier proceedings by another pursuer on similar grounds. The decision was followed in *Ward v Marine Harvest Ltd* 1997 SLT 469, where the facts were similar.

[82] In *McLeish v Glasgow Bonding Co Ltd* 1965 SLT 39 the communication was admitted for cross-examination.

[83] If the reasoning in *Rattray v Rattray* (1897) 25 R 315 is followed.

[84] *Young v National Coal Board* 1957 SC 99; *Johnstone v National Coal Board* 1968 SC 128; *More v Brown & Root Wimpey Highland Fabricators Ltd* 1983 SLT 669.

[85] RCS, Chapter 27; OCR, Chapter 21.

[86] RCS, r 36.3; OCR, r 29.11 and see Chapter 16.

[87] *Fairfield-Mabey v Shell UK Ltd* [1989] 1 All ER 576.

[88] As in *Santa Fe International Corporation v Napier Shipping SA* 1985 SLT 481, dealing with interpretation of the privilege as it applied in patent proceedings.

[89] *Wylie v Wylie* 1967 SLT (Notes) 9, unless the other parts have been withheld from that party during the discovery process, as in, *eg, Hepburn v Scottish Power* 1997 SC 80; *Anderson v Hingston* 1997 SLT 844.

[90] As read with Court of Session Practice Note No 12 of 1994 (Commercial Actions).

the *post litem motam* confidentiality in exchange for the frankness and speed of this procedure.[91]

10.4 *POST LITEM MOTAM*—APPLICATION

General

The plea of confidentiality was sustained in respect of communications between a **10.4.1** head office and one of its branches after the dispute had arisen.[92] Some judicial resistance was shown to the plea being upheld in relation to parts of communications,[93] but it is now accepted that the communication can be put to a commissioner for separation of the parts which are privileged from those that fall within one of the exceptions discussed below.[94] The exception that proves the rule occurred in an action of damages for wrongously obtaining and insisting in an interim interdict. An engineer's report was made to the defenders after the granting of the interim interdict, and this was held not to be confidential, or at least not wholly confidential, on the special ground that the state of knowledge of the defenders when they continued to insist in the interim interdict was important.[95] Efforts have been made to assimilate the position of a layman assisting a litigant to that of a solicitor, and this attempt has led to some apparent difference of judicial opinion.[96] Efforts have also been made to redefine the privilege in terms of fairness and efficacy[97] to be balanced by judicial discretion. However, these efforts have been rejected[98] in favour of the distinct privilege as traditionally understood[99] and limited exceptions which are discussed next.

Reports by employees

By an apparently arbitrary exception to the general rule,[100] reports by an employee **10.4.2**

---

[91] Lord Cullen, in his report on *Review of Business of the Outer House of the Court of Session*, Chapter 5, recommends that in all civil proceedings evidence gathered should be subject to early disclosure.
[92] *Hay, Thomson and Blair v Edinburgh and Glasgow Bank* (1858) 20 D 701; *Rose v Medical Invalid Ins Co* (1847) 10 D 156, where the defenders' local agent was called as a defender. Dickson (*Evidence* (3rd edn), para 1658) cites this case in a chapter headed "Communications between parties on the same side of the cause". This seems misleading. Communications between such parties *ante litem motam* are not necessarily confidential.
[93] In *Marks & Spencer Ltd v British Gas Corporation* 1983 SLT 196 the court rejected an offer to waive confidentiality in respect of part of a report, and in *Whitehill v Glasgow Corporation* 1915 SC 1015 the difficulty of declaring a report partially confidential was noted.
[94] *Hepburn v Scottish Power* 1997 SLT 859; *Anderson v Hingston* 1997 SLT 844.
[95] *Clippens Oil Co v Edinburgh and District Water Trustees* (1906) 8 F 731 at 740; 1907 SC (HL) 9.
[96] Dickson, *Evidence* (3rd edn), para 1666. In *Gavin v Montgomerie* (1830) 9 S 213 at 219, the then Lord President Hope expressed the view that if a litigant employs a layman to advise him or collect evidence, communications between them are confidential. In *Stuart v Miller* (1836) 14 S 837, Lord Medwyn agreed with this dictum, but Lord Justice-Clerk Boyle, Lord Meadowbank and Lord Glenlee seem to have read it as meaning that the layman was in the same position as a solicitor, and disagreed. But all the Lord President said was that communications in preparing the case are confidential, and the ground of judgment in *Stuart v Miller* was that the correspondence did not relate to the case. In an Outer House decision, *Macfarlane v Macfarlane* (1896) 4 SLT 28, communications between a party to divorce proceedings and an enquiry agent were not confidential, although they appear to meet the requirements for confidentiality *post litem motam*.
[97] Argued in the lower court in *Hepburn v Scottish Power* 1997 SLT 859.
[98] *Hepburn v Scottish Power* 1997 SLT 859.
[99] As in *Young v National Coal Board* 1957 SC 99.
[100] *Young v National Coal Board* 1957 SC 99, per Lord Mackintosh at 106, Lord Blades at 108.

present at the time of an accident made to the employer at or about the time of the accident[101] are held not to be confidential,[102] and it makes no difference that the report has been passed to the employer's insurance company.[103] If the report contains a list of witnesses, even this is not confidential, and a final effort to upset this part of the exception failed, in spite of doubts on the bench.[104] Whatever may have been the position in collisions at sea in 1900, a principal, if not the principal, purpose of the report today, after a traffic or industrial accident, is to enable the employer's insurance company to decide on their attitude to a claim of damages.[105] Doubts as to the soundness of the entire exception have been expressed,[106] and in England a House of Lords decision moved away from a situation of rule and exception as still applied here to one of recoverability unless the "dominant purpose" for which the report was obtained was to use in or in preparation for litigation.[107] However, the Scottish courts have not followed this reasoning.[108] The exception appears to rest on a theory that the purpose of the employee's report is to enable the employer to improve working methods, "presumably for no other purpose than to put the owners in possession of the true facts."[109]

Reports of destructive testing

10.4.3 The Inner House recently confirmed the existence of an exception to the rule of confidentiality *post litem motam* if the testing which the report describes has destroyed or materially altered the subject-matter of the examination, and this resulted in one party possessing information which the other was unable to acquire because of the testing itself.[110] In that situation the other party would be entitled to access to the information derived from the testing, but not to any other information contained in the report such as opinions on fault or liability, the correct procedure being to appoint a commissioner to exclude material that did not fall within the exception. This reasoning led to partial recovery, in an application by householders whose house had been destroyed by fire, of a report prepared *post litem motam* by consulting scientists appointed by the defenders into the fire having started in the electrical distribution board, of which destruction was necessary to carry out

---

[101] These words were omitted from the specification in *Stuart v Great North of Scotland Railway Co* (1896) 23 R 1005, and *Muir v Edinburgh and District Tramways Co* 1909 SC 244, in which the diligence was refused, so that technically they are distinguishable from the later cases.

[102] *Finlay v Glasgow Corporation* 1915 SC 615; *Macphee v Glasgow Corporation* 1915 SC 990; *Whitehill v Glasgow Corporation* 1915 SC 1015; *Russell v W Alexander & Sons Ltd* 1960 SLT (Notes) 92.

[103] *Russell v W Alexander & Sons Ltd* 1960 SLT (Notes) 92 (OH); *Brennan v David Lawson Ltd* 1947 SLT (Notes) 47 (OH).

[104] *McCulloch v Glasgow Corporation* 1918 SC 155.

[105] See *Young v National Coal Board* 1957 SC 99 at 105.

[106] *Anderson v St Andrews Ambulance Association* 1942 SC 555, per Lord Moncrieff at 559; Macphail, *Evidence* paras 18.25–S18.27B; Scottish Law Commission Memorandum No 46, para S.26. In *Young v National Coal Board* 1957 SC 99 at 101, 106, 108 it was observed that the exception would be unlikely to be extended.

[107] *Waugh v British Railways Board* [1980] AC 521. The Scottish Law Commission favoured this approach in Memorandum No 46, para S.26, but the case was bypassed in *Marks & Spencer Ltd v British Gas Corporation* 1983 SLT 196 and resisted in *More v Brown & Root Wimpey Highland Fabricators Ltd* 1983 SLT 669.

[108] *More v Brown & Root Wimpey Highland Fabricators Ltd* 1983 SLT 669.

[109] *Scott v Portsoy Harbour Co* (1900) 8 SLT 38 (OH), quoted in *Whitehill v Glasgow Corporation* 1915 SC 1015 and *Marks & Spencer Ltd v British Gas Corporation* 1983 SLT 196.

[110] *Hepburn v Scottish Power* 1997 SLT 859, following *Black v Bairds & Dalmellington Ltd* 1939 SC 472 (IH), a case dealing with a post mortem report.

the testing,[111] and a post mortem report has been partially recovered on similar grounds.[112]

10.5 *ANTE LITEM MOTAM*—APPLICATION

This paragraph deals with cases in which communications were said not to be **10.5.1** confidential because they were made before the litigation was in contemplation. The plea of confidentiality was repelled as regards: letters between a litigant and his agents (not law agents) before the action was contemplated[113]; the evidence of an accountant who had examined the defender's books some time before the dispute with the pursuer arose[114]; a factor's report made years before the action[115]; reports by employees before the date when the dispute arose[116]; and letters from engineers and contractors written long before the dispute arose.[117] In the last case the Lord Justice-Clerk said: "The inquiry in connection with which the diligence is asked relates to transactions alleged to have taken place at a time when, it is said, no dispute existed, or … could have existed; and when, therefore, no occasion arose for confidential communications … between employer and employed, in regard to that matter." During the reconstruction of the *Scotsman* office blasting operations were alleged to have caused damage to a neighbouring house on 15 August 1899. In an action against the proprietors, diligence was granted for recovery of reports by the contractors to the defenders from 1 March to 1 November 1899, a plea of confidentiality being repelled. The significance of the latter date does not appear from the report, but it is difficult to believe that the dispute had not arisen before then.[118]

---

[111] *Hepburn v Scottish Power* 1997 SLT 859. The facts are easily equated with those in *Marks & Spencer Ltd v British Gas Corporation* 1983 SLT 196 where disclosure was ordered of the full report on the testing of the fractured gas main. However, the reasoning employed in the Outer House was not followed in *Hepburn*. In *Marks & Spencer Ltd v British Gas Corporation* the court distinguished a report designed to recover the full facts from one prepared *post litem motam*, but also referred to factors such as accessibility of the material and expertise by both parties and the duties of the defender as statutory undertaker to find out what went wrong with the gas service. The distinctions to be sought through that reasoning were potentially elusive and thus uncertain for the parties.

[112] *Black v Bairds & Dalmellington Ltd* 1939 SC 472. However, the reasoning is mixed, with some judges considering that a post mortem report is in a special category, and others considering that the report was not in the circumstances *post litem motam*. "Equitable" consideration of the issues for and against disclosure is also mentioned, all of which is contrary to the firm application of principle and exception in *Hepburn v Scottish Power* 1997 SLT 859.

[113] *Stuart v Miller* (1836) 14 S 837. The rubric is misleading. It does not state the very limited recovery allowed, nor the grounds on which the plea was repelled.

[114] *Wright v Arthur* (1831) 10 S 139.

[115] *Mitchell v Berwick* (1845) 7 D 382. It is thought that Dickson (*Evidence* (3rd edn), para 1665, 1666) founds too sweeping propositions on these three decisions by failing to notice that the communications were *ante litem motam*.

[116] *Tannett, Walker & Co v Hannay & Sons* (1873) 11 M 931; *Morrison & Mason Ltd v Clarkson Brothers* (1896) 4 SLT 157 (OH), where recovery was allowed to the date of raising action.

[117] *Caledonian Rly Co v Symington* 1913 SC 885. This case, in argument and to some extent in the opinion, seems to have been mixed up with solicitor and client. The rubric brings out the point accurately, except that it fails to state that ultimately the Lord Ordinary repelled the objections to confidentiality and that this was acquiesced in.

[118] *Sutherland v John Ritchie & Co* (1900) 8 SLT 100 (OH).

10.6 CONFIDENTIALITY IN THE POPULAR SENSE

General

10.6.1 A person may make what is popularly called a confidential communication, only to find that in law it is not so. The particular cases dealt with in this paragraph have this in common: (i) that the recipient of the secret has an interest in maintaining it because the imparter is more likely to give a full and true account if he thinks that it can go no further, or, at any rate, that the source will not be disclosed,[119] and (ii) that breach of the duty of confidentiality may be actionable in delict, contract or agency. In considering whether to order disclosure of a communication made within this type of confidential relationship, if no privilege applies to exclude the evidence, the court will generally consider its necessity to the case, including potential alternative sources, before ordering a disclosure which will breach the confidential relationship.[120]

Banks, insurance companies, etc

10.6.2 Such institutions in the course of their business receive reports which expressly or impliedly are regarded as confidential. Reports to insurers are confidential in law if made *post litem motam*,[121] but, although judicial opinion is not uniform,[122] it is thought that reports *ante litem motam* are not. The plea was repelled when taken by a bank[123] and by a railway company.[124]

Doctors

10.6.3 A doctor's position is peculiar in that she obtains a great deal of information about the patient from observation, and there can be no doubt that, while such information is confidential in the sense that the doctor has a duty not to publish it, it is not confidential in the sense here relevant. The doctor is bound to give it in evidence if called upon,[125] and if the information is relevant to a fact in issue.[126] The question of the confidentiality of an oral or written communication to a doctor does

---

[119] This justification is also used in relation to public interest privilege: see para 10.9.

[120] As in relation to journalists in *HM Advocate v Airs* 1975 JC 64, and a doctor's records in *Rogerson v Rogerson* 1964 SLT (Notes) 89.

[121] *Wilson v Keir & Cawdor* 1947 SN 55 (OH).

[122] In a petition for disentail proof was allowed to ascertain the value of the interests of the later substitute heirs. They averred that the first substitute heir had suffered from ill health and were granted a diligence to recover medical reports made to an insurance company to which he had applied for a policy on his life, the company's plea of confidentiality being repelled: *McDonald v McDonalds* (1881) 8 R 357. The same result followed in *Elder v English and Scottish Law Life Ass Co* (1881) 19 SLR 195 (where the insurance company was defender); *cf Hope's Trs v Scottish Accident Ins Co* (1895) 3 SLT 164 (OH). In *Simcock v Scottish Imperial Ins Co* (1901) 9 SLT 234 (OH) the ground of decision is not known, and in *Macdonald v New York Life Ins Co* (1903) 11 SLT 120 (OH) the case was decided on another ground.

[123] *Foster, Alcock & Co v Grangemouth Dockyard Co* (1886) 23 SLR 713 (refusal by bank to produce correspondence). Bankers are not compellable to produce or speak to bank books or records unless the bank is a party to the proceedings, and is so ordered by the court: (criminal proceedings) Bankers Books Evidence Act 1879, s 6, and see also the Criminal Procedure (Scotland) Act 1995, Sched 3 and *Lord Advocate's Reference No1 of 1996* 1996 JC 152); (civil proceedings) Civil Evidence (Scotland) Act 1988, s 7(2). See also para 21.13.

[124] *Kinloch v Irvine* (1884) 21 SLR 685 (where, in a reduction of a will, a railway company refused to produce medical reports obtained in connection with an accident to the testator years before).

[125] *AB v CD* (1851) 14 D 177 at 180.

[126] *Higgins v Burton* 1968 SLT (Notes) 52.

not seem to have been raised, but the ordinary rule would seem to apply to it, the communication being confidential only if made *post litem motam*.[127] Since doctors and other health professionals are most frequently communicating as an employee of the local health authority, the plea of privilege in the public interest has also been taken as a subsidiary argument.[128] It would seem that a doctor claims confidentiality in the interests of the imparter of the communication, but that the records can be used without breach of confidentiality if relevant in the interest of the health authority who own and possess the records.[129]

Clergymen

The mere fact that a statement is made to a clergyman does not render it confidential.[130] Nor according to Hume[131] is a voluntary confession to a clergyman confidential unless made to relieve conscience while preparing for trial.[132] Lord Moncrieff did not have this particular point before him, but he laid down clearly that in criminal cases confidentiality attaches only to communications to spouses or solicitors, and not to other persons including relatives.[133] The position of penitent and a person whose role it is to receive penitential communications has been said to be the one most likely to support a plea of confidentiality,[134] but there is no direct reported authority,[135] perhaps because parties would not be aware that the communication had been made, or would shy away from calling for its disclosure.[136] In any event, if the privilege exists, it is that of the party, not of the clergyman.[137] **10.6.4**

Journalists

Journalists have a limited right to refuse to disclose a source of information afforded by the Contempt of Court Act 1981, s 10, but this is overidden if disclosure is necessary in the interests of justice, national security or the prevention of disorder or crime.[138] At common law a journalist had to state the name of the person from whom published information had been obtained if directed by the **10.6.5**

---

[127] In proceedings for defamation and breach of contract raised by a former patient in respect of disclosure made by her doctor while giving evidence in earlier proceedings, the court noted that the evidence of the doctor as to what she had told him *ante litem motam* had not been objected to as confidential in those earlier proceedings: *AB v CD* (1904) 7 F 72 at 74, note, per Lord Young at 83; (1905) 7 F (HL) 109.

[128] In relation to records of a child guidance clinic in *Higgins v Burton* 1968 SLT (Notes) 52.

[129] *Gibson, Petitioner* 1984 SLT 61.

[130] *McLaughlin v Douglas and Kidston* (1863) 4 Irv 273.

[131] Hume, ii, 335, 350.

[132] Macdonald, *Criminal Law* (5th edn), p 315 is more doubtful.

[133] *HM Advocate v Parker* 1944 JC 49.

[134] Wilkinson, p 106.

[135] Macphail examines comparatively the whole issue of confidentiality of relationships with the clergy at paras 18.38–S18.44. Wilkinson goes through the tangential authorities at pp 105–106; Beltrami, *The Defender*, at p 201 refers to the 1960 unreported case of *Daniels* in which it was held that a priest need not disclose what was heard in the confessional. The Scottish Law Commission considered that it was unnecessary to regulate the matter, leaving it to the exercise of judicial discretion: Macphail, para S18.44 and Scottish Law Commission Memorandum No 46, para S. 32.

[136] As Hume observes at ii, 335 and 350. See also, Cross & Tapper, *Evidence* (9th edn) p 463, and English authorities cited there which suggest that the court would be slow to force recovery in breach of a penitential confidence.

[137] Dickson, *Evidence* (3rd edn), para 1685, n (c).

[138] s 10(2).

judge to do so, but before so ordering the court did consider if such disclosure was relevant to the case, and necessary in light of the volume of other evidence of the fact.[139]

10.7 NEGOTIATION

10.7.1　Concessions made in the course of and for the furtherance of negotiation are privileged in proceedings between the parties to the negotiation[140] and include negotiations before any proceedings commenced.[141] The aim of this privilege is to encourage consensual settlement of disputes. This applies whether or not the communication carries the terms "without prejudice",[142] since it is the concessionary purpose of the communication rather than its expression "without prejudice" that attracts the privilege,[143] and the effect of the words has to be judged on the facts of each situation.[144] In considering the concessionary purpose the communication can be broken down into parts and unequivocal admissions which are made in the course of negotiations are not protected.[145] Communications made during negotiations which are not strictly related to the settlement negotiations also fall outwith the privilege.[146] The privilege can be waived[147] and it would appear that negotiating communications can be produced without consent or waiver to compare a judicial outcome with the parties' negotiating positions in order to determine judicial expenses.[148]

10.8 CONCILIATION

10.8.1　There is no general authority on the issue of communications made during a negotiation facilitated by a neutral third party, such as conciliation or mediation. English authorities in consistorial causes dating from 1949 protected the confidentiality of communications to persons who were trying to reconcile the parties to a dispute, whether the interview was with the parties together or only with

---

[139] *HM Advocate v Airs* 1975 JC 64.

[140] Dickson, *Evidence* (3rd edn), para 305; *Fyfe v Miller* (1835) 13 S 809; *Williamson v Taylor* (1845) 7 D 842; *Daks Simpson Group v Kuiper* 1994 SLT 689.

[141] As in *Assessor for Dundee v Elder* 1963 SLT (Notes) 35, but in the sense that this decision relies upon the effect of "without prejudice correspondence" it is now overtaken by the cases cited below.

[142] According to the Outer House decisions in *Daks Simpson Group v Kuiper* 1994 SLT 689; *Gordon v East Kilbride Development Corporation* 1995 SLT 62; *Watson-Towers Ltd v MacPhail* 1986 SLT 617; *Ware v Edinburgh District Council* 1976 SLT (Lands Tr) 21. *Cf* another Outer House decision, *Bell v Lothiansure Ltd* 1990 SLT 58, and also *Assessor for Dundee v Elder* 1963 SLT (Notes) 35.

[143] *Daks Simpson Group v Kuiper* 1994 SLT 689.

[144] *Richardson v Quercus Ltd* 1999 SLT 596. Those facts included the terms of other communications between the party and the issue to which the evidence is relevant, per Lord Justice-General Rodger at 600.

[145] *Daks Simpson Group v Kuiper* 1994 SLT 689; *Richardson v Quercus Ltd* 1999 SLT 596.

[146] *Burns v Burns* 1964 SLT (Sh Ct) 21; *Ware v Edinburgh District Council* 1976 SLT (Lands Tr) 21. In *Richardson v Quercus Ltd* 1999 SLT 596 there was information in a letter which, considered in all the circumstances, constituted a relevant acknowledgment of claim in terms of the Prescription and Limitation (Scotland) Act 1973, s 10(1), overriding the "without prejudice" statement.

[147] In England it is clear that such waiver must be with the consent of both parties: *Walker v Wilsher* (1889) LR 23 QBD 335, applied in *Somatra Ltd v Sinclair Roche & Temperley* [2000] 1 Lloyd's Rep 311.

[148] *Critchley v Campbell* (1884) 11 R 475 at 480; *O'Donnell v AM & G Robertson* 1965 SLT 155.

one,[149] and either party could invoke the privilege or could waive it expressly or by giving evidence about the process.[150] The reason behind the rule is the interest of the state that reconciliation should be effected, and that reconciliation is more likely if people can speak freely knowing that what they say cannot be used against them. The confidentiality arose through the nature of the discussion rather than the terms of the communication which formed part of it.[151] The rule was applied to probation officers,[152] counsel[153] and clergymen,[154] but the confidentiality belongs to the parties and the conciliator could not invoke it if both parties expressly waive it.[155] In Scotland mediation or conciliation of family disputes was considered by the Scottish Law Commission,[156] and this is now the subject of the Civil Evidence (Family Mediation) (Scotland) Act 1995. Evidence of what occurred during family mediation[157] is inadmissible[158] subject to the specified exceptions[159] which justify disclosure: to establish the fact that there was or was not a completed mediation; in subsequent child protection proceedings; in proceedings between the mediator and the parties; and if the participants agree.[160]

The position regarding conciliations or mediations other than those to which the Act relates remains undetermined, except in the case of those carried out in pending applications to the Employment Tribunal, which are protected from disclosure without the consent of the person who made the communication to the conciliator.[161] While it has been suggested that the situation in family disputes as developed in England need not be equated with commercial or reparation disputes[162] there appears to be no reason why commercial and other non-family conciliations should not be treated in the same manner as negotiations, described in the previous paragraph. If a model akin to that applied to family mediation were to apply, the permission of all participants to the mediation, excluding the mediator, would be necessary for the privilege to be waived.[163] Unlike family matters where wide-ranging disclosure in mediation is to be encouraged in the interest of fairness to the child and the parties,[164]

10.8.2

---

[149] *Mole v Mole* [1951] P 21, and whether the approach to a conciliator had come from the party or the conciliator: *Henley v Henley* [1955] P 202.

[150] *McTaggart v McTaggart* [1949] P 94.

[151] *McTaggart v McTaggart* [1949] P 94.

[152] *Mole v Mole* [1951] P 21; *McTaggart v McTaggart* [1949] P 94.

[153] *Pool v Pool* [1951] P 470; *Pais v Pais* [1971] P 119.

[154] *Henley v Henley* [1955] P 202.

[155] *Pais v Pais* [1971] P 119.

[156] Scottish Law Commission Memorandum No 46 (1980), para S.29 recommended no privilege for marriage guidance counsellors and was equivocal about mediation or conciliation at para S.28. However, in 1992 the *Report on Evidence: Protection of Family Mediation* (Scot Law Com No 136) recommended legislation.

[157] Limited to mediation carried out by a provider approved by the Lord President: s 1(2)–(6).

[158] s 1(1).

[159] s 2(1).

[160] s 2(2). The participants include any children who are the subject of the mediation even if not present during it, but not the mediator: s 2(2)(b).

[161] Trade Union and Labour Relations (Consolidation) Act 1992, s 210 and see Selwyn's *Employment Law* (9th edn), para 1.9.

[162] Macphail, para 18.31.

[163] The Scottish Law Commission in 1980 saw such a requirement as fettering the parties' right to waive unilaterally (Memorandum S.28, S.29), but by 1992 had included this in a draft bill: Scot Law Com No 136, Appendix A.

[164] Macphail, para 18.31 refers to the importance of "truth" in family proceedings. Interestingly the same concern for truth in the interests of the child in family proceedings in England has been used to justify overriding privilege: eg *Re L (A Minor) (Police Investigation: Privilege)* [1996] 2 All ER 78; *Oxfordshire County Council v M* [1994] 2 All ER 269.

as well as to facilitate agreement (and thence the broad confidentiality is subject only to express exceptions), it is suggested that in non-family disputes the privilege should be limited in a manner similar to that applying in negotiations, that is to concessions (but not unequivocal admissions) which are related to mediation of the dispute.

10.9 PUBLIC POLICY

10.9.1 Evidence may be excluded on the ground that disclosure of the facts would be contrary to public interest, otherwise termed public policy.[165] English authorities are of some relevance after the House of Lords indicated that rulings on this should be the same in Scotland and England.[166] In order to comply with Article 6(1) of the European Convention on Human Rights, the discretion to withhold evidence on this ground in a criminal case must be exercised by the trial judge.[167] The objection may be taken on the basis that the document contains information which it is contrary to the public interest to reveal. Alternatively, it may be taken on the basis the document falls within a class of item which should be immune from disclosure in the public interest, although the particular item sought may not contain information which is in need of protection.

10.9.2   In either case the court has power to overrule the objection[168] but, in considering whether to do so or not, it must accept the Minister's assessment of that public interest[169] and decide whether, in spite of that, it will allow recovery.[170] Ordinarily diligence has been refused if a Minister objects that recovery would be contrary to the public interest, but this probably applies only where the document is in the possession of the department or its agent.[171] A practice of ordering production under seal so that the court itself may consider the danger to the public interest was disapproved,[172] but has found renewed favour in England,[173] and would help to satisfy the requirements of Article 6.[174] It was difficult to see how the court could avoid forming some view as to the extent of the public danger, and there are increasing traces of this in the case law,[175] to the extent that some have seen the public interest

---

[165] This area has bred variations in terminology for what appears to be the same doctrine. English authorities refer to "public interest immunity" (*Burmah Oil Co Ltd v Bank of England* [1980] AC 1090) and "Crown privilege" (*Conway v Rimmer* [1968] AC 910). Scottish authorities refer to "public policy" or "public interest". For a discussion of the topic see Mackay of Clashfern, "The Development of the Law of Public Interest Immunity" (1983) 2 CJQ 337.

[166] *Conway v Rimmer* [1968] AC 910.

[167] *Rowe and Davis v United Kingdom* [2000] TLR 147.

[168] *Glasgow Corporation v Central Land Board* 1956 SC (HL) 1.

[169] Unless the opinion formed is patently unreasonable or erroneously reached: *Glasgow Corporation v Central Land Board* 1956 SC (HL) 1; *AB v Glasgow & West of Scotland Blood Transfusion Service* 1993 SLT 36.

[170] *Glasgow Corporation v Central Land Board* 1956 SC (HL) 1 at 18, 1955 SC 64 at 75; *AB v Glasgow & West of Scotland Blood Transfusion Service* 1993 SLT 36 at 38; *Henderson v McGown* 1916 SC 821 at 825.

[171] *Whitehall v Whitehall* 1957 SC 30. As to claims by public or quasi-public entities. See paras 10.9.4 and 10.9.5.

[172] *Rogers v Orr* 1939 SC 492 at 498; *Admiralty v Aberdeen Steam Trawling and Fishing Co Ltd* 1909 SC 335 at 340, 342, 344.

[173] *Science Research Council v Nasse; Leyland Cars v Vyas* [1980] AC 1028.

[174] *Rowe and Davis v United Kingdom* [2000] TLR 147. Production is not strictly necessary for compliance with Article 6, but the court must have sufficient information upon which to ensure that the interests of an accused are not infringed.

[175] *Glasgow Corporation v Central Land Board* 1956 SC (HL) 1 at 18, 1955 SC 64 at 77, where Lord Russell referred to the compelling reasons for the objection in the leading English case, *Science*

argument as simply a form of arguing confidentiality in the normal sense of the word.[176] Courts have observed that the circumstances in which the courts might disregard the Minister's certificate would vary, according to the grounds on which that certificate was based,[177] but that no class of documents should be assumed to be beyond recovery,[178] and that "clear and compelling evidence" is necessary for a class-based claim.[179] The trend is towards judicial expectation that the Minister will disclose the grounds for the objection, although in the past it was not normal to require this,[180] so that this can be balanced against the interest in recovery. Furthermore, the expectation is that the Minister will, to some extent, consider competing interest before deciding whether to claim immunity from disclosure, particularly on class grounds.[181]

The balancing must now be considered in terms of the fundamental rights **10.9.3** enshrined in Article 6 of the European Convention on Human Rights.[182] To date the balancing interest in recovery has been expressed as a public interest in the administration of justice more pressing or greater than that covered by the objection[183] and separately as a private interest of the litigant in having access to all information relevant to the case.[184] The outcome of the balance inevitably varies between criminal cases and civil cases, the public interest in the administration of criminal justice being a particularly strong counter-balance.[185] Clearly the items sought must be relevant to the applicant's case[186] and in criminal cases of material

---

Research Council v Nasse; Leyland Cars v Vyas [1980] AC 1028. See also *AB v Glasgow & West of Scotland Blood Transfusion Service* 1993 SLT 36, in which the court noted that it would have been useful in making the assessment to know what degree of risk to the public's willingness to give blood was anticipated to be caused by the requested disclosure of the identity of a donor to someone who received that donor's infected blood.

[176] See Macphail, para S18.54A.

[177] *Whitehall v Whitehall* 1957 SC 30; *AB v Glasgow & West of Scotland Blood Transfusion Service* 1993 SLT 36.

[178] *Burmah Oil Co Ltd v Bank of England* [1980] AC 1090.

[179] *R v Chief Constable of the West Midlands Police, ex parte Wiley* [1995] 1 AC 274, per Lord Woolf at 305.

[180] *Glasgow Corporation v Central Land Board* 1956 SC (HL) at 19, 1955 SC at 66.

[181] *R v Chief Constable of the West Midlands Police, ex parte Wiley* [1994] 3 All ER 420.

[182] See *Rowe and Davis v United Kingdom* [2000] TLR 147.

[183] Civil cases: *P Cannon (Garages) Ltd v Lord Advocate* 1983 SLT (Sh Ct) 50 (blood sample taken in driving case, for potential damages action for negligent driving), following *Friel, Petitioner* 1981 SC 1 (details of a police informant whom the petitioner wished to sue for damages for giving false information); *Parks v Tayside Regional Council* 1989 SC 38 (OH) (in which disclosure was granted on the basis of the greater public interest in the pursuer having access to social work files regarding a child whom she had fostered and from whom she averred that she had contracted hepatitis B). Criminal cases: *HM Advocate v Ward* 1993 SLT 1202; *Hemming v HM Advocate* 1997 JC 140; and the full bench decision in *McLeod v HM Advocate* 1998 JC 67.

[184] *AB v Glasgow & West of Scotland Blood Transfusion Service* 1993 SLT 36; *Higgins v Burton* 1968 SLT (Notes) 52.

[185] The authorities and the ministerial practices for claiming public interest immunity on class grounds were considered in some depth in the *Report of Inquiry into the Exports of Defence Equipment and Dual-Use Goods to Iraq and Related Prosecutions* (the Scott Inquiry), Part 3, Section G, Chapter 13 and Part 5, Section K. There it is doubted whether in criminal cases there should be the balancing of public interests, and it is suggested that if a document would be of assistance to the defence there can be no claim of immunity, whilst if the document does not appear to have potential to assist the defence the court would have to apply the balance, but that claiming immunity on a class basis cannot be justified in criminal proceedings (paras K6.11–K6.17, with conclusions summarised at K6.18).

[186] *AB v Glasgow & West of Scotland Blood Transfusion Service* 1993 SLT 36. It was noted in *Downie v HM Advocate* 1952 JC 37 that in criminal proceedings where no averments exist it is more difficult to assess whether the items which the defence seeks to recover are necessary.

assistance to the proper preparation of the defence.[187] It is clearly impossible to test materiality if the claim is made in respect of a class of documents, but it has been recommended in England and Wales that class immunity should never be claimed in criminal cases,[188] and the Lord Advocate has recently stated that class immunity will no longer be claimed in respect of prosecution records in Scotland.[189] Overall, recovery is more likely to be ordered in face of the objection if the applicant's case may be thwarted or defeated due to the absence of the information.[190]

10.9.4   An objection on grounds of Crown privilege is generally taken by the Minister,[191] not by a litigant.[192] However, objection in the public interest has been pled by litigants or havers who are not Ministers. In the case of a Blood Transfusion Service it was noted that no doubt a duty of confidentiality existed preventing voluntary disclosure by them of a donor's identity and that it could be expressed as justified in a "public interest" since donors might be lost if aware of breaches of confidentiality, but this was not in the nature of "immunity" afforded in ministerial claims of public interest.[193] Objections by a police authority to the disclosure of complaints by a member of the public against a police officer in civil proceedings by the officer against the complainer have been overruled in the absence of an objection by the Lord Advocate.[194] Different considerations would come into play in deciding whether to refuse recovery from such a body, there being greater scope for the court to balance the competing interests in confidentiality. In particular the court does not feel bound by the assessment of public interest made by the objector. A similar approach has been taken to claims of confidentiality made by local authorities.[195]

10.9.5   The objection has been taken frequently to protect information gathered by the police or other prosecuting authorities. Faced with such objection the court had refused to order recovery of Crown precognitions and communications between the procurator-fiscal and the Crown office[196]; communications by a private indi-

---

[187] *McLeod v HM Advocate* 1998 JC 67.

[188] *Report of Inquiry into the Exports of Defence Equipment and Dual-Use Goods to Iraq and Related Prosecutions* (the Scott Inquiry), para K6.16.

[189] *McLeod v HM Advocate* 1998 JC 67.

[190] *Air Canada v Secretary of State for Trade (No 2)* [1983] 2 AC 394. In *Glasgow Corporation v Central Land Board* 1993 SLT 36; *Henderson v McGown* 1916 SC 821; *Rogers v Orr* 1939 SC 492; *Caffrey v Lord Inverclyde* 1930 SC 762 the objection was not overruled and it was noted that recovery was not vital to the litigant. However, in *Science Research Council v Nasse; Leyland Cars v Vyas* [1980] AC 1028 the court considered whether the documents were necessary for disposing of the proceedings fairly.

[191] As to the appropriate Minister, account will have to be taken of devolved powers in terms of the Scotland Act 1998. It is conceivable that Ministers of both Parliaments will seek to protect an item from disclosure in the public interest.

[192] *Henderson v Robertson* (1853) 15 D 292. In *Sheridan v Peel* 1907 SC 577, although the question of the Lord Advocate's consent was mentioned, diligence was refused on other grounds. In *Muir v Edinburgh and District Tramways* 1909 SC 244, no reason was given, in the absence of objection by the Lord Advocate, for refusing recovery of police reports.

[193] *AB v Glasgow & West of Scotland Blood Transfusion Service* 1993 SLT 36 at 38D–E.

[194] As in *Anderson v Palombo* 1984 SLT 332, *Davers v Butler* 1994 SCLR 717.

[195] *Parks v Tayside Regional Council* 1989 SLT 345; *McLeod v British Railways Board* 1997 SLT 434; *Pearson v Educational Institute for Scotland* 1997 SC 245. Cf the outcome in *Strathclyde Regional Council v B*, unreported, described in Macphail at para S18.54C, a decision of the Sheriff Principal in which the facts and authorities were carefully weighed.

[196] *Arthur v Lindsay* (1895) 22 R 417; *Donald v Hart* (1844) 6 D 1255. Cf *Mills v Kelvin & James White Ltd* 1912 SC 995, where the Lord Advocate did not object. In *Cheshire County Council v C* [1995] 2 FLR 862 the Family Division noted that unlike the position in England the file of the Scottish

vidual to the police[197]; probably statements made to Post Office investigators[198]; a report by the police to a procurator-fiscal or regulatory body[199]; the identity of an informant.[200] A conviction was quashed where a police officer's refusal to disclose the name of his informant was sustained by the magistrate.[201] The objection has also been taken to a report by a naval officer to the Admiralty following a collision[202]; medical history sheets of a soldier[203]; income tax returns[204]; instructions issued to officers of excise[205]; communications between the Central Land Board and district valuers.[206] An objection to produce a telegram by the Postmaster General was upheld, not on the ground of public policy but on account of the difficulty of tracing it.[207] The objection was overruled *quoad* a Post Office Savings Bank account, and sustained *quoad* the inventory of an estate.[208] However, it appears that in criminal cases public interest will no longer be claimed on policy or class grounds in respect of police statements made by witnesses,[209] and such a claim will be made only if there is a public interest objection on a specific ground.[210] In turn the defence will be required to show that the evidence of which recovery is sought would be likely to be of material assistance to the proper presentation of the accused's defence.[211]

---

prosecuting authorities remained confidential at all times. The court made no order for recovery of the prosecution file when sought by an English local authority taking care proceedings, but it did make a request for disclosure.

[197] *Rogers v Orr* 1939 SC 492. Contrast *Sheridan v Peel* 1907 SC 577, where the Lord Advocate consented to recovery, and *Anderson v Palombo* 1984 SLT 332, 1986 SLT 46. In *Daly v Vannet* 1999 SCCR 346 the appeal court observed that the entries in a police officer's notebook immediately preceding and succeeding that relating to the accused "being confidential . . . should not be made available" to the accused's solicitor.

[198] *Downie v HM Advocate* 1952 JC 37.

[199] *Hastings v Chalmers* (1890) 18 R 244; *McKie v Western SMT Co* 1952 SC 206 (report by police officer to his superior); *Rogers v Secretary of State for the Home Department* [1978] AC 388 (report by police to Gaming Board).

[200] *Friel, Petitioner* 1981 SC 1, *Henderson v Robertson* (1853) 15 D 292 re police informers; in relation to informant of child neglect: *D v NSPCC* [1978] AC 171.

[201] *Thomson v Neilson* (1900) 3 F (J) 3.

[202] *Admiralty v Aberdeen Steam Trawling and Fishing Co Ltd* 1909 SC 335.

[203] *Caffrey v Lord Inverclyde* 1930 SC 762.

[204] *Henderson v McGown* 1916 SC 821. See *Show v Kay* (1904) 12 SLT 359 (OH).

[205] *Tierney v Ballingall & Son* (1896) 23 R 512.

[206] *Glasgow Corporation v Central Land Board* 1956 SC (HL) 1.

[207] *Somervell v Somervell* (1900) 8 SLT 112 (OH).

[208] *Forrest v MacGregor* 1913 1 SLT 372 (OH).

[209] The recovery of police statements taken from persons who did not become witnesses was considered at length by a full bench in *McLeod v HM Advocate* 1998 SCCR 77. It may be more difficult to justify such disclosure than disclosure of statements of those who appear on the prosecution witness list.

[210] *McLeod v HM Advocate (No 2)* 1998 JC 67. For the position of the Scottish Criminal Case Review Commission seeking such recovery, see para 21.8.3.

[211] *McLeod v HM Advocate (No 2)* 1998 JC 67 at 80D–F. The court also held that this requirement was consistent with the accused's right to a fair trial in terms of Art 6 of the European Convention on Human Rights, as interpreted in relation to recovery of prosecution evidence in *Edwards v United Kingdom* Series A No 247-B (1993) 15 EHRR 417.

CHAPTER 11

PROOF—WHERE EVIDENCE IS EXCLUDED

11.1 PROOF—GENERAL

Evidence, although the most important, is not the only method of establishing **11.1.1** facts. In civil causes, subject to some exceptions in family actions,[1] evidence is unnecessary and may be inadmissible if the fact to be proved has been judicially admitted by the other party, has already been adjudicated upon by a competent court (*res judicata*), or is within judicial knowledge. Judicial admissions, *res judicata* and judicial knowledge, in civil and criminal causes, are dealt with in this chapter. Presumptions, which may render evidence inadmissible[2] or unnecessary,[3] or which affect the burden of proof, are dealt with in another chapter.[4]

11.2 JUDICIAL ADMISSIONS—CIVIL CAUSES

General

In civil actions, other than family actions,[5] judicial admissions are in themselves, **11.2.1** and without anything more, conclusive against the party making them, for the purposes of the action in which they are made.[6] In order to be the equivalent of proof and to make evidence of the fact to be proved unnecessary, they must be clear and unequivocal, and must be read along with any qualifications and explanations which accompany them.[7] A qualified admission may be founded upon as the equivalent of proof by the party in whose favour it is made only if that party is able to disprove the qualification, and this is true whether the qualification is intrinsic

---

[1] See para 28.2.
[2] See para 3.2.
[3] See paras 3.3 *et seq.*
[4] See Chapter 3.
[5] See para 28.2.
[6] Stair, iv, 45, 5; Erskine, iv, 2, 33; *Scottish Marine Insurance Co v Turner* (1853) 1 Macq 334 at 340.
[7] *Lee v National Coal Board* 1955 SC 151 at 158–159; *Darnley v Kirkwood* (1845) 7 D 595; *Chrystal v Chrystal* (1900) 2 F 373; *Baikie v Glasgow Corporation* 1922 SC (HL) 144; *London & Edinburgh Steam Shipping Co v The Admiralty* 1920 SC 309; *M'Kie v Wilson* 1951 SC 15.

or extrinsic.[8] When writing is essential to the constitution, as distinct from the proof, of a contract, a judicial admission that agreement was arrived at does not take the place of a writing.[9] Judicial admissions may be made in the following ways.

Minute of admissions

11.2.2 A minute lodged in process by a party, or by the parties jointly, is a competent method of recording admissions, and is the appropriate method of bringing them to the notice of a jury, who are denied access to the written pleadings.[10] A joint minute of admissions does not exclude consideration of admissions made in the closed record or of the terms of documents admitted in the closed record to be genuine,[11] but, unless the contrary appears, it excludes all other or additional evidence on the matters admitted.[12] A joint minute may recount the facts that the parties have agreed to admit without evidence, or may recount the parties' agreement upon issues in the case in respect of which the parties seek orders of the court in terms agreed by them and set out in the joint minute.[13] A joint minute in settlement of issues in a case becomes conclusive of the matters detailed in it[14] when lodged in court although the court may not yet have interponed authority to it.[15]

Notice to admit

11.2.3 In order that preparation for proof will focus on disputed evidence, the rules of the Court of Session and the sheriff court now provide that, after the record is closed, a party may serve on the other a notice calling upon the other party to admit the facts specified in the notice, and/or calling upon that party to admit that a document lodged in process and specified in the notice is the original and properly authenticated document, or is a true copy of the original and properly authenticated.[16] The other party, if not willing to admit that fact or the authenticity of the document serves a counter-notice of non-admission.[17] In the absence of a counter-notice within the period required by the rules, the evidence (or such part of it that has not been the subject of a counter-notice) is deemed to be admitted for the purpose of

---

[8] *Picken v Arundale & Co* (1872) 10 M 987; *Chrystal v Chrystal* (1900) 2 F 373 at 375–376, 377–378; Dickson, *Evidence* (3rd edn), paras 312, 313; Bell, *Principles*, para 2218.

[9] See Chapters 22 and 23.

[10] RCS 1994, r 37.4, applying r 36.7 to jury trials. *Lee v National Coal Board* 1955 SC 151 at 159, 161.

[11] *Nisbet v Cairns* (1864) 2 M 863.

[12] *London & Edinburgh Steam Shipping Co v The Admiralty* 1920 SC 309.

[13] The terms of a joint minute may be proved *prout de jure* at common law (*Gow v Henry* (1899) 2 F 48; *Love v Marshall* (1872) 10 M 795; *Thomson v Fraser* (1868) 7 M 39; *Jaffray v Simpson* (1835) 13 S 1122), as may variation of its terms (*Hamilton & Baird v Lewis* (1893) 21 R 120; *Union Canal Co v Johnston* (1834) 12 S 304; (1835) 1 Sh & McL 117), but, although at common law this applied even if the agreement related to heritage (*Anderson v Dick* (1901) 4 F 68; *Torbat v Torbat's Trs* (1906) 14 SLT 830 (OH); *Dewar v Ainslie* (1892) 20 R 203), it is thought that the effect of the Requirements of Writing Act 1995, s 1 is to require a joint minute in writing for agreements which relate to an interest in heritage or the other obligations referred to in that section. As to the requirements for writing after the 1995 Act, see Chapter 22.

[14] Other than matters concerning the welfare of children, on which see para 28.2.

[15] *Gow v Henry* (1899) 2 F 48. The joint minute is conclusive between the parties even in family actions where the court has still to be satisfied by evidence before granting decree in terms of the joint minute: *Lothian v Lothian* 1965 SLT 368; *Jongejan v Jongejan* 1993 SLT 595.

[16] RCS, r 28A.1(1), OCR, r 29.14(1).

[17] RCS, r 28A.1(2), OCR, r 29.14(2).

those proceedings for the exclusive use of the party who served the notice.[18] However, the court may, on special cause shown, direct otherwise,[19] and in this sense the notice procedure may generate no more than a strong rebuttable presumption that the subject of the notice is admitted.[20]

Oral admissions made at the bar

In practice admissions are frequently made orally by counsel or solicitors at the **11.2.4** bar, and are acted upon by the parties and by the court. In the Court of Session, after proof has been allowed, it is expected that admissions will be made in writing.[21] An admission or consent given orally is usually noted in the interlocutor following upon it, or, if made in the course of a proof, in the notes of evidence. If an interlocutor incorrectly records an admission thought to have been made by counsel, the party may nevertheless be bound by it unless the mistake is noticed and challenged at an early stage,[22] there being limited scope for the correction of an error in an interlocutor.[23] Accordingly, it is preferred that any admission is offered to the court in writing by way of minute or uncontradicted notice described in the preceding paragraphs.

Admissions in closed record

It is unnecessary to lead evidence to prove matters which have been admitted by the **11.2.5** other party.[24] However, this is true only of admissions, and is not true of unadmitted averments, even if made by the other party. The party who wishes to found on them must prove the latter in the ordinary way.[25] Subsidiary pleas and averments, made on the assumption that the party's principal contention may be overruled, are not construed as admissions fatal to the main contention, if they are clearly stated as alternatives.[26] Admissions may be implied. Both in the Court of Session[27] and in the sheriff court[28] an averment made by one party of a fact within the knowledge of the other party[29] is held by implication to be admitted if it is not denied by the other party.[30] Averments in answer may imply admission of another fact which has not

---

[18] RCS, r 28A.2(2), OCR, r 29.14(6).

[19] RCS, r 28A.2(1), OCR, r 29.14(3).

[20] On rebuttable presumptions, see paras 3.3, 3.4.

[21] RCS, r 36.7.

[22] *Lauder v National Bank of Scotland* 1918 1 SLT 43. See also *Whyte v Whyte* (1895) 23 R 320 (consent by solicitor in sheriff court).

[23] RCS, r 4.15(6)(Outer House), r 4.16(7)(Inner House); OCR, r 12.2(2).

[24] Admissions deleted from the pleadings before the record is closed are not binding on the party, but may be the subject of cross-examination and comment by his opponent: Dickson, *Evidence* (3rd edn), para 282; *Lennox v National Coal Board* 1955 SC 438 (OH).

[25] *Lee v National Coal Board* 1955 SC 151, per Lord Russell at 158–159, Lord Sorn at 160; *Stewart v Glasgow Corporation* 1958 SC 28, per Lord President Clyde at 39, Lord Russell at 45; *Wilson v Clyde Rigging and Boiler Scaling Co Ltd* 1959 SC 328 ("believed and averred"). *Cf* Dickson, *Evidence* (3rd edn), para 417; Bell, *Principles*, para 2218.

[26] Dickson, *Evidence* (3rd edn), para 277, and cases cited; *Miller v Miller* (1898) 25 R 995.

[27] Maclaren, *Court of Session Practice*, p 375; *Pegler v Northern Agricultural Implement Co* (1877) 4 R 435 at 438; *Central Motor Engineering Co v Galbraith* 1918 SC 755 at 765, 770; *Gilmour v Scottish Clan Motorways* 1928 SN 19 (OH).

[28] OCR, r 9.7.

[29] Without that party requiring to make enquiry to establish its truth: *O'Connor v WG Auld & Co (Engineering) Ltd* 1990 SLT (Notes) 16.

[30] *Gray v Boyd* 1996 SLT 60, and see Walker, "Written Pleadings" (1963) 79 ScLR 161 at 169. In *Gray v Boyd* the court noted that a bare denial, even if apparently lacking in candour, would not, of

been specifically admitted, if the express admission supports the reasonable inference that the other fact must also be admitted.[31] The words "not admitted" or the like are not the equivalent of a denial for this purpose.[32] But the words "believed to be true" in averments in answer have been considered to amount to an admission.[33] A reference by a party to a document for its terms is not an implied admission that the document exists, unless its existence is a fact within that party's knowledge.[34]

Special case

11.2.6 This is a statutory process[35] whereby the agreed statement of facts, presented to the court for its opinion upon the law, is binding upon all the parties to it, and renders evidence both unnecessary and inadmissible.

11.3 JUDICIAL ADMISSIONS—CRIMINAL CAUSES

Plea of guilty

11.3.1 A plea of guilty to a charge or to part of a charge, which is accepted by the prosecutor, and which is not later withdrawn with the leave of the court,[36] is a judicial admission which is conclusive against the accused. It enables the prosecutor to move for, and the court to pronounce, sentence, without evidence having been led. It is tendered in open court, in solemn procedure orally by the accused or his counsel or solicitor, and in summary procedure orally by the accused if present (even if represented)[37] or by letter by the accused or the counsel or solicitor for the accused.[38] In solemn procedure, when the plea of guilty is recorded by the clerk of court, the accused, if not a company,[39] signs it, and it is countersigned by the

---

itself, constitute an implied admission (Lord Morison dissenting). See also *McManus v Speirs, Dick & Smith Ltd* 1989 SLT 806, *Sabre Leasing Ltd v Copeland* 1993 SC 345. *Cf Ellon Castle Estates Co Ltd v Macdonald* 1975 SLT (Notes) 66, *Foxley v Dunn* 1978 SLT (Notes) 35 and the practice of treating a bare denial as an implied admission when considering the relevancy of pleadings at debate.

[31] Per Lord Sorn in *Dobson v Colvilles Ltd* (opinion unreported, but excerpted in *Wilson v Clyde Rigging & Boiler Scaling Co Ltd* 1959 SC 328), applied in *Lord Advocate v Gillespie* 1969 SLT (Sh Ct) 10.

[32] *Ellis v Fraser* (1840) 3 D 264 at 271. See also *Stephen v Pirie* (1832) 10 S 279, *Clark v Clark* 1967 SC 296 at 305.

[33] Particularly when read alongside other averments of denial: *Binnie v Rederij Theodoro BV* 1993 SC 71. See also *Wilson v Clyde Rigging and Boiler Scaling Co Ltd* 1959 SC 328 ("believed and averred").

[34] *Pringle v Bremner and Stirling* (1867) 5 M (HL) 55.

[35] Court of Session Act 1988, s 27 and RCS 1994, Chap 78.

[36] Leave may be granted in appropriate circumstances before conviction and sentence. The statutory provision that existed in solemn cases (Criminal Procedure (Scotland) Act 1975, s 122) has been repealed, but the principle appears still to apply: see Renton & Brown *Criminal Procedure* (6th edn), para 16-09 and cases cited there, and para 18-32. In summary cases, at common law, the court may allow a plea of guilty to be withdrawn in exceptional circumstances: *Williams v Linton* (1878) 6 R (J) 12; *Spowart v Burr* (1895) 22 R (J) 30 at 33; *Nicol v Brown* 1951 JC 87; and see later examples cited in Renton & Brown, *Criminal Procedure* (6th edn), para 20-33.

[37] Act of Adjournal (Criminal Procedure Rules) 1996, r 18.1(1).

[38] Solemn procedure: Criminal Procedure (Scotland) Act 1995, s 77. The plea will be tendered at the first diet in a case indicted before the sheriff (s 71(6)) or at any preliminary diet, failing which at the trial in a case before the High Court (s 73(1)). Summary procedure: Criminal Procedure (Scotland) Act 1995, s 144(1) and (2), which provide that a guilty plea may be made at the first calling or any adjournment thereof (ss 144(9) and 145). The plea may also be tendered at an intermediate diet (s 148(6)), failing which at trial.

[39] Criminal Procedure (Scotland) Act 1995, s 70(7).

judge.[40] In summary procedure the plea, when recorded, is signed by the judge or by the clerk of court.[41] If a plea of guilty is not accepted by the prosecutor, who may insist on the right[42] to lead evidence in support of the charge, or, if the court has allowed the plea to be withdrawn,[43] the fact that it has been tendered must not be used against the accused or disclosed to the jury, the accused must not be questioned about it even if he or she gives evidence inconsistent with it,[44] and may be acquitted in spite of it.

Minute of admission, notice of uncontroversial evidence

Apart from the judicial admission contained in a plea of guilty, the only[45] methods in a criminal cause whereby a fact may in certain circumstances be established without evidence are regulated by statute. A minute of admissions may be signed by the accused's representative or the accused personally, or by the prosecutor in relation to defence evidence, and is accepted in lieu of evidence as proof of any fact admitted.[46] Agreed documents or copies may be the subject of such a minute, but will only be so proved if the document or an agreed copy of it accompanies the minute.[47] The statute enjoins the prosecutor and accused to attempt to agree evidence,[48] and provides a process for notice of uncontroversial[49] evidence, which if not challenged by counter-notice in accordance with the statute is treated as conclusively proved.[50] In exceptional circumstances during the trial the court may permit this presumptively conclusive proof to be contradicted.[51] A special defence, such as that of self-defence, may, logically, seem to imply an admission that the accused committed the act complained of, albeit justifiably,[52] but nothing in such a special defence has the effect of relieving the Crown of the burden of proving the commission of the act, or of preventing the accused from contending that its commission has not been proved.[53]

11.3.2

---

[40] Criminal Procedure (Scotland) Act 1995, s 77. In solemn procedure, acceptance of a partial plea of guilty ought to be signed by the prosecutor.

[41] Act of Adjournal (Criminal Procedure Rules) 1996, r 18.1(5).

[42] *Strathern v Sloan* 1937 JC 76. The proper method of recording the plea in such circumstances is indicated in the opinions.

[43] The statutory provision that existed in solemn cases (Criminal Procedure (Scotland) Act 1975, s 122) has been repealed, but the principle appears still to apply: see Renton & Brown, *Criminal Procedure* (6th edn), para 16-09 and cases cited there, and para 18-32. In summary cases, at common law, the court may allow a plea of guilty to be withdrawn in exceptional circumstances: *Williams v Linton* (1878) 6 R (J) 12; *Spowart v Burr* (1895) 22 R (J) 30 at 33; *Nicol v Brown* 1951 JC 87; and see later examples cited in Renton & Brown, *Criminal Procedure* (6th edn), para 20-33.

[44] *Strathern v Sloan* 1937 JC 76.

[45] *Tullis v Millar* (1899) 1 F (J) 75; *Brown v Macpherson* 1918 JC 3 at 8.

[46] Criminal Procedure (Scotland) Act 1995, s 256.

[47] *Evans v Wilson* 1981 SCCR 60.

[48] Criminal Procedure (Scotland) Act 1995, s 257. For a discussion of this see Duff "Intermediate Diets and the Agreement of Evidence: A Move Towards Inquisitional Culture?" (1998) 6 JR 349.

[49] Criminal Procedure (Scotland) Act 1995, s 258.

[50] Criminal Procedure (Scotland) Act 1995, s 258(3), and see, for example, *HM Advocate v Shepherd* 1997 JC 131.

[51] Criminal Procedure (Scotland) Act 1995, s 258(6).

[52] It is described in this way (as a qualified implied admission) in *HM Advocate v Brogan* 1964 SLT 204, but the conclusion was that the burden of proof remained with the Crown throughout.

[53] This was conceded by the Crown in *HM Advocate v McGlone* 1955 JC 14, and confirmed in *Lambie v HM Advocate* 1973 JC 53. See also *Owens v HM Advocate* 1946 JC 119, per Lord Justice-General Normand at 124 (commented upon in *Lambie*); Dickson, *Evidence* (3rd edn), para 374. As to burden of proof and a special defence, see para 2.12.

11.4 *RES JUDICATA*—GENERAL

11.4.1 When a matter has been the subject of judicial determination by a competent tribunal, the determination excludes any subsequent litigation in regard to the same matter between the same parties on the same grounds.[54] In the case of some determinations (decrees *in rem*), which are mentioned in the next paragraph, the exclusion applies even when the parties are not the same. The plea of *res judicata* (matter decided), so described, is a plea in bar of subsequent litigation on that matter,[55] and in Scotland it is generally so regarded.[56] On either statement the result of a successful plea of *res judicata* is that evidence is neither necessary nor admissible with regard to the issues previously determined. Since the subject is not so much part of the law of evidence as an aspect of procedure, it is dealt with only briefly[57] in this and the next paragraph with reference both to civil and criminal causes and the relationship between them.

11.5 *RES JUDICATA*—CIVIL AND CRIMINAL CAUSES

Civil causes

11.5.1 The following elements are essential for a successful plea of *res judicata*. (i) The earlier determination[58] must be made by a competent court or arbiter,[59] and the court may be a foreign[60] or an inferior court or tribunal.[61] (ii) The earlier determination must be pronounced *in foro contentioso* (in court)[62] without fraud or collusion.[63] A decree by default[64] will support the plea, but a decree in

---

[54] Dickson, *Evidence* (3rd edn), para 385.

[55] The matter need not be the case as a whole but an issue within a case: *Anderson v Wilson* 1972 SC 147 at 148. The issue should probably have been a principal, rather than subsidiary, one within the first action. See *Clink v Speyside Distillery Co Ltd* 1995 SLT 1344, in which the Lord Ordinary refused to follow the reasoning in an English case *Carl Zeiss Stiftung v Rayner and Keeler Ltd (No 2)* [1967] AC 853, an "unusual" case discussed in Cross & Tapper, *Evidence* (9th edn), pp 72–75 in the context of the use of issue estoppel in England. Any suggested adaptation of the operation of *res judicata*, which was resisted in *Clink v Speyside Distillery Co Ltd*, must have regard to the separate, but related plea of "competent and omitted", on which see Macphail, *Sheriff Court Practice* (2nd edn), paras 2.112–2.114, Beaumont, "Competent and Omitted" 1985 SLT (News) 345, and the observations in *Dickson v United Dominions Trust Ltd (No 3)* 1988 SLT 19.

[56] For the position in England, see Cross & Tapper, *Evidence* (9th edn), pp 79–88.

[57] For a fuller statement of this branch of law, see Macphail, *Sheriff Court Practice* (2nd edn), paras 2.104–2.109.

[58] Which must be judicial rather than administrative: *Milligan v Chief Constable of Glasgow* 1976 SLT (Sh Ct) 55.

[59] *Farrans v Roxburgh County Council* 1969 SLT 35.

[60] Foreign Judgments (Reciprocal Enforcement) Act 1933, s 8; Civil Jurisdiction and Judgments Act 1982, ss 2(1) and 19(1), and see Anton with Beaumont, *Private International Law* (2nd edn), pp 234–237.

[61] Stair, iv, 40, 16; *cf* Erskine, iv, 3, 7. For examples, see *Murray v Murray* 1956 SC 376 (OH); *Anderson v Wilson* 1972 SC 147 at 149; *McPhee v Heatherwick* 1977 SLT (Sh Ct) 46; *McSheehy v MacMillan* 1993 SLT (Sh Ct) 10.

[62] *Lockyer v Ferryman* (1876) 3 R 882, per Lord Gifford at 911. In a sheriff court action defences must have been lodged: *Esso Petroleum Co Ltd v Law* 1956 SC 33.

[63] *Lockyer v Ferryman* (1876) 3 R 882, per Lord Gifford at 911.

[64] *Forrest v Dunlop* (1875) 3 R 15.

absence[65] and a decree of dismissal,[66] will not. As to a decree resulting from a compromise, conflicting views have been expressed.[67] (iii) The subject-matter of the two litigations must be the same.[68] (iv) The *media concludendi* (points in controversy between the parties) in the two litigations must be the same[69] in substance rather than form.[70] Negligence arising from breach of common law duty and negligence arising from breach of statutory duty constitute one and the same *medium concludendi* for this purpose.[71] (v) Except where the earlier decree is a decree *in rem*, both litigations must be between the same parties or between their authors, successors, representatives, cedents or assignees.[72] When the earlier judgment is a judgment *in rem*, which includes for this purpose a judgment affecting status,[73] a plea of *res judicata* will be upheld not only against the original parties, but against any other person who desires to litigate with regard to the same

---

[65] Erskine, iv, 3, 6; *Mackintosh v Smith and Lowe* (1864) 2 M 1261; (1865) 3 M (HL) 6; *Fulton v Earl of Eglinton* (1895) 22 R 823, per Lord President Robertson at 824. A decree in an undefended family action is a decree in absence although pronounced after proof: *Paterson v Paterson* 1958 SC 141. In *Gibson & Simpson v Pearson* 1992 SLT 894 (OH) it was observed that although the decree in absence had been the subject of an unsuccessful reponing note it was still unable to found the plea.

[66] *Duke of Sutherland v Reed* (1890) 18 R 252; *Menzies v Menzies* (1893) 20 R (HL) 108, per Lord Watson at 111; *Waydale Ltd v DHL Holdings (UK) Ltd (No 2)* 2000 SC 172 (reversing the decision of the Lord Ordinary in *Waydale Ltd v DHL Holdings (UK) Ltd* 1999 SLT 631 to the effect that a plea of *res judicata* could be founded upon a decree of dismissal if there had been inquiry into the merits before dismissal). *Cf Malcolm Muir Ltd v Jamieson* 1947 SC 314, per Lord Mackay at 321. See also *Paterson v Paterson* 1958 SC 141; *Gallacher v Champenoy* 1987 SCLR 752; *Mason v A & R Robertson & Black* 1993 SLT 773.

[67] Maclaren, *Court of Session Practice*, p 396, founding upon *White v Lord Morton's Trs* (1866) 4 M (HL) 53; *Jenkins v Robertson* (1867) 5 M (HL) 27 (decree following a compromise will not support the plea). *Cf Young v Young's Trs* 1957 SC 318 (OH), following *Glasgow and South Western Railway Co v Boyd & Forrest* 1918 SC (HL) 14.

[68] *Leith Dock Commissioners v Miles* (1866) 4 M (HL) 14, per Lord Chelmsford at 19. For examples of differing but closely related subject-matters, see *Weissenbruch v Weissenbruch* 1965 SLT 139; *Mitchell's Trs v Aspin* 1971 SLT 29; *McPhee v Heatherwick* 1977 SLT (Sh Ct) 46; *McSheehy v MacMillan* 1993 SLT (Sh Ct) 10 applying the dicta in *Steven v Broady Norman & Co* 1928 SC 351 (and purporting not to follow *McPhee v Heatherwick* although there is no conflict in *ratios*); *Margrie Holdings Ltd v Edinburgh District Council* 1994 SC 1.

[69] *North British Railway Co v Lanarkshire & Dumbartonshire Railway Co* (1897) 24 R 564, per Lord Kinnear at 572; *Edinburgh & District Water Trs v Clippens Oil Co Ltd* (1899) 1 F 899, per Lord President Robertson at 907, Lord Kinnear at 909; *Malcolm Muir Ltd v Jamieson* 1947 SC 314. In *Gibson & Simpson v Pearson* 1992 SLT 894 (OH) the court held that the assessment of the respective *media concludendi* should be based upon consideration of the pleadings and the earlier decision, and not upon extraneous, antecedent matters. However, in *Short's Trustee v Chung (No 2)* 1999 SC 471 it was considered relevant to have regard to the fact that a material change in circumstances had occurred after the first action, *Short's Trustee v Chung* 1996 SC (HL) 14 (a decision of the House of Lords which precluded the pursuer from implementing the remedy originally sought).

[70] Maclaren, *Court of Session Practice*, p 400; *Grahame v Secretary of State for Scotland* 1951 SC 368; *Gibson & Simpson v Pearson* 1992 SLT 894 (OH); *Forrest v Hendry* 2000 SC 110 (OH).

[71] *Matuszczyk v National Coal Board* 1955 SC 418 (OH).

[72] Stair, iv, 40, 16; Erskine, iv, 3, 3; *Allen v McCombie's Trs* 1909 SC 710, per Lord President Dunedin at 715 (beneficiary); *Ryan v McBurnie* 1940 SC 173 (assignee).

[73] For actions *in rem* competent in the sheriff court, see the Sheriff Courts (Scotland) Act 1907, s 5(1), (2B), (3) and (4). Most actions concerning status (other than declarator of marriage or nullity of marriage) are now competent in the sheriff court as well as the Court of Session, and will give rise to a judgment *in rem* if a declarator on that issue is granted. See Wilkinson & Norrie, *The Law Relating to Parent and Child in Scotland* (2nd edn), para 1.61. For a recent example of shrieval concern that all interested parties should receive intimation before proceedings *in rem* are determined, see *Secretary of State for Social Security v Ainslie* 2000 SLT (Sh Ct) 35, where the pursuer was the Minister responsible for establishing paternity under statutory authority for the purposes of determining the defender's liability for child support maintenance in terms of the Child Support Act 1991.

matter.[74] In child protection proceedings before the sheriff[75] a plea of *res judicata* has been upheld only in very limited circumstances.[76] Due to the statutory requirement that the sheriff must hear evidence in order to find established a ground of referral which is not accepted, the scope for *res judicata* to apply is limited.[77]

Criminal causes

11.5.2 A conviction or an acquittal[78] in a criminal court, even where the former proceeds upon a plea of guilty without trial,[79] is *res judicata* in relation to any subsequent criminal proceedings upon the same charge.[80] A ruling on the relevance or competency[81] of a libel in the same terms will also found a plea of *res judicata*.[82] A plea cannot be founded upon a decision of the court which was fundamentally null[83] or incompetent.[84] A charge of assault and a subsequent charge of murder, as a result of death ensuing from the same assault, are regarded as different charges for this purpose,[85] as is perjury arising from evidence given in the first trial.[86] The test is whether the second charge libelled was identical in substance with the first.[87] A plea of *res judicata* may be founded on a prior conviction or acquittal in an English court,[88] but it is unsettled whether the same applies to a verdict overseas.[89] If a conviction has been quashed on appeal, and statutory authority granted for new

---

[74] *Administrator of Austrian Property v Von Lorang* 1926 SC 598, per Lord Sands at 620, 622, 627; 1927 SC (HL) 80. See also *Murray v Murray* 1956 SC 376 (OH).

[75] Under the Children (Scotland) Act 1995, Pt II, previously the Social Work (Scotland) Act 1968, Pt III.

[76] In *McGregor v H* 1983 SLT 626.

[77] See the review of the cases, and observations, in *M v Constanda* 1999 SC 348.

[78] Whether by verdict of not guilty or not proven. The trial would have to reach a conclusion: see Renton & Brown, *Criminal Procedure* (6th edn), para 9-09.

[79] *Hilson v Easson* 1914 SC (J) 99, per Lord Anderson at 107.

[80] Macdonald, *Criminal Law* (5th edn), p 272, and cases cited there.

[81] Logically, the issue here is whether the same issue *of competency* arises in the second proceedings: for example, if it were held that the sheriff court in Edinburgh lacked jurisdiction over a complaint because the libel narrated that the offence was committed outside the territory of that court, a plea of *res judicata* could be no bar to subsequent proceedings in a different court.

[82] *Longmuir v Baxter* (1858) 3 Irv 287. An example in the sheriff court is *McNab, Petitioner* 1994 SCCR 633, where the plea was sustained after the High Court had confirmed a decision of the sheriff that the first indictment was oppressive due to undue delay (without hearing argument). It is, however, competent to charge an accused in the High Court on a libel previously held irrelevant by the sheriff: *Fleming* (1866) 5 Irv 289.

[83] *Thomson, Petitioner* 1997 SLT 322.

[84] As in *Whitelaw v Dickinson* 1993 JC 68, *McGlynn v HM Advocate* 1995 JC 196.

[85] *Isabella Cobb or Fairweather* (1836) 1 Swin 354; *Stewart* (1866) 5 Irv 310; *O'Connor* (1882) 10 R (J) 40; *Tees v HM Advocate* 1994 JC 12.

[86] *HM Advocate v Cairns* 1967 JC 37.

[87] *McGlynn v HM Advocate* 1995 JC 196.

[88] *Macgregor and Inglis* (1846) Ark 49, per Lord Justice-Clerk Hope at 60; *Clements v HM Advocate* 1991 JC 62, per Lord Justice-General Hope at 71. It cannot, however, be pleaded where the English court has simply "taken into account" the crime in passing sentence on another conviction (*Hilson v Easson* 1914 SC (J) 99), which in any case would not support an equivalent plea in England either (*R v Nicholson* (1947) 32 Cr App R 98). It has been said that for a successful plea the second libel must be at the instance of the same prosecutor (*HM Advocate v Mullen* 1987 SLT 475 at 477D), but this appears to be a misreading of *Longmuir v Baxter* (1858) 3 Irv 287, per Lord Deas at 291–292.

[89] It does in England: see *R v Thomas* [1985] QB 604 and authorities cited there. Note the UK's obligations under the European Convention on the International Validity of Criminal Judgments (1970), Arts 53–55; the European Convention on the Transfer of Proceedings in Criminal Matters (1972), Arts 35–37, and the European Convention on Double Jeopardy (1987, not yet in force).

proceedings against the accused,[90] the plea will not apply to the new proceedings if they are commenced during the two-month period within which the prosecutor may act upon that authority,[91] and are not for an offence more serious than that of which the accused was convicted in the earlier proceedings.[92] After the two-month limit the plea would revive, because the outcome of the appeal is then deemed to be an acquittal for all purposes.[93]

Civil and criminal causes *inter se*

Apart from rare exceptions in which the proceedings in the criminal court were of **11.5.3** a quasi-civil character and the parties in both proceedings were the same,[94] the same matter may properly be adjudicated upon both in the criminal and in the civil court without justifying a plea of *res judicata* in either.[95] There are statutory provisions whereby an extract conviction[96] in a criminal case, on being produced in a civil case, will give rise to a presumption in the civil cause to the effect that the person named in the conviction behaved in the manner described in it.[97]

11.6 JUDICIAL KNOWLEDGE—GENERAL

It is unnecessary, and usually incompetent, to lead evidence regarding matters **11.6.1** which fall within judicial knowledge.[98] The judge will take notice of these matters, either because bound by statute to do so, or because it is customary for judges to do so. In general they are matters which can be immediately ascertained from sources of indisputable accuracy,[99] or which are so notorious as to be

---

[90] Criminal Procedure (Scotland) Act 1995, s 118(1)(c) (solemn), s 183(1)(d) (summary).

[91] Criminal Procedure (Scotland) Act 1995, s 119(1) and (5), s 185(1) and (5).

[92] Criminal Procedure (Scotland) Act 1995, ss 119(2) and 185(2). For example, if A is charged with murder and convicted of culpable homicide, successfully appeals against that conviction and authority for a retrial is granted, he can only be charged with culpable homicide and not murder. The provisions of the 1995 Act thus have the effect of overruling *HM Advocate v Boyle* 1993 JC 5 and *Boyle, Petitioner* 1993 SLT 1085.

[93] Criminal Procedure (Scotland) Act 1995, ss 119(9) and 185(9).

[94] Dickson, *Evidence* (3rd edn), para 385; *Young v Mitchell* (1874) 1 R 1011, per Lord President Inglis at 1013; *Kennedy v Wise* (1890) 17 R 1036.

[95] Hume, ii, 71, 479; Dickson, *Evidence* (3rd edn), para 385; *Wood v North British Railway Co* (1899) 1 F 562; *Faculty of Procurators of Glasgow v Colquhoun* (1900) 2 F 1192; *Wilson v Bennett* (1904) 6 F 269; *Wilson v Murphy* 1936 SLT 564 (OH).

[96] The same does not apply to an acquittal which is generally inadmissible (as irrelevant) in subsequent civil proceedings: see Macphail, *Evidence*, paras 1.18–S11.19A. *Cf Shaw v Craig* 1916 1 SLT 116; *Dennison v Chief Constable, Strathclyde Police* 1996 SLT 74. See also para 9.3.

[97] Law Reform (Miscellaneous Provisions) (Scotland) Act 1968, ss 10–12. The presumptions in ss 10 and 11 are rebuttable, but in s 12 the presumption is conclusive for limited factual purposes in support of a plea of *veritas* in defamation proceedings. See para 3.3.1.

[98] This subject has been developed more fully in the English textbooks. See Cross & Tapper, *Evidence* (9th edn), pp 67–77.

[99] For example, a dictionary or almanac. The Inner House has stated that notice may be taken of *Actuarial Tables with explanatory notes for use in Personal Injury and Fatal Accident Cases (1984)* ("Ogden's tables") (*O'Brien's Curator Bonis v British Steel Corporation* 1991 SLT 477), but evidence was required on matters concerning the applicability of the tables to the losses incurred in Scotland; notice being taken also to the effect that rates of inflation mentioned in the explanatory notes no longer applied. The rate of inflation, retail prices index or equivalent economic indicator is a matter within judicial knowledge: see *Ross v Ross* 1930 SC (HL) 1 and para 11.7.4 below.

indisputable.[100] If a matter is not immediately notorious or ascertainable the party who seeks to prove the matter should be prepared to lead evidence in direct proof of it or from which the matter will be presumed or inferred. If a matter is one which is judicially noticed, a judge may refresh his memory or supplement his knowledge regarding it by consulting recognised works of reference, such as dictionaries[101] or textbooks.[102] While it is unnecessary to prove matters within judicial knowledge, evidence may sometimes be necessary and admissible, regarding their applicability or inapplicability to the particular case,[103] and it may be necessary to have evidence as to what is within common knowledge at a particular time or place.[104]

11.6.2   Apart from the matters which are recognised as being within judicial knowledge, it is improper for a judge to proceed upon personal knowledge of the facts in issue,[105] or upon personal examination of passages in textbooks.[106] Thus the judge may not use personal observations of a locus[107] or of documents,[108] made after the conclusion of a proof, to contradict or supplement the evidence of the witnesses. Whether a judge's special knowledge may be used to *interpret* evidence led is not a matter on which there appears to be Scottish authority,[109] although commonly judicial opinions are such that they give rise to the logical inference that the judge has read more widely than the authorities cited, or has special knowledge or experience which enables skilled assessment of the evidence.[110] In statutory tribunal proceedings members are frequently selected for their experience in the

---

[100] Notoriety must, of nature, reflect social change. In *Doyle v Ruxton* 1999 SLT 487 it had been argued that evidence was necessary to prove that drinks such as McEwans Export, Guinness and Carlsberg Special Brew were of sufficient alcoholic content to fall within the terms of the Licensing (Scotland) Act 1976. The Court decided the case on another point and did not have to rule on the matter but observed, per Lord Philip at 490, that it would be reluctant to hold that the alcoholic content of brands of which the public was widely aware through extensive advertising in the media and in public places was not within judicial knowledge. The same could not be said of the Coors lager, the strength of which had been in issue in *Grieve v Hillary* 1987 SCCR 317, which had not been a well-known drink in Scotland at that time. In *Davidson v Aitchison* 1986 SLT 402 and *Valentine v McPhail* 1986 JC 131 (overruling *Knox v O'Brien* 1985 JC 32) the court took judicial notice of the fact that the "camic device" referred to by the police officers who gave evidence was a device approved by the relevant minister for the purposes of assessing level of alcohol in breath specimen, a device unknown in the days before the introduction of determinative breath testing for cases of drink driving. The name of the approved device was by then a matter of notoriety, but evidence to give rise to the inference that the notorious device rather than an unapproved one had been used was held to be necessary. The "Gatso mini radar device" to which officers had referred in *Pickard v Carmichael* 1995 SLT 675 was not sufficiently notorious to dispense with evidence of its approval status for speed testing.

[101] *eg Edinburgh Corporation v Lord Advocate* 1923 SC 112; *Rutherford & Son v Miln & Co* 1941 SC 125; *Inland Revenue v Russell* 1955 SC 237.

[102] *eg Williamson v McClelland* 1913 SC 678; *G's Trs v G* 1936 SC 837 at 847–848; *Henderson v Somers* (1876) 3 R 997 at 998; *Whyte v Whyte* (1884) 11 R 710 at 712.

[103] See, generally, *Gibb v Edinburgh and District Tramways Co Ltd* 1912 SC 580; *Dyer v Wilsons & Clyde Coal Co Ltd* 1915 SC 199.

[104] As to common knowledge, see paras 11.7.3–11.7.5.

[105] *Morrison v Monro* (1854) 1 Irv 599.

[106] *Davie v Mags of Edinburgh* 1953 SC 34 at 41.

[107] *Hattie v Leitch* (1889) 16 R 1128. With regard to inspections by jurors, see *Sutherland v Prestongrange Coal Co* (1888) 15 R 494; *Hope v Gemmell* (1898) 1 F 74. *Cf Sime v Linton* (1897) 24 R (J) 70.

[108] *McCann v Adair* 1951 JC 127. See also para 16.4.

[109] In England, *Wetherall v Harrison* [1976] QB 773 appears to condone the use of special knowledge of lay magistrates to interpret, but not supplement, evidence led.

[110] See, for example, *Oliver v Hislop* 1946 JC 20; *Cruickshank v Smith* 1949 JC 134, where judicial knowledge was taken of implements used for fishing in the particular locality of the court.

field of the tribunal's jurisdiction or for local knowledge[111]; furthermore, the designation of specialist judges for commercial actions in the Court of Session[112] and the creation of a team of specialist sheriffs for family proceedings in a sheriff court[113] all point towards an acknowledgement of the role for specialist interpretation. It has been said in relation to the situation in England that "no formula has yet been evolved" for describing the limits within which special knowledge may be used in interpretation of evidence.[114] It is clear that any such use must comply with established principles of natural justice,[115] and with the right to a fair trial enshrined in Article 6(1) of the European Convention on Human Rights.

11.7 MATTERS WITHIN JUDICIAL KNOWLEDGE

The following matters have been judicially noticed in the Scottish courts.   **11.7.1**

Acts of Parliament and statutory orders[116]

With certain exceptions, Acts of the old Scots Parliament, the United Kingdom Parliament and the Scottish Parliament must be judicially noticed, and evidence regarding them is excluded.[117] Acts of Sederunt and Acts of Adjournal are the same.[118] It is the duty of counsel and of solicitors to draw the attention of the court to the existence of any relevant statute, whether it appears to assist the party concerned or not.[119]

Law and judicial procedure[120]

Scots law, including Scottish judicial decisions in the House of Lords and the **11.7.2** lower courts, and the practice and procedure of the Scottish courts, are within judicial knowledge, and evidence regarding these matters is excluded. Failure on the part of counsel or solicitors to draw the attention of the court to a relevant authority may be reflected in the award of expenses.[121] Judicial notice is also taken, for their persuasive effect only, of decisions of the Judicial Committee of the Privy Council, of the House of Lords in English cases,[122] and of the English courts,

---

[111] For example, see the discretion afforded to licensing boards as interpreted in *Latif v Motherwell District Licensing Board* 1994 SLT 414, per Lord Allanbridge at 415J, quoted with approval in *Caledonian Nightclubs Ltd v City of Glasgow District Licensing Board* 1995 SC 177 (IH); 1996 SC (HL) 29. It may be that a distinction can be made between professional judges and lay tribunals. Authorities on this point in England are contradictory: see Cross & Tapper, *Evidence* (9th edn), pp 73–75.

[112] RCS 1994, Chap 47.2.

[113] Described at (2000) 45 JLSS 32.

[114] Cross & Tapper, *Evidence*, p 75.

[115] See, for example, *Black v Black* 1990 SLT (Sh Ct) 42, but *cf Latif v Motherwell District Licensing Board* 1994 SLT 414.

[116] These are discussed in detail in Chapter 19.

[117] See paras 19.2–19.5.

[118] See para 19.11.

[119] *Glebe Sugar Refining Co v Greenock Harbour Trs* 1921 SC (HL) 72.

[120] This is discussed in detail in Chapter 19.

[121] *Glebe Sugar Refining Co v Greenock Harbour Trs* 1921 SC (HL) 72; *Mitchell v Mackersy* (1905) 8 F 198; *Baker v Glasgow Corporation* 1916 SC 199.

[122] As to the effect of a House of Lords decision in an English case, see *Orr Ewing v Orr Ewing's Trs* (1884) 11 R 600; (1885) 13 R (HL) 1; *Glasgow Corporation v Central Land Board* 1956 SC (HL) 1.

having reference to a branch of law assimilated to Scots law, or to the interpretation of a statute which applies also to Scotland. The necessity for proof of English law and foreign law in general is dealt with later.[123]

Facts of history and public national events

11.7.3 Examples of these are the history of the unions and divisions of the Christian churches,[124] and the oath taken by the Sovereign on accession to the throne regarding the rights of the Church of Scotland.[125]

Facts of general economic and social custom and behaviour

11.7.4 Examples include the facts of the calendar,[126] general economic conditions,[127] changes in the value of money,[128] the general practices of business people and bankers,[129] the normal scope and effect of recognised classes of contracts,[130] the conditions of the local labour market and the average wages of different types of worker,[131] the prefixes used in classifying public roads,[132] the differences between the habits and equipment of legitimate anglers and salmon poachers,[133] and the accepted conventions of society.[134] These facts should be limited to matters of common knowledge,[135] although it has been accepted that common knowledge will vary from one locality to another.[136]

In *McMillan v BP Refinery (Grangemouth) Ltd* 1961 SLT (Notes) 79, it appears to have been accepted without comment by the Second Division that a decision of the Court of Session was overruled by a later House of Lords decision in an English case.

[123] See para 16.5.

[124] *Renouf's Trs v Haining* 1919 SC 497.

[125] *MacCormick v Lord Advocate* 1953 SC 396 at 410.

[126] *Goodwin* (1837) 1 Swin 431.

[127] *Naismith v Assessor for Renfrewshire* 1921 SC 615.

[128] *Ross v Ross* 1930 SC (HL) 1; *Sands v Devan* 1945 SC 380; *Kelly v Glasgow Corporation* 1949 SC 496: 1951 SC (HL) 15.

[129] *Crerar v Bank of Scotland* 1921 SC 736; 1922 SC (HL) 137. However, in *Lord Advocate's Reference (No 1 of 1992)* 1992 JC 179, it was observed that it was not within judicial knowledge that a particular major clearing bank or building society fulfilled a requirement of the Building Societies Act 1986.

[130] *Muirhead & Turnbull v Dickson* (1905) 7 F 686; *Taylor v Wylie & Lochhead Ltd* 1912 SC 978.

[131] *Keane v Mount Vernon Colliery Co Ltd* 1933 SC (HL) 1, per Lord Buckmaster at 6; *Moore v Harland & Wolff Ltd* 1937 SC 707.

[132] *Russell v Annan* 1993 SCCR 234; *Donaldson v Valentine* 1996 SLT 643.

[133] *Oliver v Hislop* 1946 JC 20; *Cruickshank v Smith* 1949 JC 134.

[134] *Bennet Clark v Bennet Clark* 1909 SC 591; *Ross v Ross* 1930 SC (HL) 1.

[135] *Naismith & Ors v Assessor for Renfrew* 1921 SC 615, per Lord Hunter at 623.

[136] A district land judge had common knowledge of housing shortages in Skye: *Martin v Shareholders in Luib Common Grazing* 1973 SLT (Land Ct) 9, following *Moyes v Assessor for Perth* 1912 SC 761. Cases to the effect that a licensing court could not take judicial knowledge of adequacy of provision of premises licensed for liquor or for gaming in a city, since this was a complex issue outwith common knowledge (*Russo v Hamilton No 2 District Licensing Court* 1962 SLT (Sh Ct) 40; *Carnie v Edinburgh Licensing Court* 1962 SLT (Sh Ct) 83; *Leckie v Ross* 1963 SLT (Sh Ct) 21) have been overtaken by the extensive discretion now afforded to licensing boards on this point by the Licensing (Scotland) Act 1976, s 17 (as amended), in which local knowledge is presumed for the purposes of determining a comparative locality and the extent of over-provision: see *Latif v Motherwell District Licensing Board* 1994 SLT 414, per Lord Allanbridge at 415J, quoted with approval in *Caledonian Nightclubs Ltd v City of Glasgow District Licensing Board* 1995 SC 177 (IH); 1996 SC (HL) 29.

Facts of nature

Examples include the normal period of human gestation,[137] fertility[138] and **11.7.5**
survivance,[139] the mischievous habits of children,[140] the vicious propensities of
animals,[141] and the elementary principles of dynamics.[142]

---

[137] See paras 28.14 and 28.15.

[138] *G's Trs v G* 1936 SC 837. The court was primarily concerned to declare, as applicable in all but a
certain class of future cases, a rebuttable *praesumptio juris* that fertility ends at 53 years. On this, see
para 3.5. The facts regarding normal capacity for childbearing, however, on which this presumption
was founded, were regarded as being within judicial knowledge.

[139] The presumption in favour of survivance (see para 3.5) has been recognised as terminating at a
hundred years from the date of birth (see, *eg*, *Bruce v Smith* (1871) 10 M 130). This recognition was
based on judicial knowledge of the ages normally attained by human beings.

[140] *Taylor v Glasgow Corporation* 1922 SC (HL) 1.

[141] *Hennigan v McVey* (1882) 9 R 411; *Harper v Great North of Scotland Railway Co* (1886) 13 R
1139. See also *McQuaker v Goddard* [1940] 1 KB 687 (CA). But *cf Dickie v Corbett* 1954 JC 57, per
Lord Sorn at 65, Lord Justice-General Cooper at 62–63.

[142] *Ballard v North British Railway Co* 1923 SC (HL) 43; *Carruthers v Macgregor* 1927 SC 816 at
819–820.

CHAPTER 12

ORAL EVIDENCE—GENERAL

12.1 THE OATH

General

Every witness must take the oath or affirm before giving evidence,[1] unless he is a **12.1.1** child[2] or mentally incapable,[3] and a witness who refuses to take the oath or affirm may be punished for contempt.[4] This applies also to evidence given in mitigation,[5] although letters in mitigation are in practice received without being sworn to as evidence.[6] If a witness is called merely to be shown to the jury he must be sworn, since the other side may wish to question him.[7] The rules governing certain tribunals allow them to take evidence without administering an oath or affirmation,[8] but no such relaxation applies in small claims procedure.[9] A witness who gives false evidence on oath or affirmation is liable to prosecution for perjury.[10]

---

[1] *McLaughlin v Douglas and Kidston* (1863) 4 Irv 273. Hume suggests that peers "whose privilege it is to be trusted in certain cases on their word of honour" (i, 370) are not required to take the oath or affirm, but Dickson takes a different view, which appears to have prevailed: Dickson, *Evidence* (3rd edn), para 1409.
[2] See para 13.2.
[3] See para 13.5.
[4] *Tweedie* (1829) Shaw 222; *Bonnar v Simpson* (1836) 1 Swin 39; *Wylie v HM Advocate* 1966 SLT 149. See also the Criminal Procedure (Scotland) Act 1995, s 155(1)(b) (a witness in a summary prosecution who "unlawfully refuses to be sworn" shall be deemed guilty of contempt of court).
[5] *Forbes v HM Advocate* 1963 JC 68.
[6] See Renton and Brown, *Criminal Procedure* (6th edn), para 22-13. The learned editor notes also that oral reports are sometimes made by social workers without them being sworn.
[7] Dickson, *Evidence* (3rd edn), para 1765; *Milne* (1866) 5 Irv 229.
[8] *Douglas v Provident Clothing Supply Co* 1969 SC 32. See, *eg*, Industrial Tribunals Rules of Procedure 1993 (SI 1993/2687), r 9(4); Lands Tribunal for Scotland Rules 1971 (SI 1971/218), r 23. In each case, the tribunal may at its discretion administer an oath or affirmation.
[9] Small Claims Rules 1988 (SI 1988/1976), r 16.13.
[10] See *Lord Advocate's Reference (No 1 of 1985)* 1986 JC 137. It is perjury to give evidence which the witness does not know to be true, even if he does not know it to be false: *Simpson v Tudhope* 1988 SLT 297.

Form of oath

12.1.2 When taking the oath, the witness should raise his right hand and repeat after the judge "I swear by Almighty God that I will tell the truth, the whole truth, and nothing but the truth."[11] If the witness states, expressly or impliedly,[12] that the manner of taking the oath is not appropriate to his religious belief, the oath is administered in the appropriate manner. If the witness objects, but it is not reasonably practicable without inconvenience or delay to administer the oath in the appropriate manner, the witness may be required to affirm.[13] Whatever form the oath is taken in, it is binding if the person taking it has accepted that form without objection[14] or has declared it to be binding upon him.[15]

Form of affirmation

12.1.3 The witness need not raise his right hand when making the affirmation,[16] but should repeat after the judge "I solemnly, sincerely and truly declare and affirm that I will tell the truth, the whole truth, and nothing but the truth."[17] Such an affirmation is of the same force and effect as an oath.[18]

Effect of failure to administer oath or affirmation

12.1.4 In *McCubbin v Turnbull*,[19] an affidavit was held invalid because a Quaker had not sworn in proper form.[20] Beyond this, there appears to be no other Scottish case dealing with the situation where evidence of an adult, capable witness is taken without an oath or affirmation, or following on an incorrectly administered oath or affirmation.[21] The English courts have taken the view that where a witness is incorrectly allowed to give evidence without taking the oath, their evidence is "not evidence" at all,[22] but by statute, a criminal conviction is now not to be taken as unsafe solely because it appears to the Court of Appeal that a witness's evidence should have been given on oath.[23]

---

[11] Act of Adjournal (Criminal Procedure Rules) 1996, rr 14.5 and 18.2 and Form 14.5-A; OCR, r 29.16 and Form G.14; RCS, rr 36.10 and 37.4 and Form 36.10-A.

[12] *eg*, a Jew may cover his head.

[13] Oaths Act 1978, s 5(2)–(3).

[14] False Oaths (Scotland) Act 1933, s 7(1)(a).

[15] False Oaths (Scotland) Act 1933, s 7(1)(a); Oaths Act 1978, s 4(1). Nor is the validity of an oath affected by the witness having had no religious belief: Oaths Act 1978, s 4(2).

[16] Macphail, *Sheriff Court Practice* (2nd edn), para 16.64.

[17] Act of Adjournal (Criminal Procedure Rules) 1996, rr 14.5 and 18.2 and Form 14.5-B; RCS, rr 36.10 and 37.4 and Form 36.10-B; OCR, r 29.16 and Form G.15. Strictly speaking, these prescribed forms are at variance with s 6(1) of the Oaths Act 1978, which requires the witness to state his name between "I" and "do solemnly".

[18] Oaths Act 1978, s 5(4).

[19] (1850) 12 D 1123.

[20] Although he *had* sworn in a form which statute had made available to non-Quakers.

[21] *Cf Jardine v Howdle* 1997 JC 163, where it seems to have been assumed that such evidence was inadmissible, but it was unnecessary to decide the issue as no timeous objection had been taken at trial. For the effect of a failure to object to evidence, see para 12.6.

[22] *R v Sharman* [1998] 1 Cr App R 406.

[23] Youth Justice and Criminal Evidence Act 1999, s 56(5).

12.2 CONDUCT OF PROOF OR TRIAL

General

Each party leads evidence in turn,[24] and usually the witnesses are cross-examined **12.2.1** and re-examined. Re-examination should be confined to matters raised in cross-examination, except where the judge grants permission for a new matter to be raised.[25] If permission is granted, it is usual for the judge to allow cross-examination on that point. The judge may put questions to "clear up ambiguities that are not being cleared up by either the examiner or the cross-examiner [and] such questions as he might regard relevant and important for the proper determination of the case", but should not take over the role of examiner or cross-examiner.[26] It is thought that if he elicits new and material evidence, he should give an opportunity for cross-examination on that point.[27] In civil cases, it is competent for parties to agree that a witness is to be held as concurring in chief and in cross with another witness, in which case the second witness will be sworn, will give his name, age, designation and (if an expert witness) his qualifications, and will express his concurrence.[28] This procedure is incompetent in criminal cases.[29]

12.3 RECALL OF WITNESS

At common law, only the judge could recall a witness,[30] and then only for the pur- **12.3.1** pose of clearing up a point left ambiguous or obscure.[31] Where the judge exercises this power, he must question the witness himself,[32] although it is thought that if any new and material evidence is elicited an opportunity to cross-examine should be granted.[33] The power can be exercised at any time.[34] It has been noted that there is no reported case of this power being exercised in a civil case in recent times.[35]

Now, by statute, it is competent for the judge to recall a witness on the motion **12.3.2**

---

[24] In criminal cases, this means that the prosecutor leads. In civil cases, the pursuer usually begins but the defender may be ordained to lead. See para 2.3.2. In criminal cases, the accused may make a submission of no case to answer at the close of the prosecution case and, if successful, will be acquitted without having to lead evidence. See Criminal Procedure (Scotland) Act 1995, ss 97 and 160.

[25] Codifying Act of Sederunt (1913) F, II, 2. The judge must have regard to the "interests of justice", including the public interest: *Gunn v Brown* 1987 SLT 94. But see *Niven v Tudhope* 1982 SCCR 365.

[26] *Tallis v HM Advocate* 1982 SCCR 91, per Lord Justice-General Emslie at 98, quoting Lord Justice-Clerk Wheatley in *Livingstone v HM Advocate*, 22 March 1974, Crown Office Circular A7/74. See also *Nisbet v HM Advocate* 1979 SLT (Notes) 5 and *Elliot v Tudhope* 1988 SLT 721.

[27] *McLeod v HM Advocate* 1939 JC 68.

[28] Macphail, *Sheriff Court Practice* (2nd edn), para 16.83 notes that the procedure is now rarely employed.

[29] *Cafferty v Cheyne* 1939 JC 1; *Black v Bairds & Dalmellington Ltd* 1939 SC 472 at 477.

[30] Although, as has been pointed out elsewhere, this could be at the request of a party: Field and Raitt, *Evidence* (2nd edn), para 10-114.

[31] *Todd v MacDonald* 1960 JC 93, per Lord Sorn at 96; *Davidson v McFadyean* 1942 JC 95, where dicta in earlier cases, which would justify such recall for wider purposes, were doubted: *Collison v Mitchell* (1897) 24 R (J) 52; *Saunders v Paterson* (1905) 7 F (J) 58. See also *Brown v Smith* 1982 SLT 301.

[32] Macphail, *Evidence* (1987), para 8.54; *Brown v Smith* 1982 SLT 301, per Lord Cameron at 303.

[33] *Cf McLeod v HM Advocate* 1939 JC 68.

[34] In *Rollo v Wilson* 1988 JC 82, a witness in a summary prosecution was recalled after the defence had started to address the sheriff on the evidence.

[35] Macphail, *Sheriff Court Practice* (2nd edn), para 16.82.

of either party.[36] Although it is not explicitly stated in the statutes, it is now accepted that such a motion is competent only before a party closes his case.[37] For example, recall was allowed to enable a witness to speak more clearly to acts of adultery,[38] and to enable the witness to be asked whether he had, on an occasion before he gave evidence, made a statement inconsistent with his evidence.[39] Recall was refused, however, where the contradictory statement was alleged to have been made after he had given evidence.[40] The decision whether or not it is in the interests of justice to grant the motion is in the discretion of the trial judge.[41]

12.4 EVIDENCE IN REPLICATION AND ADDITIONAL EVIDENCE

Evidence in replication in civil proceedings

12.4.1 In civil proceedings, it is competent, although most unusual, to allow the pursuer a proof in replication with regard to any matter of which notice has not been given on record or of which it may fairly be said, proof in anticipation could not have been expected.[42] Proof in replication was allowed where, if it had not been allowed, one party would have had no opportunity to meet his opponent's case.[43] It has also been allowed in a slander action to prove malice[44] or to meet *veritas*.[45]

Evidence in replication in criminal proceedings

12.4.2 After the close of the defence evidence but before the prosecutor proceeds to address the judge on the evidence (or, in solemn procedure, the commencement of the speeches to the jury), the prosecutor may make a motion to be allowed to lead evidence in replication.[46] This must be for the purpose of contradicting evidence given by any defence witness[47] which could not reasonably have been anticipated by the prosecutor,[48] or to prove that a witness has on a specified occasion made a

---

[36] Evidence (Scotland) Act 1852, s 4 (civil proceedings); Criminal Procedure (Scotland) Act 1995, s 263(5) (criminal proceedings).
[37] *Todd v MacDonald* 1960 JC 93, per Lord Sorn at 96; *Lindie v HM Advocate* 1974 JC 1 at 5; Macphail, *Sheriff Court Practice* (2nd edn), para 16.81. *Cf* Gordon, "*Lindie v HMA*" (1974) 19 JLSS 5 at 5–6.
[38] *A v B* (1858) 20 D 407 at 413 and 418.
[39] *Dyet v National Coal Board* 1957 SLT (Notes) 18; *Hoey v Hoey* (1884) 11 R 578; *Robertson v Steuart* (1874) 1 R 532 at 586 and 588.
[40] *Begg v Begg* (1887) 14 R 497.
[41] *HM Advocate v Maclennon* (1972) 36 JCL 247. It has been used to allow witnesses to purge a contempt of court: *Thomson v HM Advocate* 1988 JC 105; *Gall v HM Advocate* 1992 JC 115. As has been pointed out, however, the primary interest in recall is not to allow a contempt to be purged but to allow a party to lead the evidence which the witness is now willing to give: *Birrell v HM Advocate* 1993 SCCR 812 at 823A–B.
[42] *Dick & Stevenson v Mackay* (1880) 7 R 778; *Wilson v Thomas Usher & Son Ltd* 1934 SC 332 at 338; *Gairdner v Youngs* (1874) 2 R 173.
[43] *Gairdner v Youngs* (1874) 2 R 173.
[44] *Rankine v Roberts* (1873) 1 R 225.
[45] *Kessack v Kessack* (1889) 1 F 398.
[46] Criminal Procedure (Scotland) Act 1995, s 269.
[47] So, in *Campbell v Allan* 1988 JC 46, it was held incompetent to lead evidence in replication to contradict a Crown witness, even though defence witnesses had given concurring evidence on the point at issue.
[48] Criminal Procedure (Scotland) Act 1995, s 269(1)(a). See *MacGillivray v Johnston (No 2)* 1994 SLT 1012: evidence in replication could not be led where the defence agent had written to the Crown intimating the line of defence and the Crown had precognosced the relevant witnesses.

statement different from the evidence given by him at the trial.[49] The judge may permit this evidence to be led despite the fact that proper notice of the witness or a production has not been given, or that a witness must be recalled.[50]

Additional evidence in criminal proceedings

12.4.3 Before the prosecutor proceeds to address the judge on the evidence (or, in solemn procedure, the commencement of the speeches to the jury), either the prosecutor or the accused may make a motion to be allowed to lead additional evidence.[51] The judge shall only grant such permission where he considers such evidence to be *prima facie* material,[52] and that at the commencement of the trial[53] the evidence was not available and could not reasonably have been made available, or that the materiality of the evidence could not reasonably have been foreseen by the party.[54] The judge may permit this evidence to be led despite the fact that proper notice of the witness or a production has not been given, or that a witness must be recalled.[55]

12.5 QUESTIONS

General

12.5.1 Questions should be clear and unambiguous and as short as possible, each raising a single point. A long and involved question may confuse the witness and give an unjustified bad impression, or it may lead to an incomplete answer. A cross-examiner may obtain what appears to him at the time to be a favourable answer, only to find, possibly on appeal, that the question was ambiguous and that the court is unwilling to rely on the answer because the witness may have taken the other meaning from the question.

Leading questions

12.5.2 A leading question is one which suggests the answer desired. Except for introductory narrative and on non-controversial matters,[56] it is inappropriate for a party to ask leading questions of a witness favourable to its case—for example, whether certain named persons were present rather than who was present,[57] or whether she was employed to find lodgings for the pursuer and a young woman rather than

---

[49] Criminal Procedure (Scotland) Act 1995, ss 269(1)(b) and 263(4).

[50] Criminal Procedure (Scotland) Act 1995, s 269(2).

[51] Criminal Procedure (Scotland) Act 1995, s 268.

[52] Criminal Procedure (Scotland) Act 1995, s 268(2)(a). See *Brown v Smith* 1982 SLT 301.

[53] Meaning the time when the first witness for the prosecution is sworn (or, in solemn procedure, the time when the jury is sworn): Criminal Procedure (Scotland) Act 1995, s 268(5).

[54] Criminal Procedure (Scotland) Act 1995, s 268(2). See *Cushion v HM Advocate* 1994 SLT 410, where the judge refused a defence motion to lead additional evidence and it was held irrelevant to the subsequent appeal that a fuller explanation as to why it could not reasonably have been available earlier was by then available.

[55] Criminal Procedure (Scotland) Act 1995, s 268(3).

[56] See *McKenzie v McKenzie* 1943 SC 108, per Lord Justice-Clerk Cooper at 109.

[57] *Mackenzie v Murray* (1819) 2 Mur 155.

whether she had been employed to find lodgings, and, if so, for whom.[58] The effect may be such as to make the answer worthless in evidence.[59]

12.5.3   In general, this means that leading questions are inappropriate in examination in chief or re-examination,[60] but permissible in cross-examination.[61] However, if a witness proves hostile to the party calling him, or reluctant to give evidence, that party may ask leading questions without the leave of the court.[62] Leading questions on any point of importance ought to be objected to, though the mere putting of the question usually does the damage, and in a proof it is often better just to have the evidence recorded as question and answer, so as to enable the judge and any appeal court to see how the evidence was elicited. It may then be treated as of little weight.[63] Circumstances may be mentioned to the witness to direct his mind to the facts to which he is to speak. Thus a fact may be stated to remind the witness of a date.[64]

Hypothetical questions

12.5.4   This phrase has two meanings. First, the hypothesis may be that something happened which did not happen. In some cases such a question is essential—for example, in a reduction on the ground of misrepresentation. The pursuer must be asked what he would have done if he had known the truth.[65] An Outer House decision[66] disapproving of such questions cannot be of universal application and is difficult to reconcile with an earlier Inner House decision.[67] Secondly, the hypothesis may be that something has been or will be proved. Such a question should not be asked unless evidence has been led to support the hypothesis or if it is intended to lead such evidence. In any event, evidence depending on an unproved hypothesis is useless.

Double questions

12.5.5   This form of question makes an implied assumption and the witness cannot answer it directly without affirming the truth of the assumption. The hackneyed example is "Have you stopped beating your wife?" Questions of this nature are often put unintentionally by a cross-examiner so certain of his facts that he does not notice that the witness has not admitted them, and they are unfair and should be objected

---

[58] *Baillie v Bryson* (1818) 1 Mur 331. See also *King v King* (1842) 4 D 590, where the witness was asked whether she formed a certain impression rather than what impression she formed: *Hunter v Dodds* (1832) 10 S 833.

[59] *Bishop v Bryce* 1910 SC 426, per Lord President Dunedin at 431.

[60] Cf Macphail, *Evidence*, para 8.33, where "a fairly widespread practice of asking leading questions in re-examination", which the author finds objectionable, is noted.

[61] It is thought that if the witness proves favourable to the cross-examiner, leading questions in cross-examination may in certain cases be inappropriate, and will certainly diminish the weight to be given to the evidence elicited. Cf Macphail, *Sheriff Court Practice* (2nd edn), para 16.75.

[62] Dickson, *Evidence* (3rd edn), para 1773; *Gall v Gall* (1870) 9 M 177, per Lord President Inglis at 179; *Frank v HM Advocate* 1938 JC 17; *Brennan v Edinburgh Corporation* 1962 SC 36, per Lord Sorn at 42; *Avery v Cantilever Shoe Co Ltd* 1942 SC 469; *Lowe v Bristol Motor Omnibus Co* 1934 SC 1. See para 12.8.

[63] *McKenzie v McKenzie* 1943 SC 108; *Bishop v Bryce* 1910 SC 426.

[64] *Auchmutie v Ferguson* (1817) 1 Mur 212.

[65] *AW Gamage Ltd v Charlesworth's Tr* 1910 SC 257, per Lord Kinnear at 265; *Boyd & Forrest v Glasgow & South-Western Railway* 1915 SC (HL) 20 at 24, 26, 38 and 42; *McWilliams v Sir William Arrol & Co Ltd* 1961 SC 134 at 144.

[66] *AB v CD* 1957 SC 415.

[67] *Bairner v Fels* 1931 SC 674.

to. An affirmative and a negative answer may be almost equally damaging, and a perfectly honest witness may give a bad impression because he cannot answer directly, but has to enter on an explanation. Dickson gives two examples[68]: asking a person why he did something before asking whether he did it, and asking how much was paid before asking whether any payment was made.

Questions usurping function of court

In many cases the fact in issue is really a matter of inference from other facts, and **12.5.6** it is for the court, not the witnesses, to draw the inference. So it is incompetent in an action arising from a traffic accident to ask a witness, even in cross, whether in his opinion the driver was to blame.[69] It is also incompetent to ask a witness his opinion as to the meaning of a contract, that being for the court.[70] A witness may not be asked his impression from the facts known to him; it is for the court to form its impression on the whole evidence.[71] So evidence of a witness's impression that a wife's distressed conduct on a particular occasion was due to her husband's ill treatment was rejected since it was based on her knowledge of the husband's previous conduct towards his wife.[72] On the other hand, evidence of an impression produced at the moment by the facts then observed is competent.[73] Where a witness in an action of divorce for adultery had given evidence that on entering a room at midnight she found the defender and a man not her husband lying together on a sofa, it was held competent to ask her what her impression was.[74]

12.6 OBJECTIONS TO QUESTIONS

Civil cases

It is important to object timeously to evidence, as if no objection is taken a party **12.6.1** may be entitled to found on it despite the fact that it is inadmissible or there is no record.[75] Usually one advocate is heard for the objector, then one for the opposite party and finally the first advocate in reply, but in cases of difficulty and moment more than one advocate may be heard.[76] The objection, any submissions, and the court's ruling on the objection and submission should be included in the record of the evidence.[77] A very general practice is to allow the evidence under reservation as to its admissibility and leave the point for decision later,[78] and the summary

---

[68] Dickson, *Evidence* (3rd edn), para 1771.
[69] *Gunn v Gardiner* (1820) 4 Mur 194. See also para 16.1.
[70] *Milne v Samson* (1843) 6 D 355.
[71] *AB v CD* (1848) 11 D 289 at 293.
[72] *AB v CD* (1848) 11 D 289.
[73] *King v King* (1842) 4 D 590 at 596; *AB v CD* (1848) 11 D 289 at 292 and 295.
[74] *King v King* (1842) 4 D 590. The evidence is narrated at (1842) 4 D 575.
[75] *McGlone v British Railways Board* 1966 SC (HL) 1; *O'Donnell v Murdoch McKenzie & Co Ltd* 1966 SC 58; *Albacora SRL v Westcott & Laurence Line* 1966 SC (HL) 19; *Brown's Exrx v North British Steel Foundry Ltd* 1968 SLT 121. See also *Royal Bank of Scotland plc v Malcolm* 1999 SCLR 854.
[76] Codifying Act of Sederunt (1913) F, II, 3.
[77] RCS, r 36.11(2); OCR, r 29.18(5).
[78] *McDonald v Duncan* 1933 SC 737 and 744. See also *Thomson v Glasgow Corporation* 1962 SC (HL) 36.

cause rules expressly require the sheriff to follow this procedure "except where he is of the opinion that the evidence is clearly irrelevant or scandalous."[79]

12.6.2   If an objection is sustained to a line of evidence, counsel should state, if it be the fact, that that line would have been pursued with other named witnesses. This ensures that if the ruling is reversed there will be no confusion as to what additional evidence may be led.[80]

12.6.3   In the sheriff court, in the case of an objection to oral or documentary evidence on the ground of confidentiality, or to the production of a document on any ground, an incidental appeal lies to the sheriff principal with leave of the sheriff.[81]

Criminal cases

12.6.4   In solemn procedure any objection to the competency or admissibility of evidence must be recorded,[82] but failure to object does not necessarily bar an appeal on the ground that incompetent evidence was led.[83] In summary procedure any objection to the competency or admissibility of evidence must, if either party desires it, be entered in the record.[84] It is good practice to intimate a desire to have the objection noted.[85] If the accused is legally represented, it is provided by statute that no conviction may be set aside in respect of such objections unless they have been timeously stated at the trial.[86] It has been held that this is simply an application of a more general rule that "unless objection to the competency or admission of evidence is timeously taken, it cannot be subsequently taken, and, if not, such evidence becomes part of the evidence *in causa*."[87] It has been suggested that evidence which is objected to in summary procedure may be led under reservation to its admissibility,[88] but there is now some doubt as to whether this is appropriate.[89] If evidence is led under reservation, its admissibility will require to be determined at the end of the Crown case so as not to prejudice the accused's right to make a submission of no case to answer.[90] If it is necessary to hear evidence from the accused or other defence witnesses in order to make this decision, a trial within a trial is appropriate.[91]

---

[79] SCR, r 44.

[80] *Hewat v Edinburgh Corporation* 1944 SC 30.

[81] OCR, r 29.19, which is applied to summary cause proceedings by SCR, r 3(2). For the procedure, see Macphail, *Sheriff Court Practice* (2nd edn), paras 16.89–16.90, where it is submitted that leave "should be granted only in the most exceptional circumstances."

[82] Criminal Procedure (Scotland) Act 1995, s 93(5)(a)(iii).

[83] Macdonald, *Criminal Law* (5th edn), p 358; *HM Advocate v McGachy* 1991 JC 199, per Lord Sutherland at 201. See also para 1.1.

[84] Criminal Procedure (Scotland) Act 1995, s 157(2).

[85] *Macaulay v Wilson* 1995 SLT 1070.

[86] Criminal Procedure (Scotland) Act 1995, s 192(3)(b)(ii). For applications of this rule, see *Maciver v Mackenzie* 1942 JC 1; *Sutterfield v O'Brien* 1996 SLT 198; *Jardine v Howdle* 1997 JC 163. See also *Tudhope v Stewart* 1986 SLT 659, where the principle was applied without reference to the statute. But see *Robertson v Aitchison* 1981 SCCR 149, where s 192 (then s 454 of the 1975 Act) was not referred to, and a conviction was quashed because a prior conviction had been improperly disclosed to the sheriff, albeit without objection. If the objection has been timeously stated, it is no bar to the appeal that it has not been entered in the record: *McDonalds, Ltd v Adair* 1944 JC 119; *Cameron v Waugh* 1937 JC 5.

[87] *Skeen v Murphy* 1978 SLT (Notes) 2, per Lord Justice-Clerk Wheatley at 2.

[88] *Clark v Stuart* 1950 JC 8.

[89] See *Thompson v Crowe* 2000 JC 173.

[90] *Runham v Westwater* 1995 JC 70.

[91] *Thompson v Crowe* 2000 JC 173.

12.7 REFRESHING MEMORY

As a general rule a witness must speak from his own recollection, but he is usually **12.7.1** allowed to refresh his memory by looking at notes made by himself [92] at the time of the events to which he is speaking, or very shortly thereafter. The notes need not themselves be admissible in evidence.[93] It is everyday practice for police officers to refer to their notebooks for details of measurements or positions, and for any statement made by an accused person. The notes, though not themselves evidence, become part of the witness's oral testimony, and the other side is entitled to see them.[94] If the witness does not refer to them while giving evidence (even if he has referred to them beforehand), the other side is not entitled to see them.[95] The purpose of the notes or other writing is to refresh, stimulate or excite the memory of a witness. They are not a substitute for memory, and where the witness has "no recollection of the facts whatever",[96] notes cannot be used to refresh memory,[97] although they may be lodged as a production and sworn to by the witness as accurate.[98]

The privilege is primarily confined to the original notes, but in two old cases **12.7.2** witnesses were allowed to refer to secondary documents. A witness was allowed to refer to a draft minute of a meeting framed by him from notes made apparently partly by himself and partly by someone else.[99] Where a witness was using a printed report which he alleged was in substance the same as his notes, an objection was repelled on the ground that no attempt was made to discredit the statement by calling for the notes.[100] Presumably if the notes had been called for and were not available, the objection would have been sustained, and in a subsequent case the objection was sustained on that ground.[101] In that case Lord Fullerton distinguished two kinds of original note. First, there are notes of a temporary state of affairs (such as the height of a flood); second, there are notes of permanent features

---

[92] A witness may also refer to documents which were prepared under his eye, or which he perused to his satisfaction while the facts were fresh in his recollection. See Dickson, *Evidence* (3rd edn), para 1784. But a note dictated by the witness which he did not verify at the time in some way probably cannot be used: *R v McLean* (1968) 52 Cr App R 80. However, in a criminal prosecution in Scotland, the witness could adopt such a note as a prior statement under the Criminal Procedure (Scotland) Act 1995, s 260. See paras 5.4.5 and 8.6.5.

[93] In *Dickson v Taylor* (1816) 1 Mur 142, the witness was allowed to look at an unstamped document. On afterstamping, see para 21.12.

[94] *Niven v Hart* (1898) 25 R (J) 89, where Lord Justice-General Robertson observed that, if the notes contained private memoranda irrelevant to the case, they might be handed to the judge rather than the other party for examination.

[95] *Hinshelwood v Auld* 1926 JC 4; *Deb v Normand* 1997 SLT 107. See also *Bullock v HM Advocate* 1999 JC 260; *Daly v Vannet* 1999 SCCR 346.

[96] *McPherson* (1845) 2 Broun 450, per Lord Cockburn at 453.

[97] The English courts have taken a rather different view: see *R v Bryant & Dickson* (1946) 31 Cr App R 146.

[98] *McPherson* (1845) 2 Broun 450 (where the writing was not lodged); *Gibb* (1871) 2 Coup 35 (where it was). See also the Criminal Procedure (Scotland) Act 1995, s 260, which allows a witness to adopt a prior statement in a document. See para 8.6.5.

[99] *Wilson v Glasgow & South-Western Railway* (1851) 14 D 1. This ruling was excepted to, but the case was settled. As to minutes generally, see paras 19.32–19.33. In such circumstances it is advisable to have the original notes available for inspection.

[100] *MacKenzie v Horne* (1838) 16 S 1286; (1839) McL & Rob 977. In *Wilson v Glasgow & South-Western Railway* (1851) 14 D 1 the witness was not asked to produce the original notes.

[101] *Campbell v Macfarlane* (1840) 2 D 663. Another ground for refusing to allow the witness to use the report was that the copy proposed to be used had been made by a third party, who was not a witness, and had not been checked by the witness himself.

(such as the width of a bridge). Lord Fullerton thought that the former kind, if called for, must be produced, but not the latter. Presumably the distinction is that the width of the bridge can be checked at any time, whereas the height of the flood at a particular moment cannot.

12.7.3   Medical and other expert reports may be read by the witness in court, and become part of his oral evidence in this way.[102]

12.8 HOSTILE WITNESS

12.8.1   This expression has no technical meaning in Scotland. When a witness gives evidence damaging to the case of the party calling him, the counsel or solicitor of that party is free to challenge that evidence by suggesting that in specified respects it is mistaken, unreliable or untruthful, and may ask the court to disbelieve any part of it.[103] Leave of the court to do this is not required.[104] The same rule applies in a prosecution.[105] A witness may be asked, in order to explain his apparent reluctance, whether an attempt has been made to intimidate him.[106]

12.9 CROSS-EXAMINATION—GENERAL

Introductory

12.9.1   Cross-examination has two purposes: first, to test the veracity of the witness and the accuracy of his evidence, and, secondly, to obtain from him evidence on points on which he has not been questioned and which may support the cross-examiner's case.[107] It follows that insofar as the opposing advocate is satisfied that the witness is veracious and that his evidence in chief is accurate and complete, cross-examination is useless. It may even be harmful to the cross-examiner by emphasising the evidence already given or suggesting to the jury that the cross-examiner has a weak case. But if a party intends to lead evidence to contradict what a witness has said he is at least wise to challenge the witness's statements by cross-examination.[108]

Accuracy of evidence

12.9.2   Inaccuracy in evidence may be due to deliberate lying, to reckless over-confidence, or to the unconscious substitution of imagination for genuine recollection. Many a witness really believes that he is describing exactly what he has seen or heard, when in fact he only remembers certain parts, and the rest of his evidence consists of what he thinks must have happened or must have been said. Frequently, a detailed cross-examination will lead the witness (whatever the cause of his

---

[102] *McEwan v HM Advocate* 1939 JC 26, per Lord Justice-General Normand at 32; *Black v Bairds and Dalmellington Ltd* 1939 SC 472, per Lord Justice-Clerk Aitchison at 477. The observations on that opinion in *Anderson v St Andrew's Ambulance Association* 1942 SC 555 appear to relate to the question of recovery.

[103] *Avery v Cantilever Shoe Co Ltd* 1942 SC 469; *Lowe v Bristol Motor Omnibus Co* 1934 SC 1.

[104] *Avery v Cantilever Shoe Co Ltd* 1942 SC 469; *Lowe v Bristol Motor Omnibus Co* 1934 SC 1.

[105] *Frank v HM Advocate* 1938 JC 17.

[106] *Manson v HM Advocate* 1951 JC 49.

[107] See Codifying Act of Sederunt (1913), F, II, 4.

[108] On the effect of a failure to cross-examine, see para 12.15.

inaccuracy) to contradict himself or other witnesses on the same side, or to contradict some fact established by other evidence. Opinions have differed as to the proper course for the cross-examiner when there is an apparent inconsistency in the evidence of the witness. Is he entitled to leave the inconsistency and found on it, or must he give the witness an opportunity to explain it?[109] Opinions have also differed as to whether a cross-examiner, having received a general answer negativing his case, must proceed to put further detailed questions which can only be answered in the negative.[110] There appears to be some risk in omitting the additional questions in both cases.[111]

Credibility of witness

This may be tested by cross-examination as to interest—for example, relation- **12.9.3**
ship,[112] motive,[113] or prejudice.[114] Subject to privilege,[115] the witness may be cross-examined on his character[116]—for example, as to a conviction for a crime inferring dishonesty.[117] While there is authority that a witness may be questioned as to whether she is a prostitute for this purpose,[118] it may be doubted whether this would be taken to be correct as a general rule today.[119] In one case, while it was held competent to ask a witness whether she had been found fault with by previous employers for telling lies, it was said that she should be warned that she was not obliged to answer the question.[120] Where credibility is in issue, a witness may be cross-examined on the truth of any statement made by him during his evidence, even if the original statement was not strictly relevant evidence.[121] It is also competent to ask a witness whether he has made a previous statement inconsistent with his evidence, and this is discussed below.[122]

New matter

The second purpose of cross-examination is to elicit from the witness evidence on **12.9.4**
matters as to which he has not been asked in examination in chief, but which may be within his knowledge. Frequently, in a trial on a charge of careless driving, a

---

[109] *Macfarlane v Raeburn* 1946 SC 67 at 73 and 76.

[110] *Wilson v Thomas Usher & Son Ltd* 1934 SC 332 at 337 and 338.

[111] See para 12.15.

[112] *Roxburgh v Watson* (1868) 7 M 19.

[113] Whether, for example, the witness has made a claim against the defenders arising from the same accident.

[114] *King v King* (1841) 4 D 124, where it was held competent, not only to cross-examine a witness as to expressions of hostility to a party, but also to prove these by other evidence.

[115] See para 12.13.

[116] Evidence of character is dealt with in Chapter 7.

[117] It is said, however, that the extent to which the character of a witness may be attacked will be strictly limited for two reasons: first, to protect witnesses from attacks for which they are unprepared and which they are unable to meet, and to avoid the introduction of collateral issues impeding with the proper conduct of judicial proceedings. See *Dickie v HM Advocate* (1897) 24 R (J) 82, per Lord Justice-Clerk Macdonald at 83.

[118] *Webster* (1847) Ark 269. See also *Tennant v Tennant* (1883) 10 R 1187.

[119] It is certainly inconsistent with the statutory restrictions on cross-examination of complainers in sexual offence prosecutions. See the Criminal Procedure (Scotland) Act 1995, s 274 and para 7.7. *Cf* Macphail, *Evidence*, para 16.11, where the view is taken that the question is still competent but would generally be "discouraged" by the court.

[120] *King v King* (1842) 4 D 590 at 598.

[121] *Clinton v News Group Newspapers Ltd* 1999 SC 367.

[122] See para 12.10.

prosecution witness is asked in cross-examination whether there was not in the vicinity another vehicle, which he has not mentioned, but the presence of which may be important. Failure to put such a question to the appropriate witnesses is prejudicial to a defence founded on the alleged presence of the other vehicles.[123] Where the court is to be asked to draw an inference from the facts, the inference must be put in cross-examination, to that witness, if it is an inference as to the witness's actions or intentions,[124] and, if it is a scientific inference, to the expert witnesses.[125] The witness may have an explanation destroying, or at least throwing doubt on, the inference.[126] It has been held that where a witness's own conduct is called into question he ought to be given an opportunity to explain it.[127]

12.10 CROSS-EXAMINATION—PREVIOUS STATEMENTS

General

12.10.1   At common law it was competent to ask a witness whether he had on a previous occasion made a statement different from his evidence but, if he denied doing so, evidence could not be led to contradict the denial.[128] By statute, it is now competent both to put the question to the witness and to adduce evidence to prove that he made the statement alleged.[129] These provisions are now of limited importance in civil cases, since prior statements (whether consistent or inconsistent) are now of themselves admissible hearsay,[130] but remain important in criminal cases.

Prior inconsistent statements in criminal cases

12.10.2   The statutory provisions do not apply to statements made by a witness after he has given evidence.[131] Evidence cannot be led of the inconsistent statement unless the witness has been specifically asked whether he made the statement[132] and has denied making it.[133] The witness must be asked whether he made that specific statement and not simply whether he has made "an" inconsistent statement.[134] Because evidence of the statement cannot be led until after the witness has denied making it, it may be necessary to recall a witness or apply to lead evidence in

---

[123] On failure to cross-examine, see para 12.15.

[124] *Ryan v Mills* 1948 JC 28 at 35; *McCann v Adair* 1951 JC 127 at 130; *Cambo Shipping Co Ltd v Dampskibsselkabet Carl* 1920 SC 26 at 30.

[125] *Crawford v Granite City SS Co Ltd* (1906) 8 F 1013 at 1025.

[126] On failure to cross-examine, see para 12.15.

[127] *Turner v Board of Trade* (1894) 22 R 18; *Watson v Board of Trade* (1892) 19 R 1078. Both cases deal with enquiries into shipping casualties and are therefore special. In an ordinary action any explanation would normally be given in re-examination.

[128] *Livingstone v Strachan, Crerar & Jones* 1923 SC 794, per Lord Murray at 818; *Gall v Gall* (1870) 9 M 177.

[129] Evidence (Scotland) Act 1852, s 3 (civil cases); Criminal Procedure (Scotland) Act 1995, s 263(4).

[130] Civil Evidence (Scotland) Act 1988, s 3. Precognitions are specifically excluded: s 9.

[131] *Begg v Begg* (1887) 14 R 497.

[132] *Livingstone v Strachan, Crerar & Jones* 1923 SC 794; *Gall v Gall* (1870) 9 M 177; *McTaggart v HM Advocate* 1934 JC 33. *Cf Common* (1860) 3 Irv. 632, which has been doubted: *Kerr v HM Advocate* 1958 JC 14.

[133] *Ogilvie v HM Advocate* 1999 SLT 1068.

[134] *Paterson v HM Advocate* 1998 JC 182, where the detail of the witness's inconsistent statement only came to the defence agent's attention after she had given evidence. It was observed that the defence agent should have moved to recall her and that the sheriff would have been "virtually bound" to grant such a motion.

replication to utilise the provisions.[135] The prior statement is evidence as to the witness's credibility only—it is not evidence of its facts.[136] Where a witness has been questioned on part of a prior statement to show inconsistency, the consistent parts may be put to him in re-examination to show his consistency.[137] The prior statement need not be lodged as a production.[138]

12.10.3 The previous statement may, for example, have been made while giving evidence in another case, in the statutory examination of the witness as a bankrupt,[139] in answer to a questionnaire,[140] merely in conversation,[141] before a commissioner,[142] or probably in the witness's pleadings in a civil case to which he was a party.[143] It cannot, however, have been made in the form of a precognition,[144] except for a precognition on oath.[145]

12.10.4 It has been said that a statement may be used for these purposes even if it was unfairly obtained, and that it is for the jury to consider the issue of fairness in evaluating the statement.[146] That decision, however, was taken when it was considered to be for the jury to determine whether a confession was fairly obtained or not. Now that this is a question of law for the judge,[147] it may follow that the judge must rule on whether a statement which a party wishes to use in this manner was unfairly obtained and, if so obtained, exclude it.

12.11 CROSS-EXAMINATION—SEVERAL PARTIES

Civil causes

12.11.1 Cases where pursuers have conflicting interests must be rare, but in one case where salvage actions were conjoined the court expressly gave the pursuers the right to cross-examine each other's witnesses.[148] An opinion by Lord Shand that one defender has no right, save by agreement, to cross-examine a witness called for another defender, was not concurred in by the other judges, and it was held in that

---

[135] *Harlow v HM Advocate* 1993 GWD 11-727. On recall of witnesses and evidence in replication generally, see paras 12.4–12.5.

[136] *Muldoon v Herron* 1970 JC 30; *Paterson v HM Advocate* 1974 JC 35.

[137] *Coyle v HM Advocate* 1994 JC 239.

[138] *HM Advocate v Sayers* 1981 JC 98.

[139] *Emslie v Alexander* (1862) 1 M 209; *Forrests v Low's Trs* 1907 SC 1240 at 1248.

[140] *Maitland v Glasgow Corporation* 1947 SC 20. See also *Healey v A Massey & Son Ltd* 1961 SC 198.

[141] *Robertson v Steuart* (1874) 1 R 532.

[142] *Forrests v Low's Trs* 1907 SC 1240, where the evidence was taken to lie *in retentis*, and it was held that the report of the commissioner could not be used to contradict the witness, since she had appeared and given evidence at the proof.

[143] *Jackson v Glasgow Corporation* 1956 SC 354, per Lord President Clyde at 358 and Lord Russell at 362; *Stewart v Gelot* (1871) 43 Sc Jur 578, where an exception against the admission of cross on such pleadings was abandoned. But averments, like precognitions, are the pleader's version of the witness's statement.

[144] *Kerr v HM Advocate* 1958 JC 14; *McNeilie v HM Advocate* 1929 JC 50; *Binnie v Black* 1923 SLT 98; *O'Donnell and McGuire* (1855) 2 Irv 236; Macdonald, *Criminal Law* (5th edn), p 310. Earlier authorities took a different view: see *Leckie* (1895) 1 Adam 538; *Robertson* (1873) 2 Coup 495; *Inch v Inch* (1856) 18 D 997. See also *Luke* (1866) 5 Irv 293. This limitation is not set out in the statute and has been heavily criticised: see, eg, "Evidence: Contradiction by Precognition" 1959 SLT (News) 33; Macphail, *Evidence*, paras 19.47–S19.49. For the definition of a precognition, see para 17.1.

[145] *Coll, Petitioner* 1977 JC 29; *Coyle v HM Advocate* 1994 JC 239.

[146] *Young v HM Advocate* 1995 SCCR 418.

[147] *Thompson v Crowe* 2000 JC 173. See para 9.12.

[148] *Boyle v Olsen* 1912 SC 1235.

case that there was implied agreement to hold all the evidence as evidence in the cause.[149] In modern practice proofs and trials are conducted on that footing.[150]

Criminal trials

12.11.2 The right of one co-accused to cross-examine another co-accused, or a witness called by another co-accused, is discussed in the next chapter.[151]

12.12 RESTRICTIONS ON IMPROPER EXAMINATION

12.12.1 The court may prevent questions which are being put simply for the sake of insult and which are not to be backed up with any other evidence, questions which are simply irrelevant, or repeated questioning on a point which has already been answered, including a series of specific questions on a point which has already been answered with a general denial.[152] In such a case, the judge should record the refusal to allow the question and the reasons for the decision.[153] In one case, the High Court upheld a decision by the sheriff to refuse to allow any further questioning of a witness who had no relevant evidence to give and was "wholly embarrassed" by the proceedings.[154] Proposed restrictions on the right of an accused person to personally cross-examine witnesses who might be considered vulnerable are mentioned elsewhere.[155]

12.13 PRIVILEGE AGAINST SELF-INCRIMINATION

General

12.13.1 A witness is entitled to refuse to answer a question if a true answer may lead to his conviction for a crime[156] or involves an admission of adultery. The privilege is that of the witness, not of a party[157] and may therefore be waived by the witness.[158] It

---

[149] *Ayr Road Trs v Adams* (1883) 11 R 326.
[150] Macphail, *Sheriff Court Practice* (2nd edn), para 16.74. If this were not the case, there could have been no question of granting a diligence to one defender for the recovery of documents in the hands of another: *Anderson v St Andrew's Ambulance Association* 1942 SC 555.
[151] See paras 13.15–13.17.
[152] *Falconer v Brown* (1893) 1 Adam 96. See also *McAllister v Normand* 1996 SLT 622.
[153] *Falconer v Brown* (1893) 1 Adam 96.
[154] *Reid v Guild* 1991 SCCR 71.
[155] See para 13.1.
[156] This would appear to extend to the possibility of a conviction of a crime in England: *HM Advocate v Entwhistle*, unreported, Perth High Court, 1980, but see Macphail, *Evidence*, para S18.13A. There appears to be no authority on whether it is limited to crimes within the United Kingdom. Such a limitation exists in England: Civil Evidence Act 1968, s 14(1) and see *In re Westinghouse Uranium Contract* [1978] AC 547, where it was held that penalties under the EC Treaty were "penalties provided for by [United Kingdom] law" within the meaning of the 1968 Act because of the provisions of the European Communities Act 1972. It is submitted that the case is no authority on the wider issue of whether the privilege can be pleaded in respect of an offence under foreign law, but *cf* Field and Raitt, *Evidence* (2nd edn), para 12-13.
[157] See *Kirkwood v Kirkwood* (1875) 3 R 235, per Lord President Inglis at 236: "The common law interposes to protect the witness, not to give an advantage to the defender," or, it may be added, to the pursuer, the prosecutor, or the accused. As to the privilege as it applies to the accused, see para 13.11, and to a person under investigation, see paras 9.11–9.22.
[158] *Bannatyne v Bannatyne* (1886) 13 R 619.

is the duty of the judge to tell the witness that he need not answer such a question, but if the judge does not realise the situation and the witness apparently does not understand his rights, it is proper for counsel to point these out to the judge.[159] The opinion has been expressed that it is not incompetent to raise the point in the form of an objection by a party,[160] and in two criminal trials it was raised by objections by the prosecutor.[161] The privilege applies only to the particular question, and a witness has no right to be sworn or to answer any question because he anticipates an incriminating question.[162] Incriminatory affidavit evidence may be vulnerable unless the affidavit discloses *in gremio* that the deponent has been advised of their privilege.[163] Where the witness is not warned of the privilege and incriminates himself, it is an unsettled point as to whether his evidence is admissible against him in a subsequent prosecution.[164]

Incrimination as to crime

"It is a sacred and inviolable principle . . . that no man is bound to incriminate himself."[165] The privilege applies not only to a direct question as to whether he has committed a specific crime, but to examination on facts which indirectly infer guilt or may form links in a chain of evidence.[166] But there is no privilege if the witness cannot be prosecuted for the crime, either because he has been called as a witness for the prosecution in the trial of another person for the same crime,[167] or because he has already been tried for the crime.[168] If asked, the witness must state whether he has been convicted,[169] and a negative answer may be contradicted by production of an extract conviction, which must be proved to relate to that witness.[170] Since the only legitimate purpose of this type of question is to shake credibility, it is generally confined to crimes inferring dishonesty, such as theft or perjury, or possibly extreme depravity.[171] However, if any attack is made on the character of a prosecution witness the court

12.13.2

---

[159] *Kirkwood v Kirkwood* (1875) 3 R 235.

[160] *Kirkwood v Kirkwood* (1875) 3 R 235, per Lord Deas at 236.

[161] *Dickie v HM Advocate* (1897) 24 R (J) 82; *Kennedy v HM Advocate* (1896) 23 R (J) 28.

[162] *Don v Don* (1848) 10 D 1046.

[163] Compare *Sinclair v Sinclair* 1986 SLT (Sh Ct) 54, where Sheriff Principal Caplan held affidavit evidence of adultery in divorce action admissible despite no indication that the deponent had been advised of privilege, with *Cooper v Cooper* 1987 SLT (Sh Ct) 37, where Sheriff Risk held similar evidence inadmissible. See also paras 15.1–15.3.

[164] See *O'Neill v Wilson* 1983 JC 42; *Graham v HM Advocate* 1969 SLT 116.

[165] *Livingstone v Murrays* (1830) 9 S 161, per Lord Gillies at 162. In England and Wales, by virtue of statute, no person is bound to incriminate his or her spouse either: Civil Evidence Act 1968, s 14(1)(b).

[166] Dickson, *Evidence* (3rd edn), para 1789.

[167] *HM Advocate v Weatherly* (1904) 4 Adam 353; *Macmillan v Murray* 1920 JC 13; *McGinley v MacLeod* 1963 JC 11. The privilege is not removed simply because the witness is being put on trial separately: *HM Advocate v Mitchell* (1887) 1 White 321.

[168] However, if the witness had given evidence at his earlier trial, he would be entitled to refuse to answer any question where the answer might show that he had committed perjury at that trial.

[169] *Dickie v HM Advocate* (1897) 24 R (J) 82, per Lord Justice-Clerk Macdonald at 83; *Kennedy v HM Advocate* (1896) 23 R (J) 28, per Lord Justice-Clerk Macdonald at 30.

[170] There is a dictum to this effect in *Dickie v HM Advocate* (1897) 24 R (J) 82. It is not easy, however, to see how it would have been possible to prove such an extract at the time that case was decided, when the Crown were not allowed to apply to lead proof in replication. (See now para 12.4 on proof in replication and additional evidence.) See also *HM Advocate v Ashrif* 1988 SLT 567, where it was said (per Lord Dunpark at 197) that if a witness were to deny falsely (to Crown knowledge) that he had been convicted of a crime, "the Crown practice is to demonstrate the false denial in re-examination by producing, if necessary, relevant extract convictions". Parole evidence would be necessary to link the extract to the accused, but denial of a conviction probably cannot be proved by parole evidence alone.

[171] Dickson, *Evidence* (3rd edn), para 1618.

may, on application, admit evidence as to the character of the accused, and this is considered in the next chapter.[172]

Incrimination as to adultery

12.13.3   At common law a witness is not bound to answer a question tending to show that he has committed adultery. This applies both in civil causes[173] and criminal trials,[174] and is not confined to cases where adultery is the issue.[175] This rule has been established in statute.[176] Provided the witness is made fully aware of his rights, and is willing to answer, the evidence is competent.[177] If he refuses to answer, this should not be recorded,[178] and the refusal cannot be founded on.[179] If he answers in the negative, he may be cross-examined to test credibility.[180] The privilege is somewhat archaic and has been abolished in England,[181] while calls have been made for its abolition in Scotland for over a century.[182]

12.14 PRIVILEGE AGAINST DISCLOSING SPENT CONVICTIONS

12.14.1   Under the Rehabilitation of Offenders Act 1974, no evidence is admissible to prove that a person has committed, been charged with, prosecuted, convicted or sentenced for any offence which was the subject of a spent conviction, and no person shall be asked or required to answer any question relating to his past "which cannot be answered without acknowledging or referring to a spent conviction or spent convictions or any circumstances ancillary thereto."[183] This restriction does not apply in criminal proceedings,[184] service disciplinary proceedings and appeals therefrom,[185] various specified procedures relating to children,[186] and where the witness consents.[187]

12.15 FAILURE TO CROSS-EXAMINE

Civil cases

12.15.1   To quote Lord Justice-Clerk Cooper, "if it is intended later to contradict a witness

---

[172] paras 13.13 and 13.14.
[173] *Muir v Muir* (1873) 11 M 529.
[174] *Stephens* (1839) 2 Swin 348.
[175] *Stephens* (1839) 2 Swin 348.
[176] Evidence (Further Amendment) (Scotland) Act 1874, s 2.
[177] *McDougall v McDougall* 1927 SC 666; *Bannatyne v Bannatyne* (1886) 13 R 619; *Kirkwood v Kirkwood* (1875) 3 R 235. Strictly speaking, since the question cannot be put, the judge should establish first whether the witness is willing to waive privilege: *Bannatyne v Bannatyne*.
[178] *Cook v Cook* (1876) 4 R 78.
[179] *Hunt v Hunt* (1893) 1 SLT 157.
[180] *Muir v Muir* (1873) 11 M 529.
[181] Civil Evidence Act 1968, s 16(5).
[182] Lord Trayner, "The Advances of a Generation" (1886) 2 Sc L Rev 57, 89 at 91–92; Macphail, *Evidence*, para 18.18.
[183] Rehabilitation of Offenders Act 1974 ("1974 Act"), s 4(1).
[184] 1974 Act, s 7(2)(a).
[185] 1974 Act, s 7(2)(b).
[186] 1974 Act, s 7(2)(c)–(e).
[187] 1974 Act, s 7(2)(f).

upon a specific and important issue to which that witness has deponed, or to prove some critical fact to which that witness ought to have a chance of tendering an explanation or denial, the point ought normally to be put to the witness in cross-examination."[188] A failure to comply with this rule may render evidence for which the cross-examiner has not laid a proper foundation inadmissible,[189] but there does not seem to be any modern instance of the court taking such a harsh view. Where one party might be prejudiced by the other being allowed to lead such evidence, three other alternatives are available to the court[190]: first, to allow the evidence subject to the other party having a right to recall the first witness for cross-examination[191]; secondly, to allow the other party a proof in replication,[192] or thirdly, to admit the evidence subject to comment.[193]

The question is whether one party has been prejudiced by the other's failure to cross-examine properly, and, where cross-examination to "at least some of the appropriate witnesses on the other side" has given the other party an opportunity of meeting that case, this will normally be sufficient.[194] Therefore, Lord Cooper's dictum does not apply with the same force to cross-examination of defence witnesses,[195] since the pursuer's case has generally been put by the time they are led, there is normally no question of the pursuer leading evidence to contradict them later,[196] and the pursuer can put the defender's account to them in examination in chief if it is felt necessary for the pursuer's case. Hence, no question of prejudice should normally arise. However, it was held in one case that a failure to cross-examine the defender's witnesses on a crucial issue amounted to an implied admission that the contrary evidence of the pursuer's witnesses was a deliberate invention.[197] Normally, though, a failure to cross-examine the defenders' witness will be to the advantage of the defenders rather than to their prejudice,[198] and will not preclude the court from disbelieving that witness.[199] **12.15.2**

---

[188] *McKenzie v McKenzie* 1943 SC 108, per Lord Justice-Clerk Cooper at 109.

[189] *Stewart v Glasgow Corporation* 1958 SC 28, per Lord President Clyde at 38; *Bryce v British Railways Board* 1996 SLT 1378, per Lord Justice-Clerk Ross at 1378.

[190] They are outlined by Lord Justice-Clerk Ross in *Bryce v British Railways Board* 1996 SLT 1378 at 1378.

[191] *Wilson v Thomas Usher & Son Ltd* 1934 SC 332, per Lord Justice-Clerk Aitchison at 338–339. The right to recall may be subject to conditions as to expenses: *Bishop v Bryce* 1910 SC 426.

[192] *Wilson v Thomas Usher & Son Ltd* 1934 SC 332, per Lord Justice-Clerk Aitchison at 338–339.

[193] *Dawson v Dawson* 1956 SLT (Notes) 58.

[194] *McTague v LNER* [1948] CLY 4684. See also *Wilson v Thomas Usher & Son Ltd* 1934 SC 332, where the issue was considered to be whether the defence was "fully brought to the cognisance of the jury at the outset of the pursuer's case".

[195] *McTague v LNER* [1948] CLY 4684.

[196] The position is reversed, of course, where the defender is ordained to lead at the proof, as in *Bishop v Bryce* 1910 SC 426.

[197] *Keenan v Scottish Wholesale Co-operative Society Ltd* 1914 SC 959. This case, however, has now attained the status of a "special" or "exceptional" case "turning on its own facts": see *McTague v LNER* [1948] CLY 4684; *Walker v McGruther & Marshall* 1982 SLT 345.

[198] *Walker v McGruther & Marshall* 1982 SLT 345, per Lord Stott at 345.

[199] *Walker v McGruther & Marshall* 1982 SLT 345. It may, however, make the court less inclined to disbelieve the witness: *Dollar Air Services Ltd v Highland Council* 1997 GWD 28-1435, per Lord Marnoch. Prior to the Civil Evidence (Scotland) Act 1988, it was held in a number of cases that a failure to cross-examine on a crucial point did not supply corroboration. See *Stewart v Glasgow Corporation* 1958 SC 28; *Moore v Harland & Wolff Ltd* 1937 SC 707; *Prangell-O'Neill v Lady Skiffington* 1984 SLT 282.

Criminal cases

12.15.3 Since the burden of proof lies on the prosecutor throughout, the defence need not cross-examine, but may simply rely on the prosecution evidence not reaching the necessary standard. A failure to cross-examine does not supply corroboration.[200] The fact that the prosecution or the defence has not cross-examined one witness on a particular matter, though it may be the subject of comment, does not amount to an acceptance of the witness's evidence, nor does it prevent cross-examination of another witness on that matter.[201]

12.16 RECORDING OF EVIDENCE

Civil cases

12.16.1 In the Court of Session evidence in a proof or jury trial is recorded by tape recording or other mechanical means approved by the Lord President.[202] Ordinary cause evidence is recorded either by mechanical means or by a sworn shorthand writer, except where the parties agree (and the sheriff approves) that the recording of evidence be dispensed with.[203] In summary cause and small claims procedure, the sheriff makes notes for his own use and must retain them "until after the expiry of the period during which an appeal is competent."[204]

Criminal cases

12.16.2 In solemn criminal procedure, the evidence is recorded by a sworn shorthand writer or by mechanical means.[205] In addition, the sheriff must "duly authenticate and preserve the notes of evidence taken by him at the trial" and produce them or a certified copy to the High Court if called upon to do so.[206] The appeal court is not bound to accept the record as being accurate.[207] An inadvertent failure to keep a record is not necessarily fatal to a conviction.[208] In summary procedure the evidence is not recorded,[209] though the notes taken by the judge might be used to refresh his memory if occasion arose.[210]

---

[200] *Wilson v Brown* 1947 JC 81, per Lord Mackay at 94, 95 and Lord Jamieson at 96, 97; *Morton v HM Advocate* 1938 JC 50, per Lord Justice-Clerk Aitchison at 54.

[201] *McPherson v Copeland* 1961 JC 74 (defence); *Young v Guild* 1985 JC 27 (prosecution). It may, however, create a difficulty where an appeal is pursued on the basis of a matter newly coming to light which could have been uncovered through fuller cross-examination: see *Grimes v HM Advocate* 1988 SCCR 580.

[202] RCS, r 36.11 (proof); r 37.5A (jury trial). The rules also allow for evidence to be taken by a sworn shorthand writer, but since 1 April 1997 all proceedings are recorded by mechanical means: *Notice*, 6 March 1997.

[203] OCR, r 29.18.

[204] SCR, r 43(2); Small Claims Rules, r 20.

[205] Criminal Procedure (Scotland) Act 1995, s 93. Since 1 April 1997, evidence in the High Court is recorded by mechanical means rather than by a shorthand writer: *Notice*, 6 March 1997.

[206] Act of Adjournal (Criminal Procedure Rules), r 14.6. The rules do not place any similar obligation on High Court judges, who keep such notes as a matter of practice.

[207] *Kyle v HM Advocate* 1988 SLT 601 (shorthand notes).

[208] *Carroll v HM Advocate* 1999 JC 302. *Cf McLaughlan v HM Advocate* 1996 SLT 304.

[209] Criminal Procedure (Scotland) Act 1995, s 157. However, a note should be taken of any documentary evidence produced and any objection to the competency or admissibility of evidence: *ibid.*

[210] See *Davidson v McFadyean* 1942 JC 95, where the fact that the sheriff had written "sworn" after the name of a witness was held to be evidence that the witness had taken the oath.

CHAPTER 13

ORAL EVIDENCE—SPECIALTIES OF WITNESSES

13.1 INTRODUCTORY

General

A witness is competent unless excluded by a rule of law, and compellable unless **13.1.1** entitled on some legal ground to refuse to give evidence. As a general rule any person is a competent and compellable witness, but some are not competent, and some, though competent, are not compellable. Further, a witness may be competent and compellable, but the evidence that the witness can give may not be admissible for all purposes or against all the parties.[1] This chapter deals with these exceptional cases. It is thought that any exception will be considered strictly, and that unless there is express provision to the contrary a witness will be compellable.[2]

The old law

Under early practice there were numerous grounds on which persons were held to **13.1.2** be incompetent as witnesses.[3] Of these some have been abolished by, or as the result of, statute, and others have been abandoned. A party to a civil action and,

---

[1] Applied in *Patterson v HM Advocate* 1999 GWD 34–169.
[2] See the comments by Sheriff Sir Allan Walker, joint author of the first edition of this work, in *McDonnell v McShane* 1967 SLT (Sh Ct) 61 at 63.
[3] Dickson, *Evidence* (3rd edn), paras 1542–1611.

subject to limitations, the spouse of such party are competent.[4] So is an accused person and, again subject to limitations, the spouse of such person.[5] With the exception of the spousal relationship,[6] relationships of agency and partial counsel, or conviction of or punishment for an offence,[7] or interest,[8] no longer disqualify. Family members, other than spouses, are compellable.[9] There has not been a reported objection on the ground of malice and enmity[10] or of bribery[11] for more than a century, and the court refused to set aside a conviction on the ground that a witness had told another witness about to be called the answers he had given in cross-examination.[12] The development of the law is described in general terms in *Dow v MacKnight*,[13] where it is pointed out "that moral turpitude or interest is a ground of criticism not of the admissibility of the witness but of the reliability of his evidence."[14]

Penuria testium

13.1.3   The old grounds of objection to a witness were so numerous that it might be impossible to find competent witnesses to prove a case. This situation was known as *penuria testium* and justified the admission of witnesses who would normally have been incompetent.[15] Since the abolition of the old objections the phrase has now no technical meaning. Sometimes, it has been loosely used to describe a situation where in the nature of the case there must be a paucity of witnesses, with the implication that slight corroboration is sufficient, or to justify the admission of hearsay where not otherwise admissible.[16] Such situations are now catered for either by special provision,[17] or within the liberalising reforms of recent years. That liberal background militates against the application *ad hoc* of *penuria testium*,[18] except, perhaps, in approaching best evidence[19] and assessment of the weight to be attached to evidence led.[20]

---

[4]   Evidence (Scotland) Act 1853, s 3; Evidence (Further Amendment) (Scotland) Act 1874, ss 2 and 3. As to the limitations, see paras 13.7 and 13.8.

[5]   Criminal Procedure (Scotland) Act 1995, s 264. As to the limitations, see paras 13.7 and 13.8.

[6]   Which is limited to those in a lawful marriage: *Casey v HM Advocate* 1993 SLT 33.

[7]   Criminal Procedure (Scotland) Act 1995, s 265(1).

[8]   Evidence (Scotland) Act 1852, s 1; Evidence (Scotland) Act 1853, s 2.

[9]   Criminal Procedure (Scotland) Act 1995, s 265(3) and (4).

[10]   *Wilson* (1861) 4 Irv 42.

[11]   *Crighton v Fleming* (1840) 3 D 313.

[12]   *Campbell v Cadenhead* (1884) 11 R (J) 61.

[13]   *Dow v MacKnight* 1949 JC 38 at 42 and 56.

[14]   *Dow v MacKnight* 1949 JC 38 at 56 and 57. As to cross-examination, on these points, see para 12.9.

[15]   *Surtees v Wotherspoon* (1872) 10 M 866; *Dow v MacKnight* 1949 JC 38 at 53 and 56.

[16]   *Moorov v HM Advocate* 1930 JC 68 at 79; *McKie v Western Scottish Motor Traction Co* 1952 SC 206 at 209 (reclaimers' argument).

[17]   *eg* the Law Reform (Miscellaneous Provisions)(Scotland) Act 1968, s 9, now subsumed within the Civil Evidence (Scotland) Act 1988, s 1.

[18]   Implied in *Smith v Lees* 1997 JC 73, per Lord McCluskey at 103 *et seq*; and stated to be historical only in *McGregor v T* 1975 SC 14, per Lord Cameron at 25.

[19]   *eg* when an application is made to take evidence on commission as in *Tonner v FT Everard & Sons Ltd* 1994 SC 593.

[20]   As when evidence is scant due to passage of time—*eg James & Ors v McLennan* 1971 SC (HL) 77; *MacDonald of Keppoch, Petitioner (No 2)* 1994 SLT (Lyon Ct) 2.

Vulnerable and intimidated witnesses

In recent times, greater attention has been focused than in the past[21] upon address- **13.1.4**
ing the concern felt by a witness around the process of giving evidence in court.[22]
This has led to reforms in relation to children and the mentally incapacitated as
witnesses, discussed in the following paragraphs.[23] No statutory reform has
occurred at the time of writing to make special provision for evidence to be given
by victims of sexual crime,[24] or of physical abuse at the hand of a relative or
spouse, and witnesses who as a result of actual intimidation or a perceived threat
of intimidation, including racial intimidation, are in fear of giving evidence in
court, although the concerns of these witnesses have been the subject of consultation and changes in practice.[25] However, reform in Scotland is intended,[26]
including extending the availability of special arrangements for giving evidence to
a wider range of vulnerable groups, and preventing accused persons from cross-
examining the victim in person in certain cases.[27]

13.2 CHILDREN—GENERAL

A child who appears to be able to understand what he has seen or heard and to **13.2.1**
appreciate the duty to speak the truth is admissible as a witness.[28] It is for the judge
to determine whether a child meets these requirements (sometimes termed "competent" or "capable"), after a preliminary examination of the child[29] and, if necessary, after hearing other evidence.[30] It is not essential for competence that the child

---

[21] See *Second Report of the Thomson Committee on Criminal Procedure in Scotland* (Cmnd 6218, 1975) at para 43.32.

[22] *Report on Evidence of Children and Other Potentially Vulnerable Witnesses* (Scot Law Com No 125, 1990); *Towards a Just Conclusion: Vulnerable and Intimidated Witnesses in Scottish Criminal and Civil Cases* (Scottish Executive, November 1998); *Towards a Just Conclusion: An Action Plan* (Scottish Executive, 2000). In England *Speaking Up for Justice: Report of the Interdepartmental Working Group on the Treatment of Vulnerable or Intimidated Witnesses in the Criminal Justice System* (Home Office, 1998).

[23] paras 13.2–13.5.

[24] Other than limitation upon cross-examination as to sexual character (Criminal Procedure (Scotland) Act 1995, ss 274 and 275), examined at para 7.7.

[25] *Report on Evidence of Children and Other Potentially Vulnerable Witnesses* (Scot Law Com No 125, 1990), which was preceded by a discussion paper of the same name (Discussion Paper No 75); *Towards a Just Conclusion: Vulnerable and Intimidated Witnesses in Scottish Criminal and Civil Cases* (Scottish Executive, November 1998); *Towards a Just Conclusion: An Action Plan* (Scottish Executive, 2000).

[26] *Towards a Just Conclusion: An Action Plan* (Scottish Executive, 2000), paras 3.8.23 and 3.8.38.

[27] In England reforms are already on the statute book: see the Youth Justice and Criminal Evidence Act 1999, Pt II, following recommendations in *Speaking Up for Justice: Report of the Interdepartmental Working Group on the Treatment of Vulnerable or Intimidated Witnesses in the Criminal Justice System* (Home Office, 1998).

[28] Dickson, *Evidence* (3rd edn), para 1543. See also in civil cases: *M v Kennedy* 1993 SC 115, *L v L* 1996 SLT 767, 1996 SCLR 11 (OH) at 16–18; criminal cases: *Rees v Lowe* 1990 JC 96, *Kelly v Docherty* 1991 SLT 419. As to what the examination may entail, see *R, Petitioner* 1999 SC 380, also reported *sub nom R v Walker* 1999 SLT 1233 and *AR v Walker (Reporter for Aberdeenshire)* 1999 SCLR 341. This case confirms that it is inadequate merely to ask the child if he understands. The judge should ask questions from which the judge makes the assessment of understanding, after hearing other evidence if necessary, and should make a distinct admonition to tell the truth.

[29] *Rees v Lowe* 1990 JC 96; *Kelly v Docherty* 1991 SLT 419; *R, Petitioner* 1999 SC 380.

[30] Dickson, *Evidence* (3rd edn), para 1548. See also *KP v HM Advocate* 1991 SCCR 933; *M v Ferguson* 1994 SCLR 487; *R, Petitioner* 1999 SC 380.

should be able to give an account of what was witnessed.[31] It is expected that the examination of the child for purposes of assessing competency will take place in court.[32] Children of from four to seven years of age have been admitted in criminal cases,[33] but a child aged six was rejected after preliminary examination by the judge.[34] In civil cases, particularly those arising in connection with child protection, young children have been admitted.[35] However, a boy of nearly seven was rejected in an action of divorce on the ground of adultery "on account of the nature of the case".[36] Children under the age of 12 are not put on oath, but admonished to tell the truth, and children over 14 years of age are usually sworn. The oath is not administered to children between these ages unless the judge is satisfied that the child understands its nature.[37] The matter is one for the discretion of the judge.[38] The matter of receipt of evidence from children and other potentially vulnerable witnesses has been the subject of a report by the Scottish Law Commission,[39] which led to reforms detailed in the following paragraphs. If a child is a witness in any proceedings in a court,[40] and if the court so directs,[41] which it may do subject to conditions,[42] nothing[43] may be published in the media revealing the name, address or school of the child, or containing particulars calculated to lead to identification of the child. If a criminal conviction, which relied upon evidence from children, is quashed on appeal, the appeal court may refuse to grant authority for a fresh prosecution because to do so would put the child witness through additional distress.[44]

---

[31] *M v Kennedy* 1993 SC 115 at 122–125, in which the court examines this issue in depth having regard to texts which imply the need for the child to be able to give an account of what was seen. There the child was mute, but a lengthy preliminary examination established her competence and her evidence was received in the form of positive and negative gestures in response to questions, all of which was approved in the circumstances by the Inner House.

[32] Criminal: *Rees v Lowe* 1990 JC 96, *Quinn v Lees* 1994 SCCR 159; Civil: *L v L* 1996 SLT 767, *R, Petitioner* 1999 SC 380. Assessment of competence in relation to the admission of hearsay evidence is considered for criminal cases at para 13.3, and for civil cases at para 13.4.

[33] Bell's Notes, pp 246–247. A child of three was rejected in *Thomson* (1857) 2 Irv 747, a murder trial, mainly because she had not made a *de recenti* statement, while one of three-and-a-half years was admitted when she had made a *de recenti* statement, and the charge was of assault on her: *Miller* (1870) 1 Coup 430.

[34] *McBeth* (1867) 5 Irv 353.

[35] Norrie, *Children's Hearings in Scotland*, p 90.

[36] *Robertson v Robertson* (1888) 15 R 1001. On children as witnesses in family proceedings, see para 28.10.

[37] Dickson, *Evidence* (3rd edn), para 1549. See also *Quinn v Lees* 1994 SCCR 159.

[38] *Anderson v McFarlane* (1899) 1 F (J) 36; *Quinn v Lees* 1994 SCCR 159.

[39] *Report on Evidence of Children and Other Potentially Vulnerable Witnesses* (Scot Law Com No 125, 1990). The matter is subject to ongoing review: see *Towards a Just Conclusion: Vulnerable and Intimidated Witnesses in Scottish Criminal and Civil Cases* (Scottish Executive, November 1998); *Towards a Just Conclusion: An Action Plan* (Scottish Executive, 2000).

[40] Criminal Procedure (Scotland) Act 1995, s 47(1)–(3).

[41] Criminal Procedure (Scotland) Act 1995, s 47(3)(a). If the child is a party the protection applies unless the court directs otherwise: s 47(1)(a), (3)(b) and (c). Breach of an order or condition is a criminal offence. See also Renton & Brown, *Criminal Procedure* (6th edn), para 25-27, and Macphail, *Evidence*, paras 7.17–7.30.

[42] See *Caledonian Newspapers Ltd, Petitioners* 1995 JC 172.

[43] Including a picture of the child: Criminal Procedure (Scotland) Act 1995, s 47(2).

[44] *Kelly v Docherty* 1991 SLT 419; *Farooq v HM Advocate* 1993 SLT 1271.

13. 3 CHILDREN—CRIMINAL CASES

Guidelines

Guidelines issued by the Lord Justice-General in 1988[45] are designed to assist the judge in criminal cases in the exercise of discretionary powers to put child witnesses at ease.[46] In terms of those guidelines the judge is expected to give an opportunity to representatives of the Crown and accused to address him, outwith the presence of any jury, regarding arrangements for the child to give evidence, if any appear to those representatives to be necessary.[47] The arrangements must be such that they do not encroach upon the rights of the accused to a fair trial, and the child must at all times be visible to the jury, if there is one, and to the accused.[48] Having regard to the age and maturity of the child, the nature of the charge(s) and of the evidence that the child is likely to have to give, the relationship, if any, between the child and the accused, whether the case is on summary complaint or on indictment, any special factors concerning the disposition, health or physique of the child, and the practicability of departing from normal procedures, including the nature of the courtroom and available amplification,[49] the judge may, for example, require that court apparel is removed, that the court environment is made more informal by the judge coming down from the bench and sitting alongside the representatives and the witness in the well of the court, and that the child is accompanied while giving evidence by a relative or other supporting person.[50] However, the judge should not act towards the child in a way that may interfere with the perception of a fair trial.[51] The court may be cleared while a child is giving evidence in any case where the judge is satisfied that this "is necessary in order to avoid undue anxiety or distress to the child."[52] Separately, the judge may appropriately make an order to clear the court in a case involving indecency or immorality.[53] **13.3.1**

Statute

Since 1990[54] statutory provision has been made for the evidence of a child[55] to be facilitated by special arrangements authorised by the court on application being **13.3.2**

---

[45] Reproduced in Renton & Brown, *Criminal Procedure Legislation*, para C1.04. These followed upon recommendations of the Scottish Law Commission in *Report on Evidence of Children and Other Potentially Vulnerable Witnesses* (Scot Law Com No 125, 1990).

[46] The same may be done in civil cases although there is no express provision for it.

[47] Lord Justice-General's Guidelines, para 5. The wording is such that the judge should take the initiative in asking whether such arrangements are necessary.

[48] Guidelines, paras 4(f) and 8. The requirements of Article 6 may be met even if the witness cannot be seen, provided that the accused has been able to ascertain the evidence in advance and test it at trial, *X v UK* 15 EHRR CD 113.

[49] Guidelines, para 5.

[50] Guidelines, para 6. A witness in the cause cannot be the supporting person, and the person must be warned by the judge not to prompt, or seek to influence, the child.

[51] In *McKie v HM Advocate* 1997 SLT 1018, it was observed to be "unfortunate" that the sheriff rose from the bench to comfort the tearful child witness, rather than calling for a carer in court to do so.

[52] Guidelines, para 7: persons involved in the case as parties or representatives, court personnel and *bona fide* members of the press are excepted, as are others for whose presence the court has granted permission.

[53] Criminal Procedure (Scotland) Act 1995, s 50(3) and (4).

[54] Law Reform (Miscellaneous Provisions) (Scotland) Act 1990, ss 55–59, thereafter the Prisoners and Criminal Evidence (Scotland) Act 1993, ss 33–35, and now the Criminal Procedure (Scotland) Act 1995, s 271 (substituted by the Crime and Punishment (Scotland) Act 1997, s 29).

[55] Since 1997 the provisions have specified "vulnerable person" rather than "child", but a person under 16 years is deemed to be a vulnerable person: Criminal Procedure (Scotland) Act 1995, s 271(12). As to the other category of vulnerable person, see para 13.5.

made to it.[56] These work in tandem with the Lord Justice-General's Guidelines.[57] The statute allows for: evidence to be taken in court but while a screen is used to conceal the accused from the sight of the child, provided that the accused is able to see and hear the child as the evidence is given[58]; the child to give evidence from outwith the courtroom by way of a live television link[59]; and the child to give evidence before a commissioner appointed by the court, subject to the proceedings before the commissioner being video-recorded.[60]

13.3.3   The court may grant an application for these special arrangements only on cause shown, having regard to: (a) the possible effect on the child if required to give evidence if such an application were not to be granted; (b) whether it is likely that the child would be better able to give evidence if such an application were granted; and (c) the views of the child.[61] The court may also take into account, where appropriate, any of: (a) the nature of the alleged offence; (b) the nature of the evidence which the child is likely to be called upon to give; (c) the relationship, if any, between the child and the accused; and (d) the age and maturity of the child.[62] If an application is refused *in hoc statu*,[63] it may be renewed at a later stage, despite the fact that the provisions of the statute and the Act of Adjournal do not expressly

---

[56] Criminal Procedure (Scotland) Act 1995, s 271(1), (5) and (6). In respect of the appointment of a commissioner, the application may be made at any time before the jury oath is administered in solemn cases, and before the first witness is sworn in summary cases, but in exceptional circumstances during the course of the trial: s 271(1). Application for a live television link should be made not later than 14 days before the trial, except on special cause shown: Act of Adjournal (Criminal Procedure Rules) 1996, r 22.1. In *HM Advocate v Birkett* 1993 SLT 395, the court held that an application might be renewed or, in exceptional circumstances, be first made, when the trial was in progress. At that time the facilities for television link did not exist in all sheriff court buildings, and the need for a pre-trial decision ensured that the facilities would be available. Facilities are now more widely available, but, if the application would be granted but for the want of facilities, the sheriff has power to transfer a case to another court in which these are available: Criminal Procedure (Scotland) Act 1995, s 271(9) and the Act of Adjournal (Criminal Procedure Rules) 1996, r 22.2.

[57] The criteria justifying the arrangements under both are very similar.

[58] Criminal Procedure (Scotland) Act 1995, s 271(6). A video camera and television allow the accused to see and hear the child's evidence.

[59] Criminal Procedure (Scotland) Act 1995, s 271(5). The jury should be charged that they are entitled if they think fit to attach the same value to evidence given by television link as to evidence given in court by other witnesses in the case: observed in *Brotherston v HM Advocate* 1996 SLT 1154 at 1158D. The use of the live television link between 1990 and 1995 is examined in Murray, *Live Television Link: An Evaluation of its Use by Child Witnesses in Scottish Criminal Trials* (Scottish Office Central Research Unit, 1995), in which the process is described in detail at paras 1.28–1.34. The title of this report is rather misleading in that the report contains useful information and discussion on the whole range of issues concerning the evidence of a child. See also Spencer & Flin, *The Evidence of Children: The Law and the Psychology* (2nd edn).

[60] Criminal Procedure (Scotland) Act 1995, s 271(1)–(2). It is provided that "the accused shall not, except by leave of the commissioner, be present in the room where such proceedings are taking place but shall be entitled by such means as seem suitable to the commissioner to watch and hear the proceedings," and it must be implicit that this will be contemporaneous, particularly if this is read in the light of s 271(6), which requires that an accused screened from the witness must be able to see and hear the child's evidence as it is given. The general provisions regarding evidence on commission contained in s 272(2)–(6), (8) and (9) also apply. As to evidence on commission generally, see Chapter 14.

[61] Criminal Procedure (Scotland) Act 1995, s 271(7).

[62] Criminal Procedure (Scotland) Act 1995, s 271(8).

[63] As in *HM Advocate v Birkett* 1993 SLT 395. There an application was granted only in respect of one 3-year-old child victim who was frightened of the accused and in respect of whom the application was not opposed, but refused *in hoc statu* on opposed applications in respect of child witnesses aged 4, 6, 6 and 8, in support of which it was said only that they were "quiet and hesitant", that the evidence was of a traumatic nature and that they would be better able to give evidence by the live television link.

so provide,[64] which, it is suggested, must involve a change of circumstances. When the application has been granted and the evidence is being led the court may make other special provision in keeping with the authorised arrangement albeit that it is not expressly provided for in the statute,[65] subject, of course, to the need to ensure fairness to the accused. This was decided when, in a case where the child was giving evidence by live television link, the child was to be asked to identify the accused. The trial judge rejected the defence proposition that the child would have to come into court to carry out a dock identification and instead allowed for the identification to be carried out over the television link with the camera sweeping the court room in the way that a witness would do by sight from the witness box. This approach was supported on appeal, together with the general discretion to ease the process of giving evidence for the child.[66] However, it was also observed that an application for television link having been granted, it is not incompetent to dispense with it and to put the witness into the witness box, to give evidence in full, although fairness would require that once the evidence has been started by television link it will carry on to its conclusion by that process.[67]

Apart from common criteria for deciding whether the application should be **13.3.4** granted, the three special arrangements are not treated in common, and it is expected that the applicant will consider which would be most appropriate before the application is framed. Although early applications proceeded upon *ex parte* statements based on the impression which the applicant had formed about the existence of qualifying factors, later applicants have more successfully relied upon expert reports from psychiatrists and psychologists, particularly when the application is opposed.[68] Application is not restricted to the party seeking to lead the witness, although that will be the norm. However, it has been recognised that it is as much against the interest of the cross-examining party as the party who has called the witness if the child is to be distressed by giving evidence.[69]

Hearsay

The normal rules for the admission of hearsay in criminal cases both at common **13.3.5** law[70] and under statute apply to a witness who is a child,[71] but there are additional matters to consider. Hearsay may be admitted only if the maker of the statement would have been a competent witness, and in criminal cases that competence is assessed as at the date when the statement was made.[72] Evidence enabling the court to assess the competence of a child[73] who made the statement will require to be led

---

[64] They provide only for late application on special cause shown, but do not expressly prevent repeat applications: *HM Advocate v Birkett* 1993 SLT 395.

[65] *Brotherston v HM Advocate* 1996 SLT 1154.

[66] *Brotherston v HM Advocate* 1996 SLT 1154 at 1160K.

[67] *Brotherston v HM Advocate* 1996 SLT 1154 at 1158K and 1161B. However, fairness might dictate that the television link should be abandoned—*eg* if the child finds the link unsatisfactory and distressing and expresses a preference for giving evidence in court.

[68] Murray, *Live Television Link: An Evaluation of its Use by Child Witnesses in Scottish Criminal Trials* (Scottish Office Central Research Unit, 1995), paras 4.5–4.19.

[69] See *Brotherston v HM Advocate* 1996 SLT 1154 at 1161.

[70] There is no relaxation of the limitations of hearsay evidence at common law in the case of a child witness—see, *eg Farooq v HM Advocate* 1993 SLT 1271.

[71] Criminal Procedure (Scotland) Act 1995, ss 259–262, and para 8.6.

[72] Criminal Procedure (Scotland) Act 1995, s 259(1)(c). Compare the position in civil cases considered at para 13.4. See also Sheldon, "Children's Evidence, Competency and the New Hearsay Provisions" 1997 SLT (News) 1.

[73] On which see *R, Petitioner* 1999 SC 380.

before the hearsay can be admitted, unless no other party in the proceedings objects.[74] It might be possible to make an application in advance of trial for receipt of hearsay evidence of a child based upon the argument that the child is, by reason of bodily or mental condition, unfit or unable to give evidence in any competent manner,[75] but the applicant would have to explain why none of the competent manners for a child to give evidence is appropriate, supported, no doubt, by expert report.[76] A party may apply at the trial for hearsay to be admitted if the child is called to be a witness and, having been assessed as competent, refuses to accept an admonition to tell the truth or, after admonition, refuses to give evidence.[77] However, the court has stressed that refusal, as compared to mere reticence, will be necessary before hearsay can be admitted on this ground, observing that the refusal will only arise if the child has failed to comply with a direction from the judge to answer the question.[78] If an application has been granted for the child to give evidence by one of the statutory special arrangements, and the child in evidence recalls having previously identified a person alleged to have committed an offence, the evidence of a third party as to that prior identification is admissible as evidence of the identification.[79]

13.4 CHILDREN—CIVIL CASES

Guidelines and special arrangements

13.4.1   There are no general guidelines for judges in dealing with child witnesses in civil cases, but it has been suggested that special arrangements should be accessible when appropriate,[80] and that regard should be had to the possibility of using

---

[74] Criminal Procedure (Scotland) Act 1995, s 259(7).

[75] Criminal Procedure (Scotland) Act 1995, s 259(2)(a).

[76] On the face of it this provision could be used, subject to lack of notice being excused under s 259(6)(b), if a child is called to give evidence by appropriate means, but at that time is unfit or unable to give evidence due to bodily or mental condition, whether or not the judge has found the child competent after preliminary examination, provided that there is acceptable evidence that the child was competent when the hearsay statement was made. The child may not be competent, or assessable for competence, at trial due to an intervening event such as an accident or deterioration of physical or mental condition. The question was mooted but left open in a civil case (*M v Kennedy* 1993 SC 115), and closed in relation to civil cases by *L v L* 1996 SLT 767.

[77] Criminal Procedure (Scotland) Act 1995, s 259(2)(e).

[78] *MacDonald v HM Advocate* 1999 SLT 533. Whilst this is consistent with the word "refuse", it will require skill on the part of the judge to "direct" while not thereby distressing the child.

[79] Criminal Procedure (Scotland) Act 1995, s 271(11) and see *Brotherston v HM Advocate* 1996 SLT 1154 at 1158–1159. Its purpose is to incorporate the ratio of *Muldoon v Herron* 1970 JC 30 which permitted the court to receive the evidence of a third party *who saw the earlier identification of the accused* (usually a police officer) to complete the identification which the witness could not repeat in court, and indeed to contradict a statement in court that the accused is not the perpetrator. (For more discussion of this case, see paras 5.4.5 and 8.6.5.) There is separate provision for any witness to adopt prior evidence contained in a document: see the Criminal Procedure (Scotland) Act 1995, s 260, and paras 8.6.5 and 12.7.1.

[80] *Towards a Just Conclusion* (Scottish Executive 1998), Chap 7. In para 7.7 the authors of the report cite an example of a successful application to the Inner House approving the practice of allowing a television link in appropriate circumstances in the civil court. In *Towards a Just Conclusion: An Action Plan* (Scottish Executive, 2000) at para 3.10, the authors acknowledge that the recommendations made in Chapter 7 of *Towards a Just Conclusion* were underdeveloped and that this matter requires to be revisited.

hearsay evidence to avoid the need for the witness to attend court.[81] If the child would be a direct witness to an issue in a civil case, failure to lead the child's evidence may lead to failure on that issue.[82] Statutory provision exists in relation to proceedings before the sheriff arising from applications under the Children (Scotland) Act 1995, Pt II. At the discretion of the sheriff, the child to whom the proceedings relate may be excluded from the proceedings while other evidence is led,[83] and relevant persons may be excluded while the child's evidence is led,[84] subject always to preservation of the right of any party against whom that evidence may apply, to know of and respond to its content.[85] The sheriff may, on application, allow the child to give evidence by live television link.[86]

Hearsay

The general rule in civil cases allows for admission of hearsay evidence. It has **13.4.2** been held that hearsay evidence of a child will be admissible as evidence of its contents only if the court can assess and accept the competence of the child as a witness.[87] Furthermore, in the Outer House, in an action between parents concerning contact, it has been held that the assessment requires oral examination of the child at the point of proof.[88] The decision on this issue is based upon a strict interpretation of the relevant provisions of the Civil Evidence (Scotland) Act 1988, s 2. Although the case was appealed to the Inner House this issue was not considered on appeal. The judge had rejected the possibility of assessing competence through the evidence of a social worker who had worked with the child, although in earlier cases concerning compulsory measures of care for children it had been observed that the court might assess a child's capability from evidence of parents and those with professional experience of the child such as social workers or child psychologists.[89] However, the court in these cases envisaged that the evidence would be supplemental to rather than a substitute for examination of the child. If the child is examined and deemed competent the child's evidence may be led orally, but it is also then competent to lead hearsay evidence of the child in

---

[81] In a sheriff court case, *H v H* 2000 GWD 11-376, the sheriff principal accepted an affidavit from a child aged 13 in respect of whom there was professional evidence that he was competent but that giving evidence would have an adverse effect on him.

[82] In *L v L* 1996 SLT 767 children were not called as witnesses, and in the absence of their direct evidence on the issue in question, and having regard to other facts and circumstances, the burden of proof on that issue was not satisfied. On appeal the Lord Ordinary's approach to the assessment of the evidence was approved: *L v L* 1998 SLT 6720. However, in *MT v DT*, 10 July 2000 this was doubted and that case has been referred to a larger court on this point.

[83] Act of Sederunt (Child Care and Maintenance Rules) 1997 (SI 1997/291) ("Act of Sederunt"), r 3.47(5).

[84] Act of Sederunt, r 3.47(6).

[85] Act of Sederunt, r 3.47(7).

[86] Act of Sederunt, r 3.22(2). Application should be made at least 14 days before the court hearing, by application in Form 44 attached to the rules. The form requires that reasons be stated but, unlike the provisions in criminal cases, there is no indication of what the reasons should be. It is thought that the criteria for criminal cases may act as a guide, and would be particularly appropriate when the proceedings concern a ground of referral based upon criminal conduct of the child, which must meet the usual standards of criminal evidence and procedure: see para 29.5. In civil cases there is more scope for prioritising the child's interest in reaching a decision on the application, subject always to ensuring that the proceedings will be fair in accordance with Art 6 of the European Convention on Human Rights.

[87] *F v Kennedy (No 1)* 1992 SC 28.

[88] *L v L* 1996 SLT 767. This appears to close the question left open in *M v Kennedy* 1993 SC 115.

[89] *M v Ferguson* 1994 SCLR 487. For a discussion of the case and comparison with criminal cases, see Sheldon, "Children's Evidence, Competency and the New Hearsay Provisions" 1997 SLT (News) 1.

substitute for or to supplement the child's oral evidence.[90] If both are led and the two conflict, the court may accept the hearsay as the more credible and as proof of the facts contained in it.[91] The House of Lords has held that hearsay evidence of a child's comments after a visit with a parent, whilst not admissible as proof of the truth of the comments, can be of value to the court in its assessment of the child's reaction to the visit within the overall consideration of the child's best interests.[92] In general the court has indicated that the duty to have regard to the child's interests in making any decision affecting a child, and the general liberalisation of the rules of evidence, will militate against the application of any restrictive rule which might keep relevant evidence from the court.[93] In family cases, whether under Part I or Part II of the Children (Scotland) Act 1995, where the views of a child affected by the proceedings require to be sought, this may be in the form of evidence from the child as a witness, or by other means[94] in which case the issue of competence will not arise.[95]

13.5 MENTAL INCAPACITY

General

13.5.1   The effect of mental incapacity[96] upon the ability to act as a witness is a question of degree,[97] and the competence of the witness depends on the nature and extent of the incapacity,[98] which may be linked to the nature of the evidence which it is intended to take from the witness.[99] The effect of examination in court upon the witness should be kept in view,[100] but in modern practice arrangements to facilitate such examination may be made.[101] The decision as to whether the witness is competent to be a witness is for the judge, and whether the judge should note the

---

[90] Civil Evidence (Scotland) Act 1988, s 2; *F v Kennedy (No 2)* 1993 SLT 1284.

[91] *K v Kennedy* 1993 SLT 1281.

[92] *Sanderson v McManus* 1997 SC (HL) 55 at 61, and in *M v Ferguson* 1994 SCLR 487 the Inner House confirmed that the court could take account of a hearsay comment from a child as part of the overall narrative of the case, provided that it was not accepted going towards proving the truth of the comment.

[93] Per Lord President (Rodger) in *L v L* 1998 SLT 672 at 676. *Cf T v Watson* 1995 SC 57 to the effect that such reasoning cannot be used to override the clear meaning of a statutory provision.

[94] See para 28.10, and for example *Lothian Regional Council v F* 1997 SC 164. For a discussion, see Ross, "Reforms in Family Proceedings in the Sheriff Court: Raising Conflicts in Civil Justice" 1998 CIL 1.

[95] *Lothian Regional Council v F* 1997 SC 164.

[96] This term is used for continuity with the first edition of this work, and for the purpose of this paragraph the term includes any disorder, disability or disturbance of mental functioning whether permanent or temporary in nature. The term is not intended to be associated with any technical meaning which may be ascribed to it, or other terms in legislation governing mental health or criminal justice, present or, in light of substantial review in this area, future. For an examination of the terminology applying at present in the criminal justice arena, see Duff & Hutton (eds), *Criminal Justice in Scotland*, Chap 15. The limited extent of formal interaction between this topic and categorisation of mental illness under that legislation is described in para 13.5.2.

[97] *Black* (1887) 1 White 365.

[98] Dickson, *Evidence* (3rd edn), para 1550.

[99] A witness with a mental defect was rejected when she was to be asked why the title to shares had been taken in a particular way: *Buckle v Buckle's Curator* (1907) 15 SLT 98 (OH).

[100] *Tosh v Ogilvy* (1873) 1 R 254 at 257; *Kilpatrick Parish Council v Row Parish Council* 1911 2 SLT 32 (OH).

[101] Criminal Procedure (Scotland) Act 1995, s 271, examined further at para 13.5.2.

issue in the absence of objection will depend upon the circumstances.[102] In the event of objection to the witness on the ground of incapacity[103] the trial judge should call for submission, and possibly evidence,[104] from the party seeking to lead the witness. That evidence may include that of the witness,[105] and will be as to the state of the witness's mental capacity at the time of trial.[106] However, it may also be relevant to consider the witness's capacity at the date of the event witnessed,[107] at the time of any statement made[108] and during the intervening period.[109] In solemn criminal procedure witnesses may be called for this purpose although they are not on the Crown or defence lists.[110] The mere fact that the witness is a patient in a mental hospital does not exclude.[111] Mere inability to understand the oath is not an impediment to admitting the witness,[112] and, if it appears appropriate to the trial judge, the witness may be admonished to tell the truth.[113] When commission is granted to take the evidence of a witness of doubtful mental capacity, it is for the commissioner to decide whether to proceed with the examination.[114] An objection to the mental capacity of a witness is most likely to arise in criminal proceedings, to which most of the case authority relates. However, the same principles apply to such a witness in civil cases.

Special arrangements

Since 1997, the special arrangements that may be applied for in criminal cases **13.5.2** under statute extend to any "vulnerable person". This definition includes a person over 16 who: (a) is subject to an order under the mental health legislation of any

---

[102] *McAvoy v HM Advocate* 1991 JC 16 at 23.

[103] Which should be taken at the time: *McAvoy v HM Advocate* 1991 JC 16 at 23.

[104] *Black* (1887) 1 White 365; *Stott* (1894) 1 Adam 386. In *McKenzie* (1869) 1 Coup 244 such evidence was thought to be necessary, on which see also *Stott*. *Cf McAvoy v HM Advocate* 1991 JC 16.

[105] *O'Neil and Gollan* (1858) 3 Irv 93.

[106] Historically a witness insane at the time of the trial was usually rejected (Macdonald, *Criminal Law* (5th edn), p 288), but not without exception: *Stott* (1894) 1 Adam 386.

[107] This will be relevant if the witness made a statement then, and an attempt is made to have the statement admitted in evidence under an exception to the hearsay rule. It may also influence the weight to be attached to anything the witness said then.

[108] In June 1998 the Scottish Office published guidance on "Appropriate Adult Schemes" which are non-statutory but promote the practice that when a person lacking full mental capacity is interviewed by police, an appropriately qualified adult will be present to facilitate the process. Such schemes exist across Scotland. An appropriate adult may be called to give evidence concerning the interview.

[109] Hume, ii, 340, states that a witness who suffers from periodic derangements may be examined regarding any matter observed by him during a period of sanity, but that if a period of subsequent insanity has intervened before the trial, he is inadmissible for this purpose. In *McKenzie* (1869) 1 Coup 244, in which a witness was rejected because he had been insane between the incident and the trial, the judges were of the opinion that this part of the rule should be reconsidered. It is thought that, if expert evidence reveals that the witness is mentally well at the date of hearing and the intervening illness has not irretrievably affected the ability to recall matters seen or heard during prior lucidity, the witness would be admitted, all other matters going to the weight to be attached to the evidence rather than the admissibility of the witness.

[110] *Black* (1887) 1 White 365; *Stott* (1894) 1 Adam 386.

[111] *Littlejohn* (1881) 4 Coup 454.

[112] *Black* (1887) 1 White 365. Earlier judgments to the contrary, such as *Murray* (1866) 5 Irv 232 and *McGilvray* (1830) Bell's Notes 264, are not to be relied upon.

[113] *Black* (1887) 1 White 365. In *McAvoy v HM Advocate* 1991 JC 16, the witness who was said by a lay witness to be "slightly handicapped" was unable to take the oath in the normal manner but was able to say "yes" after each phrase of the oath was put to him by the trial judge, without defence objection at the trial. On appeal the process used was considered appropriate in the circumstances.

[114] *Tosh v Ogilvy* (1873) 1 R 254 at 257; *McIntyre v McIntyre* 1920 1 SLT 207 (OH).

part of the United Kingdom arising from a consequence of a finding in court that the person suffers from a mental disorder; (b) is subject to a directed transfer from prison to mental hospital under mental health legislation; or (c) otherwise appears to the court to suffer from significant impairment of intelligence and social functioning.[115] A special arrangement is available only on application and on showing cause within the criteria set out in the statute, considered in detail in an earlier paragraph.[116] Although evidence on commission may be sought within this provision, separately, it may be appropriate to take the evidence of a witness with mental incapacity within the scope for evidence on commission in general in civil or criminal cases.[117] The very limited provision for evidence by television link in civil proceedings before the sheriff arising out of the Children (Scotland) Act 1995, Pt II does not apply to persons over the age of 16.

Hearsay

13.5.3   It may be appropriate for the evidence of a mentally incapacitated witness to be received in the form of a hearsay statement, whilst bearing in mind that less weight may attach to hearsay than to evidence given orally. In criminal cases if mental incapacity gives rise to unfitness or inability to give evidence in court, an application for admission of hearsay may be made.[118] Unless no objection is taken to the competence of the witness whose hearsay statement is to be led,[119] the court will require to be satisfied that, at the time when the statement was made, the person who made it would have been a competent witness.[120] In civil cases, although hearsay evidence is generally admissible,[121] the competence of the maker of the statement, if that is in any doubt, must be established by preliminary examination of the maker of the statement by the judge, and competence is assessed as at the date of examination, not the time when the statement was made.[122]

13.6 WITNESSES UNABLE TO SPEAK AND/OR HEAR

13.6.1   A witness who is unable to speak and hear is treated as an ordinary witness, except that he or she is sworn and has evidence taken through an interpreter using a sign or other visual language known to the witness by written question and answer.[123] Where neither method is possible the witness may communicate by other signs if

---

[115] Criminal Procedure (Scotland) Act 1995 ("1995 Act"), s 271(12), as substituted by the Crime and Punishment (Scotland) Act 1997, s 29.

[116] para 13.3.

[117] On which see Chapter 14.

[118] 1995 Act, s 259(2)(a).

[119] 1995 Act, s 259(7).

[120] 1995 Act, s 259(1)(c). See also para 13.3 for commentary on situations where competence may vary after the statement having been made and before the trial date.

[121] Civil Evidence (Scotland) Act 1988, s 2.

[122] *L v L* 1996 SLT 767; but in *MT v DT*, 10 July 2000 the point decided in *L v L* was referred to a larger court. See also *M v Ferguson* 1994 SCLR 487, Sheldon, "Children's Evidence, Competency and the New Hearsay Provisions" 1997 SLT (News) 1 and para 13.4. An interesting example is to be found in *H v H* 2000 GWD 11-376 (Sh Ct) where the witness was a child and did not have full mental capacity.

[123] Dickson, *Evidence* (3rd edn), para 1556; Macdonald, *Criminal Law* (5th edn), p 289; *Martin* (1823) Shaw 101; *Reid* (1835) Bell's Notes 246.

these can be understood[124] and interpreted. An inarticulate witness[125] has been examined through a person who understood her means of expression,[126] and a child witness who was an elective mute was successfully examined for competence by the sheriff before her evidence was led.[127]

13.7 SPOUSE OF ACCUSED—WITNESS FOR DEFENCE

At common law the spouse of an accused person was not a competent defence witness.[128] Now, the spouse of an accused may be called as a witness by the accused in any criminal case.[129] Failure of the spouse to give evidence must not be the subject of comment by the prosecutor.[130] If the accused is charged jointly with another person, the co-accused may not call the spouse of another accused as a witness except with the consent of the accused.[131] Although there is not express statutory provision, the spouse of an accused has been held to be a compellable witness for the accused unless excused by some principle of common law or by statute.[132] Notice of the intention to call the spouse as a defence witness must be given to the prosecutor in the usual way.[133] The question of confidential communications between the spouses is mentioned later.[134] **13.7.1**

13.8 SPOUSE OF ACCUSED—WITNESS FOR PROSECUTION

At common law, with a single important exception, one spouse[135] is not a competent witness against the other.[136] The exception applies when the spouse is the alleged victim, in which case he or she is both a competent and a compellable witness.[137] In order to make the spouse a competent witness the crime need not **13.8.1**

---

[124] *Rice* (1864) 4 Irv 493; *Montgomery* (1855) 2 Irv 222, in neither of which was the witness put on oath. *HM Advocate v Wilson* 1942 JC 75.

[125] If the inarticulacy is coupled with a question as to mental capacity, see para 13.5. Doubt as to the cause of the inarticulacy will not necessarily render the witness inadmissible (*cf O'Neil and Gollan* (1858) 3 Irv 93), unless it is not possible to communicate for the purposes of assessing competence or receiving evidence.

[126] *Howison* (1871) 2 Coup 153. See also *Mark* (1845) 7 D 882.

[127] *M v Kennedy* 1993 SC 115.

[128] See Macphail, *Evidence*, paras 6.05–6.06.

[129] Criminal Procedure (Scotland) Act 1995 ("1995 Act"), s 264(1)(a). There is further express provision, in relation to a prosecution for bigamy, in s 264(4).

[130] 1995 Act, s 264(3).

[131] 1995 Act, s 264(1)(b).

[132] *Hunter v HM Advocate* 1984 JC 90. The excused situations envisaged are the witness's privilege against self-incrimination (see para 12.13) and the statutory right to refuse to reveal a matrimonial communication (see para 13.10).

[133] Criminal Evidence Act 1898, s 5.

[134] See para 13.10.

[135] In order to be a "spouse" there must be a marriage. If the marriage is an irregular one it must probably be instantly verifiable—*Reid* (1873) 2 Coup 415, *Muir* (1836) 1 Swin 402—*eg* by decree of the court in an action of declarator of marriage. A cohabitee is not a spouse: *Casey v HM Advocate* 1993 SLT 33.

[136] *Harper v Adair* 1945 JC 21; *Foster v HM Advocate* 1932 JC 75.

[137] *Harper v Adair* 1945 JC 21; *Foster v HM Advocate* 1932 JC 75. The common law is preserved by statute: Criminal Procedure (Scotland) Act 1995, s 264(2)(a).

involve physical injury, but the spouse should be the discernible victim.[138] A husband was competent and compellable when his wife was charged with uttering cheques on which his signature was forged,[139] and with stealing his property,[140] and a wife was competent and compellable when her husband was charged with falsely accusing her of trying to poison him.[141]

13.8.2   By statute a spouse of the accused, while not compellable,[142] is a competent witness for the prosecution or a co-accused without the consent of the accused.[143] If a spouse opts to give evidence he or she must answer all relevant questions, even if incriminating the other spouse,[144] unless they are challengeable on some other ground such as self-incrimination of the witness.[145] Furthermore, the spouse may be called as a prosecution witness without the consent of the person charged, if the offence charged is bigamy.[146] The confidentiality of communications between husband and wife is dealt with later.[147]

13.9 SPOUSE OF PARTY—CIVIL CAUSES

13.9.1   At common law the spouse of a party was not a competent witness. The Evidence (Scotland) Act 1853 provided that it should be competent to adduce the spouse of a party, but no person was compellable to answer any question tending to criminate himself or herself, and the confidentiality of communications during marriage was safeguarded.[148] The Act did not apply to consistorial actions,[149] but that limitation was removed by section 2 of the Evidence (Further Amendment) (Scotland) Act 1874, which further provided that no witness should be asked or bound to answer any question tending to show that he or she had been guilty of adultery, unless the witness had already given evidence in the same proceeding in disproof of his or her alleged adultery. Apart from the confidentiality of communications during marriage,[150] the privilege of a spouse is thus the same as that of any other witness.[151] The evidence of a spouse is admissible to prove that intercourse did or did not take place between them during any period, but neither is compellable to give such evidence.[152] It does not appear to have been decided whether one spouse

---

[138] See *Hay v McClory* 1994 SLT 520, where, in a charge of vandalism of a common door of a block of flats in which the spouse lived, the spouse was compellable when the charge named the landlord as the proprietor of the damaged property.

[139] *Foster v HM Advocate* 1932 JC 75.

[140] *Harper v Adair* 1945 JC 21 .

[141] *Millar* (1847) Ark 355.

[142] Criminal Procedure (Scotland) Act 1995 ("1995 Act"), s 264(2)(a).

[143] 1995 Act, s 264(1)(b). *Lockhart v Massie* 1989 SCCR 421, a shrieval decision to allow hearsay, in the form of evidence given by a wife in an earlier trial, at a later trial in which the wife was unwilling to give evidence and was is in any event medically unfit, is difficult to reconcile, even with the authority of *Wm Harvey* (1835) Bell's Notes 292 quoted in the commentary to the report at 424. Although rules for the admission of hearsay have since extended to cover the medical unfitness of the spouse, it is thought that there would be no basis in law for compulsion in a situation such as this.

[144] *Bates v HM Advocate* 1989 SLT 701.

[145] Considered at para 12.13.

[146] 1995 Act, s 264(4).

[147] See para 13.10.

[148] s 3. See para 13.10.

[149] s 4.

[150] See para 13.10.

[151] See paras 12.13 and 12.14.

[152] Law Reform (Miscellaneous Provisions) Act 1949, s 7.

is, as a general rule, a compellable witness against the other. The limited form of the proviso, which applies only to communications, suggests that the intention of the leading part of the section is to make such a witness compellable.[153]

13.10 HUSBAND AND WIFE—CONFIDENTIAL COMMUNICATIONS

General

The rule that communications between husband and wife during the subsistence of **13.10.1** the marriage are privileged and may not be given in evidence is not a sacred principle of the common law, but entirely the creation of the statutes which made parties and their spouses competent witnesses.[154] Accordingly its scope depends not on the underlying principle[155] but on the words of the statutes.

Civil causes

The Evidence (Scotland) Act 1853 provides that nothing in the Act "shall in any **13.10.2** proceeding render any husband competent or compellable to give against his wife evidence of any matter communicated by her to him during the marriage, or any wife competent or compellable to give against her husband[156] evidence of any matter communicated by him to her during the marriage." Since both the words "competent" and "compellable" are used, it would appear that either the party or the witness may object. The communication may be oral or written,[157] and the rule applies even if the marriage has been dissolved by death or divorce.[158] In spite of the generality of the words there is a recognised exception where the action is concerned with the conduct of the spouses towards each other, as in actions of divorce.[159] Since only the husband and wife are mentioned in the Act it is impossible to accept Dickson's view[160] that it is incompetent to examine third parties as to communications in their presence between husband and wife. The authorities cited by him have no bearing, and a communication in the presence of third parties can hardly be said to have been "confided by one of the spouses to the bosom of the other."[161] The rule does not apply to a wife examined as a witness in the bankruptcy of her husband.[162]

Criminal trials

The statute provides: "Nothing in this section shall compel a spouse to disclose any **13.10.3**

---

[153] Although it had been decided in *Leach v R* [1912] AC 305 that implication is not a safe ground for holding that the common law has been altered, and therefore that a wife though competent is not compellable. In *McDonnell v McShane* 1967 SLT (Sh Ct) 61 at 63, that implication is accepted by Sheriff Sir Allan Walker, joint author of the first edition of this work.

[154] *Sawers v Balgarnie* (1858) 21 D 153, per Lord Benholme at 157.

[155] Dickson, *Evidence* (3rd edn), para 1660.

[156] Otherwise the rule does not apply: *Sawers v Balgarnie* (1858) 21 D 153, per Lord Cowan at 156.

[157] Dickson, *Evidence* (3rd edn), para 1661: *MacKay v MacKay* 1946 SC 78 (letter to husband confessing adultery); *Gallacher v Gallacher* 1934 SC 339 (letters to wife inciting her to commit adultery).

[158] Dickson, *Evidence* (3rd edn), para 1660.

[159] Dickson, *Evidence* (3rd edn), para 1661: *MacKay v MacKay* 1946 SC 78 (letter to husband confessing adultery); *Gallacher v Gallacher* 1934 SC 339 (letters to wife inciting her to commit adultery).

[160] Dickson, *Evidence* (3rd edn), para 1660.

[161] See also *Rumping v DPP* [1964] AC 814.

[162] Bankruptcy (Scotland) Act 1985, ss 44, 46 and 47; *Sawers v Balgarnie* (1858) 21 D 153.

communication made between the spouses during the marriage."[163] In contrast
with the provision of the Evidence (Scotland) Act 1853, the words "competent or"
do not appear. The objection is therefore open only to the witness, who may opt to
disclose the communication.[164] The communication may be oral or written,[165] the
rule applies even if the marriage has been dissolved,[166] and the evidence of third
parties as to such communications is competent.[167]

13.11 ACCUSED PERSON—GENERAL

13.11.1   At common law an accused person was not a competent witness at his own trial.
Hence the former importance of a prisoner's declaration,[168] the only opportunity
of giving the accused's account of events. Under criminal statutes since 1898[169]
every person charged with an offence is a competent witness for the defence at
every stage of the case,[170] whether the accused is on trial alone or jointly with a co-
accused, that is a person named with the accused on the same libel, albeit on different charges.[171] In solemn procedure the name of the accused need not be
included in the list of witnesses for the defence.[172] The accused may be called only
on his own application[173] or in very limited other circumstances. These circumstances are: (a) if the accused consents a co-accused may call him as a witness provided that the accused has not already given evidence, in which case the
co-accused may cross-examine him[174]; and (b) if the accused no longer stands
accused and unconfessed on any charges, through pleading guilty to or being
acquitted of all charges, or desertion.[175] If the accused is to be a witness he is called
as the first defence witness unless the court, on cause shown, otherwise directs.[176]
Unless otherwise ordered by the court, the accused gives evidence from the witness box or other place from which the other witnesses in the case have given evidence.[177] An accused who is married is not bound to disclose any communication
made between the spouses during the marriage.[178] The accused may be asked in

---

[163] Criminal Procedure (Scotland) Act 1995, s 264(2)(b).
[164] *HM Advocate v HD* 1953 JC 65.
[165] Dickson, *Evidence* (3rd edn), para 1661: *MacKay v MacKay* 1946 SC 78 (letter to husband confessing adultery); *Gallacher v Gallacher* 1934 SC 339 (letters to wife inciting her to commit adultery).
[166] Dickson, *Evidence* (3rd edn), para 1660. *Cf* Clive, *The Law of Husband & Wife in Scotland* (4th
edn), para 18.019.
[167] *Rumping v DPP* [1964] AC 814.
[168] Macdonald, *Criminal Law* (5th edn), pp 201 and 328. See para 9.3.1.
[169] Criminal Evidence Act 1898, s 1; now the Criminal Procedure (Scotland) Act 1995, s 266(1).
[170] While these words were presumably inserted to cover any preliminary hearing in England, they
would include a proof as to the accused's fitness to plead or as to the admissibility of a statement by
him: *Manuel v HM Advocate* 1958 JC 41 at 49; *Thompson v Crowe* 2000 JC 173.
[171] This is the meaning of "co-accused" used throughout the following paragraphs. For comparison with
the term "accomplice", see para 13.18.
[172] *Kennedy* (1898) 1 F (J) 5.
[173] Criminal Procedure (Scotland) Act 1995 ("1995 Act"), s 266(2).
[174] 1995 Act, s 266(9).
[175] 1995 Act, s 266(10).
[176] 1995 Act, s 266(11). No doubt application for another witness to speak first should be made at the
start of the defence case. A party may apply, and show cause, to interrupt the evidence of his own witness to allow for another witness to be examined: s 263(2) and (3). There appears to be no reported case
of enforcement of this provision, and it seems unlikely that refusal to allow the accused to give evidence other than as first witness would accord with the requirements of a fair trial.
[177] 1995 Act, s 266(8).
[178] 1995 Act, s 264(2)(b).

cross-examination any question notwithstanding that it would tend to incriminate him as to the offence charged.[179]

13.12 ACCUSED PERSON—COMMENT ON FAILURE TO TESTIFY

Until 1996 the accused's failure to give evidence could not be made the subject of comment by the prosecutor.[180] Since 1 April 1996 that restriction on prosecutorial comment no longer exists,[181] although it has been observed that the situations in which the prosecutor will wish to comment will be rare, and that a prosecutor's comment is likely to be limited in the same way as that of a judge, considered next.[182] If an accused has been judicially examined and has declined to answer a question, but later gives evidence in court on a matter which might have been stated appropriately in answer to that question, the prosecutor, co-accused or judge may comment at trial.[183] If an accused has lodged a special defence and withdrawn it before trial the matter may be raised in cross-examination at trial.[184] **13.12.1**

The restriction on prosecutorial comment did not deprive the judge of the right to comment to the jury on the accused's failure to give evidence, but the judge should do so only with restraint,[185] probably only in exceptional circumstances,[186] and not with undue emphasis.[187] It has been considered proper to direct the jury that on the facts they are entitled in the absence of any explanation by the accused to draw an inference of guilt.[188] It would also seem proper, where innocent explanations for the accused's conduct have been suggested unsuccessfully in **13.12.2**

---

[179] 1995 Act, s 266(3). This provision must be read subject to limitation. See para 13.13.

[180] Criminal Procedure (Scotland) Act 1975, ss 141(1)(b) and 346(1)(b). These ceased to have effect as a result of the Criminal Justice (Scotland) Act 1995, s 32. For comment on the effect that the restriction had in summary cases, see *Ross v Boyd* (1903) 5 F (J) 64, *McAttee v Hogg* (1903) 5 F (J) 67, and in solemn cases see *Scott v HM Advocate* 1946 JC 90, *Clark v HM Advocate* (1977) SCCR Supp 162, *Upton v HM Advocate* 1986 JC 65, *McHugh v HM Advocate* 1978 JC 12, *Dempsey v HM Advocate* 1995 JC 84. Comment by a co-accused, although not expressly prohibited, was, in the opinion of the Lord Justice-Clerk (Ross) in *Collins v HM Advocate* 1991 JC 204, not allowed on the same principle. Lords Murray and Weir reserved opinion on this point, and Lord Murray was of the view that the principle underlying the prohibition on the prosecutor was the burden of proof, which did not underlie the position of the co-accused, even if incriminating the other accused. It is difficult to see on what principle any such restriction on the co-accused could now survive.

[181] For comment on its removal, see the annotations (by Robert Sheils) to the Criminal Justice (Scotland) Act 1995, s 32 in *Current Law Statutes*. The position of comment by the co-accused is unchanged.

[182] *Hansard*, HL Vol 560, col 416 and see para 13.12.2.

[183] Criminal Procedure (Scotland) Act 1995, s 36(8).

[184] *Williamson v HM Advocate* 1980 JC 22.

[185] *Scott v HM Advocate* 1946 JC 90; *Stewart v HM Advocate* 1980 JC 103.

[186] *Brown v Macpherson* 1918 JC 3, followed in *Scott v HM Advocate* 1946 JC 90 with some comment that the need for exceptional circumstances should be reconsidered, but that comment was rejected in *Knowles v HM Advocate* 1975 JC 6. See also *McIntosh v HM Advocate (No 2)* 1997 SLT 1320.

[187] As in *Dempsey v HM Advocate* 1995 JC 84, where the prosecutor had made improper comment on the accused's silence and the judge did also, to the extent that there was a miscarriage of justice. There is an interesting discussion of this issue by Lord McCluskey in *Hoekstra v HM Advocate (No 1)* 2000 JC 387, but this is of academic interest only since the judgment was recalled in full after a successful challenge to the perceived impartiality of the judge, reported in *Hoekstra v HM Advocate (No 2)* 2000 JC 391.

[188] *Hardy v HM Advocate* 1938 JC 144, *Scott v HM Advocate* 1946 JC 90, *McIlhargey v Herron* 1972 JC 38, *Sutherland v HM Advocate* 1994 JC 62, *McIntosh v HM Advocate (No 2)* 1997 SLT 1320. *Cf Dempsey v HM Advocate* 1995 JC 84. See also para 6.10.

cross-examination or suggested in the speech for the defence, for the judge to point out to the jury that such explanations would have come better from the accused, who would have been liable to cross-examination.[189]

13.13 ACCUSED WITNESS—EVIDENCE OF ANOTHER OFFENCE OR OF BAD CHARACTER—GENERAL

13.13.1 The accused must not be asked, and if asked must not be required to answer, any question tending to show that he has committed or been convicted of, or been charged with, any offence other than that with which he is then charged, or is of bad character,[190] except in one or other of three situations described in the next paragraph.[191] However, before moving to the exceptions some points should be made concerning the provision itself.

13.13.2 The mere fact that one of the exceptions applies does not necessarily establish the admissibility of a question on one of the prohibited subjects, which may be inadmissible on more general grounds.[192] Even if the accused has given evidence against another person charged with the same offence, evidence of an acquittal on another matter, if it neither affects his credibility nor bears on the offence for which he is on trial, is irrelevant, and so inadmissible,[193] but *may* be admissible as a preliminary to relevant questions—for example, as to evidence given by the accused in a previous trial when he was acquitted[194]; and if the accused has introduced a statement, cross-examination on it is not prohibited. So, if an accused gives evidence that he has never been charged,[195] he may be cross-examined on that, even although the charge resulted in an acquittal.[196]

13.13.3 The mere asking of the question may be fatal even if it is disallowed or withdrawn.[197] The judge has a discretion and the fundamental consideration is fairness.[198] The evidence which satisfies the particular exception may be so trivial, and the evidence which it is proposed to take from the accused so serious, that it would be unfair to allow it.[199] The question will not breach the provision if it could not have tended to reveal or disclose something more than was already known to the court.[200] An accused who does not object at the time normally will be deemed to have waived the right to do so.[201] Breach of the prohibition does not necessarily lead to the quashing of the conviction,[202] provided there was no miscarriage of justice.

---

[189] See observations of Lord Carmont in *Maitland v Glasgow Corporation* 1947 SC 20 at 28.

[190] As to the relevance of evidence of character, see Chapter 7.

[191] Criminal Procedure (Scotland) Act 1995, s 266(4). See para 13.4.

[192] *Maxwell v Director of Public Prosecutions* [1935] AC 309 at 319.

[193] *Maxwell v Director of Public Prosecutions* [1935] AC 309 at 319.

[194] *Maxwell v Director of Public Prosecutions* [1935] AC 309 at 320. See also *R v Z* (HL, unreported, 22 June 2000).

[195] ie accused before a court: *Stirland v Director of Public Prosecutions* [1944] AC 315 at 323 and 327.

[196] *Stirland v Director of Public Prosecutions* [1944] AC 315 at 326 and 327. See also *McIntyre v HM Advocate* 1998 JC 232. Cf *Andrew v HM Advocate* 2000 SLT 402.

[197] *Barker v Arnold* [1911] 2 KB 120.

[198] Observed in *Leggate v HM Advocate* 1988 JC 127 at 147.

[199] *Leggate v HM Advocate* 1988 JC 127 at 146.

[200] *Dodds v HM Advocate* 1988 SLT 194, following *Jones v Director of Public Prosecutions* [1962] AC 635.

[201] *Cordiner v HM Advocate* 1993 SLT 2. However, depending upon the circumstances an appeal may succeed even if no objection is taken at the trial: *Stirland v Director of Public Prosecutions* [1944] AC 315 at 327.

[202] *Stirland v Director of Public Prosecutions* [1944] AC 315 at 327.

13.14 ACCUSED WITNESS—EVIDENCE OF ANOTHER OFFENCE OR OF BAD CHARACTER—EXCEPTIONS

Admissibility as evidence of guilt

The prohibition does not apply if proof that the accused has committed or been **13.14.1** convicted of the other offence is admissible to show that he is guilty of the offence charged.[203] This may apply in situations such as proof of conviction and disqualification from driving in a subsequent charge of driving while disqualified,[204] or proof of conviction and length of sentence in a subsequent charge of prison-breaking. In certain situations, statute provides that previous convictions may be proof *in causa*. A person found in possession of tools or objects in circumstances from which it can reasonably be inferred that it was intended to commit theft can only be successfully prosecuted if proved to have two or more convictions for theft.[205]

Attempt to establish good character, or attack character of Crown witness or prosecutor

The full words of this exception are that "the accused or his counsel or solicitor **13.14.2** has personally or by his advocate asked questions of the witnesses for the prosecution with a view to establishing the accused's good character or impugning the character of the complainer, or the accused has given evidence of his own good character, or the nature or conduct of the defence is such as to involve imputations on the character of the prosecutor or of the witnesses for the prosecution or of the complainer."[206] Situations in which the accused does not give evidence but leads witnesses to the same effect are dealt with in the same terms by another section.[207]

At one time, the generality of similar words in previous statutes was restricted **13.14.3** by judicial decision to the effect that the imputations on the character of witnesses had to be in matters extraneous to the charge.[208] Imputations which were relevant to the accused's line of defence or proper cross-examination of a Crown witness were thought not to bring the exception into play.[209] However, after review of the

---

[203] Criminal Procedure (Scotland) Act 1995, s 266(4)(a).

[204] *eg Mitchell v Dean* 1979 JC 62, but the record of previous convictions produced should not exceed that necessary to prove the current charge.

[205] Civic Government (Scotland) Act 1982, s 58; *Newlands v MacPhail* 1991 SLT 642. For another example, see *Stirland v Director of Public Prosecutions* [1944] AC 315 at 321.

[206] Criminal Procedure (Scotland) Act 1995, s 266(4)(b). In *Anderson v HM Advocate* 1996 JC 29, an appeal against conviction on the ground of defective legal representation, the court examined the respective roles of legal representative and accused in the conduct of the defence. Provided that the representative conducts the defence that he has been instructed to present, how that is done, including the decision whether to attack the character of Crown witnesses, is a matter for the representative, not the accused. In *Anderson* the representative chose not to put the criminal record of a Crown witness to that witness in cross-examination, against the will of the accused who volunteered his own while giving evidence. If the converse were to be the case, *quaere* the effect of the resultant loss of the protection for the accused. See also *McIntyre v HM Advocate* 1998 JC 232.

[207] Criminal Procedure (Scotland) Act 1995, s 270(1) and (2).

[208] *O'Hara v HM Advocate* 1948 JC 90 at 98.

[209] *O'Hara v HM Advocate* 1948 JC 90. So, where a person charged with assaulting two constables pleaded self defence and gave evidence that one of the constables was the aggressor and was drunk, it was held that this formed part of the substance of the defence and was not extraneous to the charge, and did not open the way to cross-examination of the accused on his character. See, *eg, Conner v Lockhart* 1986 JC 161. On the other hand, to suggest to a constable that he had been reduced from inspector for a breach of discipline would probably have done so: *O'Hara v HM Advocate* 1948 JC 90, and see, *eg, Fielding v HM Advocate* 1959 JC 101, *Templeton v McLeod* 1985 JC 112.

authorities in Scotland and in England and close examination of the statutory provisions then applying, that approach was disapproved, and decisions based upon it
overruled, by a court of seven judges.[210] The statutory provision is drawn to pro-
hibit evidence of the accused's character, unless the exception is triggered. If the
exception is triggered the prohibition disappears, but it is then in the discretion of
the trial judge[211] to allow the cross-examination (or evidence) of character, which
must always be for the limited purpose of attacking credibility, applying a test of
fairness.[212] The requirement for permission of the court before the evidence
of character can be led under this exception is now found in the statute.[213]

Evidence against person charged with same offence

13.14.4   If an accused has given evidence against a co-accused, that co-accused may cross-
examine the accused as to character without seeking permission from the court,[214]
and indeed the court may not prevent this.[215] The most obvious example is where
A and B are charged with assault and B gives evidence that A was kicking the
victim and he (B) was trying to protect him; B may be asked whether he has previously been convicted of theft, and such question may be put by A or his agent
without permission, or by the prosecutor with permission of the court.[216] The
exception is not connected to intention of the accused,[217] and will apply whether
the evidence is expressly or impliedly[218] supportive of the prosecution case against
the co-accused or undermining of the co-accused's defence.[219] In some cases, in
order to avoid the automatic adverse effect of challenging the character of a co-
accused, the accused has applied for separation of trials, but this has been unsuccessful when the accused is merely concerned that pursuing a line of defence
through cross-examination of the co-accused will trigger a counter-attack on character, which, in light of the trial judge's role in ensuring fairness, could not be said
to leave the accused unprotected.[220]

13.15 CO-ACCUSED CALLED ON OWN APPLICATION

13.15.1   At the time when an accused had no right to cross-examine unless the evidence
incriminated him,[221] where there was a joint defence, the evidence of one of the

---

[210] *Leggate v HM Advocate* 1988 JC 127, overruling *O'Hara v HM Advocate* 1948 JC 90, *Fielding v
HM Advocate* 1959 JC 101, *Templeton v McLeod* 1985 JC 112, and *Conner v Lockhart* 1986 JC 161.
It was pointed out in *Leggate*, at 143, that the results in each of these cases would probably not have
been different if the correct approach had been taken, so they retain some value as examples of imputations and their likely effect upon introduction of evidence of the accused's character.

[211] See, *eg, Sinclair v Macdonald* 1996 JC 145.

[212] *Leggate v HM Advocate* 1988 JC 127 at 143–147.

[213] Criminal Procedure (Scotland) Act 1995 ("1995 Act"), s 266(5).

[214] 1995 Act, s 266(4)(c).

[215] *McCourtney v HM Advocate* 1977 JC 68. See also *Murdoch v Taylor* [1965] AC 574.

[216] *Hackston v Millar* (1906) 8 F (J) 52. See also *Murdoch v Taylor* [1965] AC 574.

[217] *Murdoch v Taylor* [1965] AC 574.

[218] *Burton v HM Advocate* 1979 SLT (Notes) 59; *cf Sandlan v HM Advocate* 1983 JC 22.

[219] *McCourtney v HM Advocate* 1977 JC 68.

[220] *Brown v HM Advocate* 1992 SLT 272; *Toner v HM Advocate* 1995 JC 192.

[221] *Gemmell v MacNiven* 1928 JC 5. See also *Townsend v Strathern* 1923 JC 66, and *Morrison v Adair*
1943 JC 25. The decision in *Gemmell* was alleged to follow *Hackston v Millar* (1906) 8 F (J) 52, but
goes beyond it. *Hackston* decided only that a co-accused was entitled to cross-examine if the evidence
incriminated him. It did not decide that that was the limit of his right, a point taken up by their
Lordships in the full bench decision *Todd v HM Advocate* 1984 JC 13.

co-accused was in the ordinary case admissible for and against the others.[222] A joint defence involved a single representation, so that no question of cross-examination on behalf of the other accused arose. Where there were separate defences and separate representation, the evidence of each accused was admissible against the others.[223] So long as that rule stood unqualified, the law was left in the position that if one co-accused gave evidence tending to incriminate another, however slightly, he might be fully cross-examined like any other witness; otherwise he could not be cross-examined at all,[224] but the evidence of a witness called for one co-accused, as distinct from that of the co-accused himself, was never evidence against another.

Statute has, since 1980, allowed an accused to cross-examine a co-accused, **13.15.2** whether or not that co-accused has given evidence incriminating the other,[225] and whether or not the charges against them are the same. The co-accused may be asked "any question", but this does not override normal privileges afforded to any witness, such as the privilege against self-incrimination on a matter outwith the offences charged,[226] or the right to withhold evidence of a matrimonial communication.[227] If an accused is cross-examined by a co-accused, the prosecutor is entitled to cross-examine last.[228] The prosecutor may cross-examine on a matter designed to assist the case against a co-accused.[229] The court may require to allow further cross-examination or evidence in replication, if later cross-examination for one accused reveals fresh information adverse to the defence of another.[230]

13.16 CO-ACCUSED CALLED AS WITNESS FOR ANOTHER ACCUSED

At common law it is competent for one co-accused to call another, if their trials **13.16.1** have been separated.[231] Under statute an accused can call a co-accused in any case if the co-accused consents.[232] A co-accused called as a witness by another accused is in the same position as any other witness called for the defence, and is subject to cross-examination, for example, on previous convictions. No notice is necessary.[233] If the co-accused has pled guilty or has been acquitted or the case against him has been deserted, so that there are no charges remaining for proof against him, he may be called as a witness by the co-accused or the prosecutor without notice, but subject to such adjournment or postponement as seems just.[234] An accused can,

---

[222] *Young v HM Advocate* 1932 JC 63 at 72.

[223] *Young v HM Advocate* 1932 JC 63 at 74.

[224] See *Young v HM Advocate* 1932 JC 63 at 73.

[225] Criminal Justice (Scotland) Act 1980, ss 27 and 28, now the Criminal Procedure (Scotland) Act 1995, s 266(9)(b).

[226] See para 12.13.

[227] See para 13.10.

[228] This right was expressly recognised both by the judges and by defence counsel at the trial which preceded *Young v HM Advocate* 1932 JC 63.

[229] Implicit in s 266(3) of the Criminal Procedure (Scotland) Act 1995. *Cf* the position at common law: *Young v HM Advocate* 1932 JC 63 at 74.

[230] Discussed in *Sandlan v HM Advocate* 1983 JC 22, in which the court would have preferred not to apply a formulaic approach.

[231] *Bell and Shaw v Houston* (1842) 1 Broun 49; *Morrison v Adair* 1943 JC 25. *Cf Mitchell* (1887) 1 White 320.

[232] Criminal Procedure (Scotland) Act 1995 ("1995 Act"), s 266(9).

[233] 1995 Act, s 266(9).

[234] 1995 Act, s 266(10).

in certain circumstances, lead the evidence of a hearsay statement made by a co-accused, and this is considered in another chapter.[235]

13.17 WITNESS CALLED FOR CO-ACCUSED

13.17.1   Historically, if the defence was joint, each defence witness was a witness for all the accused. But a difficulty did arise at common law if there were separate defences and two of the co-accused wished to call the same witness. The common law came to be interpreted to the effect that the evidence of a witness led for one co-accused was not evidence against another, who should therefore have had no right to cross-examine, but that interpretation was rooted in the historical situation in which an accused was not permitted to give evidence. Judges were not prepared to press that technical rule to the point of unfairness,[236] and the interpretation was abandoned by the decision in *Todd v HM Advocate*,[237] which confirms that evidence led on behalf of one accused is evidence in the cause, which the jury may use in assessment of the case against each accused.

13.18 ACCOMPLICES

13.18.1   The term "accomplice" has been applied in a variety of situations in the past; partly to distinguish from co-accused to whom the historical limitations described in previous paragraphs applied.[238] Whilst the term includes a person indicted or on trial along with others charged with committing the same or a related charge,[239] it may include a person who has previously pleaded guilty to, or been convicted of, the charge or a related charge, and a mere witness[240] who admits his own guilt of the charge or a related charge.[241] It is not settled in law whether the term applies to a person, other than an accused, who has neither admitted nor been convicted of the charge, but to whom the evidence points as an associate. If an accomplice is a co-accused the rules that are described in the previous paragraphs apply, but, if not, the accomplice is admissible either for the prosecution or the defence, but enjoys the privilege against self-incrimination.

13.18.2   At one time the evidence of an accomplice was received with suspicion, and a jury had to be specifically directed that it was their duty to apply to it "a special scrutiny over and above the general examination which a jury has to apply to all

---

[235] See para 8.6.6. See also Renton & Brown, *Criminal Procedure* (6th edn), paras 24-24 to 24-26.

[236] *Morrison v Adair* 1943 JC 25; *Lee v HM Advocate* 1968 SLT 155.

[237] 1984 JC 13.

[238] See the first edition of this work, para 363.

[239] Theft and reset of the same property are related charges: *HM Advocate v Murdoch* 1955 SLT (Notes) 57.

[240] A witness accomplice who gives self-incriminating evidence as a Crown witness called for that purpose in order to secure a conviction of the accused acquires immunity from prosecution on the crime admitted during his evidence. The limited scope of this is clear from *O'Neill v Wilson* 1983 JC 42. See also *Boyes v MacLeod (No 2)* 1998 SLT 1129.

[241] *HM Advocate v Murdoch* 1955 SLT (Notes) 57. Admission of guilt, art and part, of a statutory charge would be enough. Two accused summoned on different complaints with the offence of assault, each offence arising from a melee but in which the accused in one was the victim in the other, are not accomplices: *O'Neill v Wilson* 1983 JC 42. *Cf Boyes v MacLeod (No 2)* 1998 SLT 1129.

the material evidence."[242] However, this rule led to some difficulty[243] and comment that credibility of a witness should be dependent upon the circumstances of each case.[244] A review of the law from the time of Hume time was undertaken by a full bench in *Docherty v HM Advocate*.[245] The Court decided that no special warning was required for an accomplice, commented on the direction to be given to the jury, and observed that the judge could direct the jury that in assessing the credibility of a witness they could take into account criticisms which had been made of the witness.[246] The evidence of an accomplice, if believed, has the same effect in law as that of any other witness.[247]

13.19 PROSECUTORS

It is thought that a prosecutor can be a witness in a case in which the prosecutor **13.19.1** has played no part. While it has been laid down emphatically that a prosecutor—that is the person who conducts the prosecution—can never be a competent witness,[248] the view was less emphatic when the witness did not conduct the prosecution but it was at his instance.[249] Prosecutors commonly give evidence in cases of perjury arising from a trial in which the prosecutor was presenting, and in relation to disturbances occurring within or about the criminal courts.

13.20 JUDGES, JURORS AND ARBITERS

Supreme courts

While there is no actual decision, it is plain from the opinions in the undernoted **13.20.1** case[250] that it is incompetent to call a judge as a witness as to judicial proceedings which took place before him, though he might be a witness as to an unusual event such as a disturbance, or possibly an assault.[251]

---

[242] *HM Advocate v Murdoch* 1955 SLT (Notes) 57. This was laid down only *quoad* witnesses for the prosecution, and the question was not raised whether it is proper to give a similar direction as regards a defence witness. See also *Wallace v HM Advocate* 1952 JC 78 per Lord Justice-General Cooper at 82.

[243] *HM Advocate v Murdoch* 1955 SLT (Notes) 57; *Slowey v HM Advocate* 1965 SLT 309; *McGuinness v HM Advocate* 1971 SLT (Notes) 7. Reconsideration was called for in *Scott v HM Advocate* 1987 SLT 389.

[244] *Scott v HM Advocate* 1987 SLT 389.

[245] 1987 JC 81.

[246] *Docherty v HM Advocate* 1987 JC 81 at 95. Applied in *Casey v HM Advocate* 1993 SLT 33.

[247] Accordingly, a conviction resting entirely on the evidence of two accomplices was sustained: *Dow v MacKnight* 1949 JC 38.

[248] *Graham v McLennan* 1911 SC (J) 16.

[249] *Mackintosh v Wooster* 1919 JC 15.

[250] *Muckarsie v Wilson* (1834) Bell's Notes 99.

[251] In connection with alleged fraud in obtaining legal aid by application to a judge and sheriff, see *HM Advocate v Muirhead*, a 1983 case (reported on other points only in *The Scotsman*, 6 June), referred to in the *Stair Memorial Encylopaedia*, Vol 10, "Evidence", para 528. In view of these opinions it is thought that the following earlier cases, where judges were examined of consent, both of themselves and of parties, are now of no importance: *Stewart v Fraser* (1830) 5 Mur 166; *Gibson v Stevenson* (1822) 3 Mur 208; *Harper v Robinsons and Forbes* (1821) 2 Mur 383.

Inferior courts

13.20.2 Judges of inferior courts are competent witnesses to the proceedings before them[252] and are frequently called in trials for perjury to testify as to the evidence given in their courts.[253]

Jurors

13.20.3 Jurors in civil and criminal cases are not competent to give evidence about jury deliberations, which will most commonly be the discussion and events in the jury room, but may, unusually, take place in the jury box.[254] An exception is no doubt made of necessity when there is an enquiry into jury conduct whether during, or after, a proof or trial.[255]

Arbiters

13.20.4 The arbiter is a competent witness in an action for enforcement or reduction of the award, but only certain evidence may be taken from the arbiter. Evidence from the arbiter is competent on any matter which would entitle the court to interfere with the award.[256] The arbiter may be asked: about the procedure adopted, to find out whether the rules of natural justice were transgressed[257]; how he construed the submission, for if it was misconstrued, the award may be reduced[258]; what factors he has taken into account and dealt with, because taking into account some irrelevant factor or failing to decide a matter before him may justify reduction of the award.[259] However, the arbiter cannot be asked to give reasons for the award or to alter or contradict it, unless it is averred that he has erred in some way which entitles the court to interfere, such as those mentioned above. The mere fact that the court thinks his decision wrong is not enough.[260] On matters other than the merits of the award it is likely that the arbiter is competent, and, in the absence of express provision to the contrary, compellable,[261] on matters concerning the conduct of the parties during the arbitration and the condition of goods or property inspected, in so far as these are issues in subsequent proceedings, and the purpose is not to have the arbiter reconsider the award.[262]

13.21 FOREIGNERS AND NON-ENGLISH SPEAKERS

13.21.1 A person who is a foreigner[263] is a competent witness. It is integral to the fair trial

---

[252] *Monaghan* (1844) 2 Broun 131.

[253] eg *Davidson v McFadyean* 1942 JC 95.

[254] *Dickson* (3rd edn), paras 1118 and 1642–1636. *Pirie v Caledonian Railway Co* (1890) 17 R 1157.

[255] *McCadden v HM Advocate* 1986 SLT 138.

[256] *Black v John Williams & Co (Wishaw) Ltd* 1923 SC 510 at 512 (where the arbiter's evidence is quoted); 1924 SC (HL) 22.

[257] *Black v John Williams & Co (Wishaw) Ltd* 1923 SC 510.

[258] *Glasgow City and District Railway Co v Macgeorge, Cowan & Galloway* (1886) 13 R 609 (where the arbiter was the only witness).

[259] *Glasgow City and District Railway Co v Macgeorge, Cowan & Galloway* (1886) 13 R 609.

[260] *Rogerson v Rogerson* (1885) 12 R 583; *Johnson v Lamb* 1981 SLT 300.

[261] *McDonnell v McShane* 1967 SLT (Sh Ct) 61 at 63.

[262] See *Stair Memorial Encyclopaedia (Re-issue)*, Vol 1, para 98.

[263] Including a person who has been classed as an enemy alien in time of conflict: *Patrick Macguire* (1857) 2 Irv 620.

in terms of Article 6 of the European Convention on Human Rights that everyone charged with a criminal offence is informed promptly in a language which he understands of the nature and detail of the charge and has free assistance of an interpreter if he cannot understand or speak the language of the court.[264] A non-foreigner may, unusually, have a first language other than English. This may apply in the case of someone whose first language is Gaelic or Welsh but only if the witness cannot understand and speak the language of the court. There is no entitlement to have proceedings interpreted into that language if that is the witness's second language.[265] The interpreter for an accused or witness should be independent,[266] and swear the appropriate oath and is *pro hac vice* an officer of the court.[267] It is not appropriate for a party to interpret for another.[268] The interpreter should be available to deal with all stages of the case including procedural stages,[269] and evidence relied upon at trial such as an extra-judicial statement of a non-English-speaking accused,[270] or a hearsay statement of an absent foreign witness may be challenged on this ground. However, failure to object at an early stage, unless that too is attributable to a lack of understanding of the language or there is a clear breach of Article 6(3)(e), may be fatal to a later complaint about lack of understanding.[271] When the quality of interpreting is called into question the correct process is to adjourn without further procedure until an appropriate interpreter is available.[272] It appears that if an accused alleges during trial that interpreted material was not comprehensible, this is not fatal to the proceedings, and the witness may be recalled for evidence to be interpreted afresh by an appropriate interpreter.[273]

13.22 PRESENCE IN COURT

General

At common law a witness who had been in court and heard the evidence of other   13.22.1

---

[264] Art 6(3)(e). See *Kamasinski v Austria* (1991) 13 EHRR 36 at 66, where lack of translation of the indictment was not in the circumstances unfair to the accused who appeared to understand the accusation and did not ask for a translation.

[265] *Taylor v Haughney* 1982 SCCR 360, following *Alex McRae* (1841) Bell's Notes 270.

[266] *HM Advocate v M'Pherson* (1902) 10 SLT 216; *Liszewski v Thomson* 1942 JC 55.

[267] *HM Advocate v Olsson* 1941 JC 63; *Liszewski v Thomson* 1942 JC 55—In both cases the accused was the foreigner but it seems equally applicable in the case of a witness: Dickson, *Evidence* (3rd edn), para 1793.

[268] *Liszewski v Thomson* 1942 JC 55.

[269] Art 6(3)(e), discussed in *Kamasinski v Austria* (1991) 13 EHRR 66; see also *HM Advocate v Olsson* 1941 JC 63, *Mikhailitchenko v Normand* 1993 SLT 1138. *Cf Ucak v HM Advocate* 1999 SLT 392. It is thought that the judgment in *Montes v HM Advocate* 1990 SCCR 645 should now be treated with suspicion. There the test of fairness was applied to the issue of whether there was understanding when a statement was made by an accused without the benefit of an interpreter, but this was left to the jury, following *Balloch v HM Advocate* 1977 JC 23. The court also felt it unnecessary to consider two judgments of the European Court of Human Rights referred to in argument. The *Balloch* approach has been overruled in *Thompson v Crowe* 2000 JC 173.

[270] *HM Advocate v Olsson* 1941 JC 63.

[271] As in *Ucak v HM Advocate* 1999 SLT 392, where the test applied was one of prejudice to the accused. However, this preceded the application of the clear ECHR requirement for access to interpretation.

[272] *Mikhailitchenko v Normand* 1993 SLT 1138.

[273] *HM Advocate v Al Megrahi and Fhimah*, interlocutor of 13 June 2000, unreported, a summary of which is accessible via www.law.gla.ac.uk/lockerbie.

witnesses was thereby rendered incompetent to testify.[274] The only exception was that skilled witnesses might be allowed to hear evidence of fact, but were required to withdraw during the evidence of other skilled witnesses.[275]

Criminal cases

13.22.2 Statute provides that the court may, on application by a party, permit a witness to be in court during the proceedings or any part of them before giving evidence if it appears to the court that the presence of the witness would not be contrary to the interests of justice.[276] If a witness has been present during the proceedings without such permission or consent of the parties, where it appears to the court that the presence of the witness was not a result of culpable negligence or criminal intent *and* that the witness has not been unduly instructed or influenced by what took place during his presence in court, *or* that injustice will not be done by his examination, the court has discretion to admit the witness.[277]

Civil cases

13.22.3 It is no longer imperative in the civil cases to reject any witness against whom it is objected that he has, without the permission of the court[278] and without the consent of the party objecting, been present in court during the proceedings.[279] The court may, in its discretion, admit the witness where it appears to the court that presence in court was not the consequence of culpable negligence or criminal intent and that the witness has not been unduly instructed or influenced by what took place in his presence, or that injustice will not be done by his examination. The judge may raise the question, and need not wait for an objection. When the question is raised, it is for the party tendering the witness to satisfy the court that the statutory test for admitting the witness has been met.

Parties to the cause

13.22.4 So long as the parties themselves were not competent witnesses they no doubt attended at proofs and jury trials. This practice has continued, although they are now competent witnesses. They remain in court and are compellable witnesses.[280] They may be called by other parties without notice.[281] The fact that they have heard the earlier evidence may be taken into account in assessing the value of their own evidence.[282]

Solicitor conducting case

13.22.5 It is no objection to a solicitor as a witness that he is engaged in or even actually conducting a civil cause, and has therefore been present in court.[283] A person who

---

[274] *Docherty and Graham v McLennan* 1912 SC (J) 102.
[275] Dickson, *Evidence* (3rd edn), para 1761. On this see para 16.3.12.
[276] Criminal Procedure (Scotland) Act 1995, s 267(1).
[277] Criminal Procedure (Scotland) Act 1995, s 267(2).
[278] Provided for by RCS, r 36.9. There is no express provision in the sheriff court rules but it would be competent to seek leave of the court for a witness to be present.
[279] Evidence (Scotland) Act 1840, s 3. As to skilled witnesses, see para 16.3.12.
[280] Dickson, *Evidence* (3rd edn), para 1601; *McDonnell v McShane* 1967 SLT (Sh Ct) 61.
[281] *McDonnell v McShane* 1967 SLT (Sh Ct) 61.
[282] *Perman v Binny's Trs* 1925 SLT 123 (OH).
[283] *Campbell v Cochrane* 1928 JC 25.

is or has been an agent of the accused may be called as a witness for the accused, and, if so called, the accused may not object on the ground of solicitor–client confidentiality to any question put to the witness on a matter pertinent to the accused's guilt.[284]

13.23 BANKER'S IMMUNITY

A banker or officer of a bank[285] is not compellable in any proceedings to which the **13.23.1** bank is not a party to prove matters which can be proved by a copy of an entry in the books, unless by order of the judge made for special cause.[286] Proof of bankers' books is the subject of special provisions dealt with in another chapter.[287]

13.24 HEADS OF STATE AND DIPLOMATS

General

There are certain immunities from giving evidence which apply to heads of state, **13.24.1** diplomats, consuls and officials in such missions and recognised international organisations.

Heads of state

It is thought that the monarch is a competent witness but not compellable.[288] Heads **13.24.2** of state of other countries are brought within the provisions applying to diplomats and consuls by order under the legislation described below.

Diplomats and consular officials

The status of diplomatic agents or consular officials is determined by certificate **13.24.3** given by the Secretary of State in accordance with the relevant legislation.[289] The immunity of ambassadors, their wives and families[290] and their suites,[291] from legal process rested on comity and was part of the common law.[292] Immunity from jurisdiction in the courts of the United Kingdom in civil and criminal matters is now

---

[284] Criminal Procedure (Scotland) Act 1995, s 265(2).

[285] "Bank" means an institution authorised under the Banking Act 1987 or a municipal bank within the meaning of that Act, a Building Society within the meaning of the Building Societies Act 1986, a National Savings Bank and the Post Office (when exercising its banking functions): Bankers' Books Evidence Act 1879, s 9(1) (as amended).

[286] Bankers' Books Evidence Act 1879, s 6.

[287] para 21.13.

[288] Macphail, *Evidence*, para 3.05.

[289] Diplomatic Privileges Act 1964, s 4, adopting the process familiar from *Engelke v Musmann* [1928] AC 433.

[290] *Engelke v Musmann* [1928] AC 433, per Lord Phillimore at 450.

[291] The "suite" of an ambassador means his counsellors, secretaries and clerks and his servants, with the probable exception of servants who are nationals of the state to which he is accredited: *Engelke v Musmann* [1928] AC 433, per Lord Phillimore at 450.

[292] *Engelke v Musmann* [1928] AC 433, per Lord Dunedin at 447, Lord Warrington of Clyffe at 458. If domestic provision is not sufficiently wide to incorporate international standards, it will be interpreted in such a manner as to give effect to the requirement of comity—see, *eg, Propend Finance Pty Ltd v Sing, The Times*, 2 May 1997, 1997 TLR 238.

regulated by statute,[293] which incorporates international convention.[294] Diplomatic agents are not obliged to give evidence as a witness on any matter.[295] Members of the family, and forming part of the household, of a diplomatic agent are included if they are not nationals of the United Kingdom.[296] If they are United Kingdom nationals their immunity is limited to the exercise of diplomatic functions.[297] The extent of immunity may be reduced to reflect the extent of immunity afforded to British diplomats in the other country.[298] Immunity from jurisdiction may be waived, but that will not waive immunity from execution of a judgment for which a separate waiver is necessary.[299]

Consular officials have a more limited form of immunity which is regulated by the Consular Relations Act 1968, and status is confirmed by a certificate of the Secretary of State.[300] Members of a consular post may be called to attend as a witness but are not compellable if this (a) concerns matters connected with the exercise of consular functions[301] or (b) interferes with the performance of those functions,[302] and written evidence should be used where possible.[303] A consular employee or member of service staff is compellable, unless on matters connected with the exercise of consular functions.[304] A consular member is not a compellable expert witness on the law of the state which sent them to the United Kingdom.[305] Immunity may be waived.[306]

Others Commonwealth representatives may be given the status of diplomatic or consular representatives.[307] So, too, may the representatives of international organisations approved by Order in Council.[308]

---

[293] Diplomatic Privileges Act 1964.

[294] Vienna Convention on Diplomatic Relations (Cmnd 2565) reproduced, in so far as it is incorporated thereby, in Sched 1 to the Diplomatic Privileges Act 1964.

[295] Vienna Convention on Diplomatic Relations, Art 31, para 2. A "diplomatic agent" is a head of mission or a member of the diplomatic staff of the mission: Art 1(e).

[296] Art 37(1).

[297] Art 38.

[298] Diplomatic Privileges Act 1964, s 3.

[299] Art 32.

[300] Consular Relations Act 1968, s 11.

[301] Consular Relations Act 1968, Sched 1, Art 44, para 3.

[302] Art 44, paras 1 and 2.

[303] Art 44, para 2.

[304] Art 44, para 3.

[305] Art 44, para 3.

[306] Art 45.

[307] Diplomatic and Other Privileges Act 1971, s 12 (as amended).

[308] International Organisations Act 1968 (as amended), esp Sched 1, Pt II.

CHAPTER 14

EVIDENCE ON COMMISSION

14.1 INTRODUCTORY

It is generally the case that evidence should be led in the presence of the tribunal **14.1.1** of fact, and in the building where the tribunal normally convenes. However, it has long been accepted in civil cases that, when a witness will be unable to deliver the evidence in person and in that place, commission may be granted by the court for the evidence to be taken before a substitute appointed by the court, who will then report the evidence. The form of the commission procedure may be open, whereby an individual is appointed to hear the evidence at large as a judge would in the proceedings normally, or in the form of prescribed interrogatories and cross-interrogatories which the commissioner must put to the witness. In 1980[1] commission in these forms was introduced for criminal proceedings in the High Court and sheriff court, but not the district court.[2]

In civil cases there are two avenues for seeking an order for evidence to be taken **14.1.2** on commission. First, where for some specific reason there is a danger of evidence being lost the court may appoint a commissioner to take the evidence and report, and this power may be exercised before any averments have been remitted to proof, or even before there are any averments. Evidence so taken is said to be taken to lie *in retentis*. Secondly, after proof has been allowed, or issues approved, and a diet fixed, the court may appoint a commissioner to take the evidence of a witness who will probably not be able to attend the diet, whether because they are abroad or unable to attend because of age, infirmity or sickness. So described, these exceptions are not mutually exclusive but the broad distinction is that the first case depends on an emergency and danger of the evidence being lost and the second does not. Accordingly, the material differences[3] relate to the reasons for

---

[1] Criminal Justice (Scotland) Act 1980, s 32 following a recommendation by the Thomson Committee in *Criminal Procedure in Scotland: Second Report by the Committee appointed by the Secretary of State for Scotland and the Lord Advocate* (Cmnd 6218, 1975), paras 43.23–43.30. As to the comparison between the limited purpose of the recommendation and the broader effect of the statute, see the commentary to *HM Advocate v Lesacher* 1982 SCCR 418. At common law commission was not competent in criminal proceedings: *HM Advocate v Hunter* (1905) 7 F (J) 73.

[2] The relevant provision is now the Criminal Procedure (Scotland) Act 1995, s 272.

[3] The distinction is clearly recognised in the Court of Session Act 1988, s 10, and in OCR, r 28.10(1).

granting commission, the time at which application may be made and, in some cases, the procedure.[4] In criminal cases the procedure is akin to the second avenue in terms of reasons and procedure, but can be taken "at an appropriate time" in the criminal proceedings even before it is known in which court the trial will be held. Because it can have the practical effect of gathering evidence to lie *in retentis* it will, where relevant, be considered under both avenues. These avenues will be considered in turn.

14.2 COMMISSION FOR EVIDENCE TO LIE *IN RETENTIS*

Reasons

14.2.1   The reason is usually stated generally as risk of the loss of the evidence, but that is plainly too wide. Any prospective witness may die unexpectedly. The risk must be one peculiar to the witness, and the usual risks are that the witness is so old or infirm or unwell as to be in danger of early death. The reasons are limited to these grounds in the Court of Session.[5] In the sheriff court reasons have included that the witness is obliged to go abroad[6] permanently or for a prolonged period.[7] It has usually been assumed in civil cases that on proof that a witness is aged 70, commission should be allowed automatically.[8] As life expectancies increase the justification for such an assumption must be in doubt.[9] Age, if challenged, is proved by production of a birth certificate.[10] Nevertheless, the grant of commission to take evidence to lie *in retentis* is a matter of discretion, and commission was refused to examine two aged witnesses when plenty of younger members of the congregation were available to prove a slander alleged to have been uttered from the pulpit.[11] Infirmity or sickness is proved by production of a medical certificate,[12] and, if it is challenged, a remit may be made to a doctor appointed by the court.[13]

14.2.2   The mere fact that the witness is going abroad does not mean that his evidence is necessarily lost, since facilities exist in certain circumstances for evidence to be

---

[4]   For the procedure in commissions to take evidence furth of Scotland, see para 14.7.

[5]   Court of Session Act 1988, s 10. For a history to the present powers of the Court of Session to allow evidence to be taken on commission, see annotations to the RCS, r 35.11 in the *Parliament House Book*, Division C.

[6]   Bankton, *Institute*, iv, 30, 27, quoted in *Boettcher v Carron Co* (1861) 23 D 322 at 325; Dickson, *Evidence* (3rd edn), para 1727.

[7]   Although the rule (OCR 28.10(1)(b) simply refers to danger of the evidence being lost. In summary cause actions the motion may be granted if it desirable to do so: Summary Cause Rules, Sheriff Court 1976, r 34(1). Evidence on commission is not provided for in small claims procedure, but letters of request may be sought in terms of the Small Claims Rules 1988, r 2(1), App 2 and OCR, r 28.14.

[8]   Dickson, *Evidence* (3rd edn), para 1728; *Wilson v Young* (1896) 4 SLT 73 (OH), although many septogenarians would resist any assumption that their death is imminent.

[9]   In criminal cases it would be dangerous to rely on such an assumption, and specific infirmity should be proven.

[10]   *Watsons* (1829) 8 S 261; *Morison v Cowan* (1828) 6 S 1082.

[11]   *Dudgeon v Forbes* (1832) 10 S 810.

[12]   This requires to be "on soul and conscience" for criminal proceedings: Act of Adjournal (Criminal Procedure Rules) 1996, r 24.1(3). It appears that in civil proceedings it need not be: Court of Session Practice Note, 6 June 1968.

[13]   In *Lunn v Watt* 1911 2 SLT 279 (OH) of consent. It used to be the practice to require production of such certificates, birth and medical, before the commissioner (Dickson, *Evidence* (3rd edn), para 1738), but the more logical and convenient modern practice, if there is a question, is to produce them when the commission is applied for.

taken before a court abroad,[14] or by video link or by affidavit.[15] Hearsay evidence of that witness may also be admissible.[16] But the existence of such facilities has not been regarded as an impediment to granting commission.[17] Indeed, the fact that the witness is examined in Scotland by counsel or solicitor in the case, rather than abroad on interrogatories,[18] may outweigh the disadvantage of evidence being taken early in the case.[19] A commission for evidence to lie *in retentis* will not be granted if the witness is going abroad by choice[20] (*eg* on holiday),[21] but would be if the witness was obliged to go, for example, on public service or other employment,[22] or, in the case of a party, by inability, owing perhaps to lack of means, to remain in Scotland till proof is allowed.[23] Where the witnesses were about to go abroad in course of their employment with the party asking for the commission, the court in one case refused the application[24] and in others granted it.[25] In one exceptional case commission was granted to take the evidence of the only two possible witnesses to the facts, a situation to which the phrase *penuria testium* (scarcity of witnesses) was applied, presumably on the ground that one might die unexpectedly.[26]

Timing and procedure

The emergency justifying the application may arise before the action has been **14.2.3** raised, and in such circumstances the Court of Session has power under the *nobile officium* to grant commission.[27] The application is accordingly by petition to the Inner House,[28] or possibly in extreme urgency to the vacation judge.[29] Evidence so taken may be used in an arbitration and, it would seem to follow, in the sheriff court. After an action has been raised the application is made by motion to the Lord Ordinary or sheriff of the court in which the action has been raised,[30] which motion

---

[14] See para 14.6.

[15] Chapter 15.

[16] Criminal Procedure (Scotland) Act 1995, s 259(2)(b) and (c), and see para 8.6–8.7.

[17] In *Grant v Countess of Seafield* 1926 SC 274, a diet of proof had been fixed and the witness could have been examined on commission abroad. Yet the court would apparently have allowed her to be examined in Scotland if she had been obliged to go abroad.

[18] See para 14.4.3.

[19] *Hay v Binny* (1859) 22 D 183; *Grant v Countess of Seafield* 1926 SC 274 at 280.

[20] Although granting commission in such circumstances after proof has been fixed has been approved by the Inner House in *Tonner v FT Everard & Sons Ltd* 1994 SC 593 and see para 14.3.

[21] *Grant v Countess of Seafield* 1926 SC 274. If the witness is emigrating by choice and cannot control timing this may be sufficient, but other means of recovering the evidence should be considered.

[22] *Galloway Water Power Co v Carmichael* 1937 SC 135; *Pringle* (1905) 7 F 525; *Neill* (1911) 48 SLR 830.

[23] *Anderson* 1912 SC 1144. The court may find it hard to give due weight to the evidence of a party which is given on commission, particularly by interrogatories and cross-interrogatories: see *Barr v British Transport Corporation* 1963 SLT (Notes) 59.

[24] *Munn v Macgregor* (1854) 16 D 385.

[25] *Hansen v Donaldson* (1873) 1 R 237; *Sutter v Aberdeen Arctic Co* (1858) 30 ScJur 300.

[26] *Copland v Bethune* (1827) 5 S 272. In *Malcolm v Stewart* (1829) 7 S 715, commission was granted of consent. It was refused in *Maltman's Factor v Cook* (1867) 5 M 1076, where the *penuria testium* was not admitted. On *penuri testium* see para 13.1.

[27] *Galloway Water Power Co v Carmichael* 1937 SC 135. The Administration of Justice (Scotland) Act 1972, s 1 applies only to recovery or inspections of property, not oral evidence *per se*.

[28] *Galloway Water Power Co v Carmichael* 1937 SC 135; RCS, r 14.3(d).

[29] There are no reported decisions on this point, but for illustrations of extreme urgency, where the Lord Ordinary on the Bills exercised the *nobile officium*, see *Edgar v Fisher's Trustees* (1893) 21 R 59; *Laggan* (1890) 17 R 757; *Glasgow International Exhibition v Sosnowski* (1901) 39 SLR 28. *Cf Buchanan* 1910 SC 685, and *Aberdeen University Court* (1901) 4 F 122.

[30] RCS, r 35.11(2); OCR, r 28.10(2).

must contain a name or a proposed commissioner.[31] If the party applying for the commission is resident furth of Scotland he may be ordained to sist a mandatory before commission is granted.[32]

14.3 COMMISSION AFTER ENQUIRY ALLOWED

14.3.1 In addition to pre-existing practice allowing it to grant commission for evidence to lie *in retentis*[33] the Court of Session is statutorily empowered to grant commission to take and report in writing the evidence of any witness who is beyond the jurisdiction of the court, or who, by reason of age, infirmity or sickness, is unable to attend the diet of proof or trial,[34] and further in its Rules of Court provides for commission to be granted "on special cause shown".[35] The sheriff's power is in similar terms,[36] but with the additional ground that the witness lives within the jurisdiction, but at some place remote from the court.[37] Although on a strict construction these grounds are independent, it is not necessary to treat them as such, since the whole question is one for the discretion of the court hearing the motion,[38] and the appeal court will rarely intervene.[39] The "special cause" has been broadly interpreted in recent years in cases where no objection was taken by the other party,[40] the Inner House, on a report from the Outer House, having approved the grant of commission where the witnesses were respectively to be engaged in study for university examinations, on holiday in the Outer Hebrides, at a professional conference, and in the late stages of pregnancy.[41]

14.3.2 The fact that there may be means of compelling a witness to attend court in Scotland[42] may be a reason for refusing a commission to examine such a witness.[43] Commission has also been refused where the evidence of the witness was likely to be very important and credibility was in issue,[44] and where it was premature due to the failure to explore other possibilities.[45] Although, as a general rule, the court does not grant commission to take the evidence of a party,[46] there may be excep-

---

[31] RCS, r 35.11(2); OCR, r 28.10(2).
[32] *Hansen v Donaldson* (1873) 1 R 237; *Sandilands v Sandilands* (1848) 10 D 1091.
[33] Court of Session Act 1988, s 10 and RCS, r 35.11(1)(b).
[34] Court of Session Act 1988, s 10(b) and RCS, r 35.11(1)(a).
[35] A power which had been expressly reserved when the practice of taking proofs on commission was abolished in the Court of Session (Evidence (Scotland) 1866, s 2), although inexplicably it does not appear in the Court of Session Act 1988.
[36] OCR, r 28.10(1).
[37] OCR, r 28.10(1)(a)(ii); Summary Cause Rules, Sheriff Court 1976, r 34(2). The Small Claims Rules do not provide for evidence on commission.
[38] *Campbell v Henderson* 1948 SLT (Notes) 71; *Venter v Scottish Legal Aid Board* 1993 SLT 147 at 153F. It was stressed in *Venter v Scottish Legal Aid Board* that a party applying for evidence to be taken on commission should seek prior approval from the Board for the cost of the commission.
[39] For an example of a successful reclaiming motion, see *Nicolson v McLachlan and Brown* 1985 SLT 132.
[40] A factor relevant to the exercise of discretion: *Tonner v FT Everard & Sons Ltd* 1994 SC 593.
[41] All considered in the report of *Tonner v FT Everard & Sons Ltd* 1994 SC 593.
[42] See paras 17.7.3 and 17.8.3.
[43] *Mackintosh v Fraser* (1859) 21 D 783 at 793.
[44] *Western Ranches Ltd v Nelson's Trustees* (1898) 25 R 527; *Nicolson v McLachlan and Brown* 1985 SLT 132.
[45] *Nicolson v McLachlan and Brown* 1985 SLT 132. The process of commission with interrogatories was described in *Nicolson* as "the last resort", although the question of how this compares with the admission of hearsay might now be asked.
[46] *Sofio v Gillespie* (1867) 39 Sc Jur 268.

tions where great hardship would be caused,[47] and much depends on the nature of the evidence the party is expected to give and the extent to which it is in issue.[48]

In criminal cases a judge of the court in which the trial is to take place[49] may **14.3.3** appoint a commissioner to examine at any place in the United Kingdom, Channel Islands or Isle of Man, a witness who by reason of being ill or infirm is unable to attend the trial, or is not ordinarily resident in, and is at the time of the trial unlikely to be present in, the United Kingdom, Channel Islands or the Isle of Man. However, additional criteria apply to structure judicial discretion in criminal cases.[50] The application may be granted only if the evidence of that witness is necessary to the proper adjudication of the trial[51] and there would be no unfairness to the other party were the evidence to be received in the form of a record of examination on commission.[52] The provision has received differing interpretations,[53] but it is understandably more restrictive than the civil equivalent. The availability of alternative witnesses, the importance of the witness's testimony and credibility and the issue of fairness which are relevant to the exercise of discretion in civil cases are determining factors in the criminal test, and in particular any unfairness to the other party through receipt of the evidence in record form prevents the application from being granted.[54] A "record" is widely defined in the same terms as a "document" is now defined generally in evidence legislation to include electronic recordings of data, sound and visual images[55] but any parts of the record not already in writing must be accompanied by a transcript.[56] The application must be made before the jury is sworn in a solemn case[57] or before the first witness is sworn in a summary case,[58] unless the reason for the application only manifests during the trial.[59] The outcome of the application is not appealable except as part of a competent appeal against the final outcome of the case.[60]

14.4 THE COMMISSION

Names of witnesses

As a general rule the applicant must furnish the names of the witnesses he desires **14.4.1**

---

[47] In a case which was to hinge upon the credibility of pursuer and defender, the court nevertheless granted commission in respect of the defender's evidence, since jurisdiction here had been founded on an arrestment and the defender had deponed by affidavit that he could not afford to travel to Scotland: *Morris v Goldrich* 1953 SLT (Sh Ct) 43.

[48] *Anderson v Morrison* (1905) 7 F 561; *Samson & Co v Hough* (1886) 13 R 1154. For the reaction to a pursuer's evidence on commission at proof, see *Barr v British Transport Corporation* 1963 SLT (Notes) 59.

[49] If the judge of the court has not yet been identified the application is considered by a High Court judge: Criminal Procedure (Scotland) Act 1995 ("1995 Act"), s 272(1).

[50] 1995 Act, s 272(1)(b).

[51] 1995 Act, s 272(3)(a).

[52] 1995 Act, s 272(3)(b).

[53] *HM Advocate v Lesacher* 1982 SCCR 418 and *Muirhead, Petitioner* 1983 SLT 545.

[54] *Muirhead, Petitioner* 1983 SLT 545, an interpretation to be preferred over the liberal one taken in *HM Advocate v Lesacher* 1982 SCCR 418, and see commentary to *Lesacher* at 431.

[55] Criminal Procedure (Scotland) Act 1995 ("1995 Act"), s 272(8).

[56] 1995 Act, s 272(5).

[57] 1995 Act, s 272(7)(a).

[58] 1995 Act, s 272(7)(b).

[59] 1995 Act, s 272(7).

[60] *Lang, Petitioner* 1991 SLT 931, but the issue of fairness can be raised again in the appeal.

to examine so that they may be inserted in the commission.[61] It will generally be impossible for the court to consider the merits of the application without knowing the identity of the witness, and in criminal cases this is particularly so. Where a letter of request from a foreign court requested that evidence be obtained from a limited company in Scotland, the court ordained the company to name its representatives to be examined before the commissioner.[62]

The commissioner

14.4.2 In the Court of Session a practising advocate is usually appointed if the commission is to be executed within a reasonable distance of Edinburgh.[63] Otherwise a sheriff or solicitor may be appointed in any court. In civil cases it is the responsibility of the applicant to name a potential commissioner in the application,[64] but it is within the court's discretion to approve that appointee or name another. The court may grant commission to a judge or sheriff, and may be inclined to do so in favour of the judge who is to hear the proof or trial or who is otherwise familiar with the issues in the case.[65]

Interrogatories

14.4.3 Until 1907 examination on interrogatories was compulsory. Now the Court of Session may, on the motion of any party and on cause shown, dispense with interrogatories.[66] The matter is one of discretion. Reasons for dispensing with interrogatories are the time, expense and difficulty of framing them and the risk that they may turn out to be inadequate. The main reason for insisting on them is that a foreign commissioner abroad may allow unsatisfactory and unduly prolonged questioning to include irrelevant evidence.[67] In the sheriff court the commission proceeds without interrogatories unless the sheriff otherwise directs.[68] The interrogatories and cross-interrogatories[69] must be prepared before the commission can take place.[70] They are checked by the clerk of court, and in the event of question as to their relevance the clerk will consult the relevant judge or sheriff.[71]

14.4.4   In criminal cases there are no interrogatories unless the witness is to be examined abroad under letters of request.[72]

---

[61] *Western Ranches Ltd v Nelson's Trustees* (1898) 25 R 527; *Crawford & Law v Allan SS Co* (1908) 16 SLT 434 (OH). In some older cases commission was granted to examine witnesses, the party undertaking to give the other side notice of their names: *Hunt v Commissioners of Woods and Forests* (1856) 18 D 317.

[62] *Lord Advocate* 1925 SC 568.

[63] The Lord President described this as proceeding "in the ordinary way": *McCorquodale* 1923 SLT 520.

[64] RCS, r 35.11(2); OCR, r 28.10(2).

[65] As had occurred in the *Venters* case, which was the subject of judicial review against refusal of legal aid for the cost of the commission: *Venters v Scottish Legal Aid Board* 1993 SLT 147.

[66] RCS, r 35.11(10). The rule no longer makes a distinction between commission which will be executed abroad, where interrogatories would be required, and those to be executed at home, where instead the parties' agents would normally attend to examine the witness orally in front of the commissioner: *Dexter & Carpenter v Waugh & Robertson* 1925 SC 28.

[67] *Dexter & Carpenter v Waugh & Robertson* 1925 SC 28.

[68] OCR, r 28.10(5).

[69] An application in *Charteris v Charteris* 1966 SLT (Notes) 85 for the preparation of the cross-interrogatories to be deferred until the interrogatories had been answered was refused by the Lord Ordinary.

[70] RCS, r 33.12; OCR, r 28.11.

[71] RCS, r 35.12(3); OCR, r 28.11(3).

[72] Act of Adjournal (Criminal Procedure Rules) 1996, r 24.2(2).

14.5 EXECUTION OF COMMISSION

Civil cases

A certified copy of the interlocutor granting the commission is the warrant for **14.5.1**
citing witnesses.[73] If the witness fails to attend the commission in response to the
citation the commissioner will report accordingly and the court may, on application by the party seeking the evidence, order that the witness be apprehended for
a subsequent commission hearing or grant letters of second diligence.[74] The witness is sworn, examined, cross-examined and re-examined as at a proof and in
accordance with the appropriate rules of evidence and procedure. The evidence is
recorded. Whether or not the examination is on interrogatories and cross-interrogatories, the commissioner may put any questions he considers necessary. He
must decide any question as to the admissibility of evidence. In the Court of
Session, if his decision is not objected to, it is final. If objection is taken, the evidence should be noted on a separate paper and sealed for the decision of the
court.[75] In the sheriff court any objection is noted and determined by the court.[76]

Criminal cases

In criminal cases the commissioner does not determine issues of competency or **14.5.2**
relevancy but hears the evidence under reservation.[77]

14.6 COMMISSION FURTH OF SCOTLAND

Civil cases

The court may grant commission to take the evidence of a witness furth of **14.6.1**
Scotland if, in addition to the other criteria discussed above, the witness is willing
to attend and an appropriate commissioner is identified. However, a warrant to take
evidence on commission alone will not enable a party to enforce the attendance of
the witness outwith the United Kingdom or Ireland. In the United Kingdom or
Ireland attendance before the commissioner can be enforced to some extent. If the
witness is cited to attend in appropriate form, and if he fails to do so, an application
may be made direct to the superior court there for an order to punish the witness.[78]
If in either case he fails to obey the order, he is liable to punishment by the court.
Where the commission is granted by an arbiter, the authority of the court must be
interposed before it can be enforced.[79]

The process by which a witness can be ordered to submit to examination furth **14.6.2**
of Scotland is by application to the court for letters of request. An application
would be by minute,[80] or by petition to the Court of Session if proceedings had not

---

[73] RCS, r 35.11(4); OCR, r 28.10(3).
[74] See *Parliament House Book*, Division C, note 35.11.12; OCR, rr 28.15, 29.9, 29.10.
[75] AS, 11 March 1800.
[76] Maclaren, *Court of Session Practice*, pp 1047–1050.
[77] Act of Adjournal (Criminal Procedure Rules) 1996, r 24.4(3).
[78] Attendance of Witnesses Act 1854, ss 1–4, Evidence (Proceedings in Other Jurisdictions) Act 1975,
s 4.
[79] *John Nimmo & Son Ltd* (1905) 8 F 173; *Blaikies Brothers v Aberdeen Rly Co* (1851) 13 D 1307.
[80] RCS, r 35.15(3), Form 35.15-A; OCR, r 28.14(3) and Form G16. OCR, r 28.14 is applied to
Summary Causes by the Summary Cause Rules, Sheriff Court 1976, r 3 and the Small Claims Rules
1988, r 2(1) and App 2.

yet commenced, and in every case should be accompanied by the proposed letter of request in prescribed form.[81] It is appropriate for the court considering the application to address the issues of relevance and specification rather than leaving that to the court which will receive the letters.[82] If granted, the court issues letters of request to an appropriate court in the country where the witness is, and requests the court there to examine the witness on interrogatories or to appoint some person so to examine.[83] The letter is delivered to the appropriate court via the Foreign Office.[84] Unless the court is in a country where English is the official language or the clerk of court confirms that no translation is required, the applicant must lodge in court translations of the letter of request and interrogatories in the official language of the relevant court.[85]

14.6.3   Letters of request may be addressed to any foreign court having the appropriate jurisdiction.[86] However, if the court is in a country which is a contracting party to the Hague Convention on the Taking of Evidence Abroad in Civil and Commercial Matters[87] additional options exist for United Kingdom diplomatic or consular officials taking the evidence to which the letters refer and for compulsion of the witness to co-operate.

Criminal cases

14.6.4   In criminal cases, if a party seeks to have a witness examined outside the United Kingdom, Channel Islands or Isle of Man in advance of the trial, letters of request must be sought. The procedure for obtaining letters of request is similar to that for seeking commission[88] but the application must be accompanied by the letter of request in prescribed form.[89] The grounds upon which it can be granted are the same.[90] In deciding whether the grounds have been met the court would no doubt take account of the existence of an option available only in solemn cases, to seek that a witness outwith the United Kingdom gives evidence via live television link in terms of a letter of request to the court in the country where that witness is seeking their assistance in facilitating the link.[91] If such a television link is possible having regard to the facilities available where the witness is and where the trial is

---

[81] RCS, r 35.15(3), Form 35.15-B; OCR, r 28.14(3) and Form G17.

[82] *Stewart v Callaghan* 1996 SLT (Sh Ct) 12.

[83] RCS, r 35.15(1) and (2)(a); OCR, r 28.14(1) and (2)(a). The interrogatories are adjusted at the sight of the clerk of court. There is no express option to proceed without interrogatories, and it has been held that if the parties consider that interrogatories are inappropriate it is not appropriate to grant the application for letters of request: *Williams, Deceased (No 1)* 1992 SLT (Sh Ct) 56.

[84] RCS, r 35.15(6); OCR, r 28.14(6).

[85] RCS, r 35.15(5); OCR, r 28.14(5).

[86] RCS, r 35.15(1); OCR, r 28.14(1). Some cases have considered whether letters from a foreign court may properly be executed here, and discuss interesting issues of interpretation. See *Lord Advocate, Petitioner* 1994 SLT 852 (in which the court took the unusual step of allowing the witnesses to be represented after challenges that the questions were more for the purposes of discovery than testimony); *Morris v Lord Advocate* 1973 SLT (Notes) 62.

[87] Cmnd 6727 (1977). Ratified by the United Kingdom per the Evidence (Proceedings in Other Jurisdictions) Act 1975 which allows the Convention to be relied upon within the United Kingdom: ss 1 and 2. "Civil or commercial matters" have been said to include everything other than criminal proceedings: *Re State of Norway's Application (Nos 1 & 2)* [1990] 1 AC 723 at 806.

[88] Criminal Procedure (Scotland) Act 1995, s 272 and Act of Adjournal (Criminal Procedure Rules) 1996, Chap 23. See para 14.3.3.

[89] Act of Adjournal (Criminal Procedure Rules) 1996, r 23.1(3).

[90] Criminal Procedure (Scotland) Act 1995, s 272(3).

[91] Criminal Procedure (Scotland) Act 1995, s 273.

to be held respectively, it could be argued that letters of request should be refused because they automatically involve unfairness to the other party who, under the live video-link option, would not be restricted to interrogatories and cross-interrogatories drawn up in advance of trial.[92]

Under separate legislation designed to enable co-operation between the United **14.6.5** Kingdom and other countries in criminal proceedings and investigations, letters of request may be issued in terms of the Criminal Justice (International Co-operation) Act 1990[93] to request assistance from overseas authorities in obtaining evidence specified in the letter for use in criminal proceedings or in an investigation into an offence which has been committed or for which there are reasonable grounds to suspect that it has been committed.[94] The letters are granted primarily by a sheriff or judge[95] on application by the prosecutor, or, if the proceedings have commenced, by a person charged,[96] but the prosecutor may be authorised to issue the letters in circumstances designated by the Secretary of State.[97] If granted the letters are conveyed to the relevant country via the Secretary of State[98] but in circumstances of urgency the prosecuting authority may send them direct to the relevant court or tribunal overseas.[99] Except with the permission of the overseas authority who implement the request, the evidence may only be used for the purposes specified in the letter of request and must be returned after its use,[100] but it can be received into evidence in proceedings here without being sworn to by witnesses, if that can be done without unfairness to either party.[101] The definition of "evidence" is said to include documents and other articles.[102] It does not specify that oral evidence is included but neither is it outwith the terms of the definition.[103] Separate provisions allow for warrant to be issued to have a prisoner who is serving a period of imprisonment outwith the United Kingdom[104] brought, with his consent,[105] and with the anticipated assistance of the overseas authorities,[106] to the United Kingdom to give evidence in criminal proceedings for which he is a witness or in which the Secretary of State thinks that it is desirable to have the assistance of that person's presence.[107]

---

[92] The grounds for securing the live TV link include an "interests of justice" test, but no requirement to consider unfairness to the prosecutor if the application is by an accused: s 273(3).
[93] s 3. (The remaining references in this paragraph are to the 1990 Act unless otherwise stated.)
[94] s 3(1).
[95] s 3(1).
[96] s 3(2).
[97] s 3(3).
[98] s 3(4).
[99] s 3(5).
[100] s 3(7).
[101] s 3(9).
[102] s 3(6).
[103] In *R v Radak and Others*, *The Times*, 7 October 1998, [1998] TLR 586, in construing an application under the Criminal Justice Act 1988, s 23 for admission of the written statement of a prosecution witness who was abroad and refusing to give evidence through fear, the court, having regard to Art 6(3)(d) of the European Convention on Human Rights, refused the application when evidence could have been taken on commission under the Criminal Justice (International Co-operation) Act 1990, s 3.
[104] Which may be a sentence imposed there or transferred on repatriation from the United Kingdom or elsewhere: s 6(1) and (7).
[105] s 6(3).
[106] s 6(2).
[107] s 6(1), *eg* for identification of the prisoner.

14.7 USE OF REPORT AT TRIAL OR PROOF

Civil cases

14.7.1 The deposition may be used in evidence unless the witness becomes available to attend,[108] but the court must hear and determine any objection to its use.[109] Where evidence has been taken to lie *in retentis*, the opposite party may insist on a re-examination if the witness is available,[110] but this right is seldom, if ever, used. The party who obtained the commission is responsible for lodging it in process.[111] If the party who obtained the commission does not use it, his opponent is entitled to do so.[112] In any event, the deposition cannot be used unless it is expressly made part of the evidence at the trial or proof.[113] If the witness is examined at the proof, the evidence taken on commission should not be used for any purpose,[114] and in particular not used to contradict evidence given in court.[115] The fact that evidence is to be led in the form of a report on commission is not cause for refusing issues for jury trial.[116]

Criminal cases

14.7.2 The report can be referred to only with leave of the court,[117] but the presence of the report in the possession of the clerk of court removes the need for a party to list the name of the witness who has given evidence on commission in the list of witnesses or to list the report as a documentary production.[118]

---

[108] RCS, r 35.14(1) and (3); OCR, r 28.13(1) and (4). Compare the onus at common law to satisfy the judge that the witness cannot attend: *Willox v Farrell* (1848) 10 D 807; *Ainslie v Sutton* (1851) 14 D 184, (1852) 1 Macq 299; *Boettcher v Carron Co* (1861) 23 D 322.

[109] RCS, r 35.14(2); OCR, r 28.13(2).

[110] *Boettcher v Carron Co* (1861) 23 D 322.

[111] RCS, r 35.12(8); OCR, r 28.11(8).

[112] RCS, r 35.14(4); OCR, r 28.13(4).

[113] *Cameron v Woolfson* 1918 SC 190.

[114] RCS, r 35.14(3); OCR, r 28.13(3).

[115] *Forrests v Low's Trs* 1907 SC 1240. However, in *Webster v Simpson's Motors* 1967 SLT 287 at 288, a case dealing with liability for expenses of the commission, it is noted that the report on commission was referred to at some length during the proof at which the witness had given evidence after legal argument as to the competency of doing so.

[116] *Shearer v Bevan's Exrx* 1986 SLT 226; *Nicol v McIntosh* 1987 SLT 104; *Stevens v Cremonesi* 1988 SLT 838.

[117] Act of Adjournal (Criminal Procedure Rules) 1996, rr 23.5(4) and 24.5(4).

[118] Act of Adjournal (Criminal Procedure Rules) 1996, rr 23.5(3) and 24.5(3).

CHAPTER 15

AFFIDAVITS, REPORTS AND DYING DEPOSITIONS

15.1 AFFIDAVITS—GENERAL

An affidavit is a written *ex parte* statement made on oath or affirmation,[1] before one **15.1.1** having authority to administer oaths.[2] With one rare exception[3] affidavits are not evidence at common law.[4] However, statute provides for the use of affidavit evidence in certain circumstances. The admissibility and effect of an affidavit made in terms of a statute depends on the terms of the statute. There are specific provisions for the use of affidavits in for example family,[5] commissary[6] and commercial proceedings including bankruptcy,[7] in child abduction proceedings,[8] in declarators that a writing is signed by the person named,[9] and under the Bankers' Books Evidence Act 1879.[10]

The Court of Session has had power since 1933[11] to provide by Act of Sederunt **15.1.2** for the admission of affidavit in lieu of parole evidence in civil proceedings affecting status, and in civil proceedings in general in the sheriff court.[12] This has been strengthened by the admission of hearsay evidence in general in civil proceedings, including hearsay in written form such as affidavit evidence.[13] There is a

---

[1] Oaths Act 1888, s 1.
[2] Dickson, *Evidence* (3rd edn), paras 1534, 1537.
[3] In the *Lauderdale Peerage Case* (1885) 10 AppCas 692, an affidavit by a deceased person was accepted as evidence. In *Shields v North British Railway Co* (1874) 2 R 126, affidavits were lodged, but no importance seems to have attached to their form, and no attempt was made to use them as evidence. See also *Tennent v Tennent* (1890) 17 R 1205 at 1210, 1225.
[4] *Glyn v Johnston* (1834) 13 S 126.
[5] *eg* RCS, r 49.28; OCR, r 33.28 (undefended family actions, and in simplified divorce actions in the sheriff court parole evidence is not competent: OCR, r 33.79); RCS, r 49.71 (orders under the Matrimonial Homes (Family Protection) (Scotland) Act 1981).
[6] Act of Sederunt (Chancery Procedure Rules) 1996 (SI 1996/2184), r 5.
[7] *eg* Act of Sederunt (Disqualification of Directors etc) Rules 1986 (SI 1986/692), para 2(2); Act of Sederunt (Company Insolvency Rules) 1986 (SI 1986/2297), r 33.
[8] RCS, r 70.5(1)(c), (2)(c) and (3)(c).
[9] Requirements of Writing Act 1995, ss 4(1), (2), 5(6), Sched 1, para 2(1) or 2(2) and Sched 3, para 7 or para 14; Act of Sederunt (Requirements of Writing) 1996 (SI 1996/1534), para 7.
[10] ss 4, 5. See para 21.13.
[11] Administration of Justice (Scotland) Act 1933, s 16.
[12] Sheriff Courts (Scotland) Act 1971, s 32(1).
[13] Civil Evidence (Scotland) Act 1988, s 2; Court of Session Act 1988, s 5(e); Sheriff Courts (Scotland) Act 1971, s 32(1)(e).

difference of judicial opinion as to whether the court now has any discretion to refuse an affidavit tendered in evidence in civil proceedings.[14] There are no binding authorities.[15] It is thought that, taking a literal interpretation of the Civil Evidence (Scotland) Act 1988, s 2(1)(a), there is no discretion to refuse affidavit evidence tendered, regardless of the apparent discretion provided for by the rules of court.[16] It has been said that the affidavit may be admitted under reservation of issues of competency and relevancy,[17] particularly if objections on those grounds strike only at parts of the affidavit, but if direct oral evidence of the deponent would not have been admissible at all,[18] this would be a reason for refusing to admit the affidavit.[19] Although affidavit evidence may be admitted on the application of one party in place of attendance of the deponent, the other party may still seek to secure the attendance of the deponent in court, or recover their evidence by commission or letters of request, failing which the court will take into account in assessing the weight of the evidence the absence of the opportunity to subject it to scrutiny in court.[20]

15.1.3   In criminal cases there is no express general provision for admission of affidavit evidence in proof of a fact in a criminal trial, although there are some statutory exceptions.[21] However, the court routinely receives affidavits in an appeal based upon the ground that fresh evidence exists which was not led at the trial.[22] In that event the court receives in affidavit form the evidence which the appellant seeks to introduce in support of the appeal.[23]

15.2 BEFORE WHOM

15.2.1   Any affidavit may be made before a notary public,[24] justice of the peace, sheriff or magistrate.[25] A sheriff, who is *ex officio* a justice of the peace, or a justice of the peace may act outside his jurisdiction, even in England,[26] and an English justice of the peace may act in Scotland.[27] If the notary, magistrate or other person is entitled to act, which requires an absence of interest in the matter to which the affidavit relates, a misdescription of his office does not nullify the affidavit,[28] nor does the

---

[14] In *Ebrahem v Ebrahem* 1989 SLT 808 and *Lobban v Philip* 1995 SCLR 1104 the court said that there was discretion to refuse the application to allow affidavit evidence if it was inappropriate to allow it—*eg* because the evidence was critical to the case. In *McVinnie v McVinnie* 1995 SLT (Sh Ct) 81 and *Glaser v Glaser* 1997 SLT 456 the court held that there was no such discretion.

[15] *Ebrahem* and *Glaser* are Outer House judgments; *McVinnie* and *Lobban* are sheriff court decisions.

[16] RCS, r 36.8; OCR, r 29.3(1) is now omitted by virtue of the Act of Sederunt (Sheriff Court Rules Amendment) (Miscellaneous) 2000 (SI 2000/239), para 3(11).

[17] *McVinnie v McVinnie* 1995 SLT (Sh Ct) 81.

[18] *eg* because the deponent is not a competent witness due to mental incapacity.

[19] Civil Evidence (Scotland) Act 1988, s 2(1)(a).

[20] *McVinnie v McVinnie* 1995 SLT (Sh Ct) 81.

[21] *eg* Bankers' Books Evidence Act 1879, ss 4 and 5 which still sit alongside the provisions of the Criminal Procedure (Scotland) Act 1995, Sched 3; *Lord Advocate's Reference No 1 of 1996* 1996 JC 152. See also para 21.13.

[22] See, *eg*, *Mills v HM Advocate* 1999 SLT 680, *Campbell v HM Advocate* 1998 JC 130, *Mitchell v HM Advocate* 1996 SLT 1339, *Ralton v HM Advocate* 1994 SLT 321.

[23] It appears that affidavits for criminal cases may not be sworn before a notary public: see Solicitors (Scotland) Act 1980, s 59(2).

[24] Solicitors (Scotland) Act 1980, s 59(1), but criminal cases are expected under s 59(2).

[25] Dickson, *Evidence* (3rd edn), paras 1534, 1537.

[26] *Kerr v Marquis of Ailsa* (1854) 1 Macq 736.

[27] *Taylor v Little* (1822) 1 ShApp 254.

[28] *Paterson v Duncan* (1846) 8 D 950.

fact that his wife is an interested party.[29] Any affidavit may be made in England before a solicitor who is a commissioner for oaths[30] or abroad before a British diplomatic officer or consul[31] or someone who has authority to administer oaths there. Further, in commissary proceedings it may be made before a sheriff-clerk or depute, before a notary public in the United Kingdom, before a commissioner of oaths in England or Northern Ireland,[32] and out of the United Kingdom before a local magistrate, notary public or someone empowered to administer oaths there[33]; and in bankruptcy in the United Kingdom before any person entitled to administer an oath or affirmation, and abroad before a British diplomatic or consular official or any person authorised to administer an oath or affirmation according to the law of the place where the oath is made.[34]

15.3 FORMALITIES

The deponent must appear in person before the notary public or other person, and **15.3.1** must be put on oath[35] or affirm.[36] Each page of the deposition ought to be signed both by the deponent and by the person before whom it is sworn or affirmed.[37] If the deponent cannot write, it is sufficient that the affidavit so bears.[38] An alteration *in essentialibus* (in an essential part) nullifies the affidavit,[39] unless it is initialled both by the deponent and the notary[40] or it is plain that it was made before signing.[41] An unauthenticated marginal addition was disregarded.[42] An illegible signature alleged to be that of the deponent has been held to be set up by the notary's signature.[43] What appear to be clerical errors have sometimes been disregarded[44] and sometimes not.[45] Affidavits which are to be used in a proof should be lodged as productions.[45a]

15.4 REPORTS AND CERTIFICATES

Admission of routine evidence in the form of reports and certificates has expanded **15.4.1** greatly in recent years, particularly in criminal cases. Following the review of criminal procedure in 1993 one recommendation was to speed up admission of

---

[29] *Kerr v Marquis of Ailsa* (1854) 1 Macq 736.
[30] Solicitors Act 1974, s 81(1) and (2).
[31] Commissioners for Oaths Act 1889, s 6.
[32] Supreme Court of Judicature (Northern Ireland) Order 1921 (SI 1921/1802), Art 2.
[33] Executors (Scotland) Act 1900, s 8. This provision is due to be replaced by a declaration procedure introduced by the Law Reform (Miscellaneous Provisions) (Scotland) Act 1990, to coincide with the introduction of registered executry practitioners; however, the relevant provisions of the 1990 Act are not yet in force.
[34] Bankruptcy (Scotland) Act 1985, s 11(2).
[35] *Blair v North British and Mercantile Ins Co* (1889) 16 R 325.
[36] Oaths Act 1978, s 5.
[37] Dickson, *Evidence* (3rd edn), para 1539; *MacAlister v MacAlister* 1978 SLT (Notes) 78.
[38] *Paul v Gibson* (1834) 7 W & S 462.
[39] *Jardine v Harvey* (1848) 10 D 1501; *Miller v Lambert* (1848) 10 D 1419.
[40] *Dow & Co v Union Bank* (1875) 2 R 459.
[41] *Dyce v Paterson* (1846) 9 D 310 at 313.
[42] *Mackersy v Guthrie* (1829) 7 S 556.
[43] *Perryman v McClymont* (1852) 14 D 508.
[44] *Taylor v Manford* (1848) 10 D 967; *Foulds v Meldrum* (1851) 13 D 1357.
[45] *Anderson v Monteith* (1847) 9 D 1432.
[45a] RCS r36.8(4), OCR r 29.11 (as amended by Act of Sederunt (Sheriff Court Ordinary Cause Rules Amendment) (Miscellaneous) 2000 (SI 2000/239) para 3(12).

technical or routine evidence which was not contested by a process of admitting written reports and certificates, of which the opponent would receive notice, and would be entitled to serve a counter-notice objecting to the evidence being admitted in written form.[46]

15.5 DYING DEPOSITION

15.5.1 Where there is a risk of a material and competent witness in a criminal case, whether the injured party or not,[47] dying before the trial, his deposition may be taken so that it may be put in evidence at the trial if he dies before it.[48] In practice it is usually taken on behalf of the Crown, but the accused has the same right to secure evidence in his favour.[49] The deposition is taken on oath or affirmation, usually by a sheriff, but it may be taken by a justice of the peace or other magistrate.[50] It is not necessary that the witness should believe himself to be dying.[51] The questions are put by the sheriff or the procurator-fiscal (or, if the witness is being examined for the defence, by the accused's solicitor) and the deposition is normally recorded by the sheriff-clerk or depute.[52] It is then read over to the deponent and signed by him on each page, if he is able to write. If not, this is recorded. It is also signed by the sheriff and two witnesses, usually the doctor and the sheriff-clerk.[53] At the trial the deposition is spoken to by two witnesses, one of whom should be the sheriff, and they should establish that the deponent realised what he was doing.[54] As evidence the deposition does not have the weight of evidence given by a witness who has been cross-examined.[55] Where a deposition cannot be taken a dying declaration may be recorded by any responsible person.[56]

This common law process is not displaced by the statutory provision for evidence to be taken on commission in criminal cases which can be sought if the witness due to illness or infirmity will be unable to attend trial.[57] The latter may be the preferred option in some cases if time and circumstances permit, not least because it does not require the report on commission to be spoken to by witnesses at trial, and enables examination and cross-examination to take place while the witness is alive. However, the former is more closely associated with circumstances of extreme urgency, when the witness is near death, and some degree of veracity is inferred from the circumstances in which the deposition is made. Macphail considers the use to which the deposition might be put if the witness has not died by the time of the trial.[58] He concludes that the deposition should be admissible to the

---

[46] Criminal Procedure (Scotland) Act 1995, ss 280–284. See also para 19.16.

[47] *Stewart* (1855) 2 Irv 166. Macphail in *Evidence*, para 19.34 considers that the use of dying depositions is limited to the trial of the person accused of the killing of the deponent, but recommends that they be admissible in all civil or criminal proceedings (assuming that the statement is otherwise relevant and admissible).

[48] Macdonald, *Criminal Law* (5th edn), p 330; Dickson, *Evidence* (3rd edn), para 1754.

[49] Dickson, *Evidence* (3rd edn), para 1754.

[50] Dickson, *Evidence* (3rd edn), para 1755.

[51] *Brodie* (1846) Ark 45; *Stewart* (1855) 2 Irv 166.

[52] Dickson, *Evidence* (3rd edn), para 1755.

[53] Dickson, *Evidence* (3rd edn), para 1755.

[54] Dickson, *Evidence* (3rd edn), para 1755.

[55] *Brodie* (1846) Ark 45 .

[56] Macdonald, *Criminal Law* (5th edn), p 330.

[57] Criminal Procedure (Scotland) Act 1995, s 272(1)(b)(i).

[58] *Evidence*, para 19.33. His conclusion was adopted by the Scottish Law Commission, Memo No 46, T12.

extent that any other statement would be admissible, and gives the example of its use as a previous inconsistent statement to challenge credibility.[59] Since then scope has increased for admission of hearsay evidence if the witness is unable to attend,[60] and for a witness to adopt a prior statement into evidence,[61] and the dying deposition would meet the criteria for admission as a statement contained in a document.[62]

---

[59] *Evidence*, para 19.33.
[60] Criminal Procedure (Scotland) Act 1995 ("1995 Act"), s 259(2).
[61] 1995 Act, s 260.
[62] 1995 Act, s 262(2).

OPINION EVIDENCE

16.1 INTRODUCTORY

General

16.1.1 Testimony, which at first sight appears to be of fact, may prove to be actually of belief or opinion. Identification of a person is one instance.[1] This may range from "That is my partner" to "That is the stranger I saw in the close that night." Each statement on analysis is one of belief founded on inferences, but, while the former would normally be accepted as equivalent to a statement of fact, the latter is obviously one of belief or opinion. Cross-examination on the former is unlikely to be effective, but may greatly reduce the weight of the latter. The question is thus in practice one of degree.

16.1.2 This chapter is concerned with evidence which either bears to be of opinion or belief or at least is of that nature. Such evidence is in many cases admissible from any witness, but where the opinion depends on specialised knowledge it may be taken only from an expert in that sphere.

Limitations

16.1.3 A question is normally inadmissible if its purpose is to elicit an opinion on the actual issue before the court.[2] In an action for reduction of a will Lord Justice-Clerk Inglis directed the jury that the question whether the testator had the capacity to sign the will was a question for them, not for the medical witnesses to whom it had been put, which seems to imply that he would have sustained an objection to the questions.[3] In a trial on a charge based upon obscenity, it was held to be

---

[1] Dickson, *Evidence* (3rd edn), para 392.

[2] eg see *Kelso v HM Advocate* 1990 SCCR 9 in which the sheriff refused such a question from the defence without it being objected to by the other party. Whilst commenting that it would have been preferable for the sheriff to wait for an objection, the court on appeal confirmed that the question was directed at the very issue which the jury had to decide and was not properly framed. In *Lacey v Russell* 1966 SLT (Sh Ct) 76 the evidence of an architect was held to have been unnecessary and inadmissible since it expressed an opinion on the issue before the court, and this was reflected in the award of expenses. In England, this restriction has been abandoned, according to Cross & Tapper *Evidence* (9th edn), pp 519–520.

[3] *Morrison v Maclean's Trs* (1862) 24 D 625 at 631. However, a factual witness has been allowed to express a view on whether a testator was too weak and debilitated to be of capacity: *McNaughton v Smith* 1949 SLT (Notes) 53.

incompetent to ask a witness whether in his opinion there was obscenity,[4] for that is for the court to decide. A witness may not be asked whether the driver of a vehicle was to blame, or whether he considered conduct to be malicious.[5] There was at one time doubt as to whether in an insurance case it was competent to ask a skilled witness whether a particular fact would have influenced a prudent underwriter and was therefore material or whether this was not a matter for the court,[6] but such questions are competent.[7] In cases concerning professional negligence by a legal adviser it will be necessary to satisfy the court that expert evidence of the normal practice of a reasonably competent adviser will enhance the ability of the court to determine matters of fact and law.[8]

16.1.4   This does not always preclude the receipt in evidence of the view of a witness which is on, or very near to, an issue in the case. A question properly framed may produce an answer on an issue which is for the court to decide. The evidence of a factual witness may in some situations be incomplete, or incapable of proper evaluation, without an accompanying opinion or impression which goes directly to an issue.[9] The witness who saw or heard the event may have been much better placed to form an opinion on the facts than the court if given the bare facts only. So, for example, a witness who regularly used a stretch of road, or whose duty it was to report defects in the road, may be well placed to express an opinion upon whether the road surface was dangerous.[10] If the issues are in themselves of a technical nature, requiring evidence from an expert, it may be unavoidable for the expert witness to express an opinion on an issue, such as identification by scientific means. Hence, for example, evidence of DNA analysis contains factual reporting of the analysis and opinion as to probabilities of matching with the accused and a wider population.[11] So, too, with fingerprint evidence.[12]

16.1.5   The important point is that the court is not bound by the evidence of opinion on an issue, since the court, not the witness, must reach the decision on that issue. It is for the court to decide what evidence to accept and reject. The court may even form an opinion which is supported by the facts but which is not supported by or in common with the opinion of an expert.[13] A skilled witness whose opinion is to

---

[4]   *Galletly v Laird* 1953 JC 16 at 27; *Ingram v Macari* 1982 JC 1. See also *Campbell v Tyson* (1841) 4 D 342.

[5]   Dickson, *Evidence* (3rd edn), para 391.

[6]   *Baker and Adams v Scottish Sea Insurance Co* (1856) 18 D 691 at 699 (fourth exception).

[7]   *Dawsons Ltd v Bonnin* 1921 SC 511 at 517, 519, 521; 1922 SC (HL) 156 at 160, 166, 172. In *The Spathari* 1924 SC 182; 1925 SC (HL) 6, the facts were so clear that, if opinion evidence as to materiality was led, it was not referred to in the opinions or speeches.

[8]   There is a dearth of case law in Scotland, but this line has been taken in England, in *Bown v Gould & Swayne* [1996] PNLR 130 regarding normal English conveyancing practice, about which the expert could not have advanced the court's knowledge.

[9]   See Macphail at paras 17.03–S17.10.

[10]   *Hewat v Edinburgh Corporation* 1944 SC 30.

[11]   See, *eg, Welsh v HM Advocate* 1992 SLT 193.

[12]   See *Hamilton v HM Advocate* 1934 JC 1.

[13]   *Davie v Magistrates of Edinburgh* 1953 SC 34, *Beaton v HM Advocate* 1993 JC 35. See more recently *Stewart v HM Advocate (No 1)* 1997 SCCR 330, *Fyfe v HM Advocate* 1998 SLT 195 but *cf HM Advocate v McGinlay* 1983 SLT 562. In the former the jury were entitled to decide that the assault had led to the death although medical witnesses could not state that the libelled assault (as compared to others during a violent domestic relationship lasting 10 years) led to the brain haemorrhage from which the victim died. In the latter it was held that the inability of medical witnesses to say beyond reasonable doubt that the victim's heart attack, given a pre-existing condition, was caused by the assault libelled, prevented the jury from reaching the conclusion that the link had been proved. *McGinlay* was explained but not followed in *Hendry v HM Advocate* 1987 JC 63, and any view that a Crown expert in a criminal case should testify beyond reasonable doubt is contradicted there.

assist the court in analysing evidence does not require to be corroborated,[14] but if the evidence from the skilled witness is in proof of a crucial fact in the case the normal corroboration requirements apply.[15] So, for example, identification may be proved by analysis of fingerprints or handwriting, which in a criminal case requires two skilled witnesses, although procedures exist to save both from attending court if their joint report is not disputed.[16]

16.2 ORDINARY WITNESS

As already observed,[17] evidence which is accepted as fact may really be opinion. **16.2.1** But what is obviously opinion evidence may be admissible from an ordinary witness. Identification of handwriting[18] or of property[19] are examples. In an action of divorce on the ground of adultery a witness who had described the position of the defender and the alleged paramour when she entered a room was allowed to be asked what immediate impression she formed.[20] While that decision was expressly rested on the ground that the impression was immediate, evidence was allowed of an opinion which to some extent must have rested on reflection and special knowledge. In a written slander the names had been left blank, and a witness was allowed to be asked to whom in his opinion the slander applied.[21] Opinions have been expressed, *obiter*, that a witness who has described a depression in a pavement may be asked whether he saw anything dangerous about it.[22]

16.3 SKILLED WITNESS

Purpose

A skilled witness is a person who, through expertise or education or both, is **16.3.1** specially qualified in a recognised branch of knowledge, whether it be art, science or craft.[23] The term "expert witness" has prevailed in England.[24] However, the term "skilled witness" is retained here since it reflects the range of attributes which may qualify the witness to give opinion evidence.

It is competent to take the opinion of the skilled witness, based on special **16.3.2** knowledge, on facts that he or she has observed (including the results of tests made by himself or in his presence)[25] or spoken to by other witnesses. The opinion may

---

[14] *Davie v Magistrates of Edinburgh* 1953 SC 34.
[15] *McKillen v Barclay Curle & Co Ltd* 1967 SLT 41.
[16] Criminal Procedure (Scotland) Act 1995, ss 280, 281 and 284.
[17] See para 16.1.
[18] See para 16.4.
[19] Dickson, *Evidence* (3rd edn), para 392.
[20] *King v King* (1842) 4 D 590 at 596. Similar evidence was led without objection in *Wilson v Wilson* (1898) 25 R 788.
[21] Dickson, *Evidence* (3rd edn), para 392; *Edwards v McIntosh* (1823) 3 Mur 374.
[22] *Hewat v Edinburgh Corporation* 1944 SC 30 at 35.
[23] Dickson, *Evidence* (3rd edn), para 397.
[24] See Cross & Tapper, *Evidence* (9th edn), pp 521–525.
[25] In *Irvine v Powrie's Trs* 1915 SC 1006 it was said that both parties may have to be present, but in modern practice parties are given the opportunity to have tests carried out by their own skilled witness: *eg* Criminal Procedure (Scotland) Act 1995, s 276.

be as to the probable cause of facts[26] or their probable result.[27] So, the pathologist who has carried out a post mortem revealing detailed biological facts may be asked for a scientific opinion as to cause of death or as to whether a particular weapon could have caused an injury of which evidence was found on the body. In a case concerning professional negligence evidence will be led from a person knowledgeable and experienced in the relevant profession as to what is usual and normal practice in that profession, since proof of professional negligence requires evidence of departure from normal practice and also that the course adopted by the defender is one which no professional person of ordinary skill would have taken if acting with ordinary care.[28] In exceptional situations the court has permitted evidence as to human nature and behaviour, falling short of psychiatric condition.[29] Normally such evidence would be considered incompetent since the assessment of human nature (for example, reactions to stresses such as a partner's infidelity),[30] would be deemed to be within the experience and knowledge of a court.[31] In order to have such evidence admitted a matter of personality must be identified which is particularly relevant to proof or defence of an issue in the case,[32] and which is outwith the normal experience of the court, such as the reactions of a child to sexual abuse by an adult.[33]

Qualification and knowledge

16.3.3 If the opinion of the skilled witness is not based on the principles of some recog-

---

[26] The "Nerano" v The "Dromedary" (1895) 22 R 237.

[27] SS "Rowan" v SS "Clan Malcolm" 1923 SC 316.

[28] Hunter v Hanley 1955 SC 200.

[29] There is no clear Scottish authority, but in Green v HM Advocate 1983 SCCR 42 fresh evidence in the form of psychiatric evidence of the tendency of the victim to fantasise was admitted in support of the appeal against a conviction of rape; and in Blagojevic v HM Advocate 1995 SLT 1189 a psychologist was not permitted to give evidence about the suggestibility of the accused in police interview, not on the ground that it was incompetent but because there had been no factual evidence taken from the accused or Crown witnesses to found a basis for the opinion evidence. Although the evidence of psychiatrists as to abnormality or disorder of personality has been allowed in cases where provocation and diminished responsibility is pled (eg Carraher v HM Advocate 1946 JC 108, Connelly v HM Advocate 1990 JC 349, Williamson v HM Advocate 1994 JC 149 and Martindale v HM Advocate 1994 SLT 1093), the court has tended to withdraw from the jury a plea of diminished reponsibility which is based on evidence of personality rather than mental disorder as defined in the Mental Health (Scotland) Act 1984. The definitions of mental disorder and personality disorder are under review by the Millan Committee (Review of the Mental Health (Scotland) Act 1984), and the MacLean Committe (Review of the Treatment and Sentencing of Sexual Offenders in Scotland), both of which were set up by the Scottish Office in 1999.

[30] In R v Turner [1975] QB 834, the court refused to allow defence evidence from a psychologist, in support of a defence of provocation, to the effect that the accused was likely to be provoked to extreme violence on learning of his partner's infidelity.

[31] R v Turner [1975] QB 834. For comment upon this case, see Sheldon, "The Admissibility of Psychological and Psychiatric Expert Testimony" 1992 SLT (News) 301, Sheldon & MacLeod, "From Normative to Positive Data: Expert Psychological Evidence Re-examined" [1991] Crim LR 811.

[32] In Lowery v R [1974] AC 85 one accused blamed the other for the crime of which they were both charged, and evidence as to the dominance of their respective personalities was admitted. The case is considered special, and is frequently distinguished in England, where there is a reluctance to allow evidence from, eg, a psychologist to influence the court upon the reliability of the witness (R v Turner [1975] QB 834 and see Cross & Tapper Evidence (9th edn), pp 517–518 and cases cited there). No doubt this is why the evidence is admitted in cases of provocation or diminished responsibility cited above.

[33] This is commonly admitted in child welfare cases: eg M v Kennedy 1993 SC 115. However, in Martindale v HM Advocate 1994 SLT 1093, evidence from a psychiatrist that the accused may have reacted more violently due to delayed reaction to abuse as a child, although led, was not permitted to go to the jury in support of a plea of diminished responsibility.

nised branch of knowledge, it is useless, and probably inadmissible, because it cannot be tested by cross-examination. Accordingly, the qualification and experience of the skilled witness must first be established,[34] usually by the testimony of that witness alone, though cross-examination has been known to reduce pretensions and to remind the skilled witness to offer opinion only within that field.[35] It has been accepted in some cases that a witness may gain a particular field of knowledge through attendance at seminars or reading academic literature, albeit that they have not qualified personally in that discipline. Hence, police officers who had attended seminars on drug enforcement were allowed to give evidence regarding what they had learnt from the speakers and other participants in the process of drug control,[36] and medical witnesses who were not epidemiologists were permitted to refer to and adopt into their evidence published material on epidemiology.[37] However, these examples stand on their own facts, and the assessment of the skill of the witness will be a matter for the court to assess in each case. A party seeking to lead a witness with purported knowledge or experience outwith generally recognised fields would need to set up by investigation and evidence not only the qualifications and expertise of the individual skilled witness, but the methodology and validity of that field of knowledge or science.[38]

After the witness's own knowledge and expertise in the area has been estab- **16.3.4** lished the witness may refer to relevant books or articles which are recognised in that field,[39] and any passages adopted by the witness become part of the evidence.[40] This written material is not considered to be hearsay[41] but if not so adopted it is not evidence, and the court may not rely on it.[42] In a criminal case where published material was put to an expert in cross-examination, although not produced for him to examine, the witness stated that he knew of the material but that counter-material had since been published. An appeal on the basis that his evidence was not supported by the material put to him in cross-examination was rejected, and the court stressed that the witness's evidence had been based on his own experience, not the publication to which he had been referred.[43] If reliance is to be placed upon the published material as part of the evidence of the skilled

---

[34] Dickson, *Evidence* (3rd edn), para 98.

[35] See the warning in *R v Turner* [1975] QB 834 at 841.

[36] *Wilson v HM Advocate* 1988 SCCR 384.

[37] *Main v McAndrew Wormald Ltd* 1988 SLT 141. Similarly in *M v Kennedy* 1993 SC 115 a paediatric neurologist was permitted to give evidence regarding the gynaecological examination of a child when she had been present at the examination and concurred with the findings, albeit that her only knowledge of that specialism was from attending lectures and working together with other specialists concerned with the identification of cases of child sexual abuse. In accepting her evidence on this point the court noted that "care should be taken to avoid leading more skilled witnesses than necessary, having regard to the evidence which they can give and their experience."

[38] A point noted *obiter* in *Mearns v Smedvig Ltd* 1999 SC 243, where an order for examination of the pursuer by a consultant of the novel "Blankenship system" for assessment of the effects of injury was refused.

[39] *Main v McAndrew Wormald Ltd* 1988 SLT 141.

[40] *Davie v Magistrates of Edinburgh* 1953 SC 34. In *Williamson v McCleland* 1913 SC 678, the Lord President based his opinion partly on books never referred to.

[41] *Main v McAndrew Wormald Ltd* 1988 SLT 141, following *Davie v Magistrates of Edinburgh* 1953 SC 34, *R v Abadom* [1983] 1 WLR 126.

[42] *Davie v Magistrates of Edinburgh* 1953 SC 34.

[43] *Di Luca v HM Advocate* 1996 SLT 924. A similar distinction was made in relation to a Code of Practice to which the witness was referred in *Balmoral Group Ltd v HM Advocate* 1996 SLT 1230.

witness it should probably be lodged as a production in order to give fair notice to the opponent.[44]

16.3.5 A witness may be skilled without possessing formal qualifications. Much will depend upon the area of knowledge and the extent to which it is exclusive to those with particular educational or professional qualifications. Hence, medical and scientific witnesses will generally require to show relevant qualifications, professional experience and memberships of regulatory bodies; but, for example, a witness who speaks to an office practice or custom of trade should have appropriate experience, but not necessarily qualifications, of that trade.[45]

Basis of fact

16.3.6 (i) Since the opinion is based on a certain state of facts, it is valueless unless the facts are averred and proved. In an action for reparation evidence, including that of a skilled witness, regarding a particular process for lifting a disabled patient was inadmissible when there was no notice on record of that process,[46] and in an action where foreign law might have been relied upon skilled evidence as to that law was inadmissible when the pleadings gave no notice of the substance of that law, its relevance and effect upon the facts, and the alleged difference between the foreign law and the law of Scotland.[47] Where a pursuer sought to prove by skilled evidence that from the condition of a pole in October it must have been in a dangerously corroded state in the preceding May, she failed because she did not prove by sufficient evidence the condition of the pole in October.[48] In a criminal trial the connection of the accused with the crime depended, *inter alia*, on a comparison by a skilled witness between material used for the crime and material said to have been found in the pocket of the accused. The Crown, however, failed to establish by sufficient evidence that the material had been found there, and accordingly the opinion evidence was useless.[49] In a reparation action a report of a medical witness referring to X-ray films not produced was vitiated in so far as it relied upon those films.[50] A skilled witness for the defence in a criminal case must also have a basis in fact. Hence, the evidence of a clinical pyschologist as to the suggestibility of the

---

[44] *Main v McAndrew Wormald Ltd* 1988 SLT 141, but *cf Roberts v British Railways Board* 1998 SCLR 577 (OH). However, a flexible attitude to the reception of a late report by a skilled witness in a criminal case—*Torres v HM Advocate* 1998 SLT 811—suggests that the court will not exclude relevant material, and the matter of fairness can be dealt with by, *eg*, adjournment.

[45] The knowledge of police officers as to relative quantities of controlled drugs kept for personal use or dealing has been admitted: *Bauros v HM Advocate* 1991 SCCR 768; *Haq v HM Advocate* 1987 SCCR 433; *White v HM Advocate* 1986 SCCR 224. In *Hopes and Lavery v HM Advocate* 1960 JC 104 the typist who had transcribed the content of a tape recorded exchange between the victim and the accused was an expert witness to the process of transcription, with hesitation on the part of the majority since she had never carried out the process before.

[46] *Parker v Lanarkshire Health Board* 1996 SCLR 57.

[47] *Armour v Thyssen Edelstahlwerke AG* 1989 SLT 182 (the appeal at 1990 SLT 891 is on another point.

[48] *Stewart v Glasgow Corporation* 1958 SC. 28. See also *AB v Northern Accident Ins Co* (1896) 24 R 258, decided on similar grounds.

[49] *Forrester v HM Advocate* 1952 JC 28. See also *Carraher v HM Advocate* 1946 JC 108 at 118.

[50] *Ward v Upper Clyde Shipbuilders* 1973 SLT 182. Where in a collision case the court was asked to infer from the damage to one of the ships that the other must have been going at a high speed, the argument failed at the outset on the ground that the only evidence of the damage was that of the damaged ship's own master: *The "Nerano" v The "Dromedary"* (1895) 22 R 237 at 246. Such a case would not now require corroboration of that fact—Civil Evidence (Scotland) Act 1988, s 1—but the fact must still be established in evidence.

accused during the pressure of a police interview was not permitted when there had not been factual evidence of pressure.[51]

(ii) The experts may have failed to take all the facts into account or have pro- **16.3.7** ceeded upon inadmissible facts[52] or unjustifiable assumptions. In a collision case the experts, in drawing conclusions from marks on one of the ships, had left out of account the possibility of the ship rolling, or, to put it another way, had assumed that the sea was absolutely smooth.[53]

(iii) The alleged facts on which an opinion is based may be disproved or **16.3.8** explained so as to deprive them of significance. Where medical opinions that a testator was insane depended partly on supposed delusions and peculiar conduct, it was established that one of the supposed delusions was a fact and another probably true, and that the conduct had been characteristic of the testator before insanity was suggested.[54] In these cases the facts on which the skilled witnesses proceeded were closely connected with the facts in issue, but where they are not, enquiry into them may be refused, not on the ground that they are logically irrelevant, but on the ground that limits must be set to the enquiry.[55] When sanity is an issue, evidence of mental disorders in close relatives has been considered relevant in a civil case,[56] but generally not in criminal cases.[57] In an action of damages for slander contained in letters, where the only issue was authorship, proof was allowed of averments that the defender had written other letters as a basis for skilled evidence.[58]

Controls upon use of skilled witnesses

In the Court of Session, if an assessor is sitting,[59] limitations are put upon the **16.3.9** parties' recourse to evidence of skilled witnesses. Generally, only one skilled witness may be led on each side on a matter within the qualification of the assessor,[60] unless leave is obtained.[61] If the case arises out of a collision at sea and a nautical assessor is sitting, no skilled evidence is competent on nautical

---

[51] *Blagojevic v HM Advocate* 1995 SLT 1189. The police officers had not been cross-examined on this, and the accused elected not to give evidence. Since *Thompson v Crowe* 2000 JC 173, the correct procedure is to allow the accused to give evidence regarding the pressure in a *voirdire*.

[52] Such as hearsay, confidential or irrelevant facts; however relevance to proof of the issue and relevance to expert opinion on the issue may be two different things, as in *Gemmill v HM Advocate* 1980 JC 16, where previous convictions were referred to in the medical reports regarding diminished responsibility. See also *Macdonald v Munro* 1997 SLT 446, *Sloan v Crowe* 1996 SLT 1094. In civil cases few categories of evidence are now inadmissible, but failure to aver the basis for the factual evidence will render the expert evidence based on those facts inadmissible: see, *eg, Armour v Thyssen Edelstahlwerke AG* 1989 SLT 182 (the appeal at 1990 SLT 891 is on another point), *Parker v Lanarkshire Health Board* 1996 SCLR 57. For a discussion in relation to England see Pattenden, "Expert Opinion Evidence based on Hearsay" [1982] CrimLR 85.

[53] *SS "Rowan" v SS "Clan Malcolm"* 1923 SC 316 at 340. *Cf Gardiner v Motherwell Machinery and Scrap Co* 1961 SC (HL) 1, where the opinion evidence rested on an unproved assumption.

[54] *Morrison v Maclean's Trs* (1862) 24 D 625 at 645.

[55] *Swan v Bowie* 1948 SC 46 at 51. "Life is not long enough to allow an exhaustive inquiry into every side issue which has or may have a bearing upon the main issue": *Houston v Aitken* 1912 SC 1037 at 1038. See para 7.1.

[56] *Houston v Aitken* 1912 SC 1037.

[57] *Edmonstone* 1909 2 SLT 223; *Brown* (1855) 2 Irv 154; *Gibson* (1844) 2 Broun 332; *McClinton* (1902) 4 Adam at 1 at 13; *Paterson* (1872) 2 Coup 222; *McQue* (1860) 3 Irv 578. *Cf Galbraith* (1897) 5 SLT 65; *Dingwall* (1867) 5 Irv 466.

[58] *Swan v Bowie* 1948 SC 46.

[59] Which may be at the court's instance, although this rarely occurs, or on the application of either party: RCS, r 12.1(1).

[60] RCS, r 12.7(2).

[61] RCS, r 12.7(4).

matters.[62] In reparation proceedings in the Court of Session which are taken under the more informal and speedier optional procedure, parties are limited to one medical witness and one other skilled witness.[63] These situations apart, there is no procedural limitation[64] upon the number of skilled witnesses to be led by a party.[65] Concerns have been voiced in other jurisdictions[66] about excessive resort by parties to the evidence[67] of opinion of skilled persons, particularly in civil cases, and suggestions have been made regarding the use of court-appointed neutral experts in place of the court having to choose between conflicting evidence of experts employed by each party.[68] However, there is less evidence of particular concern in Scotland to date,[69] and the powers of the Court of Session to appoint an assessor,[70] and of the sheriff, on application, to remit to a person of skill,[71] to report on any matter of fact are powers that are rarely used in practice.

16.3.10   Procedures have been introduced to encourage disclosure and exchange of reports of skilled witnesses prior to proof or trial. In optional procedure for reparation in the Court of Session a written report of any skilled person whom a party intends to call as a skilled witness at proof must be disclosed to the other party and lodged in process all not less than 28 days before proof,[72] with the sanction that unless the report has been so disclosed the witness may not be called except on special cause shown.[73] In actions of damages for personal injury or death in the Sheriff court all medical reports on which the pursuer intends to rely must be lodged as productions with the initial writ, or the defender may move for an order for their production.[73a] In an action

---

[62] RCS, r 12.7(1).

[63] RCS, r 43.27(3).

[64] There are practical limitations such as cost and the availability of legal aid.

[65] Apart from the power of the Court of Session to appoint an assessor *ex proprio motu* under RCS, r 12.1 or in a commercial action to seek an expert report under RCS, r 47.12(2)(f), there is no provision in Scotland for a court appointed expert, a feature of the inquisitorial system.

[66] Particularly the USA and England. See Basten, "The Court Expert in Civil Trials, A Comparative Appraisal" (1977) 40 MLR 174–191; Kenny, " The Expert in Court" (1983) 99 LQR 197–216; Woolf, "Access to Justice: Interim Report to the Lord Chancellor on the Civil Justice System in England & Wales" (1995), Chapter 23; Final Report (1996), Chapter 13. In England the use of expert evidence is restricted to cases in which the court permits it, and the court may order a joint report: Civil Procedure Rules 1998 (SI 1998/3132) Chap 35. Restriction is not contrary to Art 6 provided that there is quality of arms, *Bönisch v Austria* A92 (1985) Com Rep.

[67] As compared to unobjectionable reliance upon expert opinion outwith the court room such as in preparation for a case or during settlement discussions.

[68] Basten, "The Court Expert in Civil Trials, A Comparative Appraisal" (1977) 40 MLR 174–191; Howard, "The Neutral Expert: a plausible threat to justice" [1991] CrimLR 98–105; Spencer, "The Neutral Expert; an implausible bogey" [1991] CrimLR 106–110.

[69] Macphail considers the matter at paras 17.27–17.28 and notes that concerns in America and England may be of significance here, but that within an adversarial system the present system is probably best. The Scottish Law Commission did not recommend change: Memo No 46, R.16. Lord Cullen, in his report, *Review of the Business of the Outer House* (1995) mentions only greater and earlier disclosure of reports of skilled witnesses (paras 5.23–5.24), and potentially limiting each party to one skilled witness except on cause shown (para 5.25, although this is a little unclear).

[70] RCS, r 12.1.

[71] OCR, r 29.2.

[72] RCS, r 43.27(1). Lord Cullen proposes a similar requirement for all cases—*Review of the Business of the Outer House* (1995) para 5.24—and in reparation actions, a requirement that the medical report on which the claim has been founded is attached to the summons when it is presented for signetting (para 5.23). The latter may be have been adopted into practice: see Wadia, "Judicial Case Management in Scotland" 1997 SLT (News) 255 at 258.

[73] RCS, r 43.27(2).

[73a] OCR 36.17C (introduced by Act of Sederunt (Sheriff Court Ordinary Cause Rules Amendment) (Miscellaneous) 2000 (SI 2000/239) para 3(19).

which proceeds as a commercial action in the Court of Session the parties must lodge copies of expert reports at least three days in advance of the procedural hearing,[74] and amongst the commercial judge's wide range of powers is the power to appoint a **16.3.11** skilled person to examine the issues including the reports of any skilled witnesses.[75]

Procedures to encourage disclosure and agreement of evidence now pervade both civil and criminal procedure.[76] For example, in addition to the general enjoinder to seek to agree evidence in optional[77] and commercial[78] procedures in the Court of Session, and in criminal proceedings,[79] parties may by notice call upon the other to admit evidence[80] or to accept evidence in the form of a report[81] or in testimony from only one of two forensic analysts.[82] In the event of failure to serve a counter-notice the evidence may be deemed to be admitted, evidence to contradict it may be inadmissible and, in the case of a skilled witness in civil cases, the court may refuse to certify the witness or award the expenses of calling that witness.[83]

Presence in court

Since the skilled witness is to give an opinion on the facts, it is usually helpful that **16.3.12** the witness should be in court to hear the evidence of the witnesses to fact relevant to the area of skilled testimony,[84] and as a general rule this is allowed unless objection is taken. Traditionally the skilled witness has been excluded while other skilled witnesses are giving evidence of opinion,[85] although there have been contrary examples.[86] This is thought to derive from times when the reliability of witnesses was generally doubted and it has been suggested that there should be no rule against a skilled witness who has yet to testify being present in court while another is testifying.[87] If the skilled witness is to speak to facts as well as opinion, it may be that he ought to be withdrawn while other witnesses are speaking to these facts.[88]

Cross-examination

The cross-examiner may challenge the soundness of the conclusions drawn by **16.3.13** the witness from the facts as the witness has assumed them. This may involve challenging the extent of the witness's knowledge and understanding of the facts, or it may involve challenging the professional or technical competence of the

---

[74] RCS, r 47.12.

[75] RCS, r 47.12(2)(f).

[76] In addition to the procedures mentioned in this paragraph, parties require to disclose lists of witnesses in civil proceedings in the Court of Session, and in solemn prosecutions a list of witnesses must accompany the indictment.

[77] RCS, r 43.28.

[78] RCS, r 47.10.

[79] Criminal Procedure (Scotland) Act 1995 ("1995 Act"), s 257.

[80] RCS, r 36.6; OCR, r 29.14; 1995 Act, s 258.

[81] 1995 Act, s 280.

[82] 1995 Act, s 281.

[83] *Ayton v National Coal Board* 1965 SLT (Notes) 24.

[84] Although practical considerations of the time and cost of the skilled witness frequently preclude this.

[85] *Laurie* (1889) 2 White 326; *Pritchard* (1865) 5 Irv 88; *Milne* (1863) 4 Irv 301; *Murray* (1858) 3 Irv 262.

[86] *Granger* (1878) 4 Coup 86; *Dingwall* (1867) 5 Irv 466 at 471.

[87] Macphail, paras 17.11–17.13; Scottish Law Commission Memo No 46, R.07.

[88] But even if he is not, the court may allow his evidence on fact to be taken: Evidence (Scotland) Act 1840, s 3. Macphail proposes a discretion to allow the witness to be present (para 17.12) and the Scottish Law Commission recommend that the witness be permitted to be present (Scottish Law Commission Memo No 46, R.07). The statement in Macdonald, *Criminal Law* (5th edn), p 295, that he cannot be examined on the facts, is wrong. See para 13.22.

witness.[89] Alternatively, the cross-examiner may ask the witness for his opinion on the facts as the cross-examiner hopes to establish them.[90] The witness's opinion may be the same as that of the cross-examiner's experts, which is thus reinforced and, if it is not, the cross-examiner is not open to the observation that he has failed to give the opposing experts an opportunity to state their opinions.

Necessity for skilled evidence

16.3.14   If the court is to be asked to draw an inference of a technical or scientific nature, skilled evidence must be led.[91] Where the court was asked in a collision case to infer from the marks on one ship that the speed of the other must have been high, it held itself unable to do so in the absence of skilled evidence.[92] In another collision case, where it was sought to establish the position of the ships by means of photographs taken at the time of the collision, the Privy Council held that the lower court ought not to have used this evidence because no skilled evidence had been led to explain the effects of planes, perspectives, etc.[93] However, in a charge relating to the supply of cannabis resin the lay identification of the substance by persons who purchased it was held, on appeal, to be sufficient.[94]

16.4 HANDWRITING

16.4.1   Where the genuineness of handwriting is in issue the best evidence, if it is available, is that of the purported writer.[95] This rule does not seem to have been departed from,[96] and it would probably apply in a civil case where it is averred that the party supporting the document forged it, or knows it to be forged.[97] Another class of direct evidence is that of witnesses who saw the writing carried out, such as an attesting witness.[98] Opinion evidence identifying handwriting may come either from witnesses who claim to be familiar with the handwriting of the purported writer or from skilled witnesses, who compare the questioned writing with specimens admitted or proved to be in that of the purported writer. There is old authority[99] for the view that the evidence of skilled witnesses is of little value,

---

[89] As in *Preece v HM Advocate* [1981] CrimLR 783.

[90] Dickson, *Evidence* (3rd edn), para 401, thinks this should be done in chief, but if it is not, the cross-examiner should do it: *Wilson v Thomas Usher & Son* 1934 SC 332 at 337.

[91] The court will not consider a plea of diminished responsibility without skilled evidence (*Carraher v HM Advocate* 1946 JC 108), yet difficulties arise as to whether the court is required to make a technical inference when personality rather than mental disorder is the issue: see *R v Turner* [1975] QB 834; *Connelly v HM Advocate* 1990 JC 349; *Williamson v HM Advocate* 1994 JC 149; and *Martindale v HM Advocate* 1994 SLT 1093.

[92] *The "Nerano" v The "Dromedary"* (1895) 22 R 237.

[93] *United States Shipping Board v The St Albans* [1931] AC 632, where counsel supplied the expert evidence.

[94] *McCallum v McKay* 1997 SCCR 558; and *Main v Russel* 1999 GWD 13–592 (in which the persons were three young boys).

[95] In a trial for uttering, where the Crown must prove that the document is forged, it has been held that opinion evidence is incompetent unless the purported writer is examined (Dickson, *Evidence* (3rd edn), para 200; *Humphreys* (1839) 2 Swin 356 at 374) or the writer's absence satisfactorily explained (*Wilson* (1857) 2 Irv 626 at 631).

[96] In *Richardson v Clark* 1957 JC 7, Mrs Shiells presumably denied the signatures at the trial.

[97] *Arnott v Burt* (1872) 11 M 62 at 74.

[98] *Stirling Stuart v Stirling Crawfurd's Trs* (1885) 12 R 610.

[99] eg *Forster v Forster* (1869) 7 M 797 at 804.

greatly inferior to that of persons familiar with the genuine writing and to the opinions of the court, and certainly insufficient alone to establish the point. However, the court refused to affirm these statements when the scientific study of handwriting advanced,[100] and now routinely admits evidence of witnesses skilled in examining questioned documents as sufficient evidence of identification.[101] Documents used for comparison may be written before or after the date of the questioned document, but if written afterwards it is relevant to consider whether the style of writing in the later document has been altered intentionally to influence the analysis.[102] The document used for comparison may be one which is inadmissible for any other purpose.[103]

Differing views have been expressed as to whether it is competent for the jury **16.4.2** to make their own comparison of handwriting and proceed upon that. This practice was approved in several old civil cases[104] and in a trial for uttering.[105] However, in other cases the practice was disapproved, and the jury were advised to form a view based upon the opinion evidence led.[106] The judge or jury would be entitled to examine the documents,[107] but in some cases the court did not allow that.[108] The modern approach is to lead evidence as to the handwriting from those who are directly familiar with it or from those skilled in technical comparison of handwriting, but to allow the jury to interpret and weigh that evidence by reference to the documents themselves.[109]

16.5 FOREIGN LAW

General

Except for Scots law and the laws of the European Community[110] which are within **16.5.1** judicial knowledge,[111] all other law is foreign law and is a question of fact.[112] If it

---

[100] *Richardson v Clark* 1957 JC 7.

[101] *Campbell v Mackenzie* 1974 SLT (Notes) 46.

[102] Dickson, *Evidence* (3rd edn), in para 411, states that the document used for comparison must be earlier than the questioned document, since otherwise it might be specially prepared for comparison. He cites *Cameron v Fraser & Co* (1830) 9 S 141 and *Ross v Waddell* (1837) 15 S 1219. Nowadays this would go to weight rather than admissibility of the evidence.

[103] *HM Advocate v Walsh* 1922 JC 82; *Davidson v HM Advocate* 1951 JC 33. For a civil example see *Mackenzie v Crawford* (1839) 1 D 1091, in which an unstamped document was used for comparison.

[104] eg *Paul v Harper* (1832) 10 S 486; *Bryson v Crawford* (1834) 12 S 937.

[105] *Beveridge* (1866) 3 Irv 625.

[106] *Gellatly v Jones* (1851) 13 D 961; *Robertson* (1849) J Shaw 186; *McCann v Adair* 1951 JC 127.

[107] *Slater v HM Advocate* (1899) 2 F (J) 4.

[108] *Gellatly v Jones* (1851) 13 D 961; *Robertson* (1849) J Shaw 186 at 191 not cited in *Beveridge* (1866) 3 Irv 625. It is perhaps indicative of the practice at the time that the advocate depute had told the jury that they would have an opportunity of comparing the documents.

[109] The judicial encouragement of independent scrutiny (*eg* "I am inclined to place considerable reliance on the evidence of my own eyes"; *Stirling Stuart v Stirling Crawfurd's Trs* (1885) 12 R 610 at 621; and in *National Bank of Scotland Ltd v Campbell* (1892) 19 R 885 at 887, 890) is not in accordance with the requirement that judgments are based upon interpretation of the evidence led. See Macphail, para 17.21. The court can reject the opinion evidence and base a judgment on other evidence, but should not replace the evidence with their own impression, although one may be but a short step from the other.

[110] European Communities Act 1972, s 3.

[111] See paras 11.6–11.7 and 19.2–19.6.

[112] This hardly needs authority, but see, *eg, Campbell's Trs v Campbell* (1903) 5 F 366.

is not admitted[113] or ascertained under statutory procedure or by remit to foreign counsel, it must be proved by the evidence of skilled witnesses. The court will not attempt to construe a foreign statute for itself without the aid of skilled witnesses.[114] The House of Lords, however, as the final court of appeal in civil matters from all parts of the United Kingdom, has judicial knowledge of Scots, English and Northern Irish law, and may take cognisance, without need of evidence, of matters of the law of one jurisdiction in an appeal originating in another, and that even though the foreign law has not been pleaded or argued.[115] Provision has now been made for proof of judgments of which the courts in Scotland must take account under the Human Rights Act 1998, s 2. These are not within judicial knowledge, but any authoritative and complete report of such a judgment given in any manner is sufficient evidence of it.[116]

Statutory ascertainment

16.5.2 If any court is of opinion that it is necessary or expedient to ascertain the law of any other part of Her Majesty's dominions,[117] applicable to the facts[118] of a case, it may remit to a superior court of that part for its opinion.[119] The court has a discretion and refused to exercise it where the court to which the remit was asked had concurrent jurisdiction.[120] A remit may be made although skilled evidence has been led.[121] The opinion obtained is conclusive,[122] except that the Judicial Committee and the House of Lords are not bound by the opinion of a court whose judgments they have power to review.[123]

Remit to foreign counsel

16.5.3 The court may make such a remit of consent, and the opinion is binding,[124] except that if the opinion is on English law the House of Lords may disregard it.[125] Where a remit was made to two counsel, and they differed, a remit was made to a third.[126]

---

[113] As in *Studd v Studd* (1880) 8 R 249; (1883) 10 R (HL) 53.

[114] *Higgins v Ewing's Trs* 1925 SC 440; *Kolbin & Sons v Kinnear & Co* 1930 SC 724 at 737, 748, 753; 1931 SC (HL) 128 (point not raised in HL); *R v Governor of Brixton Prison, ex parte Shuter* [1960] 2 QB 89. *Cf Great Northern Railway Co v Laing* (1848) 10 D 1408.

[115] *Elliot v Joicey* 1935 SC (HL) 57. Also, for income tax purposes only, the English law of charities must be regarded as part of the law of Scotland and not as foreign law, so that in this class of case the Scottish courts must themselves seek to interpret the English decisions as to what is or is not a "charity". This exception is justifiable by the need for a common tax code and its uniform interpretation. *Inland Revenue v Glasgow Police Athletic Association* 1953 SC (HL) 13.

[116] Act of Sederunt (Evidence of Judgements etc) (Human Rights Act 1998) 2000 (SI 2000/314); Act of Adjournal (Criminal Procedure Rules 1996) r 41.2 added by the Act of Adjournal (Criminal Procedure Rules Amendment No 2) (Human Rights Act 1998) 2000 (SI 2000/315) para 2.

[117] The Republic of Ireland is not part of Her Majesty's dominions, but it is not a foreign country for the purposes of any law in force in the United Kingdom: Ireland Act 1949, s 2(1).

[118] As ascertained by a verdict or other mode competent (which would include findings by the court) or agreed.

[119] British Law Ascertainment Act 1859 ("1859 Act"), ss 1, 5.

[120] *MacDougall v Chitnavis* 1937 SC 390. What must be necessary or expedient is not, as the Lord President said, the remit, but the ascertainment of the foreign law.

[121] *MacDougall v Chitnavis* 1937 SC 390; *De Thoren v Wall* (1876) 3 R (HL) 28.

[122] 1859 Act, s 3.

[123] 1859 Act, s 4; *De Thoren v Wall* (1876) 3 R (HL) 28.

[124] *Duchess of Buckingham v Winterbottom* (1851) 13 D 1129 at 1141; *Baird v Mitchell* (1854) 16 D 1088 at 1092.

[125] *Macpherson v Macpherson* (1852) 1 Macq 243.

[126] *Kerr v Fyffe* (1840) 2 D 1001.

The remit ought to be carefully limited to questions of law. When a remit was so framed as to ask the opinion of counsel, *inter alia*, on the construction of a will which raised no question of foreign law, the court was narrowly divided as to whether they were bound by counsel's views on construction, and by seven to six decided in the negative.[127]

Skilled witnesses

Such evidence is usually given by members of the bar, but, in spite of an *obiter* **16.5.4** dictum by Lord Young,[128] there seems to be no reason why it should not be given by solicitors or academics according to their experience and knowledge.[129] English counsel would be accepted to state the law of any country where English law prevailed. So the court remitted to English counsel for an opinion on the law of Newfoundland, which was English law.[130] Where the witnesses differ, the court is bound to weigh the evidence as in any question of fact.[131] There seems to be no reason in principle why the court should not reject the opinion, even if it is uncontradicted, as it may do in the case of any other skilled witness.[132] There is, however, no reported instance of rejection of the opinion on its merits although it has been rejected due to inadequate basis in the pleadings,[133] and the court proceeds to deal with the matter according to Scots law.[134] A number of recent examples deal with the foreign law as to formalities such as marriage or divorce.[135] If the matter of foreign law relates to the validity of an official document, the better course may be to use the statutory basis for proof of such documents.[136] In countries which are named by Order in Council[137] public records and documents taken therefrom are deemed to be regularly kept and extracted,[138] and certificates named in the order may be granted by the officials of the relevant country and constitute evidence of the facts stated in the certificate.[139]

---

[127] *Thomson's Trs v Alexander* (1851) 14 D 217. The decision would have been the other way, if Lord Dundrennan had not died before the judgment was signed and been succeeded by Lord Cowan, who took the opposite view.

[128] *Dinwoodie's Exrx v Carruthers' Exr* (1895) 23R 234 at 238. So far as the report discloses there was no dispute as to English law, but only as to whether it applied.

[129] Wilkinson cites the example of *Brailey v Rhodesia Consolidated Ltd* [1910] 2 Ch 95 in which the skilled witness was a reader in Roman-Dutch law. As to proof of foreign statutes see para 19.13.

[130] *Thomson's Trs v Alexander* (1851) 14 D 217.

[131] *Kolbin & Sons v Kinnear & Co* 1930 SC 724; *Girvin, Roper & Co v Monteith* (1895) 23 R 129, where, at 132, 135, there was discussion of the evidence.

[132] See para 16.03.

[133] *Armour v Thyssen Edelstahlwerke AG* 1989 SLT 182, (the appeal reported at 1990 SLT 891 is on another point), following *Stuart v Potter, Choate and Prentice* 1911 1 SLT 377. Examples of skilled evidence of foreign law are to be found in, eg, *Ross v HH Sir Bhagat Sinhjee* (1891) 19 R 31; *Scottish National Orchestra Society v Thomson's Exr* 1969 SLT 325; *Galbraith v Galbraith* 1971 SC 65; *Bain v Bain* 1971 SC 146; *Broit v Broit* 1972 SC 192.

[134] As occurred in *Armour v Thyssen Edelstahlwerke AG* 1989 SLT 182, *Kraus's Administrators v Sullivan* 1998 SLT 963.

[135] *Galbraith v Galbraith* 1971 SC 65; *Bain v Bain* 1971 SC 146; *Broit v Broit* 1972 SLT (Notes) 32.

[136] Evidence (Foreign, Dominion & Colonial Documents) Act 1933 ("1933 Act"), s 1.

[137] See the list attached to the text of the 1933 Act in *Parliament House Book*, vol. 1, Div B.

[138] 1933 Act, s 1(2)(a)–(c). See also para 19.31.

[139] 1933 Act, s 1(2)(d). The evidence was received by certificates in *Makouipour v Makouipour* 1967 SC 116.

CHAPTER 17

ACCESS TO WITNESSES AND SECURING THEIR ATTENDANCE

17.1 INTRODUCTORY

Historically, the scope for ascertaining the extent of oral evidence that an opponent **17.1.1** would lead and the identity of the witnesses through whom it would be led, was very limited. Such information might be obtained indirectly through commission and diligence for recovery of documents.[1] However, a combination of statutory change in civil cases, and the requirement of equality of arms under the European Convention on Human Rights, has expanded the scope for production or recovery of such information in certain circumstances, and these are examined below. Citation of witnesses for proof, trial or other tribunal and the effect of failure to answer or enforce citations is examined, not for its procedural interest but for the impact upon the proof or trial and the leading of evidence by means other than the attendance of the witness in court. Reference is made in this chapter to "precognosce" and "precognition", which mean the act of taking a statement from a person for the purpose of discovering what his evidence is to be in a cause commenced or at least decided upon,[2] and the resulting record of it.[3] The distinction between a precognition and a statement is significant in that the former is not admissible hearsay as proof of its contents in court proceedings[4] because it is assumed to contain some input from the precognition taker,[5] unless it is a

---

[1] Commented upon in *Friel v Chief Constable of Strathclyde* 1981 SC 1 at 8–9.

[2] *McNeilie v HM Advocate* 1929 JC 50, per Lord Sands at 54; *Kerr v HM Advocate* 1958 JC 14, per Lord Justice-Clerk Thomson at 19. Interpretation of the practices prior to those cases is examined, and declared to be of historical value only, in *Coll, Petitioner* 1977 JC 29.

[3] A statement made during police enquiries was held not to be made on precognition in civil proceedings connected with the same facts: *Gilmour v Hansen* 1920 SC 598.

[4] Criminal Procedure (Scotland) Act 1995, s 262(1); Civil Evidence (Scotland) Act 1988, s 9; *Kerr v HM Advocate* 1958 JC 14; *Coll, Petitioner* 1977 JC 29. A precognition has also been found to be the property of the agent who took it rather than the client for whom it was taken: *Swift v T G Bannigan & Co* 1991 SCLR 604.

[5] *Kerr v HM Advocate* 1958 JC 14; *Coll, Petitioner* 1977 JC 29. See also para 8.7.

precognition on oath,[6] and it is for the party seeking to have a statement admitted to show that it is not a precognition.[7]

17.2 DISCOVERY OF OTHER PARTY'S WITNESSES—CRIMINAL CASES

17.2.1 In criminal cases on indictment the Crown must serve, with the indictment, a list of the witnesses to be adduced.[8] This list should show the name of the witness and an address at which the witness can be contacted for precognition,[9] which may be an accommodation address. Objection may be taken by the accused to the clarity or accuracy of the details on the list, and if the court finds that the accused has not been supplied with sufficient detail to enable identification of the witness for pre-cognition before trial adjournment, postponement or other order may be made.[10] The Crown may, with leave of the court, and having given the accused two days' notice of the name and address of the witness, call a witness not named on the original list.[11] The accused must produce a list of names and addresses of witnesses whom he intends to examine at least 10 days before a High Court trial and before the first diet in a sheriff court jury trial,[12] failing which it will not be competent to call the witness except if the court directs, on cause shown.[13] All parties may call witnesses named on the list submitted by the Crown, accused or co-accused.[14] Where a witness is on the Crown list the witness should not be excused without the consent of the accused.[15]

17.2.2 In summary cases there is no requirement to intimate a list of witnesses, but as a matter of practice a list will be provided to the accused or agent of the accused on request.[16] It is common practice for each party to precognosce the intended witnesses of the other, and this will normally be done by voluntary arrangement after invitation. Defence witness lists were formerly expected at least three days before trial,[17] but that expectation no longer has a statutory footing.

---

[6]   Criminal Procedure (Scotland) Act 1995, s 262(1); *Coll, Petitioner* 1977 JC 29.

[7]   *Kerr v HM Advocate* 1958 JC 14. In *HM Advocate v McGachy* 1991 JC 199 the prosecutor was able so to prove, and in *Low v HM Advocate* 1988 SLT 97 the matter was left to the jury. It must be borne in mind that the decision cannot now be left to the jury if, in order to challenge the nature of the statement, the accused will require to give evidence, and the matter should be dealt with in *voir dire*: *Thompson v Crowe* 2000 JC 173. See para 9.12. For civil examples, see *McAvoy v Glasgow District Council* 1993 SLT 859; *Stevenson v Chief Constable of Strathclyde* 1998 GWD 18-935 and para 8.7.

[8]   Criminal Procedure (Scotland) Act 1995 ("1995 Act"), s 66(4).

[9]   1995 Act, ss 66(4) and 67(1).

[10]   1995 Act, s 67(3) and (4).

[11]   1995 Act, s 67(5).

[12]   1995 Act, s 78(4)(a).

[13]   1995 Act, s 78(4)(b). For an example in relation to an earlier version of this rule, see *Lowson v HM Advocate* 1943 JC 141. The court has stressed that these lists are intended to be definitive: *Brown v HM Advocate* 1998 SCCR 461.

[14]   1995 Act, s 67(6).

[15]   Observed in *Berry v HM Advocate* 1989 SLT 71. In *Mellors v HM Advocate* 1999 SCCR 869 the witness was still being traced while the trial proceeded, and due to lapse in communication between Crown counsel the witness was found and released without the defence being informed. This was a "serious flaw in the conduct of the case".

[16]   This practice is alluded to in *Low v MacNeill* 1981 SCCR 243 at 247.

[17]   Criminal Procedure (Scotland) Act 1975, s 82(2).

17.3 DISCOVERY OF OTHER PARTY'S WITNESSES—CIVIL CASES

Lists of witnesses

In civil cases other than commercial actions and actions for damages under the **17.3.1** optional procedure, the parties are expected to exchange lists of witnesses at least 28 days before proof or jury trial in the Court of Session, and within 28 days after allowance of proof in the Sheriff Court.[18] A party wishing to call, or present the evidence of, a witness not listed may be permitted to do so on such conditions as the court thinks fit.[19] In commercial actions[20] and actions under the optional procedure[21] the court may make orders requiring the parties to exchange witness lists.

Identifying witnesses—common law

The position at common law was that a party might apply for commission and dili- **17.3.2** gence in pending proceedings[22] to obtain details for identification of witnesses, but the court resisted the formulation of general rules and considered each case on its circumstances,[23] having regard to the position apparent from the pleadings and the *ex parte* statements made in support of the application.[24] It is considered legitimate to seek disclosure of the names or addresses of persons who represented the parties in the issue under dispute, such as employees in respect of whom defenders were averred to be vicariously liable.[25] If to deny the motion might result in "material prejudice in respect that the applicant may be unable to try to precognosce a witness, who, on the face of the pleadings, is bound to be a potential witness of importance," but to grant the motion would have no comparable prejudicial effects upon the defenders, the motion should be granted.[26]

Identifying witnesses—statute

A statutory power to apply to the court for an order for the identification of wit- **17.3.3** nesses was introduced by the Law Reform (Miscellaneous Provisions) (Scotland) Act 1985[27] and now forms part of section 1 of the Administration of Justice

---

[18] Court of Session: Practice Note (No 8 of 1994), para 1. Sheriff Court: OCR r 9. 14(1) as amended by Act of Sederunt (Sheriff Court Ordinary Cause Rules Amendment) (Miscellaneous) 2000 (SI 2000/239) para 3(4).

[19] Practice Note (No 8 of 1994), para 2; OCR 9.14(2).

[20] RCS, r 47.11(1)(b)(iv) and (vi).

[21] RCS, r 43.26.

[22] On which see further Chapter 21 in relation to recovery of documents and Chapter 18 regarding real evidence.

[23] *Henderson v Patrick Thomson Ltd* 1911 SC 246; *Clarke v Edinburgh & District Tramway Co* 1914 SC 775.

[24] As in *McGinn v Meiklejohn Ltd* 1969 SLT (Notes) 49, where the absence of prejudice to the party opposing the motion and the potential benefit to all parties were mentioned in support of the decision, which was to order the defenders to name the persons working for them on a site in which they averred that contractors were in charge of the works, to clarify the issue of vicarious liability. See also *De Luca v Sillitoe* (1935) 52 Sh Ct Rep 18; *McDade v Glasgow Corporation* 1966 SLT (Notes) 4. These cases are discussed in MacSporran & Young, *Commission and Diligence*, paras 2.68–2.69.

[25] *Henderson v Patrick Thomson Ltd* 1911 SC 246; *Clarke v Edinburgh & District Tramway Co* 1914 SC 775. The dicta to this effect in *Clarke* are followed in *Halloran v Greater Glasgow Passenger Transport Executive* 1976 SLT 77, and the court was unwilling there to consider referring the point to a larger court.

[26] *Halloran v Greater Glasgow Passenger Transport Executive* 1976 SLT 77. The court was unable to accept the defenders' submission that the grant of the motion impinged in any significant way upon the right of the defenders to select and present their own evidence working at arm's length.

[27] s 19.

(Scotland) Act 1972,[28] a section which in its generality has been considered in greater detail in other chapters.[29] The statutory power exists without prejudice to the powers at common law, and allows the Court of Session and sheriff court[30] to order any person to disclose such information as he has as to the identity of any persons who appear to the court to be persons who (a) might be witnesses in any existing civil proceedings before the court or in proceedings that are likely to be brought, or (b) might be defenders in any civil proceedings which appear to the court to be likely to be brought. The provision is subject to the normal plea of confidentiality.[31] Application is by motion in the proceedings before the Court of Session or sheriff,[32] or, if proceedings have not yet been raised, by petition in the Court of Session[33] and summary application in the sheriff court.[34] Assessment of the application proceeds upon the averments at that date,[35] or the circumstances disclosed by the application and answers, together with *ex parte* statements.

17.3.4   The terms of the statutory provision are, on their face, much broader than those applying at common law,[36] and they are premised upon tests used in the remainder of the section in relation to documents, things and premises.[37] However, an argument that the terms should be interpreted to allow all recovery after proof has been allowed, as tends to occur with documents,[38] unless the holder of the information to the contrary establishes a case, was rejected in a recent case in the Outer House.[39] The court confirmed that the test, as for all applications for recovery under that statute, requires the applicant to put forward the justifying circumstances, and the court to consider whether in those circumstances, weighed along with any counter-bearing circumstances, it is in the interests of justice that the order be made.[40] It will be relevant to consider what the party applicant has done to recover the information by agreement.[41] An argument that recovery would enable the witness list to be lodged early, although in keeping with the desirability of early disclosure, is not persuasive *per se*.[42]

---

[28] s 1(1A).

[29] See Chapters 18 and 21.

[30] Not in summary causes or small claims, which make provision only for recovery of documents.

[31] Administration of Justice (Scotland) Act 1972, s 1(4). See, *eg, Conoco (UK) Ltd v Commercial Law Practice* 1997 SLT 372. See also Chapter 10.

[32] RCS, r 35.2; OCR, r 28.2.

[33] RCS, r 64.2 as substituted by the Act of Sederunt (Rules of the Court of Session Amendment No 4) (Applications under s 1 of the Administration of Justice (Scotland) Act 1972) 2000 (SI 2000/319) para 2. Although the Act of Sederunt purports to apply to applications under s 1.

[34] Act of Sederunt (Summary Applications, Statutory Applications and Appeals etc Rules) 1999 (SI 1999/929), r 3.1.2.

[35] And it was held to be not appropriate to invoke the s1(1A) procedure to bolster inherently unspecific averments in *Boulting v Elias* 1990 SLT 596. The substituted RCS r 64.2 requires the petitioner to submit an affidavit supporting the petition.

[36] Ostensibly, they extend to orders against non-parties, orders sought before the proceedings and witnesses of any significance. RCS r 64.3(b), 64.7 and 64.12 as substituted provide additional protections for respondents and havers.

[37] Administration of Justice (Scotland) Act 1972, s 1(1) and (3), discussed in detail in para 21.7.

[38] See para 21.7.

[39] *Moffat v News Group Newspapers* 2000 SCLR 346.

[40] *Mooney v City of Glasgow District Council* 1989 SLT 863; *Boyce v Cape Contracts Ltd* 1998 SLT 889.

[41] *Mooney v City of Glasgow District Council* 1989 SLT 863.

[42] *Moffat v News Group Newspapers* 2000 SCLR 346.

17.4 WITNESS PRECOGNITION—CRIMINAL CASES

Citing for precognition by prosecutor

In summary cases the Crown is empowered by statute to cite a witness for pre- **17.4.1**
cognition, whether or not a person has been charged with an offence, and failure
by a witness to co-operate[43] with a timeous[44] citation is punishable in proceedings
for contempt.[45] The witness is expected to attend at the time and place intimated
and "provide information within his knowledge regarding a matter relevant to the
commission of the offence in relation to which such precognition is taken."[46] In
solemn cases the Crown may apply for a warrant for citation of a witness for precognition, and failure by the witness to co-operate is an offence.[47] The Crown is
entitled at common law to apply to the court for precognition on oath,[48] and this
may be done at any stage in the proceedings, including after commencement of the
trial.[49] It has been said in relation to petitions for warrant for precognition on oath
that the procedure should be reserved for the recalcitrant witness[50] who is unwilling to give evidence and cannot be relied upon to adhere to the earlier statement at
trial.[51]

Precognition for accused

There is no provision for the accused to cite for precognition except on oath.[52] In **17.4.2**
both solemn and summary cases the accused may apply to the court for warrant to
cite a witness (other than a co-accused) for precognition on oath[53]; if warrant is
granted, the citation must be served personally on the witness by an officer of
law.[54] Failure to attend is an offence, and the court may issue a warrant for apprehension of the witness to be precognosced on oath.[55] A witness who, having been
cited, attends but "(a) refuses to give information within his knowledge or to produce evidence in his possession; or (b) prevaricates in his evidence," is guilty of
an offence.[56] A claim of privilege to refrain from answering questions may be
made by the witness and will be considered on its merits by the presiding judge.[57]
A witness is not entitled to have a solicitor present during precognition on oath.[58]

---

[43] That is, "fails without reasonable excuse to attend or refuses to give relevant information within his knowledge": 1995 Act, s 155(4).
[44] *ie* 48 hours' notice of the precognition appointment: s 155(4).
[45] Criminal Procedure (Scotland) Act 1995 ("1995 Act"), s 155(1) and (4).
[46] 1995 Act, s 155(4).
[47] 1995 Act, s 67A.
[48] There is interesting commentary on this after the report of *Low v MacNeill* 1981 SCCR 243 at 248.
[49] *Kelly v Vannet* 1999 JC 109.
[50] *Low v MacNeill* 1981 SCCR 243.
[51] *Coll, Petitioner* 1977 JC 29, where early authorities regarding the destruction of precognitions at sight of the witness are considered but rejected in view of the modern practice, then clear from the cases of *McNeilie v HM Advocate* 1929 JC 50, and *Kerr v HM Advocate* 1958 JC 14.
[52] This is commented upon in *Low v MacNeill* 1981 SCCR 243 at 247.
[53] 1995 Act, s 291(1). The section heading is misleading in its reference to defence witnesses. The provisions cover any witness whom the defence wish to precognosce, whether on a Crown list or an anticipated witness for the defence.
[54] Act of Adjournal (Criminal Procedure Rules) 1996, r 2.3(3). As to "officer of law", see the Criminal
Procedure (Scotland) Act 1995, s 307 and para 17.7 below.
[55] 1995 Act, s 291(2).
[56] 1995 Act, s 291(3).
[57] *Kelly v Vannet* 1999 JC 109.
[58] *Carmichael v B* 1991 JC 177.

17.4.3   It has been observed that such applications are strictly considered,[59] although the only statutory test is whether precognition on oath is reasonable in the circumstances.[60] In some cases the sheriff has taken the line that the procedure is limited to the case of the recalcitrant witness as in applications by the prosecutor.[61] However, the appeal court observed in a case decided on another point that a precognition on oath should have been applied for when an accused who was conducting his own defence was unable, due to mild dyslexia, to note the police officer's precognition, and the officer was unwilling to be tape recorded or to speak without a senior officer present.[62]

17.4.4   A precognition on oath is within the definition of a "statement" which may be used in evidence if admissible in subsequent proceedings under an exception to the hearsay rule.[63] If a party gives notice to the other of an intention to lead hearsay evidence as proof of its contents under the statutory exception,[64] the notice must be accompanied by a copy of the statement on which it is intended to rely.[65] The witness who has given the precognition on oath will have seen it when attending to sign the transcription of it in accordance with Act of Adjournal.[66] A precognition on oath has been used in cross-examination to attack the credibility of the witness who gives evidence inconsistent with it in court, and in that event the parts of the precognition which are consistent may be put to the witness in re-examination.[67]

Recovery of statements and precognitions

17.4.5   The prosecutor has an obligation to disclose to the defence any information which supports the defence case.[68] Historically, applications by the accused for production or recovery of statements or precognitions[69] taken by the prosecutor had been met with a blanket plea of confidentiality in the public interest, for the protection of the public who report crime, and the court had, in the main, upheld the prosecutor's objection.[70] However, that approach was examined, together with a number

---

[59]   Renton & Brown, *Criminal Procedure* (6th edn), paras 13-14 and 19-21.

[60]   1995 Act, s 291(1). That test was followed in its simple terms in *Brady v Lockhart* 1985 SCCR 349.

[61]   *Low v MacNeill* 1981 SCCR 243; *Cirignaco, Petitioner* 1986 SLT (Sh Ct) 11. In *Cirignaco* the attempt to obtain warrant for precognition on oath of a rape victim to take place during the week-long continuation of a petition for further examination, while competent, was always unlikely to succeed on grounds of procedural inexpedience, but failed on its merits too.

[62]   *Drummond, Petitioner* 1998 SLT 757. See also *HM Advocate v Campbell* 1996 JC 117.

[63]   1995 Act, s 262(1).

[64]   1995 Act, s 259. See para 8.7.

[65]   s 259(5) and Act of Adjournal (Criminal Procedure Rules) 1996, r 21.3 and Form 21.3.

[66]   Act of Adjournal (Criminal Procedure Rules) 1996, r 29.4(3)(b).

[67]   *Coyle v HM Advocate* 1994 SLT 133.

[68]   *McLeod v HM Advocate (No 2)* 1998 JC 67 at 77F–79C, affirming statements in *Slater v HM Advocate* 1928 JC 94, and *Downie v HM Advocate* 1952 JC 37, but disapproving the passage to the contrary in *Higgins v HM Advocate* 1990 SCCR 268.

[69]   A distinction was made between precognitions and statements in *HM Advocate v Ward* 1993 SLT 1202, the former being subject then to blanket confidentiality, but the latter being recoverable.

[70]   Faced with such objection the court had refused to order recovery of Crown precognitions and communications between the procurator-fiscal and the Crown office, and to disclose the identity of an informant: *Arthur v Lindsay* (1895) 22 R 417; *Donald v Hart* (1844) 6 D 1255; *Friel v Chief Constable of Strathclyde* 1981 SC 1; *Henderson v Robertson* (1853) 15 D 292 (re police informers); *D v NSPCC* [1978] AC 171 (in relation to informant of child neglect). *Cf Mills v Kelvin & James White Ltd* 1912 SC 995, where the Lord Advocate did not object. In *Cheshire County Council v C* [1995] 2 FLR 862 the Family division noted that unlike the position in England the file of the Scottish prosecuting authorities remained confidential at all times, but this comment pre-dates *McLeod v HM Advocate (No 2)* 1998 JC 67.

of other aspects of defence applications for recovery, and revised in *McLeod v HM Advocate (No 2)*,[71] a case in which the accused sought to recover numerous precognition forms completed by those present in licensed premises when they were raided by police in connection with suspected drug misuse offences. An order for production[72] will be granted if it will serve a proper purpose and it is in the interests of justice to do so.[73] This will involve a question of whether the evidence of which recovery is sought would be likely to be of material assistance to the proper presentation of the accused's defence.[74] The Crown may take an objection on grounds of confidentiality and the court will examine the conflicting public interests of protecting sources of information and securing a fair trial.[75] In summary cases it is the practice for police officers' statements to be copied to the defence to limit the intrusion on police time in giving precognitions, but precognoscing the officer is not thereby precluded if circumstances indicate that it will be appropriate to preparation of the defence. Statements and precognitions taken by the defence are clearly confidential, in keeping with the accused's right to silence, but if introduced by the defence during trial, the confidentiality is lost.[76]

17.5 WITNESS PRECOGNITION—CIVIL CASES

Precognition

There is no procedure in civil cases whereby a party may cite the witnesses of the other party for precognition. This occurs as a matter of practice only by invitation and agreement. **17.5.1**

Recovery of statements and precognitions in the hands of the other party

Procedurally an application may be made at common law or under the Administration of Justice (Scotland) Act 1972 for recovery of documents relevant to current civil proceedings (or proceedings likely to be taken) in the hands of the opposite party or a third party. Such a motion, if directed to statements or precognitions, is likely to be met with a plea of confidentiality, on the basis that the document was obtained *post litem motam*.[77] Actions taken in the Court of Session under the commercial procedure are an exception, where the court may order that parties disclose or exchange witness statements.[78] If a party intends to rely on the hearsay statement of a witness in a civil case in the Court of Session, application **17.5.2**

---

[71] 1998 JC 67. See also paras 10.9 and 18.2.

[72] Which should be sought by order for production rather than commission and diligence if the items are in the possession of the prosecutor: *McLeod v HM Advocate (No 2)* 1998 JC 67 at 69F.

[73] *McLeod v HM Advocate (No 2)* 1998 JC 67 at 80E–G.

[74] *McLeod v HM Advocate (No 2)* 1998 JC 67 at 80E–G. The court also held that this requirement was consistent with the accused's right to a fair trial in terms of Art 6 of the European Convention on Human Rights, as interpreted in relation to recovery of prosecution evidence in *Edwards v United Kingdom* Series A No 247-B (1993) 15 EHRR 417.

[75] *McLeod v HM Advocate (No 2)* 1998 JC 67 at 71F–G. See also para 10.9. An application may be made for the purpose of an appeal on the grounds of fresh evidence: *Barbour v HM Advocate* 1994 GWD 37-2169; *Porter, Petitioners*, 2000 GWD 2-46.

[76] Observed in *Wotherspoon v HM Advocate (No 1)* 1999 SLT 664.

[77] See paras 10.3 and 10.4.

[78] RCS, r 47.11(1)(b)(vii).

for leave should be made to the court.[79] That application should be accompanied by the statement, which must be lodged as a production, and if the application is opposed an explanatory affidavit in support of the motion is required.[80]

17.6 CITATION—GENERAL

17.6.1 All courts have power to compel the attendance of witnesses residing within their jurisdiction.[81] Attendance is ordered by citation and, if the witness is in Scotland, may be enforced by apprehension. In civil cases all witnesses are entitled to payment of travelling expenses before answering the citation. A person cited is not entitled to disregard the citation on the ground that he is not a competent witness,[82] or that he has no relevant evidence to give, although an application might be made to the court to cancel the citation of such a witness.[83] A peer must obey a citation.[84] It is doubtful whether the lower courts may issue warrant for the apprehension of a peer, but the Court of Justiciary or the Court of Session, as the case might be, would grant the necessary authority.[85] A witness who is in prison may be cited by normal means, and may be brought to court by the prison authorities if this is desirable in the interests of justice or for a public inquiry.[86]

17.7 CITATION—CRIMINAL CASES

Solemn

17.7.1 For a trial in the High Court warrant to cite witnesses is issued by the Clerk of Justiciary; where the trial is on indictment in the sheriff court it is issued by the sheriff-clerk.[87] The warrant may be executed by an officer of law, that is a macer, messenger-at-arms, sheriff officer, constable, person commissioned by Customs and Excise or employed by the police to assist with service, a prison officer (if service is to be effected upon a person in prison),[88] or any other person or classes of persons authorised by the Lord Advocate or Secretary of State.[89] Citation may

---

[79] RCS, r 36.8(3); OCR, r 29.3. However, the court's discretion to refuse to admit the statement is of limited, if any extent. In the Outer House cases of *Ebrahem v Ebrahem* 1989 SLT 808 and *Lobban v Philip* 1995 SCLR 1104 the court said that there was discretion to refuse the application to allow affidavit evidence if it was inappropriate to allow it, for example, because the evidence was critical to the case. In *McVinnie v McVinnie* 1995 SLT (Sh Ct) 81 and *Glaser v Glaser* 1997 SLT 456 the court held that there was no such discretion. See also para 15.3.

[80] RCS, r 36.8(4). In the sheriff court there is no express requirement for production but the statement would fall within the range of document and affidavit to which OCR r 29.11 refers.

[81] A warrant of citation issued in a sheriff court may be executed in any sheriffdom without endorsation, by implication from OCR, r 5.4.

[82] *Bryce* (1844) 2 Broun 119.

[83] See *HM Advocate v McDonald* 1989 SLT 627.

[84] *Fraser v Nicholl* (1840) 2 D 1254.

[85] Dickson, *Evidence* (3rd edn), para 1691.

[86] Criminal Justice Act 1961, s 29(1).

[87] Criminal Procedure (Scotland) Act 1995 ("1995 Act"), s 66(1).

[88] As to citation and attendance of a prisoner witness, see Renton & Brown, *Criminal Procedure* (6th edn), para 11-17.

[89] 1995 Act, ss 66(9) and 307(1). The accused does have a right to the services of the police for citation of defence witnesses, although, exceptionally, this might be achieved by agreement.

also be effected by post.[90] If postal citation is ineffective officers of law may proceed to serve,[91] but postal service need not be attempted first.[92] The officers of law may serve at any place in Scotland. There is no particular time in criminal proceedings by which the prosecutor should have cited witnesses and this may occur even during the trial.[93] Where a witness regularly cited fails to appear, if the court is satisfied that the witness was aware of the citation,[94] warrant may be granted for his apprehension and detention until the trial, and the same course may be followed if a witness is likely to abscond.[95]

Summary

In a summary trial the Act is sufficient warrant for the citation of witnesses,[96] **17.7.2** which means that no other warrant is required. Citation may be by post in accordance with the requirements of postal service[97] or at any place in Scotland by any officer of law. A witness who has been cited and fails to appear may be punished for contempt of court[98] and, if the court is satisfied that the witness was aware of the citation, may order that the witness be apprehended and detained.[99] A party who persistently delays in citation or, despite non-attendance by a witness after postal service at one trial diet, uses postal service again rather than service by officer of law, may not expect another adjournment if the witness again fails to attend.[100]

Witnesses outwith Scotland

A witness in England, Wales or Northern Ireland may be cited to attend a solemn **17.7.3** trial in Scotland.[101] While failure to obey the citation may be punished by the appropriate court in that country,[102] there seems to be no power to enforce attendance. If postal service in that country has been attempted and failed a party will be expected to attempt service by an officer before seeking an adjournment on the

---

[90] 1995 Act, s 66(3); Act of Adjournal (Criminal Procedure Rules) 1996, r 2.4(1). Unfortunately the Act of Adjournal (Criminal Procedure Rules) 1996, r 2.3 read with s 141 of the 1995 Act and r 2.4 read with r 2.5 create two different requirements for postal service. It is thought that this would be interpreted to allow both, by analogy with the reasoning in *Garrow v HM Advocate* 1999 JC 209, but the confusion is unfortunate. See also Renton & Brown, *Criminal Procedure* (6th edn), para 11-14.
[91] Act of Adjournal (Criminal Procedure Rules) 1996, r 2.4(2).
[92] *Garrow v HM Advocate* 1999 JC 209.
[93] *Garrow v HM Advocate* 1999 JC 209 and, *eg*, *Mellors v HM Advocate* 1999 SCCR 869.
[94] *HM Advocate v Bell* 1936 JC 89 (narrative of earlier proceedings) and the Criminal Procedure (Scotland) Act 1995, s 66(10). For an example of proof of citation on its facts, see *Mack v HM Advocate* 1999 SCCR 181.
[95] Hume, ii, 375. See also Renton & Brown, *Criminal Procedure* (6th edn), para 11-22.
[96] Criminal Procedure (Scotland) Act 1995 ("1995 Act"), s 140(1)(b).
[97] 1995 Act, s 140(2). Unfortunately the Act of Adjournal (Criminal Procedure Rules) 1996, r 2.3 read with s 141 of the 1995 Act and r 2.4 read with r 2.5 create different requirements for postal service. It is thought that this would be interpreted to allow both, by analogy with the reasoning in *Garrow v HM Advocate* 1999 JC 209, but the confusion is unfortunate. See also Renton & Brown, *Criminal Procedure* (6th edn), para 11-14.
[98] 1995 Act, s 155. For factual examples, see *Pirie v Hawthorn* 1962 SLT 291; *Orr v Annan* 1988 SLT 251.
[99] 1995 Act, s 156(1) and (3).
[100] *Dailley v Friel* 1999 GWD 10-452. See also *Sargeant, Petitioner* 1990 SLT 286; *Timney v Cardle* 1996 SLT 376.
[101] Writ of Subpoena Act 1805, s 3. The Act mentions only the Court of Justiciary, but its terms seem wide enough to include the lower courts.
[102] Writ of Subpoena Act 1805, s 3.

ground of the witness's non-appearance at the trial diet.[103] A witness in England may be cited to attend a summary trial if the complaint is endorsed by a court of summary jurisdiction there.[104] If the witness is further abroad from Scotland recourse may be had to the arrangements provided for by the Criminal Justice (International Co-operation) Act 1990,[105] but these carry no powers of enforcement. If the witness is outwith Scotland, consideration should be given to obtaining an order for evidence to be taken on commission by letters of request,[106] or, as a last resort, making an application for admission of the hearsay statement of the witness.[107]

17.8 CITATION—CIVIL

Court of Session

17.8.1   The interlocutor fixing a proof or a jury trial is warrant to cite witnesses in Scotland.[108] The citation[109] may be by messenger-at-arms,[110] or in a sheriff court district where there is no resident messenger-at-arms or in any of the islands of Scotland, by sheriff officer,[111] or by post by an agent for the party citing the witness.[112] If the witness fails to attend, it is competent to seek apprehension on letters of second diligence, or to ask the court, on proof that citation was effected, to grant warrant to messengers-at-arms to apprehend the witness and bring him to the proof.[113] Citation by a party litigant must be by messenger-at-arms, and the party litigant must apply to the court at least 12 weeks before the proof for the court to order the amount of caution to be fixed for the expenses of the witnesses that the party litigant intends to cite.[114] The party litigant must find the caution before instructing messengers-at-arms to serve the citations.[115]

Sheriff court

17.8.2   A copy of an interlocutor certified by the sheriff clerk allowing a proof or fixing the date for a jury trial is sufficient warrant to cite witnesses.[116] It may be executed in any part of Scotland by sheriff officer personally; by sheriff officer leaving it in a prescribed manner at a residential address or place of business; or by sheriff

---

[103] Act of Adjournal (Criminal Procedure Rules) 1996, r 2.7.

[104] Summary Jurisdiction (Process) Act 1881, ss 4 and 8. This Act contemplates a warrant issued by a court, which was necessary in 1881.

[105] s 2(1)(b) and (2), which permit service outwith the United Kingdom of a document which might competently be served on a witness in Scotland.

[106] See Chapter 14.

[107] See para 8.6.

[108] RCS, r 36.2(2).

[109] A very detailed form must be used, provided for in RCS, r 36.2(1) and Form 36.2-A.

[110] RCS, r 36.2(1)(b) and rr 16.1 and 16.3.

[111] Execution of Diligence (Scotland) Act 1926, s 1.

[112] RCS, r 36.2(1)(a) and rr 16.1 and 16.4.

[113] The latter is more commonly used; see annotations to r 36.2 in Greens Annotated Rules of the Court of Session.

[114] RCS, r 36.2(5)(a). The amount will vary according to the number of witnesses detailed in the application, and the period for which they are to be required. Application for variation of the amount of caution may be made if the party decides to cite fewer witnesses: r 36.2(6). There is no express provision for a party calling more than those listed.

[115] RCS, r 36.2(5)(b).

[116] OCR, r 29.7(3).

officer or solicitor by post.[117] The court may be asked to grant a second diligence to compel the attendance of a party.[118] If a witness, after citation, fails to answer the citation the court may, on the application of a party and on production of the certificate of citation, order that the witness be apprehended and brought to court, in which case the witness will be liable for the expenses of the procedure.[119] If the witness having been cited and paid travelling expenses fails to attend the diet the court may, without application by a party, make an order for the witness to pay a penalty of up to £250 if no reasonable excuse for non-attendance is offered and sustained.[120]

Witnesses outside Scotland

If the witness is in England, Wales or Northern Ireland a special warrant may **17.8.3** be granted by the Court of Session for attendance of the witness to a proof, trial or commission in proceedings in that court.[121] The application may require to be supported by an affidavit,[122] and the grant is entirely a matter of discretion.[123] Warrant may not be granted if the witness is to opinion only.[124] A witness who does not obey the citation may be punished by the court there,[125] but attendance cannot be enforced. If the witness is required for proceedings in the sheriff court,[126] or if such a witness is unlikely to answer the citation, evidence on commission by letters of request should be used to secure the evidence of the witness.[127]

17.9 OTHER TRIBUNALS

Arbitration

Requirements for exchange of witness details or statements may be agreed **17.9.1** between the parties to an arbitration when the submission to arbitration is made. Otherwise the arbiter has no power to insist upon such exchange. It may be possible for a party to arbitration to seek a statutory order from the court for disclosure of names of witnesses.[128] Arbiters have no power to compel the attendance of witnesses. A warrant to cite must be obtained from the Court of Session or the sheriff,[129] and compliance with the citation may be enforced by the sheriff.[130] An

---

[117] OCR, r 29.7(1). If the sheriff officer deposits the citation at the witness's address or affixes it to the door there, a postal copy must also be sent: OCR, r 29.7(2).

[118] OCR, r 29.9.

[119] OCR, r 29.10(1).

[120] OCR, r 29.10(2).

[121] Attendance of Witnesses Act 1854, s 1; Evidence (Proceedings in Other Jurisdictions) Act 1975, s 4.

[122] *Macdonald v Highland Railway Co* (1892) 20 R 217 (affidavit required); *Pirie v Caledonian Railway Co* (1890) 17 R 608 (affidavit not required, but certificate by solicitor lodged).

[123] *Henderson v North British Railway Co* (1870) 8 M 833; *Gellatly v Law* (1865) 4 M 267.

[124] *Macdonald v Highland Railway Co* (1892) 20 R 217; *Gilmour v North British Railway Co* (1893) 1 SLT 370.

[125] Attendance of Witnesses Act 1854, s 3.

[126] Where there is no method for effective citation of witnesses furth of Scotland.

[127] See Chapter 14.

[128] Administration of Justice (Scotland) Act 1972, s 1(1A) and *Anderson v Gibb* 1993 SLT 726.

[129] Dickson, Evidence (3rd edn), para 1704; *Caird, Petitioner* (1865) 3 M 851.

[130] *Blaikie v Aberdeen Railway Co* (1852) 14 D 590.

application for warrant to cite a witness in England was refused, apparently on the ground that the Attendance of Witnesses Act 1854 does not apply to arbitrations.[131] Where the witness is in England, Wales or Northern Ireland the Court of Session may grant a commission to take his evidence.[132]

Church courts

17.9.2 The sheriff may grant warrant to cite witnesses to attend the courts of the Church of Scotland and, if necessary, letters of second diligence,[133] and the opinion has been expressed that the sheriff may also do so in the case of voluntary churches.[134]

Statutory tribunals

17.9.3 Most statutory tribunals have, in their rules of procedure, power to cite,[135] and may there be given power to punish failure to attend, but are unlikely to have power to order apprehension.[136] It may be that a tribunal can seek grant of letters of second diligence from the sheriff.[137] The tribunal may have discretion to limit the number of witnesses,[138] and the way in which the examination or cross-examination is conducted,[139] or may leave the matter to the parties.[140] In proceedings against a solicitor before the Scottish Solicitors' Disciplinary Tribunal lists of witnesses[141] must be exchanged by the complainer and respondent[142] and the Court of Session or the sheriff may grant warrant to cite witnesses and letters of second diligence.[143]

17.10 EVIDENCE REQUIRED FOR FOREIGN COURTS

Criminal

17.10.1 The Lord Advocate may receive a request from a foreign court or tribunal exercising criminal jurisdiction, or a foreign prosecuting authority, for assistance in obtaining evidence here in connection with criminal proceedings or a criminal investigation in the requesting country or territory.[144] If the Lord Advocate is

---

[131] *Highland Railway Co v Mitchell* (1868) 6 M 896.

[132] *John Nimmo & Son Ltd* (1905) 8 F 173. In one case the court granted commission to take evidence to lie *in retentis*: *Galloway Water Power Co v Carmichael* 1937 SC 135.

[133] *Presbytery of Lews v Fraser* (1874) 1 R 888.

[134] *Presbytery of Lews v Fraser* (1874) 1 R 888 at 894.

[135] See Cross & Tapper, *Evidence* (9th edn), p 21, MacSporran & Young, *Commission and Diligence*, paras 12.5–12.15.

[136] As to courts martial, see the Naval Discipline Act 1957; Army Act 1955; Rules of Procedure (Army) 1972 (SI 1972/316), as amended; Air Force Act 1955; Rules of Procedure (Air Force) 1972 (SI 1972/419), as amended. Evidence for a court martial abroad may be obtained in Scotland by letter of request in terms of the Criminal Justice (International Co-operation) Act 1990, s 11. See para 17.10.

[137] The main ground of the decision in *Presbytery of Lews v Fraser* (1874) 1 R 888, that the sheriff may on the application of a presbytery grant letters of second diligence, was that a presbytery is a court recognised by law. The same reasoning may be applied to statutory tribunals. The same is the case in England: *Currie v Chief Constable of Surrey* [1982] 1 All ER 89.

[138] See, *eg*, *Noorani v Merseyside TEC Ltd* [1999] IRLR 184.

[139] As in *Errington v Wilson* 1995 SC 550.

[140] *Aberdeen Steak Houses Group v Ibrahim* [1988] ICR 550.

[141] As to the calling of witnesses, see the Solicitors (Scotland) Act 1980, s 52 and Sched 4, para 11.

[142] Scottish Solicitors' Discipline Tribunal Procedure Rules 1989, r 7.

[143] Solicitors (Scotland) Act 1980, s 52 and Sched 4, para 12.

[144] Criminal Justice (International Co-operation) Act 1990 ("1990 Act"), s 4(1).

satisfied that an offence under the law of that country[145] has been committed or there are reasonable grounds for suspecting so, and that proceedings or an investigation have commenced, on which a certificate from an appropriate authority of the requesting country is conclusive,[146] he may nominate a court to hear the evidence in order to give effect to the request.[147] Although the request may be at an early stage in proceedings, it is not intended that the request be used to obtain discovery such as precognition or deposition as compared to trial testimony.[148] A witness may be cited to attend, apprehended and punished for non-attendance, in the same way as any witness in summary proceedings.[149] A witness may claim that he is not compellable according to the law in Scotland[150] or according to the law of the requesting country.[151] If the latter, the witness is excused if the claim is conceded by the requesting party,[152] failing which the evidence is heard but not transmitted until the matter is determined in the country from which the request originates.[153] A witness will not be compellable to give evidence in the capacity of Crown employee[154] or if giving evidence would be prejudicial to the security of the United Kingdom, to which a certificate of the Secretary of State is conclusive.[155]

17.10.2 The Scottish prosecutor participates in the hearing of the evidence,[156] and may be joined by, from the requesting country, the prosecutor, judge, parties and their lawyers and any other person who applies for leave of the court,[157] which leave is not granted without giving the requesting party an opportunity to be heard.[158] It is thought that the witness has no entitlement to be represented, since that would be contrary to the position of an ordinary witness,[159] but the court has on one reported occasion taken the unusual step of directing that a legal representative of the witness may be present.[160]

Civil

17.10.3 When evidence is required from a witness in Scotland for civil proceedings[161] in a

---

[145] A fiscal offence is not included unless the request is from a commonwealth country or similar conduct would constitute an offence here: 1990 Act, s 4(3).

[146] 1990 Act, s 4(4).

[147] 1990 Act, s 4(2).

[148] *Lord Advocate, Petitioner* 1994 SLT 852, following *Rio Tinto Zinc Corporation v Westinghouse Electric Corporation* [1978] AC 547 and *Re State of Norway's Application (Nos 1 & 2)* [1990] 1 AC 723.

[149] 1990 Act, s 4(6) and Sched 1, paras 1 and 2.

[150] See Chapter 13.

[151] 1990 Act, Sched 1, para 4(1).

[152] 1990 Act, Sched 1, para 4(2).

[153] 1990 Act, Sched 1, para 4(3).

[154] 1990 Act, Sched 1, para 4(5).

[155] 1990 Act, Sched 1, para 4(4).

[156] Act of Adjournal (Criminal Procedure Rules) 1996, r 36.8(1).

[157] See r 36.8(1) for the extensive list of persons who may participate.

[158] r 36.8(2).

[159] See *Carmichael v B* 1991 JC 177.

[160] *Lord Advocate, Petitioner* 1994 SLT 852, an application where the Scottish court was hearing evidence from a witness at the request of a court in the USA. A question arose as to whether the testimony was truly for the trial or akin to a deposition, and, since from the letter of request it seemed to combine the two, the representation was directed in order to ensure fairness.

[161] *ie* proceedings in any civil or commercial matter (Evidence (Proceedings in Other Jurisdictions) Act 1975, s 9(1)) determined according to the law and practice of the receiving court: *Re State of Norway's Application (Nos 1 & 2)* [1990] 1 AC 723 at 806F and see Lord Woolf's remarks in the Appeal Court reported at 775. The proceedings may be ongoing or contemplated: s 1(b).

court in another part of the United Kingdom, or a foreign court,[162] or, if included by Order in Council, in proceedings before an international tribunal,[163] the Court of Session may make appropriate provision for obtaining the evidence in Scotland for use in those proceedings.[164] This includes the examination of witnesses orally or in writing,[165] but should not be used to obtain discovery such as one would obtain through precognition or deposition.[166] The application is by petition[167] and should be accompanied by a letter of request and certificate from an officer of the requesting court if it is elsewhere in the United Kingdom, or from a duly authorised diplomatic or consular representative of another country.[168] A witness may claim that he is not compellable according to the law in Scotland,[169] or in the country of the requesting court, or if the evidence would be prejudicial to the security of the United Kingdom.[170] If the claim based on the law of the receiving country is not conceded the evidence of such a witness is taken separately and retained until the matter of the claim is determined in the requesting country, after which the evidence is sent on to that court or back to the witness if the claim is upheld.[171]

---

[162] Evidence (Proceedings in Other Jurisdictions) Act 1975 ("1975 Act"), s 1.

[163] 1975 Act, s 6. The Act also applies to the European Patent Office: Patents Act 1977, s 92(1).

[164] 1975 Act, s 2. The procedure is governed by RCS, Chap 66. This procedure does not preclude an application under the Administration of Justice (Scotland) Act 1972, s 1 for recovery of evidence in Scotland for use in proceedings outwith Scotland: *Iomega Corporation v Myrica (UK) Ltd* 1998 SC 636 (overruling *Dailey Petroleum Services Corporation v Pioneer Oil Tools Ltd* 1994 SLT 757).

[165] 1975 Act, s 2(2)(a). In England an application to record the evidence on videotape, although not expressly permitted by the rules of court, was granted against a background of very full argument of the issues in the requesting court and the receiving court: *J Barber & Sons v Lloyd's Underwriters* [1986] 2 All ER 845.

[166] *Rio Tinto Zinc Corporation v Westinghouse Electric Corporation* [1978] AC 547 and *Re State of Norway's Application (Nos 1 & 2)* [1990] 1 AC 723, the principle of which was followed in relation to the criminal legislation in *Lord Advocate, Petitioner* 1994 SLT 852.

[167] RCS, r 66.3(1).

[168] RCS, r 66.3(2). If the application is from the European Patent Office, RCS, r 66.7 applies.

[169] See Chapter 13.

[170] Evidence (Proceedings in Other Jurisdictions) Act 1975, s 3. A certificate signed by the Secretary of State is conclusive on this matter: s 3(3).

[171] RCS, r 66.6.

CHAPTER 18

REAL EVIDENCE

18.1 GENERAL

There is little profit in attempting to reach a logically impregnable definition of real **18.1.1** evidence. Such a definition either is departed from or unduly restricts the discussion of practical questions. Thus Dickson,[1] having defined real evidence as "evidence derived from things", immediately proceeds to treat the things as the evidence. In Cross & Tapper[2] it is observed that there is general agreement that the term "covers the production of material objects for inspection by the judge or jury in court, but it is debatable how much further the term should be extended." This definition excludes things upon which expert witnesses base opinions but which are not brought to court and things which the tribunal may never have any opportunity of inspecting at all because they cannot be moved or because they have perished. The term is examined here in a wider sense to include a thing, which may be a human being, any features of the thing which are significant, and the inferences to be drawn from the existence of the thing or from its significant features. It may, for example, include broken glass and dried mud left on a road after a motorcar collision, their exact positions on the road, and the inferences which arise from their existence and positions, or the cut behind the right ear of the victim of an assault and the inference that he was attacked from behind by a right-handed person, or the bloodstained clothing which can be seen by the court, but is invaluably supplemented by forensic analysis. Further, an exclamation which is part of the *res gestae* may be thought of as real evidence,[3] and so is the fact that the accused ran from the scene of the crime.

Matters which in the past might have been left to the recollection of a witness **18.1.2** may now be the subject of real evidence in the form of an automatic recording.[4] The court has been quick to admit recordings as an extension of[5] and supplement to[6] the

---

[1] Dickson, *Evidence* (3rd edn), para 1815.
[2] *Evidence* (9th edn), p 48.
[3] See para 8.5.
[4] Most automatic recordings such as audio and video tapes, and matter stored on computer disk, fall within the broad statutory definitions of "document" (Criminal Procedure (Scotland) Act 1995, s 279 and Sched 8; Civil Evidence (Scotland) Act 1988, s 9), and are considered further in Chapter 21.
[5] *Hopes and Lavery v HM Advocate* 1960 JC 104.
[6] *HM Advocate v Swift* 1983 SCCR 204.

oral evidence of a witness,[7] but preserves the right to hear oral evidence despite the existence of a recording.[8] While such evidence is physically produced in court, mere sight of the thing (*eg* a video cassette or computer disk) is not of value and may not enable the witness to identify it.[9] Its value is in it being seen, heard or analysed by a witness,[10] or viewed or heard by the court. Audio recordings are frequently accompanied by a written transcript which should be authenticated,[11] but need not be spoken to by the maker of the transcript.[12] If there are doubts as to the accuracy or clarity of the recording or the accuracy of the transcript the court reverts to the recollection of the witness.[13]

18.1.3   The question of drawing inferences from things and their features is dealt with under opinion evidence[14] and circumstantial evidence[15] and is mentioned only briefly at the end of this chapter,[16] which is mainly concerned with the recovery of the thing when it is not in the possession of the party desiring to use it,[17] the necessity for lodging it before the trial or proof,[18] and the necessity for its production at the trial or proof.[19] Recovery of evidence in general must be considered against the terms of Article 8 of the European Convention on Human Rights which enshrines the right to respect for private and family life, home and correspondence. Any interference by a public authority under Article 8(2) must be in accordance with law and necessary in a democratic society in the interests of national security, public safety or economic well-being, prevention of disorder or crime, protection of health or morals, or protection of rights and freedom of others.

18.2 RECOVERY—CRIMINAL

Person of accused

18.2.1   There is an important difference in the powers of recovery before detention or arrest, when the police do not have sufficient evidence to justify that detention or arrest, and after detention or arrest, when they are trying to obtain further evi-

---

[7]   And in the case of, *eg,* radar the recording can produce information that is better than human effort: *The Statue of Liberty* [1968] 1 WLR 739.

[8]   *HM Advocate v Swift* 1983 SCCR 204. A similar approach is taken in relation to notes made by a witness: *Deb v Normand* 1997 SLT 107, and see Chapter 21.

[9]   *Heywood v Ross* 1994 SLT 195.

[10]   As in *Bowie v Tudhope* 1986 SCCR 205, where the identification of the accused was by police officers who identified him from a CCTV video recording, although they had no direct knowledge of the crime.

[11]   As with a copy document, in terms of the Act of Adjournal Criminal Procedure Rules 1996, r 26. If the record of a judicial examination is being produced the taped record must be transcribed: Criminal Procedure (Scotland) Act 1995, ss 37(4) and 68(1).

[12]   *Cf Hopes and Lavery v HM Advocate* 1960 JC 104, in which the evidence of the transcriber was led, and admitted as that of a skilled witness.

[13]   *HM Advocate v Swift* 1983 SCCR 204.

[14]   See Chapter 16.

[15]   See Chapter 6.

[16]   See para 18.6.

[17]   See paras 18.2 and 18.3.

[18]   See para 18.4.

[19]   See para 18.5.

dence. A principle applicable to both situations is that a person is not bound to supply evidence against himself or herself.[20]

Before detention or arrest the right is limited to such observation as is pos- **18.2.2** sible without interfering with the person. So it is not at that stage competent to search[21] a person without express warrant or consent[22] or to take fingerprints[23] or scrapings from the person's fingernails.[24] The only exception might be in situations of extreme urgency where the evidence is at risk of being lost.[25] Nevertheless, valuable evidence may be obtained without interference. For example, the observed conduct or appearance of a person together with the observed circumstances often are sufficient to give rise to the necessary suspicion to justify detention.[26] On the other hand, after detention or arrest the accused who is in custody may be searched,[27] and may be required to provide relevant physical data (including prints) which it is reasonably appropriate to take given the circumstances of the offence of which the accused is suspected or charged,[28] and to have samples taken from external parts of the body,[29] all without individual warrant[30] and without consent.

A person who is not subject to these statutory grounds for search and recovery of **18.2.3** evidence[31] (normally an accused who is not in custody or a person who is not yet a suspect)[32] may nevertheless be the subject of an application for warrant to take evidence

---

[20] *Adair v McGarry* 1933 JC 72 at 88. It might be argued that this principle has been infringed in a number of respects in modern criminal procedure, such as the Criminal Procedure (Scotland) Act 1995, s 36 (the judicial examination process), s 148 (the intermediate diet), and s 257 (the duty to seek to agree evidence). In *Brown v Stott* 2000 JC 328 a distinction was made between statutory compulsion to make an incriminating statement, which was held to be contrary to Article 6 of the ECHR, and compulsion to provide real evidence which might prove incriminating, which was not. The case is under appeal to the Privy Council.
[21] Indeed if the person voluntarily co-operates with a police request for access to property or person it has been said that there is no search at all: *eg Davidson v Brown* 1990 JC 324; *Devlin v Normand* 1992 SCCR 875.
[22] *Adair v McGarry* 1933 JC 72 at 90; *McGovern v HM Advocate* 1950 JC 33 at 36.
[23] *Adamson v Martin* 1916 SC 319; *Adair v McGarry* 1933 JC 72 at 79, 90.
[24] *McGovern v HM Advocate* 1950 JC 3 .
[25] In *Bell v Hogg* 1967 JC 49 an officer took rubbings from the hands of persons suspected of being involved in the theft of copper, and this evidence was admitted despite the failure to caution the suspects, since any deposits of copper could have been disposed of by hand-washing. Whether a similar approach would be taken now that suspects can be detained and recovery warranted under the Criminal Procedure (Scotland) Act 1995, s 18(6) is not clear, but in relation to property the situation of urgency can still provide justification for recovery without warrant or detention: *Edgley v Barbour* 1995 SLT 711.
[26] Under the Criminal Procedure (Scotland) Act 1995, ss 13–15.
[27] Criminal Procedure (Scotland) Act 1995, s 14(7) re detention and arrest; *McGovern v HM Advocate* 1950 JC 33 at 36; *Adair v McGarry* 1933 JC 72 at 80 re arrest.
[28] Criminal Procedure (Scotland) Act 1995, s 18(2) and (7A); *Adair v McGarry* 1933 JC 72 and *Forrester v HM Advocate* 1952 JC 28 provided authority for post-arrest fingerprinting and limited examination of a cut arm, respectively. The purpose must be with a view to connecting the accused with the crime for which he has been arrested (or detained): *Adair v McGarry* 1933 JC 72, followed in *Namyslak v HM Advocate* 1995 SLT 528.
[29] Criminal Procedure (Scotland) Act 1995, s 18(6), samples of pubic hair excluded.
[30] Criminal Procedure (Scotland) Act 1995, s 18 is the general statutory authority, which builds upon the developments at common law in the cases cited in this paragraph.
[31] Which followed upon recommendations of the Scottish Law Commission in their report on *Blood Group Tests, DNA Tests and Related Matters* (Scot Law Com No 120), Pt II.
[32] *eg* in *Smith v Cardle* 1994 SLT 514 the person was an identical twin and the warrant was to take his precise measurements to compare with a video of the crime, but on appearance alone that person was no more the suspect than his twin. In *McGlennan v Kelly* 1989 SLT 832, the person had been committed for trial and was on bail when the warrant was sought and granted.

from the person. In deciding whether to grant a warrant in such circumstances the court must consider the balance between the public interest in the recovery of evidence relevant to the identification and prosecution of a perpetrator of crime and protection of the interest of the individual named in the warrant from undue or unnecessary invasion of person.[33] The test is not further prescribed, but it appears that the court will consider the speciality of the circumstances leading to the application[34] and the invasiveness of the process for which warrant is sought.[35] The right to privacy of person and property enshrined in Article 8 of the European Convention on Human Rights must now be taken into account, and all pre-existing authorities read with that in mind.

18.2.4   Evidence obtained from the person may be used in proof of any offence arising from the same *species facti* (precise circumstances of the event),[36] but evidence obtained under the statutory power of recovery, and any further evidence derived from that—for example, a report of forensic analysis—must be destroyed when a decision is made not to prosecute, or when proceedings are taken but the accused is not convicted.[37] An exception is made if the evidence incorporates evidential material lawfully held in relation to another person[38] or is of the same kind as record material already lawfully held by police in relation to the person.[39] The court has noted that if evidence may be retained under these provisions, there is no express limitation upon the use to which it may be put in evidence, but this was before Article 8 had direct application to the prosecuting authority.[40]

18.2.5   Sometimes a witness asked to identify the perpetrator asks that the suspect speak in order to assist the identification. Guidelines for identification parades do not provide for the witness to make such a request.[41] If such a request is made it is thought that the suspect should be cautioned, on the ground that by doing so he is supplying evidence against himself.[42] Where at the request of the police an accused gave a specimen of his handwriting, the specimen was held to be properly admitted for comparison with forged documents, but the accused had been told that he need not do so unless he wished, and that the specimen might be used in evidence.[43] In the same case it was held competent to use the accused's signature on a fingerprint form, adhibited without warning, on the ground that it was not taken for purposes of comparison and was in the same position as any casual writing by the accused. Whether a warning is necessary before consent to search or other process is obtained and acted upon will depend upon whether suspicion has fallen upon the person.[44]

---

[33] *Hay v HM Advocate* 1968 JC 40, a full bench decision, following *Adair v McGarry* 1933 JC 72. The invasion of privacy of person argument is strengthened by Art 8 of the ECHR.

[34] *Hay v HM Advocate* 1968 JC 40. In this case warrant was granted for detailed dental impressions, and photographs and examination of the mouth to be taken from one resident of an approved school, in a murder case where the victim's body bore a bite mark. Impressions taken by consent from all the school residents had eliminated all but Hay from the inquiry. See *Morris v MacNeill* 1991 SLT 607; 1991 SCCR 722 and commentary at 726. While *Hay* was a serious case, and the circumstances were special, these have not survived as requisite factors in subsequent cases: *Hughes v Normand* 1992 SCCR 908, 1993 SCCR 69 and commentary at 74.

[35] *HM Advocate v Milford* 1973 SLT 12; *Lees v Weston* 1989 JC 35.

[36] *McKie v HM Advocate* 1958 JC 24.

[37] Criminal Procedure (Scotland) Act 1995 ("1995 Act"), s 18(3).

[38] 1995 Act, s 18(4)(a).

[39] 1995 Act, s 18(4)(b).

[40] *HM Advocate v Shepherd* 1997 SLT 891.

[41] Guidelines for the Conduct of Identification Parades, Scottish Home and Health Department.

[42] *Adair v McGarry* 1933 JC 72 at 88, 89. On confessions, see Chapter 9.

[43] *Davidson v HM Advocate* 1951 JC 33.

[44] *Brown v Glen* 1998 SLT 115. This matters only if the police are not entitled to search under the Criminal Procedure (Scotland) Act 1995, s 18, or another statutory ground.

Things

In situations of urgency where the evidence is at substantial risk of disappearing **18.2.6** the police may search without a warrant.[45] The procurator-fiscal may also, by the hands of the police, take possession of an article without warrant if the custodier of it consents.[46] Apart from these two situations at common law the police are not entitled without a warrant to take possession of an article from a third party, or from an accused who is not in custody.[47] In some situations statute provides for search without warrant.[48] Such provisions are construed strictly,[49] and any attempt to fish for evidence may render the search irregular,[50] but the irregularity may be excused and the evidence admitted.[51] A person searched under a statutory power need not be asked to consent or warned before the search.[52] Warrant may be granted to search for stolen goods of a specified nature in the premises of a person who has not been apprehended or charged.[53] A warrant must be precise in the sense that it authorises search for and seizure of documents and other articles tending to establish guilt of the specified crime.[54] If the police in executing it come across an article clearly connecting the accused with another crime, they may probably seize it on the ground that, if they do not do so, the owner will dispose of it as soon as their backs are turned.[55] However, they are not entitled to carry off a mass of papers and weed through them to see if they can find evidence of another crime.[56]

It has been the practice of the Crown to make available to the defence any **18.2.7** document likely to assist the defence,[57] and indeed this is recognised to be in the nature of an obligation.[58] A bench of five judges had now confirmed that the defence are entitled to seek recovery by way of an order of the court for production by the Crown,[59] or commission and diligence for recovery from the Crown or a third party.[60] However, if such application is made it will be granted merely upon the *ex parte* motion of the defence agent. The defence must explain the basis for the request

---

[45] *HM Advocate v McGuigan* 1936 JC 16, and see, *eg, Edgley v Barbour* 1995 SLT 711.

[46] *Watson v Muir* 1938 JC 181. Much stolen property is recovered in this way.

[47] *Lawrie v Muir* 1950 JC 19; *Fairley v Fishmongers of London* 1951 JC 14.

[48] *eg* Misuse of Drugs Act 1971, s 23(2); Civic Government (Scotland) Act 1982, s 60(1).

[49] *Wither v Reid* 1980 JC 7.

[50] Although the many reported appeals arising from searches under the Misuse of Drugs Act 1971, s 23(2), when all circumstances are considered, rarely succeed, with the exception *Lucas v Lockhart* (1980) SCCR Supp 256 being frequently distinguished.

[51] Applying the test in *Lawrie v Muir* 1950 JC 19. See para 1.7.

[52] *Rees v Lees* 1997 SLT 872, following *McGovern v HM Advocate* 1950 JC 33.

[53] *Stewart v Roach* 1950 SC 318, where *Bell v Black and Morrison* (1865) 5 Irv 57, was explained. See *HM Advocate v McKay* 1961 JC 47.

[54] *Stewart v Roach* 1950 SC 318, where *Bell v Black and Morrison* (1865) 5 Irv 57, was explained. See *HM Advocate v McKay* 1961 JC 47.

[55] *HM Advocate v Hepper* 1958 JC 39. In *Drummond v HM Advocate* 1992 SCCR 290 the evidence of one police officer was to the effect that items were found incidentally while he was carrying out a search under the warrant, while the other said that he was primarily looking for goods stolen in another offence to which the warrant did not relate. The evidence of the latter was held to be inadmissible, but this did not preclude the evidence of the former being put to the jury.

[56] *HM Advocate v Turnbull* 1951 JC 96.

[57] *Downie v HM Advocate* 1952 JC 37.

[58] *McLeod v HM Advocate (No 2)* 1998 JC 67, a full bench decision. The suggestion in *Higgins v HM Advocate* 1990 SCCR 268 at 269B that there was no such obligation has been denied by successive Lords Advocate in practice and is dissapproved in *McLeod* at 79.

[59] Observed by the Lord Justice-General (Hope) in *McLeod v HM Advocate (No 2)* 1998 JC 67 at 69E.

[60] *McLeod v HM Advocate (No 2)* 1998 JC 67. This had been the effect of *Downie v HM Advocate* 1952 JC 37; *HM Advocate v Hasson* 1971 JC 35; *Hemming v HM Advocate* 1997 JC 140.

and the application will be granted only if the court is satisfied that the order will serve a proper purpose and that it is in the interest of justice to grant it. This involves an assessment of relevance to the charge and defence and materiality to the proper preparation or presentation of the accused's defence to the charge.[61] While the case law is concerned primarily with the recovery of documents there is no reason to restrict it to property of that nature and it would apply to any object, provided that the tests of materiality and relevance are satisfied. If the tests are not met and the order is therefore refused, this is not inherently unfair to the accused,[62] and if it emerges later that a material item has not been accessible to the defence the matter can be dealt with by allowing an appropriate remedy such as adjournment or desertion.[63]

18.3 RECOVERY—CIVIL

Persons

18.3.1   In an action of damages for personal injuries the court may, and, if asked, normally does, ordain the pursuer to submit for examination by a doctor selected by the defenders,[64] assuming that a request to submit voluntarily has not been fulfilled. Frequently the pursuer attends at the doctor's consulting room, but in normal circumstances will not be ordained to go far from home.[65] A pursuer has been ordained to submit to examination before the closing of the record,[66] and proceedings may be delayed to require a pursuer to submit for examination.[67] Examination is normally by an appropriate medical practitioner.[68] It may be the case that examination by another appropriate person would be ordered,[69] having regard to the defender's need to obtain the information for the proper conduct of the case, the qualifications and reputation of the person, the degree of invasion of the pursuer's privacy and the safeguards for confidentiality of medical and other information.[70]

18.3.2   In consistorial causes an order has been made for examination of a party,[71] but where proof had been allowed on the defender's plea that the action was incompetent because the pursuer was of unsound mind, it was held that no order for examination of the pursuer should be made until the defender had established a *prima facie* case.[72] In a nullity case refusal to submit to examination infers an

---

[61]   *McLeod v HM Advocate (No 2)* 1998 JC 67 at 80E.

[62]   *McLeod v HM Advocate (No 2)* 1998 JC 67 at 77C after considering Art 6 of the European Convention on Human Rights and *Edwards v United Kingdom*, 25 November 1992; Series A, No 247-B (1993) 15 EHRR 417.

[63]   *McLeod v HM Advocate* 1998 JC 67 at 80B–C.

[64]   *McDonald v Western SMT Co* 1945 SC 47.

[65]   *McDonald v Western SMT Co* 1945 SC 47.

[66]   *Smyth v Gow* (1895) 2 SLT 473.

[67]   *Junner v North British Railway Co* (1877) 4 R 686; *Starr v National Coal Board* [1977] 1 WLR 63.

[68]   And in *Rawlinson v Initial Property Maintenance Ltd* 1998 SLT (Sh Ct) 54, the sheriff considered that examination by a person who was not medically qualified was an unwarranted invasion of privacy.

[69]   Observed in *McLaren v Remploy Ltd* 1996 SLT 382.

[70]   These factors (or the absence of them) led to failure of the application in *Mearns v Smedvig Ltd* (unreported, 25 November 1998).

[71]   *X v Y* 1922 SLT 15 (OH) (an action of adherence and aliment where the defence was refusal to consummate and examination of the pursuer was ordered); *AB or D v CD* (1908) 15 SLT 911 (OH) (a declarator of nullity on the ground of impotency where examination of the defender was ordered).

[72]   *AB v CB* 1937 SC 696. In *Hardie v Hardie* 1993 SCLR 60 a sheriff's call for a report under the Matrimonial Proceedings (Children) Act 1958, s 11(1) was held to be incompetent when it called specifically for information as to a party's mental health rather than the ability of the party in the circumstances to care for the child.

admission of incapacity,[73] and in any other case would probably affect the burden of proof.

At common law no one could be compelled to give a sample of blood for test-ing,[74] and a party had to be clear as to the implications of consenting before doing so.[75] Now[76] statute provides that the court may, whether or not an application is made, request a party to provide blood or other body fluid or tissue for laboratory analysis,[77] and request a party to consent to the taking of such sample from a child.[78] The court cannot compel a party to comply with the request, but where a party fails or refuses to comply, providing the sample in or prevents its analysis, the court may draw from that refusal or failure such adverse inference, if any, in relation to the subject-matter of the proceedings, as seems appropriate.[79] This pro-vision is used most commonly in proceedings where parentage is an issue,[80] but applies in all civil proceedings. It has been decided that the court may draw an inference that perfects the opponent's case, but it is entirely within the court's dis-cretion to decide whether to draw any inference at all.[81] If evidence of blood test-ing has already been carried out for another purpose, commission and diligence may be sought for recovery of the result of that testing.[82] **18.3.3**

The court has no power to order a witness, as distinct from a party, to submit to exam-ination, and the result is that evidence founded on an examination for one side has been held inadmissible unless the witness is willing to submit to examination for the other.[83] If evidence from medical examination or blood testing is sought from a person who is outwith Scotland the court may be asked to grant letters of request[84] for such recovery addressed to a court where the person is.[85] However, these letters may only be granted in respect of recovery which the court here could order,[86] so "any person" in effect would mean "any party" since the court cannot order such recovery from a witness. **18.3.4**

Things

Things, other than documents,[87] could not be recovered by diligence under a spec-ification at common law.[88] The proper method at common law was by motion for **18.3.5**

---

[73] Fraser, *Husband and Wife* (2nd edn), Vol I, 104. Clive, *The Law of Husband and Wife in Scotland* (4th edn), para 23.065.

[74] *Whitehall v Whitehall* 1958 SC 252, followed in *Torrie v Turner* 1990 SLT 718.

[75] *Borthwick v Borthwick* 1929 SLT 57, 596; *Davidson v Davidson* (1860) 22 D 749.

[76] Following recommendations of the Scottish Law Commission in their report on *Blood Group Tests, DNA Tests and Related Matters* (Scot Law Com No 120), Pt III.

[77] Law Reform (Miscellaneous Provisions) (Scotland) Act 1990, s 70(1)(a).

[78] 1990 Act, s 70(1)(b).

[79] *Imre v Mitchell* 1958 SC 439.

[80] See Chapter 28.

[81] *Smith v Greenhill* 1993 SCLR 776.

[82] *Docherty v McGlynn* 1985 SLT 237. An earlier report at 1983 SLT 645 deals with the issue of con-sent to blood sampling from a child, a matter now governed by the Law Reform (Parent and Child) (Scotland) Act 1986, s 6 and Children (Scotland) Act 1995, s 1(3). See also Chapter 28.

[83] *Borthwick v Borthwick* 1929 SLT 57, 596; *Davidson v Davidson* (1860) 22 D 749.

[84] As to letters of request, see Chapter 14.

[85] RCS, r 35.15(2)(c) and (d), OCR, r 28.14 (c) and (d) in depending actions in the Court of Session or sheriff court respectively. In actions not yet commenced application would be by petition to the Court of Session, or summary application in the sheriff court, Act of Sederunt (Summary Applications, Statutory Application and Appeals etc Rules) 1999 (SI 1999/929) r 3.1.2.

[86] RCS, r 35.15(2); OCR, r 28.14(2).

[87] As to recovery of documents, see Chapter 21.

[88] *Mactaggart v Mackillop* 1938 SLT 559 (OH); *Lord Advocate v Fleming* (1864) 2 M 1032 at 1061.

production[89] or inspection, for example, of premises or machinery.[90] Where the order so sought was for inspection, the names of the persons who were to inspect had to be furnished. The order would be granted if necessary for the justice of the cause.[91] This method was used to obtain an order for an ergonomics expert to video-record a process within the defender's premises which the pursuer blamed for his repetitive strain injury,[92] with appropriate protection of confidentiality and under reservation of the issue of admissibility. In unusual circumstances a chemical test of documents was authorised, provided that both parties were present.[93]

18.3.6   Without prejudice to existing powers of the Court of Session or sheriff court, there is now statutory provision[94] for the court to order inspection, photographing, preservation, custody and detention of documents and other property[95] which appear to the court to be property[96] as to which any question may relevantly arise in existing civil proceedings[97] or those that are likely to be brought.[98] The court may also order production and recovery of such property, its sampling, and experimentation on or with it.[99] Application may be made by a party, minuter or any person whom the court considers to appear to have an interest to enter into the proceedings as a party or minuter,[100] in pending proceedings by motion. Before proceedings have been raised application is made by petition in the Court of Session[101] or summary application in the sheriff court.[102] In the former the party seeking the order must show that the property in respect of which the order is sought is required "to serve the purposes of the pleadings" as they stand when the application is made.[103] In the latter the person seeking the order must be likely to be a party or minuter,[104] and the application should set out in as much detail as possible the basis for the likelihood[105] that proceedings will be taken and the part that it is thought that the property will play in proof of those proceedings.[106]

---

[89] *Mactaggart v Mackillop* 1938 SLT 559 (OH); *Bell v Hamilton's Trs* (1889) 16 R 1001; *Jardine's Trs v Carron Co* (1864) 2 M 1372.

[90] *Bell v Hamilton's Trs* (1889) 16 R 1001; *Murray v The Waterproofing Co* 1914 1 SLT 46; *Stevenson v Gray & Sons* (1902) 9 SLT 489; *Clippens Oil Co Ltd v Edinburgh and District Water Trs* (1906) 8 F 731; *Routledge v Somerville & Son* (1866) 4 M 830; *Brown v Brown & Somerville* (1840) 2 D 1356; *Lowrie v Colvilles Ltd* 1961 SLT (Notes) 73; *Christie v Arthur Bell & Sons Ltd* 1989 SLT 253.

[91] *Brown v Brown & Somerville* (1840) 2 D 1356; *Christie v Arthur Bell & Sons Ltd* 1989 SLT 253. See also para 21.6.

[92] *Christie v Arthur Bell & Sons Ltd* 1989 SLT 253.

[93] *Irvine v Powrie's Trs* 1915 SC 1006. The argument that the pursuer must first establish a *prima facie* case was rejected.

[94] Administration of Justice (Scotland) Act 1972 ("1972 Act"), s 1.

[95] Including, where appropriate, land.

[96] A process of work within the defender's premises has been held not to fall within the meaning of "property"—*Christie v Arthur Bell & Sons Ltd* 1989 SLT 253—but an order was made at common law allowing inspection and video-recording of the process, on the basis that it was necessary for the justice of the cause.

[97] Which, in relation to proceedings not yet raised, may include tribunal or arbitration proceedings: *Anderson v Gibb* 1993 SLT 726.

[98] 1972 Act, s 1(1).

[99] 1972 Act, s 1(1).

[100] 1972 Act, s 1 (2)(a).

[101] RCS, r 64.2.

[102] Act of Sederunt (Sheriff Court Summary Applications, Statutory Applications and Appeals etc Rules) 1999 (sI 1999/929) r 3.1.2.

[103] *Moore v Greater Glasgow Health Board* 1978 SC 123; and see, *eg, Cole, Petitioner* 1993 SLT 894.

[104] 1972 Act, s 1(2)(b).

[105] The likelihood should exist even without the property to which the application relates: *Colquhoun, Petitioner* 1990 SLT 43.

[106] *Yau v Ogilvie & Co* 1985 SLT 91; *Dominion Technology Ltd v Gardner Cryogenics Ltd (No 1)* 1993 SLT 828; *Pearson v Educational Institute for Scotland* 1997 SC 245.

The court may make the order unless there is special reason not to do so.[107] It is not necessary to show a *prima facie* relevant case for proceedings not yet raised,[108] but when the application is in depending proceedings the averments should show a *prima facie* case.[109] If it is in the interests of justice to grant the application then this should be done unless there are special reasons for refusal.[110] The application is competent, and indeed designed to be used, before the record is closed,[111] but has not been permitted as a means of building evidence for a case, only as a means of completing relevant pleadings.[112] The same statute provides for an application to obtain an order for disclosure of the information as to the identity of persons who appear to the court to be persons who might be witnesses in existing civil proceedings or who might be witnesses or defenders in proceedings likely to be brought.[113] Any application for an order under the Administration of Justice (Scotland) Act 1972, s 1 is subject to objection on the ground of privilege or confidentiality arising under common law, practice or statute.[114] Where a thing has been recovered in some irregular way (*eg* by theft), it may nevertheless be admitted.[115]

If the evidence that it is sought to recover is outwith Scotland, letters of request **18.3.8** may be sought in the Court of Session or the sheriff court[116] for the recovery of that evidence.[117] Such letters can be granted in respect of evidence for which the court could order recovery if the evidence was in Scotland. Hence, recovery akin to that provided for in the Administration of Justice (Scotland) Act 1972, s 1 is included,[118] as is medical examination,[119] the taking and testing of blood,[120] and any other order for the taking of evidence.[121]

18.4 LODGING OF ARTICLES BEFORE TRIAL OR PROOF

General

Except in a summary criminal trial, a party (as a general rule) must lodge before- **18.4.1** hand in the hands of the clerk of court any article on which he intends to found at

---

[107] 1972 Act, s 2.

[108] *Friel, Petitioner* 1981 SC 1. See para 21.7.

[109] *Smith Petitioner* 1985 SLT 461. See para 21.7.

[110] *Moore v Greater Glasgow Health Board* 1978 SC 123; *Civil Service Building Society v MacDougall* 1988 SC 58. Earlier authorities differed as to whether the absence of special reason was a qualifying factor: *McGown v Erskine* 1978 SLT (Notes) 4; *cf Baxter v Lothian Health Board* 1976 SLT (Notes) 37.

[111] See annotations to RCS, rr 35.2.5 and 64.1 in the *Parliament House Book*, Division C, and see para 21.7.4.

[112] *Moore v Greater Glasgow Health Board* 1978 SC 123. Lord Cullen, in his report on *Review of Business of the Outer House of the Court of Session*, proposes that such restrictions should be lifted so that the process may legitimately be used to gather evidence at as early a stage as possible: paras 5.7–5.10.

[113] Administration of Justice (Scotland) Act 1972, s 1(1A), and for an example see *Conoco (UK) Ltd v The Commercial Law Practice* 1997 SLT 372. An application was competent at common law: *Halloran v Greater Glasgow Passenger Transport Executive* 1976 SLT 77.

[114] Administration of Justice (Scotland) Act 1972, s 1(4). Such a ground of objection was taken in *Conoco (UK) Ltd v The Commercial Law Practice* 1997 SLT 372.

[115] *Rattray v Rattray* (1897) 25 R 315; *MacColl v MacColl* 1946 SLT 312 (OH); *McLeish v Glasgow Bonding Co* 1965 SLT 39. See para 1.7.

[116] In the sheriff court this is possible only in a depending action: OCR, r 28.14.

[117] RCS, r 35.15, OCR, r 28.14 deal with depending actions before that court. For detail on letters of request, see para 14.6.

[118] RCS, r 35.15(2)(b), OCR, r 28.14(2)(b). In the Court of Session letters in advance of proceedings should be sought by petition, and in the sheriff court by summary application. See note 85.

[119] RCS, r 35.15(2)(c), OCR, r 28.14(2)(c).

[120] RCS, r 35.15(2)(d), OCR, r 28.14(2)(d).

[121] RCS, r 35.15(2)(e), OCR, r 28.14(2)(e).

the trial or proof. The purpose is to give his opponent an opportunity to examine the article and, if he wishes, have it examined by experts. Plaster impressions of the accused's boots were excluded when they were not in the Crown list of productions and were only brought to court by the witness,[122] and a witness was not allowed to demonstrate that a key fitted a lock, when the key was lodged and included in the Crown list, but the lock was not.[123] Lodging may be dispensed with if it is impracticable[124] or there is some good objection to it, provided that timeous notice of the intention to use the article is given to the opponent so as to enable him to examine it.[125]

Criminal

18.4.2   In solemn procedure a list of the Crown productions must be appended to the record copy indictment[126] and lodged in court on or before the date of service.[127] In practice the service copy is accompanied by a list of productions.[128] The productions themselves must be lodged with the sheriff clerk of the district where the trial is to be held, or, if the trial is before the High Court in Edinburgh, in the Justiciary Office,[129] and the accused is entitled to see these in accordance with the practice operating in that court.[130] No time by which they must be lodged is fixed by statute, and practice may vary according to locality, storage facilities and the nature of the productions. However, if the production is lodged at least eight days before the trial a presumption arises without proof that it remains in the condition it was in when examined by any witness who is to speak to that examination.[131] This may act as an incentive to lodge productions at that time. The test of whether the lodging is timeous is whether the accused has had a fair opportunity to examine the productions.[132] If the accused is to object to the use of a production on that ground, notice must be given before the jury is sworn, so that if the objection is upheld the diet can be deserted *pro loco et tempore*.[133] The prosecutor must include in the productions the record[134] of a judicial examination if one was held,[135] although this does not require to be the subject of evidence to prove its terms.[136] The accused must give notice of defence productions at least 10 clear

---

[122] *Milne* (1866) 5 Irv 229.
[123] *Goodwin* (1837) 1 Swin 431. *Smith* (1837) 1 Swin 505 is of doubtful authority. See Dickson, *Evidence* (3rd edn), para 1819.
[124] See para 18.5.
[125] *Baird v Leechman* (1903) 11 SLT 200.
[126] Except in cases where the accused has intimated an intention to plead guilty under the Criminal Procedure (Scotland) Act 1995 ("1995 Act"), s 76; see s 66(5).
[127] 1995 Act, s 66(5).
[128] Although only a list of witnesses is required by the Criminal Procedure (Scotland) Act 1995, s 66(4).
[129] Criminal Procedure (Scotland) Act 1995, s 68. Productions unsuitable to be kept in an office, such as livestock, may be lodged with a representative of the sheriff clerk or of the Clerk of Justiciary: *Stark and Smith v HM Advocate* 1938 JC 170.
[130] Criminal Procedure (Scotland) Act 1995, s 68(2).
[131] Criminal Procedure (Scotland) Act 1995, s 68(3). The accused may challenge this presumption by giving written notice at least four days before the trial diet: s 68(3) and (4).
[132] *Watt* (1859) 3 Irv 389 (bank's books available two days before trial); *Kerr* (1857) 2 Irv 608 (watch lodged at 9.30 on morning of trial); *Aymers* (1857) 2 Irv 725 (book lodged an hour before trial, but only required to compare extracts lodged ten days before).
[133] *Watt* (1859) 3 Irv 389; *Kerr* (1857) 2 Irv 608.
[134] Made under the Criminal Procedure (Scotland) Act 1995 ("1995 Act"), s 37, or a record which has been rectified under s 38.
[135] 1995 Act, s 68(1).
[136] 1995 Act, ss 37(5) and 278(1).

days before trial commences in the High Court or on or before the first diet in sheriff and jury cases, unless the court on cause shown otherwise directs.[137] The defence may without notice rely on any production shown on the Crown list,[138] but the court may on application by either party determine that all or part of the record of judicial examination will not be read to the jury.[139] If a Crown production is sealed the court may give the accused authority to open it.[140]

In summary procedure, although there is no obligation to give notice of or lodge **18.4.3** productions before the trial, the practice of the Crown is to act fairly.[141]

Civil

Rules of court provide that productions must be lodged with the court not later **18.4.4** than a specified period before the date fixed for proof and may not otherwise be referred to unless by consent of the parties, or with leave of the court; that copies should be lodged for use of the judge or sheriff[142]; and that the opponent[143] may borrow the productions provided that they are returned by noon on the day before the proof. In the Court of Session the productions[144] must be lodged 28 days beforehand.[145] In commercial actions the court may order production of relevant items at any stage in the case.[146] In an ordinary cause in the sheriff court productions must be lodged 14 days before the proof.[147] In summary cause[148] and small claim proceedings[149] the period is seven days.

18.5 PRODUCTION AT TRIAL OR PROOF

The article itself is the best evidence of its appearance at the time of the trial or **18.5.1** proof. Accordingly, an oral description of it in its absence is inadmissible, provided that it is practicable and convenient to produce it.[150] It follows that evidence

---

[137] 1995 Act, s 78(4).

[138] 1995 Act, s 78(1).

[139] 1995 Act, s 278.

[140] Hume, ii, 388. See also *Wilson* (1857) 2 Irv 626.

[141] See *Smith v HM Advocate* 1952 JC 66. If there were serious prejudice to either side, the trial might be adjourned: *Maciver v Mackenzie* 1942 JC 51 at 54.

[142] This does not apply in summary causes or small claims.

[143] But not a party litigant in summary causes or small claims.

[144] Documentary productions are dealt with at Chapter 20.

[145] RCS, rr 36.3–36.5 re proof, applied to jury trials by RCS, r 37.4.

[146] RCS, r 47.11(1).

[147] OCR, rr 29.11–29.13.

[148] Summary Cause Rules, Sheriff Court 1976, r 24.

[149] Small Claims Rules 1988, para 17(1), provided that the productions are reasonably capable of being lodged.

[150] *Maciver v Mackenzie* 1942 JC 51, where no objection was taken to oral descriptions, and consequently no explanation offered for the failure to produce; *MacLeod v Woodmuir Miners Welfare Society Social Club* 1961 JC 5; *Hughes v Skeen* 1980 SLT (Notes) 13; *Morrison v Mackenzie* 1990 JC 185. *Cf Paterson v HM Advocate* (1901) 4 F (J) 7, where adequate grounds of judgment would have been (1) that no objection was taken to the Crown evidence, and (2) that as the sheep were presumably on the Crown list of productions they could have been produced by the defence. *Cf* also *Stewart v Glasgow Corporation* 1958 SC 28, where evidence was led without objection as to the condition of a pole not produced, a fact on which two of the judges remarked at 30, 38.

of a skilled witness based on such an article would also be inadmissible.[151] Whether or not it is practical or convenient to produce an item may depend upon its own nature,[152] the importance of the item to the issues in the case[153] and upon the practicality of withholding it from the owner pending production at trial. Hence goods allegedly stolen, if recovered, may be returned to the owner, and oral[154] or photographic evidence of them may be led.[155] An accused who wishes to object to the failure to produce should do so at the first available opportunity,[156] which may be a first or preliminary diet,[157] but if the significance or otherwise of actual production can not be determined then the matter may be raised again at trial as an issue of fairness.[158] The court will consider whether production of the item is necessary for proof and whether there will be prejudice to the accused by the failure to produce.[159] Objection has been overruled where the defence sought to refer to the item not produced for assessment of credibility through cross-examination rather than for proof of an issue.[160]

18.5.2   A statutory exception to the requirement for production is also made in criminal cases for evidence of the characteristics and composition of biological material deriving from human beings and animals. This may be the subject of oral evidence without being produced in court,[161] but where neither the material nor a sample of it is to be lodged, the material or sample must have been made available for inspection by the other party before destruction unless it constitutes a hazard to health or has been destroyed in the process of analysis.[162] This reflects the approach taken at common law where a description by a witness is competent if the article is perishable[163] or the relevant feature of it is subject to fading or deterioration, and a dead body need not be produced.[164] Again, the article may be an immoveable object away from the court, which cannot be produced.[165] The question is "whether

---

[151] *McGowan v Belling & Co Ltd* 1983 JC 9 confirming a view expressed by Dickson, *Evidence* (3rd edn), paras 1817 *et seq.*

[152] The evidence in *Anderson v Laverock* 1976 SLT 62 was 26 salmon.

[153] *HM Advocate v A1 Megrahi and Fhimah.* ("The Lockerbie trial") was delayed for two days while a baggage container, described by the judge as "of critical importance" was dismantled from its position in a room in the court building and re-assembled in the court room. A summary of interlocutors is accessible via www.law.gla.ac.uk/lockerbie.

[154] In *Anderson v Laverock* 1976 SLT 62 it was said that labels or other records of the fish were not strictly necessary because the secondary evidence in place of the fish was oral evidence of witnesses.

[155] As in *Houston v HM Advocate* 1990 SLT 514; *Tudhope v Stewart* 1986 SLT 659; *Anderson v Laverock* 1976 SLT 62.

[156] *Tudhope v Stewart* 1986 SLT 659.

[157] As in *Houston v HM Advocate* 1990 SLT 514.

[158] *Houston v HM Advocate* 1990 SLT 514.

[159] *Maciver v Mackenzie* 1942 JC 51; *Tudhope v Stewart* 1986 SLT 659; *Friel v Leonard* 1997 SLT 1206.

[160] *Maciver v Mackenzie* 1942 JC 51, applied in *Tudhope v Stewart* 1986 SLT 659, and in *Friel v Leonard* 1997 SLT 1206.

[161] Criminal Procedure (Scotland) Act 1995, s 276(1).

[162] 1995 Act, s 276(2).

[163] But the opposite party should be allowed to inspect it before it perishes or is destroyed: *Anderson v Laverock* 1976 JC 9.

[164] *Punton* (1841) 2 Swin 572.

[165] In civil cases an order for its inspection or photographing might be sought under the Administration of Justice (Scotland) Act 1972, s 1, in which case the report or photographs should be produced. There is statutory provision for a party to apply for a civil jury to view any heritable or moveable property relevant to the action: Court of Session Act 1988, s 14. See *Redpath v Central SMT Co* 1947 SN 171 (OH). But a private inspection by a tribunal is incompetent (*Hattie v Leitch* (1889) 16 R 1128), at least if it is to influence the decision: *Sime v Linton* (1897) 24 R (J) 70; *Hope v Gemmell* (1898) 1 F 74. Where no evidence was led as to the weight of the stolen article produced in court, the

the production is practicable and convenient".[166] In a trial on indictment, when a witness gives evidence that he has examined a production lodged eight days before the second diet, it is not necessary to prove that he received it in the same condition as when it was taken possession of by the procurator-fiscal or the police and returned by him, unless the accused gives four days' written notice that he does not admit that it was so received or returned.[167]

18.6 USE AT TRIAL OR PROOF

The article itself is evidence only of its appearance at the time,[168] and justifies **18.6.1** simple inferences—for example, that a box has been forced open, that a witness's arm has been injured,[169] that the accused is sufficiently powerful to have committed the crime,[170] and that jewellery has been made up to deceive.[171] A bottle proved to have been found at the scene of a crime, and bearing fingerprints, provides evidence of the accused's presence at the scene, if the jury is satisfied that the fingerprints are his.[172] But the tribunal may not be entitled to draw an inference from its own examination unless the party against whom the inference is drawn has an opportunity to challenge it.[173] Where the matter is technical, lay opinion is not admissible. A police officer can only say that marks on clothing look like blood; In such matters, where skilled knowledge is required, evidence of a skilled witness is necessary.[174] However, police officers have been allowed to express an opinion as to the likelihood that a particular quantity of drugs produced in evidence was held for personal use or supply.[175] Furthermore, lay identification of cannabis resin has been admitted.[176]

---

jury were not permitted to have it brought into the jury room for them to assess its weight (*Sandells v HM Advocate* 1980 SLT (Notes) 45) since this would involve recovery of new evidence rather than mere interpretation of what had been led in evidence.

[166] *Maciver v Mackenzie* 1942 JC 51 at 55.

[167] Criminal Procedure (Scotland) Act 1995, s 68(3) and (4).

[168] Any relevant dimensions that are not obvious to the naked eye must be the subject of separate evidence, rather than assessment by a jury examining the article more closely in private: *Sandells v HM Advocate* 1980 SLT (Notes) 45.

[169] *Aitken v Wood* 1921 JC 84.

[170] *Withers v HM Advocate* 1947 JC 109.

[171] *Patterson v Landsberg* (1905) 7 F 675 at 681.

[172] *Hamilton v HM Advocate* 1934 JC 1 at 4.

[173] *McCann v Adair* 1951 JC 127. See also *Sandells v HM Advocate* 1980 SLT (Notes) 45. The trial judge has discretion to deal with the jury's request to examine productions, *Collins v HM Advocate* 1993 SLT 101.

[174] See para 16.3.

[175] eg *Bauros v HM Advocate* 1991 SCCR 768; *Haq v HM Advocate* 1987 SCCR 433.

[176] *McCallum v McKay* 1997 SCCR 558; *Main v Russell* 1999 GWD 13-592.

CHAPTER 19

PUBLIC AND OFFICIAL DOCUMENTS

19.1 SCOPE OF CHAPTER

19.1.1 This chapter deals with documents,[1] not as constituting or proving obligations, but as evidence of the facts stated in them. Various types of documents are considered from one or both of two aspects: (1) whether the document itself requires to be proved; and (2) whether and to what extent it is evidence of the facts stated in it. What is said here will have to be read in light of the new demands of proof of electronic documents, whenever the provisions of the Electronic Communications Act 2000, s 8 take full effect and are applied, by Order, to writings required by statute or statutory instrument. It appears that the principle of the Act cannot be enforced upon non-statutory situations such as those arising at common law, or by agreement of the parties.

---

[1] It also includes maps, plans and tombstones. It is, however, somewhat superfluous to state this since there now exists judicial authority for the proposition that these are documents: *Rollo v HM Advocate* 1997 JC 23 at 25E and 26G.

19.2 STATUTES

Public statutes

19.2.1 Public statutes are the Acts of the old Parliaments of Scotland down to 1707, the Acts of the Parliament of the United Kingdom at Westminster after the Act of Union in 1707 until the present, and Acts of the Scottish Parliament after its formal creation on 1 July 1999.[2] Public Acts need not be proved, since judicial notice must be taken of them.[3] Should any question arise as to the precise terms of a Public Act, the following may be referred to[4] in order to refresh judicial knowledge: the Record Edition of Acts of the old Parliaments of Scotland,[5] although it should be noted that these Acts have been revised since the publication of that edition[6]; a copy of a statute of the Westminster Parliament or the Scottish Parliament bearing to be printed by the Queen's Printer or under the authority of HM Stationery Office,[7] although a recognised version such as that found in the *Parliament House Book* or *Current Law Statutes* is likely to be acceptable.[8]

Private statutes

19.2.2 Every Act since 1850 is deemed to be a Public Act and within judicial knowledge unless the contrary is expressly provided.[9] Accordingly, it is now unnecessary, as a rule, to prove such an Act and, as in the case of a Public Act, its terms are established by production of a copy bearing to be printed by the Queen's Printer or under the authority of HM Stationery Office. A Private Act which was passed before 1850 and which does not contain a clause to the effect that it is to be judicially noticed as a Public Act should be proved by a copy sworn to be collated with the Parliament Roll.[10] Private Acts of the old Parliaments of Scotland consisted of decrees of the Parliament when acting in a judicial capacity, and of grants of land, titles and immunities or ratifications of Crown grants. It is thought that their terms are sufficiently established by the Record Edition.[11] The evidential effect of such

---

[2] See the Scotland Act 1998; Scotland Act 1998 (Commencement) Order 1998 (SI 1998/3178).

[3] For United Kingdom statutes, see the Interpretation Act 1978, s 3. This provision applies only to Acts passed after 1850 (*ibid* Sched 2, Pt I, para 2), but it is thought that the same rule applies at common law irrespective of the date of the Act: Dickson, *Evidence* (3rd edn), para 1105; *Macmillan v McConnell* 1917 JC 43, per Lord Justice-Clerk Scott Dickson at 47; *Herkes v Dickie* 1958 JC 51 at 55, 57 and 58. For Acts of the new Scottish Parliament, see the Scotland Act 1998, s 28(b).

[4] There is no need to lodge these as formal productions, but a list of statute authority should be provided to the court and one's opponent as a matter of courtesy.

[5] *The Acts of the Parliaments of Scotland* (Thomson and Innes (eds) 1844–75). *Cf Kemp v Glasgow Corporation* 1920 SC (HL) 73, where Viscount Finlay, while giving a citation to the Record Edition, chose to quote the text of APS, ii, 227, c 19 (1491) which appeared in Balfour's *Practicks* at p 45 rather than the Record Edition text.

[6] See the Statute Law Revision (Scotland) Act 1906 and the Statute Law Revision (Scotland) Act 1964. Subsequent to the 1964 Act, those pre-1707 public statutes still in force were collated and printed in *The Acts of the Parliament of Scotland 1424–1707* (2nd revised edn, HMSO, 1966). Reference to this edition will usually be sufficient in practice.

[7] Dickson, *Evidence* (3rd edn), para 1105.

[8] *Macmillan v McConnell* 1917 JC 43 refers to a reputable edition. Care should be taken with statute material which although recognised or reputable is annotated. The annotations are not part of the statute and have no greater weight than the opinion of a commentator expressed in academic material. Statements and narrative in public statutes are mentioned later.

[9] Interpretation Act 1978, ss 3, 21 and Sched 2, Pt I, para 2. Despite the general wording of these provisions, the distinction between public and private Acts subsists for other purposes. See *Bennion on Statute Law* (3rd edn), pp 18–19.

[10] Dickson, *Evidence* (3rd edn), para 1105.

[11] *The Acts of the Parliaments of Scotland* (Thomson and Innes (eds) 1844–75).

a decree is presumably the same as that of any other decree,[12] but grants were made *salvo jure cujuslibet* (reserving the rights of all others),[13] so that statements in them would appear to be of little value in evidence.

19.3 LEGISLATION OF THE DEVOLVED ASSEMBLIES OF THE UNITED KINGDOM

The Welsh Assembly has no power to make primary legislation. Its power is **19.3.1** limited to subordinate legislation applying in or to Wales.[14] The Northern Ireland Assembly will have power to make primary legislation applying to Northern Ireland if and when the relevant provisions of the Northern Ireland Act 1998 are brought into force.[15] Should a question of Welsh or Northern Irish legislation arise in a Scottish court, it will require to be proved by evidence as a matter of foreign law.[16]

19.4 PROOF IN CONSTRUCTION OF STATUTES[17]

Matters within the statute

The title, preamble and headings which introduce groups[18] of sections are all **19.4.1** regarded as part of the statute and may be used in its construction.[19] Punctuation may be taken into account, although its presence or absence cannot defeat the plain intention of the statute.[20] While older Scottish decisions held that side-notes could not be considered,[21] more recent English cases have abandoned that view in favour

---

[12] See para 19.5.

[13] APS, iv, 321, c 68 (1606); see *Earl of Lauderdale v Scrymgeour Wedderburn* 1910 SC (HL) 35 at 42.

[14] Government of Wales Act 1998, s 22. Technically, the Assembly could acquire powers to amend primary legislation by way of subordinate legislation if such powers were conferred on a Minister of the Crown by an Act of the Westminster Parliament and transferred under s 22. Such a transfer, however, is not envisaged.

[15] Northern Ireland Act 1998, s 5.

[16] See para 16.5.

[17] See, in general, *Stair Memorial Encyclopaedia*, Vol 12, "Interpretation of Statutes, Deeds and Other Documents" (1992), paras 1134–1164.

[18] The term "fasciculus" is used in some older cases: *eg Mags of Buckie v Dowager Countess of Seafield's Trs* 1928 SC 525, per Lord President Clyde at 528.

[19] For the title, see *Mags of Buckie v Dowager Countess of Seafield's Trs* 1928 SC 525, per Lord President Clyde at 528–529; *Millar & Lang Ltd v Macniven & Cameron Ltd* (1908) 16 SLT 56, per Lord Dundas at 58. For the preamble, see *Minister of Brydekirk v Minister and Heritors of Hoddam* (1877) 4 R 798, per Lord President Inglis at 800; *Tennent v Mags of Partick* (1894) 21 R 735, per Lord President Robertson at 741. For headings, see *Mags of Buckie*, above, per Lord President Clyde at 528; *Hill v Orkney Islands Council* 1983 SLT (Lands Tr) 2 at 4.

[20] *Alexander v Mackenzie* 1947 JC 155, per Lord Jamieson at 166, quoted with approval by Lord Lowry in *Hanlon v The Law Society* [1981] AC 124 at 197–198. There is some scepticism in the English authorities about reference to punctuation, but this appears to be based on the view that Acts were unpunctuated prior to 1850: see *Inland Revenue Commissioners v Hinchy* [1960] AC 748, per Lord Reid at 765. The historical accuracy of this assertion has been subjected to severe criticism, although it is not disputed that punctuation in printed versions of earlier Acts was unreliable. See Bennion, *Statutory Interpretation* (2nd edn), p 516; Mellinkoff, *The Language of the Law*, pp 157–164. In any event, it does not reflect modern practice. See *Bennion on Statute Law* (3rd edn), p 52.

[21] *Farquharson v Whyte* (1886) 13 R (J) 29, per Lord Justice-Clerk Moncreiff at 31 and Lord Young at 32; *Nelson v McPhee* (1889) 17 R (J) 1, per Lord McLaren at 2; *Mags of Buckie v Dowager Countess of Seafield's Trs* 1928 SC 525, per Lord President Clyde at 528.

of the position that a side-note may competently be referred to, although it is a poor guide to the scope of a section and will rarely be of assistance.[22]

Matters outwith the statute

19.4.2 Legislation must, so far as possible, be interpreted in such a way as to be compatible with European Community obligations and the provisions of the European Convention on Human Rights.[23] Beyond this, external aids to construction will be of most significance where a legislative provision is ambiguous, obscure, or would produce an absurd result if applied literally. In such a case, reference may now be made to a clear Parliamentary statement by a minister or promoter of a Bill which clearly describes the mischief aimed at or the legislative intention behind the ambiguous provision.[24] In such a situation, any Scottish Law Commission (or similar) report which led to the legislation in question may also be referred to.[25] In the former case, the relevant *Hansard* volume should be produced, and in the latter case there should be produced the HMSO copy of the relevant report which the Commission laid before Parliament.

19.5 STATEMENTS AND NARRATIVE IN STATUTES

19.5.1 Statements and narrative in public statutes are evidence of the facts narrated,[26] but their effect is not conclusive,[27] and consequently may be contradicted by other evidence.[28] Such matters in Private Acts, even when rendered public for the purposes of judicial knowledge either by an *in gremio* provision to that effect or by virtue of the Interpretation Act 1978,[29] are not evidence except in peerage cases, and even then only in relation to Private Acts which, as in the past, proceeded on

---

[22] *R v Schildkamp* [1971] AC 1, per Lord Reid at 10 and Lord Upjohn at 28; Bennion, *Statutory Interpretation* (2nd edn), pp 512–513. *Cf* Lord Reid's earlier comments in *Chandler v DPP* [1964] AC 763 at 789–790. Side-notes have been found to be of assistance in a number of English cases: see *Tudor Grange Holdings Ltd v Citibank NA* [1992] Ch 53, per Browne-Wilkinson V-C at 66; *Chilcott v Inland Revenue Commissioners* [1982] STC 1, per Vinelott J at 23–24; *In re Phelps, decd* [1980] Ch 275, per Buckley LJ at 281.

[23] Case C-106/89 *Marleasing SA v La Comercial Internacional de Alimentación SA* [1990] ECR I-4135 at 4159 (European Community obligations); Human Rights Act 1998, s 3 (European Convention on Human Rights). Prior to the 1998 Act, the position *quoad* the European Convention was that "when legislation is found to be ambiguous in the sense that it is capable of a meaning which either conforms to or conflicts with the Convention, Parliament is to be presumed to have legislated in conformity with the Convention, not in conflict with it": *T, Petitioner* 1997 SLT 724, per Lord President Hope at 734C–D (disapproving dicta in *Kaur v Lord Advocate* 1980 SC 319). For discussion of what is "possible", see Bennion, "What interpretation is 'possible' under section 3(1) of the Human Rights Act 1998?" [2000] PL 77; Weatherhill & Beaumont, *EU Law* (3rd edn), pp 419–423.

[24] *Pepper v Hart* [1993] AC 593, per Lord Browne-Wilkinson at 634; *Short's Tr v Keeper of the Registers of Scotland* 1994 SC 122, per Lord President Hope at 138 (decision affirmed 1996 SC (HL) 14).

[25] *Rehman v Ahmad* 1993 SLT 741, per Lord Penrose at 745E–F. See also *McWilliams v Lord Advocate* 1992 SLT 1045; *Barratt Scotland Ltd v Keith* 1993 SC 142; *Archer Car Sales (Airdrie) Ltd v Gregory's Tr* 1993 SLT 223.

[26] Not *qua* statute, but *qua* public document: Dickson, *Evidence* (3rd edn), para 1108; Phipson, *Evidence* (15th edn), para 36-04.

[27] Dickson, *Evidence* (3rd edn), para 1108; Phipson, *Evidence* (15th edn), para 36-04.

[28] *Ibid.*

[29] ss 3, 21 and Sched 2, Pt I, para 2.

evidence approved by the judges.[30] However, statements in Private Acts appear to be admissible to prove reputation in questions of public or general right.[31]

19.6 EUROPEAN COMMUNITY LAW

Judicial notice is taken of the European Treaties and the *Official Journal of the* **19.6.1** *Communities*.[32] The *Official Journal* is sufficient evidence of any Community instrument thereby communicated.[33] Should further proof, or proof of a Community instrument not published in the *Official Journal* be required, the procedures laid down by the European Communities Act 1972 may be followed.[34]

19.7 ORDERS AND PROCLAMATIONS

Orders in Council

Orders in Council are acts of subordinate legislation made by the Crown by virtue **19.7.1** of the prerogative, or by a minister of the Crown by virtue of statute. Since 1948 they have been classed as statutory instruments[35] and are proved as such.[36] Of Orders before that year *prima facie* evidence exists when a copy of the *Gazette*[37] purporting to contain the order is produced[38]; or a copy purporting to be printed by the government printer,[39] or under the superintendence of HM Stationery Office,[40] or a certified copy or extract.[41] In Scotland, apart from such *prima facie* evidence, it would appear that an Order must be proved by production of the original or of a copy sworn to be a true copy.[42] Orders in Council pursuant to statute are within judicial knowledge.[43]

Royal proclamations

Proclamations, which are used to declare war and peace, and to summon and dis- **19.7.2** solve parliament, are "valid in law" if published in the *Gazette*,[44] and are within judicial knowledge.[45]

---

[30] Dickson, *Evidence* (3rd edn), para 1108; Phipson, *Evidence* (15th edn), para 36-05 and fn 18.
[31] Dickson, *Evidence* (3rd edn), para 1108; Phipson, *Evidence* (15th edn), para 35-37. In *Wyld v Silver* [1963] 1 QB 169, it was held that in the absence of evidence to the contrary the narrative in a Private Act must be very strong evidence of the truth of a matter long beyond the reach of living memory.
[32] European Communities Act 1972, s 3(2).
[33] European Communities Act 1972, s 3(2) and (5).
[34] See the European Communities Act 1972, s 3(3)–(4).
[35] Statutory Instruments Act 1946, s 1(1).
[36] See para 19.8.
[37] See para 19.18.
[38] Documentary Evidence Act 1868, s 2(1).
[39] Documentary Evidence Act 1868, s 2(2).
[40] Documentary Evidence Act 1882, s 2.
[41] Documentary Evidence Act 1868, s 2(3).
[42] Phipson, *Evidence* (15th edn), para 41-44. For the procedures associated with warrants for production of original documents from public records, see RCS 1994, r 35.9; OCR 1993, r 28.9; Macphail, *Sheriff Court Practice* (2nd edn), Vol 1, para 15.98.
[43] *Macmillan v McConnell* 1917 JC 43; *Bradley v Arthur* (1825) 4 B & C 292, per Abbott CJ at 304; 107 ER 1068 at 1072.
[44] Crown Office Act 1877, s 3. See para 19.18.
[45] Crown Office Act 1877, s 3.

19.8 STATUTORY INSTRUMENTS

19.8.1 A statutory instrument is any document by which Her Majesty exercises a power conferred on her exercisable by Order in Council or a minister exercises a power conferred on him exercisable by statutory instrument.[46] The term also includes any document by which a rule-making authority under the Rules Publication Act 1893[47] exercised its powers after 1948.[48] As a matter of practice, it is generally thought that a statutory instrument does not require to be proved, but the authorities are not absolutely clear on this point.[49] Where necessary, the terms of a statutory instrument are established under the Documentary Evidence Acts,[50] and its date of issue by a list issued by the Stationery Office.[51]

19.9 PRE-1708 SCOTTISH SUBORDINATE LEGISLATION

19.9.1 Before its abolition in 1708,[52] the Scottish Privy Council was the principal executive organ as well as a superior judicatory, and the Acts of Privy Council were analogous to the English Orders in Council. Such Acts—and decrees when the Privy Council was acting in a judicial capacity—are, it is thought, adequately proved by production of the manuscript of the Register of the Privy Council[53] or by an extract therefrom certified by the Keeper of the Records.[54]

19.10 BYELAWS AND REGULATIONS

19.10.1 A byelaw or regulation, as presently considered, is "an ordinance affecting the public, or some portion of the public, imposed by some authority clothed with statutory powers".[55] Where the statute authorising the byelaw or regulation provides that it shall have the same effect as if it were contained in the Act,[56] or shall have the effect of an Act of Parliament,[57] no proof of it is required.[58] Statutory instruments[59] and orders founded on in a criminal prosecution[60] are mentioned

---

[46] Statutory Instruments Act 1946, s 1.

[47] s 4. This Act is now repealed: see Northern Ireland Act 1955, Sched.

[48] Statutory Instruments Act 1946, s 1(2).

[49] *Sharp v Leith* (1892) 20 R (J) 12, per Lord McLaren at 15–16; *Hutchison v Stevenson* (1902) 4 F (J) 69, per Lord McLaren at 72; *Macmillan v McConnell* 1917 JC 43, per Lord Justice-Clerk Scott Dickson at 47 and Lord Justice-General Strathclyde at 54. See also Renton & Brown, *Criminal Procedure* (6th edn), para 24-121/1; Macphail, *Evidence* (1987), paras 2.03 and 11.02. Sheriff Macphail has suggested that a statutory provision to the effect that judicial notice be taken of all statutory instruments would be desirable: see *Evidence* at para 11.02. See also Cross and Tapper, *Evidence* (9th edn), p 71. There are special provisions relating to the proof of official documents in criminal proceedings: see the Criminal Procedure (Scotland) Act 1995, s 279A, as inserted by the Crime and Punishment (Scotland) Act 1997, s 28, the presumption contained in Sched 3, para 12(a), and para 19.19.

[50] Documentary Evidence Act 1868, s 2; Documentary Evidence Act 1882, s 2.

[51] Statutory Instruments Act 1946, s 3(1).

[52] Act 6 Anne, c 6, s 1.

[53] This work has been largely calendared and printed in the *Register of the Privy Council of Scotland*.

[54] Public Records (Scotland) Act 1937, s 9.

[55] *Kruse v Johnson* [1898] 2 QB 91 at 96.

[56] *Institute of Patent-Agents v Lockwood* (1894) 21 R (HL) 61 at 67, 70 and 71.

[57] *Hamilton v Fyfe* 1907 SC (J) 79.

[58] *Herkes v Dickie* 1958 JC 51 at 55 and 57.

[59] See para 19.8.

[60] See para 19.19.

elsewhere. The statute authorising the making of an order may also provide how the terms of the order are to be proved—for example, by a certificate.[61] Where there is no statutory method of certifying the terms of a byelaw, then a copy made in terms of the Civil Evidence (Scotland) Act 1988[62] or the Criminal Procedure (Scotland) Act 1995[63] should generally be acceptable. The whole byelaw or regulation, and not simply those sections which the party relying on it considers pertinent, should be put in evidence.[64]

19.11 ACTS OF SEDERUNT AND ACTS OF ADJOURNAL

19.11.1 Acts of Sederunt and Acts of Adjournal are authenticated respectively by the signature of the Lords of Council and Session and the Lords Commissioners of Justiciary.[65] The legislation instituting the College of Justice provided for royal ratification of Acts of Sederunt,[66] but the Act of 1540 gave power to the Lords of Session to make such Acts by themselves.[67] The latter statute would appear to give an Act of Sederunt statutory effect. Acts of Sederunt and Acts of Adjournal made since 1948 are statutory instruments.[68] As such they are within judicial knowledge and do not require proof.

19.11.2 The position of these Acts before 1948 is lacking in authority.[69] Although they do not appear to come within the ambit of the Act of 1868,[70] which gives certain orders *prima facie* value, it is thought that in the absence of challenge, copies of Acts of Sederunt and Acts of Adjournal would be received without proof, but if challenged—and there appears to be no reported case of challenge—the books of sederunt or books of adjournal would be produced by their custodier or an extract given by the clerk of court or by the keeper of the records to whom the books have been transmitted for custody.

19.12 ACTS OF ASSEMBLY

19.12.1 Acts of Assembly are the vehicle of legislation of the General Assembly of the Church of Scotland. There appears to be no distinction between the legislative and other powers of the church courts (including the General Assembly) in relation to proof of an Act. This may be done by producing the original minutes, if these are

---

[61] See, *eg*, Local Government (Scotland) Act 1973, s 202B(5), as inserted by the Civic Government (Scotland) Act 1982, s 110(3); Agricultural Wages (Scotland) Act 1949, s 15. As to statutory certificates, see para 19.16.

[62] See para 20.2.

[63] See para 20.2.

[64] *Donnelly v Carmichael* 1995 JC 215 at 216I (referring to production of byelaws in a criminal prosecution, but the point is thought to be of general application).

[65] Normally the president of each court signs, and the accession of the other lords is testified by the addition of "*I.P.D.*", *in praesentia dominorum* (in the presence of the lords): *Maclean of Ardgour v Maclean* 1941 SC 613 at 708.

[66] APS, ii, 335, c 2 (1532); Act of Sederunt, 27 May, 1532.

[67] APS, ii, 371, c 10 (1540).

[68] See the Statutory Instruments Act 1946, s 1(2) (for Acts of Sederunt and Acts of Adjournal made under statutes passed prior to 1948); Law Reform (Miscellaneous Provisions) (Scotland) Act 1966, s 10 (for Acts of Sederunt and Acts of Adjournal made under statutes passed since 1948).

[69] *Cf Lane's Case* (1596) 2 Co Rep 16b; 76 ER 423.

[70] Documentary Evidence Act 1868, s 2.

authenticated according to the forms observed by the church,[71] or an extract attested by the clerk which will be received in evidence.[72] There are various church records embodying the earlier Acts of Assembly,[73] the more recent being printed by authority of the Assembly.

19.13 COLONIAL AND FOREIGN STATUTES

19.13.1 Colonial and foreign statutes are not part of the general law and therefore, unlike British statutes, do not prove themselves by mere citation.[74] Colonial statutes may be proved by copies certified by the clerk or other proper officer of a legislative body in that colony,[75] or by copies which purport to be printed by the government printer of that colony.[76] The latter method, while generally more convenient, has the disadvantage that no one but an expert can be sure that the copy tendered is the latest version of the local law.[77] The statutory provisions which allow for proof in this manner continue to apply to many former colonies due to the statutes granting or recognising their independent status, which frequently provide that existing UK law will continue to apply to them as if they had not become republics.[78] Foreign statutes may be proved in the same way as any other matter of foreign law by the evidence of witnesses skilled in the law of the country concerned.[79] Foreign, dominion and colonial documents are dealt with elsewhere.[80]

19.14 CROWN CHARTERS, ETC

19.14.1 Crown charters are grants made by the Crown usually under the great seal[81] or otherwise according to the forms prescribed by statute.[82] The variety of names (such as letters patent, pardons, commissions) given to these grants refers to the subject-matter of the grant rather than the form. A charter is a probative document

---

[71] In particular, authentication by the *timeous* subscription of the moderator and clerk is not essential: APS, viii, 585, c 4 (1686); "ordaining Interlocutors to be subscribed by the Judges" does not apply to church matters: *Fergusson v Skirving* (1850) 12 D 1145, affd 1 Macq 232 (presbytery); see also Cox, *Practice and Procedure in the Church of Scotland* (6th edn), pp 81 *et seq*. The inspection and subscription of the minutes is normally done half-yearly: see also para 19.32.

[72] As to the form, see Cox, *Practice and Procedure in the Church of Scotland* (6th edn), pp 73 *et seq*.

[73] Cox, *Practice and Procedure in the Church of Scotland* (6th edn), pp 210 *et seq*; Grant, "Presbyterian Court Records, 1560–1935" in *An Introductory Survey of the Sources and Literature of Scots Law* at pp 156–157.

[74] *R v Governor of Brixton Prison, ex parte Percival* [1907] 1 KB 696.

[75] Colonial Laws Validity Act 1865, s 6.

[76] Evidence (Colonial Statutes) Act 1907, s 1. For references to a substantial number of English cases in which this procedure has been invoked, see *Jasiewicz v Jasiewicz* [1962] 1 WLR 1426.

[77] *R v Governor of Brixton Prison, ex parte Shuter* [1960] 2 QB 89, per Lord Parker CJ at 95. *Cf Jasiewicz v Jasiewicz* [1962] 1 WLR 1426.

[78] See O'Malley and Layton, *European Civil Practice*, para 9.11.

[79] Dickson, *Evidence* (3rd edn), para 1107. See para 16.5.

[80] See para 19.31.

[81] Grants of lesser rights were normally given under the privy seal; in addition writs under the privy seal were also precepts for the execution of a grant under the great seal. The necessity for a privy seal precept was removed in 1809 by 49 Geo III c 42, s 13, and of a signature as warrant for a grant by the Titles to Land Consolidation (Scotland) Act 1868, s 63. For the former practice, see Menzies, *Conveyancing According to the Law of Scotland* (Sturrock's edn), pp 837–844.

[82] *eg* Titles to Land Consolidation (Scotland) Act 1868, s 83, as amended by the Conveyancing (Scotland) Act 1874, s 57.

if executed in the normal way. Usually, royal charters were engrossed in the Register of the Great Seal,[83] but until 1672[84] failure to register was not attended by any penalty and omissions were common.[85] The register was not probative until 1809,[86] and before then booking usually preceded sealing, thus affording *locus poenitentiae* (an opportunity for reconsideration).[87] It is admissible for a witness to testify that he has examined the register and produce his copy thereof; and an extract by an official having a commission to that effect from the Clerk Register is admissible evidence.[88] Despite their imperfections these royal registers are of great weight.

A royal charter is not always proof of the facts narrated therein. Thus a remission is not proof that a crime has been committed,[89] nor a gift of escheat that the person escheated was illegitimate,[90] although illegitimacy may be established by a legitimation.[91] British and United Kingdom peerages may also be proved by production of entries in the House of Lords Journals.[92]   **19.14.2**

Records of chancery, although granted under the great seal or the analogous "quarter seal", differ from other Crown grants under seal in that they are not special grants *de novo* of particular rights, but are deliverances or decrees in the judicial process initiated by brieve, which process was largely superseded by procedure by summons. The chief part of these records of chancery are the retours and decrees of services of heirs.[93] The retour of service was the verdict of an inquest or assize held by virtue of a brieve issued out of chancery for trying certain matters, such as the propinquity of the claimant's ancestor, and whether the ancestor was seized of lands. The verdict of the assize was "retoured," or returned, to chancery and an extract retour was given out under seal.[94] The book of engrossed retours begins in 1830, but they are often incomplete or inaccurate. However, these books and other records of chancery may be of importance in pedigree cases.[95] Extracts from chancery are equivalent to extract retours.[96]   **19.14.3**

Procedure by brieve and retour has now been superseded by petition and service[97]; and an extract registered decree of service is equivalent in effect to the former retour.   **19.14.4**

---

[83] After about 1808 this is called the *Register Magni Sigilli*. There was also a Register of the Privy or Secret Seal: Livingstone, *Guide to the Public Records of Scotland*.

[84] APS, vii, 69, c 16 (1672).

[85] McKechnie, "The Pursuit of Pedigree" (1928) 40 JR 304 at 336.

[86] 49 Geo III c 42, s 15.

[87] Erskine, iv, 1, 22; Dickson, *Evidence* (3rd edn), paras 1151 and 1302; *cf* Titles to Land Consolidation (Scotland) Act 1868, ss 78 and 87. A precept under the privy seal, which was formerly a necessary warrant for a great seal charter, does not prove such a grant under the great seal: *Mags of Sanquhar v Officers of State* (1864) 2 M 499.

[88] Titles to Land Consolidation (Scotland) Act 1868, s 87.

[89] *Baird v Baird* (1662) Mor 12630.

[90] *Cunningham v Montgomery* (1670) Mor 12637.

[91] *King's Advocate v Craw* (1669) Mor 12637.

[92] *Barony of Saye & Sele* (1848) 1 HLC 507.

[93] See, generally, Thomson, *Abridgment of Retours* (1811), Preface; Dickson, *Evidence* (3rd edn), paras 1144–1150.

[94] Originally the principal retour was given out.

[95] McKechnie, "The Pursuit of Pedigree" (1928) 40 JR 205 at 222–226.

[96] Balfour, *Practicks* (1754), p 420: "Na persoun can pretend or alledge ignorance of ony retour or evident that is past or extractit furth of the chancellarie."

[97] Service of Heirs Act 1847, s 2; Titles to Land Consolidation Act 1868, s 27.

19.15 JUDICIAL RECORDS

19.15.1 Interlocutors, decrees, verdicts and other steps in procedure are proved by the original, authenticated by the judge or the clerk of court, as the case may be, or by extracts[98] certified by the proper officer, who, in the case of records in the custody of the court, is the clerk of court or the extractor,[99] and, in the case of records which have been transmitted to his custody, the Keeper of the Records of Scotland.[100]

19.15.2   As between the parties or their successors these records, unless impugned on some extrinsic ground, are conclusive of all facts stated in them which fall properly within the record.[101] But they are not conclusive as to extraneous matters.[102] When the parties are not the same, the findings in one cause would appear to have no evidential value in another unless the first was an action *in rem*.[103]

19.15.3   Admissions on record and confessions by plea are dealt with elsewhere.[104]

19.16 STATUTORY CERTIFICATES

19.16.1 The statutory provisions which allow certificates to take the place of oral testimony are variously expressed, and since they introduce an exception to the general rule which excludes writing as evidence of the facts stated in it, their precise terms are important.[105] Where a certificate is "conclusive evidence" of the matter certified, evidence to contradict the facts to which it speaks is inadmissible,[106] although evidence may be led to challenge the validity of the certificate.[107]

19.16.2   A provision that a certificate shall be "sufficient evidence"[108] renders corroboration unnecessary, and the authorities tend towards the view that in the absence of contradictory evidence, such a certificate is conclusive.[109] While it was previously thought that the privilege attaching to such a certificate ceased if the other party required that the granter be called as a witness,[110] it has more recently been held that evidence from the granter "which did not contradict or take anything

---

[98] Dickson, *Evidence* (3rd edn), para 1286.

[99] Dickson, *Evidence* (3rd edn), paras 1286 and 1288.

[100] Public Records (Scotland) Act 1937, s 9, as amended by the Public Registers and Records (Scotland) Act 1948, s 1. As to judgments of the House of Lords, see para 19.17.

[101] See para 11.5.

[102] Persons who had been fined by magistrates for attending conventicles brought an action founded on subsequent legislation to recover the fines. The decree imposing the fines bore that the money had been applied to the use of the town. This statement was held not to be within the record and therefore not probative *per se* of the fact. It was not decided that it had no evidential value: *Stuart v Mags of Edinburgh* (1697) Mor 12536.

[103] See para 11.5.

[104] See para 9.4.

[105] *Bisset v Anderson* 1949 JC 106 at 111.

[106] *Jamieson v Dow* (1899) 2 F (J) 24; *Henderson v Wardrope* 1932 JC 18; *Walkingshaw v McLaren* 1985 SCCR 293.

[107] *Henderson v Wardrope* 1932 JC 18, per Lord Justice-General Clyde at 21. See also *Kemp v Ballachulish Estate Co Ltd* 1933 SC 478, per Lord Anderson at 491.

[108] *Quaere* as to whether "*prima facie* evidence" can be taken to mean the same as "sufficient evidence": cf *Bisset v Anderson* 1949 JC 106.

[109] *Chalmers v McMeeking* 1921 JC 54; *Inland Revenue Commissioners v Findlay McClure & Co* 1986 SLT 417 (OH). But see *Callan v MacFadyean* 1950 JC 82, per Lord Russell at 87: "I have difficulty in reading the words 'sufficient evidence' in their context as meaning 'conclusive proof'."

[110] *Callan v MacFadyean* 1950 JC 82.

away from the terms of the certificate" should not deprive the party relying on the certificate of the benefit of the presumption.[111]

It has been held that where a certificate signed by an analyst is made "evidence" of the facts therein stated it merely comes in place of the analyst's oral testimony and is therefore insufficient, unless corroborated, to establish a crucial fact.[112]   **19.16.3**

Statutory certificates are most likely to be encountered in conjunction with section 280 of the Criminal Procedure (Scotland) Act 1995, which provides that in proceedings (both summary and solemn) for any offence under certain specified enactments,[113] a certificate will be sufficient evidence as to its subject-matter[114] provided that a copy has been served on the other party not less than 14 days before the trial and that the other party has not timeously challenged its subject-matter.[115] It has been suggested that failure to timeously challenge a certificate means that the accused is barred from disputing the facts therein,[116] although this may be doubtful given that the statutory provisions do not talk of "conclusive" evidence.[117] The section also provides that in any criminal proceedings a report purporting to be signed by two authorised forensic scientists shall be sufficient evidence of any fact or conclusion as to fact contained therein, subject to the same provisions for service and challenge.[118] A report will be sufficient evidence as to its facts even if it is a matter as to which a certificate could have been given and it does not contain all the requirements which would be applicable to the appropriate certificate.[119]   **19.16.4**

A certificate is only evidence of the facts stated therein. For example, a certificate to the effect that a blood sample, delivered to an analyst for examination, contained a certain level of alcohol cannot by itself establish that the sample in question was taken from a particular person at a particular time and place,[120] just as a certificate that a speed measuring device is accurate cannot by itself establish that it was the one used to measure the speed of the accused's car.[121] Here, the question is whether the appropriate link is proved to the relevant standard on competent evidence.[122]   **19.16.5**

---

[111] *Straker v Orr* 1994 SCCR 251 at 254. *Callan v MacFadyean* was not cited. *Straker* differs from *Callan* in that it was the prosecutor who both relied on the certificate and led evidence from the granters, but it is difficult to see why this distinction should be of importance.

[112] *Bisset v Anderson* 1949 JC 106. As to crucial facts, see paras 5.3–5.6.

[113] For which, see the Criminal Procedure (Scotland) Act 1995, Sched 9, as amended by the Criminal Procedure and Investigations Act 1996, s 73(4) and the Crime and Punishment (Scotland) Act 1997, s 30.

[114] Only certain matters are capable of certification; these are specified in Sched 9 to the 1995 Act.

[115] Which challenge must be not more than seven days after the date of service, save on cause shown: Criminal Procedure (Scotland) Act 1995, s 280(6)(b).

[116] *Allan v Taylor* 1986 SCCR 202. *Meek v Vannet* 2000 SCCR 192 proceeded on the basis that a certificate was sufficient if not challenged.

[117] Compare notices of uncontroversial evidence, discussed at para 11.3.

[118] Criminal Procedure (Scotland) Act 1995, s 280(4). "Forensic scientist" is defined in s 280(5).

[119] See *O'Brien v McCreadie* 1994 SCCR 516, where a report narrated that a substance had been analysed and identified as a controlled drug. It did not narrate that the signatories had themselves analysed the substance, which would have rendered it invalid as a certificate (*Normand v Wotherspoon* 1993 JC 248). It was held that the report was nevertheless sufficient evidence. In so holding, the court stressed that reports were only competent in summary prosecutions. However, since the 1995 Act, they are also competent in proceedings on indictment.

[120] *McLeary v Douglas* 1978 JC 57.

[121] *Barbour v Normand* 1992 SCCR 331.

[122] *Tudhope v Corrigall* 1982 SCCR 558; *Williamson v Aitchison* 1982 SLT 399. See also *Lawrie v Stevenson* 1968 JC 71, which took a rather stricter view of the quality of evidence required to establish the link, but has not been followed in subsequent cases. See also para 6.3.

19.16.6   The statute will generally require that the certificate be "signed" by the granter. In such a case, a stamped facsimile rubber signature is sufficient.[123] There is no need to prove the identity of the granter.[124] Where the statute requires that the granter be qualified in a particular way (for example, that they hold a certain post, or that they have undertaken a certain relevant act such as an analysis), the certificate must narrate their qualification *in gremio*.[125] There is no need to prove the granter's qualification, but evidence may be led to show that they were in fact unqualified to grant the certificate, or that it is a fabrication or forgery.[126]

19.16.7   A provision that a certificate "shall, until the contrary is proved, be evidence"[127] seems to imply that it is sufficient, although granted by one person.

19.17 NON-LEGISLATIVE RECORDS OF PARLIAMENT

19.17.1 The non-legislative records of both houses of Parliament and devolved parliaments and assemblies include the *Journals*,[128] speeches from the throne and addresses to the Crown. These are *prima facie* evidence of the proceedings which they record. Their status as evidence of any facts they record is unclear.[129] A copy judgment of the House of Lords, if certified by the proper officer, is adequate proof.[130]

19.18 GAZETTES

19.18.1 The official organs of the state are the *Gazettes* of Edinburgh, London and Belfast (formerly Dublin).[131] These are admissible evidence of the *public* matters contained in them.[132] While judicial notice is taken of the *Gazettes*, the entire *Gazette* and not simply a cutting therefrom should be shown to the court.[133] Thus the Gazette is *prima facie* evidence of any proclamation, order or regulation issued by the Crown, the Privy Council or any of the principal departments of state,[134] but

---

[123] *Cardle v Wilkinson* 1982 JC 36.

[124] *Henderson v Wardrope* 1932 JC 18; *Cardle v Wilkinson* 1982 JC 36.

[125] *Normand v Wotherspoon* 1993 JC 248. This case was distinguished in *Donnelly v Schrikel* 1995 SLT 537, where the parties had entered into a joint minute to the effect that the certificate was a "true and accurate report". It was held that the joint minute superseded the certificate and the defect in the certificate was therefore irrelevant.

[126] This is so whether or not the statute uses the terminology "purporting to be signed", and also whether it explicitly states that no proof of the granter's handwriting or identity is required. See *Henderson v Wardrope* 1932 JC 18; see also *Cardle v Wilkinson* 1982 JC 36.

[127] See, *eg*, Solicitors (Scotland) Act 1980, s 22(1).

[128] And probably now, for these purposes, *Hansard*: see Phipson, *Evidence* (15th edn), para 36-04.

[129] Bell and Dickson took the view that they were not evidence of the facts stated in the resolutions: see Bell, *Principles*, para 2210; Dickson, *Evidence* (3rd edn), para 1110. However, there appears to be no Scottish decision in point and this view is at variance with English decisions: see Phipson, *Evidence* (15th edn), para 36-04 and authorities cited there. It is doubtful whether this position is altered by s 2 of the Civil Evidence (Scotland) Act 1988, as a resolution is probably not a statement "by a person" within the meaning of s 2(1)(b). However, where facts stated "by a person" are recorded, these should now be admissible hearsay in civil proceedings.

[130] Dickson, *Evidence* (3rd edn), para 1110; *Aberdeen Railway Co v Blaikie* (1854) 16 D 470.

[131] Documentary Evidence Act 1868, s 5; Government of Ireland (Adaptation of Enactments) (No 3) Order 1922 (SR&O 1922 No 183), para 38(2)(c).

[132] Phipson, *Evidence* (15th edn), paras 36-07 and 36-08; Dickson, *Evidence* (3rd edn), paras 1112 and 1113.

[133] Phipson, *Evidence* (15th edn), para 36-09; *R v Lowe* (1883) 15 Cox 286.

[134] Documentary Evidence Act 1868, s 2; Documentary Evidence Act 1882, s 2.

not of minor acts of officials.[135] Matters in the *Gazette* relating to questions of *private* right or affecting individuals are in a different position: the *Gazette* is primary evidence of the fact of publication, but only hearsay evidence of the facts contained in the notice,[136] unless statute enjoins otherwise.[137]

19.19 ADMINISTRATIVE DOCUMENTS IN CRIMINAL PROCEDURE

In addition to the rules already mentioned relative to the evidential effect of public documents in criminal procedure, further special rules have been made by statute.[138] Thus, any letter, minute or other official document issuing from the office or in the custody of any of the departments of state or government in the United Kingdom is, when produced, *prima facie* evidence of the matters contained in it without being produced or sworn to by any witness.[139] A copy of such document bearing to be certified by any person having authority to certify it is held as equivalent to the original. No proof of signature or of authority to certify is required.[140] Further, any order by any department of state or government or any local authority or public body made under statutory powers, or a print or copy of such order, when produced is received in evidence of the due making, confirmation and existence of such order without being sworn to by any witness and without further or other proof[141]; but the accused may challenge the order on the ground that it is *ultra vires*.[142]   **19.19.1**

When the order founded upon is one of which judicial notice is taken (principally statutory instruments), there is no need for it to be "produced" in the technical sense, or "received in evidence", because it is used merely to remind the court of what the law is.[143] The position is otherwise when the order lacks this statutory status—it must then be produced and made part of the evidence in the cause.[144] If there is any doubt as to whether judicial notice is taken of the instrument in question, the prudent course for a party wishing to found on it is to produce it in evidence.[145]   **19.19.2**

---

[135] Phipson, *Evidence* (15th edn), para 36-07.

[136] See Dickson, *Evidence* (3rd edn), paras 1112 and 1113.

[137] See, *eg*, Bank Notes (Scotland) Act 1845, s 3 (conclusive evidence).

[138] Criminal Procedure (Scotland) Act 1995, s 279A, as inserted by the Crime and Punishment (Scotland) Act 1997, s 28. Section 279A applies to both summary and solemn proceedings. Its predecessor, s 154 of the 1995 Act, applied only to summary proceedings.

[139] Criminal Procedure (Scotland) Act 1995, s 279A(1).

[140] Criminal Procedure (Scotland) Act 1995, s 279A(2).

[141] Criminal Procedure (Scotland) Act 1995, s 279A(3). See also Sched 3, para 12(a). It has been suggested that the effect of this provision is to give statutory instruments equivalent status to an Act of Parliament in criminal proceedings: Field and Raitt, *Evidence* (2nd edn), para 4-25. However, s 279A(3) still requires the document to be produced and received in evidence, which is unnecessary for Acts of Parliament.

[142] Criminal Procedure (Scotland) Act 1995, s 279A(4).

[143] *Herkes v Dickie* 1958 JC 51 at 55, 57 and 58; *Macmillan v McConnell* 1917 JC 43 at 47 and 53.

[144] *Herkes v Dickie* 1958 JC 51. It seems doubtful whether the regulations in *Macmillan v McConnell* in fact possessed this status, but in both cases the opinions cited proceeded upon the assumption that they did.

[145] Renton & Brown, *Criminal Procedure* (6th edn), para 24-121/1. Although Renton & Brown refers to production by "the prosecutor", it is competent for any party in a criminal proceeding to rely on s 279A.

19.20 REGISTERS OF DEEDS AND OTHER WRITINGS

19.20.1 Private deeds may be registered for one or more of three purposes: (1) for preservation; (2) for execution; and (3) for publication. The appropriate registers are the books of the courts and the register of sasines. Generally, an extract from these registers is probative evidence of the tenor of the original deed except in case of forgery.

19.21 REGISTRATION FOR PRESERVATION

19.21.1 Any deed of private parties, whether it contains a clause of consent for registration for preservation or not,[146] may be registered in the Books of Council and Session[147] or in the books of the sheriff court.[148] The purpose here is to guard against loss or destruction of the deed. While, historically, the principal deed was returned to the ingiver,[149] this is no longer the case with regard to the Books of Council and Session.[150] In both cases, an extract may be given out to interested parties,[151] and such an extract is probative evidence of the tenor of the deed.[152]

19.22 REGISTRATION FOR EXECUTION

19.22.1 Private deeds may be registered in the books of a court for execution.[153] The effect of such registration is to dispense in advance with an action to set up the obligation contained in the deed. An extract of the deed is equivalent to a decree of the court, and execution can be done on the extract. As with registration for preservation, the principal deed is only returned to the ingiver where it is registered in the books of the sheriff court.[154] Registration for execution requires a clause of consent for registration in the deed, except in the case of bonds in favour of the Crown.[155] As with registration for preservation, the competent court books available for registration for execution have been limited to the books of Council and Session and the sheriff court books.[156] An extract or official copy of a deed registered for execution is probative evidence of the tenor of the deed.[157]

---

[146] The common law requirement for such a clause was removed by APS, x, 149, c 4 (1698): see Dickson, *Evidence* (3rd edn), para 1140.

[147] Initiated 1554 when styled "Register of Deeds". Its full title is now the "Register of Deeds and Probative Writs in the Books of Council and Session".

[148] The former multiplicity of court books in which registration was competent was restricted by the Act, 49 Geo III c 42: Dickson, *Evidence* (3rd edn), para 1141.

[149] APS, x, 149, c 4 (1698).

[150] Writs Registration (Scotland) Act 1868, s 1.

[151] Dickson, *Evidence* (3rd edn), para 1139.

[152] APS, x, 149, c 4 (1698); Writs Execution (Scotland) Act 1877, s 5. The former statute is of general application; the latter relates only to the Books of Council and Session.

[153] For the historical development of registration for execution, see Dickson, *Evidence* (3rd edn), para 1136; Morrison, "Registration and Records" in *Encyclopaedia of the Laws of Scotland*, Vol xii, para 762.

[154] The principal deed has not been returned from the Books of Council and Session since the Writs Registration (Scotland) Act 1868, s 2, but may be given out on the order of a judge.

[155] Exchequer Court (Scotland) Act 1856, s 38.

[156] Act, 49 Geo III c 42.

[157] Writs Execution (Scotland) Act 1877, s 5. This statute relates only to the Books of Council and Session, but on principle it is thought that the same applies to extracts from the books of the sheriff court.

19.23 REGISTRATION FOR PUBLICATION

The system of registration for publication[158] of deeds creating heritable rights was **19.23.1** introduced by the Registration Act 1617,[159] which instituted a universal system of registration of deeds, consisting of a general, or nationwide, register of sasines (arranged in county divisions) and particular or local registers. Registration of the deed in the appropriate register constitutes infeftment. The principal deed is returned to the ingiver after recording, and extracts from the register are to be accepted for all purposes as sufficient evidence of the contents of the original.[160]

Under the Land Registration (Scotland) Act 1979,[161] the Keeper is required to **19.23.2** make up and maintain a title sheet of an interest in land in the register.[162] A copy of the title sheet, authenticated by the Keeper's seal, is known as a land certificate[163] and is to be accepted for all purposes as sufficient evidence of the title sheet of which it is a copy.[164] A charge certificate, which is issued by the Keeper upon completion of registration in respect of a heritable security,[165] is for all purposes sufficient evidence of the facts stated in it.[166]

19.24 REGISTER OF INHIBITIONS AND ADJUDICATIONS

Commonly known as the Personal Register or the Diligence Register, this is the **19.24.1** only diligence register now in use.[167] Inhibition is the interdiction of a person from dealing with his estate; and adjudication is the procedure whereby a creditor can obtain what amounts to a judicial security over heritable subjects.[168] Inhibitions must be recorded in this register,[169] but adjudications will only be recorded therein if the subjects are not registered in the Sasine or Land Register.[170] Extracts from this register are probative both at common law and statute.[171]

---

[158] For the historical development of registration for publication, see Morrison, "Registration and Records" in *Encyclopaedia of the Laws of Scotland*, Vol xii, para 773; McKechnie, "The Pursuit of Pedigree" (1928) 40 JR 304.

[159] APS, iv, 545, c 16.

[160] Conveyancing and Feudal Reform (Scotland) Act 1970, s 45. This gave effect to a recommendation of the Halliday Committee designed to overcome some doubts as to the value of extract deeds: *Conveyancing Legislation and Practice* (Cmnd 3118, 1966), para 66.

[161] At the time of writing, it is intended that the whole of Scotland will be operational for Land Registration purposes by 2003. See National Audit Office, *The Registers of Scotland: Service to the Public* (1994), p 19. Even after that date, however, the Sasine Register will continue in operation for properties not sold after the Land Register came into operation for the relevant area.

[162] Land Registration (Scotland) Act 1979, s 6. This section lists in detail the information which should be entered on the title sheet.

[163] Land Registration (Scotland) Act 1979, s 5(2).

[164] Land Registration (Scotland) Act 1979, s 5(4).

[165] Land Registration (Scotland) Act 1979, s 5(3).

[166] Land Registration (Scotland) Act 1979, s 5(4).

[167] Earlier registers of apprisings (or comprisings) are preserved in HM General Register House: Livingstone, *Guide to the Public Records of Scotland*; Land Registers (Scotland) Act 1868, ss 16 and 17.

[168] See Gretton, *The Law of Inhibition and Adjudication* (2nd edn) pp 1 and 4.

[169] Titles to Land (Consolidation) (Scotland) Act 1868, s 155.

[170] Gretton, *The Law of Inhibition and Adjudication* (2nd edn), p 212.

[171] *Williamson v Threapland* (1682) Mor 12548; APS, iii, 223, c 24 (1581). While these authorities are concerned only with registration of inhibition, it is thought that the same principle would apply to a registration of adjudication in this Register.

19.25 RECORDS, ETC, RELATIVE TO SHIPS

Merchant Shipping Act 1894

19.25.1 Under the Merchant Shipping Act 1894, a certificate of registry (or an endorsement thereon) purporting to be signed by the registrar or other proper officer, and any declaration made in pursuance of Part I of that Act, is sufficient evidence of the matters stated therein.[172]

Merchant Shipping Act 1995

19.25.2 Under the Merchant Shipping Act 1995, various documents are made admissible in evidence and are, "subject to all just exceptions", sufficient evidence of the matters stated therein.[173] These include documents purporting to be submissions and decisions relating to disputes about seamen's wages[174]; the official log book[175]; crew agreements, lists of crews and related documents[176]; returns or reports made under the provisions relating to returns of births and deaths in ships[177]; and documents transmitted to the Registrar-General of Shipping and Seamen by mercantile marine superintendents and customs and excise officers.[178]

19.25.3 A copy or extract is admissible and sufficient provided that (in criminal proceedings) it is proved to be an examined copy or extract, or purports to be signed and certified as a true copy or extract by the officer to whose custody the original document was entrusted,[179] or (in civil proceedings) that it is authenticated in accordance with section 6(1) of the Civil Evidence (Scotland) Act 1988.[180] Such documents are not conclusive evidence and may be rebutted.[181] The Act also contains provisions which allow for public inspection and issuance of copies of documents in the custody of the Registrar-General of Shipping and Seamen.[182]

19.26 REGISTERS OF BIRTHS, DEATHS AND MARRIAGES, ETC

Before 1854

19.26.1 Prior to the Registration of Births, Deaths and Marriages (Scotland) Act 1854, there was no statutory system of registration of life statistics. The only records were those of the parishes instituted in the sixteenth century by virtue of the legislation of the provincial council of the Catholic Church, and thereafter regulated by

---

[172] Merchant Shipping Act 1894, s 64 (as amended by the Merchant Shipping Act 1988, Sched 1).

[173] Merchant Shipping Act 1995, s 288(1)(b).

[174] Under s 33 of the Act: Merchant Shipping Act 1995, s 287(1)(a).

[175] Merchant Shipping Act 1995, s 287(1)(b). Prior to the introduction of a statutory provision requiring the keeping of an official log book (Merchant Shipping Act 1970, s 68), any log kept was not evidence but might, be reports, be used to refresh the memory of the person who made the entry or for purposes of cross-examination. The same would presumably apply to any unofficial log book today. See *Admiralty v Aberdeen Steam Trawling & Fishing Co Ltd* 1909 SC 335 at 341. See also *Palestine Transport Shipping Co v Greenock Dockyard Co* 1947 SN 162.

[176] Merchant Shipping Act 1995, s 287(1)(c).

[177] Under s 108 of the Act: Merchant Shipping Act 1995, s 287(1)(d).

[178] Under s 298 of the Act: Merchant Shipping Act 1995, s 287(1)(e).

[179] Merchant Shipping Act 1995, s 288(3).

[180] Merchant Shipping Act 1995, s 288(8). See para 20.2. This is subject to the court's discretion not to accept a copy authenticated in this manner.

[181] *Watson v Duncan* (1879) 6 R 1247. See also *Duthie v Aiken* (1893) 20 R 241.

[182] Merchant Shipping Act 1995, ss 287 and 288.

acts of assembly of the Reformed Church between 1574 and 1816.[183] This system of parish registration operated with varying degrees of accuracy and completeness. The chief defects were that: not all parishes kept registers[184]; as a rule only members of the established church were considered; and the events recorded were baptisms (not births), weddings in established churches (sometimes merely banns), and burials (rather than deaths).[185] The registers are admissible evidence of the facts contained in them, the degree of credit being proportionate to their regularity.[186] The absence of an entry relating to an event raises no presumption against its occurrence.[187]

After 1854

The 1854 Act instituted a regular public system of registration administered on the basis of registration districts, which originally corresponded to parishes.[188] A Register of Corrections, Etc was established in 1965 for the recording of corrections, amendments and particulars of events occurring subsequent to registration,[189] and a Register of Divorces was established in 1985.[190] The registers are kept by registrars, who derive their information from persons who give it under penalty for falsehood.[191] A duly authenticated[192] extract from the registers,[193] or abbreviated certificate of birth, is sufficient evidence of the birth, death, marriage, decree of divorce or declarator of nullity of marriage to which it relates.[194] Extracts are merely hearsay evidence of other facts stated therein, such as the parentage of a child, but may give rise to a presumption and may be evidence of a statement against interest by the person proved to have signed the entry.[195]

19.26.2

---

[183] Dickson, *Evidence* (3rd edn), paras 1168–1204.

[184] In 1801, only 99 out of 850 parishes had registers.

[185] It was held in *Watson v Glass* (1837) 15 S 753 that, where the age at death was stated in the recording of a burial, this was not good evidence of the fact of age. Following s 2 of the Civil Evidence (Scotland) Act 1988, it would now be admissible hearsay in civil proceedings but would probably have limited weight.

[186] Dickson, *Evidence* (3rd edn), para 1173.

[187] Dickson, *Evidence* (3rd edn), para 1173.

[188] Registration of Births, Deaths and Marriages (Scotland) Act 1854 (now repealed). The principal statute is now the Registration of Births, Deaths and Marriages (Scotland) Act 1965.

[189] Registration of Births, Deaths and Marriages (Scotland) Act 1965, s 44. All previously existing registers of corrected entries are to have effect as if they were part of this Register: s 44(2).

[190] Registration of Births, Deaths and Marriages (Scotland) Act 1965, s 28A, as inserted by the Law Reform (Miscellaneous Provisions) (Scotland) Act 1985, s 50. This register also records declarators of nullity of marriage. This gave statutory authority to the Register of Divorces which had been operated as part of the Register of Corrections Etc since 1 May 1984.

[191] Registration of Births, Deaths and Marriages (Scotland) Act 1965, s 53.

[192] Sealed or stamped with the seal of the General Register Office or signed by the district registrar: Registration of Births, Deaths and Marriages (Scotland) Act 1965, s 41(1).

[193] Excluding extracts from parochial registers.

[194] Registration of Births, Deaths and Marriages (Scotland) Act 1965, ss 28A(5) and 41(3). *Cf Keenan v Keenan* 1974 SLT (Notes) 10, where Lord Fraser held extracts not to be sufficient evidence in a consistorial action. However, this judgment was taken under reference to s 58 of the Registration of Births, Deaths and Marriages (Scotland) Act 1854, which had been repealed eight years beforehand. See the Registration of Births, Deaths and Marriages (Scotland) Act 1965, ss 58–59 and Sched 2. It would appear that the 1965 Act was not cited to the court.

[195] *Stewart v Stewart* 1930 SLT 363; *Alexander v Alexander* 1920 SC 327; *Mathieson v Mathieson* 1914 1 SLT 511; *Duncan v Duncan* (1893) 30 SLR 435. As to presumptions in this context see paras 3.5.3 and 28.15.

19.27 ADOPTED CHILDREN REGISTER

19.27.1 This register, maintained by the Registrar General for Scotland at the General Register Office, contains such entries as are directed to be made therein by adoption orders.[196] An extract from the Register is admissible as evidence of the adoption to which it relates and also as to the date of birth, or country of birth, of the adopted person, if it contains such information.[197]

19.28 PROFESSIONAL AND MILITARY REGISTERS

19.28.1 Authorised copies of registers or lists kept under statute relative to the practice of certain professions or certificates granted by persons appointed to keep these records are generally sufficient evidence (although the statutory provisions are not all uniform); the appearance of a person's name in them is evidence of his or her name having been duly registered or entered. The absence of a person's name from the list or a certificate to that effect is equally evidence of non-registration of that person. Examples of professions whose registers or rolls are in this position are architects,[198] dentists,[199] medical practitioners,[200] nurses, midwives and health visitors,[201] osteopaths,[202] pharmaceutical chemists,[203] solicitors[204] and veterinary surgeons.[205]

19.28.2 Evidential effect is given to certificates purporting to be issued by or on behalf of the Defence Council relative to the status, rank and appointment of members of HM Forces and certain other military matters, but the relevant statutory provisions only apply to proceedings under the Army Act 1955 and the Air Force Act 1955.[206]

19.29 REGISTER OF PATENTS

19.29.1 Under the Patents Act 1977, the Comptroller-General of Patents, Designs and Trade Marks is required to maintain the Register of Patents. Certified copies or extracts from that Register are sufficient evidence of their contents.[207] Furthermore, the Comptroller may issue a certificate certifying that any entry which he is authorised to make in the Register by the 1977 Act has or has not been

---

[196] Adoption (Scotland) Act 1978, s 45(1). See McNeill, *Adoption of Children in Scotland* (3rd edn), paras 11.03–11.04.

[197] Adoption (Scotland) Act 1978, s 45(2). The statute provides merely that the extract shall be "evidence", not that it shall be sufficient or conclusive.

[198] Architects Act 1997, s 3.

[199] Dentists Act 1984, s 14.

[200] Medical Act 1983, s 34.

[201] Nurses, Midwives and Health Visitors Act 1979, s 10.

[202] Osteopaths Act 1993, s 9(4).

[203] Pharmacy Act 1954, s 6(2).

[204] Solicitors (Scotland) Act 1980, s 22.

[205] Veterinary Surgeons Act 1966, ss 2–9.

[206] Army Act 1955, s 198; Air Force Act 1955, s 198, both as amended by the Army and Air Force Act 1981, Sched 2 and SI 1964/488. The use of certificates issued under the Confirmation of Executors (War Service) (Scotland) Act 1940 for purposes outwith the scope of the statute was rejected in *Robson Scott's Trs v Robson Scott* 1945 SC 52 and *Hannay, Petitioner* 1949 SC 304.

[207] Patents Act 1977, s 32(11), as amended by the Patents, Designs and Marks Act 1986, s 1 and Sched 1.

made, or that any other thing which he is authorised to do has or has not been done.[208] Such a certificate is sufficient evidence of the matters so certified.[209]

19.30 OFFICIAL RECORDS

At common law, books kept by public officials for the purpose of recording cer- **19.30.1** tain facts are admissible as *prima facie* evidence of those facts,[210] but merely hearsay evidence of extraneous matters which may have been entered.[211] For example, in *Kay v Rodger*,[212] a jail book exhibited by the clerk to the jail was evidence of the date of an execution, and an extract from the books of the War Office would have been admitted to prove where a unit was stationed at a particular time, if the person who made the extract had been adduced to prove its accuracy.[213]

19.31 FOREIGN, DOMINION AND COLONIAL DOCUMENTS

At common law the contents of public registers of countries outwith Scotland **19.31.1** require to be proved. However, where an Order in Council is made under statute,[214] an official copy of an extract in a register specified in the relevant Order may be received in evidence. Orders have been made in respect of many countries,[215] and the relevant Order should be referred to in each case for any conditions it may specify, including the proper manner of authentication.[216] Whether the official copy can be received as evidence of the facts stated therein or simply as evidence of the fact of such an entry existing will depend upon the provisions of the relevant Order in respect of that register.[217]

19.32 MINUTES OF MEETINGS—GENERAL

Introductory

Since the Civil Evidence (Scotland) Act 1988, minutes of meetings will generally **19.32.1** now be admissible hearsay evidence. However, the common law rules will continue to apply in criminal proceedings, and may also provide some guidance as to the weight to be given to such evidence in civil proceedings, and they are set out here for those purposes.

---

[208] Patents Act 1977, s 32(10).
[209] Patents Act 1977, s 32(10).
[210] For example, records of lighthouse keepers have been held admissible as evidence of the weather (*Williams v Dobbie* (1884) 11 R 982), and the appointment of a burgh official to be sufficiently proved by an entry in the burgh books (*Hunter v Hill* (1833) 11 S 989).
[211] Dickson, *Evidence* (3rd edn), para 1209.
[212] (1832) 10 S 831.
[213] *Kay v Rodger* (1832) 10 S 831. It would no longer be necessary to adduce evidence from the person who made the extract if it were certified in accordance with s 5(1) of the Civil Evidence (Scotland) Act 1988: see para 20.3.
[214] Evidence (Foreign, Dominion and Colonial Documents) Act 1933, s 1, as amended by the Oaths and Evidence (Overseas Authorities and Countries) Act 1963, s 5.
[215] For a list, see *Halsbury's Laws* (4th edn), Vol 17, *Evidence*, para 184.
[216] If the conditions laid down in the order are not satisfied, the benefit of the statutory provisions will be lost: *Motture v Motture* [1955] 1 WLR 1066.
[217] See the Evidence (Foreign, Dominion and Colonial Documents) Act 1933, s 1(2)(c)–(d).

Common law—general

19.32.2 At common law, it is thought that the best evidence of what took place at a meeting is the testimony of those who were present, and on strict principle a written account is inadmissible except as evidence against those who have accepted it as accurate. The principle has, however, been impinged upon by statute[218] and there are dicta suggesting that, even at common law, minutes may acquire general evidential value.[219] Any such value, it is thought, is confined to the minute of a corporation, or possibly of persons meeting under a common duty, such as trustees, and does not extend to that of a meeting of individuals who voluntarily meet to discuss a matter.[220] The other main distinction appears to be in the method of approving the minute. While a minute may be written and approved at the meeting, the normal practice is to compile a draft minute from notes taken at the meeting and present it for approval at the next meeting. There are thus three writings: the notes, the draft minute and the approved minute.

Common law—before approval

19.32.3 Like any other notes made at the time,[221] they may also be used to refresh the memory of the person who took them while he is giving evidence.[222] A ruling that the witness might use the draft minute for the same purpose was excepted to, with, it is thought, some justification, but the case was settled.[223]

Common law—after approval

19.32.4 Unless under statute,[224] or in matters of great antiquity[225] or in exceptional circumstances,[226] the principal (if not the only) evidential value of an approved minute is as the writ of party[227] or as a statement against interest.[228] Where the meeting was one of individuals held to discuss a common project, the minute can be evidence against one of the individuals only if he has approved it. This he may do either by signing it or assenting to its signature by the chairman of that or a subsequent meeting.[229] But a minute of meeting of a corporation or firm is evidence against it if it has been approved at a subsequent meeting, even although not

---

[218] See para 19.33.

[219] *City of Glasgow Bank Liquidators* (1880) 7 R 1196 at 1199. But it is not easy to see the value of the minute if the facts have been proved *aliunde*. *Cf Johnston v Scott* (1860) 22 D 393 at 402, where it is said that a minute is not evidence at all, but may be an adminicle of evidence. See also *A v B* (1858) 20 D 407.

[220] *Johnston v Scott* (1860) 22 D 393 at 402 and 403; Dickson, *Evidence* (3rd edn), para 1216.

[221] See para 27.7.

[222] *Wilson v Glasgow and South Western Railway Co* (1851) 14 D 1. *Cf Mathers v Laurie* (1849) 12 D 433.

[223] *Wilson v Glasgow and South Western Railway Co* (1851) 14 D 1. Use of the notes for such a purpose might be more acceptable if the witness had seen them (or possibly had them read aloud to him) at the time they were taken: *cf R v Kelsey* (1982) 74 Cr App R 213.

[224] See para 19.33.

[225] Dickson, *Evidence* (3rd edn), para 1217.

[226] *A v B* (1858) 20 D 407. The minutes incorporated hearsay of a person who died before the proof, and the tenor of a letter later lost.

[227] See para 25.5.

[228] See Chapter 9.

[229] *Devlin v McKelvie* 1915 SC 180, where the pursuer failed to prove that the defender had assented to signature by the chairman; *Cameron v Panton's Trs* (1891) 18 R 728, where the pursuer did not sign the minute; *Johnston v Scott* (1860) 22 D 393 at 399–404, where the defenders neither signed nor assented to the chairman's signature.

composed of the same individuals.[230] It is the assent, not the signature, which is vital. Signature by a chairman who has no authority has no effect,[231] and conversely an unsigned minute was held to be evidence against a firm.[232] An approved minute may, however, have a wider evidential value owing to the operation of some extrinsic rule. So, for example, the minutes of a kirk session have been admitted (1) as proof of the tenor[233] of a letter engrossed in them, the principal having been lost, and (2) as hearsay of the minister who had died, provided that they might require to support them the evidence not only of the clerk who wrote them, but also of others present at the meeting.[234]

Common law—kirk sessions and other church courts

The minutes of these bodies of the established Church[235] sometimes take the form **19.32.5** of, or include, decrees in an ecclesiastical process. Such decrees are probably admissible where they have been authenticated according to the forms of the church, which at one time seem to have been somewhat irregular.[236] In other situations it appears that these minutes are not in general admissible as evidence.[237] The records of dissenting congregations are not admissible.[238]

19.33 MINUTES OF MEETING—STATUTORY

Local authorities

The minute books of local authorities are "received in evidence" without further **19.33.1** proof.[239] This, it is thought, makes the minutes evidence of decisions and orders therein recorded. It has been held that the minutes of road trustees are the only competent evidence of their proceedings.[240] It has been doubted whether an order by road trustees was valid *quoad* third parties where the minute recording it was unsigned, though approved at a subsequent meeting.[241]

Limited companies

A company's articles may render the minutes conclusive evidence of the fact that **19.33.2**

---

[230] *Cf Hill v Lindsay* (1847) 10 D 78, where all the shareholders signed the minute and proof was allowed only because the minute was not clear.

[231] *Mackenzie v Macartney* (1831) 5 W & S 504; *Devlin v McKelvie* 1915 SC 180.

[232] *Ivison v Edinburgh Silk Yarn Co* (1846) 9 D 1039. This was a joint stock company; but the Private Act establishing it expressly excluded its incorporation.

[233] See paras 20.4 *et seq.*

[234] *A v B* (1858) 20 D 407 at 417 and 418.

[235] A kirk session is not a corporation: *Kirk Session of North Berwick v Sime* (1839) 2 D 23.

[236] *Ferguson v Skirving* (1850) 12 D 1145; affirmed (1852) 1 Macq 232; see also *Dalhousie's Tutors* (1890) 17 R 1060, where the admissibility of the minute was not in issue and it was held competent to lead evidence to explain the decree, but not to contradict it. It seems to be assumed in *Mathers v Laurie* (1849) 12 D 433 that they are admissible. As to the mode of authentication of minutes, etc, and their inspection by superior church courts, see Cox, *Practice and Procedure in the Church of Scotland* (4th edn), pp 70, 72 and 75. See also para 19.12.

[237] *A v B* (1858) 20 D 407.

[238] Dickson, *Evidence* (3rd edn), para 1216; *Mathers v Laurie* (1849) 12 D 433 (Free Church).

[239] Local Government (Scotland) Act 1973, Sched 7, para 7(1).

[240] *McGhie v McKirdy* (1850) 12 D 442. Doubted by Dickson, *Evidence* (3rd edn), para 1215.

[241] *Lord Blantyre v Dickson* (1885) 13 R 116; *Forbes v Morison* (1851) 14 D 134; *cf Ivison v Edinburgh Silk Yarn Co* (1846) 9 D 1039, where unsigned minutes of a firm were admitted against the firm.

a resolution has been carried or lost at a general meeting[242] but they may be sup-plemented by other evidence, at least so as to show that the proper procedure was followed.[243] Apart from these special provisions, the minutes of a general meeting of a company, its directors or its managers (if any), purporting to be signed by the chairman at that or the next succeeding meeting, are evidence of the proceed-ings.[244] They are not expressly either conclusive or exhaustive, and in England, while the absence of any reference to a matter in the minutes is evidence that it was not discussed, a transaction may be proved though not inserted in the minutes.[245] Where, however, a resolution for voluntary winding-up had been intimated to the Registrar and recorded in a minute, as directed by statute, and acted upon by the court, evidence to supplement the terms of the resolution, as recorded in the minute, was held inadmissible.[246]

Bankruptcy

19.33.3 The Bankruptcy (Scotland) Act 1985 requires minutes to be kept of all meetings of creditors, but there is no express provision as to their evidential effect.[247] These minutes are good *prima facie* evidence and parole proof in contradiction of them should be inadmissible,[248] unless due exertion has failed to permit production of the principals.[249] The accuracy of the minutes can be challenged only if they have not been acted upon.[250]

19.33.4   The permanent trustee must keep a sederunt book "for the purpose of providing an accurate record of the sequestration process".[251] Any entry in this book is suf-ficient evidence of the facts stated therein, except where it is founded on by the permanent trustee in his own interest.[252]

19.34 HISTORIES AND PRIVATE RECORDS

19.34.1 In ancient matters, such as peerage and pedigree cases, contemporary chronicles and histories are admissible evidence on the ground that the authors were acquainted with the facts and that their compilation was not made with a view to litigation.[253] The weight to be given to these works depends on the reputation of the historian.[254] Modern compilations, such as peerage books, because they are secondary works based on primary sources which are still extant, were not admissible at common law[255] but would now be admissible hearsay in civil

---

[242] Companies (Tables A to F) Regulations 1985 (SI 1985/805), Table A, reg 47.

[243] *Fraserburgh Commercial Co Ltd* 1946 SC 444.

[244] Companies Act 1985, s 382(2).

[245] *Re Fireproof Doors Ltd* [1916] 2 Ch 142.

[246] *City of Glasgow Bank Liquidators* (1880) 7 R 1196 at 1199.

[247] Bankruptcy (Scotland) Act 1985, s 66 and Sched 6, para 16.

[248] Goudy, *Bankruptcy* (4th edn), p 226. Goudy does state (at pp 197–198) that minutes of the first statutory meeting of creditors are the *only* legitimate evidence of proceedings, but this is not supported by the authorities cited.

[249] On which see para 20.3.

[250] *Brown v Lindsay* (1869) 7 M 595; *Lea v Landale* (1828) 6 S 350.

[251] Bankruptcy (Scotland) Act 1985, s 3(1)(e).

[252] Bankruptcy (Scotland) Act 1985, s 62(3).

[253] *Report on the Trial of Earl of Stirling,* 1839 (Swinton (ed)).

[254] Dickson, *Evidence* (3rd edn), para 1220; Stair, iv, 42, 16; Erskine, iv, 2, 7.

[255] Dickson, *Evidence* (3rd edn), para 1220. The *Statistical Accounts* of 1796 and 1845 "are not, strictly, evidence"; *Meacher v Blair-Oliphant* 1913 SC 417 at 430, 432 and 437.

proceedings.[256] Private muniments, such as cartularies, old inventories of writs and tacks of land are admissible,[257] as are entries in family bibles, memoranda in church registers, tombstone inscriptions,[258] and minutes.[259]

19.35 MAPS AND PLANS

While maps and plans are generally admissible in evidence and are now within the statutory definition of "document",[260] the weight to be attached to them is dependent upon various factors. **19.35.1**

Matters pertaining to reliability

An anonymous plan will be of little or no value, at least where it has not been previously acted upon.[261] An estate map or plan is good evidence if it can be shown that it was impartial—for example, that it was made by or for the common author of the parties—or at least that it has been so used that it would probably have been challenged if inaccurate. Where a plan had been handed by the defenders' predecessor in title to his trustees in bankruptcy during negotiations for the sale of the property, it was admitted and used as evidence against the defenders,[262] and the same was held with regard to a plan which had been used in settling a question between predecessors of the parties.[263] Ordnance Survey maps are often used, although it should be noted that nothing done under the Ordnance Survey Act 1841 is to alter any boundaries, and that all right and title remain as if the Act had not been passed.[264] Nevertheless, Ordnance Survey Maps (including the digital versions of these) form the basis for the "index map" of Scotland against which applications for land registration[265] are assessed by the Keeper.[266] **19.35.2**

Matters pertaining to accuracy

In *Morrison v McCowan*,[267] measurements of the distances between various major towns taken from an Ordnance Survey map were admissible to prove that vehicles must have exceeded the speed limit in travelling between them, but in that case the measurements could have been some 30 or 40 miles out (on journeys of less than 250 miles) before an acquittal would have been justified. Where a matter is sought to be proven with more precision, an Ordnance Survey map is unlikely to be **19.35.3**

---

[256] Civil Evidence (Scotland) Act 1988, s 2.
[257] McKechnie, "The Pursuit of Pedigree" (1928) 40 JR 304 at 315–317; see also *Mags of Sanquhar v Officers of State* (1864) 2 M 499 (charter in collection in Advocates' Library); *Proceedings before the Committee of Privileges* (HMSO): *Dudhope Peerage* (1952); *Earldom of Dundee* (1953).
[258] Dickson, *Evidence* (3rd edn), para 1222.
[259] Dickson, *Evidence* (3rd edn), para 1217. See also paras 19.32–19.33.
[260] On which see paras 19.1 and 21.1. Ordnance Survey Maps are now produced digitally.
[261] *Place v Earl of Breadalbane* (1874) 1 R 1202.
[262] *Reid v Haldane's Trs* (1891) 18 R 744. The plan would not have been evidence in favour of the defender. See Phipson, *Evidence* (15th edn), para 36-54.
[263] *Brown v North British Railway Co* (1906) 8 F 534.
[264] Ordnance Survey Act 1841, s 12, as amended by the Statute Law Revision (No 2) Act 1888.
[265] See para 19.23.
[266] Land Registration (Scotland) Rules 1980 (SI 1980/1413), r 23, explained further in the *Registration of Title Practice Book* (Law Society of Scotland & Registers of Scotland, Executive Agency), paras 4.4, 4.14 and 4.22–4.26.
[267] 1939 JC 45.

sufficient without further supporting evidence,[268] and particularly so where there is contradictory evidence.[269] Where an Ordnance Survey map is sought to be used to prove the exact position of a boundary, it will probably be necessary to lead evidence of the plotted sketch maps and rough sketches used in preparing the OS map, and probably also evidence as to the manner in which the mapping exercise is carried out, even if there is no contradictory evidence.[270] Ordnance Survey Maps are recreated regularly to reflect the outcomes of regular surveys of the country, but, clearly, evidence will be admissible to prove that the actual situation differs from that represented by the map. The weight to be attached to such evidence will depend upon the delay between the last survey and the situation arising in the proceedings, and to the accuracy of the mapping technique.

19.36 NOTARIAL INSTRUMENTS

19.36.1 A notarial instrument is a narrative under the hand of a notary detailing procedure which has been transacted by or before him in his official capacity[271] and, being a tested writ, is probative of the act which it is in the province of the notary to perform, but not of extraneous facts narrated in the instrument.[272] Notarial power has by statute been accorded to consuls-general, consuls, counsellors and holders of various other similar specified offices appointed by the Crown abroad.[273] A notarial instrument can only be contradicted by way of reduction.[274]

19.37 CITATIONS AND EXECUTIONS

19.37.1 Some documents, although not probative, self-proving or historically privileged according to the rules of execution of writs,[275] are nevertheless competent and conclusive evidence of the matters which they narrate when they have been signed by the appropriate officer—messenger-at-arms, sheriff officer or solicitor.[276] These are chiefly citations of witnesses, parties, jurors and havers,[277] and executions, which narrate the fact of citation having been carried out.[278] An *ex facie* regular execution is probative of these facts, but not of extraneous matter,[279] and is generally exclusive evidence of the citation. But there are exceptions: parole evidence

---

[268] *Ross v Beck* 1992 GWD 16-930 (Sh Ct).

[269] *Meacher v Blair-Oliphant* 1913 SC 417; *Gibson v Bonnington Sugar Refining Co* (1869) 7 M 394.

[270] *Miller v Jackson*, 15 March 1972 (OH) (reported on another point at 1972 SLT (Notes) 31). See Macphail, *Evidence*, para 12.40.

[271] Dickson, *Evidence* (3rd edn), paras 1233–1238, 1244 and 1245; Bell, *Dictionary and Digest of the Law of Scotland* (7th edn), p 744. A notice of title is now equivalent to a notarial instrument: Conveyancing (Scotland) Act 1924, s 6(1).

[272] Stair, iv, 42, 9; Erskine, ii, 3, 34; iv, 2, 5; Bell, *Principles*, para 2221; Dickson, *Evidence* (3rd edn), para 1233; *Balfour v Lyle* (1832) 10 S 853.

[273] Commissioners for Oaths Act 1889, s 6, as amended by Commissioners for Oaths Act 1891, s 2 and Oaths and Evidence (Overseas Authorities and Countries) Act 1963, s 3.

[274] Dickson, *Evidence* (3rd edn), para 1244; *Henry v Reid* (1871) 9 M 503.

[275] See Chapters 23 and 24.

[276] Dickson, *Evidence* (3rd edn), paras 1246–1247.

[277] Dickson, *Evidence* (3rd edn), paras 1253–1261.

[278] Dickson, *Evidence* (3rd edn), paras 1261–1284. Signature of the citation is probably essential: see *Blackfriars (Scotland) Ltd v John Laurie* 2000 SCLR 385 at 390E–391A.

[279] Dickson, *Evidence* (3rd edn), paras 1263 and 1279.

was allowed where the debtor had destroyed the execution of the charge necessary to constitute notour bankruptcy[280]; and the service of complaints, warrants and other proceedings in summary criminal procedure may be proved by the oath of the officer.[281]

In *Mackinnon v Virhia*,[282] a police officer's certificate of execution of service **19.37.2** narrated that he had served on the accused both a complaint and a statutory certificate as to the level of alcohol in his blood at the time of the offence. It was held that, while the certificate did prove service of the complaint,[283] it did not prove service of the certificate without its being spoken to by the officer.

---

[280] *Drummond v Clunas Tiles and Mosaics Ltd* 1909 SC 1049.
[281] Criminal Procedure (Scotland) Act 1995, s 297(2).
[282] 1980 JC 70.
[283] By virtue of the statutory provisions noted earlier, then contained in the Criminal Procedure (Scotland) Act 1975, s 326.

CHAPTER 20

PROOF OF TERMS OF DOCUMENTS NOT PRODUCED

20.1 BEST EVIDENCE—COMMON LAW

At common law secondary or substitutionary evidence is inadmissible when primary original evidence is, or ought to be, available.[1] This manifests in the rule against hearsay as proof of its facts,[2] and, of interest to us in this chapter, the exclusion of secondary evidence of a document. Except in the circumstances mentioned below[3] it is incompetent in the course of a proof or trial to establish the terms of a document not produced, by secondary evidence such as parole evidence[4] or production of a copy[5] unless of consent[6] or under statutory authority. Special rules concerning public, official and business documents are considered in another chapter.[7] **20.1.1**

What the best evidence rule excludes is secondary evidence, and it does not mean that because a fact could be proved by production of a document it cannot be proved by other primary evidence. Where an agreement could have been proved by a letter of undertaking, the pursuer was allowed to prove it by letters and entries in the defenders' books.[8] Births, deaths and marriages may be proved by parole without extracts from the register.[9] Further, it is competent to prove that the document exists[10] and also to prove a practice founded on instances occurring in documents, such as leases and insurance policies, without producing them.[11] **20.1.2**

---

[1] *Dickson, Evidence* (3rd edn), para 195.
[2] See para 8.1. Another occurs with real evidence: see para 18.5.
[3] See para 20.3.
[4] *Malley v MS Railway* 1944 SC 129, per Lord President Cooper at 138; *Aitchison v Robertson* (1846) 9 D 15; *Gibson v Anderson* (1846) 9 D 1.
[5] *Summers v Fairservice* (1842) 4 D 347; Dickson, *Evidence* (3rd edn), para 227.
[6] In *Mayor v Mayor* 1995 SLT 1097, Lord Marnoch at 1100 and *obiter*, expressed grave doubts as to the competency of the evidence of the contents of a will (in proceedings for financial provision on divorce) where the parties had led the evidence of consent.
[7] Chapter 19.
[8] *Thom v North British Banking Co* (1850) 13 D 134, per Lord Fullerton at 143.
[9] Dickson, *Evidence* (3rd edn), para 210. See also para 19.26.
[10] para 19.26.
[11] para 19.32.

20.1.3   If a document is not in a party's possession and could not have been recovered, its terms may, in certain circumstances,[12] be proved incidentally in the course of a depending action either in the Court of Session or in the sheriff court.[13] Except in these circumstances the terms of the document can be proved only in an action of proving the tenor,[14] which is competent only in the Court of Session.[15]

20.2 BEST EVIDENCE—EFFECT OF STATUTE

Civil proceedings

20.2.1   The Civil Evidence (Scotland) Act 1988 impinges generally upon the topic of best evidence in civil cases, quite apart from any specific statutory provision which may allow for a matter to which it relates to be proved other than by production of a relevant document. The effect of the Civil Evidence (Scotland) Act in relation to oral hearsay is considered in another chapter.[16] Its effect in relation to hearsay of a document is not identical.[17] Section 6 provides that for the purposes of civil proceedings a copy (including transcript or reproduction) of a document purporting to be authenticated by a person responsible for making *the copy* shall, unless the court otherwise directs, be deemed a true copy and treated for evidential purposes as if it was the document itself. This extends the scope of best documentary evidence from the original only, to the original or authenticated copy.[18] Rules of court facilitate the agreement of evidence between the parties that the document which a party intends to rely upon is the original or copy and is duly authenticated[19] (meaning that the document itself, as compared to the copy, is duly authenticated). The definition of "document" for these purposes is much broader than at common law and includes pictorial, graphical, electronic, audio and video representations.[20]

20.2.2   In section 2 the Act provides that evidence shall not be excluded solely on the ground that it is hearsay,[21] and goes on to provide that a statement made by a person other than in the course of proof shall be admissible as evidence of any matter contained in the statement of which direct oral evidence by that person would be admissible.[22] "Statement" includes any representation (however made or

---

[12] See para 20.3.

[13] *Elliott v Galpern* 1927 SC 29.

[14] See para 20.4.

[15] *Dunbar & Co v Scottish County Investment Co* 1920 SC 210. It is competent in the Teind Court (*Alexander v Oswald* (1840) 3 D 40), which is subsumed within Court of Session procedure: see RCS, r 3.6 and annotations thereto in Greens *Annotated Rules of the Court of Session* 1999/2000.

[16] para 8.4.

[17] For a comparison, see Poole, "Productions, Hearsay and the Best Evidence Rule", 1998 SLT (News) 211. Business books and documents kept for business purposes receive separate attention in s 7 and are examined at paras 21.14–21.16.

[18] This limitation was adhered to in *McIlveney v Donald (t/a MDM Design)* 1995 SCLR 802, and a motion to authenticate the copies after objection had been taken to them during the proof was refused. As to whether authentication could take place after documents are lodged but before objection see the commentary to the case at 804.

[19] RCS, r 28A.1(b); OCR, r 29.14(1)(b). They do no more than reflect the fact that the parties may agree to rely upon secondary evidence and concede that it was properly authenticated. See para 11.2.

[20] Civil Evidence (Scotland) Act 1988, s 9. It includes, in addition to writing, any map, plan, graph, drawing, photograph; disc, tape, sound track or other audio recording; film, negative, tape, disc or other video recording. The recordings must be capable of reproduction.

[21] s 2(1)(a).

[22] s 2(1)(b). See also RCS, r 36.8(3) and paras 15.1 and 17.5.

expressed) of fact or opinion.[23] In *Japan Leasing (Europe) plc v Weir's Trustee (No 2)*[24] the Inner House considered whether it was appropriate to treat the broad terms of section 2 as applying to documents, as the sheriff appeared to have done in relying upon unauthenticated copy documents despite objection having been taken to their admissibility.[25] The Inner House did not accept that an unauthenticated copy document was a "statement made by a person otherwise than in the course of the proof",[26] on the basis that section 2 was intended to deal with the past statement of a *person*, however recorded. The documents in this case were not personal but contractual. The court also stated, although it was *obiter*,[27] that "(e)ven if the copy document were to be regarded as a statement ... this would not render it admissible as evidence of the contents of the principal document, since direct oral evidence of the signatories would not be admissible (*ie* apart from the effect of s 2) as evidence of those contents. That is because the best evidence rule would entail that oral evidence as to its contents would be inadmissible." Had the copy documents been authenticated in terms of section 6, or accepted by the parties for use in place of the original,[28] the evidence would have been admissible, as they would have been had the party relying upon them been unable to recover them with all due exertion,[29] discussed in the next paragraph. Accordingly, the Civil Evidence (Scotland) Act 1988 goes only a limited distance in tempering the best evidence rule in relation to documentary evidence, and if parties have committed to writing, whether for the purpose of evidencing or constituting an obligation only the writing will be admissible as the best evidence.

Criminal proceedings[30]

The Criminal Procedure (Scotland) Act 1995[31] permits a copy (including transcript or reproduction) of a document or a material part of it, purporting to be authenticated in a manner prescribed,[32] to be deemed a true copy and treated for evidential purposes as if it were the document, or the material part of it.[33] This applies whether or not the document is still in existence,[34] and regardless of how many **20.2.3**

---

[23] s 9.

[24] 1998 SC 543.

[25] Although the sheriff was not specific on this point and appeared to admit the evidence merely because it was relevant: 1998 SC 543 at 545H–I.

[26] 1998 SC 543 at 547A. *Cf* Sheldon, *Evidence: Cases and Materials* at p 195.

[27] Given the non-acceptance of the inclusion of a document generally in the definition of "statement".

[28] 1998 SC 543 at 545D.

[29] Which the pursuers had made no effort to do: see 1998 SC 543 at 547F. Poole in "Productions, Hearsay and the Best Evidence Rule", 1998 SLT (News) 211 states, at 213, that if the documents had been destroyed or lost, rather than not produced, the copies would have been the best available evidence but would have been inadmissible because oral evidence of them would be precluded due to the requirement for best conceivable evidence in respect of documents. It is submitted that this would not be the effect, because of the co-existing scope at common law for reliance upon oral or other adminicles of evidence if the document is truly unavailable to the party who has made all due exertion to recover it. See para 20.3.

[30] Including proceedings before the sheriff under the Children (Scotland) Act 1995, s 62 in so far as they deal with a ground of referral involving commission of an offence by a child: Criminal Procedure (Scotland) Act 1995, Sched 8, para 7.

[31] Criminal Procedure (Scotland) Act 1995, s 279 and Sched 8. Much of Sched 8 is given over to business documents to which other criteria apply. These are examined at paras 21.14–21.16.

[32] Prescribed in the Act of Adjournal (Criminal Procedure Rules) 1996, r 26.1.

[33] Criminal Procedure (Scotland) Act 1995, Sched 8, para 1(1).

[34] Sched 8, para 1(1)(b).

removes there have been between the original and the copy.[35] Authentication may be by the author of the original, or by a person who is, or has been, in possession of the original or a copy of it, or that person's authorised representative.[36] "Document" carries the same broad definition as it does in civil proceedings.[37] Business documents are subject to special provisions which are examined in another chapter,[38] which, briefly, allow for evidence, oral or by certificate, in respect of business documents by a person authorised by the business or office holder who kept the documentary record.[39] Statutory provision had been called for in *Lord Advocate's Reference (No 1 of 1992)*,[40] in which the court acknowledged that modern practices of record-keeping, involving input and generation of computer data by a multiplicity of authors, made it impracticable to produce an original document spoken to by the author of it.[41]

20.3 ALLOWANCE OF PROOF OF TERMS OF A DOCUMENT NOT PRODUCED

General

20.3.1   Subject to the exception below, incidental proof of the terms of a document is usually allowed when it is not in the party's possession and could not have been recovered by the party in spite of all due exertion.[42] The extent of the exertion required varies with the nature and importance of the document,[43] but the condition of due exertion will probably be held satisfied if the document is in the possession of the opposite party, who has failed to produce it when called on to do so.[44] Such incidental proof has been allowed not only in the case of letters and other documents which were merely adminicles of evidence,[45] but also in the case of documents which formed the only competent evidence of a party's case or of part of it.[46] However, there does seem to be a distinction between these different types of document. A party who moves for proof without being able to produce a document which normally would be essential for that party's case must make

---

[35] Sched 8, para 1(2).

[36] Act of Adjournal (Criminal Procedure Rules) 1996, r 26.1(1).

[37] Criminal Procedure (Scotland) Act 1995, Sched 8, para 8. It includes, in addition to writing, any map, plan, graph, drawing, photograph; disc, tape, sound track or other audio recording; film, negative, tape, disc or other video recording. The recordings must be capable of reproduction. An electronic notepad was a "document" in *Rollo v HM Advocate* 1997 JC 23.

[38] paras 21.14–21.16.

[39] Criminal Procedure (Scotland) Act 1995, Sched 8, paras 2–4.

[40] 1992 JC 179.

[41] per the Lord Justice-General (Hope) at 193 and Lord Allanbridge at 194.

[42] *Clements v Macaulay* (1866) 4 M 543; *Dowgray v Gilmour* 1907 SC 715; *Clark v Clark's Trs* (1860) 23 D 74; *Inverclyde District Council v Carswell* 1987 SCLR 145; *Scottish & Universal Newspapers Ltd v Gherson's Trs* 1987 SC 27. In the first case due exertion was proved; in the others it was not. See also *McIntosh v Chalmers* (1883) 11 R 8, per the Lord Ordinary at 12.

[43] *Walker v Nisbet* 1915 SC 639. See further para 20.7.

[44] *Elliott v Galpern* 1927 SC 29; *Young v Thomson* 1909 SC 529; *Mitchell v Berwick* (1845) 7 D 382.

[45] *Clements v Macaulay* (1866) 4 M 543; *A v B* (1858) 20 D 407 at 415; *Ritchie v Ritchie* (1857) 19 D 505.

[46] *Young v Thomson* 1909 SC 529 (receipt for payment of money); *Drummond v Clunas Tiles and Mosaics Ltd* 1909 SC 1049 (execution of charge); *Elliott v Galpern* 1927 SC 29 (written offer and acceptance); *Viscountcy of Dudhope & Earldom of Dundee*—decision made in 1953 by the Committee of Privileges for the House of Lords, reported 1986 SLT (Lyon Ct) 2, per Lord Normand at 7C–F (a patent of 1641 establishing title to the Earldom of Dundee).

averments sufficient to show entitlement to prove its terms incidentally.[47] Proof has been refused,[48] or at least ought not to have been allowed,[49] owing to the insufficiency of such averments. On the other hand, where the document was merely an adminicle of evidence, so far as the reports show, there were no particular averments, and proof was led without notice.[50] Although this distinction has not been expressly noticed, it appears to be of some importance.

In a criminal trial the terms of a writing may be proved by parole evidence if its **20.3.2** production is impracticable.[51] In certain circumstances in criminal cases it will be necessary to prove that a documentary business record does not exist. The special statutory rules in relation to business documents[52] provide for admission of evidence, given orally or by certificate,[53] of a person authorised by a business[54] to the effect there is no document within a category of business documents,[55] or no statement within a business document, on a particular matter[56] where in the ordinary course of events the document or statement within a document might reasonably have been expected to exist.[57]

Excepted documents

If the pursuer's title is constituted by a will not produced, the tenor of the will can **20.3.3** be proved only in an action of proving the tenor.[58] This applies probably to all documents which constitute rights, as opposed to documents which are merely evidence of them.[59] In two cases the title of the claimant depended on a written contract of copartnery. In one[60] an action of proving the tenor was held necessary; in the other[61] it was not. These decisions are reconcilable on the view that in the former the writing was regarded as constituting the contract,[62] while in the latter it was regarded merely as evidence of it.[63] In an action by one granter of a promissory note, who had paid, for relief against another granter who had not, incidental proof of the terms of the note was refused. While this decision is said to rest on the ground that the note was "the basis of the pursuer's case", the opinions are open to the construction that the

---

[47] An exception might be made regarding averments in the more informal process of summary causes but the test for admissibility remains the same: see, for example, *Inverclyde District Council v Carswell* 1987 SCLR 145 (no explanation for failure to produce originals of dayworks sheets).

[48] *Walker v Nisbet* 1915 SC 639.

[49] *Mackinnon's Trustee v Bank of Scotland* 1915 SC 411, per Lord Hunter at 423.

[50] *Clements v Macaulay* (1866) 4 M 543; *A v B* (1858) 20 D 407 at 415; *Ritchie v Ritchie* (1857) 19 D 505.

[51] *MacLeod v Woodmuir Miners Welfare Society Social Club* 1961 JC 5; *Hughes v Skeen* 1980 SLT (Notes) 13 and *Lord Advocate's Reference (No 1 of 1992)* 1992 JC 179. See paras 20.2. As to practicability, see para 18.5.

[52] Found in the Criminal Procedure (Scotland) Act 1995 ("1995 Act"), Sched 8, paras 4–6; examined in paras 21.14–21.16.

[53] 1995 Act, Sched 8, para 5(1) and (3).

[54] 1995 Act, Sched 8, para 5(4).

[55] As prescribed in 1995 Act, Sched 8, para 2(1).

[56] 1995 Act, Sched 8, para 5(1)

[57] 1995 Act, Sched 8, para 5(2).

[58] *Gilchrist v Morrison* (1891) 18 R 599.

[59] *Elliott v Galpern* 1927 SC 29 at 33. Followed in *Crichton v Wood* 1981 SLT (Notes) 66 in respect of a minute of agreement concerning a right of access to heritage.

[60] *Shaw v Shaw's Trs* (1876) 3 R 813.

[61] *Clark v Clark's Trs* (1860) 23 D 74 where Lord Justice-Clerk Inglis clearly implied, and Lord Cowan expressly said, that an action of proving the tenor was unnecessary.

[62] Lord President Inglis used the word "constitute".

[63] On this distinction, see para 23.5.

true ground was the insufficiency of the explanation for the failure to produce in view of the nature of the document.[64]

20.4 ACTION OF PROVING THE TENOR

General

20.4.1 "The purpose of an action of proving the tenor is to replace a lost document by a new document [viz a decree] in precisely the same terms and with the same legal effect."[65] The action may also be used to restore parts of a document which have been destroyed, obliterated or mutilated.[66] Anyone with an interest, however slight, has a title to sue,[67] and all parties interested must be called as defenders.[68] If the pursuer alone has an interest the Lord Advocate is called as representing the public interest.[69] Where the representatives of the granter of the deed cannot be found, they have been called as "the heir and representatives of" AB, but the decree, in that event, is not *res judicata* against them.[70] The conclusion is "for declarator that [*the lost deed*] was of the tenor following [*set out the terms of the lost deed*] and that the decree to be pronounced herein shall be equivalent to the original deed."

Averments and proof

20.4.2 To obtain decree the pursuer must aver and prove (1) the execution of the document,[71] (2) its tenor or terms,[72] and (3) the *casus amissionis* (the circumstances of the loss).[73] But these three matters may not be wholly independent. For example, if it is proved that the document was destroyed by someone with an adverse interest, who had no right to destroy it (the *casus amissionis*), the burden of proving its execution and tenor may be reduced,[74] and strong evidence that a deed of the nature alleged was executed may lead the court to accept slight evidence of its tenor.[75] Clear proof of authenticity and tenor reduces the burden of proving the *casus amissionis*, and vice versa.[76] It is therefore unwise to isolate the evidence on one matter in a previous decision and assume that the same result will follow in another cause where the evidence on that matter is similar. The evidence on the other matters may be different.

---

[64] *Walker v Nisbet* 1915 SC 639. See further para 20.7.
[65] *Rannie v Ogg* (1891) 18 R 903, per Lord Kinnear at 909. The effect of a decree is considered at para 20.9.
[66] See para 20.8.
[67] *Browne v Orr* (1872) 10 M 397; *Winchester v Smith* (1863) 1 M 685.
[68] RCS, r 52.1(a).
[69] RCS, r 52.1(b).
[70] *Pollok v Jones' Heir* (1899) 1 F 394.
[71] See para 20.5.
[72] See para 20.6.
[73] See para 20.7.
[74] *Young v Thomson* 1909 SC 529 at 536; *Leckie v Leckie* (1884) 11 R 1088; *Borland v Andrew's JF* (1901) 4 F 129; *Ritchie v Ritchie* (1871) 9 M 820; *Rintoul v Boyter* (1833) 6 W & S 394. In the first three cases parole evidence of the tenor was held sufficient.
[75] *Leckie v Leckie* (1884) 11 R 1088; *Rintoul v Boyter* (1833) 6 W & S 394.
[76] *Graham v Graham* (1847) 10 D 45 at 49.

Procedure

The cause proceeds by way of summons in the normal way,[77] but additional rules[78] **20.4.3** provide that if the action is undefended there must be proof.[79] If the action is defended, it may be dismissed as irrelevant without proof.[80] Proceedings in the sheriff court, in which an issue for proving the tenor has arisen incidentally, have been sisted pending the determination of tenor proceedings in the Court of Session.[81] A conclusion for proving the tenor may be included with other conclusions in a single cause in the Court of Session, provided the additional procedural requirements[82] are met.

20.5 EXECUTION—AVERMENT AND PROOF

An averment of execution is naturally essential. Since the document *ex hypothesi* **20.5.1** cannot be produced and spoken to, the proof must be by inference.[83] Evidence that a deed of the nature alleged was executed[84] or existed[85] is sufficient. Where the pursuers had possessed property for over eighty years and there was a statement in a disposition in favour of a neighbouring proprietor suggesting that he had granted a disposition in favour of the pursuers, the Court doubted whether execution was proved, but refused decree on another ground.[86] In a case where the pursuer failed to prove the *casus amissionis* the judges differed as to whether execution was proved.[87]

20.6 TENOR—PROOF

Since the alleged terms of the document are set forth in the conclusion, they need **20.6.1** not be repeated in the condescendence. While, in general, it is not necessary to prove the *ipsissima verba* (very words) of the document, it must be established that it was substantially to the effect alleged.[88] The most satisfactory proof is by written adminicle (*eg* an extract, a draft or a copy), supported by parole evidence to connect it with the original. The rule is that written adminicles must be averred, but all this appears to mean is that, if the pursuer is relying on written adminicles, they must be averred sufficiently to disclose a relevant case.[89] There is no decision that a pursuer is not entitled to rely on a written adminicle at the proof due to failure to aver it. Where it was proved that a person had executed a will on the day he

---

[77] RCS, Chap 13.
[78] RCS, Chap 52.
[79] RCS, r 52.3. The rule is peremptory. It appears that however irrelevant the averments, the Lord Ordinary must allow proof. Until 1913 the Lord Ordinary made great avizandum.
[80] This was done in *Clyde v Clyde* 1958 SC 343.
[81] *Crichton v Wood* 1981 SLT (Notes) 66.
[82] In RCS, Chap 52.
[83] As to the possible distinction between direct and indirect evidence of the fact of execution, where a subsequent action of reduction is brought on the ground of forgery, see para 20.9.
[84] *Young v Anderson* (1904) 7 F 128 (evidence that deceased's solicitor called on him on the night of his death, and entry in the solicitor's books "getting will executed").
[85] *Leckie v Leckie* (1884) 11 R 1088; *Rintoul v Boyter* (1833) 6 W & S 394 (in both of which the will had been seen and read); *Pollok v Jones' Heir* (1899) 1 F 394 (instrument of sasine following on lost disposition).
[86] *Incorporation of Skinners and Furriers in Edinburgh v Baxter's Heir* (1897) 24 R 744.
[87] *Smith v Ferguson* (1882) 9 R 866. On *casus omissionis* see para 20.7.
[88] *Leckie v Leckie* (1884) 11 R 1088.
[89] *Jenkinson v Campbell* (1850) 12 D 854.

died and an alleged copy which bore to have been compared was produced, the copy was held sufficient proof of the tenor.[90] The terms of a disposition were held proved where the description and other clauses peculiar to the deed were taken from the instrument of sasine following on it, and the clauses of style from the forms in use at the time.[91] The terms of an ante-nuptial marriage contract and of a post-nuptial marriage contract were established from a draft of the latter and an instrument of sasine following on it.[92] In all these cases evidence was led to establish the circumstances—for example, by whom a document had been written—and evidence was also produced of entries in solicitors' books. The tenor of a report dated 1629 was proved by a copy established by expert evidence to be in seventeenth century handwriting.[93] On the other hand, decree was refused where it was doubtful whether the disposition had ever been granted and the pursuers had framed its alleged clauses from the titles of neighbouring properties.[94]

20.6.2   Although written adminicles are the most satisfactory form of proof, they are not essential. While in some cases they are to be expected (*eg* a draft of a disposition[95]), in others they are not (*eg* draft or copy of a composition contract[96]). Oral evidence proof may be sufficient if the document is of a simple nature and has been unlawfully destroyed.[97] If oral evidence alone is relied upon the terms of the document must be proved beyond mere general effect.[98]

20.7 *CASUS AMISSIONIS*—AVERMENT AND PROOF

20.7.1   The pursuer must aver and prove loss of the document "in such a manner as implied no extinction of the right of which it was the evident,"[99] and the precision of the averment and the weight of the proof required thus depend on the nature of the lost document.[100] If it is of a kind which is usually destroyed when it has served its purpose (*eg* a bill[101] or an IOU[102]), or of a kind which is revocable (*eg* a will[103]), a special *casus amissionis* must be averred and proved—that is, the pursuer must

---

[90]   *Young v Anderson* (1904) 7 F 128.
[91]   *Pollok v Jones' Heir* (1899) 1 F 394. A more extreme form of this was figured by Lord McLaren in *Rannie v Ogg* (1891) 18 R 903 at 909.
[92]   *McLeod v Leslie* (1865) 3 M 840.
[93]   *Richmond v Officers of State* (1869) 7 M 956. See also *A v B* (1858) 20 D 407 (copy of letter in kirk session minutes).
[94]   *Incorporation of Skinners and Furriers in Edinburgh v Baxter's Heir* (1897) 24 R 744. *Cf Maxwell v Reid* (1863) 1 M 932.
[95]   *Rannie v Ogg* (1891) 18 R 903 at 909.
[96]   *Winton & Co v Thomson & Co* (1862) 24 D 1094.
[97]   *Young v Thomson* 1909 SC 529; *Leckie v Leckie* (1884) 11 R 1088.
[98]   *Rannie v Ogg* (1891) 18 R 903 at 910.
[99]   *Winchester v Smith* (1863) 1 M 685 at 689, quoted in *Clyde v Clyde* 1958 SC 343 at 345, and in *Mackinnon's Tr v Bank of Scotland* 1915 SC 411 at 423, where a cautioner paid the amount due, received the bond and, as he was entitled to, destroyed it, and the Bank was not allowed to prove its terms. *Cf Drummond v Clunas Tiles and Mosaics Ltd* 1909 SC 1049, where a debtor was charged and paid and received the execution, which he destroyed, but the creditor was allowed to prove the terms of the execution. *Cf* also *Smith v Smith's Trs* (1904) 6 F 775, which is difficult to reconcile with the general rule. *Russell's Trs v Russell* (1862) 24 D 1141 provides a practical illustration of the specification required.
[100] *Walker v Nisbet* 1915 SC 639 at 643, 645. As to presumptions arising from possession or destruction of documents, see para 3.9.
[101] *Walker v Nisbet* 1915 SC 639 at 643, 645.
[102] *Borland v Andrew's JF* (1901) 4 F 129. See also *Smith v Ferguson* (1882) 9 R 866.
[103] *Clyde v Clyde* 1958 SC 343.

establish the actual, or at least probable, cause of the loss, and one not inconsistent with the continued existence of the right. The reason for this is that the granter of the IOU may have paid the money and recovered and destroyed the document, while the granter of the will may have decided to revoke it and simply burnt it. The action failed where the will was proved to have been destroyed without authority[104] or on the testator's instructions[105] and where a letter of guarantee was delivered to the cautioner after payment and destroyed by him.[106] On the other hand, a person who has taken infeftment and possessed for a long time is unlikely to destroy his or her own title.[107] In such a case a general *casus amissionis* will probably suffice, which usually means averment and proof merely that the document cannot be found.[108] But the nature of the document is not conclusive, because the circumstances may render the general rule inapplicable. Where it was proved that the testator died on the day a will was said to have been executed and his estate had been administered for over fifty years on the basis of the will, the court was satisfied with a general statement that the will could not be found.[109] When it was averred that the testator was of deteriorating mental health (although not without testamentary or revocatory, capacity) such that an inference of mere loss rather than revocation might be drawn from the circumstances, the court allowed proof before answer.[110] On the other hand, a special *casus amissionis* was required in the case of a long lease because the circumstances were suspicious.[111]

20.8 MUTILATED DOCUMENTS

An action of proving the tenor is competent to restore any obliterated part of a document.[112] Where the damage is clearly due to natural causes, wear and tear or damp, or was accidental, and there are no suspicious circumstances, there is little difficulty.[113] If there are suspicious circumstances, the opposite is true.[114] Where the document has been deliberately mutilated, the result depends on whether the mutilator had the right to do so. If not, the mutilation has no legal effect.[115] If the mutilator had the right, intention determines the effect.[116] **20.8.1**

---

[104] *Cullen's Exr v Elphinstone* 1948 SC 662 and *Falconer v Stephen* (1849) 11 D 1338 (both unauthorised destruction of a will after testator's death).

[105] *Bonthrone v Ireland* (1883) 10 R 779.

[106] *Mackinnon's Tr v Bank of Scotland* 1915 SC 411. See also para 3.9.

[107] *Pollok v Jones' Heir* (1899) 1 F 394.

[108] *Walker v Nisbet* 1915 SC 639 at 643, 645.

[109] *Young v Anderson* (1904) 7 F 128. See also *Mackenzie v Lord Dundas* (1835) 14 S 144; *Brodie v Brodie* (1901) 4 F 132, a doubtful decision (Lord Moncreiff dissented).

[110] *Lauder v Briggs* 1999 SC 453.

[111] *Paterson v Houston* (1837) 16 S 225. See also *Graham v Graham* (1847) 10 D 45; *Marquis of Annandale v Lord Hope* (1733) 1 Pat App 108.

[112] *Duke of Athole* (1880) 7 R 1195; *Winchester v Smith* (1863) 1 M 685.

[113] *Duke of Athole* (1880) 7 R 1195; *Duke of Argyll v Campbell* (1873) 11 M 611; *Cousin v Gemmill* (1862) 24 D 758.

[114] *Graham v Graham* (1847) 10 D 45 (deed of entail with a great part of the testing clause torn off, under reduction on the ground of forgery).

[115] *Cunningham v Mowat's Trs* (1851) 13 D 1376 (unauthorised deletion of signature by solicitor); *Ronald* (1830) 8 S 1008 (unauthorised deletion of clause); *Falconer v Stephen* (1849) 11 D 1338 (will destroyed by solicitor after death of testator).

[116] Indeed, it was observed that an action of proving the tenor was inapplicable to a case where issues were raised as to the right of a granter of a document to mutilate it and with what intention she had done so: *Winchester v Smith* (1863) 1 M 685 at 698.

20.9 EFFECT OF DECREE

20.9.1 The modern conclusion for declarator ends with the words "and that the decree to be pronounced herein shall be equivalent to the original deed."[117] Lord Kinnear's dictum, that the decree replaces the lost document and has the same legal effect,[118] must mean the same legal effect as the document had when executed. It is replaced only because authorised cancellation has been negatived by proof of some other *casus amissionis*. A decree proving the tenor is thought to be subject to the implied reservation of all questions of who could benefit under the deed,[119] but dicta[120] to the effect that the decree is also subject to the reservation as to whether the act of destruction was wrongful or not, are impossible to reconcile with the requirement for proof of *casus amissionis* before the decree can be granted. However, the decree is open to attack on grounds on which the document itself might have been attacked—for example, incapacity of the granter, facility and circumvention or fraud. According to Dickson[121] reduction on the ground of forgery is also competent, but there is an obvious difficulty. Decree cannot be granted in an action of proving of the tenor unless the court is satisfied that the deed was executed by the alleged granter, and *prima facie* a reduction on the ground of forgery would be met by a plea of *res judicata*, unless the decree were in absence.[122] However, Stair[123] and Erskine[124] appear to take the view that reduction would be open unless the proof of execution in the proving of the tenor was by direct evidence.

---

[117] The earlier form was for declarator that the decree "shall be in all respects as valid, and effectual a document to the pursuer, in all cases, improbation as well as others, as the original deed, if extant, would be ...": see *Smith v Smith's Trs* (1904) 6 F 775. All the decisions on this question turn on the earlier form, but it is thought that they still apply, notwithstanding the disappearance of the words "improbation as well as others".

[118] In *Rannie v Ogg* (1891) 18 R 903 at 909, and see para 20.4.

[119] *Winchester v Smith* (1863) 1 M 685 at 700.

[120] Of Lord Justice-Clerk Inglis in *Winchester v Smith* (1863) 1 M 685 at 700, appearing to overstate the view of Lord Deas, at 694, one of the seven judges of both Divisions to whom the case had been referred for consultation before judgment; *Smith v Smith's Trs* (1904) 6 F 775, per Lord Trayner at 778. The rubric in *Smith* is misleading in that none of the judges concurred in Lord Trayner's dictum to this effect.

[121] Dickson, *Evidence* (3rd edn), para 1356.

[122] See para 20.4.

[123] iv, 32, 11.

[124] iv, 1, 59.

CHAPTER 21

RECOVERY AND PRODUCTION OF DOCUMENTS

21.1 SCOPE OF "DOCUMENT"

General

This chapter concerns the requirements for recovery and production of documents **21.1.1** in order for them to be available as evidence in civil and criminal cases and before other tribunals. Although the common law has originated from consideration of documents in their traditional, written, sense, latterly the courts have accepted that records may now be made using a variety of media.[1] Statute has proceeded to take account of a variety of media by which information may be recorded, and for the purposes of both civil and criminal cases the definition of "document" includes in addition to writing, any map,[2] plan, graph or drawing; any photograph[3]; any disc, tape, sound track or other audio recording; any film (including microfilm), negative, tape, disc or other video recording. The recordings must be capable of reproduction with or without the aid of some other equipment.[4] These media are included within the definition of "document", so the remainder of this chapter relates to them in the same way that it does to writing. In some respects the courts have treated non-written media as real evidence—for example, when the original has been destroyed before exhibition to the other party[5]—so regard may be had to

---

[1] *Lord Advocate's Reference (No 1 of 1983)* 1984 JC 52 (audio tape recording of extra-judicial statement by an accused); *Lord Advocate's Reference (No 1 of 1992)* 1992 JC 179 (computer records).
[2] Examined further at para 19.35.
[3] In relation to admissibility and sufficiency of photographs, see *Patterson v Howdle* 1999 JC 56 and *Longmuir v HM Advocate* 2000 JC 378. An implied admission from photographs lodged as productions supported an order for interim damages in *Cleland v Campbell* 1998 SLT 642 (OH). As to recoverability of photographs taken in anticipation of litigation, see paras 10.3–10.4.
[4] Civil Evidence (Scotland) Act 1988, s 9; Criminal Procedure (Scotland) Act 1995, s 279 and Sched 8, para 8.
[5] See, for example, *McQuade v Vannet* 2000 SCCR 18; *Allan v Napier* 1999 GWD 29-1364.

comments which apply to real evidence in terms of presentation to the court,[6] but the issue of admissibility should be determined by reference to the statutory definitions of "document". The definition is sufficiently wide to include, for example, digital photographs, documents which have been digitally scanned, computer files and internet images or communications.

Recordings

21.1.2 While such evidence is produced in court, mere sight of the thing (*eg* a video cassette or computer disc) may not be of value and may not enable the witness to identify it,[7] other than by reference to a label.[8] Its value is in it being reproduced, heard or analysed by a witness,[9] or viewed or heard by the court. The court's assessment of it must be limited to what has been presented in evidence; care must be taken to prevent a judge or jury from extracting additional evidence not led in court upon viewing the document during deliberations.[10] Production for assessment by another party in the case is the same as that relating to documents in general.[11] Editing before production appears to be accepted,[12] and is appropriate if the recording includes material otherwise inadmissible or prejudicial to an accused in a criminal case,[13] but comments later in this chapter regarding a party's right to seek recovery of the whole when an excerpt has been offered apply equally to the recording.[14] Whether such an argument will be taken, or will succeed will no doubt depend upon an argument as to confidentiality of the remainder of, for example, files on disc, closed circuit television surveillance videotapes.[15] Audio recordings are frequently accompanied by a written transcript[16] which should be authenticated,[17] but need not be spoken to by the maker of the transcript.[18] If there are doubts as to the accuracy or clarity of the recording or the accuracy of the transcript the court reverts to the recollection of the witness, assuming that one was present during the recording process,[19] but the availability of a recording may be

---

[6]   See para 18.1.

[7]   *Heywood v Ross* 1994 SLT 195. *Cf Hudson v Hamilton* 1992 JC 162.

[8]   On label production and identification, see Renton & Brown, *Criminal Procedure* (6th edn), para 14-22.

[9]   As in *Bowie v Tudhope* 1986 SCCR 205, where the identification of the accused was by police officers who identified him from a CCTV video recording, although they had no direct knowledge of the crime. See also *Clarke v Webster* 1996 GWD 40-2266.

[10] *Gray v HM Advocate* 1999 SLT 528. However, the court's assessment of what has been viewed and spoken to in evidence prevails over expert assessment of the same, as in *Re N (A minor)(Child Abuse: Video Evidence)* [1996] 4 All ER 225, and see para 16.1.5.

[11] See paras 21.5 *et seq*, but the recording has at times been treated as real evidence: see *McQuade v Vannet* 2000 SCCR 18 and *Allan v Napier* 1999 GWD 29-1364.

[12] As in *Timney v Cardle* 1996 SLT 376, although repeated failures on the part of the prosecutor including failure to arrange facilities for editing and viewing of the video led to a successful argument of oppression on appeal.

[13] See, for example, *Tunnicliffe v HM Advocate* 1991 SCCR 623.

[14] See para 21.4.1.

[15] By analogy with the reasoning in *Daly v Vannet* 1999 SCCR 346.

[16] This is a matter of convenience and although adjournment for preparation of a transcript will be appropriate in some circumstances it will not always be so, and the court has no power to insist upon a transcript: *McGlennan v McLaughlin* 1992 SCCR 454.

[17] As with a copy document, in terms of the Act of Adjournal Criminal Procedure Rules 1996, r 26. If the record of a judicial examination is being produced the taped record must be transcribed: Criminal Procedure (Scotland) Act 1995, ss 37(4) and 68(1).

[18] *Cf Hopes and Lavery v HM Advocate* 1960 JC 104, in which the evidence of the transcriber was led, and admitted as that of a skilled witness.

[19] *HM Advocate v Swift* 1983 SCCR 204.

seen as an advantage.[20] A challenge to the admissibility of recorded evidence—for example, on the ground that it has been obtained unfairly—may require to be considered only after the tape or disc has been viewed or heard, since it may be impossible to assess the point by looking at the cassette, disc or its packaging. However, although the point has not been decided in relation to recorded material, it is thought that an examination of the contents for the purposes of admissibility should be within *voir dire* procedure in order to meet the requirements of the European Convention on Human Rights.[21]

The risk of digital adaptation of electronically stored data before recovery or **21.1.3** production, at the hands of any party who can access the digital data, must be a matter of weight rather than admissibility, and in civil cases would require to be averred for evidence of adaptation to be relevant and admissible. The court had acknowledged that computerised records, although compiled through entries of various authors who could not be expected to give evidence in relation to the authenticity of the records, should nevertheless be capable of production as admissible evidence,[22] and statute now regulates how such records are provable.[23] Such statutory provision, whilst facilitating reliance upon the contents of the document for general evidential purposes, does not assist in the case of documents which form the only competent evidence of a party's civil case or of part of it, that is in situations when only writing will suffice or where writing is self-proving.[24] That situation is being addressed by the enactment of the Electronic Communications Act 2000. While that Act creates a system for proof of electronically generated or stored material, the courts, meantime, have dealt on a case by case basis with the evidence of electronically generated documents.[25]

21.2 ELECTRONIC COMMUNICATIONS ACT 2000

General

In order to address the increasing reliance upon electronic communication and **21.2.1** storage for private, commercial and public purposes, Parliament has enacted the Electronic Communications Act 2000.[26] The potential effect of the Act, and more particularly Part II, upon the law of documentary evidence is substantial, and arises in two ways.

---

[20] *HM Advocate v Nulty* 2000 SLT 528, per Lord Abernethy at 532. *Cf* the attitude of the sheriff before the jury in *Blair-Wilson, Petitioner* 1997 SLT 621.

[21] Following the reasoning in *Thompson v Crowe* 2000 JC 173. This should be borne in mind when the observations in, *eg, Lord Advocate's Reference (No 1 of 1983)* 1984 JC 52 are considered.

[22] *Lord Advocate's Reference (No 1 of 1992)* 1992 JC 179.

[23] See paras 21.14 and 21.15.

[24] On which see Chapter 24.

[25] See, *eg, Longmuir v HM Advocate* 2000 JC 378.

[26] The explanatory notes published with the Act, *Explanatory Notes to the Electronic Communications Act 2000* and available online at www.hmso.gov.uk, explain (at paras 11–18) that it follows extensive consultation and is consistent with the EU Electronic Signatures Directive, 1999/93/EC; [2000]OJ L13/12. The Act also accords with guidelines and developments promoted by the OECD and UNCITRAL: see *Explanatory Notes*, para 19. Its aims include: the removal of legislative obstacles to the use of electronic communication and storage in place of paper; and legal recognition of electronic signatures and the process under which they are verified, generated or communicated (*Explanatory Notes*, para 7).

Electronic signature

21.2.2 The Act provides for an electronic signature to be incorporated into or legally associated with a particular electronic communication[27] or particular electronic data, and to be certified by the person whose signature it is, which shall be admissible in evidence in relation to any question as to the authenticity of the communication or data or as to the integrity of the communication or data.[28] "Authenticity" means one or more of "whether the communication or data comes from a particular person or source; whether it is accurately timed and dated; and whether it is intended to have legal effect."[29] "Integrity" refers to "whether there has been any tampering with or modification of the communication or data."[30] The provision for electronic signature[31] came into effect on 25 July 2000.[32]

Provision for writing to allow for electronic communication or storage

21.2.3 By a provision which has not come into effect at the time of writing, the appropriate Minister is empowered "to modify, by Order, the provisions of any enactment or subordinate legislation or any scheme, licence, authorisation or approval issued, granted or given by or under any enactment or subordinate legislation ... for the purpose of authorising or facilitating the use of electronic", instead of other forms of, communications or storage[33] for any purpose specified in the Act. Those purposes are very widely drawn. They are:

> "(a) the doing of anything which under any such provisions is required to be or may be done or evidenced in writing or otherwise using a document,[34] notice or instrument;
>
> (b) the doing of anything which under any such provisions is required to be or may be done by post or other specified means of delivery;
>
> (c) the doing of anything which under any such provisions is required to be or may be authorised by a person's signature or seal, or is required to be delivered as a deed or witnessed;
>
> (d) the making of any statement or declaration which under any such provisions is required to be made under oath or to be contained in a statutory declaration;
>
> (e) the keeping, maintenance or preservation, for the purposes or in pursuance of any such provisions, of any account, record, notice, instrument or other document;
>
> (f) the provision, production or publication under any such provisions of any information or other matter; and
>
> (g) the making of any payment that is required to be or may be made under any such provisions."[35]

21.2.4   Hence, it is possible for a Ministerial order to convert the requirement for

---

[27] "Communication" includes a communication comprising sounds or image or both and a communication effecting payment: s 15(1).

[28] s 7, which, together with ss 11 and 12 only, came into force on 25 July 2000: Electronic Communications Act 2000 (Commencement No 1) Order 2000 (SI 2000/1798).

[29] s 15(2).

[30] s 15(2).

[31] s 7.

[32] Electronic Communications Act 2000 (Commencement No 1) Order 2000 (SI 2000/1798).

[33] s 8(1).

[34] "Document" includes a map, plan, design, drawing, picture or other image: s 15(1).

[35] s 8(2).

writing, if contained in any statute or statutory instrument, to include an electronic form of communication or storage. The Minister shall not make such an order unless he considers that the electronic records so provided for will be no less satisfactory than records kept otherwise.[36] The Minister is empowered to regulate the manner in which those authorised electronic communications or storage may be used to establish in legal proceedings whether a thing has been done using electronic communication or storage, the time or date and place of that thing, the person who did it and the contents, authenticity or integrity of it.[37] It is said that it is "for the court to decide in a particular case whether an electronic signature has been correctly used and what weight it should be given (*eg* in relation to the authenticity or integrity of a message) against other evidence," and that parties may nevertheless contract about how they are to treat each other's electronic signatures.[38] Clearly the assessment of signature, authenticity and integrity requires that evidence other than that of the terms of the documents and the signature is admissible. This is perhaps unsurprising given that the communication will not have the familiar appearance of writing, and its authenticity or integrity cannot be assessed with the naked eye. The Act contains no presumptions, although it is possible that these might be incorporated in orders applying the electronic communication provisions to enactments which at present require writing. The terms of the Act are sufficiently wide to allow for electronic creation and transmission of self-proving documents.

21.3 GENERAL—CIVIL CASES

The court has power to compel the production of documents which may have a **21.3.1** bearing on the issues. The power has usually been exercised by approving a specification of documents[39] and granting diligence for their recovery, and is the appropriate method of recovery if the document is in the hands of a third party.[40] That

---

[36] s 8(3). For example, it may be argued that the writing which makes a document self-proving in terms of the Requirements of Writing (Scotland) Act 1995, and can be assessed by the naked eye, is more "satisfactory" than a communication the authenticity of which is not so evident, and may be dependent upon judicial admission, certificate of authenticity, or extrinsic evidence (perhaps from an expert on encryption—a process for regulation of which is set up in Part I of the Act) before it will attain self-proving status.

[37] s 8(4)(g) and (5). The Minister may also regulate: the electronic form to be taken by the communications or storage; conditions subject to which the use of these is authorised; implications of non-compliance with such conditions; provision for refusal to commit to, or accept receipt of, something in electronic form other than after due notice or in excepted situations; use of intermediaries to transmit any data or establish the authenticity or integrity of data; conditions for qualifying persons to use electronic storage; and procedures and fees for storage of, access to, and misuse of, records (s 8(4)(a)–(f), (h)–(m) and (6)).

[38] *Explanatory Notes to the Electronic Communications Act 2000* (available online at www.hmso.gov.uk), para 43.

[39] See para 21.10.

[40] As to the special procedure for bankers' books, see para 21.13. The relevant court rules are in RCS, Chap 35 and OCR, Chap 28. Commission may be sought in summary causes after the summons has been served: Summary Cause Rules 1976 (SI 1976/1860) (as amended), r 37, and OCR, r 28.2 is applied to summary causes by Summary Cause Rules, r 3(2) (1993 version). The Small Claims Rules 1988 (SI 1988/1976), r 18 provides for an order for recovery akin to commission and diligence. In summary applications the sheriff is empowered to make any order as he thinks fit for the progress of the application: Act of Sederunt (Summary Applications, Statutory Applications and Appeals etc Rules) 1999 (SI 1999/929), r 2.31, but in accordance with that rule this power must be exercised "in a manner which is not inconsistent with section 50 of the Sheriff Courts (Scotland) Act 1907", which section requires the sheriff to "summarily dispose" of the matter. It is thought that an order for production, but not for commission and diligence, would be consistent with s 50.

power to grant commission and diligence as it has operated at common law exists alongside other devices for discovery of relevant documentary[41] evidence, viz[42]: (a) voluntary disclosure; (b) rules of practice or procedure requiring that documents are produced in process in advance of reliance upon them at proof or trial (both of which are available only if the document is in the possession of, or accessible by, the other party); and (c) an order under the Administration of Justice (Scotland) Act 1972 for inspection, photographing, preservation, custody and detention of documents and other property[43] which appear to the court to be property as to which any question may relevantly arise in any existing proceedings before that court or in any civil proceedings which are likely to be brought.[44] In certain circumstances failure to disclose relevant documents to the opposite party will constitute a breach of the requirement for a fair trial in civil[45] or criminal proceedings.[46] The breach will not exist if there is a procedure which enables a party to apply for production or recovery, even if the party has not invoked that procedure.[47]

21.3.2 At common law only documents were recovered by commission and diligence, not things.[48] For the purposes of civil proceedings generally the definition of "document" has been greatly extended to include pictorial, graphical, electronic, audio and video representations.[49] At common law diligence was not granted for recovery of public documents or documents in the custody of a court, the proper procedure being to cite the custodier to exhibit them at the trial.[50] Public documents of which judicial knowledge[51] is taken will not be recoverable, and recovery of documents in the possession of some public authorities may be withheld on the grounds of confidentiality in the public interest.[52] However, in other respects commission and diligence may be sought for recovery of public documents[53] as it is for any other document, subject to intimation to the Lord Advocate if the document is in the hands of the Crown or a government department.[54]

21.3.3 The court exercises the power in accordance with rules of court and practice,

---

[41] For real evidence, see Chapter 18. For evidence of witnesses, see Chapters 12, 13 and 17.

[42] A suggestion by Macphail that proceedings for discovery rooted in civil law might be revived (see *Evidence*, paras 25.08–25.11) was overtaken by the extension of the procedure under the Administration of Justice (Scotland) Act 1972, s 1: see *Evidence*, para S25.11.

[43] The statutory process of recovery relates to "documents and other property" and hence did not apply to a defenders' work processes which a pursuer wished to videotape, although inspection of these was permissible and permitted at common law: *Christie v Arthur Bell & Sons Ltd* 1989 SLT 253. See also para 18.3.6.

[44] s 1(1).

[45] *McGinley v United Kingdom* (1999) 27 EHRR 1.

[46] *McLeod v HM Advocate (No 2)* 1998 JC 67.

[47] *McGinley v United Kingdom* (1999) 27 EHRR 1.

[48] *Mactaggart v Mackillop* 1938 SLT 559 (OH); *HM Advocate v Fleming* (1864) 2 M 1032. See para 18.3.5.

[49] Civil Evidence (Scotland) Act 1988, s 9. It includes, in addition to writing, any map, plan, graph, drawing, photograph; disc, tape, sound track or other audio recording; film (including microfilm), negative, tape, disc or other video recording. The recordings must be capable of reproduction. See para 21.1.

[50] *Maitland v Maitland* (1885) 12 R 899 at 903. As to public and official documents, see Chapter 19.

[51] See paras 11.6–11.7 and 19.2–19.6.

[52] See para 10.9.

[53] On proof of public documents, see Chapter 19.

[54] Intimation to the Lord Advocate is required, where necessary, by RCS, r 35.2(3)(c) and OCR, r 28.2(3)(c). See also *Sheridan v Peel* 1907 SC 577.

usually on the basis of *ex parte* statements after intimation,[55] but always subject to confidentiality,[56] and may refuse a diligence as a matter of discretion.[57] An application must pass the tests mentioned in the following paragraphs, and approval of it implies that it has passed them all. On the other hand, refusal may be on one of several grounds, including confidentiality and discretion, and it is not clear in some of the old decisions on which ground the court proceeded.[58] In some cases, where a document was in the possession of a third party, diligence has been refused, and the possessor had to be cited as a witness and required to bring the document to court.[59] When the documents are in the possession of a third party, that third party has no opportunity of raising any objection when the diligence is asked for, but is not compelled to produce at the commission[60] if able to establish confidentiality[61] or substantial prejudice arising from compulsion.[62] Since any documents recovered must be lodged as a production, diligence has been refused on the ground that any documents recovered could not be lodged timeously.[63] However, much will depend upon materiality of the document and the circumstances in which it has been omitted from production.[64] It has been considered competent to adjourn the trial in summary criminal proceedings in which it emerges that a recovery is required, so that an order for recovery may be sought.[65]

21.4 VOLUNTARY OR PROCEDURAL DISCLOSURE

Voluntary disclosure

It is always open for the parties to agree that they will exchange relevant docu- **21.4.1** ments at any stage prior to or during court proceedings, although there is no obligation to do so, unless under the procedures described later in this paragraph. Voluntary disclosure may be pragmatic, and may facilitate early resolution of the dispute. Acceptance of an offer of voluntary disclosure should not preclude an application for commission and diligence if the order can be shown to be necessary according to the normal tests described below, and having regard to the extent

---

[55] The circumstances may justify an order based on the *ex parte* statement of the applicant's agent, if surprise is necessary to enable recovery in the context of proceedings arising from breach of intellectual property: approved in *The British Phonographic Industry Ltd v Cohen, Cohen, Kelly, Cohen & Cohen Ltd* 1983 SLT 137 following *Piller KG v Manufacturing Processes Ltd* [1976] Ch 55. The order so awarded is known as an "Anton Piller" order.

[56] See Chapter 10.

[57] *Macqueen v Mackie & Co Distillers, Ltd* 1920 SC 544. See also *Young v National Coal Board* 1957 SC 99.

[58] A number of the reported cases were decided in Single Bills or on the Motion Roll with little or no citation of authority, and opinions are brief or non-existent.

[59] See para 21.4.

[60] See para 21.11.

[61] See Chapter 10.

[62] *North British Railway Co v R & J Garroway* (1893) 20 R 397 at 401. Under one or other of these exceptions a third party would be entitled to claim the privilege against self-incrimination, following the decision in *The British Phonographic Industry Ltd v Cohen, Cohen, Kelly, Cohen & Cohen Ltd* 1983 SLT 137. However, such a claim cannot be made in an application under the 1972 Act concerning infringement of intellectual property: Law Reform (Miscellaneous Provisions) (Scotland) Act 1985, s 15.

[63] *Murphy v Clyde Navigation Trs* (1900) 4 F 653. *Cf Baroness Gray v Richardson* (1874) 1 R 1138.

[64] See the examples given in MacSporran & Young, *Commission and Diligence*, para 3.24.

[65] *Anderson v Hingston* 1997 SLT 844 at 849.

of voluntary disclosure.[66] A party may have to withhold or refuse voluntary disclosure if the information is held on behalf of a third party to whom it is confidential[67] or to whom the haver owes a duty of confidentiality.[68]

Procedures requiring disclosure—general

21.4.2 If a party founds upon in pleadings or incorporates into pleadings a document or documents in that party's possession, court rules require that the document is lodged in court at the same time as the pleadings in which it is so mentioned.[69] A document is "founded on" if it appears from the condescendence that the pursuer's case is to any extent based on it.[70] So a summons or initial writ,[71] a petition or application,[72] or minute, defences, counterclaim or answers[73] in which a document is founded upon or adopted (as distinct from a document which will merely be an item of evidence)[74] should be accompanied by the document. The document becomes a borrowable item of process,[75] but it is probably the case that an order for production carries the implied condition that the document will be used only for the purposes of those proceedings.[76] This requirement is without prejudice to any power of the court to order production of a document[77] or to grant commission and diligence for its recovery.[78]

21.4.3 In the sheriff court,[79] within 14 days of proof or proof before answer having been allowed, each party must exchange with the other parties a list of the documents which are or have been in his possession or control which he intends to use or put in evidence at proof, and disclose the whereabouts of those documents.[80] The recipient of such a list is entitled to inspect such documents as are in the possession or control of the party listing them, at a time and place fixed by the party listing them which is reasonable to both parties.[81] A party may object to inspection on the ground of confidentiality,[82] and the right to apply for commission and

---

[66] As in *Moore v Greater Glasgow Health Board* 1978 SC 123; *Anderson v Hingston* 1997 SLT 844.
[67] *eg* CCTV footage.
[68] As in *Conoco (UK) Ltd v Commercial Law Practice* 1996 SCLR 446. See also MacSporran & Young, *Commission and Diligence*, para 1.6.
[69] RCS, r 27.1; OCR, r 21.1. See also *Western Bank of Scotland v Baird* (1863) 2 M 127; *Reavis v Clan Line Steamers Ltd* 1926 SC 215.
[70] *Western Bank of Scotland v Baird* (1863) 2 M 127.
[71] RCS, r 27(1)(a); OCR, r 21.1(a).
[72] RCS, r 27.1(b).
[73] OCR, r 21.1(b).
[74] *Western Bank of Scotland v Baird* (1863) 2 M 127.
[75] RCS, rr 4.5 and 4.12; OCR, rr 9.5 and 11.3.
[76] *Iomega Corporation v Myrica (UK) Ltd* 1998 SC 636, per Lord President Rodger at 645. An applicant for recovery before proceedings are raised must lodge an undertaking to this effect, RCS r 64.3 (b)(iii).
[77] See para 21.1.
[78] RCS, r 27.2; OCR, r 21.2. It is likely that this refers to an order for production or commission and diligence of the same document, which might be sought before its production in terms of this rule, although there may be circumstances in which such an order will be appropriate afterwards such as where the party possesses only a copy but the original might be recovered from a third party by commission and diligence. The same may apply if the party produces only an extract. If the rule is breached, at worst the party in default will be prevented from relying on the document, which may prove fatal to the pleadings at procedure roll or options hearing, and at very least that party should be penalised in expenses.
[79] The procedure does not apply in the Court of Session, except in proceedings for reparation in which the optional procedure set out in RCS, Chap 43 has been used, on which see further in para 21.4.5. Lord Cullen, in *Review of Business in the Outer House of the Court of Session* (1995) at para 5.14, proposed that it be extended to all Court of Session proceedings.
[80] OCR, r 9.13(1).
[81] OCR, r 9.13(2).
[82] OCR, r 9.13(4)(a).

diligence is not affected by the rule.[83] Producing the documents in process might satisfy this requirement but that is not necessary at this stage.

The stage at which production[84] in process is compulsory is 28 days before **21.4.4** proof or jury trial in the Court of Session,[85] and 14 days before proof in the sheriff court standard or additional procedure,[86] and seven days before summary cause or small claim proof. Failure to comply with these various requirements leaves the party seeking to rely upon the document the option of seeking the agreement of the opponent, or the authority of the court, for late disclosure or production.[87] Both may be conditional, usually in terms of expenses or adjournment.[88] This rule is not applied to documents written by a witness who is not a party and used merely to test the credibility of that witness,[89] or to refresh his memory. Such a document may be produced at the diet,[90] or the witness may be cited to produce it.[91]

Procedures requiring disclosure—specialities

The most commonly encountered specialities of procedural disclosure or recovery **21.4.5** of documents arise in commercial actions in the Court of Session, divorce actions in which financial provision is sought, and reparation actions which proceed under the optional procedure in the Court of Session.[92] In actions which are commenced or transferred to the commercial cause procedure in the Court of Session parties are expected to produce a list of all relevant documents at commencement of the proceedings, and to produce all relevant documents at the preliminary hearing or at any subsequent stage, on the order of the commercial judge.[93] In proceedings for financial provision on divorce orders may be sought under the Family Law (Scotland) Act 1985 requiring a party to produce details of resources.[94] The court may also make an incidental order in such proceedings necessary to give effect to the principles under the Act or to any order for financial provision.[95] Exceptionally, this could include an order for production of relevant documents. The court has indicated a preference for voluntary disclosure by the parties in such proceedings, particularly over the costly and inappropriately adversarial procedure

---

[83] OCR, r 9.13(4)(b).

[84] Although the obligation to produce is not subject to a plea of confidentiality, it has been held in England that confidentiality is not waived until the document is spoken to or otherwise incorporated into evidence: see para 10.3.2.

[85] RCS, rr 36.3 and 37.4. Lord Cullen, in *Review of Business in the Outer House of the Court of Session* (1995), para 5.15, proposed an extended period of eight weeks and that parties might only consent to late production if the documents were lodged not less than six weeks before proof.

[86] OCR, r 29.11.

[87] RCS, r 36.3.

[88] RCS, r 36.3(2); OCR, rr 9.13(3) and 29.11(2).

[89] *Paterson & Sons v Kit Coffee Co Ltd* (1908) 16 SLT 180. It is submitted in Macphail, *Sheriff Court Practice* (2nd edn), para 16.25, under reference to the Scottish Law Commission's *Memorandum on Evidence* (Memo No 46), para G25, that no distinction need be made between a document which is to be used to test the credibility of a witness and that which is to be used only for testing credibility of a party, both of which should be capable of production during proof.

[90] *Paterson & Sons v Kit Coffee Co Ltd* (1908) 16 SLT 180.

[91] See para 21.5.

[92] For a fuller examination of the range of special procedures, see MacSporran & Young, *Commission and Diligence*, Chap 1. See also, *eg*, *McIsaac and Wilson, Petitioners* 1995 SLT 498 (application under the Insolvency Act 1986).

[93] RCS, rr 47.11(1) and 47.12, and see Practice Note No 12 of 1994, para 11.

[94] Family Law (Scotland) Act 1985, s 20.

[95] s 14(2)(k).

of commission and diligence.[96] In reparation actions proceedings under the optional procedure in the Court of Session,[97] there is a procedure akin to that applying in all sheriff court actions and described earlier in this paragraph, whereby a list of those documents, not being confidential documents, which are or have been in the possession of the parties, must be exchanged within 14 days after the interlocutor allowing proof, together with information as to the whereabouts of those no longer in the party's control, and arrangements agreed for their inspection.[98]

21.5 APPLICATION FOR RECOVERY—GENERAL

Common law

21.5.1 At common law, although a diligence might be granted before the record is closed[99] to enable the party to make averments specific,[100] or to frame an issue,[101] the usual purpose has been to enable a party, after proof has been allowed or issues approved, to recover documents for use at the proof or trial.[102] The tests for a successful application at common law are considered below.[103] In order to obtain a diligence before proof has been allowed, to enable a party to make averments specific, it has been said that the party must first have set forth a case in general terms, and not be merely trying to discover whether he or she has a case,[104] often termed a "fishing diligence". If from the documents recovered a pursuer discovers another case, that party could not be prevented from pleading it, since the record is open, but a strictly limited recovery is the safeguard against this.[105] Diligence has been refused on the ground that the averments are already sufficiently specific,[106] but the question of recovery could then arise again at a later stage in order to deal with amendment.[107] Diligence to recover evidence before proceedings had commenced required application to the *nobile officium* of the Court of Session.[108]

---

[96] *Gould v Gould* 1966 SC 88 (per the Lord Ordinary after a report to the Inner House); *Savage v Savage* 1981 SLT (Notes) 17.

[97] RCS, Chap 43.

[98] RCS, r 43.25. Lord Cullen, in *Review of Business in the Outer House of the Court of Session* (1995) at para 5.14, proposed that it be extended to all Court of Session proceedings.

[99] See *Braby & Co v Story* (1896) 3 SLT 325 (OH) (Court of Session); *Orr v Orr* (1937) 53 Sh Ct Rep 89. See also *Boyle v Glasgow Royal Infirmary and Associated Hospitals* 1969 SC 72. Cf *Prentice v Kirkwood* (1949) 65 Sh Ct Rep 207.

[100] See para 21.6.

[101] In slander actions: *Graeme-Hunter v Glasgow Iron & Steel Co Ltd* (1908) 16 SLT 15 (OH); *Stephen v Paterson* (1865) 3 M 571.

[102] A diligence has been granted during a proof (*Baroness Gray v Richardson* (1874) 1 R 1138), and after appeal to the House of Lords, when the petition had not been served (*Tulloch v Davidson's Exrs* (1858) 20 D 1319).

[103] At para 21.4.

[104] As in *Greig v Crosbie* (1855) 18 D 193; *Boyle v Glasgow Royal Infirmary and Associated Hospitals* 1969 SC 72.

[105] See, eg, *MacRae v British Transport Commission* 1957 SC 195; *Donaldson v Bannatyne* (1828) 7 S 130.

[106] *Jamieson v Jamieson* 1928 SLT 427 (OH); *Dalgleish's Trs v Mathieson's Trs* (1902), 10 SLT 56 (OH). An example of this under the statutory procedure described below is *McInally v John Wyeth & Brother Ltd* 1996 SLT 1223.

[107] See *Thomson v Gordon* (1869) 7 M 687 (refused diligence to enable a party to make an amendment specific).

[108] Impliedly competent, although refused on the merits, in *Jennings v Glasgow Corporation* 1937 SC 180.

Statute

Under the Administration of Justice (Scotland) Act 1972[109] (hereafter "the 1972 **21.5.2**
Act") the Court of Session[110] and the sheriff court[111] are empowered to make an
order for inspection, photographing, preservation, custody and detention, recovery
or inspection of documents or other property. The power is exercisable on application by any party appearing to the court to have an interest and at any time after
commencement of civil proceedings in the Court of Session or the sheriff court.[112]
Furthermore, it may be exercised before an action has been commenced on the
application of a person who appears to the court to be likely to be a party or
minuter in civil proceedings which are likely to be brought.[113] The normal test to
be applied in considering an application under the statute is considered below.[114]

Conditions of order for recovery

Although, remarkably, there was until recently no authority on the point,[115] an **21.5.3**
order for commission and diligence at common law or under the 1972 Act, carries
an implied obligation or undertaking that the party who obtains it will not use
what is recovered, or allow its use, for any purpose other than the action or proceedings in respect of which recovery was ordered.[116] When diligence is ordered
the documents come under the protection of the court which granted the order.[117]
The court may attach express conditions[118] to regulate access to all or parts of the
documents to be recovered or require an undertaking from the party to that
effect.[119]

21.6 COMMON LAW TESTS

Averments

At common law a diligence will not be granted for the recovery of documents unless the **21.6.1**
documents will, or at least may, have a bearing on the averments remitted to proof.[120]

---

[109] s 1. Section 1(1A) was added later, when the Act was amended by the Law Reform (Miscellaneous
Provisions) (Scotland) Act 1985, s 19.

[110] For procedure, see RCS, Chap 35.

[111] For procedure, see OCR, Chap 28.

[112] s 1(2)(a).

[113] s 1(2)(b). Application before proceedings commence is by petition in the Court of Session (RCS,
r 64.2) and summary application in the sheriff court (Act of Sederunt (Summary Applications, Statutory
Applications and Appeals etc Rules) 1999 (SI 1999/929), r 3.1.2).

[114] para 21.7.

[115] Inner House in *Iomega Corporation v Myrica (UK) Ltd* 1998 SC 636.

[116] *Iomega Corporation v Myrica (UK) Ltd* 1998 SC 636, per Lord President Rodger at 645. He also
observes, at 645, that the situation need not be different if documents are simply ordered to be produced.

[117] *Iomega Corporation v Myrica (UK) Ltd* 1998 SC 636, per Lord President Rodger at 640.

[118] *Dailey Petroleum Services Corporation v Pioneer Oil Tools Ltd* 1994 SLT 757, overruled in *Iomega
Corporation v Myrica (UK) Ltd* 1998 SC 636 but this point was not criticised.

[119] *McInally v John Wyeth & Brother Ltd* 1992 SLT 344 (overturned on another point in *McInally v
John Wyeth & Brother Ltd* 1996 SLT 1223, but the requirement for an undertaking was approved).
Additional procedural requirements of this nature are contained in RCS r 64.3, substituted by Act of
Sederunt (Rules of the Court of Session Amendment No. 4) (Applications under 1 of the
Administration of Justice (Scotland) Act 1972) 2000, (SI 2000/319) para 2.

[120] *British Publishing Co v Hedderwick & Sons* (1892) 19 R 1008.

Thus the form of the interlocutor allowing proof,[121] and the issues that appear from the averments,[122] will be highly relevant to the drafting and success of the specification. Subsequent doubt about the relevancy of the averments remitted to proof is not a ground for refusing recovery if the documents bear on the averments.[123]

Purpose of recovery

21.6.2 It is suggested that the rule at common law can be stated most precisely in negative form.[124] A document is not recoverable if it has not been communicated to or by one of the parties and if it can be used only to provide material for the examination in chief or in cross of a witness who is not a party. To state the rule positively, and at the same time comprehensively, is more difficult, but it is thought that it may be stated thus. Subject to confidentiality[125] and relevancy, a document is recoverable if it is a deed granted by or in favour of a party or his predecessor in title, or a communication sent to, or by or on behalf of, a party, or a written record kept by or on behalf of a party. The distinction between what is and what is not recoverable by diligence has been assimilated to the distinction between documents which, both in the Court of Session and in the sheriff court, must be lodged in process before the proof and those which may be produced for the first time at the proof.[126] Although a document in the second category is not in general recoverable by diligence, a witness who possesses it may be cited to bring it along to the proof.[127]

Application of the rule

21.6.3 The rule has been applied to exclude documents which are in the possession of third parties who are to be no more than witnesses in the cause,[128] but it is thought that the accident of who happens to possess the document is not the sole deciding feature and that the question of who wrote it, and to whom, is of at least equal importance.[129] Documents which, subject to relevancy and confidentiality, if their

---

[121] In *Scott, Simpson & Wallis v Forrest & Turnbull* (1897) 24 R 877, where the Lord Ordinary had allowed the pursuers a proof of their averments and to the defenders a conjunct probation, the defenders, owing to the form of the interlocutor, could not recover documents bearing on a separate substantive defence. In *Brown v Evered* (1904) 12 SLT 121 (OH), a Lord Ordinary found that, owing to the form of his interlocutor allowing proof, he had to grant a diligence much against his will.

[122] *Ogston & Tennant Ltd v The "Daily Record", Glasgow, Ltd* 1909 SC 1000 is an example of close comparison between averment (or its equivalent) and the specification. For other examples see *Duke of Buccleuch v Cowan* (1866) 4 M 475; *John Watson Ltd v Caledonian Railway Co* (1901) 3 F 791; *Burrows v Corporation of Glasgow* (1916) 1 SLT 420 (OH); *Earl of Morton v Fleming* 1921 1 SLT 205 (OH); *Northern Garage Ltd v North British Motor Manufacturing Co Ltd* (1908) 16 SLT 573 (OH); *Boyle v Glasgow Royal Infirmary and Associated Hospitals Board of Management* 1969 SC 72. *Cf Robertson v Earl of Dudley* (1875) 2 R 935.

[123] *Duke of Hamilton's Trs v Woodside Coal Co* (1897) 24 R 294.

[124] For which the judgment in *Livingstone v Dinwoodie* (1860) 22 D 1333 forms the basis.

[125] See Chapter 10.

[126] See para 21.3.

[127] *Livingstone v Dinwoodie* (1860) 22 D 1333 at 1334; *Hogg v Campbell* (1864) 2 M 1158 at 1161; *Steven v Nicoll* (1875) 2 R 292 at 293; *North British Railway Co v R & J Garroway* (1893) 20 R 397 at 403; *Watson v Watson* 1934 SC 374.

[128] *Admiralty v Aberdeen Steam Trawling and Fishing Co Ltd* 1909 SC 335, per Lord Kinnear at 343; *Watson v Watson* 1934 SC 374 at 380, referring to dicta in *Livingstone v Dinwoodie* (1860) 22 D 1333.

[129] See the various circumstances in the following cases, the facts of which are considered in more detail in the first edition of this work at para 289: *Livingstone v Dinwoodie* (1860) 22 D 1333; *Sutherland v John Ritchie & Co* (1900) 8 SLT 100 (OH); *Devlin v Spinelli* (1906) 14 SLT 9 (OH);

authenticity is presumed or averred, constitute written evidence, are clearly recoverable. Other writings are recoverable in general if they have been written to or by a party. These include business books and records[130] and other writings by or on behalf of a party which may contain an extra-judicial admission or statement against interest,[131] or may throw light on the party's state of mind,[132] as, for example, mental condition[133] or fraudulent intent.[134] They also include communications received by a party which may disclose his or her state of knowledge at a particular time[135] or contain a "contemporaneous record" of events,[136] as, for example, reports received from a party's contractors[137] or employees.[138] In an action by a trustee in bankruptcy for reduction of an assignation granted by the bankrupt, diligence was granted for recovery of the bankrupt's public examination.[139] This may be explained on the view that the examination was public and that the answers were to questions by or on behalf of the pursuer. A document not uttered is in many cases not recoverable,[140] but where the defender was accused of fraud, his diary was held recoverable as possible evidence of his state of mind.[141] Although it was often said that a document to be used for cross-examination only was not recoverable by diligence,[142] this proposition was thought to be far too wide, and documents frequently have been recovered for that purpose.[143] There were conflicting judicial statements as to whether the document had to be capable

---

Steven v Nicoll (1875) 2 R 292 (*cf Porter v Phoenix Assurance Co* (1867) 5 M 533); *Hogg v Campbell* (1864) 2 M 1158; *McNeill v Campbell* (1880) 7 R 574. *Cf Fraser v Fraser's Trs* (1897) 4 SLT 228 (OH) (a doubtful decision).

[130] *Gray v Wyllie* (1904) 6 F 448; *Aitchison & Sons Ltd v McEwen* (1903) 5 F 303; *Christie v Craik* (1900) 2 F 1287; *Rhind v Kemp* (1894) 1 SLT 434 (OH); *Johnston v Caledonian Railway Co* (1892) 20 R 222, where *Craig v North British Railway Co* (1888) 15 R 808 was distinguished and the decision explained to rest on the excessive period; *Irvine v Glasgow and South Western Railway Co* (1913) 2 SLT 452 (OH).

[131] See paras 9.8 and 9.9. The decisions in *Jenkins v Glasgow Corporation* 1934 SLT 53 (OH), and *French v Purnell* 1931 SLT 85 (OH), are difficult to reconcile with principle.

[132] See paras 7.11–7.13.

[133] *Mackintosh v Fraser* (1859) 21 D 783 at 792.

[134] *Strachan v Barlas* (1894) 2 SLT 59 (OH); *Assets Co Ltd v Shirres' Trs* (1897) 24 R 418. See also *Wilson's Trs v Bank of England* 1925 SLT 81 (OH); *Dobbie v Johnston* (1860) 22 D 1113; *Tulloch v Davidson's Trs* (1858) 20 D 1319.

[135] As in *Parks v Tayside Regional Council* 1989 SLT 345, an application under the 1972 Act.

[136] This, however, is limited to medical or other scientific reports: *Black v Bairds & Dalmellington* 1939 SC 472, per Lord Justice-Clerk Aitchison at 477 and Lord Wark at 483.

[137] *Sutherland v John Ritchie & Co* (1900) 8 SLT 100 (OH); *Sneddon v Glasgow Corporation* 1935 SLT 74 (OH).

[138] *Tannett, Walker & Co v Hannay & Sons* (1873) 11 M 931.

[139] *Emslie v Alexander* (1862) 1 M 209. The report of *Fife County Council v Thoms* (1898) 25 R 1097, is obscure, but the decision is not surprising. The letters were obviously confidential, as the defender argued, and the diligence was obviously fishing and should never have been agreed to.

[140] *Watson v Watson* 1934 SC 374, per Lord Murray at 378.

[141] *Strachan v Barlas* (1894) 2 SLT 59 (OH).

[142] Dickson, *Evidence* (3rd edn), para 1361; Lewis, *Evidence*, p 191.

[143] *Johnston v South of Scotland Electricity Board* 1968 SLT (Notes) 7; *Young v National Coal Board* 1957 SC 99, per Lord Justice-Clerk Thomson at 105; *Black v Bairds & Dalmellington* 1939 SC 472, per Lord Justice-Clerk Aitchison at 478; *Admiralty v Aberdeen Steam Trawling and Fishing Co Ltd* 1909 SC 335, per Lord McLaren at 341; *Emslie v Alexander* (1862) 1 M 209, per Lord Justice-Clerk Inglis at 210. *Cf Mackinnon v National SS Co* (1904) 12 SLT 411 (OH) and *Devlin v Spinelli* (1906) 14 SLT 9 (OH) (where the reasons for refusal are unconvincing) and *Maitland v Glasgow Corporation* 1947 SC 20.

of being used in evidence.[144] In many of these cases the practical result of recovery is to provide material for the cross-examination of the person making the report.

21.7 TEST FOR APPLICATION UNDER THE ADMINISTRATION OF JUSTICE (SCOTLAND) ACT 1972

The statutory provision

21.7.1 The 1972 Act contains a procedure for recovery of evidence which is, on the face of it, considerably more extensive than the scope for recovery at common law. It exists alongside the common law procedure, although rules of court treat the procedures together for most purposes.[145] The most obvious extension in scope of the 1972 Act is the provision for an order to be made at any stage in proceedings or before proceedings are taken. In respect of all orders under the Act the court exercises a discretion in deciding whether or not to make an order. In order for the statute to apply the court must be satisfied (a) that the property in respect of which the order is sought is property as to which any question may relevantly arise,[146] (b) that the question may arise in any existing civil proceedings or in civil proceedings that are likely to be brought,[147] and (c) that the person seeking the order is a party or minuter in the proceedings or any other person who appears to the court to have an interest to be joined in current proceedings as a party or minuter or to be likely to be a party or minuter in proceedings to be brought.[148] Objections on the grounds of confidentiality are preserved.[149] The 1972 Act provides that the court may exercise the powers to order recovery "notwithstanding any rule of law or practice to the contrary" and "unless there is special reason why the application should not be granted."[150] The combination of these words and the absence of any other express test within the statute has caused the court to consider whether the statutory test is so broad that it dictates that the order shall be granted unless there is special reason otherwise, effectively reversing the burden of proof that applies at common law.[151]

---

[144] "The proper use of diligence is to recover writings of the nature of evidence, and capable of being used as evidence in the cause: we must be satisfied that the writings are of such a kind that they may be used in evidence": *Livingstone v Dinwoodie* (1860) 22 D 1333 at 1334. The decision may be more limited than they suggest: see *Admiralty v Aberdeen Steam Trawling and Fishing Co Ltd* 1909 SC 335, per Lord Kinnear at 343; *Watson v Watson* 1934 SC 374 at 380. *Cf Young v National Coal Board* 1957 SC 99, per Lord Blades at 108; *Black v Bairds & Dalmellington* 1939 SC 472; *Admiralty v Aberdeen Steam Trawling and Fishing Co Ltd* 1909 SC 335, per Lord President Dunedin at 340. There is no explanation of the meaning in this connection of the terms "of the nature of evidence", "used as evidence" and "used in evidence". Some judges contrasted the writings of the living with those of the dead: *County Council of Fife v Thoms* (1898) 25 R 1097, per Lord Justice-Clerk Macdonald at 1098; *Hogg v Campbell* (1864) 2 M 1158, per Lord Deas and Lord Ardmillan at 1161.
[145] RCS, rr 35.4–35.7; OCR, rr 28.4–28.7.
[146] Administration of Justice (Scotland) Act 1972, s 1(1).
[147] s 1(1).
[148] s 2.
[149] s 1(4) and see Chapter 10. This will include not only the privilege, confidentiality and public interest privilege referred to in the provision, but also the privilege against self-incrimination: *The British Phonographic Industry Ltd v Cohen, Cohen, Kelly, Cohen & Cohen Ltd* 1983 SLT 137. However, the privilege cannot be claimed in an application under the 1972 Act concerning infringement of intellectual property: Law Reform (Miscellaneous Provisions) (Scotland) Act 1985, s 15.
[150] The words quoted form the preamble and conclusion to s 1(2).
[151] This argument persuaded the Lord Ordinary in *McGown v Erskine* 1978 SLT (Notes) 4, but not in *Baxter v Lothian Health Board* 1976 SLT (Notes) 37. The view in *McGown* was preferred by Macphail (see *Evidence*, para 25.05), but see *Moore v Greater Glasgow Health Board* 1978 SC 123; *Civil Service Building Society v MacDougall* 1988 SC 58.

However, the opinion which has prevailed is that, despite the broad terms of the statutory provision, the onus remains with the applicant to satisfy the court according to the principle of the tests at common law.[152]

Application of test after proof allowed

In applications made after proof has been allowed, in general the tests familiar at **21.7.2** common law, based on averment and purpose, apply.[153] There is a general assumption that this is the appropriate time for recovery to be sought and ordered, but it has been noted that an underlying assumption that the court should not allow recovery before this stage operates to inhibit advancement of pleadings and early resolution of proceedings.[154]

After record closed

In applications made after the record is closed but while the cause is on the pro- **21.7.3** cedure roll in the Court of Session, or awaiting debate in the sheriff court, the court has considered whether the recovery sought will enable a party to give more effective consideration to the specification of pleadings before the cause comes to be debated,[155] particularly when the documents of which recovery is sought have been available to another of the parties in the course of pleading prior to the record having been closed.[156]

Before record closed

In applications made before the record is closed the test is whether the documents **21.7.4** of which recovery is sought are necessary[157] for the purpose of enabling the party seeking recovery to make more specific averments which have been made.[158] As at common law, recovery has not been ordered if the averments are sufficiently specific, the assessment of their specification being considered according to the circumstances at the date when the court hears the application,[159] rather than by reference to anticipated averments in answer.[160]

Before proceedings raised

In applications before proceedings are raised there can be no assessment of **21.7.5**

---

[152] *Moore v Greater Glasgow Health Board* 1978 SC 123; *Civil Service Building Society v MacDougall* 1988 SC 58.

[153] See para 21.6.

[154] Lord Cullen, *Review of Business in the Outer House of the Court of Session* (1995), para 5.9.

[155] *Graham Builders Merchants Ltd v Royal Bank of Scotland plc* 1992 SCLR 402; *Bank of East Asia Ltd v Shepherd & Wedderburn* 1994 SCLR 526. As to recovery based upon averments in a minute of amendment, see *Greens Annotated Rules of the Court of Session 1994*, annotations to RCS, r 35.2.5.

[156] Per Lord McCluskey in *Gallier v Lothian Regional Council* (unreported), excerpted in *Bank of East Asia Ltd v Shepherd & Wedderburn* 1994 SCLR 526 at 527.

[157] Necessity should be assessed in a reasonable sense: *Christie v Arthur Bell & Sons Ltd* 1989 SLT 253. The application was refused as unnecessary in *McInally v John Wyeth & Brother Ltd* 1996 SLT 1223 (IH); *Iomega Corporation v Myrica (UK) Ltd* 1998 SC 636.

[158] *Moore v Greater Glasgow Health Board* 1978 SC 123.

[159] *Moore v Greater Glasgow Health Board* 1978 SC 123, per Lord Cameron at 131.

[160] *McInally v John Wyeth & Brother Ltd* 1996 SLT 1223 (IH), reversing the decision of the Lord Ordinary made much earlier in *McInally v John Wyeth & Brother Ltd* 1992 SLT 344. In the intervening period the case had been sisted while proceedings on the same subject-matter in England were the subject of preliminary procedure and legal aid applications.

pleadings in the cause. In such a case the application should contain, and be supported by, sufficient information to enable the court to know what the action is going to be about and what assistance the documents sought would give in deciding it,[161] and the court has applied the test normally applied to pleadings, namely that the order is required to make the pleadings more pointed or specific, to the specification of the ground of action that the applicant has been able to make out in the petition for recovery under the 1972 Act.[162] The "likelihood of proceedings" must be made out[163] and is assessed at the time of application.[164] Although it is not necessary for the applicant to make out in the application what would constitute a relevant case in the subsequent proceedings,[165] if the application discloses no relevant basis for a subsequent action recovery will be refused.[166]

Proceedings/recovery outside Scotland

21.7.6 When proceedings are to be brought outside Scotland, in a country to which the Brussels or Lugano Conventions apply or in England or Northern Ireland it is competent to seek an order under the 1972 Act,[167] and an order to assist with the recovery of evidence may be made in response to letters of request under the Evidence (Proceedings in Other Jurisdictions) Act 1975.[168] The court will not grant an order under either enactment unless it is necessary, having regard to orders for recovery granted in any other court,[169] and in so doing applies the law and practice of the Scottish courts to the application.[170]

21.7.7   If the proceedings are to be in Scotland but the documents are outwith Scotland the court will consider the application in the normal way, and, if granted, the order will be for commission to take place in Scotland.[171] The order will not be enforceable against a third party haver (that is the person thought to be in possession of the documents) outwith Scotland unless a court in the relevant country grants an order for enforcement.[172]

---

[161] *Falkingham v Lothian Regional Council* 1983 SLT (Sh Ct) 2, followed in *Yau v Ogilvie & Co* 1985 SLT 91. RCS r 64.3 now requires the applicant to submit an affidavit supporting the averments in the petition.

[162] *Cole, Petitioner* 1993 SLT 894; *Thorne v Strathclyde Regional Council* 1984 SLT 161. In *Union Carbide Corporation v BP Chemicals* 1995 SC 398 the applicants' state of knowledge was such that they were able only to plead a case which met the technical requirements but not the spirit of the English Supreme Court Rules then applying, and recovery was ordered.

[163] Applications were unsuccessful on this basis in *Colquhoun, Petitioner* 1990 SLT 43 (likelihood of action, and likelihood that applicant would be a party to action, not made out); *MT Group v James Howden & Co Ltd* 1993 SLT 409 (merits to be decided in proceedings outside Scotland, hence no likelihood in Scotland).

[164] *Dominion Technology Ltd v Gardner Cryogenics Ltd (No 1)* 1993 SLT 828.

[165] *Friel, Petitioner* 1981 SLT 113; *Dominion Technology Ltd v Gardner Cryogenics Ltd (No 1)* 1993 SLT 828.

[166] *Dominion Technology Ltd v Gardner Cryogenics Ltd (No 1)* 1993 SLT 828.

[167] Civil Jurisdiction and Judgments Act 1982, s 28, considered in *Iomega Corporation v Myrica (UK) Ltd* 1998 SC 636. *Cf Dailey Petroleum Services Corporation v Pioneer Oil Tools Ltd* 1994 SLT 757 in which the Lord Ordinary relied upon the Evidence (Proceedings in Other Jurisdictions) Act 1975, ss 1 and 2, which appeared to him to preclude the use of recovered documents in foreign litigation. *Dailey* was overruled by *Iomega*, in which the competence of such an order was confirmed although it was not granted due to lack of necessity. See also para 17.10.3.

[168] s 2.

[169] *Iomega Corporation v Myrica (UK) Ltd* 1998 SC 636.

[170] s 2(3).

[171] *Maitland v Maitland* (1885) 12 R 899 at 904. See also *Baxter v Lothian Health Board* 1976 SLT (Notes) 37.

[172] For the converse of this situation, see *Union Carbide Corporation v BP Chemicals Ltd* 1995 SC 398.

Reform

The view has been expressed that the tests for recovery in terms of the Act are **21.7.8**
applied more restrictively than is appropriate in a growing climate of early disclosure to facilitate early settlement and reduced cost and delay in court. Lord Cullen,
in his *Review of Business in the Outer House of the Court of Session*[173] proposes
that the question of whether proof has been allowed should not of itself weigh
against recovery.[174] He suggests that what should matter is whether the averments
on which recovery is based will be refused probation, and whether those averments
provide an adequate foundation for the terms in which recovery is sought.[175] If
these tests are applied, the risk that a "fishing diligence" will be sought or granted,
whether before or after the record has closed, should be avoided,[176] it being possible to apply this test at any stage, "subject to the proviso that the court may exercise its discretion to refuse the recovery where it is related to averments in respect
of which there is an unresolved dispute as to whether probation should be
allowed."[177]

21.8 CRIMINAL CASES

In criminal cases under solemn procedure a list of productions should be served **21.8.1**
with the indictment[178] and usually the documents appearing on that list are lodged
with the record copy indictment.[179] In summary cases there are no specific requirements for production or lodging of documents, but the parties are enjoined to
attempt to agree evidence in the case,[180] which is not possible if the evidence has
not been disclosed.[181] The accused has a right of reasonable inspection,[182] and on
application to the court an order may be made for expert examination of a production,[183] or for recovery of the whole item if only an excerpt is produced.[184] The
Crown cannot seek an order for production from the accused, since this would contravene the accused's right to silence, nor, for the same reason, may an accused
seek recovery from another, but all may use the productions listed by the others.[185]
If an accused wishes to rely upon a document not lodged by the Crown or a co-
accused that document should be lodged in court 10 days before the jury is sworn

---

[173] Issued in December 1995.
[174] Lord Cullen's Review, para 5.9.
[175] This is an important aspect of the common law test: see para 21.6 above.
[176] Lord Cullen's Review, para 5.9.
[177] Lord Cullen's Review, para 5.10. Apparently there has been no change in procedure to this effect
and the matter is to be left to evolution of judicial attitudes: see *Greens Annotated Rules of the Court
of Session 1994*, annotations to RCS, r 35.2.6.
[178] Criminal Procedure (Scotland) Act 1995, s 66(7).
[179] Renton & Brown, *Criminal Procedure* (6th edn), para 14-24.
[180] Criminal Procedure (Scotland) Act 1995, s 258.
[181] Noted in relation to witnesses in Renton & Brown, *Criminal Procedure* (6th edn), para 20-45.
[182] See, *eg, Anderson v Hingston* 1997 SLT 844 in which it was not considered unreasonable that an
extract was taken from a document which was claimed to be commercially secret, with which the
accused was not satisfied, and a subsequent offer made by the Crown to allow the accused's agent to
view the whole document on condition that the whole was not revealed to the accused.
[183] *Davies, Petitioner* 1973 SLT (Notes) 36.
[184] *Anderson v Hingston* 1997 SLT 844. It is common practice to produce only excerpts from a police
officer's notebook (see Renton & Brown, *Criminal Procedure* (6th edn), para 24-158/2), anything not
related to the case in hand being confidential: *Daly v Vannet* 1999 SCCR 346.
[185] Criminal Procedure (Scotland) Act 1995, s 67(6).

in a High Court trial or at the first diet of a solemn case in the sheriff court.[186] Failure to lodge a document in time will not normally render it inadmissible[187] (although intimation will be expected) since to counter any perceived injustice the court can make appropriate orders in relation to adjournment, permission to lead additional evidence or desertion *pro loco et tempore*.[188]

21.8.2 The Crown has an obligation to disclose to the defence any information which supports the defence case.[189] If an accused wishes to gain access to documents not produced which are in the possession of the Crown, the appropriate procedure is to apply to the court for an order for production of a document.[190] An application for commission and diligence is competent nevertheless,[191] and is the competent[192] means of securing recovery if the document is in the hands of a third party.[193] The application for commission and diligence is to the High Court, even if trial is to be in the sheriff court.[194] Although unusual, an application for recovery for a summary trial appears to be competent, subject to possible liability for the expenses of the process if the application is unsuccessful.[195] Proceedings before the sheriff may be adjourned for the application to be presented to the High Court[196] although it is preferable for this to be dealt with sufficiently early in the proceedings for the documents recovered to be produced for trial.[197]

21.8.3 An order will be granted only if it will serve a proper purpose and it is in the interests of justice to do so.[198] This will involve a question of whether the evidence of which recovery is sought would be likely to be of material assistance to the proper presentation of the accused's defence.[199] The Crown may take an objection on grounds of confidentiality and the court will examine the conflicting public interests of protecting sources of information and securing a fair trial.[200] An application may be made for the purpose of an appeal on the grounds of fresh evidence.[201] The Scottish Cases Review Commission has a separate statutory power to seek an order from the High Court for recovery of relevant documents[202]

---

[186] Criminal Procedure (Scotland) Act 1995, s 78(4); Act of Adjournal (Criminal Procedure Rules) 1996, r 11.2. There are no specific time limits in summary cases, although the convention, based on previous statutory provision, is three days. See Renton & Brown, *Criminal Procedure* (6th edn), para 14-29.

[187] See Renton & Brown, *Criminal Procedure* (6th edn), paras 14-24 and 14-33.

[188] *McLeod v HM Advocate (No 2)* 1998 JC 67 at 80B–C.

[189] *McLeod v HM Advocate (No 2)* 1998 JC 67 at 77G–79C, affirming statements in *Slater v HM Advocate* 1928 JC 94 and *Downie v HM Advocate* 1952 JC 37, but disapproving the passage to the contrary in *Higgins v HM Advocate* 1990 SCCR 268.

[190] *McLeod v HM Advocate (No 2)* 1998 JC 67 at 69.

[191] And was the procedure used in *McLeod v HM Advocate* 1998 JC 67.

[192] *Downie v HM Advocate* 1952 JC 37; *HM Advocate v Hasson* 1971 JC 35.

[193] *McLeod v HM Advocate (No 2)* 1998 JC 67 at 69.

[194] *HM Advocate v Ashrif* 1988 SLT 567.

[195] *Gallacher, Petitioner* 1990 JC 345; *Anderson v Hingston* 1997 SLT 844.

[196] *Anderson v Hingston* 1997 SLT 844.

[197] *Anderson v Hingston* 1997 SLT 844.

[198] *McLeod v HM Advocate (No 2)* 1998 JC 67 at 80D–E.

[199] *McLeod v HM Advocate (No 2)* 1998 JC 67 at 80D–E. The court also held that this requirement was consistent with the accused's right to a fair trial in terms of Art 6 of the European Convention on Human Rights, as interpreted in relation to recovery of prosecution evidence in *Edwards v United Kingdom* Series A No 247-B (1993) 15 EHRR 417.

[200] *McLeod v HM Advocate (No 2)* 1998 JC 67 at 71F–G. See also para 10.9.

[201] *Barbour v HM Advocate* 1994 GWD 23-1396; *Porter and Smith, Petitioners*, unreported, 23 December 1999, available via www.scotscourts.gov.uk.

[202] Criminal Procedure (Scotland) Act 1995, s 194I.

and the duty to comply with that order is not affected by any obligation of secrecy or other limitation whether imposed by another enactment or otherwise.[203]

21.9 OTHER TRIBUNALS

Powers to order production or recovery of evidence in proceedings before **21.9.1** statutory tribunals may be found in the statute by which the tribunal is established or in the rules of procedure of the tribunal.[204] Even where the tribunal is not bound by the rules of evidence,[205] the protocols which are consistent with a fair trial—namely lodging productions for consideration by the other party,[206] and having a process for ordering production of material items not lodged—will be expected for compliance with the European Convention of Human Rights if the tribunal has the power to make a decision which is determinative of an issue.[207] The sheriff has power to grant warrant for the citation of witnesses to the courts of the Church of Scotland[208] and possibly to those of other churches,[209] and it is therefore presumed that there is power to grant commission and diligence for recovery of documents for use before these courts. An application for commission and diligence, both at common law and under the 1972 Act,[210] is competent in an arbitration. The proper procedure is that the arbiter, if so advised, approves the specification, and application is then made to the court for a diligence.[211] If a haver refuses to produce on the ground of confidentiality, the arbiter or the party may apply to the court, which must consider whether the objection is well founded before pronouncing an order.[212]

21.10 THE SPECIFICATION

General

The normal method of recovering documents, whether at common law or under the **21.10.1** 1972 Act, is to lodge a specification with a motion for its approval, or a petition or application if proceedings have not been raised, and for the appointment of a com-

---

[203] Criminal Procedure (Scotland) Act 1995, s 194I(2). The effect of this provision has been considered in *The Scottish Criminal Cases Review Commission, Petrs*, 29 August 2000.

[204] See, *eg*, Solicitors Discipline Tribunal Procedure Rules 1989, r 7; Pensions Appeal Tribunal (Scotland) Rules 1981 (SI 1981/500), r 6, examined in *McGinley v United Kingdom* (1999) 27 EHRR 1. A range of tribunals most commonly encountered is examined, as at 1 January 1995, in MacSporran & Young, *Commission and Diligence*, Chapter 8.

[205] In the small claims procedure in the sheriff court no enactment or rule of law relating to admissibility or corroboration of evidence (in so far as corroboration is required in civil cases after the Civil Evidence (Scotland) Act 1988, s 1) applies, but nevertheless there is a procedure akin to commission and diligence: Small Claims Rules 1988 (SI 1988/1976), r 1.

[206] The subject of comment by the Lands Tribunal in *Forest Hills Trossachs Club v Assessor for Central Region* 1991 SLT (Lands Tr) 42. See also *Edwards v United Kingdom* Series A No 247-B (1993) 15 EHRR 417.

[207] *McGinley v United Kingdom* (1999) 27 EHRR 1.

[208] *Presbytery of Lews v Fraser* (1874) 1 R 888. See para 17.9.

[209] *Presbytery of Lews v Fraser* (1874) 1 R 888 at 894. See para 17.9.

[210] *Anderson v Gibb* 1993 SLT 726.

[211] *Blaikie v Aberdeen Rly Co* (1851) 13 D 1307; *Crichton v North British Railway Co* (1888) 15 R 784.

[212] *Blaikie v Aberdeen Rly Co* (1852) 14 D 590.

missioner to execute the diligence. The specification should consist of a detailed and articulate statement of the particular documents, or classes of documents, which are sought to be recovered.[213] Where a call is for books tending to show the truth of some averment it should be "in order that excerpts may be taken therefrom at the sight of the commissioner", unless there is a special reason for requiring the books themselves.[214] The specification concludes with a call "failing principals, drafts, copies or duplicates of the above." Approval of a specification containing such a call did not, at common law, entitle the party to obtain copies, etc, until he had failed to recover the principals after a reasonable attempt had been made.[215] Although recovery of the principals is still desirable, statute now permits reliance on authenticated copies as if they were originals.[216] If the court refuses part of the specification, the deletion ought to be authenticated by the court.[217]

Special

21.10.2 In most cases involving personal injuries, when the pursuer has been in hospital, the hospital records are recovered from the relevant health authority after intimation to the Lord Advocate.[218] Although diligence for recovery of income tax returns has been refused at the instance of a party,[219] a more recent decision seems to show that it would be granted if the Lord Advocate does not object.[220] While communications made to a party are in their nature recoverable, recovery may be refused on the ground that they were made *post litem motam*, that is after the dispute had arisen, or was at least in contemplation, and are therefore confidential.[221] An exception has been made for reports where the process of examination leading to the report, obtained by the party in possession of evidence, has led to destruction of the evidence.[222] There is also an arbitrary exception in the case of reports to a party by that party's employee present at the incident, and made at or about the time of it.[223] By comparison, documents prepared *de recenti*—including entries in accident books[224]—which are prepared in accordance with a statutory duty,

---

[213] *Paterson v Paterson* (1919) 1 SLT 12 (OH).

[214] However, if the excerpts produced are considered to be insufficient it is possible to apply afresh for the whole document: see RCS, rr 35.3.12 and 35.3.14; OCR, r 28.3(9) and (11) in relation to optional procedure but the principle is of wider effect. On optional procedure, see para 21.9.

[215] *Caledonian Railway Co v Symington* 1912 SC 1033. *Cf Sleigh v Glasgow and Transvaal Options Ltd* (1903) 5 F 332.

[216] Civil Evidence (Scotland) Act 1988, s 5, and see para 21.2.

[217] *Thomson & Co v Bowater & Sons* 1918 SC 316.

[218] *Glacken v National Coal Board* 1951 SC 82. Note that documents kept by a health authority may fall within the definition of "business" records of an "undertaking" in terms of the Civil Evidence (Scotland) Act 1988. See paras 21.14–21.16.

[219] *Gray v Wyllie* (1904) 6 F 448.

[220] *Henderson v McGown* 1916 SC 821. *Cf Jenkins v Glasgow Corporation* 1934 SLT 53 (OH).

[221] See para 10.4.

[222] eg *Marks & Spencer Ltd v British Gas Corporation* 1983 SLT 196, *Hepburn v Scottish Power* 1997 SLT 859 (IH) and *Waddington v Buchan Poultry Products Ltd* 1961 SLT 428 (in which *Black v Bairds & Dalmellington* 1939 SC 472 was followed).

[223] *Young v National Coal Board* 1957 SC 99, per Lord Ordinary at 101, Lord Justice-Clerk Thomson at 105, Lord Mackintosh at 106; *Anderson v St Andrews Ambulance Association* 1942 SC 555, per Lord President Normand at 557, Lord Moncrieff at 559; *Black v Bairds & Dalmellington* 1939 SC 472, per Lord Mackay at 482, Lord Wark at 483; *Johnston v South of Scotland Electricity Board* 1968 SLT (Notes) 7. See further para 10.4.

[224] Although this may be recovered if the pleadings disclose an issue to which the accident book is material: see *Dobbie v Forth Ports Authority* 1974 SC 40 at 45 and 47; *Comer v James Scott & Co*

although arguably prepared in the public interest and of actual evidential value,[225] fall outwith that exception, and are not recoverable.[226] It has been said that a diligence will be granted to recover from the opposite party only specific documents for a specific purpose[227] and a more general call will require to be particularly justified or will fail.[228] Greater latitude has been permitted when fraud is averred.[229] Attempts to recover third parties' titles have failed.[230]

21.11 EXECUTION OF COMMISSION[231]

Optional procedure

After obtaining an order for commission and diligence a party may, before executing the commission in its entirety, opt for a shortened procedure which involves serving written notice upon a haver calling upon him to produce the documents to the clerk of court, or to certify that he has no such documents.[232] The party in whose favour the commission and diligence has been granted may inspect the documents lodged, produce them, or return them, via the clerk, to the haver, all within set time limits.[233] If not satisfied that this procedure has brought about full compliance with the order for commission and diligence the party in whose favour it has been granted may proceed to execute it. If an excerpt only has been produced the court may, on application, order recovery of the whole.[234]   **21.11.1**

Commission procedure

When the commissioner has fixed the diet, the haver is cited to it and informed of the documents of which production is expected by sending a copy of the specification, as approved, or of the part which affects that haver. The haver is put on oath by the commissioner and questioned by the solicitor who has cited him, or by counsel. The only legitimate purposes of the examination are to recover the docu-   **21.11.2**

(*Electrical Engineers*) *Ltd* 1976 SLT (Notes) 72; *Boyes v Eaton Yale & Towne Inc* 1978 SLT (Notes) 6; *McIntyre v National Coal Board* 1978 SLT (Sh Ct) 32; *Govan v National Coal Board* 1987 SLT 511.
[225] See Macphail, *Evidence*, paras 25.12–25.15, examining the dicta in *Dobbie v Forth Ports Authority* 1974 SC 40 and *Johnstone v National Coal Board* 1968 SC 128.
[226] *Johnstone v National Coal Board* 1968 SC 128; *Dobbie v Forth Ports Authority* 1974 SC 40; *McIntyre v National Coal Board* 1978 SLT (Sh Ct) 32; *More v Brown and Root Wimpey Highland Fabricators Ltd* 1983 SLT 669. *Cf Johnston v South of Scotland Electricity Board* 1968 SLT (Notes) 7.
[227] *Richardson v Fleming* (1867) 5 M 586; *Earl of Lauderdale v Scrymgeour Wedderburn* (1905) 7 F 1045 at 1048.
[228] *Riggs v Drummond* (1861) 23 D 1251; *Van Engers, Roeclofs & Co v Ellis Hughes* (1898) 6 SLT 90 (OH).
[229] As in *Strachan v Barlas* (1894) 2 SLT 59 (OH); *Assets Co Ltd v Shirres' Trs* (1897) 24 R 418; *Wilson's Trs v Bank of England* 1925 SLT 81 (OH); *Dobbie v Johnston* (1860) 22 D 1113; *Tulloch v Davidson's Trs* (1858) 20 D 1319.
[230] *Riggs v Drummond* (1861) 23 D 1251; *Fisher v Bontine* (1827) 6 S 330.
[231] Once commission has been ordered it is not competent to sist the commission process although the order may be recalled of consent: *Exal Sampling Services Ltd v Massie* 1993 SLT 1220. The divergence of authority in relation to the procedures for appeal against such an order is outwith the scope of this work, but see MacSporran & Young, *Commission and Diligence*, paras 3.65–3.69.
[232] RCS, r 35.3; OCR, r 28.3.
[233] RCS, rr 35.3.4–35.3.9; OCR, r 28.3(4)–(7). Lord Cullen, in *Review of Business in the Outer House of the Court of Session* (1995) at paras 5.11 and 5.12 proposes some streamlining of this procedure in the Court of Session.
[234] RCS, rr 35.3.12 and 35.3.14; OCR, r 28.3(9) and (11).

ment and if the haver does not have it, to discover whether he ever had it and why it is no longer in his possession. If the haver admits to having the document, and has no objection to delivering it, it is handed over to the commissioner, and that ends the matter. A haver who has destroyed the document[235] may be asked when, where, how and why; and if it has been handed to someone else, to whom.[236] Questions as to the contents of the documents[237] or as to the merits of the cause[238] are incompetent. The haver, who has had no opportunity to object to the terms of the specification, is entitled at this stage to refuse to answer or to produce, either on the ground of confidentiality[239] or on the ground that to do so will cause the haver serious prejudice.[240] It is the duty of the commissioner to decide the question and, if an appeal is taken, to seal up the documents for the decision of the court,[241] or in case of special difficulty he may report to the court.[242] Where excerpts only are to be taken, except of consent, the commissioner alone may see the books, but may have the assistance of an expert such as an accountant.[243] Rules of court govern the appointment of the commissioner, the lodging of the commissioner's report and the documents recovered, and intimation thereof.[244]

21.12 STAMPING

21.12.1 Stamping is a statutory requirement designed to raise revenue, and one of its sanctions is the inadmissibility in evidence of an instrument not duly stamped. Admissibility thus depends on the terms of the statutory provisions. Unless it is stamped while the case is in progress "an instrument executed in any part of the United Kingdom, or relating, wheresoever executed, to any property situate, or to any matter or thing done or to be done, in any part of the United Kingdom, shall not, except in criminal proceedings, be given in evidence, or be available for any purpose whatsoever, unless it is duly stamped in accordance with the law in force at the time when it was first executed."[245] Unless the document falls under the statutory description no question of stamping arises.[246] It has been held in England that if there is a trace of a stamp, the instrument will be presumed to have been duly stamped,[247] and the same presumption arises if the original document cannot be produced and its terms are proved by secondary evidence.[248] It is the duty of the

---

[235] This statement by a haver may be used as evidence at the trial: *Home v Hardy* (1842) 4 D 1184; *Falconer v Stephen* (1849) 11 D 1338.

[236] *Somervell v Somervell* (1900) 8 SLT 84 (OH) (a clear and very helpful account of how a haver should be examined); *Gordon v Davidson* (1865) 3 M 938; *Cullen v Thomson and Kerr* (1865) 1 M 284.

[237] *Somervell v Somervell* (1900) 8 SLT 84 (OH).

[238] *Dye v Reid* (1831) 9 S 342.

[239] RCS r 64.9(b) (ii) and see Chapter 10.

[240] *North British Railway Co v R & J Garroway* (1893) 20 R 397. See para 21.3.3 regarding the havers' privilege against self-incrimination. The commissioner should inform the haver that he may seek legal advice, RCS r 64. 9(c), where the application is made before proceedings are raised.

[241] *Stewart, Govan & Co v Birrell* (1897) 5 SLT 174 (OH).

[242] *North British Railway Co v R & J Garroway* (1893) 20 R 397.

[243] *Municipal Council of Johannesburg v Stewart & Co* 1911 1 SLT 359 (OH).

[244] RCS, rr 35.4–35.7; OCR, rr 28.4–28.7.

[245] Stamp Act 1891, s 14(4).

[246] Our courts do not enforce such revenue law of foreign states: *Stewart v Gelot* (1871) 9 M 1057 at 1062, 1064 and 1065; *Valery v Scott* (1876) 3 R 965 at 967.

[247] Dickson, *Evidence* (3rd edn), para 978.

[248] Dickson, *Evidence* (3rd edn), para 978; Bell, *Commentaries* (7th edn), I, 340, note 1. But it must be impossible to produce the original: *Cowan v Stewart* (1872) 10 M 735.

court to take notice of the omission,[249] but the court is likely to take a liberal interpretation of the stamping requirements.[250] Inadmissibility in evidence of the instrument is, apart from the penalty, the only sanction. The party may prove the case by any other competent evidence available.[251]

There is no doubt that an instrument not duly stamped is inadmissible to estab-   **21.12.2** lish the obligation which it was intended to constitute or prove. But under the statutes in force before 1891[252] the courts evolved a rule that "an instrument, if it contains evidence of a fact foreign to the purpose for which it was executed, may be admitted as evidence of that fact notwithstanding the terms of the Stamp Act."[253] "Unintended effect" would thus be a better description than "collateral purpose", the phrase by which this exception has been known. An instrument not duly stamped was held admissible as evidence of the state of mind of the granter,[254] and in the same case there are dicta that such an instrument might be used for a comparison of handwriting or as evidence that a signatory was alive at its date.[255] However, the statutes under which these decisions were pronounced did not contain the words "or be available for any purpose whatsoever", which suggests a deliberate intention to put an end to the "collateral purpose" exception. In Scotland that result has been hinted at *obiter*,[256] and an opinion to that effect has been expressed in England.[257] Nevertheless, it has been held that an unstamped agreement might be looked at not as an agreement but as evidence of its terms,[258] and that an insufficiently stamped promissory note could be used to extract an admission from the granter.[259]

An instrument not duly stamped may be received in evidence on payment of the   **21.12.3** duty, if it may legally be stamped after execution.[260] This course has been allowed after proof and before judgment,[261] and also on appeal.[262] Where the pursuer's case depended on an unstamped document which was not admitted, a new trial was granted, the pursuer having had the document duly stamped.[263] But if a judgment has become final, it cannot be suspended on the ground that it proceeded on a document which ought to have been stamped.[264] The Act seems to contemplate payment at the time[265] but the court has sisted process to enable payment to be

---

[249] *Cowan v Stewart* (1872) 10 M 735. But it has been said that a judge is not compelled to raise doubtful points: *Don Francesco v De Meo* 1908 SC 7, per Lord Ardwall at 11. See *Foster v Driscoll* [1929] 1 KB 470.

[250] *Dickie v Singh* 1974 SLT 129. See also *Simpson's Trs v Simpson* 1933 SC 128.

[251] *Fraser v Bruce* (1857) 20 D 115; *Greenock Bank v Darroch* (1834) 13 S 190.

[252] Stamp Act 1891.

[253] *Durie's Exrx v Fielding* (1893) 20 R 295, per Lord Kinnear at 299. On the previous decisions Lord McLaren's view seems too restricted.

[254] *Mackenzie v Crawford* (1839) 1 D 1091.

[255] *Mackenzie v Crawford* (1839) 1 D 1091 at 1094 and 1096. For other examples, see *Henning v Hewatson* (1852) 14 D 1084; *Paton v Earl of Zetland* (1843) 5 D 1049; *Matheson v Ross* (1849) 6 Bell's App 374; *Fraser v Bruce* (1857) 20 D 115.

[256] *Watson v Watson* 1934 SC 374, per Lord Murray at 378 and 379.

[257] *Fengl v Fengl* [1914] P 274.

[258] *Mason v Motor Traction Co* [1905] 1 Ch 419 at 425. No reasons were given.

[259] *Birchall v Bullough* [1896] 1 QB 325. The procedure is obscure to a Scots lawyer, and the judges seem to have overlooked the last words of s 14(4).

[260] Stamp Act 1891, s 14(1). On afterstamping, see *Dickie v Singh* 1974 SLT 129.

[261] *Weinschel* 1916 2 SLT 346 (OH).

[262] *Simpson's Trs v Simpson* 1933 SC 128.

[263] *Ivison v Edinburgh Silk Yarn Co* (1845) 8 D 236.

[264] *Napier v Carson* (1828) 6 S 500. See also *Barbour v Grierson* (1828) 6 S 860.

[265] *McTaggart v McEachern's J F* 1949 SC 503 (OH) at 504. See *Muirhead v Meikle* 1917 SC 554.

made,[266] or it may admit the instrument on an undertaking that it will be duly stamped and the penalty paid.[267]

21.13 BANKERS' BOOKS

Bankers' Books Evidence Act 1879

21.13.1 In terms of the Bankers' Books Evidence Act 1879, a copy of any entry in a banker's book is *prima facie* evidence of such entry and of the matters there recorded,[268] provided it is proved that the book was at the time of making the entry one of the ordinary books of the bank, that the entry was made in ordinary course of business, and that the book is in the custody or control of the bank. This proof may be by a partner or officer of the bank and may be oral or by affidavit.[269] It must further be proved that the copy is correct.[270] A court or judge may authorise a litigant to inspect, and take copies of, entries in a banker's book[271] for the purpose of the proceedings.[272] In criminal proceedings this has been authorised after petition but before indictment,[273] and the existence of the statutory provision has not inhibited an order for production at common law before any proceedings have been taken.[274] "Bank" and "banker" mean an institution authorised under the Banking Act 1987 or a municipal bank within the meaning of that Act, a Building Society within the meaning of the Building Societies Act 1986, a National Savings Bank and the Post Office (when exercising its banking functions).[275]

Subsequent statutory development

21.13.2 The Civil Evidence (Scotland) Act 1988 disapplies in relation to civil proceedings the requirements of sections 3 to 5 of the Bankers' Books Evidence Act 1879.[276] The Criminal Procedure (Scotland) Act 1995 establishes new processes for proof of documents in criminal proceedings.[277] There is particular provision facilitating proof of business documents.[278] The definition of "business documents" is such that bankers' books are included within in it.[279] The Act provides: "[n]othing herein shall affect the operation of the Bankers' Books Evidence Act 1879". It has been decided that where a document meets the definition both under the Criminal

---

[266] *Bankier v Robertson* (1864) 2 M 1153.

[267] *Simpson's Trs v Simpson* 1933 SC 128 at 132.

[268] Bankers' Books Evidence Act 1879, s 3.

[269] s 4.

[270] s 5.

[271] Including ledgers, daybooks, cashbooks, account books and other records used in the ordinary business of a bank, whether written, on microfilm, magnetic tape or any other form of date retrieval mechanism: s 9(2).

[272] ss 7 and 8.

[273] *Carmichael v Sexton* 1986 SLT 16.

[274] *Normand, Complainer* 1992 JC 108, following *MacNeill, Complainer* 1984 JC 1; and *Watson v Muir* 1938 JC 181.

[275] Bankers' Books Evidence Act 1879, s 9(1) as amended.

[276] s 6(3).

[277] s 279 and Sched 8.

[278] Sched 8, paras 2–6 and see paras 21.14–21.16.

[279] Sched 8, paras 2 and 7, and see *Lord Advocate's Reference (No 1 of 1996)* 1996 JC 152.

Procedure (Scotland) Act 1995 and the Bankers' Books Evidence Act 1879, either process for proof of the document may be used.[280] The provisions in the 1995 Act are the more flexible.

21.14 BUSINESS DOCUMENTS—ADMISSIBILITY AT COMMON LAW

Business books are admissible in evidence at common law if they appear to be **21.14.1** regularly kept[281] and are sworn to as an accurate record.[282] Even if not sworn as accurate, they may be evidence of a statement against interest.[283] In an 1816 case, the House of Lords held one regular entry to be sufficient proof of a transaction despite the fact that no corroborating evidence was led.[284] The common law rule certainly applies to books kept by merchants[285] and banks,[286] and may extend more generally to records of transactions kept with sufficient regularity and detail even where these are not of a commercial nature.[287] Although the cases are concerned only with records kept in paper form, there is nothing to suggest that the principle is limited in this way.

21.15 BUSINESS DOCUMENTS IN CIVIL CASES—STATUTORY PROVISIONS

Authentication

In accordance with section 5(1) of the Civil Evidence (Scotland) Act 1988, a doc- **21.15.1** ument may be taken to form part of the records of a business or undertaking if it is certified as such by a docquet purporting to be signed[288] by an officer of the business or undertaking to which the records belong. Accordingly, it will usually be unnecessary for a witness to swear to the accuracy of the record before it is admitted in evidence, although the court has the power to direct that this relaxation of the usual rule should not apply in particular cases.[289] The provisions are

---

[280] *Lord Advocate's Reference (No 1 of 1996)* 1996 JC 152, approving *HM Advocate v Fox*, unreported, Glasgow Sheriff Court, 6 Dec 1995, and recognising Scottish Law Commission Report No 137, para 3.24.

[281] As to the level of irregularity which will exclude business books from being evidence, see *Ivory & Co v Gourlay* (1816) 4 Dow 467.

[282] *Grant v Johnston* (1845) 7 D 390; *Wood v Kello* (1672) Mor 12,728; Erskine, *Institutes*, iv, 2, 4.

[283] *British Linen Co v Thomson* (1853) 15 D 314, per Lord Ivory at 320.

[284] *Ivory & Co v Gourlay* (1816) 4 Dow 467 (the two other transactions in issue in that case were held to be insufficiently proved due to the irregularity of the record). But see *Hatton v Buckmaster & Co* (1853) 15 D 574.

[285] *Wood v Kello* (1672) Mor 12,728.

[286] *British Linen Co v Thomson* (1853) 15 D 314.

[287] *Fisher's Trs v Fisher* (1850) 13 D 245 at 252 (books kept in connection with the management of an executry); *Macfarquhar v McKay* (1869) 7 M 766 (defender's account of advances of money and other disbursements on behalf of the pursuer).

[288] It is provided that, for these purposes, a facsimile of a signature shall be treated as a signature: Civil Evidence (Scotland) Act 1988, s 5(2), although this provision is, strictly speaking, superfluous: see *Cardle v Wilkinson* 1982 JC 36.

[289] Civil Evidence (Scotland) Act 1988, s 5(1).

deliberately broad in their scope: "business",[290] "undertaking"[291] and "document"[292] are all widely defined.

Admissibility

21.15.2 It should be noted that these provisions do not necessarily render business records admissible in evidence. Admissibility is dependent either upon the common law rules relating to business books or (more importantly) section 2 of the 1988 Act, which abolishes the rule against hearsay and renders "a statement made by a person otherwise than in the course of the proof ... admissible as evidence of any matter contained in the statement of which direct oral evidence by that person would be admissible."[293]

21.15.3 For example, the Inner House held in *Japan Leasing (Europe) plc v Weir's Trustee (No 2)*[294] that an unauthenticated photocopy of a contract was not admissible as evidence of the contents of the principal, since it did not amount to a "statement made by a person otherwise than in the course of the proof".[295] The photocopy in question may well have been part of Japan Leasing's "records", but certifying it as such would have been to no avail since it was inadmissible from the outset. This is because section 5 goes no further than to remove the need for a witness to swear to the accuracy of the document (which was in fact done in *Japan Leasing*[296]); it does not of itself render the document admissible.

Non-existent statements

21.15.4 The 1988 Act also provides that "the evidence of an officer of a business or undertaking that any particular statement is not contained in the records of the business or undertaking shall be admissible as evidence of that fact whether or not the whole or any part of the records have been produced in the proceedings."[297] Unless the court otherwise directs, such evidence may be given by means of the affidavit of the officer.[298]

21.16 BUSINESS DOCUMENTS IN CRIMINAL CASES—STATUTORY PROVISIONS

21.16.1 This is dealt with under Schedule 8 to the Criminal Procedure (Scotland) Act 1995. These provisions have three aspects: first, they relax the rule against hearsay to

---

[290] "Business" includes any trade or profession: Civil Evidence (Scotland) Act 1988, s 9.

[291] "Undertaking" includes "any public or statutory undertaking, any local authority and any government department": Civil Evidence (Scotland) Act 1988, s 9. This term was specifically included "so as to cover large organisations which might not fall under the definition of 'business', for example the National Health Service." See Scottish Law Commission, *Report on Corroboration, Hearsay and Related Matters in Civil Proceedings* (1986), para 3.70; *cf Docherty v McGlynn* 1985 SLT 237.

[292] See the Civil Evidence (Scotland) Act 1988, s 9. It includes, in addition to writing, any map, plan, graph, drawing, photograph; a disc, tape, sound track or other audio recording; a film, negative, tape, disc or other video recording. The recordings must be capable of reproduction. See also *Rollo v HM Advocate* 1997 JC 23 (which concerned the interpretation of another statute) at 26G: "the essential essence of a document is that it is something containing recorded information of some sort."

[293] Civil Evidence (Scotland) Act 1988, s 2(1)(b).

[294] 1998 SC 543.

[295] 1998 SC 543 at 547A. See para 20.2.

[296] See 1998 SC 543 at 545–546.

[297] Civil Evidence (Scotland) Act 1988, s 7(1).

[298] Civil Evidence (Scotland) Act 1988, s 7(2).

render statements in business documents[299] admissible subsequent to certain conditions; second, they remove the need for a witness to swear to such a document if it is appropriately certified; third they provide for the admissibility of evidence as to the non-existence of relevant statements in business documents. These three aspects will be dealt with in turn.

Admissibility

21.16.2 Paragraph 2 of Schedule 8 provides that a statement in a document will be admissible "as evidence of any fact or opinion of which direct oral evidence would be admissible", if three conditions are satisfied: "(a) the document was created or received in the course of, or for the purposes of, a business or undertaking or in pursuance of the functions of the holder of a paid or unpaid office; (b) the document is, or at any time was, kept by a business or undertaking or by or on behalf of the holder of such an office; and (c) the statement was made on the basis of information supplied by a person (whether or not the maker of the statement) who had, or may reasonably be supposed to have had, personal knowledge of the matters dealt with in it."[300] This does not apply where the information in the statement was supplied directly and "it appears to the court that any person through whom it was supplied did not both receive and supply it in the course of a business or undertaking or as or on behalf of the holder of a paid or unpaid office."[301] Nor does it apply to a statement made directly or indirectly by a person who is an accused in the proceedings if the statement "being exculpatory only, exculpates the accused",[302] but such a statement may be admissible as evidence of the fact it was made (but not of the truth of its contents) if conditions (a) and (b) above are satisfied.[303]

21.16.3 One possible difficulty with admitting statements in business documents in criminal proceedings is that there will be no opportunity to cross-examine the maker of the statement.[304] The provisions remedy this problem in part by making admissible: (a) evidence which would have been admissible as relevant to the maker's credibility, or to the credibility of any other person who supplied information on which the statement was based, had the maker or the supplier been called as a witness[305]; (b) evidence which could have been put to the maker or supplier in cross-examination as relevant to his credibility[306]; and (c) evidence tending to prove that the maker or supplier has at any point made some other

---

[299] "Document" includes, in addition to writing, any map, plan, graph, drawing, photograph; a disc, tape, sound track or other audio recording; a film, negative, tape, disc or other video recording. The recordings must be capable of reproduction. See the Criminal Procedure (Scotland) Act 1995, Sched 8, para 8. See also *Rollo v HM Advocate* 1997 JC 23 (which concerned the interpretation of another statute), at 26G: "the essential essence of a document is that it is something containing recorded information of some sort."

[300] Criminal Procedure (Scotland) Act 1995 (hereafter referred to as the "1995 Act"), Sched 8, para 2(1)(a)–(c).

[301] 1995 Act, Sched 8, para 2(2). "Business" includes a "trade, profession or other occupation", and "undertaking" includes "any public or statutory undertaking, any local authority and any government department". See Sched 8, para 8.

[302] 1995 Act, Sched 8, paras 2(1) and 3.

[303] 1995 Act, Sched 8, para 3.

[304] Note that the court has no discretion to disapply the rules relating to admissibility of statements contained in business documents, although it can direct that the statement be sworn to by a witness rather than being certified by means of a docquet.

[305] 1995 Act, Sched 8, para 2(3)(a).

[306] 1995 Act, Sched 8, para 2(3)(b).

representation inconsistent with the statement, for the purpose of showing that he has contradicted himself.[307]

Authentication

21.16.4 Unless the court otherwise directs, a document may be taken to be "a document kept by a business or undertaking or by or on behalf of the holder of a paid or unpaid office if it is certified as such by a docquet in the prescribed form and purporting to be authenticated, in such manner as may be prescribed"[308] by the relevant office-holder or a person authorised to authenticate such a docquet on behalf of the business, undertaking, or office-holder.[309]

Non-existent statements

21.16.5 Schedule 8 provides further that an authorised person[310] may give evidence that a document which meets conditions (a) and (b) as to admissibility noted above, or that no document within a category of such documents, contains a relevant statement as to a particular matter.[311] This applies whether or not all or part of such documents have been produced in evidence.[312] A "relevant statement" is one which the document(s) in question "might reasonably have been expected to contain".[313] This evidence, unless the court otherwise directs, may be given by means of a certificate by the authorised person in prescribed form.[314]

---

[307] 1995 Act, Sched 8, para 2(3)(c).

[308] 1995 Act, Sched 8, para 4. See the Act of Adjournal (Criminal Procedure Rules) 1996, r 26.1(2) and Form 26.1-B.

[309] 1995 Act, Sched 8, para 4(a)–(b).

[310] Meaning a person authorised to give evidence as an office-holder, or on behalf of a business, undertaking, or office-holder. See 1995 Act, Sched 8, para 5(4).

[311] 1995 Act, Sched 8, para 5(1).

[312] 1995 Act, Sched 8, para 5(1).

[313] 1995 Act, Sched 8, para 5(2).

[314] 1995 Act, Sched 8, para 5(3). See the Act of Adjournal (Criminal Procedure Rules) 1996, r 26.1(3) and Form 26.1-C.

CHAPTER 22

REQUIREMENTS OF WRITING FOR SELF-PROVING OR PROBATIVE DEEDS

22.1 INTRODUCTORY

Background

Prior to 1995 the law which required writing for the constitution or proof of certain **22.1.1** obligations was so uncertain and unsatisfactory that it was almost impossible to state a principle of general application.[1] It differentiated between different types of obligation and different types of writing, and irregularities in writing might lead not only to evidential difficulties but to invalidity. In attempting to state the law as it then was, it was difficult not to adopt the course, so often adopted by the courts, of dealing with each kind of obligation as if it were contained in a water-tight compartment, and without regard to the anomalies arising from the application of different rules to other analogous obligations. An attempt to deal with the subject as a whole had been made in the Whole Court case of *Paterson v Paterson*.[2] This case had been criticised as misrepresenting the earlier law,[3] but pending a restatement of the law, the decision, if not perhaps all its *obiter dicta*, was regarded as authoritative, in spite of any anomalies to which it gave rise.

---

[1] See, for example, the Scottish Law Commission's Consultative Memoranda: *Constitution and Proof of Voluntary Obligations: Formalities of Constitution and Restrictions on Proof* (No 39) (1977) and *Constitution and Proof of Voluntary Obligations and the Authentication of Writings* (No 66) (1985). These led to the Commission's *Report on Requirements of Writing* (Scot Law Com No 112) (1988) and in turn to the Requirements of Writing (Scotland) Act 1995.

[2] (1897) 25 R 144.

[3] See JJ Gow, "Constitution and Proof of Voluntary Obligations, Part II", 1961 JR 119 *et seq.*

New statutory regime for requirement of writing and self-proving status

22.1.2 The old law is now replaced by a much simpler statutory regime found in the Requirements of Writing (Scotland) Act 1995. However, that Act, which commenced on 1 August 1995, in general applies only to contracts and other obligations entered into after its commencement[4] and thus has no bearing upon events prior to commencement,[5] to which the prior law as to requirement of writing for constitution and proof still applies. Such events will continue to bear scrutiny for the foreseeable future during the examination of titles and in any dispute concerning a contract, obligation or other event entered into or occurring before 1 August 1995 which required writing for its constitution or proof. Hence, the old law distinguishing between the different types of writing and obligation must still be stated, and is to be found in the next chapter. In this chapter the present law, as stated in the Requirements of Writing (Scotland) Act 1995, is dealt with, and the aim is to concentrate upon the evidential aspects of the new regime. That regime includes new measures for the authentication of writings, the evidential aspects of which are discussed, but an in-depth study of authentication of writings is outwith the scope of this text.[6] For ease of reference and comparison the evidential aspects of the authentication requirements applying prior to 1 August 1995 are also dealt with in this chapter. It is suggested that in those situations where the Requirements of Writing (Scotland) Act 1995 does not make express provision, prior authority relative to subscription and attestation may be founded upon, and, in any event, most of the new provisions are simplified statements of the common law. The main differences are the separation of probativity from validity, the sufficiency of attestation by one person who need only sign, and not subscribe, and the new regime for subscription by non-individual persons (juridical persons).

Relaxation of evidential restrictions

22.1.3 The rules requiring writing for constitution or proof traditionally have been treated alongside the rules restricting proof of an obligation to the writ or oath of a party. The expression "proof by writ or oath," although customary and concise is misleading. The sole requirement of the law regarding restricted proof is to proof by writ.[7] Since either party to a litigation could invoke the procedure for reference to the oath of an opponent the whole cause or any disputed question of fact,[8] except an *obligatio literis* or a consistorial cause, it followed that reference to oath was always in practice an alternative to proof by the opponent's writ, subject to the overriding discretion of the court. However, despite the implication of the shorthand "proof by writ or oath" the proof by oath referred to is simply the reference to oath.[9] Reference to oath was rarely a party's chosen mode of proof, since the

---

[4] Requirements of Writing (Scotland) Act 1995, s 14(3).
[5] If the date of execution of a writing cannot be ascertained, it is presumed to have been executed after commencement of the Act: Requirements of Writing (Scotland) Act 1995, s 14(6).
[6] Halliday, *Conveyancing Law and Practice* (2nd edn, Talman), Chapter 3.
[7] Lord Young, in *Paterson v Paterson* (1897) 25 R 144 at 152, remarks on the true relationship between proof by writ and reference to oath. This relationship was demonstrated in the interlocutors pronounced in the sheriff court in *Hamilton v Hamilton's Exrx* 1950 SC 39 at 39, 40.
[8] See Chapter XXV in first edition.
[9] This interpretation is implicit in the language used by the Scottish Law Commission in their *Report on Requirements of Writing* (Scot Law Com No 112), para 3.1, although the Commission later adopts the usual coupling of "writ or oath". The Prescription Acts of 1579 (APS III, 145 c 21), 1669 (APS VII, 561 c 14) and 1685 (APS VIII, 471 c 14) (which were repealed with immediate effect by the

oath of the opponent became conclusive of the matter. Hence reference to oath, which was a relic of the days when a party was not a competent witness,[10] came to be a procedure of last resort used only if parole evidence was not admissible and no writ was available. The procedure for reference to oath was abolished with immediate effect by the Requirements of Writing (Scotland) Act 1995, s 11[11] except in proceedings which had been commenced before 1 August 1995.[12] Section 11 also provides that restriction of mode of proof to writ or reference to oath whether by rule of law or enactment shall cease to have effect.[13] Read with section 14(3), which provides that nothing in the Act shall apply to any document executed or anything done before the commencement of the Act,[14] or affect the operation, in relation to such document, of any procedure for establishing the authenticity of such a document,[15] the rule restricting proof to writ or oath may be held to continue to apply in proceedings raised after 1 August 1995 concerning an event which occurred under the old law.[16] Such was the interpretation favoured in a sheriff court case raised after 1 August 1995 for implement of an agreement allegedly made in 1983 and 1984 which had not been committed to writing nor reflected in the terms of the testator's will made in 1993.[17] However, since the procedure for reference to oath had fallen into disuse in any event it is thought that it would not survive beyond cases which had been commenced prior to 1 August 1995. Some coverage of restriction to proof by writ[18] is retained in a later chapter.

22.2 REQUIREMENTS OF WRITING (SCOTLAND) ACT 1995— GENERAL

The rules at common law[19] which, prior to 1 August 1995, required a contract, unilateral obligation or trust to be constituted in writing are abolished by the Requirements of Writing (Scotland) Act 1995, ss 1(1) and 11(3)(b). The authentication statutes[20] are also repealed.[21] There is, in place of the complex and   **22.2.1**

Prescription and Limitation (Scotland) Act 1973, s 16(2) and (3), following recommendations of the Scottish Law Commission in 1970 in their Report on *Reform of the Law Relating to Prescription and Limitation of Actions* (Scot Law Com No 15)) referred to "writ or oath", and in some of the judgments the judges proceeded upon the precise words of the statute: *eg Bertram & Co v Stewart's Trs* (1874) 2 R 255.

[10] When calling a party, including one's opponent, became competent the procedure for reference to oath was reserved: Evidence (Scotland) Act 1853, s 5; and for their respective application in context, see *Hamilton v Hamilton's Exrx* 1950 SC 39.

[11] s 11(2).

[12] s 11(4).

[13] s 11(1).

[14] s 14(3)(a).

[15] s 14(3)(b).

[16] Accordingly, material from the first edition of this text dealing with proof by writ remains, in updated form, in Chapter 25 of this edition, but material on reference to oath has not been carried forward. For the highly unusual case raised before 1 August 1995 in which reference to oath arises, readers are referred to Chapter XXV of the first edition.

[17] *McEleveen v McQuillan's Exrx* 1997 SLT (Sh Ct) 46.

[18] Restriction of proof in cases of triennial, quinquennial, sexennial and vicennial prescriptions, covered in Chapter XII of the first edition of this text, has been omitted because restriction in these circumstances was abolished with immediate effect by the Prescription and Limitation (Scotland) Act 1973, s 16(2) and (3).

[19] But not under any enactment unless expressly repealed by the Act.

[20] Subscription of Deeds Act 1540, c 117; Subscription of Deeds Act 1579, c 80; Subscription of Deeds Act 1681, c 5; Deeds Act 1696, c 15; Conveyancing and Feudal Reform (Scotland) Act 1970, s 44.

[21] Requirements of Writing (Scotland) Act 1995, s 14(2) and Sched 5.

piecemeal requirements at common law described below,[22] a statutory requirement described in the next paragraph. Only the events referred to there *require* writing for their constitution. Any other event, unless required by another enactment to be constituted or proved in writing, may be constituted orally or otherwise (*eg* by actings) and proved by parole evidence. In the civil context, where such questions most commonly arise, there is no requirement for corroboration,[23] and hearsay evidence is competent.[24]

22.2.2 A written document[25] is required for: (a) the constitution or variation[26] of (i) a contract or unilateral obligation for the creation, transfer, variation or extinction of an interest in land[27]; (ii) a gratuitous unilateral obligation except one undertaken in the course of business; and (iii) a trust whereby a person declares himself to be sole trustee of his own property or any property which he may acquire[28]; (b) the creation, transfer, variation or extinction of an interest in land otherwise than by the operation of a court decree, enactment or rule of law[29]; and (c) the making of any will, testamentary trust disposition and settlement or codicil.[30]

22.2.3 It will not be possible to prove the existence of any of the events referred to without a written document, and the only exception arises in the case of the constitution or variation of contracts, obligations or trusts referred to in (a) above, in respect of which reliance may be placed upon a statutory rule akin to *rei interventus*[31] found in the Requirements of Writing (Scotland) Act 1995, s 1(3) and (4). If there is no written document but one of the parties to the contract, a creditor in the obligation or beneficiary under the trust ("the first person") has acted or refrained from acting in reliance on the contract, obligation or trust with the knowledge and acquiescence of the other party to the contract, the debtor in the obligation or the truster ("the second person"), the second person is precluded from withdrawing, and the contract, obligation or trust is not considered invalid,[32] provided that the first person has been affected to a material extent as a result of so acting or not acting, or would be adversely affected if the second person was entitled to withdraw.[33] This statutory exception does not apply to testamentary writings or to the specific type of trust for which the Act requires writing. On one view, for constitution of these, writing will always be required.[34] However, in

---

[22] See Chapter 23.

[23] Civil Evidence (Scotland) Act 1988, s 1.

[24] Civil Evidence (Scotland) Act 1988, s 2.

[25] Which in terms of the Requirements of Writing (Scotland) Act 1995, s 12 includes any annexation incorporated in the document under s 8. A "writing" may consist, wholly or partly, of typescript, printing, or of other modes of representing or reproducing words in a visible form: Interpretation Act 1978, s 5 and Sched 1.

[26] Requirements of Writing (Scotland) Act 1995, s 1(6).

[27] As to what constitutes an "interest in land", see s 1(7) which, in summary, includes any estate, interest or right in or over land, including a right to occupy or restrict occupation, but excludes a tenancy or other right to occupy or restrict occupation which is not granted for more than a year unless it covers recurring periods more than a year apart.

[28] Requirements of Writing (Scotland) Act 1995, s 1(2)(a).

[29] s 1(2)(b).

[30] s 1(2)(c).

[31] See Chapter 26.

[32] s 1(3).

[33] s 1(4).

[34] This was the express intention of the Scottish Law Commission in relation to testamentary settlements and, by implication, in relation to interests in land: *Report on Requirements of Writing* (Scot Law Com No 112), paras 2.49–2.50.

advance of judicial interpretation, it appears that the combined effect of the various statutory provisions[35] does not rule out completely reliance upon *rei interventus* or homologation at common law in the circumstances not governed expressly by the statute. In general the statutory provisions create a more liberal regime for requirements of writing than the complex one which had developed under the old law described later in this chapter, although they are not without difficulties of interpretation.[36]

22.2.4 The "interest in land" which triggers the requirement for writing under section 1(2)(a)(i) and (b) is defined in section 1(7) to include any estate, interest or right in or over land, including a right to occupy or restrict occupation, but excludes a tenancy or other right to occupy or restrict occupation which is not granted for more than a year unless it covers recurring periods more than a year apart. Section 1(2)(a)(i) is clearly intended to govern missives and section 1(2)(b) to govern deeds, but to read the terms exclusively in this way is to limit the "interest in land" to a real one.[37] A submission to arbitration in relation to an interest in land arguably falls within section 1(2)(a)(i),[38] as would an arbitration award which introduces the variation etc of an interest in land.[39] So too would an agreement between separating spouses or joint purchasers dealing with distribution of their respective interests in land.[40]

22.3 REQUIREMENTS OF WRITING (SCOTLAND) ACT 1995— EXECUTION OF WRITINGS

22.3.1 A writing required for constitution must be validly executed. In order to be validly executed a document must be subscribed by the granter or granters,[41] and a contract may comprise a series of documents, such as an exchange of letters, each subscribed by the granter.[42] Nothing more than subscription is required to give the document formal validity,[43] unless another enactment makes different provision in respect of the formalities of execution.[44] A document which is not subscribed nevertheless may be used in evidence in relation to any right or obligation to which the document relates but if the event is one which requires a validly executed document for its formal validity an unsigned document cannot *per se* establish that validity. It might be used to support or challenge the application of the actings

---

[35] ss 1(3)–(5) and 14(3).

[36] Such as the respective effect of the saving provisions in ss 11 and 14. For detailed analysis of the Act see the annotations thereto by Kenneth Reid in Greens *Current Law Statutes*.

[37] Reid, annotation to s 1(7) in *Current Law Statutes*. This was the intention of the Scottish Law Commission: *Report on Requirements of Writing* (Scot Law Com No 112), para 2.18.

[38] Although the word "for" implies a more purposive contract than a submission for which an interest in land is an indirect or consequential issue, and this narrow focus for requirement of writing was intended by the Scottish Law Commission, *Report on Requirements of Writing* (Scot Law Com No 112), para 2.18. See also *Stair Memorial Encyclopaedia* Reissue, *Arbitration*, para 20.

[39] The award would have to be in writing to meet the form of the submission, but might conceivably raise the issue of an interest in land when this had not been included in the submission.

[40] This was considered to be *obligatio literis* under the old law in *Mulhern v Mulhern* 1987 SCLR 252, but not in *Denvir v Denvir* 1969 SLT 301.

[41] s 2(1)

[42] s 2(2). As to what constitutes subscription by an individual, see s 7, and by non-individual persons or bodies, see Sched 2. For notarial execution, see s 9 and Sched 3. Incorporation and subscription of annexations is governed by s 8.

[43] s 2(1).

[44] s 2(4).

rule,[45] or might be used to support an argument that the whole express terms of a contract have not been committed to writing.[46]

22.4 REQUIREMENTS OF WRITING (SCOTLAND) ACT 1995— EXECUTION REQUIRED FOR SELF-PROVING[47] STATUS

22.4.1 While a subscribed document is sufficient for formal validity it does not "bear on its face sufficient proof of its own authenticity".[48] The old terms "solemn writing" and "probative deed"[49] which described a writing that proved its own authenticity have no place under the new statutory regime although the reliance upon witnessing for proof of authenticity is carried over, the main difference being that one witness is now sufficient.[50] Furthermore, the "privileged" status which at common law attached to writings which were holograph or adopted as holograph[51] and writs *in re mercatoria*[52] is abolished with effect from 1 August 1995 for documents executed after that date.[53] Instead, the only means of ensuring that a document is proof of its own authenticity is by establishing the presumption that the document was subscribed by the granter. This involves proof of two basic facts, the first of which is the subscription itself. Section 7 sets out the requisites of subscription by an individual, and, by reference to Schedule 2, rules as to what constitutes subscription by partnerships, companies, local authorities, other bodies corporate and Ministers. Execution by a third party where the granter is blind or unable to write is governed by section 9. The second fact which is required to activate the presumption is witnessing of the subscription in the manner described in section 3 or, in the absence of that presumption, a certificate from the court issued in terms of section 4.[54] If these basic facts are proved the presumption is activated and gives rise to "self proving" status but it should be noted that the presumption applies to the subscription rather than the document and therefore it is possible that the presumption would apply to the subscription of one granter but not to that of another. The subscription of a granter in respect of which the presumption did not apply would require to be the subject of proof in any proceedings concerning or founding upon the document, but after the abolition of restricted modes of proof,[55] parole evidence would be competent.

---

[45] Under s 1(3) and (4). Rennie & Cusine refer to this as "a statutory form of personal bar", in *The Requirements of Writing*, para 3.03, and Talman to "personal bar and reliance" in Halliday's *Conveyancing Law and Practice* (2nd edn) Vol 1, para 3–96. As with pleas of personal bar in general the onus is on the person making the plea, but usually evidence must be led before the plea can be upheld or refused. Parole evidence is admissible in support of the plea.

[46] Under the Contract (Scotland) Act 1997, s 1(2).

[47] The term does not appear in the Act, but is used by the Scottish Law Commission in their *Report on Requirements of Writing* (Scot Law Com No 112), Part V.

[48] Words used in the Scottish Law Commission's *Report on Requirements of Writing* (Scot Law Com No 112), para 5.1.

[49] The Scottish Law Commission noted that probativity had come to have a variety of meanings: *Report*, para 5.1.

[50] This accords with the Civil Evidence (Scotland) Act 1988, s 1, by which the requirement for corroborative testimony is removed in civil cases and displays an appropriate correlation between testimony for judicial proof and attestation.

[51] See paras 23.12–23.18.

[52] See Chapter 24.

[53] Requirements of Writing (Scotland) Act 1995, s 11(3)(b) and s 14(3).

[54] And the Act of Sederunt, Requirements of Writing (SI 1996/1534).

[55] See para 24.1.

Subscription and attestation

In order to invoke the presumption arising from witnessing, the following criteria **22.4.2**
must be satisfied: the document bears to be subscribed by the granter,[56] signed on
every sheet[57] if it is a testamentary document,[58] it bears to be signed[59] by a person
witnessing the granter's subscription whose name and address are contained in the
document or the testing clause or its equivalent,[60] and that nothing in the document
or testing details indicates that it was not so subscribed or that it was not validly
witnessed.[61] Furthermore, the date or place of signing may be presumed. This
arises under section 3 in relation to a testamentary document if it bears to have
been subscribed and the document or testing clause bears a date or place of signing and there is nothing in the document or testing clause that indicates that the
date or place stated is incorrect.[62] In relation to other documents the presumption
as to date or time arises only if the presumption as to subscription by the granter
also arises.[63] The court on application by an interested party and receipt of satisfactory affidavit evidence to the effect that the document was signed by the
granter, may grant a certificate or decree which has the effect of establishing the
presumption. The court may separately establish the presumption as to date or
place of signing on application supported by satisfactory affidavit evidence.[64]

In terms of section 7, signing requires use of the full name, or surname and at **22.4.3**
least one forename or initial or familiar form of that forename.[65] Another name
description, initial or mark may be used if it is the signatory's usual method of
signing[66] but this type of signature will not form the basis for a presumption
of self-proving status, and requires proof in proceedings relating to the deed or for
a judicial endorsement of subscription.[67] A granter who is unable to see or unable
to write, may declare[68] that to a third party, and authorise the third party[69] to sign
or subscribe in the granter's presence.[70]

22.5 ALTERATIONS TO THE WRITING

If an alteration[71] is made to the document before subscription the altered term is **22.5.1**

---

[56] s 3(1)(a). Subscription is governed by s 7; see para 22.11 below.
[57] As to what constitutes a sheet, see para 22.11. Annexations are governed by s 8.
[58] s 3(2).
[59] As to signature in general, see s 7, and by a witness, s 7(5).
[60] s 3(1)(b).
[61] s 3(1)(c).
[62] s 3(10).
[63] s 3(8).
[64] s 4(1) and (3) and Act of Sederunt, Requirements of Writing (SI 1996/1534).
[65] s 7(2)(a) and (b).
[66] s 7(2)(c).
[67] Under s 4.
[68] This is the replacement for "notarial execution". Alternatively, the granter may choose to sign in the
normal way: s 9(7) and s 7.
[69] A solicitor with a current practising certificate, an advocate, justice of the peace or sheriff clerk or,
if signing in another jurisdiction, a person with equivalent authority there: s 9(6). Such person and their
spouse or direct offspring cannot benefit directly or indirectly from the deed, but if the deed does confer
benefit it is invalidated only to that extent: s 9(4).
[70] s 9(1) and (2).
[71] Defined in s 12(1) to include interlineation, marginal addition, deletion, substitution, erasure or anything written on erasure.

assumed to be part of the original document[72] but the timing of the alteration is a matter for proof by any competent means.[73] That proof may be offered in proceedings in which the document is challenged, or may be offered independently in order to support an application for a certificate to be attached to the document to the effect that alteration took place before subscription, or a decree to the same effect if the document has been registered in the Books of Council and Session or the Sheriff Court Books.[74] A certificate or decree in these terms may be issued only if a statutory presumption of alteration prior to subscription does not apply.[75] The presumption of alteration prior to subscription applies if (a) subscription is presumed by attestation[76] in accordance with the new statutory formalities, (b) the document or testing clause states that the alteration was made before subscription, and (c) nothing *ex facie* of the document or testing clause indicates that the alteration was made after subscription.[77] If the alteration was made prior to subscription but validly authenticated by the signature of the granter the alteration does not affect the validity of the document,[78] and there are statutory presumptions as to signature, date and place of subscription which come into play in that event.[79] If the alteration is proved to have been made pre-subscription it forms part of the original document. If proved to have been made post-subscription and attestation it must meet the normal formalities for a variation, which in relation to an obligation for which writing is required are the same as formalities for constitution.[80]

22.6 PATENT DEFECTS IN SUBSCRIPTION AND ATTESTATION

22.6.1 If the writing does not bear to have been subscribed in accordance with the statutory formalities[81] it will not have formal validity.[82] If properly subscribed but not attested in the manner required to invoke the statutory presumptions,[83] extrinsic evidence will be admissible in order to support a certificate giving self-proving status.[84] If proof of actual adherence with those formalities of attestation cannot be led to satisfy the requirements[85] for a certificate to that effect, the document will not be self-proving.

---

[72] s 5(1)(a). (References in following paragraphs are to the 1995 Act unless otherwise specified.)
[73] s 5(3).
[74] s 5(6).
[75] s 5(6). The procedure is the same as application for proof of subscription to achieve self-proving status set out in s 4 and Act of Sederunt, Requirements of Writing (SI 1996/1534). As to the interplay between statutory presumptions and the court certification procedure, see para 22.4 below.
[76] In terms of s 3.
[77] s 5(4) and (5).
[78] s 5(1)(b).
[79] Sched 1.
[80] s 1(6).
[81] s 7.
[82] s 2(1).
[83] ss 3, 7.
[84] s 4.
[85] Uncorroborated evidence is technically sufficient: Civil Evidence (Scotland) Act 1988, s 1; and hearsay evidence is admissible: Civil Evidence (Scotland) Act 1988, s 2.

22.7 LATENT DEFECTS IN SUBSCRIPTION AND ATTESTATION

The effect of the presumption arising from witnessing is to prevent a party relying **22.7.1** upon the document from having to prove that it was subscribed by the granter. However, if one or more of a list of latent defects[86] is established, then *in the proceedings in which that defect is established* the presumption as to the granter's subscription will not apply.[87] The list is as follows: that the subscription is not that of the granter, whether by forgery or otherwise; that the person who witnessed was a person named in the document as a granter; that the witness did not know the granter,[88] was under the age of 16 or mentally incapable of acting as a witness; that the purported witness did not sign after the granter and as part of a continuous process; that the details of the witness were added after registration of the document,[89] or are materially incorrect; or any one of the subscriptions in a testamentary document is not that of the granter, whether by forgery or otherwise. Contrary to the old law described below, such a defect does not render the document invalid, but merely prevents the presumption of authenticity from arising. The burden of proving the latent defect would rest with the party seeking to rebut the presumption of authenticity, and if the presumption is rebutted the party seeking to rely upon the document must prove that it was subscribed by the granter. A certificate in terms of section 4 can be issued only if the document bears to have been subscribed by the granter and there is no presumption under section 3, and is clearly intended for the situation where there is unattested subscription. It is anticipated that the certificates will be sought in respect of documents the subscription of which is not challenged but which require to be presumed to have been validly executed for the purpose of registration in the land registers or books of court,[90] or for support of an application for confirmation of executors.[91] However, it would be available equally if a patent defect in attestation had prevented operation of the presumption. If there was witnessing which appeared in order but the presumption has been rebutted by proof of a latent defect in it, the rebuttal applies only in the proceedings in which the latent defect has been proved, so it might be argued that there is, at least for all other purposes, a presumption under section 3, thus precluding the issue of a certificate under section 4. An application for a certificate may be made by summary application or in other proceedings,[92] and it is possible that a challenge to the witnessing presumption in proceedings might be countered by an application for a section 4 certificate.

---

[86] Set out in s 3(4).

[87] s 3(4). The words in italic were used by the Scottish Law Commission in their *Report on Requirements of Writing* (Scot Law Com No 112), para 5.25.

[88] An introduction from a credible source is sufficient: s 3(5).

[89] It is in order to add the details after subscription but before registration or before the document is founded upon in legal proceedings: s 3(3)(a).

[90] s 6.

[91] Succession (Scotland) Act 1964, s 21A.

[92] s 4(4).

Authentication prior to 1 August 1995

22.8 SOLEMN WRITINGS

22.8.1 A series of statutes enacted in the sixteenth and seventeenth centuries and sup-
plemented by a recent provision,[93] were termed "the authentication statutes" and
prescribed certain solemnities[94] for the execution of the deeds to which they
applied. Any such deed which lacked the prescribed solemnities was declared to
be null and void or to "make no faith in judgement or outwith".[95] The deeds enu-
merated in the statutes, the language of which varies, in this matter, cover a wide
range, but may be summarised as including contracts, obligations and bonds then
considered to be of great importance,[96] and writings importing heritable title. The
application of the statutes to deeds constituting or transmitting heritable title has
always been fairly clear, but until 1897 there was uncertainty and conflict of judicial opinion as to their further scope and application. As mentioned above, the distinction was made in that year by the Whole Court decision of *Paterson v
Paterson*[97] between *obligationes literis*, to which the statutes apply, and obligations which require writing only *in modum probationis*, to which they do not
apply. It was open to parties to a contract, or a testator, to agree additional solemnities, which would be given effect, although the practice was rare.[98] Reduced
solemnities might be prescribed by statute, but otherwise the only recognised convention for reduced formalities applied to testamentary writings where in a solemn
or holograph will the testator instructed that effect should be given to subsequent
informal writings.[99] Holograph writs were not mentioned at all in the authentication statutes,[100] and were accordingly not expressly authorised by the statutes as
adequate alternatives to deeds solemnly executed.[101] Nevertheless, although not
probative,[102] they were as valid for their purposes as deeds executed in accordance
with the statutory solemnities.[103]

---

[93] Subscription of Deeds Act 1540, c 117; Subscription of Deeds Act 1579, c 80; Subscription of
Deeds Act 1681, c 5; Deeds Act 1696, c 15; Conveyancing and Feudal Reform (Scotland) Act 1970,
s 44.

[94] For the nature of these solemnities as amended and still applicable, see paras 22.11 *et seq*.

[95] This is subject, however, to the effect of holograph writing (see paras 23.12–23.18), and of *rei interventus* and homologation (see Chapter 26).

[96] *ie* those concerning a sum exceeding £100 Scots (£8.33): Erskine, iii, 2, 10.

[97] (1897) 25 R 144.

[98] Examples are to be found in *Campbell's Trs v Campbell* (1903) 5F 366; *Nasmyth v Hare* (1821) 1
Shaw's App 65.

[99] *Fraser v Forbes' Trs* (1899) 1 F 513, discussed in *Waterston's Trs v St Giles Boys' Club* 1943 SC
369.

[100] See para 22.8.

[101] *Paterson v Paterson* (1897) 25 R 144, per Lord Trayner at 163.

[102] They are not probative because their authenticity, if not admitted by the opponent, must be proved
by the person founding upon them, unlike solemnly executed documents which prove themselves. See
para 23.13. One practical result of this is that a purchaser of heritage would be justified in refusing to
accept from the seller a holograph non-tested disposition, the authenticity of which he and his successors in title might be quite unable to prove.

[103] Stair, iv, 42, 6; Erskine, iii, 2, 22; Dickson, *Evidence* (3rd edn), paras 754 *et seq*. See also *Harper v
Green* 1938 SC 198; *Cranston* (1890) 17 R 410, per Lord McLaren at 415; *Anderson v Gill* (1858) 20
D 1326; XI (HL) 74; 3 Macq 180. Lord McLaren's opinion was that the authentication statutes related
only to deeds written by a person other than the granter, with the result that holograph writings, which
were effective for all purposes prior to the statutes, continued, and still continue, to be so effective. See

22.9 RELEVANCE TO LAW OF EVIDENCE

The authentication of writings made prior to 1 August 1995 in accordance with the **22.9.1** statutory solemnities, has a two-fold bearing upon the law of evidence. First, if a writing has the appearance, or bears the insignia, of having been authenticated in this way, it is probative, and the leading of evidence with regard to its genuineness is unnecessary. Secondly, the production of a writing which has been executed in accordance with the statutory solemnities was the only means[104] whereby certain matters might be founded upon in a litigation, other evidence, subject to certain exceptions, being inadmissible. However, a probative writing might be reduced in an action raised for that purpose, if, despite its appearance to the contrary, it was not in fact holograph or executed in accordance with the statutory solemnities. Finally, a writing which was not probative, or which had been executed without some of the solemnities, might nevertheless be valid as if it were a solemnly executed writing if certain matters were proved.[105] In this context, dicta and decisions in reference to testamentary writings must be read with care, since they may relate not to the rules for the solemn execution of writings but to the special rules regarding the revocation and amendment of testamentary and other undelivered unilateral deeds. Similarly, decisions regarding the execution of untested holograph writings are sometimes cited as if they were relevant to the authentication of documents solemnly executed. It is thought that in general this practice is unsafe.[106]

22.10 PROBATIVE WRITING

Meaning of "probative"

The word "probative" is frequently used in judicial pronouncements and in text-   **22.10.1** books to describe a writing which has been properly executed in accordance with the statutory solemnities or is the equivalent of such a writing. It is also sometimes used to describe an untested holograph writing, merely because, for certain purposes, a holograph writing is the equivalent of solemn writing. The better practice is to use the word, in its original and restricted sense, as applying only to the kind of writing which afforded proof of its own authenticity, and it is so used in this book. To use the word in a wider sense may lead to confusion.[107] Thus a deed which is *ex facie* solemnly executed and therefore proves itself until reduced, may not in fact have been executed in accordance with the statutory solemnities, and would therefore not be probative if that word is used in its wider sense[108]; a deed

---

McLaren, *Wills and Succession* (3rd edn), I, 276–277, and his dissenting opinion in *Macdonald v Cuthbertson* (1890) 18 R 101 at 107.

[104] See paras 23.12 *et seq.*

[105] Conveyancing (Scotland) Act 1874, s 39. And see para 22.15.

[106] So, for example, the signature "Connie", which has been held to be sufficient as the subscription of a holograph writing in *Draper v Thomason* 1954 SC 136, would not constitute a valid subscription of a writing solemnly executed, and the rules regarding the authentication of erasures and other alterations in holograph writings must not be regarded as applicable to writings solemnly executed: *Magistrates of Dundee v Morris* (1858) 3 Macq 134, per Lord Chancellor Chelmsford at 151–152; Montgomerie Bell, *Lectures* (3rd edn), I, 67.

[107] Scottish Law Commission, *Report on Requirements of Writing* (Scot Law Com No 112), para 5.1.

[108] *McBeath's Trs v McBeath* 1935 SC 471, per Lord President Clyde at 476; *McLaren v Menzies* (1876) 3 R 1151, per Lord Deas at 1156; *Hamilton v Lindsey-Bucknall* (1869) 8 M 323, per Lord Neaves at 327–328; *Ferrie v Ferrie's Trs* (1863) 1 M 291, per Lord Curriehill at 298.

which is not probative in the narrower sense, because some of the statutory solemnities are clearly lacking, may nevertheless be declared to be the equivalent of a solemnly executed deed[109]; and an untested holograph writing must be proved to be authentic by the party founding upon it, and is therefore never probative in the narrower sense.[110]

Effect of probative writing

22.10.2 A writing[111] which appears to have been executed in accordance with the statutory solemnities proves itself.[112] When produced in a judicial proceeding the genuineness of a probative writing is assumed,[113] and the attendance of the granter and the instrumentary witnesses, to prove that the granter subscribed and that they witnessed, is both unnecessary and incompetent.[114]

> "A probative document is one which, in respect that it complies on the face of it with the prescribed legal formalities, is held to prove the verity of the legal *actus* of its author. It is important to keep in mind that, in speaking of the formalities required for the purpose of the authentication of a deed, what is meant is something in the form, or shape, or expression of the deed itself, which (when presented to the intelligent eye) provides a legal test of its authenticity. The formalities, in short, are intrinsic, not extrinsic to the deed. They are, so to speak, the legally recognisable features of honesty and genuineness which the deed carries about with it on its face into whosesoever hands it may pass."[115]

Such deeds cease to be probative only when reduced by a decree of the Court of Session on proof, the burden of which rests upon the challenger, that they were not in fact executed according to the statutory solemnities, despite their appearance to the contrary.

22.11 ESSENTIAL CHARACTERISTICS OF PROBATIVE WRITING

22.11.1 A writing[116] executed after 1 October 1874[117] and before 1 August 1995[118] is probative

---

[109] See para 22.15.

[110] See para 23.12.

[111] A "writing" may consist, wholly or partly, of typescript, printing, or of other modes of representing or reproducing words in a visible form: Interpretation Act 1978, s 5 and Sched 1; *Simpson's Trs v Macharg & Son* (1902) 9 SLT 398. If not printed, a deed is usually written in ink, but if it is written in pencil, provided the whole of the body of the deed is in pencil, there seems to be no reason in principle why, merely on that account, it should not be probative. See *Simson v Simson* (1883) 10 R 1247 (tested non-holograph will, wholly in pencil, subscribed by the testatrix and witnesses in ink).

[112] The essential characteristics of such a writing are referred to in the next paragraph.

[113] *McBeath's Trs v McBeath* 1935 SC 471, per Lord President Clyde at 476; *McLaren v Menzies* (1876) 3 R 1151, per Lord Deas at 1156; *Hamilton v Lindsey-Bucknall* (1869) 8 M 323, per Lord Neaves at 327–328; *Ferrie v Ferrie's Trs* (1863) 1 M 291, per Lord Curriehill at 298.

[114] *Reid v Kedder* (1840) 1 Robin App 183; *Grant v Shepherd* (1847) 6 Bell's App 153; *Boswell v Boswell* (1852) 14 D 378 at 382, 385, 392; *Munro v Butler Johnstone* (1868) 7 M 250 at 256; Menzies, *Lectures* (Sturrock's edn), p 138; Wood, *Lectures*, p 72.

[115] *McBeath's Trs v McBeath* 1935 SC 471, per Lord President Clyde at 476.

[116] For a definition of "writing", see n 111.

[117] Conveyancing (Scotland) Act 1874, s 2. As to deeds executed before 1 October 1874, see Montgomerie Bell, *Lectures* (3rd edn), I, pp 23–34; Menzies, *Lectures* (Sturrock's edn), pp 80 *et seq*.

[118] Requirements of Writing (Scotland) Act 1995, s 14(3).

when it bears to be subscribed at the end by the granter[119] and also by two witnesses,[120] whose designations are either mentioned in a testing clause or added to their signatures,[121] provided that, if the deed is written bookwise on more than one sheet, each page must also bear to be subscribed by the granter.[122] The attested subscription of the granter and the subscriptions of the witnesses must appear at the end of the last page of the deed,[123] and not, unless linked in some way with the rest of the deed, on a following blank page.[124] A writing is also probative if it bears to have been executed in accordance with the rules for notarial execution of writings.[125] There were statutory rules for execution of a probative deed by a company registered under the Companies Acts,[126] and by a local authority,[127] and in relation to other non-individual persons the form of execution would be found in relevant statutory provisions or internal ordinances, failing which the authentication statutes applied. "Notarial execution" was competent.

Before 1 October 1874[128] the inclusion of a testing clause was an essential **22.11.2** solemnity. Thereafter, although inclusion of a testing clause was still customary, a deed did not need a testing clause in order to be probative unless it contained erasures, deletions, interlineations or other additions,[129] or unless the designations of the witnesses were not added to their signatures. If the designations of the witnesses were placed in the testing clause and not added to the subscriptions, it was unnecessary also to mention their names in the testing clause, provided that it was clear to which subscription each designation applied.[130] Although it was customary and convenient to state in the testing clause the date and place of subscription, this was not an essential solemnity.[131] It has been judicially recognised that the part of a testing clause which referred to the place and date of subscription, and the witnesses' names and designations, could not be written until after the deed had been executed, although by a legal fiction it was regarded as having been written at the time of execution.[132] Strictly speaking the part relating to alterations

---

[119] Acts, 1540 c 117; 1555 c 29; 1579 c 80; 1584 c 4. After 1584 sealing in addition to subscription fell into disuse. Only the Sovereign may authenticate by superscription: *Foley v Costello* (1904) 6 F 365 at 370; *Taylor's Exx v Thom* 1914 SC 79 at 88.

[120] Acts, 1681 c 5; 1696 c 15. The statutes speak of "witnesses", and custom established that two would be sufficient: Montgomerie Bell, *Lectures* (3rd edn), I, p 50.

[121] Conveyancing (Scotland) Act 1874, s 38. The designations need not be written by the witnesses themselves.

[122] Act, 1696 c 15. A deed written on a single sheet folded to exhibit four pages need not be subscribed by the granter on each page: *Baird's Trs v Baird* 1955 SC 286; *Ferguson* 1959 SC 56.

[123] Act, 1696 c 15.

[124] *Ferguson* 1959 SC 56; *Baird's Trs v Baird* 1955 SC 286.

[125] See para 22.14.

[126] The most recent prior to 1 August 1995 being the Companies Act 1985, s 36B, as amended by the Law Reform (Miscellaneous Provisions) (Scotland) Act 1990, s 72(1). Different methods applied in earlier versions of companies legislation. These are drawn together for reference by Reid at 1990 SLT (News) 369.

[127] The most recent prior to 1 August 1995 being the Local Government (Scotland) Act 1973, s 194.

[128] Conveyancing (Scotland) Act 1874, s 2. As to deeds executed before 1 October 1874, see Montgomerie Bell, *Lectures* (3rd edn), I, 23–34; Menzies, *Lectures* (Sturrock's edn), pp 80 *et seq*.

[129] Menzies, *Lectures* (Sturrock's edn), p 171; Burns, *Conveyancing* (4th edn), p 1. See also para 22.12.

[130] *McDougall v McDougall* (1875) 2 R 814 (name in testing clause written on erasure).

[131] Erskine, iii, 2, 18; Dickson, *Evidence* (3rd edn), paras 718, 722; Montgomerie Bell, *Lectures* (3rd edn), I, pp 64, 65; Menzies, *Lectures* (Sturrock's edn), p 125; *Cairney v Macgregor's Trs* 1916 1 SLT 357, per Lord Anderson at 359.

[132] *Walker v Whitwell* 1916 SC (HL) 75, per Lord Dunedin at 80, Lord Shaw at 87; *Blair v Assets Co* (1896) 23 R (HL) 36, per Lord Watson at 47; *Smith v Chambers' Trs* (1877) 5 R 97, per Lord Deas at 110–111, approving *Leith Bank v Walker's Trs* (1836) 14 S 332, per Lord Moncreiff (Ordinary) at 335. See also Montgomerie Bell, *Lectures* (3rd edn), I, 234; Menzies, *Lectures* (Sturrock's edn), pp 172–173.

ought to have been completed before subscription.[133] The testing clause might be completed by the person in possession of the deed at any time before it is founded upon in a litigation or recorded for preservation,[134] even after the death of the granter.[135] Because it is recognised that the testing clause is usually inserted after subscription, no words contained therein can restrict, alter or add to, the provisions of the deed.[136]

22.11.3   In order to be valid a subscription on a writing which purports to have been solemnly executed must consist of the christened name (or forename), or shortened form[137] or initial letter thereof, and the surname of the person subscribing.[138] In the subscription of a married woman the surname may be her maiden surname.[139] A surname alone, preceded by "Mr" or "Mrs" is not a valid subscription,[140] but the addition of "Mr" or "Mrs" to what would otherwise be a valid subscription does not render it invalid.[141] There are special rules for members of the nobility and their families.[142] A subscription by mark is not valid,[143] and a subscription adhibited by a stamp[144] or cyclostyle,[145] or typewritten,[146] is equally invalid. A deed on which the subscription of the granter or a witness consists only of initials is not probative, because in the exceptional cases in which it is has been held that such a deed was executed in accordance with the statutory solemnities, proof was

---

[133] See para 22.12.

[134] *Blair v Assets Co* (1896) 23 R (HL) 36, per Lord Watson at 47; Bell, *Principles*, para 2226; Dickson, *Evidence* (3rd edn), para 731.

[135] *Walker v Whitwell* 1916 SC (HL) 75, per Lord Dunedin at 80; *Veasey v Malcolm's Trs* (1875) 2 R 748. In one case a deed was held to have been validly executed when the testing clause was inserted 32 years after its subscription by the granter: *Blair v Earl of Galloway* (1827) 6 S 51.

[136] *Blair v Assets Co* (1896) 23 R (HL) 36; *Smith v Chambers' Trs* (1877) 5 R 97; *Reid v Kedder* (1840) 1 Robin App 183, per Lord Brougham at 208, 209. Lord Gordon's *obiter* opinion to the contrary in *Smith v Chambers' Trs* (1878) 5 R (HL) 151 at 168 *et seq* was disapproved in *Blair v Assets Co*.

[137] Montgomerie Bell, *Lectures* (3rd edn), I, 37; Menzies, *Lectures* (Sturrock's edn), p 98.

[138] Act, 1672 c 21. A landowner might add the designation of his lands, prefixed by the word "of". Dickson (*Evidence* (3rd edn), paras 668, 670) accepted the view that a breach of the provisions of the Act did not invalidate the deed, but merely rendered the subscriber liable to punishment. This view was not generally adopted: see Montgomerie Bell, *Lectures* (3rd edn), I, 37; Menzies, *Lectures* (Sturrock's edn), p 98. The Act has been described as a definition of the word "signature" for the purposes of the authentication statutes: *Gardner v Lucas* (1878) 5 R (HL) 105, per Lord O'Hagan at 114.

[139] *Dunlop v Greenlees' Trs* (1863) 2 M 1.

[140] *Allan and Crichton* 1933 SLT (Sh Ct) 2. "Fullarton of that Ilk", although sustained in *Gordon v Murray* (1765) M 16818, ceased to be accepted as a valid subscription: Montgomerie Bell, *Lectures* (3rd edn), I, 37; Menzies, *Lectures* (Sturrock's edn), p 98; Craigie, *Conveyancing* (2nd edn), pp 66, 68.

[141] In *Ferguson* 1959 SC 56, "Mme. Pion Roux" was accepted as a valid subscription.

[142] Noblemen might subscribe by their titles alone—Act, 1672 c 21—and this was extended in practice to include the eldest sons of peers who might subscribe by their courtesy titles: Montgomerie Bell, *Lectures* (3rd edn), I, 37. A peeress, whether in her own right or by marriage, including the wife of a peer by courtesy, subscribed by her title or that of her husband, preceded by her christened name. The Act allowed bishops also to subscribe by their titles but the Lord Lyon, writing in 1930 (*Encyclopaedia of the Laws of Scotland*, Vol X, para 298, note 4) observed that this practice was then obsolete, citing *Drummond v Farquhar* 6 August 1809, FC.

[143] *Donald v McGregor* 1926 SLT 103 (OH); *Morton v French* 1908 SC 171; *Stirling Stuart v Stirling Crawfurd's Trs* (1885) 12 R 610, per Lord McLaren (Ordinary) at 617; *Crosbie v Wilson* (1865) 3 M 870 at 874, 878; Montgomerie Bell, *Lectures* (3rd edn), I, 49; Dickson, *Evidence* (3rd edn), para 672. As to subscription by mark in connection with writs in *re mercatoria*, see para 24.3, n 22.

[144] *Stirling Stuart v Stirling Crawfurd's Trs* (1885) 12 R 610.

[145] *Whyte v Watt* (1893) 21 R 165 at 166.

[146] *McBeath's Trs v McBeath* 1935 SC 471, per Lord President Clyde at 476–477, Lord Anderson at 487.

necessary.[147] A subscription is not invalid merely because it is rude or faulty or even illegible.[148] A deed which is otherwise probative does not cease to be probative because the granter's subscription is written upon an erasure,[149] and there seems to be no reason in principle why the position should be different if the subscription written upon an erasure is that of a witness.[150] Latent defects in the subscription of the granter of a deed are mentioned later.[151]

When there were several granters of a deed, the same two witnesses, who **22.11.4** needed to subscribe only once, might attest the subscriptions of those granters who had signed at the same time and place.[152] One granter could not be a witness to the subscription of another granter even when both signed at the same time and place.[153] The designation of each witness, whether mentioned in a testing clause or added to the signature,[154] ought to provide such a description as will distinguish the individual who has acted as witness from all other individuals, and the most correct practice is to state the person's profession or occupation and residence.[155] It is customary for the word "witness" to be written immediately after the signature, either by the witness himself or by another person, but this has never been a

---

[147] Dickson, *Evidence* (3rd edn), para 671. Such a deed was also usually invalid as a solemnly executed writing, since it lacked the kind of subscription required by the authentication statutes: *Gardner v Lucas* (1878) 5 R 638; (1878) 5 R (HL) 105; except perhaps in the exceptional case of a granter (but not of a witness: *Meek v Dunlop* (1707) M 16806) who was either unable to write his full surname or was accustomed to subscribing by the use of initials alone. There were early decisions supporting the validity of deeds on these grounds, some of them dated after the Act, 1672 c 21. See, for example, *Ker v Gibson* (1693) M 16805; *Weir v Ralston* 22 June 1813, FC. In one case of a bilateral contract, the onus was even placed upon the party repudiating the contract to prove that his custom was to sign *ad longum*: *Forrest v Marshall* (1701) M 16805. In other cases, however, the court proceeded upon an admission that the granter had in fact adhibited his initials (see *Earl Traquair v Gibson* (1724) M 16809), or insisted, in addition to proof of usage, on proof, restricted to the evidence of the instrumentary witnesses, that the granter had in fact subscribed (see *Couts v Straiton* (1681) M 16804). These decisions were regarded as exceptions to the general rule: *Gardner v Lucas* (1878) 5 R (HL) 105, per Lord O'Hagan at 115. They have been described as "contrary both to the words and the spirit of the statute" (Erskine, iii, 2, 8), "led by the hardship of particular case" (Ross, *Lectures*, I, 136), but see also *Gardner v Lucas* (1878) 5 R 638, per Lord President Inglis at 645; (1878) 5 R (HL) 105, per Lord Chancellor Cairns at 107; Montgomerie Bell, *Lectures* (3rd edn), I, 49; Menzies, *Lectures* (Sturrock's edn), p 100.

[148] *Stirling Stuart v Stirling Crawfurd's Trs* (1885) 12 R 610; *Perryman v McClymont* (1852) 14 D 508.

[149] *Brown v Duncan* (1888) 15 R 511.

[150] However, in *Gibson v Walker* 16 June 1809, FC: affd (1814) 2 Dow 270, a deed was reduced because the subscription of a witness upon an erasure was regarded as a vitiation *in essentialibus*. The instrumentary witness deponed that the signature was his, that as an official he witnessed many signatures and could not remember the circumstances in which the particular deed was subscribed, but that he would not subscribe as a witness a deed which he had not seen signed by the principal party. Those objecting to the deed founded upon the facts that the word "witness" was not in the handwriting of the witness and that his subscription was written in a different ink from that used by the granter and the other witness, and upon the proposition that both witnesses must together see the granter sign or acknowledge his signature. These are no longer valid grounds of objection to a deed.

[151] See para 22.13.

[152] Dickson, *Evidence* (3rd edn), para 704; Wood, *Lectures*, 67; *Baird's Trs v Murray* (1883) 11 R 153 at 157.

[153] Montgomerie Bell, *Lectures* (3rd edn), I, 51; Dickson, *Evidence* (3rd edn), para 693; *Miller v Farquharson* (1835) 13 S 838, per Lord Corehouse (Ordinary) at 839–840.

[154] See para 22.11.2.

[155] Montgomerie Bell, *Lectures* (3rd edn), I, 58. However, in some of the older cases, very meagre designations were at times sustained by the Court: *Reid v Brown* 1700 (noted in *Rule v Craig* (1712) M 16920) ("merchant" and "surgeon" without specification of place); *Baillie v Somervel* (1672) M 16913 ("indweller in Edinburgh"); *Duncan v Scrimgeour* (1706) M 16914 ("at Auchterhouse"); *Jamieson v Sheriff* (1708) M 16916 ("at Leckie").

statutory requisite, and its absence does not affect the probative quality of the deed.[156]

22.12 ALTERATIONS IN ATTESTED DEEDS

Unauthenticated alterations

22.12.1 A writing upon which there appear erasures, deletions, interlineations or additions,[157] which do not bear to have been properly authenticated, is not probative, because, failing agreement, a judicial declarator is necessary to determine whether it, or any part of it, is nevertheless effectual as a solemnly executed deed.[158] If the existence of an erasure or other alteration is not admitted, a proof on the point is necessary, the onus of proof of the fact of erasure in an otherwise probative deed resting upon the party who asserts it.[159] If the existence of an unauthenticated alteration is proved or admitted, there is a presumption of law, which (apart from statutory exception)[160] is irrebuttable,[161] that the alteration was made after the deed was executed.[162] This does not mean that the deed is necessarily ineffectual. When the alterations consist merely of additions, such as marginal additions, interlineations or interpolations, it may be possible, by disregarding them as *pro non scriptis*, to give effect to the rest of the deed.[163] Even when words are written upon an erasure, it may similarly be possible to disregard them as *pro non scriptis* and give effect to the rest of the deed.[164] However, before this can be done two conditions must be satisfied. The words written upon the erasure must not be essential to the deed,[165] and it must be manifest, either by reading the erased words if they are legible, or from their context, that they were

---

[156] *Lord Blantyre* (1850) 13 D 40. The customary practice was a proper precaution for the witness's security, in order to indicate clearly the capacity in which he signed: Menzies, *Lectures* (Sturrock's edn), p 118.

[157] Under the new statutory system alterations include anything written on blanks. The common law in relation to blanks was unclear, and rarely referred to. It has not been covered in this edition, but for the authors' examination of the law as it stood in 1963, see the first edition, para 184.

[158] Stair, iv, 42, 19 (2); Erskine, iii, 2, 20; *Grant v Shepherd* (1847) 6 Bell's App 153, per Lord Lyndhurst at 171; *Glassford's Tr v Glassford* (1864) 2 M 1317 at 1324, 1326; *Munro v Butler Johnstone* (1868) 7 M 250, per Lord Neaves at 256; Menzies, *Lectures* (Sturrock's edn), p 138.

[159] *Hamilton v Lindsey-Bucknall* (1869) 8 M 323.

[160] The question of whether the presumption might be rebutted by parole evidence in terms of s 39 of the Conveyancing (Scotland) Act 1874 is discussed at para 22.15.

[161] *Reid v Kedder* (1840) 1 Robin App 183, per Lord Brougham at 211, Lord Chancellor Cottenham at 219; *Grant v Shepherd* (1847) 6 Bell's App 153, per Lord Lyndhurst at 171; *Boswell v Boswell* (1852) 14 D 378; *Munro v Butler Johnstone* (1868) 7 M 250, per Lord Neaves at 256.

[162] Stair, iv, 42, 19 (2); Erskine, iii, 2, 20; *Grant v Shepherd* (1847) 6 Bell's App 153, per Lord Lyndhurst at 171; *Glassford's Tr v Glassford* (1864) 2 M 1317 at 1324, 1326; *Munro v Butler Johnstone* (1868) 7 M 250, per Lord Neaves at 256; Menzies, *Lectures* (Sturrock's edn), p 138.

[163] In *Munro v Butler Johnstone* (1868) 7 M 250, the important word "not" was interpolated, without authentication in a deed of entail. The court disregarded the word as *pro non scripto*, and construed the rest of the deed. However, the deed was meaningless for its purpose without the word.

[164] In *Cattanach's Tr v Jamieson* (1884) 11 R 972, there was a reference in a bond and disposition in security to another deed for a description of the subjects which were being disponed, the date of the other deed being written upon an unauthenticated erasure. The court was able to find a sufficient description of the subjects in other clauses of the bond, which was therefore held to be effectual for its purpose. For other examples, see *McDougall v McDougall* (1875) 2 R 814; *Wilson v Taylor* (1869) 7 M 773; *Gollan v Gollan* (1863) 1 M (HL) 65; *Morrison v Nisbet* (1829) 7 S 810.

[165] *Gollan v Gollan* (1863) 1 M (HL) 65, per Lord Westbury at 66.

immaterial,[166] and that their deletion could not materially have altered the sense of the deed.[167] Moreover, it may be possible to hold that the clause vitiated by the unauthenticated alteration is separable from the other clauses, and, by disregarding it, to give effect to the rest of the deed.[168] No challenge of an instrument of sasine, notarial instrument[169] or notice of title,[170] on the ground that any part of it is written on erasure, will have effect unless it is averred and proved that the erasure was made for the purpose of fraud, or that the record in the sasine register is not conformable to the instrument as presented for registration.[171] Further, no challenge of any deed, instrument or writing recorded in any register of sasines will receive effect, on the ground that any part of the record of such deed, instrument or writing is written on erasure, unless such erasure is proved to have been made for the purpose of fraud, or the record is not conformable to the deed, instrument or writing as presented for registration.[172]

Authenticated alterations

Alterations which have been properly authenticated form part of the probative writing in which they are found, and do not deprive it of its probative quality.[173] To be properly authenticated for this purpose, the alteration must appear, from a mere reading of the deed, to have been made before the subscriptions of the granter and the witnesses were adhibited.[174] This is achieved by referring to the alteration in a testing clause[175] placed at the end of the body of the deed and before the subscriptions.[176] Erasures, writing on erasures, interlineations or interpolations, must, by the reference in the testing clause, be adopted or acknowledged as having been made before subscription, the words or letters being quoted, and their position in the text being exactly specified by reference to page and line. Marginal additions are signed by the granter with his forename or initial on one side and his surname on the other, and must be further authenticated by a reference to them in the testing clause, as in the case of other alterations, with the additional statement that the

22.12.2

---

[166] Stair, iv, 42, 19 (2); *Glassford's Tr v Glassford* (1864) 2 M 1317 at 1324. In *Reid v Kedder* (1840) 1 Robin App 183 (name of grantee), *Howden v Ferrier* (1835) 13 S 1097 (description of the subjects in an instrument of sasine), and *Kirkwood v Patrick* (1847) 9 D 1361 (date before which obligation enforceable), the erasure was held to be material, so as to invalidate either the clause in which it appeared or the whole deed. *Cf Richardson v Biggar* (1845) 8 D 315.

[167] *McDougall v McDougall* (1875) 2 R 814 at 819, 825.

[168] Dickson, *Evidence* (3rd edn), para 879; *Grant v Shepherd* (1847) 6 Bell's App 153, per Lord Lyndhurst at 172; *Howden v Ferrier* (1835) 13 S 1097; *Peddie v Doig's Trs* (1857) 19 D 820.

[169] See Titles to Land Consolidation (Scotland) Act 1868, ss 3, 144 for a definition of the various instruments covered by this provision.

[170] Conveyancing (Scotland) Act 1924, s 6 (1).

[171] Erasures in Deeds (Scotland) Act 1836; Titles to Land Consolidation (Scotland) Act 1868, ss 3, 144.

[172] Conveyancing (Scotland) Act 1874, s 54.

[173] Erskine, iii, 2, 20; Dickson, *Evidence* (3rd edn), para 729.

[174] At common law it was incompetent to prove this by parole evidence: *Grant v Shepherd* (1847) 6 Bell's App 153, per Lord Lyndhurst at 171. As to whether such a proof is competent under statute, see para 22.15. If the appearance of the deed itself suggests that the alteration may have been made after the deed was subscribed and attested, the presumption of law is that it was so made. Montgomerie Bell, *Lectures* (3rd edn), I, 68. The sense of the alteration may itself disclose this, as when the recording of a deed was said to have occurred at a date (written upon an authenticated erasure) later than the date of execution of the writing in which the alteration occurred, as disclosed by its testing clause: *Cattanach's Tr v Jamieson* (1884) 11 R 972.

[175] See para 22.11.

[176] Dickson, *Evidence* (3rd edn), para 728; Montgomerie Bell, *Lectures* (3rd edn), 1, 68; Menzies, *Lectures* (Sturrock's edn), pp 138–139, 172–173.

marginal addition was signed by the granter in the presence of the witnesses.[177] The reference in the testing clause to alterations in the deed ought to have been written before the granter and witnesses subscribed,[178] unlike the date and place of execution and the witnesses' names and designations, which, in practice, must be written afterwards. If the appearance of the deed raises an inference that the reference in the testing clause to alterations was written after the granter and the witnesses subscribed, the deed is not probative.[179] This inference might arise, if, for example, the testing clause makes reference to a date which is later than the date on which the deed is said to have been executed, or if the lines or words are so crammed together as to indicate that they were written in a space already bounded by the body of the deed above and the signatures below.[180]

22.12.3   The rules with regard to solemn authentication were the same for testamentary as for other writings,[181] but the question which more often arises is not whether the deed was properly executed in the first place, but whether, *after* its original execution, and while still undelivered and in the possession of the granter, it was validly revoked or amended, in whole or in part, by deletions or writings which the granter made upon it. This is a matter of the substantive law of wills and succession rather than the law of evidence,[182] and dicta on this topic must be read with this distinction in mind, because, although sometimes pronounced in general terms, they may refer, not to the solemn execution of testamentary writings, but to their subsequent amendment. Deletions are effective only if they are authenticated by the testator's signature or initials or are proved to have been made by him. If not thus authenticated or proved they will be ignored.[183] Marginal or interlineal additions, even if proved to be holograph of the testator, are thought to be effective only if separately authenticated by the subscription or initials of the testator.[184] Alterations to solemnly executed wills do not enjoy the relaxations extended to

---

[177] Montgomerie Bell, *Lectures* (3rd edn), I, p 75; Menzies, *Lectures* (Sturrock's edn), p 139. The weight of authority seems to support the view that the granter's signature alone, without a reference in the testing clause, was insufficient for proper authentication, since without the reference it does not appear that the signature was attested by the witnesses. See Stair, iv, 42, 19 (3); Erskine, iii, 2, 20; Dickson, *Evidence* (3rd edn), para 734; *Smith v Chambers' Trs* (1877) 5 R 97, per Lord Deas at 109. Two early decisions apparently to the contrary effect (*Cuming v Presbytery of Aberdeen* (1721) Robertson's App 364; *Spottiswood* (1741) M 16811) are discussed by Montgomerie Bell, *Lectures* at I, 76. An old practice whereby the witnesses subscribed in the margin beside the granter's signature of the marginal addition, which made it unnecessary to mention the addition in the testing clause was still sound in principle if the designations of the witnesses were added to their signatures: Montgomerie Bell, *Lectures* (3rd edn), I, 77; Conveyancing (Scotland) Act 1874, s 38.

[178] Montgomerie Bell, *Lectures* (3rd edn), I, pp 69, 234; Menzies, *Lectures* (Sturrock's edn), pp 172–173; *Encyclopaedia of the Laws of Scotland*, Vol II, para 661 (article by John Burns, WS).

[179] *Cattanach's Tr v Jamieson* (1884) 11 R 972.

[180] Montgomerie Bell, *Lectures* (3rd edn), I, 69, 234; Menzies, *Lectures* (Sturrock's edn), pp 172, 173. In *Reid v Kedder* (1834) 12 S 781; (1835) 13 S 619; (1840) 1 Robin App 183, the fact that the last three words of the testing clause were written over part of the granter's signature was mentioned as indicative that the signature was written first. See 1 Robin App, per Lord Brougham at p 209.

[181] *Macdonald v Cuthbertson* (1890) 18 R 101, per Lord President Inglis at 104–105, Lord Kinnear at 108; *Walker v Whitwell* 1916 SC (HL) 75, per Lord Dunedin at 79, Lord Shaw at 84 *et seq*.

[182] McLaren, *Wills and Succession* (3rd edn), I, para 743; *Grant v Shepherd* (1847) 6 Bell's App 153, per Lord Lyndhurst at 172; *Pattison's Trs v University of Edinburgh* (1888) 16 R 73; *Watson's Factor v Watson* (1899) 7 SLT 288 (OH).

[183] *Pattison's Trs v University of Edinburgh* (1888) 16 R 73, per Lord McLaren at 76, 77.

[184] *Pattison's Trs v University of Edinburgh* (1888) 16 R 73, per Lord McLaren at 77. Effect was given to such authenticated holograph additions in *Hogg's Exrs v Butcher* 1947 SN 141, 190; *Caledonian Banking Co v Fraser* (1874) 44 SLR 345; *Royal Infirmary of Edinburgh v Lord Advocate* (1861) 23 D 1213.

alterations to holograph wills.[185] For the effect of deletions, and subscribed additions or alterations, in the *copy* of a will, reference is made to the undernoted decisions.[186]

22.13 PROBATIVE WRITING—LATENT DEFECTS IN STATUTORY SOLEMNITIES

General—onus and standard of proof

A probative deed,[187] the genuineness of which must be assumed, may nevertheless **22.13.1** be reduced on proof that, in fact, either the granter's subscription or the attestation was invalid.[188] The evidence of instrumentary witnesses, who admit their signatures but who say that they do not remember seeing the granter sign or hearing his acknowledgement of his subscription[189] or who expressly deny that they either saw the granter sign or heard him acknowledge, was regarded with suspicion, partly because after a lapse of time the recollection of the witnesses was not usually to be preferred to the evidence afforded by their subscriptions on the document,[190] and partly, in the latter case, because it constituted an admission that they had been accessories to forgery.[191] Such evidence by the instrumentary witnesses, when not supported by other evidence—that they were not in the district when the deed was signed by the granter, for example[192]—on a number of occasions failed to satisfy the court or the jury.[193] However, evidence of this nature, even if by only one of the instrumentary witnesses, could, since the Civil Evidence (Scotland) Act 1988, be sufficient to discharge the onus of proof resting upon the pursuer even if

---

[185] *Magistrates of Dundee v Morris* (1858) 3 Macq 134, per Lord Chelmsford at 152. As to alterations to holograph wills, see para 23.18. It is doubtful whether the following authorities to the contrary would be followed: *Horsbrugh v Horsbrugh* (1848) 10 D 824; *Gibson's Trs v Lamb* 1931 SLT 22 (OH); *Gray's Trs v Dow* (1900) 3 F 79; *Grant v Stoddart* (1849) 11 D 860. See the doubt regarding *Grant v Stoddart* expressed in Menzies, *Lectures* (Sturrock's edn), p 142.

[186] *Thomson's Trs v Bowhill Baptist Church* 1956 SC 217; *Lawson v Lawson* 1954 SLT (Notes) 60; *Manson v Edinburgh Royal Institution* 1948 SLT 196 (OH); *MacKinnon's Trs v MacKinnon* (1896) 3 SLT 284.

[187] See paras 22.10, 22.11.

[188] Proof that the granter's signature was forged is, of course, another ground of reduction, with which this chapter is not concerned.

[189] *Morrison v Maclean's Trs* (1862) 24 D 625, per Lord Justice-Clerk Inglis at 629; *Donaldson v Stewart* (1842) 4 D 1215, per Lord Justice-Clerk Hope at 1217. See also *Smith v Bank of Scotland* (1824) 2 Shaw's App 265, per Lord Gifford at 287; *Frank v Frank* (1793) M 16822; Dickson, *Evidence* (3rd edn), para 903.

[190] *Sibbald v Sibbald* (1776) M 16906.

[191] See Act, 1681 c 5; *Morrison v Maclean's Trs* (1863) 1 M 304, per Lord Cowan at 304–305. The instrumentary witnesses must be warned before they give evidence that they need not answer questions tending to incriminate them: Dickson, *Evidence* (3rd edn), paras 901, 904; *Frank v Frank* (1793) M 16822; *McArthur v McArthur's Trs* 1931 SLT 463 (OH).

[192] The example in the text was suggested by *Young v Paton* 1910 SC 63, but there the independent evidence as to the non-presence of the instrumentary witnesses in the district was *preferred* to the evidence of these witnesses, who deponed that it was not their practice to attest a signature without having seen it executed or heard it acknowledged.

[193] *Morrison v Maclean's Trs* (1863) 1 M 304; *Cleland v Cleland* (1838) 1 D 254; *Condie v Buchan* (1823) 2 S 385; *Frank v Frank* (1793) M 16822. Since neither instrumentary witness necessarily corroborated the other, the proof was held to fail because of a technical absence of corroboration: *McArthur v McArthur's Trs* 1931 SLT 463 (OH), but the corroboration requirement no longer applies: Civil Evidence (Scotland) Act 1988, s 1.

unsupported by other evidence.[194] Much would depend upon the cogency and credibility of the witness's evidence. In some circumstances the question of whether the granter's signature was properly attested is of no practical importance. If the granter of an onerous deed delivered it to the grantee as such, and, when it was delivered, the granter's signature appeared to be properly attested by two witnesses, the granter was personally barred from founding upon the latent defect that the subscribing witnesses had not in fact seen him sign or received an acknowledgement of his signature.[195]

Faulty subscription by granter

22.13.2 The whole of the subscription must be adhibited by the hand of the granter, and without assistance.[196] So a deed was held invalid when the granter's hand was guided in making the subscription, although all but the last syllable was written without assistance.[197] However, it has also been held that the subscription was not invalid when the granter's hand was held about the wrist so as to support it, no guidance being given in the formation of the letters.[198] A subscription was held invalid when it was marked in ink by the granter over words scored with a pin by another person,[199] but a subscription written freehand by the granter herself, while she had before her a trial signature made by herself on a slip of paper below a copy of her signature made by another person, was sustained.[200] Retouching of the subscription by the granter himself, even after attestation, does not invalidate it, if the attested subscription was itself genuine and sufficient.[201] The other rules regarding the subscription of the granter of a deed were mentioned in an earlier paragraph.[202]

Competence of instrumentary witnesses

22.13.3 Those without capacity due to age or unsound mind[203] and blind persons[204] were not competent instrumentary witnesses. Apart from these, any person[205] might competently act as a witness. A person who had a beneficial interest in the deed was not on that account an incompetent witness,[206] and near relatives,[207] including,

---

[194] For sufficiency of evidence in civil cases generally, see Chapter 5. Contrary to the authorities at common law when corroboration was required: ie *Forrest v Low's Trs* 1907 SC 1240, per Lord Kinnear at 1253; 1909 SC (HL) 16, per Lord Dunedin and Lord Shaw at 18; *Cleland v Paterson* (1837) 15 S 1246. However, careful and precise evidence will be required to overcome the presumption of validity, see *Sereshky v Sereshky* 1988 SLT 426, *Rehman v Ahmed* 1993 SLT 741, and para 4.3.

[195] *Boyd v Shaw* 1927 SC 414; *MacLeish v The British Linen Bank* 1911 2 SLT 168 (OH); *National Bank of Scotland v Campbell* (1892) 19 R 885; *Baird's Tr v Murray* (1883) 11 R 153. See also *Young v Paton* 1910 SC 63 and, e.g. *Forsyth v Royal Bank of Scotland plc* 2000 SCLR 61. By these authorities the same rule applied if the granter handed the deed to a third party in order that it may be delivered to the grantee as an onerous deed.

[196] Montgomerie Bell, *Lectures* (3rd edn), I, 38; Menzies, *Lectures* (Sturrock's edn), pp 98, 99.

[197] *Moncrieff v Monypenny* (1710) M 15936; (1711) Robertson's App 26.

[198] *Noble v Noble* (1875) 3 R 74.

[199] *Crosbie v Picken* (1749) M 16814.

[200] *Wilson v Raeburn* (1800) Hume 912 (described in Montgomerie Bell, *Lectures* (3rd edn), I, 38–39).

[201] *Stirling Stuart v Stirling Crawfurd's Trs* (1885) 12 R 610.

[202] See para 22.11.

[203] Montgomerie Bell, *Lectures* (3rd edn), I, p 50; Menzies, *Lectures* (Sturrock's edn), p 111.

[204] *Cuningham v Spence* (1824) 3 S 144.

[205] Titles to Land Consolidation (Scotland) Act 1868, s 139; *Hannay* (1873) 1 R 246.

[206] *Simson v Simson* (1883) 10 R 1247; Erskine, iv, 2, 27.

[207] Montgomerie Bell, *Lectures* (3rd edn), I, p 50; Menzies, *Lectures* (Sturrock's edn), p 112.

it is thought, a husband or wife,[208] were not incompetent because of their relationship.

Requirements for valid attestation

The only persons who might validly attest were those receiving the assent, express **22.13.4** or implied, of the granter to sign as witnesses.[209] The deed will be executed invalidly and open to reduction,[210] unless the witness knew the granter, and either saw him subscribe or observed his acknowledgement of his subscription at the time when he himself subscribed.[211] The witness's knowledge of the granter was sufficient if he had credible information that the person executing the writing was the person designed in it,[212] which might be communicated by the granter personally[213] or from the introduction of any reliable person present.[214] The granter's acknowledgement of his subscription might be made to the witness orally, or in writing, or by his acts, or by a combination of words and acts.[215] An attestation was valid although one witness saw the granter subscribe and the other observed him acknowledge,[216] and, if neither saw him subscribe, it was valid although a separate acknowledgement was made to each witness outwith the presence of the other.[217] An attestation is not invalid because the instrumentary witnesses were unaware of the terms or nature of the deed.[218] If the pretended witnesses signed before the deed had been subscribed by the granter, the signatures do not in fact attest anything and the deed is invalid and will be reduced.[219] Questions have arisen as to where and when the instrumentary witnesses must subscribe. The subscription or acknowledgement by the granter, and the subscription by the witness, must both take place *unico contextu*[220] that is, as parts of a single continuous process.[221] What is said to have been intended by the rule is to ensure that the deed subscribed by the witnesses is that on which the granter's subscription was adhibited or acknowledged in their presence,[222] and that the granter's express or implied

---

[208] This seems to be implied in *Brownlee v Robb* 1907 SC 1302, per Lord Johnston (Ordinary) at 1310, Lord McLaren at 1312; *Tener's Trs v Tener's Trs* (1879) 6 R 1111 (overruled on another point in *Walker v Whitwell* 1916 SC (HL) 75).

[209] *Walker v Whitwell* 1914 SC 560, per Lord Guthrie at 586, Lord Skerrington at 594–595; 1916 SC (HL) 75, per Lord Dunedin at 82, Lord Shaw at 90, 91.

[210] *Smyth v Smyth* (1876) 3 R 573. Lord Young's *obiter* opinion in *Geddes v Reid* (1891) 18 R 1186, contrary to the decision in *Smyth v Smyth*, that if the granter's subscription was proved, faulty attestation did not invalidate the deed, was expressly rejected in *Forrest v Low's Trs* 1907 SC 1240 at 1252–1253 (1909 SC (HL) 16 at 18).

[211] Act, 1681 c 5. The Act must now be read in the light of later authority cited in this paragraph.

[212] Dickson, *Evidence* (3rd edn), para 697; Montgomerie Bell, *Lectures* (3rd edn), I, p 52.

[213] *Brock v Brock* 1908 SC 964 at 966; *Walker v Adamson* (1716) M 16896; *Campbell v Robertson* (1698) M 16887.

[214] *Brock v Brock* 1908 SC 964.

[215] *Cumming v Skeoch's Trs* (1879) 6 R 963; Dickson, *Evidence* (3rd edn), para 699.

[216] Montgomerie Bell, *Lectures* (3rd edn), I, 52.

[217] *Hogg v Campbell* (1864) 2 M 848.

[218] Dickson, *Evidence* (3rd edn), para 701.

[219] *Smyth v Smyth* (1876) 3 R 573. Lord Young's *obiter* opinion in *Geddes v Reid* (1891) 18 R 1186, contrary to the decision in *Smyth v Smyth*, that if the granter's subscription was proved, faulty attestation did not invalidate the deed, was expressly rejected in *Forrest v Low's Trs* 1907 SC 1240 at 1252–1253 (1909 SC (HL) 16 at 18).

[220] *Walker v Whitwell* 1914 SC 560, per Lord Skerrington at 588, 589.

[221] *Walker v Whitwell* 1914 SC 560, per Lord Johnston at 577; 1916 SC (HL) 75, per Lord Shaw at 89, 91; *Thomson v Clarkson's Trs* (1892) 20 R 59, per Lord Rutherfurd Clark at 62, Lord Kyllachy at 64.

[222] *Thomson v Clarkson's Trs* (1892) 20 R 59 at 61, 62.

assent to attestation had not been withdrawn before the witnesses subscribe.[223] In applying the rule it has been held that the witnesses need not subscribe in the presence of the granter, and the attestation was held to be valid when the witnesses, having seen the granter sign, adhibited their own subscriptions in an adjoining room, the deed having been out of their sight for a few minutes,[224] and when the witnesses, having observed the granter acknowledge his subscription in his own house, took the deed to the solicitor's office in which they were employed, where they at once adhibited their own subscriptions.[225] Since the witnesses cannot subscribe at the very moment when the granter subscribes or acknowledges his subscription, it is clear that some time must elapse between the two events, and the question of the length of time which is permissible depends upon the application of the rule to the circumstances of the particular case. Intervals of a quarter of an hour,[226] and three-quarters of an hour[227] have been held to be permissible. However, an attestation is invalid if one of the witnesses does not subscribe until after the death of the granter.[228]

22.14 NOTARIAL EXECUTION OF WRITINGS

22.14.1 After 1 January 1925,[229] any deed, instrument or writing, whether relating to land or not, might be validly executed on behalf of a granter, who for any cause, permanent or temporary, was blind[230] or unable to write, by a solicitor,[231] notary public, justice of the peace, or, as regards testamentary writings, by a parish minister acting in his own parish.[232] Any such person executing the deed on the granter's behalf is referred to as the "notary" in this paragraph, and the process was commonly known as "notarial execution". The granter had to declare that he was blind or unable to write,[233] and the onus of proving that this declaration was untrue rested upon the person seeking to reduce the deed.[234] The writing had to be read over to the granter, and it was then subscribed on his behalf, in his presence, and

---

[223] *Walker v Whitwell* 1916 SC (HL) 75, per Lord Dunedin at 81, 82, Lord Shaw at 91.

[224] *Frank v Frank* (1795) M 16824; (1809) 5 Paton's App 278. See also *Condie v Buchan* (1823) 2 S 385.

[225] *Thomson v Clarkson's Trs* (1892) 20 R 59.

[226] *Walker v Whitwell* 1916 SC (HL) 75.

[227] *Thomson v Clarkson's Trs* (1892) 20 R 59.

[228] *Walker v Whitwell* 1916 SC (HL) 75.

[229] As to deeds executed before that date, see Conveyancing (Scotland) Act 1874, s 41 and Montgomerie Bell, *Lectures* (3rd edn), I, 39 *et seq*; Menzies, *Lectures* (Sturrock's edn), pp 102 *et seq*.

[230] If a blind person could write, his deed was probably valid when executed by him personally: Burns, *Conveyancing* (4th edn), p 9; Montgomerie Bell, *Lectures* (3rd edn), I, pp 46–47.

[231] "Law agent" (the term formerly used) came to mean a solicitor enrolled, or deemed to have been enrolled, in pursuance of the relevant Solicitors (Scotland) Act and included every person entitled to practise as a solicitor in a court of law in Scotland: Conveyancing (Scotland) Act 1924, s 2 (6). The solicitor might then act as notary without having taken out an annual certificate authorising him to practise: *Stephen v Scott* 1927 SC 85.

[232] The power was also given to a minister of the Church of Scotland who had been appointed to officiate as minister to a charge without limit of time or for a period of years in any parish in which his charge, or any part of it, was situated or his assistant or colleagues and successor so acting: Church of Scotland (Property and Endowments) Amendment Act 1933, s 13; Conveyancing (Scotland) Act 1924, s 18(1).

[233] Conveyancing (Scotland) Act 1924, Sched. 1.

[234] Dickson, *Evidence* (3rd edn), para 683. The granter is personally barred from seeking reduction of his own deed on the ground that his declaration was untrue: Dickson, para 684.

by his authority, all before two witnesses, who had heard the writing read over to the granter and had heard or seen his authority given.[235] The witnesses, by subscribing, attested not only the subscription of the notary, but also the fact that the deed was read over to the granter and that authority had been given for execution by the notary.[236] A holograph docquet, in statutory form,[237] or in any words to the like effect,[238] had to precede the signatures of the notary and the witnesses.[239] The docquet had to be written on the last page of the deed, and it was unnecessary for the notary to sign above as well as below the docquet.[240] The earlier pages, if any, had to be authenticated if required in the usual manner by the subscription of the notary.[241] The designations of the witnesses, as with other solemnly executed deeds,[242] had to be mentioned in a testing clause or added to their signatures, and, if there was no testing clause,[243] a specification of the place and date of signing might be added, if desired, to the docquet. The docquet must have been written by the notary in the presence of the granter and witnesses, and the subscriptions of the notary and witnesses must have been adhibited in the presence of the granter of the deed and of each other.[244] The deed is not necessarily invalid if one notary executed on behalf of more than one party,[245] but it was preferable to use separate notaries for separate parties requiring notarial execution. A writing which appears to have been executed by a notary in accordance with the rules mentioned above is a probative writing.[246] In common with other probative writings, a notarially executed deed may be reduced on the ground that the statutory rules have not in fact been complied with. A notarially executed deed might also be reduced if the notary had a beneficial interest in it.[247] A notarially executed writing which is not probative or which has been executed without some of the solemnities may nevertheless be valid as if it had been solemnly executed if certain matters are proved.[248]

---

[235] Conveyancing (Scotland) Act 1924, s 18(1).
[236] Montgomerie Bell, *Lectures* (3rd edn), I, p 57; *Farmer v Myles* (1760) M 16849.
[237] Conveyancing (Scotland) Act 1924, Sched 1.
[238] Conveyancing (Scotland) Act 1924, s 18(1). See also *Watson v Beveridge* (1883) 11 R 40; *Atchison's Trs v Atchison* (1876) 3 R 388.
[239] Conveyancing (Scotland) Act 1924, s 18(1).
[240] Conveyancing (Scotland) Act 1924, Sched 1. The note has been regarded as explanatory of the section: *Hynd's Tr v Hynd's Trs* 1955 SC (HL) 1 at 9, 11, 27. For the proposition that the deed need not be signed above as well as below the docquet, see also *Mathieson v Hawthorns & Co Ltd* (1899) 1 F 468.
[241] See para 22.11.
[242] See para 22.11.
[243] See para 22.11.
[244] *Hynd's Tr v Hynd's Trs* 1955 SC (HL) 1.
[245] A bilateral contract, subscribed on behalf of each party by the same notary, was held invalid in *Craig v Richardson* (1610) M 16829. In *Graeme v Graeme's Trs* (1868) 7 M 14, however, the earlier case was not accepted as laying down a general rule even for contracts between strangers, and was held not to apply to a mutual will.
[246] See paras 22.10, 22.11.
[247] *Crawford's Trs v Glasgow Royal Infirmary* 1955 SC 367 (OH); *Gorrie's Tr v Stiven's Exrx* 1952 SC 1; *Finlay v Finlay's Trs* 1948 SC 16; *Newstead v Dansken* 1918 1 SLT 136 (OH). The opinion has been expressed that a deed is not invalid merely because the notary's employers had a beneficial interest in the deed: *Hynd's Tr v Hynd's Trs* 1955 SC (HL) 1 at 13–14, 21. As to the validity in Scotland of a will notarially executed in England, in accordance with English law, by a solicitor who had a beneficial interest, see *Irving v Snow* 1956 SC 257. In the last-mentioned case the opinion was expressed that some aspects of the earlier decisions may need reconsideration.
[248] Conveyancing (Scotland) Act 1874, s 39; Conveyancing (Scotland) Act 1924, s 18 (2). This subject is dealt with at para 22.15.

22.15 INFORMALITY OF EXECUTION—STATUTORY REMEDY

22.15.1 At common law a solemnly executed deed was valid for its purpose only if the solemnities of execution had been complied with. The fact that they had been complied with had to be manifest from a mere scrutiny of the writing itself. If the insignia of a probative deed were lacking, their place could not be taken by proof that the solemnities were in fact observed, such proof being incompetent.[249] A limited exception to this rule was authorised by the Conveyancing (Scotland) Act 1874,[250] to the effect that, in spite of what would otherwise be a fatal informality of execution, a deed might nevertheless be valid and effective as a solemnly executed deed if two conditions were satisfied. First, the deed had to be validly subscribed by the granter and by the two persons who bear, on the face of the deed, to attest the granter's signature.[251] Secondly there must be proof by the party upholding the deed that it was in fact subscribed by the granter and two witnesses[252] in such a way as to constitute a validly attested subscription,[253] viewed objectively rather than by reference to the subjective intention of a signatory.[254] Proof that the granter and witnesses in fact subscribed is not enough, if the purported attestation by the witnesses was invalid.[255] The absence of the designations of the witnesses, either after their signatures or in a testing clause,[256] is an informality to which the section has been held to apply, and if the proof required by the section is satisfactory, the deed is valid in spite of the lack of this solemnity.[257] The section applied similarly when: the informality was the misspelling in the testing clause of the names of one of the witnesses, provided that there was no doubt that the designation applied to the subscription of the witness whose subscription was in question[258]; when a deed which required to be signed on every sheet had not been so subscribed but there was proof to the satisfaction of the court that the earlier unauthenticated pages formed part of the "deed, instrument or writing" when the granter and the witnesses subscribed[259]; when there are unauthenticated alterations in the deed but as a result of the proof which the section requires including proof that the deed, instrument or writing which the granter and witnesses are said to have subscribed is identified by reference to its terms, the court is satisfied

---

[249] See para 22.10. For the insignia of a probative deed, see para 22.11.

[250] s 39.

[251] See para 22.11. Thus the section was of no help if the subscription of the granter or one of the witnesses was "Mr Smith" even if it were proved that Mr Smith had in fact adhibited that subscription (*Allan and Crichton* 1933 SLT (Sh Ct) 2), or if the subscriptions of the granter and witnesses appear, not on the last page of the deed itself or linked with it, but on a following blank page (*Baird's Trs v Baird* 1955 SC 286 at 293, 295).

[252] Proof of subscription by the granter is not enough: *Bisset* 1961 SLT (Sh Ct) 19.

[253] *Walker v Whitwell* 1916 SC (HL) 75.

[254] *Williamson v Williamson* 1997 SLT 1044.

[255] See para 22.07. See *Forrest v Low's Trs* 1907 SC 1240, per Lord Johnston (Ordinary) at 1246–1247, Lord Kinnear at 1252–1253; *Smyth v Smyth* (1876) 3 R 573; *Walker v Whitwell* 1916 SC (HL) 75 at 83, 90; *Williamson v Williamson* 1997 SLT 1044.

[256] For the rule as to this, see para 22.11.

[257] *Inglis' Trs v Inglis* (1901) 4 F 365; *Nisbet* (1897) 24 R 411; *Thomson's Trs v Easson* (1878) 6 R 141; *Addison* (1875) 2 R 457.

[258] *Richardson's Trs* (1891) 18 R 1131.

[259] *Inglis' Trs v Inglis* (1901) 4 F 365; *Brown* (1883) 11 R 400; *McLaren v Menzies* (1876) 3 R 1151. The underlying principle is thought to be the same as that applying to the informality of authentication of alterations. Examples of the application of the section to this kind of informality may be found in *Bisset* 1961 SLT (Sh Ct) 19; *Bogie's Exrs v Bogie* (1953) 69 Sh Ct Rep 128; *Manson v Campbell* (1948) 64 Sh Ct Rep 28; *Shiell* 1936 SLT 317.

that the unauthenticated alterations in fact formed part of the deed when the granter and witnesses subscribed.[260] The section applies not only to a deed executed by the granter, but also to a notarially executed deed, which for the purpose of the section is deemed to be a deed subscribed by the granter or maker,[261] but the deed must have been executed in accordance with the statutory formalities for notarial execution.[262] Thus the section does not apply, and the deed is invalid, if the holograph docquet, together with the signatures of the notary and the two witnesses, were not made *unico contextu* in the presence of the granter,[263] and would not apply if, in spite of what is said in the docquet, the granter did not in fact declare that he was blind or unable to write, or the writing was not read over to him in the presence of the witnesses, or the witnesses did not see or hear him authorise the notary to sign. The section has applied when there was an omission from the docquet,[264] and should apply in notarial execution to the type of omissions for which it has been used in deeds executed normally, but complete absence of the docquet probably would not be excusable.[265]

---

[260] *Elliot's Exrs* 1939 SLT 69 (OH). See also Menzies, *Lectures* (Sturrock's edn), p 133; Burns, *Conveyancing* (4th edn), p 3. There was earlier doubt on the point: *McLaren v Menzies* (1876) 3 R 1151, per Lord Curriehill, *obiter*, at 1173.

[261] Conveyancing (Scotland) Act 1924, s 18(2); *Hynd's Tr v Hynd's Trs* 1954 SC 112 at 121, 125 (affd 1955 SC (HL) 1).

[262] Conveyancing (Scotland) Act 1924, s 18(1); and see para 22.14.

[263] *Hynd's Tr v Hynd's Trs* 1955 SC (HL) 1.

[264] *Shiels v Shiels* (1951) 67 Sh Ct Rep 54; *cf Cameron v Holman* 1951 SLCR 14.

[265] See *Hynd's Tr v Hynd's Trs* 1955 SC (HL) 1. In *Watson v Beveridge* (1883) 11 R 40, where the section was not referred to, proof before answer was allowed of an averment that the deed had in fact been "read over" to the granter, although the words used in the docquet were merely that it had "been previously gone over and explained" to him. The majority did not commit themselves to a view as to whether the informality in the docquet was an insuperable flaw in the deed. Lord Rutherfurd Clark, in a strong dissenting opinion, thought that even if the notary had read every word of the deed to the granter, the correct wording of the docquet was a solemnity, the absence of which could not be cured by extraneous evidence.

CHAPTER 23

MATTERS REQUIRING WRITING FOR CONSTITUTION AND PROOF BEFORE 1 AUGUST 1995

23.1 MATTERS REQUIRING WRITING BEFORE 1 AUGUST 1995— GENERAL

Briefly put, the solemnities prescribed by the authentication statutes applied only **23.1.1** to obligations which required writing for their constitution (*obligationes literis*), and did not apply to obligations which required writing, not for their constitution, but only for their proof (*in modum probationis*).[1] For the latter, informal writings were held to be sufficient, and their speciality arose because they required to be proved by writ or oath or judicial admission. *Obligationes literis* included obligations relating to heritage, testamentary writings and contracts of service for more than a year. Contracts which the parties have committed to writing by choice and arbitral submissions and awards have been included although uncertainty attached to their status. Cautionary obligations, contracts of insurance and transfers of incorporeal rights in moveables are mentioned in the next chapter, together with writings *in re mercatoria*, which formed an exception to the rule requiring solemn or holograph writing for the constitution of *obligationes literis*.[2]

23.2 POINTS OF DISTINCTION BETWEEN *OBLIGATIONES LITERIS* AND OBLIGATIONS REQUIRING WRITING FOR THEIR PROOF

The main point of distinction, namely that the authentication statutes applied only **23.2.1**

---

[1] The proposition accepted by the majority in *Paterson v Paterson* (1897) 25 R 144.
[2] All such documents, together with *obligationes literis*, now have no special status: Requirements of Writing (Scotland) Act 1995, s 11(3).

to *obligationes literis,* was authoritatively settled by the Whole Court decision of *Paterson v Paterson.*[3] The constitution of *obligationes literis* could be established only by production of the obligatory or constitutive writing, which had to be solemnly executed[4] or holograph.[5] This was subject to the exceptions that writs *in re mercatoria,*[6] unless relating to heritage or contracts of service, could be informal, and that, when homologation or *rei interventus* followed upon oral agreements proved by writ or oath, or upon informal writings, these could be founded upon in a litigation.[7] Obligations requiring writing only for their proof, on the other hand, which had been constituted orally, might be proved by writings not obligatory in their terms, and not solemnly executed or holograph.[8] In proceedings for implement of a contract entered into before 1 August 1995 or for damages for its breach[9] the mere judicial admission[10] of an *obligatio literis* does not enable it to be founded upon in a litigation, since the admission does not take the place of the essential writing.[11] On the other hand, obligations which required writing only for their proof are held to be proved if they are judicially admitted, or proved by any other competent means.

23.3 CONTRACTS RELATING TO HERITAGE

23.3.1 Contracts relating to heritage were *obligationes literis,*[12] and could therefore be constituted only by writing which was either executed in accordance with the statutory solemnities,[13] or was holograph[14] of, or adopted[15] as holograph by, the party or parties.[16] Before such a contract entered into before 1 August 1995 can be founded upon in an action, whether for its implement or for damages for its

---

[3]   (1897) 25 R 144. This is referred to in para 22.1.
[4]   See para 22.8.
[5]   See paras 23.12–23.16.
[6]   See paras 24.1–24.2.
[7]   See para 26.1. Homologation and *rei interventus* were replaced with new provisions in the Requirements of Writing (Scotland) Act 1995, s 1(2)(a), (3)–(5).
[8]   For the requirements of proof by writ, see paras 25.4–25.6.
[9]   *Allan v Gilchrist* (1875) 2 R 587.
[10]   As to judicial admissions generally, see para 11.2.
[11]   *Jamieson v Edinburgh Mutual Investment Building Society* 1913 2 SLT 52. It may be described as an admission of a legal nonentity, or, alternatively, as an admission merely of an obligation from which the party has the right to withdraw: Gloag, *Contract* (2nd edn), p 162. For similar reasons a reference to oath of such a contract was incompetent: *Perdikou v Pattison* 1958 SLT 153 (lease), per Lord Justice-Clerk Thomson at 157, Lord Patrick at 158, Lord Mackintosh and Lord Blades at 159; *Dickson v Blair* (1871) 10 M 41; Stair, iv, 44, 5; Erskine, iii, 2, 2; iv, 2, 9.
[12]   See para 22.1.
[13]   See para 22.8.
[14]   See paras 23.12–23.18.
[15]   *Maitland's Trs v Maitland* (1871) 10 M 79, per Lord President Inglis at 88. A typewritten acceptance of an offer to purchase, enclosed with a holograph covering letter which made reference to it, was held sufficiently adopted as holograph for this purpose: *McGinn v Shearer* 1947 SC 334.
[16]   When the contract consists of an offer and acceptance, each, if not solemnly executed, must be signed by, and holograph of, or adopted as holograph by, its granter: Erskine, iii, 2, 2; More's Notes to Stair, lxv; Dickson, *Evidence* (3rd edn), para 549; *Goldston v Young* (1868) 7 M 188; *Scottish Lands and Building Co v Shaw* (1880) 7 R 756. If one of the writings is solemnly executed or holograph, but the other is not, neither party is bound: *Malcolm v Campbell* (1891) 19 R 278. A unilateral promise or letter of obligation, on the other hand, not requiring acceptance, is by itself valid and binding, if it is solemnly executed, holograph or adopted as holograph: Bell, *Principles,* para 889; Erskine, iii, 3, 88; Gloag, *Contract* (2nd edn), p 166; *Sichi v Biagi* 1946 SN 66.

breach,[17] a writing of the kind described above must be produced. A mere judicial admission that such a contract was agreed is useless, and a reference of it to oath always has been incompetent. The contracts entered into before 1 August 1995 to which the general rule applies include all forms of purchase or sale of heritable subjects,[18] and all contracts regarding subordinate rights in heritable property, such as heritable securities.[19] The general rule also applies to all leases, with the exception of leases for not more than a year which might be proved by parole evidence.[20] Positive servitudes may be proved to have been constituted by prescription,[21] implied grant or reservation[22] or acquiescence,[23] as well as by express grant, but negative servitudes require formal writing for constitution.[24] There are a number of cases in which oral evidence or informal writing was held to be admissible in a matter involving heritage, and the common feature in these exceptional cases appears to be that the contract related only incidentally, or to a minor extent, to heritage[25]: for example, a contract that neither party should buy certain heritage without allowing the other to join in the purchase[26] and a compromise of a litigation although its terms concerned heritable property.[27] The absence of formal writing in relation to heritage could be overcome when homologation or *rei interventus* had followed upon an oral agreement or upon an informal writing.[28]

23.4 CONTRACTS OF SERVICE

Contracts of service for not more than one year could be constituted orally, and **23.4.1** proved *prout de jure*.[29] Apart from these, such contracts were *obligationes literis* and could therefore be constituted only by writing which was either executed by both parties in accordance with the statutory solemnities,[30] or was holograph[31] of, or adopted as holograph by, both of them. The general rule did not apply to a

---

[17] See para 23.2.

[18] A sale by public roup being no exception: *Shiell v Guthrie's Trs* (1874) 1 R 1083.

[19] Gloag, *Contract* (2nd edn), p 163.

[20] Stair, ii, 9, 4; Erskine, iii, 2, 2.

[21] Stair, ii, 7, 2; Erskine, ii, 9, 3.

[22] *Ewart v Cochrane* (1861) 4 Macq 117; *Menzies v Marquis of Breadalbane* (1901) 4 F 59.

[23] *Macgregor v Balfour* (1899) 2 F 345, per Lord President Balfour at 351.

[24] Gloag, *Contract* (2nd edn), p 163; *Dundas v Blair* (1886) 13 R 759; *Inglis v Clark* (1901) 4 F 288; *Metcalfe v Purdon* (1902) 4 F 507. Cf *Heron v Gray* (1880) 8 R 155; Bell, *Principles* (10th edn), para 994, note (g).

[25] *Allan v Gilchrist* (1875) 2 R 587; *Gibson v Adams* (1875) 3 R 144; *Dickson v Blair* (1871) 10 M 41 at 45; *Walker v Flint* (1863) 1 M 417; *Stewart v Ferguson* (1841) 3 D 668, per Lord Ivory (Ordinary) at 674; *Bathie v Lord Wharncliffe* (1873) 11 M 490; *Kinninmont v Paxton* (1892) 20 R 128; *Moncrieff v Seivwright* (1896) 33 SLR 456; *Rigg v Mather* (1902) 10 SLT 426 (OH); *Hamilton v Lochrane* (1899) 1 F 478; *Woddrop v Speirs* (1906) SLR 22 (OH); *Mackay v Rodger* (1907) 15 SLT 42 (OH). See also *Bell v Bell* (1841) 3 D 1201; *Allan v Millar* 1932 SC 620; *William Masson Ltd v Scottish Brewers Ltd* 1966 SC 9; *Denvir v Denvir* 1969 SLT 301.

[26] *Mungall v Bowhill Coal Co* (1904) 12 SLT 80.

[27] *Anderson v Dick* (1901) 4 F 68; *Torbat v Torbat's Trs* (1906) 14 SLT 830 (OH) (the latter is questioned in *Cook v Grubb* 1963 SLT 78).

[28] See paras 26.3–26.6.

[29] Bell, *Principles*, para 173; Dickson, *Evidence* (3rd edn), para 567; Gloag, *Contract* (2nd edn), p 179; *Cook v Grubb* 1963 SLT 78 at 81, 84, 86, 88; *Murray v Roussel Laboratories Ltd* 1960 SLT (Notes) 31 (OH); *Nisbet v Percy* 1951 SC 350, per Lord President Cooper at 355; *Stewart v McCall* (1869) 7 M 544.

[30] See para 22.8.

[31] See paras 23.12–23.18.

contract of undefined duration to do a particular piece of work,[32] and was held not to apply to an engagement for five years at an annual salary and a commission on goods sold,[33] and, when services had in fact been rendered from year to year for a period of years, without remuneration having been received, proof *prout de jure* was allowed of the facts from which a right to remuneration may be inferred.[34] The absence of the requisite formal writing might be overcome when homologation or *rei interventus* had followed upon an oral agreement or upon an informal writing.[35] These evidential requirements were separate from any statutory obligation to provide written details of employment terms under employment legislation.

23.5 CONTRACTS WHICH PARTIES AGREED TO COMMIT TO WRITING—GENERAL

23.5.1 The parties to a contract might reduce it to formal writing by choice rather than requirement for one or other of two purposes.[36] They might intend the writing to constitute the agreement, so that, without the writing, there was no agreement, or at least there was *locus poenitentiae*. On the other hand, they might intend the writing to be merely a record or formal confirmation of a binding contract, which had already been constituted orally or by informal writing. It is only the first of these alternatives, it is thought, which gave rise to *obligationes literis*.[37] In *Paterson v Paterson*[38] there are dicta which might be read as suggesting that the category into which the contract is to be placed depends not upon the intention of the parties but upon the terms of the writing. The distinction is made between writings which contain express words of obligation and those which merely record facts from which obligations may be inferred, and there are suggestions that the former relate to *obligationes literis*,[39] while the latter do not.[40] "Obligatory writing" is spoken of as providing the test.[41] It is thought that this distinction was intended to relate rather to the authentication of the writing, and the use which was made of it, than to the nature of the obligations themselves. Thus a party to an

---

[32] In *Dumbarton Glass Co v Coatsworth* (1847) 9 D 732 at 736, Lord Jeffrey speaks of the possibility of the contract being admitted and of its being provable *scripto* which implied that a reference to oath might have been competent. However, this was before the decision of *Paterson v Paterson*. See para 23.1; Gloag, *Contract* (2nd edn), p 180.

[33] *Pickin v Hawkes* (1878) 5 R 676. See the comments in Gloag, *Contract* (2nd edn), p 180, on this not very illuminating case.

[34] *Thomson v Thomson's Tr* (1889) 16 R 333; *Anderson v Halley* (1847) 9 D 1222; *Smellie v Gillespie* (1833) 12 S 125. See also *Davies v City of Glasgow Friendly Society* 1935 SC 224.

[35] See paras 26.3–26.8 for the general principles. For the decisions on the application of *rei interventus* to contracts of service, see Gloag, *Contract* (2nd edn), p 179. See also *Cook v Grubb* 1963 SLT 78.

[36] See *Van Laun & Co v Neilson Reid & Co* (1904) 6 F 644, per Lord Kinnear at 652; *Rederi Aktiebolaget Nordstjernan v Salvesen & Co* (1903) 6 F 64, per Lord Moncrieff at 75 (revd on another point (1905) 7 F (HL) 101); *Paterson v Paterson* (1897) 25 R 144, per Lord Kyllachy at 174.

[37] See para 23.1.

[38] (1897) 25 R 144.

[39] (1897) 25 R 144, per Lord Kyllachy at 172, 173, 177.

[40] "The distinction . . . depends . . . on the character of the writing": (1897) 25 R 144, per Lord Kyllachy at 174. See also the approval by Lord Trayner (at 163), Lord Kyllachy (at 173), Lord Kincairney (at 181), of Lord Benholme's dictum in *Thoms v Thoms* (1867) 6 M 174 at 176: "The scope of the statutes is confined to those writings by which a person becomes directly bound, and which form the substantive *vincula* upon which action may be raised." Lord Kincairney (at 181) remarks upon the shadowy and technical nature of the distinction.

[41] (1897) 25 R 144, per Lord Pearson at 183.

obligatory writing might found upon it as the sole basis of his action[42] only if it was solemnly executed or holograph or one of the exceptions applied, even if he might alternatively have sued upon an antecedent binding oral agreement, in support of which the writing, whether properly authenticated or not, might have been used as evidence. But whether or not the obligations of the parties are to be regarded as having been *obligationes literis* must depend, it is thought, upon proof of their agreement, and not solely upon the terms of the writing,[43] for which extrinsic evidence would have to be admitted. Only if this is the test can it be truly said that "by ... agreement of the parties obligations or rights require writing for their constitution",[44] or that "the parties have mutually selected the writing as the proof and measure of their contract, its existence and terms".[45]

23.6 CONTRACTS—*OBLIGATIONES LITERIS*

When the parties to a contract made prior to 1 August 1995, which might then have been constituted orally, agreed expressly or by implication that they would not be bound until a written contract had been executed, the resulting obligations are to be regarded as *obligationes literis*,[46] with all the consequences flowing therefrom.[47] The authentication statutes applied to the writing unless it was holograph,[48] the contract can be founded upon in a litigation only if the writing is produced, and a judicial admission cannot take the place of its production.[49] It would appear that a contract of this kind could be constituted in an informal writing if it was *in re mercatoria*.[50] No question of using the writing as evidence of an earlier oral bargain can arise because, *ex hypothesi*, no bargain ever existed.

23.6.1

---

[42] It ought to be made clear in the condescendence whether or not the document is being founded upon as the substantive cause of action.. The distinction between the alternative methods of stating the pursuer's claim is mentioned by Lord President Dunedin in *Hope v Derwent Rolling Mills Co Ltd* (1905) 7 F 837 at 844.

[43] In *Van Laun & Co v Neilson, Reid & Co* (1904) 6 F 644 at 652, Lord Kinnear said that when parties agree that their arrangements are to be embodied in a formal written contract, there is *locus poenitentiae* until the written contract is executed. This statement of the law has been criticised as too wide: Gloag, *Contract* (2nd edn), p 43. It is thought to be valid only if the whole circumstances warrant an inference that the parties so intended.

[44] *Paterson v Paterson* (1897) 25 R 144, per Lord Moncreiff at 168.

[45] Dickson, *Evidence* (3rd edn), para 206. On extrinsic evidence see Chapter 27.

[46] See para 23.1.

[47] See para 23.2.

[48] In *Hutchinson v Ferrier* (1851) 13 D 837; (1852) 1 Macq 196, which is difficult to understand, a lease from year to year, which could have been constituted orally, was confirmed annually by missive letters, which were presumably holograph. In the Court of Session it was held that the letters were rightly rejected, when tendered in evidence, because they were unstamped. The opinion was also expressed that the lease could be proved in no other way, presumably on the footing that the contract was of the kind to which this paragraph refers. It seems likely, however, that Lord Fullerton's dissenting opinion states the true position.

[49] As with other *obligationes literis* if homologation or *rei interventus* follows upon an oral or informal written agreement, that agreement might be proved by writ: see *Clark v Clark's Trs* (1860) 23 D 74—where *rei interventus* had followed upon a written contract of co-partnery which was defective in form, it was held that the partnership could be established only by production of the writing. It is thought that, had the other party to the contract not been dead, reference to his oath would have been a permissible alternative. As to homologation and *rei interventus* generally, see paras 26.3–26.8.

[50] See, for example, *Buttery & Co v Inglis* (1877) 5 R 58; (1878) 5 R (HL) 87. The deed embodying the contract was informally executed, but was agreed to be *in re mercatoria*. See (1877) 5 R (HL) at 87 (note). It was held by the House of Lords that only the written contract could be looked at.

23.7 CONTRACTS WHICH ARE NOT *OBLIGATIONES LITERIS*

23.7.1 When an agreement had been constituted orally or by informal writings, and the parties decided to execute a formal written contract which they intended to be merely a record or formal confirmation of the earlier binding agreement, the resulting obligations were *not* to be regarded as *obligationes literis*, with the consequences previously mentioned.[51] They might be proved *prout de jure* unless they were obligations then provable only by writing.[52] In neither case was production of a formal written contract essential. These considerations ceased to be of practical importance if both parties to such an agreement in fact executed a formal and effective written contract with the intention that it should take the place of the earlier agreement. In that event, the formal contract became the measure of the rights and obligations of the parties, and was presumed to contain all the express terms of the contract, unless the contrary could be proved.[53] Before such a formal contract might be founded upon by either party in a litigation as a liquid document of debt or as the sole foundation of the case,[54] it must have been solemnly executed or holograph, unless it was *in re mercatoria*.[55]

23.8 ASCERTAINMENT OF INTENTION OF PARTIES

23.8.1 When an oral or informal agreement had been negotiated, which the parties agreed would be embodied in a formal written contract, the question as to whether *locus poenitentiae* existed until the formal writing was executed, in which case their obligations were *obligationes literis*, or whether, on the other hand, the obligations, orally or informally constituted, were instantly binding, and were not *obligationes literis*,[56] had to be answered in the light of the whole circumstances in each case.[57]

> "It is perfectly possible for the parties to an apparent contract to provide that there shall be *locus poenitentiae*, until the terms of their agreement have been reduced to a formal contract; but the bare fact that the parties to a completed agreement stipulate that it shall be embodied in a formal contract does not necessarily import that they are still in the stage of negotiation. In each instance it is a matter of the construction of the correspondence in the light of the facts, proved or averred, on which side of the border line the case lies."[58]

Locus poenitentiae was held to exist, and the contract was therefore *obligatio literis*, in the following circumstances. The defenders agreed, "subject to contract,"

---

[51] See para 23.6.
[52] For the matters which might be proved only by writ, see Chapter 25.
[53] See paras 27.7, 27.9.
[54] See n 42 above.
[55] *Thoms v Thoms* (1867) 6 M 174, per Lord Benholme at 176; *Paterson v Paterson* (1897) 25 R 144, per Lord Trayner at 163, Lord Kyllachy at 173, Lord Kincairney at 181.
[56] See paras 23.6–23.7. See also para 23.2.
[57] *Stobo Ltd v Morrisons (Gowns) Ltd* 1949 SC 184; *Rederi Aktiebolaget Nordstjernan v Salvesen & Co* (1903) 6 F 64, per Lord Moncreiff at 75 (revd on another point (1905) 7 F (HL) 101); Bell, *Principles*, para 25. For a comment on Lord Kinnear's statement in *Van Laun & Co v Neilson Reid & Co* (1904) 6 F 644 at 652, see para 23.5.
[58] *Stobo Ltd v Morrisons (Gowns) Ltd* 1949 SC 184, per Lord President Cooper at 192.

that if they bought two shops from the owners, they would sell one of them to the pursuers. The decision was based *inter alia* upon the unlikelihood that the parties intended to be conclusively bound before the conditions of purchase from the original proprietors, particularly with regard to servitudes and rights in common with neighbouring properties, were adjusted.[59] The pursuers sued for commission said to be due under an oral contract, in which was incorporated an unsigned memorandum setting forth its terms, the opening words of which were: "The undersigned firms agree that they will enter into a proper legal contract, when prepared, with [the pursuers]." The decision in this instance turned mainly upon a construction of the words quoted.[60] *Locus poenitentiae* was held *not* to exist, and the contract was therefore *not obligatio literis*, in the following circumstances. The pursuer made to the defenders, who were Police Commissioners, an offer to compromise a claim, one of the conditions being "that a formal deed of agreement embodying the stipulations ... above written and other necessary formal clauses shall be prepared by the Commissioners' agent and revised by the agent of [the pursuer], and shall be executed by the Commissioners and [the pursuer] within fourteen days." The Commissioners accepted the offer, with one alteration, which, in turn, was accepted by the pursuer. It was held that the purpose of the proposed deed was merely to put the concluded agreement into formal terms.[61] A similar decision, it is thought, would follow if, in an oral or informal contract for the transfer of shares in a company or in a ship, where statute requires that the transfer itself must be in formal writing,[62] there were included the words "subject to transfer (or bill of sale) drawn out in due form".[63] The inclusion of these words in the acceptance of an offer cannot infer *locus poenitentiae* until the transfers or bills of sale are executed, "merely because the acceptor puts into words what the law would imply as the method in which an agreement, *ex hypothesi* complete, would be carried into legal effect."[64]

23.9 UNILATERAL WRITTEN OBLIGATIONS

It is thought that a unilateral obligation, which, prior to 1 August 1995, might be constituted orally, became an *obligatio literis* only in the comparatively rare event of its being constituted for the first time in a personal bond or similar obligatory document. If, for example, without prior communings between them, one person executed, and sent to another person, a bond in which he obliged himself to pay money or to perform some act in the future, the obligation thereby undertaken was an *obligatio literis*, with all the consequences flowing therefrom.[65] The authentication statutes applied to the bond unless it was holograph or *in re mercatoria*,[66] and the obligation might be founded upon in a litigation only if the bond was produced, judicial admission or restricted mode of proof being incompetent. **23.9.1**

[59] *Stobo Ltd v Morrisons (Gowns) Ltd* 1949 SC 184.
[60] *Van Laun & Co v Neilson Reid & Co* (1904) 6 F 644.
[61] *Smeaton v St Andrews Police Commissioners* (1871) 9 M (HL) 24.
[62] See para 24.11.
[63] This is on the analogy of *Erskine v Glendinning* (1871) 9 M 656, per Lord President Inglis at 659. That case is itself not in point as an example, since it related to a lease of heritage, and was therefore necessarily concerned with *obligationes literis*.
[64] *Stobo Ltd v Morrisons (Gowns) Ltd* 1949 SC 184, per Lord President Cooper at 191–192.
[65] See para 22.4.
[66] As an example of such a bond which was held to be *in re mercatoria*, see *Beardmore & Co v Barry* 1928 SC 101; 1928 SC (HL) 47.

However, if the bond was defective in form, it might probably, as with other *obligationes literis*, be founded upon by the creditor if it was followed by homologation or *rei interventus*.[67] However, most bonds were granted as liquid documents of debt in order to facilitate the recovery or enforcement of obligations already incurred. In these circumstances the mere granting of a bond by the debtor could not convert the existing obligation into an *obligatio literis*, and thereby compel the creditor to found upon the bond as the only method of constituting his right.[68] If a debtor under a joint and several obligation paid the whole debt, or a cautioner paid the principal debtor's debt, whereby the law implies an immediate right of relief,[69] if the bond had been solemnly executed or holograph,[70] the creditor might found upon it as a liquid document of debt.[71] But the granting of an obligatory document did not necessarily extinguish the original obligation,[72] and if the obligatory document was defective, or for some reason the creditor chose not to found upon it, the antecedent obligation might be proved by competent evidence.[73] Although there have been judicial doubts on the point,[74] there seems to be no reason why the bond, whether defective in form or not, should not be used as part of that evidence, if it contains admissions of the antecedent obligation.[75] However, when a bond is accepted by the creditor as taking the place of the original obligation, or is founded upon by the creditor in a litigation as a liquid document of debt, it then becomes the measure of the rights and obligations of the parties, and is presumed to contain the express terms of the contract, the onus being on the challenger to prove the contrary by reference to the earlier transaction.[76]

23.10 ARBITRATION

23.10.1 Submission to arbitration, including remit to a man of skill,[77] while generally in

---

[67] As to homologation and *rei interventus* generally, see paras 26.3–26.6.

[68] When A granted a bond in respect of a loan from B (which was provable only by writ), it could not be the presumed intention of the parties that if B lost the bond, or it was in some way defective in form, A need not repay the money.

[69] Stair, i, 8, 9; Erskine, iii, 3, 74.

[70] *Thoms v Thoms* (1867) 6 M 174, per Lord Benholme at 176; *Paterson v Paterson* (1897) 25 R 144, per Lord Trayner at 163, Lord Kyllachy at 173, Lord Kincairney at 181.

[71] As to the distinction between the alternative methods of stating the pursuer's claim, see para 23.5. See also Lord Pearson's reference in *Paterson v Paterson* (1897) 25 R 144 at 183–184 to the way in which a bond, although unnecessary for the constitution of loan, might be used to found an action for its repayment.

[72] *Thom v North British Banking Co* (1850) 13 D 134, per Lord Fullerton at 143; Gloag, *Contract* (2nd edn), p 187.

[73] *Hope v Derwent Rolling Mills Co Ltd* (1905) 7 F 837; *Duncan's Trs v Shand* (1872) 10 M 984.

[74] *Paterson v Paterson* (1897) 25 R 144, per Lord Kyllachy at 174, Lord Kincairney at 181, Lord Pearson at 187.

[75] *Paterson v Paterson* (1897) 25 R 144, per Lord Kyllachy at 177–178. This view avoids the anomaly, inherent in the contrary view, that if a debtor signs a typed note "I have received on loan from John Smith £100", the creditor can use the note as proof by writ, but if the further words "and I promise to repay it" are included, he cannot. The anomaly is mentioned by Lord Young in *Paterson v Paterson* at 151.

[76] The Scottish Law Commission in their *Report on Requirements of Writing* (Scot Law Com No 112) found this a difficult topic to plan for in revision of the law (see paras 4.36–4.38) and came down in favour of making no express provision, so that writing is not required and such a document would be of strong evidential value only. See also Chapter 27 re extrinsic evidence.

[77] *McLaren v Aikman* 1939 SC 222, per Lord Justice-Clerk Aitchison at 228, Lord Wark at 229; *Stewart v Williamson* 1909 SC 1254, per Lord President Dunedin at 1258, Lord Kinnear at 1258; 1910 SC (HL) 47.

writing, did not require formal writing, except submissions concerning heritage which, with some exceptions, were clearly *obligationes literis*.[78] The contract of submission in an arbitration relating to heritage had to be constituted by writing which was executed by the parties in accordance with the statutory solemnities, or was holograph of or adopted as holograph by them.[79] It followed from this that the decree-arbitral had to be contained in a similar writing. It also followed that the production of such writing was the only means by which a submission or decree-arbitral might be founded upon in a litigation. In arbitrations regarding agricultural leases,[80] whether they related to heritage such as buildings and fences,[81] or to the valuation of moveables such as crops, manure, and implements,[82] the submission and the decree-arbitral, though they had to be in writing and signed by the granters, did not require to be solemnly executed or holograph.[83] The same rule applied to a submission and a decree-arbitral *in re mercatoria*, which could be contained in informal documents.[84] Any submission which did not fall into one or other of these categories possibly required solemnly executed or holograph writing for its constitution,[85] unless the sum involved was less than £100 Scots (£8.33),[86] but submissions which were in fact reduced by the parties to writing usually had to be regarded as *obligationes literis* for all purposes. If the genuineness of the documents was disputed, it might be proved *prout de jure*.[87] When the submission in any arbitration was solemnly executed by, or was holograph of, the parties, then, unless it related to an agricultural lease or a mercantile transaction, the decree-arbitral, in order to be binding, had to be in writing similarly authenticated, and such writing was the only evidence by which it might be proved.[88] In any case in

---

[78] It was thought that submissions regarding moveables, to which one or other of the numerous exceptions did not apply, were to be similarly regarded, but the many conflicting decisions as to what is required to constitute or prove submissions and decrees-arbitral (awards) make it difficult to deduce general principles: see Bell, *Arbitration* (2nd edn), paras 61, 62, 67, 81, 86–88, 91, 93, 94; Dickson, *Evidence* (3rd edn), paras 553, 562, 789, 792; Irons and Melville, *Arbitration*, pp 51, 52; Guild, *Arbitration*, pp 18–22, 77, 82. For more recent coverage, see *Stair Memorial Encyclopaedia* Reissue, *Arbitration*.

[79] Bell, *Arbitration* (2nd edn), paras 93, 94; Dickson, *Evidence* (3rd edn), para 553; *Robertson v Boyd and Winans* (1885) 12 R 419, per Lord Rutherfurd Clark at 427; *McLaren v Aikman* 1939 SC 222. As to contracts relating to heritage generally, see para 23.3.

[80] And remit to a man of skill about an agricultural lease: *Cameron v Nicol* 1930 SC 1, per Lord Sands at 15; *Davidson v Logan* 1908 SC 350, per Lord Low at 366–367; *Nivison v Howat* (1883) 11 R 182.

[81] *McGregor v Stevenson* (1847) 9 D 1056.

[82] *Cameron v Nicol* 1930 SC 1, Lord Sands at 15 (award not tested); *Gibson v Fotheringham* 1914 SC 987, per Lord Hunter (Ordinary) at 993–994, Lord Justice-Clerk Macdonald at 996; *Davidson v Logan* 1908 SC 350, per Lord Low at 366–367, Lord Stormonth-Darling at 368; *Nivison v Howat* (1883) 11 R 182, per Lord Craighill at 191 (both submission and award informal).

[83] *McLaren v Aikman* 1939 SC 222, per Lord Justice-Clerk Aitchison at 227–228, Lord Wark at 229–230, Lord Carmont at 231.

[84] *McLaren v Aikman* 1939 SC 222, per Lord Justice-Clerk Aitchison at 227–228; *Dykes v Roy* (1869) 7 M 357, per Lord Neaves at 360; *Hope v Crookston Bros* (1890) 17 R 868. As to writings *in re mercatoria* generally, see paras 24.1 *et seq.*

[85] Bell, *Arbitration* (2nd edn), paras 61, 62 and 67; Guild, *Arbitration*, p 20; Gloag, *Contract* (2nd edn), p 185; Erskine, iii, 2, 6; *Paterson v Paterson* (1897) 25 R 144, per Lord Pearson at 183. See also *Fraser v Williamson* (1773) M 8476; *Ferrie v Mitchell* (1824) 3 S 75. However, cf Bell, *Arbitration* (2nd edn), paras 93 and 94; Guild, *Arbitration*, p 21.

[86] *A v B* (1746) M 8475; Bell, *Arbitration* (2nd edn), paras 81–88, 91; Guild, *Arbitration*, pp 19, 21. *Cf* Dickson, *Evidence* (3rd edn), para 562.

[87] Dickson, *Evidence* (3rd edn), para 793.

[88] *McLaren v Aikman* 1939 SC 222, per Lord Justice-Clerk Aitchison at 227, Lord Wark at 229; *Dykes v Roy* (1869) 7 M 357, per Lord Neaves at 360; *Lang v Brown* (1852) 15 D 38, per Lord Fullerton at 44; affd (1855) 2 Macq 93; *Earl of Hopetoun v Scots Mines Co* (1856) 18 D 739, per Lord Curriehill at 748, Lord Benholme at 757.

which the submission and decree arbitral required to be solemnly executed or holograph, informal documents would bind the parties if they had been followed by *rei interventus*,[89] homologation[90] or adoption.[91] In such a case the acts constituting *rei interventus,* homologation or adoption could be proved by parole evidence, but the terms of the submission had to be proved by writ.[92] An opinion of counsel on a joint memorial, which stated that the parties had agreed to be bound by the opinion, was as binding as a decree-arbitral, and it was sufficient both for constitution and for proof of the submission and the award that the memorial and the opinion were signed without witnesses in accordance with normal practice.[93] A judicial reference, which was signed without witnesses by the parties or their counsel or solicitors,[94] became irrevocable when the court had interposed authority to it,[95] and the referee's report or award following thereon, which might also be signed by him without witnesses,[96] was sufficient foundation, if not challenged on some matter of substance, for the pronouncement of a decree in conformity therewith.[97]

23.11 TESTAMENTARY SETTLEMENTS

23.11.1 With one unimportant exception, rights and obligations arising under testamentary settlements made in Scotland had to be constituted in writings which were either executed in accordance with the statutory solemnities,[98] or holograph of[99] or adopted as holograph and subscribed[100] by, the testator.[101] If holograph or adopted as holograph the will is not probative of the testator's signature and, before granting confirmation on the testator's estate, the court requires affidavit evidence to the effect that the writing and signature are that of the testator.[102] The exception was a

---

[89] Bell, *Arbitration* (2nd edn), para 62; *Otto v Weir* (1871) 9 M 660, per Lord Justice-Clerk Moncrieff at 661 (heritage).

[90] Bell, *Arbitration* (2nd edn), para 62; *Robertson v Boyd and Winans* (1885) 12 R 419 (heritage); *Dykes v Roy* (1869) 7 M 357 at 359, 360 (moveables). In connection with a disputed claim to pasturage, two of the three parties signed a submission to a named arbiter, who issued a decree-arbitral. One of the signatories claimed the right to resile because the third party had not signed the submission. It was held that, although the submission was invalid, all were bound by it because it had been homologated by the third party in respect of his appearing and leading evidence before the arbiter: *Brown v Gardner* (1739) M 5659, 8474.

[91] *Dykes v Roy* (1869) 7 M 357 at 359, 360. For *rei interventus*, homologation and adoption generally, see paras 26.3–26.6.

[92] *Procurator Fiscal of Roxburgh v Ker* (1672) M 12410; Dickson, *Evidence* (3rd edn), para 832.

[93] Bell, *Arbitration* (2nd edn), para 69; Dickson, *Evidence* (3rd edn), para 792; *Dykes v Roy* (1869) 7 M 357, per Lord Cowan at 360; *Fraser v Lord Lovat* (1850) 7 Bell's App 171.

[94] Bell, *Arbitration* (2nd edn), para 513.

[95] Bell, *Arbitration* (2nd edn), para 519; Dickson, *Evidence* (3rd edn), para 563; *Reid v Henderson* (1841) 3 D 1102; *Walker & Co v Stewart* (1855) 2 Macq 424.

[96] Bell, *Arbitration* (2nd edn), paras 533, 535; Dickson, *Evidence* (3rd edn), para 792.

[97] Bell, *Arbitration* (2nd edn), paras 533, 535; Dickson, *Evidence* (3rd edn), para 792.

[98] paras 22.8, 23.11.

[99] paras 23.12–23.18.

[100] *Robbie v Carr* 1959 SLT (Notes) 16; *McLay v Farrell* 1950 SC 149; *Stenhouse v Stenhouse* 1922 SC 370; *Taylor's Exx v Thom* 1914 SC 79; *Foley v Costello* (1904) 6 F 365; *Goldie v Shedden* (1885) 13 R 138; *Skinner v Forbes* (1883) 11 R 88; *Dunlop v Dunlop* (1839) 1 D 912. Cf *Fraser's Exrx v Fraser's CB* 1931 SC 536.

[101] McLaren, *Wills and Succession* (3rd edn), I, 273 *et seq.* Any writing on which confirmation of executors was issued prior to 1 July 1938 is deemed to be probative: Conveyancing Amendment (Scotland) Act 1938, s 11.

[102] Succession (Scotland) Act 1964, s 21.

bequest of moveables of a value not exceeding £8.33 which might be nuncupative (expressed orally), and proved by parole evidence.[103] If a bequest of more than that sum was made orally it was valid only to the extent of £8.33, but a person might make a number of such bequests, each of which would be valid to the extent of £8.33.[104] An oral direction to a residuary or universal legatee to pay a legacy of any amount was effective as a trust, and might be proved as such,[105] but this did not apply to a direction given to an executor-nominate or testamentary trustee who had no beneficial interest in the estate.[106] It is doubtful whether the relaxation in formality of execution allowed by Roman law for a soldier's will (*testamentum militare*), which has been incorporated by statute[107] into English law, has ever formed part of the law of Scotland.[108] The rules regarding a testamentary settlement made outside Scotland are outwith the scope of this text.

23.12 UNTESTED HOLOGRAPH WRITING

Until 1 August 1995 a valid holograph writing, or a writing adopted by the granter **23.12.1** as holograph, although not executed in accordance with the statutory solemnities,[109] was the equivalent of a writing so executed. Since 1 August 1995 no privilege has attached to holograph writings made after 31 July 1995.[110] The reason for this relaxation of the rules for the authentication of solemnly executed documents was that the forgery of the whole of a handwritten deed was thought to be more difficult, and less likely to be attempted, than the forgery of a mere signature.[111] Unlike a solemnly executed writing, an untested holograph writing made prior to 1 August 1995 is not probative.[112] Unless its genuineness is admitted, it must be proved to be holograph before it can be founded upon.[113]

23.13 CHARACTERISTICS AND PROOF OF HOLOGRAPH WRITING

Deeds holograph of the granter

In order to be the equivalent of a solemnly executed writing an untested holograph **23.13.1** writing must be proved by the person founding upon it to be wholly, or in the

---

[103] Stair, iii, 8, 36; Erskine, iii, 9, 7; Bell, *Principles*, para 1869; McLaren, *Wills and Succession* (3rd edn), I, 573; *Kelly v Kelly* (1861) 23 D 703.

[104] Bell, *Principles*, para 1874; McLaren, *Wills and Succession* (3rd edn), I, 573.

[105] Erskine, iii, 9, 7; Bell, *Principles*, para 1869; McLaren, *Wills and Succession* (3rd edn), I, 573.

[106] Bell, *Principles*, para 1869; McLaren, *Wills and Succession* (3rd edn), I, 573; *Forsyth's Trs v McLean* (1854) 16 D 343. Such a direction might, of course, be proved to be effective as a nuncupative legacy to the extent of £8.33.

[107] Wills Act 1837, s 11; Wills (Soldiers and Sailors) Act 1918.

[108] *Stuart v Stuart* 1942 SC 510.

[109] As to the nature of the solemnities, see paras 22.8 *et seq.*

[110] Requirements of Writing (Scotland) Act 1995, s 11(3).

[111] Stair, iv, 42, 6; Erskine, iii, 2, 22; Montgomerie Bell, *Lectures* (3rd edn), I, 78; Bell, *Dictionary* (7th edn), 509; *Callander v Callander's Trs* (1863) 2 M 291, per Lord Cowan at 301.

[112] For the meaning of "probative", see para 22.10. A holograph writing was sometimes so described: *Cranston* (1890) 17 R 410, per Lord McLaren at 415.

[113] *Harper v Green* 1938 SC 198; *Cranston* (1890) 17 R 410; *Anderson v Gill* (1858) 20 D 1326; (1858) 20 D (HL) 7; (1858) 3 Macq 180. *Cf Maitland's Trs v Maitland* (1871) 10 M 79.

essential parts,[114] written by the granter and subscribed by him.[115] A writing which complies with the rule does not cease to be valid merely because it is written in pencil,[116] or partly in pencil and partly in ink,[117] unless the pencil writing consists only of unauthenticated alterations to a document written originally in ink, which, if construed as merely deliberative, are ignored.[118] A writing which purports to be solemnly executed, but is defective in some of the solemnities, will nevertheless be sustained as a valid holograph writing if it complies with the rule mentioned above.[119] And an otherwise valid holograph writing was held not to be invalid merely because it concluded with the words "before these witnesses", and was not in fact attested.[120] A document written by a partner, and signed by him with the firm name, bound the firm,[121] and a document holograph of, and signed by, a duly authorised agent on behalf of his principal, bound the principal.[122]

23.13.2   Except in the case of testamentary writings,[123] and of a holograph acceptance of intimation of an assignation,[124] untested holograph writings, although proved to be genuine, are not probative of the dates they bear.[125] When the date is of importance, it must be proved to be the true date by the party founding upon the writing.[126] However, the right of challenging the date is open only to third parties, since the granter and grantee are personally barred from challenging it on that ground.[127]

---

[114] A testamentary writing, subscribed by the testator, of which only the introductory words "To my Executors," were holograph, was held not to be holograph in the essentials.

[115] Bell, *Principles*, para 20; approved in *Tucker v Canch's Tr* 1953 SC 270 at 274, 276; *Bridgeford's Exr v Bridgeford* 1948 SC 416 at 419–420; *Macdonald v Cuthbertson* (1890) 18 R 101 at 106. As to what constitutes an adequate subscription, see para 23.17. For the statutory provisions regarding proof of holograph testamentary writings, see para 23.16 below. In *McBeath's Trs v McBeath* 1935 SC 471 a will which was wholly in typewriting except for the testator's signature, and which was untested, was held to be valid as a holograph will in the following circumstances: (1) the will was admittedly type-written by the testator himself and subscribed in his handwriting; (2) it contained a statement, also in typewriting, that it was typed by the testator and accepted as holograph by him; (3) it was admitted that owing to physical infirmity the testator's handwriting had become indecipherable, and that he invari-ably used a typewriter for all communications. The decision to uphold the validity of the deed was by a majority of Seven Judges, the dissenting minority consisting of the Lord President (Clyde), the Lord Justice-Clerk (Aitchison) and Lord Murray, and Lord Morison, in an addendum to his opinion, appeared to concede that, apart from the very special circumstances of the particular case, the minority view was correct. This decision has since been held to rule only in cases where the essential facts are identical. In *Chisholm v Chisholm* 1949 SC 434 (OH), the averment that the will was valid as a holo-graph document because it had been typed by the testator was held to be irrelevant, and the action, in so far as founded on this averment, was dismissed.

[116] *Muir's Trs* (1869) 8 M 53; *Tait's Trs v Chiene* 1911 SC 743.

[117] *Manson v Edinburgh Royal Institution for the Education of Deaf and Dumb Children* 1948 SLT 196 (OH).

[118] See para 23.18.

[119] *Yeats v Yeats' Trs* (1833) 11 S 915; *Lorimer's Exrs v Hird* 1959 SLT (Notes) 8 (OH).

[120] *Gunnell's Trs' v Jones* 1915 1 SLT 166 (OH).

[121] *Nisbet v Neil's Tr* (1869) 7 M 1097; *Buchanan v Dennistoun* (1835) 13 S 841. In *Littlejohn v MacKay* 1974 SLT (Sh Ct) 82 it was said that an employee could not bind the firm in this way, but see the following footnote, and (1991) 36 JLSS 73.

[122] *Whyte v Lee* (1879) 6 R 699 at 704, 705. *Cf Scottish Lands and Buildings Co Ltd v Shaw* (1880) 7 R 756 (offer to purchase heritage, purporting to be written and signed by offerer, but in fact written and signed by his brother with his authority, held not binding).

[123] See para 23.16 below.

[124] Bell, *Principles*, para 1465; Dickson, *Evidence* (3rd edn), para 775.

[125] Erskine, iii, 2, 22; Dickson, *Evidence* (3rd edn), para 770.

[126] *Dyce v Paterson* (1847) 9 D 1141 (sequestration); *Waddell v Waddell's Trs* (1845) 7 D 605 (insan-ity). The date appearing in the writing is not to be disregarded. It is an item of evidence to be considered in relation to the whole circumstances: Dickson, *Evidence* (3rd edn), para 772.

[127] Dickson, *Evidence* (3rd edn), para 774.

23.14 DEEDS PARTLY PRINTED AND PARTLY HOLOGRAPH[128]

The general rule is that a deed drawn prior to 1 August 1995 may be valid as a **23.14.1**
holograph writing if *in the essential parts* it is written by the granter.[129] In order
that a testamentary deed may be valid as a holograph writing all the essential parts
must be in the testator's writing.[130] The printed parts must be purely formal or
superfluous so that, if they are struck out or disregarded, there still remains a complete expression of the writer's intention.[131] But the printed parts must not be
entirely disregarded. However clear the expression of intention in the written parts
may seem to be, no effect can be given to them if any of the printed parts add to,
detract from or qualify what is expressed by the written words.[132] It would seem
that once it is held that a writing is essentially holograph because it complies with
these principles, effect may properly be given to the whole document, printed and
written.[133]

The principles are easy to state, but their application is frequently difficult. The **23.14.2**
question of whether a particular deed is essentially holograph is said to be one of
fact,[134] which must be decided in the first place by construing the holograph parts
of the deed.[135] Deeds were held to be holograph when the portions in the testator's
writing consisted of the following: (i) "[testator's name and address]"—"to my sis-
ters [A and B] £40 each: to Mr. and Mrs. [C] £10 each"—"Residue divided into 4
equal parts to [D, E, G, F]" "Reverend [H]"—"[the date]"—"[testator's signa-
ture]"[136]; (ii) "[testator's name and address and the date]"—"[a name and
address]"—"[a name and address]"—"house at 19 Upper Grove Place,"
"Furniture, bed and table linen in fact everything in the house, also my insurances,
and pay all my debts at my death, all other money left by me to be divided among
the family." "[testator's signature], 19 Upper Grove Place, Edinburgh"[137]; (iii)
"[testator's name and address and the date]"—"[two names and addresses]"—
"Jane Carmichael (nee Clark), as long as she remains a faithful and dutiful wife,
all my houses, lands, all money that is or may be mine [and an enumeration of
household goods]. I desire at the decease of my wife and myself that the whole of
the estate be divided as follows: [exact instructions for the division of the capital
of the estate, appointment of executors, and testator's signature]".[138] Deeds were

---

[128] All the reported decisions on deeds of this kind relate to the difficulties which have arisen when a
testator completes the blanks in a printed form of will, in ignorance of the fact that, unless the deed is
solemnly executed, there is a grave risk that it will be invalid. What is said here, therefore, refers in
terms only to testamentary writings, but there seems no reason why the principles underlying the
decisions should not apply to other untested deeds which are partly holograph and partly printed. They
apply also to a deed which is partly holograph and partly typewritten or written by the hand of another
person: *Macdonald v Cuthbertson* (1890) 18 R 101 at 109.

[129] See para 23.13 above.

[130] *Gillies v Glasgow Royal Infirmary* 1960 SC 439, per Lord President Clyde at 442.

[131] *Macdonald v Cuthbertson* (1890) 18 R 101, per Lord Kinnear at 108; approved in *Bridgeford's Exr
v Bridgeford* 1948 SC 416 at 420, 437; *Tucker v Canch's Tr* 1953 SC 270 at 274, 277.

[132] *Bridgeford's Exr v Bridgeford* 1948 SC 416 at 420, 421, 438.

[133] *Tucker v Canch's Tr* 1953 SC 270 at 278; *Bridgeford's Exr v Bridgeford* 1948 SC 416 at 438.

[134] *Macdonald v Cuthbertson* (1890) 18 R 101, per Lord Kinnear at 108; approved in *Bridgeford's Exr
v Bridgeford* 1948 SC 416 at 420, 437; *Tucker v Canch's Tr* 1953 SC 270 at 274, 277.

[135] For a discussion of what may, and what may not, be read into incompleted sentences in the testator's handwriting, see *Cameron's Trs v Mackenzie* 1915 SC 313, per Lord President Strathclyde at
318–319; *Gillies v Glasgow Royal Infirmary* 1960 SC 439 at 442, 443.

[136] *Gillies v Glasgow Royal Infirmary* 1960 SC 439.

[137] *Bridgeford's Exr v Bridgeford* 1948 SC 416.

[138] *Carmichael's Exrs v Carmichael* 1909 SC 1387.

held *not* to be holograph when the portions in the testator's writing consisted of the following: (i) "[testator's name and address]"—"to my daughter Enid ... Revoke former will," "[testator's signature]"—"[the date]"—"[testator's signature]"[139]; (ii) "[testator's name and address]"—"my two brothers [naming them] equally and jointly, if one deceased to the survivor only"—"their"—"[a name and address]"— "[the testator's name]"—"[the date]"—"[testator's signature]".[140]

23.15 ADOPTION AS HOLOGRAPH

Express adoption as holograph

23.15.1 A deed which was printed, typewritten or written by the handwriting of another, might become the equivalent of a deed holograph of the granter if the granter had added below it, in his own handwriting, the words "adopted as holograph" and his signature.[141] This would apply even when the holograph docquet appears immediately after the signature, instead of immediately before it.[142] The operative part of such a deed is the holograph docquet,[143] by which the granter has agreed to be bound by a writing which would not otherwise be binding upon him.[144] The use of such docquets made it possible for all the parties to a deed to be bound by it as if it were holograph of each of them. It might be written and subscribed by one of the parties and adopted as holograph by the other, or it might be printed, typewritten or written by another person, and adopted as holograph by each of the parties by a docquet written and subscribed by himself.[145]

Implied adoption as holograph

23.15.2 Although not expressly adopted as holograph, a deed which is printed, or typewritten or written by the hand of another, may have been adopted as holograph by implication if it is referred to and recognised in a later holograph writing as a valid

---

[139] *Tucker v Canch's Tr* 1953 SC 270. It was contended that, even if the holograph portion of the deed failed to dispone anything to the person named, the will at least effectively revoked earlier wills. This contention was unsuccessful. Such a deed must receive effect as a whole, or not at all.

[140] *Macdonald v Cuthbertson* (1890) 18 R 101.

[141] *Gavine's Tr v Lee* (1883) 10 R 448. Other words accepting or adopting what appears above the docquet, such as "I agree to the above", produced the same result. See Dickson, *Evidence* (3rd edn), para 756; *Maitland's Trs v Maitland* (1871) 10 M 79, per Lord Kinloch at 84.

[142] *Gavine's Tr v Lee* (1883) 10 R 448.

[143] *McBeath's Trs v McBeath* 1935 SC 471, per Lord President Clyde at 477.

[144] *Campbell's Trs v Campbell* (1903) 5 F 366, per Lord McLaren at 372. In *Harvey v Smith* (1904) 6 F 511, an offer was signed in circumstances which cast grave doubts upon the serious intention of the offeror to enter into a contract. It was held that the writing and subscribing of the words "adopted as holograph" was not binding unless the offeror understood that, by so doing, he made the deed irrevocably binding upon him. For doubts about this decision, see Gloag, *Contract* (2nd edn), pp 95–96. Whatever the *ratio decidendi* may have been, it is thought that it cannot mean that a person is not bound by such a docquet unless he understands the literal meaning of the words "adopted as holograph". A person entering into a contract which is unintelligible to him, is bound by its true construction as ascertained by the court: *Laing v Provincial Homes Investment Co Ltd* 1909 SC 812. See also *Bell Bros (HP) Ltd v Reynolds* 1945 SC 213 at 221.

[145] Dickson, *Evidence* (3rd edn), para 756. The authorities cited by Dickson are not exactly in point, but the statement seems to be clearly right in principle. A deed holograph of one of the parties is not holograph of the others who merely sign it: *Miller v Farquharson* (1835) 13 S 838. (Opinions to the contrary in *Dickson v Blair* (1871) 10 M 41, per Lord Deas at 46, and *Weir v Robertson* (1872) 10 M 438 are thought to be wrong in principle.) And it is not binding even upon the party who wrote it, if his liability depends upon all being bound: Gloag, *Contract* (2nd edn), p 201.

and subsisting writ.[146] The principle is the same as that applicable to solemnly executed deeds which make reference to earlier improbative writings as if they were valid.[147] So a non-holograph acceptance of an offer to purchase heritage was given holograph effect by the covering holograph letter with which it was enclosed, in which reference was made to "my acceptance of your offer".[148] What remained of a solemnly executed will, after parts had been deleted, and most of the testing clause and the signatures of the testator and witnesses had been cut off, was held to be valid as if it were holograph, because a holograph note, written in the margin and subscribed by the testator, mentioned certain of its provisions in such a way as to show that they were still effective.[149] A will, written to the testator's dictation by his wife, was held to be valid as a holograph writing because in a holograph note, subscribed by the testator, at the top of the other side of the page, there was a reference to "my Trustees", which was construed as a recognition of the valid appointment of trustees, and of the trust purposes, in the non-holograph writing.[150] A non-holograph will, in which *inter alia* each grandchild was given a legacy of £25, was held to have been impliedly adopted as holograph, because in a holograph codicil, subscribed by the testator, one of the grandchildren was "fined" £12 for his failure to repay a loan, "leaving balance £13 as his share".[151]

A similar principle applied to a holograph writing invalid due to lack of sub-   **23.15.3**
scription which may, by implication, have been adopted as holograph, if it is unmistakably identified by, and incorporated by reference in, another writing which is both holograph and subscribed.[152] So an unsigned holograph will was held to have been adopted as valid by a later subscribed holograph writing, which commenced with the words "In addition to will made before my father's death"[153]; and by a subscribed holograph docquet, on the back of one of the pages, which appointed two named executors "of this my Will".[154] However, the adoption is effective only in so far as the unsigned document is consistent with the terms of the adopting document.[155] A mere subscription on the envelope containing the unsigned writing is not sufficient to render the latter valid as a holograph writing.[156]

23.16 PROOF AND DATE OF TESTAMENTARY WRITINGS— STATUTORY PROVISIONS

Any testamentary writing on which confirmation of executors nominate was issued   **23.16.1**
prior to 1 July 1938 is deemed to be probative.[157] Any other testamentary writing may be proved to be in the proper handwriting of, and signed with the proper signature of, the deceased testator in an action in the sheriff court for declarator

---

[146] *McGinn v Shearer* 1947 SC 334 at 344, 346.
[147] See the reference to *Callander v Callander's Trs* (1863) 2 M 291 in *McGinn v Shearer* 1947 SC 334.
[148] *McGinn v Shearer* 1947 SC 334.
[149] *Liddle v Liddle* (1898) 6 SLT 218 (OH).
[150] *Cross's Trs v Cross* 1921 1 SLT 244 (OH).
[151] *Craik's Exrx v Samson* 1929 SLT 592 (OH).
[152] *Stenhouse v Stenhouse* 1922 SC 370, per Lord President Clyde at 372–373.
[153] *Fraser's Exrx v Fraser's CB* 1931 SC 536.
[154] *Campbell's Exrs v Maudslay* 1934 SLT 420 (OH). See also *Muir v Muir* 1950 SLT (Notes) 40 (OH).
[155] *Macphail's Trs v Macphail* 1940 SC 560.
[156] *Macphail's Trs v Macphail* 1940 SC 560 at 567. See also *Stenhouse v Stenhouse* 1922 SC 370 ("will and testament of Joseph Stenhouse" on the envelope).
[157] Conveyancing Amendment (Scotland) Act 1938, s 11.

that the writing is holograph of the testator, in the course of which the sheriff may accept affidavit evidence. The deponent should be well acquainted with the handwriting and signature of the testator.[158] Persons may so depone although they have a patrimonial interest in the estate.[159] The Act of Sederunt provides for affidavits of at least two witnesses or the equivalent oral, additional or other evidence.[160] Since the proceedings to which the Act refers are civil it may be argued that the Civil Evidence (Scotland) Act 1988 removes the need for corroboration, and one affidavit would be sufficient. On the other hand, subscription of probative writings required to be witnessed by two persons until 1 August 1995, and it would be prudent to produce two affidavits in support of a holograph writing made before that date. The affidavits may be endorsed on the testamentary writing or an extract thereof, or may be contained in separate documents referring *in gremio* to the testamentary writing or extract.[161] The affidavits may be taken before a magistrate, commissioner for oaths, justice of the peace or notary public, not being the solicitor for the pursuer or one of his partners or servants, or before any commissioner whom the sheriff may appoint.[162] In the absence of evidence to the contrary, every holograph writing of a testamentary character is deemed to have been executed or made of the date it bears.[163]

23.17 SUBSCRIPTION OF HOLOGRAPH WRITING

23.17.1 A holograph writing must have been subscribed by the granter, since without subscription the writing is understood to be an incomplete act from which he has resiled.[164] So when a holograph writing was only superscribed,[165] or bore the granter's signature down the left side of the last page,[166] the whole deed was ineffectual and, when there was writing both above and below the signature, only the writing above the signature was effectual.[167] Subscription of the last page of the writing is sufficient and, if it is not clear from the writing itself to which pages the subscription applies, this may be established by parole evidence.[168] An exception to the general rule was sustained when an unsubscribed holograph offer was delivered for the purpose of being acted upon, and was met by a subscribed holograph acceptance[169] or its equivalent.[170] It was held that in these circumstances a contract had been validly concluded and was binding on both parties.

---

[158] AS, 19 July 1935 (SR&O 1935 No 756), S 1 (2). Apart from the exceptional procedure provided by the Act of Sederunt, the action proceeds as an ordinary action: S 1(4). The initial writ must be served on the heir at law, and on such other interested persons as the sheriff may direct: S 1(1).
[159] S 1(2).
[160] S 1(2).
[161] S 1(3).
[162] S 1(2). As to affidavits generally see Chapter 15.
[163] Conveyancing (Scotland) Act 1874, s 40. This is an exception to the general rule regarding the dates of holograph writings.
[164] Stair, iv, 42, 6. See also para 23.13.
[165] *Taylor's Exrx v Thom* 1914 SC 79; *Foley v Costello* (1904) 6 F 365.
[166] *Robbie v Carr* 1959 SLT (Notes) 16 (OH).
[167] *McLay v Farrell* 1950 SC 149. *Cf Fraser's Exrx v Fraser's CB* 1931 SC 536 (mentioned with doubt in *McLay v Farrell*), where the writing after the signature was preceded by the letters "P.S."
[168] *Cranston* (1890) 17 R 410 at 411, 415; *Speirs v Home Speirs* (1879) 6 R 1359.
[169] *Caithness Flagstone Quarrying Co v Sinclair* (1880) 7 R 1117 (the opinions on the point were *obiter*).
[170] *Weir v Robertson* (1872) 10 M 438.

Since valid holograph writings may include such informal documents as letters, **23.17.2** notes or jottings, a corresponding informality is permitted in their subscription, and the rule for solemnly executed documents does not apply.[171] A subscription of a holograph writing is valid if it is the form of subscription ordinarily used by the granter for the kind of writing in question. So a holograph letter was held to be validly subscribed in one case by initials alone,[172] and in another case by a shortened form of the christened name without the surname,[173] it being proved or admitted in each case that the writer was accustomed to signing letters in that way.[174]

23.18 ALTERATIONS TO HOLOGRAPH WRITING

Non-holograph alterations

An alteration, whether it be a deletion or an addition, made or written by a person **23.18.1** other than the granter of the deed, is of no effect and will be ignored.[175] The only possible exception to this statement would be an alteration *aliena manu* (in another hand) which was subscribed by the granter of the holograph writing and attested in accordance with the statutory solemnities, which would be, in effect, a solemnly executed codicil to a holograph writing.

Holograph alterations

When a holograph testamentary writing is found to contain deletions or erasures **23.18.2** which appear to have been made by the testator, or holograph additions, the date when these were made is usually of little importance.[176] In particular it is usually of little moment whether they were made before or after the subscription of the deed.[177] What must be proved by the party founding upon the writing in its altered form is that the alterations were in fact made by the hand of the testator, and that they were made with the deliberate intention of revoking or amending the parts of the deed to which they refer. That they were made with this intention will be assumed if they are separately authenticated by the testator's signature or initials, but such authentication is not essential. In this respect alterations to holograph writings, consisting of writing on erasure, interpolations, interlineations and marginal additions, are to be distinguished from similar alterations to solemnly executed writings,[178] and unauthenticated alterations made by the testator in his own handwriting to a holograph deed are in the same position as alterations in a solemnly executed writing which are authenticated by being mentioned in the test-

---

[171] *Draper v Thomason* 1954 SC 136 at 140.

[172] *Speirs v Home Speirs* (1879) 6 R 1359.

[173] *Draper v Thomason* 1954 SC 136 ("Connie").

[174] It has been said that "yr. loving mother" is not a valid subscription: *Pentland v Pentland's Trs* (1908) 16 SLT 480 (OH), per Lord Skerrington at 481.

[175] This seems too obvious to require authority, but if authority is necessary it can be found in *Pattison's Trs v University of Edinburgh* (1888) 16 R 73, per Lord McLaren at 77 (proposition (2)).

[176] If the date is important it must be proved, because the date of the alteration is not presumed to be that of the original writing: Dickson, *Evidence* (3rd edn), para 760.

[177] In *Reid's Exrs v Reid* 1953 SLT (Notes) 51 (OH), effect was given to an unauthenticated holograph addition above the signature of a holograph will, which was manifestly made more than two years after the signature was adhibited. The testator had added the dates both of the original writing and of the addition.

[178] *Magistrates of Dundee v Morris* (1858) 3 Macq 134, per Lord Chelmsford at 152. As to alterations of solemnly executed wills, see para 22.12.

ing clause.[179] Whether a deletion was made by the testator accidentally or deliberately is a question of fact to be ascertained by evidence.[180] Subject to any doubt on this question, however, there is a presumption of fact, when holograph testamentary writings containing alterations are found apparently undisturbed in the repositories of the testator, that the alterations were made by him with testamentary intention.[181] This presumption does not apply when the original writing is in ink and the alterations are in pencil. In these circumstances the pencil alterations are presumed to be merely deliberative in character and effect will not be given to them,[182] unless this presumption can be rebutted by evidence.[183] It has been said that a word which has been deleted, but is still legible, may be looked at in order to see what the testator originally intended, and to give a meaning to the parts of the writing left undeleted.[184]

23.18.3   *Inter vivos* deeds are thought to be in a different position from testamentary writings from this point of view. Since the writing was intended to leave the granter's possession during his lifetime, there is no room for the presumption that unauthenticated alterations were made by him before the deed became effective by delivery. It is thought that deletions, to be effective, must be authenticated by the granter's subscription or initials, that additions, even if holograph, must be similarly authenticated, and that unauthenticated erasures are fatal to the deed, or to the clause in which they occur.[185]

---

[179] *Robertson v Ogilvie's Trs* (1844) 7 D 236, per Lord Mackenzie at 242 (approved in *Magistrates of Dundee v Morris* (1858) 3 Macq 134; *Hogg's Exrs v Butcher* 1947 SN 141, per Lord Mackintosh (Ordinary) at 142–143 (affd 1947 SN 190). See also McLaren, *Wills and Succession* (3rd edn), I, 288.

[180] *Magistrates of Dundee v Morris* (1858) 3 Macq 134 at 153.

[181] *Milne's Exr v Waugh* 1913 SC 203, per Lord President Dunedin at 208; *Allan's Exrx v Allan* 1920 SC 732.

[182] *Currie's Trs v Currie* (1904) 7 F 364; *Munro's Exrs v Munro* (1890) 18 R 122; *Lamont v Magistrates of Glasgow* (1887) 14 R 603 at 607, 609.

[183] *Lamont v Magistrates of Glasgow* (1887) 14 R 603, per Lord Shand at 608, Lord Adam at 609.

[184] *Magistrates of Dundee v Morris* (1858) 3 Macq 134, per Lord Cranworth at 164, followed reluctantly in *Chapman v Macbean* (1860) 22 D 745, per Lord Justice-Clerk Inglis at 747.

[185] See Montgomerie Bell, *Lectures* (3rd edn), I, 73. It may be possible to hold that the clause in which the vitiation occurs is separable from the other clauses and, by disregarding it, to give effect to the rest of the deed. See para 22.12.

CHAPTER 24

INFORMAL WRITINGS IN COMMERCIAL MATTERS AND IN PROOF OF OBLIGATIONS GENERALLY

24.1 WRITINGS *IN RE MERCATORIA*

The privilege attaching to these writings prior to 1 August 1995 had no signifi- **24.1.1** cance apart from the application of the authentication statutes.[1] A writing *in re mercatoria* could be informally executed in circumstances where, were it not *in re mercatoria*, it had to be solemnly executed or holograph in order to comply with the authentication statutes.[2] The exception relating to writings *in re mercatoria,* however, did not apply to contracts relating to heritage[3] or contracts of service for more than a year,[4] which because of their subject-matter were *obligationes literis*,[5] even if they were in some way associated with a mercantile transaction. It would appear, accordingly, that, whatever may have been the original importance of writings *in re mercatoria*, their practical application prior to 1 August 1995 became very limited. They are thought to have been relevant only to an obligation which, although it could have been constituted orally, was agreed by the parties to be binding only when a formal written contract had been executed in respect of it,[6] or which was constituted for the first time in a unilateral written obligation such as a bond.[7] In such a case the writing had to be solemnly executed or holograph unless it was *in re mercatoria*, when it could be informally executed. The

---

[1] See para 22.8.
[2] Erskine, iii, 2, 24; Bell, *Commentaries*, I, 342; Bell, *Principles*, para 21; Dickson, *Evidence* (3rd edn), para 793; Gloag, *Contract* (2nd edn), p 185; *McLaren v Aikman* 1939 SC 222, per Lord Justice-Clerk Aitchison at 228.
[3] Gloag, *Contract* (2nd edn), p 185. In *Danish Dairy Co v Gillespie* 1922 SC 656 (lease of business premises for a term of years), it was not argued that the writing was *in re mercatoria*.
[4] Gloag, *Contract* (2nd edn), p 185; *Stewart v McCall* (1869) 7 M 544.
[5] As to these, see para 23.6.
[6] See para 23.6.
[7] See para 23.9.

position of cautionary obligations[8] and of the writings referred to in the statutes dealing with hire-purchase and credit sale agreements[9] was so obscure that it cannot be said with certainty whether or not the exception for writings *in re mercatoria* was relevant to them.[10] There were judicial indications of an opinion that an obligation, which *ex facie* was *res mercatoria*, might lose its normal privilege and need solemn or holograph writing for its constitution if it was shown to be granted for some ulterior purpose—in order, for example, to provide security for a loan.[11]

24.1.2   The privilege attaching to writings *in re mercatoria* was removed by the Requirements of Writing (Scotland) Act 1995,[12] but the old law is saved in relation to documents executed or things done before 1 August 1995.[13] The Act maintains some distinction in relation to events of a commercial nature in that there is exempted from the requirement for writing for constitution or variation of a gratuitous unilateral obligation "an obligation undertaken in the course of business".[14]

24.2 DEFINITION OF *RES MERCATORIA*

24.2.1   The expression had to be given a wide interpretation.[15] It related to what were properly "mercantile dealings", and was defined in general as including "all the variety of engagements or mandates or acknowledgments which the infinite occasions of trade may require."[16] Such obligations included bills of exchange,[17] promissory notes[18] and bank cheques, orders for goods, mandates and procurations, guarantees,[19] offers to sell or buy merchandise or to transport it from place to place, and acceptances thereof.[20]

---

[8]   See para 24.8.

[9]   See para 24.9.

[10]   An informally executed guarantee was held to be *in re mercatoria* in *BOCM Silcock Ltd v Hunter* 1976 SLT 217.

[11]   See *Commercial Bank v Kennard* (1859) 21 D 864, per Lord President McNeill at 870; *McAdie v McAdie's Exrx* (1883) 10 R 741, per Lord Justice-Clerk Moncrieff at 744. Lord Rutherfurd Clark dissented in the last-mentioned case, which Gloag, *Contract* (2nd edn), p 186 considered to be of doubtful authority.

[12]   s 11(3)(b)(ii).

[13]   s 14(3).

[14]   s 1(2)(a)(ii). Many such obligations are now constituted electronically. On proof of electronic communications see para 21.2, and business documents paras 21.14–21.16.

[15]   *Beardmore & Co v Barry* 1928 SC 101, per Lord Justice-Clerk Alness at 110; 1928 SC (HL) 47; Gloag, *Contract* (2nd edn), p 185.

[16]   The definition and these examples are from Bell, *Commentaries*, I, 342.

[17]   As to bills of exchange, bank cheques and promissory notes, see paras 24.5 *et seq.*

[18]   A letter acknowledging that one of the obligants under a promissory note, granted of even date therewith, was truly a cautioner, was itself held to be a writing *in re mercatoria*: *Thoms v Thoms* (1867) 6 M 174.

[19]   eg *BOCM Silcock Ltd v Hunter* 1976 SLT 217. As to cautionary obligations, see para 24.8.

[20]   The following are examples: *BOCM Silcock Ltd v Hunter* 1976 SLT 217; *Beardmore & Co v Barry* 1928 SC 101; *Henry v Strachan & Spence* (1897) 24 R 1045; *Kinninmont v Paxton* (1892) 20 R 128; *United Kingdom Advertising Co v Glasgow Bag-Wash Laundry* 1926 SC 303; *Dykes v Roy* (1869) 7 M 357; *Paterson v Wright* 31 January 1810, FC; (1814) 6 Paton 38; *Stuart v Potter, Choate & Prentice* 1911 1 SLT 377.

24.3 AUTHENTICATION, MODE OF PROOF AND DATE OF THE INFORMAL WRITING

A writing *in re mercatoria* was sufficiently authenticated if it had been **24.3.1** subscribed[21] by the parties, or initialled[22] by them. The genuineness of the subscription or of the initials, if disputed, had to be proved, and the proof might be by parole evidence.[23] The date of an informal writing *in re mercatoria*, which was admitted or proved to be subscribed or initialled by the obligant, did not need to be independently proved,[24] at least for the mercantile purpose for which the writing was granted.[25] When the date was of importance for some other purpose, as in a question with a trustee in bankruptcy, for example, independent evidence of its accuracy might be necessary.[26]

24.4 DOCQUETS ON ACCOUNTS

Docquets of approval, adjustment, acknowledgement or discharge, written upon **24.4.1** business books or mercantile accounts, and subscribed by the person interested, were admissible in the same way as documents solemnly executed or holograph,[27] and were in the same position with regard to authentication and proof as other mercantile writings.[28] Although it has been said that the ordinary solemnities are necessary in connection with docquets on accounts which are not truly mercantile,[29] accounts of a character similar to mercantile accounts, although not necessarily between merchants, were in practice regarded by the courts for this purpose as if they were mercantile accounts.[30] The effect given to a docquet depended upon its terms and the whole surrounding circumstances. The docquet might be reduced on the ground that its signature was induced by fraud or misrepresentation

---

[21] Bell, *Commentaries*, I, 342; Dickson, *Evidence* (3rd edn), para 793.

[22] Bell, *Commentaries*, I, 343; Dickson, *Evidence* (3rd edn), para 793. Authentication by cross or mark might also be sufficient (Dickson, paras 672, 793), at least when it is proved to be the party's accustomed mode of transacting business (Bell, *Commentaries*, I, 343; *Rose v Johnston* (1878) 5 R 600, per Lord Ormidale at 604), but perhaps only if the writing was read over to and orally adopted by the party before he made the cross or mark *(Rose v Johnston* per Lord Justice-Clerk Moncreiff at 603–604). As to authentication by cross or mark, see also *Morton v French* 1908 SC 171; *Forbes' Exrs v Western Bank* (1856) 16 D 242, 807; *Craig v Scobie* (1832) 10 S 510; and Cusine & Meston, "Execution of Deeds by a Mark" (1993) 38 JLSS 270.

[23] Erskine, iii, 2, 24; Bell, *Commentaries*, I, 342; Bell, *Principles*, para 21; Dickson, *Evidence* (3rd edn), para 793.

[24] Bell, *Commentaries*, I, 343.

[25] Dickson, *Evidence* (3rd edn), para 794. See also *Purvis v Dowie* (1869) 7 M 764.

[26] Dickson, *Evidence* (3rd edn), para 794. See also *Purvis v Dowie* (1869) 7 M 764.

[27] *McLaren v Liddell's Trs* (1860) 22 D 373, per Lord Cowan at 378; Dickson, *Evidence* (3rd edn), para 797.

[28] See para 24.2. There is also authority for the view that such docquets, if holograph, are effective although not subscribed: Stair, iv, 42, 6; Dickson, *Evidence* (3rd edn), para 799.

[29] Erskine, iii, 2, 24; Dickson, *Evidence* (3rd edn), para 798.

[30] So, for example, an acknowledgement by a farmer, subscribed by him, and written upon an account for deliveries of farm stock and advances of money made to him by his uncle, who was also a farmer, during the period of a year, was regarded as being "of the nature of a mercantile transaction": *Stephen v Pirie* (1832) 10 S 279, per Lord Balgray at 281. The other judges, although not regarding the transaction as being *in re mercatoria*, concurred in regarding the acknowledgement as effective. See, for examples of docquets admitted as *res mercatoria*: *Elder v Smith* (1829) 7 S 656; *Walker v Drummond* (1836) 14 S 780; *Boswell v Montgomerie* (1836) 14 S 554; *Laing v Laing* (1862) 24 D 1362. However, compare *Laidlaw v Wilson* (1844) 6 D 530 and *McAdie v McAdie's Exrx* (1883) 10 R 741.

or on some other competent ground. If it was not reduced, the court would usually allow any error which appeared on the face of the account, such as an arithmetical error[31] or an error of accounting,[32] to be corrected, but would not allow an enquiry into matters extrinsic to the account, which might have been alleged to affect its accuracy.[33] The party challenging a docquetted account had to aver specific objections to it and, if proof of the objections was allowed, had the onus of proving them, there being no onus upon the other party, at least at the outset, to prove that the account was accurate.[34]

24.5 NEGOTIABLE INSTRUMENTS AS WRITINGS *IN RE MERCATORIA*

24.5.1 At common law negotiable instruments in the form of bills of exchange, cheques and promissory notes were recognised as writings *in re mercatoria*,[35] and they could accordingly be authenticated in the same way as other writings *in re mercatoria*.[36] These are now largely governed by statute from which it is clear that a bill of exchange requires writing[37] for its form. The bill is inchoate and unenforceable unless subscribed.[38] As in the case of other mercantile documents, if the signature on a bill of exchange is disputed, the onus of proving that it is genuine rests upon the party founding upon it.[39] The following are statutory specialties with regard to the signature of bills of exchange: when a bill is wanting in any material particular, the person in possession of it has a *prima facie* authority to fill up the omission in any way he thinks fit[40]; a person whose signature to a bill is required need not sign by his own hand, and it is sufficient if his signature is written thereon by some other person by or under his authority[41]; when a bill must be signed by a corporation it is sufficient if it is sealed with the corporate seal,[42] but this is not essential,

---

[31] *McLaren v Liddell's Trs* (1862) 24 D 577, per Lord Justice-Clerk Inglis at 584.

[32] *McLaren v Liddell's Trs* (1862) 24 D 577, per Lord Benholme at 585.

[33] *Walker v Drummond* (1836) 14 S 780. The only error alleged in the docquetted accounts did not appear *ex facie* of the accounts or of the ledger from which they were compiled, but was said to be discoverable from an examination of certain private books of the bank. See the Lord Ordinary's findings at 784. The bank's claim, based upon a correction of the accounts, was refused without enquiry.

[34] *Laing v Laing* (1862) 24 D 1362, per Lord Justice-Clerk Inglis at 1366, Lord Cowan at 1367; *Struthers v Smith* 1913 SC 1116, per Lord President Dunedin at 1119–1120.

[35] Dickson, *Evidence* (3rd edn), para 801.

[36] See Bills of Exchange Act 1882, ss 3(1), 17(2), 32(1). As to execution of a bill of exchange by initials and by mark, see Dickson, *Evidence* (3rd edn), para 802; Cusine & Meston, "Execution of Deeds by a Mark" (1993) 38 JLSS 270.

[37] Bills of Exchange Act 1882, s 2. Some electronic communication suffices now, see Deregulation (Bills of Exchange) Order 1996 (SI 1996/2993), and Electronics Communications Act 2000 discussed at para 21.2.

[38] Bell, *Principles*, para 323. The earlier rule that a bill of exchange is sufficiently signed by the drawer if the document is in his own handwriting and his name is in the body of it (see Bell, *Principles*, para 311; Dickson, *Evidence* (3rd edn), para 805)) would not now be followed since a bill of exchange must be signed: Bills of Exchange Act 1882, s 3. "Signed" is now interpreted as meaning "subscribed": see *Waterson's Trs v St Giles Boys' Club* 1943 SC 369, per Lord Justice-Clerk Cooper at 374. The validity of a bill of exchange signed by the executor of the drawer after the latter's death has been doubted: *Lawson's Exrs v Watson* 1907 SC 1353, per Lord McLaren at 1357, Lord Pearson at 1358.

[39] *McIntyre v National Bank of Scotland* 1910 SC 150.

[40] Bills of Exchange Act 1882, s 20(1). It has been held that the drawer may sign even after the acceptor and payee are dead, and at any time before the bill is produced in judgment: *Shaw v Farquhar* (1761) M 1444; *Cathcart v Dick's Reps* (1748) M 1439; Bell, *Commentaries*, I, 421; Bell, *Principles*, para 311.

[41] Bills of Exchange Act 1882 ("1882 Act"), s 91(1).

[42] 1882 Act, s 91(2).

and the company's signature may be effected by another person adhibiting his own signature for or on behalf of the company[43]; signature of a bill by procuration operates as a notice that the agent has only a limited authority to sign, and the principal is only bound by such signature if the agent in so signing was acting within the actual limits of his authority[44]; a person signing a bill who adds to his signature words indicating that he signs for or on behalf of a principal, or in a representative character, is not personally liable thereon,[45] but, if a signatory intends to bind a third party and not himself, the obligation must unambiguously bear that meaning,[46] the onus of proving that the alleged principal only is bound being on those who assert it,[47] and the mere addition to the signature of words describing the signatory as agent, or as filling a representative character, does not exempt him from personal liability[48]; when a person signs a bill in a trade name, or an assumed name, he is liable thereon as if he had signed it in his own name, and the signature of the name of a firm is equivalent to the signature by the person signing of the names of all persons liable as partners in that firm.[49] When a bill, or an acceptance or indorsement thereon, is dated, the date is deemed to be the true date unless the contrary is proved.[50] A bill is not invalid because it is undated,[51] or ante-dated or post-dated,[52] and when a bill payable at a fixed period after date is issued undated, any holder may insert the true date, and the bill is payable accordingly.[53] If a wrong date is inserted and the bill subsequently comes into the hands of a holder in due course, the bill operates and is payable as if the date so inserted was the true date.[54]

24.6 SUMMARY DILIGENCE ON NEGOTIABLE INSTRUMENTS

The Scottish law and practice with regard to summary diligence upon a bill of **24.6.1** exchange was not in any way altered or affected by the Bills of Exchange Act 1882, or by any repeal affected thereby.[55] In order that summary diligence may be competent, the bill must be complete, and in particular must be dated,[56] and

---

[43] 1882 Act, s 25, 26. See also Companies Act 1985, s 349 and *Brebner v Henderson* 1925 SC 643; *Scottish & Newcastle Breweries Ltd v Blair* 1967 SLT 72.

[44] 1882 Act, s 25.

[45] 1882 Act, s 26 (1). The question of whether words added to the signature are merely descriptive of the signatory or, on the other hand, have the effect of relieving the signatory of liability, is one which must be answered by interpretation of the document as a whole: *Brebner v Henderson* 1925 SC 643.

[46] *Brebner v Henderson* 1925 SC 643, per Lord President Clyde at 647.

[47] *Brebner v Henderson* 1925 SC 643, per Lord Sands at 648.

[48] 1882 Act, s 26 (1). The question of whether words added to the signature are merely descriptive of the signatory or, on the other hand, have the effect of relieving the signatory of liability, is one which must be answered by interpretation of the document as a whole: *Brebner v Henderson* 1925 SC 643.

[49] 1882 Act, s 23(1), (2).

[50] 1882 Act, s 13(1).

[51] 1882 Act, s 3(4) (a).

[52] 1882 Act, s 13(2).

[53] 1882 Act, s 12.

[54] 1882 Act, s 12.

[55] 1882 Act, s 98.

[56] Dickson, *Evidence* (3rd edn), para 802; *Cameron v Morrison* (1869) 7 M 382. The Mercantile Law Amendment (Scotland) Act 1856, s 10, which made this explicit, and to which the opinions in *Cameron v Morrison* referred, was repealed by the Bills of Exchange Act 1882, but it is thought that, in terms of s 98 of that Act, the existing law on this point remained unchanged.

subscribed[57] by the drawer. Authentication by initials[58] or by mark[59] is not sufficient for this purpose, but a signature per procuration would appear to be unobjectionable.[60] If the bill is complete at the time when it is sought to do summary diligence upon it, it is immaterial that it was originally signed on a blank stamped paper, or was otherwise incomplete when originally delivered, and that it was subsequently completed as authorised by statute.[61]

24.7 PAROLE EVIDENCE AS TO LIABILITY ON NEGOTIABLE INSTRUMENTS

24.7.1 Section 100 of the Bills of Exchange Act 1882 provides that, in any judicial proceeding in Scotland, any fact relating to a bill of exchange, bank cheque or promissory note, which is relevant to any question of liability thereon, may be proved by parole evidence. This section, although applied in some cases,[62] was apparently received without enthusiasm by the Scottish courts and there are a number of decisions, including a decision of the House of Lords,[63] which ignore this and adhere to the rule at common law which provided that performance, discharges or variations of an obligation constituted by writing might not be proved by parole evidence.[64] However, the section has been said to apply, but only as between the drawer and acceptor,[65] in order to allow proof by parole evidence that the bill was granted for the accommodation of the drawer, and that, although the apparent creditor, he is in truth the debtor.[66] Moreover, parole evidence has been held to be admissible to prove either that the bill of exchange, although bearing to be granted for an onerous consideration, was not in fact so granted,[67] or that a contractual undertaking, which represented the onerous consideration for the bill, was not, or could not be, implemented. A person, *ex facie* liable under a bill of exchange, was allowed to prove by parole evidence, and so to escape liability, that the bill was granted in terms of a contract under which goods were to be delivered when the bill became payable, and that the goods were not tendered when payment was demanded,[68] or were properly rejected as disconform to contract.[69] Similarly

---

[57] Bell, *Principles*, para 311; Dickson, *Evidence* (3rd edn), paras 802, 807. See also *Lawson's Exrs v Watson* 1907 SC 1353, and para 24.5, n 38.

[58] Dickson, *Evidence* (3rd edn), paras 671, 802.

[59] Dickson, *Evidence* (3rd edn), paras 673, 802.

[60] *Summers v Marianski* (1843) 6 D 286; *Turnbull v McKie* (1822) 1 S 331.

[61] *Cameron v Morrison* (1869) 7 M 382. Authority for completion of an inchoate or incomplete bill is given by the Bills of Exchange Act 1882, s 20.

[62] *Viani & Co v Gunn & Co* (1904) 6 F 989; *Drybrough & Co Ltd v Roy* (1903) 5 F 665. These cases were commented upon with disapproval in *Nicol's Trs v Sutherland* 1951 SC (HL) 21.

[63] *Nicol's Trs v Sutherland* 1951 SC (HL) 21.

[64] *Robertson v Thomson* (1900) 3 F 5; *National Bank of Australasia v Turnbull & Co* (1891) 18 R 629, per Lord President Inglis at 634, Lord McLaren at 638; *Gibson's Trs v Galloway* (1896) 23 R 414, per Lord McLaren at 416; *Stagg & Robson Ltd v Stirling* 1908 SC 675. These decisions were approved in *Nicol's Trs v Sutherland* 1951 SC (HL) 21, per Lord Simonds at 26–27, Lord Normand at 32, Lord Reid at 43–44. See also *Manchester & Liverpool District Banking Co v Ferguson & Co* (1905) 7 F 865; *Gibson's Trs v Galloway* (1896) 23 R 414.

[65] *National Bank of Australasia v Turnbull & Co* (1891) 18 R 629, per Lord President Inglis at 635.

[66] *Nicol's Trs v Sutherland* 1951 SC (HL) 21, per Lord Simonds at 27; *Stagg & Robson Ltd v Stirling* 1908 SC 675, per Lord President Dunedin at 679.

[67] *Marr & Sons v Lindsay* (1881) 18 SLR 721, per Lord President Inglis at 723.

[68] *Marr & Sons v Lindsay* (1881) 18 SLR 721.

[69] *Wallace & Brown v Robinson, Fleming & Co* (1885) 22 SLR 830.

parole evidence was regarded as admissible to prove that a bill was granted as part of a partnership agreement from which the debtor under the bill resiled, with the result that, implement of a partnership agreement being in law unenforceable, payment of the bill could not be insisted in.[70] Quite apart from section 100 of the Bills of Exchange Act, a bill of exchange is incomplete and revocable until it is delivered,[71] and the fact of delivery as well as the purpose for which it is made, may be proved by parole evidence.[72] Delivery of a bill of exchange will constitute proof of payment, but, although evidence of an obligation,[73] in the face of denial of that obligation the bill is not proof of it *per se*.[74] It has been decided in the sheriff court that a countermanded cheque, although valuable evidence in the payee's hands, does not absolve the payee from proving the obligation to pay.[75] These cases predated the removal of the corroboration requirement in civil cases by the Civil Evidence (Scotland) Act 1988, s 1, but the principle remains that the bill is no more than an adminicle of evidence in relation to the underlying obligation.

24.8 CAUTIONARY OBLIGATIONS

Prior to 1 August 1995, all cautionary obligations, unless implied by law, had to be in writing and subscribed by the person undertaking the obligation, otherwise they had no effect.[76] This applied to all guarantees, securities or cautionary obligations made or granted by any person for any other person, and all representations and assurances as to the character, conduct, credit, ability,[77] trade or dealings of any person, made or granted to the effect or for the purpose of enabling such person to obtain credit, money, goods, or postponement of payment of any debt, or of any other obligation demandable from him.[78] The writing was necessary whether the obligation was to be relied upon as a cause of action or as the basis of a defence,[79] and even when the obligation was alleged to have been undertaken fraudulently.[80] There was doubt[81] as to whether the writing required

24.8.1

---

[70] *Pert v Bruce* 1937 SLT 475.

[71] Bills of Exchange Act 1882, s 21. The giving of notice of acceptance may be the equivalent of delivery.

[72] *National Bank of Australasia v Turnbull & Co* (1891) 18 R 629.

[73] Chalmers & Guest, *Bills of Exchange* (15th edn), paras 370–383.

[74] *NV Devos Gebroeder v Sunderland Sportswear Ltd* 1987 SLT 331 (OH).

[75] *Williams v Williams* 1980 SLT (Sh Ct) 25.

[76] Mercantile Law Amendment (Scotland) Act 1856, s 6.

[77] This has been construed as meaning ability to pay: *Irving v Burns* 1915 SC 260.

[78] Mercantile Law Amendment (Scotland) Act 1856, s 6. The terms of the statutory provision seem to indicate fairly clearly that writing was necessary for the constitution of the obligation, and not merely for its proof. "Shall have no effect" seems to produce the same result as "shall be null and void and make no faith"—the expression used in the authentication statutes, which have been held to deal with the constitution of obligations. But contrary views have been expressed, as in Bell, *Principles*, para 249A; *Walker's Trs v McKinlay* (1880) 7 R (HL) 85, per Lord Blackburn at 88; *Wallace v Gibson* (1895) 22 R (HL) 56, per Lord Wellwood (Ordinary) at 59. It was conceded that the terms of the statute indicated that the writing was necessary for constitution, but it was argued that, since the purpose of the statute was to assimilate the law of Scotland to that of England, and in England the writing was needed only as evidence of the obligation, the opposite construction ought to be placed upon it. As to the Scottish law on the point prior to the passing of the 1856 Act, opinions have differed, but the weight of authority favoured the view that writing was required as evidence, but not for constitution: Erskine, iv, 2, 20; Bell, *Principles*, para 18; Dickson, *Evidence* (3rd edn), para 600; Gloag and Irvine, *Rights in Security*, pp 684 *et seq*. *Cf Church of England Life Assurance Co v Hodges* (1857) 19 D 414, per Lord Justice-Clerk Hope at 421–422, per Lord Cowan at 425.

[79] *Union Bank of Scotland v Taylor* 1925 SC 835.

[80] *Clydesdale Bank v Paton* (1896) 23 R (HL) 22.

[81] See Gloag and Irvine, *Rights in Security*, pp 684 et *seq*, 721 *et seq*; Gloag, *Contract* (2nd edn), p 184.

authentication.[82] If it did so require, this was mitigated in the usual way when the writing was *in re mercatoria*,[83] or when *rei interventus* had occurred, as, for example, by the making of advances on the faith of the obligation,[84] in both of which cases a writing subscribed by the granter without witnesses would be sufficient on either view of the law.[85] However, it is thought that the statutory provisions then applying which provided that a writing subscribed by the granter was the only essential requirement, would prevail. In any event, the statutory requirement for writing to constitute cautionary obligations was repealed by the Requirements of Writing (Scotland) Act 1995,[86] and a cautionary obligation, unless a gratuitous unilateral obligation not undertaken in the course of business,[87] does not require writing for constitution.[88] Writing for proof is, of course, prudent and desirable.

24.9 HIRE-PURCHASE AND CREDIT SALE AGREEMENTS

24.9.1 A statutory rule applies to any hire-purchase or credit sale contract in respect of hire payments not exceeding £25,000[89] where the hirer is not a limited company.[90] No such contract, and no contract of cautionry for, or guarantee of, the performance of any obligation under such a contract, is binding on any person as hirer, purchaser, cautioner or guarantor, unless the contract is signed by such person,[91] and

---

[82] If the authentication statutes are regarded as applying, then, in order that it may be founded upon, the writing in which the obligation is expressed must be solemnly executed or holograph and there is authority for the view that such authentication is required: Bell, *Principles*, paras 248, 249A; Dickson, *Evidence*, (3rd edn), para 603.

[83] *Johnston v Grant* (1844) 6 D 875; *National Bank of Scotland v Campbell* (1892) 19 R 885. In both these cases the writing was held to have been validated *rei interventu*, but it was assumed that, if the writing had been *in re mercatoria*, it would have been valid on that ground also. See also Bell, *Principles*, para 249A; Dickson, *Evidence* (3rd edn), para 604; Gloag, *Contract* (2nd edn), p 184. As to writings *in re mercatoria* generally, see paras 24.1 *et seq*.

[84] *Johnston v Grant* (1844) 6 D 875; *National Bank of Scotland v Campbell* (1892) 19 R 885; *Snaddon v London, Edinburgh and Glasgow Assurance Co* (1902) 5 F 182, per Lord Trayner at 186. As to *rei interventus* generally, see paras 26.3 *et seq*.

[85] The state of the law before 1856 is so doubtful that it seems impossible to state with certainty what changes the Mercantile Law Amendment (Scotland) Act effected or was intended to effect. See Bell, *Principles*, para 249A; *Walker's Trs v McKinlay* (1880) 7 R (HL) 85, per Lord Blackburn at 88; *Wallace v Gibson* (1895) 22 R (HL) 56, per Lord Wellwood (Ordinary) at 59. It was conceded that the terms of the statute indicated that the writing was necessary for constitution, but it was argued that, since the purpose of the statute was to assimilate the law of Scotland to that of England, and in England the writing was needed only as evidence of the obligation, the opposite construction ought to be placed upon it. As to the Scottish law on the point prior to the passing of the 1856 Act, opinions have differed, but the weight of authority favoured the view that writing was required as evidence, but not for constitution: Erskine, iv, 2, 20; Bell, *Principles*, para 18; Dickson, *Evidence* (3rd edn), para 600; Gloag and Irvine, *Rights in Security*, pp 684 *et seq*. Cf *Church of England Life Assurance Co v Hodges* (1857) 19 D 414, per Lord Justice-Clerk Hope at 421–422, per Lord Cowan at 425.

[86] s 14(2) and Sched 5.

[87] s 1(2)(a)(ii).

[88] s 1(1).

[89] Consumer Credit Act 1974, ss 8, 9, 15(1) and 189(1).

[90] ss 8 and 189(1).

[91] In relation to earlier statutory regulation of such agreements it has been held that the subscription need not be witnessed: *United Dominions Trust (Commercial) Ltd v Lindsay* 1959 SLT (Sh Ct) 58. It was also doubted by the sheriff-substitute whether *rei interventus* (or homologation) could cure the defect arising from the absence of the purchaser's subscription. *English v Donnelly* 1959 SLT 2 decided that the provisions are mandatory, but was not otherwise concerned with this question.

the agreement is not considered to be properly executed unless the requisite disclosure of information has been made to the hirer in advance.[92] The purchaser's subscription of a printed form in which the essential details, later completed by the vendors, were blank, was held not to be a subscription of the contract.[93]

24.10 CONTRACTS OF INSURANCE

By statute[94] a contract of marine insurance is not admissible in evidence unless it **24.10.1** is embodied in a marine policy containing certain statutory requirements,[95] but the contract is deemed to have been concluded when the proposal of the assured was accepted by the insurer,[96] and, if a duly stamped policy has been issued, reference may be made to the slip or covering note[97] for the purpose *inter alia* of discovering the date when the contract was concluded. At common law the position with regard to the contract of insurance generally was uncertain. It had been stated that a contract of insurance could only be made in writing, and that the only admissible evidence of such a contract was a policy or an informal writing followed by *rei interventus*, such as, for example, acceptance of a premium.[98] When that statement was made, however, the attention of the court was not called to an early case[99] where opinions were expressed that an oral contract of insurance could be proved by parole evidence, and in an Outer House[100] case it had been accepted by the defenders and by the court that a contract of insurance could be constituted orally and proved by parole evidence.[101] There is no requirement now for writing to constitute a contract of insurance, and such contracts are often made orally.[102] However, proof of the terms of an insurance contract, particularly if the terms are complex, will be difficult without some writing in the form of proposal documents or at least a policy of insurance.[103] Assignation of a policy of life assurance must be made in writing.[104]

---

[92] Consumer Credit Act 1974, Part IV.

[93] *United Dominions Trust (Commercial) Ltd v Lindsay* 1959 SLT (Sh Ct) 58, interpreting an earlier statute with similar effect. It was also doubted by the sheriff-substitute whether *rei interventus* (or homologation) could cure the defect arising from the absence of the purchaser's subscription. *English v Donnelly* 1959 SLT 2 decided that the provisions are mandatory, but was not otherwise concerned with this question.

[94] Marine Insurance Act 1906 ("1906 Act").

[95] 1906 Act, s 22. As to a form of policy and the statutory meaning of customary terms and expressions, see s 31, Sched 1.

[96] 1906 Act, s 21.

[97] 1906 Act, s 89.

[98] *McElroy v London Assurance Corporation* (1897) 24 R 287, per Lord McLaren at 290–291. In Gloag, *Contract* (2nd edn), p 181, this is preferred as a correct statement of the law. Erskine (iii, 3, 17) mentions the matter only incidentally in relation to the consensual contract of affreightment, and refers to an obligation in writing styled a policy of insurance. Bell (*Principles*, paras 465, 467) describes the contract as consensual, but says that it is invariably embodied in a policy.

[99] *Christie v North British Insurance Co* (1825) 3 S 360 at 362.

[100] *Parker & Co (Sandbank) Ltd v Western Assurance Co* 1925 SLT 131 (OH).

[101] See also Scottish Law Commission, *Report on Requirements of Writing* (Scot Law Com No 112), para 2.30.

[102] See Forte (ed), *Scots Commercial Law*, pp 118–119.

[103] It has been noted that general principles governing marine insurance are frequently applied across the whole field of insurance: see Forte (ed), *Scots Commercial Law*, p 113.

[104] Policies of Assurance Act 1867, s 5.

24.11 TRANSFERS OF INCORPOREAL RIGHTS IN MOVEABLES

24.11.1 A distinction must be made between an actual assignation or transfer of an incorporeal right in moveables[105] and a contract which merely creates an obligation to assign or transfer. The latter might be constituted orally or by informal writing and proved by parole evidence. It was thought that, as a general rule at common law, an actual transfer of such rights,[106] at least when the rights themselves were constituted in writing,[107] could be constituted only in writing solemnly executed[108] or holograph[109] or in an informal writing followed by *rei interventus* or homologation.[110] However, writing is no longer required for assignation of incorporeal moveables[111] unless required by specific statutory provision such as those applying to assignations of patents[112] and life insurance policies.[113] Nevertheless, for the assignation to be enforceable against third parties there must be intimation and, unless implied from the circumstances, this should be in writing.[114]

---

[105] An assignation pertaining to an interest in land generally does require to be in writing, whether by virtue of the Requirements of Writing (Scotland) Act 1995, s 1(2)(a)(i) or (b), or another enactment such as the Conveyancing and Feudal Reform (Scotland) Act 1970, s 14.

[106] Dickson, *Evidence* (3rd edn), para 560.

[107] *McMurrich's Trs v McMurrich's Trs* (1903) 6 F 121, per Lord McLaren at 126; Bell, *Commentaries*, I, 345. The cases cited in Gloag, *Contract* (2nd edn), p 180, in support of the opinion that writing is required only for proof and not for constitution, seem to refer not to an actual transfer or assignation but to an agreement to transfer or assign.

[108] See paras 90, 176 *et seq*.

[109] See paras 91, 188 *et seq*.

[110] *Jeffreys v Kyle* (1856) 18 D 906, per Lord Curriehill at 912; (1859) 3 Macq 611.

[111] Requirements of Writing (Scotland) Act 1995, s 11(3)(a).

[112] Patents Act 1977, s 31(6), as amended by the Requirements of Writing (Scotland) Act 1995, Sched 4.

[113] Policies of Assurance Act 1867, s 5.

[114] Transmission of Moveable Property (Scotland) Act 1862, s 2.

CHAPTER 25

PROOF BY RESTRICTED MODE

25.1 INTRODUCTORY

Any event which occurred after 1 August 1995 may be proved *prout de jure*. If the **25.1.1** event is one requiring writing for constitution in terms of the Requirements of Writing (Scotland) Act 1995, s 1 the writing must be produced in evidence, and whether evidence extrinsic to the writing is admissible will depend upon the application of exceptions and presumptions which are described in detail in another chapter.[1] In the absence of writing the event (including the informal agreement upon which the actings are said to have been based) may be proved by evidence of actings,[2] to which no restriction in mode of proof applies. In proceedings raised prior to 1 August 1995 restricted proof is still competent,[3] and a court may still be asked in such proceedings to restrict proof of a matter to writ or to the oath of the other party, or may be asked to fix a proof *habili modo* (in the manner competent) to be determined as appropriate by the judge hearing the proof.[4]

It was clearly the intention of the Scottish Law Commission that restricted **25.1.2** modes of proof would be abolished for proceedings other than those which had been commenced prior to 1 August 1995,[5] but the effect of the provision saving the old law in relation to documents executed and things done prior to 1 August 1995 may be to retain the restricted modes of proof in relation to those documents and events.[6] It is attractive to follow the Scottish Law Commission's proposals that

---

[1] Chapter 27.
[2] Requirements of Writing (Scotland) Act 1995, s 1(3) and (4).
[3] 1995 Act, s 11(4).
[4] See para 1.3.
[5] See *Report on Requirements of Writing* (Scot Law Com No 112) at paras 3.17–3.19, *Report on Three Bad Rules in Contract Law* (Scot Law Com No 152), para 2.17 and *Report on Interpretation in Private Law* (Scot Law Com No 160), para 8.6.
[6] This appears to be the consequence of s 14(3), which overrides the abolition for all future proceedings implied by s 11(4), particularly when it is compared to the clearer abolition in the context of proof of trusts, set out in s 14(4).

restrictive rules of evidence can be reformed with immediate effect, except in relation to proceedings already commenced, but in the context of proof of obligations, it ignores the interaction of the restricted mode of proof and the substantive law. The latter was, and still is, designed to promote certainty of contract by concentrating upon the parties' writings, and the admission of certain evidence only in the form of writ or oath exemplified that concentration. It must be assumed, in law at least, that when deciding how to record their dealings some parties were aware that the absence of writing might result in proof of the matter as a whole (such as loan) or an element in the matter (such as the oral agreement preceding *rei interventus* or homologation) being restricted. On this premise, it would be appropriate to save the operation of restricted modes of proof in relation to documents or events occurring prior to 1 August 1995, whether this was the true intention of the draftsmen. There is also a question over the effect of the removal of the restriction. Is it to admit proof at large in all situations where there was previously restriction to writ or oath, or must the court assess carefully the relevance and admissibility of the proposed evidence (which assessment in the past was usurped by the delineation of the circumstances in which the restrictions applied)? In time there may be authoritative rulings on these matters but in the absence of such rulings the following material on proof by writ is repeated in updated form in this edition in the expectation that it may be required in proceedings where the restriction is applied and, furthermore, because the discussion of what constituted the "writ" of a party may assist in determining, if not relevance and admissibility, at least the weight which the myriad forms of writ may carry. The material on reference to oath has not been retained, on the ground that the procedure had fallen into disuse even before the Scottish Law Commission's reforms and there have been no developments of the common law as it is fully described in the first edition of this text.[7]

25.2 RESTRICTION OF MODE OF PROOF—GENERAL

25.2.1 This chapter is concerned with matters which, as a general rule, could be constituted orally, but which could be proved only by the writ of the other party. These were distinguishable, on the one hand, from *obligationes literis*, which required solemn or holograph writing for their constitution,[8] and, on the other hand, from matters, such as consensual contracts, which could be both constituted orally and proved by parole evidence.[9] Since either party to a litigation was entitled to refer to the oath of his opponent the whole cause or any disputed question of fact,[10] except an *obligatio literis*[11] or a consistorial cause,[12] it followed that until 1 August 1995 a reference to oath was always an alternative to proof by the opponent's writ. Hence frequently a matter was said to be restricted to "proof by writ or oath," although this could be misleading.[13] This did not alter the fact that

---

[7] Chapter XXV.
[8] As to these, see paras 23.1–23.6.
[9] For examples of this group, see paras 144 *et seq* of the first edition.
[10] See first edition, Chapter XXV.
[11] See first edition, para 92.
[12] See first edition, paras 156, 317.
[13] Lord Young in *Paterson v Paterson* (1897) 25 R 144 at 152 remarks on the true relationship between proof by writ and reference to oath. This relationship is demonstrated in the interlocutors pronounced in the sheriff court in *Hamilton v Hamilton's Exrx* 1950 SC 39 at 39, 40. See para 22.2.

the sole requirement of the law was proof by writ.[14] A party seeking to have the mode of proof restricted should have stated a plea to that effect and the court would normally rule on the plea before allowing proof. A difference of opinion arose in *Clark's Executrix v Brown*[15] as to the correct form of interlocutor.[16] The majority held that the appropriate interlocutor sanctioned by practice was to allow proof *habili modo*, and this was followed by the Inner House in a very recent case,[17] provided that the pleadings disclosed some extrinsic matters which might be proved by parole.[18] This form of interlocutor leaves all questions of admissibility to be settled at the proof or, more usually, to be reserved until its conclusion. If proof *habili modo* had been allowed, the proper course appeared to be to object to parole evidence during the proof as and when it was being presented for an incompetent purpose,[19] which would normally lead to its admission under reservation as to competency. Failure to object to parole evidence as it is led is not necessarily fatal to insistence upon restriction of proof, provided that the objection is taken in closing submissions.[20] However, if, through a failure to state a plea for restricted proof, a proof *prout de jure* has been allowed, the court has refused to limit the mode of proof at the point of hearing,[21] and has, in fairness to the party who has prepared for proof *prout de jure*, decided the case upon all evidence heard.[22] When the matter on which proof fell to be restricted was judicially admitted without qualification, the admission might be founded upon, and further proof of it was unnecessary.[23] If the qualification strikes not at the existence of the obligation but to quantification of it, the requirement for writ may have been satisfied.[24]

25.3 PAROLE EVIDENCE IN ADDITION TO WRIT

In addition to proving that the writ was actually[25] or constructively that of the **25.3.1** debtor, there appear to have been four purposes for which parole evidence was competent,[26] viz: (a) once the existence of the obligation had been established by

---

[14] By interpreting ss 11 and 14 together; see also *McEleveen v McQuillan's Exrx* 1997 SLT (Sh Ct) 46.

[15] 1935 SC 110 (loan). See also observations in *Gill v Gill* 1907 SC 532 (loan).

[16] The Lord Justice-Clerk (Aitchison) strongly dissented, holding that the interlocutor ought to specify what the parole proof was to be about. It is true that practice did sanction the general form, though in at least two cases the court pronounced a precise interlocutor: *Christie's Trs v Muirhead* (1870) 8 M 461 (loan); *Johnston v Scott* (1860) 22 D 393 at 395. *Cf Hope v Derwent Rolling Mills Co Ltd* (1905) 7 F 837, where a proof, apparently *prout de jure*, was allowed, and at the end the court picked out the writs on which loan was held proved. See also *Hamilton v Hamilton's Exrx* 1950 SC 39 (prescription).

[17] *Royal Bank of Scotland Plc v Malcolm* 1999 SCLR 854.

[18] *Dunn's Tr v Hardy* (1895) 23 R 621, followed in *Royal Bank of Scotland Plc v Malcolm* 1999 SCLR 854. See also *Inverfleet Ltd v Woelfell* 1977 SLT (Sh Ct) 44.

[19] *Jackson v Ogilvie's Exr* 1935 SC 154; *Gill v Gill* 1907 SC 532.

[20] *Royal Bank of Scotland Plc v Malcolm* 1999 SCLR 854.

[21] *Kerr's Trs v Woods* (1832) 10 S 774; *Wyse v Wyse* (1847) 9 D 1405; *Simpson v Stewart* (1875) 2 R 673; *Kerr's Trs v Ker* (1883) 11 R 108.

[22] Recent examples in the sheriff court are: *Dick's Exrx v Dick* 1964 SLT (Sh Ct) 41; *Cuthbertson v Paterson* 1968 SLT (Sh Ct) 21; *McLellan v Kelly* 1981 SLT (Sh Ct) 100.

[23] See paras 25.4–25.6.

[24] *Royal Bank of Scotland Plc v Malcolm* 1999 SCLR 854.

[25] See para 25.5.

[26] The phrase "writ sufficient to let in parole proof" (or similar words) is used in some of the cases: *eg* by Lord Deas in *Williamson v Allan* (1882) 9 R 859 at 865 (loan), but was misleading. This decision

writ, the amount of the debt might be proved by parole evidence[27]—where the writ admitted some debt, and there was no debt other than that sued for to which the admission could apply, the identification was sufficient[28]; (b) the date of the writ might be proved by parole evidence[29]; (c) where necessary, delivery of the writ might be proved by parole evidence[30]; and (d) the circumstances surrounding the writ might be proved by parole evidence if, for example, it was impossible to understand the effect of the writ without proof of those circumstances[31] or it was necessary to establish whether it had been in that state when signed by the defender.[32]

25.4 NATURE OF WRIT

25.4.1 Proof of an obligation by writ of party meant proof of the obligation by unequiv-ocal[33] inference from documents which were actually[34] or constructively[35] that of the party.[36] Accordingly, even after admission or proof that the writ or writs were those of the party, the question remained whether they were sufficient to justify the inference. In drawing the inference it might be necessary to take into account the relevant circumstances surrounding the writ,[37] and account might be taken of

---

is explained in *Dunn's Tr v Hardy* (1896) 23 R 621, per Lord Kinnear at 633–634. As to the form of interlocutor allowing proof see para 25.2.

[27] *Royal Bank of Scotland Plc v Malcolm* 1999 SCLR 854 *Borland v Macdonald Ltd* 1940 SC 124 at 130, 138 (prescription); *Johnson v Tillie, Whyte & Co* 1917 SC 211 (prescription); *Wilson v Scott* (1908) 15 SLT 948 (OH) (prescription); *Stevenson v Kyle* (1850) 12 D 673 (prescription); *Rutherford's Exrs v Marshall* (1861) 23 D 1276 (loan), in which no opinions are reported, seems to be a contrary decision.

[28] *Rennie v Urquhart* (1880) 7 R 1030 (prescription); *Fiske v Walpole* (1860) 22 D 1488 (prescription). Contrast *Blair v Horn* (1859) 21 D 1004 (prescription), where there were other debts to which the writ could have applied.

[29] *Williamson v Allan* (1882) 9 R 859, where an IOU bore an incorrect date and the true date was proved; *Evans v Craig* (1871) 9 M 801 at 803 (loan).

[30] *Dunn's Tr v Hardy* (1896) 23 R 621 at 633.

[31] *Robb & Co v Stornoway Pier and Harbour Commission* 1932 SC 290, per Lord President Clyde at 296. It is not easy to illustrate the extent of the rule. In *Robb & Co* the parole evidence appears to have been used to establish (1) that the letters were actually or constructively those of the defender and (2) that they had passed between the parties. In *Jackson v Ogilvie's Exr* 1935 SC 154, where the inventory of a deceased's estate signed by the executor was held to be the writ of the executor as an individual, the only disputed circumstance appears to have been whether the execu-tor acquiesced in the inclusion of his debt in the inventory, and understood the effect of so doing. This suggests that if the solicitors had included the debt without saying anything to the executor, and he had signed without noticing it, the inventory would, or at least might, not have been held to be his personal writ.

[32] *Christie's Trs v Muirhead* (1870) 8 M 461 (loan); *Johnston v Scott* (1860) 22 D 393 at 395. *Cf Hope v Derwent Rolling Mills Co Ltd* (1905) 7 F 837, where a proof, apparently *prout de jure*, was allowed, and at the end the court picked out the writs on which loan was held proved.

[33] A word stressed in *Seth v Hain* (1855) 17 D 1117 (proof of loan).

[34] See para 25.5.

[35] See para 25.5.

[36] *Robb & Co v Stornoway Pier and Harbour Commission* 1932 SC 290, per Lord President Clyde at 297, Lord Blackburn at 298.

[37] Each reported decision was given in relation to a particular statute or rule of the common law (noted after the citation) some of which, such as prescription limiting proof, have no current or future effect (Prescription and Limitation (Scotland) Act 1973, s 16). In some cases the court founded on the words of the relevant statute, but, generally speaking, decisions under one statute or common law rule have been cited, both in argument and by the court, in cases under another: *MacBain v MacBain* 1930 SC

another document if that document was expressly referred to in the writ.[38] Hence a receipt which referred to interest due to the defenders jointly "in terms of will" could be read with the will to constitute a clear and unequivocal basis from which the obligation to sell a farm could be inferred.[39] It is thought that in the absence of express statutory provision as to the form of writing required to constitute a particular obligation the following statements hold good as to the inferences that may be drawn from various forms of writing and the examples are illustrative as to forms of writing which were, in the restrictive and complex regime applying before 1 August 1995, held to constitute the writ of the party.

25.5 WRIT OF PARTY—ACTUAL OR CONSTRUCTIVE

The party's signature may be admitted or proved[40] but if it is not admitted that the **25.5.1** party appended his or her signature to the words appearing on the document, parole proof of this is competent,[41] as is parole evidence to show the authenticity of the signature or the fact that the writing was holograph.[42] The following are examples of the writ of a party: entries in the party's business books[43] or cash books that he kept as a factor,[44] markings on the back of a bill of interest paid,[45] and a minute of meeting approved by the party.[46] If the debtor is in a sense acting on behalf of the creditor, any writ issued while acting in that capacity may be that of the creditor. Where the defender had signed and delivered an unqualified acknowledgement of receipt of money, a proof was allowed before answer of his averment that he was acting only as an agent.[47] In a matter where an estate in trust or executry is a party, the trustee or executor is in place of the party[48] and the writ of the trustee or executor would be the writ of the estate.[49]

(HL) 72, per Lord Chancellor Hailsham at 75 (prescription); *Paterson v Paterson* (1897) 25 R 144 at 168, 174, 175, 190 (loan); *Fisher v Fisher & Ors* 1952 SC 347, where, in a case concerning a contract relating to heritage, reference was made to a decision on loan.

[38] *Stewart's Exrs v Stewart* 1994 SLT 466.

[39] *Stewart's Exrs v Stewart* 1994 SLT 466.

[40] And if so the writ did not require to be holograph or tested: *Paterson v Paterson* (1897) 25 R 144 (loan).

[41] *Christie's Trs v Muirhead* (1870) 8 M 461 (loan); *Mackenzie v Stewart* (1848) 9 D 611 at 633, 639, 641, 645 (proof of promise of marriage), referred to in *Thoms v Thoms* (1867) 6 M 174 at 177 (relief).

[42] *Borland v Macdonald Ltd* 1940 SC 124 at 137, 138 (prescription); *Dunn's Tr v Hardy* (1896) 23 R 621 at 633 (loan).

[43] *Jackson v Ogilvie's Exr* 1935 SC 154 at 163 (prescription); *Hope v Derwent Rolling Mills Co Ltd* (1905) 7 F 837 (loan); *Thomson v Lindsay* (1873) 1 R 65 (trust); *Walker v Buchanan, Kennedy & Co* (1857) 20 D 259 (trust); *Seth v Hain* (1855) 17 D 1117 (trust: the proof failed). Unsigned jottings in books might be writ if admitted or proved to be holograph: *Storeys v Paxton* (1878) 6 R 293 (prescription: the proof failed); *Wink v Speirs* (1868) 6 M 657 (loan: the proof failed).

[44] *Drummond v Lees* (1880) 7 R 452 (prescription).

[45] *Drummond v Lees* (1880) 7 R 452 (prescription).

[46] *Devlin v McKelvie* 1915 SC 180 (relief). As to minutes, see paras 19.32 and 19.33.

[47] *Welsh's Trs v Forbes* (1885) 12 R 851 (loan): but see Lord Rutherfurd Clark at 862, Lord Craighill at 863. *Cf Laidlaw v Shaw* (1886) 13 R 724 (loan).

[48] *Briggs v Swan's Exrs* (1854) 16 D 385, per Lord Justice-Clerk Hope at 389 (interruption of long negative prescription).

[49] There does not seem to be any reported decision to that effect, but an executor was held to have homologated an informal acknowledgement of loan by the deceased: *McCalman v McArthur* (1864) 2 M 678 (loan). Since the decision in *Paterson v Paterson* (1897) 25 R 144 (loan) the informal writing would have been enough without homologation.

25.5.2 A document written by another person may be the writ of the party, and parole evidence is competent to show that it is. The most obvious example is the writ of an authorised agent, solicitor,[50] banker,[51] factor,[52] partner[53] or cashier.[54] But the agent's authority, if not admitted, must be proved,[55] and it must be shown that his authority was either specific or otherwise sufficient to bind the principal.[56] While an express admission on record of the subsistence of the obligation renders proof unnecessary, pleadings signed by counsel or solicitor are not, unless specially authorised, the writ of the party, so they cannot be used as a basis for an inference.[57] Documents granted by the creditor and received and retained by the debtor, such as receipts[58] and correspondence[59] became constructively the debtor's writ, the debtor being taken to have retained them for his own proper purposes. Diligence has been granted to recover the creditor's letter to which the debtor's is an answer.[60]

25.6 DELIVERY OF WRIT

25.6.1 Whether delivery of the writ was necessary depended on the terms of the writ. If it was merely an unqualified acknowledgement of receipt of money, no inference of liability to repay arose without delivery.[61] But if it actually acknowledged the obligation or was so expressed as to justify an inference of liability, delivery was unnecessary. Entries in an alleged debtor's books might be his writ, although the creditor knew nothing about them until long after they were made.[62] A letter written by a landlord to the inspector of taxes was held to be his writ in a question with a person claiming the tenancy of a farm.[63] Although delivery of a writ is not necessary, it must be clear from the writ itself and the surrounding circumstances that the writer is committing himself seriously[64] to a statement from which the

---

[50] *Dryburgh v Macpherson* 1944 SLT 116 (OH) (loan), approved and distinguished in *Fisher v Fisher & Ors* 1952 SC 347 (heritage: unusual and innominate contract). See also *Turner v MacMillan-Douglas* 1989 SLT 293 (doubted by the Outer House in *Miller Construction Ltd v Trent Concrete Cladding Ltd* 1996 GWD 2-69 but not on this point).
[51] *Clark's Exrx v Brown* 1935 SC 110 at 116, 118, 122 (loan).
[52] *Smith v Falconer* (1831) 9 S 474 (prescription).
[53] *Bryan v Butters Bros & Co* (1892) 19 R 490 (loan).
[54] *Bryan v Butters Bros & Co* (1892) 19 R 490 (loan).
[55] *Smith v Smith* (1869) 8 M 239 (loan).
[56] *McGregor v McGregor* (1860) 22 D 1264 (prescription).
[57] *Darnley v Kirkwood* (1845) 7 D 595 at 598, 600, 602 (prescription); *Campbell v Grierson* (1848) 10 D 361 (prescription); *Cullen v Smeal* (1853) 15 D 868 at 879.
[58] *Campbell's Trs v Hudson's Exr* (1895) 22 R 943 at 948, 953; *Wood v Howden* (1843) 5 D 507.
[59] *Thomson v Lindsay* (1873) 1 R 65 (trust); *MacBain v MacBain* 1930 SC (HL) 72; *Rennie v Urquhart* (1880) 7 R 1030. As to the importance of producing the whole correspondence, see *McKeen v Adair* (1864) 2 M 392 (loan).
[60] *Stevenson v Kyle* (1849) 11 D 1086. See *Fiske v Walpole* (1860) 22 D 1488.
[61] See para 3.9.
[62] *Hope v Derwent Rolling Mills Co Ltd* (1905) 7 F 837 (loan); *Walker v Buchanan, Kennedy & Co* (1857) 20 D 259 (trust). As to diligence, see *Paterson v Paterson* (1897) 25 R 144 at 184; *Walker v Buchanan, Kennedy & Co* at 260; *Seth v Hain* (1855) 17 D 1117 at 1118 (trust); and the creditor may obtain a diligence for recovery of writs on which he hopes to rely.
[63] *Emslie v Duff* (1865) 3 M 854 (lease). See also *Wilson v Scott* (1908) 15 SLT 948 (OH). Cf *Wink v Speirs* (1868) 6 M 657, per Lord Neaves at 658; *Jackson v Ogilvie's Exr* 1935 SC 154.
[64] "For the purpose of being acted on as true debts": *Briggs v Swan's Exrs* (1854) 16 D 385, per Lord Wood at 394.

relevant admission of liability or of the obligation may be inferred.[65] Entries in regularly kept books, taken into account in balancing, are better evidence than an isolated note.[66]

25.7 RESTRICTION OF PROOF—LOAN

The receipt on loan of money exceeding £100 Scots (£8.33),[67] if received prior to **25.7.1** 1 August 1995, and not judicially admitted without qualification,[68] could be proved only by the writ of the alleged borrower.[69] When the judicial admission, or written acknowledgement[70] upon which the pursuer relied as proof of loan, was qualified by an assertion of repayment, the proof of loan failed. However, when a loan of money had been proved in one or other of the ways mentioned, the burden of proving repayment by the lender's writ rested upon the borrower.[71] The rule was not applied in circumstances which, although pled as loan, were truly based upon a different ground of action.[72] In an action for payment of a sum of money representing a few individual loans of £5 each, and some larger sums said to have been expended by the pursuer on the defender's behalf, a proof *habili modo* was allowed on the footing that if the pursuer was able to prove that the larger payments were made by him as the defender's agent, the proof need not be restricted to writ.[73] However, the mere fact that the loan to be proved was one of a series of similar loans between the parties has not prevented the application of the general rule.[74]

25.8 INFERENCE OF LOAN FROM WRITINGS

If a proof of loan by writ of party was allowed, a writing granted by the alleged **25.8.1**

---

[65] A letter from the alleged debtor to his brother saying, "I am sorry I cannot help you, as I already owe Aunt Mary £1,000 myself", is much stronger proof of the debt to Aunt Mary than a holograph scrap of paper bearing the words, "I owe Aunt Mary £1,000", found in a box of Christmas decorations and possibly a relic of a family game.

[66] *Storeys v Paxton* (1878) 6 R 293 (prescription).

[67] A loan not exceeding £8.33 might be proved *prout de jure*: Erskine, iv, 2, 20; *Annand's Trs v Annand* (1869) 7 M 526. Proof by writ is required if the original loan exceeded £8.33, even if the balance sued for is less: *Clark v Glen* (1836) 14 S 966.

[68] When the judicial admission is qualified, the qualification must be disproved by the writ of the defender before the pursuer may found upon the admission: *Walker v Garlick* 1940 SLT 208 (OH) (averment that loan repaid); *Kerr's Trs v Ker* (1883) 11 R 108, per Lord President Inglis at 116 (averment that claim abandoned); *McKie v Wilson* 1951 SC 15 (averment that money received for services rendered). A judicial admission of the mere receipt of money, as distinct from a judicial admission of loan, does not usually raise a presumption of loan so as to relieve the pursuer of the burden of proving loan by writ, unless the admission is coupled with an averment that the money was received as a gift. As to this, see para 11.2.

[69] Stair, iv, 43, 4; Erskine, iv, 2, 20; Bell, *Principles*, para 2257; Gloag, *Contract* (2nd edn), p 192; *Haldane v Speirs* (1872) 10 M 537. The rule does not apply to a loan of corporeal moveables, which may be proved *prout de jure*: *Scot v Fletcher* (1665) M 11616; *Geddes v Geddes* (1678) M 12730.

[70] See Lord Trayner's illustration in *Patrick v Patrick's Trs* (1904) 6 F 836 at 839.

[71] *Thiem's Trs v Collie* (1899) 1 F 764; *Fraser v Bruce* (1857) 20 D 115. As to proof of discharge or payment, see paras 25.11, 25.12.

[72] See, for example, *Robb v Robb's Trs* (1884) 11 R 881; *Smith's Tr v Smith* 1911 SC 653, the *ratio decidendi* of which was explained by Lord President Cooper in *McKie v Wilson* 1951 SC 15 at 20.

[73] *Boyd v Millar* 1933 SN 106; 1934 SN 7. Cf *Grant's Exrx v Grant* 1922 SLT 156 (OH).

[74] *McKie v Wilson* 1951 SC 15. See also *Smith's Tr v Smith* 1911 SC 653, per Lord President Dunedin at 659.

debtor, which expressly acknowledged the loan as such, would normally discharge the onus of proof resting upon the party who alleged loan, and this might be true even if the writing was signed, not by the borrower, but by another person on his behalf, who was proved to have signed on his instructions.[75] However, when the writing founded upon did not expressly refer to loan, the question then to be decided was whether a sufficient presumption or inference arose, from the terms of the writing founded upon, to discharge the burden of proof. An unqualified written acknowledgement of the receipt of money, signed by the granter and delivered to the grantee, raised a presumption that the money was received on loan, or on some other footing inferring an obligation to repay, and placed upon the recipient the onus of proving that it was not so received,[76] and a bill of exchange, although inoperative as such due to absence of execution, has been used as written evidence of the loan, in respect of which it had been granted as additional security, in the course of a proof by writ.[77] The following are examples of writings which have been held sufficient to raise a presumption that money was received by the alleged debtor from the alleged creditor, by way of loan or under an obligation to repay: receipts importing a reference to repayment,[78] IOUs,[79] an unqualified acknowledgement of the receipt of money contained in a letter or letters addressed by the debtor,[80] or by his solicitor[81] or agent[82] with his authority,[83] to the creditor, the correspondence of which the letters form part, being relevant to the interpretation of the acknowledgement in question.[84]

25.8.2 The following are examples of writings which have been held *not* to raise a presumption that money was received by the alleged debtor from the alleged creditor by way of loan: the debtor's endorsement on a cheque in his favour for the amount

---

[75] *Bryan v Butters Bros & Co* (1892) 19 R 490.

[76] This presumption, and the authorities relating to it, have already been discussed: see para 3.12.

[77] *Lawson's Exrs v Watson* (1907) SC 1353.

[78] *Thomson v Geekie* (1861) 23 D 693; *Gill v Gill* 1907 SC 532.

[79] *Thiem's Trs v Collie* (1899) 1 F 764; *Black v Gibb* 1940 SC 24. If the transaction with which it is associated is real and not fictitious, an IOU is an acknowledgement of debt which imports an obligation to repay, and it is immaterial that no money passes at the time when the IOU is granted: Lord President Normand at 26–27, Lord Moncrieff at 28–29. See also *Paterson v Wilson* (1883) 21 SLR 272. *Cf Bishop v Bryce* 1910 SC 426; *Dinesmann & Co v John Mair & Co* 1912 1 SLT 217 (OH).

[80] *McKeen v Adair* (1864) 2 M 392. The letter need not have been contemporaneous with the constitution of the debt: *Carmichael's Tr v Carmichael* 1929 SC 265, per Lord President Clyde at 268, but was valueless if granted after the debtor's sequestration.

[81] *Dryburgh v Macpherson* 1944 SLT 116; *Fisher v Fisher & Ors* 1952 SC 347, per Lord President Cooper at 351. In *Laidlaw v Shaw* (1886) 13 R 724, a letter addressed by the debtor's solicitor, not to the creditor, but to his own client, in which the sum in question was expressly referred to as having been borrowed from the creditor, was held to be a sufficient writing for the purposes of establishing the loan.

[82] *Clark's Exrx v Brown* 1935 SC 110, per Lord Hunter at 116, Lord Murray at 118; *McGregor v McGregor* (1860) 22 D 1264 (letters by debtor's bank-agent to creditor, referring to the loan).

[83] In *Smith v Smith* (1869) 8 M 239, an admission of the receipt of money contained in a letter by the debtor's solicitor was held not to be the constructive writ of the debtor because it was not proved to have been written with his authority. For general dicta as to writings which may be proved to be constructively the writs of the debtor, see *McGregor v McGregor* (1860) 22 D 1264, per Lord President McNeill at 1268, Lord Deas at 1271; *Paterson v Paterson* (1897) 25 R 144, per Lord Trayner at 164, Lord Pearson at 184; *Clark's Exrx v Brown* 1935 SC 100, per Lord Hunter at 116, Lord Justice-Clerk Aitchison at 122.

[84] *McKeen v Adair* (1864) 2 M 392; *Duncan's Trs v Shand* (1873) 11 M 254, per Lord Cowan at 258; *MacBain v MacBain* 1930 SC (HL) 72, per Lord Hailsham at 75, Lord Dunedin at 75; *Dryburgh v Macpherson* 1944 SLT 116.

of the sum sued for,[85] or on a deposit receipt for that amount[86]; a letter written by the debtor to the creditor referring to a debt owed by him or to a payment received by him, without reference to any particular loan or sum of money,[87] or such a letter which refers only to a loan received in the past without admitting indebtedness at the date of the letter[88]; a letter by the debtor, written in answer to a letter by the creditor requesting repayment of a loan, in which the debt was neither expressly admitted nor repudiated[89]; and a letter by the debtor, addressed not to the creditor, but to a third party, which acknowledged only the receipt of money.[90]

The effect of entries in the debtor's books was uncertain. A jotting "Borrowed from Rob £215", written in pencil in the debtor's pocket-book, was held not sufficient to prove loan.[91] It has been said that entries in regularly kept business books might raise an inference of loan,[92] and such entries coupled with other writings have in fact been held sufficient to prove loan,[93] but there seems to be no decided case in which such entries by themselves have been held sufficient for that purpose. The presumption of loan arose, not from the mere receipt of money, but because a written acknowledgement had been granted as a document of debt and was in the creditor's possession when payment was demanded, and a mere entry in the debtor's business books was not the equivalent of the granting of such an acknowledgement.[94] An entry in a solicitor's business books was not to be regarded as constructively the writ of his client.[95] An entry made by the cashier or book-keeper of a firm in the firm's business books, coupled with his written acknowledgement to the creditor of the loan, might have been sufficient to establish loan in an action against the firm and its partners,[96] and the position with regard to a company was similar.[97]

25.8.3

---

[85] *Haldane v Speirs* (1872) 10 M 537; *Dunn's Tr v Hardy* (1896) 23 R 621; *Scotland v Scotland* 1909 SC 505. Such an endorsement proved only the passing of money and raised no presumption as to the purpose of the payment.

[86] *Nimmo v Nimmo* (1873) 11 M 446, per Lord Neaves at 449, Lord Cowan at 450.

[87] *Rutherford's Exrs v Marshall* (1861) 23 D 1276; *Morison's Trs v Mitchell* 1925 SLT 231 (OH).

[88] *Patrick v Patrick's Trs* (1904) 6 F 836.

[89] *MacBain v MacBain* 1929 SC 213; 1930 SC (HL) 72.

[90] *Wink v Speirs* (1868) 6 M 657, per Lord Neaves at 658; *Haldane v Speirs* (1872) 10 M 537, per Lord President Inglis at 541; *Dunn's Tr v Hardy* (1896) 23 R 621. Cf *Wilson v Scott* (1908) 15 SLT 948 (OH) (triennial prescription). For the position when the letter to the third party acknowledged the debt, see *Emslie v Duff* (1865) 3 M 854 and para 25.6.

[91] *Wink v Speirs* (1868) 6 M 657.

[92] *Wink v Speirs* (1868) 6 M 657, per Lord Neaves at 658. In *McRae v Williamson Bros* (1877) 14 SLR 562, where entries in the business books of the defending firm were held to relate only to payments received for the personal benefit of one of the partners, it seems to have been implied that if the entries had related to the receipt of money by and for the firm, otherwise than in payment of debts due to the firm, a loan of money to the firm would have been sufficiently proved.

[93] *Muir v Goldie's Trs* (1898) 6 SLT 188 (endorsements, some in debtor's handwriting and some in creditor's, upon the back of a prescribed bill for the same debt, noting payments of interest on the debt, coupled with entries in debtor's books relating to similar payments); *Hope v Derwent Rolling Mills Co Ltd* (1905) 7 F 837 (a cheque, which vouched the passing of a sum of money, coupled with a post entry in pencil in the debtor's cash book crediting the pursuer with that sum, and a similar entry in the account kept with the pursuer in the debtor's books: the defence, being very technical, was treated critically by the court (per Lord President Dunedin at 842), and the decision is not to be regarded as of general application); *Kenney v Walker* (1836) 14 S 803 (letter to creditor by firm's cashier acknowledging loan, coupled with entry, expressly referring to loan, made by him in firm's business books).

[94] See para 3.12.

[95] *Fisher v Fisher & Ors* 1952 SC 347.

[96] *Kenney v Walker* (1836) 14 S 803; *Bryan v Butters Bros & Co* (1892) 19 R 490.

[97] *Field v RH Thomson & Co* (1902) 10 SLT 261 (OH). See also *Hope v Derwent Rolling Mills Co Ltd* (1905) 7 F 837.

25.9 DECLARATOR OF TRUST

25.9.1 When a deed declared in absolute terms that a right of property, whether heritable[98] or moveable,[99] existed in one person, and the right was claimed by another person in an appropriate action, the trust could be proved only by the writ of the alleged trustee.[100] The rule and its application resulted from judicial interpretation of the Blank Bonds and Trusts Act 1696 which provided: "that no action of declarator of trust shall be sustained as to any deed of trust made for hereafter except upon a declaration or back-bond of trust lawfully subscribed by the person alleged to be the trustee, and against whom, or his heirs or assignees, the declarator shall be intended, or unless the same be referred to the oath of party *simpliciter*; declaring that this Act shall not extend to the indorsation of bills of exchange or the notes of any trading company." In spite of the terms of the statute, unsigned writings were in certain circumstances regarded as the writ of the alleged trustee.[101] Proof by writ was unnecessary if the existence of the trust was judicially admitted.[102] If the existence of a trust was proved by writ or was judicially admitted, its terms could be proved *prout de jure*,[103] but only if the writ was ambiguous was it appropriate for the court to examine parole evidence for consistency with the writ.[104] Whether there was "deed of trust" to bring a case within the operation of the statute was debatable,[105] and depended primarily upon the pursuer's averments, whether the word "trust" appeared in the pleadings or not.[106] The rule was interpreted as subject to certain limitations which, if applicable, enabled the pursuer to prove the case *prout de jure*.[107] The effects of the rule and its limitations upon proof of trusts have been described as "arbitrary"[108] and unprincipled[109] and when the law on requirements of writing was reviewed the Blank Bonds and Trusts Act 1696 was repealed,[110] with savings *quoad* restriction of proof[111] only in proceedings

---

[98] Dickson, *Evidence* (3rd edn), para 579.
[99] Dickson, *Evidence* (3rd edn), para 579.
[100] *Laird & Co v Laird and Rutherfurd* (1884) 12 R 294, per Lord President Inglis at 297.
[101] *Thomson v Lindsay* (1873) 1 R 65; *Seth v Hain* (1855) 17 D 1117, per Lord Justice-Clerk Hope at 1124, Lord Wood at 1125; *Knox v Martin* (1850) 12 D 719. See McLaren, *Wills and Succession* (3rd edn), II, 1066. *Cf Walker v Buchanan, Kennedy & Co* (1857) 20 D 259, per Lord Deas at 269.
[102] *Seth v Hain* (1855) 17 D 1117.
[103] *Livingstone v Allan* (1900) 3 F 233, per Lord President Balfour at 237; *National Bank of Scotland v Mackie's Trs* (1905) 13 SLT 383 (OH); Dickson, *Evidence* (3rd edn), para 587. See also *Cairns v Davidson* 1913 SC 1054, per Lord Skerrington (Ordinary) at 1055, Lord Guthrie at 1058–1059; *Grant v Grant* (1898) 6 SLT 203 (OH).
[104] *Pickard v Pickard, Pickard v Rice* 1963 SLT 56, per Lord President Clyde at 62.
[105] Bell, *Principles*, para 1995 (1), note (l); Mackenzie Stuart, *Trusts*, pp 14, 15; *Dunn v Pratt* (1898) 25 R 461, per Lord Kinnear (dissenting) at 469; *Anderson v Yorston* (1906) 14 SLT 54 (OH); *Cairns v Davidson* 1913 SC 1054, per Lord Salvesen at 1057–1058; *McConnachie v Geddes* 1918 SC 391, per Lord Salvesen at 399–400; *Newton v Newton* 1923 SC 15, per Lord Sands at 25; *Beveridge v Beveridge* 1925 SLT 234 (OH). The preferred view seems to have been that expressed in the dissenting opinion of Lord Kinnear in *Dunn v Pratt*.
[106] *McNairn's Exrx v Litster* 1939 SC 72, per Lord Fleming at 77.
[107] Which are detailed in the first edition of this text at para 123.
[108] Scottish Law Commission, *Report on Requirements of Writing* (Scot Law Com No 112), paras 2.34, 2.36.
[109] Scottish Law Commission, *Report on Requirements of Writing* (Scot Law Com No 112), para 2.36.
[110] Requirements of Writing (Scotland) Act 1995, s 14(2) and Sched 5.
[111] For *constitution* of trusts the old rules apply to trusts created prior to 1 August 1995, and trusts now require writing for constitution only if they involve heritage or a declaration by a person that he is sole trustee of his own property or any property that he may acquire: Requirements of Writing (Scotland) Act 1995, s 1(2)(a)(i) and (iii).

commenced prior to 1 August 1995 in which a question arises as to the deed of trust.[112]

25.10 OBLIGATIONS OF RELIEF

Express obligations of relief might be proved only by the writ of the party said to **25.10.1** have undertaken the obligation.[113] When an obligation of relief arose by force of law, nothing was to be proved other than the facts from which the obligation emerged, and these might be proved *prout de jure*.[114] So, for example, it might be proved by parole evidence that the pursuer, although bound as a principal to the creditor, is in fact a cautioner in relation to his co-debtor, the defender, and that he has paid the debt, and, if he proves these facts, the defender's obligation to relieve him arises by force of law.[115] There was also authority for the proposition that when, as between co-cautioners, the normal rights of relief had been varied by agreement, the true relationship between the co-obligants might be proved by parole evidence.[116] It has been said that an obligation of relief might be proved by parole evidence "when it forms part of a transaction which may be established by that means".[117]

25.11 PERFORMANCE AND DISCHARGE OF OBLIGATIONS CONSTITUTED OR VOUCHED BY WRITING

When an obligation has been constituted in writing prior to 1 August 1995,[118] or is **25.11.1** vouched by a document of debt drawn prior to that date,[119] its discharge or performance might be proved only by the writ of the other party. The rule is said to be in accordance with the maxim *unumquodque eodem modo dissolvitur quo colligatur*[120] (an obligation is discharged in the same manner as that in which it was constituted).[121] The rule appears to have been firmly established at least in relation

---

[112] Requirements of Writing (Scotland) Act 1995, s 14(4).

[113] *Devlin v McKelvie* 1915 SC 180; Gloag, *Contract* (2nd edn), p 195; Erskine, iv, 2, 20. The rule was assumed in *Clark v Callender* 9 Mar 1819, FC; (1819) 6 Paton 422; *Maconochie v Stirling* (1864) 2 M 1104; *Thoms v Thoms* (1867) 6 M 174; *Woddrop v Speirs* (1906) 14 SLT 319 (OH).

[114] Gloag, *Contract* (2nd edn), p 195.

[115] Bell, *Principles*, para 267; *Lindsay v Barmcotte* (1851) 13 D 718, per Lord Cuninghame at 725; *Thow's Tr v Young* 1910 SC 588, per Lord Skerrington at 593, per Lord President Dunedin at 595.

[116] *Hamilton & Co v Freeth* (1889) 16 R 1022; *Crosbie v Brown* (1900) 3 F 83. For the principle applicable, see para 27.14.

[117] Dickson, *Evidence* (3rd edn), para 606. The passage was held to apply only to cases where the obligation of relief is an integral part of a contract regarding moveables: *Devlin v McKelvie* 1915 SC 180, per Lord Salvesen at 187, Lord Guthrie at 189.

[118] Stair, iv, 43, 4; Erskine, iv, 2, 21; Dickson, *Evidence* (3rd edn), para 610; *Keanie v Keanie* 1940 SC 549; *Nicol's Trs v Sutherland* 1951 SC (HL) 21 (approving *Robertson v Thomson* (1900) 3 F 5).

[119] *Thiem's Trs v Collie* (1899) 1 F 764, per Lord Trayner at 774, 778, Lord Moncreiff at 780; Gloag, *Contract* (2nd edn), p 715. For the different rule when the written acknowledgement is qualified by an assertion that the debt has been paid or satisfied, or when a judicial admission founded upon is similarly qualified, see paras 3.12, 25.7.

[120] See, for example, *Nicol's Trs v Sutherland* 1951 SC (HL) 21, per Lord Simonds at 26, Lord Normand at 29.

[121] If the maxim was truly the basis of the rule, one would have expected the requirement that the discharge be embodied in a writing having the same solemnities as that which constituted the original obligation, with the usual exception where there is *rei interventus* or homologation, and that, apart from this exception, reference of an oral discharge to oath would have been regarded as incompetent. For a discussion of a similar question regarding an agreement to rescind a written obligation, see Gloag, *Contract* (2nd edn), pp 392–393.

to payment of money.[122] When the creditor under a written obligation denied the validity of the obligation and the debtor sought to prove that he had made payments in respect of it, not for the purpose of discharging it, but for some other purpose—as, for example, to establish *rei interventus*—the opinion was expressed that the rule did not apply, and that the fact of payment might be proved *prout de jure*.[123] Other exceptions to the rule allowed for proof *prout de jure* in cases concerning, for example, the performance of obligations *ad factum praestandum*,[124] averments of fraud,[125] and reliance by the creditor upon proof of payment.[126] An exception made for proof *prout de jure* in respect of circumstantial evidence of performance[127] to be proved beyond reasonable doubt[128] was outmoded even in relation to events occurring prior to 1 August 1995.[129]

25.12 PAYMENT OF MONEY UNDER ANTECEDENT OBLIGATIONS

25.12.1 The payment of a sum of money in implement of an antecedent obligation, even if the obligation was not expressed in writing, might as a general rule be proved only by the writ of the creditor,[130] unless the sum was £8.33 or less.[131] The rule applied to payment of the price of goods sold on credit[132]; payment of rent under an oral

---

[122] So, for example, if a creditor sued upon a bill of exchange as in *Nicol's Trs v Sutherland* 1951 SC (HL) 21; *Robertson v Thomson* (1900) 3 F 5; *Patrick v Watt* (1859) 21 D 637 (the rule applied in spite of the Bills of Exchange Act 1882, s 100); or an IOU as in *Thiem's Trs v Collie* (1899) 1 F 764, or for payment of a debt vouched by an incomplete bill of exchange as in *Lawson's Exrs v Watson* 1907 SC 1353, per the sheriff at 1357 (approved by the Inner House), and was met by a defence of payment, the defender had to prove payment by the pursuer's writ. The rule applied even if the payments alleged to have been made were each less than £8.33: *Robertson v Thomson* (1900) 3 F 5; Dickson, *Evidence* (3rd edn), para 610. Some of the examples given above were also subject to the rule which provided that payment of money under an antecedent obligation required proof by the creditor's writ: see para 25.12.
[123] *Foggo v Hill* (1840) 2 D 1322, per Lord Fullerton at 1334; Dickson, *Evidence* (3rd edn), para 614.
[124] Stair, iv, 43, 4; Erskine, iv, 2, 21; Gloag, *Contract* (2nd edn), p 720. As to a tenant delivering produce in terms of the lease, see Rankine, *Leases* (3rd edn), pp 319, 320.
[125] See Erskine, iv, ii, 21. The converse is also true. When a receipt was sent to the debtor merely as a reminder that payment was due and was retained and founded on by him as a true receipt, proof *prout de jure* of the circumstances in which the receipt came into the debtor's hands was allowed: *Henry v Miller* (1884) 11 R 713. See also *Kirkwood v Bryce* (1871) 8 SLR 435.
[126] Erskine, iii, 3, 50; *Chalmers v Lord Craigievar* (1628) M 12368; *Ross v Elliot* (1630) M 12369; *Foggo v Hill* (1840) 2 D 1322.
[127] *A & A Campbell v Campbell's Exrs* 1910 2 SLT 240, per Lord Skerrington at 241; *Mackintosh v Mackintosh* 1928 SC 83, per Lord Constable at 88; *Chrystal v Chrystal* (1900) 2 F 373, per Lord McLaren at 379; *Bishop v Bryce* 1910 SC 426, per Lord Johnston at 435–436—see also Lord President Dunedin at 430. These dicta were quoted with approval in *McKenzie's Exrx v Morrison's Trs* 1930 SC 830, per Lord Justice-Clerk Alness at 834.
[128] *Thiem's Trs v Collie* (1899) 1 F 764, per Lord Moncreiff at 780; approved in *Chrystal v Chrystal* (1900) 2 F 373, per Lord McLaren at 379; *McKenzie's Exrx v Morrison's Trs* 1930 SC 830, per Lord Justice-Clerk Alness at 834, 836.
[129] The matter was considered at some length in para 126(d) of the first edition of this text. The main cases cited there are cited in the two preceding footnotes, and their facts, together with the other examples given in the text of para 126(d) are illustrative of the type of circumstantial evidence which can constitute proof of performance, albeit that the restrictive rule and its particular exception no longer apply.
[130] *Burt v Laing* 1925 SC 181, per Lord President Clyde at 183–184, Lord Sands at 185; Dickson, *Evidence* (3rd edn), para 615. See also Bell, *Principles*, para 2257.
[131] Erskine, iv, 2, 21; Dickson, *Evidence* (3rd edn), para 615.
[132] *Shaw v Wright* (1877) 5 R 245; *Young v Thomson* 1909 SC 529, per Lord Dundas at 536; *Tod v Flockhart* (1799) Hume 498. As to the competency of proving the terms of a receipt or similar document, which has been lost or destroyed, as part of the defence to an action for payment, see *Young v Thomson* 1909 SC 529; *James Scott & Co (Electrical Engineers) Ltd v McIntosh* 1960 SLT (Sh Ct) 15.

lease[133]; payment by a solicitor to his client of money in his hands belonging to the client[134]; repayment of a loan of money[135]; and payment by a builder to a sub-contractor of sums to account of the contract price, which, in terms of the contract, ought to have been paid weekly as the work progressed.[136] The rule was not applicable unless the obligation was antecedent. So it did not apply when the payment was alleged to have been an integral part of an obligation constituted orally,[137] and to have been made at the same time as the creation of the obligation and *unico contextu* with it (as part of a single continuous act),[138] because in such circumstances writing was not expected on either side.[139] It did not apply, therefore, to the price of goods sold for ready money when payment was alleged to have been made at the time of the purchase or of the delivery of the goods[140] and was the immediate counterpart of delivery.[141] It was also held not to apply to the payment by a mandant to a mandatory of a sum of money at the same time as the giving of the instructions for its investment which constituted the mandate.[142] In such cases the payment, like the contract of which it forms part, might be proved *prout de jure*. The rule did not apply to proof of the performance of obligations *ad factum praestandum*.[143] Proof *prout de jure* was also allowed where the relationship between the payer was merely the "hand" of the payee in connection with the day-to-day administration of the payee's affairs, and that the practice, as proved or as presumed from the circumstances, was to account daily or weekly for his intromissions without obtaining receipts.[144]

---

[133] Rankine, *Leases* (3rd edn), p 320. *Earl of Lauderdale v Tenants* (1662) M 12362.

[134] *Mackenzie v Brodie* (1859) 21 D 1048 at 1052. See also *Cairns v Garroch's Creditors* (1747) M 11389 (factor). The position is different when the person who must prove payment is merely the "hand" of the owner of the money. See *Tosh v Ogilvy* (1873) 1 R 254 (proof by parole allowed but held insufficient).

[135] *Thiem's Trs v Collie* (1899) 1 F 764, per Lord Trayner at 778; *Jackson v Ogilvie's Exr* 1935 SC 154, per Lord Moncrieff (Ordinary) at 160. In practice repayment of a loan of money was usually subject to the rule which required discharge of an obligation vouched by writing to be proved by writ. See para 25.7.

[136] *Hope Brothers v Morrison* 1960 SC 1 (OH). The Lord Ordinary observed that had the rule not applied the evidence would have favoured a contrary result, and that reform of it was overdue.

[137] Bell, *Principles*, para 565. See also Dickson, *Evidence* (3rd edn), para 616; Gloag, *Contract* (2nd edn), p 717.

[138] *Burt v Laing* 1925 SC 181, per Lord Sands at 185.

[139] Dickson, *Evidence* (3rd edn), para 616.

[140] Dickson, *Evidence* (3rd edn), para 616; Gloag, *Contract* (2nd edn), p 717; *Stewart v Gordon* (1831) 9 S 466. In *Macdonald v Callender* (1786) M 12366, parole proof of payment a few days after delivery was allowed, but this decision was regarded as doubtful by Baron Hume (*sub voce Tod v Flockhart* (1799) Hume 498 at 499), Dickson, *Evidence* (3rd edn), para 616, and Lord Gifford in *Shaw v Wright* (1877) 5 R 245 at 247, although it is cited without disapproval in Gloag, *Contract* (2nd edn), p 717.

[141] *Shaw v Wright* (1877) 5 R 245, per Lord Gifford at 247.

[142] *Burt v Laing* 1925 SC 181.

[143] See para 25.11.

[144] For example, the brother of a farmer who was compelled to retire from active work through ill health lived with him and acted as farm overseer under him until his death four years later, and during the period reported all transactions orally to him from day to day: *Russell's Trs v Russell* (1885) 13 R 331 (see also *Stuart v Maconochie* (1836) 14 S 412); a son, residing with his father, intromitted with his property and accounted to him without taking receipts, until his death: *Lord Saltoun v Fraser* (1722) M 11425; and a son managing his father's affairs when he became incapax, was not sued by his younger brothers until 13 years later: *Wilson v Wilson* (1783) M 11646; a domestic servant, who collected his employer's rents and sold her corn under her oral instructions, left her employment without quarrel with her and after receiving all his wages, no action for an accounting being raised until after his death: *Irvine v Falconer* (1671) M 11424; a taverner who, in accordance with custom, was presumed to account to his employer for the takings nightly or weekly, left the employer's service and continued to live in the same city for nine months before an action for accounting was raised by the employer: *Couts v Couts* (1636) M 11423.

25.13 RENUNCIATION[145] OF RIGHTS

25.13.1 As a general rule the renunciation of rights constituted in writing, without payment or performance by the obligant, might be proved only by the writ of the creditor.[146] As distinct from the similar rule regarding proof of performance and discharge of such obligations, which was mentioned earlier,[147] the rule in this case may perhaps be justified by regarding such unilateral renunciations as gratuitous obligations, for the proof of which writ was always appropriate.[148] The rule was applied to the renunciation of an acknowledgement of trust,[149] a decree-arbitral,[150] a written lease,[151] a decree of removal,[152] the right to do diligence on a decree,[153] and a stipulation in a feu charter as to the vassal's use of the subjects.[154] A difference of opinion existed as to whether there was a restriction on mode of proof of renunciation when the right had been constituted orally. One view was that it could be proved by parole evidence.[155] The other view was that the renunciation, if it took place not at the time of the making of the contract but after an interval, could be proved only by the writ of the creditor.[156] The former view prevailed[157] up to the time of the abolition of the rule in relation to contracts entered into after 1 August 1995. Exceptions to the rule allowed proof *prout de jure* of actings by the creditor which give rise to an inevitable inference that the right has been renounced by him.[158] Similarly, proof *prout de jure* might be allowed of actings by the debtor with the consent of the creditor,[159] which were inconsistent with or

---

[145] Also acceptilation or *acceptilatio* ("discharge of an obligation by complete or partial remission of performance": *Glossary of Scottish Legal Terms etc.*, Butterworths).

[146] Erskine, iii, 4, 8; Dickson, *Evidence* (3rd edn), para 627; Gloag, *Contract* (2nd edn), p 722.

[147] See para 25.11.

[148] See para 25.15.

[149] *Keanie v Keanie* 1940 SC 549.

[150] Dickson, *Evidence* (3rd edn), para 627.

[151] *Lord Shaw v Palmer* (1605) M 12301; *Lord Craigmillar v Chalmers* (1639) M 12308.

[152] *Countess of Argyle v Sheriff of Moray* (1583) M 12300.

[153] *Reid v Gow & Sons* (1903) 10 SLT 606 (OH).

[154] *Scot v Cairns* (1830) 9 S 246.

[155] Erskine, iii, 4, 8; Gloag, *Contract* (2nd edn), p 722, n 4. This is the view preferred by the Scottish Law Commission in their *Report on Requirements of Writing* (Scot Law Com No 112), para 3.9.

[156] Dickson, *Evidence* (3rd edn), para 629; *Kilpatrick v Dunlop* 1909 2 SLT 307 (OH). This was the view preferred by the authors in the first edition of this text, on the basis that a renunciation of this kind was a gratuitous obligation. This did not apply to sums of £8.33 or less, or to rights which are both constituted and renounced on the same occasion, when parole evidence is sufficient.

[157] *Armia Ltd v Daejan Developments Ltd* 1979 SC (HL) 56, and see Scottish Law Commission *Report on Requirements of Writing* (Scot Law Com No 112), para 3.9.

[158] Dickson, *Evidence* (3rd edn), para 628. So, for example, proof *prout de jure* was allowed of averments that obligatory documents had been destroyed or given up, as when an IOU was handed by the creditor to the debtor for destruction in her presence: *Anderson's Trs v Webster* (1883) 11 R 35; or that the creditor had entered into a new contract with the debtor regarding the same subject-matter: Gloag, *Contract* (2nd edn), pp 392, 722; Erskine, ii, 6, 44 (new lease); *Campbeltown Coal Co v Duke of Argyll* 1926 SC 126 (new lease), per Lord President Clyde at 131; *Edinburgh Entertainments Ltd v Stevenson* 1926 SC 363 (new lease), per Lord Justice-Clerk Alness at 378. A bill of exchange or promissory note, if delivered up to the acceptor, need not be renounced in writing: Bills of Exchange Act 1882, s 62(1). As to the presumption arising from a creditor's inability to produce the document of debt, see para 3.9.

[159] This part of the statement in the text is based upon the terms of the issue directed by the House of Lords in *Wark v Bargaddie Coal Co* (1859) 3 Macq 467 (at 488) for the trial of the cause: "Whether the barrier coal worked ... by the defenders was so worked ... with the consent of the pursuer."

contradictory of the right, and which justified an inference that the right had been renounced.[160]

25.14 INNOMINATE AND UNUSUAL CONTRACTS

Such contracts might be proved only by the writ of the other party.[161] The restric-   **25.14.1**
tion of proof did not apply merely because the contract was innominate (*ie* not one of the recognised consensual contracts), and earlier statements to the contrary effect[162] were disapproved.[163] In order that the restriction might apply, the contract, in addition to being innominate, also had to be of an unusual, anomalous or peculiar character.[164] It was for the court in each case to decide whether or not the contract, as described in the averments of the party alleging it, was of this character.[165] Proof was restricted to writ on this ground in relation to the following contracts: an agreement by a landlord that if the tenant of the farm would remain in occupancy to the end of the lease, and pay the rent, he would repay the whole loss incurred by the tenant during the 19 years of the lease[166]; an agreement by a person negotiating for a feu charter from a landowner, that he would pay the latter's legal expenses whether the negotiations were successful or not[167]; a confused and complex oral agreement between merchants, said to be the basis of all future business between them, that the pursuers would purport to purchase goods from the defenders, but would in fact receive only a commission on a resale by them to a named purchaser[168]; an agreement between two managing directors of a limited company that if one would vote for an increase in the salary of the other, the latter would pay to the former half the increase obtained[169]; an agreement by a guarantor of his son-in-law's bank overdraft that the son-in-law need relieve him of payments made under the guarantee only if his financial circumstances allowed, and that if they did not, the payments would be regarded as having been made to account of

---

[160] *Keanie v Keanie* 1940 SC 549, per Lord Wark at 559; *Lavan v Gavin Aird & Co* 1919 SC 345, per Lord Justice-Clerk Scott Dickson at 348, Lord Dundas at 350; *Kirkpatrick v Allanshaw Coal Co* (1880) 8 R 327, per Lord President Inglis at 334. This part of the statement in the text is thought to be justified by the dicta cited in this note. It seems irrelevant to consider whether an express oral renunciation, followed by actings of the kind described, might itself be proved by parole evidence, since, if the required actings themselves had to justify an inference of renunciation, it was immaterial whether there was an express oral renunciation or not.

[161] *Smith v Reekie* 1920 SC 188; *Allison v Allison's Trs* (1904) 6 F 496, per Lord President Kinross at 500; *Hendry v Cowie & Son & Co* (1904) 12 SLT 31, 261; *Forbes v Caird* (1877) 4 R 1141, per Lord Deas at 1142; *Thomson v Fraser* (1868) 7 M 39, per Lord Neaves at 41.

[162] Erskine, iv, 2, 20; *McFadzean's Exr v Robert McAlpine & Sons* 1907 SC 1269, Lord President Dunedin at 1273; *Cochrane v Traill & Sons* (1900) 2 F 794, per Lord Young at 799.

[163] *Smith v Reekie* 1920 SC 188; *Allison v Allison's Trs* (1904) 6 F 496, per Lord President Kinross at 500; *Hendry v Cowie & Son & Co* (1904) 12 SLT 31, 261; *Forbes v Caird* (1877) 4 R 1141, per Lord Deas at 1142; *Thomson v Fraser* (1868) 7 M 39, per Lord Neaves at 41.

[164] *Smith v Reekie* 1920 SC 188; *Allison v Allison's Trs* (1904) 6 F 496, per Lord President Kinross at 500; *Hendry v Cowie & Son & Co* (1904) 12 SLT 31, 261; *Forbes v Caird* (1877) 4 R 1141, per Lord Deas at 1142; *Thomson v Fraser* (1868) 7 M 39, per Lord Neaves at 41.

[165] For example, an observation to the effect that a contract was not in this category was made in *McEleveen v McQuillan's Exrx* 1997 SLT (Sh Ct) 46. See also the facts of *Denvir v Denvir* 1969 SLT 301.

[166] *Garden v Earl of Aberdeen* (1893) 20 R 896.

[167] *Woddrop v Speirs* (1906) 44 SLR 22 (OH).

[168] *Muller & Co v Weber & Schaer* (1901) 3 F 401, per Lord Ordinary (Kincairney) at 404. The First Division adhered on different grounds.

[169] *Jackson v Elphick* (1902) 10 SLT 146 (OH).

his wife's interest in the guarantor's estate.[170] In respect of the following contracts the restriction of proof was not applied, and proof *prout de jure* was allowed: an agreement by an innkeeper to stable horses for a horse-drawn bus free of charge on condition that the bus called at the inn on its way to and from the railway station[171]; an agreement by owners of a drifter to pay a daily bonus to the crew, over and above wages paid by the Admiralty, while the crew and the drifter remained in Admiralty service[172]; an agreement by a defender to pay £2000 and judicial expenses on condition that the pursuer publicly abandoned his case at the conclusion of the defence evidence, so that the defender might obtain a verdict,[173] and an agreement for the compromise of a litigation by a person who was not a party, but had a material interest in it[174]; an agreement by a prospective partner to advance a sum of money to the firm on condition that it would be repaid if he decided not to become a partner[175]; an agreement to act as manager of a business for a yearly salary and a share of profits,[176] and to act as a debt collector without remuneration apart from what could be extracted from the debtors.[177] A contract to bequeath money or property by testamentary settlement might, after the testator's death, be proved only by writ, partly because it was innominate and unusual,[178] and partly because to hold otherwise would have had the practical result of allowing a testamentary settlement to be proved by parole evidence.[179] A contract by a solicitor to charge only in the event of success had been held to be anomalous and unusual, and to be provable only by writ,[180] but speculative actions are now well known in practice having repeatedly received judicial recognition[181] and, more recently, statutory recognition.[182]

25.15 GRATUITOUS OBLIGATION

25.15.1 A unilateral gratuitous obligation or promise, for which no return was asked, as distinct from a bilateral contract in which obligations were undertaken on both

---

[170] *Williamson v Foulds* 1927 SN 164 (OH). See also *Cook v Grubb* 1963 SLT 78 at 81, 85, 87, 89 ("permanent employment" of motor mechanic).

[171] *Forbes v Caird* (1877) 4 R 1141.

[172] *Smith v Reekie* 1920 SC 188.

[173] *Jaffray v Simpson* (1835) 13 S 1122.

[174] *Thomson v Fraser* (1868) 7 M 39.

[175] *Hendry v Cowie & Son & Co* (1904) 12 SLT 31, 261.

[176] *Allison v Allison's Trs* (1904) 6 F 496.

[177] *Fisher v Fisher & Ors* 1952 SC 347; *McMurrich's Trs v McMurrich's Trs* (1903) 6 F 121, per Lord Kincairney (Ordinary) at 123; *Johnston v Goodlet* (1868) 6 M 1067, per Lord Justice-Clerk Patton at 1072; *Edmondston v Edmondston* (1861) 23 D 995.

[178] *Edmondston v Edmondston* (1861) 23 D 995, per Lord Jerviswoode (Ordinary) at 1000; *Johnston v Goodlet* (1868) 6 M 1067, per Lord Justice-Clerk Patton at 1072; *Hallet v Ryrie* (1907) 15 SLT 367 (OH); *Smith v Oliver* 1911 SC 103, per Lord President Dunedin at 111–112; *Gray v Johnston* 1928 SC 659, per Lord Hunter at 668, Lord Ormidale at 670; *Jackson v Ogilvie* 1933 SLT 533 (OH). With regard to some of these decisions, see para 25.15.

[179] *Taylor v Forbes* (1853) 24 D 19 (note). See also *Forbes v Caird* (1877) 4 R 1141, per Lord Deas at 1142.

[180] *X Insurance Co v A and B* 1936 SC 225, per Lord President Normand at 239, Lord Fleming at 250.

[181] *Jacobs v McMillan* (1899) 2 F 79, per Lord Kincairney (Ordinary). It was unnecessary for the Second Division to consider the mode of proof allowed, and no opinions on it were expressed. See also *A & A Campbell v Campbell's Exrs* 1910 2 SLT 240 (per Lord Skerrington (Ordinary) quoted at 241).

[182] Solicitors (Scotland) Act 1980, s 61A.

sides, might be proved only by writ of the obligant or reference to oath.[183] The restriction of proof applied even when the creditor had subsequently incurred expenditure, or otherwise altered his position in the expectation that the obligation would be implemented.[184] When an obligation, while *ex facie* unilateral and gratuitous, was in fact part of a bilateral onerous contract which might be proved by parole evidence, the obligation also might be so proved.[185]

---

[183] Erskine, iv, 2, 20; Dickson, *Evidence* (3rd edn), para 598; Gloag, *Contract* (2nd edn), p 50, and see, for example, *Jackson v Ogilvie* 1933 SLT 533 (OH).

[184] Gloag, *Contract* (2nd edn), p 51, and see *Smith v Oliver* 1911 SC 103; *Gray v Johnston* 1928 SC 659; *Millar v Tremamondo* (1771) M 12395.

[185] *Hawick Heritable Investment Bank v Hoggan* (1902) 5 F 75; Dickson, *Evidence* (3rd edn), para 598; Gloag, *Contract* (2nd edn), p 52.

CHAPTER 26

PROOF OF ACTINGS TO PERFECT PROOF OF OBLIGATIONS—PERSONAL BAR, *REI INTERVENTUS* AND HOMOLOGATION

26.1 INTRODUCTORY

At common law if an agreement or obligation which required formal writing for **26.1.1** its constitution had not been so constituted there was *locus poenitentia*, and either party might resile. But if the agreement or obligation was established by judicial admission, or by writ, and actings had followed on it the agreement or obligation might become binding. When the actings were those of the person seeking to enforce the agreement or obligation they were known as *rei interventus*; when they were those of the person seeking to resile they were known as homologation.[1] Not infrequently both parties took some action following on an imperfect agreement, and both *rei interventus* and homologation were pleaded and might support each other.[2]

Since 1 August 1995 the requirement for formal writing to constitute certain **26.1.2** forms of obligation, contract or trust has been regulated by the Requirements of Writing (Scotland) Act 1995, s 1. This section also requires writing for the creation, transfer, variation or extinction of an interest in land and for the making of a will or other testamentary settlement. Apart from other statutory requirements for writing for the constitution of matters to which the particular statute refers, there is no requirement for an obligation to be put in writing for its formal validity or proof. The Requirements of Writing (Scotland) Act 1995 also prescribes a statutory means of perfecting the contract, obligation or trust, if it has not been committed to writing in the form required by the legislation, by proof of acts or omissions by the parties to a contract, the creditor or beneficiary as the case may be.[3] That statutory provision expressly replaces the common law rules of *rei interventus* and homologation in relation to the constitution or variation of the contracts, obligations and trusts for which the Act requires writing,[4] but the saving provisions are such that the statutory rule applies only to matters occurring after

---

[1] *Mitchell v The Stornoway Trs* 1936 SC (HL) 56 at 63; *McCalman v McArthur* (1864) 2 M 678 at 682.
[2] *Bathie v Lord Wharncliffe* (1873) 11 M 490 at 496; *Kinnear v Young* 1936 SLT 574.
[3] s 1(3) and (4).
[4] s 1(5).

the commencement of the Act.[5] Clearly the old rules still apply in relation to occurrences before commencement of the Act. However, there remains the question as to whether the common law rules are preserved for the future in relation to other matters requiring writing in terms of the statute, namely the creation etc of an interest in land such as sale or lease or a testamentary settlement. One view is that the common law rules do not survive; such obligations must be constituted in writing[6] and cannot be perfected by *rei interventus* or homologation.[7] The other view, and the one which accords with a standard approach to statutory interpretation, is that the common law is altered only in so far as can be taken from the express words of the statute, and that the common law rules of *rei interventus* and homologation in so far as they applied in such circumstances remain in existence.[8] This chapter looks first at the nature and extent of the statutory rule, and then examines the common law in the same way. In so far as an issue arises in relation to the interpretation or application of the statutory rule it is thought that the interpretations of the common law rules may be called upon.

26.2 STATUTORY *REI INTERVENTUS*

26.2.1 The provisions of the Requirements of Writing (Scotland) Act 1995, s 1(3) and 1(4) come into play when a contract, obligation or trust which in terms of section 1(2)(a) requires writing for its constitution or variation, is not constituted or varied in a written document complying with section 2.[9] "[I]f a party to the contract, a creditor in the obligation or a beneficiary under the trust ('the first person') has acted or refrained from acting in reliance of the contract, obligation or trust with the knowledge or acquiescence of the other party, the debtor in the obligation or the truster ('the second person')—(a) the second person shall not be entitled to withdraw from the contract, obligation or trust; and (b) the contract, obligation or trust shall not be regarded as invalid, on the ground that it is not so constituted".[10] However, there is a further condition which must be satisfied before that provision can apply, viz that the position of the first person (a) as a result of so acting or so refraining from acting has been affected to a material extent; and (b) as a result of such a withdrawal would be adversely affected to a material extent.[11] Hence the elements required for the statutory rule to apply are: (a) a preceding contract, obligation or trust which the Act requires to be put in writing; (b) an absence of writing in the form required by the Act; (c) actings or omissions *in reliance of* the contract, obligation or trust; (d) acquiescence by the other party in relation to those actings; (e) material effect to the person who relied upon the contract, obligation or trust as

---

[5] s 14(3). Commencement date is 1 August 1995.

[6] In terms of s 1(2)(b).

[7] Reid, annotations to Requirements of Writing (Scotland) Act 1995, s 1(5), supported by Scottish Law Commission, *Report on Requirements of Writing* (Scot Law Com No 112), para 2.50, although he notes that this is not necessarily desirable in policy terms.

[8] Cusine & Rennie, *The Requirements of Writing*, para 3.08, consider that homologation is not lost altogether for the future, despite the intention of the Scottish Law Commission that it should be: *Report on Requirements of Writing* (Scot Law Com No 112), para 2.40. They make no comment as to the possible continuing effect of *rei interventus* at common law, although they note the limited scope of the new provisions: see para 3.03.

[9] For the requirements of such a writing, see paras 22.2–22.4.

[10] s 1(3).

[11] s 1(4).

a result of the acts or omissions; and (f) adverse effect to that party to a material extent if withdrawal was permitted.

There is no express requirement as to the nature of proof of the contract, obli- **26.2.2** gation or trust. At common law there had to be competent evidence in the form of a writ or admission[12] in proof of the invalid contract or obligation before the invalidity could be cured by *rei interventus* or homologation. The restriction of proof of a matter to writ was removed by the Requirements of Writing (Scotland) Act 1995[13] although expressly saved in relation to proceedings which had commenced before 1 August 1995.[14] However, the prospective effect of the Act in general has been interpreted to retain the restriction in so far as it applied to contracts or obligations entered into prior to 1 August 1995 but raised in proceedings after 1 August 1995.[15] There can be no doubt that in proceedings raised after 1 August 1995 relating to a contract, obligation or trust created after 1 August 1995 to which the Requirements of Writing (Scotland) Act 1995 applies, no restriction on proof applies, and proof *prout de jure*, including parole proof, applies.[16] In terms of the Civil Evidence (Scotland) Act 1988 hearsay evidence would be admissible, if the evidence could competently be given orally, and corroboration is not required (although it must surely be desirable if the elements of the statutory test are to be proved).

The statutory rule replaces both *rei interventus* and homologation[17] which **26.2.3** together encompassed the actings of both parties, and offered a remedy to either party. At the time of writing there is little reported case law in relation to the application of the statutory form of *rei interventus*,[18] which is open to either party in the case of contractual matters, but only to the beneficiary in matters of trust or gratuitous unilateral obligations. However, in so far as the elements of the statutory rule are broadly consistent with elements of the common law rules the case law in relation to the common law rules should be of value in interpreting and applying the statutory rule.

26.3 *REI INTERVENTUS*—GENERAL

Rei interventus or homologation might have the effect of completing an agree- **26.3.1** ment, although the parties had not expressly agreed to all the terms[19] or making binding an informal agreement to vary a written contract.[20] Although the term is sometimes used in a wide sense to cover the whole principle, viz the agreement and the actings following thereon, its precise meaning is a real change of position[21]

---

[12] See para 26.1.1. Proof of the obligation by reference to oath was also possible, but was removed as a procedure by the Requirements of Writing (Scotland) Act 1995, s 11(1), (2) and (4). This does not prevent a party from calling the other as a witness: *McDonnell v McShane* 1967 SLT (Sh Ct) 61.

[13] s 11(1).

[14] s 11(4).

[15] *McEleveen v McQuillan's Exrx* 1997 SLT (Sh Ct) 46.

[16] See, for example, *Bryce v Marwick* unreported, Aberdeen Sh Ct, 19 Mar 1999 (A2342/97).

[17] Cusine & Rennie consider that homologation might still be pled at common law as personal bar: see *The Requirements of Writing*, para 3.08.

[18] In *Super (Tom) Printing and Supplies Ltd v South Lanarkshire Council (No 2)*, 1999 GWD 38-1856 (OH), an attempt to rely on s 1(3) and (4) to establish variation failed at debate *inter alia* on specification and relevancy of the actings. See also 1999 GWD 31-1496.

[19] The cases are discussed at para 26.4.3.

[20] See, for example, *BP Oil Ltd v Caledonian Heritable Estates Ltd* 1990 SLT 114.

[21] Bell, *Principles*, para 27A.

by the creditor. Bell's description has frequently been approved. *"Rei interventus* raises a personal exception, which excludes the plea of *locus poenitentiae*. It is inferred from any proceedings not unimportant on the part of the obligee, known to and permitted by the obligor to take place on the faith of the contract as if it were perfect,[22] provided they are unequivocally referable to the agreement and productive of alteration of circumstances, loss or inconvenience, though not irretrievable."[23] Although Bell referred only to contract, the principle applied also to unilateral obligations such as a cautionary obligation,[24] provided that all the cautioners had signed.[25] It also applied to prevent the granter of a deed from founding on the fact that his signature was not properly attested.[26] Since *rei interventus* raises a personal exception the doctrine is really part of the general doctrine of personal bar.[27]

26.4 PROOF OF AGREEMENT

General

26.4.1 Subject to the exception mentioned below, no amount of *rei interventus* would be of any avail unless the agreement, or obligation, was established by competent evidence.[28] Although it had frequently been laid down that the agreement could be established only by writ or oath,[29] this was not exhaustive. It could also be established by admission on record[30] or by a combination of these. Thus a partial admission on record might be completed by writ.[31] If the new rule is invoked in relation to an obligation entered into after 1 August 1995 the restriction of mode of proof does not apply and parole evidence of the obligation is competent.[32] If the common law rule is invoked in relation to an obligation entered into before 1 August 1995 the restriction upon mode of proof of the original agreement may

---

[22] *ie* executed with the necessary formalities.

[23] Bell, *Principles*, para 27.26. For the use of the phrase to mean actings from which a new agreement must be inferred, see para 26.4.4.

[24] *National Bank of Scotland v Campbell* (1892) 19 R 885; *Church of England Fire and Life Assurance Co v Wink* (1857) 19 D 1079.

[25] *Paterson v Bonar* (1844) 6 D 987. But *cf Craig v Paton* (1865) 4 M 192, where a cautioner signed and delivered the bond knowing that a co-cautioner refused to sign, and was held liable. Attestation may not be necessary: see para 24.8.

[26] *National Bank of Scotland v Campbell* (1892) 19 R 885. See also *Baird's Tr v Murray* (1883) 11 R 153.

[27] *Boyd v Shaw* 1927 SC 414 and *Baird's Tr v Murray* (1883) 11 R 153 raised substantially the same question as *National Bank of Scotland v Campbell* (1892) 19 R 885 and *Church of England Fire and Life Assurance Co v Wink* (1857) 19 D 1079 but they were decided on general pleas of personal bar.

[28] *Stobo Ltd v Morrisons (Gowns) Ltd* 1949 SC 184; *East Kilbride Development Corporation v Pollok* 1953 SC 370; *Buchanan v Duke of Hamilton* (1878) 5 R (HL) 69 (where it turned out that there was no *consensus in idem*). If the agreement was made by an agent, his authority must be implied, admitted or proved: *Pratt v Abercromby* (1858) 21 D 19. For the exception see para 26.4.3.

[29] *Sutherland's Tr v Miller's Tr* (1888) 16 R 10 (decided in the sheriff court on oath and in the Division on writ); *Gibson v Adams* (1875) 3 R 144; *Philip v Gordon Cumming's Exrs* (1869) 7 M 859 (the rubric is misleading); *Walker v Flint* (1863) 1 M 417. Reference to oath was abolished in all proceedings other than those raised prior to 1 August 1995 by the Requirements of Writing (Scotland) Act 1995, s 11(1), (2) and (4).

[30] *Church of England Fire and Life Assurance Co v Wink* (1857) 19 D 1057.

[31] *Paterson v Earl of Fife* (1865) 3 M 423.

[32] The combined effect of the Requirements of Writing (Scotland) Act 1995, s 11(1) and s 14(3).

have been saved.[33] However, some authority exists for proof of the original agreement to be completed by parole evidence[34] despite clear authority to the contrary.[35]

Proof by writ[36]

In so far as the agreement required to be proved by writ, the writ founded upon did **26.4.2** not require to be one to which the opponent was a party,[37] and some of the terms might be proved by one writ and some by another writ[38] or document referred to in the writ.[39] The following have been held sufficient: a docquet in a building plan,[40] a return under the Valuation Acts,[41] entries in the landlord's books,[42] an offer from the tenant,[43] an adjusted draft[44] and a receipt for feu-duty which stated the area of the ground.[45]

Incomplete agreement

Express agreement on every term was, generally speaking, not necessary. In lease, **26.4.3** for example, if the four essentials—parties, subjects, duration and rent—could be established by writ or judicial admission, and nothing had been said about the other terms, the lease was binding if *rei interventus* or homologation had followed; and the clauses usual and necessary in a lease of its kind were added by the court,[46] after a remit, if necessary, to a conveyancer.[47] The same course was competent in a sale of heritage,[48] where there required to be evidence of *consensus in idem*[49] but

---

[33] See the Requirements of Writing (Scotland) Act 1995, s 14(3) and *McEleveen v McQuillan's Exrx* 1997 SLT (Sh Ct) 46.

[34] *Errol v Walker* 1966 SC 93, the reasoning in which, although widely criticised, drew no adverse comment from the House of Lords in *Morrison-Low v Paterson* 1985 SC (HL) 49. The reasoning was founded upon a passage in Gloag, *Contract* (2nd edn) at pp 46–47 which in turn was based upon *Colquhoun v Wilson's Trs* (1860) 22 D 1035. For criticism of the decision in *Errol v Walker*, see Stewart (1966) 11 JLSS 263, Smith, "*Rei Interventus* revisited" 1986 SLT (News) 137, McBryde, para 27–44, Cusine & Rennie, *Missives*, para 3.36. However, see Gretton & Reid in *Conveyancing*, (2nd edn) para 3.14 and the Scottish Law Commission in *Report on Requirements of Writing* (Scot Law Com No 112), para 3.13.

[35] In *Mitchell v The Stornoway Trustees* 1936 SC (HL) 56, Lord Macmillan (at 66) criticised an earlier judgment to this effect: *Seller v Aiton* (1875) 2 R 381, per Lord Shand at 390.

[36] As to proof by writ generally, see Chapter 25.

[37] *Emslie v Duff* (1865) 3 M 854.

[38] *Wilson v Mann* (1876) 3 R 527.

[39] *Stewart's Exrs v Stewart* 1994 SLT 466.

[40] *Mitchell v The Stornoway Trustees* 1936 SC (HL) 56.

[41] *Emslie v Duff* (1865) 3 M 854.

[42] *Wares v Duff Dunbar's Trs* 1920 SC 5.

[43] *Forbes v Wilson* (1873) 11 M 454.

[44] *Bathie v Lord Wharncliffe* (1873) 11 M 490. See also *Lang v Lang's Trs* (1889) 16 R 590.

[45] *Stodart v Dalzell* (1876) 4 R 236. However, a receipt for a year's rent must be distinguished from the last example, since it does not indicate the endurance of the lease: *Gowans' Trs v Carstairs* (1862) 24 D 1382.

[46] See *Shetland Islands Council v BP Petroleum Development Ltd* 1990 SLT 82 (OH), where the court would not dictate a term for a long lease, but might have applied a term if an annual tenancy had been found to exist but where the parties had not agreed upon an ish.

[47] *Wight v Newton* 1911 SC 762 at 772, 775; *Erskine v Glendinning* (1871) 9 M 656.

[48] *Westren v Millar* (1879) 7 R 173 at 178.

[49] *Grant v Peter G Gauld & Co Ltd* 1985 SLT 545. In *Barratt Scotland v Keith* 1994 SLT 1337 the land to be sold was specified only "as agreed", the extent having allegedly been the subject of prior informal agreement, but proof before answer was permitted on a plea of *rei interventus* and homologation.

the date of entry was not essential to agreement.[50] However, it could not be followed if, in the circumstances, more than the usual and necessary clauses required to be added, or if there was insufficient averment of agreement or even negotiation of lease.[51] Where the essentials of sale of heritage were agreed, but it was clear that various reservations and servitudes would be required, which had not been discussed, it was held that there was no sufficient agreement.[52] If, on the other hand, an additional term had been discussed, but there was no competent evidence that it had been agreed to, the result appeared to depend upon the importance attached to the term by the parties in their communings, "a question of degree, of the relative importance of the point left unsettled."[53] In a sale of heritage the question of the servitudes to be imposed on the ground, described by Lord Deas as "of vital importance", and by Lord Shand as "of vital consequence", had been discussed, but no agreement reached, and it was held that there was no contract.[54] However, where only "petty details" remained unsettled, the bargain was held complete, the details being left for subsequent settlement.[55]

Actings in proof of the underlying agreement

26.4.4 The decision of the Inner House in *Errol v Walker*[56] constituted a departure from the understood requirement that the underlying agreement required to be proved by writ or judicial admission. In that case a holograph offer to purchase subjects previously occupied under a long lease was not accepted in writing, but there were actings of the pursuer's wife acquiesced in by the pursuer and improvements made by the defender of which the pursuer was aware.[57] There was no dispute between the parties in that case as to *consensus in idem* and, after reviewing the authorities, including the decision of the House of Lords in *Mitchell v The Stornoway Trustees*[58] the Inner House, relying upon a passage in Gloag,[59] came to a contrary conclusion, to the effect that parole proof of actings was competent even where the actings were in support of the existence, as compared to the formalisation, of the underlying agreement. The decision has been widely criticised,[60] and although

---

[50] *Secretary of State for Scotland v Ravenstone Securities Ltd* 1976 SC 171, followed in the Outer House in *Gordon District Council v Wimpey Homes Holdings Ltd* 1988 SLT 481. *Cf Law v Thomson* 1978 SC 343, an Outer House case in which *Secretary of State for Scotland v Ravenstone Securities Ltd* was not cited.

[51] See, for example, *Pickard v Ritchie* 1986 SLT 466 (OH).

[52] *Stobo Ltd v Morrisons (Gowns) Ltd* 1949 SC 184.

[53] Gloag, *Contract* (2nd edn), p 40.

[54] *Heiton v Waverley Hydropathic Company* (1877) 4 R 830. *Cf Colquhoun v Wilson's Trs* (1860) 22 D 1035, doubted in so far as it proceeded on the view that the actings are evidence of the contract in *Mitchell v The Stornoway Trustees* 1936 SC (HL) 56, per Lord Macmillan at 66, and in *East Kilbride Development Corporation v Pollok* 1953 SC 370 at 374, but followed on this point in *Errol v Walker* 1966 SC 93.

[55] *Westren v Millar* (1879) 7 R 173.

[56] 1966 SLT 159.

[57] *Errol v Walker* 1966 SC 93.

[58] 1936 SC (HL) 56.

[59] *Contract* (2nd edn), pp 46–47, together with *Ballantine v Stevenson* (1881) 8 R 959 and *Keir v Duke of Atholl* (1815) 6 Paton 130.

[60] See Stewart (1966) 11 JLSS 263, Smith "*Rei Interventus* revisited" 1986 SLT (News) 137, McBryde, para 27-44, Cusine & Rennie, *Missives*, para 3.36. However, see also Gretton & Reid *Conveyancing*, (2nd edn) para 3.14 and the Scottish Law Commission in *Report on Requirements of Writing* (Scot Law Com No 112), para 3.13.

adopted in some instances,[61] it has been carefully distinguished in others.[62] The matter was of relevance at common law because of the restriction of mode of proof of the underlying agreement. Under the statutory regime the underlying agreement would not per se require to be in writing, and in any event restricted modes of proof are expressly abolished for the future.[63]

26.5 THE ACTINGS

General

The actings, or the abstention from action, which might be equally effective,[64] **26.5.1** might be judicially admitted[65] or proved by parole evidence.[66] But they did not constitute *rei interventus* so as to render the agreement effectual unless they were performed in reliance on the agreement, known to the obligor to be so performed, and productive of some loss to the obligee. Although all three conditions must be proved, at common law they might have a bearing on each other.[67] The more extensive the actings, the more likely they were to be known to the obligor, and the more expensive they were, the more likely they were to have been performed in reliance on the agreement. Under statute the actings must be in reliance of the agreement, but the material effect of these is a separate condition of the rule, and although the effect must be as a result of the actings there is no requirement for direct connection between the effect and the reliance. In all cases the averments must be sufficiently specific to show that the actings fulfilled the conditions.[68]

Reliance on agreement

At common law, and under statute, the actings must be such as would not have **26.5.2** been done except in reliance on the agreement. "Unequivocally referable to the agreement" are Bell's words, and the phrase "not unimportant" refers, not to the extent of the acts, but to their nature or significance[69] in showing reliance on the agreement.[70] In comparison the statutory rule requires actings which are in reliance upon the agreement and, separately, that those actings had "material effect". Accordingly it is not necessary that the effects are themselves directly referable to the reliance. Obviously the acts must be subsequent in date to the agreement.[71]

---

[61] By the House of Lords in *Morrison-Low v Paterson* 1985 SC (HL) 49.

[62] *eg* in the Inner House in *Stewart's Exrs v Stewart* 1993 SC 427, *Cumming v Quartzag Ltd* 1980 SC 276, by Lord Cullen in the Outer House in *Shetland Islands Council v BP Petroleum Development Ltd* 1990 SLT 82, and in *Mulhern v Mulhern* 1987 SLT (Sh Ct) 62.

[63] Requirements of Writing (Scotland) Act 1995, s 11, but see s 14(3) as to possible continuing effect in relation to agreements made prior to 1 August 1995 and *McEleveen v McQuillan's Exrx* 1997 SLT (Sh Ct) 46.

[64] *Danish Dairy Co v Gillespie* 1922 SC 656 at 666, 670, 672.

[65] *Beardmore & Co v Barry* 1928 SC 101; point not raised in House of Lords, 1928 SC (HL) 47.

[66] *Mitchell v The Stornoway Trustees* 1936 SC (HL) 56 at 63.

[67] *Buchanan v Harris & Shelden* (1900) 2 F 935 at 939; *Danish Dairy Co v Gillespie* 1922 SC 656.

[68] *Van Laun & Co v Neilson Reid & Co* (1904) 6 F 644 at 653. But somewhat vague averments passed in *National Benefit Trust Ltd v Coulter* 1911 SC 544.

[69] The word used by the Lord President in *Bathie v Lord Wharncliffe* (1873) 11 M 490 at 496, and by Lord Macmillan in *Mitchell v The Stornoway Trustees* 1936 SC (HL) 56 at 66.

[70] *Buchanan v Harris & Shelden* (1900) 2 F 935.

[71] *Pollok v Whiteford* 1936 SC 402; *Van Laun & Co v Neilson Reid & Co* (1904) 6 F 644; *Mowat v Caledonian Banking Co* (1895) 23 R 270.

Most of the cases deal with leases, and it must be plain that the acts are referable to a lease[72] for a term of years and not equally referable to a lease for a year.[73] When a tenant pulled down buildings and drove tiles for draining, both obligations mentioned in a draft lease, and also spent a considerable amount on lime and manure, these actings were held to have been done in reliance on the draft lease for 19 years.[74] Where there was an informal agreement for a lease, followed by a probative lease, which was reduced, the tenant's entry and other actings were held to be referable to the lease and not to the informal agreement.[75] Where there was a binding agreement for renewal of a lease, and the tenant sought to establish an additional oral agreement, it was held that the acts founded on were ordinary acts of tenancy and so referable to the lease.[76] Where a farm had been leased to the father of the current occupiers by a lease which continued by tacit relocation until his death, the continued occupation by his sons after his death, although mistakenly believed by both the landowner and occupiers to be founded upon continued tacit relocation of the father's lease, was held to be referable to a lease in favour of the sons.[77]

Obligor's knowledge and possession

26.5.3   The actings must be permitted to take place on the faith of the contract as if it were perfect. The statutory language is "with the knowledge and acquiescence" of the other party. It is necessary, accordingly, either that the obligor should know of the actings and allow them to take place as if there was a binding contract,[78] or at least that the actings should be such as would naturally be expected to follow on the agreement.[79] Thus it was held irrelevant to aver that the obligee had given up a business in order to take possession under a lease, without averring knowledge by the obligor.[80] Knowledge and permission by an agent are sufficient, but only if the agent has implied or express authority to enter into the agreement,[81] or to permit the acts.[82] It may be more difficult to establish knowledge of abstention from acting than knowledge of positive acts.[83] A singular successor may be bound not only by knowledge of the informal agreement, but also by knowledge of facts which should put him on his inquiry.[84]

---

[72]   As compared to a personal obligation between the parties, as in *BP Oil Ltd v Caledonian Heritable Estates Ltd* 1990 SLT 114 (OH).

[73]   *Pollok v Whiteford* 1936 SC 402; *Mowat v Caledonian Banking Co* (1895) 23 R 270; *Buchanan v Nicoll* 1966 SLT (Sh Ct) 62.

[74]   *Bathie v Lord Wharncliffe* (1873) 11 M 490; *Sutherland's Tr v Miller's Tr* (1888) 16 R 10.

[75]   *Gardner v Lucas* (1878) 5 R 638; point not raised in House of Lords (1878) 5 R (HL) 105.

[76]   *Philip v Gordon Cumming's Exrs* (1869) 7 M 859. The rubric is misleading. See also *Mitchell v The Stornoway Trustees* 1936 SC (HL) 56.

[77]   *Morrison-Low v Paterson* 1985 SC (HL) 49.

[78]   *Bell v Goodall* (1883) 10 R 905; *Stewart v Burns* (1877) 4 R 427, where the pursuer (the seller) warned out a tenant at the defender's request.

[79]   *Gardner v Lucas* (1878) 5 R 638 at 650, 656; *Danish Dairy Co v Gillespie* 1922 SC 656 at 666, 670; *National Bank of Scotland v Campbell* (1892) 19 R 885; *Boyd v Shaw* 1927 SC 414 (pleaded as personal bar, but similar to *National Bank of Scotland v Campbell*).

[80]   *Gardner v Lucas* (1878) 5 R 638.

[81]   *Danish Dairy Co v Gillespie* 1922 SC 656.

[82]   *Heiton v Waverley Hydropathic Co* (1877) 4 R 830.

[83]   *Danish Dairy Co v Gillespie* 1922 SC 656.

[84]   *Stodart v Dalzell* (1876) 4 R 236. In *Wilson v Mann* (1876) 3 R 527, it was held that a lease constituted by informal writ and *rei interventus* was good against a singular successor, whether he knew of the *rei interventus* or not. But knowledge of a mere personal right is irrelevant: *Wallace v Simmers* 1961 SLT 34; *Morier v Brownlie & Watson* (1895) 23 R 67.

Consequent loss or inconvenience

In the common law rule the entire phrase is "productive of alteration of circum- **26.5.4** stances, loss or inconvenience, though not irretrievable", and with it is coupled in many opinions the earlier words "proceedings not unimportant". Under statute the equivalent is the requirement of "material effect".[85] The effect upon the obligee required to be more than as a result of their own misunderstanding of the situation.[86] The importance depended upon the size of the transaction,[87] and in most of the cases the point was clear one way or the other.[88] The seller or landlord withdrawing the subjects from the market, and the purchaser or tenant taking possession and expending money on the subjects are frequent examples.[89]

26.6 HOMOLOGATION

It is unclear whether the statutory rule has the effect of abolishing homologation **26.6.1** in circumstances other than those to which the replacement statutory *rei interventus* applies.[90] Homologation had a wider scope than *rei interventus*. Not only might it exclude *locus poenitentia* from an imperfectly constituted agreement, but it might also bar reduction of a properly constituted agreement voidable on some extrinsic ground such as error.[91] Bell's definition of homologation is "an act approbatory of a preceding engagement, which is itself defective or informal, either confirming it or adopting it as binding. It may be express or inferred from circumstances. It must be absolute and not compulsory, nor proceeding on error or fraud, and unequivocally referable to the engagement; and must imply assent to it, with full knowledge of its extent, and of all the relative interests of the homologator."[92] Homologation thus differs from *rei interventus* in one important respect. No prejudice to anyone need be established, except the loss of the right to resile.[93]

---

[85] Requirements of Writing (Scotland) Act 1995, s 1(4).
[86] *Cumming v Quartzag Ltd* 1980 SC 276, but misunderstanding by both parties did not prevent the rule from applying in *Morrison-Low v Paterson* 1985 SC (HL) 49.
[87] *Kinnear v Young* 1936 SLT 574 (OH).
[88] In *Mitchell v The Stornoway Trustees* 1936 SC (HL) 56 there was considerable debate about this point.
[89] See, for example, the facts in *Morrison-Low v Paterson* 1985 SC (HL) 49.
[90] Cusine & Rennie think that it might still be pled in personal bar: see *The Requirements of Writing*, para 3.08.
[91] Gloag, *Contract* (2nd edn) deals with the first application of homologation at pp 171 *et seq* and with the second at pp 544 *et seq*. Although this latter application of homologation falls outside the law of evidence, the decisions are used interchangeably as authorities in both branches; in *Danish Dairy Co v Gillespie* 1922 SC 656 (defective writings relating to lease), Lord President Clyde (at 664) cited *Gardner v Gardner* (1830) 9 S 138 (reduction *ex capite lecti*).
[92] *Principles*, para 27. Bell also refers there to "adoption" which differs from homologation. An imperfectly constituted obligation may be adopted, and so validated, if it is repeated, confirmed or corroborated in a properly authenticated writing, which is in effect a new obligation. No knowledge of the original defect is necessary, and the obligation takes effect from the date of the adoption, not, as in homologation, from the date of the imperfect obligation. See, for example, *Callander v Callander's Trs* (1863) 2 M 291. Gloag, *Contract* (2nd edn), p 171, seems to treat this as a case of homologation. This is essentially a matter of construction and effect of later contracts rather than evidence. Evidence may be of importance where it is pled that a void deed, *eg* a forged deed, has been adopted; see *Muir's Exrs v Craig's Trs* 1913 SC 349.
[93] *Mitchell v The Stornoway Trustees* 1936 SC (HL) 56 at 67. Professor Rankine's statement, *Personal Bar* at p 144, is at least misleading.

Where the deed is a conveyance defective *in substantialibus* there seems to have been no room for homologation.[94]

26.6.2   The preceding engagement had to be established by writ[95] or judicial admission.[96] The following have been held to be sufficient proof by writ: the docquetting of building plans[97]; an acknowledgement of loan neither holograph nor tested[98]; an informal offer to lease[99]; an informal submission and award[100]; an improbative award[101]; improbative offer and acceptance of a lease.[102] Naturally, the approbatory act had to be subsequent to the engagement.[103] Since the act was evidence of consent it had to be that of one capable of consenting. A person without legal capacity could not homologate.[104] Further, the party had to know of a right to resile.[105] An act after an action had been raised probably had no effect,[106] nor had one done under reservation or protest.[107] If the act was that of an agent it had no effect unless the agent had authority to conclude the contract or the principal authorised the act.[108]

---

[94] *Boswell v Boswell* (1852) 14 D 378; *Robertson v Ogilvie's Trs* (1844) 7 D 236 at 242, 244; *Grant v Shepherd* (1847) 6 Bell's App 153.

[95] *Mitchell v The Stornoway Trustees* 1936 SC (HL) 56 at 64 (where this is taken for granted).

[96] There is no direct authority for this, but it seems sound in principle.

[97] *Mitchell v The Stornoway Trustees* 1936 SC (HL) 56. The docquet followed on other writings.

[98] *M'Calman v M'Arthur* (1864) 2 M 678. Since the decision in *Paterson v Paterson* (1897) 25 R 144, the document alone would have sufficed without proof of homologation. See para 25.7.

[99] *Forbes v Wilson* (1873) 11 M 454.

[100] *Bremner v Elder* (1875) 2 R (HL) 136. The criticism in the House of Lords of the interlocutor of the Court of Session is difficult to reconcile with its own action in sustaining the appellant's fifth plea.

[101] *Robertson v Boyd and Winans* (1885) 12 R 419; *Danish Dairy Co v Gillespie* 1922 SC 656.

[102] *Danish Dairy Co v Gillespie* 1922 SC 656.

[103] *Mitchell v The Stornoway Trustees* 1936 SC (HL) 56 at 62, 63.

[104] Erskine, iii, 3, 47.

[105] *Shaw v Shaw* (1851) 13 D 877 (defective execution of missive of lease); not an easy report to follow, but Lord Cockburn states the principle clearly. Where an heir performed acts apparently approbatory of a deed of entail it was held in a reduction *ex capite lecti* that he had not homologated because he did not know that the deed was reducible: *Gardner v Gardner* (1830) 9 S 138, cited by Lord President Clyde in *Danish Dairy Co v Gillespie* 1922 SC 656. For another example, where the facts were contrary to the requirements for homologation, see *Clark's Exr v Cameron* 1982 SLT 68.

[106] *Harkness v Graham* (1833) 11 S 760 (reduction on the ground of minority and lesion). There was ratification, not homologation, by the minor after he attained majority and after the action had been raised. Apparently the minor was bankrupt and had no interest in the outcome of the case. A litigant is not likely to perform an approbatory act against his own interest, and one in his own favour could not be taken into account.

[107] *Miller & Son v Oliver & Boyd* (1906) 8 F 390, where the pursuers were held not to have consented to the enlargement of the scope of a reference because they had protested timeously.

[108] *Danish Dairy Co v Gillespie* 1922 SC 656. In *Forbes v Wilson* (1873) 11 M 454 the agent had authority, but in addition the landlord had knowledge. See also *Clark's Exr v Cameron* 1982 SLT 68.

CHAPTER 27

EVIDENCE EXTRINSIC TO WRITINGS

27.1 INTRODUCTORY—THE GENERAL RULE

As a general rule, at common law it is incompetent to contradict, modify or explain **27.1.1**
writings by parole or other extrinsic evidence.[1] The traditional statement of the
rule emphasises the important principle that the court, when seeking the intention
of the writer, should find it in the words which are used in the writing. "The duty
of the court in dealing with the document is not to discover the abstract or secret
intention of the parties as contradistinguished from what they have expressed but
to construe and give effect to the words in which they have deliberately set forth
their final intention."[2] The rule has been considered to be an exclusionary rule
preventing admissibility of relevant evidence on the ground that it is not best
evidence,[3] but it may also be rooted in relevancy[4]; the existence of a document

---

[1]   Dickson, *Evidence* (3rd edn), para 1015. The equivalent English rule provides that extrinsic evidence is inadmissible to contradict, vary, add to or subtract from the terms of a writing: *Bank of Australasia v Palmer* [1897] AC 540, per Lord Morris at 545; Cross & Tapper, pp 765–769, but, subject to exceptions, it admits extrinsic evidence for the purpose of explaining or interpreting a writing.
[2]   Dickson, *Evidence* (3rd edn), para 1043. See also para 27.19.
[3]   Lewis, *Manual of the Law of Evidence in Scotland*, p 91.
[4]   Noted by Cross & Tapper, *Evidence* (9th edn) pp 651–652 in relation to the equivalent English rule, citing *Lambert v Lewis* [1982] AC 225 at 263, and by the Scottish Law Commission, *Report on Three Bad Rules in Contract Law* (Scot Law Com No 152), para 2.16 in relation to proof of additional terms, and in *Report on*

which purports to be the deliberate expression of the parties' intentions in most circumstances renders irrelevant evidence of other intention, prior communings, additions or variations. Exceptions have evolved through case law in a fragmented yet overlapping fashion,[5] and in some cases it is by no means clear whether the court considers that the rule applied but that there was an applicable exception, or that the rule did not apply in the first place. Statutory exceptions have been added at the suggestion of the Scottish Law Commission, for rectification of a document agreed to be defective,[6] for proof of additional terms of a contract or unilateral voluntary obligation,[7] and for proof of continuing effect of missives in relation to heritable property in respect of which a disposition has been delivered.[8] Proposals of the Scottish Law Commission for the admission of extrinsic evidence where relevant to interpretation[9] were published in 1997[10] but are not yet implemented. In this chapter there is an attempt to state the present extent of the general rule,[11] the classes of writing to which the rule does and does not apply, and the extent of the exceptions at common law and under statute. Suggestions that the rule be abolished completely[12] have not been put into effect,[13] despite comment that courts tend to overlook it in favour of the receipt of all relevant evidence, at least allowing discovery and proof before answer as to the relevance and admissibility of the extrinsic evidence.[14] Certainty of contract and writings is cited as the prevailing reason for continuation of the rule itself,[15] and it is impossible to

---

Interpretation in Private Law (Scot Law Com No 160), paras 8.10–8.17, in relation to extrinsic evidence in aid of interpretation.

[5] Many cases will appear in more than one of the exception categories set out below.

[6] Scottish Law Commission, *Obligations. Report on Rectification of Contractual and other Documents* (Scot Law Com No 79).

[7] Scottish Law Commission, *Report on Three Bad Rules in Contract Law* (Scot Law Com No 152), Part II.

[8] Scottish Law Commission, *Report on Three Bad Rules in Contract Law* (Scot Law Com No 152), Part III.

[9] The proposal is not limited to interpretation of a writing, but to any act of will or intention which is intended by the maker of that act "a juridical act" to have legal effect: see draft bill attached to *Report on Interpretation in Private Law* (Scot Law Com No 160).

[10] Scottish Law Commission, *Report on Interpretation in Private Law* (Scot Law Com No 160), preceded by Discussion Paper No 101, *Interpretation in Private Law* (1996).

[11] There are conflicting views as to whether the admissibility of extrinsic evidence is part of the law of evidence, or whether, since it relates to construction, it is part of substantive law. For a discussion of the subject, see Phipson, "Evidence in Aid of Interpretation" (1904) 20 LQR 245 at pp 246–247.

[12] Macphail, *Evidence*, at para 15.38 re the rule in general, and raised again by the Scottish Law Commission in their Discussion Paper No 97, para 2.41 in relation to additional terms. In *Report on Interpretation in Private Law* (Scot Law Com No 160) there is no discussion of complete abolition of the extrinsic evidence rule, only of its many overlapping exceptions in the context of interpretation, despite the criticisms made at para 1.2 and the acknowledgement at para 8.8 that the trend in practice is towards admission of all relevant extrinsic evidence in aid of interpretation.

[13] Macphail, *Evidence*, para S15.39. The Scottish Law Commission in their Memorandum No 46, paras P.06–P.07 sought comments on the possibility of abolition or a presumption in place of the exclusionary rule, and the latter was preferred by respondents: see Scottish Law Commission *Report on Three Bad Rules in Contract Law* (Scot Law Com No 152), para 2.27. The same reaction was received to the Commission's suggestion in relation to proof of additional terms: *Report on Three Bad Rules in Contract Law*, para 2.28.

[14] Scottish Law Commission, *Report on Interpretation in Private Law* (Scot Law Com No 160), para 8.8. Despite the comments of the Commission's Advisory group, cases in which extrinsic evidence is disregarded after proof are hard to track down or monitor.

[15] As in *Inglis v Buttery & Co* (1877) 5 R 58. Macphail, *Evidence*, paras 15.34 and 15.36, re the rule in general. Scottish Law Commission, *Report on Three Bad Rules in Contract Law* (Scot Law Com No 152), paras 2.19 and 2.34 re the prohibition against proof of additional terms. See also in relation to evidence of subsequent actings, *Miller & Partners Ltd v Whitworth Street Estates (Manchester) Ltd*

measure the extent to which the existence of such a rule exerts indirect pressure upon parties to carefully express and adhere to the terms of writings. It is suggested that certainty could be achieved without a rule excluding evidence extrinsic to the writing,[16] thus admitting extrinsic evidence either subject to specified exceptions or subject to careful application of the relevance test to the writing and the averments in the context of the applicable substantive law.

27.2 MEANING OF EXTRINSIC EVIDENCE

"Extrinsic evidence", as used in the general rule, includes parole evidence[17] but is **27.2.1** not confined to it. It extends to all evidence, documentary,[18] oral or real, extraneous to the document. Thus it includes parole testimony given by the parties themselves or by any other witness to relevant fact or opinion, hearsay evidence, including evidence of statements which they have made orally or in writing by way of extra-judicial admission, or as to their intention in executing the document, or as to their understanding of its meaning and effect, and evidence of the actings of the parties or course of dealing before and after the execution of the document, including the evidence of any writings dealing with these actings.

27.3 WRITINGS TO WHICH GENERAL RULE APPLIES

The writings to which the common law rule applies have been described as those **27.3.1** which the parties have constituted as the only outward and visible expression of their meaning, and deliberately prepared as the record of a transaction[19] or unilateral voluntary obligation.[20] The definition includes the discharge, as well as the creation, of obligations. The general rule applies to documents which have been drawn up because required by law and also to those drawn up by choice. Accordingly it applies to events which the law requires to be constituted, varied or

---

[1970] AC 583, per Lord Reid at 603E: "I must say that I had thought that it was now well settled that it is not legitimate to use as an aid in the construction of the contract anything which the parties said or did after it was made. Otherwise one might have the result that a contract meant one thing the day it was signed, but by reason of subsequent events meant something different a month or a year later." A historical wariness of parole evidence was influential in the development of the rule, but is of no current influence: Scottish Law Commission, *Report on Three Bad Rules in Contract Law* (Scot Law Com No 152), paras 2.17 and 2.21.

[16] Of course, there is a move away from writing as a means of constituting and recording an obligation or event, which is reflected in the terminology used by the Scottish Law Commission in the most recent of their reports impacting on this topic, *Report on Interpretation in Private Law* (Scot Law Com No 160). Macphail advocated abolition of the rule in 1988: Macphail, *Evidence*, para 15.39.

[17] A mistrust of parole evidence has been cited as one of the justifications for the rule: Scottish Law Commission, *Report on Three Bad Rules in Contract Law* (Scot Law Com No 152), paras 2.17 and 2.21.

[18] For the wide definition of "document" to include material recorded electronically, orally or visually, see Civil Evidence (Scotland) Act 1988, s 9, and para 21.1.

[19] Dickson, *Evidence* (3rd edn), paras 1015, 1016 and 1043. "The whole doctrine of the exclusion of parole testimony with regard to … a written document rests upon this, that the document is intended to be a final and conclusive statement of the whole transaction between the parties." *McAdam v Scott* (1912) 50 SLR 264, per Lord Kinnear at 266–267. However, it should not preclude the parties from reaching and proving subsequent separate agreements upon the same or similar subject-matter: *How Group Northern Ltd v Sun Ventilating Co Ltd* 1979 SLT 277 at 279 (OH).

[20] Contract (Scotland) Act 1997, s 1(1).

discharged in writing, that is the transactions referred to in the Requirements of Writing (Scotland) Act 1995, s 1, those for which writing is required by any other enactment,[21] and those requiring writing not for constitution but enforcement, such as cautionary obligations.[22] The rule also applies to informal documents such as commercial writings[23] or receipts and to a joint minute for the settlement of an action[24] and generally to writings which have been drawn up by choice rather than requirement.[25] It also applies to a writing which would be ineffective but for homologation, *rei interventus*[26] or statutory personal bar.[27]

Unilateral writings

27.3.2 The general rule applies[28] to unilateral writings which constitute, create or discharge obligations on the part of the granter,[29] or from which such obligations or their discharge are inferred. It thus applies to personal and heritable bonds and discharges,[30] to bills of exchange,[31] cheques and promissory notes,[32] and to cautionary obligations.[33] It has been applied to a discharge by creditors of all debts due to them prior to a certain date,[34] and by an employer of all sums due by his factor,[35] and to receipts for payment of sums due to the granters, such as receipts

---

[21] As to matters for which writing is now required, see Chapter 22.

[22] *eg McPherson v Haggart* (1881) 9 R 306. See para 24.8.

[23] It applied to writings *in re mercatoria*, as in, *eg, Inglis v Buttery & Co* (1878) 5 R (HL) 87. Any privilege attaching to writings *in re mercatoria* was removed by the Requirements of Writing (Scotland) Act 1995, s 11(3)(b), but informal commercial writings, in so far as they appear to embody the contract or obligation, are still subject to the general rule or one of its exceptions. If they appear to contain all of the terms of the contract, there is a presumption that they do so, but, unless the contract states expressly that it contains all the terms of the agreement between the parties the completeness may be rebutted by evidence to the effect that there was an additional term: Contract (Scotland) Act 1997, s 2.

[24] *Hamilton & Baird v Lewis* (1893) 21 R 120. Proof of an oral agreement to vary the terms of the joint minute was refused.

[25] *Riemann v John Young & Co Ltd* (1895) 2 SLT 426 (OH) (contract of employment terminable at short notice).

[26] For example, *Pratt v Abercromby* (1858) 21 D 19; *Wight v Newton* 1911 SC 762; *Campbell v Western Islands Council* 1988 SLT (Lands Tr) 4. See also *Bathie v Lord Wharncliffe* (1873) 11 M 490.

[27] In terms of the Requirements of Writing (Scotland) Act 1995, s 1(4) and (5).

[28] Dickson, *Evidence* (3rd edn), para 1016.

[29] As to these generally, see para 23.9. In *Walker v Hendry* 1925 SC 855 and *Graham v Stirling* 1922 SC 90 relating to a notice to remove from, or a notice of intention to leave, a farm it was contended that the general rule applied to the document. It was held that parole evidence was admissible to prove that one co-proprietor or co-tenant signed, not only on his own behalf, but also on behalf of the other proprietor or tenant, but it was not made clear in the opinions whether this was regarded as an exception to the general rule, or whether the general rule was regarded as not applicable to such a document. These cases should probably be regarded merely as examples of the rule of the law of principal and agent which allows the authority of a principal to be proved by parole evidence. See para 27.14.

[30] *Wallace v Henderson* (1867) 5 M 270; *Drysdale v Johnstone* (1839) 1 D 409.

[31] *National Bank of Australasia v Turnbull & Co* (1891) 18 R 629, per Lord President Inglis at 634, Lord McLaren at 638. For a statutory exception to the application of the general rule to bills of exchange, see para 24.5.

[32] As to the application of the general rule to bills of exchange, cheques and promissory notes, and the exceptions thereto, see para 24.5.

[33] See also *Hilson v Otto* (1870) 9 M 18 (deed for appointment of a factor); *Stevenson v Manson* (1840) 2 D 1204 (mandate to buy shares from which an obligation to pay stockbroker's commission was implied); *Mackenzie v Dunlop* (1853) 16 D 129 (scrip notes obliging the granter to deliver iron to bearer).

[34] *Harris v Churchill* (1822) 1 S 348.

[35] *Spence v Duncan* (1706) M 12333.

written on the back of a bill of exchange for payments to account of the sum due under it,[36] a receipt for payment of a sum due by the insurers under a policy of insurance,[37] and a receipt in the body of a disposition of heritage in respect of payment of the price.[38]

Statute, judicial decree and similar writings

The general rule applies to rights and obligations constituted by official and public **27.3.3** writings as it does to those constituted by private writings. It was applied to an obligation imposed by statute upon a railway company to accept a lease of a railway line on terms and conditions specified in the statute,[39] and to a right of inheritance constituted by statute[40]; to a right to a lump sum payment under a small debt decree[41]; to a liquidator's right to remuneration in terms of a resolution recorded in a minute, the making of which was directed by statute[42]; and to the boundaries of a glebe as fixed by a decree or minute of a presbytery.[43]

27.4 INCORPORATION OF OTHER WRITINGS BY REFERENCE

General

The application of the general rule to a particular document has not excluded con- **27.4.1** sideration by the court of other writings, if the terms of the document show, by express reference or clear implication,[44] that the other writings are intended to be incorporated in it, or to be looked at in construing it.[45] In accordance with this principle the courts have considered, in conjunction with the terms of the principal document, plans,[46] schedules or specifications,[47] standard conditions applying at the date of the contract,[48] estate rules in connection with leases,[49] and the rules of

---

[36] *Macfarlane v Watt* (1828) 6 S 556.

[37] *Anderson v Forth Marine Insurance Co* (1845) 7 D 268.

[38] *Gordon v Trotter* (1833) 11 S 696. It has also been applied to a receipt which acknowledged, not only the payment of money, but also the terms of a bilateral contract in respect of which the payment was made, such as a receipt for a sum of money "in payment of purchase price of 150 shares ... the transfer for which will be sent you for signature in due course": *Lindsay v Craig* 1919 SC 139.

[39] *Stirling & Dunfermline Railway Co v Edinburgh & Glasgow Railway Co* (1852) 14 D 747; (1853) 15 D (HL) 48.

[40] *McMurrich's Trs v McMurrich's Trs* (1903) 6 F 121, per Lord McLaren at 125–126.

[41] *Lavan v Gavin Aird & Co* 1919 SC 345. See also *Watson v Gardner* (1834) 12 S 588.

[42] *City of Glasgow Bank Liquidators* (1880) 7 R 1196; Companies Act 1862, s 67; now Companies Act 1985, s 382(1).

[43] *Dalhousie's Tutors v Minister of Lochlee* (1890) 17 R 1060; affd (1891) 18 R (HL) 72.

[44] See McBryde, *Contract*, paras 13-26 to 13-30.

[45] Dickson, *Evidence* (3rd edn), para 1047.

[46] *Burrell & Son v Russell & Co* (1900) 2 F (HL) 80, per Lord Chancellor Halsbury at 84 (express incorporation); *Edinburgh Tramways Co v Black* (1873) 11 M (HL) 57, per Lord Chelmsford at 58 (private Act—implied incorporation); *Shearer v Peddie* (1899) 1 F 1201; *Boyd v Hamilton* 1907 SC 912 (feu disposition—implied incorporation).

[47] *Aberdeen Railway Co v Blaikie* (1851) 13 D 527 (schedule expressly incorporated in contract); *Wilson v Glasgow and South-Western Railway Co* (1851) 14 D 1 (specification expressly incorporated in contract); *D Cameron & Son v McLeod* 1999 GWD 20-918 (Sh Ct) (schedule and plans incorporated in estimate verbally accepted).

[48] *Smith v UMB Chrysler (Scotland) Ltd* 1978 SC (HL) 1.

[49] *Lyon v Irvine* (1873) 1 R 512 (general regulations expressly incorporated); *Pratt v Abercromby* (1858) 21 D 19 (general regulations expressly incorporated for limited purpose). For other cases, see Rankine, *Leases* (3rd edn), p 108.

an association of which only one of the contracting parties was a member.[50] In some cases it was held that the other writing was incorporated in the principal document for a limited purpose only.[51] If another writing is held to have been incorporated by express reference or clear implication in the principal document, extrinsic evidence is admissible to identify the other writing.[52] The mere exhibition by one of the parties to the other of a writing such as a plan,[53] or a list of articles to be used in connection with the contract,[54] does not necessarily incorporate it in the written contract subsequently executed, and estate regulations which were expressly incorporated in the lease of a sitting tenant were held not to be incorporated by implication in missives of lease of the same property to the same tenant, which were to take effect on the expiry of the existing lease.[55] And the mere reference in the principal document to an earlier holograph agreement, even when it is expressly stated to be in implement of that agreement, does not have the effect of incorporating the earlier agreement in the principal document, or of allowing it to be founded upon as controlling or qualifying the terms of that document.[56] The admissibility of the earlier document would depend upon it falling within one of the recognised exceptions at common law or under statute.

Testamentary writings

27.4.2   The principle applicable to testamentary writings is similar to that applying to other writings, although what was described in the last paragraph as "the principal document" may, in the case of testamentary writings, consist of several documents. All the unrevoked testamentary writings, or parts of testamentary writings, of the testator must be read together as if they were one document.[57] The testator may, by reference to it in his testamentary writings, incorporate therein another writing, which may be informal, and parole evidence is admissible to identify the other writing to which the testamentary writings refer.[58] A reference

---

[50] *Stewart, Brown & Co v Grime* (1897) 24 R 414: distinguished in *McConnell & Reid v Smith* 1911 SC 635 at 638.

[51] *Barr v Robertson* (1854) 16 D 1049 (plan); *Pratt v Abercromby* (1858) 21 D 19 (estate rules); *Shearer v Peddie* (1899) 1 F 1201 (plan); *Boyd v Hamilton* 1907 SC 912 at 919 (plan); *Goodwins Jardine & Co Ltd v Brand & Son* (1905) 7 F 995 (arbitration clause in contract between one of parties and a third party).

[52] Dickson, *Evidence* (3rd edn), para 1049; *Burroughs Machines Ltd v Timmoney* 1977 SC 393.

[53] *Boyd v Hamilton* 1907 SC 912; *Gordon v Marjoribanks* (1818) 6 Dow 87 at 112; *Heriot's Hospital v Gibson* (1814) 2 Dow 301 at 306, 311–312. In the two House of Lords decisions cited, the earlier speech of Lord Mansfield to the contrary effect in *Deas v Magistrates of Edinburgh* (1772) 2 Pat 259 was found unacceptable.

[54] *Walker v Caledonian Railway Co* (1858) 20 D 1102.

[55] *Stewart v Maclaine* (1899) 37 SLR 623 (HL).

[56] *Lee v Alexander* (1883) 10 R (HL) 91, per Lord Watson at 96. *Cf Davidson v Magistrates of Anstruther Easter* (1845) 7 D 342 at 352, 353, per Lord Fullerton (354–355) dissenting; *Renton v North British Railway Co* (1847) 9 D 1209—Lord Fullerton (1217) dissented in this case also. In *Leith Heritages Co v Edinburgh & Leith Glass Co* (1876) 3 R 789 (action of damages for breach of warrandice), Lord Gifford (at 794) stated that a minute of sale was "embodied" in a disposition because it was referred to in the narrative. In Lord Ormidale's opinion (at 799) the earlier deed could be looked at only because of an ambiguity in the dispositive clause of the disposition, and Lord Neaves and the Lord Justice-Clerk proceeded upon other and special grounds of decision.

[57] *Magistrates of Dundee v Morris* (1858) 3 Macq 134; *Horsbrugh v Horsbrugh* (1847) 9 D 329 at 340–341, 353, 359–360; *Tronson v Tronson* (1884) 12 R 155 at 157, 158. See also *Wingate v Wingate's Trs* 1921 SC 857. Whether a testamentary writing revokes or qualifies all the earlier testamentary writings, or only some of them, depends upon the construction of the writings by the court: *Bankes v Bankes' Trs* (1882) 9 R 1046.

[58] *Inglis v Harper* (1831) 5 W & S 785.

to "such bequests as I may instruct . . . in a letter signed by me this date" was held to have the effect of incorporating the letter in the will. The question of whether it is competent to look at testamentary writings which have been revoked is discussed later in this chapter.[59]

27.5 IMPLIED TERMS

The general rule applies not only to the express terms of a writing but also to terms **27.5.1** which, apart from express stipulation in the writing itself, are implied by law.[60] When a deed, which *ex facie* is solemnly executed, is delivered by the granter, implied authority is thereby given to the grantee to insert a testing clause when necessary, and proof of an intention that there should be no testing clause is incompetent.[61] The conveyance of a building having a mutual gable which overlapped a neighbouring building stance gave to the disponee an implied right to recover half the value of the gable from the owner of the stance when he came to build upon it.[62]

27.6 WRITINGS FALLING OUTWITH GENERAL RULE

Since the general rule applies to all writings in which, by agreement of the parties, **27.6.1** their obligations have been constituted or an earlier oral informal agreement has been subsequently embodied in a formal and effective written contract with the intention that it should take the place of the earlier agreement,[63] it follows that a writing which is not the embodiment of the contract or obligation falls outwith the general rule. When a contract is intended by the parties to be partly oral and partly in writing,[64] or is an oral contract in which a writing is incorporated,[65] the oral stipulations may be proved by parole evidence. So, in a case which concerned a contract for the supply of iron pipes of certain dimensions at a specified price per

---

[59] See para 27.22.

[60] *Barclay v Neilson* (1878) 5 R 909. See also *Wight v Newton* 1911 SC 762. It was held to be an implied term of a joint minute in which two defenders undertook to pay a sum of money to the pursuer in settlement of an action, all questions of relief between the co-obligants being expressly reserved, that each defender should be liable for half, and proof of an oral agreement to the contrary was refused: *Union Canal Co v Johnston* (1834) 12 S 304; (1835) 1 Sh & Macl 117. It is thought that the decision would have been otherwise but for the express reference in the joint minute to the obligations of the co-obligants *inter se*, which made it necessary for the court to decide this matter on a construction of the writing. In general the liabilities of co-obligants *inter se* may be proved *prout de jure*. See para 27.14.

[61] *Shaw v Shaw* (1851) 13 D 877 at 879. For documents requiring writing drawn after 1 August 1995 there is express authority for this in the Requirements of Writing (Scotland) Act 1995, s 3(3)(b).

[62] *Baird v Alexander* (1898) 25 R (HL) 35, per Lord Chancellor Halsbury at 37; Lord Herschell, at 39, reserved his opinion; Lord Shand, at 41, thought the missives might be looked at to see if they contained a discharge of the right. Reference is made later in the chapter to implied terms arising in special circumstances, which, by an exception to the general rule, may be proved by extrinsic evidence. See para 27.21.

[63] *Inglis v Buttery & Co* (1877) 5 R 58, per Lord Gifford at 69; approved (1878) 5 R (HL) 87, per Lord Blackburn at 102; *Walker v Caledonian Railway Co* (1858) 20 D 1102.

[64] See the examples in Dickson, *Evidence* (3rd edn), para 1033, and in *H Widdop & Co Ltd v J & J Hay Ltd* 1961 SLT (Notes) 35, Lord Kilbrandon noted "Nothing is commoner in business, and nothing would be less reasonable than to select out of the communings between parties those which happen to be in writing and to maintain that that there, and there only, is the contract to be found."

[65] Dickson, *Evidence* (3rd edn), para 1037.

yard, all specified in writing, proof of an oral stipulation as to the quantity to be supplied would have been allowed if the court had been satisfied that the writing was intended only to give particulars of dimensions and price, in relation to a contract, the obligatory provisions of which had been agreed upon orally.[66] It is apparent from the contract's silence on quantity that it did not comprise all express terms. The general rule extends to a written offer which is completed by an unqualified oral acceptance,[67] or by actings from which an unqualified acceptance is implied,[68] if it was averred that, instead of an unqualified acceptance of a written offer, there was an acceptance subject only to verbal conditions, or a counter offer. In that situation, provided that the pleadings and an examination of the documents supported the implication that the writing was not accepted unconditionally, the general rule could not apply, since the terms of the contract must then be sought, not in the writing alone, but partly in the writing and partly in the oral communings to be proved by parole evidence.[69]

27.6.2   When it was averred that, during the execution of an oral contract, invoices or similar documents had passed between the parties containing printed or written conditions which contradicted some of the conditions of the contract, the court had to consider the whole history of the transaction in order to discover whether the contract was fundamentally oral or fundamentally written. In such circumstances proof before answer is usually necessary.[70] A sale note, correctly recording the terms of an oral contract, has been held not to convert the oral contract into a written contract so as to make the general rule apply.[71] The general rule is also

---

[66] *Pollock & Dickson v McAndrew* (1828) 7 S 189 per Lord Glenlee at 191; see also *H Widdop & Co Ltd v J & J Hay Ltd* 1961 SLT (Notes) 35.

[67] *Pollock & Dickson v McAndrew* (1828) 7 S 189 (argued on both sides on footing that the contract was in writing). In *D Cameron & Son v McLeod* 1999 GWD 20-918 (Sh Ct) the general rule was applied when one side argued that the contract was constituted by an estimate and verbal acceptance (the acceptor also having signed the estimate) although there was a separate oral contract for the construction of a garage, but the other claimed that additional terms to the written estimate were agreed verbally. On the basis of the pleadings and the detail contained in the estimate there was "no rational basis on which it could be held that such a detailed document was intended to include only certain of the works".

[68] *Muller & Co v Weber & Schaer* (1901) 3 F 401 (sold-notes, granted by pursuers and admittedly retained by defenders without timeous rejection, which pursuers themselves sought to qualify by reference to an earlier oral agreement). See also *Croudace v Annandale SS Co* 1925 SLT 449 (OH), where a letter confirming an oral contract was ambiguous, and it was not clear whether the contract ever ceased to be oral, and proof of the conversations between the parties was allowed.

[69] Gloag, *Contract* (2nd edn), p 364, however, does not make this distinction. In *Thomson v Garioch* (1841) 3 D 625, the general rule was applied, although it was averred by the defender that the oral acceptance of the written offer was subject to additional provision which the pursuers in turn accepted orally. The terms of the interlocutor, however, indicate that parole proof was held to be incompetent because what the defender wished to prove was illegal. A similar point arose in *Cuthbertson v Lowes* (1870) 8 M 1073. See also *D Cameron & Son v McLeod* 1999 GWD 20-918 (Sh Ct) where the general rule was applied where the contract was so detailed that one could not rationally conclude that it was intended to include only some of the contract works in it, and the averments regarding additional works "were repugnant to earlier admissions".

[70] In *Buchanan & Co v Macdonald* (1895) 23 R 264, a printed notice as to terms of credit on the invoice sent with each consignment of goods, was said to conflict with the oral contract, in terms of which all the consignments were supplied. After proof it was held that the invoices were intended only to indicate the quantity of goods despatched, and not to vary or express the terms of the contract, which remained oral throughout. In *Woodrow v Patterson* (1845) 7 D 385, proof before answer was allowed of an averment that invoices accompanying goods, which stated that they had been "bought" at the price indicated, were not intended to vary or qualify the underlying oral agreement that the goods were supplied on sale or return.

[71] *Ireland & Son v Rosewell Gas Coal Co* (1900) 37 SLR 521, per Lord Kyllachy (Ordinary) at 522 approved. A sale by public roup, during which the auctioneer read excerpts from a document described

thought not to apply when a written offer is met by an oral acceptance which is subject to conditions or which constitutes a counter offer.[72] When two bilateral written contracts had been executed by the same parties, each providing for the sale of a ship, it was held competent to prove that the written contracts were intended merely as pieces of machinery for the implementing of an earlier oral agreement for the sale of both ships together, and not as superseding that agreement.[73]

27.7 WRITINGS *EX FACIE* COMPLETE

The general rule applied to exclude extrinsic evidence in relation to a writing **27.7.1** which was apparently a complete record of an obligation or contract between the parties.[74] Similarly contradiction or variation of an apparently complete writing could not be the subject of extrinsic evidence. A party seeking to establish by extrinsic evidence that there was an additional term of the contract could do so only if the other party admitted the error or omission,[75] or if the other term was considered by the court to be a separate but collateral agreement.[76] These were, in effect, categories of exception to the general rule, which are considered in more detail later in this chapter.[77] The limited nature of the exceptions at common law for proof of additional or contradictory terms was perceived to create injustice[78] and statutory reform proposed by the Scottish Law Commission[79] received strong

---

as an agreement of sale, which had been signed only by the exposer, was held to be essentially an oral contract, and proof of an additional stipulation, said to have been announced by the auctioneer, was accordingly allowed: *Christie v Hunter* (1880) 7R 729. Such a case may be distinguished from a sale regulated by formal articles of roup, which are properly authenticated at every stage and are finally executed by both exposer and purchaser. For examples of sales regulated by articles of roup, which were held to be written contracts, see *Stevenson v Moncrieff* (1845) 7 D 418 (sale of heritage); *Lang v Bruce* (1832) 10 S 777 (sale of cattle).

[72] See para 27.6.

[73] Before bills of sale could be executed in implement of the written contracts, one of the ships was requisitioned by the government, and the purchasers were held entitled to refuse to accept a bill of sale of the other ship in spite of the separate written contract regarding it: *Claddagh Steamship Co v Steven & Co* 1919 SC (HL) 132; cf *Duke of Fife v Great North of Scotland Railway Co* (1901) 3 F (HL) 2.

[74] Extrinsic evidence was disallowed or disregarded of the following suggested additions to written contracts: an obligation upon a landlord to execute fencing and draining, which was provided for in an earlier informal agreement but was not mentioned in the written lease, *Norval v Abbey* 1939 SC 724; an obligation to pay a landlord the cost of cultivating the summer fallow left upon the farm by the former tenant, said to have been agreed to orally by the new tenant, but not mentioned in his lease, *Alexander v Gillon* (1847) 9 D 524; an alleged condition in a sale of heritage that the price was to be wholly paid within six years, which was not mentioned in the missives, *General Assembly of Baptist Churches v Taylor* (1841) 3 D 1030; and provision, said to have been agreed to orally, but not mentioned in the written contract, that a specified number of pipes were to be delivered in terms of the contract, *Pollock & Dickson v McAndrew* (1828) 7 S 189. See also *Walker v Caledonian Railway Co* (1858) 20 D 1102.

[75] *Grant v Mackenzie* (1899) 1 F 889 at 894; *Irons v Partick Thistle Football Club Ltd* 1997 SLT 983 (OH), the admission having been clear in evidence during the proof and could be inferred from the pleadings (987F–I). If the parties are agreed that the writing contains an error an application may be made for rectification under the Law Reform (Miscellaneous Provisions) (Scotland) Act 1985, s 8, in which case evidence extrinsic to the writing may be led in relation to the application: see para 27.12

[76] *Renison v Bryce* (1898) 25 R 521; *Garden v Earl of Aberdeen* (1893) 20 R 896. See also *British Workman's etc, Assurance Co Ltd* (1900) 8 SLT 67 (OH).

[77] At paras 27.12 and 27.16.

[78] Scottish Law Commission, *Report on Three Bad Rules in Contract Law* (Scot Law Com No 152), para 2.20.

[79] In their Discussion Paper No 97.

support.[80] Reform to allow the court to rectify, rather than merely reduce, a writing that had defectively expressed the terms of an agreement had also been made at the suggestion of the Scottish Law Commission.[81]

27.7.2   The Contract (Scotland) Act 1997, s 1 establishes a rebuttable presumption that a document which appears to contain all the express terms of a contract or unilateral voluntary obligation does contain all the express terms.[82] Extrinsic evidence, whether oral or documentary, is admissible in order to rebut the presumption, that is to prove that there are additional express terms (whether in writing or not).[83] However, if the document contains a term to the effect that the document comprises all the express terms of the contract or unilateral voluntary obligation that term is conclusive of the matter.[84]

27.7.3   This statutory provision as drawn does not sweep away the rule completely; the Scottish Law Commission, after consultation, having rejected the option of abolishing the general rule in relation to additional terms.[85] Outwith the precise situation for which the statute makes provision the common law rule and its exceptions still apply: that is, to writings other than contracts and voluntary obligations (for example, documents of transfer which the granter is obliged to execute by law or prior contractual obligation[86]); and to contracts and unilateral voluntary obligations which do *not* appear to contain all of their terms, although in that situation[87] extrinsic evidence normally would be admissible either because the contract or obligation is partly oral, or because one of the common law exceptions would support the admission of extrinsic evidence. This statutory exception is limited to additional terms, which would not normally include contradiction[88] or variation,[89] of which extrinsic evidence is generally excluded at common law. Other statutory reforms have eased proof of variation.[90]

---

[80] Scottish Law Commission, *Report on Three Bad Rules in Contract Law* (Scot Law Com No 152), para 2.28.

[81] Scottish Law Commission, *Obligations: Report on Rectification of Contractual and other Documents* (Scot Law Com No 79) and see para 27.12.

[82] s 1(1). The provisions of s 1 are without prejudice to any enactment making provision for constitution and execution of a contract or unilateral voluntary obligation: s 1(4).

[83] s 1(2).

[84] s 1(3); although such a term may be challengeable on substantive grounds such as the Unfair Contract Terms Act 1977 and could not exclude the operation of terms implied by the substantive law.

[85] Scottish Law Commission, *Report on Three Bad Rules in Contract Law* (Scot Law Com No 152), paras 2.25–2.36.

[86] Accordingly, while the statutory provisions would apply to missives they do not apply to the subsequent disposition, nor, for example, to a standard security or a share transfer document although both may be preceded by a contractual arrangement to which the statutory provisions do apply.

[87] Covered in more detail in para 27.8.

[88] For example *Muller & Co v Weber & Schaer* (1901) 3 F 401; *Wallace v Henderson* (1867) 5 M 270; *McGregor v Lord Strathallan* (1862) 24 D 1006; *Pattinson v Robertson* (1844) 6 D 944; affd (1846) 5 Bell's App 259; *Gregson v Alsop* (1897) 24 R 1081; *Shaw Stewart v Macaulay* (1864) 3 M 16; *Reimann v John Young & Co Ltd* (1895) 2 SLT 426 (OH); *Hilson v Otto* (1870) 9 M 18; *Lawson v Murray* (1825) 3 S 371; *Harris v Churchill* (1822) 1 S 348; *Spence v Duncan* (1706) M 12 333; *Anderson v Forth Marine Insurance Co* (1845) 7 D 268. *Cf Smith v Kerr* (1869) 7 M 863; *Macfarlane v Watt* (1828) 6 S 556. For the exception to the general rule which allows the liability of co-obligants *inter se* to be proved by extrinsic evidence, see para 27.14.

[89] For example *Skinner v Lord Saltoun* (1886) 13 R 823; *Barr's Trs v Barr & Shearer* (1886) 13 R 1055; *Lavan v Gavin Aird & Co* 1919 SC 345; *Dumbarton Glass Co v Coatsworth* (1847) 9 D 732; *Turnbull v Oliver* (1891) 19 R 154; *Law v Gibsone* (1835) 13 S 396; and *Hamilton & Baird v Lewis* (1893) 21 R 120. As to the possible exceptions at common law and statutory reforms affecting variation, see paras 27.26–27.28.

[90] See para 27.28.

27.8 WRITINGS *EX FACIE* INCOMPLETE OR DEFECTIVE

Common law

The operation of the rule at common law in relation to writings *ex facie* incomplete **27.8.1**
or defective is as described in this paragraph, but is now the subject of a related
statutory exception which is described thereafter. When a writing, founded upon
by one of the parties as constituting a right, was construed by the court as incomplete or defective for this purpose, this did not of itself render admissible evidence
of facts extrinsic to the writing, purporting to show that the right was nevertheless
constituted. The position was different when the court was unable, from a mere
perusal of the terms of the writing, to decide whether or not a binding contract had
been effected.[91] In such cases, if the surrounding circumstances were not admitted
or within judicial knowledge, they had to be proved.[92] When from the terms of
what is alleged to be a testamentary writing it is not clear whether it is intended as
a will, or merely as a draft or note of instructions for the preparation of a will,
extrinsic evidence of the surrounding circumstances is admissible.[93] However,
when no doubt arises on the face of the will, and it bears to express a completed
testamentary intention, proof of an averment that it was delivered to a solicitor for
some purpose other than as a valid will, or for cancellation or destruction, is at
present incompetent.[94] When missives and a disposition had been completed,
neither of which identified adequately one of the boundaries of the property being
conveyed, extrinsic evidence was admitted to show that the parties had reached
agreement on this important matter which was not reflected in the missives or disposition.[95] When a contract for supply of petrol made no reference to payment
other than reference to "Esso's terms of settlement" proof of a verbal agreement as
to payment terms was admitted since the contract was so lacking in specification
that it could not have been intended to be conclusive of the matter.[96]

Furthermore, when a written contract has been acted upon,[97] and it appeared, **27.8.2**
as construed by the court, that one of the terms essential for its fulfilment as a
concluded contract was not expressed in the writing,[98] or was expressed only

---

[91] When, for example, a contract of sale is alleged to have been made by written offer and acceptance,
the question may turn upon whether or not the offer was accepted within a reasonable time. What is a
reasonable time in a particular case may depend upon the nature of the article sold and whether its
market price fluctuated quickly or was relatively static.

[92] *Wylie & Lochhead v McElroy* (1873) 1 R 41; *Glasgow, etc Steam Shipping Co v Watson* (1873) 1
R 189.

[93] *Young's Trs v Henderson* 1925 SC 749; *Wilson v Hovell* 1924 SC 1; *Sprot's Trs v Sprot* 1909 SC
272; *Whyte v Hamilton* (1882) 9 R (HL) 53. Applied in *Barker's Exrs and Scottish Rights of Way
Society Ltd* 1996 SC 396.

[94] *Robb's Trs v Robb* (1872) 10 M 692, per Lord President Inglis, Lord Deas at 697; *Wilson v Hovell*
1924 SC 1, per Lord Constable (Ordinary) at 5–6. See also *MacLaren's Trs v Mitchell & Brattan* 1959
SC 183 (OH). This position is affected by the Scottish Law Commission's proposed legislation
allowing extrinsic evidence to enable interpretation of a writing. See para 27.19.

[95] *McClymont v McCubbin* 1994 SC 573. Although the action is for rectification of the disposition
under the Law Reform (Miscellaneous Provisions) (Scotland) Act 1985, s 8(1)(b) the admission of evidence extrinsic to the missives was justified by application of the reasoning as to error in *Anderson v
Lambie* 1954 SC (HL) 43.

[96] *McInally v Esso Petroleum Co* 1965 SLT (Notes) 13 (OH). The Lord Ordinary seemed to prefer this
ground for admitting the evidence to the "collateral agreement" ground which had been argued, on
which see para 27.16.

[97] The actings of parties are themselves extrinsic evidence. Cases in which the actings of parties may
be proved in order to explain the contract are mentioned later: see para 27.23.

[98] *McAllister v McGallagley* 1911 SC 112.

imperfectly or incompletely,[99] and must necessarily have been the subject of oral agreement between the parties, the missing or incompletely expressed term might be proved by parole or other extrinsic evidence.[100] So, for example, in a lease of land it was essential to know the date of entry and thus the date of termination of the lease, and when neither was stated in the writing, parole evidence as to the date of entry agreed upon by the parties was admitted,[101] and when a contract provided for the transfer of businesses and plant in consideration of the allotment of a specified number of shares in "your proposed limited company" it was held that "your proposed limited company" required elucidation, and that since the capital of the proposed company was a matter of great importance in relation to the value of the shares to be allotted to the defender, and had not been specified in the writing, proof of the oral agreement was permissible.[102] By comparison, in a written contract for the supply of iron pipes of certain dimensions at specified price per yard, no reference was made to minimum or maximum quantities. The purchasers averred that the sellers had agreed orally to supply a specified quantity. Proof of the oral agreement was refused on the ground that there was nothing "palpably defective" about the contract which would prevent it being carried into effect without explanation, and that the court must not make a new contract for the parties in place of their own written contract, which left each party free to stop the contract when he chose.[103]

27.8.3   These cases are difficult to categorise, in that they might be said to be examples of an exception applying when the writing is *ex facie* incomplete or defective in respect of a term which is either deemed to be inherently essential to its operation or, by reference to the actings of the parties, clearly missing from the contract. However, this is difficult to distinguish from finding that a contract was intended to be partly oral and partly in writing.[104] Furthermore, as the Scottish Law

---

[99] *Renison v Bryce* (1898) 25 R 521.

[100] At common law an unexpressed term which was *not* essential for the fulfilment of the contract, even if oral agreement upon it would seem to be probable, might not be proved: *Walker v Caledonian Railway Co* (1858) 20 D 1102. The parties are bound by the true construction of the terms of the contract as ascertained by the court: *Laing v Provincial Homes Investment Co Ltd* 1909 SC 812 at 822, 826. However, this restriction does not now apply to an additional term, which may be proved by extrinsic evidence, to rebut the statutory presumption that a contract which appears to contain all the contract terms does so: Contract (Scotland) Act 1997, s 2, and see para 27.7.

[101] *Watters v Hunter* 1927 SC 310. For a similar example, see *Russell v Freen* (1835) 13 S 752. See, in particular, the opinion of Lord Corehouse (Ordinary) at 754. For another similar example, see *McLeod v Urquhart* (1808) Hume 840, explained by Lord President Dunedin in *McAllister v McGallagley* 1911 SC 112 at 117–118.

[102] *Renison v Bryce* (1898) 25 R 521.

[103] *Pollock & Dickson v McAndrew* (1828) 7 S 189. In *Walker v Caledonian Railway Co* (1858) 20 D 1102, where the written contract was for the performance of the horse haulage work on a railway company's lines for three years, at a specified rate per day for each horse and man, the contract to be worked to the satisfaction of the company's goods manager, the contract did not provide for any particular number of horses. The contractor averred that the contract was executed with special reference to a list of the number of horses to be supplied at each station which had been shown to him. Proof of the prior communings of the parties and of the list was refused, apparently on the ground that the missing term was not essential to the execution of the contract. It was observed that "if such evidence is to be admitted, there would be an end to the rule of written contracts altogether. It would be open to any party to raise questions as to the construction of a contract he found to be working against him. If the pursuer stipulated for the constant employment of a certain number of horses ... that was a most important part of the stipulation, and ought to have been embodied in the contract." (Lord Justice-Clerk Hope at 1105.)

[104] Dealt with at para 27.7.

Commission point out,[105] it was difficult for the parties to predict whether a court would hold that the terms of the contract showed that it was incomplete or defective.

Statutory exception

The rule excluding extrinsic evidence to prove an additional term of a contract has **27.8.4** now been moderated by the statutory exception contained in the Contract (Scotland) Act 1997, s 1, which applies in proceedings raised after the commencement of the Act regardless of the date of the contract. Section 1 admits extrinsic evidence to rebut the statutory presumption of completeness attaching to a contract or unilateral voluntary obligation which appears to contain all of its terms. This removes from the general exclusionary rule the situations described above where extrinsic evidence of missing terms had been ruled inadmissible because the writing was not clearly defective or the missing term not clearly essential.[106] When the writing does *not* appear to contain all of its terms because it is *ex facie* incomplete or defective the statutory provision does not apply but the extrinsic evidence is admissible at common law. Furthermore, a writing *ex facie* incomplete or defective may be the subject of extrinsic evidence because of a drafting error in light of which reduction or rectification is sought[107] or because the parties are agreed that it is defective.[108]

27.9 CONVEYANCES OF HERITAGE—RELATIONSHIP BETWEEN PRIOR COMMUNINGS AND FORMAL CONVEYANCES

At common law deeds conveying heritage were subject to what may be termed a **27.9.1** special extension of the general rule or may be deemed a separate rule of substantive law. Before a purchaser of heritage obtains a conveyance of the property it is usual for the parties to enter into a written contract, which may have consisted of solemnly executed articles or memorandum of sale or, more commonly now, an interchange of letters (missives). However, it is an express or implied condition of all such contracts that the seller shall grant to the purchaser a disposition which, when recorded in the Land Register or the Register of Sasines, gives the purchaser a real, instead of merely a personal, title to the property. At common law, when such a disposition had been delivered to and accepted by the purchaser, in implement of the obligations of the contract, the original contract was at an end, and was superseded by the disposition which became the sole measure of the contracting parties' rights. It was not then competent to lead evidence extrinsic to the deed,[109] including evidence of the informal contract, since the contract is both extrinsic to

---

[105] *Report on Three Bad Rules in Contract Law* (Scot Law Com No 152), para 2.6.

[106] Such as *Pollock & Dickson v McAndrew* (1828) 7 S 189; *Walker v Caledonian Railway Co* (1858) 20 D 1102.

[107] Law Reform (Miscellaneous Provisions) (Scotland) Act 1985, ss 8 and 9, and see para 27.12.

[108] See para 27.18.

[109] *Edinburgh United Breweries Ltd v Molleson* (1894) 21 R (HL) 10, per Lord Watson at 16; *Orr v Mitchell* (1893) 20 R (HL) 27, per Lord Watson at 29; *Lee v Alexander* (1883) 10 R (HL) 91 at 96–98, 100. This statement was reaffirmed in *Butter v Foster* 1912 SC 1218 at 1225, and by Lord Reid in *Anderson v Lambie* 1954 SC (HL) 43 at 62. In *King's College of Aberdeen v Lady Hay* (1852) 14 D 675 the result was achieved by reading the feu charter and the preceding personal bond together. It is thought that, since the decision of *Lee v Alexander*, the same result would be reached without considering the terms of the earlier documents, which the feu-contract would be regarded as superseding.

the deed (and thus excluded by the rule of evidence) and superseded by it (by operation of the substantive law).[110]

27.9.2   However, evidence of the contract might be admissible at common law if the contract provided for obligations beyond the conveyance of heritage.[111] Therefore multiple contracts and, more commonly, contracts which dealt with moveable property as well as the heritage, have not been superseded completely by the delivery of the disposition.[112] At common law the disposition had been held to be final and conclusive in regard only to the rights which it was intended and adapted to carry, namely the heritage.[113] With regard to the other matters, the granting of the disposition did not "exhaust the contract between the parties".[114] So, when a contract provided for the performance of building work on,[115] or the sale of moveable fittings in,[116] the premises sold, as well as for the sale of the premises themselves, it was held that the acceptance of the disposition did not preclude the purchaser from enforcing that part of the contract which dealt with performance of work or sale of moveables. So, too, in a contract for sale of ground which provided for a right of access over the ground in favour of the sellers the route of which could not be determined before the property had been developed by the purchasers, the access condition was deemed to be collateral and not superseded by the disposition.[117] The parties may expressly provide in the contract, or in the deed or in another document, for a personal obligation in the contract to continue in operation after delivery of the deed,[118] sometimes restricting the period during which the personal obligation is to be enforceable.[119]

27.9.3   However, in *Winston v Patrick*[120] the Inner House decided that a clause in the

---

[110] As described in the Scottish Law Commission's *Report on Three Bad Rules in Contract Law* (Scot Law Com No 152), para 3.16, n 2. This extended form of the general rule has been applied to a feu charter and a formal lease which was regarded as superseding earlier less formal missives of lease: *Robertson's Trs v Lindsay* (1873) 1 R 323, per Lord Deas at 327. In *Widdowson v Hunter* 1989 SLT 478 the transaction was the sale of a business which included heritage. For a discussion of the rule, see Talman, Halliday's, *Conveyancing Law and Practice* (2nd edn), Vol 2, paras 30-130 to 30-138 and 33-03.

[111] Indeed there is authority for admission of evidence of an oral agreement in relation to the Inn sign on the public house being sold which did not belong to the sellers and therefore could not be covered by the missives or the disposition: *William Masson Ltd v Scottish Brewers Ltd* 1966 SC 9.

[112] *McKillop v Mutual Securities Ltd* 1945 SC 166, per Lord Moncrieff at 172; *King v Gebbie* 1993 SLT 512 (OH) at 517F–I. For another example of a multiple contract, see *Gibb v Cunningham & Robertson* 1925 SLT 608 (OH) (contract for sale of both shares and heritage).

[113] *Jamieson v Welsh* (1900) 3 F 176, per Lord Kinnear at 182. The other rights are thought to arise from collateral agreements, properly so described. As to these, see para 27.16.

[114] *Butter v Foster* 1912 SC 1218, per Lord Mackenzie at 1225; and see *Bradley v Scott* 1966 SLT (Sh Ct) 25.

[115] *McKillop v Mutual Securities Ltd* 1945 SC 166; *King v Gebbie* 1993 SLT 512 (OH).

[116] *Jamieson v Welsh* (1900) 3 F 176. The same principle was mentioned with approval in *Forth Bridge Railway Co v Incorporation of the Guildry of Dunfermline* 1909 SC 493 at 502, where it was observed that a disposition might be regarded as only partly implementing a decree-arbitral, if that document dealt also with other matters not covered by the disposition. *Wann v Gray & Son* 1935 SN 8 (OH), which is difficult to understand, may also be partly explicable on the same principle. *Wann v Gray & Son* was disapproved in *Winston v Patrick* 1981 SLT 41, and although difficulties with the reasoning and outcome in the latter led to reform of the law, the disapproval of *Wann v Gray & Son* is unobjectionable.

[117] *Callander v Midlothian District Council* 1997 SLT 865 (OH).

[118] *Lee v Alexander* (1883) 10 R (HL) 91 at 96; *Winston v Patrick* 1980 SC 246 at 249, and see, for example, *Jamieson v Stewart* 1989 SLT (Sh Ct) 13; *Fraser v Cox* 1938 SC 506; *Young v McKellar Ltd* 1909 SC 1340; *Wood v Magistrates of Edinburgh* (1886) 13 R 1006. See also Lord Wark in *Norval v Abbey* 1939 SC 724 at 730.

[119] As in *Pena v Ray* 1987 SLT 609 (OH), where the time limit was held to apply to a collateral obligation which had not been superseded by the disposition.

[120] 1980 SC 246.

contract, in which the seller warranted that all statutory requirements in connection with alterations and extensions to the property had been fulfilled, was one which did not incorporate any personal or collateral obligation and was superseded by the delivery and acceptance of the disposition.[121] The Inner House in that case adhered to the general supersession rule and noted that the circumstances did not fit any one of the three situations in which evidence of the terms of the missives would outlive the delivery of the disposition, namely (a) where the missives incorporated obligations in relation to moveables which would not be appropriate to be included in a disposition of heritage, (b) where in the missives there was a collateral obligation distinct from the obligation to convey the heritage, or (c) where there was an agreement in writing either in the missives or in a separate document or in the disposition itself that a personal obligation included in the missives would subsist and remain in force even if it was not included in terms in the disposition.[122] These categories were later treated as an exhaustive list in some cases[123] but judicial opinion differed as to whether a warranty in the missives could be deemed to be a personal or collateral obligation and in various quarters doubt was expressed as to what these terms meant.[124] The basic proposition that supersession applied only in so far as the disposition exhausted the contract[125] appeared to have been overlooked. It was further decided in *Winston v Patrick* that if it is the intention of the parties to create an ongoing personal or collateral obligation, this should be apparent from the terms of the writings themselves,[126] and the court would not depart from the general rule excluding parole evidence merely to allow parole evidence of the parties' unexpressed intentions.[127] The strictness of application of the supersession rule and, to a lesser extent, the extrinsic evidence rule in that case caused confusion in practice and generated academic criticism,[128] and the Scottish Law Commission ultimately reviewed the supersession rule during its review of "Three Bad Rules in Contract Law".[129] A statutory provision proposed by the Scottish

---

[121] *Cf Taylor v McLeod* 1990 SLT 194 (OH). The matter rested upon interpretation of the terms of the missives and disposition in each case, as noted in *Porch v Macleod* 1992 SLT 661 (OH) where the facts could not be distinguished from *Winston v Patrick*. Although in *Porch v Macleod* the clause warranting the condition of the property was held to apply to its condition as at the date of the missives, and the obligation to deliver evidence of fulfilment of that warranty was a personal and collateral obligation, both were held to have terminated with delivery of the disposition since the circumstances did not fall within one of the three exceptions noted in *Winston v Patrick*.

[122] *Winston v Patrick* 1980 SC 246 at 249.

[123] See *Greaves v Abercromby* 1989 SCLR 11 (Sh Ct); *Taylor v McLeod* 1990 SLT 194 (OH); *Porch v Macleod* 1992 SLT 661 (OH).

[124] An analysis of the three categories and their interpretation in cases and academic commentaries is contained in the Scottish Law Commission's *Report on Three Bad Rules in Contract Law* (Scot Law Com No 152), paras 3.11–3.17.

[125] *Butter v Foster* 1912 SC 1218, per Lord Mackenzie at 1225.

[126] It was unclear whether this meant that the missives had to be kept alive through a clause in the disposition. In *Taylor v McLeod* 1990 SLT 194 (OH), on a construction of the clause regarding the condition of the central heating system and other appliances in the property, it was held to be intended to come into effect as an ongoing personal obligation only upon delivery of the disposition.

[127] *Winston v Patrick* 1980 SC 246 at 249. In some later cases it was said that this required the obligation or a clause preserving the effect of the missives to be contained in the disposition.

[128] Reid, "Prior Communings and Conveyancing Practice" (1981) 26 JLSS 414; Cusine & Rennie, *Missives*, Chapter 7; Gretton & Reid, *Conveyancing*, pp 334–343 (and to a lesser extent *Conveyancing* (2nd edn), paras 18.02 and 18.03); *Stair Memorial Encyclopaedia*, Vol 18, para 641.

[129] Discussion Paper No 97, *Contract Law: Extrinsic Evidence, Supersession and the Actio Quanti Minoris* (1994) and *Report on Three Bad Rules in Contract Law* (Scot Law Com No 152), Part III. The Commission in the same papers reviewed the extrinsic evidence rule in so far as it related to additional terms of contracts and unilateral voluntary obligations (*Report*, Part II) and recommended

Law Commission[130] now replaces the supersession rule with a "survival" rule[131] which applies to contracts entered into after the commencement of the Contract (Scotland) Act 1997.[132] Contracts entered into before commencement are subject to the old rule and exceptions. The new rule provides that an unimplemented or otherwise unfulfilled term of the contract is not superseded by mere delivery and acceptance of the deed,[133] but the parties may opt out of or restrict the terms of operation of that survival, since the new rule is without prejudice to any agreement which the parties may reach as to supersession, whether or not that agreement is incorporated in the contract.[134]

27.10 EXCEPTIONS TO THE GENERAL RULE

27.10.1 The rest of this chapter is concerned with the many exceptions to the general rule. The more important common law exceptions acquired subsidiary rules of their own and are confusing and overlapping. The new statutory exceptions for proof of additional terms, and for rectification of an incorrectly expressed document are of broader[135] and more consistent application than the exceptions at common law, but in situations outwith the scope of the statutory exceptions the old rule and exceptions still apply. If a situation does not fall within any of the exceptions, the general rule still applies to exclude extrinsic evidence. The exceptions now fall into three broad categories, namely (1) where there is substantive challenge to the validity, expression or completeness of the writing; (2) where the writing is ambiguous and it is necessary to look beyond the writing for explanation or interpretation of it; and (3) where variation of a writing is said to have been effected by waiver, acquiescence or authorisation.

Substantive challenge to the validity, expression or completeness of the writing

27.11 DEFECTIVE AUTHENTICATION, FRAUD, ESSENTIAL ERROR OR ILLEGALITY

27.11.1 The law permits challenge to the authentication of a document which was probative under the rules applying prior to 1 August 1995, or self-proving under the

---

that to overcome the effect of *Winston v Patrick*, the two reforms should be effected at the same time, although the exceptions at common law would continue to afford a ground for admission of evidence extrinsic to the disposition: see *Report*, para 3.31.

[130] Scottish Law Commission, *Report on Three Bad Rules in Contract Law* (Scot Law Com No 152), para 3.29.

[131] The Scottish Law Commission preferred this to a clarified statutory "non-survival" rule: *Report on Three Bad Rules in Contract Law* (Scot Law Com No 152), para 3.24.

[132] 21 June 1997.

[133] Contract (Scotland) Act 1997, s 2(1).

[134] Contract (Scotland) Act 1997, s 2(2). For a description of the position immediately before and after the commencement of the Act, see Talman, "Endureth Forever" 1997 SLT (News) 309.

[135] It is not appropriate in this text to deal with statutory exceptions which admit parole evidence in connection with specific documents such as bills of exchange, although this is touched upon earlier at para 24.7.

Requirements of Writing (Scotland) Act 1995. If it is alleged that the subscription is not that of the granter, whether by forgery or otherwise; that the person who witnessed was a person named in the document as a granter; that the witness did not know the granter,[136] was under 16 years or mentally incapable of acting as a witness; that the purported witness did not sign after the granter and as part of a continuous process; that the details of the witness were added after registration of the document,[137] or are materially incorrect; or any one of the subscriptions in a testamentary document is not that of the granter, whether by forgery or otherwise, extrinsic evidence to support the allegation will be admissible.

The general rule does not apply when it is sought to reduce a writing on the **27.11.2** ground of fraud,[138] essential error[139] or illegality.[140] In these cases the question is not whether the written contract can be construed, contradicted or modified by extrinsic evidence, but whether it is binding upon parties.[141] Thus extrinsic evidence was admitted of a conversation with the granter of a conveyance of heritage, in an action of reduction of the deed on the ground that it had been impetrated by circumvention when he was of weak and facile mind[142]; of false statements said to have been made by employees of the owners of two motor cars as to the roadworthiness of vehicles, in a reduction *ope exceptionis* of a written hire-purchase agreement which included an acknowledgement by the hirer that he had examined the vehicles, and had satisfied himself as to their roadworthiness[143]; of communications between solicitors and two lending institutions whereby error arose as to which of the recorded securities over the debtors' property should be discharged[144]; of the circumstances surrounding the conclusion of missives and correspondence thereafter all to establish whether the disposition which described five areas of ground should be reduced because the subjects for sale extended to only four areas of ground.[145]

27.12 DEFECTIVE EXPRESSION

At common law, when one party to a written contract averred that, as a result of **27.12.1** a drafting error, the writing misrepresented the agreement and intention of both parties the averment might be proved by parole or other extrinsic evidence. A

---

[136] An introduction from a credible source is sufficient: s 3(5).

[137] It is in order to add the details after subscription but before registration.

[138] See para 27.11. This includes written contracts induced by misrepresentation: *Bell Brothers (HP) Ltd v Aitken* 1939 SC 577, per Lord President Normand at 585.

[139] *Steuart's Trs v Hart* (1875) 3 R 192 at 201; *Stewart v Kennedy* (1890) 17 R (HL) 25; *Security Pacific Finance Ltd v T & I Filshie's Tr* 1994 SCLR 1100; 1995 SCLR 1171.

[140] This includes writings, which, in themselves innocent, were executed to promote an illegal or immoral purpose. See Dickson, *Evidence* (3rd edn), paras 1038–1040; Gloag, *Contract* (2nd edn), p 563.

[141] Gloag, *Contract* (2nd edn), p 365.

[142] *Napier v Sharp* (1851) 14 D 313.

[143] *Bell Brothers (HP) Ltd v Aitken* 1939 SC 577.

[144] *Security Pacific Finance Ltd v T & I Filshie's Tr* 1994 SCLR 1100; 1995 SCLR 1171. For further examples, see *Steuart's Trs v Hart* (1875) 3 R 192; *Stewart v Kennedy* (1890) 17 R (HL) 25.

[145] *Aberdeen Rubber Ltd v Knowles & Sons (Fruiterers) Ltd* 1994 SC 440 (affirmed by the House of Lords at 1995 SC (HL) 8). Proof before answer was allowed by the Lord Ordinary, but the Inner House held that the error could be inferred from the admitted averments as to the circumstances extrinsic to the disposition. An alternative conclusion for rectification under the Law Reform (Miscellaneous Provisions) (Scotland) Act 1985, s 8 required proof that the error was one of expression which arose after the conclusion of missives.

disposition of heritage, which conveyed a farm and a neighbouring colliery, was reduced as a result of extrinsic evidence which established that the parties had only the farm in mind when they made their bargain, and that the colliery was included because of a conveyancing blunder on the part of both the solicitors concerned.[146] A feu contract was reduced in so far as it imposed an obligation on the superiors to form certain roads coloured brown on a plan appended to the deed, because it was proved by extrinsic evidence that these roads had been coloured brown erroneously, and contrary to the agreement of the parties as disclosed by the missives.[147]

27.12.2   At common law, in connection with recorded titles to heritage, a Scottish court appeared to have no power to make a new bargain for the parties or to alter the deed in order to make it conform to the missives or to the real intention of the parties.[148] The reduction of the deed was the only competent remedy,[149] although partial reduction was competent if the reduced part was clearly severable from the rest,[150] and the court did, in some cases, secure a positive outcome without reducing the deed,[151] or coupled reduction with declarator or other order which would have the effect of securing rectification by the parties.[152]

27.12.3   The law in relation to rectification of defectively expressed documents was considered by the Scottish Law Commission in a memorandum published in 1979[153] and in a report published in 1983,[154] as a consequence of which a procedure for rectification of documents defectively expressed was enacted in the Law Reform (Miscellaneous Provisions) (Scotland) Act 1985, ss 8 and 9. The legislation provides that (a) a document which is intended to give effect to an agreement, which fails to express accurately the common intention[155] of the parties to the

---

[146] *Anderson v Lambie* 1954 SC (HL) 43.

[147] *Glasgow Feuing & Building Company v Watson's Trs* (1887) 14 R 610.

[148] *Anderson v Lambie* 1954 SC (HL) 43, per Lord Morton at 50, Lord Reid at 61, Lord Keith at 67; *Steuart's Trs v Hart* (1873) 3 R 192 at 200. See also *Equitable Loan Company of Scotland Ltd v Storie* 1972 SLT (Notes) 20 (OH). However, in *Russell's Exr v Russell's Exrs* 1983 SLT 385 (OH), the court took the view that there was no express authority declaring it incompetent for the court to make an order which would rectify the situation when a document failed to express the proved intention of the parties.

[149] *Hunter v Bradford Property Trust Ltd* 1970 SLT 173 at 194 (HL).

[150] *Anderson v Lambie* 1954 SC (HL) 43, per Lord Reid at 60–61. See also *Glasgow Feuing & Building Company v Watson's Trs* (1887) 14 R 610; *Waddell v Waddell* (1863) 1 M 635.

[151] Proof was allowed of an averment that in a formal minute of agreement for *inter alia* the payment to a hotel manager of one-fifth part of the profits of the hotel, "one-fifth" had been inserted, by an arithmetical error on the part of a clerk, as being the half of one-tenth: *Krupp v Menzies* 1907 SC 903. See also *Carricks v Saunders* (1850) 12 D 812. And the opinion was expressed that an insurance company could competently be proved to have made a clerical blunder in the terms of an insurance policy which failed to give effect to the instructions of the insured who had requested the policy: *North British Insurance Co v Tunnock & Fraser* (1864) 3 M 1, per Lord Justice-Clerk Inglis at 5.

[152] When a deed by which an irrevocable discretionary trust had been set up failed to provide for the truster's issue and spouse because a schedule of beneficiaries prepared by the truster's solicitor was incomplete, the court, after reviewing the authorities, decided that it was appropriate to order partial deduction and declarator as to the true schedule of beneficiaries, both with retrospective effect: *Hudson v St John* 1977 SC 255 (OH), also reported as *Hudson v Hudson's Trs* 1978 SLT 88. And in *Russell's Exr v Russell's Exrs* 1983 SLT 385 (OH), after a review of the authorities the court held that an order to ordain a third party to execute a deed in place of that which the pursuer sought to have reduced would have been competent, had there been evidence to support the reduction and the true terms of the agreement.

[153] Scottish Law Commission, *Voluntary Obligations, Defective Expression and its Correction* (Memorandum No 43).

[154] Scottish Law Commission, *Obligations: Report on Rectification of Contractual and other Documents* (Scot Law Com No 79).

[155] Which should be viewed objectively: *Rehman v Ahmad* 1993 SLT 741, adopting *Thomson v James* (1855) 18 D 1 and *Muirhead & Turnbull v Dickson* (1905) 7 F 686. For an exception at common law when parties agreed that a writing was inaccurate see para 27.18.

agreement at the time when it was made, or (b) a document intended to create, transfer, vary or renounce a right, not being a document falling within paragraph (a),[156] which fails to express the intention of the granter at the date when it was executed, may be rectified by order of the Court of Session or the sheriff court.[157] Rectification may be ordered if it would give effect to the intention as proved[158] and is retroactive[159] but the procedure requires consideration to be given to the interests of third parties who may have acted or failed to act in reliance of the document as originally expressed.[160] Evidence extrinsic to the document which is allegedly defectively expressed is admissible in order to prove the matters necessary to justify rectification,[161] namely:

> "(1) that there is a document to be rectified; (2) that that document was intended to express or give effect to an already existing agreement arrived at between two (or more) parties; (3) that there was, when the document was executed, such a pre-existing agreement—whether or not enforceable; (4) that that agreement itself embodied and was an expression of one or more intentions common to (that is to say, shared by) the parties; (5) that the intentions were actual (not deemed) intentions; (6) that the agreement itself must have been reached at a definite point in time (*cf* 'the date when it was made')."[162]

27.13 REAL NATURE OF WRITTEN CONTRACT IN ISSUE

General

The general rule does not apply, and extrinsic evidence is admissible, when it is **27.13.1** alleged that the writing was not intended to be a true record of the contract, but was merely a cover for some ulterior transaction of a different nature.[163] Although in a Scottish case in the House of Lords[164] it was said that a Court of Equity may always give effect to a transaction different from what the deeds represent its character to be, such a general statement of the exception appears to leave no content

---

[156] Testamentary writings are excluded from these provisions: s 8(5).

[157] s 8(1).

[158] s 8(1). If there is not common intention at the time the error occurs, rectification is not appropriate, but the error may lead to reduction at common law.

[159] s 8(4) and (5), but subject to s 9(4).

[160] s 9.

[161] s 8(2).

[162] *Shaw v William Grant (Minerals) Ltd* 1989 SLT 121 (OH), followed in *Huewind Ltd v Clydesdale Bank plc* 1995 SLT 392 (OH). Lord Penrose in *Rehman v Ahmad* 1993 SLT 741 (OH) at 751 required "proof of an agreement made independently of, and at or prior to the date of, the document or documents intended to give effect to it, coupled with proof that the writing failed to express accurately the common intention of the parties at the point at which the agreement was made". As to the pleadings required, see *MAC Electrical and Heating Engineers Ltd v Calscot Electrical (Distributors) Ltd* 1989 SCLR 498 (OH) and *Huewind Ltd v Clydesdale Bank plc.* As to whose intention should be proved, see *Belhaven Brewery Co Ltd v Swift* 1996 SLT (Sh Ct) 127; *Bank of Scotland v Brunswick Developments (1987) Ltd* 1995 SC 272; *Bank of Scotland v Brunswick Developments (1987) Ltd (No 2)* (IH) 1997 SC 226; *Bank of Scotland v Brunswick Developments (1987) Ltd* 2000 SCLR 30 (HL).

[163] Dickson, Evidence (3rd edn), para 1038.

[164] *Scottish Union Insurance Co v Marquis of Queensberry* (1842) 1 Bell's App 18. *Ex facie* absolute assignations were held to be truly in security only. It was later said, however, that the real nature of the transaction was implied by the terms of the deeds themselves, and to be "stamped from the beginning as a transaction of loan": *Anderson v Lambie* 1954 SC (HL) 43 per Lord Keith at 68–69.

to the general rule and it was not followed in a subsequent case,[165] where such an exception, had it been of general application, ought to have been allowed. In that case a written contract for the sale of goods was alleged to be only *pro forma*, the true contract being that the consignees accepted the goods as agents on a commission basis for sale to a third party. Despite this allegation, the general rule was applied and extrinsic evidence was disallowed.[166]

27.13.2   It is thought that this exception must in general be restricted to transactions where there is an element of collusion or deceit.[167] The exception which allows extrinsic evidence in relation to fraud or illegality, which has been mentioned earlier,[168] is an example of the same principle.[169] In two cases concerning receipts, where the circumstances were rather special but where an element of collusion or deceit existed, extrinsic evidence was allowed when it was alleged: that a receipt by a minor, with the consent of her curators, was granted for the purpose, not of acknowledging the receipt of money, but of enabling the trustees to settle the duties on her father's estate[170]; that a receipt for payment of rent in the tenant's possession, which he founded upon as a valid receipt, had been sent to him by the landlord merely as a reminder that the rent was due, and not as an acknowledgement of payment.[171] In the statutory examples mentioned in the next paragraph, an element of collusion is present in most cases.

Statutory

27.13.3   When a transaction in the form of a contract of sale of goods, whether oral[172] or written,[173] is alleged to have been intended to operate by way of mortgage, pledge, charge or any other security, without delivery of the goods to the creditor, the court must receive evidence to establish the true nature of the contract. A contract intended to create a security rather than a sale cannot be established without delivery.[174] "The reality of the transaction must be inquired into, and if, contrary to the form of the contract, and even the declaration of the parties, it appears from the whole circumstances that a true sale was not intended, it will be held that the property has not passed, and that no effectual security has been acquired."[175] Extrinsic

---

[165] *Muller & Co v Weber & Schaer* (1901) 3 F 401.

[166] *Muller & Co v Weber & Schaer* (1901) 3 F 401.

[167] Dickson, *Evidence* (3rd edn), para 1038.

[168] See para 27.11.

[169] Dickson, *Evidence* (3rd edn), para 1038. The main examples arise in relation to proof of marriage: *Imrie v Imrie* (1891) 19 R 185; *Maloy v Macadam* (1885) 12 R 431; *Fleming v Corbet* (1859) 21 D 1034, per Lord Justice-Clerk Inglis at 1044; *Orlandi v Castelli* 1961 SC 113 (OH).

[170] *Smith v Kerr* (1869) 7 M 863. *Cf Anderson v Forth Marine Insurance Co* (1845) 7 D 268.

[171] *Henry v Miller* (1884) 11 R 713. The proof was said to be allowed in order to discover whether the receipt came into the debtor's possession as a "delivered evident", *ie* as an effective receipt: per Lord President Inglis at 716. This case may perhaps also be regarded as an example of a condition attached to the delivery of a writing, which may be proved by extrinsic evidence. As to this, see para 27.17.

[172] *Scottish Transit Trust v Scottish Land Cultivators* 1955 SC 254; *Newbigging v Ritchie's Tr* 1930 SC 273. Although these cases are concerned with oral contracts, the opinions are thought to apply also to written contracts. The same statutory provision governs both.

[173] *Gavin's Tr v Fraser* 1920 SC 674; *Hepburn v Law* 1914 SC 918; *Rennet v Mathieson* (1903) 5 F 591; *Jones & Co's Tr v Allan* (1901) 4 F 374; *Robertson v Hall's Tr* (1896) 24 R 120.

[174] Sale of Goods Act 1979, s 62(4).

[175] *Robertson v Hall's Tr* (1896) 24 R 120, per Lord Moncreiff at 134. On these grounds extrinsic evidence was admitted in the following circumstances: by a written contract the owner of certain horses and wagons purported to sell them subject to a condition that he could buy them back within a year at the original purchase price with interest, and the goods remained in the seller's possession, *Gavin's Tr v Fraser* 1920 SC 674 (held after proof that the agreement was in fact a contract of sale); a debtor in a

evidence was also admitted in cases where the contract of sale was in writing but the question arose as to whether the goods had in fact been sold but not delivered to the purchaser, with the result that the subsequent sequestration of the seller did not defeat the purchaser's right to delivery, or whether the transaction was in reality an unsuccessful attempt to grant a security *retenta possessione* (possession being retained).[176] These cases were decided before the Sale of Goods Acts, and it is possible to regard these as additional examples, apart from statute, of the exception described generally in the last sub-paragraph. On the other hand, Lord Watson doubted whether in such a case, when the writing was unambiguous, it was competent to consider extrinsic evidence,[177] and more recently the relevance and admissibility of evidence of intention outwith the written contract has been queried in the context of sale and lease-back agreements.[178]

Another statutory exception to the general rule allows parole evidence in **27.13.4** relation to bills of exchange. Section 100 of the Bills of Exchange Act 1882 provides that, in any judicial proceeding in Scotland, any fact relating to a bill of exchange, bank cheque or promissory note, which is relevant to any question of liability thereon, may be proved by parole evidence. This section was received without enthusiasm by the Scottish courts and examples of circumstances in which it has been judicially held to apply are few, presumably because it conflicted with the common law rule that then provided that performance, discharges or variations of an obligation constituted by writing might not be proved by parole evidence.[179]

27.14 INTERACTION OF PRINCIPAL AND AGENT, CO-OBLIGANTS AND CO-CREDITORS *INTER SE*

Liability of apparent principal

When a person, who has signed a contract ostensibly on his own behalf, alleges **27.14.1** that he was acting for an undisclosed principal and is accordingly not liable, the general rule applies in a question between himself and the creditor in the obligation. Solicitors who signed missives for the sale of heritage,[180] and a chartered accountant who signed a receipt for the price of shares,[181] were not allowed to

---

sum of money granted a receipt for that sum which bore to be the price of a certain article of furniture, and it was averred that no money passed and that the furniture remained in the debtor's possession, *Hepburn v Law* 1914 SC 918 (held not to be a sale); a receipt was granted for £79 which bore to be the price of certain machinery, and on the same day the machinery was hired back to the purported seller at a rent equal to interest at 4½ per cent on £79 (with mutual rights of redemption), *Rennet v Mathieson* (1903) 5 F 591 (held not to be a sale); the recipient of a loan of money gave the creditor a receipted invoice for bicycles at a specified price which was averred not to have been paid, *Jones & Co's Tr v Allan* (1901) 4 F 374 (held not to be a sale).

[176] *McBain v Wallace* (1881) 8 R (HL) 106 and *Liddell's Tr v Warr* (1893) 20 R 989. See also *Pattison's Tr v Liston* (1893) 20 R 806.

[177] *McBain v Wallace* (1881) 8 R (HL) 106, per Lord Watson at 114–115. It has been suggested that s 61(4) of the Sale of Goods Act 1893 (now s 62(4) of the 1979 Act) was enacted because of doubts such as those expressed by Lord Watson, and to provide that, in spite of the form of the contract, the intention of the parties might be proved by extrinsic evidence: see *Robertson v Hall's Tr* (1896) 24 R 120, per Lord Moncreiff at 135.

[178] Styles, "Debtor-to-Creditor Sales and the Sale of Goods Act 1979", 1995 JR 365, founding upon the Sale of Goods Act 1979, s 62(4) and *Gavin's Tr v Fraser* 1920 SC 674.

[179] Examples of decisions contrary to the terms of this provision are given at para 24.07.

[180] *Gibb v Cunningham & Robertson* 1925 SLT 608 (OH).

[181] *Lindsay v Craig* 1919 SC 139. In *Welsh's Trs v Forbes* (1885) 12 R 851, where proof in similar circumstances was allowed, it is thought that Lord Rutherfurd Clark's dissenting opinion, at 862, was correct.

prove by extrinsic evidence that, in spite of the unqualified terms of their written obligations, they had acted only as agents for other persons. However, by an exception to the general rule it is competent to prove that a person who was not signatory of a writing was in fact the principal of one of the signatories, and is entitled to sue or is liable to be sued upon it.[182] When notice to a tenant to remove was given by only one of two co-proprietors, the other co-proprietor was held entitled to prove that the notice had been signed on his behalf and with his authority.[183] Conversely, when one of two co-tenants gave notice of intention to remove, the proprietors were allowed to prove that the notice had been given on behalf of, and with the authority of, the other tenant.[184] This exception is said to be justified because it does not discharge any liability appearing *ex facie* of the writing, but merely adds a party to it.[185] This is not an adequate justification at common law because the general rule excludes additions to the writing as well as contradictions. In reality the position here appears to be that a rule of the law of principal and agent conflicts with, and takes precedence over, the general rule of the law of evidence.[186]

Co-obligants and co-creditors *inter se*

27.14.2 Extrinsic evidence is admissible to establish that the contractual relationship between co-obligants is different from that expressed or implied in the writing which constitutes their contractual relationship with the creditor.[187] However, such evidence is not competent in a question between the co-obligants and the creditor.[188] Thus a co-cautioner was allowed to prove an agreement, contrary to the implied term of a cautionary obligation, that he was not bound to communicate to his co-cautioners the benefit of a security which he had obtained from the principal debtor[189]; a co-acceptor of a bill of exchange was allowed to prove, contrary to the presumption that two co-obligants *inter se* are each liable for half, that she was a cautioner only in relation to the other acceptor and was entitled to relief against him for the whole sum due under the bill which she had paid to the creditor[190]; and extrinsic evidence was allowed to prove that, as between two joint tenants only one

---

[182] Gloag, *Contract* (2nd edn), p 121. There are exceptions to the exception, for which see Gloag.

[183] *Walker v Hendry* 1925 SC 855.

[184] *Graham v Stirling* 1922 SC 90.

[185] Gloag, *Contract* (2nd edn), p 127; *Graham v Stirling* 1922 SC 90, per Lord Ashmore (Ordinary) at 98.

[186] *Anderson v Gordon* (1830) 8 S 304, where the general rule was applied in these circumstances, would presumably not now be followed.

[187] *Hamilton & Co v Freeth* (1889) 16 R 1022. See also *Thow's Tr v Young* 1910 SC 588, per Lord Skerrington (Ordinary) at 593, Lord President Dunedin at 595–596. The same principle was applied to a case of co-creditors under an insurance policy: *North British Insurance Co v Tunnock & Fraser* (1864) 3 M 1, per Lord Benholme at 5. Two persons in contemplation of marriage agreed to effect an insurance on their joint lives, the proceeds to be payable to the survivor on death of either of them. The insurance policy, when issued, made the proceeds payable not to the survivor but to the "executors, administrators and assigns" of the two assured. The opinion was expressed that it was competent to prove the insured persons' own agreement *inter se* as to the disposal of the proceeds of the policy in respect of which they were joint creditors. Lord Benholme described the agreement between the spouses as a "collateral contract". However, this was not a collateral agreement in accordance with Dickson's definition (Dickson, *Evidence* (3rd edn), para 1033), because, in a question between the insured and the insurance company, it clearly contradicted the terms of the written contract. As to collateral agreements, see para 27.16.

[188] *Drysdale v Johnstone* (1839) 1 D 409.

[189] *Hamilton & Co v Freeth* (1889) 16 R 1022. See also *Thow's Tr v Young* 1910 SC 588, per Lord Skerrington (Ordinary) at 593, Lord President Dunedin at 595–596.

[190] *Crosbie v Brown* (1900) 3 F 83.

of them owned the crop and stock on the farm,[191] or was concerned in the active working of the quarries which were the subject of the lease.[192]

27.15 QUESTIONS WITH THIRD PARTIES

It has been held in certain circumstances that the general rule does not apply in a question between persons who are not parties to the writing but have an interest, or between such persons and one of the parties.[193] A third party with an interest may prove *prout de jure* that subjects held on an *ex facie* absolute title by one party are really held in trust for another,[194] and the acceptor of a bill was held entitled, as a third party to the transaction, to prove against an assignee who had charged him on it, that the assignee held the bill in trust for another person who had discharged his claim in respect of it.[195] For the purpose of this exception a person deriving title from a party to the writing is not, in general, a third party.[196] Differing opinions have been expressed as to whether a trustee on the sequestrated estate of one of the parties to the writing, as representing his creditors, can be regarded as a third party for this purpose.[197]

27.15.1

27.16 COLLATERAL AGREEMENTS

By an exception to the general rule, agreements which are collateral to a writing may be proved by extrinsic evidence. However, "collateral agreements" must be carefully defined. Some of the cases appear to indicate that any agreement may be proved as collateral which is not found in the writing, and is not directly contradictory of anything found there, but this has been said to leave very little content to the general rule.[198] In conveyancing transactions, obligations in missives were in some cases said to be "collateral" if they regulated a matter intended to be of future effect, that is to survive the delivery of the disposition.[199] Dickson defined the word "collateral" in relation to this exception in the following terms:

27.16.1

---

[191] *Kilpatrick v Kilpatrick* (1841) 4 D 109.
[192] *Moore v Dempster* (1879) 6 R 930; *Union Canal Co v Johnston* (1834) 12 S 304; (1835) 1 Sh & McL 117, where proof was refused of an oral agreement between two defenders as to the allocation *inter se* of their liability under a joint minute for payment of a sum of money to the pursuers, is thought to be distinguishable, because the question of relief between the co-obligants was expressly mentioned in the joint minute and fell, therefore, to be decided on a construction of its terms. In *McPherson v Haggart* (1881) 9 R 306, where proof of such an agreement was also held to be inadmissible, it was observed that there was no relevant averment that the other co-cautioner had been a party to it.
[193] Gloag, *Contract* (2nd edn), pp 377, 390.
[194] *Hastie v Steel* (1886) 13 R 843; *Lord Advocate v McNeill* (1864) 2 M 626, per Lord Deas at 634; *Lord Elibank v Hamilton* (1827) 6 S 69. In *Scott v Miller* (1832) 11 S 21, there were conflicting opinions. The cases are discussed in McLaren, *Wills and Succession* (3rd edn), II, 1070–1071. In one case proof *prout de jure* was allowed in a declarator of trust between the trustees on the sequestrated estates of the two parties to the writing: *Wallace v Sharp* (1885) 12 R 687.
[195] *Middleton v Rutherglen* (1861) 23 D 526.
[196] Gloag, *Contract* (2nd edn), p 377. In *Norval v Abbey* 1939 SC 724, the general rule was applied between one party and the singular successors of the other.
[197] *Wink v Speirs* (1867) 6 M 77. The trustee in a sequestration is at the same time an agent of the general body of creditors and a representative of the bankrupt, taking his estate *tantum et tale* as it stood in him. See Goudy, *Bankruptcy* (4th edn), pp 336, 249.
[198] Gloag, *Contract* (2nd edn), p 371.
[199] See Gretton & Reid, *Conveyancing*, pp 341–343 and *Conveyancing* (2nd edn), para 18.02; *Taylor v McLeod* 1990 SLT 194; *Bourton v Claydon* 1990 SLT (Sh Ct) 7.

"The rule by which extrinsic evidence is inadmissible to add to the stipulations of a deed does not apply to matters collateral to the document; because on these there is no written agreement between the parties. In such questions, therefore, the nature and object of the writing must be considered, so that on the one hand obligations or conditions may not be added to a deed designed for recording all the agreement which the parties made on a particular subject, while, on the other hand, a writing intended to embrace only certain branches or stipulations of an agreement ought not to be stretched to matters beyond its purview; for, if it were, extrinsic evidence would be excluded on matters which the parties purposely left to be expiscated by that means."[200]

What are described by Dickson as the "most prominent" illustrations of this exception are cases where the writing is a short memorandum in which only certain points of the contract are recorded: for example, a pencil note "Six weeks at two guineas," which was regarded as recording only some of the terms of a contract for the hire of a horse, leaving the remaining terms to be proved by parole evidence.[201]

27.16.2   So defined, the scope of this exception is rightly to be regarded as very limited indeed.[202] It includes only agreements between the parties or their successors in title which are shown by the terms of the writing, as construed by the court, not to form part of the matter with which the writing was properly concerned. One example, mentioned above, is a writing which was clearly intended to record only some of the terms of a contract. Another is a conveyance of heritage following upon a multiple contract, which provides not only for a sale of heritage but also for other matters, such as the performance of work or the sale of moveables, or the transfer of a fixture not owned by the seller.[203] Since these other matters do not properly fall to be mentioned in a conveyance of heritage, they may be proved by extrinsic evidence.[204] Another example is an agreement, entered into during the currency of a lease, in terms of which the landlord, on the termination of the lease, must pay to the tenant all his loss during the 19 years of his tenancy.[205] Proof of

---

[200] Dickson, *Evidence* (3rd edn), para 1033. See *Norval v Abbey* 1939 SC 724, per Lord Wark at 730, Lord Jamieson at 734. Many of the examples given by Dickson do not fall within his own general definition.

[201] As to this kind of writing, see para 27.8.

[202] Examples of agreements which fall outside this definition: An oral agreement, confirmed in writing, was entered into between landlords and prospective tenants with regard to fencing, on the strength of which the tenants accepted a lease which did not refer to the agreement. In a question between the original tenant and disponees of the original landlords, the tenants' averments with regard to the agreement were held to be irrelevant, because proof of them would result in adding to the lease terms which were not, but which ought to have been, contained in it: *Norval v Abbey* 1939 SC 724. An oral agreement was said to have been made *unico contextu* (as parts of a single continuous process) with the execution of a formal lease of certain premises for a period of five years. The oral agreement provided for payment by the tenants to the landlords of the sums which the latter would have had to disburse in respect of owners' rates and property tax during the currency of the lease. The landlord's averments regarding the oral agreement were held irrelevant because they related not to a collateral agreement but to an agreement which purported to add to, or to alter, the express stipulations of the lease regarding the payments to be made by the tenants: *Perdikou v Pattison* 1958 SLT 153 (see also *McGregor v Lord Strathallan* (1862) 24 D 1006 ("an attempt to engraft on the lease a clause not to be found in it": per Lord Justice-Clerk Inglis at 1010); *Stewart v Clark* (1871) 9 M 616).

[203] *William Masson Ltd v Scottish Brewers Ltd* 1966 SC 9.

[204] For an examination of the common law in this context, see para 27.9, which is now affected by the Contract (Scotland) Act 1997, s 2, see also para 27.9, and see Talman, Halliday's, *Conveyancing Law and Practice* (2nd edn), paras 30-130 to 30-138 and 33-03.

[205] *Garden v Earl of Aberdeen* (1893) 20 R 896. See also *British Workman's etc, Assurance Co Ltd v Wilkinson* (1900) 8 SLT 67 (OH), where the collateral agreement did not take effect until the termination of the written contract. The case is difficult to fit into one of the recognised exceptions.

the agreement was allowed because (a) it could not have been included in the lease, since it was entered into after the lease had commenced, and (b) it did not seek to contradict or vary the lease, since it did not commence to operate until after the lease had terminated. An example of this kind has been described as "the constitution of an original and independent agreement by parole".[206] In proceedings arising out of building works for which a written estimate had been accepted verbally, an agreement for construction of a garage not referred to in the estimate was accepted to be collateral, but additional terms in relation to the main works which, if agreed, one would have expected to find set out in the agreement, were excluded.[207] When footballers' contracts contained provision for payment, an oral agreement for "signing on" fees and promotion bonuses could not be deemed collateral since it related to, and contradicted, a matter covered in the contracts.[208]

27.17 CONDITIONAL DELIVERY OR EXECUTION

In a few cases extrinsic evidence has been admitted to prove that a writing was **27.17.1** executed or delivered only on a condition.[209] The only purpose for which such a proof can be allowed is to suspend the operation of the whole contract until the condition is fulfilled[210]—for example, when it was averred that a written contract to take advertising space from advertising contractors for a period of two years was signed by the defender's managing director subject to the orally expressed condition that the contract was not to be regarded as binding until it was approved by his co-directors[211]; when it was averred that a cheque, *ex facie* unqualified, was delivered subject to the condition that it would be stopped unless the drawer received on that day a cheque for the same amount from a named person[212]; when a receipt was sent by a landlord to a tenant merely as a reminder that the rent was due, and subject to the condition that he should either send the money or return the receipt.[213] When a

---

[206] *Kirkpatrick v Allanshaw Coal Co* (1880) 8 R 327, per Lord President Inglis at 332, quoted by Lord Trayner in *Garden v Earl of Aberdeen* (1893) 20 R 896 at 899. Another example of a collateral agreement may be found in *McAlister v Gemmil* (1862) 24 D 956; affd (1863) 1 M (HL) 1, and possibly in *Merrow & Fell v Hutchison & Brown* (1873) 10 SLR 338.

[207] *D Cameron & Son v McLeod* 1999 GWD 20-918 (Sh Ct). In *Lithoprint (Scotland) Ltd v Summit Leasing Ltd* 1998 GWD 38-1956 (OH) Lord Milligan allowed a proof before answer in respect of interest arrangements contained in a side letter which one might have expected to be intrinsic to leases signed later that day.

[208] *Irons v Partick Thistle Football Club Ltd* 1997 SLT 983 (OH). Evidence of the oral agreement was admitted on the basis that the contract was admittedly incorrect in this respect (the admission having been clear in evidence during the proof and could be inferred from the pleadings): 987F–I.

[209] Gloag, *Contract* (2nd edn), p 371. See also Lord Bramwell, obiter, in *North British Railway Co v Wood* (1891) 18 R (HL) 27 at 36–37. This exception is of English origin: Cross & Tapper, *Evidence* (9th edn) p 656.

[210] *Norval v Abbey* 1939 SC 724, per Lord Wark at 731.

[211] *Abrahams & Sons v Robert Miller (Denny) Ltd* 1933 SC 171. For another similar example, see *Dodds v Walker* (1822) 2 S 73 (acceptance by agent of offer to take a lease to be binding only if approved by principal).

[212] *Semple v Kyle* (1902) 4 F 421. The condition was held proved, and the drawer, who was sued on the cheque by an endorsee for value who had known that the cheque was dishonoured, was assoilzied. Despite Lord Kinnear's opinion to the contrary (at 424) it is thought that the condition did qualify the meaning and effect of the writing, and that it was not, accordingly, a collateral agreement. As to collateral agreements, see para 27.16.

[213] *Henry v Miller* (1884) 11 R 713, as described by Lord Shand at 718. This case is also mentioned in para 27.13.

written contract of employment followed upon a written application by the employee, in which he undertook not to interfere with the employer's business on the termination of the employment, it was held that the undertaking, which was not mentioned in the contract, was a collateral undertaking on the faith of which the applicant obtained employment.[214]

27.18 WRITING ADMITTEDLY INACCURATE

27.18.1   When the party founding upon a writing admits on record or in writing that it does not contain a true account of the transaction the door is opened to extrinsic proof of the facts.[215] "When both parties are agreed that the writing does not express the contract, and yet differ as what the real contract is, then, unless evidence were admissible, there would be a complete impasse—no solution being possible."[216] When the creditor in a bond and disposition in security for £900, who had charged on the bond, admitted that only £300 had been advanced, extrinsic evidence was admitted to prove the amount actually advanced.[217] Employers, who were bound under a written contract of employment to pay a specified weekly wage, averred that by oral agreement between the parties this had been reduced. When the employee admitted the reduction, subject to the explanation that the balance was to be accumulated to provide a retirement pension, it was held that proof of the true terms of the oral agreement was permissible.[218]

---

[214] *British Workman's etc Assurance Co Ltd v Wilkinson* (1900) 8 SLT 67 (OH). This was a departure from the general rule which is difficult to fit into one of the recognised exceptions.

[215] Dickson, *Evidence* (3rd edn), para 1035; *Norval v Abbey* 1939 SC 724, per Lord Wark at 730. For situations when one party alleges defective expression see para 27.12.

[216] *Grant v Mackenzie* (1899) 1 F 889 at 894.

[217] *Hotson v Paul* (1831) 9 S 685. See also *Miller v Oliphant* (1843) 5 D 856 where a person who had some years earlier granted a disposition containing a discharge for the price of £120, which was stated to have been paid, sued the disponee for £80 on an averment that only £40 of the price had in fact been paid. Since the disponer had admitted that the statements in the disposition were inaccurate, the disponee was allowed to prove by extrinsic evidence that, although *ex facie* absolute, the disposition was truly in security for advances made to the disponer which were still outstanding. Conversely when a disponee admitted that the price actually paid by him was not the price which was stated in the disposition to have been paid, the disponer was allowed to prove by extrinsic evidence that the disposition, although *ex facie* absolute, was truly in security only: *Miller v Miller* (1905) 12 SLT 743 (OH). See also *Grant's Trs v Morison* (1875) 2 R 377. *Cf Leckie v Leckie* (1854) 17 D 77.

[218] *Campbell v Arbuthnot* (1904) 12 SLT 438. For additional examples, see *Blackwood v Hay* (1858) 20 D 631 and *Miller v Wilson* 1919 1 SLT 223 (OH). Prior to the abolition of reference to oath in civil cases, when a party founding upon a writing admitted on reference to oath that the true contract differed from the writing extrinsic evidence to prove the true terms of the contract became admissible. Dickson, *Evidence* (3rd edn), para 1035; Gloag, *Contract* (2nd edn), p 377. See also *Aikman* (1665) M 12311; *Kinnaird v McDougal* (1694) 4 Brown's Supp 184. *Sim v Inglish* (1674) M 12321, the first report of which supports the statement in the text, whereas the second report appears to contradict it, is difficult to understand. It has been said that this exception applies if the admission is contained in a writing subsequent to the date of the writing in question: Gloag, *Contract* (2nd edn), pp 376–377.

Explanation or interpretation of writing

27.19 EXPLANATION OF THE WRITING

General[219]

In accordance with the general rule, the intention of the parties to a writing must **27.19.1** be discovered from the writing itself, and from it alone.[220] When the language of the writing is clear and applies without doubt or difficulty to the facts of the case, extrinsic evidence is neither necessary nor admissible for its interpretation.[221] Even when, because there is an ambiguity,[222] the exception applies, the purpose of extrinsic evidence is not to discover the writer's intention apart from the words used in the writing, but to ascertain the proper meaning of these words.[223] "We must seek the meaning of the writer, but we must find it in his words; and we must seek the meaning of the words, but they must be *his* words, the words as he used them, the meaning of which they have in his mouth."[224] The Scottish Law Commission, in their consideration of interpretation in private law, propose that all evidence relevant to interpretation should be admitted notwithstanding that it is extrinsic evidence,[225] but their proposals have not been implemented at the time of writing. Their proposals are prompted by the uncertainty of the present position in which through case law, some of which adopts English concepts, many exceptions to the rule have evolved in order to explain or interpret writings. These exceptions evolved against the background of general rules of construction of writings. The present situation is described by the Commission as "complex, obscure and unsatisfactory".[226] The Scottish Law Commission have reviewed the whole area of interpretation in private law, proposing a statutory statement of rules of interpretation and rules of preference in cases of doubt, not only for application to writings but to any act of will or intention which has or is intended to have, legal effect (thus including contracts, conveyances and testamentary writings, but excluding legislation and acts of a court or tribunal).[227] However, until these proposals, or any other changes, are enacted, the "complex and obscure" workings of the rule and its exceptions in this area must be stated against the general background of construction of writings.

Basic rules of construction

Before it can be decided in a particular case whether extrinsic evidence is admissible **27.19.2**

---

[219] See McBryde, Chapter 19.
[220] See para 27.1.
[221] Bell, *Commentaries* (7th edn), I, 456; *Blair v Blair* (1849) 12 D 97, per Lord Moncreiff at 107; *Higgins v Dawson* [1902] AC 1. See also *Nasmyth's Trs v National Society for Prevention of Cruelty to Children* 1914 SC (HL) 76, per Lord Loreburn at 82, Lord Atkinson and Lord Shaw at 83, Lord Parmoor at 84: dub Lord Dunedin at 82–83.
[222] "Ambiguity" is used in this chapter to mean any doubt as to the meaning of the words or their application to the facts, including inaccuracies and misdescriptions.
[223] Dickson, *Evidence* (3rd edn), para 1043.
[224] Graves, 28 AmerLRev 323.
[225] Scottish Law Commission, *Report on Interpretation in Private Law* (Scot Law Com No 160), para 8.20.
[226] *Report on Interpretation in Private Law*, notes to Clause 2 in Appendix A.
[227] *Report on Interpretation in Private Law*, Part 1.

or not, certain basic rules of construction may have to be considered.[228] There is a presumption that the words of a writing are to be understood according to their plain, ordinary and obvious acceptation,[229] unless the law has attached to them a recognised meaning,[230] in which case they are presumed to bear that meaning.[231] The words are to be construed neither by strictly etymological nor by vulgar and inaccurate standards, but in accordance with the meaning which persons of ordinary intelligence would naturally attribute to them.[232] However, if it is clear from some parts of the writing[233] under construction that the writer has used certain words in a particular sense, or even in a peculiar or inaccurate sense, they will be so construed in each part of the writing in which they occur in the same connection or apparently with the same signification.[234] If by applying these basic rules of construction the court has been able to give an intelligible meaning to the writing, then failing a relevant averment that the writing, so construed, cannot reasonably be applied to the facts,[235] extrinsic evidence purporting to show that some other meaning was intended is inadmissible. The following are some examples of extrinsic evidence being held inadmissible on these grounds: in a commercial contract, because "acre" was defined by statute to mean imperial acre, evidence of an oral agreement that it should mean a Scotch acre was excluded[236]; the word "interest" in a lease was held to have a definite, unambiguous and well-known meaning, both in common and legal parlance, and evidence that it was used by landlords and tenants to mean annual rent-charges, including repayments of capital, was held to be inadmissible[237]; the word "residue" in a will, although capable of including heritage, was construed by reference to other parts of the will as being intended to exclude it, and evidence of the testator's instructions to his solicitors, purporting to show an intention contrary to the construction placed upon the word by the court, was held to be inadmissible[238]; in a question as to whether

---

[228] There are conflicting views as to whether the admissibility of extrinsic evidence is part of the law of evidence, or whether, since it relates to construction, it is part of substantive law. For a discussion of the subject, see Phipson, *Extrinsic Evidence in Aid of Interpretation* (1904) 20 LQR 245 at 246–247.
[229] Bell, *Principles*, para 524; Dickson, *Evidence* (3rd edn), para 1052; Wigram's First Proposition (Wigram, *Extrinsic Evidence in Aid of the Interpretation of Wills* (5th edn), p 11). This was repeated by Lord Hoffmann in an English case, *Investors Compensation Scheme Ltd v West Bromwich Building Society* [1998] 1 All ER 98.
[230] For example, in a statutory context or, in the case of words in statutes, by the Interpretation Act 1978.
[231] Bell, *Principles*, para 1694; *Blair v Blair* (1849) 12 D 97 at 109–111; *Brand v Scott's Trs* (1892) 19 R 768 (recognised rule of construction). The presumption may be irrebuttable if the meaning has been prescribed by statute. See *Thomson v Garioch* (1841) 3 D 625; *McDowall & Neilson's Tr v JB Snowball & Co Ltd* (1904) 7 F 35 at 44, 45.
[232] Bell, *Commentaries* (7th edn), I, 456; Dickson, *Evidence* (3rd edn), para 1052. In *Investors Compensation Scheme Ltd v West Bromwich Building Society* [1998] 1 All ER 98 Lord Hoffmann opined that evidence of the background to the parties' use of the words (excluding evidence of prior negotiations and declarations of subjective intention) would be admissible to clarify the meaning that would be attached to them.
[233] Or writings. See para 27.4.
[234] Dickson, *Evidence* (3rd edn), para 1053; *Lee v Alexander* (1883) 10 R (HL) 91 at 93; Wigram's First Proposition (Wigram, *Extrinsic Evidence in Aid of the Interpretation of Wills* (5th edn), pp 11–12). See also *Hunter v Nisbett* (1839) 2 D 16; *Anderson v Anderson* (1829) 7 S 743; *Easson v Thomson's Trs* (1879) 7 R 251; *Dunsmure v Dunsmure* (1879) 7 R 261.
[235] See, for example, *Hunter v Fox* 1964 SC (HL) 95.
[236] *Thomson v Garioch* (1841) 3 D 625. Cf *Miller v Mair* (1860) 22 D 660.
[237] *Sinclair v McBeath* (1868) 7 M 273 at 277, 278.
[238] *Farquhar v Farquhar's Exrs* (1875) 3 R 71. Cf *Cathcart's Trs v Bruce* 1923 SLT 722 (OH), where a letter of instructions was looked at only for the purpose of discovering the testator's state of knowledge.

a disposition of *inter alia* "all other lands and others" included a particular mid-superiority, it was held, on a proper construction of the deed as a whole, that there was no ambiguity, and evidence of prior communings between the parties was held to be inadmissible[239]; when a bequest in a will named two public houses, it was considered, on reading the will as a whole, not to be ambiguous and thus extrinsic evidence was not admissible to the effect that the testator had intended to include in the bequests the flats above the tied houses.[240]

Unusual use or meaning of words and phrases

As stated earlier, the words used in a writing are to be understood according to **27.19.3** their plain, ordinary and accepted meaning, or according to any recognised meaning attached to them by law. It may be necessary to examine the circumstances pertaining at the date of execution to ascertain what the plain meaning was then.[241] In England this background has been described as "the matrix of fact"[242] and more broadly to include anything which would have affected the way in which the language of the document would have been understood at the time of execution.[243] However, when the characters in which the document is written are difficult to decipher, or are in a foreign language, expert evidence is admissible to declare what the characters are or to translate the foreign words.[244] The same principle applies when the words used, although decipherable and apparently in English, are peculiar[245] or are used in a peculiar way.[246] If the peculiar use or meaning of the word is not obvious, it must be specially averred before extrinsic evidence becomes admissible to establish it.[247] So extrinsic evidence was admissible

---

[239] *Lee v Alexander* (1883) 10 R (HL) 91. See also *Barclay v Neilson* (1878) 5 R 909, where the court felt able to put a construction upon a blundered clause in an agricultural lease relating to new buildings and repairs, and where evidence of an oral agreement upon the matter was held inadmissible. As to the inadmissibility of evidence of possession to contradict or explain an unambiguous bounding title in a disposition or similar deed, see *Dalhousie's Tutors v Minister of Lochlee* (1890) 17 R 1060; *North British Railway Co v Moon's Trs* (1879) 6 R 640.

[240] *Fortunato's JF v Fortunato* 1981 SLT 277 (OH). For other examples in which extrinsic evidence was not admitted to explain unambiguous terms, see: *Butter v Foster* 1912 SC 1218 (re asssignation of rents); *Blair v Blair* (1849) 12 D 97 (re meaning of "heirs"); *Stevenson v Moncrieff* (1845) 7 D 418 (re the expression "rents falling due from and after Martinmas"; *Towill & Co v The British Agricultural Association* (1875) 3 R 117 and *Haigh & Ringrose Ltd v Barrhead Builders Ltd* 1981 SLT 157 (OH) (re payment terms in commercial contracts); *Parochial Board of Greenock v Coghill & Son* (1878) 5 R 732 (re "sharp freshwater sand"); *Highland Railway Co v Great North of Scotland Railway Co* (1896) 23 R (HL) 80 (re "traffic"). See also *Miller v Miller* (1822) 1 Shaw's App 308, per Lord Chancellor Eldon at 317.

[241] See, for example, *Retail Parks Investments Ltd v The Royal Bank of Scotland (No 2)* 1996 SC 227 in relation to what the parties would have contemplated at the date of execution in referring to a branch of a bank, and *Bank of Scotland v Junior* 8 January 1999 (IH).

[242] Per Lord Wilberforce in *Prenn v Simmonds* [1971] 1WLR 1381 at 1384–1386.

[243] One of the five detailed propositions for admission of evidence for interpretation of documents proposed by Lord Hoffmann in *Investors Compensation Scheme Ltd v West Bromwich Building Society* [1998] 1 All ER 98, and commented upon in *Bank of Scotland v Dunedin Property Investment Co Ltd* 1998 SC 657 and *Bank of Scotland v Junior* 8 January 1999 (IH).

[244] Wigram's Fourth Proposition (Wigram, *Extrinsic Evidence in Aid of the Interpretation of Wills* (5th edn), p 13); Dickson, *Evidence* (3rd edn), para 1058.

[245] Dickson, *Evidence* (3rd edn), paras 1058, 1059.

[246] Dickson, *Evidence* (3rd edn), para 1060.

[247] *Sutton & Co v Ciceri & Co* (1890) 17 R (HL) 40 at 43; Dickson, *Evidence* (3rd edn), para 1063. Extrinsic evidence, to show that the word "effects" in a will was intended to include heritage, was disallowed because it was not averred that the word had a technical meaning in the country where the will was made: *Griffith's JF v Griffith's Exrs* (1905) 7 F 470.

to provide the meaning of trade or technical terms,[248] such as "soum" in connection with an area of pasture,[249] "cutting-shop" in the glasscutting trade,[250] "statuary" in the carrying trade,[251] "Scotch iron of best quality" in the iron casting trade,[252] "St. Lawrence" in a contract of marine insurance,[253] and "stone" in connection with the local price of cheese, used as a means of fixing the rent in a lease.[254] It seems probable that evidence would be admitted to show that the writer was in the habit of designating certain persons or things by peculiar terms or nicknames, as in a case where a legacy was left to "Mrs. G."[255]

Explanation of deeds and obligations relating to heritage

27.19.4 If the conveyance of heritage is unclear in its terms then extrinsic evidence may be admitted to explain its terms or to apply the terms to the reality of the heritage, such as where the nature of a boundary description is unclear[256] or a servitude is implied or its extent is not precisely specified.[257] In one case, where a disposition was granted in implement of a decree-arbitral,[258] the opinion was expressed that, the governing instrument being the decree-arbitral and the disposition having been granted for the sole purpose of constituting a feudal title, the terms of the former deed, which the disposition purported to repeat but repeated inaccurately, continued to regulate the obligations of the parties.[259] If the deed contains a special destination, then unless the terms are such that they narrate who paid the purchase price and therefore relate a contract between the disponees, breach of which may be proved by extrinsic evidence, the terms of the special destination, if unambiguous, are conclusive. Accordingly, extrinsic evidence of revocation of the special

---

[248] *Buttery & Co v Inglis* (1877) 5 R 58 at 67; (1878) 5 R (HL) 87 at 90; Gloag, *Contract* (2nd edn), p 365.

[249] *McKenzie v McCrae* (1825) 4 S 147.

[250] *Watson v Kidston & Co* (1839) 1 D 1254.

[251] *Sutton & Co v Ciceri & Co* (1890) 17 R (HL) 40 at 40–41.

[252] *Fleming & Co v Airdrie Iron Co* (1882) 9 R 473.

[253] *Birrell v Dryer* (1884) 11 R (HL) 41. The evidence being inconclusive as to whether the river or the gulf was intended, the House of Lords construed the words in the light of the extrinsic facts known to both parties.

[254] *Miller v Mair* (1860) 22 D 660. *Cf Thomson v Garioch* (1841) 3 D 625.

[255] Dickson, *Evidence* (3rd edn), para 1059; McLaren, *Wills and Succession* (3rd edn), I, 382.

[256] eg *Butt v Galloway Motor Co Ltd* 1996 SC 261.

[257] eg *Houldsworth v Gordon Cumming* 1910 SC (HL) 49, *Robson v Chalmers Property Investment Co Ltd* 1965 SLT 381 (OH). For detailed description of the use of extrinsic evidence in relation to the explanation of writings in which servitudes are established (including identification of the dominant and servient tenement), see Cusine & Paisley, *Servitudes and Rights of Way*, paras 2.17, 2.24–2.38, *Stair Memorial Encyclopaedia*, Vol 18, para 450; and in relation to admission of extrinsic evidence to supplement the terms of the written servitude, see Cusine & Paisley, paras 2.80–2.83.

[258] In Gloag, *Contract* (2nd edn), p 369, it is doubted whether, or to what extent, the rule applies to conveyances which follow decrees-arbitral. See *Guthrie v Glasgow and South-Western Railway Co* (1858) 20 D 825.

[259] *Duke of Fife v Great North of Scotland Railway Co* (1901) 3 F (HL) 2, per Lord Macnaughten at 12–13. It is thought that the true ground of decision in this case was that the clause in the disposition was an "ungrammatical and ... unintelligible" sentence, and that it was therefore permissible to look at the decree-arbitral in order to discover its meaning. See Lord Low's opinion (at 4–5), which was substantially affirmed by the House of Lords, and the comments of Lord Dundas (Ordinary) thereon in *Forth Bridge Railway Co v Incorporation of the Guildry of Dunfermline* 1909 SC 493 at 497–498. An analogous exception to the general rule was permitted in connection with an oral contract for the sale of two ships, which was held to govern the two written contracts, each relating to one ship, which followed upon it: *Claddagh Steamship Co v Steven & Co* 1919 SC (HL) 132, mentioned more fully at para 27.6.

destination by testamentary writing or other unilateral document, or of facts contradicting the implication of equal contribution to the purchase price, will not be admitted[260] unless there is a judicial admission that the special destination is inaccurate.[261]

When a solemn lease was executed after the tenant had been in possession for some time under an informal agreement, and the solemn lease was said to differ in its provisions from the informal agreement, the solemn lease was not applied to anything done by the parties prior to the date of its execution although it bore to be effective retrospectively from the date of entry. In such a case the party founding upon the informal agreement is allowed to prove that it differs in its terms from the subsequent lease, and that the question at issue between the parties relates to the period prior to execution of that lease.[262] **27.19.5**

27.20 AMBIGUITY OR EQUIVOCATION

If, after the basic rules of construction have been applied,[263] the language of a writing still requires elucidation, either because it appears to the court or because it is averred by the parties that its meaning is uncertain, or that there is uncertainty about its application to the facts, extrinsic evidence, subject to one qualification, is in general admissible to explain and clarify.[264] The qualification relates to evidence of direct declarations of intention or understanding, which, in general, is inadmissible.[265] It is thought to be immaterial whether the ambiguity is patent or latent, extrinsic evidence generally being admissible in both cases.[266] A patent ambiguity is apparent on the face of the writing, whereas a latent ambiguity arises, not from the words of the writing, which are clear and comprehensible, but from their attempted application to the facts.[267] In practice the distinction appears never to have been applied in Scotland, and in a number of reported cases patent ambiguities have been resolved by the admission of extrinsic evidence.[268] **27.20.1**

---

[260] *Gordon-Rogers v Thomson's Exrs* 1988 SLT 618 (OH); *Smith v Mackintosh* 1989 SCLR 83.

[261] *Hay's Tr v Hay's Trs* 1951 SC 329.

[262] *Korner v Shennan* 1950 SC 285.

[263] For the basic rules of construction, see para 27.19.

[264] Wigram's Fifth Proposition (Wigram, *Extrinsic Evidence in Aid of the Interpretation of Wills* (5th edn), p 14).

[265] See para 27.21.

[266] Except perhaps in connection with direct declarations of intention or understanding, which are mentioned in para 27.20.2.

[267] Apparently, in England there had been a rule that a latent ambiguity might competently be resolved by extrinsic evidence, whereas a patent ambiguity might not, but this ceased to be the case: *Watcham v East African Protectorate* [1919] AC 533. In two early House of Lords decisions in Scottish cases, Lord Chancellor Brougham pronounced this English distinction to be part of the law of Scotland—*Morton v Hunter & Co* (1830) 4 W & S 379 at 386–387; *Logan v Wright* (1831) 5 W & S 242 at 247—although he conceded in both cases that extrinsic evidence was admissible when there was a doubt as to the identity of the subject-matter of the writing. The distinction was adopted by Bell, *Principles*, paras 524, 1871 and in *Ritchie v Whish* (1880) 8 R 101, per Lord President Inglis at 104, but the distinction has been described as not always very satisfactory or easy to apply: Gloag, *Contract* (2nd edn), p 372.

[268] *Robertson's Tr v Riddell* 1911 SC 14; *Anderson v McCracken Brothers* (1900) 2 F 780; *Brownlee v Robb* 1907 SC 1302 at 1311, 1313, 1314; *Von Mehren & Co v Edinburgh Roperie & Sailcloth Ltd* (1901) 4 F 232; *Blackstock v Macarthur* 1919 SC 57; *Trustees of the Free Church of Scotland v Maitland* (1887) 14 R 333 at 338, 341, 343, 344. For a similar case, where even a direct declaration of intention was apparently considered, see *Livingston v Livingston* (1864) 3 M 20.

27.20.2   Evidence of direct statements by the writer as to what he intended the writing
to mean, or as to his understanding of its meaning, is in general inadmissible.[269]
In a Scottish case in the House of Lords it was said that the irrelevancy of averments regarding statements of this kind is too obvious to need argument,[270] but
more recently in an English case in the House of Lords there has been criticism of
the distinction between direct and circumstantial evidence of intention, and a preference for the admission of relevant evidence of either kind.[271] It was thought that
there would be a risk, if such statements were admitted, that the parole evidence
of the parties to a written contract might take the place of the writing, or that
hearsay evidence of what a testator said might take the place of the will, whereas
this risk did not arise to the same extent from the admission of circumstantial evidence of the granter's intention, which, when there is an ambiguity, is always
accepted.[272] The distinction at one time recognised between patent and latent
ambiguities appears to have been replaced by a distinction, relevant only in
connection with direct declarations of intention, between the particular kind of
latent ambiguity known in England as an equivocation[273] and all other ambiguities, whether latent or patent.[274] An equivocation arises when the language of the
writing, though intended to apply to one person or one thing only, is equally
applicable in all its parts to two or more, and it is impossible to gather from the
context which was intended.[275] When there is an equivocation, it is said, direct
declarations of the granter's intention are admissible to solve it,[276] while in the
case of ambiguity or equivocation, circumstantial evidence of intention is

---

[269] *Devlin's Trs v Breen* 1943 SC 556 at 570, 582, 586; affd 1945 SC (HL) 27; *Campbell's Trs v
Adamson* 1911 SC 1111; *Brownlee v Robb* 1907 SC 1302 at 1311, 1314; *Johnstone v Haviland* (1896)
23 R (HL) 6, per Lord Watson at 6, Lord Shand at 11; *Trustees of the Free Church of Scotland v
Maitland* (1887) 14 R 333, per Lord President Inglis at 338, Lord Shand at 343, Lord Adam at 344;
Farquhar v Farquhar's Exrs (1875) 3 R 71, per Lord Gifford at 74; *cf* Lord Justice-Clerk Moncreiff at
73. In only one case (*Livingston v Livingston* (1864) 3 M 20), a letter expressly declaratory of a testator's intention was considered by the court.

[270] *Devlin's Trs v Breen* 1945 SC (HL) 27, per Lord Macmillan at 38.

[271] *Wickman Machine Tool Sales Ltd v Lord Schuler AG* [1974] AC 235 at 268, but the objection to
admission of direct statement of intent was carried forward by Lord Hoffmann in his statement of principles relevant to interpretation in *Investors Compensation Scheme Ltd v West Bromwich Building
Society* [1998] 1 All ER 98. The former approach is preferred by the Scottish Law Commission in their
Report on Interpretation in Private Law (Scot Law Com No 160), Part 8.

[272] See para 27.21.

[273] *Devlin's Trs v Breen* 1943 SC 556 at 570, 582, 586 (affd 1945 SC (HL) 27), applied the English
case of *Charter v Charter* (1874) LR 7 HL 364, per Lord Chancellor Cairns at 376–377.

[274] Although any distinction between forms of ambiguity has been criticised in the House of Lords in
an English case: *Wickman Machine Tool Sales Ltd v Lord Schuler AG* [1974] AC 235 at 268.

[275] Dickson, *Evidence* (3rd edn), paras 1075, 1077, 1078 defines latent ambiguity as if it meant equivocation. In *Fortunato's JF v Fortunato* 1981 SLT 277 an attempt to argue that there was "latent ambiguity" fell on a construction that the words in context were unambiguous, but the Lord Ordinary
stressed that evidence of the testator's expression of intention would only be admitted in the most
exceptional circumstances, such as in *Devlin's Trs v Breen* 1943 SC 556 (affd 1945 SC (HL) 27). For
earlier statements to this effect, see *Brownlee v Robb* 1907 SC 1302; *Trustees of the Free Church of
Scotland v Maitland* (1887) 14 R 333; *Farquhar v Farquhar's Exrs* (1875) 3 R 71 at 74 ("conversations of the testator . . . are not admissible").

[276] Wigram's Seventh Proposition (Wigram, *Extrinsic Evidence in Aid of the Interpretation of Wills*
(5th edn), p 14). The distinction in England is said to have been due to "special reasons, which are
partly historical and partly precautionary, but wholly arbitrary": Phipson, *Extrinsic Evidence in Aid of
Interpretation* (1904) 20 LQR 245 at 253. The English rule has been moderated by the Interpretation
of Wills Act 1982, s 2. For the current English position regarding interpretation of wills, see Cross &
Tapper *Evidence* (9th edn), pp 662–665.

admissible.[277] The purpose of the evidence is not to establish intention apart from the writing, but to discover the meaning of the words which the granter used in the writing, and the evidence is admissible only when there is an ambiguity. Circumstantial or indirect evidence has consisted of evidence of special or technical meanings of words or of the granter's habits of speech, of the circumstances antecedent to and surrounding the execution of the writing, of the granter's actings subsequent to the execution of the writing, and of custom or usage of trade. The admissibility of revoked or superseded writings or clauses is doubtful. The purpose of the evidence is to resolve the ambiguity and to identify the thing or the person or the nature or extent of the right or liability about which there is a doubt. All of these examples of circumstantial evidence of intention are considered in the following paragraphs.

27.21 AMBIGUITY—CIRCUMSTANCES SURROUNDING EXECUTION OF WRITING

General

When there is an ambiguity[278] in a writing, extrinsic evidence is admissible to show the circumstances which surrounded the granter when he subscribed it, as well as those which were antecedent to or coincident with its execution.[279] The purpose of the evidence is to enable the court to examine the writing as nearly as possible from the point of view from which the granter saw it, and to learn the appropriate meaning of the words when used by a person in that situation.[280] The evidence is relevant only in so far as the circumstances were known to the granter, or are presumed to have been known to him, at the date of the execution of the writing.

27.21.1

---

[277] Dickson, *Evidence* (3rd edn), paras 1079, 1081, 1083; McLaren, *Wills and Succession* (3rd edn), I, paras 717, 720, 723; Gloag, *Contract* (2nd edn), p 372. The examples given by Gloag of extrinsic evidence held admissible in cases of latent ambiguities, are examples of circumstantial evidence which would have been equally admissible if the ambiguities had been patent. In one of them *(Robertson's Tr v Riddell* 1911 SC 14) the ambiguity was in fact patent and not latent. For examples to the contrary in which evidence of declaration of intention appears to have been admitted as part of a series of testamentary writings, see *Livingston v Livingston* (1864) 3 M 20; *Campbell's Trs v Adamson* 1911 SC 1111, per Lord Johnston at 1117; *Ritchie v Whish* (1880) 8 R 101. Another very early example, *Weir v Steele* (1745) M 11359, was later described as contrary to all legal principle: *Blair v Blair* (1849) 12 D 97 at 108, 109.

[278] For the meaning of "ambiguity," see para 27.19. Evidence is inadmissible if there is no ambiguity: see para 27.19, but *Fortunato's JF v Fortunato* 1981 SLT 277. It may be appropriate to hear the evidence in a proof before answer.

[279] Dickson, *Evidence* (3rd edn), para 1067; Wigram's Fifth Proposition (Wigram, *Extrinsic Evidence in Aid of the Interpretation of Wills* (5th edn), p 14). In *Bovis Construction (Scotland) Ltd v Whatlings Construction Ltd* 1994 SC 351 correspondence prior to the agreement regarding a limit upon liability was admitted only to aid interpretation of the limitation as expressed in the agreement, and not to contradict or modify it.

[280] Dickson, *Evidence* (3rd edn), para 1067; Wigram's Fifth Proposition (Wigram, *Extrinsic Evidence in Aid of the Interpretation of Wills* (5th edn), p 14). *Bovis Construction (Scotland) Ltd v Whatlings Construction Ltd* 1994 SC 351. In *Investors Compensation Scheme Ltd v West Bromwich Building Society* [1998] 1 All ER 98, Lord Hoffmann's criteria for admission of extrinsic evidence to show background circumstances "indicate a very wide scope for enquiry into the background knowledge of a party entering into a contract": per Lord Penrose in *Bank of Scotland v Junior* 8 January 1999 (IH).

Contracts

27.21.2 "Where a term which might have two or more meanings is used in a mercantile contract, it is competent to prove the circumstances surrounding the parties, the character of their business, and the previous course of dealing, if any, between them, for the purpose of determining the true construction of the language used."[281] This principle was applied to a contract for the supply, for a fixed period and at a fixed price, of "your usual requirements" or "all your requirements" of a commodity, when there was a dispute as to whether the words quoted included requirements resulting from an expansion of the purchaser's business.[282] In connection with unilateral discharges of obligations it has been said that "the general words in a release are limited always to that thing or those things which were specially in the contemplation of the parties at the time when the release was given."[283] The principle was applied in construing the words "I hand over" in a deed relating to a policy of insurance,[284] in construing what level of banking provision was necessary to constitute a branch of a bank at the date of execution of the contract,[285] and was also said to apply to a clause in a disposition of heritage which reserved the right to work, win and carry away coal, there being a doubt as to whether this allowed the owner of the coal to bring down the surface.[286] There is some authority for the view that, although earlier communings or negotiations are superseded by the execution of a written contract,[287] and are inadmissible for the purpose of showing *intention*, they may legitimately be looked at in order to discover the *knowledge* of the parties as to the then existing facts or circumstances, in the light of which they executed the contract.[288]

---

[281] *Von Mehren & Co v Edinburgh Roperie & Sailcloth Ltd* (1901) 4 F 232 at 239. See *also Buttery & Co v Inglis* (1877) 5 R 58, per Lord Ormidale at 67; approved (1878) 5 R (HL) 87 at 102.

[282] *Blacklock & Macarthur v Kirk* 1919 SC 57; *Von Mehren & Co v Edinburgh Roperie & Sailcloth Ltd* (1901) 4 F 232. See also *MacKill & Co v Wright Brothers & Co* (1888) 16 R (HL) 1, in which it was held (at 6) "competent to investigate the whole facts and circumstances attendant upon the execution of the charter-party, with the view of ascertaining what particular kind of goods, if any, it was then in the contemplation of both parties should be shipped and carried, that being the cargo with reference to which it must be presumed, in the absence of express or implied stipulation to the contrary, that the guarantee was given and accepted." See also *McInally v Esso Petroleum Co* 1965 SLT (Notes) 13 (OH).

[283] *London & South Western Railway Co v Blackmore* (1870) 4 E & I App 610, per Lord Westbury at 623, quoted with approval by Lord Kinnear in *McAdam v Scott* (1912) 50 SLR 264, where proof was allowed in order to define and identify the claims mentioned in a discharge, which were said to be ambiguously described.

[284] *Brownlee v Robb* 1907 SC 1302.

[285] In relation to the tenant's obligation to operate a branch of a bank in a shopping centre: *Retail Parks Investments Ltd v The Royal Bank of Scotland (No 2)* 1996 SC 227.

[286] *Bank of Scotland v Stewart* (1891) 18 R 957, per Lord President Inglis at 960. However, the First Division ignored the proof which had been led, and construed the deed without its assistance.

[287] See para 27.9.

[288] Dickson, *Evidence* (3rd edn), para 1069. This was said with regard to prior correspondence between the parties to a marriage contract, in a question as to whether the husband's estate was liable to make good an annuity from a military pension fund which, under the rules of that fund, had ceased on a widow's second marriage. It was said that the earlier documents might be looked at in order to discover what the pension was and what knowledge the parties had of it: *Forlong v Taylor's Exrs* (1838) 3 Sh & Macl 177, per Lord Cottenham at 210. In *Leith Heritages Co v Edinburgh & Leith Glass Co* (1876) 3 R 789, Lord Ormidale, at 797, thought that the mere existence of an ambiguity in a disposition entitled the court to look at an earlier minute, which was superseded by the disposition, in order to learn the true meaning of the ambiguous words. This case was mentioned earlier, along with other special cases, at para 27.4.

Testamentary writings

In every case of ambiguity in a testamentary writing the court has a right to ascer- **27.21.3**
tain all the facts which were known to the testator at the time of making the will,
and thus to place itself in the testator's position, in order to ascertain the bearing
and application of the language used, and in order to ascertain whether there exists
any person or thing to which the whole description given in the will can, reasonably and with sufficient certainty, be applied.[289] The court has been held entitled
to know the amount of the estate at each relevant period according to the testator's
own estimate,[290] the relationship of the persons claiming to be legatees and the way
in which the testator was accustomed to design them,[291] the circumstances of the
testator's family and the history of his provision for them,[292] the testator's knowledge that his daughter had only one illegitimate child and was beyond the age of
child bearing,[293] the fact that, when his will was made, a Scottish testator's bequest
to the National Society for Prevention of Cruelty to Children, an English institution, would, by an agreement between the two institutions subsequently departed
from, have been handed over to the Scottish National Society for the Prevention of
Cruelty to Children[294] and, in a question as to whether heritage held under a special
destination has been carried by a subsequent general testamentary disposition, the
testator's actings in relation to his estate and with his succession generally.[295] In
general, direct declarations of the testator's intention as distinct from circumstantial evidence as to the meaning of the words used in the writing, are inadmissible
in evidence.[296] Except perhaps in the case of equivocation,[297] it seems clear that the
evidence not only of oral statements by the testator, but also of letters of instructions to a solicitor, or drafts or copies of wills, is inadmissible for the purpose of
explaining what the will is intended to mean.[298] Where a description in the will did
not apply to any known person, but was an apparent misdescription of one of
two persons, evidence of the testator's letter of instructions to his solicitor was

---

[289] *Charter v Charter* (1874) LR 7 (HL) 364, Cairns at 377: applied in *Devlin's Trs v Breen* 1943 SC
556 at 570, 582, 586 (affd 1945 SC (HL) 27). See also *Fortunato's JF v Fortunato* 1981 SLT 277;
McLaren, *Wills and Succession* (3rd edn), I, 388.

[290] *Trustees of the Free Church of Scotland v Maitland* (1887) 14 R 333, per Lord President Inglis at
338. See also *Craw's Trs v Blacklock* 1920 SC 22 (relative values of moveable and heritable estate);
McGowan v Anstruther's Trs (1827) 5 S 276 (gradual increase of testator's wealth); *Livingston v
Livingston* (1864) 3 M 20 (purchase of heritage).

[291] *Cathcart's Trs v Bruce* 1923 SLT 722 (OH).

[292] *Milne v Scott* (1880) 8 R 83 at 86, 88.

[293] *Scott's Trs v Smart* 1954 SC 12 (meaning of "children").

[294] *Nasmyth's Trs v National Society for Prevention of Cruelty to Children* 1914 SC (HL) 76. The
Second Division (77–81) decided in favour of the Scottish Society on these and similar considerations.
The House of Lords reversed, largely on the view that, since there was no ambiguity, the evidence was
irrelevant or, in the case of Lord Dunedin, since the words used exactly described the English Society,
and did not describe the Scottish Society with complete accuracy, the evidence was insufficient to displace the obvious and natural meaning to be attributed to the words.

[295] *Gray v Gray's Trs* (1878) 5 R 820, per Lord President Inglis at 824. On this topic, which at one time
gave rise to much conflict of judicial opinion, see also *Campbell v Campbell* (1878) 6 R 310; (1880) 7
R (HL) 100; *Glendonwyn v Gordon* (1870) 8 M 1075; (1873) 11 M (HL) 33; *Catton v Mackenzie*
(1870) 8 M 1049.

[296] See para 27.20.

[297] McLaren, *Wills and Succession*, I, 396. As to declarations of intention and equivocation, see para
27.20.

[298] *Blair v Blair* (1849) 12 D 97, per Lord Moncreiff at 107 *et seq,* Lord Cockburn at 112; *Farquhar v
Farquhar's Exrs* (1875) 3 R 71 at 73.

admitted in order to discover the testator's state of knowledge of the two persons and their families.[299]

Implied term of contract or testamentary writing

27.21.4 Extrinsic evidence is inadmissible to contradict, modify or explain a term of a writing which is implied by law.[300] However, conversely, an implied term may arise only because of the extrinsic circumstances and, in this event, it is competent to allow proof of these circumstances. For example, in a written contract for sale of goods, it is a condition implied by statute, where the buyer expressly or by implication makes known to the seller the particular purpose for which the goods are required, and the goods are of a description which it is in the course of the seller's business to supply, that the goods shall be reasonably fit for that purpose.[301] When it is averred that the facts giving rise to the implied condition existed, proof of them is admissible.[302] Similarly, in the case of a testamentary writing, the question of whether it is impliedly revoked by the subsequent birth of a child, in virtue of the *conditio si testator sine liberis decesserit* (the condition if the testator dies childless), is "one wholly dependent upon the circumstances of the case"[303] and the extrinsic circumstances may therefore be proved.[304]

27.22 AMBIGUITY—REFERENCE TO REVOKED OR REJECTED CLAUSES

General

27.22.1 When there is ambiguity in connection with a writing, evidence of the surrounding circumstances is in general admissible,[305] but there is doubt as to whether the court may legitimately take cognisance of the fact that clauses suggested for inclusion in the writing were deliberately cancelled or rejected by the parties before the writing was executed. In a written contract shipbuilders undertook, for a lump sum payment, to *repair* the hull plating of a ship. In the specification the words "but if any new plating is required the same to be paid for extra" had been deleted before the contract was executed.[306] The question at issue was whether the obligation to repair included an obligation to *renew* defective plating when this was found to be necessary.[307] The

---

[299] *Cathcart's Trs v Bruce* 1923 SLT 722 (OH).
[300] See para 27.5.
[301] Sale of Goods Act 1979, s 14(3).
[302] *Jacobs v Scott & Co* (1899) 2 F (HL) 70 at 78, 80.
[303] *Hughes v Edwardes* (1892) 19 R (HL) 33, per Lord Watson at 35.
[304] *Stuart-Gordon v Stuart-Gordon* (1899) 1 F 1005; *McKie's Tutor v McKie* (1897), 24 R 526; *Elder's Trs v Elder* (1895) 21 R 704; *Millar's Trs v Millar* (1893) 20 R 1040. The rule with regard to the *conditio si institus sine liberis decesserit* may well be different. See *Devlin's Trs v Breen* 1945 SC (HL) 27 at 32, 33, 35, 38.
[305] See paras 27.19–27.20.
[306] *Inglis v Buttery & Co* (1877) 5 R 58; (1878) 5 R (HL) 87.
[307] The Lord Justice-Clerk was of the opinion that the court was entitled to consider, as part of the antecedent circumstances, the fact that the quoted words had been deliberately deleted, and also to look at the correspondence between the parties relating to the deletion. In reliance upon this evidence he construed the obligation to repair as including an obligation to renew without additional charge. Lord Ormidale construed the contract without reference to the evidence but was of opinion that, if it were admissible, it pointed in the same direction. It seems probable that he considered the deleted words and the communings between the parties to be inadmissible. Lord Gifford thought that reference to the deleted words and the communings was wholly inadmissible.

House of Lords was unanimously of opinion that it was quite improper, in attempting to discover the meaning of the contract, to consider the deleted words or any part of the antecedent communings between the parties.[308] However, in circumstances which appear to be almost identical, the majority in the Court of Session found themselves able to distinguish the earlier case and, in a charter-party, they construed the standard exception for "restraint of princes" in the light of the fact that the words "including interferences of Government Authorities" had been deliberately deleted by the parties before the deed was executed.[309]

Testamentary Writings

It has been said that, while a revoked will cannot be referred to as having any testa- **27.22.2** mentary intention, "it may be used to show what the testator knew when he wrote it, and also what was his will at the time, though he has since revoked it."[310] This was applied in a subsequent case where the question at issue was whether a bequest was intended as a mere repetition of a legacy for the same amount in an earlier and still effective will, or whether two legacies were intended. In resolving the ambiguity, the court held itself entitled to look at the whole history of the bequest, including the reference to it in a number of revoked wills.[311] And, to resolve a doubt as to whether "failing such children" meant failing their coming into existence or failing their survival of the parent, it was held legitimate to use a revoked will as a glossary, in order to determine the meaning of the words used in the effective deed.[312] These cases were later said to show that there are "certain strictly limited purposes for which a court of construction may look at a revoked Will",[313] these purposes being the identification of the subject-matter of the gift and the identification of the beneficiary.[314] However, in the House of Lords it was doubted whether, even for these purposes, reference to a revoked will is admissible.[315]

27.23 AMBIGUITY—SUBSEQUENT ACTINGS OF PARTIES

General

Even when there is an ambiguity,[316] evidence regarding the actings of the parties, or **27.23.1** of the granter, *after* the execution of the writing is, strictly speaking, irrelevant, except in so far as it throws light retrospectively upon the circumstances prevailing at the time of execution. The purpose of extrinsic evidence is to discover the meaning the writer intended the words to have at the time when the words were used, which is the

---

[308] (1877) 5 R (HL) 87 at 90, 96–99, 102, 105. The same view was taken in *Baird v Drumpellier & Mount Vernon Estates Ltd* 2000 SC 103.

[309] *Taylor v John Lewis Ltd* 1927 SC 891, per Lord Justice-Clerk Alness at 897–898, Lord Anderson at 901; Lord Hunter, *contra*, at 899–900.

[310] *Magistrates of Dundee v Morris* (1858) 3 Macq 134, per Lord Wensleydale at 171. A contrary opinion was expressed by Lord Watson in *Gordon v Gordon's Trs* (1882) 9 R (HL) 101 at 105.

[311] *McLachlan v Seton's Trs* 1937 SC 206 at 223–224, 236–237.

[312] *Currie's Trs v Collier* 1939 SC 247. See Lord Watson, *contra*, in *Gordon v Gordon's Trs* (1882) 9 R (HL) 101.

[313] *Devlin's Trs v Breen* 1943 SC 556, per Lord Justice-Clerk Cooper at 571.

[314] *Devlin's Trs v Breen* 1943 SC 556, per Lord Wark at 582–583, Lord Jamieson at 586.

[315] *Devlin's Trs v Breen* 1945 SC (HL) 27, per Lord Thankerton at 32. The doubt was *obiter* because the case was decided on another ground.

[316] For the meaning of "ambiguity," see para 27.19. As with other extrinsic evidence, evidence of subsequent actings is inadmissible if there is no ambiguity. See *Scott v Howard* (1881) 8 R (HL) 59, per Lord Watson at 67.

time when the writing was executed.[317] Subsequent actings which merely reflect a
change of circumstances, a change in the writer's intention, or a party's subsequent
understanding of its terms are of course irrelevant.[318] Evidence of subsequent actings
has been admitted in construing old writings, contracts and testamentary writings.
The proposition that subsequent actings should not be admissible as an aid to construction has been restated in general terms on a number of occasions,[319] although
there are examples to the contrary.[320] A distinction has been made between actings
which are inadmissible and subsequent writ of the party which has been admitted.[321]

Old writings

27.23.2 "It is a well established principle of law that writings, even Acts of Parliament, more
especially those of ancient date, the terms of which leave their true meaning and
effect doubtful or obscure, may be cleared up and interpreted, not controlled or
altered, by the usage or possession which has followed upon them."[322] In so far as
Acts of Parliament are concerned, the principle applies only to those enacted "one
or two centuries ago".[323] The principle has been applied, not only to the identification of the subject-matter of the writing, but also to ambiguities regarding the
extent of the obligations undertaken, even when a presumptive rule of construction
applies.[324] The justification for the principle is that the actings following the
writing, being the parties' own exposition of their language and intentions, is
the best mode of explaining obscure or obsolete expressions.[325] Evidence of subsequent actings has been admitted and considered in construing the following: ancient
charters and statutes relating to a university in order to discover whether women had
a right of membership[326]; a lease granted 100 years earlier and a sub-lease granted

---

[317] See para 27.19.
[318] *Miller Construction Ltd v Trent Concrete Cladding Ltd* 1996 GWD 2-69 (OH).
[319] *Inland Revenue v Ferguson* 1968 SC 135 at 142; *Turner v MacMillan-Douglas* 1989 SLT 293 (OH).
In the latter case the court adopted the general statement to this effect made by the House of Lords in
the English appeal *James Miller & Partners Ltd v Whitworth Street Estates (Manchester) Ltd* [1970]
AC 583 and similar comments were made in *Wickman Machine Tool Sales Ltd v Lord Schuler AG*
[1974] AC 235 at 261 and 268–269.
[320] *McAllister v McGallagley* 1911 SC 112, per Lord President Dunedin at 119, Lord Kinnear at 120,
Lord Johnston at 122; *Macgill v Park* (1899) 2 F 272; *Boyle & Co v Morton & Sons* (1903) 5 F 416,
per Lord Justice-Clerk Macdonald at 421, Lord Young at 422, Lord Trayner at 422–423, Lord
Moncreiff at 423; *Hunter v Barron's Trs* (1886) 13 R 883. In a question under a feu contract as to
whether a feuar had a permanent right of access from a lane which was the boundary of her feu, the
interlocutor found that "under the terms of the feu-contract libelled, as explained by the subsequent actings of the parties," she had such a right: *Boyd v Hamilton* 1907 SC 912. It was said that "the true
interpretation of a boundary description ... is to be arrived at, not only from the terms of the description in reference to the other clauses of the grant, but also with reference to facts and circumstances at
the time when the grant was made, and the conduct of the parties immediately after the grant": per Lord
Kinnear at 923.
[321] *Turner v MacMillan-Douglas* 1989 SLT 293, applying a statement of Gloag, *Contract* (2nd edn), at
p 376, but this is doubted in *Miller Construction Ltd v Trent Concrete Cladding Ltd* 1996 GWD 2-69
(OH) and *Baird v Drumpellier & Mount Vernon Estates Ltd* 2000 SC 103.
[322] *Jex-Blake v Senatus of Edinburgh University* (1873) 11 M 784 at 813, 820–821, 825. This exception remains limited to ancient writings, despite calls for its extension or clarification, mentioned by
Macphail, *Evidence* at para 15.26.
[323] *Clyde Navigation Trs v Laird & Son* (1883) 10 R (HL) 77, per Lord Watson at 83.
[324] *Welwood's Trs v Mungall* 1921 SC 911, per Lord President Clyde at 926; *North British Railway Co
v Magistrates of Edinburgh* 1920 SC 409, per Lord President Strathclyde at 428. See also *Jopp's Trs v
Edmond* (1888) 15 R 271.
[325] Dickson, *Evidence* (3rd edn), para 1087.
[326] *Jex-Blake v Senatus of Edinburgh University* (1873) 11 M 784.

30 years earlier, to resolve an ambiguity as to the nature of the public burdens in respect of which one of the parties was entitled to relief[327]; a feu contract granted 184 years earlier, to resolve an ambiguity as to whether an obligation to relieve from teind duties included an obligation to relieve from augmentations of stipend[328]; a disposition granted 140 years earlier for behoof of the poor of the parish, in order to discover whether this meant the legal poor or the occasional poor[329]; a feu charter granted 67 years earlier, in order to discover whether an obligation to relieve from all burdens included an obligation to relieve from minister's stipend.[330]

Testamentary writings

Direct statements by a testator, made orally or in notes or correspondence after the date **27.23.3** of his will, are in general[331] inadmissible in order to show his intention, or his understanding of its meaning.[332] The subsequent actings of the testator, however, as distinct from his direct statements, are thought to be admissible in evidence.[333] When the question in issue was whether, on the assumption that an entail was invalid, the testator, who was the heir in possession, intended to include the entailed subjects in the conveyance of his whole property, heritable and moveable, contained in his general disposition and settlement, Lord President Inglis said: "We are entitled to look at every deed executed by him, dealing with the entailed and unentailed lands, to see whether it was in his mind to convey the entailed estate by the general words of conveyance, or whether, *after the deed was made*, it was in his mind that he had conveyed it."[334] The court, largely on the evidence of the testator's whole dealings with the entailed lands before and after the general settlement, and of the deeds relating thereto, held that it was not his intention to include the entailed lands in the general conveyance. The same principle has been applied when the question in issue was whether a special destination in a title to heritage was revoked by a general disposition of the whole estate in the testator's will.[335]

27.24 AMBIGUITY—IDENTIFICATION OF SUBJECT OR PERSON OR NATURE OF OBLIGATION OR RIGHT

When there is an ambiguity,[336] the purpose of admitting circumstantial evidence[337] **27.24.1**

---

[327] *Jopp's Trs v Edmond* (1888) 15 R 271; *North British Railway Co v Magistrates of Edinburgh* 1920 SC 409; *Masters of Dundee v Wedderburn* (1830) 8 S 547.

[328] *Welwood's Trs v Mungall* 1921 SC 911.

[329] *Inspector of Kinglassie v Kirk Session of Kinglassie* (1867) 5 M 869. See also *Flockhart v Kirk Session of Aberdour* (1869) 8 M 176; *University of Aberdeen v Irvine* (1868) 6 M (HL) 29.

[330] *Heriot's Hospital v McDonald* (1830) 4 W & S 98.

[331] The only occasion on which direct declarations of intention or understanding may be admissible in evidence is mentioned at para 27.21.

[332] *Trustees of the Free Church of Scotland v Maitland* (1887) 14 R 333, per Lord President Inglis at 338, Lord Shand at 343; *Farquhar v Farquhar's Exrs* (1875) 3 R 71, per Lord Gilford at 74: *cf* Lord Justice-Clerk Moncreiff at 73; *Catton v Mackenzie* (1870) 8 M 1049, per Lord Kinloch at 1062. The admissibility of correspondence for this purpose was doubted in *Glendonwyn v Gordon* (1873) 11 M (HL) 33, per Lord Colonsay at 42.

[333] *Catton v Mackenzie* (1870) 8 M 1049 at 1055, 1059, 1060, 1062; *Glendonwyn v Gordon* (1873) 11 M (HL) 33, per Lord Colonsay at 42; *contra* Lord Chancellor Selborne at 42; *Farquhar v Farquhar's Exrs* (1875) 3 R 71, per Lord Gifford at 73–74.

[334] *Catton v Mackenzie* (1870) 8 M 1049 at 1055. See also *Thoms v Thoms* (1868) 6 M 704.

[335] *Glendonwyn v Gordon* (1873) 11 M (HL) 33.

[336] For the meaning of "ambiguity", see para 27.19. When there is no ambiguity extrinsic evidence is inadmissible.

[337] See para 27.21.

is to resolve the ambiguity and this may be necessary to identify the subject of the writing, the person mentioned in it, or the nature and extent of any obligation or right created by it, about which there is a doubt.[338] The party who desires to lead evidence must specify the words which are claimed to be ambiguous and the precise meaning which he desires to attribute to them.[339] It is probably unnecessary to state that when the writing itself refers to extrinsic matters in order to identify a thing, person or right, proof of the extrinsic matter is not only admissible but essential, not because the writing is ambiguous, but because the extrinsic facts are incorporated by reference in it. So when, in a lease, the subjects let were described by reference to what was "tenanted by" a previous tenant, proof was necessary of what in fact the previous tenant tenanted,[340] and the same principle applied when in a feu-contract there were reserved to the adjoining feuars the whole rights and privileges "which they at present possess".[341]

27.24.2   When an estate is described in the title deeds by a general name or in general terms, so that its extent and boundaries cannot be ascertained from the title deeds themselves, extrinsic evidence is admissible to establish what has been possessed under the general name or general descriptive words for the prescriptive period.[342] When the boundaries of land disponed were described partly by reference to a pier in one case[343] and to a driveway in another,[344] evidence as to the extent of the pier and the driveway was held admissible.[345] In testamentary writings extrinsic circumstantial evidence has been regarded as admissible to identify the beneficiary, or the person with reference to whom the beneficiary was identified in the writing, when the following ambiguous expressions were used: "heirs"[346] and "children",[347] which have a variety of possible meanings; nicknames such as "Mrs. G."[348]; and "my late brother James's son", when the brother James had only a daughter.[349] In a number of cases, when a will contained a bequest to a particular beneficiary, and it was doubtful, after full effect had been given to every indication of intention arising from the terms of the deed itself, whether this was intended to be in addition to, or in substitution of, a bequest of an identical sum of money

[338] Wigram's Fifth Proposition (Wigram, *Extrinsic Evidence in Aid of the Interpretation of Wills* (5th edn), pp 13–14). See also Dickson, *Evidence* (3rd edn), para 1070; McLaren, *Wills and Succession* (3rd edn), I, 378 *et seq*; Gloag, *Contract* (2nd edn), p 372. Wigram adds to what is stated in the text: "The same is true, it is conceived, of every other disputed point respecting which it can be shown that a knowledge of extrinsic facts can in any way be made ancillary to the right interpretation of a testator's words."
[339] *Sutton & Co v Ciceri & Co* (1890) 17 R (HL) 40, per Lord Watson at 43.
[340] *Earl of Ancaster v Doig* 1960 SC 203. See also *Gregson v Alsop* (1897) 24 R 1081.
[341] *Argyllshire Commissioners of Supply v Campbell* (1885) 12 R 1255.
[342] *North British Railway Co v Hutton* (1896) 23 R 522, per Lord McLaren at 525. See also *Brown v North British Railway Co* (1906) 8 F 534, per Lord Kyllachy at 543.
[343] *Davidson v Magistrates of Anstruther* (1845) 7 D 342.
[344] *Butt v Galloway Motor Co Ltd* 1996 SC 261.
[345] For other examples of extrinsic evidence admitted to identify the subject of ambiguous words or expressions see *Craw's Trs v Blacklock* 1920 SC 22; *Bruce's Trs v Bruce* (1875) 2 R 775; *Logan v Wright* (1831) 5 W & S 242; *Renison v Bryce* (1898) 25 R 521; *Birrell v Dryer* (1884) 11 R (HL) 41, and examples at para 27.19.
[346] Erskine, iii, 8, 47; Dickson, *Evidence* (3rd edn), para 1083.
[347] *Scott's Trs v Smart* 1954 SC 12.
[348] Dickson, *Evidence* (3rd edn), para 1059; McLaren, *Wills and Succession* (3rd edn), I, 382.
[349] *Macfarlane's Trs v Henderson* (1878) 6 R 288. For further examples, see *Cathcart's Trs v Bruce* 1923 SLT 722 (OH); *Keiller v Thomson's Trs* (1826) 4 S 730 and *Keiller v Thomson's Trs* (1824) 3 S 279 (Dickson, *Evidence* (3rd edn), para 1073 thought that the descriptions in these cases were so erroneous that the court, in effect, made a bequest which the testator intended, but had not expressed); *Nasmyth's Trs v National Society for the Prevention of Cruelty to Children* 1914 SC (HL) 76.

in an earlier unrevoked will, extrinsic circumstantial evidence was admitted to resolve the ambiguity.[350]

If after all admissible extrinsic evidence has been led, the court is unable to **27.24.3** determine what the granter intended by the words used, the writing will be held void from uncertainty.[351] "A court cannot construe a contract which is so vague as to be no contract at all",[352] and further extrinsic evidence is thus inadmissible for the purpose of filling in a name left blank, of reconciling conflicting clauses in a will, or where the language used is so imperfect that to admit further evidence would be not to interpret the document but virtually to make a new one.[353]

27.25 EXPLANATION—CUSTOM OR USAGE OF TRADE

Evidence of custom or usage is admissible in four cases: (1) where the writing **27.25.1** expressly refers to and incorporates the custom[354]; (2) on a point for which the writing makes no provision, express or implied[335]; (3) where it is averred that words or phrases are used with an unusual meaning and there is some ambiguity[356]; and (4) to modify the rights and obligations which the law would normally infer.[357] However, it must be admitted that it is difficult to distinguish

---

[350] *McLachlan v Seton's Trs* 1937 SC 206; *Royal Infirmary of Edinburgh v Muir's Trs* (1881) 9 R 352, per Lord President Inglis and Lord Mure at 356; *Milne v Scott* (1880) 8 R 83, per Lord President Inglis at 86, Lord Mure at 88, Lord Shand at 88; *McGowan v Anstruther's Trs* (1827) 5 S 276. See also Dickson, *Evidence* (3rd edn), para 1085. Cf *Arres' Trs v Mather* (1881) 9 R 107; *Horsbrugh v Horsbrugh* (1847) 9 D 329. For a further example, see *Forlong v Taylor's Exrs* (1838) 3 Sh & Macl 177.

[351] Dickson, *Evidence* (3rd edn), para 1076; Wigram's Sixth Proposition (Wigram, *Extrinsic Evidence in Aid of the Interpretation of Wills* (5th edn), p 14).

[352] Quoted in Bell, *Principles*, para 524. A party cannot, however, escape liability under a contract by saying merely that it was unintelligible to him. He is bound by the true construction of the terms of the contract as these shall be ascertained by the court. See *Laing v Provincial Homes Investment Co Ltd* 1909 SC 812, at 822, 826.

[353] Dickson, *Evidence* (3rd edn), para 1076.

[354] *Strathlorne SS Co Ltd v Hugh Baird & Sons Ltd* 1915 SC 956 at 973, 981, reversed on the ground that the custom was not proved, 1916 SC (HL) 134, but the four cases were founded upon without question in *Stirling Park & Co v Digby Brown & Co* 1996 SLT (Sh Ct) 17.

[355] See, for example, *Sturrock v Murray* 1952 SC 454; *William Morton & Co v Muir Brothers & Co* 1907 SC 1211. But if the writing does provide for the point, evidence of custom is inadmissible, as in *Hogarth & Sons v Leith Cotton Seed Oil Co* 1909 SC 955. See also *Duthie & Co v Merson & Gerry* 1947 SC 43; *P & W MacLellan Ltd v Peattie's Trs* (1903) 5 F 1031. Even if the writing is not express, it may deal with the matters to which the custom relates so fully as to negative the suggestion that the parties contracted with reference to the custom: *Buchanan v Riddell* (1900) 2 F 544 at 549; *Gordon v Thomson* (1831) 9 S 735; Dickson, *Evidence* (3rd edn), para 1092.

[356] *Mackenzie v Dunlop* (1853) 3 Macq 22; *Armstrong & Co v McGregor & Co* (1875) 2 R 339. See, for example, *Blackstock v Macarthur* 1919 SC 57; *Von Mehren & Co v Edinburgh Roperie & Sailcloth Ltd* (1901) 4 F 232; *Fleming & Co v Airdrie Iron Co* (1882) 9 R 473; *Sutton & Co v Ciceri & Co* (1890) 17 R (HL) 40. As to the meaning of "ambiguity", see para 27.19. But if the word or phrase is unambiguous, proof of modifying custom is not allowed: *Sworn Securities Ltd v Chilcott* 1977 SC 53. See also *Sinclair v McBeath* (1868) 7 M 273; *McDowall & Neilson's Tr v JB Snowball & Co Ltd* (1904) 7 F 35. It would probably also be refused if the word is defined by statute: *Hunter v Barron's Trs* (1886) 13 R 883 at 890, but not concurred in by the other judges.

[357] In the case of sale it is expressly provided that where any right, duty or liability would arise by implication of law it may be negatived or varied by usage: Sale of Goods Act 1979, s 55. This rule is thought to be of general application: Gloag, *Contract* (2nd edn), p 379. Where a tenant repaired his house, effect was given to an admitted local custom under which the landlord was bound at the end of the lease to pay him the value of the wood used: *Learmonth v Sinclair's Trs* (1875) 5 R 548. An averment that articles heritable in law were by a local custom not included in a sale of heritage, if relevantly stated, might have been remitted to proof: *Nisbet v Mitchell-Innes* (1880) 7 R 575.

cases which have been held to fall under one of those classes from others which have not. While no effect can be given to a custom which would render a contract *pactum illicitum* (an illegal contract)[358] or which contradicts an express statutory enactment,[359] a custom must often to some extent run counter to the general law.[360] Otherwise proof of it would be useless. The custom must be clearly and precisely averred.[361] To render a custom binding the evidence must show that it is certain, uniform, reasonable and, except in the first class of case referred to,[362] known to both parties or at least so notorious that they must be taken to have known of it.[363]

Variation of writings

27.26 VARIATION OF THE WRITING—GENERAL

27.26.1 Proof of the variation of contract is an area which overlaps with the substantive law of contract,[364] and it has been suggested that any reform of the law in this area should form part of a reform of contract law rather than evidence.[365] Reforms of the law in relation to requirements of writing, rectification of documents and proof of additional terms of a contract all made at the instance of the Scottish Law Commission have impinged significantly upon this area, but whether the problems of admissibility of extrinsic evidence of variation at common law are completely resolved remains a little unclear.

---

[358] *Ronaldson v Drummond & Reid* (1881) 8 R 956.

[359] *Magistrates of Dunbar v Duchess of Roxburghe* (1835) 1 Sh & Macl 134, per Lord Brougham at 195.

[360] Gloag's statement to the contrary (*Contract* (2nd edn), p 379) is not supported by the authorities cited. Lord Rutherfurd-Clark thought such proof admissible: *Nisbet v Mitchell-Innes* (1880) 7 R 575 at 578.

[361] *Nisbet v Mitchell-Innes* (1880) 7 R 575; *Sutton & Co v Ciceri & Co* (1890) 17 R (HL) 40, per Lord Watson at 43.

[362] *Mackenzie v Dunlop* (1853) 3 Macq 22; *Armstrong & Co v McGregor & Co* (1875) 2 R 339. See, for example, *Blackstock v Macarthur* 1919 SC 57; *Von Mehren & Co v Edinburgh Roperie & Sailcloth Ltd* (1901) 4 F 232; *Fleming & Co v Airdrie Iron Co* (1882) 9 R 473; *Sutton & Co v Ciceri & Co* (1890) 17 R (HL) 40. As to the meaning of "ambiguity", see para 27.19. But if the word or phrase is unambiguous, proof of modifying custom is not allowed: *Sworn Securities Ltd v Chilcott* 1977 SC 53. See also *Sinclair v McBeath* (1868) 7 M 273; *McDowall & Neilson's Tr v JB Snowball & Co Ltd* (1904) 7 F 35. It would probably also be refused if the word is defined by statute: *Hunter v Barron's Trs* (1886) 13 R 883 at 890, but not concurred in by the other judges.

[363] *Strathlorne SS Co Ltd v Hugh Baird & Sons Ltd* 1916 SC (HL) 134 at 135, 136, applied in *Stirling Park & Co v Digby Brown & Co* 1996 SLT (Sh Ct) 17 and observed in *Trans Barwil Agencies (UK) Ltd v John S Braid & Co Ltd* 1989 SLT 73. Proof of what generally happens is not necessarily a proof of usage: *Brown v McConnell* (1876) 3 R 788 at 788, 789; *Cazalet v Morris & Co* 1916 SC 952.

[364] For example, if averments of acquiescence are made in defence of an action of breach of contract, extrinsic evidence of the alleged acquiescence will be relevant and admissible: *Wark v Bargaddie Coal Co* (1859) 3 Macq 467; *Sutherland v Montrose Shipbuilding Co* (1860) 22 D 665 at 671; *Walker v Flint* (1863) 1 M 421, per Lord Benholme at 422, Lord Neaves at 423; *Kirkpatrick v Allanshaw Coal Co* (1880) 8 R 327 at 334, 336; *Carron Co v Henderson's Trs* (1896) 23 R 1042, per Lord McLaren at 1054. See McBryde, Chapter 23. Furthermore, if the contract is one which anticipates variation in detail according to circumstances certified by a third party, such as by an architect in a construction contract, extrinsic evidence will be relevant and admissible to prove the variation provided that the variation is in keeping with the broad terms of the original contract: *Forrest v Scottish County Investment Co* 1915 SC 115; affd 1916 SC (HL) 28. See McBryde, *Contract*, paras 6-26–6-36.

[365] Macphail, *Evidence*, para 15.32.

If a written contract is varied by a new written contract the problem of resorting **27.26.2** to extrinsic evidence is avoided.[366] There is authority for the view that when it is admitted on record that some variation of the written contract was agreed upon, proof of the exact terms of the agreement is admissible.[367] Matters which do not require writing for constitution but which the parties choose to put in writing will require writing for variation if the parties so provide in the writing itself. The Scottish Law Commission has proposed that parole proof of variation should be admissible in all other circumstances,[368] but no express statutory provision to this particular effect has been made. However, this may have been achieved by the combined effect of statutory reforms and a liberal interpretation of the application of the rule and its exceptions prior to 1 August 1995. There is as yet no authority to support that interpretation. If the combined effect of the statutory provisions in a given situation is not to remove completely the restrictions upon proof of variation by extrinsic evidence the general rule and common law exceptions as to proof of variation will still apply.

Unfortunately the decisions regarding these exceptions to the rule are difficult **27.26.3** to reconcile, and it is not easy to deduce general principles from them. Here they are considered under the following headings: (a) contracts which required writing for constitution or proof (*obligationes literis*)[369]; (b) contracts which did not require writing for constitution or proof but which the parties had committed to writing; and (c) contracts of both types where the variation was alleged to have arisen by implication from the actings of the parties and acquiescence. This categorisation was adopted by Scottish Law Commission when considering the requirements of writing.[370]

27.27 EXTRINSIC EVIDENCE IN PROOF OF VARIATION AT COMMON LAW

Variation of contracts requiring writing for their constitution

When a party averred that a contract which required writing had been perma- **27.27.1** nently altered by oral agreement, not only was parole evidence of the agreement inadmissible, but a reference of the agreement to the oath of the other party was incompetent,[371] unless there were also averments of actings consequent upon the oral agreement which were relevant to infer *rei interventus*[372] or homologation.[373] From the point of view of proof the oral agreement was regarded as if it were a

---

[366] Examples of the general rule, which excludes extrinsic evidence for the purpose of proving an oral agreement to vary the terms of a written contract, have been given earlier: see para 27.3.

[367] *Campbell v Arbuthnot* (1904) 12 SLT 438.

[368] Scottish Law Commission, *Constitution and Proof of Voluntary Obligations and the Authentication of Writings* (Memorandum No 66), para 5.11. Macphail notes that this was without prejudice to the extrinsic rule per se: para S15.32.

[369] As to *obligationes literis*, see Chapter 23.

[370] Scottish Law Commission, *Report on Requirements of Writing* (Scot Law Com No 112) (1988), para 3.12.

[371] *Perdikou v Pattison* 1958 SLT 153 (lease of heritage), per Lord Justice-Clerk Thomson at 157, Lord Patrick at 158, Lord Mackintosh and Lord Blades at 159.

[372] See paras 26.1, 26.3.

[373] See para 26.6. See also Dickson, *Evidence* (3rd edn), para 1103.

new and independent contract which requires writing for its constitution.[374] If the oral agreement could be established by writ or oath or judicial admission, the averments of *rei interventus* or homologation might then be proved *prout de jure*. This principle was applied when a tenant under a written lease for a term of years averred that the landlord had agreed orally to construct a new road, and that on the faith of this agreement the tenant had incurred expenditure in reclaiming certain moorland to which the new road was intended to give access[375]; and when a tenant under a written lease averred an oral agreement by the landlord to provide steam for heating purposes on the faith of which the tenant incurred expenditure in the installation of plant and machinery.[376] Variation of this kind of contract might also be proved as an inference from facts and circumstances as described below.

Variation when writing was not required for the original contract

27.27.2 When a contract was in writing, although the law did not require writing for its constitution, an oral agreement to vary it required to be proved by writ or oath, but it was not necessary, in addition, to establish *rei interventus* or homologation.[377] When it was averred that a beneficiary, who was entitled to the whole of an estate in terms of a private Act of Parliament, had agreed to modify his claim to a half share, it was held that the alleged oral agreement could be proved by writ or oath,[378] and the same rule was applied when it was alleged that written instructions to a stockbroker were later altered orally.[379] Variation of this kind of contract might also be proved as an inference from facts and circumstances as described below.

Agreement inferred from facts and circumstances

27.27.3 When there was no express oral agreement to vary a written contract, or when it was impossible to prove such an agreement by writ or oath, it was sometimes possible to aver facts and circumstances which were explicable only on the assumption that such an agreement, express or implied, in fact existed,[380] and such facts could be proved by parole evidence.[381] In such a case the written contract was said to be

---

[374] *Carron Co v Henderson's Trs* (1896) 23 R 1042, per Lord Kyllachy (Ordinary) at 1048–1049, Lord McLaren at 1054. Dicta in *Wark v Bargaddie Coal Co* (1859) 3 Macq 467, per Lord Chelmsford at 477 *et seq*, are confusing in relation to the elements of proof of such a contract by oral agreement and *rei interventus*.

[375] *Philip v Gordon Cumming's Exrs* (1869) 7 M 859. In spite of a suggestion in the Lord Justice-Clerk's opinion that the averments of *rei interventus* were irrelevant, the court adhered to the Lord Ordinary's interlocutor, which allowed proof of the oral agreement by writ or oath on the assumption that there were relevant averments of *rei interventus*.

[376] *Stewart v Clark* (1871) 9 M 616. The reference in the argument, and in the Lord Ordinary's opinion, to *Walker v Flint*, (1863) 1 M 417, seems to make it clear that proof of the agreement by writ or oath was allowed on the footing that *rei interventus* was relevantly averred. The principle was also applied in the following cases although due to failure of proof of the oral agreement by writ or oath, the question of *rei interventus* or homologation could not arise: *Rattray v Leslie's Tr* (1892) 19 R 853; *Turnbull v Oliver* (1891) 19 R 154; *Law v Gibsone* (1835) 13 S 396; *Gibb v Winning* (1829) 7 S 677; *Scot v Cairns* (1830) 9 S 246; *Dumbarton Glass Co v Coatsworth* (1847) 9 D 732.

[377] Dickson, *Evidence* (3rd edn), para 1103.

[378] *McMurrich's Trs v McMurrich's Trs* (1903) 6 F 121.

[379] *Stevenson v Manson* (1840) 2 D 1204. It is implied by the Lord Ordinary's opinion that it is unnecessary to prove *rei interventus* or homologation as well.

[380] Dickson, *Evidence* (3rd edn), para 1029; Erskine (Nicolson's edn), iii, 2, 3, note (d).

[381] *Carron Co v Henderson's Trs* (1896) 23 R 1042.

"altered *rebus et factis* for the past and for the future by acts of the parties necessarily and unequivocally importing an agreement to alter".[382] Of necessity the actings relied upon for this purpose must be at variance with the terms of the written contract.[383] Unlike averments of *rei interventus*, the actings must, by their own nature, manifest the intention to vary the written contract in a particular respect and support the inference of intentional departure from the original contract.[384] If the facts and circumstances themselves establish that a written contract has been varied in a particular way, it is immaterial whether or not they are preceded by an express oral agreement. The parole proof of such an express agreement, if it existed, as an incident of the proof of facts and circumstances, is therefore unobjectionable.[385] The success of the proof in these circumstances depends primarily upon the cogency of the inferences arising from the actings of the parties, and only incidentally from the existence of the earlier oral agreement.[386]

27.28 VARIATION—ADMISSION OF EXTRINSIC EVIDENCE UNDER STATUTE

Additional terms; rectification

If a party now alleges that a contract or unilateral voluntary obligation has express **27.28.1** terms beyond those set out in a writing which is apparently complete, extrinsic evidence will be admissible to rebut the presumption of the completeness of the writing.[387] This statutory exception might in some circumstances aid the admission of extrinsic evidence of variation of the contract if the variation took the form of an addition which had been agreed at or around the date of execution, although proof of variations contradictory to the express terms of the contract and those which post-date the execution of the contract were not the mischief to which that statutory exception was directed. Similarly, an argument that the writing is an inaccurate expression of the contract because the parties had agreed to vary it before it was executed, but executed it nevertheless, could be the subject of extrinsic evidence in an application for rectification under the Law Reform (Miscellaneous Provisions) (Scotland) Act 1985.[388]

Requirements of writing

The common law on variation of writings is affected by the Requirements of **27.28.2**

---

[382] *Carron Co v Henderson's Trs* (1896) 23 R 1042, per Lord Kyllachy (Ordinary) at 1049: "It is a delicate thing to infringe on the terms of a written contract, but when the parties have been acting so as to alter it by their conduct, then we must give effect to the change." *Baillie v Fraser* (1853) 15 D 747, per Lord Robertson at 750.

[383] Gloag, *Contract* (2nd edn), p 396; *Kirkpatrick v Allanshaw Coal Co* (1880) 8 R 327, per Lord Mure at 337, 338; *Lavan v Gavin Aird & Co* 1919 SC 345. In these opinions actings of this kind are sometimes described as *rei interventus*.

[384] *Kirkpatrick v Allanshaw Coal Co* (1880) 8 R 327, per Lord Mure at 337, 338; *Lavan v Gavin Aird & Co* 1919 SC 345.

[385] *Sutherland v Montrose Shipbuilding Co* (1860) 22 D 665, per Lord Justice-Clerk Inglis at 673.

[386] In *Baillie v Fraser* (1853) 15 D 747, where a variation of a written lease was held proved by the actings of the parties, it is made clear in the Lord Ordinary's opinion that no express agreement had taken place. Had there been such an agreement, however, it could competently have been proved along with the actings. See the comment on this case in Gloag, *Contract* (2nd edn), p 393, note 2.

[387] Contract (Scotland) Act 1997, s 1.

[388] ss 8 and 9.

Writing (Scotland) Act 1995 which regulates matters requiring writing for validity with effect from 1 August 1995. If the subject of the writing is a matter which in terms of the Requirements of Writing (Scotland) Act 1995 requires subscribed writing for constitution,[389] other than a will or testamentary settlement,[390] such writing is also required for variation.[391] In the absence of subscribed writing as required by the Act,[392] the contract, trust or obligation may be constituted or varied by proof of actings or omissions in reliance thereof to which there has been acquiescence and which have material effect.[393] An unsubscribed writing, although not itself capable of validly constituting or varying the matter, nevertheless may be used in evidence.[394] Unless provided for by some other enactment no other contract, trust or unilateral obligation requires writing for constitution[395] or variation.[396] The same Act abolishes the restriction of proof to the writ, or reference to oath, of the party.[397]

27.28.3   The provisions in relation to requirements of writing apply to contracts entered into on or after the commencement of the Act on 1 August 1995. The old law applies to "any document executed or anything done"[398] prior to that date. Accordingly, if the variation was said to have occurred prior to 1 August 1995 the old law would apply, as described above.[399] However, the provisions which abolish the restricted modes of proof are said not to apply to proceedings commenced before the commencement of the Act and, by implication, apply in relation to all proceedings raised after the commencement of the Act,[400] regardless of the date of the document or actings on which the proceedings may be founded. However, in one case, a sheriff principal has interpreted the statutory provisions to the effect that proof restricted to writ[401] must still be ordered when the document pre-dates the commencement of the Act.[402] This interpretation was taken because the later provision states that the new law shall not apply (a) "to any document executed or anything done after that date" and will not (b) "affect the operation, in relation to any document executed before such commencement, of any procedure for establishing the authenticity of such a document."[403] It is thought that this interpretation

---

[389] Requirements of Writing (Scotland) Act 1995, s 1(2)(a) and (b). See Chapter 22.

[390] s 1(2)(c).

[391] s 1(2)(a) and (b) and (6). The making of a will is not subject to variation as such and so, although writing is required for making the will or other testamentary settlement, there is no reference to variation.

[392] s 2.

[393] s 1(3) and (4), and eg *Super (Tom) Printing and Supplies Ltd v South Lanarkshire Council (No 2)*, 1999 GWD 38-1856 (OH). See also Chapter 22.

[394] s 2(3).

[395] s 1(1).

[396] s 1(6).

[397] s 11(1) and (2).

[398] s 14(3)(a).

[399] para 27.27.

[400] 1995 Act, s 11(2)–(4). It was clearly intended by the Scottish Law Commission that this would be the effect: see *Report on Requirements of Writing* (Scot Law Com No 112) at para 3.1, *Report on Three Bad Rules in Contract Law* (Scot Law Com No 152), para 2.17 and *Report on Interpretation in Private Law* (Scot Law Com No 160), para 8.6, although it is noted there that some doubt has arisen in relation to the effect of the abolition, at least in the context of interpretation of contracts.

[401] It is thought a distinction may be made between the abolition of proof by reference to oath, and proof restricted to writ: see para 22.1.

[402] See *McEleveen v McQuillan's Exrx* 1997 SLT (Sh Ct) 46 as to the combined effect of s 11(1) and (4) and s 14(3); and Chapter 22.

[403] Requirements of Writing (Scotland) Act 1995, s 14(3)(b).

is correct in principle vis-à-vis (a) but that the saving provision (b) would be misinterpreted if used to preserve a procedure for establishing the *existence, meaning* or *variation* of a document, when it explicitly saves only procedures for *authentication*.

CHAPTER 28

PROOF IN FAMILY ACTIONS

28.1 GENERAL

This chapter deals with the specialities of proof and evidence which apply to **28.1.1** family actions in private law[1] and the next chapter deals with family proceedings encountered most commonly in public law, viz the children's hearing, proceedings in the sheriff court under Part II of the Children (Scotland) Act 1995, and proceedings within the child support regime. These chapters also deal more fully with the application to family proceedings of the general rules of evidence which have been mentioned elsewhere. Actions of declarator of marriage, declarator of nullity of marriage and an action of reduction of a decree of divorce, are the family actions which are competent only in the Court of Session.[2] The Court of Session has inherent jurisdiction to deal with these and any other action affecting the status of the parties with regard to marriage.[3] However, actions of divorce, separation, declarator of legitimacy, illegitimacy and legitimation, declarator of parentage and non-parentage, actions concerning parental responsibilities and rights, actions of

---

[1] Family actions are subject to particular rules of court which are supplementary to the general rules of court. They are found in the Rules of the Court of Session 1994 (as amended), Chapter 49, and the Sheriff Court Ordinary Cause Rules 1993 (as amended), Chapter 33, and the list of family actions to which those rules relate is found in rr 49.1 and 33.1 respectively.

[2] Sheriff Courts (Scotland) Act 1907, s 5(1).

[3] *Acutt v Acutt* 1935 SC 525. Actions between husband and wife affecting status are also termed "consistorial causes" but the term is now largely subsumed within the broader category of family actions.

affiliation and aliment, actions for aliment[4] and actions for orders under specific enactments regulating conduct between family members are all now within the concurrent jurisdiction of the Court of Session and the sheriff court.[5] These family actions cover the remedies which exist at private law only. The field of public law in relation to children has grown in recent years and leads to a variety of proceedings in which issues of evidence arise.

28.2 NECESSITY FOR EVIDENCE—TAKING AND RECORDING OF EVIDENCE

28.2.1 A decree in a family action may affect the status, not only of the parties to the action, but also of their children, and of other persons whom they may have purported to marry. It is the policy of the law, therefore, to prevent such a decree being obtained by agreement between the parties, on what may be improper or insufficient grounds. Generally, a decree may not be pronounced in a family action, even if the action is undefended,[6] until the grounds of action are substantiated by sufficient evidence, including evidence independent of the parties.[7] If the proceedings are for an order in relation to parental responsibilities and rights under the Children (Scotland) Act 1995, s 11, or, if in an action of divorce, separation or nullity of marriage there is a child in respect of whom such an order might be made,[8] evidence regarding the arrangements for the child must be provided, including evidence from a source other than a parent or party to the action.[9] The evidence in undefended family actions is normally received in affidavit form unless the court directs otherwise.[10] If oral evidence is received because the action is defended, the evidence will be recorded by shorthand writer or approved mechanical means,[11] but in the sheriff court the parties may, with the approval of the court, dispense with recording,[12] and if evidence is ordered in undefended proceedings in the sheriff court it will not be recorded.[13] It is competent to grant a commission to examine witnesses[14] even though their evidence may be the whole evidence adduced in the case.[15] In defended actions it is competent to tender evidence in

---

[4] In so far as the court still has jurisdiction over aliment, see the Child Support Act 1981, s 8, as amended.

[5] Domicile and Matrimonial Proceedings Act 1973, s 8; Sheriff Courts (Scotland) Act 1907, s 5, as amended by, *inter alia*, the Divorce Jurisdiction, Court Fees and Legal Aid (Scotland) Act 1983, s 1.

[6] Civil Evidence (Scotland) Act 1988, s 8(1) and (2) so requires for actions for divorce, separation or declarator of marriage, nullity of marriage, legitimacy, illegitimacy, legitimation, parentage or non-parentage.

[7] For the limited range of family actions in which decree can be obtained without leading evidence, see RCS, r 49.28 (1), OCR, r 33.28(1).

[8] Children (Scotland) Act 1995, s 12.

[9] RCS, r 49.28(3); OCR, r 33.28(3).

[10] RCS, r 49.28; OCR, r 33.28.

[11] RCS, r 36.11; OCR, r 29.18. Normally evidence will be taken at a proof only, but if oral evidence is received at any other stage of the proceedings it too should be recorded unless agreed otherwise: see *Hartnett v Hartnett* 1997 SCLR 525 (Sh Ct). "Evidence" has been assumed to mean oral evidence or sworn equivalent, as in *Henderson v Adamson* 1998 SCLR 365 (Sh Ct), but see the commentary to that case at 370G.

[12] OCR, r 29.18(1).

[13] OCR, r 33.32.

[14] RCS, rr 35.11–35.15; OCR, rr 28.10–28.15.

[15] *AB v CB* 1911 1 SLT 264 (OH); *Lawson v Lawson* 1930 SC 18. See Chapter 14.

affidavit form,[16] provided that the witness would have been competent to give oral evidence and it would appear that the court has no discretion to refuse the evidence in that form.[17] However, in defended proceedings the affidavit evidence may carry less weight than other oral evidence which has been open to cross-examination.[18]

28.3 BURDEN OF PROOF

The burden of proof rests upon the pursuer in family actions. The effect of this rule **28.3.1** and the requirement for leading evidence in most family actions is that, for example, even if the defender admits a ground of divorce on record but avers a particular defence such as condonation of adultery, the pursuer must lead at the proof and establish the ground of divorce before the defence arises.[19] Many aspects of family law are now governed by statute provisions, which embody principles under which the court must exercise a discretion. Leading examples are the Children (Scotland) Act 1995, Part I which governs the making of orders in respect of parental responsibilities and rights within families, and the Family Law (Scotland) Act 1985 which governs financial provision and the division of matrimonial property on divorce. In such proceedings substantive orders may be sought by pursuer, defender[20] or any other party upon whom intimation has been made and who enters process by minute.

In common with other civil actions the party seeking an order bears a burden of **28.3.2** proof on that issue, but the court has had to consider the extent of that burden. In proceedings regarding parental responsibilities and rights the court must ultimately decide whether any order sought will safeguard and promote the interests of the child, and that issue must be given paramount consideration.[21] In relation to the legislation which preceded this Act the court stated that a parent who had parental rights by virtue of that parentage nevertheless had to satisfy the evidential burden of bringing some evidence to the court to enable that parent's claim to be considered.[22] The court may have regard to conventional thinking such as a very young child's need for maternal care, and a child's need for contact with a father figure, but such matters do not have the strength of presumptions of law or fact.[23] When the evidential burden has been satisfied the court's obligation to assess whether the order sought is in the child's best interests comes into play. The court is entitled to raise an issue in relation to a child *ex proprio motu*,[24] in which case the parties should be given an opportunity to produce evidence on that issue if that evidence has not been presented already.[25]

Where an order for financial provision under the Family Law (Scotland) Act **28.3.3**

---

[16] RCS, r 36.8. OCR, r 29.3, in similar terms is now omitted by virtue of the Act of Sederunt (Ordinary Cause Rules Amendment) (Miscellaneous) 2000 (SI 2000/239) para 3(11).

[17] See *McVinnie v McVinnie* 1995 SLT (Sh Ct) 81; *Glaser v Glaser* 1997 SLT 456 but *cf Lobban v Philip* 1995 SCLR 1104 (Sh Ct).

[18] *McVinnie v McVinnie* 1995 SLT (Sh Ct) 81 at 85; and *Smith v Alexander Baird Ltd* 1993 SCLR 563 at 565.

[19] *Paterson v Paterson* 1938 SC 251, per Lord Mackay at 256, Lord Justice-Clerk Aitchison at 272. See also *Bird v Bird* 1931 SC 731.

[20] RCS, r 49.31(2)(b); OCR, r 33.34(2)(b).

[21] Children (Scotland) Act 1995, s 11(7)(a).

[22] *Sanderson v McManus* 1997 SC (HL) 55.

[23] *Brixey v Lynas* 1997 SC (HL) 1; *Sanderson v McManus* 1997 SCLR 281.

[24] Children (Scotland) Act 1995, s 12.

[25] Under RCS, r 49.28(3) or OCR, r 33.28(3).

1985 is sought by a party to divorce, although that Act entitles a party to fair division of matrimonial property, a burden still lies upon the party seeking such provision to formulate and prove the entitlement.[26] If information on the issue in dispute is exclusively within the knowledge of one party, such as information regarding his or her own assets or liabilities, then, subject to the other party having taken reasonable steps to obtain that information,[27] the party who has the information may have to lead at the proof,[28] and failure to lead such evidence may justify the drawing of inferences most favourable to the opponent.[29]

28.4 STANDARD OF PROOF

28.4.1 In all issues in family actions the burden of proof may be discharged on a balance of probabilities[30] and corroboration is not necessary, although a source of evidence independent of the parties will be necessary in relation to divorce, separation, legitimacy, illegitimacy, legitimation or nullity of marriage,[31] and in relation to arrangements for a child.[32] Historically adultery[33] and illegitimacy, if in the face of a presumption of legitimacy,[34] had to be proved beyond reasonable doubt but now these too are subject to the normal civil standard of balance of probabilities.[35] Criminal conduct which is averred in a family action need not be proved to the criminal standard of beyond reasonable doubt as in a criminal cause, but to the normal civil standard of balance of probabilities.[36]

28.5 JUDICIAL ADMISSIONS

Express

28.5.1 In family actions affecting status and those where an order is sought in relation to a child, because evidence must be presented in support of the decree,[37] it may not be granted solely because the pursuer's averments are judicially admitted.[38] In this

---

[26] *Williamson v Williamson* 1989 SLT 866 (OH); *George v George* 1991 SLT (Sh Ct) 8.

[27] By seeking an order for disclosure under the Family Law (Scotland) Act 1985, s 20 or by commission and diligence, on which see Chapter 21.

[28] *Williamson v Williamson* 1989 SLT 866 (OH).

[29] *Berry v Berry* 1991 SLT 42.

[30] As to the meaning of "balance of probabilities", see para 4.2.

[31] Civil Evidence (Scotland) Act 1988, s 8(2).

[32] RCS, r 49.28(3); OCR, r 33.28(3).

[33] *Burnett v Burnett* 1955 SC 183, per Lord President Clyde at 186–187; *Currie v Currie* 1950 SC 10 (OH) at 14–15; Walton, *Husband and Wife* (3rd edn), p 58. Adultery carried the stigma of an "offence". It was thought that sodomy or bestiality, which were introduced as grounds of divorce under the Divorce (Scotland) Act 1938, s 1(1)(d), would also have had to be proved to that standard if a criminal conviction for such an offence could not be produced to the court under s 1(2).

[34] *Mackay v Mackay* (1855) 17 D 494; *Brown v Brown* 1972 SLT 143; *Docherty v McGlynn* 1983 SLT 645.

[35] Divorce (Scotland) Act 1976, s 1(5) and the Law Reform (Parent and Child) (Scotland) Act 1986, s 5(4) respectively.

[36] *Mullan v Anderson* 1993 SLT 835 and as to proof of criminal conduct in civil proceedings generally, see para 4.3.

[37] Civil Evidence (Scotland) Act 1988, s 8(2); RCS, r 49.28; OCR, r 33.28.

[38] *Smith v Smith* 1929 SC 75, per Lord Justice-Clerk Alness at 82, Lord Anderson at 87–88; *Muirhead v Muirhead* (1846) 8 D 786; Civil Evidence (Scotland) Act 1988, s 8(1) and (2); Children (Scotland) Act 1995, s 12.

respect a family action differs from other civil causes. However, in actions for aliment only, and in respect of orders ancillary to status issues, such as financial provision on divorce, evidence is not an essential prerequisite to a decree. Judicial admissions in the form of joint minutes are commonly used in family actions, particularly in relation to ancillary issues, and the court can grant decree for an issue contained in a joint minute although it has not been claimed by either party.[39] Although binding between the parties,[40] in so far as they relate to issues upon which evidence must be led they are subject to the court's acceptance of the evidence which must be led in support of the orders claimed.[41] If they include matters affecting a child, the court must first give the opportunity for the child's views to be expressed and give due weight to those views having regard to the child's age and maturity[42] and ultimately must consider whether the order sought is necessary to safeguard and promote the interests of the child. An early *obiter dictum*,[43] which suggested that, in assessing the sufficiency of the evidence, a judicial admission must be completely disregarded, is no longer approved.[44] Such an admission may assist towards proof of the case.[45] However, the evidence and admissions of the parties alone will be insufficient, except in cases where the court does not have to receive evidence independent of the parties or consider overarching issues.

In civil actions generally there is no longer a requirement for corroboration,[46] **28.5.2** but in any action for divorce,[47] separation or declarator of marriage or nullity of marriage evidence must consist of or include evidence other than that of a party to the marriage.[48] It is thought that the basis for this lies in preventing the possibility of collusion between the parties and emphasising the wider importance of issues of status. Decree of divorce for adultery has been refused when the only evidence was that of the pursuer, supported by a judicial admission of adultery by the defender, although the pursuer's evidence, which demonstrated that he could not have been the father of the defender's child, was believed, and the defender's admission of adultery was clearly not collusive.[49] The value to be given to an admission, and the extent to which independent testimony is needed, depends upon the nature of the cause and the apparent risk of collusion which is associated with it, and in some cases very slight independent evidence may be

---

[39] RCS, r 49.27; OCR, r 33.26.

[40] *Lothian v Lothian* 1965 SLT 368 (OH); *Jongejan v Jongejan* 1993 SLT 595.

[41] *Patterson v Patterson* 1994 SCLR 166 (Sh Ct).

[42] Children (Scotland) Act 1995, s 11(7)(b) and RCS, r 49.20(1) and (3) and OCR, r 33.19(1) and (3); and see para 28.10 re child's views and evidence.

[43] *Muirhead v Muirhead* (1846) 8 D 786, per Lord Mackenzie at 786.

[44] *Macfarlane v Macfarlane* 1956 SC 472, per Lord President Clyde at 481, Lord Sorn at 483; Dickson, *Evidence* (3rd edn), para 284.

[45] *Macfarlane v Macfarlane* 1956 SC 472, per Lord Mackintosh (Ordinary) at 476; *Smith v Smith* 1929 SC 75, per Lord Moncrieff (Ordinary) at 77, Lord Justice-Clerk Alness at 80; *Barnes v Barnes* 1935 SC 646. In *Smith v Smith* and *Barnes v Barnes* the admission was extra-judicial, but in *Macfarlane v Macfarlane* the same principle was regarded as applicable to both kinds of admission.

[46] Civil Evidence (Scotland) Act 1988, s 1.

[47] An exception is made in the case of divorces based on non-cohabitation where there are no children under 16 years, no ancillary orders sought and no mental disorder. If such a divorce is sought using the simplified procedure (RCS, rr 49.72–49.80; OCR, rr 33.73–33.82) affidavit evidence from the pursuer alone is sufficient for decree to be granted: Evidence in Divorce Actions (Scotland) Order 1989 (SI 1989/582), Arts 2 and 3.

[48] Civil Evidence (Scotland) Act 1988, s 8(2). This carries forward the requirements of the Court of Session Act 1830, s 36 and the Divorce Jurisdiction, Court Fees and Legal Aid (Scotland) Act 1983, Sched 1, para 2(b).

[49] *Macfarlane v Macfarlane* 1956 SC 472.

enough.[50] Evidence from a paramour admitting adultery with the defender is technically sufficient to satisfy the requirement of evidence from an independent source but whether that will be sufficiently independent to rule out the risk of collusion is likely to depend upon the facts of the case.[51] Collusion is an express bar to the granting of decree of divorce,[52] but may also arise in relation to other issues of fact before the court.[53] Collusion involves parties together putting forward a false case or suppressing a valid defence[54] and it is not enough for collusion that parties simply agree to facilitate the progress of the litigation.[55] Collusion might be raised as a substantive defence, although that is unlikely. However, it is *pars judicis* (in the part or duty of the judge) to raise the issue of collusion and refuse to grant an order based upon collusive evidence.

Implied

28.5.3 The failure of a defender to enter appearance and to lodge defences at one time was said to constitute an implied admission of the pursuer's averments, and to afford some degree of support for the evidence led on his behalf.[56] These judicial dicta have been disapproved,[57] and do not detract from the requirement for evidence, including evidence independent of the parties for the actions described above. However, in the absence of contrary evidence the inferences most favourable to the pursuer may well be drawn.[58]

28.6 EXTRA-JUDICIAL ADMISSIONS

General

28.6.1 The general rules regarding extra-judicial admissions in civil causes[59] apply also to family actions. In family actions the court has been concerned, not only with the relevancy, authorship, interpretation and evidential value of an admission, but also

---

[50] Dickson, *Evidence* (3rd edn), para 284; *Macfarlane v Macfarlane* 1956 SC 472, per Lord Sorn at 483–484.
[51] For conflicting views in the sheriff court, see *Sinclair v Sinclair* 1986 SLT (Sh Ct) 54 and *Cooper v Cooper* 1987 SLT (Sh Ct) 37.
[52] Divorce (Scotland) Act 1976, s 9.
[53] *Society of Solicitors before the Supreme Courts v Officer* (1893) 20 R 1106; *Lindsay v Lindsay* 1927 SC 395.
[54] *Walker v Walker* 1911 SC 163.
[55] As occurred in *Lindsay v Lindsay* 1927 SC 395; *Fairgrieve v Chalmers* 1912 SC 745 and *McKenzie v McKenzie* 1935 SLT 198.
[56] *McDougall v McDougall* 1927 SC 666, per Lord Anderson at 670; *Smith v Smith* 1929 SC 75, per Lord Justice-Clerk Alness at 80.
[57] *Barr v Barr* 1939 SC 696, per Lord President Normand at 700, Lord Moncrieff at 701, Lord Carmont at 702. *Cf* Walton, *Husband and Wife* (3rd edn), p 65. As to the failure of a defender to lead evidence, or to give evidence explaining conduct which may be suspicious, as the foundation of an implied admission, see para 28.6.2.
[58] *Berry v Berry* 1991 SLT 42. This is the attitude of the court in other civil actions, such as *Binnie v Rederij Theodoro BV* 1993 SC 71, per Lord President Hope at 87; *O'Donnell v Murdoch McKenzie & Co* 1967 SC (HL) 63 (following *Ross v Associated Portland Cement Manufacturers* [1964] 1 WLR 768). It is thought that in issues involving children the overarching requirement to safeguard and promote the welfare of the child (Children (Scotland) Act 1995, s 11(7)(a)) would also influence the assessment of the evidence.
[59] See Chapter 9.

with the possibility that it may have been made collusively.[60] When free from collusion, however, an admission by a defender may be an important element in the pursuer's proof,[61] and even an admission in a letter written after service of the summons, and for the purposes of the litigation, has been so regarded.[62] Other examples of written admissions which have been accepted by the court include a torn-up draft letter from a defender to a paramour,[63] a letter written by the defender to the paramour which had been stolen by the pursuer,[64] and entries in a defender's private diary.[65] Evidence of an extra-judicial admission is not necessarily inadmissible because it has not been made the subject of express averment.[66] An extra-judicial admission alone is an insufficient basis for a decree in cases where there is the requirement for evidence independent of the parties, but it may provide support for other evidence which, by itself, would be weak.[67] At common law, an extra-judicial admission by a party, as distinct from a party's evidence *in causa*, is admissible only against the person who makes it. So an admission by the defender, made outwith the paramour's presence, of adultery committed with the paramour, was not admissible in evidence against the latter, and similarly an admission by a paramour was not admissible in evidence against a defender.[68] However, this must now be read in conjunction with the Civil Evidence (Scotland) Act 1988 which states that a statement made otherwise than in the course of a proof shall be admissible as evidence of any matter contained in the statement of which direct oral evidence would have been admissible.[69] This implies that an extra-judicial statement admitted as hearsay evidence is evidence in the case which can be used for or against any party.

Implied extra-judicial admissions

The same general principles apply to family as to other civil causes.[70] In effect **28.6.2** inferences may be drawn from facts and circumstances and the combination of such circumstances is infinitely variable. Proof of adultery has been the area most susceptible to trends of conduct giving rise to implied extra-judicial admissions.[71]

---

[60] Collusion as a bar to divorce has been said to be "an empty concept" (Clive, *Husband and Wife*, para 22.028, and see the Scottish Law Commission, *Report on Family Law* (Scot Law Com No 135, paras 13.5–13.8)) but the good faith of the parties in presenting a true case is still expected.

[61] Fraser, *Husband and Wife*, II, 1170; Dickson, *Evidence* (3rd edn), para 301; *Fullerton v Fullerton* (1873) 11 M 720. In relation to admissions made during the course of negotiations or mediation, see para 28.7 below.

[62] *Lindsay v Lindsay* 1927 SC 395 (declarator of marriage); *Smith v Smith* 1929 SC 75; *Barnes v Barnes* 1935 SC 646 (divorce for adultery).

[63] *Watson v Watson* 1934 SC 374.

[64] *Rattray v Rattray* (1897) 25 R 315; *MacColl v MacColl* 1946 SN 80, 1946 SLT 312.

[65] *Creasey v Creasey* 1931 SC 9.

[66] *MacColl v MacColl* 1948 SC 500 (oral admission).

[67] *MacKay v MacKay* 1946 SC 78. And see para 28.5.

[68] *Creasey v Creasey* 1931 SC 9; *Swapp v Swapp* 1931 SLT 199 (OH); *Rattray v Rattray* (1897) 25 R 315, per Lord Trayner at 319, Lord Moncreiff at 321.

[69] s 2(1)(b).

[70] Chapter 9.

[71] In *McInnes v McInnes* 1954 SC 396 the only evidence adduced by the pursuer was of regular meetings at lunch time between the defender and the paramour in the pursuer's house during his absence, and latterly without his knowledge. The meetings for some years were concerned with the discussion of trade union business, in which the defender and the paramour had a common interest, but they continued for about a year after this common interest had ended. Although there was no evidence of familiarities between the defender and the paramour, their false denial in the witness box of the

In general, the failure of a defender to provide an alternative interpretation of circumstances proved by the pursuer is not to be regarded as an implied admission,[72] since the burden of proof is on the pursuer. However, such failure can lead to the court interpreting the evidence in the manner most favourable to the party leading it.[73] It is thought that the same is to be said of any persons upon whom intimation of family proceedings has been made and who have sought to enter process as a party.

28.7 EVIDENCE FROM MEDIATION OR NEGOTIATION

28.7.1 If the parties have engaged in family mediation,[74] evidence of what occurred during the mediation, whilst possibly attracting some privilege at common law as a process in aid of litigation,[75] is now protected by statute.[76] The protection applies only to mediation provided by a service approved for the purposes of the statute by order of the Lord President.[77] No information as to what occurred during family mediation is admissible in civil proceedings[78] unless all participants[79] to the mediation agree, or the situation falls within an exception set out in section 2 of the Civil Evidence (Family Mediation) (Scotland) Act 1995. These exceptions include admission of the final outcome of the mediation, whether in the form of a contract or the fact that no agreement was reached[80] and, in proceedings in which the contract is challenged, evidence relevant to that challenge.[81] Excluded from the range of civil proceedings to which the Act relates are care proceedings under the Children (Scotland) Act 1995, Part II and proceedings under the Adoption (Scotland) Act 1978.[82]

28.7.2 Evidence of negotiation prior to the initiation or culmination of family proceedings is, in theory, subject to the same privilege as that attaching in non-family proceedings, viz evidence may not be led regarding concessions made to further negotiation, but may be led in respect of unequivocal admissions made during

---

continuation of the meetings after their initial purpose had ended, and their consequent inability to provide an innocent explanation for this continuation, was regarded as raising an inference that a guilty relationship had developed between them, and that adultery had taken place. A similar inference was drawn in *Hall v Hall* 1958 SC 206. But *cf Burnett v Burnett* 1955 SC 183 and see Clive, *The Law of Husband and Wife in Scotland* (4th edn), para 25-039 and the cases cited there for examples of attempts to prove adultery by inference from opportunity and related circumstances.

[72] *Bird v Bird* 1931 SC 731. As to whether a failure to lodge defences may be regarded as an implied admission, see para 28.5.3.

[73] *Berry v Berry* 1991 SLT 42; and in parentage actions if a party has been requested to provide or consent to the provision of a sample for scientific analysis, refusal or failure to do so may lead to the court drawing inferences adverse to that party: see para 28.15.

[74] Whether by their own choice or by order of the court under RCS, r 49.23 or OCR, r 33.22.

[75] Concessions made in the course of negotiations are privileged, but not unequivocal admissions made in the course of negotiations: *Daks Simpson Group plc v Kuiper* 1994 SLT 689; 1994 SCLR 373, followed in *Richardson v Quercus Ltd* 1999 SLT 596. See also para 10.8.

[76] Civil Evidence (Family Mediation) (Scotland) Act 1995, s 1.

[77] Civil Evidence (Family Mediation) (Scotland) Act 1995, s 1(2)–(6).

[78] The protection does not extend to care proceedings.

[79] "Participant" excludes the mediator, but includes any child who is the subject of the mediation whether or not the child was present during mediation if at the time of mediation the child could understand the matters on which evidence is now sought: Civil Evidence (Family Mediation) (Scotland) Act 1995, s 2(1)(c) and (2).

[80] s 2(1)(a).

[81] s 2(1)(b).

[82] s 2(d)(i)–(iv). Also excluded are proceedings for damages arising out of some occurrence at the mediation, and proceedings to which the mediator is a party: s 2(d)(v) and (vi).

negotiation.[83] However, there may be situations where the court will want to have the fullest information regarding negotiations between the parties. For example, the Family Law (Scotland) Act 1985, s 16 requires that any agreement entered into between parties to resolve any issues concerning financial provision to which the Act relates must be fair and reasonable. The court may be required to rule upon the fairness of an agreement contained in a joint minute before interponing authority to it,[84] or may be asked to reduce the terms of an agreement which one party now contends to have been unfair or unreasonable.[85] It is thought that evidence of concessions made would be relevant and admissible, not in the sense of an extra-judicial admission but as a factor in the assessment of all the circumstances surrounding the making of the agreement.[86] Similarly, in matters affecting the welfare of children the court may be unwilling to declare relevant evidence inadmissible and may incline to the view that rules of law "should obtrude as little as possible into the process".[87]

28.8 EVIDENCE FROM OTHER PROCEEDINGS

As in other civil causes,[88] a judicial admission in an earlier criminal cause, such as **28.8.1** a plea of guilty to assault or to a charge of rape, or a judicial admission of paternity in an action of affiliation and aliment, may be founded upon by the other party in a subsequent family cause as an extra-judicial admission. The fact that a conviction has occurred or a decree has been pronounced in an earlier cause, is, at common law, irrelevant and inadmissible in evidence in a later civil cause.[89] The principle is that, apart from the statutory exceptions mentioned below and *res judicata*,[90] a court must have regard only to the evidence before it, and ought not to be influenced by the decision of another court pronounced on evidence of which it has no knowledge.

However, there are certain statutory exceptions to the common law rule. In any **28.8.2** action of divorce, the pursuer in which has previously been granted a decree of separation upon the same or substantially the same facts as those averred in support of the action of divorce, the court may treat the decree of separation as sufficient proof of the ground of action (other than adultery) in respect of which the separation decree was granted.[91] The pursuer must give evidence[92] as to the relationship between the parties at the date of the proceedings for divorce.[93] A finding of adultery in any matrimonial proceedings in the United Kingdom may be founded upon in subsequent civil proceedings and creates a rebuttable presumption that the

---

[83] *Daks Simpson Group plc v Kuiper* 1994 SLT 689; 1994 SCLR 373.
[84] But not afterwards as in *Jongejan v Jongejan* 1993 SLT 595.
[85] As in *McAfee v McAfee* 1990 SCLR 805; *Gillon v Gillon (No 3)* 1995 SLT 678.
[86] *McAfee v McAfee* 1990 SCLR 805; *Gillon v Gillon (No 3)* 1995 SLT 678. An analogous situation is found in the Civil Evidence (Family Mediation) (Scotland) Act 1995, s 2(1)(b): if a contract entered into following mediation is challenged, evidence relevant to the challenge becomes admissible.
[87] Per Lord President Rodger in *L v L* 1998 SLT 672 at 676H–I.
[88] See para 9.4.
[89] There were anomalous decisions at common law such as *Galbraith v Galbraith* (1902), 9 SLT 346 (OH); *Mathieson v Mathieson* 1914 1 SLT 511 (OH); *McDougall v McDougall* 1927 SC 666.
[90] See Chapter 11.
[91] Divorce (Scotland) Act 1976, s 3(1).
[92] Divorce (Scotland) Act 1976, s 3(2).
[93] *McFarlane v McFarlane* 1951 SC 530 (OH); *Wilson v Wilson* 1939 SC 102.

adultery was committed.[94] In any civil proceedings in which conduct amounting to a criminal offence has been averred production of an extract conviction in respect of the criminal conduct, together with proof that the person named in the conviction is the person against whom the averment has been made,[95] creates a rebuttable presumption that the offence was committed.[96]

28.9 PARTIES AS WITNESSES

28.9.1 The parties to a family cause and their spouses are competent and probably compellable witnesses.[97] However, in common with all witnesses, neither they nor an alleged paramour are liable to be asked or bound to answer any question tending to show that he or she has committed a criminal offence,[98] nor that he or she has committed adultery, unless the witness has already given evidence in the same proceeding in disproof of his or her adultery.[99] Decree in actions of divorce, separation or declarator of marriage or nullity of marriage may not be granted solely on the evidence of the pursuer and the defender.[100] The practice of calling the defender as the first witness for the pursuer on the question of adultery, in an undefended proof, in an action of divorce met with criticism.[101] It is now the norm for undefended actions to proceed by way of affidavit evidence[102] and it is not unusual to find that the defender and the paramour offer the evidence to prove the case. This has met with conflicting shrieval reactions[103] and it has been suggested that because an affidavit is given voluntarily rather than in response to questioning the protection against admission of adultery does not apply.[104] Despite earlier dicta to the contrary, evidence of the spouses to establish that intercourse between them did not occur is admissible.[105]

28.9.2 Frequently, family actions must be intimated to persons other than the defender, such as a child affected by a matter in the proceedings,[106] the next of kin if a defender's whereabouts are unknown,[107] a person with whom the defender is alleged to have committed adultery[108] or had an improper sexual relationship,[109] or a person with an interest in the matrimonial home such as a landlord[110] or heritable creditor.[111] These persons are not parties to the proceedings unless they take steps to

---

[94] Law Reform (Miscellaneous Provisions) (Scotland) Act 1968, s 11; and see para 3.3.1.
[95] *Andrews v Andrews* 1971 SLT (Notes) 44.
[96] Law Reform (Miscellaneous Provisions) (Scotland) Act 1968, s 10.
[97] Evidence (Scotland) Act 1853, s 3; and see para 13.9.
[98] Evidence (Scotland) Act 1853, s 3.
[99] Evidence Further Amendment (Scotland) Act 1874, s 2; and para 12.13.
[100] Civil Evidence (Scotland) Act 1988, s 8(3). This was thought to be the case at common law— *Macfarlane v Macfarlane* 1956 SC 472—but there were conflicting decisions (*Burrell v Burrell* 1947 SC 569).
[101] *Chatman v Chatman* 1944 SC 494 (OH).
[102] RCS, r 49.28; OCR, r 33.28.
[103] In *Sinclair v Sinclair* 1986 SLT (Sh Ct) 54 and *Cooper v Cooper* 1987 SLT (Sh Ct) 37.
[104] *Sinclair v Sinclair* 1986 SLT (Sh Ct) 45; and see Clive, *The Law of Husband and Wife in Scotland* (4th edn), para 23-034.
[105] *Lennie v Lennie* 1948 SC 466.
[106] RCS, r 49.8(8); OCR, r 33.7(1)(h).
[107] RCS, r 49.8(1)(a)(ii); OCR, r 33.79(1)(a)(ii).
[108] RCS, r 49.8(1)(b); OCR, r 33.7(1)(b).
[109] RCS, r 49.9; OCR, r 3.8.
[110] RCS, r 49.8(1)(k)(ii); OCR, r 33.7(1)(k)(ii).
[111] RCS, r 49.8(1)(i)(ii); OCR, r 33.7(1)(i)(ii). A list of those to whom intimation is commonly required is contained in RCS, r 49.8 and OCR, r 33.7, and the court may order intimation upon any other person: RCS, r 49.15; OCR, r 33.15.

enter process by minute.[112] Unless incapable of giving evidence due to age or mental incapacity they are competent and compellable witnesses whether parties or not.

28.10 CHILDREN AS WITNESSES AND THE VIEWS OF CHILDREN

A child is a competent witness in any family proceedings, as in any other pro- **28.10.1** ceedings, if capable of being a trustworthy witness.[113] It is for the judge to assess the child's ability to distinguish truth from lies, and to appreciate that only the truth must be told in evidence. This assessment is made at the time of the proceedings.[114] Traditionally, to use a child as a witness in family proceedings has been considered undesirable by the court[115] and by the parties.[116] However, the child may be a direct witness to an issue in the case and failure to lead the child's evidence may lead to failure on that issue.[117]

The general rule in civil cases allows for admission of hearsay evidence. It has **28.10.2** been held that hearsay evidence of a child will be admissible as evidence of its contents only if the court can assess and accept the competence of the child as a witness.[118] Furthermore, in the Outer House, in an action between parents concerning contact, it has been held that the assessment requires oral examination of the child at the point of proof.[119] The decision on this issue is based upon a strict interpretation of the relevant provisions of the Civil Evidence (Scotland) Act 1988, s 2. Although the case was appealed to the Inner House, this issue was not considered on appeal. The judge had rejected the possibility of assessing competence through the evidence of a social worker who had worked with the child, although in earlier cases concerning compulsory measures of care for children it had been observed that the court might assess a child's capability from evidence of parents and those with professional experience of the child such as social workers or child psychologists.[120] If the child is examined and deemed competent the child's evidence may be led orally, but it is also then competent to lead hearsay evidence of the child in substitute for or to supplement the child's oral evidence.[121] If both are led and the two conflict, the court may accept the hearsay as the more credible and proof of the facts contained in it.[122] The House of Lords has held that hearsay evidence of a child's comments after a visit with a parent, whilst not admissible as

---

[112] RCS, r 49.16; OCR, r 33.16.
[113] *M v Kennedy* 1993 SC 115; *Rees v Lowe* 1990 JC 96; and see generally re children as witnesses, paras 13.2–13.4.
[114] *L v L* 1996 SLT 767 at 770K.
[115] *eg Robertson v Robertson* (1888) 15 R 1001 (child of seven re seeing parent with an apparent paramour).
[116] Acknowledged by the Lord Ordinary in *L v L* 1996 SLT 767.
[117] In *L v L* 1996 SLT 767 children were not called as witnesses and, in the absence of their direct evidence on the issue in question and having regard to other facts and circumstances, the burden of proof on that issue was not satisfied. On appeal the Lord Ordinary's approach to the assessment of the evidence was approved: *L v L* 1998 SLT 672.
[118] *F v Kennedy (No 1)* 1992 SC 28; *R, Petitioner* 1999 SC 280.
[119] *L v L* 1996 SLT 767. In *MT v DT*, 10 July 2000 this point was referred by the Inner House to a larger court.
[120] *M v Ferguson* 1994 SCLR 487. It should be noted that these cases did involve children with a disability from whom assessment of capability had been difficult, and the third party evidence envisaged would have been supplemental rather than a substitute for some examination of the child. For a discussion of the case and comparison with criminal cases, see Sheldon, "Children's Evidence, Competency and the New Hearsay Provisions" 1997 SLT (News) 1.
[121] Civil Evidence (Scotland) Act 1988, s 2; *F v Kennedy (No 2)* 1993 SLT 1284.
[122] *K v Kennedy* 1993 SLT 128.

proof of the truth of the comments, can be of value to the court in its assessment of the child's reaction to the visit within the overall consideration of the child's best interests.[123] In general the court has indicated that the duty to have regard to the child's interests in making any decision affecting a child, and the general liberalisation of the rules of evidence, will militate against the application of any restrictive rule which might keep relevant evidence from the court.[124]

28.10.3 A child who is likely to be affected by the family proceedings either because the pursuer seeks an order in relation to the child[125] or because the defender or other party intends to do so,[126] or because the court is considering making such an order,[127] must be given the opportunity to state a view in relation to the order sought unless the child is, in the court's view, of insufficient age or maturity to express a view. The child's right to do so stems from Article 12 of the United Nations Convention on the Rights of the Child[128] and has been incorporated into domestic law[129] and procedure.[130] The child's intimation differs from that sent to other parties in that it is not accompanied by the relevant copy pleadings but instead contains a brief statement of the order sought in language a child is capable of understanding, together with information as to how the child's view may be communicated to the court.[131] This may be done by the child communicating orally or in writing with the clerk of court, or nominating a lay or legal representative[132] to do so. If the child indicates a desire to communicate a view to the court, but not what that view is, the court must make appropriate arrangements to obtain the child's view.[133] How this will be done is in the court's discretion,[134] but options include to arrange for the child to attend the child welfare hearing (if the proceedings are in the sheriff court)[135] or to appoint a reporter or curator to obtain the child's view. Interviewing the child in chambers outwith the presence of the parties has been undertaken in some courts[136] but this has been criticised as inappropriate substitution of inquisitorial methods in an adversarial system.[137] While judges in family actions are now charged with a proactive role, care has to be taken to ensure fairness to the parties. It is clear that the court is not obliged to

---

[123] *Sanderson v McManus* 1997 SC (HL) 55 at 61; applied in *Lothian Regional Council v F* 1997 SC 164. In *M v Ferguson* 1994 SCLR 487 the Inner House confirmed that the court could take account of a hearsay comment from a child as part of the overall narrative of the case, provided that it was not accepted as going towards proving the truth of the comment.

[124] Per Lord President Rodger in *L v L* 1998 SLT 672.

[125] RCS, r 49.8(1)(h); OCR, r 33.7(1)(h).

[126] RCS, r 49.15(3); OCR, rr 33.15(3) and 33.34(3).

[127] RCS, r 49.15(2); OCR, r 33.15(2).

[128] Concluded 28 November 1989; ratified by the United Kingdom on 16 December 1991. A European Convention on the Exercise of Children's Rights was signed at Strasbourg on 25 January 1996 but is not yet ratified.

[129] Children (Scotland) Act 1995, s 11(7).

[130] RCS, r 49.20(1); OCR, rr 33.15 and 33.19(1).

[131] RCS, Form 49.8N; OCR, Form F9.

[132] Instructing a legal representative is within a child's capacity: Age of Legal Capacity (Scotland) Act 1991, s 2(1)(a). There is no requirement upon a child to have a legal representative: Children (Scotland) Act 1995, s 11(9).

[133] RCS, r 49.20(2); OCR, r 33.19(2).

[134] If the child enters process as a party any legal representative may communicate the view by *ex parte* statements or may choose to lead evidence from the child.

[135] OCR, rr 33.19(2) and 33.22A.

[136] *eg Blance v Blance* 1978 SLT 74 (children aged 13 and 12); *Cosh v Cosh* 1979 SLT (Notes) 72 (children interviewed re proposed termination of access).

[137] *MacDonald v MacDonald* 1985 SLT 244.

obtain the child's view in the form of evidence. This is implicit in the wide discretion afforded to the court for obtaining the child's view and furthermore, in the sheriff court, the sheriff may direct that the record of the child's view be kept confidential to the sheriff, with no other person having access to it.[138] Withholding the information from the parties has been challenged, with varying outcomes in first instance judgments.[139] The basis for challenge is the party's entitlement to equality of arms under Human Rights jurisprudence, and the relationship between that right and the court's obligation to give paramount consideration to the interests of the child. Although the view will rarely be open to cross-examination and may be kept from the parties completely,[140] the court, in making any decision affecting the child, must give due weight to the view having due regard to the child's age and maturity.[141] A child is presumed to be of sufficient age and maturity to form a view at age 12,[142] but this does not fetter the court's discretion to have regard to the views of a younger child.

28.11 IDENTIFICATION OF DEFENDER

When the defender in a family action is not present at the proof, and it is necessary **28.11.1** that he should be identified as the person to whom the evidence of the witnesses refers, this may be done by producing and proving the authenticity of a photograph, and showing it to the witnesses.[143] The court no longer insists upon the defender being ordered to appear, and, if necessary, apprehended.[144]

28.12 EVIDENCE OF SIMILAR ACTS

Adultery

Although corroboration is no longer a requirement in civil actions, the court must **28.12.1** still be satisfied that facts have been established in order to meet the burden of proof.[145] One or more witnesses each speaking to a single act of adultery between the defender and another person, whether the other person is the same[146] or different[147] on each occasion, may prove the case. However, as an exception to the normal application of the rule of relevancy, the evidence of a single witness to an

---

[138] OCR, r 33.20(2).

[139] *Dosoo v Dosoo* 1999 SLT (Sh Ct) 86; *McGrath v McGrath* 1999 SLT (Sh Ct) 90.

[140] Withholding information from a party in care proceedings has been held to contravene the European Convention on Human Rights: *McMichael v UK* (1995) 20 EHRR 205. For a discussion of the respective interests of child and parties in family actions, see Ross, "Reforms in Family Proceedings in the Sheriff Court: Raising Conflicts in Civil Justice" 1998 CIL 1.

[141] RCS, r 49.19(3); OCR, r 33.19(3).

[142] Children (Scotland) Act 1995, s 11(10).

[143] Lewis, *Evidence*, p 281; Walton, *Husband and Wife* (3rd edn), p 301; Clive, *The Law of Husband and Wife in Scotland* (4th edn), para 23-010. This occurs commonly in actions of adultery where evidence is provided by enquiry agents who observed the conduct of the defender with a person other than the pursuer.

[144] See *Grieve v Grieve* (1885) 12 R 969.

[145] Civil Evidence (Scotland) Act 1988, s 1(1). *Cf* the old law in which one witness would not suffice: *Robertson v Robertson* (1888) 15 R 1001; *Wilson v Wilson* (1898) 25 R 788.

[146] Dickson, *Evidence* (3rd edn), para 1808; *Murray v Murray* (1847) 9 D 1556.

[147] Dickson, *Evidence* (3rd edn), para 1808; *Whyte v Whyte* (1884) 11 R 710, per Lord Lee (Ordinary) at 711 (approved on appeal).

act of adultery with a paramour may be supported by evidence of the defender's attempted adultery or indecent conduct with another woman.[148] The exception is anomalous, and would not be extended to other situations.[149]

Behaviour

28.12.2 A course of conduct described by a pursuer which includes a number of assaults and related incidents, if they all occur during a relatively short space of time and are attributable to some common cause or stimulus, may be sufficiently proved by the evidence of witnesses who speak only to some of the individual incidents. The individual incidents may for this purpose be regarded as manifestations of a continuing underlying cause, such as the defender's jealousy, drunkenness or uncontrollable temper. If against the background of the parties' married life these incidents form an apt and coherent whole, the requirements of the independent evidence may be satisfied, even if some of the incidents are spoken to by only one witness.[150]

28.13 CIRCUMSTANTIAL EVIDENCE OF SEXUAL RELATIONS FOR DIVORCE ACTIONS

28.13.1 The general principles of circumstantial evidence, which are mentioned earlier,[151] apply also to family actions. When a sexual relationship is averred in actions of divorce on the ground of adultery, while direct evidence is sometimes obtainable, the court is usually asked to find the relationship proved as an inference from facts and circumstances.[152] The same would no doubt arise if a homosexual relationship or acts of sodomy or bestiality are founded upon in a family action. Examples of the use of circumstantial evidence in cases of adultery include: the defender's visits to a brothel[153]; proof that the defender has contracted a sexually transmitted disease which could not have been passed on by the pursuer[154]; evidence that the defender and paramour shared a bed or bedroom in circumstances which exclude any other reasonable inference, or of opportunity and circumstances indicating that advantage was taken of the opportunity. Each case must be decided upon its own facts, there being no rigidly normal standard by which the actions of all human beings may be judged.[155] The cases which have caused most difficulty are those in which there has been a long, and possibly indiscreet, association between a defender and a paramour, with frequent opportunities for adultery, but with no evidence of familiarities or other indications of the existence of a passionate attachment. There can be a close friendship between a man and a woman without adultery,[156] and this has been the consideration which weighed with the court in some of the reported decisions.[157] In these cases the background was regarded as

---

[148] *Whyte v Whyte* (1884) 11 R 710; *Wilson v Wilson* 1955 SLT (Notes) 81 (OH); *Duff v Duff* 1969 SLT (Notes) 53.
[149] *Duff v Duff* 1969 SLT (Notes) 53.
[150] *Walker v Walker* 1953 SC 297; *Tullis v Tullis* 1953 SC 312.
[151] See Chapter 6.
[152] *Walker v Walker* (1871) 9 M 1091.
[153] See *Edward v Edward* (1879) 6 R 1255; *Marshall v Marshall* (1881) 8 R 702.
[154] Walton, *Husband and Wife* (3rd edn), pp 60–61.
[155] See *Bennet Clark v Bennet Clark* 1909 SC 591, per Lord Kinnear at 609.
[156] See *Bennet Clark v Bennet Clark* 1909 SC 591, per Lord Kinnear at 609.
[157] *Bennet Clark v Bennet Clark* 1909 SC 591; *Ross v Ross* 1930 SC (HL) 1; *Burnett v Burnett* 1955 SC 183.

being neutral, so that without evidence of familiarities the court was unable to accept a sinister interpretation of the association.[158] However, such conduct, although not amounting to adultery, may be such that it brought to an end the prospect of the parties' cohabitation and thus would support a divorce sought on the behaviour ground.

Adultery may be inferred from proof that one spouse had a child by another part- **28.13.2** ner. In the absence of admission this may be proved by production of an extract of the child's birth entry, but the details of the parents so recorded will do no more than raise a presumption of parentage which may be rebutted by other evidence. Proof that the child has been born to the wife during the marriage or has been conceived during the marriage[159] raises a presumption that the husband is the father, but this may be rebutted by evidence that the father was not available to have or capable of having fertile sexual intercourse with the mother at the likely time of conception. While the courts are regarded as having judicial knowledge of the normal period of gestation,[160] the question of whether a clearly abnormal period is a possible one is decided in each case in the light of the medical evidence led and the gestation age of the child at birth.[161] On a question of whether marital intercourse did or did not take place during any period, the evidence of the spouses is admissible, and this and the question of their compellability is mentioned in another chapter.[162] Even if the parties were engaging in sexual relations at the likely time of conception it has become easier to prove that the child could not be the child of the parties by scientific analysis of samples taken from the parties and the child.

28.14 ACTIONS CONCERNING PARENTAGE AND LEGITIMACY— GENERAL

In actions of declarator of parentage, non-parentage, legitimacy, legitimation, ille- **28.14.1** gitimacy and affiliation and aliment, as in other actions, the initial onus of proof rests upon the pursuer[163] and it must be discharged by sufficient evidence.[164] The standard of proof is balance of probabilities.[165] Generally such actions involve

---

[158] See *Hall v Hall* 1958 SC 206, per Lord Justice-Clerk Thomson at 207. But *cf McInnes v McInnes* 1954 SC 396. In these cases the fact that the defender and the paramour denied some of the suspicious meetings which were proved to have occurred, and were therefore unable to provide an innocent explanation of them, was regarded by the court as helping to cast a sinister light upon the association. It must be noted that false denial cannot constitute corroborative evidence (Civil Evidence (Scotland) Act 1988, s 1(2)), but it probably can still influence the assessment of credibility of other evidence.

[159] Law Reform (Parent and Child) (Scotland) Act 1986, s 5(1)(a).

[160] *Williamson v McClelland* 1913 SC 678 at 680; *Preston-Jones v Preston-Jones* [1951] AC 391 at 401, 406, 407, 412, 419. (The older authorities accepted the arbitrary periods of six lunar months as the minimum and ten (probably calendar: Dickson, *Evidence* (3rd edn), para 136) months as the maximum—Stair, iii, 3, 42; Erskine, i, 6, 50—but this rule has been departed from.)

[161] There are numerous old cases dealing with this issue (*eg Currie v Currie* 1950 SC 10 (OH); *McIntosh v McIntosh* 1947 SN 23; *Jamieson v Dobie* 1935 SC 415; *Doherty v Doherty* 1922 SLT 245 (OH); *Gray v Gray* 1919 1 SLT 163 (OH); and earlier cases are given in Dickson, *Evidence* (3rd edn), paras 136–137. However, now the matter would commonly be determined by biological evidence: see para 28.16.

[162] See para 13.9.

[163] *McBayne v Davidson* (1860) 22 D 738; *Young v Nicol* (1893) 20 R 768.

[164] Civil Evidence (Scotland) Act 1988, ss 1 and 8(2).

[165] That was always the case at common law unless a presumption of legitimacy was being challenged, in which case the standard was "beyond reasonable doubt" until the Law Reform (Parent and Child) (Scotland) Act 1986, s 5(4).

proof of paternity, since maternity is usually clear.[166] Only the increase in assisted reproductive techniques and surrogacy arrangements has led to statutory consideration of the issue of maternity, but the statutory provision deems maternity to derive from carrying and giving birth to the child.[167] Proof of paternity has always been problematic. Assistance derives from presumptions at common law and now under statute, whereby proof of certain basic facts raises a presumption of paternity which falls to be rebutted by contrary evidence from the defender. If there is no presumption to rely upon or if a presumption is successfully rebutted, the pursuer must normally rely upon inferences from facts and circumstances, since rarely will there be direct evidence of the conception of the child concerned.[168] Undoubtedly, proof has been made simpler by the access to scientific analysis of biological material which may prove or disprove genetic parentage. Actions concerning parentage and legitimacy must be distinguished from actions concerning parental responsibilities and rights under the Children (Scotland) Act 1995, Part I or actions of affiliation. The award of parental responsibilities to a putative parent claiming interest under the 1995 Act or an order of affiliation and aliment, even if it contains a finding in fact that the pursuer is a parent of the child, does not determine the issue of parentage other than for the purposes of those proceedings.[169] If parentage is to be determined per se there must be a separate conclusion, crave or action for declarator of parentage or legitimacy.[170] In terms of the Law Reform (Parent and Child) (Scotland) Act 1986, parentage determined by such declarator, whether in the Court of Session or sheriff court,[171] creates a presumption to the same effect as the decree, which displaces any contrary presumption.[172] This statutory presumption in favour of an existing decree for parentage was introduced because the common law regarding the applicability of such decrees beyond the parties to that action was somewhat unclear.[173] The statutory provision is said to be without prejudice to the effect of a declarator under any rule of law[174] which would preserve the plea of res judicata if the issue was raised in subsequent proceedings between the same parties.[175] However, the statutory presumption in favour of the terms of a decree of declarator leaves open the possibility of rebuttal in subsequent proceedings between different parties by contrary factual evidence,[176] such as biological evidence, although not by contrary presumption.

---

[166] Proof of maternity was required in the unusual case of *Douglas v Duke of Hamilton* (1769) 2 Pat 143.

[167] Human Fertilisation and Embryology Act 1990, s 27.

[168] Such evidence is likely to be available only in cases of assisted reproduction.

[169] And it is competent to make an incidental finding for those purposes only: Law Reform (Parent and Child) (Scotland) Act 1986, s 7(5). At one time an order for affiliation gave rise to a rebuttable presumption which could be relied upon in subsequent proceedings but this was removed from the Law Reform (Miscellaneous Provisions) (Scotland) Act 1968, s 11 by the 1986 Act, s 10(2) and Sched 2.

[170] Or non-parentage, illegitimacy or legitimation.

[171] 1986 Act, s 7(1).

[172] 1986 Act, s 5(3).

[173] For a discussion of the difficulties, see the Scottish Law Commission *Report on Family Law: Illegitimacy* (Scot Law Com No 82), paras 6.25–6.28.

[174] 1986 Act, s 5(3).

[175] But cf *Silver v Walker* 1938 SC 595.

[176] This was clearly the intention of the Scottish Law Commission, Report No 82 (n 173, above), para 6.28.

28.15 PARENTAGE AND LEGITIMACY—PRESUMPTIONS

Under the Law Reform (Parent and Child) (Scotland) Act 1986 a man is presumed **28.15.1**
to be the father of a child if he was married[177] to the mother at any time in the
period beginning with the child's conception and ending with the child's birth.[178]
There was a similar presumption at common law—*pater est quem nuptiae demonstrant* (he is the father whom the marriage indicates to be so)—but for that
presumption to operate the mother had to be married at the time of the child's
birth.[179] If this presumption does not apply, a man is presumed to be the father if
both he and the child's mother have acknowledged that to be the case, and the man
has been registered as the father in the child's birth entry in the Register of Births,
Marriages and Deaths.[180] The effect of these presumptions is not to establish
parentage in themselves, but to assist a party who seeks to prove parentage. The
presumptions are rebuttable by evidence as to the fact of parentage or non-
parentage and proof is on the balance of probabilities.[181]

28.16 PARENTAGE AND LEGITIMACY—BIOLOGICAL EVIDENCE

Scientific analysis of biological samples taken from the child and the parties may **28.16.1**
rule out the possibility of parentage or may enable parentage to be established.
Blood sample analysis has been used in particular to determine whether a person
is of a compatible blood group by which they could have been the parent of the
child, and thus it has been used generally to rebut a presumption of parentage or to
exclude the possibility of a particular person being parent. By analysis of the DNA
from blood or other sample of body fluid or tissue it is now possible to compare
directly the DNA of the child with that of other persons tested and to identify similarities between individuals such as may positively establish parentage.[182]

At common law no person may be ordered to submit to the removal of a sample **28.16.2**
of blood or other body fluid for evidential purposes in civil cases.[183] Now statute[184]
empowers the court to request a party to provide a sample of blood or other body
fluid or tissue for the purpose of laboratory analysis,[185] or to consent to the taking

---

[177] Even if the marriage is irregular, void or voidable: s 5(2).

[178] s 5(1)(a).

[179] The more liberal terms of the statutory presumption give rise to the possibility that more than one
man will meet the criteria. For a discussion of this and other issues arising from presumptions of
parentage and their interaction with the deeming provisions of the Human Fertilisation and Embryology
Act 1990, see Wilkinson and Norrie, *Parent and Child* (2nd edn), paras 3.13–3.41.

[180] Law Reform (Parent and Child) (Scotland) Act 1986, s 5(1)(b). For a man to be so registered
requires fulfilment of the conditions in the Registration of Births, Deaths and Marriages (Scotland) Act
1965, s 18, which in themselves require the acknowledgement, attendance and signature of both parties.

[181] Law Reform (Parent and Child) (Scotland) Act 1986, s 5(4).

[182] It has been held in a criminal case that the assessment of the degree of similarity needed to establish a connection is one for the court, informed by the scientific evidence accompanying the analysis:
see *Welsh v HM Advocate* 1992 SLT 193.

[183] *Whitehall v Whitehall* 1958 SC 252; *Torrie v Turner* 1990 SLT 718. For a discussion of the reasons
for this prohibition and the difficulties arising, see Wilkinson and Norrie, *Parent and Child*,
pp 152–153 and Scottish Law Commission, *Report on Evidence, Blood Group Tests, DNA Tests and
Related Matters* (Scot Law Com No 120), Chapters 1 and 3.

[184] Law Reform (Miscellaneous Provisions) (Scotland) Act 1990, s 70.

[185] As in *Petrie v Petrie* 1993 SCLR 391.

of such a sample from a child in respect of whom that person has the power to consent,[186] but does not go so far as to order that a sample be provided. However, if the court has made a request for provision of a sample and the person requested fails or refuses to implement the request, the court is empowered to draw from that failure or refusal such adverse inference as its appears to the court appropriate to make in the circumstances of the case.[187] The drawing of adverse inference is entirely within the discretion of the court: there is no obligation to draw an adverse inference, and if any inference is drawn it need not be an inference which perfects the other party's claim.[188]

28.16.3   In cases of assisted reproduction[189] involving donated embryo, eggs or sperm, biological evidence would link the child with the donor, rather than with the parties who have sought such assistance. However, as a matter of policy, parentage of a child born as a result of such assisted reproduction is determined by statute.[190] If a couple were married when the assistance was obtained the husband is deemed to be the father of the child born as a result of the assistance.[191] This applies only if the father consented to the assistance.[192] If it is proved that no consent was given the deeming provision regarding paternity would not come into effect. However, the deeming of paternity itself is final and irrebuttable. So, too, is the deemed maternity of the carrier of a child in a surrogacy arrangement, although the egg may have been donated by the woman seeking assistance to have a child.[193]

28.17 INFERENCES FROM OPPORTUNITY FOR SEXUAL RELATIONS

28.17.1   Evidence that the parties had opportunities for intercourse at or about the relevant times may assist the pursuer's case. Opportunity, to be of positive assistance to the pursuer, must amount to something more than the fact that the parties both resided in the same town or village.[194] When corroboration was required, opportunity was not in itself sufficient corroboration,[195] unless the circumstances or the localities of the opportunities were such as themselves to raise an inference that intercourse occurred,[196] as, for example, in clandestine meetings at unreasonable hours or in suspicious circumstances.[197] It is thought that for opportunity to carry any weight in evidence it would have to raise such an inference.

---

[186] Power to consent is determined by the Law Reform (Parent and Child) (Scotland) Act 1986, s 6 and the Age of Legal Capacity (Scotland) Act, s 2(4).

[187] Law Reform (Miscellaneous Provisions) (Scotland) Act 1990, s 70(2).

[188] *Smith v Greenhill* 1993 SCLR 776.

[189] For a discussion of proof in these situations and the interaction with presumptions of parentage under the 1986 Act, see Wilkinson and Norrie, *Parent and Child* (2nd edn), paras 3.13–3.41.

[190] Human Fertilisation and Embryology Act 1990 ("1990 Act").

[191] 1990 Act, s 28.

[192] 1990 Act, s 28(2).

[193] 1990 Act, s 27.

[194] *Buchanan v Finlayson* (1900) 3 F 245, per Lord Trayner at 251.

[195] *Dawson v McKenzie* 1908 SC 648; *Gray v Marshall* (1875) 2 R 907.

[196] *Dawson v McKenzie* 1908 SC 648, per Lord President Dunedin at 649, Lord Kinnear at 651.

[197] *Gray v Marshall* (1875) 2 R 907, per Lord Justice-Clerk Moncreiff at 908.

28.18 INFERENCES FROM ACTS OF INTERCOURSE OTHER THAN THOSE FOUNDED UPON

Between the parties

Evidence of acts of intercourse between the parties, other than those alleged to **28.18.1** have resulted in pregnancy, is admissible and may be relevant as throwing light on the probable relationship between the parties at the date of the conception of the child.[198] This is a relaxation of the general rule[199] which makes evidence of similar acts inadmissible. An act of intercourse, which is admitted or proved to have occurred either before or after the probable date of conception, may sometimes afford support of the pursuer's evidence if opportunity at the date of conception is also proved. It will have to be assessed in light of the whole circumstances of the case, including the relationship between the parties, the nature and character of the opportunities open to them, the length of time between the act and the date of conception, and the particular circumstances in which the intercourse took place.[200] When the act of intercourse occurs *before* the date of conception, and meetings between the parties continue thereafter, ordinary experience is said to have shown that intercourse, once commenced, will probably be repeated when opportunity for it is afforded, and little else will be needed to prove the case.[201] The position is different when the act of intercourse occurs *after* the date of conception.[202] In some early decisions it was said that if intercourse occurred within the period of gestation, and there was opportunity at the time of conception, little or no further corroboration was required.[203] This is not now accepted as a general rule,[204] although intercourse very soon after the probable date of conception may throw a significant light on the relationship between the parties at the relevant date.[205] In general, the act of intercourse after conception will support the pursuer only if it occurs in circumstances which indicate the probability of an earlier illicit association between the parties.[206]

Between the pursuer and another man[207]

Evidence of such acts of intercourse is admissible because it is relevant to the **28.18.2** question of whether the defender is the father of the child.[208] If it is proved that

---

[198] *Lawson v Eddie* (1861) 23 D 876; *Ross v Fraser* (1863) 1 M 783; *McDonald v Glass* (1883) 11 R 57; *Scott v Dawson* (1884) 11 R 518; *Buchanan v Finlayson* (1900) 3 F 245; *Havery v Brownlee* 1908 SC 424; *Florence v Smith* 1913 SC 978; *Roy v Pairman* 1958 SC 334.

[199] See Chapter 7.

[200] *Roy v Pairman* 1958 SC 334, per Lord Justice-Clerk Thomson at 336.

[201] *Buchanan v Finlayson* (1900) 3 F 245, per Lord Trayner at 251. See also Lord Justice-Clerk Macdonald at 249.

[202] *Ross v Fraser* (1863) 1 M 783, per Lord Neaves at 786.

[203] *Lawson v Eddie* (1861) 23 D 876, per Lord Benholme at 880; *Ross v Fraser* (1863) 1 M 783, per Lord Justice-Clerk Inglis at 785; *McDonald v Glass* (1883) 11 R 57, per Lord Justice-Clerk Moncreiff at 58, Lord Young at 59.

[204] *Florence v Smith* 1913 SC 978, per Lord Dundas at 985–986.

[205] *Buchanan v Finlayson* (1900) 3 F 245, per Lord Justice-Clerk Macdonald at 249, Lord Trayner at 251.

[206] See *Roy v Pairman* 1958 SC 334.

[207] A judicial suggestion that evidence of acts of intercourse between the defender and another woman might be relevant and admissible has not been adopted in practice: *Whyte v Whyte* (1884) 11 R 710, per Lord Mure at 711.

[208] *Butter v McLaren* 1909 SC 786. The averment regarding these acts of intercourse ought to specify the times and places and the names of the men: *Barr v Bain* (1896) 23 R 1090.

the defender and another man had intercourse with the pursuer at or about the probable time of conception, and the evidence indicates that either of them might be the father, the pursuer fails.[209] If, on the other hand, there is evidence which makes it more probable that the defender is the father, the pursuer can succeed. An example of such evidence is that menstruation took place after intercourse with the other man, and before intercourse with the defender.[210] The court has no power to request a third party to provide a sample for scientific analysis.[211]

28.19 DEFENDER'S ACTIONS AND EXPRESS OR IMPLIED ADMISSIONS

28.19.1 The defender's words or acts before, or at about, the time of conception, may be important as indicating the probable relationship between the parties at that time. Thus evidence of familiarities which are inconsistent with an innocent relationship, or of the defender's references to such familiarities in conversation or in letters written by him, may help provide support. When evidence of contemporary acts is lacking evidence may derive from what the defender does or says when informed of the pursuer's pregnancy, and indicated to be the cause of it. The defender's suggestions for maintaining the child, or that the pursuer should have an abortion, or offer the child for adoption, may be consistent only with the advice to be expected from a disinterested friend or may disclose a personal and interest, consistent with implied admission of paternity. Unless the surrounding circumstances suggest otherwise such evidence is probably neutral. Intercourse with the mother, after the possibility of paternity has been raised, is unlikely to be of much evidential value in the present day[212] but may constitute an adminicle of evidence which combines with others to create an inference of paternity. An express admission of paternity, if sufficiently proved, will be convincing evidence, even if it is subsequently denied, unless the admission was made on the basis of false assumption.[213]

28.20 DEFENDER'S DENIALS AND DEFENDER AS A WITNESS

28.20.1 Peculiar to actions of affiliation and aliment,[214] was a rule that the false denial by a defender in the witness box of a material fact which was proved to be true, might be accepted as corroboration of the pursuer's evidence as to the defender's paternity of her child. That rule was abolished by the Civil Evidence (Scotland) Act 1988, s 1(2) and any authorities[215] referring to such a rule cannot now be founded upon in that respect. Since the defender's admissions or denials in the witness box were of great importance to the pursuer's case, it was not unusual for the pursuer to cite the defender and to call him as one of her witnesses, in order to ensure that he gave evidence. Such a practice was unobjectionable[216] and that is probably still

---

[209] Robertson v Hutchison 1935 SC 708.

[210] Sinclair v Rankin 1921 SC 933.

[211] The power in the Law Reform (Miscellaneous Provisions) (Scotland) Act 1990, s 70 extends to parties and the relevant child only.

[212] Cf Roy v Pairman 1958 SC 334.

[213] See Havery v Brownlee 1908 SC 424, per Lord Justice-Clerk Macdonald at 425.

[214] Macpherson v Beaton 1955 SC 100.

[215] Such as those referred to in para 174 of the first edition of this text.

[216] Faddes v McNeish 1923 SC 443, per Lord Ormidale at 448.

the case.[217] The courts did criticise a practice of calling the defender as the *first* witness for the pursuer,[218] but there is no procedural or ethical reason why this should not be done.[219]

---

[217] It is in civil cases in general: *McDonnell v McShane* 1967 SLT (Sh Ct) 61.
[218] *McArthur v McQueen* (1901) 3 F 1010; *McWhirter v Lynch* 1909 SC 112; *Faddes v McNeish* 1923 SC 443, per Lord Ormidale at 448; *Fraser v Smith* 1937 SN 67, per Lord President Normand and Lord Moncrieff. *Cf Darroch v Kerr* (1901) 4 F 396.
[219] See *McWhirter v Lynch* 1909 SC 112, per Lord President Dunedin at 113.

CHAPTER 29

PROOF IN PROCEEDINGS CONCERNING CHILDREN—PUBLIC LAW

29.1 INTRODUCTORY

29.1.1 This chapter deals briefly with proceedings relating to the family in which a department or agency of central or local government plays a part.[1] Principally these are proceedings before the children's hearing and the sheriff under the Children (Scotland) Act 1995, Part II, which has replaced the Social Work (Scotland) Act 1968 in providing the framework for the exercise by local authorities of their obligations to look after children in their area. However, proceedings may now arise before tribunals in respect of aliment for children under the Child Support Act 1991, since the court has no jurisdiction over aliment in most cases.[2] Generally, in family proceedings at public law, the rules of evidence have been applied as in other civil proceedings, but certain specialities do arise.[3]

29.2 CHILDREN'S HEARINGS AND RELATED PROCEEDINGS BEFORE THE SHERIFF—GENERAL

29.2.1 The children's hearing is not concerned with the establishment by evidence of the grounds upon which a child has been referred to the hearing by the reporter, since that is a matter for the sheriff if the grounds are not accepted by a party to the proceedings or if the child is unable to understand the grounds.[4] However, the hearing will have to assess facts in order to be satisfied that compulsory measures of supervision are necessary and generally to consider and determine the merits of the

---

[1] Adoption proceedings, which involve aspects of private and public law, will not be covered specifically, but the evidential issues raised in such proceedings may be dealt with in accordance with the principles contained in the preceding chapter, although the Act of Sederunt (Child Care and Maintenance) Rules 1997 (SI 1997/291) mentioned in this chapter also regulate adoption proceedings.

[2] Child Support Act 1991, s 8, as amended.

[3] For an examination of proof within the context of detailed study of the substantive law, see Wilkinson and Norrie (2nd edn), paras 19.67–19.72.

[4] Children (Scotland) Act 1995 ("1995 Act"), s 65(7) and (9) and s 68.

child's case.[5] Special rules govern the procedures of a children's hearing[6] and related proceedings in the sheriff court,[7] although a substantial degree of discretion is afforded to the chairman of the hearing[8] and to the sheriff.[9] The persons normally involved in such proceedings (hereafter referred to as "parties") are the Principal Reporter or assistant (hereafter referred to as "the reporter"), the child, any "relevant person", being a parent or other person with parental responsibilities and rights in relation to the child and any person who appears to have *de facto* charge of and control over the child[10] and any safeguarder appointed by the court or hearing.[11] A party is entitled to be represented either by a legal representative or a lay representative.[12]

29.3 PROCEEDINGS BY REPORTER BEFORE THE SHERIFF UNDER THE CHILDREN (SCOTLAND) ACT 1995—APPLICATION OF RULES OF EVIDENCE

29.3.1 It has been stressed by the courts that proceedings before the sheriff for proof of grounds of referral are civil proceedings *sui generis*,[13] in which normal adversarial techniques are not appropriate[14] and observed that the overall purpose of determining what is necessary in the child's interest must not be hindered by rigid application of the rules of evidence.[15] So, for example, the court admitted evidence of an extra-judicial admission of criminal conduct towards a child which had been made for the purposes of criminal proceedings albeit that the normal rules of evidence would operate to exclude this in any proceedings other than that for which it was made.[16] However, by comparison, a regulation, now revoked, which prevented a relevant person from having access to information available to the hearing, was held to be in breach of the European Convention on Human Rights since it did not afford proper access to evidence for preparation of a contradictory case.[17] At very least "the basic rules of evidence" have been said by the courts to apply in such proceedings[18] and decisions in such proceedings have raised a number of interesting points in relation to application of the rules of evidence, some specific to these proceedings and some of general application. The range of proceedings before the sheriff under Part II is wider than under the Social Work (Scotland) Act

---

[5]   1995 Act, s 65(1).
[6]   Children's Hearing (Scotland) Rules 1996 (SI 1996/3261).
[7]   Act of Sederunt (Child Care and Maintenance Rules) 1997 (SI 1997/291) (hereafter "Act of Sederunt").
[8]   Children's Hearing (Scotland) Rules 1996, r 10(3).
[9]   Act of Sederunt, r 3.23.
[10] 1995 Act, s 93(2)(b). A father who is living with the child's mother (all as defined in the 1995 Act, s 15(1) and Act of Sederunt, r 5(3)(b)) but who does not fit the definition of a relevant person may become involved at the chairman's discretion: Act of Sederunt, r 12(1).
[11] 1995 Act, s 41.
[12] Children's Hearing (Scotland) Rules 1996, r 11; Children (Scotland) Act 1995, s 68(4); Act of Sederunt, r 3.21.
[13] *McGregor v D* 1977 SC 330 per Lord President Emslie in relation to the regime introduced by the Social Work (Scotland) Act 1968. There is no reason to expect that the amended form of regime contained in the Children (Scotland) Act 1995 will be considered differently.
[14] *F v Kennedy (No 2)* 1992 SCLR 750.
[15] *W v Kennedy* 1988 SCLR 236.
[16] *W v Kennedy* 1988 SCLR 236.
[17] *McMichael v UK*, ECHR, 24 February 1995.
[18] Act of Sederunt, r 3.47; 1995 Act, s 65(7).

1968,[19] and now includes applications by the reporter for a child assessment order or a parental responsibility order.[20] All such proceedings are subject to a similar procedural regime including the rules for receipt of evidence. It is thought that the case law that arose under the 1968 Act, unless contradicted by the 1995 Act or the Act of Sederunt would apply to all court proceedings taken by the reporter.

The burden of proving the grounds of referral lies upon the reporter who has **29.3.2** instituted the proceedings,[21] and in relation to any other issues arising the normal rule applies that the person asserting carries the burden of proof.[22] Since the proceedings are civil there is no requirement of corroboration and proof is on the balance of probabilities. The one exception to this is where commission of an offence by the child is a ground of referral.[23] Such a ground must be proved to the standard required in criminal proceedings,[24] and by implication requires corroboration. However, if the ground of referral requires proof of criminal conduct by any other person, such as abuse of the child by a parent, there is no such exception and the civil standard of proof still applies.[25] At the conclusion of the evidence led by the reporter the sheriff must consider whether sufficient evidence has been led.[26] This requirement of a *prima facie* case will be met easily in most cases provided that the reporter has led any evidence to support the ground of referral, but if an offence by the child is alleged it will operate akin to the no case to answer procedure in criminal cases, and the case will fall if there is not evidence from two sources. When evidence of any criminal conduct is led the sheriff is not limited to the offence named in the ground of referral, but may find another offence to have been established.[27]

The sheriff may, in certain circumstances, decide at the hearing to dispense **29.3.3** with receipt of evidence in relation to a ground or grounds of referral and deem the ground to be established.[28] This is limited to specified situations in which at the time of the hearing there is no substantive challenge to the grounds and, even if the specified situation pertains, the sheriff may nevertheless decide that in all the circumstances evidence should be led.[29] When evidence is led the proceedings are summary in nature[30]; therefore there is no requirement to record evidence by shorthand writer or mechanical means and the proceedings resemble a proof in a summary cause, or, if offending by the child is in issue, a summary trial. The oath or affirmation is administered to those giving evidence,[31] who are open to cross-examination and re-examination by the parties present or their

---

[19] Act of Sederunt, r 3.56(b).

[20] The right of appeal to the sheriff on the merits of a children's hearing decision has also been extended by the 1995 Act, s 51(5)(c), enabling the sheriff who overturns a decision of a hearing to substitute his own decision. There is scope for evidence to be heard at the appeal hearing in certain circumstances or if considered by the sheriff to be appropriate: Act of Sederunt, r 3.56(3).

[21] This is inferred from the statutory provisions requiring the reporter to support the grounds of referral and the court to consider whether sufficient evidence has been led after conclusion of the reporter's case: 1995 Act, ss 67 and 68; Act of Sederunt, r 3.47(1) and (2).

[22] rule 2.4.

[23] 1995 Act, s 52(2)(i).

[24] 1995 Act, s 68(3)(b).

[25] *McGregor v D* 1977 SLT 182; *Harris v F* 1991 SLT 242.

[26] Act of Sederunt, r 3.47(2) and (3).

[27] Act of Sederunt, r 3.50.

[28] 1995 Act, s 68(8).

[29] 1995 Act, s 68(8); Act of Sederunt, r 3.47(1).

[30] Act of Sederunt, r 3.20.

[31] A child would be admonished to tell the truth.

representatives.[32] The sheriff may interpret the overarching requirement to safe-guard the child's interest by adopting an inquisitorial or interventionist role. The rules for admission of documentary evidence and hearsay apply as in other civil proceedings, but when an offence by the child is alleged it is thought that the court would apply the basic rules of evidence as pertaining in criminal pro-ceedings, such as limiting the admission of hearsay to situations in which it is admissible in criminal trials,[33] adopting the traditional non-interventionist role of the sheriff and entitling the child, or the child's representative, to speak last.[34]

29.4 PROCEEDINGS BY REPORTER UNDER THE CHILDREN (SCOTLAND) ACT 1995, PART II—EVIDENCE OF CHILDREN

29.4.1 As in other civil proceedings a child may give evidence if assessed by the sheriff to be capable of being a trustworthy witness.[35] In the context of such proceedings the court has established that this can be done even when the child cannot speak[36] and that evidence of third parties can be heard to assist in the assessment.[37] Hearsay of the child—for example in the form of an allegation of child abuse made on an earlier occasion—may be admitted as proof of its contents[38] if, and only if, the child is capable of being a witness,[39] assessed by oral examination of the child in court,[40] and may be preferred to a conflicting statement made by the child in oral evidence.[41] In the discretion of the sheriff the child to whom the proceedings relate may be excluded from the proceedings while other evidence is led,[42] and relevant persons may be excluded while the child's evidence is led,[43] subject always to pres-ervation of the right of any party against whom that evidence may apply, to know of and respond to its content.[44] The sheriff may on application allow the child to give evidence by live television link.[45] The foregoing relates to any child as a witness, and is without prejudice to (a) the court's power to hear a statement from or on behalf of a child who is a party spoken from the table[46]; and (b) the court's obligation to afford any child to whom the proceedings relate, the opportunity to

---

[32] A relevant person who is alleged to have committed an offence against the child is nevertheless a competent and compellable witness: *McGregor v T* 1975 SLT 76.

[33] Criminal Procedure (Scotland) Act 1995, ss 259–262.

[34] Criminal Procedure (Scotland) Act 1995, ss 69 and 161.

[35] *M v Kennedy* 1993 SCLR 69, following *Rees v Lowe* 1989 SCCR 664.

[36] *M v Kennedy* 1993 SCLR 69.

[37] *M v Kennedy* 1993 SCLR 69; *M v Ferguson* 1994 SCLR 487.

[38] Civil Evidence (Scotland) Act 1988, s 2. The following qualifications apply only to hearsay which is to prove its contents. It may be received merely as proof that the statement was made or as part of the narrative of the case without satisfying any such qualifications: *M v Ferguson* 1994 SCLR 487; *Sanderson v McManus* 1997 SCLR 281.

[39] *F v Kennedy (No 1)* 1992 SCLR 139 (IH).

[40] *L v L* 1996 SCLR 11 (OH); *R, Petitioner* 1999 SC 380 considers the extent of the examination required. See further para 13.2.

[41] *K v Kennedy* 1992 SCLR 386.

[42] Act of Sederunt, r 3.47(5).

[43] Act of Sederunt, r 3.47(6).

[44] Act of Sederunt, r 3.47(7).

[45] Act of Sederunt, r 3.22.

[46] The party may make a submission, or the court may adopt an inquisitorial role and ask questions of a party who is not a witness. It is suggested that if a party wishes to speak about factual issues which are in contention the proper approach would be to put the party on oath, affirmation or admonition as appropriate, before hearing evidence, and to afford other parties the opportunity to cross-examine.

express a view and to have that view heard.[47] The sheriff may receive the child's views direct or through a safeguarder, curator or representative chosen by the child.[48] The sheriff may withhold access to the record of the child's views.[49] If a ground of referral is found to be proved, in subsequent applications based on similar or relative grounds those same grounds will not normally be *res judicata*.[50]

29.5 PROCEEDINGS INVOLVING LOCAL AUTHORITY UNDER THE CHILDREN (SCOTLAND) ACT 1995, PART II AND OTHER ENACTMENTS

An application by the local authority for a parental responsibilities order under the **29.5.1** Children (Scotland) Act 1995 is governed by procedures[51] which are similar to those applying in applications by adoption agencies for freeing for adoption and by individuals for adoption[52] under the Adoption (Scotland) Act 1978 and applications by individuals under the Human Fertilisation and Embryology Act 1990.[53] These proceedings are all primarily disposed of by way of reports and other documents submitted in support of the application, but the court may order a hearing in which oral, documentary and affidavit evidence may be received. While not directly in point with the case law arising from cases initiated by the reporter, the court has indicated that it will not let rigid application of rules of evidence and procedure thwart a decision which is in the best interests of the child.[54] However, in all other respects these are civil proceedings to which the normal rules of civil evidence apply. Whilst the sheriff has wide discretion as to procedure, the proceedings are not expressly summary in nature, and may be conducted in a manner similar to proof in ordinary civil proceedings in the sheriff court. In addition, persons engaged in or reporting in such proceedings are expressly required to maintain confidentiality.[55]

29.6 CHILD SUPPORT—APPEAL TRIBUNAL PROCEEDINGS

The Child Support Act 1991 introduced an entirely new process for the determi- **29.6.1** nation and assessment of alimentary liability for children throughout the United Kingdom, whereby jurisdiction in the matter of aliment was, in the majority of situations, removed from the court and vested in the Secretary of State for Social Security.[56] The powers and duties of the Secretary of State in relation to the assessment and recovery of aliment are implemented by Child Support Officers on the basis of evidence provided by the applicant for a child support assessment, usually

---

47 Act of Sederunt, r 3.5.
48 Act of Sederunt, r 3.21. The safeguarder may choose to enter the proceedings as a party, and is entitled to examine and cross-examine in the same way as any other party.
49 Act of Sederunt, r 3.5(4).
50 *McGregor v H* 1983 SLT 626; *Kennedy v S* 1986 SLT 679; *M v Constanda* 1999 SC 348, and see Wilkinson and Norrie, *Parent and Child* (2nd edn), para 19.71.
51 Act of Sederunt, rr 2.37–2.44.
52 Act of Sederunt, rr 2.5–2.36.
53 Act of Sederunt, rr 2.45–2.59.
54 *L v L* 1998 SLT 672 at 676.
55 Act of Sederunt, rr 2.12(2), 2.30(2), 2.47 (2).
56 Child Support Act 1991 ("1991 Act"), ss 1–6 and 8.

the parent with care of the child, and evidence provided by the parent against whom the assessment is sought.[57] Decisions of child support officers are, in common with many other administrative decisions, appealable on the merits to an administrative tribunal,[58] the Child Support Appeal Tribunal,[59] and from there, on a point of law only, to the Child Support Commissioners,[60] and further, with leave, to the Inner House of the Court of Session.[61] Separately the decisions may be judicially reviewed. Within this appeal process only the hearing before the Child Support Appeal Tribunal is an evidential one, and it involves a rehearing of the merits of the application, including evidence not presented at the time of application and evidence of subsequent changes of circumstances.[62]

29.6.2   The parties to the tribunal are the appellant, who disputes the assessment made by the Child Support Officer, the other parent, and a representative of the Child Support Officer. In Scotland, but not in England and Wales, the child is entitled to seek an assessment[63] and a child who did so would be a party to any subsequent appeal proceedings. In tribunal proceedings it may be thought that the persuasive burden of proof is upon the appellant, and otherwise upon a party making a positive assertion. For example, if a party asserted that the income of one party differed from that accepted by the child support officer in calculating the assessment the party so asserting would carry the burden of proof on that issue. However, the assertion that the appellant bears the burden of proof must be questioned for two reasons. First, the tribunal is rehearing the evidence in relation to the application and it might therefore be said that the burden of proof is on the original applicant or, since it is up to the child support officer to make the assessment, that the burden of proof is upon the child support officer to show that an assessment was properly made. Secondly, the tribunal has an inquisitorial role, and may therefore identify relevant issues not raised by the parties, or elicit evidence additional to that presented by the parties, although it is not for the tribunal to satisfy the burden of proof per se. Since appeals often relate to a particular stage or aspect of the process of child support assessment, burden of proof may be determined by interpretation of the relevant provisions of statute or regulation. The tribunal will, at the conclusion of the hearing, consider all the issues and evidence before it and assess where the persuasive burdens of proof lie and whether these have been satisfied.

29.6.3   The standard of proof is on the balance of probabilities. Parties may waive the right to an oral hearing, but one will take place unless all parties so waive. Parties are entitled to legal representation or lay representation.[64] Parties are entitled to lead evidence at the tribunal hearing even if no prior notice of it has been given. Although the proceedings are informal, the oath may be administered,[65] and should be administered if disputed issues of fact exist. Evidence is not recorded verbatim

[57] 1991 Act, ss 4 and 6; Child Support (Information, Evidence and Disclosure) Regulations 1992 (SI 1992/1812); Child Support (Maintenance Assessment and Procedure) Regulations 1992 (SI 1992/1813); Child Support (Maintenance Assessments and Special Cases) Regulations 1992 (SI 1992/1815).
[58] 1991 Act, s 20.
[59] 1991 Act, s 21 and Sched 3.
[60] 1991 Act, s 24.
[61] 1991 Act, s 25(1).
[62] 1991 Act, s 20(2A).
[63] 1991 Act, s 7.
[64] Child Support Appeal Tribunal (Procedure) Regulations 1992 (SI 1992/2641) ("1992 Regulations"), reg 9.
[65] 1992 Regulations, reg 11(5).

or by mechanical means, but the chairman of the tribunal is obliged to keep notes of the evidence and arguments, to which a party may later seek access. The conduct of the proceedings is in the discretion of the chairman[66] and parties who attend are entitled to give evidence, examine or cross-examine witnesses and to direct questions to another party or their representative.[67] A tribunal chairman may cite a person to appear as a witness at a tribunal and to bring supporting papers, subject to normal restrictions upon compellability of witnesses, confidentiality, and privilege.[68] It is thought that for tribunal proceedings an application could be made to the court under the Administration of Justice (Scotland) Act 1972[69] for the recovery etc of evidence for a tribunal. It has been held that in proceedings before a tribunal the exclusionary rules of evidence should not normally apply[70] and that all relevant evidence should be admissible. However, a tribunal chairman may refuse to admit irrelevant or superfluous evidence. The weight to attach to the evidence is a matter for the tribunal.

29.7 CHILD SUPPORT—RELATIONSHIP WITH COURTS

Whilst in the majority of situations assessment of aliment will be within the jurisdiction of the child support officer, the court retains jurisdiction situations which fall outwith that jurisdiction (for example, where a parent is not resident in the United Kingdom or the assessment is sought against a step-parent) and, on a transitional basis, in cases where there is a pre-existing court order or agreement.[71] Furthermore, if in the course of consideration of an application for child support a dispute as to parentage arises, this will be a matter for the court, unless parentage can be assumed. Parentage can be assumed for child support purposes if the alleged parent is named in an adoption order or an order under the Human Fertilisation and Embryology Act 1990, and, assuming no subsequent adoption, if there is a declarator of parentage, a presumption of parentage under the Law Reform (Parent and Child) (Scotland) Act 1986, s 5 (1), or an order for affiliation and aliment.[72] If a situation falls outwith these criteria, proceedings for declarator of parentage may be initiated by a party or initiated or defended by the Secretary of State.[73] If in an appeal to a Child Support Appeal Tribunal the ground of appeal is that a person is or is not the parent of the child, the appeal must be referred to the court.[74] However, a determination in such an appeal does not constitute a declarator of parentage or non-parentage.[75]

29.7.1

---

[66] 1992 Regulations, reg 11(1D).

[67] 1992 Regulations, reg 11(4).

[68] 1992 Regulations, reg 10.

[69] s 1. See also Chapters 17, 18 and 21 for recovery of witness details, real evidence and documentary evidence respectively.

[70] *Wednesbury Corporation v Ministry of Housing and Local Government (No 2)* [1965] 3 All ER 571 at 579.

[71] 1991 Act, s 8, as amended; Child Support (Maintenance Arrangements and Jurisdiction) Regulations 1992 (SI 1992/2645).

[72] 1991 Act, s 26, Cases A, B, C, E and F.

[73] 1991 Act, s 28. See, for example, *Secretary of State for Social Security v Ainslie* 2000 SLT (Sh Ct) 35. In that case, the sheriff expressed concern that all interested parties should receive intimation before proceedings *in rem*. For proof of parentage before the courts, see paras 28.14–28.16.

[74] 1991 Act, s 45 and the Child Support Appeals (Jurisdiction of Courts) Order 1993 (SI 1993/961).

[75] Law Reform (Parent and Child) (Scotland) Act 1986, s 8, as amended by the Child Support Appeals (Jurisdiction of Courts) Order 1993, art 8.

BIBLIOGRAPHY

Alison	*Principles of Criminal Law* (Blackwood, 1823)
Alison	*Practice of the Criminal Law of Scotland* (Blackwood, 1833)
Balfour	*Practicks* (Kinnaird and Donaldson, 1754)
Bankton	*An Institute of the Laws of Scotland in Civil Rights* (Kincaid & Donaldson, 1751–1753)
Bell	*Treatise on the Law of Arbitration in Scotland* (2nd edn) (T & T Clark, 1877)
Bell	*Commentaries on the Law of Scotland and Principles of Mercantile Jurisprudence* (7th edn) (T & T Clark, 1870)
Bell	*Principles of the Law of Scotland* (10th edn) (T & T Clark, 1899)
Bell	*Dictionary and Digest of the Law of Scotland* (7th edn) (Bell & Bradfute, 1890)
Bennion	*Bennion on Statute Law* (3rd edn) (Longman, 1990)
Bennion	*Statutory Interpretation* (2nd edn) (Butterworths, 1992)
Burnett	*A Treatise on various branches of the Criminal Law of Scotland* (Constable, 1811)
Burns	*Conveyancing Practice according to the Law of Scotland* (4th edn) (W Green, 1957)
Chalmers & Guest	*Bills of Exchange* (15th edn) (Sweet & Maxwell, 1998)
Clive	*The Law of Husband Wife in Scotland* (4th edn) (W Green, 1997)
Connell	*A Treatise respecting . . . Parishes etc* (Edinburgh, 1818)
Cox	*Practice and Procedure in the Church of Scotland* (6th edn) (Church of Scotland, 1976)
Craigie	*Scottish Law of Conveyancing* (3rd edn) (Bell & Bradfute, 1899)
Cross & Tapper	*Cross and Tapper on Evidence* (9th edn) (Butterworths, 1999).
Cusine & Paisley	*Servitudes and Rights of Way* (W Green, 1998)
Cusine & Rennie	*Missives* (2nd edn) (Law Society of Scotland & Butterworths, 1999)
Cusine & Rennie	*The Requirements of Writing* (Butterworths, 1995)
Dickson	*Evidence* (3rd edn) (T & T Clark, 1887)
Dobie	*Sheriff Court Practice* (Hodge, 1948)
Erskine	*An Institute of the Law of Scotland* (8th edn) (Bell & Bradfute, 1871)
Field & Raitt	*The Law of Evidence in Scotland* (2nd edn) (W Green, 1996)
Forte (ed)	*Scots Commercial Law* (Butterworths, 1997)
Fraser	*Husband and Wife according to the Law of Scotland* (2nd edn) T & T Clark, 1876–1878)
Gloag	*The Law of Contract: A Treatise on the principles of Contract in the Law of Scotland* (2nd edn) (W Green, 1929)

Gloag and Irvine	*Law of Rights in Security, Heritable and Movable, including Cautionary Obligations* (W Green 1897)
Gordon	*The Criminal Law of Scotland* (2nd edn) (W Green, 1978)
Goudy	*A Treatise on the Law of Bankruptcy in Scotland* (4th edn) (T & T Clark, 1914)
Gretton	*The Law of Inhibition and Adjudication* (2nd edn) (Butterworths, 1996)
Griffiths	*Confessions* (Butterworths, 1994)
Guild	*The Law of Arbitration in Scotland* (W Green, 1936)
Halliday	*Conveyancing Law and Practice* (2nd edn (Talman)) (W Green, 1996-1997)
Hume	*Commentaries on the Law of Scotland Respecting Crimes* (4th edn) (Bell & Bradfute, 1844)
Hunter (ed)	*Justice and Crime: Essays in Honour of the Rt Hon Lord Emslie* (T & T Clark, 1993)
Irons & Melville	*Treatise on the Law of Arbitration in Scotland* (W Green, 1903)
Lewis	*Manual of the Law of Evidence in Scotland* (Hodge, 1925)
Macdonald	*Criminal Law of Scotland* (5th edn) (W Green, 1948)
Maclaren	Court of Session Practice (W Green, 1916)
Macphail	*Evidence: A revised version of a Research Paper on the law of evidence in Scotland* (Law Society of Scotland, 1987)
Macphail	*Sheriff Court Practice* (2nd edn (Nicholson and Stewart)) (W Green, 1998)
MacSporran & Young	*Commission and Diligence* (W Green, 1995)
McBryde	*The Law of Contract in Scotland* (W Green, 1987)
McLaren	*The Law of Scotland in Relation to Wills and Succession* (3rd edn) (Bell & Bradfute, 1894)
Menzies	*Conveyancing according to the Law of Scotland* (Bell & Bradfute, 1900)
Montgomerie Bell	*Lectures on Conveyancing* (3rd edn) (Bell & Bradfute, 1882)
Phipson	*Phipson on Evidence* (15th edn (Howard)) (Sweet & Maxwell, 2000)
Rankine	*A Treatise on the Law of Leases in Scotland* (3rd edn) (W Green, 1916)
Renton & Brown	*Criminal Procedure according to the Law of Scotland* (6th edn (Gordon and Gane)) (W Green, 1996 et seq)
Ross	*Lectures on the History and Practice of Law of Scotland* (2nd edn) (Bell & Bradfute, 1822)
Sheldon	*Evidence: Cases and Materials* (W Green, 1996)
Stair	The Institutions of the Law of Scotland (4th edn) (Bell & Bradfute, 1832)
Stair Memorial Encylopaedia	*The Laws of Scotland* (Butterworths, 1988 et seq, Reissue, 1999 et seq)
Stewart	*The Law of Restitution in Scotland* (W Green, 1992)
Walton	A Handbook on Husband and Wife according to the Law of Scotland (3rd edn) (W Green, 1951)
Wilkinson	*The Scottish Law of Evidence* (Butterworths, 1986)
Wilkinson & Norrie	*The Law Relating to Parent and Child in Scotland* (2nd edn) (W Green, 1999)
Wills	Circumstantial Evidence (6th edn) (Butterworths, 1912)

INDEX

Index entries refer to paragraph numbers. Entries relating to notes are shown under the relevant paragraph numbers.